American Government and Politics

Deliberation, Democracy, and Citizenship

Second Edition

JOSEPH M. BESSETTE
Claremont McKenna College

JOHN J. PITNEY, JR.
Claremont McKenna College

Australia • Brazil • Japan • Korea • Mexico • Singapore • Spain • United Kingdom • United States

American Government and Politics: Deliberation, Democracy and Citizenship, 2nd Edition
Joseph M. Bessette
John J. Pitney

Publisher: Suzanne Jeans

Executive Editor: Carolyn Merrill

Development Editor: Lauren Athmer—LEAP Publishing Services

Assistant Editor: Scott Greenan

Editorial Assistant: Eireann Aspell

Media Editor: Laura Hildebrand

Brand Manager: Lydia LeStar

Content Project Manager: Alison Eigel Zade

Senior Art Director: Linda May

Manufacturing Planner: Fola Orekoya

Rights Acquisition Specialist: Jennifer Meyer-Dare

Production Service and Compositor: S4Carlisle Publishing Services

Text Designer: Rokusek Design

Cover Designer: cmiller design

Cover Images: Capital building: © Rudy Sulgan/Corbis

Martin Luther King, Jr.: © Bob Adleman/Corbis

Barack Obama: © Ken Sedeno/Corbis

Mitt Romney: © Rick Friednman/Corbis

John F. Kennedy: © Bettmann/Corbis

Ronald Reagan: © Wally McNammee/Corbis

Nancy Pelosi: © J. Scott Applewhite/AP/Corbis

For product information and technology assistance, contact us at
Cengage Learning Customer & Sales Support, 1-800-354-9706

For permission to use material from this text or product, submit all requests online at **www.cengage.com/permissions**. Further permissions questions can be emailed to **permissionrequest@cengage.com**.

Library of Congress Control Number: 2012952602

Student Edition:

ISBN-13: 978-1-133-58789-7
ISBN-10: 1-133-58789-5

Wadsworth
20 Channel Center Street
Boston, MA 02210
USA

Cengage Learning is a leading provider of customized learning solutions with office locations around the globe, including Singapore, the United Kingdom, Australia, Mexico, Brazil and Japan. Locate your local office at **international.cengage.com/region**

Cengage Learning products are represented in Canada by Nelson Education, Ltd.

For your course and learning solutions, visit **www.cengage.com**.

Purchase any of our products at your local college store or at our preferred online store **www.cengagebrain.com**.

Instructors: Please visit **login.cengage.com** and log in to access instructor-specific resources.

Dedication

This book, twelve years in the making, was made possible by the extraordinary patience and understanding of our families. And so with love and gratitude, we dedicate it to our wives—Lisa Minshew Pitney and Anne Nutter Bessette—and our children and stepchildren—Joshua Lawrence Pitney, Hannah Rose Pitney, Joseph Timothy Bessette, Rebecca Anne Bessette, Margaret Hanway Nones, William Couch Nones, and Elizabeth Calvert Nones.

We especially dedicate this second edition to the memory of loved-ones lost: John J. Pitney (1922–1987), Lawrence J. Friedman (1922–2010), Joseph A. Bessette (1923–2010), and Anne Nutter Bessette (1954–2011).

Brief Contents

Chapter 1: © iStockphoto.com/Joseph C. Justice Jr.; Chapter 2: The Signing of the Constitution of the United States in 1787, 1940 (oil on canvas), Christy, Howard Chandler (1873–1952)/Hall of Representatives, Washington D.C., USA/The Bridgeman Art Library; Chapter 3: Office of the Attorney General of Texas; Chapter 4: USCIS

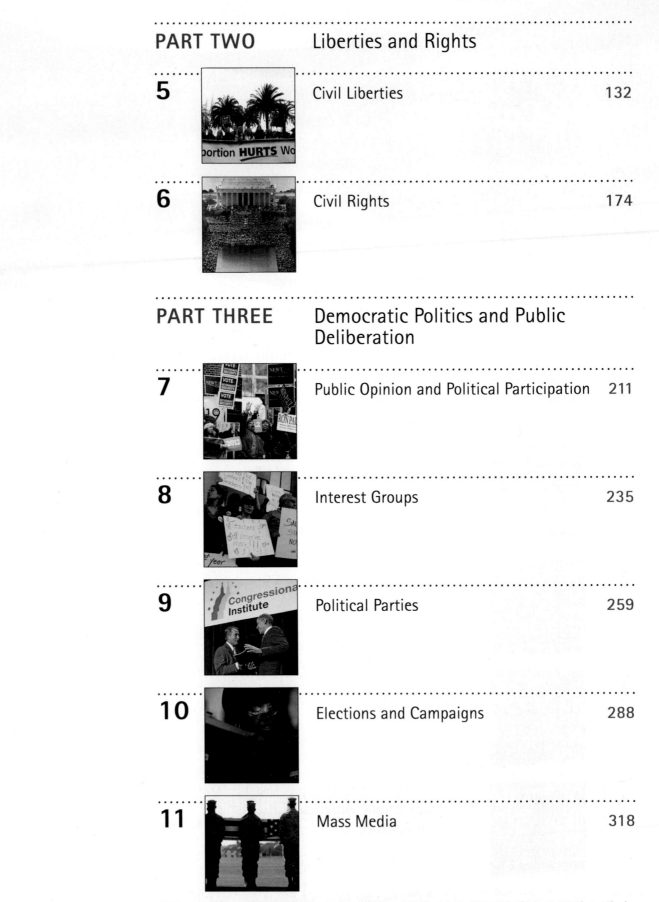
Chapter 5: Courtesy of Thomas Aquinas College; Chapter 6: © Flip Schulke/CORBIS; Chapter 7: AP Photo/Charles Dharapak; Chapter 8: Joe Raedle/Getty Images; Chapter 9: SAUL LOEB; Chapter 10: © Linda Davidson/The Washington Post via Getty Images; Chapter 11: Mark Wilson/Getty Images

Contents

© iStockphoto.com/Joseph C. Justice Jr.

2 THE AMERICAN CONSTITUTION   29

The Signing of the Constitution of the United States in 1787, 1940 (oil on canvas), Christy, Howard Chandler (1873–1952)/Hall of Representatives, Washington D.C., USA/The Bridgeman Art Library

3 FEDERALISM   64

Office of the Attorney General of Texas

USCIS

4 E PLURIBUS UNUM: AMERICAN CITIZENSHIP AND CIVIC CULTURE

Courtesy of Thomas Aquinas College

PART THREE   Democratic Politics and Public Deliberation

8 INTEREST GROUPS   **235**

Joe Raedle/Getty Images

SAUL LOEB

9   POLITICAL PARTIES   259

10 ELECTIONS AND CAMPAIGNS 288

© Linda Davidson/The Washington Post via Getty Images

11 MASS MEDIA 318

Mark Wilson/Getty Images

PART FOUR   Governing Institutions

12 CONGRESS   344

MANDEL NGAN/Getty Images

13   THE PRESIDENCY   375

Vacclav/Shutterstock.com

14 BUREAUCRACY AND THE ADMINISTRATIVE STATE   410

Courtesy of the Federal Bureau of Investigation

15 THE JUDICIARY 436

Jonathan Larsen/Shutterstock.com

PART FIVE   The Issues of American Politics

Doug Mills/The New York Times/Redux

16 SOCIAL POLICY AND THE WELFARE STATE   474

Joe Raedle/Getty Iamges

© Musa Farman/EPA/Corbis

Preface

The basic premise of this textbook is that Americans believe in ideals greater than their own self-interests—especially the principles of freedom and equality articulated in the Declaration of Independence—and that as citizens, voters, and public officials, they often act on those ideals. When they appraise how government is performing and what they should do about it, they do not just think, "What's in it for me?" They also ask themselves, "What's the right or just thing to do?" or "What's good for our community or for the country as a whole?"

As longtime students of American government and politics and as former government staffers in Chicago, Albany, and Washington, DC, we are hardly naive about the power of self-interest in government and politics. During breaks in our academic careers, we spent a total of 16 years working full-time in public affairs, including a big city prosecutor's office, a mayoral campaign staff, a state legislature, the U.S. Congress, a national party committee, and a federal statistics agency. From our study and experience, we well recognize that to some degree politics is about "who gets what, when, and how" and that political actors often focus their energies on their private interests—what scholars call "maximizing their utility."

A powerful strain of political science emphasizes self-interest, or "utility maximization," above all else, minimizing the pursuit of justice or the public interest. Scholars in this tradition view themselves as realists and dismiss serious consideration of idealism as a "goody two-shoes" approach. We believe that this view is shortsighted and fails to do justice to the range of forces and motives that drive American politics. That is why we wrote this text.

In our view, no description of American government and politics is complete without attention to the pursuit of both self-interest and public interest.

As we shall explain in the chapters ahead, there is much that self-interest cannot explain. Every day, elected officials make decisions that do not directly advance their careers. Some take politically risky stands on such emotional issues as abortion and the death penalty, while many others spend long hours on issues that may have little electoral payoff, such as prison reform. Every day, public servants in uniforms and civilian clothes make sacrifices for their fellow Americans. Firefighters, police officers, and members of the armed forces put their lives on the line, while teachers and social workers often endure poor working conditions and heartbreaking frustrations. Every day, citizens make judgments about how well their government advances justice or the broader public interest. In open meetings and in the privacy of the voting booth, they often support policies or programs whose benefits flow to others. In our view, no description of American government and politics is complete without attention to the pursuit of both self-interest and public interest.

The concept of "deliberative democracy"—which one of us began writing about three decades ago and which we elaborate in the first chapter—captures this sometimes messy combination of common good and self-interest, of collective reason and power politics. Deliberative democracy holds that democracy works best when people embrace the duties of citizenship and when informed citizens and public officials deliberate to identify and promote the common good. Citizenship, deliberation, and the relationship between the two are the themes of this book and they inform each of the following 18 chapters. We look at how public officials and ordinary Americans try to reason on the merits of public policy, and how they try to serve the public interest. No current American government textbook places as much emphasis on deliberation and citizenship.

We understand citizenship as both a legal status and as an idea that encompasses *civic virtues*. As we detail in Chapter 1, these virtues include self-restraint (or law-abidingness), self-reliance, civic knowledge, and civic participation and service. President Barack Obama captured this idea eloquently in his 2009 inaugural address. He honored men and women in the military "not only because they are the guardians of our liberty, but because they embody the spirit of service—a willingness to find meaning in something greater than themselves." Saying that this spirit must inhabit all Americans, he added that "there is nothing so satisfying to the spirit, so defining of our character than giving our all to a difficult task. This is the price and the promise of citizenship."[1]

Deliberative democracy holds that democracy works best when people embrace the duties of citizenship and when informed citizens and public officials deliberate to identify and promote the common good.

Some argue that American politics is not deliberative enough; that much political rhetoric in the United States is little more than partisan sniping and that Congress and the president too often fail to identify and promote the public good. Here the ideal of deliberative democracy serves as a standard by which to judge the political system. After reading this textbook, students will be better able to appraise policies, institutions, and public figures. They will be equipped to deliberate on contemporary issues and to meet the obligations of citizenship.

ORGANIZATION OF THE BOOK

This book has five parts, each consisting of several chapters. Part I, "Principles and Foundations of American Democracy," examines basic ideas of the American system. As one might expect, it includes a discussion of the Declaration of Independence, the Constitution, and federalism, in Chapters 1 through 3, respectively. Nevertheless, it differs from other textbooks in its breadth of coverage of the principles of the founding and in its emphasis on *The Federalist* and other writings of the founding era.

Part I includes a unique chapter. Chapter 4, "E Pluribus Unum: American Citizenship and Civic Culture," focuses on both the legal status of American citizenship and the deeper sense of national unity that ties together a large and diverse population. The chapter links citizenship to broader ideas about attachments and duties. It shows, for example, how the naturalization process highlights both the rights and obligations of American citizenship. The chapter describes the unique set of beliefs that Americans have about their relationship to government, their country's place in the world, and their duties to one another. These beliefs show up in distinctively American traditions and include individualism, religion, patriotism, and community service. One can find these things in other countries, of course, but they have special force in American political life.

Many American government textbooks overlook these subjects, which is unfortunate. Because immigration has risen sharply in recent years, about one out of every eight residents of the United States was born in another country. In some states, the ratio is much higher: in California, it is at least one out of four.[2] Accordingly, a large number of students are not yet citizens or have parents who are not yet citizens. For these students, questions surrounding the legal status of citizens and resident aliens are central to their lives, and for all people in the United States, whether they were born here or elsewhere, immigration remains a key public policy issue. Similarly, civic culture both touches students individually and shapes the country in which they live. Readers of this text will learn how the American tradition of community service has influenced issues ranging from tax law to welfare reform.[3]

Part II, "Rights and Liberties," includes a chapter each on civil liberties and civil rights. Each chapter roots its topic in the founding principles and draws attention to how those principles unfolded over time. Chapter 5, "Civil Liberties," includes an extensive treatment of the tension between civil liberties and the demands of war, with particular attention to the war on terrorism. Chapter 6, "Civil Rights," elaborates key debates on major contemporary issues and focuses attention on whether the Constitution and laws should be "color-blind."

Part III, "Democratic Politics and Public Deliberation," looks at the structures that enable ordinary Americans to take part in politics. Although the topics are the usual ones found in most American government texts, as the titles of Chapters 7 through 11 suggest—"Public Opinion and Political Participation," "Interest Groups," "Political Parties," "Elections and Campaigns," and "Mass Media"—the treatment is strongly tied to our particular themes of civic responsibility and deliberation.

Part IV, "Governing Institutions," has chapters on Congress, the presidency, the bureaucracy, and the courts. These chapters give special attention to deliberative processes, showing how presidents, bureaucrats, lawmakers, and judges reason on the merits of law and public policy. More often than many people acknowledge, the decisions of public officials are the product of reasoned judgments about the public interest, not simply the result of political pressures.

Part V, "The Issues of American Politics," looks at public policy in the fields of social welfare, economics, and national security. Responsible citizenship requires knowledge of the content of American public policy and the issues at stake in major policy debates. In American deliberative democracy, public opinion about social welfare, economic regulation, and national security both informs and constrains deliberation by the governing institutions. As Abraham Lincoln once wrote, "In this and like communities, public sentiment is everything. With public sentiment, nothing can fail; without it, nothing can succeed."[4]

INSTRUCTIONAL FEATURES

Most chapters have the following boxed features:

Myths and Misinformation examines beliefs—often widely shared—that turn out not to be true. Deliberation hinges on good information and accurate history, and these boxes try to sweep away some of the misconceptions that get in the way. For example, we examine legends about what political candidates are supposed to have said of claimed (Chapter 10) and protests against nonexistent legislation (Chapter 12).

International Perspectives compares the United States with other nations and consider the viewpoints of people across the globe. In some respects, there are similarities; but the boxes show many ways in which this country differs from the rest of the world. For instance, we consider how other countries look at the influence of religion in the United States (Chapter 5) and the role of political parties in parliamentary systems (Chapter 10).

The Impact of Social Media and Communications Technology is new to this edition and provides students with examples of how media sources influence politics, policy decisions, political parties, individuals, and day-to-day government activities. This boxed feature addresses topics such the impact of Facebook on voter mobilization (Chapter 7) and the potential impact of the massive Wikileaks document release on national security (Chapter 18).

Each chapter also includes the following features:

- Chapter outline
- Chapter learning objectives
- Critical thinking questions called "Major Issues" at the beginning of each section that frame the material
- Chapter summary
- "Test Your Knowledge" quiz
- Glossary of key terms
- Suggestions for further reading
- Web sources

UPDATED CHAPTERS: WHAT'S NEW IN THE SECOND EDITION

American Government and Politics: Deliberation, Democracy, and Citizenship gives special attention to political developments since 2010. To include descriptions and analyses of recent events and policy changes, we have updated the narrative. Topics given special attention include, by chapter:

Chapter 1: Deliberation and Citizenship in Service of Freedom and Democracy

- Coverage of the "Arab Spring" of 2011 and the prospects that freedom and democracy will spread in North Africa and the Middle East.
- An assessment of the ways in which social media empower citizens in tyrannical regimes and can contribute to democratic revolutions.

Chapter 2: The American Constitution

- Streamlined treatment of the events leading up to the Constitutional Convention and the debates that occurred there, with a sharpened contrast of the differences between the three major plans presented to the delegates.
- An overall reduction in the length of the chapter to highlight the key information and issues.
- A new focus on the importance of written media—newspapers and pamphlets—in the ratification debate to encourage thinking about how the forms of communications technology affect political deliberation.

Chapter 3: Federalism

- Analysis of the federalism implications of the Affordable Care Act of 2010 and the subsequent 2012 decision of the Supreme Court.
- Discussion of developments in issues such as gun control, same-sex marriage, and higher education.

Chapter 4: Citizenship and Civic Culture

- Demographic information from the 2010 census.
- Examination of recent action on immigration, including the controversial Arizona law and the Supreme Court decision striking down some of its provisions.
- New survey results on religion, patriotism, and other aspects of American civic culture.

Chapter 5: Civil Liberties

- Coverage of new Supreme Court cases on religious groups at public universities, the right of religious organizations to hire and fire ministers, demonstrations at military funerals, student protest activities at school-sponsored events, videos depicting animal cruelty, violent video games, and the placement by police of GPS devices on automobiles to track criminal suspects.
- Treatment of the religious freedom issues raised by regulations of the Obama administration on mandatory health insurance coverage of birth control drugs and sterilization operations.
- A new section on the right to keep and bear arms.
- Updated coverage of civil liberties issues raised by Obama administration actions in the war against al Qaeda.

Chapter 6: Civil Rights

- Updated information on EEOC actions to enforce laws that prohibit discrimination against the elderly and the disabled.
- New material on how federal laws require schools to accommodate the needs of students with disabilities.
- Updated information on the legal status of same-sex marriage in the United States and on the opening of military service to openly gay men and women.

Chapter 7: Public Opinion and Political Participation

- New public opinion data on economic, environmental, and other issues.
- Discussion of an innovative "deliberative poll" in California.
- Analysis of the role of social media in political mobilization.

Chapter 8: Interest Groups

- Discussion of American Crossroads and Crossroads GPS, outside-spending groups that Karl Rove helped organize.
- A look at the Internet both as a medium of interest group pressure and an object of government regulation.

Chapter 9: Political Parties

- New data on generational changes in party identification.
- Discussion of recent legal changes affecting the role of parties in candidate selection.
- Examination of how parties use the Internet and how they raise money in the post–*Citizens United* world.

Chapter 10: Elections and Campaigns

- Discussion of Super PACs and other outside spending groups.
- Analysis of new election procedures such as instant-runoff voting.
- A look at the early stages of the 2012 campaign.

Chapter 11: Mass Media

- Explanation of how a major news organization botched early coverage of the Supreme Court decision on health care.
- Analysis of how the new media continue to reshape the news business.
- Fresh data on media ownership and audiences.

Chapter 12: Congress

- Discussion of impact of the 2010 GOP takeover of the House.
- The effect of the 2012 congressional elections on leadership positions in the House and Senate.
- Analysis of how technology increases transparency in Congress.
- New information on the great variety of occupations represented by the members of Congress.

Chapter 13: Presidency

- Examination of the impact of divided government in the second half of President Obama's 2009–2013 term.
- Expanded analysis of President Obama's use of signing statements, executive orders, recess appointments, executive privilege, and other tools of presidential power.

Chapter 14: Bureaucracy and the Administrative State

- Discussion of recent scandals and their implications for control and oversight of administration.
- A look at the role of public employee unions in policymaking.

Chapter 15: Judiciary

- Coverage of the importance of the Supreme Court's 2012 decision on the Affordable Care Act.
- Updated information on the Supreme Court workload.
- Treatment of the impact of social media on how the Supreme Court is covered and whether justices themselves should use social media to educate the public about the workings of the Court.

Chapter 16: Social Policy and the Welfare State

- Updated information on the nature and extent of social welfare programs in the United States.
- Major new section on the passage of the Affordable Care Act of 2010 and the continuing controversy over its implementation.
- New material on how American civic values affect social programs in the United States.
- Updated coverage on the expansion of school-choice programs.

Chapter 17: Economic Policy

- Expanded analysis of how the federal government is coping with economic stagnation and mounting debt.
- Updated discussion of the tax burden and its relationship to income inequality.

Chapter 18: National Security and Foreign Policy

- A look at Obama administration policies in Libya, Afghanistan, and Iraq.
- Recent data on global attitudes toward the United States and American attitudes toward international relations.

NEW TO THE SECOND EDITION

Statistics and citations throughout have been carefully updated, and dozens of new photographs have been added. All the graphs and tables present the most current data available. In addition, Chapters 4 and 5 from the first edition have been combined, reducing the overall length of the book. New material on important developments of the past two years includes the following: the connection between the "Arab Spring" of 2011 and the principles of freedom and democracy that inspired the American founders (Chapter 1); the impact of the Supreme Court's decision on the Affordable Care Act, known to many as "Obamacare," on American federalism (Chapter 3); demographic data from the 2010 census and how it connects to immigration, citizenship, and assimilation, as well as new survey results on religion, patriotism, and other aspects of American civic culture (Chapter 4); coverage of new Supreme Court cases on a range of important civil liberties issues, including freedom of religion, freedom of speech, and police behavior (Chapter 5); updated information on the legal status of same-sex marriage in the United States and on the opening of military service to openly gay men and women (Chapter 6); coverage of innovative "deliberative polls" to promote citizens' deliberation on public issues (Chapter 7); discussion of the importance of new Super PACS in American politics (Chapter 8); examination of how political parties now use the Internet to get out their message and raise money (Chapter 9); analysis of new election procedures such as instant-runoff voting (Chapter 10); analysis of the growing influence of social media in American politics (Chapter 11); discussion of the impact of the 2012 GOP takeover of the House and of how technology is increasing the transparency of Congress (Chapter 12); analysis of the controversy over President Obama's assertion of independent presidential power through military actions, signing statements, executive orders, recess appointments, and assertions of executive privilege (Chapter 13); the growing impact of public employee unions in policymaking (Chapter 14); coverage of the importance of the Supreme Court's 2012 decision on the Affordable Care Act (Chapter 15); extensive treatment of the passage of the Affordable Care Act by Congress in 2010 and the continuing controversy over its implementation (Chapter 16); expanded analysis of how the federal government is coping with economic stagnation and mounting debt (Chapter 17); and coverage of Obama administration policies in Libya, Afghanistan, and Iraq (Chapter 18).

SUPPLEMENTS FOR INSTRUCTORS

Instructor's Edition for Bessette & Pitney's *American Government and Politics*, 2e

ISBN-13: 9781133940234

PowerLecture DVD with ExamView® and JoinIn® for Bessette & Pitney's *American Government and Politics*, 2e

ISBN-13: 9781133940180

An all-in-one multimedia resource for class preparation, presentation, and testing, this DVD includes Microsoft® PowerPoint® slides, a Test Bank in both Microsoft® Word and ExamView® formats, online polling and JoinIn™ clicker questions, an Instructor's Manual, and a Resource Integration Guide. The book-specific slides of lecture outlines, as well as photos, figures, and tables from the text, make it easy for you to assemble lectures for your course; the media-enhanced slides help bring your lecture to life with audio and video clips, with animated learning modules illustrating key concepts, tables, statistical charts, graphs, and photos from the book as well as outside sources. The Test Bank, offered in Microsoft Word® and ExamView® formats, includes 60+ multiple-choice questions with answers and page references along with 10 essay questions for each chapter. ExamView® features a user-friendly testing environment that allows you to not only publish traditional paper and computer-based tests, but also Web-deliverable exams. The Instructor's Manual includes learning objectives, chapter outlines, summaries, discussion questions, class activities and lecture-launching suggestions, key terms and definitions, and suggested readings and Web resources. JoinIn™ offers "clicker" questions covering key concepts, enabling instructors to incorporate student response systems into their classroom lectures.

A Resource Integration Guide provides a chapter-by-chapter outline of all available resources to supplement and optimize learning. Contact your Cengage representative to receive a copy upon adoption.

Companion Web Site for Bessette & Pitney's *American Government and Politics,* 2e

ISBN-13: 9781133939023

This password-protected Web site for instructors features all of the free student assets plus an instructor's manual, book-specific PowerPoint® presentations, JoinIn™ "clicker" questions, Resource Integration Guide, and a Test Bank. Access your resources by logging into your account at www.cengage.com/login.

Political Science CourseMate for Bessette & Pitney's *American Government and Politics,* 2e

ISBN-13: 9781285475974 PAC (Text plus Printed Access card)
ISBN-13: 9781133944874 IAC (Instant Access card)
ISBN-13: 9781133944973 SSO (Single Sign On: Access this resource by logging on to your account at: www.cengage.com/login.)

Cengage Learning's Political Science CourseMate brings course concepts to life with interactive learning, study tools, and exam preparation tools that support the printed textbook. Use Engagement Tracker to assess student preparation and engagement in the course, and watch student comprehension soar as your class works with the textbook-specific Web site. An interactive eBook allows students to take notes, highlight, search, and interact with embedded media. Other resources include video activities, animated learning modules, simulations, case studies, interactive quizzes, and timelines. The American Government NewsWatch is a real-time news and information resource, updated daily, that includes interactive maps, videos, podcasts, and hundreds of articles from leading journals, magazines, and newspapers from the United States and the world. Also included is the KnowNow! American Government Blog, which highlights three current events stories per week and consists of a succinct analysis of the story, multimedia, and discussion-starter questions. Access your course via www.cengage.com/login.

CourseReader: American Government 0-30 Selections

ISBN-13: 9781111479954 PAC (Printed Access Card)
ISBN-13: 9781111479978 IAC (Instant Access Card)

CourseReader: American Government allows you to create your reader, your way, in just minutes. This affordable, fully customizable online reader provides access to thousands of permissions-cleared readings, articles, primary sources, and audio and video selections from the regularly updated Gale Research Library database. This easy-to-use solution allows you to search for and select just the material you want for your courses. Each selection opens with a descriptive introduction to provide context, and concludes with critical-thinking and multiple-choice questions to reinforce key points. CourseReader: American Government is loaded with convenient tools like highlighting, printing, note-taking, and downloadable MP3 audio files for each reading. CourseReader: American Government is the perfect complement to any Political Science course. It can be bundled with your current textbook, sold alone, or integrated into your learning management system. CourseReader: American Government 0-30 allows access to up to 30 selections in the reader. Please contact your Cengage sales representative for details.

Election 2012: An American Government Supplement

ISBN-13: 9781285090931 (Printed Access card; available in bundle)
ISBN-13: 9781285420080 (Instant Access card)
ISBN-13: 9781285090924 (Single Sign On)

Written by John Clark and Brian Schaffner, this booklet addresses the 2012 congressional and presidential races, with real-time analysis and references. Access your course via www.cengage.com/login

Custom Enrichment Module: Latino-American Politics Supplement

ISBN-13: 9781285184296

This revised and updated thirty-two-page supplement uses real examples to detail politics related to Latino Americans and can be added to your text via our custom publishing solutions.

The Wadsworth News DVD for American Government 2014

ISBN-13: 9781285053455

This collection of two- to five-minute video clips on relevant political issues serves as a great lecture or discussion launcher.

SUPPLEMENTS FOR STUDENTS, IF REQUESTED BY YOUR INSTRUCTOR

Access your online American Government study tools by going directly to www.cengagebrain.com.

Political Science CourseMate for Bessette & Pitney's *American Government and Politics*, 2e

ISBN-13: 9781133944874 IAC (Instant Access card)

The more you study, the better the results. Make the most of your study time by accessing everything you need to succeed in one place. Read your textbook, take notes, watch videos, read case studies, take practice quizzes, and more—online with CourseMate. CourseMate also gives you access to the American Government NewsWatch Web site—a real-time news and information resource updated daily, and KnowNow!—the go-to blog about current events in American Government.

Companion Web Site for Bessette & Pitney's *American Government and Politics*, 2e

Access chapter-specific interactive learning tools, including flashcards, quizzes, and more in your companion Web site, accessed through www.CengageBrain.com.

REVIEWERS IN PREPARATION OF THE SECOND EDITION

MANAR ELKHALDI
University of Central Florida

FRANK J. GARRAHAN
Austin Community College

ANDREA ALEMAN
The University of Texas at San Antonio

MATTHEW GREEN
Catholic University of America

CELIA CARROLL JONES
Hampden-Sydney College

MARK SMITH
Cedarville University

JUSTIN DYER
University of Missouri

ERIK ROOT
West Liberty University

STEPHEN FRANTZICH
U.S. Naval Academy

REVIEWERS OF THE FIRST EDITION

RANDALL ADKINS
University of Nebraska at Omaha

JEFFREY ANDERSON
U.S. Air Force Academy

JOHN L. ANDERSON
University of Nebraska at Kearney

ALAN ARWINE
University of Illinois at Champaign, Urbana

AUGUSTINE AYUK
Clayton State University

JODI BALMA
Fullerton College

DANIEL BARACSKAY
Valdosta State University

KRIS BECK
Gordon College

RICHARD BILSKER
College of Southern Maryland

AMY BLACK
Wheaton College

TIMOTHY S. BOYLAN
Winthrop University

DONALD BRAND
College of Holy Cross

ANTHONY BROWN
Oklahoma State University

HEATH BROWN
Roanoke College

STEPHANIE BURKHALTER
Humboldt State University

MICHAEL BURTON
Ohio University

JOHN CARHART
Texas A&M University at Galveston

GEORGE CARSON
Central Bible College

MATTHEW CLARY
The University of Georgia

CORNELL CLAYTON
Washington State University

HAROLD CLINE
Middle Georgia College-Dublin Center

RAY MICHAEL COLLINS
University of Memphis

SCOTT COMPARATO
Southern Illinois University

WILLIAM F. CONNELLY
Washington and Lee University

PAUL COOKE
Lonestar College Cy Fair

JAMES COTTRILL
Santa Clara University

DAVID CROCKETT
Trinity University

JOHN CROSBY
California State University, Chico

KEVIN DAVIS
North Central Texas College-Corinth

LAURA DE LA CRUZ
El Paso Community College

JENNIFER DEMAIO
California State University, Northridge

JOHN DINAN
Wake Forest University

TOM DOLAN
Columbus State University

NELSON C. DOMETRIUS
Texas Tech University

VICKIE EDWARDS
University of Georgia

WALLE ENGEDAYEHU, PH.D.
Prairie View A&M University

JOHN T. FIELDING
Mount Wachusett Community College

GLEN FINDLEY
Odessa College

DANIEL W. FLEITAS
University of North Carolina Charlotte

LYNNE FORD
College of Charleston

STEVE FRANTZICH
U.S. Naval Academy

GREGORY FREELAND
California Lutheran University

EILEEN GAGE
Central Florida Community College

CRYSTAL GARRETT
Georgia Perimeter College

MICHAEL A. GATTIS M.A
Gulf Coast Community College

MARTHA GINN
Augusta State University

JEANNIE GRUSSENDORF
Georgia State University

MEL HAILEY
Abilene Christian University

AUGUSTINE HAMMOND
Augusta State University

LORI COX HAN
Chapman University

KENNETH N. HANSEN
University of Arkansas

JOSEPH P. HEIM
University of Wisconsin-La Crosse

JOHN HOWELL
Southern Utah University

WILLIAM HUDSON
Providence College

KEN HUX
Rockingham Community College

TSEGGAI ISAAC
University of Missouri – Rolla

BRIAN P. JANISKEE
California State University, Bakersfield

KAREN JOYCE
Norwich University

ANDREAS KARRAS
John Jay College

WILLIAM KELLY
Auburn University

ANDERS MICHAEL KINNEY
Calhoun Community College

REBECCA TATMAN KLASE
Greensboro College

JULIE LESTER
Macon State College

JOEL LIESKE
Cleveland State University

ROLIN G. MAINUDDIN
North Carolina Central University

DAN MARINE
U.S. Air Force Academy

THOMAS MARSHALL
University of Texas - Arlington

SEAN MATTIE
Clayton State University

LAUREL MAYER
Sinclair Community College

TERRY MAYS
The Citadel

HEATHER MBAYE
Univ of West Georgia

JOHN MCADAMS
Marquette University

LEE MCGRIGGS
Prairie View A&M University

WILL MILLER
Ohio University

STACIA MUNROE
Lincoln Land Community College

DAVID K. NICHOLS
Baylor University

MICHAEL J. NOJEIM
Prairie View A/M University

ANTHONY O'REGAN
Los Angeles Valley College

JEFF PARKEY
Clemson University

MOLLY PATTERSON
Aquinas College

MICHELLE C. PAUTZ
University of Dayton

PAUL PHILIPS
Navarro College

JAMES PONTUSO
Hampden-Sydney College

SHELLIANN POWELL
University of Georgia

ROBERT PRESS
University of Southern
Mississippi

DAVID RICHARDS
Texas Lutheran University

JACK RILEY
Coastal Carolina
University

A. PHOENIX ROUSSEAU
Eastfield College, Dallas
County Community College
District

ERIC SAPHIR
Pima Community College

TIM SCHORN
University of South Dakota

RONNEE SCHREIBER
San Diego State University

BECKI SCOLA
St. Joseph's University

SAID SEWELL
The University of West
Georgia

JAMES D SLACK
University of Alabama-
Birmingham

CHRIS SOPER
Pepperdine University

DENNIS SOUTHER
Stanly Community College

LISA SPEROW
California Polytechnic
University at San Luis Obispo

CRAIG STAPLEY
Kansas State University

STEPHEN D. STEHR
Washington State University

ROBERT STERKEN
University of Texas at Tyler

CATHY TRECEK
Iowa Western Community
College

MICHAEL TURNER
U.S. Coast Guard
Academy

JAMES VAN ARSDALL
Metropolitan Community
College

LAWSON VEASEY
Jacksonville State
University

CHARLES WALCOTT
Virginia Tech University

JENNIFER WALSH
Azusa Pacific University

JEFF WALZ
Concordia University

ROBERT WARREN
University of St Thomas-
Houston

CHRIS WHALEY
Roane State Community
College

W. CLIF WILKINSON
Georgia College and
State University,
Milledgeville

JONATHAN WILLIAMS
Kellogg Community College

MATTHEW WILSON
Southern Methodist
University

CHARLES TREY WILSON
North Georgia College &
State University

STEPHEN P. WITHAM
Liberty University

TERRY YOUNG
Patrick Henry Community
College

KEVIN WOOTEN
Angelina College

The following reviewers attended focus groups:

AUGUSTINE AYUK
Clayton State University

EVELYN BALLARD
Houston Community
College, Southeast College

DAN BARACKSAY
Valdosta State University

KRIS BECK
Gordon College

TOM DOLAN
Columbus State University

VICKIE EDWARDS
University of Georgia

CRYSTAL GARRETT
Georgia Perimeter College

CRAIG GREATHOUSE
North Georgia College &
State University

AUGUSTINE HAMMOND
Augusta State University

**MANOUCHER
KHOSROWSHAHI**
Tyler Junior College

MICHAEL KINNEY
Calhoun Community
College

JACK LAMPE
Southwest Texas Junior
College

HEATHER MBAYE
University of West Georgia

CHAD MUELLER
Vernon College, Wichita
Falls Campus

SONDRA RICHARDS
Midland College

CLIF WILKINSON
North Georgia College &
State
University

CHARLES H. WILSON III
North Georgia College and
State University

Acknowledgments

We are deeply indebted to a host of individuals for stimulating our interest in this project, moving it along at crucial stages, and ushering it to completion. James Headley, then of Bedford/St. Martin's Press, persuaded us some years ago that there was a place for a new American government textbook that emphasized deliberation and citizenship. Later, under the capable hands of Marilea Polk Fried at Bedford and then David Tatom at Wadsworth, the book began to take shape. In these early stages we benefited from the editorial assistance of Adam Beroud, Melissa Mashburn, Stacy Sims, and Beth Welch.

More recently, Carolyn Merrill of Wadsworth guided the book through completion with a steady and firm hand. For the first edition, we worked especially closely and productively with Jen Jacobson Blumenthal of Ohlinger Publishing Services. We are now equally indebted to Lauren Athmer of LEAP Publishing Services, Inc., for ushering this second edition to completion. Others who have assisted with the myriad of tasks that such a project entails include Lori Hazzard, Marcy Ross, Sarah Bonner, Laura Hildebrand, Joshua Allen, Angela Hodge, Elizabeth Kendall, Megan Lessard, Tracy Metivier, and Lydia Lestar. We have been impressed throughout with the dedication and professionalism of the Cengage/Wadsworth staff.

We are especially grateful to the approximately 150 reviewers, many anonymous, whose helpful comments shaped the final product. Carolyn Merrill did an outstanding job in identifying reviewers and persuading them to assess and critique our various drafts. One reviewer, Michael Burton of Ohio University, agreed to read and comment in detail on every chapter of the first edition. Our thanks to Mike and all the others for sharing their insights and expertise. The book is much stronger as a result of the first edition.

Friends and colleagues who provided helpful comments or assisted in other ways include William Connelly, Zachary Courser, John Gardner, Lloyd Green, Fred Lynch, Jim Pinkerton, Jeremy Shane, and Steven Schier. We especially thank Jay Speakman for preparing the first draft of Chapter 18: National Security and Foreign Policy.

We have also been assisted by several students at Claremont McKenna College and the Claremont Graduate University. These include Andrew Bluebond, Christiana Dominguez, Rhett Francisco, David Frisk, Matthew Glover, Takako Mino, and Anna Eames. Many more students in our sections of "Introduction to American Politics" at Claremont McKenna College provided helpful comments on draft chapters.

Finally, we would like to thank Tom Karako for preparing the original Test Bank in the weeks after receiving his PhD at the Claremont Graduate University and Jennifer Walsh of Azusa Pacific University for writing the Instructor's Guide for the text.

About the Authors

Joseph M. Bessette is the Alice Tweed Tuohy Professor of Government and Ethics at Claremont McKenna College in Claremont, California, where he has been on the faculty since 1990. He also teaches courses in the Department of Politics and Policy at the Claremont Graduate University. He received a B.S. in physics from Boston College and an M.A. and PhD in political science from the University of Chicago. Prior to coming to CMC he served as deputy director and acting director of the Bureau of Justice Statistics in the U.S. Department of Justice from 1985 to 1990, and as Director of Planning, Training, and Management for the Cook County, Illinois, State's Attorney's Office from 1980 to 1984. He was "Issues Coordinator" for State's Attorney Richard M. Daley's campaign for mayor of Chicago in 1983. He has also held full-time teaching positions at the University of Virginia and The Catholic University of America. He is the author of, among other works, *The Mild Voice of Reason: Deliberative Democracy and American National Government* (University of Chicago Press, 1994); coeditor and contributor to *The Presidency in the Constitutional Order* (Louisiana State University Press, 1981, reissued by Transaction Publishers in 2010);and *The Constitutional Presidency* (Johns Hopkins University Press, 2009). He is currently working on books on the death penalty and the creation and powers of the American presidency.

John J. Pitney Jr., is the Roy P. Crocker Professor of American Politics at Claremont McKenna College, where he is a four-time winner of campus-wide teaching awards. He received his B.A. in political science from Union College, where he was co-valedictorian. He earned his PhD in political science at Yale, where he was a National Science Foundation Fellow. From 1978 to 1980, he worked in the New York State Senate. From 1983 to 1984, as a Congressional Fellow of the American Political Science Association, he worked for Senator Alfonse D'Amato of New York and the House Republican Policy Committee, chaired by Representative Dick Cheney of Wyoming. From 1984 to 1986, he was senior domestic policy analyst for the House Republican Research Committee. He joined the Claremont McKenna College faculty in 1986. From 1989 to 1991, during a leave of absence, he worked at the Research Department of the Republican National Committee, first as deputy director, then as acting director. He has written articles for *The New Republic*, *The Weekly Standard*, the *Wall Street Journal*, the *Los Angeles Times*, and *Roll Call*, among others. His scholarly works include *The Art of Political Warfare*, published in 2000 by the University of Oklahoma Press. With James W. Ceaser and Andrew E. Busch, he is coauthor of *Epic Journey: The 2008 Elections and American Politics*, published in 2009 by Rowman and Littlefield.

Deliberation and Citizenship in Service of Freedom and Democracy

1

OBJECTIVES

After reading this chapter, you should be able to

- Explain the difference between a "deliberative" democracy and one based entirely on self-interest.

- Define *democracy* and describe the various forms it can take.

- Analyze the Declaration of Independence by identifying and describing its key principles.

- Describe how the principles of the Declaration have influenced American history.

- Identify the major characteristics of liberal democracies and contrast liberal democracies to other kinds of political systems in the modern world.

- Explain the knowledge that citizens should have to be able to contribute to decisions about the common good in the United States.

INTRODUCTION

Political scientists typically view politics as the balancing of interests. One famous definition of politics is: "Who gets what, when, how."[1] According to this image, people and groups participate in politics to get something for themselves:

- Citizens ask their elected representatives for money for local projects (often called "pork").
- Interest groups vie for grants and tax breaks.
- Politicians seek reelection and power.

The resulting picture is a vast web of bargains and games, where the players weigh costs against benefits and then make their moves accordingly. When they speak of higher principles, such as justice or the common good, they are just trying to trick others or cover their own tracks.

As political scientists, we have spent many years studying the literature of the "who gets what" tradition. As former government staffers in Chicago, Albany, and Washington, DC, we have touched the grubbier edges of practical politics, and because of this study and experience, we think that self-interest explains a good deal about political life. But we have also learned that it does not explain everything.

Lawmakers regularly make decisions that do not directly advance their careers, such as voting on obscure bills that have no effect on reelection. Executive officials often work long hours to advance the public interest, even when no personal benefits result. Federal judges work hard to get the law right in dozens, perhaps hundreds, of cases each year, even though such diligence has no effect on salary or tenure, since all serve life terms.

Americans—public officials and citizens—believe in more than their own self-interests, and they often act on those beliefs. They believe in and often seek to promote a broader "public interest," which includes principles of justice, the rights of others, and the good of the larger community (often called the "common good"). Yes, people disagree about the public interest, and self-interest often colors their disagreements, but unless you stretch the idea of "self-interest" beyond all sensible meaning, it fails to account for the ideals and passions that drive so much of American politics. As two military analysts write of the self-interest assumption: "The refusal of some theorists to acknowledge the possibility that people might act on the basis of motivations such as duty, honor, or community spirit flies in the face of history and, perhaps, personal experience. Those who have committed themselves to serve their communities or to defend their country in war may be entitled to find this proposition offensive."[2]

The pursuit of the public interest, or common good, works in several different ways. First, it affects all kinds of direct political activity from voting to high-level decision making. When judging candidates for national office, a voter will often consider how they will serve the entire nation. In his book *Profiles in Courage*, John F. Kennedy wrote of politicians who defied public opinion for the sake of principle: "Some were ultimately vindicated by a return to popularity; many were not."[3] Later, in his inaugural address, Kennedy famously said, "Ask not what your country can do for you; ask what you can do for your country." If Americans cared only about self-interest, they would have found that passage incomprehensible, not inspiring. A few weeks later, Kennedy established the Peace Corps by executive order, and thousands followed his call to serve a good greater than themselves.

Second, public policy depends on voluntary compliance with the law. Enforcement is necessary, and compliance is imperfect, as a few minutes on the roads will remind us. But studies show that fear of punishment is not the main reason for law-abiding behavior.[4] Americans generally stay close to the law's boundaries because they think it is the right thing to do.

Third, a successful and healthy political community requires voluntary activity beyond compliance. Government social services would fail without the private safety net of charity and voluntarism. For most of American history, the military has relied on voluntary enlistment. That reliance is remarkable, because joining the military means a willingness to lay down one's life on a battlefield. Nobody has a rational self-interest in violent, painful death. In fact, the United States came into being as an independent nation because thousands of young men voluntarily risked life and limb (25,000 died) between 1775 and 1781.

So while this book will address the "low politics" of self-interest and bargaining, it will keep returning to the "high politics" of *citizenship* and *deliberation*. These and related terms deserve some discussion.

Citizenship and Deliberation

Citizenship is a legal status that accords full membership in a political community, but it is also an idea that encompasses **civic virtues**. These virtues are essential elements of good citizenship and include the following:

- *Self-restraint*, the control of selfish impulses for the sake of the law or the public good
- *Self-reliance*, the achievement of goals through the efforts of individuals, families, and voluntary associations
- *Civic knowledge*, an understanding of government processes, public issues, and social conditions
- *Civic participation and service*, activity for the public good, ranging from voting to enlisting in the armed forces

Underlying these specific virtues is *patriotism*, both an emotional and a rational attachment to the nation. Some writers equate patriotism with mindless approval of government policies. Here we use it in a different sense, denoting a public spirit strong enough to inspire sacrifice. As we shall see in subsequent chapters, patriotism in the United States is grounded on beliefs about natural rights, human equality, and self-government. It is a key element of American civic culture.

Deliberation consists of reasoning on the merits of public policy, searching for the public interest or common good. Citizenship and deliberation have an intimate connection. Long ago Aristotle defined a citizen as anyone "who has the power to take part in the deliberative or judicial administration of any state."[5] Most Americans would likely agree that citizens in a democracy have an obligation, a **civic duty**, to contribute to deliberations about the common good. Such contributions can range from informal postings on Internet message boards to formal testimony before congressional committees.

Americans also expect their governing institutions to deliberate about the public interest on their behalf. They expect the members of the House of Representatives and Senate to reason together in committees, during floor debate, and informally to fashion laws that promote the nation's well-being. They expect the president and his advisers to think long and hard about how to secure the nation's interests in a dangerous world. And they expect the nine members of the Supreme Court to deliberate together about the meaning of the nation's Constitution and laws, free from personal interest or bias.

Nevertheless, some argue that American politics is not deliberative enough. Critics fault Congress for taking legislative shortcuts at the expense of policy discussion. Political rhetoric in Congress and elsewhere sometimes seems to be little more than name-calling and partisan sniping. In televised campaign debates, candidates often recite prepared sound bites instead of exchanging views. Campaign ads often cast more heat than light.

Although genuine reasoning on the merits of public policy sometimes seems lacking, deliberation is common enough and consequential enough that we can describe American government as a **deliberative democracy**, however imperfect. As we will show, those who built America's governing institutions sought to promote rule by reasoned and informed majorities operating through representative institutions. When American democracy does not work as well as it should, the ideal of deliberative democracy provides a standard for judging the political system.

Theories of American Democracy

The study of American government as a deliberative democracy is a relatively new approach within political science. Until the middle of the twentieth century, political scientists emphasized constitutions and laws when analyzing government. They gave short shrift to actual political behavior. But the decades after World War II ushered in a "behavioral

Citizenship—a legal status that accords full membership in a political community.

Civic virtue—a virtue that is an essential element of good citizenship, including self-restraint, self-reliance, civic knowledge, and civic participation and service.

Deliberation—reasoning on the merits of public policy, searching for the public interest or common good.

Civic duty—any obligation that citizens owe to the broader political community.

Deliberative democracy—a democracy whose institutions are designed to promote the rule of reasoned and informed majorities, usually through representative institutions.

Logrolling—when legislators (or others) trade support for one another's proposals.

Group theory—the view that a large number of diverse groups control government and politics and promote policies to serve their particular interests. (Also called "pluralist theory.")

Pluralist theory—the view that a large number of diverse groups control government and politics and promote policies to serve their particular interests. (Also called *group theory*.)

Elite theory—the view that government is controlled by a relative handful of elites in government, business, the professions, and the media who often think alike and work together to promote their mutual interests.

Rational choice theory—a theory of politics based on the premise that citizens and public officials act rationally to serve their personal interests.

FOCUS
QUESTION

Does the concept of a "public interest," or "common good," have real meaning; or are these just terms that people use to justify political preferences that serve their personal interests?

Duties of citizenship—the obligations that citizens owe to one another or the community as a whole, such as obeying the law.

revolution" within political science. New studies appeared that measured public opinion and voting behavior and linked them to broader theories of American democracy. Scholars examined why men and women sought to serve in government and how they behaved once they got there. Political scientists especially highlighted the power of organized interest groups in influencing legislators and bureaucrats.

The leading interpretations of Congress at the time reduced lawmaking to bargaining among groups, with legislators trading support for each other's proposals (a practice called **logrolling**). As one of the leading works on American politics noted, "The very essence of the legislative process is the willingness to accept trading as a means."[6] Interest groups were the fundamental elements of American politics, and vote trading was the only way to accommodate their competing desires. In the end, there was no *public* interest, just *group* interests: "In developing a group interpretation of politics, therefore, we do not need to account for a totally inclusive interest, because one does not exist."[7]

Not all political scientists accepted the accuracy of the **group theory** of politics, also called the **pluralist theory** of American democracy. Some believed that the decisive influences in American politics were not interest groups, which often gave voice to the desires of large numbers of Americans, but rather a relative handful of elites in government, business, the professions, and the media. These elites often thought alike and worked together to promote their mutual interests. Some scholars developed an **elite theory** of politics as an alternative to pluralist theory. More recently, many social scientists, adopting methods used in the study of economics, have focused on how voters and public officials act rationally to achieve their interests. Citizens, legislators, and executive officials are all presumed to be "rational actors" who use government and politics to "maximize their utility." Thus, this approach is called **rational choice theory**.

Under this view, citizens vote for candidates whom they believe will directly benefit them (usually economically); and individuals seek office for the salary, perquisites, distinction, or personal power, but not from a desire to serve the public. Once elected, legislators focus their efforts on getting reelected and discover that the best way to do this is to "bring home the bacon" from Washington or to help constituents deal with the bureaucracy. Consequently, the members of Congress "display only a modest interest in what goes into bills or what their passage accomplishes."[8] Another scholar concluded that "the general, long-term welfare of the United States is no more than an incidental by-product of the system."[9] When applied to political executives, such as the president of the United States, rational choice theory emphasizes gaining, keeping, and wielding power, often with little regard for whether or how this benefits the broader political community.

The deliberative democracy approach to American government and politics does not reject the insights of these earlier theories but denies that they tell the whole story.[10] Here is a capsule summary of the theme of this book—a theme that we will use to shed light on the topics covered in the following chapters:

> Americans believe in more than their own self-interests. They often act politically on those beliefs by exhibiting the civic virtues of self-restraint, self-reliance, civic knowledge, and civic participation. Through their own efforts and those of their elected leaders, they often search for the public interest, or common good, by reasoning on the merits of public policy. Here the public interest includes ideals such as justice and rights. We present this approach as part of what happens in American government and politics every day. Another part of politics is not so lofty: citizens, groups, and politicians use politics to promote their narrow self-interests. American politics is a messy combination of common good and self-interest, of collective reason and power politics. We believe that democracy works best when the people embrace the **duties of citizenship** (obligations that one owes to other citizens or the community as a whole) and when informed citizens and public officials deliberate to identify and promote the common good.

Consider, for example, the effort by the Congress and executive branch to fashion a national response to the growing economic crisis in the first weeks of Barack Obama's presidency in 2009. Strong opinions divided Democrats from Republicans, members of the

House from those in the Senate, and legislators from executive officials. Yet only a hardened cynic would say that the key players had no concern for the nation's well-being and sought only to advance their private interests. At the same time, many charged that Congress rushed ahead with massive new spending without detailed and careful deliberation. Indeed, some legislators complained that they did not even have time to read through the final version of the bill before they had to vote. Similarly, when Democrats and Republicans split over the president's ambitious health care proposal, which passed in 2010 with no Republican votes, few doubted that the partisan split reflected genuine differences of view as to how best to promote the health and well-being of Americans (see Chapter 16).

Consider also the Obama administration's decisions regarding how to fight the war on terror inherited from the George W. Bush administration. Within a few weeks of taking office, the new president took steps to revise or undo several Bush policies. Through executive orders and other actions, the president suspended military trials of suspected terrorists (though these were later reinstated), prohibited waterboarding and other coercive interrogation techniques, ordered the CIA to close secret detention facilities abroad, announced that the American detention facility at Guantánamo Bay in Cuba would close within a year (which congressional opposition eventually prevented), decided that most American troops would be removed from Iraq within 18 months, and authorized that an additional 17,000 troops be sent to Afghanistan.

Although Presidents Obama and Bush (and their advisers) reached some different judgments about how best to fight the war on terror, few would argue that self-interest explains their decisions. The American people expect their presidents to be the custodians of the nation's security and would be appalled to learn that a president had made key security decisions to promote his personal or political advantage.

By analyzing American government as a deliberative democracy, we are able to recognize the role that reasoning about the public interest plays in national policy making, to spot deficiencies in the deliberative process, and to evaluate how well our governing institutions meet their high responsibilities.

In this book, we will examine the core concepts, principles, practices, and institutions that constitute American government and politics, paying close attention to the role of the individual citizen and the processes of deliberation that influence public policy. In this chapter, we will lay the groundwork for that discussion by explaining the concepts of democracy and freedom, by showing how they inspired and guided the founding of the United States, by elaborating the founding principles as set forth in the Declaration of Independence, and by placing American democracy within the broader context of liberal democracies in the modern world. We conclude by detailing the kinds of civic knowledge we seek to convey in this book.

DEMOCRACY

MAJOR ISSUES

- What does "democracy" mean, and what different forms can it take?
- What kind of democracy did the founding generation choose for the United States?
- What institutional and political arrangements does every genuine democracy require?

This book is about American democracy. **Democracy** means simply "rule by the people." The term comes from the ancient Greek city-states of about 2,500 years ago, in which the free adult male citizens met periodically in the "assembly" to debate and vote on such matters as taxes, domestic legislation, choice of public officials, foreign alliances, and even war and peace. In Athens, the largest of the city-states, up to 10,000 or more would gather. The major alternative to democracy was oligarchy, which usually took the form of rule by wealthy families. (The box below lists other forms of political rule in the ancient world.) Outside the Greek city-states, monarchy was common.

Democracy—a form of government in which the people rule themselves either directly or through freely elected representatives.

Types of Rule in the Ancient World

Aristocracy	Technically, rule by "the best," but usually understood to mean rule by the nobility
Democracy	Rule by the people
Monarchy	Rule by one, such as a king
Oligarchy	Rule by the few, usually wealthy families
Plutocracy	Rule by the wealthy
Theocracy	Rule by religious leaders who seek to enforce the will of God
Timocracy	Rule based on principles of honor or ownership of property
Tyranny	Selfish rule by a single individual or small group with absolute power, unrestrained by the law or other institutions

Direct democracy—a form of government, originally found in ancient Greece, in which the people directly pass laws and make other key decisions.

Representative democracy—a form of government in which the people choose their leaders through free elections in which candidates and political parties compete for popular support and in which elected officials are held accountable for their conduct.

When the people directly make the key decisions, we call this **direct democracy**. The alternative, which is much more common in the modern world, is **representative democracy**, where the people elect officials to make the laws and other important decisions on their behalf.

The Democratic Tradition in the United States

The principles and practices of democracy did not spring forth suddenly at the nation's birth in 1776. When the British settled the American colonies, they brought with them democratic ideals and practices. Particularly in New England, the citizens governed themselves to a considerable degree from the very beginning. The Mayflower Compact of 1620, through which the Pilgrims formally organized themselves into a political society, was the beginning of self-government in New England:

> We whose names are underwritten . . . having undertaken for the glory of God, and advancement of the Christian faith, and the honor of our king and country a voyage to plant the first colony in the northern parts of Virginia, do by these presents solemnly and mutually, in the presence of God and one another, covenant and combine ourselves together into a civil body politic, for our better ordering and preservation, and furtherance of the ends aforesaid; and by virtue hereof, do enact, constitute, and frame such just and equal laws, ordinances, acts, constitutions, and officers, from time to time, as shall be thought most meet and convenient for the general good of the colony, unto which we promise all due submission and obedience.[11]

Although the settlers had emigrated from a land where the king and lords wielded enormous power, they assumed the right to govern themselves in their new local communities. This principle of local self-government spread throughout the colonies.

In New England, the adult male citizens met periodically in "town meetings" to debate and vote on common concerns. (This form of direct democracy, now open to all adult residents, still exists in some small New England towns.) Nineteenth-century philosopher and poet Ralph Waldo Emerson celebrated this type of government in 1835, on the 200th anniversary of Concord, Massachusetts. Emerson praised "this open democracy" in which "every opinion had utterance." Here, citizens learned to govern themselves by laying taxes, choosing their deputies to the state legislature, disposing of town lands, establishing schools, and providing for the poor. The success of these governments, Emerson believed, gave "assurance of man's capacity for self-government."[12]

Whatever the virtues of direct democracy at the local level, it was not possible for the people throughout a colony to assemble and pass laws. Instead, they elected representatives to an assembly, which in most of the colonies shared power with a governor appointed by the king. These assemblies imposed taxes, fashioned the criminal code, adopted policies toward religion, and addressed many other matters. Often, the assemblies clashed with the royal governors for control of policy.

These early efforts at self-government in the colonies were not full-fledged democracies in the modern sense of the term. All the colonies restricted the vote to men who owned some specified amount of property, either in real estate or the cash equivalent. In some colonies, free black men could vote along with whites, but in others they could not. John Adams, one of the most influential of the American founders, expressed a common view when he wrote that those without any property would be "too dependent on other men to have a will of their own . . . [and would] vote as they are directed by some man of property."[13] Because all voting at this time was done publicly—secret ballots were not common in the United States until the 1880s—the wealthy could intimidate those dependent on them for their livelihood to vote as they wished. Nonetheless, property qualifications for voting were modest enough that the percentage of free males who could vote ranged from a low of 50% in some colonies to as high as 80% in others.[14] (We return to the issue of voting qualifications later in the chapter.)

Despite these restrictions on voting, by 1776 democratic principles and practices were deeply rooted in the American colonies.

Why the Framers Chose Representative Democracy

From its inception, American national government has been exclusively a representative democracy. Unlike the ancient Athenians, Americans cannot make their own national laws, decide whether to go to war, choose military leaders, or form alliances with other countries. Of course, in 1787, when the Constitution was written, there was no real choice: direct democracy at the national level was not an option because the nation was too large and transportation too primitive for the citizens to gather together to debate and vote. Citizens would have to go through representatives to make their views known. The American founders called this kind of government a **republic**, where the people rule themselves through elected representatives, and distinguished it from a "pure democracy," where the people "assemble and administer the government in person."[15]

The founders believed that direct, or pure, democracy was not only impractical for the new nation but also dangerous. James Madison, the Virginian who is sometimes called the "Father of the Constitution," explained why in *The Federalist Papers* (also called *The Federalist*), essays he coauthored urging the ratification of the Constitution in 1787 and 1788. "In the ancient republics," Madison wrote, "where the whole body of the people assembled in person, a single orator, or an artful statesman, was generally seen to rule with as complete a sway as if a scepter had been placed in his single hand."[16] Although ultimate power resided with the people, too often skilled orators were able to manipulate public opinion to their own views.

Another problem was that majorities in the Greek democracies sometimes used their political power to oppress minorities and violate their rights. Madison called this the problem of **majority faction**. As he explained in his famous tenth essay in *The Federalist*, a faction is a group of citizens "who are united and actuated by some common impulse of passion, or of interest, adverse to the rights of other citizens, or to the permanent and aggregate interests of the community."[17] Direct democracies cannot solve the problem of faction because majorities can easily have their way. History shows that such democracies have been "spectacles of turbulence and contention" and "incompatible with personal security or the rights of property."[18]

Madison argued that representative democracy, or republican government, had two great advantages over direct democracy. First, if properly designed, it could "refine and enlarge the public views, by passing them through the medium of a chosen body of citizens, whose wisdom may best discern the true interest of their country and whose patriotism and love of justice will be least likely to sacrifice it to temporary or partial considerations."[19] Elected representatives should neither defer to public opinion nor simply replace public views with their own judgments. Instead, they should "refine and enlarge" public opinion with their own wisdom, patriotism, and love of justice.

Republic—as the American founders used the term, equivalent to a representative democracy.

Majority faction—defined by James Madison in *Federalist 10* as a majority of the people brought together by a common passion or interest adverse to the rights of other citizens or to the permanent and aggregate interests of the community.

In effect, representatives would deliberate *for their constituents*, giving voice to "the cool and deliberate sense of the community" that ought to rule in free governments.[20] "[I]t may well happen," Madison explained, "that the public voice, pronounced by the representatives of the people, will be more consonant to the public good than if pronounced by the people themselves, convened for the purpose."[21] A properly designed representative body of elected and accountable officials would generally make sounder judgments about the public good, while remaining true to underlying public desires, than would the people themselves acting directly.

Another advantage of a representative democracy is that it can extend over a much larger territory than can a direct democracy. Consequently, it can include "a greater variety of parties and interests," making it less likely that a majority will come together to oppress a minority.[22] Madison believed that a majority would seldom come together in such a large country, except on principles "of justice and the general good."[23] Contrary to some modern interpretations, those who designed American democracy did not reduce politics to the mere clash of interests.

To achieve justice and the general good, political leaders would sometimes have to defend the people "against their own temporary errors and delusions."[24] Alexander Hamilton, coauthor of *The Federalist Papers* and Madison's close ally in the ratification struggle, wrote that although "the people commonly *intend* the public good," they do not "always *reason right* about the *means* of promoting it." At these times, public officials have a "duty . . . to withstand the temporary delusion in order to give [the people] time and opportunity for more cool and sedate reflection."[25] Note that Madison and Hamilton were advocating a *temporary* resistance to unwise public desires, not long-standing opposition. They wanted the leaders to give the people a chance to deliberate more fully, to engage in "more cool and sedate reflection."[26] Ideally, "reason, justice, and truth" would eventually "regain their authority over the public mind."[27]

Direct Democracy in Modern American Politics

Despite the complete absence of direct democracy from American national government, some kinds of direct democracy exist today in the United States. As noted earlier, in some small New England towns, citizens still gather to debate and decide such matters as the town budget, property tax rates, public school financing, police and fire protection, and street repair.

A more common form of direct democracy is the use of initiatives and referenda, allowed in about half of the states, mostly in the West. Through these devices, citizens make their own laws. Although the terms are often used interchangeably, an **initiative** allows the citizens to draft a proposed law or constitutional amendment and place it on the ballot if enough registered voters sign petitions requesting it. A **referendum** is a proposed law or constitutional amendment, usually written by legislators, that is sent to the people for a vote. For both initiatives and referenda, the measure becomes law if a majority of voters approve. (A few states require supermajorities, such as three-fifths or two-thirds, to pass some measures, such as tax increases.) Between 1898, when South Dakota became the first state to allow its citizens to make laws directly, and 2007, citizens placed 2,236 initiatives on the ballot in 24 states and passed 908 (41%).[28]

These devices of direct democracy owe their origin to the **progressive movement** of the late nineteenth and early twentieth centuries that attacked political corruption and the failure of government to address social ills. Progressives sought to empower citizens to combat "political machines" and unresponsive government. Many of their proposals were never enacted, but initiatives and referenda remain their lasting legacy.

Applying the Definition: Rule by the People

Not every nation that calls itself a democracy allows the people to rule. A striking example is North Korea, whose official name is the Democratic People's Republic of Korea. Yet, as one of the few remaining Communist countries in the world, North Korea bars opposition parties, free elections, or any kind of public opposition to the regime. To isolate its people, the government prohibits them from owning cell phones, accessing the Internet, or even

**FOCUS
QUESTION**

Can a representative democracy be a genuine democracy? Can the people truly rule themselves if the governing power is held not by them directly but by elected officials?

Initiative—a proposed state law or constitutional amendment that appears on the ballot for a popular vote if enough registered voters sign petitions so requesting. (See also **Referendum**.)

Referendum—a proposed law or constitutional amendment, usually written by legislators, that is sent to the people for a vote. (See also **Initiative**.)

Progressive movement—a political reform movement of the late nineteenth and early twentieth centuries that attacked political corruption and the failure of government to address social ills.

listening to foreign radio stations.[29] How, then, can the leaders of North Korea possibly consider it a democracy? They do so because they claim that the government serves the true interests of the people—even though the people have no say in the decision-making process.

This understanding of democracy is a far cry from what is perhaps the best short definition, penned by Abraham Lincoln at the end of his Gettysburg Address of 1863: "government of the people, by the people, for the people." Democracy requires more than that some ruling elite govern *for* the people. Democratic government must also emerge out *of* the people and be exercised *by* the people.

This is the principle of **popular sovereignty**: that all political power derives from the people. The United States was the first modern nation to embrace it. As the Declaration of Independence famously states, "Governments are instituted among Men, deriving their just Powers from the Consent of the Governed." And, as the Preamble to the Constitution announced in 1787, "We, the people of the United States . . . do ordain and establish this Constitution for the United States of America." Today, many nations in the world ground their governing institutions on the principle of popular sovereignty, and others give it at least lip service.

The words of Abraham Lincoln's Gettysburg Address, delivered on November 19, 1863, are etched on the wall of the Lincoln Memorial in Washington, DC. The speech contains perhaps the best-known short definition of democracy: government of the people, by the people, for the people.

Popular sovereignty—the principle that all political power derives from the people.

Free Elections and Democratic Accountability

In a genuine democracy, the people can form political parties to advance their goals, try to persuade their fellow citizens through a free press and media, and vote for candidates of their choice without fear or intimidation. No government that denies these freedoms is a true democracy, even if it carries out elections of some sort. If government bans opposition parties or denies them access to the airwaves to spread their message, it undermines true self-government.

Also, democratic peoples use open communications and free elections to hold their officials accountable for their actions. "Every magistrate," Hamilton wrote, "ought to be personally responsible for his behavior in office."[30] Elected officials are directly accountable when they present themselves for reelection. Top appointed officials are indirectly accountable to the people through their elected superiors.

Democracies can face danger from elected leaders who subvert the system to prolong their power. An infamous case is Adolf Hitler, who democratically gained power in Germany in the 1930s but then made himself an all-powerful "Führer" and dictator. More recently, a U.S. State Department official warned of "those who would use the democratic process to come to power, only to destroy that very process in order to retain power and political dominance. While we believe in the principle 'one person, one vote,' we do not support 'one person, one vote, one time.'"[31] It is not enough to elect leaders one time. Democracy requires a process of ongoing accountability to the people.

Democracy, then, refers broadly to the *means*, or mechanisms, of government by which the people rule themselves. It requires free elections in which candidates and political parties compete for popular support and in which public officials are held accountable for their conduct. The term *democracy* does not, itself, specify the *ends* or purposes of government. These can differ from one democracy to another, and they can change over time. We begin with the goals of American democracy and then examine democracies elsewhere.

FREEDOM AND AMERICAN DEMOCRACY

MAJOR ISSUES

- What are the key principles and goals of American democracy as stated in the nation's founding document, the Declaration of Independence?
- How have these principles influenced American history?

Declaration of Independence— document approved by the Second Continental Congress on July 4, 1776, that articulated the principles of natural rights and consent of the governed, detailed the numerous ways in which King George III of Britain had violated the colonists' rights, and declared the former 13 colonies to be independent of Britain.

The United States was founded on a creed, or set of beliefs, about the foundations and purpose of government. That creed is set forth in the **Declaration of Independence** of July 4, 1776, which announced to the world that the 13 united colonies were casting off British rule and forming an independent nation because the king had undermined the very purpose of government: to secure the people's rights to life, liberty, and the pursuit of happiness. As we shall see throughout this book, Americans still define the purposes of government in light of the goals articulated in the Declaration. (For the United States at the time of the founding, see Figure 1-1.)

Choosing Independence

Serious fighting between the American colonists and British troops broke out at Lexington and Concord in April 1775. This was the culmination of a decade of conflict in which King George III had imposed taxes on the colonists without their consent, undermined the right to trial by jury, forced colonists to house British troops, closed the port of Boston, restricted colonial trade to Britain and the British West Indies, and closed the North Atlantic fishing grounds to American vessels.

In May, delegates from the colonies met as the Second Continental Congress in Philadelphia. A month later, they authorized the raising of a Continental Army and made George Washington of Virginia, who had distinguished himself as an officer in the French and Indian War (1754–1763), its commander in chief. Then, on June 17, colonial and British forces fought the bloody Battle of Bunker Hill (actually fought on Breed's Hill) in Charlestown, Massachusetts, next to Boston. The British won the engagement but at a surprisingly heavy cost: over 200 killed and more than 800 wounded. Americans suffered half as many casualties.

In August 1775, the king issued a proclamation accusing the Americans of "open and avowed rebellion" and later announced his willingness to use foreign troops to put down the rebellion. Parliament then passed, and the king signed, a law prohibiting all commerce with the colonies, making American vessels subject to forfeit to the Crown, and authorizing the impressment (forced recruitment) of American sailors into the Royal Navy. John Adams, serving in the Continental Congress, greeted the news

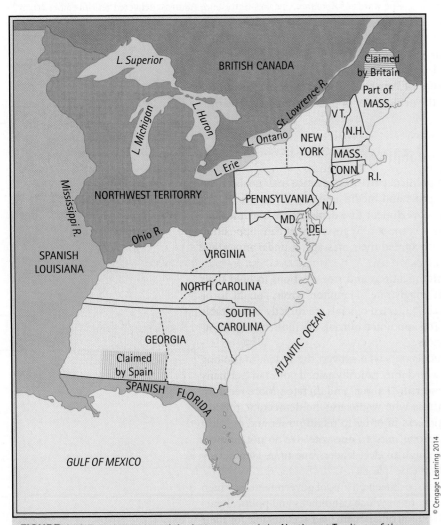

FIGURE 1-1 This shows the original 13 states and the Northwest Territory of the new nation. The four southernmost states later ceded lands to their west that became separate states.

© Cengage Learning 2014

as "a compleat Dismemberment of the British Empire. It throws thirteen Colonies out of the Royal Protection."[32]

Relations continued to deteriorate during the last half of 1775 and the first half of 1776. Serious fighting broke out in Virginia, and its royal governor burned Norfolk. Farther north, colonial troops failed to take Quebec, but colonists captured heavy guns from Fort Ticonderoga in New York and brought them to Dorchester Heights, overlooking Boston Harbor. This forced the British fleet and army to evacuate Boston in March 1776. But the king did not back down: in June, large British fleets with thousands of troops arrived off New York City and Charleston, South Carolina.

The publication of the pamphlet *Common Sense* in Philadelphia the previous January had helped prepare

On April 19, 1775, colonial militia confronted British regular forces in the town of Lexington, eight miles northwest of Boston. No one knows who fired "the shot heard around the world."

the public mind for a complete break with Britain. Published anonymously, the author was Thomas Paine, who had migrated to the colonies from England in 1774. Paine had been in the colonies for only a year when he took up the task of persuading the still reluctant Americans to break with Britain. *Common Sense* proved to be hugely popular, with sales eventually reaching half a million—a phenomenal number in colonies with about three million free people.

Unlike most American colonists, who denounced the abuses of the king and Parliament but generally respected the British system of government, Paine attacked the very nature of monarchy and aristocracy. The hereditary principle, he wrote, often placed government in the hands of "the most ignorant and unfit." In pursuing power and glory, monarchs had too often "laid . . . the world in blood and ashes."[33] Paine insisted that America did not need Britain to prosper and that the colonies, if united, had sufficient strength to achieve independence. By the spring and summer of 1776, many colonists had come to agree. On July 2, the Continental Congress voted for independence and two days later approved the document announcing its decision to the world (see Myths and Misinformation on the fate of the signers of the Declaration).

Common Sense—an influential pamphlet written by Thomas Paine and published in Philadelphia in January 1776 that urged the American colonists to break away from British rule and become an independent nation.

Expressing the American Mind: The Declaration of Independence

Reflecting on the Declaration of Independence half a century later, Thomas Jefferson, its principal author, wrote that its purpose was not "to find out new principles, or new arguments, never before thought of," but "to place before mankind the common sense of the subject, in terms so plain and firm as to command their assent." The Declaration, Jefferson said, "was intended to be an expression of the American mind, and to give to that expression the proper tone and spirit called for by the occasion."[35] In 1776, Americans believed most fundamentally that the purpose of government was to secure rights to which all were entitled by their nature as human beings. Here we examine and explain the key principles of the nation's founding document (see Myths and Misinformation on the fate of the signers of the Declaration).

We Hold These Truths to Be Self-Evident

Perhaps the best-known and most important words ever written or spoken by an American are those that begin the second paragraph of the Declaration of Independence: "We hold these truths to be self-evident, that all men are created equal, that they are endowed by

MYTHS AND MISINFORMATION

The Fate of the Signers of the Declaration of Independence

The 56 men who signed the Declaration of Independence were fully aware that their act would be viewed by British authorities as nothing less than treason, for which the common penalty was death. Thus the quip attributed to Benjamin Franklin—"We must all hang together, or assuredly we shall all hang separately"—had a very serious point.

What price did the signers of the Declaration pay for their revolt against the king? Around Independence Day in 2000, a story spread through newspaper columns and the Internet that purported to catalog the fate of the signers of the Declaration. It has now become part of the folklore about the American founders. The following table highlights in the left column key elements of this story and in the right column the facts of the case.

Internet Story	Fact
Five signers were captured by the British as traitors and tortured before they died. Twelve had their homes ransacked and burned. Two lost their sons who served in the Revolutionary Army. Another two had sons captured. Nine of the 56 fought and died from wounds or hardships of the Revolutionary War.	Although five signers were captured by the British, mainly during battle, none was killed or tortured in captivity. One, however, was released in ill health, which may have hastened his death. Contrary to the claim that nine died from wounds or hardships of the war, only two were wounded in action, and neither died of the wounds.
Carter Braxton of Virginia, a wealthy planter and trader, saw his ships swept from the seas by the British Navy. He sold his home and properties to pay his debts, and he died in rags.	Braxton did suffer financially as a result of the war but still owned the home he had built in 1767 (and perhaps another) when he died in 1797 at the age of 61.
Thomas McKean was so hounded by the British that he was forced to move his family constantly. . . . His possessions were taken, and poverty was his reward.	McKean did have to move his family several times during the war, but if "poverty was his reward," it was only temporary. Later to serve 22 years as chief justice of the Pennsylvania Superior Court and 9 years as governor, he died in 1817 at the age of 83 with a large estate of stocks, bonds, and tracts of land.
The home of Francis Lewis was destroyed. The enemy jailed his wife, and she died within a few months.	Although Francis Lewis's home was indeed destroyed by the British and his wife captured, she was eventually freed through an exchange for the wives of British officials and died more than two years after her capture—although the hardships of captivity may have contributed to her death.

None of this, of course, denies the real hardships of the war—25,000 Americans died—or the risks that the signers took in publicly committing themselves to opposing the king. (See the discussion below of the solemn oath that the signers of the Declaration took.)[34]

their Creator with certain inalienable Rights, that among these are Life, Liberty, and the Pursuit of Happiness." What does it mean to call truths "self-evident"? The dictionary tells us that *self-evident* means "evident without proof or reasoning."[36] In the words of Alexander Hamilton, a self-evident truth is one that "carries its own evidence along with it, and may be obscured, but cannot be made plainer by argument or reasoning."[37] For the American founders, the fundamental truths articulated by the Declaration were the essential starting point in political reasoning.

Three-fourths of a century later, Abraham Lincoln compared the statements of the Declaration to geometry. Although you could teach "any sane child that the simpler propositions of Euclid are true," you "would fail, utterly, with one who should deny the definitions and axioms." "The principles of Jefferson," Lincoln held, "are the definitions and axioms of free society."[38] The authors of the Declaration knew that although most Americans accepted the truths of the Declaration, most people elsewhere probably did not; but, as we shall see, they hoped that enlightenment on these essential political principles would spread widely.

That All Men Are Created Equal

The first and most fundamental truth is "that all men are created equal." To say that this is a self-evident truth is to say that equality is a fundamental characteristic of what it means to be a man. This raises two important questions: What did the authors mean by "all men," and what did they mean by "created equal"?

Decades later, some argued that because most blacks in the new nation were held in slavery and because women and poor men could not vote in the new states, the founders must have understood the principles of the Declaration to apply only to whites, or only to white men, or perhaps only to white men who owned property. Yet, the founders themselves said no such thing, and when they discussed rights, they commonly used language that referred to all human beings, such as "rights of mankind," "rights of humanity," "rights of human nature," "human rights," and "rights of nature." As Hamilton wrote in 1775, "Natural liberty is a gift of the beneficent Creator to the whole human race."[39]

When the Declaration was written, it was quite common to use the word *man* or *men* for human beings generally; and there is no evidence in the document itself that females or nonwhite races were excluded. For example, the Declaration uses the word *men* twice but the word *people* eight times, once in the phrase "the rights of the people." *Men* and *people* seem to be used synonymously to refer to human beings generally. We sometimes forget just how common it used to be to use the words *man* and *men* in this way. As recently as the 1960s, the U.S. Supreme Court used the phrases "one man, one vote" and "one person, one vote" interchangeably. *Man* in the phrase "one man, one vote" meant simply "person" or "human being."

It is important to distinguish between asserting a right and claiming that everyone is actually enjoying it. As Lincoln explained in an important speech in 1857, the authors of the Declaration "did not mean to assert the obvious untruth, that all were then actually enjoying that equality, nor yet, that they were about to confer it immediately upon them. . . . They meant

COMMON SENSE;

ADDRESSED TO THE

INHABITANTS

OF

AMERICA,

On the following interesting

SUBJECTS.

I. Of the Origin and Design of Government in general, with concise Remarks on the English Constitution.

II. Of Monarchy and Hereditary Succession.

III. Thoughts on the present State of American Affairs.

IV. Of the present Ability of America, with some miscellaneous Reflections.

Man knows no Master save creating HEAVEN,
Or those whom choice and common good ordain.
THOMSON.

PHILADELPHIA;

Printed, and Sold, by R. BELL, in Third-Street.

MDCCLXXVI.

Library of Congress

Thomas Paine's *Common Sense* was published in Philadelphia in January 1776. It was an immediate hit, eventually selling half a million copies.

The Second Paragraph of the Declaration of Independence

We hold these truths to be self-evident, that all men are created equal, that they are endowed by their Creator with certain inalienable Rights, that among these are Life, Liberty and the pursuit of Happiness. —That to secure these rights, Governments are instituted among Men, deriving their just powers from the consent of the governed, —That whenever any Form of Government becomes destructive of these ends, it is the Right of the People to alter or to abolish it, and to institute new Government, laying its foundation on such principles and organizing its powers in such form, as to them shall seem most likely to effect their Safety and Happiness. Prudence, indeed, will dictate that Governments long established should not be changed for light and transient causes; and accordingly all experience hath shewn, that mankind are more disposed to suffer, while evils are sufferable, than to right themselves by abolishing the forms to which they are accustomed. But when a long train of abuses and usurpations, pursuing invariably the same Object evinces a design to reduce them under absolute Despotism, it is their right, it is their duty, to throw off such Government, and to provide new Guards for their future security. —Such has been the patient sufferance of these Colonies; and such is now the necessity which constrains them to alter their former Systems of Government. The history of the present King of Great Britain is a history of repeated injuries and usurpations, all having in direct object the establishment of an absolute Tyranny over these States. To prove this, let Facts be submitted to a candid world.

In 1819, John Trumbull completed this 12' × 18' oil-on-canvas painting of the presentation of the draft of the Declaration of Independence to the Second Continental Congress. The five-member drafting committee faces John Hancock, the president of the Congress. Jefferson is the tall redhead, and John Adams is the third to his left. The painting has hung in the Rotunda of the Capitol Building in Washington, DC, since 1826. The event depicted is often mistaken for the signing of the Declaration.

simply to declare the *right*, so that the *enforcement* of it might follow as fast as circumstances should permit."[40]

On the second point—the meaning of "created equal"—the Declaration itself is clear: all are equal in that "they are endowed by their Creator with certain inalienable Rights." All have an equal claim to these rights; no one by birth, talent, or wealth has a greater claim to these rights than does any other.

What does it mean, then, to call these rights "inalienable"? (*Inalienable* was changed to *unalienable* in the printed version of the Declaration.) To *alienate* is to transfer or withdraw. "Inalienable Rights" are those that government cannot take away and that the people themselves cannot give away. The adjective *inalienable*, however, does not mean that the rights are absolute or cannot be legitimately regulated by the state, as we discuss later.

Life, Liberty, and the Pursuit of Happiness

What, then, are these inalienable rights? According to the Declaration, "among these are Life, Liberty, and the Pursuit of Happiness." Because all persons are entitled to these by their very nature as human beings, we call these **natural rights**. Almost a century before the American founding, the influential English philosopher John Locke (1632–1704) had written, in his *Second Treatise of Government,* that the purpose of government was to secure "the Lives, Liberties, and Estates of the People."[41] Locke held that the right to rule derived from popular consent and that the very purpose of government was to secure the people's rights. His writings on government were so highly regarded in the American colonies that Jefferson prominently displayed his portrait at his home, Monticello, and called him one "of the three greatest men the world had ever produced."[42]

Many of the new states wrote their own declarations of rights and used language similar to that in the Declaration of Independence. The Virginia Declaration of Rights, adopted in June of 1776, asserted that "all men are by nature equally free and independent and have certain inherent rights, . . . namely, the enjoyment of life and liberty, with the means of acquiring and possessing property, and pursuing and obtaining happiness and safety." The Massachusetts Constitution of 1780 identified "the right of enjoying and defending their lives and liberties; that of acquiring, possessing, and protecting property; in fine, that of seeking and obtaining their safety and happiness." Other states employed comparable language.

Unlike Locke's *Second Treatise* and the stated declarations of rights, the Declaration of Independence does not specifically mention the right to acquire or possess property. Nonetheless, it was widely believed by early Americans that one of man's most important liberties was the right to gain and hold property. And few would have disputed the idea in the Massachusetts Constitution that "acquiring, possessing, and protecting property" may be necessary for "safety and happiness."

To Secure These Rights, Governments Are Instituted among Men

This passage is the first mention of government in the Declaration. Men possess rights by their very nature, but these rights are not secure without government. Why not? Although

Natural rights—rights to which all people are entitled by their very nature as human beings, such as those cited in the Declaration of Independence: "Life, Liberty, and the Pursuit of Happiness."

FOCUS
QUESTION

The Declaration of Independence says that everyone has a right to pursue happiness, but it does not say that everyone has the right to achieve happiness. How important is this difference? Would modern Americans think of the obligations of government any differently if the Declaration had said that everyone had the right to achieve happiness?

the Declaration does not expressly say, we know that the leading thinkers in the colonies were influenced by the doctrine of a **state of nature** that preceded civil society, formulated initially by the English philosopher Thomas Hobbes (1588–1679) and later elaborated by Locke.

In the state of nature, there is no common authority to settle disputes and thus no one to protect the weaker from the stronger. In such a state, Hobbes famously wrote, the life of man is "solitary, poore, nasty, brutish, and short."[43] And according to Locke, "To avoid this State of War . . . is one great *reason of Mens putting themselves into Society*, and quitting the State of Nature."[44] Thus, the Declaration of Independence, written to justify a revolution against a government that was undermining rights, affirms that government itself is necessary to secure rights.

Deriving Their Just Powers from the Consent of the Governed

Just powers depend on the **consent of the governed** because no one has the right to govern another without that person's consent. But what form must or should consent take? The Declaration does not say. At the time of the founding, political thinkers often distinguished between active consent and tacit consent. **Active consent** occurs when the people show their acceptance of government by participating in the political system by voting, running for office, and in other ways. **Tacit consent**, on the other hand, might include the people agreeing to vest executive powers in a king for whom they could not vote, as most British citizens probably did at the time of the American Revolution. The British king was, nonetheless, limited by the various legal rights secured to British citizens and by the need to get Parliament's approval to raise revenues and to pass new laws. We call this type of government a **constitutional monarchy**.

Although Thomas Paine had opposed all hereditary government as illegitimate and dangerous, the Declaration does not go this far. It was not George III's *status* as king that justified revolution, but rather his *behavior* as king: the "long train of abuses and usurpations" for which he was responsible. The Declaration's lengthy indictment against the king (about one-half of the document) makes it clear that if a monarch is to wield power, he must be constrained by (1) a legislative branch that controls taxes, (2) an independent judiciary, (3) civilian control of the military, and (4) respect for the rights of the citizens.

It Is the Right of the People to Alter or Abolish It

Because the very purpose of government is to secure the rights to life, liberty, and the pursuit of happiness, it is legitimate to "alter" or "abolish" government if it "becomes destructive of these ends." The people may then establish new government that will better promote their "safety and happiness." In a mere 110 words, the authors of the Declaration laid the philosophical foundations for their revolution. (Interestingly, the words *revolt* and *revolution* do not appear in the Declaration.) But before the Declaration presents the evidence that the king's actions justify revolution, it adds some qualifying language.

Prudence, Indeed, Will Dictate

Prudence dictates "that Governments long established should not be changed for light and transient causes." What is "prudence," and why does it so dictate? Although to the modern ear *prudence* implies merely caution or circumspection, its older meaning, going back to ancient Greece, is broader: *practical wisdom*.

The ancient philosophers distinguished between practical wisdom—which is wisdom about such practical matters as government, politics, and ethics—and theoretical wisdom—which is deep knowledge about such subjects as metaphysics, physics, and mathematics. Practical wisdom, or prudence, is the key virtue of the statesman. Although we care little whether our political leaders are experts in metaphysics, science, or math, we very much value their ability to make sound practical judgments. George Washington's contemporaries, for example, recognized that though he had little formal education and was not particularly well read, he was a man of great wisdom about practical affairs: "no judgment was ever sounder," Jefferson wrote.[45] Why, then, does wisdom about practical matters weigh against revolting for "light and transient causes"?

State of nature—the doctrine developed particularly by English philosophers Thomas Hobbes and John Locke that refers to a state of society that preceded civil society. In a state of nature, there is no common authority to settle disputes and thus no one to protect the weaker from the stronger.

Consent of the governed—the principle that no one has the right to govern another without that other person's consent.

Active consent—the consent to government that people demonstrate in democracies by participating in the political system, especially by voting.

Tacit consent—the consent that people may give to government even if they do not actively participate.

Constitutional monarchy—rule by a monarch, such as a king, who is restrained by a constitution that defines his powers.

Prudence—as used in the Declaration of Independence, refers to wisdom about practical affairs. It is the virtue associated with having good judgment and making sound decisions in government and politics.

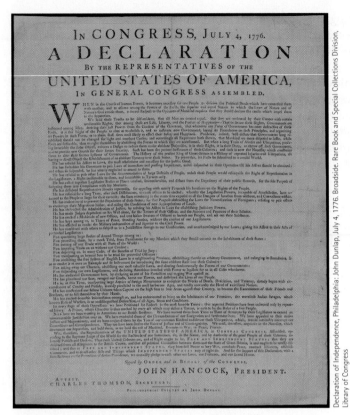

This is the first printed version of the Declaration of Independence, as it was distributed to the states by the Second Continental Congress.

The founders knew that revolutions are serious matters that lead to misery and death. They often fail and can result in political repression worse than what caused them. Frequent revolutions could lead to anarchy, throwing people back into the warlike "state of nature" that led to the creation of government in the first place. It follows that if the government's abuses are "light"—not a serious deprivation of rights—and "transient"—not likely to last long—then the wise course of action is to endure the hardship until it passes or work to address it in other less radical, ways. Indeed, as the Declaration notes, this is how people tend to react in such situations. But when they face "a long train of abuses and usurpations" directed toward the establishment of an "absolute despotism," then they have the "right" and even the "duty" to revolt.

The Concluding Oath

The delegates concluded their document with a solemn oath:

> And for the support of this Declaration, with a firm reliance on the protection of divine Providence, we mutually pledge to each other our Lives, our Fortunes and our sacred Honor.

The 56 men who signed the Declaration of Independence (after it had been handwritten on parchment some weeks later) understood full well the jeopardy they faced for an act the king would consider treason, a crime punishable by death. Although the first printed copies of the Declaration included only the names of John Hancock, a delegate from Massachusetts who was the president of the Congress, and Charles Thomson, the Congress's secretary, in January 1777 the Congress ordered another printing for a wider distribution. This copy had the list of all the signers.

Notice that the delegates did not say they would support the Declaration as long as it was in their interest to do so. They pledged to sacrifice their lives and fortunes, if necessary, for the cause of independence and the principles that justified it. Some things, they believed, were worth dying for. In politics, as in life more generally, people sometimes act out of principle and moral commitment, rather than mere self-interest.

Universal Principles

In 1859, Abraham Lincoln honored Thomas Jefferson for having had "the coolness, forecast, and capacity to introduce into a merely revolutionary document, an abstract truth, applicable to all men and all times."[46] The Declaration does not just defend the revolution of 1776; it sets forth a standard of justice against which we can judge *any* government. As Lincoln put it:

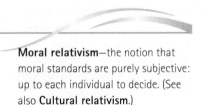

Moral relativism—the notion that moral standards are purely subjective: up to each individual to decide. (See also **Cultural relativism**.)

Cultural relativism—the notion that moral standards are purely derivative from the values of a particular culture or society: no society's standards can be said to be "better" or "worse" than those of another. (See also **Moral relativism**.)

> They meant to set up a standard maxim for free society, which should be familiar to all, and revered by all; constantly looked to, constantly labored for, and even though never perfectly attained, constantly approximated, and thereby constantly spreading and deepening its influence, and augmenting the happiness and value of life to all people of all colors everywhere.[47]

Thus, in the view of the American founders, the fundamental principles do not change over time, are not merely subjective values, and do not vary from one culture to another. This understanding is quite different from the common modern concepts of **moral relativism** and **cultural relativism**, which hold that moral standards are, respectively, either purely subjective—up to each individual to decide—or are purely derivative from the values of a particular culture.

Through their principles, the founders established a direction and goal for American politics. In many ways, American history can be seen as a record of extending the promises of the Declaration to ever larger groups of Americans (see especially Chapters 5 and 6). It is the belief in the universality of the principles of the Declaration that explains their influence beyond the confines of the conflict that split the American colonies from Britain in the 1770s.

In the 1850s, for example, a new political party formed, called the Republican Party, that opposed the extension of slavery into the federal territories by calling for a return to "the principles of Washington and Jefferson." "[W]e hold it to be a self-evident truth," the new party resolved at its convention in 1856, "that all men are endowed with the inalienable right to life, liberty, and the pursuit of happiness, and that the primary object and ulterior design of our Federal Government were to secure these rights to all persons under its exclusive jurisdiction."[48] As Lincoln put it two years before, "If the negro is a man, why then my ancient faith teaches me that 'all men are created equal'; and that there can be no moral right in connection with one man's making a slave of another."[49] Lincoln understood the Civil War to be at bottom a conflict over the meaning and application of the principles of the Declaration. The Thirteenth Amendment of 1865, which abolished slavery, was a vindication of those principles.

A century later, the civil rights struggles of the 1950s and 1960s again focused attention on the meaning and application of the principles of the Declaration. As Martin Luther King, Jr., told an audience of over 200,000 at the Lincoln Memorial in Washington, DC, on August 28, 1963 (with millions more following the event on radio or television):

> When the architects of our republic wrote the magnificent words of the Constitution and the Declaration of Independence, they were signing a promissory note to which every American was to fall heir. This note was a promise that all men, yes, black men as well as white men, would be guaranteed the inalienable rights of life, liberty, and the pursuit of happiness.

King called for the nation to "rise up and live out the true meaning of its creed—we hold these truths to be self-evident that all men are created equal."[50]

In King's view, the words of the Declaration of Independence, written to justify the overthrow of a tyrannical king, also justified the overthrow within the United States of racial oppression and state-imposed segregation nearly two centuries later. King understood "all men" in the Declaration to encompass all races, and he accepted the universality of the principles of human equality and human rights. The success of the Civil Rights Movement in ending legally enforced segregation and in attaining for black Americans the right to vote is testimony to the persuasiveness of King's appeal to "the true meaning" of the American creed. (For more on the Civil Rights Movement, see Chapter 6.)

The founders expected the principles of the Declaration to influence politics well beyond the confines of the United States. In his last letter, written just 10 days before his death on July 4, 1826, the Fiftieth anniversary of the Declaration of Independence, Jefferson described the Declaration as "an instrument pregnant with our own, and the fate of the world." He hoped it would be to all a "signal of arousing men to burst the chains [of oppression] . . . and to assume the blessings and security of self-government." "All eyes are opened, or opening," he wrote, "to the rights of man."[51] Jefferson would not have been surprised that pro-democracy demonstrators in Eastern Europe in 1989–1991 quoted the words of the Declaration in their struggle to end Communist rule. Nor would he have been surprised how, in March 2004, a leading Iraqi political figure defended his nation's new interim constitution against the charge that the rights it secured were distinctively Western: "These rights are not the exclusive property of the West, but are universal values. They should be followed in every time and place."[52]

Different Levels of Rights

To understand this spreading of rights, we should recognize that the founders distinguished between different levels, or kinds, of rights. Natural rights, as we have seen, are the fundamental rights to life, liberty, and the pursuit of happiness with which all men "are endowed

Civil rights—the rights that are accorded to citizens in a particular political community and that are regulated by the state, such as the right to sue in court, to defend one's person and property, to drive an automobile, etc.

by their Creator." But what happens to natural rights in civil society? Every person, for example, has a natural right to defend himself or herself from imminent danger. Yet in civil society, governments regulate this right through law, thereby translating the natural right to self-defense into a **civil right**. If citizens of the United States want to know when they can legally use deadly force against a robber or burglar who breaks into their home but does not immediately threaten their safety, they had better know the state law where they live, because in most states, but not all, lethal force cannot be used against a home invader unless the occupant is in imminent danger.

Also, one could argue that the natural right to liberty includes the right to travel and that any government that prohibits its citizens from traveling within the country is violating a natural right. Yet even the freest governments regulate travel in some ways. Speed limits, traffic lights, the rules of the road, and licensing requirements to use automobiles all regulate travel. We do not think of these restrictions as violating the natural right to travel because their very purpose is to promote *safe* travel. Thus, the use of an automobile is a civil right legitimately regulated by the state. In this respect, civil rights are a kind of practical approximation of natural rights.

So even though natural rights are "inalienable"—they cannot be taken away by government—they may be regulated in the interests of social order and to promote the effective enjoyment of the right itself. Yet the underlying source of the right is not government. According to the Declaration, human beings are born with rights, and government's job is to secure them. People have a right to defend themselves and to travel (and many other rights) not because government grants them permission to defend themselves and travel, but because they have a natural right to their life and liberty.

Political rights—the rights to influence governmental decisions in a democracy by voting for representatives and holding office. One can be a citizen (such as a convicted felon or a minor) without enjoying political rights.

Yet another category of rights, as understood by the founders, is **political rights**. These are the rights to influence governmental decisions by voting for representatives and holding office. One can be a citizen without enjoying political rights. Americans who are convicted felons, for example, are citizens but in many states today do not have the right to vote. Minors are also citizens who do not vote. At the time of the founding, women and the poorest Americans were citizens who enjoyed many of the rights of citizenship—such as the protections detailed in the Bill of Rights—but they could not vote.

Poor men, but not women, gained the vote during the founding era. By the 1790s, several states had abolished property qualifications for voting altogether, and in most states at least 90% of the free white males could vote. By the 1820s, property qualifications for voting were abolished in nearly all the states.[53] We recount the much longer struggle for full political equality for women in Chapter 6.

We have reviewed the nation's founding principles, but what is the status of freedom and democracy in the modern world? In the next section, we expand the focus to examine the growth of democratic institutions, the conditions that promote freedom in democratic governments, and the forces that threaten freedom and democracy.

DEMOCRACY AND FREEDOM IN THE MODERN WORLD

MAJOR ISSUES

- What are the essential characteristics of liberal democracies?
- What is the status of freedom and democracy in the modern world?

Liberal democracy—a democracy that works to secure the rights of its citizens and thus to promote their liberty, or freedoms.

When democracies work to secure the rights of their citizens, and thus to promote their freedoms, we call them **liberal democracies**. Democracy, as we have said, refers to the *means* or mechanisms of government by which the people rule themselves. *Liberal* refers to the *end* of government: liberty or freedom. Although the citizens of liberal democracies often disagree about exactly what liberties government should promote, there is, as we shall see, widespread agreement on many of the essential elements.

There is no guarantee that democracies will promote freedom as their principal goal. In this sense, democracies need not be liberal democracies. Indeed, many of the earliest settlements in New England, founded by Puritans, were democracies that sought to promote a certain brand of Christianity and strict personal morality. Nathaniel Hawthorne's widely read novel, *The Scarlet Letter,* presents a vivid portrait of Puritan Boston in the mid-seventeenth century, where the people embraced laws that sharply restricted personal freedom in the name of religion and morality. In fact, the modern adjective *puritanical* refers to attitudes or acts that unnecessarily restrict freedom in order to promote a rigid morality.

In addition, majorities may use their power to oppress minorities and violate their rights. One racial, ethnic, or language group might suppress the rights of another. One large region of a country might extract disproportionate benefits from government at the expense of a smaller one. The majority poor might confiscate the property of a wealthy few. One of the major problems that democracies face is how to get the majority who rule to promote the rights and interests of all. As we shall see in the next chapter, it was a key issue that faced the framers of the U.S. Constitution in 1787. It is also a major issue in the world today as more nations embrace democratic institutions and procedures. A different kind of problem is getting the relative few who wield the formal power in democratic nations to govern in the interests of the broader community.

The Growth of Democratic Institutions

The end of the **Cold War** in the late 1980s and early 1990s dramatically accelerated the growth of democratic institutions throughout the world. For nearly half a century, beginning after World War II ended in 1945, world politics was dominated by the clash between liberal democracies, led by the United States, and Communist nations, led by the Soviet Union. During this period, **Communism** was the governing philosophy in the Soviet Union, the states of Eastern Europe, mainland China (since 1949), and a few other smaller countries. Modern Communism owes its origins to the writings and activities of Karl Marx (1818–1883). His hugely influential *Communist Manifesto* of 1848, coauthored with Friedrich Engels, concluded by urging the world's workers to "forcibl[y] overthrow . . . all existing social conditions. Let the ruling classes tremble at a Communistic revolution. The proletarians have nothing to lose but their chains. They have a world to win. Working Men of All Countries, Unite!"[54]

Beginning with the Soviet Union in 1917, Communist states took ownership of "the means of production" (industry and agriculture); outlawed political parties other than the Communist Party; suppressed, to varying degrees, religious worship; and prohibited public opposition to the regime—all in the name of the "dictatorship of the proletariat." As the leader of Vietnam's Communist Party said in 1999, starkly clarifying the difference between Communism and liberal democracy, "Our people won't allow any political power-sharing with any other forces. Any ideas to promote 'absolute democracy,' to put human rights above sovereignty, or support multi-party or political pluralism, are lies and cheating."[55] In such regimes, a relative handful of party officials, heavily influenced by Communist ideology, conduct the key deliberations for the government. Opposing views—"political pluralism"—are not welcome and are typically outlawed.

Communism lost its hold in much of the world in the late 1980s. In a few short years, the Berlin Wall that divided Communist East Berlin from democratic West Berlin was torn down (1989); Germany reunified as formerly Communist East Germany was incorporated into democratic West Germany (1990); the Soviet Union dissolved into 15 separate nations (1991); and Communists were driven from power in the countries of Eastern Europe and the former Soviet Union. To varying degrees, these nations adopted the institutions and practices of liberal democracy. Despite this upheaval, Communism remains in control of the People's Republic of China (with one-fifth of the world's people) and such small nations as Cuba, Vietnam, and North Korea.

Besides genuine democracies and Communist nations, other forms of government in the modern world include rule by powerful individuals—such as civilian dictators, military strongmen, and monarchs—and by religious leaders. Some countries have no

Cold War—the period between the end of World War II (1945) and the collapse of Communism in Eastern Europe and the Soviet Union (1989–1991) when world politics was dominated by the clash between liberal democracies, led by the United States, and Communist nations, led by the Soviet Union.

Communism—an ideology and form of government in which the state takes ownership of "the means of production" (industry and agriculture); outlaws political parties other than the Communist Party; suppresses religious worship to various degrees; and prohibits public opposition to the regime.

FOCUS QUESTION

Is there anything inevitable about the spread of freedom and democracy throughout the world? Should we expect that a century from now more of the world's peoples will live in free and democratic nations than now do? What forces, if any, might slow, or perhaps reverse, the spread of freedom and democracy?

International Perspectives

The "Arab Spring" and the Challenge of Promoting Freedom and Democracy

Thousands of Egyptians demonstrate in Tahrir Square in Cairo, Egypt in September, 2011.

On December 17, 2010, a street vendor in a town in Tunisia in North Africa set himself on fire to protest continued harassment and demands for bribes by local officials. This sparked public protests throughout the country by Tunisians fed up with poverty and political repression. Similar protests then spread to countries throughout North Africa and the Middle East. This political movement, in which millions demanded economic reforms and an end to political repression, became known as the "Arab Spring." It had its greatest effects in Tunisia, Egypt, Libya, Yemen, and Syria.

In January 2011, the autocratic leader of Tunisia fled the nation. By the end of the year, he had been replaced by a freely elected president and prime minister. By February 2011, Egyptian president Hosni Mubarak was forced from office, leaving a military council temporarily in charge. Parliamentary elections took place in November, and a new People's Assembly met for the first time in January 2012. By the end of 2011, Yemen's leader transferred power to his vice president, who was elected president in his own right in February 2012. In Libya, opponents of dictator Moammar Kadafi took up arms against the regime. In March 2011, NATO forces launched a campaign of air strikes to assist the rebels, who had been on the verge of defeat. Kadafi was forced from power in August and was killed by rebel forces in October. A provisional government with international support took power. In Syria, protests against the repressive regime of President Bashar al-Assad spread throughout the country in 2011 and 2012. Assad responded with a brutal crackdown and managed to hold onto power. Protests in other North African and

Middle Eastern countries, such as Morocco, Algeria, Jordan, Oman, and Bahrain, led to a variety of reforms including, in some cases, constitutional change.

It is too soon to know whether the protests that began in December 2010 will result in stable democracies that promote human freedom. As one commentator put it, "The experiment has only begun in the Middle East." Perhaps the greatest question mark is the future of Egypt, the most populous and powerful of the countries in the region. In the elections for the new parliament, the party representing the Muslim Brotherhood won about half of the seats and the Al-Nour Party a quarter. The Muslim Brotherhood was founded in 1928 to promote the implementation of Islamic law in all aspects of life. The Al-Nour Party, founded as a political organization in 2011, represents fundamentalist Salafists who embrace, if anything, an even stricter approach to the fusion of politics and Islam. Tunisia's government outlaws Salafist political parties because of their refusal to accept the principles of electoral democracy.

As noted in the text, there is no guarantee that democracies will promote freedom. Just as the democracy of Puritan Massachusetts suppressed freedom in the mid-1600s in order to promote a particular religion and a strict moral code, so also might the new Egyptian democracy of the early twenty-first century. Concerned observers point to a poll conducted by the Pew Research Center in 2010 that found that 54% of Egyptians support the segregation of men and women in the workplace, 82% favor stoning adulterers, and 84% support executing those who leave the Muslim religion. Nonetheless, it is also possible that the Egyptian people, now enjoying the fruits of genuine self-government, may demand the kinds of political freedoms and civil liberties common in advanced democracies throughout the world.[56]

CRITICAL THINKING QUESTION

One of the troubling possibilities that face newly democratizing nations is that parties and groups may gain power through democratic means and then suppress or subvert democracy and freedom in the name of religion, virtue, or some other end. In light of this possibility, should these new governments give all parties and groups the opportunity to win elections and gain power, or should ballot access be limited to those committed to the principles of freedom and electoral democracy?

representative institutions at all, such as Saudi Arabia (a monarchy). In others, elected bodies are little more than puppets of powerful individuals or, as in Iran, are subordinate to religious leaders who wield the real power. Countries without effective representative institutions are those in which rights and liberties are most in jeopardy. In these countries, political deliberation is concentrated in a small number of elites, divorced from public opinion and public desires.

How many nations, then, promote freedom? Each year, an independent, nongovernmental organization called Freedom House publishes *Freedom in the World*, which analyzes the extent to which the world's 195 nations secure and promote political rights (such as voting and organizing political parties) and civil liberties (such as freedom of speech and religious worship). For 2011, it found that 87 nations (with 43% of the world's population) were free, 60 nations (with 22% of the world's population) were partly free, and 48 nations (with 35% of the world's population) were not free. The long-term trends were strongly positive. From 1976 to 2011, the number of free nations more than doubled from 42 to 87, and the number of nations not free dropped from 68 to 48. In just the 19-year period from 1992 to 2011, the number of people

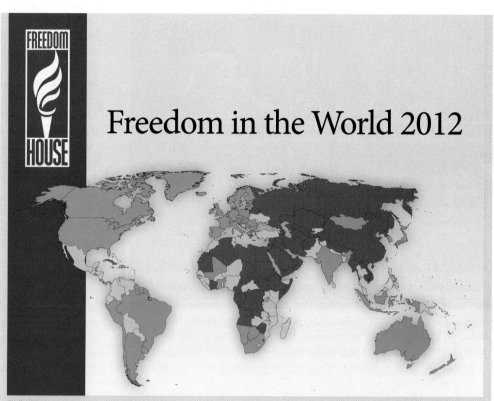

FIGURE 1-2 Each year Freedom House publishes a detailed report and map showing the status of political rights and civil liberties throughout the world. Freedom House classifies the countries in green as "free" because they allow open political competition, respect civil liberties, and have independent media. Countries in yellow are "partly free" because there is only limited respect for political rights and civil liberties due to corruption, weak rule of law, single-party dominance, or other factors. Countries in purple are "not free" because they deny basic political rights and civil liberties. SOURCE: Courtesy of www.freedomhouse.org

living in free nations grew from 1.4 billion to 3.0 billion, and the proportion of the world's population living in free nations grew from 25% to 43%.[57] (See the Freedom House map in Figure 1-2 and the International Perspectives feature on page 20.)

Terrorism, Freedom, and Democracy

Since the demise of the Cold War, a new threat to freedom and democracy has arisen: radical Islam and the terrorism that promotes it. Operating through **al Qaeda** and associated groups and appealing to just a tiny fraction of believing Muslims around the world, it is responsible for thousands of deaths in the past decade, including the following attacks:

- At the U.S. embassies in Kenya and Tanzania on August 7, 1998 (killing over 200 and wounding over 4,000)
- In the United States on September 11, 2001 (killing nearly 3,000)
- On the Indonesian island of Bali on October 12, 2002 (killing 202 and wounding 209), and on October 1, 2005 (killing 20 and wounding 129)
- On the railroads in Madrid, Spain, on March 11, 2004 (killing 191 and wounding 2,050)
- In the London subway system on July 7, 2005 (killing 52 and wounding 700)
- In Mumbai, India, in late November 2008 (killing 164 people and wounding over 300)

Al Qaeda—an international terrorist organization based on extremist Islamic beliefs and founded in the late 1980s by Osama bin Laden. It was responsible for the attacks on the United States of September 11, 2001.

Radicals and terrorists associated with al Qaeda publicly denounce democracy and freedom. One of these is a radical cleric in Indonesia who had served time in prison for his involvement in the bombing on Bali in 2002: "There is no democracy in Islam," he insisted. "God's law comes first. It is not up to the will of the people to decide what is right and how

A member of the religious police under the Taliban in Afghanistan beats a woman in the capital of Kabul in August 2001 for removing her burqa in public. American-led forces toppled the regime a few months later.

to live. Rather the will of the people . . . [must] be bent to suit the will of God. It is not democracy that we want, but Allah-cracy!"[58]

Despite such views of a few, two of the world's largest democracies have a majority Muslim population: Indonesia (with 248 million people—86% Muslim) and Turkey (with 80 million people—more than 99% Muslim). Radicals, such as the Indonesian cleric, vehemently oppose democratic institutions in such nations. Instead, they prefer regimes like the Taliban government in Afghanistan (1996–2001), which repressed and brutalized the Afghan people, especially women, and provided a safe haven to Osama bin Laden and his al Qaeda organization. After the attacks of September 11, 2001, the United States and allies assisted local forces in overthrowing the regime.

Although terrorist Islamic groups and their radical ideology pose the greatest threat in Muslim countries, they jeopardize public safety throughout the world. They also challenge liberal democracies to find ways to deal with the threat without undermining the very liberties these countries seek to promote. We say more about this last point in Chapter 5.

Public and Private Spheres

Totalitarian—a political system or ideology that places no limits on the reach of governmental power over the individual.

Both Communism and radical Islam are **totalitarian** ideologies. Because they embrace other goals as more important, they reject freedom as the purpose of government, and they reject any limits on the power of government to regulate the private lives of citizens. In liberal democracies, by contrast, the people largely control how they live. For the most part, government does not tell them where to live, whether or where they can travel, what occupation to pursue, with whom they can associate, what types of entertainment to enjoy, or whether and how to worship God. Nor does government, if true to its purposes, prohibit the mere expression of political views or subject citizens to arbitrary arrest and punishment.

Many in liberal democracies take these freedoms for granted, especially if they have not lived under repressive regimes. Yet, when government does *not* reach deeply into the private lives of citizens, that is itself the result of a political decision: a decision that government should have certain limited ends and that private citizens should decide for themselves what kind of life they will lead. In this respect, liberal democracies, unlike many of the alternatives, distinguish between the *private* and *public* spheres: the individual, not the state, is ultimately sovereign over much personal behavior.

Those who live in liberal democracies often disagree about where to draw the line between the public and the private. Views change over time (most Americans once thought that the government should prohibit the consumption of alcoholic beverages) and can differ from one country to another (broadcast television is racier in Europe than in the United States). Nonetheless, within liberal democracies most agree that there is a point beyond which government should not go in regulating personal behavior.

The Rule of Law

To be secure in their rights, individuals must be protected from arbitrary power. "The very definition of a republic," John Adams wrote in 1776, "is 'an empire of laws, and not of men.'" [59] By this Adams meant that law should replace the arbitrary will of political leaders. A few years later Adams helped to write a new constitution for his home state. The Massachusetts Constitution of 1780, the oldest written constitution still in effect anywhere in the world, famously expressed the rule-of-law principle after insisting on a separation of the powers of government into three distinct branches: "to the end it may be a government of laws and not of men."[60] Laws should be formally and publicly enacted by a proper legislative body, enforced by an accountable executive, and adjudicated in individual cases by independent courts. In 2011, the people of Kenya, in central Africa, adopted a new constitution to strengthen the rule of law and thereby constrain arbitrary executive power. As one of its leaders said, "The basic or core idea of the rule of law . . . is that the Government must be able to point to some basis for its actions that is regarded as valid by the relevant legal system."[61]

The **rule of law** is a necessary, but not sufficient, condition for securing rights. Liberal democracies themselves may have unjust laws, and tyrannies often use harsh laws to oppress the people and stifle dissent. Nonetheless, without the rule of law, rights cannot be secure, for they will be sacrificed to the whims of leaders; to arbitrary distinctions based on class, race, or ethnicity; and to the attitude that government itself is the source of rights. In the United States, the fundamental law is the Constitution of 1787 and its 27 amendments, the topic of the next chapter.

Why Not Freedom?

Given the widespread desire of men and women to be free, why do governments ever fail or refuse to promote freedom? One reason, as we have seen, is that some rulers and governing ideologies value other ends as more important. Communist nations sacrificed economic freedoms to the "dictatorship of the proletariat" and the creation of a "new man" who would place the public good over self-interest. Other regimes restrict personal behavior to promote religion or morality, and still others rank national security, public safety, or social order as more important than personal freedom.

Another reason rulers suppress freedom is simply to stay in power. They know that their rule would be short-lived if the people could communicate and organize freely. So they suppress freedom and rule through fear. In the mid–eighteenth century, the Baron de Montesquieu (1689–1755), a French political theorist, wrote that fear is the ruling principle of despotic governments:

> Just as there must be *virtue* in a republic and *honor* in a monarchy, there must be FEAR in a despotic government. . . . *[F]ear* must beat down everyone's courage and extinguish even the slightest feeling of ambition. . . . [W]hen in a despotic government the prince ceases for a moment to raise his arm, when he cannot instantly destroy those in the highest places, all is lost.[62]

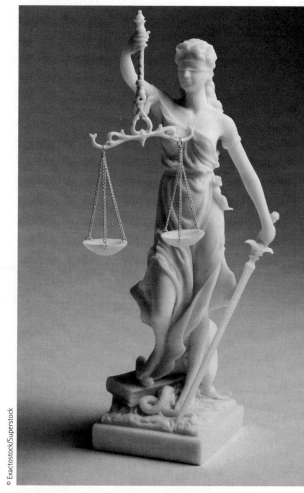

The rule of law is often depicted by the statue of Lady Justice. The scales represent the balancing necessary to assess legal claims. The blindfold shows that "justice is blind," not favoring some claimants over others. The sword represents the power of the state to enforce its judgments. Her right foot rests on a book of laws, next to which is a defeated serpent.

© Exactostock/Superstock

If the fear is intense enough to stifle opposition, then the rulers can be secure in their power, at least from a popular uprising. But when the fear subsides, the people can sometimes act quickly to depose a tyrant, as the Romanian people did in 1989 when they overthrew the iron rule of longtime Communist leader Nicolae Ceaușescu after he had brutally suppressed demonstrations for human rights. Similarly, Moammar Kadafi's tyrannical regime in Libya came tumbling down once the people ceased to fear him. "Kadafi's biggest mistake was that he built his whole regime on pure fear," said a member of the Libyan Youth Movement in 2011, citing the public torturing and execution of political dissidents. "But the fear that Kadafi built his empire with is gone, and that was his last shelter."[63] An older resister gave tribute to the young: "We fought fear; the revolution's youth taught us courage."[64]

Rule of law—the principle that rulers should govern through law and not arbitrarily, that all persons should be treated equally before the law, and that individual rights are the foundation of the law and not the creation of the law.

Embracing New Goals

Although the threat of terrorism, especially since the attacks of September 11, 2001, reminds us that government's job is to protect public safety and secure personal rights, the United States and other modern democracies embrace other goals as well. As we will see,

Social welfare—the function of government to foster a healthy economy and to enhance the material well-being of citizens, both the poor and the nonpoor.

Social welfare state—a society and government that make it a high priority to promote the social welfare of the people (see **Social welfare**).

Welfare state—see **Social welfare state**.

particularly in Chapters 16 and 17, American government now extensively regulates commerce, seeks to foster a healthy economy, and works to promote the material well-being of Americans, both the poor and the nonpoor. This is the **social welfare** function of modern government, which results in what many call the **social welfare state**, or simply the **welfare state**. Few Americans today take issue with laws that mandate a minimum hourly wage; regulate workplace safety; ensure the quality of food and the safety and effectiveness of prescription drugs; provide income support and medical assistance to the elderly; assist students with the costs of attending college; and help the poor with temporary income assistance, housing aid, food stamps, and job training.

Yet for most of American history, the national government did not act so directly to foster the material well-being of Americans. That changed dramatically with President Franklin Roosevelt's New Deal programs of the 1930s and President Lyndon Johnson's Great Society programs of the 1960s. Some now wonder whether President Barack Obama's ambitious domestic agenda, and especially the passage of his health care plan in 2010, will eventually rank alongside that of Roosevelt and Johnson.

Roosevelt defended the New Deal as necessary to fulfill the promises of the Declaration of Independence. In the modern era, he argued, people could not truly enjoy their rights to life, liberty, and the pursuit of happiness without new programs to regulate the economy and assist people with their material needs. As Chapter 16 details, more than half of the federal budget is now devoted to income support (mostly for seniors) and medical coverage (mainly for the elderly and the poor). The growth of the welfare state raises important issues about the size of government, its effect on economic growth and prosperity, how government assesses and seeks to meet human needs, what role individual initiative and the private sector should play, and how revenues should be generated to fund social programs. President Obama's domestic policy initiatives refocused public attention on the purposes, size, and cost of American national government.

CITIZENSHIP AND DELIBERATIVE DEMOCRACY

We have said that democracy works best when the people embrace the duties of citizenship and when informed citizens and public officials deliberate to identify and promote the common good. The authors of the Constitution identified five key elements of the common good that a "more perfect Union" would help achieve: justice, domestic tranquility, the common defense, the general welfare, and the blessings of liberty. American government has not always achieved these goals. Yet, throughout American history, informed and energized citizens, inspired by the ideals of the Founders, have worked to spread their influence.

The founders were keenly aware that American democracy would not work well without an educated citizenry. In his "Farewell Address" of 1796 announcing his intention to retire from public life, President George Washington urged Americans to "promote, then, as an object of primary importance, institutions for the general diffusion of knowledge. In proportion as the structure of a government gives force to public opinion, it is essential that public opinion should be enlightened."[65] Similarly, Thomas Jefferson wrote that "the basis of our governments being the opinion of the people, the very first object

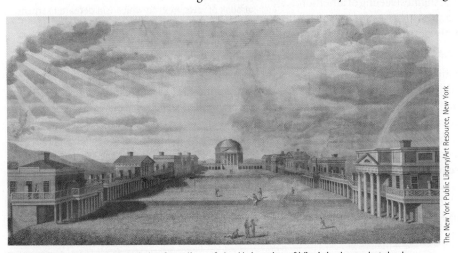

The New York Public Library/Art Resource, New York

Thomas Jefferson considered the founding of the University of Virginia, here sketched in 1826, as one of his greatest accomplishments, even more important than serving as president of the United States. The university was to be the apex of a system of public education that would provide the knowledge needed by citizens and statesmen in the new American democracy.

should be to keep that right."[66] Years later, he helped found the University of Virginia to promote the knowledge necessary for good citizenship and sound leadership. Among its essential purposes: "To instruct the mass of our citizens in . . . their rights, interests and duties, as men and citizens. . . . [and] to expound the principles and structure of government, the laws which regulate the intercourse of nations, those formed municipally for our own government, and a sound spirit of legislation."[67] And as Jefferson's friend and protégé, James Madison, famously wrote in 1822: "A popular Government, without popular information, or the means of acquiring it, is but a Prologue to a Farce or a Tragedy; or, perhaps both. Knowledge will forever govern ignorance: And a people who mean to be their own Governors, must arm themselves with the power which knowledge gives."[68]

We agree with Washington, Jefferson, and Madison that citizens cannot truly govern themselves without civic knowledge. If a democracy is to work well, its citizens must know and act on their rights and duties and must responsibly exercise their political influence, especially in voting for candidates for public office. Here is a list of what we believe a conscientious American should know about government and politics in the United States to be an effective and responsible citizen. This list reflects much of what we try to convey in this text:

- The principles of self-government and just rule that informed the creation of the American nation, decisively influenced its history, and continue to affect its government and politics
- The rights that American government seeks to secure, including those specified in the Declaration of Independence, the Constitution of 1787, the Bill of Rights, and later Amendments
- The provisions, principles, and purposes of the U.S. Constitution, including limited government, federalism, separation of powers, and checks and balances
- The nature and functioning of the major institutions of American national government—especially the Congress, presidency, and federal courts—and whether they effectively meet their broad constitutional responsibilities or display serious deficiencies

IMPACT
of Social Media and Communications Technology

Deliberation and American Democracy

The term "social media" has existed only since 2004. It refers to interactive communications made possible by the Internet and related technologies and includes the use of weblogs (or blogging), Internet forums, podcasts, wikis (Web sites like Wikipedia, where users can add and modify content), YouTube, methods to share bookmarks, and social networking sites and services such as MySpace, Facebook, and Twitter. Facebook alone has more than 800 million active users.

Although the social media are quite new, protestors in north Africa during the "Arab Spring" of 2011 used Twitter, Facebook, and YouTube to spread information and accelerate demands for political change. But what about stable democracies like the United States? How might the new social media affect government and politics? And will it be for good or for ill?

In March of 2012, a think tank in Palo Alto, California, hosted a creative brainstorming session on the impact of social media on governance. (See the summary on the Bessette/Pitney blog for March 14, 2012, and the link to the longer report.) The participants focused particularly on how social media could promote citizen deliberation, turning a "dumb mob" into a "smart mob," but also on whether popular pressure applied through social media might actually harm deliberation within governing institutions.

One fascinating innovation the group proposed was using social media "[t]o bring deliberative polling to cyberspace." A deliberative poll is when several hundred people, selected to represent some larger group, are brought together for several days to hear from experts and interact with each other about some public issue. Ideally, the participants in these exercises will develop a more informed and deliberative opinion on the issue at hand and will reach the same conclusions that the larger group would have if everyone had gone through the same experience. (For details on deliberative polls, see the Bessette/Pitney blog for December 11, 2010; May 31, 2011; June 25, 2011; and June 29, 2011. And for more on direct democracy, see the blog for February 1, 2011; March 7, 2011; and May 7, 2011.)

CRITICAL THINKING

QUESTION

In the decades ahead will the new social media be good for American democracy?

- The substance of domestic, economic, and national security policy and the issues at stake in debates over the course of national policy
- The duties and responsibilities of American citizenship, such as respecting the rights of others, obeying the law, and exercising an informed vote

SUMMARY

- Although political scientists often view politics as a struggle over who gets what, when, and how, Americans believe in more than their own self-interests, and they often act on those beliefs. They believe in and often seek to promote a broader "public interest," which includes principles of justice, the rights of others, and the good of the larger community.
- American democracy works best when the people embrace such civic virtues as self-restraint, self-reliance, civic knowledge, and civic participation and service, and when informed citizens and public officials deliberate to identify and promote the common good. We call this understanding deliberative democracy.
- Democracy, which means rule by the people, originated about 2,500 years ago in the Greek city-states. Although these were direct democracies, all modern democracies are essentially representative democracies.
- The American founders believed that representative democracy in a large nation would allow elected officials to "refine and enlarge the public views" and diminish the likelihood of majority factions.
- In all genuine democracies, the people can form political parties to advance their goals, try to persuade their fellow citizens through a free press and media, and vote for candidates of their choice without fear or intimidation.

- The United States was founded on the principles that all human beings have rights to life, liberty, and the pursuit of happiness; that the purpose of government is to secure these rights; and that government derives its just powers from the consent of the governed.
- The universal principles articulated in the Declaration of Independence set forth a standard of justice against which we can judge all governments. In many ways, American history can be seen as a record of extending the promises of the Declaration to ever larger groups of Americans.
- When democracies work to secure the rights of their citizens, and thus to promote their freedoms, we call them liberal democracies.
- Although growing numbers of nations embrace the principles and practices of liberal democracy, a significant proportion of the world's population lives under governments that do not promote freedom.
- Over the past century or so, modern democracies have increasingly embraced goals beyond public safety and securing personal rights. They now devote substantial resources to promoting a healthy economy and enhancing the people's material well-being.
- Successful democracy requires an educated citizenry. In particular, citizens must know and act on their rights and duties and must responsibly exercise their political influence, especially in voting for candidates for public office.

KEY TERMS

TEST YOUR KNOWLEDGE

1. Which of the following most accurately describes the concept of deliberation? Deliberation is
   a. not generally considered a civic duty.
   b. reasoning on the merits of public policy.
   c. only effective when it is a formal process.
   d. best left to politicians.
   e. impossible to expect from legislators.

2. According to the Founders, which of the following pose the greatest dangers in a direct democracy?
   a. landlords and wealthy men
   b. skillful orators and wealthy men
   c. majority faction and landlords
   d. landlords and skillful orators
   e. skillful orators and majority faction

3. The political corruption that plagued the late nineteenth and early twentieth centuries gave rise to
   a. the progressive movement.
   b. a representative democracy.
   c. a deliberative democracy.
   d. the rational choice theory of politics.
   e. the Socialist movement.

4. What action was taken at the Second Continental Congress in 1775?
   a. The Constitution was drafted.
   b. Delegates signed the Declaration of Independence.
   c. Delegates authorized the raising of a Continental Army.
   d. George Washington was proclaimed the first president.
   e. King George declared the colonies in open rebellion.

5. In the context of the Declaration of Independence, what is prudence?
   a. circumspection
   b. freedom
   c. intelligence
   d. practical wisdom
   e. theoretical wisdom

6. Abraham Lincoln understood the Civil War to be a(n)
   a. cultural conflict between the North and the South.
   b. political skirmish between two opposing parties.
   c. economic conflict between the manufacturing and farming industries.
   d. conflict over the meaning and application of the Declaration of Independence.
   e. unavoidable occurrence in such a large and diverse nation.

7. The right to _____ is an example of a political right.
   a. vote
   b. the pursuit of happiness
   c. defend oneself with deadly force
   d. a fair trial
   e. marry

8. Which statement best describes the "Arab Spring" political movement in North Africa and the Middle East that began in December of 2010?
   a. Islamic parties won elections to take power in Tunisia, Libya, Egypt, and Yemen and in this way forced tyrants from power.
   b. Leaders in Tunisia, Libya, and Egypt were removed from power through the impeachment provisions of those nations' constitutions.
   c. Resistance movements in five nations allied with NATO to use force to remove tyrannical leaders.
   d. Widespread protests throughout the region failed to result in significant regime change outside of Tunisia, where the movement began.
   e. Widespread protests resulted in regime change in Tunisia, Libya, Egypt, and Yemen.

9. According to Freedom House,
   a. most of the world's population is not free.
   b. the number of free countries in the world has remained about the same in the last 30 years.
   c. freedom has been in decline for the last 30 years.
   d. the number of countries that are not free is increasing.
   e. the number of free countries has increased in the last few decades.

10. Which of the following is one of the essential elements of the rule of law?
    a. Individual rights are understood to be the foundation of law rather than the creation of law.
    b. Public interests are understood to be the foundation of law rather than the creation of law.
    c. Individual rights are the creation of law while public interests are the foundation of law.
    d. Decisions by those in power predominate over existing laws.
    e. Those in power are not subject to the law.

FURTHER READING

Bailyn, Bernard. *The Ideological Origins of the American Revolution.* Enlarged edition. Cambridge, MA: Belknap Press of Harvard University Press, 1992.

Commager, Henry Steele, and Richard B. Morris, eds. *The Spirit of Seventy-Six: The Story of the American Revolution as Told by Participants.* New York: Harper & Row, 1967.

Ferris, Robert G., ed. *Signers of the Declaration*. Washington, DC: U.S. Department of the Interior, National Park Service, 1975.

Frohnen, Bruce, ed. *The American Republic: Primary Sources*. Indianapolis, IN: Liberty Fund, 2002.

Gwartney, James, and Robert Lawson. *Economic Freedom of the World: 2004 Annual Report*. Washington, DC: Cato Institute, 2004.

Horowitz, Robert H., ed. *The Moral Foundations of the American Republic*. 2nd ed. Charlottesville: University Press of Virginia, 1979.

Journal of Democracy. Published by the National Endowment for Democracy, Washington, DC; www.journalofdemocracy.org.

Maier, Pauline. *American Scripture: Making the Declaration of Independence*. New York: Vintage Books, 1998.

Marshall, Paul. *Religious Freedom in the World: A Global Report on Freedom and Persecution*. Nashville, TN: Broadman & Holman, 2000.

Marx, Karl, and Friedrich Engels. *The Communist Manifesto of Marx and Engels: With the Original Text and Prefaces*. Ed. Harold Joseph Laski. New York: Simon & Schuster, 1975.

McDonald, Forrest. *E Pluribus Unum: The Formation of the American Republic, 1776–1790*. Indianapolis, IN: Liberty Fund, 1979.

Morrison, Samuel Eliot, ed. *Sources and Documents Illustrating the American Revolution, 1764–1788*. 2nd ed. London: Oxford University Press, 1965.

Tocqueville, Alexis de. *Democracy in America*. Ed. J. P. Mayer and trans. George Lawrence. Garden City, NY: Doubleday, Anchor Books, 1969.

West, Thomas G. *Vindicating the Founders: Race, Sex, Class, and Justice in the Origins of America*. Lanham, MD: Rowman & Littlefield, 1997.

Wood, Gordon S. *The Radicalism of the American Revolution*. New York: Vintage Books, 1991.

WEB SOURCES

American Revolution.org: www.americanrevolution.org/home.html—an extensive collection of materials related to the American Revolution.

BBC: Greeks: The Democratic Experiment: www.bbc.co.uk/history/ancient/greeks/greekdemocracy_01.shtml—information on ancient Greek democracy.

Freedom House: www.freedomhouse.org—the private, nongovernmental organization that tracks the status of freedom and democracy around the world.

Institute for American Liberty: www.liberty1.org—a collection of original materials on the American founding.

Liberty Fund: www.libertyfund.org—a private, educational foundation that promotes "the ideal of a society of free and responsible individuals."

National Archives: Charters of Freedom: www.archives.gov/national_archives_experience/charters/declaration.html—the National Archives Web site on the Declaration of Independence, the Constitution, and the Bill of Rights.

National Archives Digital Classroom: www.archives.gov/digital_classroom/teaching_with_documents.html#revolution—National Archives gateway for educational resources.

National Endowment for Democracy: www.ned.org—a private organization devoted to strengthening democratic institutions around the world.

PBS: Liberty—The American Revolution: www.pbs.org/ktca/liberty—PBS's Web site for its television series on the American Revolution.

United Nations: Human Rights: www.un.org/rights—the United Nations' Web site on its efforts to promote human rights throughout the world.

User's Guide to the Declaration of Independence: www.founding.com—an extensive collection of materials on the American founding maintained by the Claremont Institute in California.

United States Commission on International Religious Freedom: www.uscirf.gov—a bipartisan body created by the federal government to promote freedom of thought, conscience, and religion.

U.S. Department of State: Human Rights Reports: www.state.gov/g/drl/rls/hrrpt/—the collection of "Country Reports on Human Rights Practices" submitted by the Department of State annually to Congress.

Virtual Marching Tour of the American Revolution: www.ushistory.org/—an extensive collection of materials on the American founding.

This famous painting of the signing of the Constitution on September 17, 1787, was commissioned by Congress and completed by Howard Chandler Christy in 1940. It is a 20 × 30-foot oil on canvas and hangs in the U.S. Capitol. (Only part of the painting is shown here.)

The Signing of the Constitution of the United States in 1787, 1940 (oil on canvas), Christy, Howard Chandler (1873–1952)/Hall of Representatives, Washington D.C., USA/The Bridgeman Art Library

The American Constitution

2

OBJECTIVES

After reading this chapter, you should be able to:

- Describe the lessons the early Americans learned about establishing effective democratic government during the first decade of independence.
- Explain the key controversies that divided the delegates at the Constitutional Convention.
- Contrast the political views of the Federalists and Anti-Federalists.
- Assess the extent to which the addition of the Bill of Rights to the Constitution served the goals of both Anti-Federalists and Federalists.
- Evaluate whether the original Constitution was pro-slavery or anti-slavery.

INTRODUCTION

It is one thing to overthrow an existing political order, but quite another to establish a successful new one. The Second Continental Congress had declared independence from Britain in 1776 and managed national affairs in the first years of self-government, but its legal authority was uncertain and it lacked clearly defined powers and responsibilities. Also, the 11 colonies that had royal governors (all but Connecticut and Rhode Island) needed new constitutions. In establishing their new governments, Americans worked to design institutions that would govern with popular consent and effectively secure the people's rights.

It took just over a decade to fashion and adopt a charter for an effective new national government, titled the Constitution of the United States of America. It remains the oldest written national constitution still in force. Although crafted by a relatively small group of men, it was ratified by popularly elected assemblies in all the states. Then, within a few years, Congress proposed and the state legislatures ratified ten amendments: the Bill of Rights.

This process of creating and adopting a new national government, though often contentious, was remarkably peaceful. "[I]t seems to have been reserved to the people of this country," Alexander Hamilton wrote at the beginning of the ratification debate, "to decide the important question, whether societies of men are really capable or not of establishing good government from reflection and choice, or whether they are forever destined to depend for their political constitutions on accident and force."[1] And two years later, President George Washington noted "the peaceable and rational manner in which we have been enabled to establish constitutions of government for our safety and happiness."[2]

The creation of the U.S. Constitution owed much to the lessons learned at the state and national levels during the period between independence (1776) and the convening of the Constitutional Convention (1787). In this chapter, we examine how these lessons influenced the writing of the Constitution, what issues divided the proponents and opponents of the Constitution, and how a bill of rights was added to broaden popular support for the new national government. We conclude by showing how those who wrote the Constitution grappled with the issue of slavery and made compromises with that institution.

In this process of establishing new governing institutions, the founders also drew on ancient and modern examples, the teachings of political philosophers, experiences with their own colonial governments, and British constitutional and legal history. This was a dramatic example of deliberative democracy in action, accommodating both broad principles and competing interests.

THE LESSONS OF THE FIRST DECADE
MAJOR ISSUE

- How did the events in the first decade after independence illustrate the deficiencies of the state constitutions and the Articles of Confederation?

State—the name given to the former American colonies when they collectively declared independence from British rule in 1776.

The first attempts to establish effective governments for the nation and the **states** were not entirely successful. The state experience in particular revealed the potential tension between the two great principles of the Declaration of Independence: that the purpose of government is to secure rights and that the just powers of government come from popular consent.

State Constitutions

Eleven of the 13 states adopted new constitutions to replace their colonial governments. (Connecticut and Rhode Island, which had not had royal governors, did not write new constitutions until many decades later.) South Carolina was first, in March 1776, and then adopted a new constitution in November 1778. Six other states adopted constitutions in

1776 and two did so in 1777. Massachusetts followed in 1780 (after an earlier one met stiff opposition in the towns of the state), and New Hampshire took until 1784.

The early state constitutions shared certain common features:

- *Separation of powers:* All the constitutions created distinct legislative, executive, and judicial branches.
- *Bicameral legislature:* All except Pennsylvania created a **bicameral legislature** with two houses, with elections for the lower branch typically every year and elections for the upper branch every two to five years.
- *Weak governors:* With the exception of New York and, to a lesser extent, Massachusetts, the new constitutions kept governors weak by providing for one-year terms, strict limits on how many years they could serve, no veto power, election by the legislature, and a salary that the legislature could alter at any time.
- *Property qualifications:* All imposed property qualifications for voting (but usually low enough that most free men could vote in most states) and for holding office (typically higher than for voting and higher for governor than for a legislator).

The authors of these constitutions were suspicious of executive power and looked to powerful legislatures to secure the people's rights. This is not surprising. For decades elected colonial assemblies had clashed with royal governors, and the revolution itself was fought against a tyrannical king. But as we will see in the following sections, these first efforts to establish effective representative democracies in the states were less than fully successful.

Articles of Confederation

After declaring independence in early July 1776, the delegates to the Second Continental Congress began the task of creating a formal national government for the new nation. Within a few weeks, a committee proposed "Articles of confederation and perpetual union," but it took until November 1777 before the Congress could agree on the details. The Congress then submitted the **Articles of Confederation** to the states, stipulating that all 13 state legislatures must concur before the new government would go into effect.

The Articles created a weak central authority acting on behalf of powerful states. It provided:

- *State sovereignty:* The states would retain all powers not "expressly delegated" to the national Congress.
- *Single governing institution:* National power would reside in a Congress, with no separate executive or judicial branch.
- *State equality:* Each state would have one vote in Congress, with each state legislature selecting between two and seven delegates to serve for one-year terms and who could be recalled and replaced at any time.
- *Limited powers:* The Congress could not raise taxes or establish a military on its own authority (but had to requisition these from the states), or regulate foreign commerce (except through treaties) or commerce between the states.
- *Supermajority requirement:* On the most important matters—such as going to war, entering into treaties, requisitioning revenues and military forces, and coining and borrowing money—9 of the 13 states had to agree.
- *Amendments:* Changes to the Articles required the unanimous consent of the 13 state legislatures.

We call this type of system, in which a limited national government acts on behalf of sovereign states, a **confederation** (see Chapter 3). State supremacy was made clear in the first substantive provision of the Articles: "Each State retains its sovereignty, freedom and independence, and every power, jurisdiction and right, which is not by this confederation expressly delegated to the United States, in Congress assembled." The Articles created "a firm league of friendship" to secure the "common defence" of the states, "the security of their liberties," and "their mutual and general welfare." Despite the supremacy of the states

Bicameral legislature—a legislative body that has two separate chambers or houses, often with equal authority to pass or amend legislation.

Articles of Confederation—the first national constitution for the United States. In force from 1781 to 1789, it created a single-branch national government (Congress) in which each state had one vote.

Confederation—a system of government in which a weak central authority acts on behalf of powerful independent states.

in the new plan, the Articles described the "Union" as "perpetual" five times, highlighting the importance of a permanent association of the states for broad common purposes.

Within 18 months of receiving the new plan, 12 states had ratified the document. Maryland, however, held out for nearly two more years, objecting to claims by other states to lands west of the Appalachians (the mountain range at the western border of most of the states on the east coast). After several states ceded their territorial claims to the national government, Maryland ratified the articles in March 1781—just seven months before the Battle of Yorktown effectively ended the Revolutionary War.

The new state constitutions and the Articles of Confederation took shape under the most trying of circumstances: during a war against a preeminent military power. It is not surprising that everything did not go smoothly. Even after peace was formally achieved in 1783, serious economic and political problems gripped the new nation in what came to be called the **"critical period."** Eventually many Americans came to believe that the nation needed a more powerful national government and new restrictions on the states.

Weaknesses of the National Government

It became painfully clear during the first decade of independence that the weak central authority—initially the Second Continental Congress and then the Congress under the Articles of Confederation (which is called the **Confederation Congress**)—could not govern the new nation effectively. Dependent on the states for revenues and an army, the national government was perennially short of cash and fielded an undermanned and underequipped fighting force during the war. Commander in Chief George Washington implored the states time and again to meet their obligations. In 1780, he predicted that the army would soon disband or, even worse, "subsist upon the plunder of the people" if the states did not take "very vigorous and immediate measures . . . to comply with the requisitions made upon them."[3] Even after the war ended, the states failed to provide the revenues requested by the Congress, leaving the Confederation perennially on the verge of bankruptcy.

Equally serious was the refusal of the states to defer to the Congress on foreign policy, making it impossible for the nation to speak with one voice overseas. Some states conducted their own foreign policies, striking separate commercial deals with other countries, and sometimes even ignored treaties approved by Congress. Many states, for example, refused to respect the rights of **Loyalists** (Americans who had supported Britain during the war) that were guaranteed by the Treaty of Paris of 1783, which ended the war. According to one historian, this treatment of Loyalists reflected "the light-hearted way in which treaties were regarded by the states."[4] By the mid-1780s, the national government was virtually bankrupt, lacked respect overseas, and was often unable even to gather a quorum of delegates to do business. The government seemed unable to achieve the very purposes for which it was created.

Conflicts between the States

Because the states set their own commercial policies, those with natural harbors—such as Massachusetts, Rhode Island, New York, Maryland, Virginia, and South Carolina—made their neighbors pay duties on foreign goods that came through their ports. The states hurt by these policies retaliated as best they could with regulations that favored their own citizens. This commercial warfare was

Critical period—the period of economic, financial, and political distress between the effective end of the Revolutionary War (1781) and the establishment of a new government under the Constitution (1789).

Confederation Congress—the name often given to the Congress established by the Articles of Confederation in 1781 to distinguish it from the Continental Congress, which it replaced.

Loyalists—Americans who remained loyal to the British government during the Revolutionary War.

Library of Congress Prints and Photographs Division

General George Washington and the Marquis de Lafayette visit suffering soldiers in the encampment of the Continental Army at Valley Forge, Pennsylvania, during the winter of 1777–1778. Congress's inability to provision the army with adequate food and clothing undermined the war effort.

bad for economic development, exacerbated tensions among the states, and undermined a sense of common nationhood.

Territorial conflicts were another source of tension. Many of the states had conflicting claims to western lands, and in some cases the borders between the states were in dispute. Most serious was the conflict between the settlers of Vermont, who desired to be a separate state, and New York, which claimed sovereignty over the territory. Sporadic fighting occurred throughout this period. The dispute did not end until Vermont was admitted to the Union in 1791 as the fourteenth state after the national government compensated New York financially. Farther south, violence erupted between settlers from Connecticut and citizens of Pennsylvania over an area called the Wyoming Valley, contiguous to Pennsylvania. The dispute was resolved after a special court appointed by the Congress sided with Pennsylvania.

Problems within the States

As troublesome as these problems were, many of the founders were even more disturbed by events within the states themselves. Weak governors and courts often could not prevent legislatures from overstepping their constitutional bounds. Thomas Jefferson, who served as governor of Virginia from 1779 to 1781, called the concentration of power in the state legislature "precisely the definition of despotic government." It did not matter that the "despots" were all elected: "an *elective despotism* was not the government we fought for."[5] Jefferson faulted provisions in the state constitution that gave the legislature control over the salaries of the governor and judges and over the election and reelection of the governor.

Shays's Rebellion

One of the most alarming events of this period was **Shays's Rebellion** in Massachusetts. In the late summer and fall of 1786, mobs of debt-ridden farmers, angry with the Massachusetts legislature for refusing to issue paper money or to take other actions to relieve high taxes or to stop farm foreclosures, prevented courts from operating in several towns. Daniel Shays, a destitute farmer and former captain in the revolutionary army, gathered some 1,200 men, who camped for two months in Worcester, 40 miles west of Boston. Including other forces allied with Shays, about 3,000 men took up arms against the lawful authority. In December, the rebels marched on the arsenal at Springfield, in the western part of the state.

At first, Governor James Bowdoin lacked a military force sufficient to meet the threat. He called on Congress for assistance, but the national government was essentially bankrupt and unable to help. After borrowing money from wealthy Bostonians, the governor raised a force of 4,400 men. It assembled at Boston, marched to Springfield, and defeated and scattered the rebels. Later, Bowdoin's successor, John Hancock, pardoned them all.

Although limited to Massachusetts, Shays's Rebellion had a powerful effect throughout the nation. Responsible leaders were appalled at the rebellion itself but also at the initial weakness of the state and federal governments in responding to it. Washington wrote to James Madison that "we are fast verging to anarchy and confusion";[6] and Abigail Adams, wife of John Adams, wrote to Jefferson that "these mobish insurgents are for sapping the foundation, and destroying the whole fabrick at once."[7] Shays's Rebellion did much to prepare the public mind for a new, more powerful national government.

Shays's Rebellion—a forcible uprising of mainly poor farmers in central and western Massachusetts between August 1786 and February 1787. The rebels, led by former Continental Army officer Daniel Shays, closed courts to prevent the foreclosure of farms or the imprisonment of farmers for debt.

© Topham/The Image Works

On January 25, 1787, Daniel Shays and his rebels attacked the armory at Springfield, Massachusetts, which was successfully defended by local militia. This violent effort to undermine lawful authority prepared the public mind for a stronger national government.

Deficiencies of State Laws

Finally, leaders such as Madison complained of the "multiplicity," "mutability," and "injustice" of state laws. According to the Virginian, the sheer number of laws and the rapidity with which they were "repealed or superseded" was "a nuisance of the most pestilent kind," causing confusion and instability within the states.[8] But even worse was the "injustice" of state laws, which, as Madison wrote to his friend Jefferson, "has been so frequent and so flagrant as to alarm the most steadfast friends of Republicanism."[9] Madison was thinking of such laws as those that burdened commerce, that denied trial by jury, that disenfranchised the Quakers in Pennsylvania, and that violated constitutional distributions of power in state governments. Even more troubling was what he called "the general rage for paper money" that spread throughout the states in 1785 and 1786.

Rage for Paper Money

Depressed economic conditions, heavy debt, high taxes, and the scarcity of specie (gold and silver coin) led many to call on their states to issue paper money. Farmers and others could then borrow the paper money from the government, with their property as security, to pay their taxes and debts. Increasingly, the voters elected officials who favored using the printing presses to relieve economic distress. When several states issued large amounts of paper currency, it depreciated rapidly and was shunned by merchants and creditors. Rhode Island suffered the most disastrous effects.

In March 1786, more than two-thirds of the legislators in Rhode Island voted against a request from six towns to issue paper money. Elections a month later, however, gave advocates of paper money a commanding majority in the legislature. Within a few weeks, the state issued a large amount of paper money. Property owners could borrow the paper for up to half the value of their land. It was made legal tender in all commercial transactions and in payment for all debts, past, present, or future.

Realizing that creditors who had previously lent gold or silver would not freely accept the new paper in repayment, the legislature stipulated that anyone could pay off his debts with paper money at a court. Because so much paper money began circulating, it fell to one-fourth of its face value in just three months. When merchants refused to accept the currency at anything like its face value, the legislature, meeting in special session, made it a criminal offense to refuse it. Trial would be within three days of the offense before a panel of three judges, no jury allowed. The judgment of a majority of the panel was to be final and without appeal.

These measures ruined the economy in Rhode Island. Merchants closed their shops, and producers from neighboring states and foreign nations refused to bring their goods for fear of having to accept relatively worthless paper in return. Further controversy arose when the supreme court of Rhode Island ruled that the legislature could not deny a jury trial to those who refused to accept the paper money. Outraged by the court's decision, the legislature called in the judges to explain themselves. Although the lawmakers did not remove the judges, the people refused to reelect all but one. Soon thereafter, the legislature bowed to economic reality and repealed the "forcing acts" and the requirement that the much depreciated paper be treated as legal tender. These events were closely watched throughout the nation.

Questions about Majority Rule

In some respects, Madison and other leaders were more troubled by the events in Rhode Island than by the uprising in Massachusetts. Shays's Rebellion was an illegal activity of a small minority that the state eventually put down. But the issuance of large quantities of paper money in Rhode Island was a legal, if unwise, act that responded to majority desires. Through its various **paper money laws**, the state had violated the property rights of creditors and merchants, ruined the economy, and undermined public confidence in the government. According to Madison, such unjust laws brought "into question the fundamental principle of republican Government, that the majority who rule in such Governments are the safest Guardians both of public Good and of private rights."[10]

FOCUS

QUESTION

Besides the events during the "critical period," have there been other times in American history when majorities in the nation or the states violated the rights of citizens? If so, what explains these violations?

Paper money laws—laws passed by several states during the 1780s that allowed citizens to borrow paper money from the government and use it as legal tender, especially to pay taxes and debts.

In a powerful way, then, the state experience demonstrated the challenge that faced the founding generation. It was one thing to give the people the power to rule, but it was quite another to ensure the wise use of that power. Thus, the state experience revealed a potential tension between the two great principles of the Declaration of Independence: that the purpose of government is to secure natural rights and that the just powers of government come from popular consent.

The Road to Philadelphia

Even before the Articles of Confederation went into effect in March of 1781, national leaders realized that the central government needed its own taxing power to fund the war and to pay off the public debt. In February, the Continental Congress proposed an amendment that would authorize it to impose a 5% duty on most imported goods. Twelve states ratified the amendment, but Rhode Island refused. Two years later, the Confederation Congress proposed a similar amendment, but several states opposed it. Then, in 1784, Congress sought new authority to regulate foreign commerce. Only through a unified policy, it said, could the nation "command reciprocal advantages in trade." Just two states agreed.

After representatives from Virginia and Maryland had success in addressing common commercial concerns at a meeting at Mount Vernon (George Washington's home) in March 1785, the Virginia legislature called on the states to send delegates to a convention on commercial problems at Annapolis, Maryland, in September 1786. Although nine of the state legislatures agreed and appointed delegates, only those from New York, New Jersey, Delaware, Pennsylvania, and Virginia arrived in time. The principal accomplishment of the **Annapolis Convention** was to issue a call for a constitutional convention "to render the constitution of the Federal Government adequate to the exigencies [urgent needs] of the Union."

On February 21, 1787, the Congress endorsed the call for a general convention as "the most probable means of establishing in these states a firm national government." It called on all the states to appoint delegates to meet in Philadelphia in May "for the sole and express purpose of revising the Articles of Confederation" so as to "render the federal constitution adequate to the exigencies of Government & the preservation of the Union."

By 1787, Americans had learned that their national government was much too weak to achieve the purposes of union and that state governments often placed their parochial interests over the common good or violated the rights of their own citizens. The national and state governments in the United States needed to be more deliberative and more effective at achieving the goals for which the Revolution had been fought. (See Figure 2-1 for forms of government throughout the world at the time of the American founding.)

Annapolis Convention—a gathering of delegates from five states that met in Annapolis, Maryland, in September 1786 to address commercial problems. It called on Congress to convene a constitutional convention to provide for a more effective national government.

THE CONSTITUTIONAL CONVENTION
MAJOR ISSUES

- What conflicts arose at the Constitutional Convention, and how were they resolved?
- How did the authors of the Constitution seek to establish just and effective republican government in the United States?

By May 25, 1787, delegates from seven states (a majority of the thirteen) arrived at Philadelphia in response to Congress's call. Adopting a rule of secrecy to screen out political pressures and to make it easier for delegates to change their minds as the arguments developed, they met in the same building and room where the Continental Congress had debated and approved the Declaration of Independence. Within a few days, the number of states in attendance was up to 11. New Hampshire's delegates did not arrive until late July; Rhode Island never sent delegates. Altogether, 55 men attended at least some portion of the

Forms of Government Throughout the World in 1790

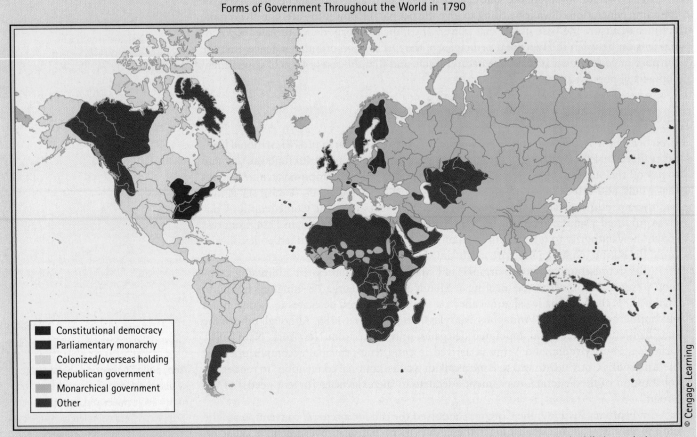

Legend:
- Constitutional democracy
- Parliamentary monarchy
- Colonized/overseas holding
- Republican government
- Monarchical government
- Other

© Cengage Learning

FIGURE 2–1 The United States was the first constitutional democracy. In most of the world at the time, the people had little say in how they were governed.

Comstock

The Assembly Room of the Pennsylvania State House, later renamed Independence Hall, is where the Second Continental Congress debated and approved the Declaration of Independence in July 1776, and where the Constitutional Convention fashioned the Constitution in the summer of 1787.

Constitutional Convention; 42 were present at the end, September 17; and 39 signed the document.

The framers of the Constitution were men of broad practical experience. Eight were signers of the Declaration, 9 were or had been governor of a state, and 36 had served in the Continental Congress or the Congress under the Articles of Confederation. More than half the delegates had served in the Continental Army or state militia during the Revolutionary War, most as officers. Many had also served in their state legislatures or in other high-level government positions. Some had been intimately involved in drafting their own states' constitutions.

The two most famous Americans attended the Convention: George Washington and Benjamin Franklin. Washington had earned the nation's enduring gratitude by his services in the Revolutionary War. Franklin, the oldest of the delegates at age 81 and in ill health, was renowned as a scientist, inventor, statesman, and diplomat not only in his native land but in Europe as well. By lending their prestige to the meeting, Washington and Franklin enhanced its credibility with their countrymen.

The delegates chose Washington to be the presiding officer, but neither he nor Franklin contributed much to the debates. Washington apparently addressed no matter of substance until the very last day, and Franklin's few speeches seemed to have little impact. The delegates who were most important to the actual drafting of the Constitution were, instead, James Madison of Virginia, just 36 years old and a leader in the movement to strengthen the national government (and the delegate who took the most extensive notes on the debates); James Wilson, an eminent expert on the law who had come to the colonies in 1763 from Scotland and settled in Pennsylvania; and Gouverneur Morris, a Pennsylvanian who had relocated from New York, where he had helped to draft that state's constitution in 1777.

Some prominent political figures, however, were absent. Thomas Jefferson was in Paris serving as envoy to France, and John Adams was in London serving as envoy to Britain. John Adams's cousin Samuel was back in Massachusetts, too ill to attend. Finally, Patrick Henry, the political leader and famous orator ("Give me liberty, or give me death") was selected as one of Virginia's delegates but refused to attend. An ardent foe of a strong central government, he reportedly said, "I smelt a rat."

Constitutional Convention—the gathering of delegates from 12 states (all but Rhode Island) that met in Philadelphia from May 25 to September 17, 1787, and wrote the Constitution.

The Nationalists Set the Agenda: The Virginia Plan

Prior to the Convention, the Virginia delegates prepared a plan for a new national government. On May 29, the first day of substantive debates, Edmund Randolph, the governor of Virginia, presented it to the Convention. It contained 15 resolutions and is commonly called the **Virginia Plan**.[11] Randolph told the delegates that the country faced a grave crisis. He cited the failure of the states to provide sufficient revenues to the national government, commercial conflicts among the states, rebellion in Massachusetts, the growing debt to foreign nations, paper money laws, and the violation of treaties.

The federal government had too little authority and too few resources. It was unable to punish treaty violations, to quell disputes between states, and to defend itself against encroachments by the states. Nor could it promote America's commercial interests with other nations. Beyond these specific defects, Randolph called attention to "the prospect of anarchy from the laxity of government every where." What was needed was a new national government "paramount to the state constitutions" and based on "the republican principle."[12]

Randolph then read the details of the Virginia Plan (see Table 2-1). What is most striking about these proposals is that they completely rejected the state-based Articles of Confederation. The Virginia delegates believed that no amendments to the existing national government could make it adequate to the needs of the nation. A wholly new government was necessary.

The proposed new government would have three independent branches, a bicameral legislature, substantial new powers, and the right to veto state laws. No longer would the states have an equal vote in the national government or would representatives serve merely as delegates of the state legislatures. Instead, representation would be based on state population (in both houses of the legislature), and the state legislatures would neither elect national representatives nor be able to recall them. Finally, by requiring popularly elected assemblies in the states to approve the new constitution, the foundations of the national government would be sunk deeper into the people than were the Articles of Confederation, which had been approved only by the state legislatures.

Some of the opponents of a strong central government—both inside the Convention and later during the ratification debates—complained that the work of the Convention was illegal because the Congress had authorized the delegates to meet only for "the sole and express purpose of revising the Articles of Confederation." Those who favored fundamental change gave two responses. First, they pointed out that the delegates were also charged with "render[ing] the federal constitution adequate to the exigencies of Government & the preservation of the Union." Merely revising the articles, they insisted, could not achieve this end. Thus, they could not fulfill their charge without proposing an entirely new national government. Second, they argued that even if the delegates went beyond their formal legal authority, the product of their deliberations was no more than a proposal that the American people could accept or reject. The people, they insisted, had the right to replace a defective government with a new one better able to promote "their safety and happiness."[13]

Virginia Plan—the plan for a strong national government of three independent branches—legislature, executive, and judiciary—introduced by Virginia governor Edmund Randolph at the beginning of the Constitutional Convention. It rejected amending the Articles of Confederation and proposed instead a wholly new government.

TABLE 2-1	PLANS OF GOVERNMENT INTRODUCED AT THE CONSTITUTIONAL CONVENTION

Virginia Plan

- **Bicameral legislature with broad powers.** The national legislature would have broad authority to deal with national concerns and the right to veto state laws that violated the new national constitution. Representation in both branches would be based on population. The members of the first branch would be popularly elected. Those of the second branch would be elected by the members of the first from nominations made by the state legislatures.
- **National executive.** The executive would be elected by the legislature and serve a single term. The plan left open the duration of the term and whether the executive would be a single person. The executive would have "a general authority to execute the National laws" and to exercise the executive powers vested in the Congress by the Articles of Confederation.
- **National judiciary.** Federal judges would serve "during good behaviour" (meaning for life unless impeached and removed) and would decide such matters as "piracies & felonies on the high seas," "captures from an enemy," cases involving foreigners or citizens from different states, and "impeachments of any National officers."
- **Council of revision.** This body would include the executive and some number of federal judges. It would have authority to veto acts of the national legislature, unless overridden by an unspecified proportion of each house.
- **Limits on the legislature's control of salaries.** To foster the independence of the executive and the judiciary, the legislature was prohibited from increasing or diminishing the salaries of executive and judicial officers while they served.
- **Guarantees to states.** The national government would guarantee each state its territory and a "Republican Government."
- **Oath.** State officers would take an oath "to support the articles of Union."
- **Ratification procedure.** The new constitution would be submitted first to Congress and then to assemblies of popularly elected representatives within the states for ratification.

New Jersey Plan

- **Congress unchanged.** The Congress of the Articles of Confederation with equal state vote would remain unchanged.
- **New powers.** Congress would receive new powers to regulate foreign and interstate trade and to raise revenues by taxing imports, requiring stamps on paper, and collecting postage on letters or packages.
- **National executive.** The Congress would elect an executive to carry out the laws and direct military operations. The number of executives and the term of office were not specified. The executive could be removed from office by Congress if a majority of the state governors requested.
- **National judiciary.** The executive would appoint a "supreme Tribunal" whose members would serve life terms.
- **Supremacy of federal law.** Laws passed by Congress and treaties would be "the supreme law" to which state judges would be bound.
- **Use of force against states.** The national executive would be authorized to use the force of the confederacy against any state or persons who opposed national laws or treaties.

Alexander Hamilton's Plan

- **Bicameral Congress with general legislative power.** The national legislature would have "power to pass all laws whatsoever." The members of the lower branch would be elected by the people for three-year terms; and those of the higher branch would be selected by special electors and would serve life terms.
- **Chief executive.** He would be chosen by electors and serve a life term. He would execute national laws, direct the operations of war, make treaties (with the Senate's approval), and appoint the heads of the executive departments. He would have an absolute veto over bills passed by the legislature and could pardon all offenses except treason.
- **Supreme Court.** Its members, nominated by the chief executive and confirmed by the Senate, would serve life terms.
- **State governors.** They would be appointed by the national government and have an absolute veto over state laws.
- **Impeachment.** Governors and all officeholders in the national government would be subject to impeachment and removal for "mal- and corrupt conduct."
- **Supremacy of national law.** All state laws contrary to "the Constitution or laws of the United States" would be "utterly void."

© Cengage Learning 2014

The Small States Counterattack: The New Jersey Plan

For two weeks the Virginia Plan dominated the discussions, as the delegates debated, modified, and voted (provisionally) on each of its 15 resolutions. Some delegates, however, thought the convention was going too far in the direction of a powerful national government. Acting on their behalf, William Paterson, a former attorney general of New Jersey who had helped to write its constitution, introduced an alternative plan on June 15. This is commonly called the **New Jersey Plan** (see Table 2-1).

The authors of this alternative were willing to increase the powers of the national government but not to alter the basic structure of the national Congress, with each state having one vote and delegates chosen and recallable by the state legislatures. Thus, the Virginia and New Jersey plans differed in several key respects. The Virginia Plan established a national government with (1) more extensive powers, essentially a general legislative power over matters of national concern; (2) the right to veto state laws; (3) a true separation of powers system with a constitutionally independent executive and judiciary; and (4) governing institutions that would represent the people—not the states.

Hamilton's Speech

Three days after Paterson introduced the New Jersey Plan, Alexander Hamilton of New York, the brilliant 32-year-old lawyer and former aide to General Washington, addressed the convention for its entire five- to six-hour session. Gouverneur Morris later told Madison that Hamilton's speech was "the most able and impressive he had ever heard."[14] Hamilton, who had not previously spoken, told the delegates that he was "unfriendly to both plans," for neither created a sufficiently strong and energetic national government. He then outlined the kind of government he would like to see (see Table 2-1).

Hamilton knew that several features of his plan went beyond what his colleagues were willing to consider, including (1) life terms for the chief executive and the members of one branch of the national legislature and (2) the appointment by the national government of state governors who would have an absolute veto power over state laws. Consequently, he did not formally propose his plan (and the delegates never formally considered it) but described it "only to give a more correct view of his ideas."[15] Eleven days after making his speech, Hamilton left for home and did not return until the final weeks.

Why did Hamilton give this speech? One possibility is that he wanted to make the Virginia Plan look moderate by comparison, thereby assisting his nationalist allies. Another

New Jersey Plan—a plan of government supported by the small states at the Constitutional Convention as a counterproposal to the Virginia Plan. It preserved the basic structure of the government under the Articles of Confederation (with equal state vote) but added new powers to regulate trade, raise revenues, and allow the Congress to create executive and judicial branches.

Sometimes called the "Father of the Constitution," James Madison of Virginia is more responsible than any other single person for replacing the defective Articles of Confederation with a more powerful and effective national government. His efforts were vital to the calling of the Convention, to the drafting of the Constitution at Philadelphia, to the success of the ratification contest, and to the addition of a sound Bill of Rights.

Alexander Hamilton, a brilliant 32-year-old lawyer and former aide to General Washington in the Revolutionary War, gave a famous speech at the Constitutional Convention on June 18 calling for a central government even stronger than that proposed in the Virginia Plan. Later, he worked tirelessly to secure ratification by New York by writing most of the *Federalist* essays and leading the pro-Constitution forces in the state ratifying convention.

James Wilson of Pennsylvania, an eminent expert on law, was a signer of the Declaration of Independence, highly influential member of the Constitutional Convention (perhaps second only to Madison in importance), and one of the six original members of the U.S. Supreme Court. He became the nation's second professor of law at an academic institution.

Although not well known to modern Americans, Gouverneur Morris of New York and Pennsylvania was one of the most influential members of the Constitutional Convention. He gave the most speeches, was a vigorous proponent of a strong national executive power, and as a member of the Committee of Style was responsible for giving the final form and polish to the Constitution. He is credited with drafting the Constitution's now famous Preamble.

is simply that he felt strongly about what needed to be done and had an obligation to speak his mind. "[W]e owe . . . it to our Country," he told the delegates, "to do on this emergency whatever we should deem essential to its happiness."[16]

The Great Compromise

The day after Hamilton gave his speech, a majority of states voted for the Virginia Plan over the New Jersey Plan. The delegates from the small states, however, were not ready to give up: they insisted that the states have equal weight in at least one branch of the new national legislature. Madison records that John Dickinson of Delaware, one of the most eminent and accomplished of the delegates, told him that the nationalists were "pushing things too far."[17] On June 30, probably the low point of the debates, Gunning Bedford of Delaware threatened that if the large states did not compromise, the confederation would dissolve and "the small ones will find some foreign ally of more honor and good faith, who will take them by the hand and do them justice."[18] Subsequent speakers denounced Bedford's "intemperance" and his "warm & rash language."[19]

For two weeks the convention was stalemated over this issue. Finally, on July 2, the delegates appointed a committee with one member from each state to fashion a compromise. On July 5, it made its recommendation:

- Representation in the first branch of the legislature to be based on population, with one representative for every 40,000 inhabitants.
- All bills for raising revenues, appropriating money, and setting salaries of federal officers to originate in the first branch and not be amendable by the second.
- No money to be drawn from the public treasury without an appropriation that originated in the first branch of the legislature.
- Each state to have an equal vote in the second branch of the legislature.

Although the committee agreed to state equality in one branch of the legislature (later named the Senate), it also enhanced the power of the more popular branch (later named the

House of Representatives) by requiring that all taxing and spending bills begin there and be unamendable by the other branch.

Debate continued through July 16, when, with 10 states in attendance, the delegates voted five to four, with one state divided, to accept the compromise. This became known as the **Great Compromise** or the **Connecticut Compromise** (because two delegates from Connecticut were instrumental in forging it). Later the delegates altered a few of its provisions. They allowed the Senate to (1) originate appropriation bills and bills setting federal salaries and (2) to amend all bills, including revenue bills, passed by the House.

Although the delegates from the small states were satisfied with this result, being willing to accept an inferior position in one branch of the legislature, many leading nationalists were not. Madison and James Wilson denounced the injustice of giving states with dramatically different populations the same weight in any organ of the new government. "Can we forget for whom we are forming a Government?" Wilson asked his colleagues. "Is it for *men*, or for the imaginary beings called *States*?"[20] Madison compared this decision to the fatal flaw of the Articles of Confederation: "I would compromise on this question, if I could do it on correct principles, but otherwise not—if the old fabric of the confederation must be the ground-work of the new, we must fail."[21]

Others, however, who favored a strong national government accepted the use of two different principles of representation. "We were partly national; partly federal," said Oliver Ellsworth of Connecticut. Representation in the first branch would follow "the national principle," and the equality of states in the second would respect "the federal principle."[22] Similarly, William Davie of North Carolina held that "we were partly federal, partly national in our Union."[23] (The federal character of American government is the subject of Chapter 3.) Thus, supporters of a strong national government disagreed over the merits of the compromise. Some considered the equality of states in even one branch of the legislature such a serious defect that it would be better for the Convention to split into two groups, with each proposing a new scheme of government. Others, however, thought either that the compromise was a reasonable accommodation or that it was better to yield to the small states and send a single plan to the people, even if imperfect.[24]

Completing the Constitution

In late July the delegates appointed a five-member **Committee of Detail** to prepare a draft constitution based on the decisions to date. The committee made its report on August 6 and distributed copies of a draft constitution to all the delegates. The committee's proposal detailed specific powers for the legislative and executive branches and specified the kinds of cases that the federal courts would hear. And for the first time we have the names *Congress*, *House of Representatives*, *Senate*, *Presidency*, and *Supreme Court* for the new governing institutions.

The plan vested Congress with substantial new powers, including

- to raise its own revenues (no more requisitions from the states),
- to regulate interstate and foreign commerce,
- to coin money,
- to borrow money,
- to establish lower federal courts, and
- to "make war" (later changed to "declare war").

It also authorized Congress "to make all laws that shall be necessary and proper for carrying into execution the foregoing powers." The new government would no longer act through the state governments but would deal directly with the citizens.

The draft constitution also imposed restrictions on state power. The states could not under any circumstances enter into treaties or alliances or grant titles of nobility. And they could not, without the consent of Congress:

- emit bills of credit,
- make anything but gold or silver legal tender in payment of debts (making a repeat of the "paper money" episode in the states impossible),

Great Compromise—the compromise between the large and small states at the Constitutional Convention, according to which population would be the basis for representation in the first branch of the new national legislature and equality of the states in the second. It also required that bills for raising revenues and appropriating funds originate in the first branch. Also called the **Connecticut Compromise**.

Connecticut Compromise—see Great Compromise.

Committee of Detail—the five-member committee of the Constitutional Convention that met in late July and early August 1787 to fashion the resolutions passed by the Convention, up to that point, into a draft constitution. Along with the Committee of Style, it was one of the two most important committees at the Convention.

FOCUS QUESTION

If you had served at the Constitutional Convention in 1787, would you have supported the Virginia Plan, the New Jersey Plan, or Hamilton's Plan (or perhaps another of your own devising)? Would you have supported the Great Compromise? Why?

- lay duties on imports,
- keep troops or ships of war in time of peace,
- enter into any agreement or compact with another state or a foreign power, or
- engage in war unless actually invaded.

For five weeks the delegates worked through the 23 articles of the draft constitution with great care, often creating special committees to address particularly thorny issues.

Presidency

In the weeks before the appointment of the Committee of Detail, the delegates had overwhelmingly agreed that the new national executive should be a single person with a fixed salary and the power to veto statutes passed by the legislature (subject to a two-thirds override). Throughout their deliberations, however, they struggled to find some way to make the president both independent of the legislature (unlike most of the state governors) and eligible to run for reelection. Initially seeing no alternative to election by Congress, they feared that if the president were reeligible, he would have too strong an incentive to curry favor with Congress, undermining his independence. But they also worried that if the president could not seek reelection, he would lack, in Gouverneur Morris's colorful language, "the great motive to good behavior, the hope of being rewarded by a re-appointment. It was saying to him, make hay while the sun shines."[25]

Some delegates, including such leading figures as Madison, Wilson, and Morris, proposed solving this problem by having the people elect the president directly, but others raised objections to direct popular election. Some feared that the people, knowing little about leaders in other states, would usually vote for a local favorite, thereby dividing up the vote among many candidates and giving the large states an unfair advantage. Others, such as Elbridge Gerry of Massachusetts, worried that "[t]he people are uninformed, and would be misled by a few designing men."[26] He particularly mentioned the Society of Cincinnati, an organization of Revolutionary War officers whose first president was George Washington. Such an influential group, he warned, could act in concert and "delude" the people.[27] Because the delegates assumed that there would be no political parties to regulate the selection process and nominate candidates, a private group like the Society of Cincinnati might dominate the process. Others, such as George Mason of Virginia, said that the country was too large for citizens to know the qualifications of the candidates. Having the people choose the president was like "refer[ing] a trial of colours to a blind man."[28]

In the end, the delegates solved their quandary by having specially appointed electors—equal to the number of representatives and senators within each state—select the president for a four-year term. Chosen as the state legislatures saw fit, the electors would meet within their state and vote for two persons for president, one of whom at least could not be from their state. If one person received the votes of a majority of the electors appointed, he became president. Whoever came in second became vice president. If no one received votes from a majority of the electors, or if two did but tied (this was possible because each elector cast two votes), then the House of Representatives would decide, with each state having one vote. (Almost two decades later, in 1804, the states ratified the Twelfth Amendment to the Constitution, which required separate votes for president and vice president. This was a reaction to the 1800 election in which Thomas Jefferson and Aaron Burr tied in the electoral vote, even though the new Jeffersonian-Republican Party had slated Jefferson as the presidential candidate and Burr as the vice-presidential candidate. It took 36 ballots before the House of Representatives settled on Jefferson.)

Although we commonly call the presidential selection system the "**electoral college**," the Constitution itself does not use the term, which originated in the early 1800s. Also, the term *college* implies that the electors all meet together, but this only happens in their individual states. Every four years we actually have many electoral colleges.

Although the delegates had rejected direct popular election of the president, they recognized that public opinion would influence presidential elections under their scheme. This was because either the state legislatures would choose electors broadly representative of

Electoral College—the name later given to the method of electing presidents outlined in the Constitution of 1787 whereby electors, equal to the number of representatives and senators in each state, would be appointed as the state legislature saw fit and would meet in their states to vote for two persons for president, one of whom could not be a resident of their state (modified by the Twelfth Amendment in 1804).

public opinion in the state or they would allow the people to choose the electors directly. In the first presidential election, almost half the states gave the people the right to elect the electors; by the 1830s, all the states but South Carolina did. Since 1860, all presidential electors have been chosen within the states directly by the people.

Once the delegates had freed the president from legislative election, they removed all limits on reelection. (The Twenty-Second Amendment, ratified in 1951, now limits presidents to two full terms.) The new president, the delegates hoped, would have an incentive to do a good job and to fight to preserve the independence of the executive branch. (For a comparison of "presidential government" with "parliamentary government," see the International Perspectives feature.)

Congress

A key feature of the new Congress was its bicameral (two-house) design. Some think that bicameralism was invented at the Convention to give the small states equal weight in one legislative branch. As we have seen, however, the original Virginia Plan proposed a bicameral legislature with neither branch based on state equality. Thus, even apart from the issue of representation, the delegates saw the virtues of requiring two distinct bodies to deliberate and agree on legislation.

With its members elected directly by the people for two-year terms, the House of Representatives would be, in the words of George Mason, "the grand depository of the democratic principle of the Govt. . . . It ought to know & sympathise with every part of the community."[29] Yet the delegates feared that as the body grew to several hundred members (it began with 65), passion and disorder might corrupt its deliberations, as often happened in large legislative bodies. Also, they worried that the House would be filled with part-time lawmakers coming and going in rapid succession who would not have time to learn about national and international affairs. Finally, short terms of office might incline representatives to do what was immediately popular, even if unwise.

To counteract these potential defects of the House, the new Senate would be much smaller (originally 26) and would have members chosen by the state legislatures to serve six-year terms. These provisions would, ideally, diminish the pressure on senators to do what was immediately popular and thus encourage a long-term view of the common good. Also, to promote consistent policies elections would be staggered so that only one-third of senators would face reelection every two years. The new Senate, Madison predicted, would function "with more coolness, with more system, & with more wisdom, than the popular branch."[30] The Senate was to be a preeminently deliberative institution.

Judiciary

The creation of a national judiciary was uncontroversial. From the very beginning, the delegates agreed that separate federal courts were needed to resolve disputes that might arise under the new constitution and federal laws. To insulate federal judges from political pressures, they should serve for life, subject to impeachment and removal by Congress for serious misbehavior. Although the original Virginia Plan had prohibited Congress from increasing or decreasing judicial salaries, the delegates changed this to allow increases (presumably to account for long-term inflation). The Committee on Detail proposed a Supreme Court to head the federal judiciary with Congress retaining authority to create lower federal courts. In this plan, the Senate would appoint the members of the Supreme Court. Later the delegates gave the president the authority to appoint federal judges, subject to Senate approval.

Controversy arose over the Virginia Plan's proposal to join the chief executive with some number of federal judges in a "council of revision" with authority to veto acts of the national legislature. Madison in particular pressed this proposal again and again, but every time the delegates soundly defeated it. They especially did not like the idea of asking judges to decide on the wisdom of public policy. As Nathaniel Gorham of Massachusetts put it, "As Judges they are not to be presumed to possess any particular knowledge of the mere policy of public measures."[31]

Parliamentary Democracy versus Presidential Government

The United States Constitution is based on the separation of powers into three distinct branches: legislative (Congress), executive (presidency), and judicial (Supreme Court and lower federal courts). No member of Congress is allowed to serve in the executive or judicial branches at the same time. The branches are "coequal" in that each is supreme within its own sphere, but no branch is supreme over the others. All three are equally the creation of the American people through the Constitution. Another name for the American system is **presidential government**, because the president is independently elected and cannot be dismissed by the legislature. This means that different political parties may run the legislative and executive branches. We call this division of power between the parties **divided government**, which is quite common in the United States. Most nations in the Western Hemisphere have presidential governments, as do a few nations in Asia and Africa.

Among democracies, the chief alternative to presidential government is **parliamentary government**, which has its roots in medieval England where the Parliament, composed of a House of Lords and a House of Commons, shared power with the monarch. By the nineteenth century, the monarchy had become little more than a figurehead; and by the twentieth century the effective political power had become concentrated in the elected House of Commons. Most European democracies have a parliamentary government, as do other large democracies such as India, Japan, and Australia.

In parliamentary governments, the people vote for representatives to the lawmaking body, however named (e.g., Parliament in Britain, Knesset in Israel, and Diet in Japan). If one party gains a majority in the legislature, its leader, often called the prime minister, becomes the head of the executive branch (usually called "the government"). Other leaders in the party become members of the cabinet and run the executive departments or serve in subcabinet positions. Most of the officials who run the executive branch serve also in the legislature. Thus, dozens of individuals may serve in the parliament and in high-level executive office simultaneously.

If no single party gains a majority in the legislature, then the largest party usually seeks to form a majority coalition with one or more smaller parties, as the Conservative Party in the United Kingdom did with the smaller Liberal Democrats in May of 2010 after it won a plurality, but not a majority, of the seats in the parliamentary election. The smaller parties typically bargain for high-level executive branch appointments and, sometimes, assurances that the largest party will support one or more of their legislative priorities. In most parliamentary democracies, new elections must take place at least every five to six years; but elections may be called sooner if the ruling party sees political advantage in doing so. Also, new elections may be called if a majority in the legislature casts a "vote of no confidence" in the leadership, although such votes are rare.

What are the virtues and vices of the two systems? A parliamentary system, according to its defenders, offers clear choices to the voters in elections, smoothly transfers public opinion into the governing institutions, and then efficiently translates these views into public policy. Presidential government, they contend, provides too many independent decision makers who are often at odds with one another, frequently leads to stalemate or deadlock since different people (and sometimes different parties) run the legislative and executive branches, and provides no easy way for public opinion to move governing institutions.

Advocates of presidential government tout its great number and variety of access points for individuals and groups to make their views known, praise its ability to resist immediate public desires by refining and enlarging public opinion through distinct institutions, and especially admire the independence and energy of its executive branch, which cannot be brought down between regularly scheduled elections by losing favor in the legislature or with the public.

Although most liberal democracies have either parliamentary or presidential governments, some are hybrids. In 1958, for example, France changed its constitution to add an independently elected president with a seven-year term (later reduced to five years). This hybrid form has been adopted by some formerly Communist countries, such as Russia, Poland, and Ukraine. Although these are not true separation of powers systems—because the leaders of the majority party in the parliament exercise important executive functions—popular election of the president makes for a more independent executive than in a pure parliamentary system.

CRITICAL THINKING
QUESTION

Would the United States be better governed by a parliamentary system?

Final Form

With the great controversies behind them (we discuss the controversy over slavery later), the delegates appointed a five-member **Committee of Style** on September 8 to give final form to the constitution. The committee reorganized the 23 articles of the Committee of Detail's much modified draft into 7, introduced by a revised preamble, and made a variety of stylistic changes. The first and longest of the articles was on Congress (just over half of the entire document); the next in order and length was on the presidency; and the third was on the judiciary. Articles IV–VII covered a variety of miscellaneous topics. The committee presented its report and distributed copies of its constitution on September 12.

Over the next several days, the delegates made final revisions. Weary from more than three months of work and eager to return to their homes, they were impatient with proposals for significant changes. When Elbridge Gerry and George Mason proposed adding a bill of rights, they were quickly turned down by a vote of 10 states to none. When Madison and Charles Pinckney proposed vesting Congress with the power to establish a national university, they lost six states to four. And when Randolph proposed another national convention to consider amendments that might be recommended by the state conventions, every state voted against. Immediately thereafter, at the end of the day on September 15, every state voted to approve the Constitution, and it was ordered to be engrossed (professionally handwritten on parchment).

The Constitution was then read to the delegates on September 17, the final day of the convention. But even then, they were not quite done. For the first time, George Washington spoke on a substantive matter. He endorsed a proposal from Gorham of Massachusetts to change the ratio of representation for the House of Representatives from no more than one representative for every 40,000 persons to every 30,000. Washington argued that this change, which could significantly increase the future size of the House, would promote "security for the rights & interests of the people."[32] Although the delegates had defeated previous attempts to increase the size of the House, the combination of the lateness of the hour and the respect for Washington silenced any opposition. The change passed unanimously.

To promote adherence to a new national constitution, the original Virginia Plan had required that all state officials take an oath to support it. In its final form the Constitution went further, with three separate requirements for oaths:

- when the Senate conducts an impeachment trial (Article I, Section 3);
- by a president to "faithfully execute the office of President" and to "preserve, protect and defend the Constitution" (discussed in Chapter 13) (Article II, Section 1); and
- by all representatives, executive officials, and judges in the national government and the states "to support this Constitution" (Article VI).

At the time of the American founding, oaths were understood to be promises before God. As Noah Webster defined the term in the first American dictionary, an oath is a "solemn affirmation or declaration, made with an appeal to God for the truth of what is affirmed." If a person falsely swears an oath, he or she "invokes the vengeance of God."[33] That the Constitution requires oaths in three places is evidence of the importance that the founding generation attached to these public promises. Officeholders, they believed, were more likely to perform their duties properly if they formally, solemnly, and publicly promised to do so before God. Moral and religious obligations could encourage responsible political behavior. (The Constitution allows officeholders to "affirm" or make an "Affirmation" rather than swear an oath in deference particularly to

Presidential government—the American system of representative democracy (also called a separation of powers system) in which the chief executive is independently elected and cannot be dismissed by the legislature. No executive official may also serve in the legislature.

Divided government—when different political parties control the executive branch and at least one chamber of the legislature in a separation of powers, or presidential, system of government.

Parliamentary government—the type of representative democracy in which the people vote for representatives to the lawmaking body and then the head of the majority party (or coalition of parties) becomes the chief executive. Many of the top executive officials also serve in the legislature.

Committee of Style—the five-member committee of the Constitutional Convention that met during the last week of the Convention in September 1787 to give final form to the Constitution. Along with the Committee of Detail, it was one of the two most important committees at the Convention.

© Bettmann/CORBIS

The British House of Commons wields the effective lawmaking power in the British Parliament, with the House of Lords limited to advising and proposing amendments to legislation. In the House of Commons, the opposition parties sit facing each other, with their leaders in the front row. Nonleaders are called "backbenchers."

Today's Oath to Support the Constitution

Through statute, Congress specifies the exact language of the oath that all state and national officials take to support the Constitution, as it did in the very first law it passed on June 1, 1789. Congress last revised the oath in 1884. Millions of Americans have now taken the following oath:

I, [name], do solemnly swear (or affirm) that I will support and defend the Constitution of the United States against all enemies, foreign and domestic; that I will bear true faith and allegiance to the same; that I take this obligation freely, without any mental reservation or purpose of evasion; and that I will well and faithfully discharge the duties of the office on which I am about to enter. So help me God. (5 U.S.C. sec. 3331) [34]

© Joseph Sohm/Visions of America/Corbis

This is the chair in which George Washington sat while presiding over the Constitutional Convention.

Quakers, who refused to swear oaths before God but were willing to make public affirmations. In the colonies, Quakers had sometimes been denied the right to hold office, serve on juries, testify in court, or vote because of their refusal to take oaths.)

Madison concluded his detailed notes on the debates in the Constitutional Convention with the following story about the signing of the Constitution:

Whilst the last members were signing it Doctr. Franklin looking towards the Presidents Chair, at the back of which a rising sun happened to be painted, observed to a few members near him, that Painters had found it difficult to distinguish in their art a rising sun from a setting sun. I have, said he, often and often in the course of the Session, and the vicissitudes of my hopes and fears as to its issue, looked at that behind the President without being able to tell whether it was rising or setting: But now at length I have the happiness to know that it is a rising and not a setting Sun. [35]

With this, the convention adjourned. Washington transmitted the Constitution to the Congress with the recommendation that Congress send it to the states for their consideration.

RATIFYING THE CONSTITUTION

MAJOR ISSUE

- What were the principal issues in the debate over the ratification of the Constitution?

The Constitution was the product of the deliberations of the 55 men who served at Philadelphia; its fate would turn on the deliberations of hundreds of individuals elected to serve in their state ratifying conventions.

The Course of Ratification

Ratification—the process by which popularly elected conventions in the states formally approved the proposed Constitution of 1787.

The struggle over **ratification** began at the Constitutional Convention itself with the debate over the method of ratification. Had the delegates followed the rules for amending the Articles of Confederation, the Constitution would have required the approval of all 13 state legislatures. All the states would have been at the mercy of any one that refused approval.

"But will any one say," asked Nathaniel Gorham of Massachusetts, "that all the States are to suffer themselves to be ruined, if Rho. Island should persist in her opposition to general measures."[36] (Recall that Rhode Island refused even to attend the Convention.) Similarly, Pierce Butler of South Carolina "revolted at the idea, that one or two States should restrain the rest from consulting their safety."[37] Thus, to insist on unanimous approval would have made the adoption of the Constitution quite unlikely and would have been unfair to the majority of the states and the people.

Consequently, the delegates came up with an alternative method of ratification: approval by at least nine popularly elected state ratifying conventions. This would have the added benefit of giving the new government the strength of a popular ratification. "We must," James Wilson argued, "go to the original powers of Society."[38] To the legalistic objection that this ratification method violated the Articles of Confederation, Madison countered, "The people were in fact, the fountain of all power, and by resorting to them, all difficulties were got over. They could alter constitutions as they pleased."[39]

A final advantage of this ratification method was that it would combine public opinion and deliberation. Because their members were to be popularly elected, the state ratifying conventions would broadly represent popular attitudes. Still, this was not a direct popular vote on the Constitution. The delegates to the state conventions could debate and reason together about the best course to take, even if this deviated from the original desires of their constituents.

Just 11 days after the Constitutional Convention adjourned, the Confederation Congress adopted a resolution, without a recommendation one way or the other, transmitting the proposed Constitution to the states and calling for them to arrange for conventions to consider ratification. As events were to show, the Constitution was popular in some states—three ratified by unanimous votes—and controversial in others, including such large states as Massachusetts, New York, and Virginia.

On December 7, 1787, Delaware became the first state to ratify by the unanimous vote of 30–0. Within two weeks, Pennsylvania and New Jersey followed, the former by a 2–1 vote and the latter 38–0. Then, in the first two weeks of the new year, Georgia approved the Constitution 26–0, and Connecticut by the lopsided vote of 128–40.

The movement for a quick ratification then stalled in Massachusetts, where opposition to the Constitution was strong among those who represented rural areas. Opponents criticized the absence of a bill of rights and of protections for state powers. The friends of the new Constitution responded by promising to support amendments, including a bill of rights, once the new government began operating. With this understanding, the delegates ratified the Constitution on February 6, 1788, by a vote of 187–168. Proponents of ratification then used this formula—ratify now with the promise of amendments to come later—in the remaining states.

With six states now on board, only three more were required to make the Constitution legally effective. In late April, Maryland approved by a 6–1 majority; South Carolina followed a month later by a 2–1 margin; and New Hampshire became the ninth state to ratify on June 21 by the fairly close vote of 57–47. Although the requisite nine states had now ratified, neither New York nor Virginia had yet done so. Given their population (Virginia ranked first and New York fifth), location, and commercial importance, few thought that the new government would be successful if these states refused to join. Indeed, if neither joined, the territory to be governed by the Constitution would be in three separate pieces.

In both states, able leaders led the opposing sides. James Madison and Patrick Henry faced off in Virginia, while Alexander Hamilton and the popular governor George Clinton did so in New York. Close votes decided both contests: on June 25, Virginia ratified 89–79; and on July 26, New York followed, 30–27. With only North Carolina and Rhode Island still outside the fold, the Confederation Congress called for the first national elections under the new Constitution. On March 4, 1789, the new Congress, with representatives and senators from 11 states, convened in New York City; and on April 30, George Washington, the unanimous choice of the presidential electors, took the oath of office as the first president of the United States. North Carolina ratified later that year (194–77 on November 21); but it was not until May 29, 1790, that Rhode Island finally joined the other states. Even at this late date, ratification nearly lost: 34 in favor; 32 opposed.

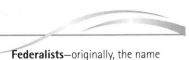

Federalists—originally, the name given to those who supported the ratification of the Constitution of 1787. Later, it was the name for members of one of the first two political parties in the United States.

Anti-Federalists—the name given to those who opposed the ratification of the Constitution of 1787.

Federalist Papers—85 essays in defense of the proposed Constitution and published in New York City newspapers between October 1787 and May 1788 under the pseudonym "Publius." They were written by Alexander Hamilton, James Madison, and John Jay and were originally titled *The Federalist.*

FOCUS QUESTION

In your view, which single argument during the ratification debates made the strongest case for the proposed new Constitution? Which was the strongest argument against? Why?

Separation of powers—an essential principle of the first American state constitutions and the U.S. Constitution according to which the legislative, executive, and judicial powers of government are assigned to three distinct institutions.

Debating the Constitution

During the ratification debates, the proponents of the Constitution took on the name **Federalists** and their opponents became known as **Anti-Federalists**. A few years later, Federalists also became the name of one of the two major political parties (see Chapter 9).

The Federalist (also called *The **Federalist Papers***) is also the name of the lengthiest and most comprehensive defense of the Constitution written during the ratification struggle. This was a series of 85 essays published in New York City newspapers between October 1787 and May 1788 under the pseudonym "Publius" (a reference to "one of the founders and saviors of republican Rome").[40] "Publius" was actually three different people—Alexander Hamilton, who wrote about three-fifths of the essays; James Madison, who wrote most of the rest (including many of the best-known essays); and John Jay, a prominent political figure from New York, who wrote only five because of illness.

In the years after ratification of the Constitution, *The Federalist* quickly became accepted as virtually a definitive interpretation of the meaning of the Constitution. Jefferson, for one, called it "the best commentary on the principles of government, which ever was written."[41] Two hundred years later, reformers in Eastern Europe were reading *The Federalist* for insight into how to establish democratic institutions. In fact, Vojislav Kostunica, the former professor who was elected as a reformer to the presidency of Yugoslavia in 2000, had translated *The Federalist* into Serbo-Croatian.

How Powerful a National Government?

Some of the opponents of the Constitution objected that they were the true "federalists" because they supported a federal system of relatively autonomous states that joined together for certain limited national purposes. In this kind of system, the states were the highest authority. Many opponents of the Constitution feared that under the new national government the states would eventually be annihilated or become mere agencies of the national government. A powerful central authority, they warned, would lose touch with the people, develop aristocratic and monarchical tendencies, amass uncontrollable power, and eventually undermine the liberties of the people.

Although the Federalists denied that they wished to abolish the states or the state governments, they insisted that the Confederation experience proved that an effective Union required an efficient national government with the authority to operate directly on the people and with sufficient powers to achieve its goals. The national government, according to Publius, ought to have "an unconfined authority in respect to all those objects which are intrusted to its management." These objects included common defense, the preservation of peace against both external and internal threats, the regulation of interstate and foreign commerce, and the conduct of foreign relations.[42]

On national security, Federalists and Anti-Federalists disagreed strongly on the need for standing armies in time of peace. Anti-Federalists denounced them—and the Constitution for allowing them—because they could be turned against the people. Federalists countered that it was impossible to foresee all possible threats that the nation might someday face. If a foreign nation invaded, there likely would not be enough time to raise an army from scratch; and it was too much to expect state militias, manned by part-time soldiers, to succeed against a well-trained professional army. "War," Publius wrote, "is a science to be acquired and perfected by diligence, by perseverance, by time, and by practice."[43]

It was irresponsible, Federalists insisted, to deny the national government the powers necessary for national defense. To the charge that these powers could be dangerous, Publius responded that safety came not from limiting power (which was dangerous in its own way) but from structuring the institutions so that power would be exercised properly.

Institutional Design

The key to the framers' institutional design is captured in the phrases "separation of powers" and "checks and balances." Although these phrases are often used interchangeably, they do not mean the same thing. **Separation of powers** refers to dividing governmental power into three basic types—making laws, executing the laws, and adjudicating controversies that arise under the laws—and assigning each to a separate institution designed for this purpose. So the word *powers* here means both the functions and the institutions. **Checks and balances** refers to the ability of each branch to control partially the power exercised by another, largely to resist encroachments on its own powers.

The presidential veto power is a classic example of these principles in action. Although separation of powers gives the lawmaking power to Congress and the law-executing power to the president, the principle of checks and balances justifies giving the president some partial check on Congress's legislative power. Wielding his veto, the president can defend his office from congressional encroachments and, at times, protect the community from bad laws (though two-thirds of the House and Senate can override a veto). Thus, the principle of checks and balances allows for some intermixture of powers—some partial violation of pure separation of powers—to help preserve the fundamental separation itself and to promote responsible policies.

As we saw earlier, all the new state constitutions had provided for separation of powers. The problem was that they did not give the executive and judicial branches sufficient means, or checks, to resist encroachments by the legislature, and thus preserve the balance of the constitution.

Yet, as Publius famously wrote in *Federalist* 51, checks would only be effective if public officials had both the "constitutional means" and the "personal motives" to resist encroachments and stand up for the rights and powers of their office: "Ambition must be made to counteract ambition. The interest of the man must be connected with the constitutional rights of the place."[44] In an ideal world, officeholders would do their duty without regard for their personal interests. But as Publius bluntly put it, "If men were angels, no government would be necessary. If angels were to govern men, neither external nor internal controls on government would be necessary." The Constitution makes up for "the defect of better motives" by relying in part on "opposite and rival interests."[45] If, for example, a president tried to usurp the legitimate powers of Congress, representatives and senators would, it was hoped, feel a personal interest in protecting the powers of their institution. Similarly, a president, possessing substantial powers, a fixed salary, a four-year term, and not beholden to Congress for reelection, would have strong motives to protect his office from congressional attack. So, although the framers did not believe that self-interest was the only motive in human affairs, they understood its power and sought to attach the personal interest of officeholders to the responsibilities of their office.

The Anti-Federalists accepted the principle of separation of powers but had serious reservations about important aspects of the constitutional design. A major objection, first voiced by George Mason in the Constitutional Convention itself, was that the Constitution vested too much power in the aristocratic Senate and monarchical presidency. He also believed, as did many opponents of the Constitution, that the more democratic House of Representatives was too small to properly represent some 3 million Americans. According to Mason, it had "not the substance but the shadow only of representation." Over time, Mason predicted, the less democratic branches would predominate in the new government, resulting "either in monarchy, or a tyrannical aristocracy." He could not say which it would be, "but one or the other, he was sure."[46]

The Anti-Federalists put their faith less in institutional structure than in responsibility, or accountability, to a virtuous citizenry. (Here the Anti-Federalists emphasized some of the duties that citizens must embrace in a successful democracy, a major theme of this book.) Effective accountability required short terms of office (many insisted on one-year terms for the House), relatively small legislative districts, and a fairly simple structure of government. The people should be able to monitor public officials effectively and deny them reelection after short terms of office. And one Anti-Federalist sharply attacked the Federalists' reliance on the self-interest of officeholders: "If the administrators of every government are actuated by views of private interest and ambition, how is the welfare and happiness of the community to be the result of such jarring adverse interests?"[47]

The Small Republic and Civic Virtue

This last quotation points to one of the deepest divisions between Federalists and Anti-Federalists and why the opponents of the Constitution preferred small republics over large

Checks and balances—the principle of the U.S. Constitution that gives each of the three major branches of government the means to control partially the power exercised by another, largely to resist encroachments on its own powers.

This is how the famous *Federalist* 10 essay appeared in the *New York Daily Advertiser* on November 22, 1787.

ones. Anti-Federalists such as Brutus, a leading New York critic of the Constitution, denied that a successful republic could be as large as the United States. For support, Brutus quoted the philosopher Montesquieu, who was well known for making the argument that a republic must be small, and he cited history that "furnishes no example of a free republic, any thing like the extent of the United States."[48]

Following Montesquieu, the Anti-Federalists believed that republican government depends for its success on civic virtue, which includes a public-spirited devotion to the common good, moderation of desires (or self-control), and law-abidingness. "Political virtue," Montesquieu wrote, "is a renunciation of oneself, which is always a very painful thing. One can define this virtue as love of the laws and the homeland. This love, requiring a continuous preference of the public interest over one's own, produces all the individual virtues."[49] In large nations, the citizens tend to think less about the common good and more about their private interests. Extremes of wealth are more common, and, as a result, desires are less restrained.

Many of the Anti-Federalists charged that the proposed new constitutional order relied too much on the self-interest of leaders and citizens; did too little to inculcate civic virtue; and by promoting commerce and acquisitiveness, threatened to undermine the human qualities necessary to sustain republican government. In the words of Mercy Warren, one of the most thoughtful critics of the proposed Constitution, "most of the inhabitants of America were too proud for monarchy, yet too poor for nobility, and it is to be feared, too selfish and avaricious for a virtuous republic."[50]

The Case for the Large Republic

In *Federalists* 9 and 10, Publius directly challenged the Anti-Federalists' preference for small republics. In the former, Publius made the telling point that when Montesquieu argued for small republics, he had in mind political communities much smaller even than most of the American states. Thus, if Montesquieu was right, Americans would have to choose between monarchy and, as Publius colorfully put it, "splitting ourselves into an infinity of little, jealous, clashing, tumultuous commonwealths, the wretched nurseries of unceasing discord and the miserable objects of universal pity or contempt."[51] Genuine small republics were not a realistic option in the United States.

Publius also argued that the historical record of republican governments, whatever their size, was rather dismal. Ever since the ancient world, republics had been unstable and torn apart by disorder and revolutions. Even in the new state governments established after independence, self-interested majorities too often undermined "the public good," ignored "the rules of justice," and violated "the rights of the minor party." The "great object" before the American people was to "secure the public good and private rights against the danger of . . . a [majority] faction, and at the same time to preserve the spirit and the form of popular government."[52]

This issue was the focus of Madison's famous argument in *Federalist* 10, which we summarized in the previous chapter. Wherever there is freedom, people will have different opinions concerning religion and government, will attach themselves to different leaders, and will have conflicting interests because of the different types and amount of property they own. They form groups based on these opinions and interests, and sometimes these groups take actions "adverse to the rights of other citizens, or to the permanent and aggregate interests of the community."[53]

National Archives

IMPACT
of Social Media and Communications Technology

The Debate over the Constitution

Communications were vital to the ratification of the Constitution. Because the Constitutional Convention met in secret, the American people had no opportunity to witness and evaluate the arguments in Philadelphia for and against the plan as a whole or its specific provisions. Today we can read Madison's detailed notes of the Convention debates, but these were not published until 1840, four years after Madison died and more than half a century after the Constitution was written. But once the proposed Constitution was sent to the states in late September 1787, partisans on both sides rushed to make their case using the cutting-edge communications technology of the day: newspapers and pamphlets.

The 85 *Federalist* essays, as we have seen, appeared in New York City newspapers. They served a similar function as modern op-ed pieces but were much longer. The famous *Federalist* 10, for example, was over 3,000 words, about four times longer than an opinion piece in a newspaper today. And, as the nearby photo illustrates, no attempt was made to add interest to the layout to attract the attention of the reader. Other defenders of the proposed Constitution made their arguments in specially printed pamphlets, as did most of the Anti-Federalist writers.

Frequently in the Bessette–Pitney blog we have called attention to the impact of social media on campaigns and debates in modern American politics. See, especially, the entries for October 9, 2011; October 14, 2011; October 30, 2011; November 5, 2011; January 17, 2012; January 22, 2012; March 12, 2012; March 14, 2012; March 17, 2012; and March 19, 2012.

CRITICAL THINKING QUESTION

Evaluate how the existence of social media in 1787 and 1788 would have impacted the ratification debates. Would the result have been different?

Madison believed that property differences were "the most common and durable source of factions."[54] Some have a lot of property; others have little or none. Some are creditors who lend money; others are debtors. Some are farmers; others make their living through manufacturing or trade. The problem in a republican government is that legislators may see themselves as advocates of a particular interest and pass laws that advance that interest in a way that unfairly harms others or undermines the good of the whole country. Unfortunately, according to Madison, "neither moral nor religious motives" will generally keep an interested majority from acting unjustly. What, then, is the solution?

The key, Madison maintained, was to have a large republic, which had two great advantages over a small one. First, in large republics the actual governing is done by representatives elected by the people. As we saw in Chapter 1, the framers hoped that elected representatives would use their "wisdom," "patriotism," and "love of justice" to "refine and enlarge the public views." The resulting laws would better promote the public good than if the people had made them directly. For this reason, representative democracies are preferable to direct democracies. Also, large representative democracies are better than small ones because they are more likely to have a sufficient number of "fit characters" to serve in the legislature.[55]

The other advantage of a large territory is that it can take in a greater diversity of groups and interests, making it unlikely that a majority of citizens would share an unjust desire or be able to act upon it.[56] As Madison elaborated in *Federalist* 51, "the society itself will be broken into so many parts, interests and classes of citizens, that the rights of individuals, or of the minority, will be in little danger from interested combinations of the majority."[57]

Thus, it is not so much republican virtue that keeps the majority from acting unjustly as it is the sheer number and variety of groups within the society and the logistical difficulties of fashioning a majority for some sinister end. Madison believed that majorities devoted to just ends would have an easier time of it than those with unjust goals: "a coalition of a majority of the whole society could seldom take place on any other principles than those of justice and the general good."[58] But he did not completely rule out unjust majorities; for to say that they would "seldom" occur is not to say that they would never occur.

Although Madison extolled the benefits of a large republic, he also recognized the importance of the states in the new system. The Constitution did not establish a single

Amending the Constitution

Prominent founders disagreed about how easy it ought to be to change constitutions. Thomas Jefferson, for one, cautioned against treating constitutions "with sanctimonious reverence" and as "too sacred to be touched." "[L]aws and institutions," he urged, "must go hand in hand with the progress of the human mind." Thus, it should be easy to change a constitution; and every generation should have an opportunity to choose its own form of government. Drawing on mortality tables, Jefferson calculated that this meant every 19–20 years.[65] James Madison disagreed. Frequent consideration of constitutional amendments would undermine "veneration" of the Constitution and would "disturb . . . the public tranquility by interesting too strongly the public passions." Revisions of the fundamental law, Madison held, are "experiments . . . of too ticklish a nature to be unnecessarily multiplied."[66]

Although most of the framers of the Constitution sided with Madison, they also believed that the people ought to have some means to alter their charter of government. Republican theory, after all, held that because government was the creation of the people it served, they were free to modify or replace it to promote their safety and happiness. "The people," Madison said at the Constitutional Convention, "could alter constitutions as they pleased." President George Washington made the same point in his Farewell Address of September 17, 1796: "The basis of our political systems is the right of the people to make and to alter their constitutions of government."[67] This right would exist whether or not the Constitution of 1787 provided a particular means for amending the document.

Recognizing this fundamental right and wishing to provide a way for the people to change the fundamental law without resorting to revolutionary actions, the framers spelled out specific steps for amending the Constitution. This would be a two-stage process, with each stage having two alternatives (see Figure 2-2) and every alternative requiring supermajorities. Only a widely shared desire to alter the Constitution would be successful.

Proposing Amendments

1. By a two-thirds vote of the House and Senate, or
2. By a convention called for by Congress when two-thirds of the state legislatures request it.

Ratifying Amendments

1. Three-fourths of the state legislatures, or
2. Three-fourths of ratifying conventions in the states, with Congress deciding on the method of ratification.

Of the 27 amendments that have been added to the Constitution, all but one resulted from Congress proposing the amendment and the state legislatures ratifying it. The exception is the repeal of Prohibition (Twenty-first), which Congress proposed but stipulated that ratification must result from conventions in the states, which happened in 1933. Another six proposed amendments passed Congress but failed in the states. The most recent was Congress's effort to amend the Constitution in 1978 to give Washington, DC, voting members in the House and Senate, as if it were a state.[68]

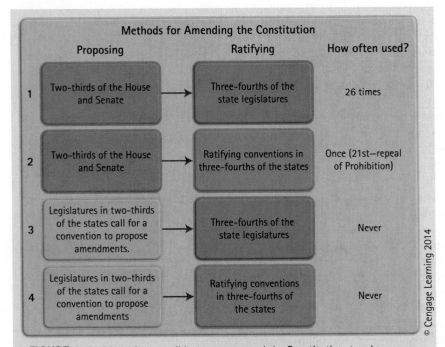

FIGURE 2-2 Of the four possible ways to amend the Constitution, two have never been used, and another has been used only once. Under the Constitution, Congress decides on the method of ratification.

consolidated republic but a federal system in which the states retained substantial powers (see especially the next chapter). As Publius explained in *Federalist* 39, the jurisdiction of the new national government "extends to certain enumerated objects only, and leaves to the several States a residuary and inviolable sovereignty over all other objects."[59] Nonetheless, everyone understood that the states would be less powerful under the Constitution than they had been under the Articles of Confederation.

The Federalists and Virtue

Although the Federalists did not rely ultimately on republican virtue to ensure just government, they still considered it essential. As Publius wrote, "The aim of every political constitution is, or ought to be, first to obtain for rulers men who possess most wisdom to discern, and most virtue to pursue, the common good of the society; and in the next place, to take the most effectual precautions for keeping them virtuous while they continue to hold their public trust."[60] Publius believed that the election of senators by state legislators and of presidents by specially chosen electors was likely to result in officeholders "most distinguished by their abilities and virtue."[61] As for the citizenry itself, Publius acknowledged that republican government more than any other kind presumes that people have "sufficient virtue . . . for self-government."[62]

In the last *Federalist* essay, Publius reminded his readers that the practices of the state governments had "undermined the foundations of property and credit," "planted mutual distrust in the breasts of all classes of citizens," and "occasioned an almost universal prostration of morals."[63] Simply put, ineffective and unjust policies had undermined public morality. By contrast, effective and just government that secured the people's rights, promoted their safety and happiness, and punished those who refused to respect the rights of others would be an indispensable aid to virtue and morality. Such a government would attract popular support and perhaps even "that veneration which time bestows on everything, and without which perhaps the wisest and freest governments would not possess the requisite stability."[64]

Although the Federalists succeeded in the ratification campaign, they still had to make good on their promise, dating back to the ratification debate in Massachusetts, to amend the Constitution. In the next section, we explore how Madison and other Federalists succeeded in adding key rights without restricting essential national powers.

ADDING A BILL OF RIGHTS
MAJOR ISSUE

- How and why did the Bill of Rights become part of the U.S. Constitution?

The addition of 10 amendments to the Constitution in 1789–1791, commonly called the **Bill of Rights**, completed the establishment of the new national government. Together with the Declaration of Independence and the Constitution, the Bill of Rights stands as one of the nation's three essential founding documents.

Bill of Rights—the first 10 amendments to the U.S. Constitution, which became effective in 1791.

Protecting Rights in the Original Constitution

Because modern Americans tend to look to the Bill of Rights for an enumeration of their freedoms, they often fail to realize that the original Constitution, despite the absence of a formal bill of rights, did protect several specific rights from federal and state action (see nearby box). Key protections included the writ of habeas corpus and prohibitions on bills of attainder and on ex post facto laws.

The **writ of habeas corpus**, sometimes called the Great Writ, protects individuals from arbitrary arrest by authorizing a judge to free someone if there are not sufficient legal grounds to hold him or her. The British Parliament codified the right in the **Habeas Corpus Act of 1679**, and American colonists considered it a fundamental protection against a tyrannical executive. Under the U.S. Constitution, habeas corpus can be suspended only if the "Public Safety" requires it during a "Rebellion or Invasion." This has happened only a few times, most extensively and controversially during the Civil War (see Chapters 5 and 13).

A **bill of attainder** is an act by a legislature convicting someone of a crime and imposing a punishment without a trial before a court of law. Although most Americans today have probably not heard the term, the British Parliament passed bills of attainder for several hundred years (the last time in 1798), and many of the new American states used them during the Revolution to confiscate the property of Loyalists. Because bills of attainder resulted in convictions and punishment without proper judicial procedures, the authors of the Constitution believed that they violated separation of powers and were procedurally unfair.

An **ex post facto law** is a law that makes an action criminal or increases its punishment after the fact. Without this prohibition, a legislature could pass a law to punish an unpopular person by making his or her actions criminal even though they were legal when they were done.

Writ of habeas corpus—protects individuals from arbitrary arrest by authorizing a judge to free someone from confinement if there are not sufficient legal grounds for holding him or her.

Habeas Corpus Act of 1679—a law passed by the British Parliament that codified the right to a writ of habeas corpus.

Bill of attainder—an act by a legislature convicting someone of a crime and imposing a punishment without a trial before a court.

Ex post facto law—a law that makes an act criminal after it was committed or increases the penalty after the fact.

Provisions Protecting Rights in the Constitution of 1787

Rights protected from federal action:

- Writ of habeas corpus—unless public safety requires its suspension during a rebellion or invasion
- Prohibition on a bill of attainder
- Prohibition against an ex post facto law
- Trial by jury in criminal cases
- No conviction for treason without the testimony of two witnesses or a confession in court

Rights protected from state action:

- Prohibition on a bill of attainder
- Prohibition against an ex post facto law
- Prohibition on coining money, emitting bills of credit, or making anything but gold and silver coin a tender in payment of debts
- Prohibition on passing any law impairing the obligation of contracts

As noted earlier, the Constitution also prohibited the states from issuing their own currency, paper or otherwise, with the potential for causing massive inflation. Nor could they, in this or other ways, violate the obligations of the parties to a contract (no law "impairing the Obligation of Contracts") such as the obligation of someone who had borrowed money to pay it back. The Constitution did not, however, place these restrictions on the federal government. The new Congress could establish a currency, borrow money, and through bankruptcy legislation affect the obligations of contracts. Reflecting Madison's argument in *Federalist* 10, the framers believed that the Congress representing the entire nation would better protect property rights than the legislatures in the much smaller states.

Fashioning the Bill of Rights

To the Anti-Federalists and some others, these rights were not enough. Many looked to the bills of rights in seven of the state constitutions as models of what should be added to the U.S. Constitution. Typically, these were quite extensive, ranging from 16 provisions in Virginia and Pennsylvania to 42 in Maryland. Not only were they longer than what would become the federal Bill of Rights; they tended to be much broader in coverage, including many items that we would not normally think of as rights, such as philosophical and governmental principles and even duties imposed on citizens.[69]

Although not himself an Anti-Federalist, Thomas Jefferson strongly criticized the absence of a bill of rights in the Constitution. In France when the Constitution was written, he received a copy from Madison. He wrote back supporting the plan as a whole but urged the addition of a formal bill of rights: "[A] bill of rights is what the people are entitled to against every government on earth, general or particular, & what no just government should refuse, or rest on inferences."[70]

Sharing Jefferson's concerns, seven state ratifying conventions proposed 157 amendments to the Constitution, although because of duplication the number of distinct amendments was much smaller. Many of these were traditional legal rights of the sort that ended up in the federal Bill of Rights. But some were attempts to weaken the new national authority by, for example, limiting the power of Congress to tax citizens directly, to create commercial monopolies, or to establish a standing army in time of peace.

Why had the framers failed to include a bill of rights in the document they wrote in Philadelphia in 1787? During the ratification debates, supporters of the Constitution gave a variety of arguments for opposing a bill of rights:

- Because the new government would have only certain delegated powers, a bill of rights was not necessary (Congress, for example, was not given any power to limit freedom of speech or freedom of the press).
- Any effort to list certain rights would imply that others did not exist, yet a complete listing was impossible.
- Bills of rights were traditionally the product of struggles between the people and a monarchy, yet the people were themselves the source of power in the new national government.

- Finally, as Alexander Hamilton argued in *Federalist* 84, the new Constitution, by defining the power and authority of the people and by structuring and limiting the power of government, "[was] itself, in every rational sense, and to every useful purpose, a BILL OF RIGHTS."[71]

Despite these initial objections, the Federalists eventually agreed to add a bill of rights, as long as it did not limit the essential powers of the new national government or significantly alter its structure.

To prevent the passage of dangerous amendments and to promote support for the new government, Madison, serving in the new House of Representatives, seized the initiative in the first months of the First Congress. On June 8, 1789, he proposed a series of amendments to the Constitution that would "expressly declare the great rights of mankind secured under this constitution,"[72] including all that would become the Bill of Rights (and some others). He recommended that they be written into the relevant sections of the Constitution rather than placed together at the beginning, as was common in the states, or at the end, as eventually happened. Thus, had Madison gotten his way, no Bill of Rights as such would have emerged separate from the original Constitution.

Madison acted when he did because Virginia and New York had formally asked Congress to call a convention for considering amendments. Had two-thirds of the states made such a request, Congress would have had to call a convention under Article V of the Constitution. The friends of the new Constitution dreaded what a second constitutional convention might propose.

Although Anti-Federalists had insisted on amendments, not all were pleased with Madison's proposals. One serving in the First Congress complained that they would not satisfy his constituents: "they are not those solid and substantial amendments which the people expect." He called them "little better than whip-syllabub, frothy and full of wind, formed only to please the palate."[73] He and others tried again and again to expand Madison's list to include new restrictions on national powers, shorter terms of office, limits on reelection, and requirements that representatives vote as instructed by their constituents.

Some also tried to amend what became the Tenth Amendment—"The powers not delegated to the United States by this Constitution, nor prohibited by it to the States, are reserved to the States respectively, or to the people"—by adding the word *expressly* before *delegated*, thereby following the language in the Articles of Confederation. Madison responded that every government needed "powers by implication," for no constitution could detail every possible necessary exercise of power.[74] In rejecting the adverb *expressly*, the First Congress seemed to endorse the doctrine of "implied powers" (see Chapter 3 for more on implied powers).

Congress turned down all attempts to weaken national power and sent 12 amendments to the states in late September. The first two, which did not become part of the Bill of Rights, were (1) a provision to alter representation in the House of Representatives so that it would grow faster than it otherwise might, and (2) a prohibition on Congress increasing the salaries of its members until a new election intervened. Thus, what is now the First Amendment was actually the third in the list sent to the states.

Ratifying the Bill of Rights

Although some Anti-Federalists opposed the amendments when they were before the states because they did not go far enough to limit federal power, the necessary three-fourths of the state legislatures ratified all but the first two by December 1791. (The original second amendment, on congressional raises, was eventually ratified by three-fourths of the states on May 7, 1992—203 years after Congress had proposed it. It became the Twenty-seventh Amendment, the last to be added. In the modern era, Congress typically gives a seven-year limit for ratification, although it can extend this if it wishes.)

Thomas Jefferson, who was the secretary of state when the amendments were ratified, notified the state governors of the passage of the 10 amendments in a brief note that first mentioned the passage of laws on the regulation of fishermen and the establishment of post offices and post roads.[75] As the author of the leading book on the drafting of the Bill of Rights notes, "The Bill of Rights slipped quietly into the Constitution and passed from sight and public consciousness until given a new and very different life by the Supreme Court more than a century later."[76]

Madison's strategy had succeeded. The Federalists made good on their promise to amend the Constitution without allowing structural changes or limits on essential governmental powers, and although some Anti-Federalists remained unsatisfied, the people seemed content that the Constitution now listed fundamental rights. In any case, the adoption of the Bill or Rights ended organized opposition to the Constitution. No anti-Constitution party arose to lend instability to American politics. Instead, as we shall see, when political parties arose in the United States, they argued not over the merits of the Constitution but over how to interpret it (see Chapter 9). (We discuss the Bill of Rights in more detail in Chapter 5.)

Despite the framers' success in fashioning a new government for a large and diverse nation, slavery would eventually drive a wedge between the states and lead to a full-scale civil war. Here we review the controversy over slavery at the time of the founding and how the Constitution dealt with it. We address other aspects of the slavery issue in Chapter 4 on citizenship and Chapter 6 on civil rights.

SLAVERY AND THE CONSTITUTION
MAJOR ISSUES

- How did the Constitution deal with the issue of slavery?
- What can we conclude about the concessions that the framers made to slavery?

African slavery was introduced into the American colonies by Dutch traders in 1619 at Jamestown, Virginia. For most of the seventeenth century, slavery grew slowly in the colonies, with only a few thousand slaves in Virginia by 1680. In the eighteenth century, however, the slave trade from the west coast of Africa to the Western Hemisphere grew steadily. Half of the slaves were carried to South America and most of the rest to the Caribbean. About 5%–6% of the slaves transported from Africa ended up in what became the United States.

At first the exact legal status of slaves was unclear. Some were even treated as indentured servants who were freed after a certain number of years. Eventually the slaves brought from Africa and their children were consigned by law to lifetime servitude. By the middle of the eighteenth century, slavery was recognized by law in each of the 13 colonies.

This period saw occasional efforts to restrict or prohibit the slave trade, even in colonies that developed large slave populations.[77] The original proprietors of Georgia, for example, prohibited trafficking in slaves because it was "against the Gospel as well as the fundamental law of England."[78] In 1749, however, they lifted this restriction in response to requests from the colonists.

In South Carolina, which had the most extensive slave trade of any of the colonies, concerns grew in the early eighteenth century that slavery was discouraging the immigration of free laborers and that public safety might be threatened by slave insurrections. A slave revolt in 1740 led the colony to impose a duty on imported slaves that was so high that it ended importation for a time. In 1760, the colonial assembly prohibited the slave trade outright, but the King's Privy Council vetoed the act. In 1764, the assembly responded with another prohibitory duty.

In Virginia, the colonial assembly passed a series of acts beginning in 1723 and continuing down to the Revolution to limit the slave trade through import duties. Some of these limits were vetoed by the royal governor, and others were rescinded by the assembly itself. In 1772, the assembly petitioned the king to allow his colonial governor to assent "to such laws as might check so very pernicious a commerce." The petition cited both the "great inhumanity" of the slave trade and the colonists' fear that it would "endanger the very existence of your Majesty's American dominions."[79] Opposition to the slave trade gained in force during the revolutionary period.

In the years after the Declaration of Independence asserted that "all men are created equal," more states restricted the foreign slave trade and the northern states began to abolish slavery. By the time the Constitutional Convention convened in 1787, only Georgia still allowed the importation of slaves from overseas, and slavery was outlawed or on its way out through "gradual emancipation" laws (such as laws that said that children born to slaves after a certain date would be free) in New Hampshire, Massachusetts, Rhode Island, Connecticut, and Pennsylvania. (New York and New Jersey followed suit in 1799 and 1804, respectively, and Vermont entered the Union as a free state in 1791.)

According to the 1790 census, more than nine-tenths of the slave population lived in the five states from Maryland southward, where most worked on farms and plantations. At that time there were 697,624 slaves in the United States; 59,557 free blacks; and 3,172,444 whites. Thus, slaves constituted 18% of the total population and free blacks, 1.5%. South Carolina had the highest percentage of its population enslaved (43%), followed by Virginia (39%), Georgia (35%), Maryland (32%), and North Carolina (26%).

Some slaves were freed through voluntary emancipations. As a result, the free black population in the South more than tripled between 1790 and 1810 (from 32,000 to 108,000). George Washington, for example, provided in his will that on his death and that of his wife, all 124 slaves that he owned outright would be emancipated. He stipulated that funds be set aside to provide for those too old or too young to support themselves and that the young "be taught to read & write; and . . . brought up to some useful occupation."[80]

This newspaper advertisement for newly arrived slaves from Africa appeared in the *South Carolina Gazette* in the 1740s.

Debating Slavery at the Constitutional Convention

As we saw earlier, both deliberation over the common good and compromise over powerful interests played a part in fashioning the Constitution. This was also apparent when the delegates tackled three contentious issues regarding slavery: (1) whether to count slaves for the purpose of determining how many representatives each state would get in the new House of Representatives, (2) whether to allow the new Congress to prohibit the importation of slaves into the United States, and (3) whether to obligate the states to return runaway slaves.

Southern delegates set the tone early on by, in effect, threatening the collapse of the Union if the new constitution did not protect slavery. In late July, General Charles Pinckney of South Carolina told the convention that he would not support any plan that failed to protect the southern states against "an emancipation of slaves."[81] Others, however, denounced slavery and the slave trade as "iniquitous," "a nefarious institution," "the curse of heaven on the States where it prevailed," and "inconsistent with the principles of the revolution." To this John Rutledge of South Carolina responded that "[r]eligion & humanity had nothing to do with this question—Interest alone is the governing principle with Nations—The true question at present is whether the Southn. States shall or shall not be parties to the Union."[82]

The most wide-ranging debate on slavery occurred in late August. Some delegates, such as Roger Sherman of Connecticut, were personally anti-slavery but willing to make concessions because abolition seemed to be well under way and "the good sense of the several States would probably by degrees compleat it."[83] George Mason of Virginia, himself a slaveholder, delivered a lengthy denunciation of slavery for discouraging "arts & manufactures"; leading the poor to "despise labor performed by slaves"; and creating tyrants of "every master of slaves."[84] Charles Pinckney of South Carolina, General Pinckney's cousin, responded that "[i]f slavery be wrong, it is justified by the example of all the world. . . . In all ages one half of mankind have been slaves."[85] This was the closest any of the delegates came to defending slavery on moral grounds. General Pinckney then added that the entire country benefited from slaves and the goods they produced.[86]

When a Georgia delegate insisted that slavery was a local issue that should not even be before the Convention, John Dickinson of Delaware countered that the slave trade affected "the national happiness" and was therefore properly a matter of national concern.[87] Near the end of the debate, Rutledge again sharpened the political issue: "If the Convention thinks that N.C.; S.C. & Georgia will ever agree to the plan, unless their right to import slaves be untouched, the expectation is vain. The people of those States will never be such fools as to give up so important an interest."[88] Because antislavery delegates would not rupture the union over slavery—potentially resulting in two nations: one slave and one free—the delegates would have to forge a compromise.

The Compromises of the Constitution

The words *slave* and *slavery* appear nowhere in the Constitution, even though the document addresses slavery in three places. This omission was quite intentional; for as James Madison told the delegates, "it [was] wrong to admit in the Constitution the idea that there could be property in men."[89] While it might have been necessary to address slavery in this Constitution for a free people, it was not necessary to taint the document with words such as *slave* and *slavery* that implied that one man could own another.

Three clauses of the Constitution deal with slavery. The first is the so-called **three-fifths clause**, which stipulates that

> Representatives and direct Taxes shall be apportioned among the several States which may be included within this Union, according to their respective Numbers, which shall be determined by adding to the whole Number of free Persons, including those bound to Service for a Term of Years, and excluding Indians not taxed, three fifths of all other Persons. (Article I, Section 2)

The phrase "all other Persons" here refers to slaves. For purposes of computing the number of representatives that each state would have in the House of Representatives and the direct taxes that the national government could impose within the states (such as a tax on property), five slaves would count as three free persons. Because it was expected that the federal government would raise most of its revenues through the indirect tax of duties on imports (as it later did), this provision was mainly important for determining representation.

What does the three-fifths clause tell us, if anything, about the framers' views toward slaves and blacks? Despite the claim of some that the Constitution categorized blacks as "three-fifths of a person,"[90] anti-slavery Northerners did not want slaves, who could not vote, to count at all for determining representation, and pro-slavery Southerners wanted the ratio at one-to-one. The higher the ratio, the more representatives the slave states would have in the new House of Representatives.

Thus, the three-fifths ratio, which had been used by the Confederation Congress to determine requisitions on the states, was a compromise between the two positions (Madison later called it a "compromising expedient"[91]), not a moral statement about the value or worth of blacks versus whites. It was the Southerners, after all, who wanted slaves to count as equal to free persons. And what of the nearly 60,000 free blacks then living in the United States? For purposes of determining representation, all of these were to count as equal to free whites.

Second, the **importation of slaves clause** limits the power of Congress to end the foreign slave trade:

> The Migration or Importation of such Persons as any of the States now existing shall think proper to admit, shall not be prohibited by the Congress prior to the Year one thousand eight hundred and eight, but a Tax or duty may be imposed on such Importation, not exceeding ten dollars for each Person. (Article I, Section 9)

Three-fifths clause—the provision of the Constitution (Article I, Section 2) that stipulated that slaves would count as three-fifths of a person when determining population for apportioning seats in the House of Representatives and direct taxes among the states.

Importation of slaves clause—the provision of the Constitution (Article I, Section 9) that prevented Congress from prohibiting the importation of slaves before 1808.

Here "such Persons" refers to slaves. Congress could not prohibit their importation until 1808 but could tax them up to $10 each. As noted earlier, when the Convention met, only Georgia still allowed the importation of slaves. North Carolina had placed a prohibitive duty on slave imports the year before, and South Carolina had outlawed the importation of slaves two months before the Convention convened. The 1808 date was a compromise between an immediate cessation of the foreign slave trade, which many delegates desired (including some from southern states), and a permanent ban on Congress's authority to prohibit it.

Indisputably, this provision was a partial concession to the Deep South and especially to Georgia, which was short of laborers and had less than a third as many slaves as any of the other southern states. Moreover, it allowed states that had prohibited the slave trade to reauthorize it anytime before 1808, as South Carolina did in 1803. But note that the phrasing of the clause seems to presume that without the prohibition, Congress would end the slave trade earlier than 1808, perhaps as soon as it could. In fact, Congress passed a law in March 1807 prohibiting the importation of slaves effective January 1, 1808—the earliest moment allowed by the Constitution.

The third provision on slavery is the **fugitive slave clause**:

> No Person held to Service or Labour in one State, under the Laws thereof, escaping into another, shall, in Consequence of any Law or Regulation therein, be discharged from such Service or Labour, but shall be delivered up on Claim of the Party to whom such Service or Labour may be due. (Article IV, Section 2)

Fugitive slave clause—the provision of the Constitution (Article IV, Section 2) that stipulated that slaves who escaped to another state must be returned to their masters.

Americans Debate Slavery and the Constitution

In the decades before the Civil War, abolitionists such as William Lloyd Garrison denounced the Constitution as "a pact with the devil," "a covenant with death," and "an agreement with hell" for its concessions to slavery. Abraham Lincoln emphatically rejected this view in his important Cooper Union Address in 1860:

> [N]either the word "slave" nor "slavery" is to be found in the Constitution, nor the word "property" even, in any connection with language alluding to the things slave, or slavery; and that wherever in that instrument the slave is alluded to, he is called a "person;" - and wherever his master's legal right in relation to him is alluded to, it is spoken of as "service or labor which may be due," - as a debt payable in service or labor. . . . [T]his mode of alluding to slaves and slavery, instead of speaking of them, was employed on purpose to exclude from the Constitution the idea that there could be property in man.[93]

Frederick Douglass, a former slave who became the foremost black leader and orator of his time, initially accepted Garrison's interpretation of the Constitution. Speaking in England in the 1840s, he denounced the Constitution for protecting slavery and said that he wished to see it "shivered in a thousand fragments."[94] By the early 1850s, however, Douglass had come to believe that the Constitution was fundamentally anti-slavery. Noting that "neither slavery, slaveholding, nor slave can anywhere be found in it," he held that the Constitution "contain[ed] principles and purposes, entirely hostile to the existence of slavery."[95] A decade later, in the midst of the Civil War, he held that "in its essence" the federal government was "an anti-slavery government. . . . It was purposely so framed as to give no claim, no sanction to the claim, of property in man. If in its origin slavery had any relation to the government, it was only as the scaffolding to the magnificent structure, to be removed as soon as the building was completed."[96]

This debate continues today. Speaking about the 200th anniversary of the Constitution in 1987, Justice Thurgood Marshall, the first African American to serve on the U.S. Supreme Court, criticized the framers for compromising with slavery. He particularly cited the decision to allow southern states to continue importing slaves until 1808. In so doing, the framers "trade[d] moral principles for self interest." Faulting the authors of the Constitution for their "outdated notions of 'liberty,' 'justice,' and 'equality,'" Marshall praised the "new, more promising basis for justice and equality" ushered in by the amendments to the Constitution that came after the Civil War.[97] (We address these matters further in Chapter 6.)

Yet, Marshall's successor on the Court and the second African American to serve there, Clarence Thomas, has a very different view. According to Thomas, if the framers had tried to abolish slavery in the new Constitution, the southern states would have broken off to form their own pro-slavery confederacy. This would have further entrenched slavery on the North American continent and made its eventual extinction even more difficult. "In other words," Thomas told a gathering celebrating Abraham Lincoln's birthday in 1999, "the Founders made the political judgment that, given the circumstances of the time, the best defense of the Declaration's principles and, ironically, the most beneficial course for the slaves themselves was to compromise with slavery while, at the same time, establishing a union that, at its root, was devoted to the principle of human equality." For Thomas, the key is "to distinguish between the compromises of the Constitution and its principles."[98]

This provision required that slaves who escaped to another state be returned to their masters. It was a real concession to the slave interests, especially in states like Maryland and Virginia, which bordered Pennsylvania where anti-slavery sentiment ran deep. Although the delegates agreed to make this concession to slavery, they grappled with the exact language. The first version, proposed by Pierce Butler of South Carolina on August 29, referred to those "bound to service or labor" being "delivered up to the person justly claiming their service or labor." The Committee of Style then replaced the phrase "justly claiming" with "no person legally held," thereby avoiding any inference that slavery was just. But even this change was not good enough. Madison records that on September 15, just two days before the Convention adjourned, "the term 'legally' was struck out, and 'under the laws thereof' inserted . . . in compliance with the wish of some who thought the term <legal> equivocal, and favoring the idea that slavery was legal in a moral view."[92]

Because the framers of the Constitution made concessions to slavery for the sake of union but chose language to avoid any suggestion that slavery was just or moral, later Americans differed sharply on the relationship of slavery to the Constitution (see the nearby box).

THE CONSTITUTION AND DELIBERATIVE DEMOCRACY

A few months after the Constitution was completed, John Adams said that it was "the greatest single effort of national deliberation that the world has ever seen."[99] Others have described it in less flattering terms as a "bundle of compromises." Yet, the framers maintained that even the compromises were fashioned to serve a larger public good. "In all our deliberations," Washington wrote in his letter submitting the Constitution to the Confederation Congress, "we have kept steadily in our view, that which appears to us the greatest interest of every true American, the consolidation of our Union, in which is involved our prosperity, felicity, safety, perhaps our national existence."[100] A few months later, he wrote to his friend the Marquis de Lafayette, the French military officer who served with distinction in the Continental Army during the Revolutionary War, that getting the delegates from so many different states to agree on a system of government was "little short of a miracle."[101]

Just as the drafting and adoption of the Constitution resulted from the deliberations—the "reflection and choice"—of those who served in the Constitutional Convention and the state ratifying conventions, so also the Constitution itself established the foundations for future deliberations about national policy. Yet the carefully crafted institutions established by the Constitution do not operate in a vacuum. In the next two chapters, we examine other fundamental features of the American political system that influence and constrain deliberative democracy in the United States: the role of the states in American democracy (Chapter 3) and the meaning and nature of American citizenship and American civic culture (Chapter 4).

SUMMARY

- After independence from Britain, Americans wrote constitutions for 11 of the 13 states and for the country as a whole. The Articles of Confederation proved too weak to govern successfully, and in the new states powerful legislatures exceeded their constitutional authority and often passed unwise or unjust measures.
- By 1787, the central government was effectively bankrupt and unable to conduct an effective foreign policy; the states were immersed in commercial and territorial

conflicts; and economic and social distress was spreading throughout the nation. In February 1787, the Confederation Congress called for a convention to amend the Articles of Confederation so as to "render the federal constitution adequate to the exigencies of Government & the preservation of the Union."
- The Constitutional Convention met from late May through mid-September 1787. Most large state delegates supported the Virginia Plan, which scrapped the

Articles of Confederation in favor of a wholly new and more powerful national government; and most small state delegates lined up behind the New Jersey Plan, which added new powers but kept the Congress of the Articles with its equal state representation.

- The final product, modeled on the Virginia Plan, established a bicameral Congress (with one house based on population and one on state equality) and also independent executive and judicial branches. It added substantial new powers to the national government and imposed numerous restrictions on the states.

- Federalists and Anti-Federalists debated whether the new national government was too powerful, whether national leaders would be sufficiently accountable to the citizenry, whether the government would degenerate into an aristocracy or monarchy, whether a republic could succeed in such a large country, and whether the new arrangements did enough to promote civic virtue.

- After supporters of the new Constitution agreed to add amendments once the new government began operating, the necessary number of states ratified the Constitution by the summer of 1788. In March of 1789, the new Congress met for the first time, and in April George Washington became president.

- By 1791 the Bill of Rights was added to the Constitution, identifying key rights but not weakening national powers.

- At the Convention, Southern delegates insisted that slaves be counted toward representation in the House of Representatives, that no federal limits be placed on the importation of slaves, and that escaped slaves be returned to their masters. After heated debates, the delegates struck compromises that satisfied the pro-slavery delegates but also (1) did not count slaves as equal to free persons when computing representation, (2) allowed the federal government to prohibit the importation of slaves by 1808, and (3) avoided any suggestion in the Constitution that slavery was moral or just.

KEY TERMS

Annapolis Convention p. 35
Anti-Federalists p. 48
Articles of Confederation p. 31
Bicameral legislature p. 31
Bill of attainder p. 53
Bill of Rights p. 53
Checks and balances p. 49
Committee of Detail p. 41
Committee of Style p. 45
Confederation p. 31
Confederation Congress p. 32
Connecticut Compromise p. 41

Constitutional Convention p. 37
Critical period p. 32
Divided government p. 45
Electoral College p. 42
Ex post facto law p. 53
Federalist Papers p. 48
Federalists p. 48
Fugitive slave clause p. 59
Great Compromise p. 41
Habeas Corpus Act of 1679 p. 53
Importation of slaves clause p. 58
Loyalists p. 32

New Jersey Plan p. 39
Paper money laws p. 34
Parliamentary government p. 45
Presidential government p. 45
Ratification p. 46
Separation of powers p. 48
Shays's Rebellion p. 33
State p. 30
Three-fifths clause p. 58
Virginia Plan p. 37
Writ of habeas corpus p. 53

TEST YOUR KNOWLEDGE

1. The "critical period" that influenced the formation of the Constitution was the
   a. Revolutionary War.
   b. years between the First and Second Continental Congress.
   c. years between the battles of Bunker Hill and Valley Forge.
   d. years between the Declaration of Independence and the end of the war.
   e. years between the end of the Revolutionary War and the establishment of a new government under the Constitution.

2. What was the cause of Shays's Rebellion?
   a. a pro-British insurgency
   b. an election dispute
   c. economic strife among poor farmers
   d. rampant crime
   e. a whiskey tax imposed by the new federal government

3. Which three men were most important to the actual drafting of the Constitution?
   a. Benjamin Franklin, Thomas Jefferson, and George Washington
   b. George Washington, John Adams, and James Madison
   c. James Madison, James Wilson, and Gouverneur Morris
   d. James Madison, John Jay, and Alexander Hamilton
   e. John Adams, Samuel Adams, and James Madison

4. When Alexander Hamilton spoke for the first time at the Constitutional Convention, what was his assessment of the Virginia and New Jersey Plans?
   a. He wished that the best of each plan could be adopted.
   b. He believed neither plan was sufficient to correct the problems of the Articles of Confederation.
   c. He preferred the Virginia Plan.
   d. He preferred the New Jersey Plan.
   e. He preferred to keep the Articles of Confederation.

5. What did the delegates hope to achieve by removing all limits on presidential reelection?
   a. The prospect of reelection would give the president an incentive to do a good job.
   b. George Washington would remain president for the remainder of his life.
   c. The executive branch would become more powerful than the legislative branch.
   d. More people would be encouraged to run for president.
   e. The legislature would be encouraged to assume a dominant role in government.

6. Under the original Constitution, members of the Senate were
   a. appointed by the president.
   b. chosen by the state legislatures.
   c. elected directly by the people.
   d. selected by special committees within each state.
   e. selected by the Senate.

7. What was a major complaint of those who opposed the ratification of the Constitution?
   a. the failure to address slavery
   b. the large bicameral legislature
   c. the president's authority as commander in chief
   d. life terms of federal judges and short terms of representatives
   e. the absence of a bill of rights and express protections for state powers

8. In the debate over ratification, the name given to those who urged adoption of the Constitution was
   a. Federalists.
   b. Anti-Federalists.
   c. Constitutionalists.
   d. Jeffersonians.
   e. Hamiltonians.

9. James Madison believed that _____ were "the most common and durable sources of factions."
   a. property disputes
   b. industry interests
   c. agricultural needs
   d. taxes
   e. family conflicts

10. An act of the legislature convicting someone of a crime and imposing a punishment without a trial is called a(n)
    a. bill of attainder.
    b. ex post facto law.
    c. initiative.
    d. referendum.
    e. writ of habeas corpus.

FURTHER READING

Bowen, Catherine Drinker. *Miracle at Philadelphia: The Story of the Constitutional Convention, May to September 1787*. Boston: Little, Brown, 1966.

Bradford, M. E. *Founding Fathers: Brief Lives of the Framers of the United States Constitution*. 2nd rev. ed. Lawrence: University Press of Kansas, 1994.

Brookhiser, Richard. *Founding Father: Rediscovering George Washington*. New York: Simon & Schuster, 1996.

Goldwin, Robert A. *Why Blacks, Women, and Jews Are Not Mentioned in the Constitution, and Other Unorthodox Views*. Washington, DC: AEI Press, 1990.

Jensen, Merrill. *The New Nation: A History of the United States during the Confederation, 1781–1789*. New York: Knopf, 1950.

Madison, James. "Vices of the Political System of the United States." In *The Mind of the Founder: Sources of the Political Thought of James Madison*, ed. Marvin Meyers. Indianapolis, IN: Bobbs-Merrill, 1973.

Maier, Pauline, *Ratification: The People Debate the Constitution, 1787–1788*. New York: Simon and Schuster, 2010.

McLaughlin, Andrew C. *The Confederation and the Constitution, 1783–1789*. New York: Harper, 1905.

Nevins, Allan. *The American States during and after the Revolution, 1775–1789*. New York: Macmillan, 1924.

Rakove, Jack N. *Original Meanings: Politics and Ideas in the Making of the Constitution*. New York: Knopf, 1996.

Sheehan, Colleen A., and Gary L. McDowell, eds. *Friends of the Constitution: Writings of the "Other" Federalists, 1787–1788.* Indianapolis, IN: Liberty Fund, 1998.

Storing, Herbert J. *What the Anti-Federalists Were For: The Political Thought of the Opponents of the Constitution.* Chicago: University of Chicago Press, 1981.

Storing, Herbert J., ed. *The Anti-Federalist.* Chicago: University of Chicago Press, 1985.

Wood, Gordon S. *The Creation of the American Republic, 1776–1787.* New York: Norton, 1969.

WEB SOURCES

Avalon Project: avalon.law.yale.edu/subject_menus/constpap.asp—an extensive collection of documents related to the development of the federal and state constitutions in the United States, maintained by the Yale Law School.

Constitution Finder: confinder.richmond.edu/—an index to constitutions around the world, maintained by the University of Richmond.

Constitution of the United States of America: www.law.cornell.edu/constitution/constitution.overview.html—an online version of the U.S. Constitution and its 27 amendments with extensive notes, maintained by Legal Information Institute of the Cornell University Law School.

Liberty Library of Constitutional Classics: www.constitution.org/liberlib.htm—classic books and other works on constitutional government.

National Archives: Charters of Freedom: www.archives.gov/national_archives_experience/charters/charters.html—the National Archives Web site on the Declaration of Independence, the Constitution, and the Bill of Rights.

National Constitution Center: www.constitutioncenter.org—a Web site for the museum within Independence National Historic Park in Philadelphia devoted to the U.S. Constitution.

The Founders' Constitution: press-pubs.uchicago.edu/founders/—an extensive collection of materials related to the writing and meaning of the U.S. Constitution, maintained by the Liberty Fund and the University of Chicago Press.

Twenty-six state attorneys general joined a legal challenge to President Obama's health care plan. After the second day of oral arguments before the U.S. Supreme Court, Greg Abbott of Texas comments on the proceedings.

Office of the Attorney General of Texas

3 Federalism

OBJECTIVES

After reading this chapter, you should be able to

- Describe briefly how the federal–state balance of power has shifted over the years.
- Explain why this balance has often tipped in favor of the federal government.
- Articulate the advantages and disadvantages of America's complex system of federalism.
- Analyze how federalism affects policy deliberation.
- Understand ways in which federalism may encourage or hamper active citizenship.

INTRODUCTION

On July 14, 1948, Minneapolis mayor Hubert Humphrey addressed the Democratic National Convention. Humphrey, who would serve later as a United States senator and vice president, urged the delegates to back civil rights. "To those who say that this civil-rights program is an infringement on states' rights, I say this: the time has arrived in America for the Democratic Party to get out of the shadow of states' rights and walk forthrightly into the bright sunshine of human rights!"[1]

Sixty-one years later, in a different context, the first African-American president spoke of "states' rights" not as a barrier to overcome, but as a principle to uphold. Criticizing a federal law defining marriage as the union of a man and a woman, President Obama said: "I believe it's discriminatory, I think it interferes with states' rights, and we will work with Congress to overturn it."[2]

As these passages suggest, the relationship between the states and the federal government has involved dramatic issues. In 1860 and 1861, 11 states seceded rather than accept a president who wanted to curb slavery. In the middle of the twentieth century, lawmakers deliberated passionately about the federal government's authority to end racial segregation. More recently, the balance of state and federal power has come up in debates over same-sex marriage, assisted suicide, and medical marijuana.

These passages also show that the question of federal–state balance cuts across partisan and ideological lines. Although liberal Democrats have a reputation for promoting federal power, they sometimes favor the states on issues such as same-sex marriage. Conservative Republicans endorse a strong federal role in certain issues such as product liability.

The political lines are complex because the system is complex. As in about two dozen other countries, the United States has a **federal system**.[3] Such a system means a division of powers in which the national government dominates certain policy issues (e.g., defense and foreign policy), while regional governments dominate others (e.g., education). The American arrangement is especially intricate. In addition to the government in Washington and the 50 state governments, the United States has 3,033 counties, 19,492 municipalities, 16,519 towns and townships, and 50,432 districts for purposes ranging from education to irrigation.[4] On many issues, no bright line distinguishes the jobs of each level. Although education has long been a state and local function, for example, the federal government influences what goes on in classrooms.

Rules and policies vary from state to state. Some spend much more than others on higher education (see Figure 3-1). Utah forbids gambling, whereas neighboring Nevada encourages it. Similar crimes have different punishments. Texas has put hundreds of prisoners to death, whereas 17 states and the District of Columbia have no capital punishment at all.[5] Variations may create new problems. As of 2010, a pack of cigarettes cost up to $13.00 in New York City because of high state and city taxes. A few hours' drive away, in Richmond, Virginia, low taxes meant that the same pack cost only $5.00. For just one case of cigarettes (typically containing 12,000 cigarettes), the tax difference between the two cities was over $3,000, creating incentives for illegal smuggling and resale—a practice called "buttlegging."[6]

Even when laws are similar, jurisdiction may be unclear. Sale of certain drugs may simultaneously violate both state and federal laws, and drug gangs usually commit other state crimes (e.g., murder) and federal crimes (e.g., money laundering). Moreover, both state and local authorities enforce state laws. Accordingly, federal, state, and local agencies may suffer from feuds and miscommunication. One mother in Boston, who lost two sons in separate murders, reacted this way on learning of such friction: "None of this helps me or the justice system, it helps the bad guys."[7]

France and many other countries have **unitary systems**, which consolidate most power in the national government. In some unitary systems, the national government delegates certain duties to local or regional governments, but it usually retains the ultimate authority. By adopting such a system, the United States might reduce duplication, overlap, and inconsistency. Yet ever since the founding, such a move has had little support. Why?

Federal system—a political system in which a national government shares powers with states or provinces. Each level has definite powers and may act directly on individuals within its jurisdiction. Examples include the contemporary United States, Germany, and Canada.

Unitary system—a political system in which all authority lies in a central government, and other governments within the nation can do only what the central government allows. Examples include France and Japan.

Confederal system—a political system in which states delegate a limited range of powers to a central government for certain purposes, such as the issuing of money. Examples include the United States under the Articles of Confederation and the contemporary European Union.

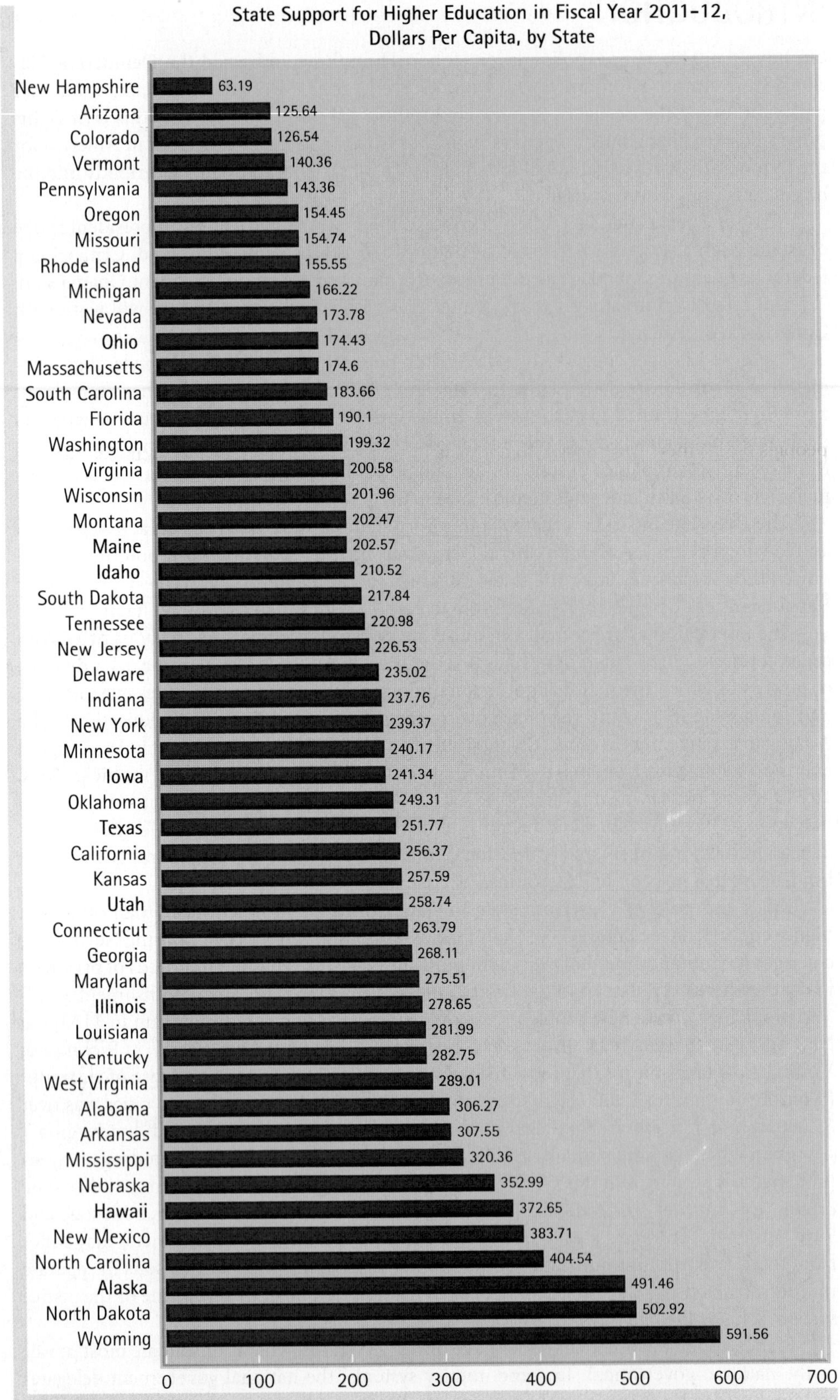

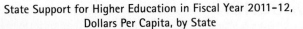

State Support for Higher Education in Fiscal Year 2011–12, Dollars Per Capita, by State

State	Dollars Per Capita
New Hampshire	63.19
Arizona	125.64
Colorado	126.54
Vermont	140.36
Pennsylvania	143.36
Oregon	154.45
Missouri	154.74
Rhode Island	155.55
Michigan	166.22
Nevada	173.78
Ohio	174.43
Massachusetts	174.6
South Carolina	183.66
Florida	190.1
Washington	199.32
Virginia	200.58
Wisconsin	201.96
Montana	202.47
Maine	202.57
Idaho	210.52
South Dakota	217.84
Tennessee	220.98
New Jersey	226.53
Delaware	235.02
Indiana	237.76
New York	239.37
Minnesota	240.17
Iowa	241.34
Oklahoma	249.31
Texas	251.77
California	256.37
Kansas	257.59
Utah	258.74
Connecticut	263.79
Georgia	268.11
Maryland	275.51
Illinois	278.65
Louisiana	281.99
Kentucky	282.75
West Virginia	289.01
Alabama	306.27
Arkansas	307.55
Mississippi	320.36
Nebraska	352.99
Hawaii	372.65
New Mexico	383.71
North Carolina	404.54
Alaska	491.46
North Dakota	502.92
Wyoming	591.56

FIGURE 3–1 States vary greatly in fiscal support for higher education: in fiscal year 2011–2012, Wyoming spent nine times as much per person as New Hampshire. But do not jump to the conclusion that the lower-spending states are stingier. Differences may reflect such things as income and the availability of private alternatives. Figures are in dollars and include state funds only. SOURCE: http://grapevine.illinoisstate.edu/tables/FY12/Revised_March13/Table%205%20Revised.xlsx

Under the Articles of Confederation, the United States had a **confederal system,** a league of states with a weak central government. The Articles ran into trouble, as we saw in Chapter 2, but Americans had fought a long war against the strong central power of the British government, and they did not want to go back. To the framers of the Constitution, a federal system avoided both extremes.[8] As James Madison wrote, dividing power between the state and federal levels means a "double security" for the people. "The different governments will control each other, at the same time that each will be controlled by itself."[9]

Over the past two centuries, other advantages of federalism have emerged. States compete for business and population. Each offers a different "package" of rules and services, each with a different "price tag" in the form of taxes and fees. In a mobile society, people and businesses can move to the states that suit them best.[10]

Each of the nation's 89,527 governments represents a gateway for citizens to speak out at public meetings, stage demonstrations, talk to officials, and run for office themselves. As Alexis de Tocqueville observed, federalism thus gives Americans an education in citizenship. "Local institutions are to liberty what primary schools are to science; they put it within the people's reach; they teach people to appreciate its peaceful enjoyment and accustom them to make use of it."[11]

FOCUS QUESTION

What are the major advantages and disadvantages of federal, confederal, and unitary governments? Does the answer depend on the characteristics of the country in question? If so, which characteristics?

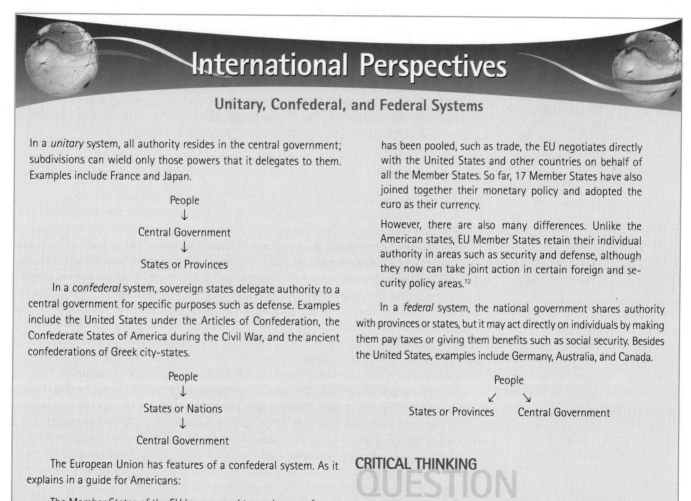

International Perspectives

Unitary, Confederal, and Federal Systems

In a *unitary* system, all authority resides in the central government; subdivisions can wield only those powers that it delegates to them. Examples include France and Japan.

People
↓
Central Government
↓
States or Provinces

In a *confederal* system, sovereign states delegate authority to a central government for specific purposes such as defense. Examples include the United States under the Articles of Confederation, the Confederate States of America during the Civil War, and the ancient confederations of Greek city-states.

People
↓
States or Nations
↓
Central Government

The European Union has features of a confederal system. As it explains in a guide for Americans:

The Member States of the EU have agreed to pool some of their sovereign powers for the sake of unity and promotion of shared values, just as American states did to create a federal republic. In the fields where national sovereignty

has been pooled, such as trade, the EU negotiates directly with the United States and other countries on behalf of all the Member States. So far, 17 Member States have also joined together their monetary policy and adopted the euro as their currency.

However, there are also many differences. Unlike the American states, EU Member States retain their individual authority in areas such as security and defense, although they now can take joint action in certain foreign and security policy areas.[12]

In a *federal* system, the national government shares authority with provinces or states, but it may act directly on individuals by making them pay taxes or giving them benefits such as social security. Besides the United States, examples include Germany, Australia, and Canada.

People
↙   ↘
States or Provinces   Central Government

CRITICAL THINKING QUESTION

What are the advantages and disadvantages of unitary, federal, and confederal systems? Under what circumstances does each work best?

In 2010, New Jersey governor Chris Christie (left) and Newark mayor Cory Booker (right) received national attention for efforts at education reform and fiscal restraint. In the center is Kim Guadagno, who was elected New Jersey's first-ever lieutenant governor in 2009.

Deliberation also benefits from the nation's federal structure. Major domestic issues undergo debate not only by Congress but also by the 50 state legislatures. With a total of 99 chambers and more than 7,000 members in all, the state legislatures can look at each issue from many angles, making it more likely that relevant ideas and details will get an airing. Justice Louis Brandeis wrote, "It is one of the happy incidents of the federal system that a single courageous state may, if its citizens choose, serve as a laboratory; and try novel social and economic experiments without risk to the rest of the country."[13]

Critics of federalism argue that these advantages are not what they seem. They point to cases where deliberation falls short of the ideal and where interstate competition stalls progress instead of fostering it. But before exploring this debate, we need to look at the history of the federal system.

GROWTH AND CHANGE

MAJOR ISSUE

- Why and how has the balance of federal–state power shifted over the years?

The relationship between the federal government and the states has involved elements of both continuity and change. The 1787 Constitution remains relevant, but amendments and historical developments have also left a profound mark on the federal system.

At the Founding

During the Constitutional Convention and the ratification debates, the issue was not whether the central government should absorb the states, but whether the states were yielding too much to the central government.

The Federalists argued that the states would remain vigorous. James Madison said that Americans' first attachment would be to their own states.[14] This notion may sound odd today, but it was normal in his time. At the Constitutional Convention, Madison wrote, another delegate looked "for the preservation of his rights to the State Governments."[15] The Constitution did give the federal government specific, or **enumerated, powers**. Among other things, Congress could impose taxes, coin money, and declare war. But the framers denied Congress certain powers, such as placing duties on exports from any state. "The powers delegated by the proposed Constitution to the federal government are few and defined," wrote Madison. "Those which are to remain in the State governments are numerous and indefinite."[16]

Anti-Federalists thought that the federal government would threaten individual liberty and civic virtue. Republican government, they believed, could thrive only in small societies where citizens knew their neighbors and where farm work cultivated character.[17] The new system would expand unfettered interstate commerce, opening the door to corrupt materialism. One Anti-Federalist said that a national capital would teem with vices: "treason—perfidy—violation of engagements—contempt of civil duties—hope from the magistrate's weakness; but above all, the perpetual ridicule of virtue."[18]

Historian Walter A. McDougall says that the Anti-Federalists were right to worry that "a federal establishment mighty enough to defend America's interests against great foreign powers would ipso facto threaten the liberty of American citizens and states."[19] Although the federal system has had many problems, it is hard to picture how the United States could have prospered if the Anti-Federalists had won. As the Federalists argued, other countries

Enumerated powers—the 17 express powers that Article I, Section 8, of the Constitution specifically grants to Congress.

TABLE 3-1	FEDERALISM: EARLY CONSTITUTIONAL PROVISIONS

- **Commerce Clause:** Article I, Section 8, gives Congress the power to "regulate Commerce with foreign Nations, and among the several States, and with the Indian Tribes."
- **Necessary and Proper Clause:** Article I, Section 8, gives Congress the power to "make all Laws which shall be necessary and proper for carrying into Execution the foregoing Powers, and all other Powers vested by this Constitution in the Government of the United States, or in any Department or Officer thereof."
- **Supremacy Clause:** Article VI, paragraph 2, establishes the Constitution, federal statutes, and treaties as "the supreme Law of the Land; and the Judges in every State shall be bound thereby, any Thing in the Constitution or Laws of any State to the Contrary notwithstanding."
- **Tenth Amendment:** "The powers not delegated to the United States by the Constitution, nor prohibited by it to the States, are reserved to the States respectively, or to the people."

© Cengage Learning 2014

could have exploited internal disagreements to pry apart the Union, and without a dynamic economy, free Americans would have been poorer.

Federalism from Chief Justices Marshall to Taney

The Anti-Federalists did win a key battle. The Bill of Rights was a response to their argument that the Constitution did not protect the people's liberty and the states' authority. Under the Tenth Amendment, "[t]he powers not delegated to the United States by the Constitution, nor prohibited by it to the States, are reserved to the States respectively, or to the people." (See Table 3-1.) This amendment spelled out the idea of **reserved powers**. Under this principle, the states (or the people) may do anything that the Constitution does not forbid, and the federal government may not intrude. The meaning of this amendment has long been in dispute. Some dismiss it as a restatement of the obvious; others see it as an important safeguard. Chief Justice John Marshall acknowledged that in a complex federal system, "contests respecting power must arise."[20]

Early in the nineteenth century, Marshall wrote historic decisions on federalism. In *McCulloch v. Maryland* (1819), the Supreme Court ruled that Congress could charter a national bank and that Maryland could not tax it. Marshall pointed to the **"necessary and proper" clause** (Article I, Section 8), allowing Congress to "make all Laws which shall be necessary and proper for carrying into Execution the foregoing Powers." Although bank chartering was not an enumerated power, wrote Marshall, Congress could consider this power "necessary and proper" for carrying out enumerated powers such as borrowing. Marshall spurned Maryland's argument that *necessary* must mean "absolutely indispensable." He laid out the idea of **implied powers**, under which Congress could take actions that had a reasonable link to its enumerated powers. "Let the end be legitimate, let it be within the scope of the constitution, and all means which are appropriate, which are plainly adapted to that end, which are not prohibited, but consist with the letter and spirit of the constitution, are constitutional."[21]

Marshall also relied on the **supremacy clause** (Article VI), which declares that the Constitution, as well as all treaties and federal laws, "shall be the supreme Law of the Land." Accordingly, Marshall said, states cannot hamper "the operations of the constitutional laws enacted by Congress to carry into execution the powers vested in the general government."[22]

Another case involved the **commerce clause** (Article I, Section 8), which empowers Congress to "regulate Commerce with foreign Nations, and among the several States." In *Gibbons v. Ogden* (1824), a dispute over navigation on the Hudson River between New York and New Jersey, Marshall said that this clause gives the federal government exclusive jurisdiction over interstate commerce. Marshall said that the clause does not involve just the exchange of goods but a variety of activities, including navigation. As for matters not involving interstate commerce, such as trade and travel within a single state, "[n]o direct general power over these objects is granted to Congress; and, consequently, they remain subject

Reserved powers—under the Tenth Amendment, the powers not delegated to the United States by the Constitution, or prohibited by it to the States, that are reserved to the states or to the people.

"Necessary and proper" clause—the final clause of Article I, Section 8, of the Constitution, which empowers Congress to make all laws "necessary and proper" in order to carry out the federal government's duties. This "elastic clause" is the constitutional basis for implied powers.

Implied powers—powers of the national government that the Constitution does not directly mention but that one may reasonably infer from the enumerated powers.

Supremacy clause—the portion of Article VI saying that the Constitution, as well as all treaties and federal laws, "shall be the supreme Law of the Land."

Commerce clause—Article I, Section 8, of the Constitution, empowering Congress to regulate commerce with foreign nations and among the states. It has supplied the basis for federal regulation of business as well as other domestic policy initiatives.

Dual federalism—an arrangement whereby the national government would focus on foreign affairs, national security, interstate relations and other topics of national reach, leaving many domestic policy issues to the states.

Nullification—the idea that a state may refuse to acknowledge or enforce federal laws within its boundaries.

to State legislation."[23] During the twentieth century, courts would note the development of an integrated national economy and expand the definition of "interstate commerce."

Although the *Gibbons* and *McCulloch* cases broadened the federal government's *potential* power, its *actual* reach remained modest. In 1816, the federal government had one civilian employee for every 1,933 people (in 2010 the ratio was one for every 109[24]). Apart from the post office, an ordinary American living in the early nineteenth century might go years without any direct contact with the federal government. During this period, the dominant view held that each level had distinct tasks and that the states alone would deal with most matters that affected everyday life. Scholars call this idea **dual federalism**.

What happened if the federal government allegedly overstepped its bounds? In response to the Alien and Sedition Acts of 1798, the Kentucky legislature passed resolutions declaring that each state could decide for itself whether federal acts were unconstitutional and therefore void. Thomas Jefferson anonymously authored these resolutions. James Madison, meanwhile, drafted resolutions for the Virginia legislature affirming that states could "interpose for arresting the progress of the evil" but without going as far as the Kentucky resolutions.[25] In 1800, Jefferson's election as president put an end to the immediate conflict, but the resolutions would fuel later debate.

In the 1830s, some political leaders cited the resolutions to support **nullification**, the idea that each state could invalidate federal laws within its own boundaries. (Madison, now an elderly former president, opposed nullification.) In 1832, reacting to unpopular tariffs, the South Carolina legislature called a special state convention, which declared the tariffs not "binding upon this State, its officers or citizens."[26] The measure threatened secession if the federal government used force to collect the duties. President Andrew Jackson declared nullification "incompatible with the existence of the Union."[27]

Under Article VI, all federal and state officials "shall be bound by Oath or Affirmation, to support this Constitution." In *The Federalist*, Publius said that "the sanctity of an oath" would ensure that states "will be incorporated into the operations of the national government *as far as its just and constitutional authority extends*; and will be rendered auxiliary to the enforcement of its laws" (emphasis in original).[28] So when the South Carolina legislature voted for nullification, Jackson thundered, "Vile profanation of oaths!"[29]

Congress authorized Jackson to use the military, while offering an olive branch by reducing the duties. The South Carolina convention rescinded the measure, and then symbolically maintained its defiance by declaring the force bill void.

This confrontation ended in victory for the federal government, but it also stiffened Southern resistance. Tocqueville wrote in 1835: "Unless I am strangely mistaken, the federal government of the United States is tending to get daily weaker.... On the other hand, I think I have seen the feeling of independence becoming more and more lively in the states."[30]

The slavery issue fueled Southern talk of secession, which Congress tried to quell by passing the Fugitive Slave Act, making it easier for slave owners to enlist federal help in capturing runaways. When the Wisconsin Supreme Court in 1855 declared the act unconstitutional, the U.S. Supreme Court reversed the decision. Writing for the majority, Chief Justice Roger Taney said that the supremacy clause was "too plain to admit of doubt or to need comment."[31] This time, it was the abolitionists who turned to nullification, and the Wisconsin legislature declared the Supreme Court decision null and void. In 1860, South Carolina cited the Wisconsin measure as well as similar acts in other northern states as a reason for secession.[32]

The Civil War and National Identity

Ten other Southern states followed South Carolina out of the Union. The resulting civil war led to the end of slavery and the transformation of American society, including federalism. Several such effects of the Civil War stand out.

First, the Union victory ended serious discussion of secession and nullification, burying the old confederal idea. Ironically, the example of the Confederacy reinforced the argument for an effective central government. After seceding, Southern states balked at ceding authority to the regime in Richmond. Thinking that he lacked sufficient power to wage war,

1862 Land Grant Colleges and Universities

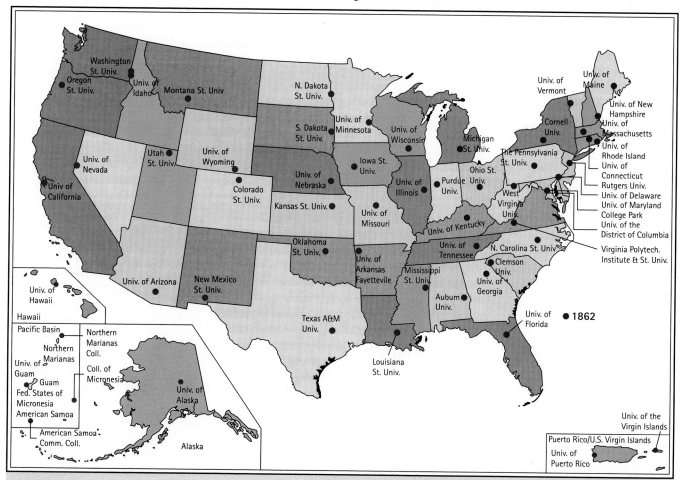

FIGURE 3-2 A number of American colleges and universities came into existence because of the 1862 Morrill Act.
SOURCE: U.S. Department of Agriculture Cooperative State Research, Education, and Extension Service Washington, D.C.

Confederate president Jefferson Davis feared that the Confederacy's epitaph would read, "Died of a Theory." Not all historians agree with Davis's diagnosis, but it became conventional wisdom after the Civil War.[33]

Second, the war effort strengthened the federal government. To supply manpower and money, Congress passed the first draft law and federal income tax, imposed consumption taxes, and established a uniform currency. With southern seats vacant, northern Republicans in Congress enacted a higher tariff, a homestead act to provide free land in the West, and legislation providing loans and land grants for a transcontinental railroad.[34] The Morrill Act of 1862 made land grants to states to support public institutions of higher education (see Figure 3-2). At the end of the war, Congress sought to help former slaves by setting up Freedmen's Bureau, the first national agency for social welfare. The bureau, however, died during Reconstruction, the period after the Civil War (see Chapter 7).

Third, the Civil War amendments to the Constitution limited the states' power and laid a foundation for growth of federal power (see Table 3-2). The Thirteenth Amendment abolished slavery. The Fourteenth Amendment said that states could not "deprive any person of life, liberty, or property, without due process of law; nor deny any person within its jurisdiction the equal protection of the laws." The Fifteenth Amendment guaranteed the right to vote. Although all three authorized Congress to pass enforcement legislation—that is, laws necessary to carry them out—for a long time judges and lawmakers read the enforcement clauses very narrowly. By the late twentieth century, however, they opened the way for federal legislation on civil rights. In 1980, the Supreme Court said, "Principles of federalism

TABLE 3-2	CIVIL WAR AMENDMENTS

- **Thirteenth Amendment:** Neither slavery nor involuntary servitude, except as a punishment for crime whereof the party shall have been duly convicted, shall exist within the United States, or any place subject to their jurisdiction. Congress shall have power to enforce this article by appropriate legislation.
- **Fourteenth Amendment (Sections 1 and 5):** All persons born or naturalized in the United States, and subject to the jurisdiction thereof, are citizens of the United States and of the State wherein they reside. No State shall make or enforce any law which shall abridge the privileges or immunities of citizens of the United States; nor shall any State deprive any person of life, liberty, or property, without due process of law; nor deny to any person within its jurisdiction the equal protection of the laws. The Congress shall have power to enforce, by appropriate legislation, the provisions of this article.
- **Fifteenth Amendment:** The right of citizens of the United States to vote shall not be denied or abridged by the United States or by any State on account of race, color, or previous condition of servitude. The Congress shall have power to enforce this article by appropriate legislation.

© Cengage Learning 2014

that might otherwise be an obstacle to congressional authority are necessarily overridden by the power to enforce the Civil War Amendments."[35]

Finally, the war helped change the way Americans saw their country. For decades after the founding, Americans typically spoke of the "United States" in the plural. With the Civil War, a spirit of national unity changed the language: *United States* was now more often singular. Usage of the word *nation* reflected the shift. Delegates to the Constitutional Convention sometimes spoke of the "nation" or "the national government." But because of a belief that these words implied a unitary regime, the delegates kept them out of the Constitution. Instead, the document referred to the United States as the "Union," which long remained the preferred term. When *United States* changed from plural to singular, *Nation* began to replace *Union* in American speech. In his first inaugural, Lincoln spoke of "Union," whereas in the Gettysburg Address two years later, he spoke of the "nation."[36] By the twentieth century, Americans called their country a "union" only in specific circumstances, such as the State of the Union Address.

Federalism in Flux

After the Civil War, federalism was in flux. Some trends favored a stronger national government, while others hampered federal "intrusions." James Bryce, a British observer, wrote in 1888 that railroads, telegraph lines, and newspapers were replacing state spirit with a national one. Each state, he said, "is attached by a hundred always tightening ties to other states, and touched by their weal or woe as nearly as by what befalls within its own limits."[37]

As interstate commerce grew, public concern about corporate power prompted Congress to pass laws regulating business practices. The Supreme Court upheld some of these laws, but in other ways it crimped federal authority. For example, the Civil Rights Act of 1875 had outlawed racial segregation in theaters and other public accommodations. But the Court found that the Fourteenth Amendment allowed Congress to regulate only the actions of state governments, not private individuals and organizations.[38] Well into the 1930s, the Court took a narrow reading of the commerce clause and a broad reading of the Tenth Amendment. It voided measures ranging from a child labor law to a tax on the sale of grain futures. While such decisions were buttressing dual federalism, Congress and the states were adding new constitutional amendments that would undercut it.

In response to an 1895 Supreme Court ruling that the federal government lacked the power to impose a direct tax on incomes (notwithstanding the Civil War levy), the Sixteenth Amendment (1913) allowed such taxes (see Table 3-3). The income tax eventually financed federal grants entailing enormous leverage over state and local policy, and it let the federal government dominate revenue sources that the states had once had to themselves. It also changed how states raise money. Most came to adopt their own income taxes, which they based on the federal income tax. (State income tax returns usually ask filers to enter information from their federal returns.) As more people had to pay federal income tax, the federal government came to play a direct role in daily life.

The Constitution originally empowered state legislatures to elect United States senators, who would presumably represent the interests of state governments. The

TABLE 3-3	FEDERALISM: TWENTIETH-CENTURY CONSTITUTIONAL AMENDMENTS

- **Sixteenth Amendment:** The Congress shall have power to lay and collect taxes on incomes, from whatever source derived, without apportionment among the several States, and without regard to any census or enumeration.
- **Seventeenth Amendment:** The Senate of the United States shall be composed of two Senators from each State, elected by the people thereof, for six years; and each Senator shall have one vote. The electors in each State shall have the qualifications requisite for electors of the most numerous branch of the State legislatures. When vacancies happen in the representation of any State in the Senate, the executive authority of such State shall issue writs of election to fill such vacancies: Provided, That the legislature of any State may empower the executive thereof to make temporary appointments until the people fill the vacancies by election as the legislature may direct. This amendment shall not be so construed as to affect the election or term of any Senator chosen before it becomes valid as part of the Constitution.
- **Eighteenth Amendment:** After one year from the ratification of this article the manufacture, sale, or transportation of intoxicating liquors within, the importation thereof into, or the exportation thereof from the United States and all territory subject to the jurisdiction thereof for beverage purposes is hereby prohibited. The Congress and the several States shall have concurrent power to enforce this article by appropriate legislation. This article shall be inoperative unless it shall have been ratified as an amendment to the Constitution by the legislatures of the several States, as provided in the Constitution, within seven years from the date of the submission hereof to the States by the Congress.
- **Twenty-first Amendment:** The eighteenth article of amendment to the Constitution of the United States is hereby repealed. The transportation or importation into any State, Territory, or possession of the United States for delivery or use therein of intoxicating liquors, in violation of the laws thereof, is hereby prohibited. The article shall be inoperative unless it shall have been ratified as an amendment to the Constitution by conventions in the several States, as provided in the Constitution, within seven years from the date of the submission hereof to the States by the Congress.

© Cengage Learning 2014

framers thought that this mechanism would serve as federalism's main shield.[39] During the nineteenth century, senators often fulfilled this role, but support for more direct democracy eventually trumped federalism. News stories about corrupt senators further eroded confidence in indirect election, even though misconduct was rare.[40] By 1911, more than half the states had provided for popular election polls to advise the legislators on choosing senators.[41] In 1913, the Seventeenth Amendment provided for direct elections. State governments no longer had a direct role in choosing federal lawmakers. (Governors could appoint senators to fill vacancies but only temporarily.) So when electoral pressures favored the federal government over the states, senators and House members alike would respond accordingly. State and local officials found that they had to represent themselves in Washington through either individual offices or groups such as the National Governors Association.

The Eighteenth Amendment (1919) provided for Prohibition, the national ban on alcoholic beverages. It took effect in 1920 and continued until the Twenty-first Amendment repealed it in 1933. Prior to Prohibition, the federal government had only a small role in law enforcement, apart from efforts to stop smuggling and counterfeiting. Now federal law enforcement stretched to include the Customs Ser-

AP Photo/File

The Eighteenth Amendment, which launched Prohibition, enabled criminals to get rich from selling alcoholic beverages. One such criminal was Chicago's Al Capone. The Sixteenth Amendment helped bring him down, however, as the federal government imprisoned him for income tax evasion. Here Capone consults with a lawyer.

vice, Coast Guard, Department of Justice, and the Bureau of Internal Revenue's Prohibition Unit, which later became a separate Bureau of Prohibition—the home of the legendary "Untouchables." Federal spending for law enforcement rose nearly 400% in the 1920s, and Congress passed new crime laws.[42] The trend toward greater federal involvement did not end with repeal of Prohibition. In 1934, Congress enacted the National Firearms Act (NFA), banning machine guns and sawed-off shotguns.

New Deal, War, and New Powers for the Federal Government

The administration of Franklin D. Roosevelt (1933–1945) marked another turning point. To fight the Great Depression, the national government started major programs in areas that had once been the domain of states and localities. In addition to benefits for seniors, the Social Security Act of 1935 included unemployment insurance, grants to the states for medical care, and aid to dependent children. The last provision, which drafters saw as a humble program for widows, evolved into Aid to Families with Dependent Children, the complex federal–state program that Americans came to identify as "welfare."

In Roosevelt's first term, the Supreme Court stuck to dual federalism, striking down key New Deal initiatives such as the National Industrial Recovery Act. In 1937, however, justices found that Congress could regulate intrastate activities "if they have such a close and substantial relation to interstate commerce that control is essential, or appropriate, to protect commerce from burdens and obstructions."[43] In *Wickard v. Filburn* (1942), the Court went further. Congress could make laws even on local, noncommercial activities if they have "a substantial economic effect on interstate commerce," whether direct or indirect.[44] Other decisions, meanwhile, shrank the reach of the Tenth Amendment. In 1941, the Court found that it "states but a truism that all is retained which has not been surrendered."[45]

In that year, the United States entered World War II. Because of the war effort, federal spending rose nearly tenfold between 1940 and 1945. Military spending plunged after the victory but started rising again because of tension with the Soviet Union. The war not only launched a large, permanent military establishment but also deepened federal involvement in domestic affairs. The era of dual federalism was over.

Categorical grant—grant that spells out in detail the specific categories in which state and local governments must spend the money.

New Federalism—President Nixon's plan to turn more authority over to state and local governments. Other presidents have also used the term.

The Federal Government Assumes a Dominant Position

In the decades after World War II, lawmakers often framed new domestic measures as efforts to strengthen national security. Congress noted that good roads were vital for the movement of military personnel and equipment. Hence, the official title of the interstate highway system was the "National System of Interstate and Defense Highways." Likewise, a major program of federal financial aid to public schools was the "National Defense Education Act" of 1958.

In the 1960s, the federal government gave more and more aid to states and localities—not only to augment their resources but to shape their policies. Federal policymakers hesitated to give governors or state legislators free rein to spend money, worrying that they would squander it.[46] In the early 1960s, most state legislatures spent little time in session and lacked professional staff support.[47] Stories of corruption and poor administration often emerged from state capitals and city halls. Consequently, Congress enacted hundreds of **categorical grant** programs, which directed the funds to very specific purposes. Categorical grants went to popular purposes such as education and health care, but opponents said they encouraged state and local policymakers to respond less to their own constituents and more to Washington bureaucrats.[48] Their complexity also sparked complaints. Federal nondefense spending was about equal to state and local spending until the late 1960s (see Figure 3-3). The federal government outstripped the states with the implementation of Medicare and the growth of other social programs. By this time, liberals

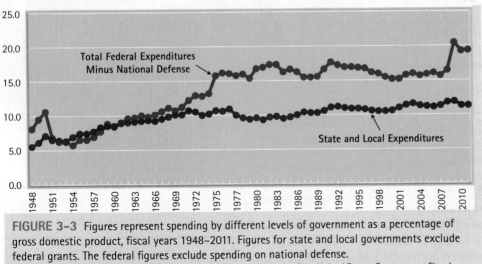

FIGURE 3-3 Figures represent spending by different levels of government as a percentage of gross domestic product, fiscal years 1948–2011. Figures for state and local governments exclude federal grants. The federal figures exclude spending on national defense.
SOURCE: United States Office of Management and Budget, *Budget of the United States Government Fiscal Year 2013* at http://www.whitehouse.gov/sites/default/files/omb/budget/fy2013/assets/hist03z1.xls and http://www.whitehouse.gov/sites/default/files/omb/budget/fy2013/assets/hist15z3.xls.

such as Robert Kennedy and conservatives such as Ronald Reagan were saying that centralization of power had gone too far.

New Federalism: Revival and Turmoil

In 1969, President Nixon declared "it is time for a **New Federalism** in which power, funds, and responsibility will flow from the federal government to the States and to the people."[49] Noting that "Washington has taken for its own the best sources of revenue," he proposed **general revenue sharing**. Under this program, the federal government would send tax money directly back to the states and localities with minimal red tape. After long debate, Congress enacted the proposal, which delivered $83 billion to states and localities during its 14-year life.

The 1970s also saw the emergence of **block grants**. More flexible than categorical grants, block grants distribute funds within a broad policy area, such as community development. In his first

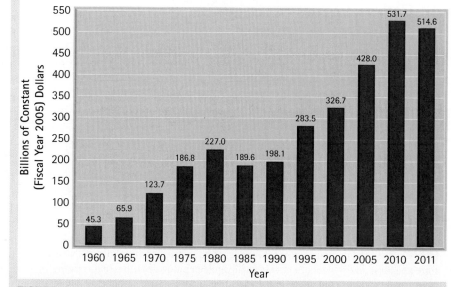

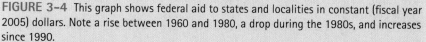

FIGURE 3-4 This graph shows federal aid to states and localities in constant (fiscal year 2005) dollars. Note a rise between 1960 and 1980, a drop during the 1980s, and increases since 1990.

SOURCE: United States Office of Management and Budget, *Budget of the United States* Government Fiscal Year 2013 at http://www.whitehouse.gov/sites/default/files/omb/budget/fy2013/assets/hist12z1.xls

year in office, President Reagan won passage of legislation combining 57 categorical grants into nine block grants. Although total federal funding for grants declined during the Reagan years, the president and his supporters argued that greater flexibility allowed the states to maintain the same level of service.[50] Critics said that his policies weakened the fight against poverty.

In some ways, state and local governments did not benefit from the trends of the 1980s. As the federal deficit increased, Congress and the president looked for programs to cut. One was revenue sharing. Reagan said, "How can we afford revenue sharing when we have no revenues to share?"[51] Congress scrapped the program.

Despite the deficit, lawmakers wanted to supply more services. One way out of this bind consisted of **mandates**—requirements that states or localities take certain actions lest they face penalties. Mandates had long been part of American federalism, but they now became more common. Often they lacked provisions to pay for compliance. State and local officials complained that these "**unfunded mandates**" let federal officials take credit for services while shifting costs. During the 1990s, declining federal deficits enabled the federal government to send more money to states and localities (see Figure 3-4). In principle, most political leaders praised the idea of decentralizing power; in important ways, however, centralization persisted. The economic crisis that started in 2008 led to an even bigger role for the central government, with a large spike in federal spending.

General revenue sharing—a program to distribute federal tax money to states and localities with few restrictions. The program ended in 1986.

Block grant—grant in which the federal government lays out broad terms on how the state and local governments should spend the money.

Mandate—federal requirement that state and local governments take certain actions.

Unfunded mandate—law or rule requiring states and localities, or the private sector, to perform functions for which the federal government does not supply funding.

CONTEMPORARY ISSUES IN FEDERALISM

MAJOR ISSUE

- Most federal policymakers endorse the idea of transferring power to the states. Why do their policy decisions so often go in the opposite direction?

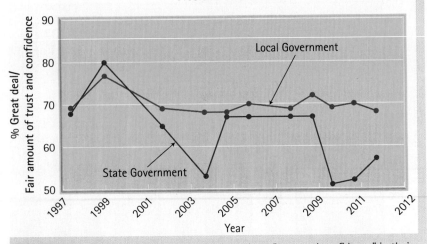

Trust and Confidence in Each Type of Government to Handle Problems—Recent Trend

FIGURE 3-5 Gallup finds that most Americans have "trust and confidence" in their state and local governments to handle public problems. But since the 1990s, they have usually had less confidence in the executive and legislative branches of the federal government.

SOURCE: http://www.gallup.com/poll/149888/Local-State-Governments-Retain-Positive-Ratings.aspx

One might refer to recent years as an era of "zigzag federalism." In some policy areas, states and localities gained greater flexibility to experiment with new approaches. At the same time, the federal government took certain actions that limited this flexibility and arguably hindered policy innovation.

Of Two Minds: Devolution and Preemption

During recent decades, Americans have favored the states in some ways. Between 1960 and 1972, no current or former governor won a major-party presidential nomination. But between 1976 and 2012, every race for the White House included at least one presidential or vice presidential candidate who had served as governor. In 1988, for instance, Michael Dukakis of Massachusetts won the Democratic nomination in part because of national praise for his jobs programs. Four years later, Bill Clinton of Arkansas stressed his record on education and welfare reform. In 2000, George W. Bush used his accomplishments in Texas to argue that he could be a bipartisan problem solver.

Survey data suggest that the appeal of governors is no fluke. Americans have more confidence in state and local government than in the federal government (see Figure 3-5). Vietnam and the Watergate scandal exposed the federal government's shortcomings. Meanwhile, state legislatures "professionalized," with more time in session, larger staffs, and longer legislative careers. (In some states, voters later thought these trends were going too far, and they passed term limits.) In the 1990s, mayors such as Rudolph Giuliani of New York and Richard M. Daley of Chicago got credit for dramatic drops in crime rates. Accordingly, many politicians called for shifting power, funds, and responsibility from the federal government to the states and people. Instead of "new federalism," they now referred to this shift as **devolution**. In 1994, Republicans won control of Congress, with devolution as part of their campaign message. The new majority passed a law requiring the Congressional Budget Office to estimate the cost of proposed mandates and making it harder to enact them without funding.

However, there was less to devolution than met the eye. While the Unfunded Mandates Reform Act of 1995 did provide more information, it had limited impact.[52] Meanwhile, Congress backed away from devolution by passing **preemption statutes**, which override state and local authority. For instance, the Internet Tax Freedom Act forbids states and localities to tax Internet access

What accounts for the apparent inconsistency? To most Americans, federalism is an abstract concept that gives way to more concrete concerns. Liberals have sometimes favored decentralization—and conservatives have opposed it—when it has advanced a progressive agenda. In the gun rights case of *McDonald v. Chicago*, for instance, liberal activists argued that state and local governments should have the flexibility to restrict gun ownership, while lawyers on the other side sought successfully to make the Second Amendment apply to the states.[53] Journalist Damon Root concludes: "In other words, there's nothing inherently liberal or conservative about making an appeal to federalism. It's a legal and rhetorical tool used— sometimes correctly, sometimes not—by both sides of the political aisle."[54] When people on either side of the spectrum break with the normal position on the balance of state and federal

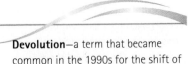

Devolution—a term that became common in the 1990s for the shift of power from the federal government to states and localities.

Preemption statute—federal law that empowers the national government to override state and local authority over a public policy issue.

power, they are not necessarily being unprincipled. Instead, they may just be managing tensions between federalism and other principles that they hold dear: equality, liberty, enterprise, or limited government.

The Health Care Law

During the 1990s, some conservatives supported an alternative to liberal proposals for national health insurance: legislation to prompt the purchase of health insurance by everyone who could afford it. A more stringent version of this idea was the centerpiece of the comprehensive health care law that President Obama signed in 2010. For those who could not afford to buy insurance, the law expanded the federal–state Medicaid program. States had to take part in this expansion, or lose all their federal funding for Medicaid, the federal government's largest grant program.

A number of states sued, arguing that this requirement unconstitutionally violated the principles of federalism. The brief that they submitted to the U.S. Supreme Court contended that the law was an act of coercion, not persuasion:

> Congress answered the coercion question itself by tying Medicaid to the individual mandate and premising its comprehensive health insurance reform scheme on the understanding that States had no realistic option but to expand Medicaid. The individual mandate gives low-income individuals no choice but to obtain insurance. And the Act provides no means for those individuals to obtain such insurance save Medicaid. A program necessary to satisfy a mandate cannot be understood as anything other than mandatory.[55]

During oral argument, Justice Elena Kagan expressed skepticism:

> So that really reduces to the question of why is a big gift from the Federal Government a matter of coercion? In other words, the Federal Government is here saying, we are giving you a boatload of money. There are no–there's no matching funds requirement, there are no extraneous conditions attached to it, it's just a boatload of federal money for you to take and spend on poor people's healthcare. It doesn't sound coercive to me, I have to tell you.[56]

Although the Court upheld the individual mandate to buy insurance, it struck down the Medicaid provision. The Court said that Congress can attach strings to aid, provided that the financial inducements are not so coercive as to turn pressure into compulsion. In his opinion for the majority, however, Chief Justice Roberts wrote that the health care law crossed this line:

> In this case, the financial "inducement" Congress has chosen is much more than "relatively mild encouragement"—it is a gun to the head. Section 1396c of the Medicaid Act provides that if a State's Medicaid plan does not comply with the Act's requirements, the Secretary of Health and Human Services may declare that "further payments will not be made to the State. A State that opts out of the Affordable Care Act's expansion in health care coverage thus stands to lose not merely "a relatively small percentage" of its existing Medicaid funding, but *all* of it.[57]

But although Congress cannot withhold *all* Medicaid funding from states that do not meet the new eligibility requirements, it can still withhold *additional* Medicaid funding that comes with the law. So while the Court limited the federal government's leverage over the states, it did eliminate it completely.

Regulation

Regulatory issues supply vivid examples of such tensions. In 1976, the Supreme Court ruled on a law extending the federal minimum wage to state and local employees. The majority said that the law invaded the states' "traditional governmental functions" and

FOCUS QUESTION

For certain kinds of businesses, such as insurance, most regulation takes place at the state level. Who benefits from this kind of decentralized regulation: consumers or the regulated industry?

Alex Wong/Getty Images

President Obama signs a memorandum to extend benefits to same-sex partners of federal employees. During the ceremony, the president said that he would work to repeal the Defense of Marriage Act. "I believe it's discriminatory, I think it interferes with states' rights, and we will work with Congress to overturn it."

was outside the authority of the commerce clause.[58] Nine years later, in *Garcia v. San Antonio Metropolitan Transit Authority,* the Court overturned that decision, holding that federal wage and hour rules *did* apply to state and local employees. The states do not need the protection of the federal judiciary, said the Court, since the "political process ensures that laws that unduly burden the States will not be promulgated."[59]

During the George W. Bush administration, new federal laws preempted state laws or rules on public health, the environment, and other issues. Democrats accused the Republican White House and Congress of usurping state powers.

During the Obama administration, Democrats sometimes invoked federalism in an effort to expand the regulatory power of state governments. In 2011, Senator Sheldon Whitehouse (D-RI) and several colleagues sponsored legislation to let states limit interest rates on credit cards and other forms of consumer lending. "It is pure States rights," he said. "We should go back to the historic States rights norm, the way the Founding Fathers saw things under the doctrine of federalism and close this modern bureaucratic loophole that allows big Wall Street banks a special deal to gouge our constituents."[60] During debate in 2010 on an earlier version of the measure, Senator Johnny Isakson (R-GA) voiced opposition: "[Y]ou will put an end to credit in the housing business and in many other types of instruments in the United States, and you will have 50 different usury regimens in 50 different States."[61]

Welfare and Education

In 1996, Congress backed devolution by ending Aid to Families with Dependent Children (AFDC), the welfare program that had started as part of the 1935 Social Security Act. The

Key Supreme Court Decisions on Federalism

McCulloch v. Maryland (1819)—Congress could enact all laws "necessary and proper" to carry out enumerated constitutional powers.

Gibbons v. Ogden (1824)—Congress could regulate a wide range of matters of interstate commerce, not just direct exchange of goods, as long as there is a commercial connection with another state.

Wickard v. Filburn (1942)—Congress could regulate intrastate, noncommercial activity if it would have a substantial effect on interstate commerce.

Garcia v. San Antonio Metropolitan Transit Authority (1985)—Congress could apply minimum wage requirements to state and local governments. The decision overruled a previous decision holding that such regulation would violate the Tenth Amendment.

United States v. Lopez (1995)—Congress could not regulate firearms in school zones. The decision was the first in decades to limit congressional power under the commerce clause.

Printz v. United States (1997)—Congress could not require local law enforcement officials to make criminal background checks of people seeking to buy handguns.

United States v. Morrison (2000)—Congress lacked power under the Commerce Clause to enact federal civil remedies for victims of gender-based violence.

Kelo v. City of New London (2005)—States and localities could use eminent domain to further private economic development.

Florida et al. v. U.S. Dept. of Health and Human Services et al. (2012)—Whether the federal government could force states to expand their Medicaid programs to comply with the national health care law.

1996 welfare reform law replaced AFDC with block grants. The new law made other major changes, such as work requirements for able-bodied recipients and limits on how long families could receive cash welfare. Within three years of the law's enactment, welfare caseloads fell by nearly half. Supporters of the law argue that it moved people from welfare to work, whereas skeptics contend that it pushed the needy into destitution or dead-end, low-wage jobs. Both sides agree that at least some of the reduction stemmed from general economic growth, and both agree that the law did shift authority to the states. Before the law, the federal government had set eligibility guidelines and then funded specific programs at certain levels. But with the block grant, the states have more say over whom to help and how. The federal role consists mainly of setting goals and then rewarding or penalizing states according to their performance.

On another issue, however, Congress enhanced federal authority when it passed President George W. Bush's education proposal, the No Child Left Behind Act (NCLB). To receive federal aid, states would now have to meet major new requirements that aimed at improving outcomes. Although the law was the initiative of a Republican president, some in his own party fault it as a federal intrusion. "What we want is to make a real firm stand for local control," said a Republican state senator in Minnesota when he proposed ending the state's participation in NCLB. "We've had five years of the No Child Left Behind regime, and I think it's safe to call it a failure now. We're giving it an F and trying to take back our schools."[62] Supporters say that the new requirements ensure improvements in education and that it provides enough flexibility.

In 2009, President Obama's economic stimulus legislation provided $4.35 billion for the Race to the Top Fund. This competitive grant fund rewards states that have improved student achievement and have crafted the best plans for speeding up their reforms in the future. The idea is that the winning states will offer models for others to follow. Explaining why Texas did not compete for the funds, Governor Rick Perry said: "Texas is on the right path toward improved education, and we would be foolish and irresponsible to place our children's future in the hands of unelected bureaucrats and special interest groups thousands of miles away in Washington, virtually eliminating parents' participation in their children's education."[66]

IMPACT
of Social Media and Communications Technology

Online Education

Nearly every state supports online elementary and secondary education. Opportunities range from supplementing traditional classroom teaching to offering full-time programs.[63] One example is the North Carolina Virtual Public School (NCPVS), which describes its goal as providing courses that students cannot take at their local schools.

> In other words NCVPS will provide courses that augment a student's local school's program of study. For example a student may wish to take an AP course the local school does not offer. Another student may want to complete the remaining requirement for graduation this semester yet the course needed at the student's school is already full this semester. Another student may be home bound or hospital bound due to illness or injury and wish to remain on schedule to graduate on time. Yet another student may wish to graduate from high school in three years.[64]

Online learning is increasingly important in higher education. About six million students were taking at least one online course in the Fall 2010 semester, an increase of half a million from the year before.[65] Many of these students are using social media to connect with one another and collaborate on class projects.

State policymakers wrote regulations for higher education when nearly all instruction took place at bricks-and-mortar institutions. Schools that focus on distance learning across state lines often have a hard time getting the necessary approvals. (See the Bessette–Pitney blog of January 21, 2011, for a discussion of these issues.) The Council of State Governments is working on an interstate compact to allow greater reciprocity in online education among the states.

CRITICAL THINKING QUESTION

As more and more schooling goes on-line, does it still make sense to regulate education at the state and local levels?

Crime

Alexander Hamilton wrote of a "transcendent advantage belonging to the province of the State governments . . . I mean the ordinary administration of criminal and civil justice. This, of all others, is the most powerful, most universal, and most attractive source of popular obedience and attachment."[67] Until Prohibition, as we have seen, federal authorities had only a slight role in crime control. In the 1960s and 1970s, surging crime created a public demand for action, and Congress responded by extending federal jurisdiction, and often duplicating state laws. By "federalizing" crimes such as carjacking, Congress allowed federal law enforcement officers and prosecutors to go after offenses that would otherwise be in the domain of state and local authorities. The federalization of crime has continued, increasing the burden on federal agents and courts. "Why should there be a Federal offense of carjacking?" asks Rep. Bobby Scott (D-VA). "State and local laws have been investigating and prosecuting those cases long before Congress made it a Federal crime, and they have been doing the job much better. In fact, when you are a victim of carjacking, you do not call the FBI; you call the local police."[68]

In the 1990s, the Supreme Court considered federalism issues arising from several anticrime measures that Congress had passed. In the 1995 case of *United States v. Lopez*, the Court reviewed a law making it a federal crime to have a firearm within 1,000 feet of a school. The Court voided the law, saying that the mere act of bringing a weapon near a school had little to do with interstate or foreign commerce, so Congress could not ban it. In the majority opinion, Chief Justice William Rehnquist wrote that upholding the law would require the Court to accept "that there never will be a distinction between what is truly national and what is truly local."[69] The following year, the Court considered another firearms law. One provision required local law enforcement officials to make criminal background checks of people seeking to buy handguns. In *Printz v. United States*, the Court declared the provision unconstitutional. "The Federal Government may neither issue directives requiring the States to address particular problems, nor command the States' officers, or those of their political subdivisions, to administer or enforce a federal regulatory program."[70]

Dealing with an even more sensitive case, *United States v. Morrison*, the Court in 2000 struck legislation allowing victims of sexual assault to sue their alleged attackers in either federal or state court. Supporters of the measure justified its constitutionality under the commerce clause, arguing that such violence diminishes the victims' productivity. The Court's majority disagreed. "Gender-motivated crimes of violence are not, in any sense of the phrase, economic activity."[71]

Lethal and Medicinal Drugs

In 1994, Oregon voters passed the Death with Dignity Act (DWDA), the first state law allowing physician-assisted suicide for terminally ill adults. After court battles and the defeat of a ballot measure that would have repealed it, the law went into effect in 1997. In 2001, Attorney General John Ashcroft ordered the Drug Enforcement Administration to consider the lethal administration of drugs to be a violation of the federal Controlled Substances Act. A group of Oregon residents fought this interpretation, and the U.S. Supreme Court agreed

Robert Nickelsberg/Getty Images

Agents of U.S. Immigration and Customs Enforcement (ICE) work with local law enforcement officers to arrest a suspected gang member. When gangs smuggle illegal aliens, traffic in drugs, or commit other federal crimes, federal agents already have the authority to go after them. Proposed legislation would broaden this authority.

with them. Writing for a majority that included the Court's liberal members, Justice Anthony Kennedy said that the federal law did not regulate the practice of medicine in general. "The silence is understandable given the structure and limitations of federalism," which give the states great leeway in protecting health and safety.[72] In dissent, Justice Antonin Scalia, a conservative, wrote that from early national history, "the Federal Government has used its enumerated powers, such as its power to regulate interstate commerce, for the purpose of protecting public morality—for example, by banning the interstate shipment of lottery tickets. . . . . [U]sing the federal commerce power to prevent assisted suicide is unquestionably permissible."[73]

A different outcome came from an earlier case involving the same federal law. In 1996, California voters passed a ballot measure legalizing medical marijuana, but federal agents continued to enforce the Controlled Substance Act even when patients claimed the protection of the state law. This time, the Supreme Court sided with the federal government. The majority opinion relied on the *Wickard*

Protesters in wheelchairs demonstrate outside the U.S. Supreme Court as the justices take up the issue of physician-assisted suicide. "Not Dead Yet" is a group that opposes this practice on the grounds that it may endanger people with disabilities.

precedent: "In both cases, the regulation is squarely within Congress' commerce power because production of the commodity meant for home consumption, be it wheat or marijuana, has a substantial effect on supply and demand in the national market for that commodity."[74] In *U.S. v. Morrison*, by contrast, the justices found that violence against women did not involve interstate market activity. Although the Obama administration initially indicated that it would give a low priority to prosecuting medical marijuana dispensaries that follow state laws, it pursued them vigorously. One commentator said that the federal government had become arguably tougher on medical marijuana operations than it was under George W. Bush.[75]

Lawsuits

In 1793, the Supreme Court accepted jurisdiction of a lawsuit against one state by a citizen of another. Seeing an apparent encroachment on state powers, Congress and the states responded with the Eleventh Amendment (passed by Congress in March 1794 and ratified in February 1795). It provides that federal judicial power shall not extend to lawsuits "against one of the United States by Citizens of another State, or by Citizens or Subjects of any Foreign State." (See Table 3–4.)

Recent Supreme Court decisions have renewed the prominence of this long-obscure amendment. In 1999, the Court ruled that Congress could not subject states to lawsuits in their own courts for violations of federal laws.[76] In 2002, the Court found that states enjoyed similar

TABLE 3-4   INTERSTATE RELATIONS

- **Eleventh Amendment:** The Judicial power of the United States shall not be construed to extend to any suit in law or equity, commenced or prosecuted against one of the United States by Citizens of another State, or by Citizens or Subjects of any Foreign State.
- **"Full Faith and Credit" Clause:** According to Article IV, section 1, "Full Faith and Credit shall be given in each State to the public Acts, Records, and judicial Proceedings of every other State. And the Congress may by general Laws prescribe the Manner in which such Acts, Records and Proceedings shall be proved, and the Effect thereof."

© Cengage Learning 2014

JASON REED/Reuters /Landov

protections from private complaints before federal agencies.[77] In these cases, the Court did not rely on the Eleventh Amendment alone but on the Constitution's original structure. These cases seemed to strengthen the states' hand, but meanwhile, Congress was preempting their authority over other kinds of lawsuits. The Protection of Lawful Commerce in Arms Act is one example. Starting in the late 1990s, dozens of local governments sued firearm manufacturers and distributors, seeking millions of dollars in damages for gun violence. They charged negligence on the part of the industry, which responded that it should not be liable when others use their products to commit crimes. In 2005, Congress voted to shield firearm makers and dealers from such lawsuits in state and federal courts. The chair of the House Judiciary Committee quoted a Supreme Court decision: "[O]ne State's power to impose burdens on the interstate market . . . is not only subordinate to the Federal power over interstate commerce but is also constrained by the need to respect the interests of other States."[78] Sheila Jackson Lee (D-TX) disagreed: "[T]he leadership of the House is all too eager to ignore principles of federalism when it suits their ideological needs."[79]

Same-Sex Marriage

"Full faith and credit" clause—Article IV, Section 1, of the Constitution, which requires each state to recognize and honor the actions of the other states.

The Constitution's **"full faith and credit" clause** requires each state to recognize the others' laws, records, and judicial proceedings. Under this clause, you can use your home-state license to drive anywhere in the country. If you successfully sue someone, that person cannot escape the judgment by moving because it is enforceable in out-of-state courts.

The clause also allows Congress to "prescribe the Manner in which such Acts, Records and Proceedings shall be proved, and the Effect thereof." In 1996, reacting to the prospect that some states might legalize same-sex marriages, Congress passed and President Clinton signed legislation specifying that other states need not recognize such marriages. Supporters of the Defense of Marriage Act cited this clause as their constitutional basis. Opponents said that Congress may only set out procedures for carrying out the "full faith and credit" clause, not make exceptions.

In 2003, a Massachusetts court ruled that the state's constitution required official recognition of same-sex marriages. Some conservatives sought to amend the U.S. Constitution to stop same-sex marriages. Liberals objected to the proposal, saying that it violated the principle of federalism. "I, like everyone else in the Senate, took an oath when I joined this body to support and defend the Constitution," said Russ Feingold (D-WI). "The Framers of our Constitution granted limited, enumerated powers to the Federal Government, while reserving the remaining powers of government, including family law, to State governments."[80] Conservatives replied that marriage had long been a matter of federal jurisdiction. They cited nineteenth-century laws banning polygamy in territories and twentieth-century court rulings striking down state laws on marriage and divorce.[81]

As suggested at the start of this chapter, the Defense of Marriage Act has prompted similar lines of argument, with conservatives supporting federal action and liberals supporting states' rights. Yet when federal courts overturned California's ban on same-sex marriage, the two sides switched places, with conservatives saying that the rulings violated states' rights and liberals defending the courts' actions as an appropriate exercise of federal power. In criticizing the Defense of Marriage Act, President Obama said that marriage was a matter for the states, although he also opposed the California law. When he endorsed same-sex marriage in 2012, he said:

> At a certain point, I've just concluded that—for me personally, it is important for me to go ahead and affirm that—I think same-sex couples should be able to get married. Now—I have to tell you that part of my hesitation on this has also been I didn't want to nationalize the issue. There's a tendency when I weigh in to think suddenly it becomes political and it becomes polarized. . . . And I continue to believe that this is an issue that is gonna be worked out at the local level, because historically, this has not been a federal issue, what's recognized as a marriage.[82]

The National Guard

By federal law (10 USC 311), the "unorganized militia" includes all other able-bodied males between the ages of 17 and 45.[83] The National Guard constitutes the "organized" militia and consists mainly of civilians who serve part-time. It has both federal and state roles. Each governor commands Guard forces through the state adjutant general and can call them into action during emergencies such as riots and floods. Congress provides funding for the Guard, and the president can activate it for federal missions, including overseas duty.[84] In such cases, the president serves as its commander in chief.

The overlap of state and federal authority has sometimes caused political tension. In 1957, the segregationist governor of Arkansas, Democrat Orval Faubus, tried to block the integration of a Little Rock high school by sending the Arkansas National Guard. Because the attempted integration was the result of federal court rulings, Faubus's action defied federal authority. A court order forced him to withdraw the Guardsmen, but when anti-integration violence erupted, President Dwight Eisenhower sent regular army troops to keep order; and to block Faubus from interfering, he put the Arkansas National Guard under federal control.

Thirty years later, Governor Rudy Perpich of Minnesota sued when the Reagan administration sent members of his state's Guard to Central America for active-duty training. Perpich, along with other governors who opposed the administration's foreign policy,

Photo by Mario Tama/Getty Images

National Guard troops help victims of Hurricane Katrina outside the New Orleans convention center.

said that the federal government had no right to take such action without gubernatorial consent. The Supreme Court unanimously disagreed, citing a 1933 law providing that all members of state National Guard units were members of the National Guard of the United States.[85]

When Hurricane Katrina devastated New Orleans in 2005, relief efforts suffered from lack of coordination between the regular military and National Guard.[86] Critics accused the Bush administration of straining the National Guard by sending units to Iraq and Afghanistan. Five years later, the BP oil spill in the Gulf of Mexico reignited conflicts between the federal and state governments. According to one poll, people in Louisiana approved of their state's response but disapproved of the federal response.[87] Wrote columnist David Brooks: "Some of this rage is unavoidable when you have a crisis that no one can control. But it's also clear that we have a federalism problem. All around the region there are local officials who think they know their towns best. They feel insulted by a distant and opaque bureaucracy lurking above."[88]

DEBATING FEDERALISM

MAJOR ISSUE

- What are the advantages and disadvantages of America's complex system of federalism?

As we have just seen, federalism involves complicated choices. On the one hand, there is broad support for decentralization in the abstract. On the other hand, specific issues often create pressure for a strong federal response. These tensions raise questions about the value of federalism itself.

Double Security

Admirers of the federal system say that the federal and state governments make up two layers of protection for Americans' rights and interests. The Seventeenth Amendment deprived legislatures of a role in choosing senators. Nevertheless, states and localities have other ways of influencing federal policy. Most states and many cities have Washington lobbying offices or contract with lobby firms. Dozens of organizations represent state and local officials from across the country. Here are a few:

- The Council of State Governments
- The National Council of State Legislatures
- The National Governors Association
- The National Association of Counties
- The National League of Cities

In 2010, state and local governments spent more than $77 million lobbying the federal government, down from an all-time high of $83 million the year before.[89] State and local officials tend to see lobby expenditures as a wise investment. The most dramatic example is Galena, Alaska, which spent $60,000 on federal lobbying in 2010, or $127.66 for each of its 470 residents. It got about $1.5 million in grants, representing a 25:1 return on its lobbying outlay.[90] But not all governments can win. "We are all asking for the same thing, unfortunately," said Los Angeles County's head lobbyist in 2010. "No matter where you stand on issues like the jobs bill or the healthcare bill, there are definitely competing state and local interests competing for money.[91] "In the end," added an official of the National Taxpayers Union, "taxpayers come back losing. Even if the aid comes back in federal dollars, the dollars are deficit financed, fueled by more taxpayer money."[92]

Federalism may provide a "double security" in another way: by providing "backup systems." When citizens try and fail to get action from the federal government, they may turn to state governments. In August 2001, President George W. Bush announced that for the first time federal funds could support research on human embryonic stem cells, but under limited conditions. Many researchers deemed the limits too narrow. A number of states then launched efforts to foster embryonic stem cell research. By a 2004 ballot measure, Californians set up a research institute and will generate $3 billion in bond funding for embryonic stem cell research. (In 2009, President Obama revoked President Bush's executive order on stem cell research.)

Another example of relying on state governments to further efforts arose from *Kelo v. City of New London*. This Supreme Court case involved eminent domain, the power of governments to take private property in exchange for payment, even if the owner objects. The Court said that the U.S. Constitution does not bar states and localities from transferring private property to new private owners for the purpose of economic development. The decision disturbed many property owners, who feared that governments could seize their land to enrich developers. But writing for the majority, Justice Stevens practically invited states to supply their own remedy: "We emphasize that nothing in our opinion precludes any State from placing further restrictions on its exercise of the takings power."[93] As of 2011, 42 had done so.[94]

One could view both cases from different perspectives. From the standpoint of those who oppose embryonic stem cell research, state action means double danger, not double security. That is, critics must win at two levels, not just one. In the case of eminent domain, one could argue that the states created the problem in the first place and that the legislative responses were often weak. Noting that state and local officials can be at least as oppressive as their federal colleagues, they cite cases where state and local authorities have misused tax dollars, silenced dissent, shut down honest businesses, and invaded privacy.[95]

"Race to the Bottom" or Healthy Competition?

States compete for jobs and people. One state may even run ads in a neighboring state in order to persuade businesses to relocate. When a state loses business and population to others, it has an incentive to change its services, rules, or taxes. As in any marketplace, say federalism enthusiasts, choice and competition result in efficiency and responsiveness.

Others argue that this competition has harmful effects. States try to attract businesses by giving them tax breaks and other advantages that ordinary citizens have to pay for. Seeking to curb expenses and limit burdens on big corporations, the states cut services and skimp on protections for labor and the environment. In the case of poverty policy, said the late senator Daniel Patrick Moynihan (D-NY, served 1977–2001) in 1995, "The hidden agenda of the Devolution Revolution is a large-scale withdrawal of support for social welfare, no matter how well conceived. The result would be a race to the bottom, as states, deprived of Federal matching funds, compete with one other to reduce spending by depriving their own dependent population of help."[96]

One counterargument holds that there is little evidence of a "race to the bottom." The quest for new business is just one of many driving forces behind state policy, and pressure from citizens and interest groups may boost spending. And although businesses may like lower taxes and less regulation, they also have an interest in such things as good roads and well-educated workforces, which may prompt them to back more activist state governments. As for poverty, Senator (and former governor) Tom Carper (D-DE) observed in 2002, "In most states . . . the feared race to the bottom turned out to be a race to the top. States have used waivers from the federal government and the flexibility granted them by the 1996 welfare reform law to ensure that the majority of families who move from welfare rolls to payrolls are truly on their way to becoming better off."[97]

In the same vein, a study found that many states exceed federal clean air standards. Instead of weakening their programs in the face of economic pressures, state lawmakers strengthen them in response to citizen demands.[98] Even more striking has been action on climate change. The costs to each state are immediate and potentially large, while the benefits lie in the future and apply broadly to the whole world. If states responded only to economic cost-benefit analyses, they would never consider such action. Yet by 2011, 23 states had adopted statewide emission targets and goals, while 36 had either completed comprehensive climate action plans or were in the process of doing so.[99]

In 2010, the Environmental Protection Agency (EPA) set the first national greenhouse gas standards, which will control emissions from new cars and light trucks. The Obama administration crafted an agreement with California to harmonize state-level standards, so that auto makers would have one national set of standards.

Closer to the People or Closed to the People?

Several other countries with large land areas (e.g., Canada, Australia, and Germany) also have federal systems. That is no coincidence, say the advocates of federalism. In big countries, the seat of the central government may lie far from many of the people—both physically and politically. Although technological advances have shrunk the globe in many ways, problems of communication and understanding still tend to increase with distance, especially when different regions have diverse interests. With a federal system, the officials at lower levels of government can more easily deal with regional issues, and the people can more easily hold them to account.

In 2012, former California assemblyman Chuck DeVore left his home state for Texas. He cited California's fiscal policies and economic climate as reasons for his move.

President Obama makes brief remarks about the regulation of greenhouse gases. Left to right: Transportation Secretary Ray LaHood, President Obama, and EPA Administrator Lisa Jackson.

FOCUS
QUESTION

Which level of government—federal, state, local—provides the greatest opportunities for political participation and other forms of active citizenship?

In the United States, citizens benefit from the sheer multiplicity of offices. It may be confusing to have more than 89,000 units of government, but more units mean more gateways to civic participation. More than half a million Americans hold elected offices ranging from school board member to state legislator. With so many places to turn, citizens with ideas or problems can usually get at least one politician to listen.

The Internet has been a boon to citizens who want to study and influence their state governments. They may now identify their legislators online and get in touch with them by e-mail. Many public documents are easily accessible, and state residents may download applications for citizen advisory boards.

Critics of federalism counter that state and local governments are "closer" only in a strict geographic sense. These governments vary greatly in the extent to which they require records and meetings to be open to the public.[100] It may be hard for citizens to find out what their state governments are doing, much less have a hand in policy. The media do not always fill in the gap, as coverage of statehouses and city halls ranges from commendable in some places to scant in others. As a result, people may know less about the "closer" levels of government than about Washington (see Myths and Information: Knowledge of State Government). In 2010, for instance, the American National Election Studies found that while most Americans knew which party controlled the U.S. House and Senate, they did not know which side controlled their state legislature.[101] Few would deny that citizens might have a spotty understanding of state and local government. When Americans need information, however, they can learn a great deal by word of mouth or personal contact with the officials. In 29 of 49 lower chambers of state legislatures (Nebraska is unicameral), districts have fewer than 50,000 people.[102] Districts for school boards and city councils are often much smaller. People can reach elected officials through a variety of formal and informal means, including chance encounters at the supermarket checkout line. According to a Minnesota state senator, "I have 66,000 constituents and so when an issue of controversy comes up and my constituents communicate their views on that to me, I do still have time to write back to them and say, well, what about this aspect of the argument or what about another aspect of the argument. . . . [A]nd then if I get a response back from the constituent, I do get a real dialogue rather than an opinion poll about an issue."[103]

MYTHS AND MISINFORMATION

Knowledge of State Government

Nearly all Americans can name the president. But things are different with the states' chief executives. In a 2007 national survey, 66% of Americans could recall their own governor's name.[104] While it is encouraging that most answered correctly, the figure had dropped from 74% in 1989 and 86% in 1970.[105]

California's Arnold Schwarzenegger was one exception to the relatively low profile of American governors. In a 2007 survey, 93% of Californians could recall his name. But as a bodybuilder and movie star, he had global fame long before he ever ran for office. Other state officials lacked that advantage, so only 8% could name the state's assembly speaker, and only 3% could name the state senate's leader. A national poll at the same time found that 49% could identify Nancy Pelosi as Speaker of the House.[106] (The figures are not strictly comparable. The state poll provided the names and asked respondents to identify the positions. The national poll did the reverse.)

Americans also have spotty knowledge of the states' finances. For instance, one-third of Oregonians thought that property taxes were their state's main source of revenue, even though the state received no property tax revenues.[107] A January 2012 poll of Californians was even more revealing. The state's deep fiscal problems had been in the news for several years, yet fewer than one in four adults (16%) knew that K–12 education was the largest area of state spending. Less than a third correctly named the personal income tax as the state's largest state revenue source, with most incorrectly naming the sales tax, corporate taxes, or motor vehicle fees.[108]

By learning more about state governments, Americans could overcome many misconceptions and become better citizens. Where should they turn?

- The U.S. General Services Administration posts links to each state's official Web page at www.usa.gov/Agencies/State_and_Territories.shtml.
- Stateline.org (www.stateline.org) is a nonprofit online news site that reports on emerging trends and issues in state policy and politics.
- The Pew Center on the States (www.pewcenteronthestates.org) produces in-depth analyses of a variety of state policy issues.

FEDERALISM AND DELIBERATIVE DEMOCRACY

Perhaps the greatest advantage of federalism, say its defenders, is that it fosters deliberation. Intergovernmental organizations serve as clearinghouses of state and local government knowledge. For instance, the National Governors Association has a Center for Best Practices (www.nga.org/cms/center), which helps state executives share ideas and experiences.

Scholar Alan Rosenthal finds that state lawmakers learn from many sources and can examine local effects in greater detail than their federal counterparts. "Throughout the lawmaking process, the merits get studied, discussed, and argued back and forth. On that basis—and with the understanding that this encompasses both substantive and political considerations—the respective merits essentially account for most of the votes of most of the members most of the time."[109] As we noted at the beginning of this chapter, one may think of states as laboratories of democracy. "There is ever more interest and states are imitating and learning from each other," says Judi Greenwald of the Pew Center on Global Climate Change.[110] States can also learn from policy failure. In 2000 and 2001, California suffered severe electricity disruptions stemming from an unhappy mix of regulation and deregulation. Other states can study California's experience to avoid its mistakes.[111]

Successful state innovations may influence Congress and the White House. Franklin D. Roosevelt said of the New Deal, "Practically all the things we've done in the federal government are like things Al Smith did as governor of New York."[112] In the same vein, President Clinton said, "If something is working in a State I try to steal it."[113] For decades, lawmakers in Washington and the state capitals studied and debated the best ways to reduce dependency. In the 1990s, states applied for federal waivers so they could try their own innovations in the AFDC program. The results of these innovations supplied material for the 1996 welfare reform bill.

There are limits to the states' ability to serve as laboratories of democracy. Poorer states often cannot pay for expensive innovations, and even the richer states are sometimes unable to afford them. In 2007, California governor Arnold Schwarzenegger proposed an ambitious health care reform. At first, prospects for passage seemed bright. But the costly plan stalled when the state's budget deficit grew.

Most state legislators, skeptics claim, serve only part-time and can seldom gain the expertise that genuine deliberation requires. The situation is especially stark in the states with legislative term limits, they add, because lawmakers have to leave office before they can even start to learn the issues. States also vary greatly in their ability and willingness to make government information public.[114] In some places, data are abundant, but in others, policymakers and interested citizens are flying blind, and the availability of information is no guarantee that it will go to good use. When lawmakers get analysis by the crateful, they have a hard time digesting it all. Even in "professional" legislatures without term limits, reasoned debate may be in short supply. A 2004 report by the Brennan Center concluded that New York's legislature was the least deliberative and most dysfunctional in the nation.[115] Subsequent reforms improved the institution's capabilities only a little. Supporters of federalism criticize this example as unrepresentative, arguing that debate is extensive in most state capitols. To say that all levels of government should be "professional" is to miss the point, they would contend. What matters is that a wide variety of perspectives may come into play. Yale law professor Heather Gerken acknowledges that liberals are often skeptical of federalism, "and with good reason. States' rights

AP Photo/Haraz N. Ghanbari

President Obama and Arizona governor Jan Brewer have a brief, heated discussion on immigration policy as he arrives in Phoenix.

have been invoked to defend some of the most despicable institutions in American history, most notably slavery and Jim Crow." Nevertheless, she argues, federalism enables liberals to get a hearing for their ideas when the doors of Washington are closed to them:

> Decentralization gives political outliers one of the most important powers a dissenter can enjoy—the power to force the majority to engage. It thus helps generate the deliberative froth needed to prevent national politics from becoming ossified or frozen by political elites uninterested in debating the hard questions that matter most to everyday voters.[116]

Tocqueville praised America's decentralized structure: "Democracy does not provide a people with the most skillful of governments, but it does that which the most skillful government cannot do: it spreads throughout the body social a restless activity, superabundant force, and energy never found elsewhere, which, however little favored by circumstance, can do wonders. Those are its true advantages."[117]

SUMMARY

- The United States has a complicated federal system that divides authority between the states and the federal government.
- Most important domestic policy issues involve that division of authority.
- Since the founding, power has shifted from the states to the federal government. The Civil War, two world wars, and the Cold War all increased the federal government's authority, as did the Sixteenth and Seventeenth Amendments. In recent decades, federal policymakers have often spoken of transferring power to the states. But their policy decisions have often gone the opposite way because public opinion and political pressure tend to put other goals ahead of preserving federalism.
- In spite of the long-term trend toward centralization, however, the states still retain substantial authority.
- Madison said that the division of power between the federal and state levels adds security for individual

rights, whereas some contemporary observers contend that states may actually threaten liberties and interests that Americans hold dear.
- Although conservatives tend to favor devolution of power to the states and liberals tend to support an active federal government, certain key issues are exceptions to this pattern.
- There is also disagreement as to whether interstate competition fosters a "race to the bottom" or governmental excellence.
- In principle, a complex federal system expands opportunities for active citizenship. In practice, however, citizens may lack the necessary information to take advantage of such opportunities.
- States provide multiple forums for reasoning on the merits of issues and experimenting with new public policies, but there is debate about the quality of the resulting deliberation.

KEY TERMS

Block grant p. 75
Categorical grant p. 74
Commerce clause p. 69
Confederal system p. 65
Devolution p. 76
Dual federalism p. 70
Enumerated powers p. 68

Federal system p. 65
"Full faith and credit" clause p. 82
General revenue sharing p. 75
Implied powers p. 69
Mandate p. 75
"Necessary and proper" clause p. 69
New Federalism p. 74

Nullification p. 70
Preemption statute p. 76
Reserved powers p. 69
Supremacy clause p. 69
Unfunded mandate p. 75
Unitary system p. 65

TEST YOUR KNOWLEDGE

1. A system in which the national government dominates certain policy areas while regional governments dominate others is called a _____ government.
   a. divided
   b. federal
   c. liberal
   d. progressive
   e. unitary

2. Which of the following is NOT generally considered an advantage of federalism?
   a. a "double security" for the people's liberties
   b. competition between states
   c. increased opportunities for citizens to involve themselves in government
   d. more and better deliberation
   e. more overlap of state and federal laws

3. _____ anonymously authored a resolution for Kentucky which declared that states had the right to declare federal acts unconstitutional, and therefore void.
   a. Alexander Hamilton
   b. Benjamin Franklin
   c. James Madison
   d. Thomas Jefferson
   e. Thomas Paine

4. The amendment that was concerned with _____ marked the beginning of a federal role in law enforcement.
   a. direct election of senators
   b. income tax
   c. prohibition
   d. sovereign immunity
   e. women's suffrage

5. Survey data and presidential election statistics indicate that since 1976, voting Americans have tended to favor
   a. businesspeople over career politicians.
   b. federal government over state and local governments.
   c. senatorial candidates over former governors.
   d. state and local governments over the federal government.
   e. unitary governments over federal governments.

6. *United States v. Lopez* and *Printz v. United States* both dealt with
   a. firearms.
   b. interstate commerce.

   c. minimum wage.
   d. slavery.
   e. street gangs.

7. How do states and cities influence federal policy in contemporary politics?
   a. State legislatures elect senators to Congress.
   b. State legislatures pass preemption statutes.
   c. States and cities bring cases to the attention of the Supreme Court.
   d. States and cities control the salaries of representatives.
   e. States and cities hire lobbyists.

8. The history of which of the following cases illustrates the "double security" of federalism by which the states can take up issues when the federal government cannot or will not help?
   a. *Kelo v. City of New London*
   b. *McCulloch v. Maryland*
   c. *United States v. Lopez*
   d. *United States v. Morrison*
   e. *Wickard v. Filburn*

9. Which of the following is most likely to contribute to the fact that Americans tend to know more about their federal government than their local government?
   a. poor quality of the education system
   b. tendency of media networks to provide more coverage of federal proceedings
   c. laws passed by Congress requiring state meetings to be closed to the public
   d. corruption at the local level
   e. interference from the federal government

10. Why has there often been conflict between the state and federal governments regarding the National Guard?
    a. States resent a prominent presence of federal forces.
    b. National Guard forces are less restricted by federal law and can therefore be used against a state government more easily.
    c. The National Guard has both state and federal roles, which sometimes results in an overlap of authority.
    d. Other branches of the military are more closely monitored, causing tension with the National Guard.
    e. There are too few laws governing the role of the National Guard.

FURTHER READING

Bolick, Clint. *Grassroots Tyranny: The Limits of Federalism.* Washington, DC: Cato Institute, 1993.

Epstein, Richard A., and Michael S. Greve, eds. *Federal Preemption: States' Powers, National Interests.* Washington, DC: AEI Press, 2007.

Gerken, Heather K. "A New Progressive Federalism," *Democracy: A Journal of Ideas* 24 (Spring 2012), at www.democracyjournal.org/24/a-new-progressive-federalism.php.

McPherson, James B. *Abraham Lincoln and the Second American Revolution.* New York: Oxford University Press, 1991.

Osborne, David. *Laboratories of Democracy: A New Breed of Governor Creates Models for National Growth.* Boston: Harvard Business School Press, 1990.

Rosenthal, Alan. *Heavy Lifting: The Job of the American Legislature.* Washington, DC: CQ Press, 2004.

Rossum, Ralph A. *Federalism, the Supreme Court, and the Seventeenth Amendment: The Irony of Constitutional Democracy.* Lanham, MD: Rowman & Littlefield, 2001.

WEB SOURCES

National Conference of State Legislatures: www.ncsl.org—the organization of state-level lawmakers.

National Governors Association: www.nga.org—an organization of state governors.

Pew Center on the States: www.pewcenteronthestates.org—studies of state policy initiatives.

Stateline: www.stateline.org/live/—news and information on state government.

StateMaster: www.statemaster.com/index.php—statistical data on states.

New citizens from 19 nations take the Oath of Allegiance on July 1, 2010, at Independence National Historical Park, the site of Independence Hall in Philadelphia where both the Declaration of Independence and the Constitution were written.

E Pluribus Unum
American Citizenship and Civic Culture

4

OBJECTIVES

After reading this chapter, you should be able to:

- Describe the role of ideals and beliefs in what it means to be an American citizen.

- Evaluate immigration controversies in light of the meaning of American citizenship.

- Compare the controversies over the citizenship of free blacks before the Civil War and the citizenship of Native Americans.

- Describe the requirements that Congress has imposed for the naturalization of foreigners and assess how these requirements relate to the duties of citizenship.

- Compare American civic culture to that in other industrial democracies and evaluate the importance of civic culture to American government and politics.

INTRODUCTION

Citizens are full-fledged members of a political community, with both rights and responsibilities. In democracies, they contribute to deliberations about the common good by participating in the political process in various ways, as we describe in later chapters. In particular, only citizens (typically) have the right to vote and hold office. Every democracy must determine the legal rights and duties of citizens and decide who should enjoy this legal status.

Controversies over citizenship have been common in the United States because of its character as a nation of immigrants and the great diversity of its people. Since 1782, the **Great Seal of the United States**—which is used on official government documents— has included on it a bald eagle that carries in its beak a scroll with the Latin phrase, "**E pluribus unum,**" which means "From many, one." This motto implies that being an American is something more than just a legal status. The citizens of the country are more than just a collection of disparate individuals or groups pursuing their private interests.

The very notion of a "common good" would be meaningless if Americans did not identify with something larger than their private or group interests. What, then, does it means to be an American? What is the "unum"—if there is one—that ties together the "pluribus" of the more than 300 million residents of the United States? The answers to these questions have profound consequences for American deliberative democracy.

We begin this chapter, then, with the American ideal that a commitment to common principles ties together a large and diverse population. From there we address the history of American immigration and the controversies that it has spawned; the policies and practices that govern becoming an American citizen; the rights and privileges that citizenship confers; the contemporary debate over assimilation; the responsibilities of citizenship; and the unique set of beliefs that Americans share about their relationship to government, their country's place in the world, and their duties to one another.

Great Seal of the United States— adopted by the Congress of the Articles of Confederation in 1782 for use on official government documents. It includes the Latin motto "E pluribus unum."

E pluribus unum—Latin motto on the scroll carried in the mouth of the eagle on the Great Seal of the United States: "Out of many, one."

© Bettmann/CORBIS

The Great Seal of the United States, designed in 1782, shows the Latin motto: "E pluribus unum." The two sides of the Great Seal appear on the back of the dollar bill.

E PLURIBUS UNUM
MAJOR ISSUE

- What makes the large, diverse population of the United States "one united people"?

In July 1776, the Declaration of Independence announced that "one People"—the colonists— was dissolving its political connection "with another"—the British. But what made the 3 million individuals scattered along a thousand miles of the North American coast truly one people with the right to be a separate nation? This issue—what makes a group of individuals a people in a political sense—has profound practical implications.

In just the past few decades, the former Soviet Union broke up into 15 separate nations and the former Yugoslavia into 6. Two countries became 21. If those living in the old Soviet Union and Yugoslavia had thought of themselves as one people, they would not have split into so many different countries. Similarly, Czechoslovakia, which had been one country since the end of World War I, peacefully divided into two on January 1, 1993—the Czech Republic and Slovakia—because of the widespread view that the old boundaries really incorporated two different peoples, each of which deserved its own nation. And in 2011, after decades of conflict, the African country of Sudan split in two, resulting in the new country of South Sudan. Separatist movements continue to this day. Palestinians in the Middle East press their claim for nationhood, as do many Kurds who live in a territory that overlaps Iraq, Iran, and Turkey.

Characteristics of Early Americans

Writing in *The Federalist Papers* in 1787, John Jay explained what made Americans "one united people." In addition to possessing "one connected, fertile, wide-spreading country," the Americans were "descended from the same ancestors, speaking the same language, professing the same religion, attached to the same principles of government, very similar in their manners and customs, and who, by their joint counsels, arms, and efforts, fighting side by side throughout a long and bloody war, have nobly established their general liberty and independence."[1] Common territory, ancestors, language, religion, political principles, manners and customs, and the joint revolutionary war effort—all of these bound Americans together as one people.

Jay did not say that *all* these commonalities were necessary. A common territory seems required, but what about similarities in nationality (common ancestors), language, religion, manners and customs, and principles of government? Jay exaggerated the commonalities. He failed to note that nearly one-fifth of the population was enslaved; that American Indians in the new country did not have much in common with those of European ancestry; that religious differences among the mainly Christian population had often been divisive; and that there were pockets where the common language was Dutch, German, Swedish, or Scottish Gaelic.

The Declaration of Independence is silent on whether any of these characteristics is necessary for nationhood except one: political principles. What those who separated from Britain in July 1776 had in common was a belief in human equality, natural rights, and consent of the governed—"Truths" held to be "self-evident." It is hard to see how a group of individuals could found a new nation if some believed that kings or aristocrats should rule while others were committed to self-government; or if some held that government's main purpose should be promoting religious belief, while others thought that it should be securing rights.

The Diversity of Modern Americans

Modern Americans are a diverse people. Of the just over 300 million persons now living in the United States, 66% are white, 16% are Hispanic, and 13% are black. Asians are 5% of the population; and American Indians, Alaskan Natives, Native Hawaiians, and Pacific Islanders make up another 1.6% (see Table 4-1). Although 88% of residents are citizens by virtue of being born in the United States, another 5% (16 million) were born elsewhere and later became American citizens (naturalized citizens), and 7% (22 million) were born elsewhere and are not citizens (including those in the country legally and illegally) (see Table 4-2).

Of the 38 million foreign-born residents, just over half come from Latin America (20 million), and most of the rest are from Asia (11 million). Europe, from which most American immigrants originally came, is now the origin of only 5 million (about one in eight) of foreign-born persons. A fifth of the population speaks a language other than, or in addition to, English at home, with Spanish (35 million) being the most common. In addition, over 2 million speak Chinese at home; and over a million each speak Tagalog (the national language of the Philippines), French, Vietnamese, German, or Korean.

The United States is also the home to many faiths. In a large-scale survey conducted in 2008, 76% of respondents identified themselves as Christians (see Table 4-3). Of these, the largest groups were Catholics (57.2 million), Baptists (36.1 million), and Methodists (11.4 million). Other denominations with at least 3 million members were Lutheran (8.7 million), Pentecostal (5.4 million), Presbyterian (4.7 million), and Mormon/Latter-day Saints

TABLE 4-1	AMERICAN PEOPLE: DEMOGRAPHIC CHARACTERISTICS	
	Number	Percentage
Population (2010)	308,746,000	100%
Sex (2010)		
Male	151,781,000	49%
Female	156,964,000	51
Age (2010)		
Under 20	83,267,000	27%
20–39	82,830,000	27
40–59	85,563,000	28
60–74	38,531,000	12
75 and older	18,554,000	6
Race and ethnicity (2009)*		
Non-Hispanic		
White	203,800,000	66%
Black	39,495,000	13
Asian	15,437,000	5
American Indian and Alaska Native	3,874,000	1
Native Hawaiian and Pacific Islander	918,000	<0.5
Hispanic	48,419,000	16
Education (those 25 and older) (2010)		
Not a high school graduate	25,790,000	13%
High school graduate (or equivalent)	62,377,000	31
Some college, no degree	33,588,000	17
Associate's degree	18,193,000	9
Bachelor's degree	38,786,000	19
Advanced degree	20,992,000	11
Family income (2009)		
Less than $20,000	10,094,000	13%
$20,000–$39,999	15,716,000	20
$40,000–$59,999	13,554,000	17
$60,000–$74,999	8,677,000	11
$75,000–$99,999	10,668,000	14
$100,000 and above	20,157,000	26

*Percentages add up to more than 100% because about 4 million individuals listed more than one race.

SOURCE: U.S. Census Bureau, *The 2010 Statistical Abstract, The National Data Book*, Tables 1, 6, 7, 231, 695, at http://www.census.gov/compendia/statab/2012edition.html, accessed April 19, 2012.

(3.2 million). Another 8.8 million persons identified themselves with a non-Christian religion, including Judaism (2.7 million), Islam (1.3 million), and Buddhism (1.2 million). Twenty percent of respondents professed no religion or did not answer the question.

This picture shows both diversity and commonality. Most Americans are descendants of Europeans, but a third are not. A large majority speak English at home, but a fifth speak another language along with, or instead of, English. Most consider themselves Christians, but almost a fourth identify with other religions, no religion, or refuse to say.

TABLE 4-2	AMERICAN PEOPLE: FOREIGN BIRTH AND USE OF FOREIGN LANGUAGES		
		Number	Percentage
Foreign Born (2010)		37,606,000	12%
Citizenship status			
Naturalized U.S. citizen		16,024,000	5%
Not U.S. citizen		21,581,000	7
Region (2009)			
Latin America		20,456,000	7%
Mexico		11,478,000	4
Caribbean		3,466,000	1
South America		2,596,000	1
Central America (not Mexico)		2,916,000	1
Asia		10,652,000	3
Europe		4,887,000	2
Africa		1,492,000	<0.5
Other		1,030,000	<0.5

Language spoken at home*
(those 5 years and older, with
at least 1 million) (2009)

	Number	Percentage
English only	228,700,000	80%
Spanish	35,469,000	12
Chinese	2,600,000	1
Tagalog	1,514,000	1
French	1,306,000	<0.5
Vietnamese	1,251,000	<0.5
German	1,109,000	<0.5
Korean	1,039,000	<0.5

*In addition to, or instead of, English.

SOURCE: Tables 40, 42, and 53 in the source cited in Table 4-1 above; accessed April 19, 2012.

Does any of this matter to what it means to be an American? In the 1820s, a naturalized Englishwoman (an immigrant from England who had become an American citizen) asked, "For what is it to be American? Is it to have drawn the first breath in Maine, in Pennsylvania, in Florida, or in Missouri?" No, she answered, "*[t]hey* are American who, having complied with the constitutional regulations of the United States . . . wed the principles of America's Declaration to their hearts and render the duties of American citizens practically in their lives."[2] For this new American, citizenship derived not from blood or geography but from a commitment to embrace the nation's legal and political principles and to carry out the duties of citizenship.

Three decades later, Abraham Lincoln made a similar point in an address to an ethnically diverse audience of Chicagoans. He noted that perhaps half the American people in 1858 were not descended from the generation that fought the Revolutionary War and founded the nation. They had come from Europe or were children of immigrants from Europe. How, then, were they connected with the American body politic?

[W]hen they look through that old Declaration of Independence they find that those old men say that "We hold these truths to be self-evident, that all men are created equal," and then they feel that that moral sentiment taught in that day evidences their relation to those men, that it is the father of all moral principle in them, and that they have a right to claim it as though they were blood of the blood, and flesh of the flesh of the men who wrote that Declaration, . . . and so they are.[3]

TABLE 4-3　AMERICAN PEOPLE: RELIGIOUS AFFILIATION

	Number	Percentage
Religious identification of adults (2008)		
Christian	173,402,000	76.0%
Catholic	57,199,000	25.1
Baptist	36,148,000	15.8
Protestant or Christian, no denomination specified	32,441,000	14.2
Methodist	11,336,000	5.0
Lutheran	8,674,000	3.8
Pentecostal, unspecified	5,416,000	2.4
Presbyterian	4,723,000	2.1
Mormon/Latter-day Saints	3,158,000	1.4
Episcopalian/Anglican	2,405,000	1.1
Churches of Christ	1,921,000	0.8
Jehovah's Witnesses	1,914,000	0.8
Other	8,065,000	3.5
Jewish	2,680,000	1.2
Muslim/Islamic	1,349,000	0.6
Buddhist	1,189,000	0.5
Other religions	3,576,000	1.6
No religion or refused to answer	45,984,000	20.2

SOURCE: *American Religious Identification Survey, Summary Report*, March 2009, Barry A. Kosmin and Ariela Keysar, Trinity College, Hartford, Connecticut, Table 1, p. 3, and Table 3, p. 5, at http://commons.trincoll.edu/aris/files/2011/08/ARIS_Report_2008.pdf, accessed July 10, 2012.

According to this view, the core of American identity and citizenship is a freely chosen commitment to the principles of the Declaration and Constitution. "To the eighteenth-century founders," one historian writes, "an American was a bundle of rights, freely chosen." Thus, "[t]he tie that has united Americans is not ancestry, soil, church, soul, or folk; it is civic belief."[4] In this respect, American citizenship embraces ideas and choice in a way that one does not find in most other countries. As President Woodrow Wilson said to 5,000 new citizens at a naturalization ceremony in Philadelphia in 1915, "You have taken an oath of allegiance to a great ideal, to a great body of principles, to a great hope of the human race."[5] President Barack Obama said in 2011: "America is not defined by ethnicity. It's not defined by geography. We are a nation born of an idea, a commitment to human freedom."[6]

A 2001 incident sheds light on this understanding. Li Shaomin, a naturalized American citizen and professor at City College of Hong Kong, was detained by Chinese authorities (and later convicted of espionage) when he attempted to enter China for an overnight visit. Early on, one of the interrogators said to Shaomin, "Don't hope that the American government will help you. You are Chinese, born in China. You are not a real American."[7] For this official, citizenship was defined by blood, ethnicity, or race. Yet Shaomin was a naturalized American citizen, like 16 million other Americans. According to the American creed, each of these **naturalized citizens** is as much a "real American" as someone whose ancestors stepped off the *Mayflower*.

Most of today's Americans gained their citizenship at birth. They did not *choose* citizenship, nor did they have to affirm belief in certain political principles in order to enjoy the rights and privileges of citizenship. Yet some beliefs are so central to what the nation stands for that to believe otherwise seems "un-American." These core beliefs include human equality, human rights, democracy, and the rule of law.

Children in the United States are taught these principles at an early age. A teacher at a public school would likely not last long if he or she taught impressionable first graders that Americans had no rights that government was duty bound to respect, that one race was

Naturalized citizen—someone who moves from one country to another and becomes a citizen of the new country.

intended by God to rule another, that we would all be better off if forced to worship God through a federally funded national church, or that Americans should bow to a dictator. In this respect, beliefs in certain fundamental principles are central to American identity—whether or not Americans ever formally profess them.

Even if American identity at its core is defined by a commitment to certain political principles, some have insisted that "one united people" must share other characteristics as well, such as race, religion, or language. For this reason, large-scale immigration to the United States has frequently led to controversies over **assimilation**—the blending of diverse immigrant groups into one American people.

Assimilation—the blending of diverse immigrant groups into one people by the adoption of common language, customs, and values.

IMMIGRATION
MAJOR ISSUES

- How has immigration policy changed over the course of American history?
- What challenges has large-scale immigration presented for assimilating newcomers into the American political community?

From 1820, when the federal government began counting immigrants, through 2010, more than 76 million individuals voluntarily moved to the United States (see Figure 4-1). This number is about 20 times the entire population of the country at its beginning. Of all the voluntary migrations throughout the world during the past two centuries, an estimated 60% were to the United States, followed far behind by Canada (12%), Argentina (10%), Brazil (7%), Australia (5%), New Zealand (3%), and South Africa (2%). As one expert notes, "The peopling of America during the nineteenth and twentieth centuries adds up to the largest migration in recorded history."[8]

Immigration and the Founding

The new nation signaled its openness to large-scale immigration in the Declaration of Independence itself when it attacked King George III for trying "to prevent the Population of these States" by "obstructing the Laws for Naturalization of Foreigners" and "refusing to pass others to encourage their Migrations hither." Eleven years later, James Madison expressed his wish that the United States continue "to invite foreigners of merit & republican principles."[9]

A few prominent founders, however, wondered whether the new nation could successfully assimilate all who wanted to come. Even before independence, Benjamin Franklin had raised concerns about the influx of Germans into Pennsylvania: "Why should *Pennsylvania*," he asked, "founded by the *English*, become a Colony of *Aliens*, who will shortly be so numerous as to Germanize us instead of our Anglifying them?"[10]

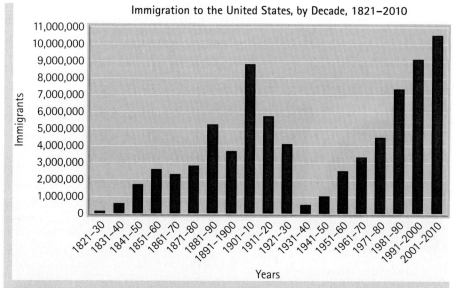

FIGURE 4-1 Immigration to the United States has varied greatly since the federal government began collecting the data in 1820.
SOURCE: Data for 1820–2000 are from Department of Homeland Security, "Fiscal Year 2000 Statistical Yearbook," Table 1, at http://www.dhs.gov/files/statistics/publications/YrBk00lm.shtm, accessed April 19, 2012; data for 2001–2010 are from Department of Homeland Security, "Yearbook of Immigration Statistics, 2010," Table 1, at http://www.dhs.gov/files/statistics/publications/LPR10.shtm, accessed April 19, 2012.

A few years after independence, Thomas Jefferson expressed his own doubts. He feared that European immigrants, most of whom had lived under monarchies, would either bring monarchical principles with them and pass them along to their children or, having thrown off monarchy, embrace "unbounded licentiousness, passing, as is usual, from one extreme to another."[11] In either case, large-scale immigration might not be good for the United States.

Unrestricted Immigration

Despite the concerns of some, the new nation placed no limits of any sort on voluntary immigration until 1875. (As noted in Chapter 2, Congress prohibited the importation of slaves, effective January 1, 1808.) During the nation's first century, there seemed to be more land than people to fill it and more jobs than people to work them. States competed for immigrants by advertising in European newspapers, sending agents to Europe, and in some cases recruiting newcomers at the east coast docks.[12] Five million Germans arrived in the nineteenth century, followed by a million Irish and thousands of Scandinavians and Danes. Texas had so many Germans in 1843 (about a fifth of its white population) that it published a German edition of its laws; and by 1900, more than 750 German-language newspapers were published in the United States.[13]

One exception to this policy of welcoming foreigners came in the 1790s. Many in Congress worried that European immigrants would bring with them radical and dangerous ideas inspired by the French Revolution (which had begun in 1789). As a result, in 1798 Congress authorized the president, then John Adams, to deport dangerous aliens (Alien Act) and to apprehend, confine, and possibly deport aliens who were citizens of a foreign nation at war with the United States (Alien Enemies Act). But even this Congress did not limit immigration, and the president deported no one for dangerous activities.

Although the official open-borders policy did not change before 1875, opposition to unrestricted immigration grew in the 1840s and 1850s. The principal target was Irish Catholics. In this largely Protestant nation, some believed that Roman Catholicism was incompatible with American institutions. As one study described this attitude, "[I]f Catholics 'took over' America, the pope in Rome would rule and religious and political liberty would be destroyed."[14] As recently as 1960, Democratic (and Catholic) presidential candidate John F. Kennedy addressed this very concern. In a major address, he told Protestant ministers in Houston, Texas, that no official of the Catholic Church could tell him "how to act." "I do not speak for my church on public matters," Kennedy reassured his audience, "and the church does not speak for me."[15] In the 2011–2012 Republican presidential primary campaign, candidate Rick Santorum of Pennsylvania made news when he denounced Kennedy for "say[ing] that people of faith have no role in the public square. . . . What kind of country do we live [in] that says only people of non-faith can come into the public square and make their case?"[16] (See more on religion and politics later in this chapter and in Chapter 5.)

The political focus of the anti-Catholic and anti-immigrant movement was the so-called **Know-Nothing Party** of the 1850s, which arose out of several secret anti-Catholic societies. The odd nickname came from the vow that members took to answer "I know nothing" if asked about the organization. The peak of its political influence came in the 1854 elections, when it gained control of the Massachusetts legislature, polled 40% of the vote in

Know-Nothing Party—an anti-Catholic and anti-immigrant party of the 1850s (also known as the American Party). It opposed Catholic candidates for political office because of their supposed ties to the pope in Rome, and it proposed requiring immigrants to wait 21 years before applying for citizenship.

Courtesy of the Milwaukee County Historical Society

A flag of the anti-Catholic and anti-immigrant Know Nothing Party, which was a powerful force in American politics in the 1850s.

Pennsylvania, and elected several dozen congressmen. This was the first large-scale nativist movement in the United States. *Nativism* is the term often used to describe efforts by native-born Americans to restrict immigration.

Restricting Immigration

As the nation's cities and farmlands filled up and as more immigrants arrived from diverse cultural backgrounds, the policy of unrestricted immigration came to an end. In 1875, Congress for the first time restricted some individuals (prostitutes and convicts) from entering the United States. Other restrictions soon followed.

The Chinese Exclusion Act of 1882, which prohibited the entry of Chinese laborers and remained in effect in some form until 1943, was the first time the federal government based exclusion on ethnicity. Although the Chinese had been welcomed in the West a few decades earlier to work the gold mines and help build the transcontinental railroad, opposition to them grew in the 1870s as jobs became scarce. Also, many Americans came to believe that assimilation was impossible because of cultural and racial differences.[17] Pressure from western states led Congress to pass the restrictive law, which also included a prohibition on naturalization: "no State court or court of the United States shall admit Chinese to citizenship."[18]

Restrictions on Immigration, 1875–1917

In 1875, Congress for the first time prohibited some individuals from voluntarily entering the United States. Here are the major restrictions from 1875 to 1917:

- prostitutes and convicts (1875);
- Chinese laborers, the mentally impaired, and those likely to be unable to provide for themselves (1882);
- contract laborers (1885);
- those with a dangerous contagious disease, those previously convicted of a crime involving moral turpitude, and polygamists (1891);
- anarchists and those who advocated the violent overthrow of the government of the United States (1903—in response to President William McKinley's assassination in 1901 by a Polish anarchist, Leon Czolgosz);
- those with serious mental or intellectual disabilities, paupers, and professional beggars (1907); and
- most immigrants from Asia (1917—also requiring for the first time a literacy requirement for immigrants).

Around the turn of the century, prejudice grew toward the Japanese population, especially in California. In 1906, the San Francisco Board of Education ordered Asian students segregated from the white population. Faced with growing national concern over the "yellow peril," President Theodore Roosevelt negotiated the **Gentleman's Agreement of 1907** with the Japanese government. Japan agreed to restrict passports for its citizens to work in the United States, and the United States agreed to allow the Japanese already in the country to remain and to bring in their families. In this way Roosevelt circumvented pressure for a possible Japanese Exclusion Act.

To gain greater control over immigration, Congress established the **Bureau of Immigration** within the Treasury Department in 1891. For the first time, federal law required the commanders of vessels bringing immigrants to report to government officials the "name, nationality, last residence, and destination of all such aliens." The following year, the government opened the immigrant processing center at **Ellis Island** in New York Harbor. Between 1892 and 1924, when Ellis Island was last used for general immigration processing, some 12 million immigrants passed through its facilities for medical and legal examinations. This was about 70% of the nation's immigrant population during this period. Approximately 2% failed the examinations and were returned to their home countries.

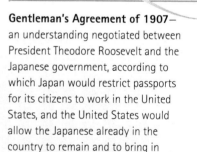

Nativism—opposition to immigration by native-born Americans, giving rise to such movements as the Know-Nothing Party of the 1850s.

Gentleman's Agreement of 1907—an understanding negotiated between President Theodore Roosevelt and the Japanese government, according to which Japan would restrict passports for its citizens to work in the United States, and the United States would allow the Japanese already in the country to remain and to bring in their families.

Bureau of Immigration—the agency created within the Treasury Department in 1891 to gain greater control over immigration into the United States.

Ellis Island—site of the federal government's first immigrant processing center through which 12 million immigrants passed between 1892, when it opened, and 1924, when it was last used for the mass processing of immigrants.

Between 1892 and 1924, more than 12 million immigrants entered the United States through the Ellis Island Immigration Center in New York Harbor for medical and legal examinations.

National origins quota system—the policy adopted in the Immigration Act of 1924 that limited immigration of each nationality group to 2% of the number residing in the United States in 1890, thus favoring immigrants from northern and western Europe.

During this period, the immigrant population shifted from predominantly northern and western European to southern and eastern European. Many fled political repression, and others sought economic opportunity. Italians led the way, with an average of 300,000 entering each year in the early twentieth century, followed by Jews (especially from Russia) and Slavs (predominantly Poles, a million of whom arrived before World War I).[19] By 1910, nearly 15% of the nation's population was foreign born, the highest level before or since (see Figure 4-2). In that same year, over half of all those living in many major cities of the Northeast and Midwest were immigrants or their children.[20]

Some Americans considered the new immigrants "hostile or indifferent to American values" and responsible for overcrowding and crime in the nation's cities.[21] Pressure grew to restrict immigration. Congress responded with the Immigration Act of 1924, which established a **national origins quota system**. This measure capped total immigration and tried to preserve the country's basic ethnic makeup by limiting the immigration of each nationality to 2% of the number residing in the country in 1890, thus favoring immigrants from northern and western Europe. The act also established preferences for family unification involving spouses and children.

The new restrictions, combined with the economic collapse of the 1930s and the disruption of World War II, substantially reduced immigration. During the Depression, pressure also grew to deport Mexican immigrants, who competed for jobs in the Southwest. Eventually, between 300,000 and 500,000 had to return to their homes in this **Mexican Repatriation**. About half of those affected were children born in the United States and thus American citizens. By 1970, less than 5% of the nation's population was foreign born— only a third of the proportion 60 years earlier. Nonetheless, trends were underway that would again boost immigration.

Modern Immigration Law

In 1943, in the middle of World War II, Congress repealed the outright ban on Chinese immigrants (but limited them to 105 per year). Cold War conflicts such as the Hungarian Revolution of 1956 created large numbers of political refugees, and the United States accepted many. In 1963, President John Kennedy called on Congress to abolish the quota system because it "neither satisfies a national need nor accomplishes an international purpose."[22] Congress complied two years later. It also increased the total numbers of permitted immigrants and allowed for the entry and settlement of large numbers of refugees. From 1960 to 2010, legal immigration grew from 265,000 to about a million a year.

Recent immigrants have been much less likely to come from Europe than was true in

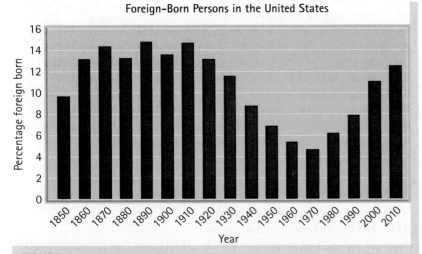

Foreign-Born Persons in the United States

FIGURE 4–2 The percentage of American residents born in other countries was highest a century ago.

SOURCE: Dianne A. Schmidley, U.S. Census Bureau, Current Population Reports, Series P23–206, *Profile of the Foreign-Born Population in the United States: 2000* (Washington, DC: U.S. Government Printing Office, 2001), Figure 1-1, p. 9, at http://www.census.gov/prod/2002pubs/p23-206.pdf, accessed April 20, 2012; and Tables 1 and 2 in the text.

the past. In 2010, only 13% of the foreign-born residents of the United States (legal and illegal) were from Europe, compared with 75% in 1960 and 86% in 1900 (see Figure 4-3). Also in 2010, more than four times as many immigrants came from Asia (410,209) and from Latin America (407,536) as from Europe (95,379).[23] The foreign-born population reached 37.6 million—the highest number ever but not the highest percentage. The 12.0% of the nation's population that was foreign born in 2010 was more than twice as high as the 1970 figure (4.7%) but less than the 13%–15% foreign born between 1860 and 1920 (see Figure 4-2).[24]

When Congress abolished the national origins quota system in the 1960s, it established several new categories of legal immigrants.[25] (Refugees are handled separately; see the later discussion.) The largest category, at 480,000 per year, is for family members sponsored by citizens and, in some cases, by permanent residents. Priority goes to spouses, minor children, and parents of U.S. citizens. The next largest category, now 140,000 per year, is employment based. Preferences go to those with "extraordinary" or "exceptional" ability in the sciences, arts, and business, and those with advanced degrees or special skills. The final category is "diversity immigrants," who now number 55,000 per year. This last category was created in 1990 for persons from countries with historically low rates of immigration to the United States. Immigrants are chosen by a lottery among applicants from eligible countries. For the 2012 lottery, almost 15 million foreigners applied, representing 20 million when family members are included. (In May of 2011, a serious computer glitch resulted in nearly all the winners being chosen from those who applied in the first two days of the month-long application process. The State Department issued a public apology for the computer error, rescinded the winning notices sent to 20,000 applicants, and re-ran the lottery.)[26]

In addition to admitting these immigrants, the United States accepts and resettles **refugees** from around the world. **U.S Citizenship and Immigration Services**, a bureau in the **Department of Homeland Security**, defines a refugee as:

> a person who has fled his or her country of origin because of past persecution or a fear of future persecution based upon race, religion, nationality, political opinion, or membership in a particular social group. . . . A refugee does not include a person who has left his or her home only to seek a more prosperous life, also known as an economic migrant.[27]

The number admitted varies, depending on world events. Between 1980 and 2010, the United States

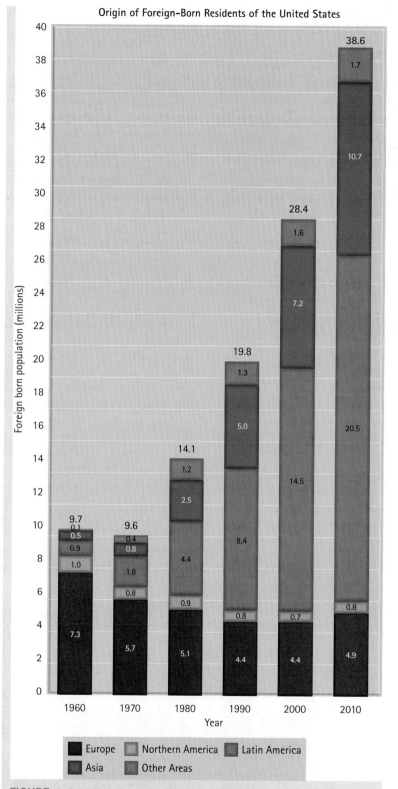

FIGURE 4-3 Half a century ago, Europe was the origin of most foreign-born Americans. Now it is Latin America (about half) and Asia (one-quarter). (Latin America includes Mexico and the Caribbean.)
SOURCE: Dianne A. Schmidley, U.S. Census Bureau, Current Population Reports, Series P23-206, *Profile of the Foreign-Born Population in the United States: 2000* (Washington, DC: U.S. Government Printing Office, 2001), p. 11, at www.census.gov/prod/2002pubs/p23-206.pdf; accessed April 20, 2012; and Table 4-2 in the text.

Mexican repatriation—policy adopted during the Great Depression to force between 300,000 and 500,000 Mexican immigrants to return to their homes.

Refugee—someone who has fled his or her country because of the fear of persecution.

U.S. Citizenship and Immigration Services—the bureau within the Department of Homeland Security that adjudicates immigration and naturalization issues and provides services to immigrants.

Department of Homeland Security—the federal agency created in 2002 to defend the nation from threats such as terrorism and natural disasters.

Illegal immigrant—a foreigner who is illegally in the United States because (1) he or she entered the country illegally or (2) after a legal entry overstayed he or she visa. Also called *illegal alien, undocumented immigrant,* and *undocumented worker.*

Border Patrol—the agency within the U.S. Department of Homeland Security that enforces immigration laws at the borders of the United States.

admitted a total of 2.56 million refugees, an average of 82,000 each year. In 2010, it admitted about 73,000.[28]

The Controversy over Illegal Immigration

The foreign-born population includes those in the country legally and illegally. In 2011, the U.S. Census Bureau estimated that there were 11.5 million **illegal immigrants** in the country. These include both those who entered the country illegally and those who entered legally but overstayed their temporary visas. Of all illegal immigrants in the United States, 6.8 million (59%) came from Mexico, and another 1.56 million (14%) came from either El Salvador, Guatemala, or Honduras.[29]

The U.S. **Border Patrol** of the Department of Homeland Security has the responsibility to prevent illegal entries. In 2010, its 20,000 agents (a doubling since 2004) apprehended about 463,000 individuals (see Table 4-4). Of these, almost 97% were caught at the border with Mexico, and 87% were natives of Mexico. It is no surprise, then, that the illegal immigration controversy has focused on securing the 2,000-mile U.S.–Mexico border.

Apprehensions in 2010 were down 72% from the 1,676,000 in 2000. What explains this dramatic drop? Since there is no reason to believe that the Border Patrol was less likely to catch those entering the country illegally in 2010 than in 2000 (especially with so many more agents), it follows that far fewer individuals tried to cross. Some of this drop was likely due to worsening economic conditions in the United States; but would-be immigrants may also have been deterred by enhanced physical barriers at the border, a greater likelihood of apprehension by the Border Patrol, or new state efforts to combat illegal immigration (see below).

Policymakers, activists, researchers, and scholars disagree as to whether illegal immigration is good or bad for the United States. State and local officials, especially in states with large illegal immigrant populations, highlight the costs of educating the children of those in the country illegally; of providing health care to a population that is not likely to have insurance; and of investigating, arresting, prosecuting, and incarcerating those who turn to crime.

A key question for many researchers is whether illegal immigrants contribute more to the economy—by working jobs that many Americans shun, paying taxes, and consuming products and services—than they cost in social services. In 2007, the Congressional Budget Office (CBO) of the U.S. Congress reviewed 29 studies comparing what illegal immigrants paid in taxes with what they cost in services. The CBO concluded that the services provided to illegal immigrants by state and local governments exceeded the tax revenues that the immigrants generated, even accounting for federal programs that helped to meet these costs.[30] However, not all agree, and a lively debate continues.

TABLE 4-4	APPREHENSIONS OF THOSE ATTEMPTING TO ENTER THE UNITED STATES ILLEGALLY, 2010	
Border	**Number of Apprehensions**	**Percentage**
Total	463,382	100.0%
Southwest	447,731	96.6
Coastal	8,220	1.8
Northern	7,431	1.6
Country of Origin		
Mexico	404,365	87.3%
Guatemala	18,406	4.0
El Salvador	13,723	3.0
Honduras	13,580	2.9
Other	13,308	2.9

SOURCE: Office of Immigration Statistics, Department of Homeland Security, *Apprehensions by the U.S. Border Patrol: 2005–2010, Fact Sheet, July 2011,* at http://www.dhs.gov/xlibrary/assets/statistics/publications/ois-apprehensions-fs-2005-2010.pdf, accessed April 23, 2012.

In recent years the debate over illegal immigration has focused on three issues: (a) whether to construct new physical barriers, or enhance existing ones, at the border between the United States and Mexico; (b) whether to provide illegal immigrants, or at least their minor children born elsewhere, a path to citizenship; and (c) whether to enhance the powers of state and local officials to combat illegal immigration.

In 2006, Congress authorized the building of 700 miles of fence between the United States and Mexico (The Secure Fence Act). In April of 2010, the Commissioner of U.S. Customs and Border Protection reported to Congress that the agency had completed 646 miles of fence along the southern border, supplemented by a "virtual fence" of "sensors, command and control systems, and communications."[31]

More controversial have been proposals to provide illegal immigrants a path to citizenship. President Barack Obama urged Congress to "provide a legal pathway so [those in the country illegally] can get out of the shadows and contribute to society."[32] But critics responded that those who broke the law to enter the country should not be rewarded with citizenship and that this would encourage others to engage in similar behavior. Although Congress has not come close in recent years to passing a comprehensive law to give illegal immigrants a path to citizenship, it nearly passed the DREAM (Development, Relief, and Education for Alien Minors) Act in 2011, which would have provided an opportunity for permanent residency (and later citizenship) to children brought to the United States illegally who later earned a college degree or served in the military. (Note that children born within the United States to illegal immigrants become citizens at birth. This is the principle of **birthright citizenship**. See the discussion of the Fourteenth Amendment below.)

In recent years, a number of states have passed new laws to combat illegal immigration. The first was Arizona's 2010 law that authorizes state and local law enforcement officers to check the immigration status of anyone subject to a "lawful stop, detention, or arrest" if the officer has a "reasonable suspicion . . . that the person is an alien who is unlawfully present in the United States." Other provisions prohibit "sanctuary" cities and towns and allow officers to ask for the immigration papers that federal law requires legal immigrants to possess. Alabama, Georgia, Indiana, South Carolina, and Utah followed with their own strict laws. Among the new provisions were harsh sanctions on companies that hire illegal aliens, the exclusion of illegal immigrants from public colleges and universities, and criminalizing the transportation or harboring of illegal immigrants.

President Obama's Department of Justice challenged several of these laws in federal court, primarily on the ground that immigration control was a federal responsibility under the Constitution and could not be preempted by the states. Federal judges blocked enforcement of some provisions of these laws but upheld others. In 2012 the U.S. Supreme Court ruled on four of the provisions of the Arizona law. It overturned three on the grounds that the Constitution gave Congress exclusive authority in these areas. The voided provisions (1) made it a misdemeanor to be an illegal immigrant in Arizona, (2) made it a misdemeanor for an illegal immigrant to work or seek work in Arizona, and (3) authorized police officers in the state to arrest without a warrant anyone who the officer had probable cause to believe had committed any offense that would make the person deportable. Nonetheless, the Court did uphold the most controversial provision of the law, which required police officers to make a reasonable attempt to determine the immigration status of anyone they stop, detain, or arrest if they had a reasonable suspicion that the person was an illegal immigrant. The Court made clear that other constitutional challenges might be appropriate once the law was actually enforced and interpreted by the state courts.[33]

Allowing foreigners to enter the United States and establish residency is not the same as granting them citizenship. For that they must go through a process of **naturalization** defined in federal law. Before we turn to naturalization law and practice, we review citizenship controversies over two groups that were present in the United States at the time of the founding: free blacks and Native Americans. These controversies reveal ambiguities in the Constitution on citizenship; they show how early Americans thought about the openness of the nation to non-European groups; and they illustrate how Americans insisted on undivided loyalty from those who wanted citizenship.

Birthright citizenship—when a nation automatically grants citizenship to everyone born in the country (except for the children of foreign diplomats).

FOCUS QUESTION

Critics of current U.S. immigration policy attack it from both sides. Some prefer no restrictions on immigration (the policy before the late 1800s) and others prefer suspending, or dramatically decreasing, legal immigration until the nation can properly assimilate its current foreign-born population. Would either of these be better than current policy?

Naturalization—the process by which a foreigner becomes a citizen of a nation.

EARLY CITIZENSHIP CONTROVERSIES

MAJOR ISSUE

- What was the citizenship status of free blacks and Native Americans under the Constitution, and what policies led to citizenship for all members of the two groups?

The Articles of Confederation referred to the "free citizens in the several states" but made no mention of national citizenship. The Constitution, by contrast, required that every member of Congress be "a Citizen of the United States": House members for seven years and senators for nine. It also stipulated that the president be "a natural born Citizen, or a citizen of the United States, at the time of the Adoption of this Constitution." Yet in defining the jurisdiction of the Supreme Court, the Constitution refers to individuals as "Citizens of . . . States." Also, Article IV, Section 2, requires that "the Citizens of each State shall be entitled to all Privileges and Immunities of Citizens in the several States."

The Constitution does not explain or define these different phrases. Is there a difference between being a citizen of the United States and being a citizen of a state? The Constitution seems to presume, although it does not actually say, that the citizens of the individual states were also citizens of the United States. Did this mean, then, that free blacks, who were citizens in some of the states, were also citizens of the United States? In one respect, national citizenship was a broader category than state citizenship because those who lived in the Northwest Territory (now the American Midwest) were citizens of the United States but not of any particular state. The same would be true for future residents of the nation's capital.

One thing is clear: under the Constitution, the national government would set the rules for foreigners to become national citizens. Under the Articles of Confederation, each state had passed its own naturalization laws, with some making it easy to become a citizen and others making it hard. The Constitution moved this power to the new national government by giving Congress the power "To establish an uniform Rule of Naturalization." Although some states continued to naturalize foreigners after the Constitution was ratified, in 1795 Congress asserted its exclusive authority to naturalize, and in 1817 the Supreme Court agreed: "the power of naturalization is exclusively in congress."[34]

The Citizenship of Free Blacks before the Civil War

When the Constitution was ratified, about 700,000 black slaves and nearly 60,000 free blacks lived in the United States. Although the slaves were not citizens with legal rights, what about the free blacks? Were they citizens of the states in which they lived? Were they citizens of the United States? If they were citizens of their states, did the other states have to respect their rights under the "Privileges and Immunities" clause of the Constitution?

Although the new national government did not formally address the citizenship status of free blacks during the first decades, in the 1790s it began issuing documents called **seamen's protection certificates** to American sailors, regardless of race, to certify that they were U.S. citizens. The purpose of these documents was to protect American sailors on the high seas from being forced into the service of a European navy (especially Britain or France) if they were suspected of being a former subject of that nation. (This common practice of "impressment" was one of the grievances that led to the War of 1812.) Because free blacks during this period were about a fifth of all American seamen, many had received the certificates. When traveling within the United States, they often used them to prove that they were not runaway slaves.

Congress confronted the citizenship status of free blacks during the rancorous debates that surrounded the **Missouri Compromise of 1820** (discussed in more detail in Chapter 6). The territory of Missouri sought admission to the Union as a slave state with a constitutional provision that required the new state legislature to pass laws "to prevent free negroes and mulattos from coming to and settling in [Missouri] under any pretext whatsoever."[35]

Seamen's protection certificates—documents issued by the federal government to sailors, both white and black, to certify that they were citizens of the United States.

Missouri Compromise of 1820—a national compromise over the slavery issue in 1820 whereby Missouri entered the Union as a slave state, Maine entered as a free state, and slavery was "forever prohibited" in the remaining territory of the Louisiana Purchase north of the latitude line 36°30', which was the southern border of Missouri.

When some members of Congress objected that under the "Privileges and Immunities" clause of the Constitution free blacks should be able to travel and settle wherever they wished within the United States, southerners responded that blacks were never intended to be members of the American political community, whether free or not. As evidence they cited the laws in several states that denied free blacks the right to vote, hold political office, or serve on juries. One senator said that these restrictions "furnish a mass of evidence, which nobody could doubt but a skeptic, that free negroes and mulattoes have never been considered as part of the body politic."[36] But not all agreed. A congressman from Massachusetts pointed out that when his state ratified the federal Constitution in 1788, free blacks could vote. In helping to select representatives to the ratifying convention that adopted the federal Constitution, blacks were part of "We the People" who "ordain[ed] and establish[ed]" the Constitution.[37] It was not until the 1850s in the *Dred Scott* case that the U.S. Supreme Court finally confronted the issue of the citizenship of free blacks.

Dred Scott Case

In 1834, Dr. John Emerson took a slave named Dred Scott with him from Missouri to the free state of Illinois. After two years, Emerson moved with Scott to the Wisconsin Territory, where slavery was illegal under the 1820 Missouri Compromise. There Scott married another slave. After more than two years in the Wisconsin Territory, Emerson moved back to Missouri with the Scotts. Later, Emerson sold the Scotts to John Sanford. Scott and his wife then sued for their freedom on the grounds that extended residence on free soil had made them free persons. The case eventually made its way to the U.S. Supreme Court.[38] On March 6, 1857, the Court issued its ruling in *Scott v. Sandford.* (The Court misspelled the defendant's name.) Chief Justice Roger B. Taney wrote the official "opinion of the Court" holding against Scott's claim for freedom. Six others wrote separate opinions concurring with the result, but not necessarily with all of Taney's arguments. Two—John McLean and Benjamin Curtis—wrote forceful dissents.

Taney reached three controversial conclusions.

- First, although the broad language of the Declaration of Independence "would seem to embrace the whole human family," it did not "embrace the negro race, which, by common consent, had been excluded from civilized Governments and the family of nations, and doomed to slavery."[39] Blacks, consequently, "had no rights which the white man was bound to respect."[40]

- Second, because blacks were no part of "the People" who "ordain[ed] and establish[ed]" the Constitution, they could not be citizens of the United States, whatever rights or privileges they might have in the individual states. It followed that they could not have access to the federal courts and they had no federally enforceable rights under the privileges and immunities clause of the U.S. Constitution.

- Finally, the U.S. Congress had no authority to prohibit slavery in any federal territory, rendering the Missouri Compromise of 1820 (subsequently superseded by the Kansas-Nebraska Act of 1854) unconstitutional. (This was only the second time that the Supreme Court had ruled a congressional statute unconstitutional.)

The two dissenters strongly disagreed on all three points. Justice Curtis presented evidence that in five states at the time of the founding free blacks "were not only citizens of those States" but were also able to vote "on equal terms with other citizens" if they had the necessary qualifications (such as property).[41] Although three of these states later denied the vote to free blacks or imposed special qualifications on them, New Hampshire and Massachusetts

A portrait of Dred and Harriett Scott, whose legal effort to achieve their freedom led to the infamous Supreme Court decision, *Dred Scott v. Sandford*, in 1857.

still allowed blacks to vote on an equal basis with whites. Curtis also pointed out that voting rights were not necessary to show citizenship. Women and minors, for example, were citizens even though they could not vote.

Public reaction to the *Dred Scott* decision was fierce on both sides. Horace Greeley's New York *Tribune* denounced the decision as "atrocious," "wicked," "abominable," and "detestable." Southern papers, by contrast, embraced the decision. One proclaimed that "opposition to southern opinion upon this subject is now opposition to the Constitution, and morally treason against the Government." Northern newspapers allied with the Democratic Party also endorsed the decision and castigated Republicans for "revolution and anarchy" for opposing it."[42]

Fourteenth Amendment

Although the Thirteenth Amendment of 1865, ratified eight months after the conclusion of the Civil War, officially ended slavery throughout the United States, it did not address the citizenship status of the now four million free blacks. Despite the Union victory, the *Dred Scott* decision remained binding constitutional law, raising the possibility that state governments could still deny citizenship rights to blacks or that federal courts might deny them access.

To address this problem, Congress proposed the Fourteenth Amendment in 1866, and the states ratified it two years later. It began by defining American citizenship in a way that overruled a central holding of *Dred Scott*: "All persons born or naturalized in the United States and subject to the jurisdiction thereof, are citizens of the United States and of the State wherein they reside." From now on, blacks would be recognized as citizens of the United States and of the state where they lived. (Because Indians born on reservations and children born to foreign diplomats stationed in the United States were not legally "subject to the jurisdiction" of the nation, they were not covered by the amendment.)

The citizenship provision of the Fourteenth Amendment had another far-reaching effect, perhaps not fully recognized by its drafters. As we will see, the first naturalization laws under the Constitution, which specified how foreigners could become citizens, limited this privilege to whites. Congress extended eligibility to blacks in 1870 but did not open up naturalization to all races until 1952. Yet by extending citizenship to the American-born children of foreigners (excluding diplomats) regardless of their race, the Fourteenth Amendment opened up citizenship to Asians.

The Supreme Court confirmed this in 1898 when it ruled in *U.S. v. Wong Kim Ark* that a young man born in San Francisco to Chinese laborers legally in the country was an American citizen who could not be denied readmission to the country after a temporary visit to China.[43] As we will see in Chapter 5, when the government interned those of Japanese ancestry on the west coast during World War II, about 70,000 of these were American citizens because they had been born in the United States to Japanese parents. Although the Supreme Court has never ruled directly on the citizenship status of children born to those in the country illegally, national policy is that the legal status of the parents does not affect the citizenship of children born in the United States.[44]

The Citizenship of Native Americans

In the 2000 census, 4.3 million Americans (1.5% of the population) identified themselves as "American Indian and Alaskan Native." About 2.5 million listed this as their only race; the others included another race. Of the total, 875,000 identified themselves as Cherokee, followed by Navajo (310,000), Choctaw (173,000), Sioux (168,000), Chippewa (160,000), and Apache (105,000). (Other tribes totaled another 301,000.) About one-third of American Indians live on one of about 300 Indian reservations, and in 2010 the federal government recognized 565 tribal governments.[45] (Not every tribe has a reservation.) Although all American Indians are now citizens, and thus full members of the American political community, this was not always the case.

In the new American nation, Indian affairs were an important responsibility of the national government. The Constitution gave Congress the power to regulate commerce "with the Indian tribes," and implicitly left it to the president to manage other aspects of Indian relations. For about 80 years, presidents regularly negotiated treaties with Indian tribes, subject to Senate approval. Forty such treaties were enacted in the first two decades under the Constitution, and there were 360 by 1868, the year of the last Indian treaty.

In the early 1830s, a controversy arose over the legal status of Indian tribes. Could they gain access to the federal courts under the provision of the Constitution that allowed "foreign States" to sue American states or their citizens (Article III, Section 2)? This issue came to a head when the Cherokee Nation tried to stop Georgia from exercising jurisdiction over tribal lands and effectively "annihilat[ing] the Cherokees as a political society."[46] In *Cherokee Nation v. Georgia* (1831), the majority of the Supreme Court held that Indian tribes were not "foreign nations" as that term was used in the Constitution, but rather "domestic dependent nations. . . . [who] are in a state of pupilage. Their relation to the United States resembles that of a ward to his guardian."[47] Indian tribes, then, had no constitutional right to access the federal courts, even if Georgia had violated their legal rights.

Just a year later, however, in *Worcester v. Georgia*, the Court ruled as null and void acts of the state of Georgia that seized Cherokee lands, imposed state jurisdiction over the Cherokee Nation, and effectively "abolish[ed] its institutions and its laws." This time the Court maintained that Indian tribes, such as the Cherokee Nation, were "distinct political communities, having territorial boundaries, within which their authority is exclusive."[48] The tribe had rights guaranteed by the national government that the state of Georgia must respect. This did not mean, however, that the tribes were equivalent to foreign nations. They could not, for example, enter into treaties with any country other than the United States or freely dispose of their land to foreigners. They had a kind of semi-sovereign status: neither fully a part of the American political community nor as autonomous as a foreign nation.

In the end, this decision proved of no value to the Cherokee. The state of Georgia ignored it, and President Andrew Jackson refused to assist the Court in enforcing it, reportedly saying, "[Chief Justice] John Marshall has made his decision; now let him enforce it."[49]

A few years before, Jackson had supported passage of the Indian Removal Act of 1830, which authorized the president to reach agreements with Indian tribes in eastern states to exchange their lands for land west of the Mississippi River. The act also provided funds to assist with the removal. While some of the subsequent agreements were voluntary, others resulted from fraud, bribery, or coercion. Tribes began moving west in 1830, but because of insufficient food and resources, many Indians suffered and died during the journey. In 1836, the Senate ratified a removal treaty that had been negotiated with an unrepresentative group of Cherokee Indians. When most Cherokee refused to relocate, the U.S. army forcibly removed about 16,000 of them from the Southeast to what is now Oklahoma. Four thousand died in what became known as the "Trail of Tears."

Some of the nineteenth-century Indian treaties provided land grants to the heads of Indian families who wished to leave tribal lands and become American citizens.[50] Other treaties allowed for whole tribes to disband and divide the land in exchange for citizenship. By the 1880s, however, only about 3,000 Indians had become American citizens in this way.

One purpose of these citizenship provisions was to promote the voluntary assimilation of some Native Americans into the broader civil and political community. In 1887, Congress made a major effort to foster assimilation with the Dawes Severalty Act. This law offered citizenship to Indians if their tribes dissolved as legal entities and then divided their lands into privately owned plots of typically 160 acres. "The objective," writes one historian, "was the creation of independent persons who regarded themselves as Americans."[51] By the early 1900s, the Dawes Act and related laws had resulted in about half of American Indians becoming citizens. About 90 million acres of land passed from Indian to non-Indian ownership, at least some through fraud that enriched unscrupulous settlers and speculators.

© CORBIS

American Indians have served in America's wars since the War of 1812. Perhaps their most famous contribution was as "code talkers" in World War II where Navajos used their distinctive unwritten language to code military communications in the Pacific theater in a way that proved unbreakable by the Japanese. Although this program was kept secret for several decades after the war ended, the military honored the contribution of the code talkers in a public ceremony at the Pentagon on September 17, 1992.

In 1903, the U.S. Supreme Court unanimously affirmed the near-absolute power of Congress over Indian lands and Indian affairs in *Lone Wolf v. Hitchcock*. In holding that the Congress was not obligated to respect two 1868 treaties with Indian tribes, the Court held that "[p]lenary authority over the tribal relations of the Indians has been exercised by Congress from the beginning, and the power has always been deemed a political one, not subject to be controlled by the judicial department of the government."[52] Also, beginning in the late nineteenth century, government and private associations sought to assimilate or "Americanize" Indians by raising the children in boarding schools where they were immersed in the English language and American culture.

In the early years of the twentieth century, pressure grew for citizenship for all American Indians, especially after thousands served ably in World War I in 1917–18. "Ironically," writes one expert on Indian citizenship, "they were fighting for freedoms abroad that they did not possess at home."[53] Congress responded in 1919 by declaring that all Indians could become citizens if they served in the war and were honorably discharged. The following year women gained the vote. Four years later, Congress passed the Indian Citizenship Act of 1924, which rejected assimilation as a condition and granted citizenship to all Indians born within the territorial limits of the United States, whether or not they lived on reservations.

Since the 1930s, federal policy has downplayed assimilation and instead worked to strengthen tribes and foster a sense of Indian identity. In recent decades, Congress has passed laws to protect Indian religious sites and archeological artifacts, to increase the authority of tribal governments (facilitating the expansion of commercial gambling on Indian reservations), and to protect American Indian culture by making it harder for non-Indians to adopt Indian children.

Although Congress retains ultimate authority over Indian tribes, it "recognizes a special kind of Indian sovereign authority to govern themselves, subject to an overriding federal authority."[54] This gives tribes some independence from state control but not from Congress's ultimate legislative authority.

Most Americans today are descended not from slaves brought to the United States against their will or from the native peoples of the New World, but from foreigners who voluntarily immigrated in search of a better life. As we will see, except during a few early years, the nation has made it relatively easy for immigrants to become citizens.

ACQUIRING AMERICAN CITIZENSHIP

MAJOR ISSUES

- What are the ways in which persons legally in the United States can acquire citizenship?
- What are the rights, privileges, and duties of American citizenship?

A fundamental power of sovereign nations is the right to decide who may become a full-fledged member of the political community. Under federal law, foreigners legally within the country may apply for citizenship. If they succeed, they become naturalized citizens with all the rights, privileges, and duties of those who are citizens by birth except for one: they cannot become president of the United States. However, as we have seen with the history of American Indians, individual naturalizations are not always necessary: treaties and laws can also confer citizenship on groups of individuals.

Citizenship through Law or Treaties

The first time the federal government conferred citizenship on a class of persons, without requiring individual naturalizations, was through the Louisiana Purchase Treaty of 1803, which provided that the inhabitants of the Louisiana Territory would gain U.S. citizenship.

Similarly, the **Treaty of Guadalupe Hidalgo**, which ended the Mexican-American War in 1848, provided that the approximately 100,000 residents of the lands ceded by Mexico (the present states of Arizona, California, Nevada, and Utah, and parts of New Mexico, Colorado, and Wyoming) would become American citizens unless they decided to retain their Mexican citizenship. This treaty extended citizenship to a large group of individuals we would now classify as Hispanics or Latinos. Several times in the nineteenth century, the Supreme Court upheld the government's authority to vest citizenship collectively through treaties or laws.

In 1917, Congress exercised this authority when it granted citizenship to the residents of Puerto Rico, the island in the Caribbean that came under U.S. control after the Spanish-American War of 1898. Puerto Ricans may travel on U.S. passports into and out of the country, travel freely within the United States (no passport or visa required), and, like other Americans, permanently relocate to another part of the country. Although Puerto Rico functions in many ways like a U.S. state with its own elected governor and legislature, its citizens do not vote in presidential elections, are not represented in the U.S. Senate, and have only a single nonvoting delegate in the House of Representatives. (If Puerto Rico were a state, its population of almost four million would give it at least six members in the House.) Like other citizens, Puerto Ricans are the beneficiaries of federal programs. They pay no federal income tax but do pay Social Security taxes. In a popular referendum in November of 2012, 54% of voters expressed a preference not to continue the island's current territorial status; and then 61% expressed a preference for statehood over "sovereign free associated state" (33%) or "independence" (6%). Almost half a million voters answered the first question but not the second. Puerto Ricans themselves disagreed as to whether these results demonstrated that a majority of islanders supported statehood.

Citizenship through Naturalization

The more common method by which foreigners become citizens is through the naturalization process. As noted earlier, under the Articles of Confederation the states had retained control over naturalizations. Some encouraged immigration by making it easy for foreigners to become citizens; others erected high barriers. The Constitution, however, empowered Congress to "establish an uniform Rule of Naturalization."

In its first naturalization law, the Naturalization Act of 1790, Congress provided a fairly easy route to citizenship. An alien—that is, a foreigner living in the United States—who was a "free white person" and "of good character" and who had lived in the United States for two years could become a citizen by filing a petition for naturalization in a court of law and taking an oath "to support the constitution of the United States." Despite the racial restriction, which was apparently intended to exclude free blacks born overseas from becoming citizens (immigration from Asia was not then an issue), a major work on American citizenship describes this law as "the most liberal naturalization law then in existence."[55]

Congress made changes in 1795. It increased the residency requirement to five years and stipulated that, in addition to "good moral character," the applicant must be "attached to the principles of the Constitution of the United States, and well-disposed to the good order and happiness of the same." It also expanded the oath to require that the applicant "absolutely and entirely renounce and abjure all allegiance and fidelity to any foreign prince, potentate, state, or sovereignty." Finally, the would-be citizen must renounce any hereditary titles. Although the Federalist Congress, fearful of foreign influence, increased the residency requirement for citizenship to 14 years in 1798, the new Republican Congress of President Jefferson's first term restored the five-year residency rule in 1802. It has remained five years ever since.

With a few exceptions, the basic requirements for naturalization are the same now as established in 1795. Among the important changes are the following:

- In 1870, Congress expanded eligibility to "persons of African nativity and African descent"; and in 1952, it eliminated race altogether as a bar to immigration or naturalization.
- In 1906, Congress for the first time required proficiency in English for naturalization; but in 1990, it added new grounds for waiving the English requirement (particularly for older applicants who had lived in the United States as legal residents for many years).

Treaty of Guadalupe Hidalgo—the treaty between the United States and Mexico that ended the Mexican-American War in 1848. It provided that the approximately 100,000 residents of the lands ceded by Mexico would become American citizens unless they decided to retain their Mexican citizenship.

Citizenship oath—the oath of allegiance to the United States that candidates for naturalization must take in a public ceremony.

- Finally, the **citizenship oath** was expanded, requiring new citizens to promise "to support and defend the Constitution and the laws of the United States against all enemies, foreign and domestic; . . . to bear true faith and allegiance to the same; and . . . to bear arms on behalf of the United States when required by law, or . . . to perform noncombatant service in the Armed Forces of the United States when required by law" (with exceptions for conscientious objectors).

Although the first immigration laws stipulated the basic elements of the citizenship oath, they did not spell out a specific oath. For over a century, the exact wording was left up to the judges or other public officials who carried out the naturalization process. In 1906, the federal government began to standardize naturalization procedures, and in 1929, it adopted an official oath through administrative regulations. Current regulations stipulate that an applicant for citizenship take and sign a copy of the oath "in a public ceremony held within the United States."

Citizenship Oath ("The Oath of Allegiance")

I hereby declare, on oath, that I absolutely and entirely renounce and abjure all allegiance and fidelity to any foreign prince, potentate, state, or sovereignty, of whom or which I have heretofore been a subject or citizen; that I will support and defend the Constitution and laws of the United States of America against all enemies, foreign and domestic; that I will bear true faith and allegiance to the same; that I will bear arms on behalf of the United States when required by the law; that I will perform noncombatant service in the Armed Forces of the United States when required by the law; that I will perform work of national importance under civilian direction when required by the law; and that I take this obligation freely, without any mental reservation or purpose of evasion; so help me God. (*Code of Federal Regulations*, Title 8, Volume 1—8CFR337.1)

In recent years some have proposed amending the oath to remove unfamiliar and archaic words like *abjure* and *potentate*. Others, who favor dual citizenship, would simply drop the renunciation of allegiance to foreign powers; and still others would add a fuller statement of the duties that new citizens owe the United States. In 2003, the Department of Homeland Security proposed a simpler, more modern version of the oath, but officials killed the plan when members of Congress, veterans, and others complained about dropping the phrases "I will bear true faith and allegiance to the same" and "I will bear arms on behalf of the United States" from the traditional oath.

Current naturalization law makes one major exception to the five-year residency requirement: military service. Prior to 2002, legal residents could apply for citizenship after three years in the U.S. military. Congress then reduced the requirement to one year. The law also allows presidents to designate periods of war when the residency requirement is eliminated altogether for legal residents on active duty. Presidents have regularly done so. At the beginning of the Iraq war in 2003, about 37,000 noncitizen legal residents were serving in the U.S. military. One of the first marines killed in combat in Iraq, Lance Corporal Jose Gutierrez, was a legal U.S. resident from Guatemala. He was awarded citizenship posthumously.[56]

The Rights and Privileges of Citizenship

Green card—a federally issued identification card (which used to be green but is no longer) that attests to the permanent legal status of an alien, or foreigner, within the United States.

Citizens of the United States are full members of the political community. Noncitizen residents, such as "permanent residents" who hold "**green cards**" (which, by the way, are no longer green), are not. Permanent residents are those who are allowed to stay in the United States indefinitely. Many are family members of a U.S. citizen. A key difference between citizens and permanent residents is that citizens are entitled to vote in all local, state, and federal elections for which they meet the basic requirements (age, residency, etc.). Also, only citizens can hold public offices that directly affect public policy. The Constitution itself, as noted earlier, requires citizenship in order to be a member of Congress or president.

TABLE 4-5	THE RIGHTS AND RESPONSIBILITIES OF U.S. CITIZENSHIP

Rights	Responsibilities
Freedom to express yourself.	Support and defend the Constitution.
Freedom to worship as you wish.	Stay informed of the issues affecting your community.
Right to a prompt, fair trial by jury.	Participate in the democratic process.
Right to vote in elections for public officials.	Respect and obey federal, state, and local laws.
Right to apply for federal employment requiring U.S. citizenship.	Respect the rights, beliefs, and opinions of others.
Right to run for elected office.	Participate in your local community.
Freedom to pursue "life, liberty, and the pursuit of happiness."	Pay income and other taxes honestly, and on time, to federal, state, and local authorities.
	Serve on a jury when called upon.
	Defend the country if the need should arise.

SOURCE: U.S. Citizenship and Immigration Services, "Citizenship Rights and Responsibilities," at http://www.uscis .gov/portal/site/uscis/menuitem.749cabd81f5ffc8fba713d10526e0aa0/?vgnextoid=39d2df6bdd42a210VgnVCM100 000b92ca60aRCRD&vgnextchannel=39d2df6bdd42a210VgnVCM100000b92ca60aRCRD, accessed April 24, 2012.

Table 4-5 displays a more complete list of the rights and responsibilities of citizenship, as described by U.S. Citizenship and Immigration Services in the Department of Homeland Security.

Despite the benefits of citizenship, the federal courts have curbed the power of government to discriminate between citizens and permanent legal residents in some areas, including welfare benefits, the right to practice law, and the right to hold state and local jobs that do not affect public policy. But when it comes to those in the country illegally, the courts have allowed lawmakers more discretion in denying the rights, privileges, and public benefits that are accorded to citizens. The principal exceptions are health care (most emergency rooms must treat anyone who shows up regardless of ability to pay or immigration status) and public schooling (in 1982 the Supreme Court ruled that illegal immigrants may not be denied a public education through the twelfth grade).

While millions have sought to obtain the rights, privileges, and duties of American citizenship, a few Americans have voluntarily renounced their allegiance to the United States, and still others have committed acts that have put their citizenship in jeopardy. Can citizenship be given up or taken away?

EXPATRIATION

MAJOR ISSUES

- What is the right of expatriation?
- Are there any circumstances under which the government may strip an American of citizenship?

The common view in Europe at the time of the American founding was that men and women owed perpetual allegiance to their country of birth. They were not free without the consent of the sovereign to renounce that allegiance and to take on the citizenship of another country, even if they permanently relocated to it. Early Americans believed, however, that political communities were voluntary associations of free individuals seeking to secure their natural rights. This meant both (a) that the community would decide whether and how to allow foreigners to become citizens and (b) that citizens had the right to renounce their allegiance and move elsewhere.

Voluntarily Giving Up Citizenship

To the American founders, the **right of expatriation**—that is, the right to renounce one's citizenship—followed from the social contract principles of the Declaration of Independence. Federal law, however, was silent on this subject until just after the Civil War. In 1868, Congress responded to the refusal of the British government to recognize the right of its Irish subjects to renounce allegiance to Britain and become American citizens by passing the Expatriation Act. This law declared that "the right of expatriation is a natural and inherent right of all people, indispensable to the enjoyment of the rights of life, liberty, and the pursuit of happiness."[57] This was the first time a national government had affirmed the right of expatriation.

In accordance with this right, federal law and regulations establish procedures, administered by the State Department, by which Americans may renounce their citizenship. "**Renunciates**" must appear in person before a U.S. consular or diplomatic officer in a foreign country and sign an "oath of renunciation." In reporting the number of renunciates, the government does not distinguish between Americans who renounce citizenship and foreign nationals who renounce permanent U.S. residency. In recent years, the number in these two categories has jumped from several hundred per year to more than a thousand, many (perhaps most) for tax reasons.[58] In May of 2012, naturalized U.S. citizen Eduardo Severin, one of the cofounders of Facebook, made news when he renounced his citizenship just days before the initial public offering of Facebook, which made him a billionaire. He explained his decision by saying that he planned to spend most of his time in Singapore, but skeptics noted that he would likely save a considerable amount in taxes.[59]

Taking Citizenship Away

Americans may voluntarily renounce their citizenship, but may the government ever take it away? Federal statutes list a variety of acts that shall result in the loss of citizenship if "voluntarily perform[ed] . . . with the intention of relinquishing United States nationality." These include:

- obtaining naturalization in a foreign state;
- declaring allegiance to a foreign state;
- serving in the armed forces of a foreign state (1) engaged in hostilities against the United States or (2) as an officer;
- serving in office in a foreign state if (1) one has or acquires the nationality of that state or (2) such office requires an oath of allegiance to the foreign state; and
- committing treason against, attempting to overthrow by force, or bearing arms against the United States.

Prior to several important Supreme Court decisions in the last half of the twentieth century, federal statutes had also required loss of citizenship for other acts deemed inconsistent with the duties of citizenship. Starting in 1958, however, the U.S. Supreme Court began to cut back on Congress's power over forced expatriation. It has ruled that the government could not take citizenship away from (a) a soldier who deserts from the military in wartime, (b) a civilian who flees the country to evade military service, (c) a naturalized citizen who returns to his or her native country and resides there for at least three years, and (d) a U.S. citizen who relocates to another country and votes in its elections. The Court based these decisions on the citizenship clause of the Fourteenth Amendment. Every American, it ruled, has "a constitutional right to remain a citizen in a free country unless he voluntarily relinquishes that citizenship."[60] The government may not take citizenship away unless the individual actually "intended to relinquish his citizenship."[61]

These were controversial decisions, with most decided by 5–4 votes. Opponents charged that the Court was sapping citizenship of its meaning and of the obligations it places on Americans. Certain virtues and behaviors, they insisted, were essential to full membership in the American political community. Unless the Supreme Court rethinks the matter, apparently nothing done by an American-born citizen—including taking up arms against the United States—can result in forced expatriation.

Right of expatriation—the right of men and women to renounce their allegiance to a nation and move elsewhere.

Renunciate—someone who voluntarily renounces his or her American citizenship.

These Supreme Court decisions partly explain the growth in **dual citizenship** among Americans. Until the twentieth century, American public policy consistently prohibited dual citizenship (also called *dual nationality*). Since 1795, federal law has required that applicants for naturalization "absolutely and entirely renounce and abjure" allegiance to their native land and any other foreign power. That requirement remains an integral element of the citizenship oath, officially titled the "Oath of Renunciation and Allegiance." Until the twentieth century, American Indians could be citizens of their tribes or of the United States, but not both. At the end of the Mexican-American War in 1848, those living in the lands ceded by Mexico to the United States had to choose between becoming American citizens or retaining their Mexican citizenship. And in the early twentieth century, federal law stipulated that Americans who obtained citizenship or declared allegiance to a foreign state would be subject to expatriation.

Now, however, Americans can become citizens of another country without losing their American citizenship. Here are other ways in which Americans can be dual citizens: (a) if a child is born on U.S. soil to foreign visitors, the child is a U.S. citizen and likely also a citizen of the parents' country; (b) a child born to one American parent and one foreign parent will likely be a citizen of both countries; (c) in some cases the native countries of foreigners who become naturalized U.S. citizens do not recognize the renunciation of prior allegiance that new citizens take.

Unlike natural-born citizens, those who become U.S. citizens through naturalization may in some cases lose their citizenship against their will. **Denaturalization** can occur if the person originally obtained citizenship through fraud or illegality. Most notably, in recent decades the government has taken American citizenship away from (and usually deported) former Nazis who engaged in war crimes during World War II and lied about these activities either when they entered the United States after the war or when they applied for citizenship. More than 100 former Nazis have lost their American citizenship in this way.[62] The courts have generally upheld such actions but have placed a high standard of proof on the government.

Earlier we quoted the naturalized American citizen from Britain who said that Americans are those who "wed the principles of America's Declaration to their hearts and render the duties of American citizens practically in their lives." As we have seen, those unwilling to embrace the duties of citizenship have a legal right to renounce it; but if they do not exercise that right, government can no longer take it away.

There is no guarantee that immigrants to the United States will embrace the rights and duties of citizenship and come to think of themselves more as Americans than as members of a particular racial, ethnic, or nationality group. In the next section, we examine the issues involved in the assimilation debate.

Dual citizenship—citizenship in two nations simultaneously. It is sometimes called "dual nationality."

Denaturalization—the process by which naturalized American citizens lose their citizenship because they obtained their original naturalization through fraud or illegality.

FOCUS
QUESTION

Should American citizens lose their citizenship if they (a) leave the U.S. to become the citizen of another country, (b) desert during wartime, (c) serve in the armed forces of a country at war with the United States, or (d) commit treason against the United States? Should the Constitution be amended to authorize Congress to pass such laws?

IMPACT
of Social Media and Communications Technology

Citizenship, Patriotism, and Contacts with Foreigners

Until a few decades ago, it was rare for average Americans to have regular contact with citizens of other countries. Unless one had a job that involved overseas travel, met foreigners regularly through professional organizations, or, perhaps, enjoyed the hobby of amateur radio, there were few opportunities to communicate directly with foreigners. The Internet, e-mail, and the budding social media have changed all that. Facebook alone had over 800 million users worldwide in March 2012. Of these, 233 million were in Europe, 195 million in Asia, 173 million in North America, and 154 million in Central and South America. Except when repressive governments clamp down on Internet communications, citizens can communicate across national boundaries at will.

CRITICAL THINKING

Drawing upon your personal experience with modern communications technology and studies on the use of social media that we highlight in the Bessette–Pitney blog (see entries for November 16, 2011; December 23, 2011; and March 14, 2012), evaluate the impact of social media and modern communications on two important issues we cover in this chapter: patriotism versus cosmopolitanism and dual citizenship. Will the new technology decisively affect how we think about these issues?

ASSIMILATION

MAJOR ISSUE

- What is required for large numbers of new immigrants to assimilate successfully into American civic culture?

Since the earliest days of the republic, Americans have debated assimilation. From Ben Franklin's concerns about Germans moving into Pennsylvania, to the Know-Nothing opposition to Irish Catholics, to the exclusion of Asians, and to the debate over illegal immigration, Americans have disagreed about the effects of racial, ethnic, religious, and language differences on the American political community. Over time, the country has rejected all racial, ethnic, and nationality criteria for citizenship, requiring instead a commitment to the universal principles of freedom and democracy. Nonetheless, intelligent observers of the American scene still disagree on whether the nation can successfully assimilate all those now entering the country.

The Assimilation Debate

Two prominent antagonists in the immigration and assimilation debate are Michael Barone and John Fonte.[63] Barone, a journalist and political analyst, defends large-scale immigration by noting that throughout American history, immigrant groups have successfully assimilated into American civic culture. Latino immigrants, for example, participate in the labor force at very high rates, are more likely than native-born whites to live with both their mother and father, and have divorce rates below average. Asians, another major immigrant group, are passionate about education and have started thousands of small businesses.

Barone continues:

> [O]pponents of immigration argue that today's minorities are bringing habits of mind inimical to America's traditions of tolerance, civic involvement, and voluntary associations. But that was also true of the immigrants of 100 years ago. Fortunately, most people come to America not to replicate their home country but to leave it behind and become Americans. And America, with its long history as a multiethnic society, has so far found ways to productively absorb them all.

Researcher and immigration expert John Fonte disagrees: "To put things simply: It's not 1900 anymore." Fonte explains that a century ago, "we had self-confident patriotic elites in politics, education, business, religion, and civic associations who insisted that new immigrants Americanize." But no longer: "Now, we have diffident and divided elites who are either actively promoting anti-Americanization policies such as 'multiculturalism' or doing little to encourage assimilation." "Back then," he continues, "the federal government promoted Americanism and individual rights. Now it promotes ethnic consciousness and group rights."

When social scientists study assimilation of immigrant groups, they look at such indicators as income levels, labor force participation, educational attainment, home ownership, intermarriage with someone born in the United States, ability to speak English, naturalization, and military service. Some distinguish between *economic assimilation* (whether immigrants reach economic parity with native-born Americans), *cultural assimilation* (especially whether immigrants intermarry with non-immigrants and learn English), and *civic assimilation* (whether immigrants become naturalized citizens).[64]

A recent major study found that although immigrants who had arrived since 1990 were more distinct from the American population than those who arrived a century ago, they assimilated more rapidly than the earlier immigrants.[65] Others emphasize that even if some new arrivals assimilate slowly, their children and grandchildren fully assimilate into American society and civic culture. According to one academic expert, "By the third generation, it's over. English wins. Even among Mexicans in Southern California." His research found that "more than 95% of third- and later-generation California Mexicans prefer to speak English at home."[66]

The issue that Fonte and other critics raise is whether these standard measures of assimilation capture the kind of "patriotic assimilation" that they believe is necessary. One organization concedes that "[m]ost immigrants will undergo a superficial assimilation," but denies that this is enough: "[T]here is more to Americanization than learning English and getting a job. The development of a visceral, emotional attachment to America and its history, or 'patriotic assimilation,' is increasingly unlikely when the schools and the culture at large are skeptical, even hostile, to patriotism and when technology enables immigrants to maintain strong psychological and physical ties to their countries of origin."[67]

The old **melting pot** metaphor captured the notion that newcomers should leave behind old identities and adopt a new one, that many different peoples would blend together into a single people: "E pluribus unum." Critics of the metaphor promote instead **multiculturalism**, the view that American society is best thought of as a collection of different cultures, each with its own values, traditions, and practices, and that no one culture should dominate.

In his inaugural address in January 2009, President Barack Obama discussed both aspects of American nationality. "We are a nation of Christians and Muslims, Jews and Hindus, and non-believers," he told the vast crowd in attendance and the millions more watching on television. The United States, he said, is "shaped by every language and culture, drawn from every end of this Earth." But the nation is more than just a collection of disparate groups: "America [is] bigger than the sum of our individual ambitions, greater than all the differences of birth or wealth or faction."[68]

Americans have a unique set of beliefs about their relationship to government, their country's place in the world, and their duties to one another. These beliefs show up in distinctively American traditions. Although scholars sometimes refer to such attitudes and practices as **political culture**, we use a broader term: **civic culture**. Civic culture shapes the issues that Americans deliberate about and the ways in which they deliberate. Accordingly, it influences what government does—and does not even try.

Melting pot—the metaphor that conveys the notion that newcomers to the United States should leave behind old identities and adopt new ones; that many diverse peoples should blend together into a single American people.

Multiculturalism—the view that American society is best thought of as a collection of different cultures, each with its own values, traditions, and practices, and that no one culture should dominate.

Political culture—a distinctive and widely shared set of beliefs on how to practice governmental and political activities.

Civic culture—a widely shared set of beliefs and traditions concerning political activity and community service.

AMERICAN CIVIC CULTURE

MAJOR ISSUE

- How have the essential elements of American civic culture influenced deliberations about the role of government?

American civic culture has many different elements, and it would take a shelf of books to describe them all. Here we look at four of the most important: individualism, religion, patriotism, and community service.

Individualism

The United States began in violent revolution against central authority. The Declaration of Independence warned that whenever any government works against the inalienable rights of individuals, "it is the Right of the People to alter or to abolish it." Self-reliance and personal independence—what scholars call **individualism**—naturally became a key part of the civic culture.

In surveys, Americans are much more likely than Europeans to prefer that individuals be free to seek their goals without government interference than that government ensure that no one is in need.[69] Americans are also more likely to view economic competition as good.[70] Many want to join that competition. A survey of 23 nations found that 70% of Americans would prefer to be self-employed. The United States ranked third in this survey, just behind Poland and Portugal, and ahead of all other major industrial countries.[71]

Individualism—self-reliance and personal independence, usually in preference to government action.

The power of individualism helps to explain an extraordinary feature of American political history. Of the major democracies, only the United States has never had a major socialist movement or labor party.[72] Even when political leaders such as President Obama have called for greater government activism, they have stressed their basic support for free markets. As the president said when the federal government assumed majority ownership of General Motors in 2009 to forestall bankruptcy, "Our goal is to get GM back on its feet, take a hands-off approach, and get out quickly."[73]

Why, then, is there *any* support for an activist federal government in the United States? One reason is that Americans are suspicious of the concentration of power, and its threat to individual freedom, wherever they find it. Government can be a counterweight to the concentration of power elsewhere.

In the first half of the nineteenth century, suspicions about influential financiers helped doom the First and Second Banks of the United States. By the latter part of the century, political party machines had gained enormous political power in many states and cities. Meanwhile, large business corporations had accumulated immense economic power. The Progressive movement rose in opposition. Progressives argued that such concentrations of power—not the federal government—were bigger threats to the individual. They promoted the adoption of the ballot initiative through which voters could make their own laws. They got Congress to adopt campaign finance laws that banned corporate contributions to federal candidates.

To cleanse government of corruption and deprive the machines of patronage, Progressives transferred more government jobs from political appointees to civil servants. At all levels of government, they sought to put administrative decisions in the hands of politically neutral experts, who would deliberate according to scientific principles instead of making decisions on the basis of political favoritism.[74] In the early twentieth century, under Presidents Theodore Roosevelt and Woodrow Wilson, the federal government sought to curb corporate power with antitrust laws and new regulatory agencies.

Americans still voice their distrust of concentrations of power. In 2010, 77% said that too much power was "concentrated in the hands of a few big companies," and large majorities favored tighter regulation of financial institutions.[75] In 2011, however, 64% said that big government was the biggest threat to the country in the future, compared with 26% who cited big business and just 8% who mentioned big labor.[76]

Religion

Among the largest advanced industrial democracies, the United States is the most religious. A 2012 analysis of 30 countries found that that United States has a higher rate of strong belief in God than all but four (Poland, Israel, Chile, and the Philippines) and a lower rate of atheism than all but three (Chile, Cyprus, and the Philippines).[77] In a 2011 survey, half of Americans said that religion was very important in their lives. Less than a quarter of respondents in Spain (22%), Germany (21%), Britain (17%), and France (13%) said the same.[78] The same survey showed that most Americans think that it is necessary to believe in God to be moral, while most Europeans disagree.

In the 1830s, Tocqueville wrote about Americans' faith, concluding that religion is "the first of their political institutions."[79] Obviously, religion plays a part in current issues such as abortion and gay rights, but throughout American history it has affected many other debates. Some have argued that the political system could scarcely work without it. President John Adams suggested that the Constitution's limited government could not constrain a people who acted only out of self-interest. "[W]e have no government armed with power capable of contending with human passions unbridled by morality and religion."[80] In some ways, religious belief and practice counteract individualism because, as Tocqueville wrote, religion "imposes on each man some obligations toward mankind, to be performed in common with the rest of mankind, and so draws him away, from time to time, from thinking about himself."[81]

How can religion exert such influence? After all, the establishment clause of the First Amendment forbids an official church. (Although this prohibition did not originally apply

MYTHS AND MISINFORMATION

Tocqueville

Politicians have frequently quoted Alexis de Tocqueville on American character:

> I sought for the greatness and genius of America in her commodious harbors and her ample rivers—and it was not there . . . in her fertile fields and boundless forests and it was not there . . . in her rich mines and her vast world commerce—and it was not there . . . in her democratic Congress and her matchless Constitution—and it was not there. Not until I went into the churches of America and heard her pulpits flame with righteousness did I understand the secret of her genius and power. America is great because she is good, and if America ever ceases to be good, she will cease to be great.[82]

In his 1940 farewell speech, Senator Henry Ashurst (D-Arizona) attributed the first several lines of that passage to Tocqueville, then offered the last line as his own summation.[83] Tocqueville, however, wrote no such thing. Nevertheless, generations of writers and speechmakers repeated and embellished the false quotation. Instead of checking it against original sources, authors merely copied it from one another, and it spread like a virus. The quotation has found its way into the works of Republicans and Democrats, liberals and conservatives. Presidents Reagan and Clinton were equally fond of using it.

Adaptability is a key to its appeal. One may invoke it for many diverse causes. In November 2003, one House member used it to condemn plans for war in Iraq:

> There was a French man by the name of Alexis de Tocqueville that years ago as he was traveling through our Nation, our country, made the observation that America is great because America is good. And implicit in that observation is the acknowledgment that the United States respects the rule of law. If we do not have the rule of law, we have a jungle.[84]

Another attacked a court decision to remove "under God" from the Pledge:

> Alexis de Tocqueville, after watching us for 5 years, concluded that the secret of our greatness and power did not lie in any of these great harbors or grain fields or military, not in our matchless Constitution, our Declaration of Independence, but he said, "but not until I went into the churches of America and heard her pulpits flame with righteousness did I understand the secret of her genius and power. America is great because America is good; and if America ever ceases to be good, America will cease to be great." Do you think, Mr. Speaker, that taking the words "under God" out of our Pledge of Allegiance to the Flag will make us a better people?[85]

to state governments, the states abolished official religions in the decades before and after the founding. Massachusetts was the last to do so, in 1833.) In Chapter 5, we examine how the establishment clause, as interpreted by the modern Supreme Court, limits government action respecting religion.

However, the rules that limit government do not apply to private citizens or organizations. Nothing in the Constitution bans religious motivations for political action. As then-senator Barack Obama said in 2006:

> Frederick Douglass, Abraham Lincoln, Williams Jennings Bryan, Dorothy Day, Martin Luther King—indeed, the majority of great reformers in American history—were not only motivated by faith, but repeatedly used religious language to argue for their cause. So to say that men and women should not inject their "personal morality" into public policy debates is a practical absurdity. Our law is by definition a codification of morality, much of it grounded in the Judeo-Christian tradition.[86]

So in spite of the nation's historic commitment to the separation of church and state, religion is an essential part of American civic culture. As we shall see, however, Americans have not always put religion to high purposes.

Born in Mission

Whereas some colonists came to North America to make their fortunes, others were seeking religious freedom. A group that we call **Pilgrims** had faced hardships for breaking from the Church of England. Along with crewmen and others outside their faith, they left England in

Pilgrims—Calvinists who had broken with the Church of England and who settled in Massachusetts after arriving on the Mayflower in 1620.

Mayflower Compact—the Pilgrims' covenant for governing the Plymouth colony. Although neither a declaration of independence nor a constitution, it did come to symbolize how Americans could join for common purposes.

Puritans—Calvinists who wanted to "purify" the Church of England without immediately abandoning it. Puritans settled in the northeastern United States. Their strict moral code and emphasis on education left lasting marks on American thought.

First Great Awakening—a religious revival of the 1700s that stressed a personal experience of God and helped develop a national identity among the American colonists.

Enlightenment—an intellectual movement of the 1700s that stressed the power of reason and took a scientific approach to morality.

Deism—a belief that God created the world but does not intervene in its affairs.

Second Great Awakening—a religious revival of the late 1700s and early 1800s. In contrast to the First Great Awakening, this movement stressed social improvement in addition to personal conversion. It inspired efforts to curb alcohol abuse and end slavery.

1620 aboard the *Mayflower*. Their purpose, as they announced in the **Mayflower Compact** (see Chapter 1), was to promote "the glory of God, and the advancement of the Christian faith, and the honor of our king and country."[87] The adult male passengers pledged mutual support and established "a civill body politick." This document came to symbolize how Americans could join for common purposes under God's watchful eye. In 1621, the Pilgrims thanked God for their survival by holding a feast with local Indians. Theirs was not the "first Thanksgiving," as Spanish settlers had held such observances. Still, the Pilgrims' Thanksgiving, featuring turkey and an abundance of other foods, would become the model for the holiday we celebrate today.

Despite their symbolic importance as religious settlers, the Pilgrims were a small group. Following them came a larger influx of **Puritans**, who wanted to "purify" the Church of England without abandoning it. A reform movement rather than a distinct church, Puritanism spawned many denominations, including the Baptists and Presbyterians. By the American Revolution, most churchgoing colonists identified with one of these groups.[88] Puritanism left lasting marks on the American mind.[89] One was a concern for morality. Many think of the word *puritanical* as a slur, recalling the Salem witch trials. Because of this prudish tradition, the argument goes, the United States has always been more likely than Europe to censor popular culture. To others, however, Puritanism stands for moral idealism.

Revolution and Founding

The **First Great Awakening**, a mid-1700s revival movement that stressed the personal experience of religion, had profound effects. Until this time, people thought of themselves as residents of their home colonies, but the Great Awakening stirred a common American identity. George Whitefield, who preached the movement up and down the Atlantic coast, was probably the first "American" public figure famous in all the colonies.[90] Disdaining hierarchy, preachers of the Great Awakening undercut the authority of the Church of England—and, indirectly, of England itself.

By the time of the founding, the Great Awakening had cooled. The dominant intellectual current was the **Enlightenment**, which stressed that political deliberations should rely on reason instead of faith. Revolutionary hero Ethan Allen and pamphleteer Thomas Paine openly criticized Christianity as a form of superstition. Many other public figures believed in **deism**, the idea that a divine power created the universe and natural laws but stays out of human events.[91]

Nevertheless, religious colors kept showing through. In political writings of the founding era (1760–1805), the most cited book was the Bible, particularly the Book of Deuteronomy.[92] (The fifth book of the Old Testament, Deuteronomy completes and explains the law by which the Israelites were to live.) Of the 55 men who served at the Constitutional Convention, at least 50 belonged to a major Christian denomination.[93] Some may have been members in name only, but others were devout. Two of them, Charles Pinckney and John Langdon, later served as founders of the American Bible Society. The Society's second president was John Jay, author of five of *The Federalist Papers* and first chief justice of the United States.

Slavery and Civil Rights

Religion was part of one of the issues that came before the First Congress. In 1790, Quakers presented the House with petitions to halt the slave trade.[94] Arguing that Congress should ignore the request, Representative James Jackson of Georgia said, "But sir, is the whole morality of the United States confined to the Quakers? Are they the only people whose feelings are to be consulted on this occasion?" The House rejected the petitions, declaring that it lacked the power to "interfere" with slavery.

Soon afterward came a religious revival that helped sustain the national debate. The **Second Great Awakening** started in New England in the late 1790s and soon spread widely. In contrast to the First Great Awakening, this movement stressed social improvement and inspired voluntary associations to advance education and moral betterment. For many, the abolition of slavery was the centerpiece of social reform. William Lloyd Garrison, leader of the American Anti-Slavery Society, condemned slavery as a sin. Inspired by biblical stories—especially that of Moses, who led his people out of bondage—black preachers organized major slave uprisings. Three such leaders were Gabriel Prosser (1800), Denmark Vesey (1822), and Nat Turner (1831).[95]

The religious fight against slavery met resistance. In 1854, Senator Stephen A. Douglas of Illinois fumed when some 3,000 New England clergy signed a petition against the expansion of slavery. "It is an attempt to establish a theocracy to take charge of our politics and our legislation," he said. "It is an attempt to make the legislative power of this country subordinate to the church."[96]

American churches were hardly unanimous. Many kept silent, and many in slave states cited religious reasons for supporting slavery. One pro-slavery tract quoted many biblical passages and concluded "that African slavery is a Divine institution."[97] Frederick Douglass, an escaped slave and abolitionist leader, attacked the latter position as a "horrible blasphemy."[98] Several Protestant denominations broke into northern and southern wings. And after the war began, each side invoked faith.

For decades after the Civil War, religion was central to African-American life because the black church was the one institution that black people could control without white interference.[99] In the mid-twentieth century, Reverend Adam Clayton Powell Jr. pastor of the Abyssinian Baptist Church in Harlem, became the nation's most powerful black official. After winning a House seat in 1944, he eventually chaired the House Committee on Education and Labor, where he helped pass landmark social legislation.

During the 1950s, Reverend Dr. Martin Luther King Jr. emerged as a national leader by leading a church-based boycott of Montgomery's segregated buses and by helping found a major civil rights organization, the Southern Christian Leadership Conference. Like many in the movement, King relied on religious rhetoric. In his 1963 "I Have a Dream" speech, he drew upon Isaiah (40:4–5): "I have a dream that one day . . . the glory of the Lord shall be revealed and all flesh shall see it together."[100] In his last speech before his 1968 murder, King alluded to Moses: "I've seen the promised land. I may not get there with you. But I want you to know tonight, that we, as a people, will get to the promised land." He closed with the words that Julia Ward Howe wrote during the Civil War: "Mine eyes have seen the glory of the coming of the Lord!"[101] The civil rights movement extended beyond black Protestant churches. Jewish theologian Abraham Heschel marched with King and linked civil rights to biblical teaching.[102]

As early as 1956, the Catholic archbishop of New Orleans threatened to excommunicate Catholic state lawmakers who backed legislation to segregate private schools.[103] Not all denominations joined the movement. Some churches even supported segregation, though such views are rare today, and, as is often the case, some politicians objected to the involvement of religion in politics. In closing his unsuccessful fight against the 1964 Civil Rights Act, Senator Richard Russell (D-GA) said, "I have observed with profound sorrow the role that many religious leaders have played in urging passage of this bill, because I cannot make their activities jibe with my concept of the proper place of religious leaders in our national life."[104]

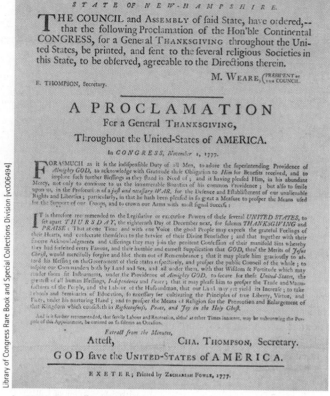

Library of Congress Rare Book and Special Collections Division [vc006494]

In 1777, Congress celebrated the victory at Saratoga by issuing the first national Thanksgiving Proclamation, which asked forgiveness through "the merits of Jesus Christ" and beseeched God "to prosper the means of Religion for the Promotion and Enlargement of that Kingdom which confideth in Righteousness, Peace, and Joy in the Holy Ghost."

Individual Conduct

By the 1830s, alcohol consumption had reached record levels,[105] so one element of the Second Great Awakening was a fight against drunkenness. Temperance activists persuaded many of their fellow citizens to drink less, and they also pressured state legislatures to curb liquor sales. In the 1840s and 1850s, another sentiment stoked temperance agitation: prejudice

President Barack Obama and First Lady Michelle Obama bow their heads in prayer during the National Prayer Breakfast in Washington, DC, February 2, 2012. In his remarks, the president said that this annual event was "a chance to step back for a moment, for us to come together as brothers and sisters and seek God's face together. . . . We can all benefit from turning to our Creator, listening to Him."

against Catholic immigrants from Ireland and Germany, who reputedly drank more than Protestant natives.[106] More restrictive legislation followed. By the Civil War, alcohol abuse had plunged. Drinking later rose, though it never again reached the levels of the early 1830s.

In the early twentieth century, religious activists helped win the passage of the Eighteenth Amendment, establishing Prohibition. Although massive defiance led to its repeal in 1933, religion has continued to fight alcoholism. Alcoholics Anonymous (AA) features a 12-step program involving reliance on God or "a Power greater than ourselves."[107] For years, probation agencies made convicted drunk drivers take part in AA. Federal courts, however, have ruled that AA must not be the only therapy available to probationers because the program is "deeply religious."[108]

In the nineteenth century, plural marriage was a major issue. The Church of Jesus Christ of Latter-day Saints (the Mormon Church) initially believed that its male members should have multiple wives. Members of the church faced harsh reactions, and in 1844 an Illinois mob killed Joseph Smith, the church's founder. Members then moved to Mexican territory around the Great Salt Lake Basin. As a result of the Mexican-American War, the area became United States territory. In 1862, Congress banned polygamy in territories. Upholding the law, the Court said, "Laws are made for the government of actions, and while they cannot interfere with mere religious belief and opinions, they may with practices."[109] The issue remained a point of contention until 1890, when the church's leader announced that he had a revelation that plural marriage was not necessary and that church members should obey laws forbidding it. Six years later, Congress admitted the area as the state of Utah.

During the late twentieth century, harsh political battles involved abortion. In the 1973 case of *Roe v. Wade*, the Supreme Court removed legal barriers to most abortions. The Catholic Church, which opposes abortion, mobilized against the decision, and other religious groups also joined the fight. But many denominations faced divisions over the issue, and a number of public officials said that although they personally opposed abortion for religious reasons, they did not want to legislate on the matter. Religious pro-life groups compared themselves to the abolitionists of the nineteenth century, while pro-choice groups accused them of seeking to impose their faith on others. According to the American Civil Liberties Union, a victory by abortion opponents would mean that "theocracy, not democracy, will soon hold sway over a nation."[110]

In later chapters we address the impact of religion on social issues such as education and welfare. Although religion affects American politics in many ways, it is not the only force that directs Americans away from the pure pursuit of self-interest. Patriotism also helps define the national character. As we shall now see, patriotism involves a kind of religion of its own.

Patriotism

Patriotism—both an emotional and a rational attachment to the nation, a public spirit strong enough to inspire sacrifice.

Patriotism refers to support of and pride in the country and its way of life. In a 2005 survey of 33 nations, the United States ranked highest in general national pride.[111] About nine-tenths of Americans consider themselves very patriotic (see Figure 4-4), and in 2011 most Americans said that the United States either stands above all other nations (38%) or is one of the greatest (53%). Just 8% said there are other countries that are better.[112] Americans attach great importance to patriotic symbols and rituals, so Congress and the courts have grappled with disputes involving flag burning and the Pledge of Allegiance. Similar fights seldom occur in other large industrial democracies.

Patriotism is more than a warm feeling; it also entails a willingness to sacrifice for the country. The government has always relied on patriotic appeals to recruit for the armed forces. Although economic incentives have also been necessary, military service has never been just about the money. As one young infantry platoon leader blogged from Afghanistan in 2007: "I am an American. I'm here to fight for the United States; to eliminate those people who would do us harm, and to prevent them from spreading their beliefs to others who would do the same."[113]

REUTERS/Jonathan Ernst

A woman walks to a "tea party" Tax Day rally at the National Mall in Washington on April 15, 2010. The "Don't Tread on Me" symbol, which comes from the Revolutionary-era "Gadsden flag," illustrates the individualist strain in American life.

Patriotism and Civil Religion

Patriotism is connected to what many call the nation's **civil religion**. This concept refers not to any religious denomination or theological doctrine but to beliefs about the country's place in the universe.[114] There is no single definition of *civil religion*, but the term generally involves an acceptance of natural law (fundamental principles of right and wrong) and a conviction that Americans should seek the protection and guidance of a higher power. The civil religion also includes **American exceptionalism**, the belief that the United States is different from other countries in its founding principles, that it should serve as an example to other nations—"a city on a hill," as Presidents Kennedy and Reagan put it—and that it has a special mission to spread freedom and democracy throughout the world.[115]

The American civil religion has roots in the Judeo-Christian tradition, and references to its writings are commonplace. The "city on a hill" image comes first from the New Testament and then from a 1630 sermon by Puritan colonist John Winthrop.[116] Kennedy's inaugural provides another example. He urged both sides in the Cold War to heed "the command of Isaiah to 'undo the heavy burdens . . . and to let the oppressed go free.'" He proclaimed "that the rights of man come not from the generosity of the state but from the hand of God." He concluded by "asking His blessing and His help, but knowing that here on earth God's work must truly be our own."[117]

Civil religion—a nondenominational belief that accepts the existence of fundamental principles of right and wrong and embraces a conviction that Americans should seek the protection of a higher power. It also includes the notion of American exceptionalism and a special attachment to national rituals and symbols. (See also **American exceptionalism**.)

Although the federal Constitution does not mention God, all state constitutions do.[118] Rhode Island is typical, expressing gratitude "to Almighty God for the civil and religious liberty which He hath so long permitted us to enjoy, and looking to Him for a blessing upon our endeavors."[119] Several state mottoes mention divinity. Ohio's motto, "With God all things are possible," provoked legal challenge under the First Amendment, with opponents noting that it is a quotation from the New Testament (Matthew 19:26). A federal court upheld its constitutionality. In 1956 the U.S. Congress adopted "In God we trust" as the nation's official motto. It

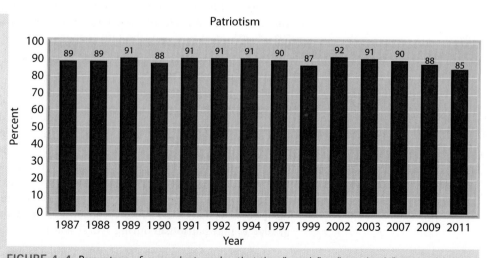

Patriotism

Year	Percent
1987	89
1988	89
1989	91
1990	88
1991	91
1992	91
1994	91
1997	90
1999	87
2002	92
2003	91
2007	90
2009	88
2011	85

FIGURE 4–4 Percentage of respondents saying that they "mostly" or "completely" agree with the statement "I am very patriotic."
SOURCE: Pew Research Center for the People and the Press, "The Generation Gap and the 2012 Election," November 3, 2011, http://www.people-press.org/files/legacy-pdf/11-3-11%20Generations%20Release.pdf, accessed May 23, 2012.

National Guard A-10 jets fly over Boston's Fenway Park during the singing of the National Anthem on July 4, 2007.

AP Photo/Winslow Townson

American exceptionalism—the belief that the United States is different from other countries in its founding principles, that it should serve as an example to other nations, and that it has a special mission to spread freedom and democracy throughout the world.

had been appearing on coins and currency off and on since just after the end of the Civil War.

In the American civil religion, official references to God now tend to be nondenominational. Presidents often speak of "The Almighty" but seldom mention Jesus Christ in public statements.

Symbols and Rituals

Americans attach great importance to patriotic symbols and rituals. Many sporting events feature color guards, the display of the flag, and the singing of the National Anthem. Such signs and expressions abound with references to religious tradition. On the reverse side of the Great Seal of the United States, you will see a pyramid beneath an eye within a triangle and the Latin phrase *Annuit Coeptis*, or "He [God] has favored our undertakings." The seal's designer said, "The Pyramid signifies strength and duration. The eye over it and the motto allude to the many signal interpositions of providence in favour of the American cause."[120]

The seal appears on the back of the dollar bill. If you look closely at the seal's obverse side, you will notice a field of 13 stars above the eagle's head. It forms a Star of David.

The Liberty Bell, which rang for the first public reading of the Declaration of Independence, bears an inscription from the Book of Leviticus (25:10): "Proclaim LIBERTY throughout all the Land unto all the inhabitants thereof." Prayers begin many official activities, including presidential inaugurations and congressional floor sessions. The U.S. Supreme Court begins its daily public business with the words "God save the United States and this Honorable Court."

Even when patriotic symbols and rituals do not have overt religious content, Americans treat them as if they did. Historian Pauline Maier points out that the National Archives displays the Declaration of Independence in a structure that looks like an altar.[121] The Lincoln Memorial bears this inscription: "In this temple, as in the hearts of the people for whom he saved the Union, the memory of Abraham Lincoln is enshrined forever."

Perhaps the nation's preeminent patriotic symbol is the flag. More than people in most other countries, Americans have deep feelings about their flag: a 2010 survey shows that 59% display it at home, in the office, or in the car.[122] Such sentiment explains why flag burning is a more emotional issue in the United States than in other developed countries. As we discuss in Chapter 5, the Supreme Court has overruled both state and federal laws against flag burning. Members of Congress have responded by trying to amend the Constitution to authorize Congress "to prohibit the physical desecration of the flag of the United States."[123] The single word *desecration* speaks volumes about Americans attitudes. William Safire, an expert on political language, has written, "Desecration is a noun steeped in the violation of religious belief. It is rooted in the Latin *sacrare* or *secrare*, source of 'sacred' and 'sacrifice,' dealing through the millenniums with worship of a deity. To *desecrate* is to profane what is holy."[124]

The importance of the flag to American civic culture is evident in the words of the Pledge of Allegiance, first written by a Baptist minister in 1892 and recognized by Congress in 1942 to rally patriotism during World War II. Modified in 1954, it now reads:

> I pledge allegiance to the Flag of the United States of America, and to the Republic for which it stands, one Nation under God, indivisible, with liberty and justice for all. (1954)

The pledge has come to embody the relationship of community, religion, and military service. Many associations start their meetings with a recitation of the pledge, both as a bonding ritual and as an affirmation of patriotism.

Patriotism and Military Service

Two federal holidays, Memorial Day and Veterans Day, honor those who have worn the uniform. On those days and other official occasions, speeches invoke battlefield deaths. In his first inaugural, President Lincoln spoke of the "mystic chords of memory, stretching from every battlefield and patriot grave to every living heart and hearthstone all over this broad land."[125] He delivered the Gettysburg Address to dedicate a battlefield cemetery and to resolve "that these dead shall not have died in vain."[126] In 1961, President Kennedy said in his inaugural address, "The graves of young Americans who answered the call to service surround the globe."[127]

Although the United States has sometimes resorted to the draft in wartime, the government has usually relied on volunteers to answer this "call to service." Throughout history, many have enlisted for material reasons, such as job training and veterans' benefits, but patriotism has always been an important motive. Even as casualties mounted in Iraq, economist Gary Becker notes, Americans continued to enlist at higher rates than military pay could explain. "One compelling other reason would be patriotism on their part, and a resulting desire to serve their country."[128] In a 2011 survey, 68% of Iraq veterans and 69% of Afghanistan veterans considered themselves more patriotic than most other people in the country. Just 37% of Americans overall said the same.[129]

African Americans enlisted even when the army officially segregated people by race. General Colin Powell, secretary of state under President George W. Bush, explains that the motive was not just the absence of civilian opportunities. "It was a way to demonstrate patriotism, to show that even though you do this to me, even though you treat me this way, I am still an American and I will demonstrate that patriotism and if the only place you will allow me to do it is on the field of battle by shedding my blood, I will do it."[130]

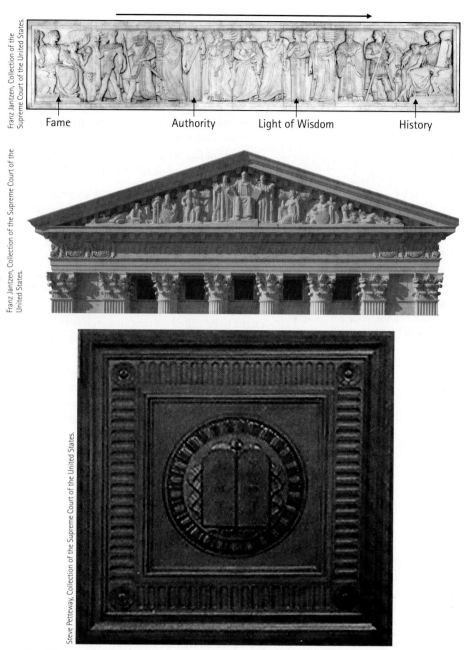

Fame   Authority   Light of Wisdom   History

Should the Ten Commandments appear on public property? Those in favor point to the Supreme Court building. Both the South Wall Frieze (top photo, figure immediately to the left of "Authority") and East Pediment (middle photo, central figure) include depictions of Moses holding the tablets. Moreover, the oak doors to the courtroom (bottom photo) feature engravings of tablets bearing Roman numerals I through X. Those who back public display of the Commandments say that this artwork clearly represents the Decalogue. Opponents are skeptical, noting that Moses appears among other historical figures (e.g., Confucius, Hammurabi, Draco, and Solon) as well as allegorical figures representing ideas such as philosophy. They also say that the tablets above do not mention the Commandments and could instead represent the Bill of Rights.

Franz Jantzen, Collection of the Supreme Court of the United States.

Franz Jantzen, Collection of the Supreme Court of the United States.

Steve Petteway, Collection of the Supreme Court of the United States.

Problems of Patriotism

Many observers have noted abuses of patriotism. In a 2008 campaign speech, presidential candidate Barack Obama said:

> Thomas Jefferson was accused by the Federalists of selling out to the French. The anti-Federalists were just as convinced that John Adams was in cahoots with the British and intent on restoring monarchal rule. Likewise, even our wisest Presidents have sought to justify questionable policies on the basis of patriotism. Adams' Alien and Sedition Act, Lincoln's suspension of habeas corpus, Roosevelt's internment of Japanese Americans—all were defended as expressions of patriotism, and those who disagreed with their policies were sometimes labeled as unpatriotic.[131]

When he faced criticism for not wearing a flag pin during his campaign for the White House, Barack Obama said that such symbols can become a "substitute for, I think, true patriotism."[132]

Some people question the concept of patriotism itself. Legal scholar Martha Nussbaum says that it wrongly places one nation ahead of others. She favors **cosmopolitanism**, where "primary allegiance is to the community of human beings in the entire world."[133] Columnist Richard Cohen says that American exceptionalism "discourages compromise, for what God has made exceptional, man must not alter." He adds that the phrase "reeks of arrogance" and "ought to be called American narcissism."[134] Political philosopher George Kateb argues that patriotism clashes with deliberative democracy. Because of patriotism, he says, people "lend their energies to a state that sooner or later embarks on an inherently unjust imperialist career and thus gets constantly engaged in policies that are deliberated in secrecy, and sustained by secrecy and propaganda, and removed from meaningful public deliberation."[135]

Critics charge that patriotic fervor allowed such excesses as (a) President Wilson's suppression of dissent during World War I through the Espionage Act of 1917 and the Sedition Act of 1918; (b) President Roosevelt's internment of Japanese Americans during World War II; and (c) Senator Joseph McCarthy's false accusations during the Cold War that many American officials had Communist ties.

Supporters of patriotism acknowledge such abuses. What is more important, they say, is that it inspires heroism.[136] Could any country survive if citizens were not wiling to die for it? Advocates of patriotism also wonder whether an allegiance to the whole world even makes sense. At the Constitutional Convention, Gouverneur Morris said that he would not trust "Citizens of the World." He explained, "The men who can shake off their attachments to their own Country can never love any other. These attachments are the wholesome prejudices which uphold all Governments."[137] In our time, political scientist Walter Berns asks, "Where is this world community—in the Balkans, Sri Lanka, Indonesia, China, Iraq, Iran, the West Bank?"[138] Defenders of American patriotism add that allegiance to the United States does not exclude the rest of the world because the founding was about the Declaration of Independence's universal principles. In that way, they say the United States serves as an example to other nations. They also note that patriotism encourages peaceful works of service and selflessness.

Community Service

Just as the United States leads major industrial democracies in religious practice and patriotism, it ranks first in charitable giving as a percentage of gross domestic product.[139] Data on volunteering are harder to interpret because of differences in defining voluntary activity and pricing volunteers' time, but studies place the United States at or near the top.

The American emphasis on service has a long history. In the years leading up to the Revolution, colonists resisted English domination with groups such as the Sons of Liberty and the Daughters of Liberty. They fought the war with their all-volunteer Continental Army, along with state and local militias. Civilians, women in particular, provided support on the home front by providing supplies and caring for wounded soldiers.[140] Historian Arthur Schlesinger Sr. summed up the impact of the period: "The philosophy of natural rights underlying the Revolution exalted the individual's capacity to act for himself; the military struggle taught men from different sections valuable lessons in practical cooperation."[141]

Cosmopolitanism—in contrast to patriotism, the belief that one's main allegiance should not be to one country but to the world community.

On a much larger scale, the Civil War engaged the spirit of voluntarism. The Young Men's Christian Association (YMCA) established a Christian Commission to support military chaplains, furnish troops with Bibles and other reading materials, and arrange exchanges of gifts and letters between soldiers and their families.[142] The United States Sanitary Commission organized a network of volunteers to supply soldiers with food and medical care. In 1881, Clara Barton and others who had worked in the Sanitary Commission joined to found the American Red Cross. In the decades after the Civil War, new national associations began, while existing groups surged in membership.[143] The first half of the next century gave them much to do, especially during World War II. The government got voluntary associations to help with drives to collect scrap metal and rubber, which were in short supply. Millions of Americans helped with air raid drills and manned observation posts.

Membership rates in volunteer organizations peaked in 1960, the year of Kennedy's election to the presidency. Then these numbers declined, as did certain other signs of civic virtue such as the share of national income going to charity.[144] Although it is hard to identify the causes for such a broad trend, the passing of "the Greatest Generation" (which fought World War II) may have had much to do with it. Watergate and the Vietnam War may have made Americans more cynical, and the latter may have temporarily diminished public regard for military service. Some also suggest that television drew Americans away from common pursuits.

Giving and Volunteering

Evidence exists that civic virtue has not fallen as badly as it may seem. In the past decade, charitable giving has ticked upward (see Table 4-6), and although historical data are scarce, large numbers of Americans take part in volunteer work. About 64.3 million people volunteered through or for an organization at least once between September 2010 and September 2011.[145] This figure amounted to just over a quarter of the population over age 16, roughly the same as in recent years. Americans are still working for the common good, and in new and different ways.[146] For instance, informal local groups and Internet communities may be taking the place of the older, chapter-based organizations.

The United States fares well in comparison with other countries. In 2011, a survey asked people in 153 countries whether they had donated money to a charity, volunteered time to an organization, or given help to a stranger. The Charities Aid Foundation calculated a "World Giving Index" for each country by averaging its responses for the three questions. The United States led the world with a score of 60%.[147] These findings reflect other themes in this chapter. Americans tend to be more patriotic than people in other developed nations, and many express these attitudes through charity and community service. Surveys suggest that students are particularly likely to put volunteerism at the core of their patriotism.[148] Religious involvement also helps account for the nation's high level of voluntary effort. Americans who regularly attend worship services are more likely than others to give time and money.[149] Much of the money and labor goes to religious organizations. Many faiths have provided social services ranging from job training to hospital care. The Salvation Army has become so familiar through its Christmas kettles that many do not even know that it is a religious denomination. Similarly, Habitat for Humanity has received more attention for its home building than for its religious origins.

Private Effort and Public Policy

In a variety of ways, public policy encourages the voluntary sector. Shortly after taking office, President Obama created the **White House Office of Faith-Based and Neighborhood Partnerships**, a successor to a similar office that President Bush had established. Under the

STAN HONDA/AFP/Getty Images

Michelle Obama helps volunteers with Operation Gratitude on National Service Day on January 19, 2009, at RFK Stadium in Washington, DC. Operation Gratitude assembles and sends packages to U.S. troops overseas.

White House Office of Faith-Based and Neighborhood Partnerships— an office that President Obama established to assist religious organizations and secular nonprofits in providing social services.

TABLE 4-6 RECIPIENTS OF GIVING AND VOLUNTEERING

Religious organizations continue to receive the biggest share of donations and volunteer effort.

Where Americans Donate Money (2010)

Religious organizations	$100.63 billion	35%
Education	$41.67 billion	14%
Grant-making foundations	$33 billion	11%
Human services	$26.49 billion	9%
Public-society benefit (United Way, etc.)	$24.24 billion	8%
Health	$22.83 billion	8%
International affairs	$15.77 billion	5%
Arts, culture, humanities	$13.28 billion	5%
Environment and animals	$6.66 billion	2%
Other	$6.32 billion	3%
TOTAL	$290.89 billion	100%

Where Americans Volunteer (2011)

Religious organizations	21,332,000	33.2%
Education or youth service	16,513,000	25.7%
Social or community service	9,188,000	14.3%
Hospital or other health	4,947,000	7.7%
Civic, political, professional, international	3,470,000	5.4%
Sports, hobbies, arts	2,442,000	3.8%
Environmental, animal care	1,478,000	2.3%
Public safety	835,000	1.3%
Other, not determined	4,048,000	6.3%
TOTAL	64,252,000	100%

SOURCES: Giving USA, "U.S. Charitable Giving Shows Modest Uptick In 2010 Following Two Years Of Declines," at www.givingusa.org/press_releases/gusa/GUSA-2011-Final-Release.pdf, accessed May 16, 2012; volunteer data are for September 2011, Bureau of Labor Statistics, U.S. Department of Labor, "Volunteering in the United States, 2011," February 22, 2012, Table 4, at www.bls.gov/news.release/pdf/volun.pdf, accessed April 30, 2012.

leadership of a former associate pastor, the office was to help religious and secular groups make a bigger impact. Supporters argue that faith-based initiatives can be more effective than secular ones, particularly on matters of personal conduct. Critics question the evidence for this claim. Critics also worry that it is often hard to separate their social services from religious preaching, particularly when they deal with problems such as substance abuse; and debate exists over whether grant recipients should be able to hire only believers.

Other federal programs to encourage voluntarism have been less controversial. Using the Quakers' American Friends Service Committee as his model, Senator Hubert Humphrey (D-MN), in 1960 introduced legislation to create the **Peace Corps**.[150] The proposal drew praise from students and other young people, and John Kennedy embraced it late in his presidential campaign. Shortly after taking office, he signed an executive order establishing the Peace Corps on a temporary basis. Congress soon made it permanent. The Peace Corps has since enabled some 170,000 Americans to do volunteer work all over the world, and in turn it has also inspired domestic counterparts. The Corporation for National and Community Service runs three programs to help people engage in community service. The best-known program, AmeriCorps (created in 1993 by Bill Clinton), provides participants with money for tuition or student loans.

In 1994, the Departments of Defense and Education launched Troops to Teachers. This program has helped thousands of retiring military and civilian Department of Defense personnel become teachers. "There are many ways to serve. Troops to Teachers helped me to transition to a new career. After four years at West Point and twenty years in the Army,

Peace Corps—a federal agency that sends civilian volunteers to help people in poor countries with education, agriculture, public health, and economic development.

FOCUS QUESTION

How effective are religion, patriotism, and community service at counteracting, or balancing, the force of individualism in American civic culture?

I have found a new, fulfilling yet still patriotic job teaching 4th grade gifted students in Killeen, Texas," said Kelly Synder.[151] "It's not based on economics," says George F. Gabb, a retired naval officer who teaches in Chesapeake, Virginia. "That's not the driving force for us. The driving force is something else: We want to give back."[152]

Public policy encourages citizens to donate to nonprofit organizations by exempting the donations from federal income tax. In 2010, these deductions totaled $158 billion.[153] Usually, such tax treatment is uncontroversial, but the Internal Revenue Service sometimes withdraws tax-exempt status if it believes that the organization is violating public policy by, for example, discriminating against minorities.

Experts debate whether the social costs of tax preferences exceed the social benefits. Those who would scrap the charitable deduction say that it has little impact on giving, and that the tax advantages go mainly to rich people. They argue that its elimination would add billions to federal revenue without substantially harming voluntary organizations. Others reply that ending the deduction would reduce charitable giving, creating a greater need for government services.

CITIZENSHIP, CIVIC CULTURE, AND DELIBERATIVE DEMOCRACY

Good citizenship is necessary for the success of American deliberative democracy. As we have seen, federal law has long required that candidates for citizenship be "of good moral character, attached to the principles of the Constitution of the United States, and well disposed to the good order and happiness of the same." Thus, a good citizen behaves morally, embraces the principles of the Constitution, and is committed to the well-being of the nation. Although current naturalization law does not detail the "principles of the Constitution," it expressly denies citizenship to anarchists (anyone "who advocates or teaches . . . opposition to all organized government"); to those who advocate Communism or the establishment of a "totalitarian dictatorship" in the United States; and to anyone who favors "the overthrow by force or violence or other unconstitutional means of the Government of the United States."[154]

A good citizen, then, recognizes the need for government, rejects totalitarianism, and respects the rule of law. The official citizenship oath adds that citizens must have undivided loyalty to the United States and be willing to defend the Constitution and laws against all enemies, including by force of arms if necessary (although federal law allows conscientious objectors to substitute noncombatant service).

Citizens in a political community dedicated to securing rights must respect the rights of others. Rights necessarily imply duties. All Americans, then, have an obligation to allow others to exercise their legitimate rights unless, in so doing, they interfere with the rights of others or the broader public good. Because the United States was founded to secure rights and because the Bill of Rights is such an important feature of the constitutional order, Americans may sometimes forget that all rights impose corresponding duties.

Democracy requires even more. It is not enough to obey the law and respect rights. Citizens in a democracy have an obligation to participate

REUTERS/Rebecca Cook

A Muslim American student holds the U.S. flag during a "Children of the World" student pageant at the Islamic Center of America in Dearborn, Michigan, March 26, 2010.

QUESTION

Should public and private institutions in the United States do more to promote good citizenship? If so, what?

in the political process by, at the very least, responsibly choosing their leaders. If no one voted, democracy would cease. If only a tiny fraction voted, we could hardly say that the people were ruling themselves. Voting means making choices, and responsible choices call for information.

Citizens, therefore, must learn about candidates and issues. There would be no point in having elections if voters failed to explore candidates' qualifications and what they would likely do in office. And because candidates are often incumbents, citizens have some obligation to follow public affairs and make judgments about what government is doing in their name. Seeking out and acting on such knowledge is an essential element of civic virtue.

In American democracy, citizens must be willing to engage in public affairs to promote the widespread enjoyment of rights and the broader public good. No civic obligation is more important than the commitment of citizens and their representatives to reason together about how best to achieve such ends.

Key aspects of American civic culture reinforce these points. In particular, religion, patriotism, and community service combat the tendency to individualism that is unavoidable in a nation devoted to securing individual rights. The motto "E pluribus unum" continues to capture the belief that a genuine American identity and community can be (and has been) forged out of the disparate and sometimes conflicting elements of a large and diverse population.

SUMMARY

- The motto "E pluribus unum" implies that being an American is something more than just a legal status. Citizenship is defined not by blood, ethnicity, or race but, by a commitment to the principles of freedom and democracy. Through their engagement in the deliberative process, Americans contribute to a larger public good.

- Until 1875, the national government placed no restrictions on voluntary immigration. During the following years, it restricted such groups as prostitutes, convicts, paupers, anarchists, and most Asians. In the 1920s, Congress imposed a quota system that limited total immigration and favored those from northern and western Europe. It abolished this system in 1965, after which legal immigration grew to about one million per year.

- In 1857, the Supreme Court ruled that free blacks could not be citizens of the United States. It took the Civil War and the Fourteenth Amendment to overturn this.

- Until the 1920s, Indians who remained on reservations could not be American citizens. Congress changed this in 1924, when it granted citizenship to all Indians born within the territorial limits of the United States.

- The first naturalization laws imposed relatively few requirements for becoming a citizen: good moral character, five years of residency (initially two years), attachment to the principles of the Constitution, and renunciation of any foreign allegiance. These requirements continue to this day. Individual naturalizations were restricted to whites until 1870, when black immigrants were added.

- Race was removed entirely as a condition of naturalization in 1952.

- In recent decades, the federal courts have curbed the power of government to discriminate between citizens and permanent residents in accessing public benefits and obtaining public jobs in state and local governments. The courts have been friendlier to federal laws restricting public benefits to illegal immigrants.

- Current Supreme Court rulings prohibit the government from removing citizenship unless the person intends to give it up. The one exception is denaturalizing those who obtained their original naturalization through fraud or illegality. These rulings and other factors have resulted in growing numbers of Americans with dual citizenship.

- Americans continue to debate whether the nation can successfully assimilate large numbers of diverse immigrants. Some argue that past success promises future success as well, but others worry that the modern emphasis on diversity, multiculturalism, ethnic consciousness, and group rights will undermine true patriotic assimilation.

- Good citizenship is necessary for the success of American deliberative democracy. Americans must be willing to engage in public affairs to promote the widespread enjoyment of rights and the broader public good. Religion, patriotism, and community service help to combat the tendency to individualism that is unavoidable in a nation devoted to securing individual rights.

KEY TERMS

American exceptionalism p. 122
Assimilation p. 97
Birthright citizenship p. 103
Border Patrol p. 102
Bureau of Immigration p. 99
Citizenship oath p. 110
Civic culture p. 115
Civil religion p. 121
Cosmopolitanism p. 124
Deism p. 118
Denaturalization p. 113
Dual citizenship p. 113
E pluribus unum p. 92
Ellis Island p. 99
Enlightenment p. 118
First Great Awakening p. 118
Gentleman's Agreement of 1907 p. 99

Great Seal of the United States p. 92
Green card p. 110
Homeland Security, Department of p. 102
Illegal immigrant p. 102
Individualism p. 115
Know-Nothing Party p. 98
Mayflower Compact p. 118
Melting pot p. 115
Mexican repatriation p. 102
Missouri Compromise of 1820 p. 104
Multiculturalism p. 115
National origins quota system p. 100
Nativism p. 99
Naturalization p. 103
Naturalized citizen p. 96
Patriotism p. 120

Peace Corps p. 126
Pilgrims p. 117
Political culture p. 115
Puritans p. 118
Refugee p. 102
Renunciate p. 112
Right of expatriation p. 112
Seamen's protection certificates p. 104
Second Great Awakening p. 118
Treaty of Guadalupe Hidalgo p. 109
U.S. Citizenship and Immigration Services p. 102
White House Office of Faith-Based and Neighborhood Partnerships p. 125

TEST YOUR KNOWLEDGE

1. Americans tend to believe that they are mainly united by
   a. birth.
   b. ideals.
   c. language.
   d. religion.
   e. geography.

2. Restrictions were first placed on voluntary immigration to the United States
   a. at the Constitutional Convention.
   b. at the adoption of the Bill of Rights.
   c. in 1808.
   d. almost 50 years after the founding.
   e. nearly 100 years after the founding.

3. During the early twentieth century, immigrant population shifted from predominantly northern and western European to
   a. African.
   b. Latin American.
   c. Middle Eastern.
   d. Russian.
   e. southern and eastern European.

4. How does an economic migrant differ from a refugee?
   a. A refugee is given a lower preference for immigration to America than an economic migrant.
   b. A refugee must be fleeing persecution, while an economic migrant is seeking a more prosperous life.
   c. An economic migrant is a refugee who enters the United States without means to support himself or herself.
   d. An economic migrant is fleeing persecution of his or her assets.
   e. Refugees and economic migrants are the same.

5. Under the Constitution, Congress has the power to
   a. apprehend and detain leaders of Indian tribes.
   b. deport Indians not living on official tribal lands.
   c. manage all affairs with Indian tribes.
   d. regulate commerce with Indian tribes.
   e. treat Indian leaders as enemy combatants.

6. Federal policies since the 1930s have
   a. destroyed nearly one-third of all Indian reservations.
   b. disbanded all major tribes.
   c. emphasized a sense of Indian identity.
   d. stressed assimilation.
   e. undercut movements to allow Indians full citizenship.

7. The right of expatriation gives people the right to
   a. become full citizens of the United States.
   b. be deported from their country.
   c. be stripped of citizenship.
   d. renounce citizenship.
   e. take on dual citizenship.

8. Most signers of the Constitution were
   a. atheists.
   b. former preachers.
   c. members of a major Christian denomination.
   d. participants in revival meetings of the First Great Awakening.
   e. strict adherents of the Enlightenment.

9. How did the First and Second Great Awakenings differ?
   a. The Second Great Awakening was distinctly less religious in nature.
   b. The First Great Awakening was distinctly less religious in nature.
   c. The First Great Awakening placed the greatest emphasis on abolition.
   d. The second stressed a personal experience, while the first emphasized social improvement and moral reform.
   e. The first stressed personal experience, while the second emphasized social improvement and moral reform.

10. America ranks _____ when compared to other industrial democracies in charitable giving as a percentage of gross domestic product.
    a. just above average
    b. well below average
    c. right at average
    d. first
    e. last

FURTHER READING

Aleinikoff, Thomas Alexander, David A. Martin, and Hiroshi Motomura. *Immigration and Citizenship: Process and Policy*. 4th ed. St. Paul, MN: West Group, 1998.

Berns, Walter. *Making Patriots*. Chicago: University of Chicago Press, 2001.

Brooks, Arthur C. *Who Really Cares?* New York: Basic Books, 2006.

Dinnerstein, Leonard, and David M. Reimers. *Ethnic Americans: A History of Immigration*. 4th ed. New York: Columbia University Press, 1999.

Easterlin, Richard A., David Ward, William S. Bernard, and Reed Ueda. *Immigration*. Cambridge, MA: Belknap Press of Harvard University Press, 1982.

Fehrenbacher, Don E. *Slavery, Law, and Politics: The Dred Scott Case in Historical Perspective*. Oxford, UK: Oxford University Press, 1981.

Franklin, Frank George. *The Legislative History of Naturalization in the United States: From the Revolutionary War to 1861*. Chicago: University of Chicago Press, 1906.

Kettner, James H. *The Development of American Citizenship, 1608–1870*. Chapel Hill: University of North Carolina Press, 1978.

Jacobsohn, Gary Jeffrey, and Susan Dunn, eds. *Diversity and Citizenship: Rediscovering American Nationhood*. Lanham, MD: Rowman & Littlefield, 1996.

Jones, Jeffrey Owen, and Peter Meyer. *The Pledge: A History of the Pledge of Allegiance*. New York: St. Martin's Press, Thomas Dunne Books, 2010.

Kohut, Andrew, and Bruce Stokes. *America against the World*. New York: Times Books, 2006.

Mann, Arthur. *The One and the Many: Reflections on the American Identity*. Chicago: University of Chicago Press, 1979.

Pickus, Noah M. J., ed. *Immigration and Citizenship in the Twenty-first Century*. Lanham, MD: Rowman & Littlefield, 1998.

Putnam, Robert D. *Bowling Alone: The Collapse and Revival of American Community*. New York: Simon and Schuster, 2000.

Schuck, Peter H. *Citizens, Strangers, and In-Betweens: Essays on Immigration and Citizenship*. Boulder, CO: Westview Press, 2000.

Schuck, Peter H., and Rogers M. Smith. *Citizenship without Consent: Illegal Aliens in the American Polity*. New Haven, CT: Yale University Press, 1985.

Shields, Jon A. *The Democratic Virtues of the Christian Right*. Princeton, NJ: Princeton University Press, 2009.

Smith, Rogers M. *Civic Ideals: Conflicting Visions of Citizenship in U.S. History*. New Haven, CT: Yale University Press, 1997.

WEB SOURCES

American Rhetoric: www.americanrhetoric.com—audio, video, and text of great speeches.

Center for Democracy and Citizenship: www.publicwork.org—a program at Augsburg College in Minneapolis, MN, that promotes the theory and practice of citizenship and democracy.

Center for Immigration Studies: www.cis.org—an independent research organization that favors reducing immigration to the United States.

Civic Life in America: civic.serve.gov—data and analysis from the Corporation for National and Community Service and the National Conference on Citizenship.

Faithful Citizenship: A Catholic Call to Political Responsibility: www.usccb.org/faithfulcitizenship—a site on citizenship of the United States Conference of Catholic Bishops.

Federation for American Immigration Reform: www.fairus.org—a nonprofit organization that works to stop illegal immigration and to reduce legal immigration to about 300,000 per year.

National Council of La Raza: www.nclr.org—the nation's largest Latino advocacy and civil rights organization.

National Immigration Forum: www.immigrationforum.org—a pro-immigration research and advocacy group.

Office of Immigration Statistics: www.dhs.gov/files/statistics/immigration.shtm—official statistics on immigration from the Department of Homeland Security.

Pew Global Attitudes Project: www.pewglobal.org—international survey data.

Religion and the Founding of the American Republic: www.loc.gov/exhibits/religion/—documents posted by the Library of Congress.

U.S. Census Bureau: www.census.gov—links to an extensive collection of census data since 1790.

U.S. Citizenship and Immigration Services: www.uscis.gov—a Web site for the agency in the Department of Homeland Security that adjudicates immigration and naturalization issues and provides services to immigrants.

U.S. English: www.us-english.org—a citizens' organization dedicated to preserving English as the unifying language of the United States.

U.S. Immigration and Customs Enforcement: www.ice.gov/index.htm—a Web site for the agency in the Department of Homeland Security that enforces immigration laws.

Both sides in the abortion controversy ground their arguments in the protections of the U.S. Constitution and exercise their constitutional right to free speech by engaging in public demonstrations. Here, pro-life advocates march in the "Walk for Life West Coast" in January, 2012, in remembrance of the 39th anniversary of *Roe v. Wade*.

Courtesy of Thomas Aquinas College

5

Civil Liberties

OBJECTIVES

After reading this chapter, you should be able to

- Describe the kinds of rights secured in the Constitution of 1787, the Bill of Rights, the Civil War amendments, and subsequent amendments.

- Explain the process and rationale by which the federal Bill of Rights became applicable to state and local governments.

- Contrast the arguments that the Supreme Court has made (a) to allow some government recognition of God or religion and (b) to overturn other acts as an improper establishment of religion.

- Analyze the difference between protected and unprotected speech under the First Amendment, and assess how this distinction applies to political speech.

- Explain how the Court has reacted to government regulation of morality and sexual behavior.

- Appraise the Supreme Court's expansion of the key constitutional rights of criminal defendants in the United States during the last half of the twentieth century.

OBJECTIVES (continued)

- Assess how the federal government has justified restricting civil liberties in wartime and how the Supreme Court has responded to such restrictions, by drawing on examples from American history.

- Evaluate the claim that the history of civil liberties in the United States demonstrates that constitutional rights are not absolute.

INTRODUCTION

As we saw in the opening chapters, those who founded the United States believed that the very purpose of government was to secure the rights and liberties to which all were entitled. Without government, the strong can tyrannize the weak. Yet, government itself can be the oppressor, as King George III showed; and even in democratic systems, as the founders quickly learned, the majority can use government to violate the rights of a minority. Thus, rights and liberties face danger from all sides: from too weak a government, from too strong a government, and from a government that becomes an instrument through which some oppress others. It is little wonder, then, that even in nations formally devoted to securing rights, so many attempts to achieve this end fail.

To complicate matters, the rights of some may conflict with the rights of others or with important governmental responsibilities. Laws that prohibit the press from covering grand jury proceedings give greater weight to a potential criminal defendant's "due process" rights (guaranteed by the Fifth and Fourteenth Amendments) than to freedom of the press (guaranteed by the First Amendment). Similarly, the rules of Congress that bar the press and public from committee meetings that deal with national security secrets restrict press freedom in the name of national defense. In some cases, one person's speech may conflict with the free speech rights of another. In September 2011, for example, 10 Muslim college students were convicted of misdemeanors for frequently interrupting and shouting questions at the Israeli ambassador to the United States as he tried to give a speech at the University of California at Irvine. This case illustrated the principle that one person does not have a free speech right to prevent another from speaking.

The common definition of a right is "something to which one has a just claim" or "something that one may properly claim as due."[1] Rights in this sense depend on a particular notion of justice or morality. To say that everyone has a right to life is to say that it is unjust or immoral for one person to kill another without due cause, such as self-defense. Thus, as we have seen in previous chapters, rights imply duties: if you have a right to something, then everyone else has a duty not to interfere with your exercise of that right without a compelling reason. When all have rights, all also have duties to respect the rights of others. Thus, when Americans learn about their rights, they also learn about their duties.

Rights, then, are more fundamental than wishes. Although we may all have a right to speak freely about political matters, as guaranteed by the First Amendment, we do not, in the absence of sufficient resources, have a right to own a radio or television station so that our voice can reach a mass audience. One of the principal purposes of deliberation in a liberal democracy is defining the nature and scope of the rights of citizens. This means thinking seriously about the purposes of free government, about how to resolve conflicts among rights, and about whether and how government may properly restrict rights in order to secure domestic peace, public order, and national security. While the federal courts play an essential role in defining rights, the public, Congress, and the presidency all make a contribution.

Although it is common to use the terms *rights*, *liberties*, and *freedoms* interchangeably, scholars differentiate between **civil liberties** (the subject of this chapter) and **civil rights**

Civil liberties—personal freedoms that government may not legitimately infringe on, such as practicing one's religion, speaking freely, communicating opinions through print and electronic media, and being secure in one's person and property from arbitrary or oppressive government action.

Civil rights—the rights to live one's life and engage in the political process free from discrimination on such grounds as race, sex, religion, age, or disability.

(the subject of Chapter 6). As these terms are now used, *civil liberties* refers to the personal freedoms on which government may not legitimately infringe. In the United States, they are found mainly in the original Constitution and the Bill of Rights. They include, among others, the freedom to practice one's religion, to speak freely, to communicate opinions through print and electronic media, and to be secure in one's person and property from arbitrary or oppressive government action.

Thus, civil liberties debates focus on when government may curb the freedom of individuals to do as they wish. A thorny issue is distinguishing genuine personal freedoms whose protection is central to liberal democracy from behaviors that might be legitimately forbidden. In the United States, for example, no state allows the possession or consumption of heroin or cocaine or the production and sale of child pornography. Most Americans believe that these are not liberty interests that government ought to respect.

Civil rights refers to the freedom to live one's life and engage in the political process free from discrimination. To secure civil rights, government action may be necessary to prevent some individuals, groups, or organizations from discriminating against others. Civil rights include the rights to travel and use public accommodations without discrimination; to be considered for employment and promotions based on one's individual merits; and to participate in the political process equally with others by, for example, voting and holding office. As we will see in Chapter 6, civil rights debates focus on whether government is doing enough to prevent some from discriminating against others because of characteristics such as race, sex, religion, age, or disability.

In this chapter, we examine the civil liberties of Americans in five areas: religious freedom, freedom of speech and press, morality and sexual behavior, the right to own and carry firearms, and the rights of criminal defendants. We conclude with a brief history of how government has regulated or restricted civil liberties during wartime and how the Supreme Court ruled on such restrictions. We focus throughout the chapter on the tension between government's obligation to secure rights and to meet other important responsibilities.

AMERICANS' CONSTITUTIONAL RIGHTS
MAJOR ISSUE

- What rights does the Constitution guarantee to the people of the United States?

The constitutional rights of Americans are detailed in the Constitution of 1787, in the Bill of Rights added in 1791, and in subsequent amendments. These rights are summarized on page 135.

As we noted in Chapter 2, the framers of the Constitution provided for several key protections in the original document but did not believe that a formal bill of rights was necessary. They tended to view bills of rights as protections that the people secured against monarchs. The Constitution itself, Alexander Hamilton argued in *The Federalist*, would achieve the purposes of a bill of rights by fashioning a responsible and accountable government with limited powers. A well-structured republican government, many founders believed, would more effectively secure the people's rights than mere "parchment barriers" listed in a constitution.

Nonetheless, the proponents of the Constitution, responding to a widespread desire for a bill of rights, came to believe that specifying additional rights in amendments would effectively end opposition to the Constitution and might have other beneficial effects. James Madison, for example, though originally skeptical about the value of a bill of rights, acknowledged that "[t]he political truths declared in that solemn manner acquire by degrees the character of fundamental maxims of free Government." These truths might "become incorporated with the national sentiment" and thereby "counteract the impulses of interest and passion."[2]

Rights Protected by the U.S. Constitution

Constitution of 1787

- Writ of habeas corpus may not be suspended unless public safety requires it during a rebellion or invasion (Art. I, Sec. 9).
- No bill of attainder may be passed by the federal or state governments (Art. I, Sec. 9 and 10).
- No ex post facto law may be passed by the federal or state governments (Art. I, Sec. 9 and 10).
- States may not make anything but gold or silver coin a tender in payment of debts (Art. I, Sec. 10).
- States may not pass a law impairing the obligation of contracts (Art. I, Sec. 10).
- Trial by jury is required in criminal cases (Art. III, Sec. 2).
- No conviction for treason is possible without the testimony of two witnesses to the same act or a confession in open court (Art. III, Sec. 3).
- The citizens in each state shall be entitled to all the privileges and immunities of citizens in the several states (Art. IV, Sec. 2).
- No religious test may be required as a condition for holding federal office (Art. VI).

Bill of Rights

- No establishment of religion (First Amendment)
- Free exercise of religion (First Amendment)
- Freedom of speech (First Amendment)
- Freedom of the press (First Amendment)
- To assemble peaceably and petition the government for redress of grievances (First Amendment)
- To keep and bear arms (Second Amendment)
- No quartering of soldiers in homes in peacetime without the owner's consent, or in wartime unless in a manner prescribed by law (Third Amendment)
- No unreasonable searches and seizures of persons, houses, papers, and effects, and no warrants without probable cause (Fourth Amendment)
- Grand jury indictment required to hold or try someone for a serious crime (Fifth Amendment)
- No one may be tried twice for the same crime (Fifth Amendment).

- No one may be compelled to be a witness against himself in a criminal case (Fifth Amendment).
- No one may be deprived of life, liberty, or property without due process of law (Fifth Amendment).
- Private property may not be taken for public use without just compensation (Fifth Amendment).
- In a criminal prosecution: to a speedy and public trial by an impartial jury from the area where the crime was committed; to be informed of the nature and cause of the accusation; to be confronted with the witnesses against him; to have compulsory process for obtaining witnesses; and to have the assistance of counsel (Sixth Amendment).
- Trial by jury in civil cases for more than $20 (Seventh Amendment).
- No excessive bail or fines or cruel and unusual punishment (Eighth Amendment).
- The people retain other rights not listed (Ninth Amendment).

Subsequent Amendments

- Freedom from slavery (Thirteenth Amendment)
- Citizenship for all those born in the United States and subject to its jurisdiction (Fourteenth Amendment)
- No state may abridge the privileges and immunities of American citizens (Fourteenth Amendment).
- No state may deprive any person of life, liberty, or property without due process of law (Fourteenth Amendment).
- No state may deny any person the equal protection of the laws (Fourteenth Amendment).
- Neither the federal nor state governments may deny anyone the right to vote on account of race, color, or previous condition of servitude (Fifteenth Amendment).
- Neither the federal nor state governments may deny anyone the right to vote on account of sex (Nineteenth Amendment).
- No poll tax may be imposed in any election for federal officials (Twenty-fourth Amendment).
- Neither the federal nor state governments may deny the right to vote to anyone at least 18 years old on account of age (Twenty-sixth Amendment).

Perhaps the best known of the amendments in the Bill of Rights is the First Amendment, which protects five distinct freedoms. The first two are about religion: freedom from an established church and freedom to worship. The next two relate to personal expression and the communication of ideas: freedom of speech and freedom of the press. The fifth guarantees the people's right to peaceably assemble and call on government to redress their grievances.

The Second Amendment, which protects "the right of the people to keep and bear Arms," is among the most controversial in the Bill of Rights. Some argue that it only protects the right of states to arm their National Guard units, as reflected in the opening phrase— "A well regulated Militia, being necessary to the security of a free State." But in two recent landmark cases discussed below, the Supreme Court ruled that the amendment vests a personal right that the federal, state, and local governments may not deny, although they may enforce reasonable regulations. Unlike the Second Amendment, the Third Amendment on quartering troops has never been at issue in a Supreme Court case.

The nation's founding documents—Declaration of Independence, Constitution, and Bill of Rights—are displayed (center of photo) in the Rotunda of the National Archives Building on Pennsylvania Avenue in Washington, DC. They are in a specially designed case that protects the documents from the effects of light and air. At night, and if necessary during an emergency, the documents descend into a fireproof and bombproof vault 20 feet below the floor of the exhibition hall.

Due process of law—procedural protections that the Fifth and Fourteenth amendments require government to follow before depriving anyone of life, liberty, or property. These include at least fair notice and an opportunity to contest charges before a neutral tribunal.

With just a few important exceptions, the Fourth, Fifth, Sixth, and Eighth amendments focus on the rights of those suspected, accused, or convicted of crimes. These amendments supplement the right to trial by jury in criminal cases guaranteed in the original Constitution. They prohibit unreasonable searches and seizures, require grand jury indictments for serious crimes, prohibit trying someone twice for the same crime or compelling a defendant to testify against herself or himself, provide detailed rights regarding criminal trials, stipulate that no one can be deprived of life, liberty, or property "without **due process of law**," and prohibit "cruel and unusual punishments." In the mid-twentieth century, the Supreme Court interpreted these provisions broadly to expand the rights of criminal defendants in far-reaching ways. These were among the most controversial actions of the Court under the leadership of Chief Justice Earl Warren (1953–1969).

The Fifth Amendment also contains provisions that apply outside criminal prosecutions. The due process clause applies not just to the deprivation of "life" and "liberty" (which relate to criminal matters) but also to "property." The courts have used it to restrict government actions affecting property rights. In addition, the Fifth Amendment ends with the "just compensation" clause: "nor shall private property be taken for public use, without just compensation." This means that if the government takes private property for a public purpose, such as a highway, it must pay the owners at least market value for the property. In recent decades, federal courts have grappled with two related issues under the just compensation clause: does it limit the power of government to decrease the value of private property without compensation through environmental regulations, and does it prohibit government from transferring private property to commercial developers even with compensation? The Supreme Court answered "no" to the latter question in 2005, in an important case on property rights from New London, Connecticut.[3]

The Seventh Amendment, which guarantees the right to a jury trial in civil suits for more than $20, was a response to the complaints of many Anti-Federalists that it was wrong to limit jury trials to criminal cases.

One of the fears of those who wrote and supported the original Constitution of 1787 was that listing some rights would imply that others do not exist. Yet Madison and others believed that it was not possible to list all rights. The Ninth Amendment—"The enumeration in the Constitution, of certain rights, shall not be construed to deny or disparage others retained by the people"—made it clear that the rights in the original Constitution and the Bill of Rights were not a complete list. The Tenth Amendment, though considered part of the Bill of Rights, addresses powers reserved to the states and the people, not rights. (See the discussion in Chapter 3 on federalism.)

The engrossed (or handwritten) Bill of Rights lists the 12 amendments that Congress passed and sent to the states for ratification, the first two of which the states did not ratify at the time.

The three great Civil War amendments, ratified between 1865 (the year the war ended) and 1870, were devised to extend full membership in the political community to the 4 million former slaves and the nearly half a million blacks who had been free men and women before the Civil War. The Thirteenth formally ended slavery throughout the nation (thus going beyond Lincoln's Emancipation Proclamation of 1863, which freed only those slaves behind Confederate lines). The Fourteenth overturned the *Dred Scott* decision (see Chapter 4) by extending national and state citizenship to everyone born in the United States and subject to its jurisdiction. It also prohibited the states from denying anyone "due process of law" and "the equal protection of the laws." The Fifteenth prohibited the denial of the vote on the basis of race. As we will see, the due process clause of the Fourteenth Amendment became quite important in the twentieth century as the provision through which most of the guarantees in the Bill of Rights, written to restrict the federal government, became applicable to the states.

In the years since the Fifteenth Amendment was added, all amendments defining or securing rights except for the repeal of prohibition (Twenty-first) have dealt with voting. The Nineteenth Amendment (1920) extended the right to vote to women in all elections; the Twenty-fourth Amendment (1964) prohibited poll taxes in federal elections; and the Twenty-sixth Amendment (1971) extended the right to vote to those at least 18 years old in all elections. In addition, the Twenty-third Amendment, ratified in 1961, gave the District of Columbia three electoral votes in presidential elections, with the electors to be chosen "as the Congress may direct." And just as the state legislators in all the states now allow the people to vote for electors, Congress did the same for the District of Columbia.

In this and the next chapter, we address in more detail many of the issues and controversies that have arisen over the interpretation of these constitutional rights, especially how courts and policymakers have had to balance personal liberties against public goods such as personal safety or public order. Striking this balance is one of the principal tasks of deliberation in a liberal democracy.

As we will see, over the past century federal courts have expanded personal liberties and contracted governmental power across a wide range of issues, including government recognition of God or religion, the free exercise of religion, the regulation of political speech (including symbolic speech), limits on pornography and censorship, and the rights of criminal defendants. In the process, the key deliberations over civil liberties have shifted from elected legislators and executives to federal judges. We begin by detailing how the provisions of the Bill of Rights, written to restrict federal power, became applicable to state and local governments.

THE NATIONALIZATION OF THE BILL OF RIGHTS
MAJOR ISSUE

- How did the Bill of Rights, which originally limited only the federal government, come to limit the states as well?

Until the early twentieth century, the Bill of Rights had little direct impact in American government and politics. When the 10 amendments were ratified in 1791 by the necessary three-fourths of the states and became part of the Constitution, there was no public celebration. As one scholar notes, "The Bill of Rights slipped quietly into the Constitution and passed from sight and public consciousness."[4] For more than a century, few court cases challenged a government action as violating the Bill of Rights, and not once before 1925 did the Supreme Court overturn an act of Congress as contrary to the First Amendment.[5]

One reason that the federal Bill of Rights is now so prominent is that the Supreme Court used it to strike down numerous state laws throughout the twentieth century. Controversial decisions prohibiting school prayer, expanding the rights of criminal defendants, and providing abortion rights all overturned laws or practices in the 50 states. Yet, during the first century under the Constitution, the federal courts held that the protections in the Bill of Rights did not apply against state or local governments. Supreme Court interpretations of the Fourteenth Amendment, ratified in 1868, eventually applied nearly all of the Bill of Rights to state actions.

Barron v. Baltimore

The question of whether the federal Bill of Rights limited state and local governments first arose in 1833 when a wharf owner in Baltimore sued the city for economic damages he suffered when city projects lowered the water level around his wharfs. He claimed that this violated the Fifth Amendment's requirement that "just compensation" be paid when private property is taken for public use.

Writing for a unanimous Court in *Barron v. Baltimore*, Chief Justice John Marshall held that the Bill of Rights applied only to the national government. The Constitution of 1787 had specified, in Article I, Section 10, what restrictions applied to the states, including no bills of attainder, ex post facto laws, and laws impairing the obligation of contracts. Had the authors of the Bill of Rights intended to restrict state governments, Marshall wrote, they would have done so "in direct words" as they did in the Constitution itself.[6] Marshall's ruling, however, did not prevent aggrieved citizens from seeking redress in state courts for violations of their rights, especially in those states that had their own bill of rights.

The Incorporation Doctrine

Thirty-five years after the Supreme Court ruled in *Barron v. Baltimore*, the Fourteenth Amendment became part of the U.S. Constitution. As we have seen, one of its provisions required the states to provide all persons due process of law before depriving them of life, liberty, or property. What exactly does "due process" require of the states?

Because this language is identical to that in the Fifth Amendment, the Court initially took the view that "due process" referred to procedural safeguards such as advance notice when government acts to deprive individuals of life, liberty, or property and an opportunity to have cases decided before a neutral tribunal. It was not thought that "due process" in the Fifth Amendment referred to the other substantive protections in the Bill of Rights, such as religious liberty, freedom of speech and press, or protection against unreasonable searches and seizures. If "due process" meant the same in the Fourteenth Amendment as in the Fifth, then it seemed to include just basic procedural protections.

In 1897, however, the Supreme Court ruled that the Fifth Amendment prohibition on the taking of private property for public use without just compensation applied to the states as part of the due process guarantee of the Fourteenth Amendment.[7] Then, in 1925, the Court for the first time held that due process required the states to respect the freedom of speech guaranteed in the First Amendment.[8] Over the following decades, the Court incorporated more and more of the specific provisions of the Bill of Rights against the states. This is referred to both as the **incorporation doctrine** and as the **nationalization of the Bill of Rights**. As more rights were incorporated, the federal courts acquired more power to strike down state laws, thereby shifting the key deliberations from state and local elected officials to federal judges.

As this process unfolded, the Supreme Court sought to spell out standards for determining which of the rights in the federal Bill of Rights also applied to the states. In *Palko v. Connecticut* in 1937, Justice Benjamin Cardozo, writing for the majority, maintained that some rights, such as freedom of speech and of the press, were so fundamental that they were "implicit in the concept of ordered liberty." States may not infringe "fundamental principles of liberty and justice which lie at the base of all our civil and political institutions."[9] This doctrine, however, did not save Palko, who had been convicted in state court of murder after two trials for the same crime. The protection against double jeopardy in the Fifth Amendment, the Court maintained, was not a fundamental right. Three decades later, the

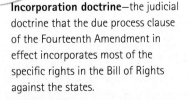

Incorporation doctrine—the judicial doctrine that the due process clause of the Fourteenth Amendment in effect incorporates most of the specific rights in the Bill of Rights against the states.

Nationalization of the Bill of Rights—refers to the incorporation of the Bill of Rights against the states as a result of Supreme Court decisions in the twentieth century.

Supreme Court overruled itself, holding that due process did include the protection against double jeopardy.[10]

As the Court expanded the meaning of due process, some members argued that the entire Bill of Rights applied to the states. Yet the Court never formally accepted the "total incorporation" view. Although incorporation was nearly complete by the mid– to late twentieth century, a few provisions were excepted, including the Fifth Amendment requirement of grand jury indictments for serious crimes and the Seventh Amendment guarantee of jury trials in civil cases. The Second Amendment right to keep and bear arms was one of those exceptions until the Court ruled in 2010 that it also applied to the states. The doctrine that much, but not all, of the Bill of Rights applies to the states is called **selective incorporation**.

Much of the following discussion is about court cases. As we will see, key civil liberties controversies in the United States are increasingly decided by courts, especially the Supreme Court, rather than by elected officials. Of course, the justices themselves often disagree as to how to strike the balance between the rights asserted by individuals and government's responsibility to secure domestic peace, public order, and national security. Although it is impossible here to analyze cases in great detail, we frequently summarize the arguments from both sides to highlight the issues that focused the Court's deliberations.

Selective incorporation—the doctrine that much, but not all, of the Bill of Rights applies to the states.

RELIGIOUS FREEDOM

MAJOR ISSUES

- What does it mean to say that the First Amendment created a "wall of separation" between church and state?
- May government ever regulate or prohibit behavior that some claim is required or justified by their religion?

The original Constitution explicitly mentioned religion only once, forbidding a "religious Test" as a qualification for federal office (Article VI). Yet it implicitly referred to religion, or belief in God, in (a) its requirements for oaths of office (oaths were understood to be promises before God), (b) its provision giving the president 10 days to sign a bill passed by Congress, "Sundays excepted" (referring to the Christian Sabbath), and (c) its conclusion that it was written "in the Year of our Lord one thousand seven hundred and Eighty seven." It also showed respect for the diversity of religious beliefs in the new nation by allowing officeholders to "affirm," or make an "affirmation," rather than swear an oath. As we noted in Chapter 2, Quakers thought it was sinful to swear oaths to God but were willing to make affirmations with the same force.[11]

The authors of the Bill of Rights added new language on the federal government's relationship to religion. The first words of the First Amendment provide that "Congress shall make no law respecting an establishment of religion, or prohibiting the free exercise thereof." These are two separate stipulations: Congress may not, at the very least, establish a national religion (the **establishment clause**); and Congress may not prohibit Americans from freely practicing their religion (the **free exercise clause**).

These words on religion grew out of arguments that had been under way for years. In the mid-1780s, Virginia debated government support for Christian religious instruction. James Madison, later the main author of the First Amendment, successfully fought the proposal with a document he submitted to the state legislature, commonly called the *Memorial and Remonstrance*. Madison argued that established churches were bad for Christianity by causing "pride and indolence in the Clergy, ignorance and servility in the laity, in both, superstition, bigotry and persecution."[12] Public support for religious instruction also violated individual conscience. The duty that men and women owe their Creator, Madison insisted, is a deeply personal matter that should be exempt from government control.

Establishment clause—provision of the First Amendment that prohibits Congress from making a law "respecting an establishment of religion."

Free exercise clause—provision of the First Amendment that prohibits Congress from "prohibiting the free exercise" of religion.

Memorial and Remonstrance—document written by James Madison in 1785 opposing the use of tax money to support Christian religious instruction and making the case for freedom of religion.

Wall of Separation

Although Thomas Jefferson had no direct hand in the establishment clause (he was secretary of state when it was written and ratified), history has linked him to it because of an 1802 letter he wrote while president to the Baptist Association of Danbury, Connecticut. The First Amendment, he famously said, built "a **wall of separation** between Church & State."[13] In 1879, the Supreme Court called the phrase "almost an authoritative declaration of the scope and effect of the amendment,"[14] and it is now so familiar that many Americans mistakenly believe that it is part of the Constitution itself.

Jefferson's metaphor is more complex than it seems. For one thing, the First Amendment did not build a "wall of separation" between church and the *state* governments, for, as we have seen, the Bill of Rights originally restricted only the federal government. In Jefferson's time, several states gave public support to religion, and some state constitutions required religious belief to hold office. For example, the Massachusetts Constitution of 1780 maintained that "good order" depends on "piety, religion, and morality." It required local governments to provide for "the public worship of God" and support "Protestant teachers of piety, religion, and morality."[15] And it required all elected officials to take an oath affirming their belief in the truth of Christianity.[16] So, not all political leaders at the time of the American founding believed there should be a wall between church and all government authority.[17]

Another problem with Jefferson's metaphor is that it does not tell us how high the wall should be. Although Jefferson did not think he should issue religious proclamations as president, other early presidents had no such qualms. In his first year in office, President George Washington, at the behest of Congress, called for "a day of public thanksgiving and prayer" so that the American people could fulfill their duty "to acknowledge the providence of Almighty God, to obey his will, to be grateful for his benefits, and humbly to implore his protection and favor."[18] Later, at the start of the War of 1812, President Madison proclaimed a day "of rendering the Sovereign of the Universe and the Benefactor of Mankind the public homage due to His holy attributes."[19]

For generations, Americans tended to think that the wall between church and state was low, so official statements favored religion in ways that would be controversial today. In an 1892 case, the Supreme Court said, "This is a Christian nation."[20] In 1947, President Harry Truman wrote Pope Pius XII: "Your Holiness, this is a Christian Nation. More than a half century ago that declaration was written into the decrees of the highest court in this land." Truman praised the American colonists who "declared their faith in the Christian religion and made ample provision for its practice and for its support."[21]

That same year, in *Everson v. Board of Education*, the Supreme Court upheld a New Jersey law that authorized local governments to reimburse parents for the cost of transporting their children to parochial schools. In so doing, however, it held that neither a state nor the federal government could "aid one religion, aid all religions, or prefer one religion over another." "The First Amendment," it concluded, "has erected a wall between church and state. That wall must be kept high and impregnable. We could not approve the slightest breach"[22] (see Figure 5-1).

Two Representations of Jefferson's "Wall of Separation between Church and State"

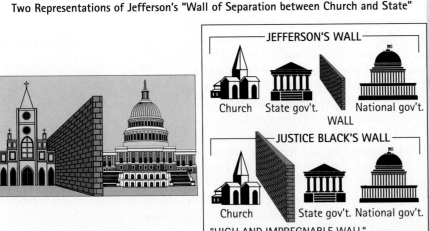

FIGURE 5-1 The first image, from an atheist group, emphasizes the absolute separation between church and state. The second, from a Christian group, conveys three messages: (1) that Jefferson's wall was not intended to separate the state government from the church or religion, but just the federal government; (2) that in the *Everson* case (1947), Supreme Court justice Hugo Black incorrectly placed the wall between all government and the church or religion; and (3) that Black's wall is higher and more impregnable than Jefferson's. SOURCE: (Left) Copyright © 2009 by American Atheists. Reprinted with permission. (Right) "'Freedom Rally' to Dispel Separation Myth" by Allie Martin, April 17, 2006, www.headlines.agapepress.org/archive/4/172006c.asp. Copyright © 2008 Agape Press—All Rights Reserved. Reprinted with permission.

Five years later, in 1952, the Supreme Court, holding that "we are a religious people whose institutions presuppose a Supreme Being," upheld release time for public school students to attend religious classes or services. By encouraging religious instruction, the majority explained, government "respects the religious nature of our people and accommodates the public service to their spiritual needs." This is in "the best of our traditions."[23]

The Wall Gets Higher

In the 1960s, the federal judiciary began to apply tougher standards to relations between religion and government. In the 1962 case of *Engel v. Vitale*, the Supreme Court struck down a nondenominational prayer—"Almighty God, we acknowledge our dependence upon Thee, and we beg Thy blessings upon us, our parents, our teachers and our Country"—that the New York State Board of Regents had written for classroom recitation in public schools.[24] The following year, in *Abington School District v. Schempp*, it ruled against requirements that school days begin with Bible readings and the Lord's Prayer.[25]

In 1971, in *Lemon v. Kurtzman*, the Court elaborated a three-part rule of thumb to govern establishment clause cases. Legal scholars call it simply the **Lemon test**. The Court held that a law that appears to aid or endorse religion may withstand challenge only if

- it has a secular legislative purpose,
- its main effect neither advances nor inhibits religion, and
- it does not foster an excessive government entanglement with religion.[26]

The test is easy to describe but hard to apply, and the Court has not used it in all cases involving religion and state. Its overall effect, however, has been to restrict official recognition of God or religion.

In 1992, for example, the Court said, in *Lee v. Weisman*, that a public middle school's graduation ceremony should not include prayers by clergy "because the State has in every practical sense compelled attendance and participation in an explicit religious exercise at an event of singular importance to every student."[27] Then, eight years later, in *Santa Fe Independent School District v. Doe*, the Court overturned a school district policy in Santa Fe, Texas, that allowed public high school students to vote whether to have a student message or prayer before varsity football games and then, if this passed, to vote on the student who would deliver it.

Writing for the majority in the *Santa Fe* case, Justice John Paul Stevens held that "the delivery of a pregame prayer has the improper effect of coercing those present to participate in an act of religious worship." Chief Justice William Rehnquist, writing in dissent, accused the majority of distorting the Court's precedents and of showing "hostility to all things religious in public life." He then pointed out that the same Congress that passed the Bill of Rights requested that President Washington issue a call for a national day of thanksgiving to God.[28]

What Does the Wall Allow?

Despite these decisions prohibiting any official endorsement of religion in public schools, the Court ruled in 1995 that the University of Virginia (a public institution) could not deny a student-run religious newspaper financial support from mandatory student fees. Then, in 2001, it said that a public school had to allow a private Christian group to hold after-hours meetings in classrooms if it made such facilities available to other groups.[29] Both cases involved the establishment clause as well as First Amendment free speech issues. In an important case in 2002 (discussed in Chapters 5 and 16), the Court allowed the state of Ohio to provide tuition vouchers to high school–age students in Cleveland that could be used at religiously affiliated private schools.[30]

Yet in 2010, the Court ruled in a highly contested 5–4 decision that the Hastings College of Law (part of the University of California) could require that all officially recognized student groups open their membership to "all-comers." This meant that a small group of Christian law students, which required that its members sign a statement of faith and conduct their lives accordingly, could not gain official recognition. The majority held that the school's policy was "a reasonable, viewpoint-neutral condition on access to the

Lemon test—the legal test promulgated by the Supreme Court in 1971 that held that a law that raises establishment clause issues may withstand challenge only if

- it has a secular legislative purpose,
- its main effect neither advances nor inhibits religion, and
- it does not foster an excessive government entanglement with religion.

student-organization forum." The dissenters countered that the "all-comers" policy was apparently created specifically to justify denying official recognition to the Christian group and that the school's policy unconstitutionally discriminated against views that were unpopular with those who ran the school.[31]

In 2012, a similar controversy arose at Vanderbilt University in Tennessee when the administration refused official recognition to several religious groups because these groups limited membership on religious grounds. The Vanderbilt case, however, did not raise constitutional issues because, unlike Hastings Law School, it is a private university. Generally, private institutions may limit speech or religious practice as long as they do not violate federal or state antidiscrimination laws.

A federal appeals court in San Francisco attracted widespread public attention in 2002 when it ruled that the phrase "under God" in the Pledge of Allegiance was an unconstitutional establishment of religion when recited in public schools. In 2004, the U.S. Supreme Court reversed the decision on technical grounds.[32] Six years later the case was back before the federal appeals court. This time it ruled that there was no violation of the establishment clause.

In what situations, then, may government constitutionally recognize or promote belief in God? The box below details the many ways in which American government seems to endorse belief in God (some of these were noted in Chapter 4). Although the Supreme Court has insisted that public schools, with their audience of young, impressionable minds, not endorse or promote belief in God, it has not extended this prohibition to all types of government activity.

Moreover, as legal scholar Stephen Carter points out, the establishment clause "is designed to limit what the state can do, not what the church can do."[33] Nothing in the Constitution prohibits citizens, such as the abolitionists in the nineteenth century and civil rights advocates in the twentieth, from basing political decisions on religious principles. As we saw in Chapter 4, American history is filled with examples of Americans pushing for social change based on deeply felt religious conviction.

How American Government Seems to Endorse Belief in God

- Both the House of Representatives and Senate employ chaplains who open each legislative session with a prayer.
- The Armed Forces employ chaplains (from a variety of faiths) to meet the religious needs of service men and women.
- The Supreme Court opens each session with an appeal to the Almighty: "God save the United States and this Honorable Court."
- Two federal holidays have religious elements. Christmas celebrates the birth of Christ, and Thanksgiving, as we have seen, is a day set aside to give thanks to God for all blessings. Since President Lincoln revived the practice of presidents issuing Thanksgiving Day proclamations in 1863, every president has done so each November.
- By Act of Congress during the Civil War, "In God we trust" began appearing on U.S. coins in 1864. It began to appear on paper currency in 1957. In 1956, Congress passed a joint resolution, signed by President Dwight Eisenhower, that made "In God we trust" the national motto.
- The Great Seal of the United States, adopted in 1782, shows on its reverse side a 13-step pyramid watched over by an eye under the Latin phrase "Annuit Coeptis." The State Department, the official custodian of the seal, translates this as "He [God] has favored our undertakings." As the final designer of the seal, Secretary of Congress Charles Thomson, explained in 1782, "The Pyramid signifies Strength and Duration: The eye over it and the

Motto allude to the many signal interpositions of providence in favour of the American cause."[36] (The seal, which is placed on presidential proclamations and other official documents such as treaties, appears also on the back of the $1 bill.)

- The Pledge of Allegiance, first officially sanctioned by Congress in 1942, was amended in 1954 by adding the words "under God."
- In 1931, Congress made Francis Scott Key's "The Star-Spangled Banner," written in 1814, the national anthem. Its fourth verse, though rarely heard, includes the lines "Praise the Power that hath made and preserved us a nation" and "And this be our motto: 'In God is our trust.'"
- Federal law includes the phrase "So help me God" at the end of the oaths required to be taken by elected and appointed officers of the government. The presidential oath, the only one spelled out in the Constitution, does not include the phrase; but beginning with Washington, all presidents have added it on their own.
- Public officials frequently deliver overtly religious messages. President Obama, for example, hosted an Easter Prayer Breakfast at the White House in April 2011 at which he celebrated "the resurrection of our savior, Jesus Christ" who "took on the sins of the world" and "extended to us that unfathomable gift of grace and salvation through his death and resurrection."[37]

In 2000, a federal court articulated this principle when loggers sued the U.S. Forest Service and two environmental groups. The loggers reasoned that limits on timber sales resulted from pressure by religiously motivated environmentalists and so were an establishment of religion. The judge dismissed the suit, saying that the right to petition is not "restricted to citizens whose motivation is only secular." The judge added, "Freedom of belief is not a passive right: citizens are not limited to merely sitting idly thinking about their political, moral, and religious beliefs; democracy is founded upon them acting upon those beliefs in efforts to effect change."[34]

Free Exercise of Religion

The First Amendment stipulates that Congress may not prohibit "the free exercise" of religion. At the beginning, everyone understood that this statement prevented the federal government from interfering with religious belief and worship. The problem comes when religious belief results in behaviors that violate laws of general applicability.

The first such case to reach the Supreme Court was *Reynolds v. U.S.* in 1879. Convicted of polygamy in the federal territory of Utah in violation of federal law, George Reynolds argued that he had a religious duty, as a member of the Church of Jesus Christ of Latter-day Saints (Mormon Church), to practice polygamy. In upholding Reynolds's conviction, the Court sharply distinguished belief from actions.[35] Religious people may believe what they wish, but that belief does not exempt them from general laws that regulate personal behavior.

According to the U.S. Department of State's description of the Great Seal, "The pyramid signifies strength and duration: The eye over it and the motto, *Annuit Coeptis* (He [God] has favored our undertakings), allude to the many interventions of Providence in favor of the American cause. The date underneath is that of the Declaration of Independence, and the words under it, *Novus Ordo Seclorum* (A new order of the ages), signify the beginning of the new American era in 1776."

Following this belief–conduct distinction, the Court in the twentieth century upheld mandatory vaccination laws over religious objections (1905); allowed the military to prohibit an Orthodox Jewish psychologist from wearing a yarmulke while in uniform on duty at a military hospital (1986); and upheld the right of the state of Oregon to deny unemployment benefits to individuals fired for using peyote, despite their claim that they used this illegal drug in rituals in the Native American Church (1990).

Yet in other cases, the Court used a balancing test that compared the importance of the government policy to the burden placed on religiously motivated conduct. In 1963, for example, the Court overruled a decision of the South Carolina government that denied a Seventh-Day Adventist unemployment compensation after she quit one job and refused others that required her to work on Saturday, her Sabbath. Nine years later, the Court held that Wisconsin's interest in compelling all children to attend school until age 16 was outweighed by the beliefs of the Amish people that school attendance beyond the eighth grade— that is, into high school—"was contrary to the Amish religion and way of life. . . . [and would] endanger their own salvation and that of their children."[38] In addition, in 1993, the Court overturned an ordinance of the city of Hialeah, Florida, that prohibited the adherents of the Santeria religion from engaging in animal sacrifice during worship ceremonies.

The Court's 1990 decision that upheld Oregon's laws and regulations against the use of peyote (*Employment Division v. Smith*) was particularly controversial because it rejected the balancing test of recent cases in favor of the belief–conduct distinction first enunciated in *Reynolds v. U.S.* in 1879. Justice Antonin Scalia, writing for the majority, insisted that an individual's religious beliefs alone could not "excuse him from compliance with an otherwise valid law prohibiting conduct that the State is free to regulate."[39]

Congress responded to this controversial ruling in 1993 by passing the Religious Freedom Restoration Act (RFRA). The law prohibited government from "substantially burden[ing] a person's exercise of religion even if the burden results from a rule of general

FOCUS
QUESTION

Is a useful civic purpose served by the many ways in which the national government endorses belief in God, such as the national motto, "In God we trust?" Would the nation be better served if all such references to God by government were eliminated, including overtly religious statements by public officials at government-sponsored events?

©Stefano Bianchetti/Corbis

applicability." Only if the burden furthered "a compelling governmental interest" using "the least restrictive means" could it be justified.[40]

In 1997, the Court struck down RFRA as applied to the states, ruling that Congress could not through legislation expand the constitutional right to free exercise of religion. Then, in 2006, it upheld RFRA as applied to the federal government when it overturned the interdiction by U.S. Customs agents of 30 gallons of tea from the Amazon rain forest that contained a hallucinogen that was illegal under federal law. The tea was headed for the New Mexican branch of a Brazilian church that used the tea in religious services. A lower federal court had ruled that the government had not met its burden under RFRA of showing a compelling interest in preventing the importation of the tea. The Supreme Court agreed.[41]

The Supreme Court also overruled the executive branch early in 2012 when it unanimously held that employment discrimination laws could not interfere with the right of a religious organization—here a Lutheran elementary school in Michigan—to hire and fire ministers, even if these "called teachers" spent most of their time on nonreligious instruction.[42] Also, controversy flared when the Obama administration issued a rule in 2012 that required religiously affiliated organizations, such as hospitals and schools, to cover in their health insurance plans birth control drugs and sterilization operations at no additional cost. The American Catholic bishops sharply criticized the rule for requiring religious organizations to fund acts they considered immoral (including the provision of some drugs that may cause an abortion). The rule, they said, violated their First Amendment guarantee to the "free exercise" of religion. A revised plan that placed the funding burden on the insurance companies satisfied some heads of Catholic health care organizations, but not the bishops. This controversy highlighted an important question: Is the "free exercise of religion" broader than just "freedom of worship"? If so, what activities does it protect beyond the freedom of Americans to worship as they please in their homes, churches, synagogues, and mosques?

After prohibiting Congress from establishing a religion or prohibiting its free exercise, the First Amendment guarantees the rights to freedom of speech and press.

FREEDOM OF SPEECH AND PRESS

MAJOR ISSUES

- May government ever restrict political speech in peacetime?
- Does "symbolic speech" have the same protections as actual speech?
- What kinds of speech, according to the Supreme Court, are not protected by the First Amendment?

The First Amendment says, in part, that "Congress shall make no law . . . abridging the freedom of speech, or of the press." A few jurists have taken the view that this means *absolutely no law*, but most members of the Supreme Court who have addressed the issue have maintained that the protections of the First Amendment must be balanced against the important responsibilities of federal, state, and local governments.

Protected and Unprotected Speech

Prior restraint—prohibiting the publication of materials because of their harmful effects. Under English common law, government could not prevent the publication of materials but could punish the publisher after the fact.

The founders were not of one mind on the meaning of the First Amendment. Some believed that the prohibition on Congress "abridging the freedom of speech, or of the press" referred to existing English common law. By that standard, government could not prevent publications—called **prior restraint**—but could punish the publisher or speaker after the fact. Influential British jurist William Blackstone had written that "[e]very freeman has an undoubted right to lay what sentiments he pleases before the public: . . . but if he publishes what is improper, mischievous, or illegal, he must take the consequence of his own temerity."[43]

Other founders, such as Thomas Jefferson, read the First Amendment as barring all speech and press restrictions by the federal government, but not by the states. In 1925, however, the Supreme Court ruled that the speech and press protections of the First Amendment applied to the states as well. From then on, all public authorities in the United States (including local governments, which are the legal creations of their state governments) had to respect freedom of speech and the press.

What, then, is **protected speech** and what is **unprotected speech** under the First Amendment? The Supreme Court has consistently held that some kinds of speech fall outside the amendment's protections. Justice Oliver Wendell Holmes famously argued in *Schenck v. United States* (1919) that no one had a right falsely to shout "Fire!" in a theater "causing a panic."[44] It is, after all, an essential purpose of government to protect the people's health and safety.

Later, in *Chaplinsky v. New Hampshire* (1942), the Court upheld the conviction of a man who, in the midst of a public disturbance on the streets of Rochester, New Hampshire, denounced the city marshall as "a God damned racketeer" and "a damned Fascist." Insisting that "the right of free speech is not absolute," a unanimous Court held that "[t]here are certain well-defined and narrowly limited classes of speech, the prevention and punishment of which has never been thought to raise any Constitutional problem. These include the lewd and obscene, the profane, the libelous, and the insulting or 'fighting' words—those which by their very utterance inflict injury or tend to incite an immediate breach of the peace." "**Fighting words**" in particular form "no essential part of any exposition of ideas," and any possible social value they might have "is clearly outweighed by the social interest in order and morality."[45] The expression of ideas, the Court argued, and especially of political ideas, most emphatically falls under the protection of the First Amendment.

The Regulation of Political Speech

The very purpose of the First Amendment was to promote community-wide deliberation about public affairs. Does this mean, then, that government may never restrict political speech? As we will see later in the chapter, in three important cases from World War I, the Supreme Court upheld the authority of the federal government to restrict political speech in wartime. As a unanimous Court maintained in one of those cases: "When a nation is at war many things that might be said in time of peace are such a hindrance to its effort that their utterance will not be endured so long as men fight and that no Court could regard them as protected by any constitutional right." The Court held that the key issue was whether the circumstances are such that the words "create a clear and present danger that they will bring about the substantive evils that Congress has a right to prevent."[46] This is called the **clear and present danger test**.

What, then, about restricting political speech in peacetime? Is this ever justified? The Court addressed this issue in *Gitlow v. New York* in 1925. This was the case in which the Court first ruled that the First Amendment applied to the states. Here a 7–2 majority upheld the conviction of a Socialist for violating the New York Criminal Anarchy Law of 1902 by writing, publishing, and distributing a pamphlet that urged "revolutionary mass action" to promote the Communist Revolution. The majority held that "a State may penalize utterances which openly advocate the overthrow of the representative and constitutional form of government of the United States and the several States, by violence or other unlawful means." In dissent, Justice Holmes denied that the activities in question created a "present danger of an attempt to overthrow the government by force." Holmes admitted that the manifesto "was an incitement," but, he argued, "[e]very idea is an incitement."[47]

A few years later (1931), however, the Court struck down an attempt by a county attorney in Minnesota to stop the publication of "malicious, scandalous and defamatory articles" on political corruption by a Minneapolis magazine. Such prior restraint, the majority argued, strikes at the core of the freedom of the press. Only in exceptional cases might prior restraint be permitted, such as those involving wartime military secrets, obscene publications, and **direct incitements** to violence.[48]

Protected speech—speech that government may not prohibit or punish under the First Amendment guarantee of "freedom of speech."

Unprotected speech—speech that the government may prohibit or punish because it is not included in the First Amendment guarantee of "freedom of speech," such as obscenity, libelous speech, and "fighting words."

Fighting words—words that, according to the Supreme Court (1942), "tend to incite an immediate breach of the peace" and thus are not protected by the First Amendment.

Clear and present danger test—a doctrine promulgated by the Supreme Court in 1919, according to which the government may restrict speech when the words "create a clear and present danger that they will bring about the substantive evils that Congress has a right to prevent."

Direct incitement test—a doctrine promulgated by the Supreme Court in the twentieth century, according to which the government may suppress political speech that directly incites violence, but not the "advocacy of forcible overthrow as an abstract doctrine."

In 1951, the Court returned to the issue it first addressed in *Gitlow* regarding how far the government could go in suppressing the advocacy of a Communist revolution in the United States. Fearful of Communist subversion, Congress had passed the Alien Registration Act in 1940, commonly called the Smith Act after its author, Representative Howard W. Smith (D-VA). The act had made it illegal for anyone "to knowingly or willfully advocate, abet, advise, or teach the duty, necessity, desirability, or propriety of overthrowing or destroying any government in the United States by force or violence."[49]

In 1948, the Department of Justice obtained indictments of the 11 members of the governing board of the Communist Party in the United States under the Smith Act. After a nine-month trial, a jury convicted them all. They appealed on the grounds that their conviction violated the free speech protection of the First Amendment.

In *Dennis v. United States*, the Court upheld by a 6–2 vote the constitutionality of the Smith Act. The plurality opinion (signed by four of the justices) reaffirmed the clear and present danger test but insisted that these words "cannot mean that before the Government may act, it must wait until the putsch is about to be executed, the plans have been laid and the signal is awaited." The defendants had organized the Communist Party to promote the overthrow of the lawful government of the United States and thus "were properly and constitutionally convicted."[50]

This was a time of great concern about the Soviet and Communist threat. In the few short years between 1948 and 1950, the Soviet Union blockaded Berlin; China fell to Communism; the Soviet Union successfully tested an atomic bomb; atomic physicist Klaus Fuchs confessed to being an agent for the Soviet Union; Alger Hiss, a high-ranking State Department official, was convicted of perjury for denying before a congressional committee that he had spied for the Soviet Union; and Communist North Korea invaded U.S. ally South Korea. From 1950 to 1954, Senator Joseph McCarthy (R-WI) dominated headlines with unsupported charges that hundreds of Communists were serving in the State Department and elsewhere in the federal government. Censured in 1954 by his Senate colleagues (67–22) for bringing the Senate "into dishonor and disrepute," McCarthy quickly lost his influence and died of an alcohol-related illness in 1957. (But his name lives on in the pejorative term *McCarthyism*, which refers to the public and unjustified smearing of others for disloyalty.)

Just six years after *Dennis*, the Court made it harder to prosecute Communist Party leaders. In *Yates v. United States* (1957), it overturned the conviction of 14 Communist Party leaders by drawing a sharp distinction between "advocacy of forcible overthrow as an abstract doctrine" and "advocacy of action to that end."[51] The Smith Act, it held, had prohibited only advocating action to overthrow the government, not the abstract doctrine itself. On this, the trial judge had improperly instructed the jury. This decision effectively ended prosecutions under the Smith Act, which had resulted in indictments of 141 persons and prison sentences for 29.

Finally, in *Brandenburg v. Ohio* (1969), the Court further limited the grounds on which government could restrict speech that advocates violence. The state of Ohio had convicted a Ku Klux Klan leader for advocating violence. In unanimously overturning the conviction, the Supreme Court ruled that a state may only prohibit speech that advocates violence or lawlessness if "such advocacy is directed to inciting or producing imminent lawless action and is likely to incite or produce such action."[52] As a result of these decisions—*Brandenburg* remains the governing case—nearly all political speech short of direct incitement to lawless action is now protected by the First Amendment.

The Court reaffirmed its broad understanding of political speech in 2011 when it overturned a civil court's ruling against a small religious group that picketed the funeral of a soldier killed in Iraq. The group, which believes that God hates the United States because it tolerates homosexuality, particularly in the military, had picketed hundreds of military funerals with offensive signs such as "Thank God for Dead Soldiers" and "Fags Doom Nations." A civil jury had awarded the dead soldier's father millions of dollars in damages for the intentional infliction of emotional harm. Ruling 8–1, the Court held that First Amendment protections applied because the demonstration was peaceful, took place on public land, and addressed "broad issues of interest to society at large." Quoting an earlier flag burning case, the Court emphasized that "the government may not prohibit the expression

FOCUS QUESTION

Should the federal government have the authority to prevent Americans from using the Internet to endorse the goals and means of al Qaeda and to call on others to do the same? Is such speech protected by the First Amendment?

of an idea simply because society finds the idea itself offensive or disagreeable." Under this principle of "content neutrality," the government may not pick and choose which messages to allow. In his lone dissent, Justice Samuel Alito insisted that "[o]ur profound national commitment to free and open debate is not a license for the vicious verbal assault that occurred in this case." Family members in this situation have a right to "a few hours of peace without harassment" and respecting that right "does not undermine public debate."[53]

"Symbolic Speech" and "Expressive Conduct"

Although these landmark cases involved political speech, sometimes citizens express political feelings through conduct, such as burning a draft card or the American flag, that does not entail speech as such. Those who defend a broad reading of the First Amendment say that it protects **freedom of expression**, which includes both speech and other kinds of political conduct. In the twentieth century, the Court ruled that the First Amendment does protect **symbolic speech** or **expressive conduct**, but within limits.

The Supreme Court first addressed this issue in 1931 when it overturned a California law that made it a felony to display a red flag (such as the Communist flag) "as a sign, symbol or emblem of opposition to organized government."[54] Because opposition to government might be peaceful, the state went too far in banning symbolic speech that promoted such opposition.

In 1969, the issue of symbolic speech in public schools reached the Court in *Tinker v. Des Moines School District,* when five junior high and high school students were suspended for wearing black armbands to class to protest the Vietnam War. Holding that students and teachers do not "shed their constitutional rights to freedom of speech or expression at the schoolhouse gate," the Court overturned the suspensions. Because the students wore the armbands to convey a political viewpoint, their actions involved the freedom of speech protected by the First Amendment. The Court suggested, however, that restrictions on speech or expressive conduct might be legitimate if necessary to prevent "disturbances," "disorders," or "substantial disruption" of school activities.[55] Later, the Court clarified that "the constitutional rights of students in public schools are not automatically coextensive with the rights of adults in other settings."[56] In 2007, for example, it ruled that administrators of a public high school in Juneau, Alaska, could properly punish students for unfurling a 14-foot banner at a school-sponsored event that read "BONG HiTS 4 JESUS." Despite the cryptic meaning, the school principal (and the Court's majority) read the banner as promoting drug use, a clear violation of school policy that justified punishing an act that in other circumstances would have been protected by the First Amendment. In schools, the Court wrote, "First Amendment rights were circumscribed 'in light of the special characteristics of the school environment.'"[57]

As we noted in Chapter 4, Americans have deep feelings about the American flag and its desecration. In 1984, outside the meeting of the Republican National Convention in Dallas, Texas, a member of the Revolutionary Communist Youth Brigade burned the flag while fellow demonstrators denounced the country and its policies. Having violated Texas law, similar to that in most other states, the perpetrator was convicted, sentenced to a year in prison, and fined $2,000. In *Texas v. Johnson* (1989), a sharply divided Supreme Court overturned the conviction by extending First Amendment protection to burning the American flag as a political protest. The five-member majority held that "the government may not prohibit the expression of an idea simply because society finds the idea itself offensive or disagreeable." To the criticism that allowing flag burning might jeopardize the flag's symbolic role, the majority responded that "the flag's deservedly cherished place in our community will be strengthened, not weakened, by our holding today." Writing in dissent, Chief Justice Rehnquist noted the symbolic importance of the flag as "embodying our Nation." He wondered how the government could draft men into the military to "fight and perhaps die for the flag, but . . . may not prohibit the public burning of the banner under which they fight."[58]

Overwhelming public disapproval of the Court's decision prompted Congress to pass by large majorities the Flag Protection Act of 1989. The law held that "whoever knowingly

Freedom of expression—a broad term to characterize what many believe the First Amendment was designed to protect, incorporating freedom of speech and press as well as expressive conduct.

Symbolic speech—conduct by which people sometimes express their political feelings without using speech as such; for example, burning the American flag as a sign of protest. Also called "expressive conduct."

Expressive conduct—conduct by which people sometimes express their political feelings without using speech as such; for example, burning the American flag as a sign of protest. Also called "symbolic speech."

BRENDAN MCDERMID/Reuters/Landov

The Occupy Wall Street protest of November 2011 in Zuccotti Park, NYC.

mutilates, defaces, physically defiles, burns, maintains on the floor or ground, or tramples upon any flag of the United States" could be fined and imprisoned for up to a year. In June 1990, the Supreme Court, by the same 5–4 vote as in *Texas v. Johnson*, struck down the federal statute. During this same period, efforts to amend the Constitution to prohibit flag desecration failed when the Senate came up short of the required two-thirds vote.

In 2003, the Court considered whether cross burnings by the Ku Klux Klan were symbolic speech with First Amendment protections. In *Virginia v. Black*, it overturned a Virginia statute that in effect made all cross burnings illegal. The Court noted that while cross burnings are often intended to intimidate, "sometimes the cross burning is a statement of ideology, a symbol of group solidarity." States may legitimately criminalize cross burnings intended to intimidate, but they may not prohibit cross burnings that symbolically express an ideology or group solidarity.[59]

Despite these cases, the Court has upheld some restrictions on expressive conduct. In *United States v. O'Brien* (1968), the Court let stand the conviction of a young man who had burned his draft card on the steps of a courthouse in Boston as a political protest. A federal appeals court had overturned the conviction on the grounds that the applicable federal law, which made it a crime to alter, destroy, or mutilate a draft card, unconstitutionally abridged freedom of speech.

In holding otherwise, the Supreme Court noted that the federal government had a legitimate interest in effectively administering the nation's draft laws. An important interest of this sort could "justify incidental limitations on First Amendment freedoms." The Court then elaborated a four-part test for determining whether a governmental regulation of expressive conduct would be allowed by the First Amendment:

- if it is within the constitutional power of the government,
- if it furthers an important or substantial governmental interest,
- if the governmental interest is unrelated to the suppression of free expression, and
- if the incidental restriction on alleged First Amendment freedoms is no greater than is essential to the furtherance of that interest.[60]

O'Brien remains the governing case for determining whether the law may restrict expressive conduct that interferes with some important government interest.

Libel Law and *New York Times v. Sullivan*

Slander—a defamatory statement made through speech (see also **Libel**).

Libel—a defamatory statement made in writing (see also **Slander**).

Although government regulation is the principal means of restricting the freedom of speech and of the press, suits by private parties for **slander** (a defamatory statement made through speech) or **libel** (a defamatory statement made in writing) can also have a considerable impact. Although the Court had long held that libel did not enjoy First Amendment protection, it had not before 1964 addressed the use of libel laws in cases involving the criticism of public officials.

In 1960, the *New York Times* ran a full-page advertisement paid for by civil rights groups that attacked the police and public officials in Montgomery, Alabama, for instigating "an unprecedented wave of terror" against civil rights activists in that city. A city commissioner brought suit in Alabama courts against the newspaper and those who paid for the advertisement, charging that it was full of factual errors and defamed him, although he was not specifically named in it. He won his case before a civil jury, which awarded him $500,000. The Alabama Supreme Court upheld the award. In *New York Times v. Sullivan*, the U.S. Supreme Court overturned on the ground that the Alabama libel law as applied to public officials inhibited the kind of free and open public debate that the First Amendment was designed to protect.

The majority held that because erroneous statements are inevitable in free debate, newspapers that criticized public officials could not be held legally responsible for libel unless they engaged in "actual malice." *Actual malice* meant knowledge that an accusation was false or "reckless disregard of whether it was false or not."[61] This rule has made it extremely difficult for public officials to prove libel. Subsequently, the Court extended the new rule to cover "public figures," such as athletes and movie stars, but not other private individuals.

MORALITY AND SEXUAL BEHAVIOR
MAJOR ISSUE

- In what ways have governments in the United States sought to regulate morality, and how has the Supreme Court limited or thwarted such regulations?

"Our society prohibits, and all human societies have prohibited, certain activities not because they harm others but because they are considered, in the traditional phrase, 'contra bonos mores,' i.e., immoral. In American society, such prohibitions have included, for example, sadomasochism, cockfighting, bestiality, suicide, drug use, prostitution, and sodomy."[62] So wrote Justice Antonin Scalia in a 1991 case that upheld an Indiana law that prohibited totally nude dancing. Although Scalia was on the winning side in this case, none of the other four members of the majority embraced his specific argument. Indeed, since the middle of the twentieth century, the Court has made it increasingly difficult for popular majorities to promote or enforce through law their view of appropriate morality.

Here we examine three areas in which the modern Supreme Court has decisively influenced public policy on issues of moral controversy: abortion, homosexuality, and pornography and censorship. All of these involve conflicts between private rights and what is sometimes called "public morality."

Abortion and the Right to Privacy

One of the Supreme Court's most controversial decisions was its ruling, in 1973, in *Roe v. Wade* (1973) that a woman had a constitutional right to an abortion. This overturned abortion laws in most of the states. Although at one time all the states had prohibited abortion, more than a dozen had liberalized their laws in the 1960s, allowing abortion if the woman's life or health was in danger, if the fetus had a severe physical defect, or if the pregnancy was the result of rape or incest. Four states allowed abortion whenever the woman and her physician agreed.

In an opinion written by Justice Harry Blackmun, the Court held, 7–2, that a woman had an essentially unrestricted right to an abortion in the first trimester. Because the medical risks of an abortion increased in the second trimester, states could impose regulations on the abortion procedure reasonably related to protecting the woman's health, such as who may perform the abortion and in what kind of facility. In the third trimester, the state's interest in the potential life of the fetus could justify more severe restrictions.[63]

Abortion is not mentioned in the Constitution. The majority argued, however, that abortion was part of a broader "right to privacy," which the Court had first articulated eight years earlier in *Griswold v. Connecticut* (1965) when it overturned Connecticut's law prohibiting the use of contraceptives. In the famous words of Justice William O. Douglas, who wrote for five members of the Court in *Griswold*, the specific guarantees of the Bill of Rights "have penumbras, formed by emanations from those guarantees that help give them life and substance." The First, Third, Fourth, Fifth, Ninth, and Fourteenth amendments imply "zones of privacy" that extend beyond the specific guarantees themselves. The right to abortion is within these zones.[64]

The two dissenting justices objected that the majority was inventing new rights nowhere mentioned in the Constitution itself. They feared that this "great unconstitutional shift of power to the courts" would be "bad for the courts and worse for the country."[65] Similarly, in the companion case to *Roe*, *Doe v. Bolton*, two dissenters called the Court's actions an exercise of "raw judicial power," with the Court deciding matters that should be left to the people and to the political processes that the people have devised to govern their affairs."[66]

Ever since *Roe*, abortion has remained highly controversial. Frequently an issue in political campaigns, it sharply divides the Democratic and Republican parties. Consider the positions stated in the official party platforms in 2008. According to its platform, the Democratic Party "strongly and unequivocally supports *Roe v. Wade* and a woman's right to choose a safe and legal abortion, regardless of ability to pay, and we oppose any and all efforts to weaken or undermine that right." By contrast, in its platform the Republican Party "assert[s] the inherent dignity and sanctity of all human life and affirm[s] that the unborn child has a fundamental individual right to life which cannot be infringed."[67] Despite these party positions, however, there are pro-life Democrats in elective office as well as pro-choice Republicans.

Public demonstrations are common on the anniversary each year of *Roe v. Wade*, decided on January 22, 1973. This pro-choice event was in San Francisco on the 32nd anniversary. See the opening chapter photo for a pro-life demonstration on the 39th anniversary.

State legislatures have sought to restrict abortions in various ways. The Supreme Court has upheld some of these and overturned others. In the 1989 case *Webster v. Reproductive Health Services*, the Supreme Court upheld a series of restrictions imposed by the state of Missouri, including prohibiting abortions on state property (the Court had previously upheld a congressional ban on public funding of abortions) and requiring physicians to perform tests to determine the viability of a fetus at least 20 weeks old.[68] Although *Webster* did not overturn *Roe*, the language of the plurality opinion by Chief Justice Rehnquist suggested to many that this was a real possibility. Accordingly, several states read *Webster* as a green light for passing more restrictions.

One state to do so was Pennsylvania, whose actions came before the Court in 1992 in *Planned Parenthood v. Casey*. A majority of justices upheld the requirement that physicians provide women seeking an abortion information about the risks of an abortion and the age of the fetus, a 24-hour waiting period after the receipt of the information, and the stipulation that a woman under age 18 seeking an abortion receive the permission of one parent or of a court acting on her behalf. But they struck down as an "undue burden" on women the requirement that a woman notify her spouse before obtaining an abortion.[69] Although the Court upheld most of the regulations, proponents of *Roe* scored a major victory in the Court's reaffirmation of a woman's right to choose an abortion. *Casey* signaled that *Roe* would stand for the foreseeable future. What remained unclear was what other restrictions might be judged an "undue burden" on abortion rights.

Although the U.S. Congress has little influence over national abortion policy, it acted three times to prohibit a particular type of late-term abortion whose technical name is "dilation and extraction." In this procedure, commonly called *partial birth abortion*, "the doctor pulls the fetal body through the cervix, collapses the skull, and extracts the fetus through the cervix."[70] Congress passed national bans on this procedure in 1996 and 1997, but President Bill Clinton vetoed them. It acted again in 2003 with the Partial Birth Abortion Ban Act, which President George W. Bush signed. The Supreme Court upheld the act in April 2007 in *Gonzales v. Carhart*.[71] Congress also addressed abortion in 2002, when it passed the Born Alive Infants Protection Act, which affirmed that any infant that is "born alive" at any stage of development shall be considered a "person" or "human being" under federal law whether the birth results from "natural or induced labor, cesarean section, or induced abortion."

Since 1961, federal law has prohibited organizations from using federal funds to pay for abortions overseas as part of family planning. Although presidents have little direct influence on abortion policy, Republican president Ronald Reagan broadened the federal restriction in 1984 by announcing that the United States also would not fund organizations that promoted abortions overseas, even if they did not perform or pay for them. This is called the "Mexico City Policy," after the city that hosted the United Nations Conference on Population where it was announced. Its critics call it the "global gag rule."

Democratic president Bill Clinton rescinded the policy within days of taking office in January 1993, and Republican president George W. Bush reinstated it as one of his first official acts in January 2001. On January 23, 2009, his third day in office, Democratic president Barack Obama overturned Bush's actions and revoked the Mexico City Policy for its "excessively broad conditions on grants and assistance awards" that "have undermined efforts to promote safe and effective voluntary family planning programs in foreign nations."[72] These reversals of policy as the presidency shifted from one party to the other demonstrate just how far apart the Democratic and Republican parties are on the abortion issue and how little deliberation there is across the party divide.

Abortion remains a highly controversial issue in American politics and is likely to remain so for some time. It raises the deepest questions about when life begins, whether constitutional protections apply to a developing fetus, whether elected officials or courts should decide such controversial matters, and what role religious beliefs and institutions ought to play in setting public policy. Until 1973, the deliberations of the people's elected representatives in the states controlled abortion policy; but since then, the reasoning of the nine members of the Supreme Court has been decisive, largely removing this contentious issue from normal political resolution. In Chapter 15 we address at some length the role of the Supreme Court in American deliberative democracy.

Homosexuality

A second area in which the modern Supreme Court has decisively influenced public policy on issues of moral controversy is homosexuality. Reflecting the view, articulated by Justice Scalia earlier in this chapter, that the majority may prohibit behavior it considers immoral, every state outlawed sodomy until the 1960s. By the mid-1980s, however, half the states had removed these bans. Many believed that when this issue reached the highest court in a case from Georgia in 1986, the justices would see this as a privacy issue and strike down state sodomy laws. Instead, a 5–4 majority refused to do so in *Bowers v. Hardwick*. Writing for the majority, Justice Byron White denied that the Constitution "confers a fundamental right upon homosexuals to engage in sodomy." To the charge that the Georgia law allowed the majority to legislate its moral beliefs, White responded that the law "is constantly based on notions of morality."[73]

The Court also ruled against attempts by gay individuals and groups to use state public accommodations statutes to prohibit their exclusion from private organizations and events. In 1995, the Court held that the organizers of the annual St. Patrick's Day parade in Boston could exclude an Irish gay, lesbian, and bisexual group from marching with its organization's banner. Because the gay group's purpose was "to celebrate its members' identity as openly gay, lesbian, and bisexual descendants of the Irish immigrants," the private group organizing the parade had its own First Amendment right to freedom of expression to exclude the gay organization. "[A] speaker," the Court ruled, "has the autonomy to choose the content of his own message."[74]

Five years later, the Court issued a similar ruling in a case involving the Boy Scouts. The New Jersey Supreme Court had ruled that the Boy Scouts of America was a public accommodation under state law and could not lawfully discriminate against homosexuals. In overturning this decision by a 5–4 vote, the U.S. Supreme Court held that the Boy Scouts had a First Amendment right to exclude gays as members and scoutmasters. Forcing a group to include a person it does not want, Chief Justice Rehnquist argued, could undermine "the group's freedom of expressive association if the presence of that person affects in a significant way the group's ability to advocate public or private viewpoints."[75] The four dissenters disputed the claim that the Boy Scouts had a record of teaching that homosexuality was wrong. Moreover, they held that the state of New Jersey had the right to combat the "prejudices . . . that have caused serious and tangible harm" to many individuals.[76]

Despite these setbacks, gays scored major victories before the Court in 1996 and 2003. In the first case, *Romer v. Evans*, the Court overturned an amendment to the constitution of Colorado adopted by a statewide referendum overturning ordinances passed by several Colorado cities that banned discrimination against homosexuals. The Court's majority maintained that the amendment violated the equal protection clause of the Fourteenth Amendment. The three dissenters viewed it as "a modest attempt" by the majority of Coloradans "to preserve traditional sexual mores."[77]

Then, in 2003, the Supreme Court overturned its *Bowers* precedent from 17 years before by ruling that a Texas law that criminalized sexual acts between persons of the same sex violated the U.S. Constitution. In *Lawrence v. Texas*, Justice Anthony Kennedy, writing for the majority, maintained that "the petitioners are entitled to respect for their private lives. The State cannot demean their existence or control their destiny by making their private sexual conduct a crime. Their right to liberty under the Due Process Clause gives them the full right to engage in their conduct without intervention of the government." Justice Scalia, writing the leading dissent, charged that "the Court has taken sides in the culture war, departing from its role of assuring, as neutral observer, that the democratic rules of engagement are observed."[78] (In the next chapter, we address the controversy over same-sex marriage.)

Pornography, Obscenity, and Censorship

As noted earlier in the discussion of *Chaplinsky v. New Hampshire*, "lewd and obscene" materials do not enjoy First Amendment protection, but to say that government may suppress obscenity does not settle the question as to what is obscene and what is not. Prior to the 1950s, the federal courts essentially left this matter to local communities and, under federal law, to the postmaster general when determining what materials may not be sent through the U.S. mails.

In 1957, in *Roth v. United States*, the Supreme Court for the first time ruled directly on the issue of constitutional protections for obscene materials. This was the first of a series of cases in which the Court attempted to give a legal definition of **obscenity**. "Pornography" is a broader category than obscenity and refers to any depiction of erotic behavior in pictures or writing that is intended to cause sexual excitement. Under Court rulings, pornography that is not obscene is protected under the First Amendment. Writing for the majority in *Roth*, Justice William Brennan formulated a test for defining what is obscene and may be censored by government: "whether to the average person, applying contemporary community standards, the dominant theme of the material taken as a whole appeals to the prurient interest."[79]

As the sexual revolution of the 1960s changed the face of American popular culture, the creators and purveyors of sexually explicit materials increasingly sought the protection

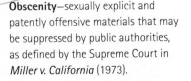

Obscenity—sexually explicit and patently offensive materials that may be suppressed by public authorities, as defined by the Supreme Court in *Miller v. California* (1973).

of the courts. In the 1960s, the Supreme Court expanded constitutional protections by adding to the *Roth* test of obscenity the requirements that the material must be "patently offensive because it affronts contemporary community standards" and that it must be "utterly without redeeming social value."[80]

This made successful prosecutions for obscenity extremely difficult because defendants were often able to find an academic expert to testify that the material in question, no matter how crude, had some "redeeming social value." Even when convictions occurred, appellate courts often made their own decisions whether the materials could be legally censored. As Supreme Court justice Potter Stewart famously noted in a censorship case in 1964, he might not be able to define "hard-core pornography" (which he believed was obscene and could be legally suppressed) but "I know it when I see it."[81]

In upholding a state obscenity conviction in 1973, the Court formulated a revised, three-part test for obscenity in *Miller v. California*:

- the average person, applying contemporary community standards, would find that the work, taken as a whole, appeals to the prurient interest;
- the work depicts or describes, in a patently offensive way, sexual conduct specifically defined by the applicable state law; and
- the work, taken as a whole, lacks serious literary, artistic, political, or scientific value.

Note that the third part of the test replaced the "utterly without redeeming social value" standard with one that evaluated the work "as a whole," returning to the standard in *Roth*. Also, the Court made clear in its opinion that the "contemporary community standards" referred to in the first part of the test could be local standards, which might vary greatly across the country. The First Amendment, said the majority, does not require "that the people of Maine or Mississippi accept public depiction of conduct found tolerable in Las Vegas, or New York City."[82]

Although the new *Miller* standards seemed to open the way for more local obscenity prosecutions, later decisions reined in the reach of *Miller*. In 1974, the Court ruled that the movie *Carnal Knowledge* could not be suppressed as obscene even if a local jury in Georgia judged it so. The Court viewed the film and concluded that it "could not be found under the Miller standards to depict sexual conduct in a patently offensive way."[83] In subsequent decisions, the Court held that the "literary, artistic, political, or scientific value" of a work had to be determined by national standards. As a result of these decisions, relatively few prosecutions for obscenity now involve adult subjects.

In two areas, however, the Supreme Court has been more tolerant of governmental efforts to regulate the display or distribution of sexual materials. First, it has allowed communities to use their zoning power to prohibit sexually oriented entertainment, such as adult bookstores and movie theaters, within a certain distance of residential zones, churches, parks, and schools.[84] Second, in *New York v. Ferber* (1982), the Court unanimously held that government may ban the dissemination of pornographic materials that involve the sexual display of minors.[85]

In upholding New York's ban on disseminating child pornography, the Supreme Court deferred to the state legislature's deliberation and judgment "that the use of children as subjects of pornographic materials is harmful to the physiological, emotional, and mental health of the child."[86] Twenty years later, however, the Court overturned a congressional statute that sought to ban virtual child pornography, which is created at a computer keyboard rather than by filming real children. It disagreed with the government that the generation and distribution of such materials was "intrinsically related" to the sexual abuse of children.[87]

Congress has been no more successful in attempting to ban the distribution of obscene materials to minors through the Internet. Neither the Child Pornography Prevention Act of 1996 nor the Child Online Protection Act of 1998 passed muster in the federal courts. The key problem was that these laws potentially restricted access by adults to materials protected by the First Amendment.[88]

Fights over pornography and obscenity in the United States typically involve conservatives, on the one side, arguing the legitimacy of community regulations to promote morality, and liberals, on the other, seeking to maximize freedom of expression. In recent decades, however, some feminist legal scholars, who on most issues are politically liberal, have added a new twist. They maintain that pornography is essentially an assault on women and thus violates the equal rights of women.

In 1984, the city of Indianapolis embraced this view when it passed an anti pornography ordinance that authorized women to file civil rights suits against pornographers. The ordinance defined pornography as a discriminatory practice that "den[ied] women equal opportunities in society" and promoted their exploitation and subordination.[89] Lower federal courts overturned the ordinance for attempting to silence speech about women that the city disapproved of regardless of its possible literary, artistic, or political value. "The state may not," said a federal appellate court, "ordain preferred viewpoints in this way. The Constitution forbids the state to declare one perspective right and silence opponents."[90]

In recent years, the Supreme Court has addressed two new controversial issues: videos depicting animal cruelty and violent video games. In April 2010, it overturned a federal law that criminalized the commercial creation, sale, or possession of depictions (such as printed matter or videos) "in which a living animal is intentionally maimed, mutilated, tortured, wounded, or killed." Although the law had been written largely to prohibit "crush videos"—in which women slowly crush helpless animals to death with high-heel shoes—the case at hand involved videos of dogs fighting. Eight of the nine members of the Court held that because the law as written could extend to speech protected by the First Amendment, such as hunting magazines and videos, it must be struck down. The Court left open the possibility that "a statute limited to crush videos or other depictions of extreme animal cruelty" might pass scrutiny.[91] By the end of the year, Congress enacted, and President Obama signed, the Animal Crush Video Prohibition Act, which imposed a criminal penalty of up to seven years in prison for creating or distributing videos in which animals are "intentionally crushed, burned, drowned, suffocated, impaled, or otherwise subjected to serious bodily injury."[92]

The following year, the Court decided for the first time whether a state could prohibit the sale of violent video games to minors. California had prohibited the sale to minors of games that depicted the "killing, maiming, dismembering, or sexually assaulting an image of a human being" if the game as a whole "appeals to a deviant or morbid interest of minors" and lacks "serious literary, artistic, political, or scientific value for minors." Writing for the five-member majority (two additional justices agreed with the holding but not with the majority's opinion), Justice Scalia held that because "video games communicate ideas—and even social messages," they cannot be prohibited by government. Under the principle of content neutrality, "government has no power to restrict expression because of its message, its ideas, its subject matter, or its content."[93]

In his concurring opinion, Justice Alito (joined by Chief Justice John Roberts) agreed with the result because he believed the statute was too broadly drawn. He emphasized, however, that in many of the games "the violence is outstanding." Players kill "with every imaginable implement"; victims "cry out in agony and beg for mercy"; "[b]lood gushes, splatters, and pools"; and "[s]evered body parts and gobs of human remains are graphically shown." In one game the objective is "to rape a mother and her daughters; in another, the goal is to rape Native American women." There is even a game in which players engage in "ethnic cleansing" by gunning down "African-Americans, Latinos, or Jews." He concluded that he "would not squelch legislative efforts [in a more precisely written statute] to deal with what is perceived

Courtesy of the Human Society of the United States

THE HUMANE SOCIETY
OF THE UNITED STATES

The Humane Society of the United States, the nation's largest organization devoted to the well-being of animals with 11 million members, was a major force behind the passage of the Animal Crush Video Prohibition Act.

by some to be a significant and developing social problem."[94] The two dissenters—justices Clarence Thomas and Stephen Breyer—would have upheld the statute as a reasonable means to assist parents in raising their children by restricting access to dangerous or unwholesome materials.

RIGHT TO KEEP AND BEAR ARMS
MAJOR ISSUE

- May the federal or state governments prohibit the private ownership of firearms?

Perhaps the most controversial right in the Bill of Rights is the one stated in the Second Amendment. It reads in full: "A well regulated Militia, being necessary to the security of a free State, the right of the people to keep and bear Arms, shall not be infringed." Two key questions arise in interpreting this right. First, does the opening clause mean that the only purpose of the amendment is to protect the right of states to arm their militias (now called the National Guard); or does the amendment protect a broader right of individual citizens to own firearms? Second, if the amendment does protect an individual's right to own firearms, does it restrict only the federal government or also states and localities? Strikingly, the U.S. Supreme Court did not rule directly on the first issue until 2008 (although justices and scholars dispute the relevance of a 1939 decision) and on the second until 2010.

Dick Heller was a special police officer in the District of Columbia who was authorized to carry a handgun when on duty at the Federal Judicial Center. He applied for a permit to keep a handgun at home for self-defense but was turned down because the city prohibits the private ownership of handguns. He sued in federal court in 2003 to overturn the ban as a violation of the Second Amendment. In *District of Columbia v. Heller*, announced in June 2008, the Supreme Court issued a landmark ruling in a sharply contested 5–4 decision.

Writing for the majority, Justice Scalia concluded from an analysis of British history and founding-era materials that the Second Amendment codified a preexisting right to carry weapons for self-defense. "It was clearly an individual right," he wrote, and was not limited to service in a citizen militia. The Constitution did not grant the right, but recognized that free people had the right to defend themselves with firearms. This meant that the District of Columbia could not prohibit the keeping of handguns in the home. Yet, "the right secured by the Second Amendment is not unlimited." The majority held that the government could prohibit felons or the mentally ill from possessing firearms and could forbid the carrying of firearms in schools or government buildings. It could also ban certain types of weapons such as sawed-off shotguns and fully automatic machine guns.[95]

In a sharply worded dissent, four justices charged the majority with completely misreading the founding materials and later court precedents. The Anti-Federalists, they explained, had feared that the new federal government would disarm the state militias; the Second Amendment was adopted to make that impossible. Neither the members of the First Congress nor the state legislators who voted to ratify the Bill of Rights had "the slightest interest in limiting any legislature's authority to regulate private citizen uses of firearms." The dissenters also embraced an "interest-balancing" approach where the Court would balance the burden of a gun control regulation against the public benefits it was meant to promote. It concluded that the District of Columbia's ban on the private possession of handguns was a reasonable response to a serious gun crime problem.[96] Two years later, in *McDonald v. City of Chicago*, the same five-member majority that overturned the DC ban overturned a similar ban in the city of Chicago, ruling that the Second Amendment right identified in *Heller* also restricted state and local governments.[97]

FOCUS QUESTION

Is the Second Amendment an anachronism that should be repealed?

When the founders identified the rights that the federal government was required to respect, they focused much of their attention on the protections that should be afforded those suspected, accused, or convicted of crimes. In the twentieth century, the Supreme Court made nearly all of these rights applicable to the states and, in the process, expanded the rights of criminal defendants in far-reaching and controversial ways.

RIGHTS OF CRIMINAL DEFENDANTS

MAJOR ISSUES

- How does the Constitution explicitly protect the rights of criminal defendants?
- How has the Supreme Court interpreted these protections in the modern era?

Five provisions of the original Constitution—on habeas corpus, bills of attainder, ex post facto laws, trial by jury in criminal cases, and convictions for treason—and part or all of four amendments—the Fourth, Fifth, Sixth, and Eighth—protect those accused or convicted of crimes. Why so much attention to the rights of criminal defendants?

Two reasons stand out. First, the founders believed that everyone was entitled to fair procedures for determining guilt or innocence. Simple justice demanded, for example, that defendants receive due process of law, that they be given fair notice of the charges against them, and that they be able to confront their accusers in open court. Guilty or innocent, the accused deserve certain basic procedural protections.

Second, and equally important, the founders identified essential rights of criminal defendants in order to thwart tyrannical or unjust acts. It was well known at the time, and has been confirmed many times since, that tyrants often use the criminal law and the criminal courts to oppress their enemies and quell opposition. Indeed, the authors of the Declaration of Independence charged that the king perverted the criminal process both by using "mock Trial[s]" to protect British officials and soldiers accused of crimes against the colonists and by sending colonists accused of crimes against the king for trial in Britain, violating their right to be judged by a local jury.

The constitutional rights themselves point to the various ways in which tyrants or dangerous rulers may abuse the criminal process. They may arrest and hold individuals without proper legal grounds (denying habeas corpus), convict and punish unpopular persons through a legislative process rather than a proper trial (bill of attainder), write a new law to punish someone for doing something that was not illegal when done (ex post facto law), retry someone for the same offense despite acquittals (double jeopardy), or impose cruel and unusual punishments on those convicted of crimes.

These can be powerful tools in the hands of those who would use the power of the state against political opponents. Besides prohibiting these acts, the original Constitution and the Bill of Rights gave the citizens themselves the power to block serious criminal charges through service on grand juries (Fifth Amendment) and to decide on guilt or innocence through service on trial juries (Article III). Because trial juries typically need unanimity to convict, juries could sometimes protect individuals even from unjust majorities.

About nine-tenths of criminal cases in the United States involve violations of state law, not federal law. Typically, local police make an arrest, county prosecutors decide whether to file charges in court, grand juries or judges determine whether there is sufficient evidence to warrant a trial, and county trial courts determine guilt or innocence. Until the twentieth century, these local and state procedures were little influenced by the federal courts. Through a series of landmark decisions, the Supreme Court has now required that the states and their political subdivisions abide by all the protections for criminal defendants in the Bill of Rights, with the sole exception of grand jury indictments in serious cases (Fifth Amendment). (As an alternative to grand jury indictments, many states allow cases to go to trial after a judge determines in a preliminary hearing that there is "probable cause" that the defendant is guilty of the crime. The Supreme Court has ruled that this is sufficient to meet the due process requirements of the Fourteenth Amendment.)

Here we review the Court's actions in four important areas: search and seizure, self-incrimination, right to counsel, and cruel and unusual punishments.

Search and Seizure

The Fourth Amendment prohibits "unreasonable searches and seizures" and requires that all warrants be based on "probable cause." The Court has interpreted this to mean that in most cases the police cannot conduct a search and seize materials without a warrant issued by a judge and supported by evidence of probable criminal activity. Even the placing of a GPS device on the automobile of a suspected criminal, the Court ruled in 2012, is a search that requires a proper warrant. Yet, the Court has permitted the following exceptions to the warrant requirement: a search or seizure incident to a lawful arrest, when contraband or other evidence of criminal activity is in the plain view of the police, the search of a vehicle if probable cause of illegal activity exists, the search of students in schools if reasonable given the circumstances, when in "hot pursuit" of a fleeing suspect, when engaging in the "stop and frisk" of a suspicious individual, drug testing of public employees in some circumstances, upon entering the country or boarding airplanes, and upon entering some public buildings such as courts.[98]

How are these exceptions determined? What standards or principles does the Court use to decide which searches are "reasonable" without a warrant? The Court addressed this point in *Pennsylvania v. Mimms* in 1977. In this case, the Pennsylvania Supreme Court had thrown out a criminal conviction that resulted from a police seizure of a loaded 38-caliber handgun from the driver of a car with an expired license plate. The police had ordered the driver to pull over and exit the vehicle, whereupon they observed a large bulge under the driver's jacket. After searching him, they discovered the gun. The driver was subsequently convicted of carrying a concealed deadly weapon without a license and sentenced to prison.

In reinstating the conviction, the U.S. Supreme Court held that the key issue was whether the "governmental invasion of a citizen's personal security" was reasonable given "all the circumstances." "Reasonableness," it said, "depends 'on a balance between the public interest and the individual's right to personal security free from arbitrary interference by law officers.'"[99] As it had said in an earlier case, "what the Constitution forbids is not all searches and seizures, but unreasonable searches and seizures."[100] The Supreme Court ruled that given all the circumstances in the Pennsylvania case, the search was reasonable and therefore not a violation of the Fourth Amendment.

Rules on seizures are especially important because Court rulings prohibit the use in court of evidence improperly obtained, no matter how relevant to demonstrating guilt. This is the so-called **exclusionary rule**. In the *Mimms* case, for example, it was obvious that the defendant was guilty of violating the state law that prohibited carrying a concealed deadly weapon without a license. Yet, had the Court ruled that the seizure was illegal (as did the Pennsylvania Supreme Court), the evidence would have been thrown out and the defendant freed.

The exclusionary rule was first promulgated by the U.S. Supreme Court for federal criminal cases in 1914. Prior to this time, federal courts had followed the common law rule, derived from British legal practice, that allowed all relevant evidence to be used in trial,

AP Photo/Jack Dempsey

Although law enforcement officials usually need a warrant issued by a court to search someone, screening and searches at airports are an exception. Courts have judged them to be reasonable given the needs of public safety. Here personnel of the Transportation Safety Administration (TSA) inspect passengers and their baggage at Denver International Airport.

Exclusionary rule—the rule imposed by the Supreme Court that prohibits the use in court of evidence improperly obtained, no matter how relevant to demonstrating guilt.

regardless how it was obtained. Although the Fourth Amendment prohibited unreasonable seizures, it did not in itself indicate what could be done with evidence wrongly procured.

In 1961, the Court extended the exclusionary rule to the state courts in *Mapp v. Ohio*, basing its decision not on a constitutional right but on the need to deter improper police behavior. Later decisions affirmed the holding and reiterated the deterrence rationale, but also carved out exceptions such as the "good faith exception" articulated in 1984. In this case, the Court held that if the police were acting in "good faith" on the basis of a warrant that was later shown to be improperly issued, the evidence could stand. After all, no deterrent effect to improper police behavior would be served by throwing out evidence that the police believed they had a legal right to obtain.

The exclusionary rule, unique to the United States, remains controversial. Opponents complain that it frees the guilty and actually does little to deter police misconduct. They propose using all relevant evidence in court and deterring police misconduct through administrative punishment or civil suits by victims of improper searches. Advocates maintain that the exclusionary rule does deter some police misbehavior. Perhaps more importantly, they object to tainting the judicial process with illegally obtained evidence.

Self-incrimination and Miranda Warnings

The Fifth Amendment stipulates that no one "shall be compelled in any criminal case to be a witness against himself." Originally, the Supreme Court held that this prohibited only extreme coercive measures such as torture to compel confessions. In overturning a conviction in Mississippi in 1936 based on confessions coerced through physical torture, the Court said that "[t]he rack and torture chamber may not be substituted for the witness stand."[101] Over the subsequent decades, the Court applied a "totality of the circumstances" rule, determining on a case-by-case basis whether given all the circumstances—such as the age and maturity of the defendant and the length and nature of the interrogation—the confession was coerced.

In its landmark ruling in *Miranda v. Arizona* in 1966, however, the Court replaced the "totality of the circumstances" standard with the requirement that the police give all criminal suspects specific warnings (commonly called **Miranda warnings**), now quite familiar to Americans, before questioning them:

> He must be warned prior to any questioning that he has the right to remain silent, that anything he says can be used against him in a court of law, that he has the right to the presence of an attorney, and that if he cannot afford an attorney one will be appointed for him prior to any questioning if he so desires.

Once a suspect has received these warnings, he can "knowingly and intelligently waive these rights and agree to answer questions or make a statement." But unless he does so, "no evidence obtained as a result of interrogation can be used against him."[102]

Chief Justice Earl Warren, writing for the narrow five-member majority, maintained that even when brutality or "third degree" tactics are not used by the police, "the very fact of custodial interrogation exacts a heavy toll on individual liberty and trades on the weakness of individuals." Police interrogation is so intrinsically coercive that unless these special warnings are given, "no statement obtained from the defendant can truly be the product of his free choice."[103]

The dissenters countered that the Fifth Amendment's protection against self-incrimination required only that confessions be truly voluntary. They noted that Miranda himself, suspected of kidnapping and raping an 18-year-old girl near Phoenix, Arizona, in 1963, had been picked out of a lineup and interrogated for two hours or less "without any force, threats or promises." During the interrogation, Miranda "gave a detailed oral confession" and then wrote out and signed a statement describing the details of the crime. "One is entitled to feel astonished," Justice John Marshall Harlan wrote in dissent, "that the Constitution can be read to produce this result" of throwing out Miranda's confession.[104]

Miranda proved highly controversial. In 1968, Congress tried to restore the "totality of the circumstances" test in the Omnibus Safe Streets and Crime Control Act, but no

Miranda warnings—the warnings required by the Supreme Court that police must give when arresting a suspect: particularly the right to remain silent and to have the assistance of an attorney (also called "Miranda rights").

administration has invoked the provision. The more conservative Supreme Court under Chief Justices Warren Burger (1969–1986) and William Rehnquist (1986–2005) refused to overturn *Miranda*, but it did allow variation from the exact form of the warnings when the police officer "touched all of the bases required by Miranda." More importantly, the Court allowed statements otherwise inadmissible under *Miranda* to be used to impeach the credibility of a defendant who took the stand on his own behalf.[105]

Right to Counsel

The Sixth Amendment provides that "[i]n all criminal prosecutions, the accused shall enjoy the right . . . to have the Assistance of Counsel for his defence." As originally understood, this guaranteed only that an accused person could have a counsel of his or her choice assist phrase at trial. It was not thought that this right placed any obligation on the government to pay for legal services for defendants who could not afford them. This began to change in the 1930s, when the Supreme Court, relying not on the Sixth Amendment but on the due process clauses of the Fifth and Fourteenth amendments, required state courts to provide indigent defendants the assistance of counsel in capital cases and federal courts to do so in all criminal cases. Then in 1963, in the landmark case *Gideon v. Wainwright*, a unanimous Supreme Court ruled that the Sixth Amendment required that in all felony cases the state must provide all indigent defendants with counsel.

Clarence Earl Gideon had been convicted in Florida courts in 1961 for breaking into a pool hall and stealing beer, wine, and change from a vending machine. At his trial he asked for an appointed attorney but was turned down by the court because it was not a capital case. Unable to hire an attorney, Gideon defended himself. After his conviction, the court sentenced him to five years in state prison. Gideon used the prison's law library to research and write a habeas corpus petition arguing that the refusal of the state to provide an attorney violated the U.S. Constitution. When the handwritten petition reached Washington, the Court assigned the case to prominent attorney Abe Fortas, who would later serve on the Supreme Court.

The Court held that in the American adversary system of criminal justice, lawyers "are necessities, not luxuries." The "noble ideal [of fair trials] cannot be realized if the poor man charged with a crime has to face his accusers without a lawyer to assist him."[106] This case dealt with felonies, serious crimes that typically can result in imprisonment for a year or longer. Later the Court ruled that the right to a publicly provided attorney also covered indigent defendants charged with misdemeanors if imprisonment could result.

A series of other decisions extended the right beyond the trial itself to lineups, pretrial arraignments, preliminary hearings, and sentencing. But the Court has not extended the right to grand jury proceedings, probation and parole revocation hearings, or most appeals.

The first page of Clarence Earl Gideon's petition to the Supreme Court arguing that his constitutional rights were violated when the state of Florida refused to provide him with an attorney at public expense.

Cruel and Unusual Punishment

The Eighth Amendment forbids the infliction of "cruel and unusual punishments," language derived from the English Bill of Rights of 1689. The Supreme Court first addressed the meaning of the prohibition in 1878, when it upheld the sentence of a murderer in the Utah Territory to death by shooting. What the Eighth Amendment prohibited, the Court held, were "punishments of torture" and those of "unnecessary cruelty," including such punishments as being emboweled alive, dissected in public, or burned alive.[107]

Key Rulings by the U.S. Supreme Court on Whether Severe Punishments Other Than the Death Penalty Are "Cruel and Unusual"

- Overturned a sentence in the Philippines, then under U.S. control, of 15 years at hard labor in prison while in chains for falsifying a public record (*Weems v. United States*, 1910)
- Invalidated a California law that made it a criminal offense to be addicted to narcotics (*Robinson v. California*, 1962)
- Allowed a sentence of life in prison with the possibility of parole for someone who committed three property offenses involving credit cards and bad checks (*Rummel v. Estelle*, 1980)
- Allowed sentences of two consecutive terms of 20 years in prison for possession with intent to distribute marijuana and distribution of marijuana (*Hutto v. Davis*, 1982)
- Overturned a sentence of life in prison without the possibility of parole for writing a bad check for $100, the offender's seventh felony conviction (three for burglary and one each for obtaining money under false pretenses, grand larceny, and driving while intoxicated) (*Solem v. Helm*, 1983)
- Upheld a sentence of life in prison without the possibility of parole for a first-time offender convicted of possession of 672 grams of cocaine (*Harmelin v. Michigan*, 1991)
- Upheld sentences of 25 years to life under California's three-strikes law for offenders with two prior convictions for violent or serious crimes who committed relatively minor felonies on the third strike, such as stealing golf clubs or videotapes (*Ewing v. California* and *Lockyer v. Andrade*, 2003)
- Ruled that a juvenile offender may not be sentenced to life without parole for any crime other than murder (*Graham v. Florida*, 2010) and then ruled that even for murder, states may not mandate life without parole for juveniles (*Miller v. Alabama*, 2012)

In the twentieth century, the Court for the first time considered whether punishments otherwise unobjectionable, such as lengthy prison terms, might be so disproportionate to the offense as to constitute cruel and unusual punishment. The key rulings are detailed in the box above.

These cases raise important questions. Must punishments be proportional to the seriousness of offenses? And if so, who decides: legislatures or courts? Although the modern Supreme Court has embraced the proportionality requirement, members have disagreed as to how strict that requirement is and what standards judges should use to determine excessive punishments. Also, the justices recognize that legislatures ought to be generally free to adopt their own principles of punishment, including some, such as deterrence and incapacitation, that might mandate very long sentences for repeat offenders, even if the offenses are not especially serious. Several justices now on the court, however, insist that the Eighth Amendment imposes no proportionality requirement at all but simply outlaws punishments that involve torture or the needless infliction of pain.

In an important noncriminal case in 1958, *Trop v. Dulles*, the Supreme Court held in a 5–4 decision that taking away someone's citizenship for deserting during wartime was a cruel and unusual punishment in violation of the Eighth Amendment. The case was important not only in the development of citizenship law (see Chapter 4), but also in promulgating a principle about how to interpret "cruel and unusual" in the modern world. According to Chief Justice Earl Warren, "the Amendment must draw its meaning from the evolving standards of decency that mark the progress of a maturing society."[108] This principle of "evolving standards of decency" became particularly important in decisions on the death penalty.

In 1972, in *Furman v. Georgia*, a sharply divided Court overturned the death penalty as then applied throughout the states. Although several in the majority thought that the death penalty in itself violated the nation's evolving standards of decency, others saw a constitutional problem only in the capricious way in which it was administered. In the words of Justice Potter Stewart, "These death sentences are cruel and unusual in the same way that being struck by lightning is cruel and unusual. For, of all the people convicted of rapes and murders in 1967 and 1968, many just as reprehensible as these, the petitioners are among a capriciously selected random handful upon whom the sentence of death has in fact been imposed."[109]

In reaction to *Furman*, most states rewrote their death penalty statutes to provide both more specificity in defining the kinds of homicides that could result in capital punishment and also special procedures for juries to weigh aggravating and mitigating factors. Four years later, in *Gregg v. Georgia*, the Court upheld the imposition of the death penalty under such a new statute.[110] Eventually, 38 states adopted constitutionally sound death penalty laws. However, legislatures in several states have abolished the death penalty in recent years: New Jersey in 2007, New Mexico in 2009, Illinois in 2011, and Connecticut in 2012. (Also, New York State's highest court effectively overturned the death penalty in 2007.)

Despite holding that the death penalty, in itself, is not cruel and unusual punishment, the U.S. Supreme Court has ruled that it is if applied to rapists who do not murder their victims (whether the victims are adults or children), to the mentally retarded, and to those under 18 at the time of the crime.[111] In the 2008 case on the rape of a child, the five-member majority held that the death penalty may not be applied to any crime against an individual that does not result in death. It left open the possibility that the death penalty might be constitutional for serious crimes against the state—such as treason, espionage, and terrorism—even if these do not result in death.

To this point we have addressed civil liberties in normal, peacetime conditions. But as American history shows, civil liberties are most under stress during wartime or other national emergencies. Actions taken in the war against al Qaeda since the attacks of September 11, 2001, remind us of the tension between civil liberties and national security.

CIVIL LIBERTIES IN WARTIME
MAJOR ISSUE

- In what ways has the government regulated or restricted the civil liberties of Americans during wartime, and how has the Supreme Court ruled on such restrictions?

Former chief justice Charles Evans Hughes once wrote that the Constitution gives the national government "the power to wage war successfully."[112] Later, Justice Robert Jackson famously wrote that the Bill of Rights is not "a suicide pact."[113] Accordingly, the Court has recognized that war may justify restrictions on personal freedoms that would not be permitted in peacetime. Yet, as Justice Sandra Day O'Connor wrote for the Supreme Court in a landmark 2004 decision, "a state of war is not a blank check for the President when it comes to the rights of the Nation's citizens."[114] If these statements are correct, then an essential purpose of political deliberation in American democracy is determining where and how to strike the balance between security and freedom.

Alien and Sedition Acts

Conflicts between war making and civil liberties extend back to the earliest days of the American republic. From 1798 to 1800, the new nation and France engaged in a naval conflict on the high seas that Congress authorized but did not formally "declare." This "Quasi War" inflamed domestic passions. The new Federalist Party, which controlled the presidency and both houses of Congress, urged the vigorous prosecution of the war. The opposition Democratic-Republican Party, which included many who had warm feelings toward France, advocated a more conciliatory approach to the nation's former Revolutionary War ally.

In 1798, the Federalist Congress, with the tacit approval of President John Adams, passed four measures, called collectively the Alien and Sedition Acts, to combat what the Federalists judged to be dangerous foreign influence. One measure, the Naturalization Act, made it harder for immigrants to become American citizens. Another, the

Alien Act, gave the president the authority to deport aliens that he judged to be dangerous. A related act, the Alien Enemies Act, authorized the president to deport or confine aliens who were citizens of a foreign nation at war with the United States. Finally, and most controversially, the Sedition Act, which was directed against outspoken critics of the undeclared war against France, whether foreigners or citizens, made it a crime to conspire to

- impede the operation of any law of the United States[;]
- write, print, utter, or publish . . . any false, scandalous and malicious writings or writings against the government of the United States; [or]
- aid, encourage or abet any hostile designs of any foreign nation against the United States.

Traditionally, the crime of sedition involved inciting resistance or insurrection against the lawful authority. The Sedition Act of 1798 essentially codified the English common law crime of **seditious libel**, according to which it was illegal to criticize the government in a way that undermined public support and respect. Under the common law it did not matter if the criticism was true. Indeed, because true charges would likely be more damaging, the doctrine of the law was "the greater the truth, the greater the libel."

Seditious libel—the crime under British law that made it illegal to criticize the government in a way that undermined public support and respect; the truth of the charges was not a defense.

Although prosecutions for seditious libel had been rare in the American colonies, in a famous case in 1735 authorities in New York prosecuted newspaper printer John Peter Zenger for criticizing the royal governor. Despite the doctrine that truth was no defense in such cases, Zenger argued that he should not be convicted because his criticisms had been accurate. The jury agreed. The Sedition Act of 1798 deviated from the common law by making truth a defense.

Although the government deported no one under the Alien Act, it prosecuted 26 and convicted 10, all Democratic-Republicans, under the Sedition Act. (Thomas Jefferson pardoned them all after becoming president in 1801.) Jefferson, Madison, and other Democratic-Republican leaders denounced the Alien and Sedition Acts as unconstitutional extensions of federal power, most famously in the **Virginia Resolutions** (authored by Madison) and the **Kentucky Resolutions** (authored by Jefferson) of 1798.

Virginia Resolutions—resolutions authored by James Madison and passed by the Virginia legislature in 1798 that criticized the Alien and Sedition Acts.

Kentucky Resolutions—resolutions authored by Thomas Jefferson and passed by the Kentucky legislature in 1798 that criticized the Alien and Sedition Acts.

These critics charged that the Sedition Act exceeded the enumerated powers of the federal government and violated the First Amendment guarantee of speech and press freedom. Nonetheless, they believed that the states could legitimately suppress seditious libel. As Jefferson wrote in the Kentucky Resolutions, "the States or the people . . . retain to themselves the right of judging how far the licentiousness of speech and of the press may be abridged without lessening their useful freedom." Indeed, after the Democratic-Republicans came to power in 1800, they prosecuted several Federalist editors in state courts "for seditious libel against state governments."[115]

By their own terms the Alien Act expired in 1800 and the Sedition Act in 1801. The Naturalization Act was radically amended in 1802 (see Chapter 4). The Alien Enemies Act, however, remains part of federal law and was upheld by the Supreme Court in 1948.[116]

Martial Law and General Andrew Jackson

Martial law—rule by military authorities (in place of civilian officials) in time of war or civil disorder.

The first declaration of **martial law** in the United States occurred at the end of the War of 1812, which was the first declared war under the Constitution. Under martial law, normal rule by civilian authorities gives way to rule by the military. General Andrew Jackson, commanding American troops at New Orleans, declared martial law throughout the city in December 1814 and continued it for two months after American forces defeated the British in the Battle of New Orleans in early January.

When a writer in a local newspaper called for an end to martial law, Jackson imprisoned him. When a judge issued a writ of habeas corpus calling on Jackson to justify the writer's detention, Jackson imprisoned him as well. Later, after martial law had been revoked, the judge found Jackson in contempt of court and fined him $1,000, a considerable sum in 1815. Jackson paid the fine out of his own pocket but was reimbursed by Congress 30 years later, as he lay on his deathbed.

Despite this episode, which occurred without the authorization of President James Madison, federal authorities made little effort elsewhere to stifle criticism of the war effort, even though a few political leaders in the Northeast, where the war was unpopular, actually called for states opposed to the war to secede from the Union.

The Civil War

Conflicts between civil liberties and warmaking were much more extensive during the Civil War, from 1861 to 1865. After the fall of Fort Sumter to Confederate forces in April 1861, President Abraham Lincoln, with Congress not in session, authorized the military to suspend habeas corpus around railroad lines used to bring troops from loyal states to Washington, DC. Lincoln was responding to rioting and the burning of railroad bridges in Baltimore, Maryland, north of the nation's capital, by Southern sympathizers.

When the military imprisoned John Merryman, a Marylander believed to be involved in the burning of the bridges, Merryman's attorney petitioned Chief Justice of the Supreme Court Roger B. Taney for a writ of habeas corpus. Taney issued the writ. When the authorities failed to produce the prisoner, Taney ordered him released. After the commanding general refused, the justice communicated all relevant materials to President Lincoln with an opinion (*Ex parte Merryman*) asserting that, under the Constitution, only Congress can suspend the writ of habeas corpus.[117]

Lincoln ignored Taney's mandate, and Merryman remained in military custody. Just over a month later, Lincoln defended his suspension of habeas corpus in the message he sent to Congress when it convened in a special session on July 4, 1861. Quoting the Constitution, he noted that the document itself allows for the suspension of habeas corpus "when in Cases of Rebellion or Invasion the public Safety may require it." Although the Constitution is silent as to who can suspend habeas corpus, "the provision was plainly made for a dangerous emergency" like the one that faced the nation in 1861. It made no sense, Lincoln explained, to wait for Congress to convene to suspend the writ when the rebels might even manage to prevent Congress from assembling.[118] (For more on Lincoln's understanding of the president's war powers, see Chapter 13.)

As the Civil War continued, Lincoln issued more orders suspending habeas corpus until the military could suspend the right anywhere in the country. Then, in March 1863, Congress passed the Habeas Corpus Act authorizing the president to suspend habeas corpus "whenever, in his judgment, the public safety may require it ... throughout the United States." The act also required, however, that the executive branch identify those detained to federal judges and release them if not indicted under the criminal laws.[119]

Under suspension of habeas corpus, military authorities arrested more than 14,000 civilians during the Civil War. Most of these arrests occurred near the front lines and involved civilian interference with the war effort—such as blockade running, resisting the draft, and selling liquor to soldiers—and had nothing to do with traditional civil liberties, such as freedom of speech or press.[120]

One famous case that did was that of Clement L. Vallandigham, a prominent Democratic political figure and ex-congressman from Ohio who opposed Lincoln's prosecution of the war. Military authorities arrested Vallandigham in May 1863, after he gave a speech denouncing the war and "King Lincoln." A military commission, acting without instructions from Washington, tried Vallandigham for violating a military order banning "declaring sympathies with the enemy." It convicted him and sentenced him to imprisonment until the war ended. Lincoln subsequently changed the sentence to banishment into the Confederacy. When Vallandigham tried to get the Supreme Court to overturn his conviction, the Court ruled in *Ex parte Vallandigham* that it had no authority to consider appeals from military courts.[121] The Vallandigham episode seemed to establish that at least some political speech that would otherwise be protected under the First Amendment during peacetime could be prohibited if detrimental to the nation's war efforts.

More successful in challenging his military trial and sentence was Lambdin P. Milligan, an Indiana citizen who was arrested by military authorities in October 1864. Several weeks later, a military commission convicted Milligan of conspiring as a member of the secret society, Sons of Liberty, to foment an insurrection against the government and forcibly to free Confederate prisoners of war held in Illinois. The commission sentenced Milligan to be hanged. Milligan challenged his conviction and sentence in the federal courts as a violation of the Habeas Corpus Act of 1863.

Nearly a year after the Civil War ended, the Supreme Court decided *Ex parte Milligan*. All nine justices agreed that under the terms of the Habeas Corpus Act, the military commission had no authority to try, convict, and punish Milligan. Despite this agreement, the justices split 5–4 on the rationale. In the ringing language of Justice David Davis, the majority held that "the Constitution of the United States is a law for rulers and people, equally in war and in peace, and covers with the shield of its protection all classes of men, at all times, and under all circumstances."[122] Thus, if the regular civil courts are open, as they were in Indiana during the Civil War, and no invasion has occurred or is imminent, then military commissions could have no authority to try civilians. Even Congress "could grant no such power" to military commissions.[123]

Chief Justice Salmon P. Chase and three others strongly disagreed on this last point. They insisted that Congress under the Constitution had the authority to pass all laws "essential to the prosecution of war with vigor and success." During a war, the federal courts might be "wholly incompetent to avert threatened danger, or to punish, with adequate promptitude and certainty, the guilty conspirators."[124] In this situation, military commissions might be necessary and thus would be lawful. As we will see, the Court revisited the issue of military commissions during World War II and in the current war on terror.

World War I

The government's authority to restrict civil liberties in wartime next became a major issue during World War I (in which the United States participated from April 1917 to November 1918), when Congress passed the Espionage Act of 1917 and the Sedition Act of 1918. Two of the provisions of the Espionage Act affected freedom of speech. One made it a crime to make false statements that interfered with the war effort or that promoted the success of the enemy; to promote insubordination or disloyalty among the troops; and to obstruct military recruitment or enlistment. The other provision denied the federal mails to materials of any kind that advocated "treason, insurrection, or forcible resistance to any law of the United States." The Sedition Act a year later broadened these provisions and made it unlawful "by word or act [to] oppose the cause of the United States."

Between 1917 and 1921, when Congress repealed these laws, prosecutors charged more than 2,000 individuals with violations and convicted about half. Several of these convictions made their way to the U.S. Supreme Court, where they were upheld. The first was that of Charles T. Schenck, who had been convicted of printing and distributing leaflets urging resistance to the draft. Schenck argued that his conviction violated his First Amendment right to freedom of speech, but in *Schenck v. United States* (1919) the Court unanimously disagreed.

This is the case, mentioned earlier, in which Oliver Wendell Holmes famously maintained that freedom of speech does not "protect a man in falsely shouting fire in a theatre." The key issue, said the Court, is whether the words someone uses "create a clear and present danger that they will bring about the substantive evils that Congress has a right to prevent." The government might legitimately suppress certain words in wartime that it could not in peacetime: "When a nation is at war many things that might be said in time of peace are such a hindrance to its effort that their utterance will not be endured so long as men fight and that no Court could regard them as protected by any constitutional right."[125]

The most famous of the prosecutions under the Espionage Act was that of Eugene V. Debs, who received nearly a million votes as Socialist Party candidate for president in 1912. Debs was convicted and sentenced to 10 years in prison in 1918 for a speech made to the Ohio State Socialist Party in which he praised three individuals convicted of failing to register for the draft and one person who was convicted of obstructing the draft. Writing for a unanimous Court in *Debs v. United States* (1919), Justice Holmes maintained that a jury could reasonably find "that the opposition [to the war] was so expressed that its natural and intended effect would be to obstruct recruiting."[126] While serving time in federal prison, Debs ran again for president in 1920 and received more than 900,000 votes. The following year President Warren G. Harding pardoned him.

In the same year as *Debs*, the Court in *Abrams v. United States* upheld the conviction under the Espionage Act of a Russian immigrant and anarchist for distributing leaflets in New York City condemning President Woodrow Wilson for intervening militarily in the Russian civil war. The pamphlets called for a general strike to oppose Wilson's policies. In refusing to overturn the conviction, the majority held that the purpose of the pamphlets "was to excite . . . disaffection, sedition, riots, and . . . revolution, in this country."[127] In opposition, Justice Holmes wrote an influential and now famous dissent. "[T]he best test of truth," he wrote, "is the power of the thought to get itself accepted in the competition of the market." Even "opinions that we loathe" need to be protected "unless they so imminently threaten immediate interference with the lawful and pressing purposes of the law that an immediate check is required to save the country."[128]

Warmaking in both the Civil War and World War I impinged on Americans' freedoms, yet important differences stand out. In World War I, unlike during the Civil War, habeas corpus was not suspended, laws passed by Congress were more important than independent presidential actions, and the federal courts were more active in litigating complaints of governmental interference with civil liberties.[129]

Courtesy of auction site Old Politicals (www.oldpoliticals.com)

A campaign button for Eugene Debs's presidential campaign in 1920 as the candidate of the Socialist Party. Debs conducted his campaign from federal prison, where he was serving a sentence for sedition.

World War II

The most controversial deprivation of civil liberties to occur in the United States during wartime was the relocation and internment of ethnic Japanese on the West Coast during World War II. In the months after the December 7, 1941, attack on Pearl Harbor, local and state officials on the West Coast feared that the Japanese military would strike, and possibly invade, the mainland (especially after a Japanese submarine shelled oil installations near Santa Barbara, California, in February 1942). Concerned about the loyalty of Japanese living on the west coast, they called on the federal government to relocate those of Japanese ancestry inland.

After initially resisting these calls, officials in Franklin Roosevelt's administration persuaded the president to endorse the plan. On February 19, Roosevelt issued Executive Order 9066 authorizing the relocation by allowing the commanding general for the region to designate areas "from which any or all persons may be excluded." Congress added its support a few weeks

American Photographer, (20th century)/Private Collection/Peter Newark American Pictures/ The Bridgeman Art Library

American residents of Japanese ancestry (some foreign aliens and some American citizens, especially the children) arrive at Camp Harmony Assembly Center, Puyallup, Washington State, in 1942.

later when it made it a criminal offense to violate regulations implementing the plan. Eventually, more than 110,000 ethnic Japanese were sent to 10 relocation centers. About 40,000 of these were aliens—that is, citizens of Japan who had immigrated to the United States—and 70,000, mainly their children, were American citizens by virtue of their birth in the United States. (Under Japanese law, those in this second group were also considered citizens of Japan, even though born in the United States.)

The Supreme Court reviewed the legality of the relocation program in three important decisions, all involving American citizens of Japanese ancestry. In the first, *Hirabayashi v. United States*, decided in June 1943, the Court ruled unanimously that the president and Congress acting together had constitutional authority during wartime to authorize the military to impose a curfew on ethnic Japanese on the west coast. (It did not rule on the relocation itself until the next year.) Writing for the Court, Chief Justice Harlan Stone maintained that the Constitution vested in the Congress and president the responsibility to wage war successfully, and it was not appropriate "for any court to sit in review of the wisdom of their action or substitute its judgment for theirs." The military orders at issue were intended to safeguard the west coast "at a time of threatened air raids and invasion by the Japanese forces, from the danger of sabotage and espionage."[130]

The second and best known of the three cases was *Korematsu v. United States*, decided in December 1944. Here the Court, by a 6–3 vote, upheld the conviction of Fred Korematsu for refusing to leave the designated military area in California in which he lived. Although the majority maintained that it was upholding only the exclusion order and not any subsequent relocation to internment camps, the dissenters insisted that this amounted to the same thing.

In his opinion for the Court, Justice Hugo Black held that only "[p]ressing public necessity" could justify a policy that "curtail[ed] the civil rights of a single racial group." Civil and military authorities had determined that the risk of espionage and sabotage by some of Japanese descent presented "the gravest imminent danger to public safety." It was not the business of the Court when the nation was at war to second guess the judgment of those responsible for waging war successfully.[131]

The final case, decided the same day as *Korematsu*, was *Ex parte Endo*. Here the Court unanimously ruled that the government had no authority to continue to detain Mitsuye Endo, a young Japanese-American woman who, the Department of Justice conceded, was a loyal citizen. The Court insisted that if the whole purpose of the internment program was to protect the nation from espionage and sabotage, then there could be no justification for holding a loyal American citizen.[132]

Soon after these decisions were handed down, the government ended the internment program, but the controversy continued over its wisdom and legality. More than four decades later, Congress passed and President Ronald Reagan signed the Civil Liberties Act of 1988, which recognized the "grave injustice" of the internment program, offered a formal apology to those who had suffered under it, and granted surviving internees a payment of $20,000 each.

A much less controversial exercise of warmaking power during World War II was the trial of eight German saboteurs by a military commission in 1942. The eight Germans, all of whom had lived for some time in the United States and later returned to Germany, trained to conduct sabotage against American industry. They arrived in two separate submarines on Long Island, New York, and Ponte Vedra Beach, Florida. After discarding their uniforms, they made their way to American cities. The FBI apprehended all eight after one of them informed on the others.

President Roosevelt appointed a military commission to try the eight "for offenses against the law of war and the Articles of War." All were convicted and six were executed, including one who had become an American citizen as a child when his parents were naturalized in the United States. The defendants challenged the authority of the military commission to try them by filing habeas corpus petitions in federal court.

In *Ex parte Quirin* (1942), the Supreme Court unanimously upheld the authority of the military commission.[133] According to the Court, the Articles of War passed by Congress, together with the president's constitutional authority as commander in chief, provided ample grounds for trying "unlawful combatants," such as spies and saboteurs, by military commission. Although the broad language of the *Milligan* decision of 1866 had suggested that American civilians could never be tried by military commissions if the civil courts were functioning, *Quirin* established a significant exception. Unlike Lambdin Milligan, the Nazi saboteurs, including the American citizen, were combatants for an enemy nation and their actions were unlawful under the rules of war.

The Vietnam War and Freedom of the Press

Perhaps the most important freedom-of-the-press controversy to arise during wartime occurred in 1971, during the final years of the Vietnam War. The executive branch sought to prohibit the *New York Times* and the *Washington Post* from publishing excerpts from classified Department of Defense materials on the history of the war. Daniel Ellsberg, a former Pentagon analyst, had provided the materials to the two newspapers. After the papers began publishing excerpts in mid-June, the administration got preliminary injunctions to prevent further releases until the Supreme Court could hear the issue. Within two weeks, the Court ruled 6–3 in *New York Times v. United States* (often called the "Pentagon Papers" case) that the government had not met its "heavy burden" to justify a prior restraint on the publication of the information.[134]

The members of the majority, however, presented very different rationales. Two argued that the government may never prevent the publication of news. Another held that an exception can be made for militarily sensitive information, such as troop movements in war. Two others recognized the need for confidentiality in international relations and national defense but could not conclude that the disclosures in this case would cause irreparable harm. Although these two justices would not prevent the newspapers from publishing the classified documents, they suggested that they might be subject to criminal sanctions after the fact if they violated federal law. Finally, one member of the majority argued that the real power to restrict publications that might impair the national security lay with Congress, not the president, and that no law was directly applicable in this case. The three dissenters complained of the decision's haste and articulated a very narrow view of the Court's right to review executive branch decisions in foreign affairs. They would have continued the restriction on publication until there were more extensive judicial proceedings.[135]

Although the newspapers won the day and continued publishing the materials, all but two members of the Court embraced the view that certain circumstances might justify prior restraint on the press in wartime. Moreover, five justices (the three dissenters and two from the majority) indicated that the Court should generally defer to the judgments of the executive branch about materials affecting national security. Because the Pentagon Papers were several years old, the majority of the Court did not believe that their publication harmed national security.

War on Terrorism

The war on terrorism, launched in the months and years after the attacks of September 11, 2001, has renewed the debate over warmaking and civil liberties. Civil libertarians have challenged many aspects of government policy, including the following:

- The USA Patriot Act, passed in 2001 and later amended, which enhanced the government's ability to electronically monitor suspected terrorists, to access their medical and business records, to detain and deport them, and to share sensitive information among intelligence and law enforcement agencies
- Wiretapping electronic communications between suspected terrorists overseas and citizens and permanent residents in the United States
- Detaining for the duration of the conflict American citizens captured in the war on terrorism and denying them access to the courts

- Detaining for the duration of the conflict foreigners suspected of terrorism as "unlawful enemy combatants" (mainly at the U.S. naval base at Guantánamo Bay, Cuba) and trying some of them before military tribunals
- Using coercive techniques to interrogate suspected foreign terrorists
- Killing Americans overseas who are believed to be involved in terrorist activities directed against the United States

These controversies have spawned numerous court cases, three of which resulted in landmark Supreme Court decisions. The first involved an American citizen, Yaser Esam Hamdi, who had been born in the United States to citizens of Saudi Arabia. His parents moved him as a child to Saudi Arabia, and by 2001 he lived in Afghanistan. Hamdi was captured, according to authorities, fighting against Afghan forces allied with the United States during the war in Afghanistan in the fall of 2001. The government took the position that though an American citizen, Hamdi had no right to counsel or to contest his detention in American courts.

In *Hamdi v. Rumsfeld* (2004), the Supreme Court disagreed. It held that even in wartime Americans have due process rights. Hamdi must have immediate access to counsel and must gain the opportunity "to challenge meaningfully the Government's case and to be heard by an impartial adjudicator."[136] Despite its defeat on the broad principle, the administration scored two victories. First, the Court said that in the hearing to determine the legitimacy of his detention, Hamdi need not receive all the rights normally accorded those subject to civil or criminal process. For example, hearsay evidence and a presumption in favor of the government's evidence could be allowed, as long as Hamdi could rebut the evidence.

Second, the Court held that Congress had effectively authorized long-term detention of enemy combatants in the joint resolution of September 18, 2001, which authorized the president to use "all necessary and appropriate force" against those responsible for the attacks of September 11, 2001. The Court's job, according to Justice Sandra Day O'Connor, was to strike "the proper constitutional balance" between the due process rights of American citizens and the government's need to effectively combat terrorism, including preventing captured enemy from returning "to battle against the United States."[137]

In the second case, *Hamdan v. Rumsfeld* (2006), the Court ruled 5–3 that President George W. Bush did not have authority to set up a military tribunal to try Salim Ahmed Hamdan, the former driver and bodyguard for Osama bin Laden who was captured in Afghanistan. Despite the precedent of *Ex parte Quirin*, which allowed a military tribunal to try Nazi saboteurs, the Court found that the Uniform Code of Military Justice implicitly incorporated into American law the protections of the Geneva Conventions of 1949. One of these protections, the Court said, required someone like Hamdan to be tried and sentenced only by "a regularly constituted court affording all the judicial guarantees which are recognized as indispensable by civilized peoples." Military tribunals did not meet this standard. The majority also held that the offense with which Hamdan was charged—conspiracy to commit war crimes—was not itself a violation of the law of war and could not be tried before a military tribunal.[138]

The three dissenters challenged the majority on all these points. More generally, Justice Clarence Thomas criticized the majority for "flout[ing] our well-established duty to respect the Executive's judgment in matters of military operations and foreign affairs." The Court, Thomas wrote, seemed to think that it was better qualified than the commander in chief to determine what was militarily necessary. Although the administration lost the case, a majority of the Court seemed to acknowledge that Congress had full authority to authorize military tribunals to try Hamdan and others like him. Congress did so four months later when it passed the Military Commissions Act of 2006.

The third case, *Boumediene v. Bush*, involved the habeas corpus rights of foreign detainees held at the U.S. naval base at Guantánamo Bay, Cuba. The administration maintained that the detainees, who were combatants captured abroad in an authorized war and were being held outside the United States, had no constitutional right to the writ of habeas corpus. In June 2008, a five-member majority of the Court disagreed, thereby granting the more than 200 prisoners at Guantánamo the right to challenge their detention in federal court.[139]

Despite these setbacks, some legal experts noted that the Bush administration was largely successful in employing the legal and investigative tools it believed necessary to fight the war against those responsible for the attacks of September 11, 2001. Nonetheless, in his first days in office, President Obama took steps to revise or undo some of the Bush policies. Through executive orders and other actions, the president

An artist's rendering of Khalid Sheikh Mohammed and four codefendants during a hearing before the U.S. Military Commissions court for war crimes at the U.S. Naval Base in Guantánamo Bay, Cuba, on January 19, 2009.

- suspended the military trials of suspected terrorists at the U.S. naval base at Guantánamo for four months until the administration could decide how to proceed;
- prohibited any federal employee from using interrogation techniques with captured prisoners that are not authorized in the Army field manual (thus prohibiting waterboarding, stress positions, sleep deprivation, and other coercive techniques);
- ordered the CIA to close any secret detention facilities where foreign captives were being held;
- ordered a review of practices transferring captives to other nations to ensure that they would not be tortured or denied humane treatment;
- ordered a prompt review of the factual and legal basis for holding foreign detainees at the U.S. naval base at Guantánamo so that they could be returned to their home country, transferred to a third country, or transferred to a detention facility in the United States; and
- ordered that the detention facility at Guantánamo be closed within a year.[140]

These actions did not, however, reverse the full range of legal tools developed during the Bush administration to fight the war on terrorism. The Patriot Act remained on the books, and President Obama signed a four-year extension of key provisions in May 2011. Military tribunals, though suspended for a time, were reauthorized by the Obama administration under revised rules of procedure. In May 2012, the government charged Khalid Sheikh Mohammed, suspected of masterminding the attacks of September 11, 2011, and four others with murder and terrorism before a military tribunal at Guantánamo. The president accepted the Bush administration position that some of those captured in the war against al Qaeda and its affiliated organizations might not be prosecuted either in federal courts or before military commissions, but instead would undergo "prolonged detention." And despite the president's commitment to close the detention facility at Guantánamo, it remained open throughout his first term. The administration also disappointed some civil libertarians when it continued the Bush administration practice of sometimes invoking the "state secrets" privilege to argue that federal courts should not hear some challenges to federal authority if a trial might expose intelligence secrets or methods. Finally, the Obama administration asserted the authority to kill Americans overseas who were believed to be involved in terrorist activities directed against the United States. (We discuss the killing of foreign enemies, such as Osama bin Laden, in Chapter 13.) Defending the administration's fatal drone attack in Yemen in 2011 on American citizen Anwar al-Awlaki, a Muslim cleric and suspected leader of al Qaeda in the Arabian Peninsula, Attorney General Eric Holder asserted that "our government has the clear authority to defend the United States with lethal force" when it is not feasible to capture "a United States citizen terrorist who presents an imminent threat of violent attack."[141]

Although the war against al Qaeda has raised new issues created by modern surveillance and military technologies (such as unmanned drone attacks overseas), every major conflict forces Americans to think hard about the inherent tension between civil liberties and national security. The conflict appears unavoidable. The issue is where and how to strike the proper balance.

FOCUS QUESTION

Should the president have the authority to order the killing of Americans overseas who are suspected of direct involvement in terrorist activities? Should he or she need the prior approval of a federal court or of select members of Congress?

IMPACT
of Social Media and Communications Technology

Government Monitoring of Social Media

The widespread use of social media by Americans raises new privacy and civil liberties issues. In May 2012, Maryland became the first state to pass a law prohibiting employers, including state agencies, from requiring job applicants to give access to their social media accounts such as Facebook and Twitter. Several months earlier, media accounts disclosed that the FBI and DARPA (the Defense Department's Defense Advanced Research Projects Agency) were soliciting proposals for new tracking technologies that would monitor social media sites. (See the Bessette–Pitney blog of May 24, 2012.) Congressman Patrick Meehan (R-PA), chairman of the House Homeland Security Subcommittee on Counterterrorism and Intelligence, responded that "[t]he concept that the government would somehow be monitoring and storing inquiries of individual Web activities—many would find that disconcerting." However, even civil libertarians agree that government monitoring of social media can be beneficial for some purposes, such as responding to a natural disaster.

CRITICAL THINKING QUESTION

Should there be any restrictions on the authority of government to monitor social media? Should government have greater leeway to monitor for national security purposes? Should government be allowed to keep electronic dossiers on Americans based on social media communications? Where, if anywhere, should the line be drawn between legitimate and improper monitoring?

CIVIL LIBERTIES AND DELIBERATIVE DEMOCRACY

The history of civil liberties in the United States demonstrates the important lesson that the rights of citizens are not absolute. One person's rights might infringe on the rights of others, or they might interfere with legitimate and important responsibilities of government. This is perhaps most obvious when the nation is at war. As we have seen, in the Civil War, World War I, World War II, and the war on terrorism, presidents and Congress have judged that national security justified some restriction of the rights that Americans normally enjoy. Yet in peacetime also, the courts have recognized public goods—such as personal safety, public order, protection against libel and slander, and the security of children—that require some moderation or restriction of personal liberties.

Nonetheless, over the past century the courts have expanded personal liberties and contracted governmental power across a wide range of issues, including government recognition of God or religion, the free exercise of religion, the regulation of political speech (including symbolic speech), limits on pornography and censorship, and the rights of criminal defendants. Where once the deliberations of legislators and executives, state and federal, were decisive in determining where to strike the balance between liberty and power, now it is mainly judges who decide, deliberating on the facts at issue, case by case.

Executives, legislators, and judges do not necessarily reason the same way about how to balance liberty and power. Each brings a particular perspective to the process. Presidents are likely to think first about national security, and the members of Congress will often reflect broad public desires on these matters. Although federal courts by their nature are likely to be attuned to individual rights, they lack the national security perspective and expertise of the executive branch and the responsiveness to majority opinion that often motivates Congress. Thus, no one branch seems perfectly suited to strike the balance between liberty and power. In Chapter 15, we will explore more fully the role of the judiciary in American deliberative democracy.

SUMMARY

- The Bill of Rights had little direct impact on American government and politics until the twentieth century. In 1897, the U.S. Supreme Court began to apply provisions of the Bill of Rights to the states through the due process clause of the Fourteenth Amendment. Now, nearly the entire Bill of Rights restricts state and local governments, as well as the federal government.

- Under Supreme Court rulings, government may neither advance nor inhibit religion. The Court has banned officially sponsored prayers in public schools, including prayers conducted at graduation ceremonies and athletic events; however, it has not prohibited governmental recognition of God, such as in the national motto ("In God we trust") and in the Pledge of Allegiance ("one nation, under God").

- In deciding cases involving the "free exercise" of religion, the Court has sometimes ruled that government may outlaw religiously motivated actions (such as polygamy or opposition to mandatory vaccinations) that violate generally applicable laws. Other times, it has overturned government policies (such as mandatory school attendance until age 16) by using a balancing test to compare the importance of the policy to the burden placed on religiously motivated conduct.

- The Court has never held that the First Amendment prohibits all restrictions on speech. Government may prohibit the lewd and obscene, the profane, the libelous, and insulting or "fighting" words. However, nearly all political speech short of direct incitement to lawless action is protected. Also, the First Amendment protects such "expressive conduct" or "symbolic speech" as flag burning.

- In the area of morality and sexual behavior, the Court has limited government power by prohibiting laws against abortion and homosexual conduct, by restricting controls over sexually explicit materials, and by thwarting congressional efforts to deny minors access to indecent materials on the Internet.

- In cases decided in 2008 and 2010, the Court ruled that the Second Amendment recognizes the right of individuals, and not just state militias, to possess firearms for self-defense and that this right restricts federal, state, and local governments.

- The Warren Court (1953–1969) expanded the rights of those suspected, accused, or convicted of crimes. It was particularly active in the areas of search and seizure, self-incrimination, right to counsel, and cruel and unusual punishments.

- The president and Congress have restricted civil liberties in wartime in various ways, including suspending habeas corpus, instituting military tribunals, restricting speech, interning American citizens and aliens, and monitoring communications between Americans and the enemy. There is an inherent tension between civil liberties and national security that makes conflict unavoidable.

- The history of civil liberties in the United States demonstrates that rights are not absolute. One person's rights might infringe on those of another, or they might interfere with legitimate and important responsibilities of government.

KEY TERMS

Civil liberties p. 133
Civil rights p. 133
Clear and present danger test p. 145
Direct incitement test p. 145
Due process of law p. 136
Establishment clause p. 139
Exclusionary rule p. 157
Expressive conduct p. 147
Fighting words p. 145
Free exercise clause p. 139

Freedom of expression p. 147
Incorporation doctrine p. 138
Kentucky Resolutions p. 162
Lemon test p. 141
Libel p. 148
Martial law p. 162
Memorial and Remonstrance p. 139
Miranda warnings p. 158
Nationalization of the Bill of
    Rights p. 138

Obscenity p. 152
Prior restraint p. 144
Protected speech p. 145
Seditious libel p. 162
Selective incorporation p. 139
Slander p. 148
Symbolic speech p. 147
Unprotected speech p. 145
Virginia Resolutions p. 162
Wall of separation p. 140

TEST YOUR KNOWLEDGE

1. How do civil liberties differ from civil rights?
   a. Civil liberties are personal freedoms, while civil rights concern freedom from discrimination.
   b. Civil liberties are rights granted by Congress, while civil rights are those due to all people without legislation.
   c. Civil liberties are those rights listed in the original Constitution, while civil rights are outlined in the Bill of Rights.
   d. Civil rights are listed in the original Constitution, while civil liberties are outlined in the Bill of Rights.
   e. Civil rights are personal freedoms, while civil liberties concern freedom from discrimination.

2. The procedural protections that government must follow before depriving anyone of life, liberty, or property are called
   a. civil liberties.
   b. due process of law.
   c. Miranda rights.
   d. prior restraint.
   e. the Bill of Rights.

3. What is the incorporation doctrine?
   a. the doctrine that prohibited speech critical of the government without concern for the truth of the accusations
   b. the doctrine that the due process clause of the Fourteenth Amendment extends most specific rights in the Bill of Rights to states and localities
   c. the doctrine that the government can restrict freedom of speech when it directly incites violence
   d. procedural protections the government is required to follow before depriving anyone of life, liberty, or property
   e. a rule that prohibits the use of evidence improperly obtained, regardless of its relevance to the guilt of the defendant

4. The three rules of thumb regarding challenges to the Establishment Clause are called the _____ test.
   a. Establishment
   b. Expressive
   c. Free Exercise
   d. Kurtzman
   e. Lemon

5. What does the belief–conduct distinction state?
   a. Citizens must conduct themselves in alignment with religious beliefs regardless of personal belief.
   b. Religious ceremonies are subject to the scrutiny of federal investigators.
   c. Religious conduct should not conflict with religious beliefs.
   d. Religious people may believe what they wish, but they must still adhere to state or federal laws that regulate personal behavior.
   e. Religious people may believe what they wish, provided it is within the federal laws.

6. The Smith Act banned
   a. allowing illegal aliens to register to vote.
   b. associating with known or suspected Communists.
   c. permitting students to hold prayer services on public school grounds.
   d. printing religious newspapers.
   e. teaching or advocating the duty to overthrow any government in the United States by force or violence.

7. In its recent Second Amendment rulings, the Supreme Court held that
   a. the right to keep and bear arms means only to the right of states to arm their militias.
   b. the amendment is no longer relevant to modern conditions.
   c. the amendment protects an individual's right to own firearms for self-defense but does not limit state and local authority to ban private ownership of handguns in high crime areas.
   d. the amendment accords an individual right to own firearms but that this must be balanced against the legitimate government interest in combating gun crimes.
   e. the amendment protects an individual right to own firearms that applies to the federal government and the states.

8. A man is accused of owning an illegal weapon that was discovered by the police during a search of the defendant's home without a warrant or probable cause. The case is most likely dismissed due to lack of evidence because
   a. only federal laws deal with gun ownership and the police acted on local authority only.
   b. seizures are illegal unless the suspect is given prior warning.
   c. the exclusionary rule prohibits the prosecution from presenting the weapon as evidence since it was unlawfully seized.
   d. the laws governing what constitutes an illegal weapon are unclear and have not been thoroughly tested in the courts.
   e. the police did not follow the basic rules of the clear and present danger test.

9. In what way did the effects on civil liberties differ in the Civil War and World War I?
   a. President Wilson issued more orders regarding civil liberties than President Lincoln.
   b. Laws passed by Congress were more influential during the Civil War than during World War I.
   c. Federal courts were more active and effective in litigating civil liberties cases during World War I than during the Civil War.
   d. Federal courts addressed more civil liberties complaints during the Civil War than during World War I.
   e. During the Civil War, habeas corpus was not suspended as it was in World War I.

10. Which of the following anti-terrorism policies of the George W. Bush administration did the Barack Obama administration NOT endorse or continue?
    a. military trials for suspected terrorists
    b. the use of interrogation techniques such as waterboarding, stress positions, and sleep deprivation
    c. the use of the "state secrets" doctrine in court to prevent the exposure of intelligence secrets or methods
    d. the prolonged detention of some suspected terrorists who would not be tried in federal courts or before military tribunals
    e. the Patriot Act

FURTHER READING

Carter, Stephen L. *God's Name in Vain: The Wrongs and Rights of Religion in Politics.* New York: Basic Books, 2001.

Clor, Harry M. *Public Morality and Liberal Society: Essays on Decency, Law, and Pornography.* Notre Dame, IN: University of Notre Dame Press, 1996.

Goldwin, Robert A. *From Parchment to Power: How James Madison Used the Bill of Rights to Save the Constitution.* Washington, DC: AEI Press, 1997.

Hamburger, Philip. *Separation of Church and State.* Cambridge, MA: Harvard University Press, 2002.

Hickok, Eugene W. Jr., ed. *The Bill of Rights: Original Meaning and Current Understanding.* Charlottesville: University Press of Virginia, 1991.

Hutson, James H., ed. *Religion and the New Republic: Faith in the Founding of America.* Lanham, MD: Rowman and Littlefield, 2000.

Kelly, Alfred H., Winfred A. Harbison, and Herman Belz. *The American Constitution: Its Origins and Development.* 2 vols., 7th ed. New York: Norton, 1991.

Levy, Leonard W. *Origins of the Bill of Rights.* New Haven, CT: Yale University Press, 1999.

Neely, Mark E. Jr. *The Fate of Liberty: Abraham Lincoln and Civil Liberties.* New York: Oxford University Press, 1991.

Rehnquist, William H. *All the Laws but One: Civil Liberties in Wartime.* New York: Knopf, 1998.

Rossum, Ralph A., and G. Alan Tarr. *American Constitutional Law: Volume II. The Bill of Rights and Subsequent Amendments.* 5th ed. New York: St. Martin's/Worth, 1999.

Storing, Herbert J. "The Constitution and the Bill of Rights." In *Toward a More Perfect Union: Writings of Herbert J. Storing,* ed. Joseph M. Bessette. Washington, DC: AEI Press, 1995.

Veit, Helen E., Kenneth R. Bowling, and Charlene Bangs Bickford, eds. *Creating the Bill of Rights: The Documentary Record from the First Federal Congress.* Baltimore, MD: Johns Hopkins University Press, 1991.

WEB SOURCES

American Center for Law and Justice: www.aclj.org—an organization that litigates on First Amendment issues, focusing on religious freedom.

American Civil Liberties Union: www.aclu.org—an organization of nearly 200 attorneys who litigate on civil liberties issues.

Americans United for Life: www.aul.org—a public interest law and policy organization that seeks to influence public policy on abortion, euthanasia, stem-cell research, and other issues.

Americans United for Separation of Church and State: www.au.org—a group that focuses on church–state separation issues.

Becket Fund for Religious Liberty: www.becketfund.org—a Washington-based public interest law firm that focuses on religious freedom.

Cato Institute: www.cato.org/civil-liberties—a libertarian organization that promotes individual liberty and free markets.

Center for Democracy & Technology: www.cdt.org—a Washington-based nonprofit public policy organization that promotes online free speech.

First Amendment Center: www.firstamendmentcenter.org—an extensive collection of online materials on the First Amendment maintained by Vanderbilt University.

Institute for Justice: www.ij.org—a libertarian public interest law firm.

Liberty Counsel: www.lc.org—a nonprofit organization "dedicated to advancing religious freedom, the sanctity of human life and the traditional family."

NARAL Pro-Choice America: www.naral.org—an organization devoted to protecting a woman's right to an abortion.

National Right to Life: www.nrlc.org—a nationwide organization opposed to abortion and euthanasia.

National Security Archive: www.gwu.edu/~nsarchiv—a depository of declassified government records on national security, foreign policy, and intelligence matters, housed at George Washington University.

Reporters Committee for Freedom of the Press: www.rcfp.org—a group that promotes press freedom and provides free legal assistance to journalists.

Rutherford Institute: www.rutherford.org—a litigation and educational group that promotes religious freedom and civil liberties.

Part of the crowd gathered around the Lincoln Memorial in Washington, DC, to hear from Reverend Martin Luther King Jr. during the March on Washington for Jobs and Freedom, August 28, 1963.

© Flip Schulke/CORBIS

6

Civil Rights

OBJECTIVES

After reading this chapter, you should be able to:

- Describe the history of the civil rights struggle in the United States.
- Assess the importance of the landmark Civil Rights Act of 1964 and the Voting Rights Act of 1965.
- Evaluate the key issues in the contemporary debates over school desegregation, voting rights, and affirmative action.
- Compare the struggle by women to achieve legal and political equality with men in the United States with the civil rights movement.
- Summarize federal efforts to eliminate discrimination against older Americans and those with disabilities.
- Compare the roles played by the U.S. Congress, state courts, state legislatures, and voter-approved initiatives in the controversy over same-sex marriage in the United States.

INTRODUCTION

The United States was founded on the principles that all human beings equally possess the rights to life, liberty, and the pursuit of happiness and that the purpose of government is to secure these rights. The nation's great moral leaders have urged Americans to recognize their obligation to secure the rights of all. Yet, as everyone knows, politics involves more than justice and the common good, for no one denies the power of self-interest and power politics. The clash between the pursuit of self-interest and deliberation about the common good is painfully obvious in the efforts of Americans to achieve their civil rights.

The self-interest of slave owners, slave traders, and others may explain why slavery persisted in the American colonies and nation from 1619 to 1865, but can it explain why it ended? Self-interest, or at least perceived self-interest, may explain why white majorities in the South after the Civil War denied blacks political power and constructed a segregated society, but can it explain why federal courts and national majorities dismantled legal **segregation** a century later? Self-interest may explain why male state legislatures in the new nation denied women the right to vote and denied married women the right to own property in their own name, but can it explain why they extended property rights to married women in the nineteenth century and why they joined men in Congress in the early twentieth century to give all women the right to vote?

Those who led the struggle for civil rights understood that connecting their cause to the nation's founding principles strengthened the moral case for change. Their efforts are testimony to the belief that despite the power of self-interest in politics, the American people and their elected officials also respond to moral appeals and in so doing reason together about the common good.

When William Lloyd Garrison and others founded the American Anti-Slavery Society in 1833, they quoted the Declaration of Independence and insisted that "the principles of natural justice, of our republican form of government, and of the Christian religion" all called for an end to slavery. They devoted their efforts to molding public opinion by appealing "to the consciences, hearts, and interests of the people."[1]

When 250 women and 40 men met at Seneca Falls, New York, in 1848 to inaugurate a movement for achieving the "social, civil and religious rights of women," they connected their cause to the principles of the Declaration of Independence, affirming in their "Declaration of Sentiments" that "[w]e hold these truths to be self-evident: that all men and women are created equal."[2]

When political leaders established the new Republican Party in the 1850s to oppose the extension of slavery into the territories, they devoted their organization to recovering the principles of freedom in the Declaration of Independence. Abraham Lincoln, an early Republican, grounded his opposition to slavery on "my ancient faith [that] teaches me that 'all men are created equal;' and that there can be no moral right in connection with one man's making a slave of another."[3]

As we saw in Chapter 1, Martin Luther King Jr. connected the cause of black Americans in the 1950s and 1960s with "the magnificent words of the Constitution and the Declaration of Independence," which "promise[d] that all men, yes, black men as well as white men, would be guaranteed the 'unalienable Rights of Life, Liberty, and the pursuit of Happiness.'"[4]

And when President Lyndon Johnson urged Congress to pass the Voting Rights Act of 1965, he cited the words of the Declaration of Independence—"All men are created equal" and "government by consent of the governed"—as evidence of the "promise to every citizen that he shall share in the dignity of man" and "be treated as a man equal in opportunity to all others."[5]

As we discussed in the previous chapter, the term *civil rights* in its modern sense refers to the freedom to live one's life and engage in the political process free from **discrimination**. In this chapter, we begin with the civil rights struggle by black Americans, including the ending of slavery in the nineteenth century and the achievement of legal equality in the twentieth. We then analyze three key contemporary issues and controversies: school desegregation and busing, voting rights, and affirmative action. In the next section, we focus on the effort by women to achieve legal and political equality with men, with particular

Segregation—a term referring to the separation of the races in housing, the use of public accommodations, employment, or education. See *De facto* segregation and *De jure* segregation.

Civil rights—in the modern understanding (and as distinguished from *civil liberties*), a term that refers to the freedom to live one's life and engage in the political process free from discrimination, especially because of race, ethnicity, or gender.

Discrimination—treating individuals differently and unfairly because of characteristics over which they have no control, such as race, ethnicity, or gender.

emphasis on voting rights and current legal controversies. Finally, we examine civil rights issues regarding older Americans, individuals with disabilities, and gays and lesbians. Although it is easy to focus on how long it took for African Americans, women, and others to achieve their rights, we should also consider why it happened at all. As we will see, congressional laws, presidential acts, constitutional amendments, and court decisions all made an important contribution.

EQUALITY FOR BLACK AMERICANS
MAJOR ISSUE

- How did the movement for black freedom and equality lead to the end of slavery, the dismantling of government-enforced segregation, and the passage of national laws to guarantee civil rights to black Americans?

The civil rights struggle for black Americans occurred in three distinct stages: the contest over limiting and ending slavery, the conflict after the Civil War between national efforts to guarantee blacks their citizenship rights and state policies to maintain a segregated society, and the twentieth-century movement to dismantle segregation and guarantee all Americans their civil rights.

Ending Slavery

In Chapter 2, we reviewed the introduction of slavery into the American colonies, the controversies over the foreign slave trade, and the compromises with slavery in the Constitution. Although early Americans knew that slavery violated the principles of the revolution, many were willing to compromise with it because they believed that it was a temporary institution that would die out in the new nation. Several trends seemed to point in that direction.

Early Policy toward Slavery

By 1787, every state except Georgia had abolished the importation of slaves from overseas. Although South Carolina reauthorized the slave trade in 1803, four years later Congress passed a law prohibiting the importation of slaves effective January 1, 1808—the earliest moment allowed by the Constitution. Also in 1787, the Confederation Congress passed the Northwest Ordinance prohibiting slavery in the only territories then fully under federal control: what are now the states of Ohio, Indiana, Illinois, Michigan, and Wisconsin. Two years later, the First Congress under the new Constitution reaffirmed the Northwest Ordinance.

Although slavery was legal in every state in 1776, by 1804 all the northern states—New Hampshire, Vermont (which entered the Union in 1791), Massachusetts, Rhode Island, Connecticut, New York, New Jersey, and Pennsylvania—had abolished slavery outright or passed laws providing for gradual emancipation. Even many southerners during this period expected to see slavery die out. As George Washington wrote in a letter to the Marquis de Lafayette, "The prevailing opinion in Virginia is against the spread of slavery in our new Territories, and I trust we shall have a confederation of free States."[6] (For a discussion of how religious attitudes motivated antislavery efforts during this period, see Chapter 4.)

Also, during the 1780s the price of slaves declined because of a downturn in the tobacco market, the principal crop in much of the South. This reinforced the belief that slavery would gradually disappear. Eli Whitney's invention of the cotton gin in 1793, however, made the production of cotton much more profitable and slavery along with it. Slavery expanded westward into the new states of Kentucky (1792), Tennessee (1796), Louisiana (1812), Mississippi (1817), and Alabama (1819). According to the 1820 census, 1.5 million slaves and about 230,000 free blacks lived in the United States. Slaves constituted 16% of the U.S. population.

The Missouri Compromise

The Louisiana Purchase of 1803 vastly increased the size of the United States. In 1820, the nation faced a crisis over whether to allow slavery in the states that would be carved out of the new lands. Because slavery had already existed in the southern part of the new territory when it was under Spanish and French control, Louisiana was allowed to enter the Union as a slave state in 1812.

In 1819, the citizens of the territory of Missouri applied for statehood as a slave state, while the citizens of Maine, formerly part of Massachusetts, applied to enter the Union as a free state. This would have preserved the balance of free and slave states in the nation and in the Senate. Although a majority of the House of Representatives voted to prohibit the introduction of additional slaves into Missouri and

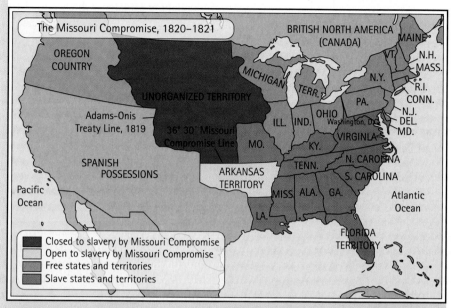

The United States at the Time of the Missouri Compromise of 1820

FIGURE 6–1 The large territory northwest of the state of Missouri was part of the Louisiana Purchase of 1803. According to the Missouri Compromise, slavery would be "forever prohibited" in this territory.
SOURCE: www.teachingamericanhistory.org/neh/interactives/sectionalism/lesson1/.

to require that slaves already there become free at age 25, the Senate rejected the measure. Congress then passed several laws that became known collectively as the Missouri Compromise of 1820. This compromise allowed Maine to enter the Union as a free state and Missouri as a slave state, but it also stipulated that slavery would be "forever prohibited" in the remaining territory of the Louisiana Purchase north of Missouri's southern border (36°30′ latitude; see Figure 6-1). Because many free states would likely enter the Union from this territory, the nation seemed committed to eventually having a majority of free states.

Growing Divisions on Slavery

Although this compromise quieted the debate over slavery for awhile, the controversy heated up again in the 1830s. In 1831, William Lloyd Garrison founded the *Liberator*, which became the leading abolitionist newspaper. He and others then established the American Anti-Slavery Society in 1833, which provided energy and direction to the growing abolitionist movement. A young escaped slave from Maryland, Frederick Douglass, added his considerable rhetorical skills to the antislavery cause through speeches and an autobiography that recounted the brutality of slavery. First published in 1845, *Narrative of the Life of Frederick Douglass* documented Douglass's life in slavery until his escape in 1838 at the age of 20. From the 1840s until his death in 1895, Douglass was the nation's leading black orator and leader.

Prior to the 1830s, southerners had defended their "peculiar institution" as at best a "necessary evil." But in 1837, Senator John C. Calhoun of South Carolina took to the Senate floor to defend slavery as "instead of an evil, a good—a positive good." "[T]here never has yet existed a wealthy and civilized society," Calhoun asserted, "in which one portion of the community did not, in point of fact, live on the labor of the other."[7] Over the coming decades, more and more southerners defended slavery as good for American society, deepening the chasm between northern and southern opinion.

The Consequences of the Mexican–American War

The debate over the extension of slavery into the territories heated up in 1846 when Democratic congressman David Wilmot of Pennsylvania proposed legislation to prohibit slavery in any territory acquired by the United States as a result of the Mexican–American War

(1846–1848). The Wilmot Proviso twice passed the House but failed in the Senate. In the Treaty of Guadalupe Hidalgo, which ended the war in 1848, the United States gained a vast new territory from Mexico, which included the present states of Arizona, California, Nevada, and Utah, and parts of New Mexico, Colorado, and Wyoming. The defeat of the Wilmot Proviso left unresolved whether slavery would be allowed into this new territory.

When California applied for statehood as a free state in 1850, a great debate broke out in the Senate over the fate of slavery in the new territories. Under the Compromise of 1850, Congress admitted California as a free state, allowed slavery in the territories of New Mexico and Utah if the local residents approved, enacted a new and more effective Fugitive Slave Act, and prohibited the slave trade in Washington, DC.

Although this compromise seemed to settle the immediate controversy, many northerners adamantly opposed the new fugitive slave law, which replaced the original Fugitive Slave Act of 1793. The new law gave the federal government exclusive jurisdiction over fugitive slave cases, provided for special U.S. commissioners to hear cases and make decisions, denied those accused of being fugitive slaves a jury trial and prohibited them from testifying on their own behalf, and authorized a payment of $10 to commissioners when they ruled against the alleged fugitive slave but only $5 when they ruled in his or her favor.

Many northerners refused to cooperate with federal agents enforcing the law, and some state legislatures passed "personal liberty laws" that prohibited their officials from cooperating with the federal law. During this period, thousands of slaves safely made their way to Canada through the so-called **Underground Railroad**—an informal network of secret routes, safe houses, and transportation run by abolitionists.

Underground Railroad—an informal network of secret routes, safe houses, and transportation run by abolitionists to help slaves escape from the South to Canada in the period before the Civil War.

The Repeal of the Missouri Compromise

As the population of the old Louisiana Territory grew, settlers pressed Congress to create territorial governments as a precursor to statehood. With slavery "forever prohibited" in most of this territory under the Missouri Compromise of 1820, southerners feared the admission of many new free states into the Union. Senator Stephen Douglas of Illinois and other leaders of the Democratic Party, hoping to quell growing sectional strife, pushed through Congress the Kansas-Nebraska Act of 1854. This law organized the territories of Kansas and Nebraska (which later became all or part of seven states) and allowed the residents of these territories to vote on slavery. This measure effectively repealed the Missouri Compromise of 1820.

Supporters of the law defended it as embracing the principle of "popular sovereignty": the people of the territories should decide for themselves whether to allow slavery. Lincoln, then a politically active lawyer in Illinois, denounced the law as a perversion of self-government: "When the white man governs himself, and also governs *another* man, that is *more* than self-government—that is despotism."[8]

In response to the repeal of the Missouri Compromise and the failure of either of the two major parties (Democratic and Whig) to take a stand against the extension of slavery, political leaders throughout the North and West organized the Republican Party, which soon replaced the Whig Party as one of the nation's two major parties. It dedicated itself to preserving the principles of freedom "promulgated in the Declaration of Independence, and embodied in the Federal Constitution." These principles demanded that slavery not be introduced into any new territories.[9]

With so much at stake, pro- and antislavery forces fought for control of the Kansas Territory in 1854–1857. Violent clashes occurred throughout the territory, leading Horace Greeley of the *New York Tribune* to coin the term "bleeding Kansas." Through deceit and fraud, slavery advocates wrote a state constitution at Lecompton (the Lecompton Constitution) in 1857 embracing slavery, but the U.S. Congress refused to accept it. Kansas eventually entered the Union as a free state in 1861.

The Supreme Court entered the fray in 1857 when it handed down *Dred Scott v. Sandford* (see Chapter 4). The majority ruled that the principles of the Declaration of Independence did not include blacks, that free blacks (then about 450,000) could not be citizens of the United States with access to the federal courts, and that Congress lacked authority to prohibit slavery in the federal territories. This last holding meant that in the view of the Court the Missouri Compromise of 1820 had been unconstitutional. Thus the *Dred Scott* decision made it impossible for Congress to reinstate the Missouri Compromise or to impose any restrictions on the spread of slavery to the territories. In a major speech on the decision, Lincoln reaffirmed the Republican Party position that "the Declaration of Independence includes *all* men, black as well as white."[10]

The Lincoln–Douglas Debates

A year later, Lincoln and incumbent Stephen Douglas, candidates for the U.S. Senate from Illinois, engaged in seven debates, called the **Lincoln–Douglas debates**. They contended over the extension of slavery into the federal territories, the meaning of the principles of the Declaration of Independence and popular sovereignty, and the importance and consequences of the *Dred Scott* decision. The candidates faced large and enthusiastic crowds throughout the state and employed a debate format unheard of today: the first speaker addressed the audience for one hour, the other responded for an hour and a half, and the original speaker wrapped up for a half hour. (Who went first alternated from one debate to the next.)

Lincoln–Douglas debates—seven debates held throughout Illinois in the Senate contest of 1858 between Democratic incumbent Stephen Douglas and Republican challenger Abraham Lincoln.

Douglas used the debates to defend the Kansas-Nebraska Act, which allowed the people of the territories to adopt slavery if they wished, by denying that blacks had any God-given rights that whites must respect: "Now, I do not believe that the Almighty ever intended the negro to be the equal of the white man." The United States, he insisted, was founded only for whites: "I believe this Government was made on the white basis. I believe it was made by white men for the benefit of white men and their posterity for ever." Lincoln countered by reaffirming the universality of the principles of freedom in the Declaration of Independence. By encouraging Americans to be indifferent toward the extension of slavery, Douglas was "blowing out the moral lights around us." He was "penetrating the human soul and eradicating the light of reason and the love of liberty in this American people."[11]

The Outbreak of War

Although Lincoln lost the Senate election, the debates helped to establish his reputation as a national leader on the slavery issue. Two years later, he was the Republican nominee for president. In a four-way race, he won the presidency with 40% of the popular vote and 59% of the electoral votes.

In response to the Republican victory, the legislature of South Carolina called for a state convention to consider secession. In December, the convention voted unanimously to secede from the Union. Before Lincoln took office on March 4, 1861, six more states followed: Mississippi, Florida, Alabama, Georgia, Louisiana, and Texas. Six weeks later, Confederate forces fired on Fort Sumter in Charleston (SC) Harbor, and the Civil War began. Four more slave states joined the Confederacy: Virginia, Arkansas, Tennessee, and North Carolina. Four slave states, however, also called the "border states," remained loyal to the Union: Delaware, Maryland, Kentucky, and Missouri.

The End of Slavery

In the early stages of the war, the aim of the federal government was to restore the Union, not to free the slaves. But in the second year of the war, the Congress, now dominated by antislavery northerners, began to move against slavery. In April 1862, it abolished slavery in the District of Columbia; in June, it prohibited slavery in the federal territories (thus defying the

© Bettmann/CORBIS

Abraham Lincoln and Senator Stephen Douglas debate the extension of slavery to the territories in the U.S. Senate campaign in Illinois in 1858. Their seven debates attracted large, festive crowds.

Supreme Court's *Dred Scott* decision); and in July, it passed a law freeing the slaves of anyone found guilty of treason against the United States and also any slaves from rebellious areas who escaped to, or were liberated by, the Union army. Also in July, Congress authorized the employment of blacks into the military, granting freedom to those who joined.

Abolitionists and others pushed President Lincoln to free all the slaves, but he denied that he had such authority. By late 1862, however, he came to see the military value of emancipating the slaves in rebel territory as a way to weaken the enemy. He deemed that his constitutional authority as commander in chief gave him the power. Accordingly, he issued the **Emancipation Proclamation** on January 1, 1863, freeing all slaves then behind Confederate lines. He defended his move as "an act of justice, warranted by the Constitution upon military necessity."[12] (Note that the proclamation did not affect slavery in the four border states loyal to the Union.) After the Emancipation Proclamation, thousands of escaped or liberated slaves joined the Union military forces. By the end of the war, nearly 200,000 blacks were serving in the army and navy.

In 1863, counties in the western portion of Virginia, a region that had remained loyal to the Union, were admitted as the new state of West Virginia. Its constitution freed slaves over the age of 21 and younger slaves once they reached that age. Two years later the state abolished slavery altogether. In 1864, pro-Union southerners established new antislavery constitutions in Arkansas and Louisiana. Maryland abolished slavery late in the year, and Missouri and Tennessee followed in early 1865. In January 1865, the House and Senate approved a constitutional amendment abolishing slavery throughout the nation. On December 6, 1865, the twenty-seventh state (making three-fourths of all the states) ratified the Thirteenth Amendment. Slavery was now illegal throughout the United States.

Reconstruction and Jim Crow

In 1860, 4 million slaves and almost half a million free blacks lived in the United States (constituting 14% of the population). By the end of 1865, all were free. The great issue in the years ahead was whether the newly freed population would enjoy the rights and responsibilities of citizenship and be treated as equal members of the political community. (Even in the North only a few states had allowed free blacks to vote, hold office, or serve on juries.) As we will see, national majorities passed laws and constitutional amendments to extend legal protections to blacks; state and local majorities in the South denied blacks political influence and mandated social segregation by law; and the Supreme Court limited the reach of federal power, especially over private discrimination. We begin with the 12-year period immediately after the Civil War, commonly called **Reconstruction** (1865–1877).

As the Civil War was coming to a close in March 1865, Congress created the **Freedmen's Bureau** in the Department of War to promote the welfare and legal rights of the newly freed slaves. The bureau's field operations continued until 1868 and its educational program until 1872. Despite this national effort, many of the reorganized southern state governments passed **Black Codes** in 1865 and 1866 that restricted the rights and freedom of the former slaves, tied them to the soil, and imposed more severe criminal punishments on blacks than on whites.

Federal Efforts to Promote Black Equality

To counteract the Black Codes, Congress passed the Civil Rights Act of 1866, which stipulated that all citizens, regardless of any previous condition of servitude, were to have the same rights to make and enforce contracts, to sue in court, to inherit property, and to hold and sell property. Other provisions outlawed different criminal punishments for blacks and whites. The law extended national citizenship to all those "born or naturalized in the United States and not subject to any foreign power, except Indians not taxed." This act overturned the *Dred Scott* decision, which had held that free blacks could not be citizens of the United States.

That same year, Confederate veterans founded the **Ku Klux Klan**, a white supremacist group, in Pulaski, Tennessee, to terrorize and intimidate southern blacks and their white

Emancipation Proclamation—President Abraham Lincoln's executive order, effective January 1, 1863, that freed all the slaves then behind Confederate lines.

Reconstruction—the 12 years after the Civil War (1865–1877) when national policy, directed principally by the Republican-dominated Congress, sought to reintegrate the 11 states of the Confederacy back into the Union and to provide for the civil and political rights of the newly freed slaves.

Freedmen's Bureau—an agency in the Department of War created by Congress in 1865 to promote the welfare and legal rights of the newly freed slaves.

Black Codes—laws passed by many of the southern states immediately after the Civil War to restrict the rights and freedom of the former slaves, tying them to the soil, and imposing more severe criminal punishments on blacks than on whites.

Ku Klux Klan—the name for both (1) a white supremacist organization founded in Tennessee in 1866 to terrorize and intimidate southern blacks and their white sympathizers and (2) an organization founded in Georgia in 1915 to promote white supremacy, anti-Catholicism, anti-immigration, and anti-Semitism.

sympathizers. It spread terror through lynchings, by hanging their victims or killing them by other means. Congress strengthened federal control over the South by passing the Reconstruction Acts of 1867 and 1868. These laws placed 10 of the former Confederate states under direct military control, subject to martial law. Up to 20,000 federal troops enforced federal law and protected the voting rights of the black population.

Because of concerns about the constitutionality of the Civil Rights Act of 1866, Congress passed the Fourteenth Amendment, which the states ratified in 1868. With language almost identical to the Civil Rights Act, it affirmed the national citizenship of the freed slaves and added that they were also citizens "of the State wherein they reside." It also prohibited states from

- abridging "the privileges or immunities of citizens of the United States,"
- depriving "any person of life, liberty, or property, without due process of law," or
- denying anyone "the equal protection of the laws."

In the twentieth century, the equal protection clause became central to the civil rights struggle.

Although the Fourteenth Amendment did not formally give blacks the right to vote, it stipulated that the representation of any state in the House of Representatives would be reduced in proportion to the number of male citizens at least 21 years of age who were denied the right to vote (a provision that was never enforced).

Fears that southerners would disenfranchise blacks, who constituted just over 40% of the population in the 11 states of the Confederacy, led to the passage of the Fifteenth Amendment in 1870. This amendment provided that neither the United States nor any state could deny the right to vote based on "race, color, or previous condition of servitude." (In 1867, Congress had granted voting rights to blacks in the nation's capital and in the federal territories.)

Congress Addresses Private Discrimination

In 1870 and 1871, Congress passed the Enforcement Acts and the Ku Klux Klan Act to make the Fourteenth and Fifteenth amendments more effective. These acts covered not only state action but also acts by private individuals to deny blacks their civil and political rights. Under authority of the Ku Klux Klan Act, President Ulysses S. Grant suspended habeas corpus and imposed martial law in parts of South Carolina in 1871. Federal authorities prosecuted, convicted, and sent to prison several hundred Klansmen. In 1872, the Klan disbanded.

In the Civil Rights Act of 1875, Congress went beyond prior law by prohibiting discrimination in what are commonly called public accommodations: "inns, public conveyances on land or water, theaters, and other places of public amusement." The law did not, however, address or require school **desegregation**.

Jim Crow Laws

In April 1877, one month after taking office, the new president Rutherford B. Hayes ordered the withdrawal of federal troops from the South, essentially ending Reconstruction. Hayes's decision made good on a promise to southern Democrats to remove the troops in exchange for their acceptance of his victory over Democrat Samuel Tilden in the disputed 1876 presidential election. Southern states quickly passed so-called **Jim Crow laws** (the term comes from a minstrel song) mandating the segregation of the races in virtually all social relations, such as transportation, housing, restaurants, churches, hospitals, cemeteries, and entertainment.

The states also sought to restrict black political power by requiring **literacy tests**, often imposed in a biased way, to keep uneducated former slaves from voting, and by imposing **poll taxes**, which many blacks could not afford. Because these same requirements might keep poor and uneducated whites from voting, states adopted **grandfather clauses**, which exempted an individual from literacy tests or poll taxes if his grandfather or any ancestor could vote before the passage of the Fifteenth Amendment. In addition, the Democratic

Desegregation—legal and other efforts to undo segregation of races or ethnic groups.

Jim Crow laws—laws passed in the South in the 1870s and 1880s that mandated the segregation of the races in virtually all social relations, such as transportation, housing, restaurants, churches, hospitals, cemeteries, and entertainment.

Literacy tests—tests once used to determine whether a person could read well enough to qualify for voting.

Poll tax—a tax assessed before someone can vote.

Grandfather clauses—laws passed in the South in the late nineteenth century that exempted an individual from literacy tests or poll taxes if his grandfather or any ancestor could vote before the passage of the Fifteenth Amendment (1870). These were designed to enfranchise poor and illiterate whites.

White primary–a primary election introduced in southern states in the late nineteenth century limited to white voters.

Party in the South introduced **white primaries**, which prohibited blacks from voting in primary elections that chose party candidates for federal and state office. As the South became solidly Democratic, white primaries denied those blacks who could vote any real opportunity to influence elections.

Key Supreme Court Decisions

Beginning in 1873, the Supreme Court issued several key decisions that limited the power of the federal government to combat discrimination. These decisions

- narrowly interpreted the "privileges or immunities" clause of the Fourteenth Amendment, giving the states priority in defining the usual rights of citizenship;[13]
- prohibited the Congress from outlawing violence against blacks unless it could be shown that racism was the cause (thus overturning the conviction of several white men for joining in the massacre of more than 100 blacks in a dispute over a contested election in Louisiana);[14] and
- struck down as unconstitutional the provisions of the Civil Rights Act of 1875 that prohibited discrimination by private individuals in public accommodations.[15]

In these last two decisions, the Court held that the Fourteenth Amendment reaches only state action, not discrimination by private individuals.

Then in 1896, in *Plessy v. Ferguson*, the Court ruled, 7–1, that Louisiana's law mandating the separation of the races on railroads did not violate the equal protection clause of the Fourteenth Amendment as long as blacks had the same access to railroads as whites. This was the beginning of the **separate but equal doctrine** that would govern federal court decisions for half a century. In a now famous dissent, Justice John Marshall Harlan insisted that the statute should be overturned because "[o]ur Constitution is color-blind, and neither knows nor tolerates classes among citizens. In respect of civil rights, all citizens are equal before the law."[16]

Separate but equal doctrine–the doctrine promulgated by the Supreme Court in *Plessy v. Ferguson* that under the equal protection clause of the Fourteenth Amendment, state governments could separate the races as long as they had access to equal facilities.

Although the Court later upheld the constitutionality of literacy tests and poll taxes (1898), it also overturned some state and local segregation laws, including laws that excluded blacks from juries (1880), grandfather clauses (1915), and city ordinances that prevented blacks from moving into white neighborhoods (1917). Later the Court struck down white primaries established by state laws (1927) and white primaries run by political parties when state law was silent on the subject (1944).

The Struggle for Civil Rights in the Twentieth Century

Two important African Americans led the struggle for black equality in the late nineteenth and early twentieth centuries. One was Booker T. Washington, the founding president in 1881 of the Tuskegee Normal and Industrial Institute in Tuskegee, Alabama. The Tuskegee Institute (later Tuskegee University) became a leading black institution for higher education in the United States. In 1901, Washington published his autobiography, *Up from Slavery*. Until his death in 1915 at age 59, Washington was the nation's foremost black educator and proponent of self-reliance and hard work.

The other early civil rights leader was W. E. B. Du Bois, the first black American to earn a PhD (from Harvard in 1895). In 1909, Du Bois and a group of white and black intellectuals founded the National Association for the Advancement of Colored People (NAACP) in New York City. Du Bois edited the NAACP's magazine *Crisis* for 24 years and wrote 20 books. He was the nation's leading black intellectual during the first half of the twentieth century. The NAACP went on to become the nation's most influential civil rights organization.

Early Setbacks

In the second decade of the twentieth century, the cause of black equality suffered several setbacks. In 1915, a second Ku Klux Klan was founded in Georgia. It promoted white supremacy, as well as anti-Catholicism, anti-immigration, and anti-Semitism. Also, during the administration of President Woodrow Wilson (1913–1921) the federal departments of the Treasury and Post Office became segregated, including separate lunch counters and bathrooms for white and black employees. The Post Office began segregated counter service to the public, and the federal civil service began requiring photographs with job applications to facilitate discrimination against blacks.

More than 300,000 African Americans served in the nation's military during World War I (1917–1918). When they returned from Europe, they felt a new urgency to improve their condition back home. As an editorial in the NAACP's *Crisis* magazine implored, "Make way for Democracy! We saved it in France, and by the Great Jehovah, we will save it in the U.S.A., or know the reason why."[17] But racial harmony and racial justice proved elusive.

Southern blacks began moving to northern cities in large numbers, the resurgent Klan spread violence and intimidation, and the NAACP and other organizations stepped up efforts to highlight the plight of blacks. A race riot in Chicago in 1919 lasted 13 days and resulted in the deaths of 15 whites and 23 blacks, with injuries to more than 500 others. Despite documenting more than 3,000 lynchings in three decades, the NAACP was unable in 1921 to convince Congress to pass a law making lynching a federal crime. Similar efforts also failed in 1935 and 1940.

Presidents Franklin Roosevelt and Harry Truman

The Great Depression of the 1930s hit blacks especially hard because most were unskilled. Many embraced President Franklin Roosevelt's leadership and New Deal programs and switched their allegiance from the Republican Party (the party of Lincoln) to the Democratic Party. In 1934, the first black Democrat was elected to Congress.

In 1940 and 1941, however, blacks became frustrated by their exclusion from employment in much of the burgeoning defense industry. When black leaders threatened a massive march on Washington, DC, in 1941, President Roosevelt issued an executive order that prohibited discrimination in federal agencies and defense industries and established the Fair Employment Practices Committee to monitor enforcement.

Then in 1948, President Harry S Truman issued an executive order ending segregation in the military by mandating "equality of treatment and opportunity for all persons in the armed services without regard to race, color, religion or national origin."[18] When the Democratic Party adopted a strong civil rights plank as part of its 1948 platform, many southern delegates bolted from the convention and established the States Rights Party, commonly called the Dixiecrats. Strongly endorsing segregation, the new party nominated South Carolina governor Strom Thurmond for president, and he carried four states in the November election.

Civil Rights in the Courts

During this period, the legal arm of the NAACP, the Legal Defense Fund, adopted an aggressive litigation strategy to combat segregation. In a series of cases, the Supreme Court began to dismantle the legal foundations of segregation. Relying on federal statutes and the equal protection clause of the Fourteenth Amendment, the Court prohibited states from segregating students in public law schools, overturned segregation in railroads and buses used in interstate transportation, and prohibited the use of restrictive covenants that required property owners to sell only to whites.

Most dramatically, in 1954, the Court unanimously ruled in *Brown v. Board of Education* that "in the field of public education, the doctrine of 'separate but equal' has no place. Separate educational facilities are inherently unequal."[19] A year later it ordered the federal district courts to see to it that the public schools were desegregated "with all deliberate speed."[20]

In response to these decisions, 100 southern members of the United States Congress issued the Southern Manifesto in 1956. It castigated the Court for its exercise of "naked judicial power" and pledged "to use all lawful means to bring about a reversal of this decision . . . and to prevent the use of force in its implementation."[21] The Court was unswayed.

AP Photo/Gene Herrick

Rosa Parks was arrested and fingerprinted after refusing to give up her bus seat to a white in Montgomery, Alabama, on December 1, 1955. Her courageous action inspired the Montgomery bus boycott, which launched the modern civil rights movement in the South.

Civil rights movement—in the broadest sense, the efforts dating back to the abolitionists of the early nineteenth century to secure equal rights for blacks in the United States. In the modern era, this term refers to the broad-based social movement that began with the Montgomery bus boycott of 1955 and involved such nonviolent "direct action" techniques as marches, demonstrations, boycotts, and sit-ins at segregated lunch counters.

Montgomery bus boycott—a boycott of city buses in Montgomery, Alabama, in 1955 to protest segregated seating. This action launched the modern civil rights movement.

Civil disobedience—the nonviolent breaking of a law to protest injustice and to press for social or political change.

In subsequent cases, it prohibited the segregation of the races in public parks and other recreational facilities, public transportation, public auditoriums, and jails.

The Modern Civil Rights Movement

The modern **civil rights movement** was launched by the **Montgomery bus boycott** of 1955. The boycott began when authorities arrested Rosa Parks, a 42-year-old black seamstress and secretary to the local chapter of the NAACP, for refusing to give up her seat on a city bus to a white in Montgomery, Alabama. The Reverend Martin Luther King, Jr. organized a black boycott of the city bus system that lasted a year. After the Supreme Court upheld a lower federal court ruling that the segregation of local bus systems was unconstitutional, blacks returned to the now-integrated buses. Shortly after the successful effort, King and others founded the Southern Christian Leadership Conference (SCLC) to promote nonviolent protest throughout the South.

Congress then passed the Civil Rights Act of 1957, the first federal civil rights legislation in more than 80 years. The law made it a federal offense to interfere with the right to vote and created the U.S. Commission on Civil Rights to investigate racial discrimination in voting rights. The law was less important for its concrete accomplishments than for its symbolic value in reasserting the federal government's responsibility for ensuring black voting rights.

Just weeks later, President Dwight Eisenhower sent 1,000 federal troops to Little Rock, Arkansas, to preserve order when an angry crowd tried to prevent the integration of the high school. In Eisenhower's last year in office, Congress passed the Civil Rights Act of 1960, modestly increasing federal power to enforce voting rights. It authorized federal judges to appoint "referees" to investigate complaints about violations of voting rights.

Throughout this period, blacks and their white allies pushed their cause through such nonviolent "direct action" techniques as marches, demonstrations, boycotts, and "sit-ins" at segregated lunch counters. Martin Luther King gave a classic defense of such actions in his "Letter from Birmingham Jail," written in April 1963 when he was serving a nine-day sentence for engaging in an unlawful demonstration:

> You may well ask: "Why direct action? Why sit ins, marches and so forth? Isn't negotiation a better path?" You are quite right in calling for negotiation. Indeed, this is the very purpose of direct action. Nonviolent direct action seeks to create such a crisis and foster such a tension that a community which has constantly refused to negotiate is forced to confront the issue. It seeks so to dramatize the issue that it can no longer be ignored.[22]

When direct action took the form of breaking a law, it became **civil disobedience**—the nonviolent breaking of a law to protest injustice and to press for social or political change. Southern white clergy, sympathetic to King's cause, had asked how he could justify breaking the law when blacks had insisted that southern segregationists obey the Supreme Court's *Brown* decision. King responded that "there are two types of laws: just and unjust. . . . One has not only a legal but a moral responsibility to obey just laws. Conversely, one has a moral responsibility to disobey unjust laws." But when disobeying unjust laws, one must do so "openly, lovingly, and with a willingness to accept the penalty." By acting nonviolently and accepting the punishment, the protestor could "arouse the conscience of the community" and in the process express "the highest respect for law."[23]

Owing his slim electoral victory in 1960 to votes from the segregationist South, President John F. Kennedy initially moved slowly on civil rights. This began to change in September 1962 when a mob of several thousand attacked federal law enforcement officials who were enforcing the integration of the University of Mississippi. Kennedy sent 16,000 federal troops to the campus to restore order. Then, after civil rights leader Medgar Evers was assassinated in Jackson, Mississippi, in June 1963, the president proposed a new civil rights bill. In August, more than 250,000 persons, mostly black Americans, attended the **March on Washington for Jobs and Freedom** in the nation's capital to press for civil rights and economic opportunity. It was at the time the largest demonstration to occur in Washington, DC. On August 28, Martin Luther King delivered his now famous "I Have a Dream" speech.

© O. J. Rapp/CORBIS

On July 2, 1964, President Johnson signed the Civil Rights Act into law in a public ceremony. He told the assembled dignitaries and a national television and radio audience that the law's "purpose is to promote a more abiding commitment to freedom, a more constant pursuit of justice, and a deeper respect for human dignity."

Landmark Civil Rights Laws

In January 1964, the states ratified the Twenty-fourth Amendment to the Constitution prohibiting poll taxes in federal elections; and in July, Congress passed the landmark Civil Rights Act of 1964. The act banned discrimination in public accommodations and strengthened federal enforcement of voting rights. Title VI ("title" refers to a major section of the law) prohibited discrimination in any program that received federal funds, and Title VII prohibited discrimination on the basis of "race, color, religion, sex, or national origin" in companies with at least 25 employees in hiring, promotion, and terms of employment. Six months after the passage of the act, the Supreme Court upheld the ban on discrimination in public accommodations as a valid exercise of Congress's power over interstate commerce. (See the key language in Titles VI and VII in the discussion of affirmative action below.)

Despite the importance of the new law, many in the civil rights movement did not believe that it went far enough in protecting and securing voting rights. When 600 individuals started a march from Selma to Montgomery, Alabama, to demonstrate for voting rights in March 1965, state and local police attacked them with clubs and tear gas. A few weeks later, under the protection of the National Guard, 3,000 set out on the 54-mile march, their ranks swelling to 25,000 by the time they reached Montgomery.

Five months later, President Lyndon Johnson signed into law the Voting Rights Act of 1965. "The most basic right of all," Johnson had told Congress a few months before, was "the right to choose your own leaders."[24] The law

- expanded the authority of the federal courts to prohibit discriminatory practices regarding the right to vote;
- effectively prohibited the use of literacy tests;
- authorized the federal government to appoint examiners with the power to register citizens to vote; and
- in jurisdictions with a history of discrimination, required preapproval from the Justice Department before any changes could be made to electoral laws or practices.

On April 4, 1968, Martin Luther King Jr. was assassinated in Memphis, Tennessee. Riots followed in cities throughout the country. Just a week after King's death, Congress passed the Civil Rights Act of 1968 (also called the Fair Housing Act), prohibiting discrimination in the sale and rental of real estate.

March on Washington for Jobs and Freedom—a peaceful mass demonstration for civil rights and economic opportunity in Washington, DC, in August 1963 attended by more than 250,000 individuals, mostly black Americans.

FOCUS QUESTION

What did President Johnson mean when he said that the right to vote for leaders was "the most basic right of all"? Was Johnson saying the same thing as the Declaration of Independence, or something different?

Congress amended and extended the Voting Rights Act in 1970, 1975, 1982, and 2006. The 1975 amendments extended voting rights protection to four "language minorities": "persons who are American Indian, Asian American, Alaskan Natives or of Spanish heritage." The Voting Rights Act Amendments of 1982 overturned Supreme Court decisions that interpreted the act to require evidence of intentional discrimination for a violation. In the future, the test would not be the intention of the lawmaker, but the "results" of any "standard, practice, or procedure" imposed by a state or its political subdivision.

In the next decade, Congress again reacted against Supreme Court decisions by passing the Civil Rights Act of 1991. This act amended Title VII of the Civil Rights Act of 1964 to make it easier to prove discrimination in so-called "disparate impact cases." These were cases where a practice or policy of a company might result in whites benefiting more than minorities even if that was not the intent. Also, the law for the first time authorized jury trials in these job-related discrimination cases and the recovery of compensation for emotional distress and punitive damages (payments assessed to punish a company for misbehavior separate from the actual damages to the person bringing the suit).

As this history illustrates, in the last half of the twentieth century, the nation committed itself to dismantling segregation imposed by law, to guaranteeing black Americans equality before the law and full voting rights, and to opening up economic and educational opportunities previously denied by private discrimination. In 2004, the U.S. Census Bureau reported on the progress that blacks had made in the four decades after the passage of the landmark Civil Rights Act of 1964. The data are summarized in Table 6-1. Family income almost doubled in real terms, the poverty rate declined by two-fifths, the number of black elected officials increased by a factor of six, and much greater numbers completed high school and college. Yet, as Table 6-2 shows, black Americans have still not reached parity with the majority white population (or with Asians in the United States), especially in terms of college education and family income.

Despite the accomplishments of the civil rights movement, legal and constitutional issues remain. In the next section, we examine three major contemporary controversies.

TABLE 6-1   CENSUS DATA COMMEMORATING THE FORTIETH ANNIVERSARY OF THE CIVIL RIGHTS ACT OF 1964

Status of Blacks in the United States

	1964	2001–2003
Population	20.7 million	38.7 million
Median family income*	$18,859	$33,634
Poverty rate	41.8%	23.9%
Black elected officials	1,469	9,101
Education		
High school degree†		
Percent	26%	80%
Number	2.4 million	16.4 million
In college	306,000	2,300,000
College degree†		
Percent	4%	17%
Number	365,000	3,600,000

*In inflation-adjusted 2002 dollars.

†For those 25 and older.

SOURCE: U.S. Census Bureau, "Special Edition: Civil Rights Act of 1964, 40th Anniversary," available at www.docstoc.com/docs/397239/Civil-Rights-Act-Of-1964-40th-Anniversary

TABLE 6-2	COMPARISON OF GROUPS WITHIN THE UNITED STATES				
	Whites	Blacks	Asians	American Indians*	Hispanics
Population	221,331,507	37,051,483	13,100,095	2,369,431	44,252,278
Median age	39.0 years	31.4 years	35.2 years	31.2 years	27.3 years
Educational attainment†					
High school grad, or higher	86.5%	79.4%	85.6%	76.2%	60.2%
College grad, or higher	28.6%	16.9%	49.2%	12.7%	12.3%
With a disability‡	15.4%	17.4%	8.7%	20.6%	10.9%
Labor force participation§	65.0%	62.9%	65.7%	59.6%	68.1%
Median household income	$51,429	$32,372	$63,642	$33,762	$38,747
Receiving public assistance					
Cash	1.8%	5.1%	2.0%	7.0%	3.7%
Food stamps	6.0%	19.8%	4.3%	18.4%	13.3%
Poverty rate					
All families	7.2%	21.6%	8.2%	22.5%	19.3%
All people	10.5%	25.3%	10.7%	26.6%	21.5%
Those 65 and older	8.4%	21.1%	12.3%	20.0%	19.7%
Residence is owned by occupier	72.3%	46.3%	60.3%	56.0%	49.3%
Home value (median)	$186,200	$130,400	$396,700	$108,700	$208,100

*Includes Alaskan Natives.

†Those 25 and older.

‡Those 5 and older.

§Those 16 and older.

NOTE: For Census Bureau data, "White," "Black," "Asian," and "American Indian" are racial categories, and "Hispanic" is an ethnic category. Hispanics may be of any race.

SOURCE: Data are for 2006 and are derived from U.S. Census Bureau, 2006 American Community Survey, Selected Population Profile www.factfinder.census.gov/servlet/IPCharIterationServlet?_ts=220383377062

KEY CIVIL RIGHTS CONTROVERSIES

MAJOR ISSUE

- What are the key issues in the contemporary debates over school desegregation, voting rights, and affirmative action?

In recent decades, three issues have dominated legal controversies over the civil rights of African Americans and other racial/ethnic minorities: school desegregation, voting rights, and affirmative action. All three raise important questions about the principles and policies that ought to govern race relations in the United States. One of the key questions is whether American government should limit its efforts to ensuring **equality of opportunity**—a level playing field on which all can compete—or whether it should seek **equality of results** in such areas as education, public contracting, and economic success.

School Desegregation and Busing

The famous *Brown v. Board of Education* decision of 1954 held that laws that mandated segregated public schools violated the "equal protection" guarantee of the Fourteenth Amendment. This is **de jure segregation**. *De jure* is a Latin phrase that means "by law." **De facto segregation**, or segregation "in fact," refers to segregation that occurs in society even though not caused by law.

In the years following *Brown*, local and state officials throughout the South resisted integration and even went so far as to close some public school systems. A decade and a half after *Brown*, most southern children still attended segregated schools. In 1971, the Supreme

Equality of opportunity—the principle that laws and government programs should seek to provide men and women of all races and ethnic groups an equal chance to succeed.

Equality of results—the principle that government should concern itself not just with equality of opportunity, but with whether men and women of different races and ethnic groups have equal educational and economic success.

De jure segregation—segregation mandated by law or official governmental policy.

De facto segregation—segregation of races or ethnic groups that occurs in society even though not caused by law or official governmental policy.

Court held that it was not enough simply to stop assigning students to segregated schools. Districts with a history of discrimination had to eliminate "all vestiges of state-imposed segregation," by, for example, redrawing attendance zones or busing students throughout a district to achieve integration or racial balance.[25]

What, then, of schools in the North that were segregated mainly because of housing patterns? In 1973, the Court ruled in a case from Denver, Colorado, a city that had never engaged in *de jure* segregation, that district courts could order widespread busing to achieve integrated schools if a school board employed any policies or practices, such as drawing attendance zones and locating new schools, that maintained or fostered segregated schools anywhere in the district. In the 1970s and 1980s, federal courts required many other northern cities to embrace school busing.

In some areas, however, most of the children in the city schools were minorities, whereas most in the neighboring suburbs were white. Could federal courts order busing between a central city and its suburbs? In 1974, the Supreme Court ruled in *Milliken v. Bradley* that lower federal courts could not order interdistrict busing between the city of Detroit and 53 suburban school districts because the separate school districts had not been created to maintain or promote segregated schools.[26]

This case limited how much federal judges could affect the integration of city schools. Many cities simply did not have enough white students to make much of a difference when busing redistributed them around the city's schools. Also, busing orders in some cities hastened "white flight" from the public schools as parents moved to the suburbs or enrolled their children in private schools, making it even more difficult to integrate the public schools.

For example, when a federal judge in 1974 ordered widescale busing across Boston's ethnic neighborhoods, the city's public schools were 49% white, 39% black, 9% Hispanic, and 3% Asian. Twenty-five years later, when busing for racial balance came to an end, the white proportion of public school students was a mere 15%, with blacks at 49%, Hispanics at 26%, and Asians at 9%. Once a city's minority school population reaches 85%, judges or policymakers cannot do much to bring about racial balance in the schools.

The busing cases point to a fundamental issue. What is the constitutional right that the equal protection clause guarantees with respect to public schools? Is it (a) a right not to be forced by public authorities to attend a segregated school or (b) a right to attend an integrated school? There is an important difference. The plaintiffs in *Brown v. Board of Education* had been forced because of their race to attend a segregated school. In *Brown*, the Supreme Court prohibited such *de jure* segregation. But what of students who live in a community where nearly everyone is in the same minority group? If they attend the neighborhood school, nearly every student in the school will be a minority student. Does this situation, which may result simply from *de facto* segregation, deny minority students the equal protection of the laws? Do these students have a constitutional right to attend an integrated school?

Although a few members of the Supreme Court and other federal judges have urged doing away with the *de jure/de facto* distinction, the majority of the Court has always required some element of state action promoting segregated schools before ordering remedies. In a 1995 case, Justice Clarence Thomas, the only current black member of the highest court, addressed this issue in a forceful concurring opinion:

The mere fact that a school is black does not mean that it is the product of a constitutional violation. . . . This position appears to rest upon the idea that any school that is black is inferior, and that blacks cannot succeed without the benefit of the company of

Police escort students to Boston's Hyde Park High School at the height of the busing controversy in that city in 1974.

© Bettmann/CORBIS

whites. . . . At the heart of . . . the Equal Protection Clause lies the principle that the Government must treat citizens as individuals, and not as members of racial, ethnic or religious groups. . . . [T]here is no reason to think that black students cannot learn as well when surrounded by members of their own race as when they are in an integrated environment. . . . "Racial isolation" itself is not a harm; only state-enforced segregation. . . . The point of the Equal Protection Clause is not to enforce strict race mixing, but to ensure that blacks and whites are treated equally by the State without regard to their skin color.[27]

In recent decades, the busing controversy has waned. More and more school districts, previously under federal court desegregation orders, have successfully petitioned to regain full control of their schools. According to the Supreme Court, once school districts have desegregated and ended any official action that promotes discrimination, they are not "required to make year-by-year adjustments of the racial composition of student bodies."[28]

But what if public school officials voluntarily promote racial balance in the schools by taking account of race when assigning students? In June 2007, the Supreme Court overturned such policies in Seattle, Washington (which had never segregated by race), and Jefferson County, Kentucky (which, a federal court ruled, had successfully desegregated its schools several years before). Writing for a plurality of four justices in *Parents Involved in Community Schools v. Seattle School District No. 1*, Chief Justice John Roberts held that classifying people by race in order to achieve racial balance or racial diversity cannot be a legitimate purpose of government. If it were, this would justify "the imposition of racial proportionality throughout American society." Such a practice would contradict the constitutional command "'that the Government must treat citizens as individuals, not as simply components of a racial, religious, sexual or national class.'" "The way to stop discrimination on the basis of race," he concluded, "is to stop discriminating on the basis of race."[29]

In a lengthy dissent, Justice Stephen Breyer, writing for four members of the Court, defended the policies of the two school boards. Despite "great strides toward racial equality," he argued, "we have not yet realized the promise of *Brown*. . . . The plurality's position, I fear, would break that promise."[30] Although Justice Anthony Kennedy agreed with Chief Justice Roberts and three others to strike down the two programs because they were not sufficiently "narrowly tailored," he expressed a greater willingness than the plurality to allow school officials in some cases to take race into account to promote diversity.[31] Kennedy's concurrence suggested that some voluntary school plans to promote racial diversity in public schools might well pass muster with the Court in the future.

Voting Rights

The purpose of the landmark Voting Rights Act of 1965 was to end policies and practices that suppressed black registration and voting. Within two years after passage, black voting registration in the Deep South rose from 7% to 60% in Mississippi, 19% to 52% in Alabama, 27% to 54% in Georgia, and 32% to 59% in Louisiana[32] (see Table 6-3).

Controversy soon arose over proposed changes in election laws that did not affect the right of blacks to register or vote but might affect their political influence. Mississippi, for example, proposed changing the way county supervisors were elected. In its previous "district system," voters within geographic subdivisions in the counties elected their own representatives to the county board. In its proposed "at-large system," the supervisors would be the top vote-getters countywide. Because many people tend to vote for someone of their own race or ethnicity ("bloc voting"), this change in voting procedures had the potential of hurting black candidates who could win in a majority black district but would likely lose in a county that had a majority of white voters. It was not obvious from the language of the Voting Rights Act that it extended to laws such as these that did not directly affect the right to vote.

The Supreme Court responded in two ways. First, it ruled that the Department of Justice must "pre-clear" election law changes that might reduce the political effectiveness of blacks, which it called a "dilution of voting power." Second, in a 1980 case it curbed the potential reach of this interpretation by ruling that in such cases the Voting Rights Act is violated only if the public officials *intended* to discriminate.

TABLE 6-3	IMPACT OF THE VOTING RIGHTS ACT OF 1965 ON SOUTHERN STATES	
Covered States	**Registered Black Voters**	
	March 1965	**September 1967**
Alabama	19.3%	51.6%
Georgia	27.4	52.6
Louisiana	31.6	58.9
Mississippi	6.7	59.8
North Carolina	46.8	51.3
South Carolina	37.3	51.2
Virginia	38.3	55.6
Total	29.3	52.1

SOURCE: U.S. Commission on Civil Rights, *The Voting Rights Act: Ten Years After,* January 1975, Table 3, p. 43.

Congress disagreed with this "intent to discriminate" standard and overruled it with the Voting Rights Act Amendments of 1982 (which extended the act for 25 years). In the future, the *results* of election law changes would be the issue, not the *intent* of the lawmaker. The amended act prohibited any electoral process or procedure that was not "equally open to participation by [racial minorities] . . . in that its members have less opportunity than other members of the electorate to participate in the political process and to elect representatives of their choice." A political compromise between liberals and conservatives in Congress resulted in a key qualification: "Provided, That nothing in this section establishes a right to have members of a protected class elected in numbers equal to their proportion in the population."[33]

What does this language require of public officials? Every decade, after the national census takes place, states must redraw congressional and state legislative districts so that they will have nearly identical populations (see Chapter 10). Does the Voting Rights Act require that districts be drawn to maximize the number of minority representatives? Must states create as many districts as they can in which minorities are a majority of the voters (so called **majority-minority districts**)?

Majority–minority district—voting district in which minorities represent a majority of the residents.

Reading the Voting Rights Act broadly, the U.S. Department of Justice (under both Democratic and Republican administrations) has pressured the states to maximize the number of minority representatives. In several cases, this demand has resulted in bizarrely shaped districts, such as the 12th Congressional District proposed by North Carolina in 1991 (see Chapter 10). In 1993 in *Shaw v. Reno*, the U.S. Supreme Court voted 5–4 to strike down the redistricting plan because the proposed district was "so extremely irregular on its face that it rationally can be viewed only as an effort to segregate the races for purposes of voting."[34] According to Justice Sandra Day O'Connor, who wrote the majority opinion, race could be considered when district lines were drawn, but it could not be the "predominant" factor.

Using similar reasoning in 1995, the Court struck down a majority-black congressional district in Georgia, which had been created in response to pressure by the U.S. Department of Justice. The following year, it struck down three majority-minority congressional districts in Texas. In 2001, however, the Court upheld, by a 5–4 vote, a redrawn, but still oddly shaped, 12th Congressional District in North Carolina in which the black population had shrunk to 47%. Here it ruled that traditional political considerations—favoring one political party (here the Democratic Party) over the other—had motivated the way the district was drawn. Partisan redistricting, long a staple of American politics, was not in itself unconstitutional.

These decisions confused many public officials, civil rights advocates, and scholars. As one study concluded, "the Court has yet to elucidate the difference between 'constitutional' and 'unconstitutional' *political* gerrymandering *or* the difference, if any, between racial and political gerrymanders." The authors faulted the Supreme Court for "fail[ing] to promulgate standards of adjudication."[35]

More recently, in a complicated case from Georgia in 2003, the Court overruled the Department of Justice when the department refused to approve a plan pushed by the state's Democrats, who controlled the legislature, that would have slightly reduced black majorities in three state senate districts. Democrats had hoped that moving some blacks into neighboring majority-white districts would help Democratic candidates win in those districts as well. Nearly all the state's black Democratic legislators had supported the plan. In sending the case back to the lower federal court, the Supreme Court noted that the redistricting plan as a whole did not reduce the effectiveness of the black vote.

Then in 2009, the Court ruled that the Voting Rights Act did not require the state of North Carolina to redraw the lines of a state legislative district in which minorities had fallen to 35% of the voters so that in the new district they would constitute 39% of the voters. Defenders of the redrawn district had argued that at 39%, minorities had a better chance of joining with others to elect a representative of their choice.

Also, in a highly watched case in 2009, the Supreme Court considered the question whether Section 5 of the Voting Rights Act remains constitutional. This provision requires all changes in election laws and procedures, even something as simple as moving a polling place, to be preapproved by the U.S. Department of Justice in nine southern states and some other counties with a history of low voter registration. This was intended to be a temporary provision—it was originally limited to five years—that would not be needed after states eliminated discriminatory practices. Yet, this provision, along with the rest of the act, was extended numerous times, including for 25 years in 2006.

In the 2009 case, a small utility district in Texas that was created in 1987 (22 years after the passage of the Voting Rights Act) and had never discriminated in its elections for its five-member board, sued to be freed from the preclearance requirements of Section 5. It argued that either it had a statutory right under the "bailout" provisions of the Voting Rights Act to be exempted from Section 5, or, if not, Section 5 as applied to it was unconstitutional. In *Northwest Austin Municipal Utility District Number One v. Holder*, the Supreme Court skirted the constitutional issue by interpreting the bailout provisions broadly to include all political subdivisions. The Court noted that "we are now a very different Nation" than when the Voting Rights Act was passed and when its preclearance provisions were first upheld. "Whether conditions continue to justify such legislation," wrote Chief Justice Roberts for the eight-member majority, "is a difficult constitutional question we do not answer today."[36]

The voting rights cases raise a fundamental question: Should the government simply ensure that racial and ethnic minorities enjoy the right to vote, or should policies maximize the likelihood that minorities will elect members of their own group? Justice Sandra Day O'Connor, who wrote several of the leading decisions on voting rights and supported some consideration of race in drawing district lines, warned of the dangers of racial classifications:

> Racial classifications of any sort pose the risk of lasting harm to our society. They reinforce the belief, held by too many for too much of our history, that individuals should be judged by the color of their skin. Racial classifications with respect to voting carry particular dangers. Racial gerrymandering, even for remedial purposes, may balkanize us into competing racial factions; it threatens to carry us further from the goal of a political system in which race no longer matters—a goal that the Fourteenth and Fifteenth Amendments embody, and to which the Nation continues to aspire.[37]

Other justices, however, have concluded that there is no constitutional violation as long as the purpose of the policy is to benefit a minority group. As we will see, a similar issue arises in affirmative action debates.

Price/CNP/Getty Images

Former Justice Sandra Day O'Connor, nominated by President Ronald Reagan in 1981 to be the first woman to serve on the Supreme Court, wrote many important decisions on voting rights and affirmative action. She retired in 2006.

FOCUS QUESTION

If the Supreme Court placed no restrictions on how voting districts are drawn, would it be a good or bad idea to use race and ethnicity as the predominant factor?

Kathleen Galligan/Detroit Free Press/ZUMA Press/Newscom

Jennifer Gratz, who became the lead plaintiff in *Gratz v. Bollinger* after she was turned down for admission to the College of Literature, Science, and the Arts at the University of Michigan, went on to head the Michigan Civil Rights Initiative. Here she celebrates the success of Amendment 2, which overturned preferential treatment in public employment, public school admissions, and public contracting, in November 2006.

Affirmative action—governmental policies that either (1) require special efforts to recruit minorities or women in employment, education, or public contracts or (2) grant preferences to minorities or women in employment, education, or public contracts.

Affirmative Action

In June 2003, the U.S. Supreme Court handed down two opinions from Michigan on the controversial subject of **affirmative action**. Although the term has no single settled definition, it means (at least) programs or policies that take race, ethnicity, or gender into account to increase opportunities in employment, education, or public contracting. Some of these programs or policies are uncontroversial, such as sending college admissions officers to minority high schools to generate interest in particular educational institutions. Others are quite controversial, such as giving minorities preferences over whites in admission to public colleges and universities. Two such preference programs were at stake in 2003.

In one case, *Grutter v. Bollinger*, the Court upheld an admission program at the University of Michigan Law School that gave significant preferences to minority applicants so that the school could enroll a "critical mass" of underrepresented minorities, defined as African American, Hispanic, and Native American. In the other, *Gratz v. Bollinger*, the Court overturned the formula used by the university's College of Literature, Science, and the Arts that automatically awarded to every African American, Hispanic, and Native American applicant 20 of the 100 points needed to guarantee admission. According to the Court, the 20-point bonus had made the factor of race "decisive."[38]

In both cases, the university had argued that the educational benefits of a racially and ethnically diverse student body justified giving admission preferences to members of minority groups. The white applicants who had brought the suits claimed that the university's preference policies violated the clear language of Title VI of the Civil Rights Act of 1964:

> No person in the United States shall, on the ground of race, color, or national origin, be excluded from participation in, be denied the benefits of, or be subjected to discrimination under any program or activity receiving Federal financial assistance.

The University of Michigan, like nearly all colleges and universities in the United States, is covered by Title VI because it receives federal financial assistance in the form of federally guaranteed student loans and federally funded research.

Prior to these Michigan decisions, most affirmative action cases had involved preferences in employment, involving hiring, training, or promotions. These decisions had turned on the Court's interpretation of Title VII of the Civil Rights Act, specifically the following language:

> It shall be an unlawful employment practice for an employer—[t]o fail or refuse to hire or to discharge any individual, or otherwise to discriminate against any individual with respect to his compensation, terms, conditions, or privileges of employment, because of such individual's race, color, religion, sex, or national origin.

Proponents of affirmative action hold that minority preferences are legal even though they seem to violate the letter of the Civil Rights Act of 1964. Congress passed the law, they contend, to improve the condition of minorities. Benign discrimination—that is, discrimination designed to improve the lot of blacks or other minorities—is consistent with the broad purposes of the act. Affirmative action policies can make up for past discrimination and can ensure that blacks and other minorities receive the employment and educational opportunities they deserve. It is not enough simply to remove legal barriers.

Here proponents cite President Lyndon Johnson's classic statement in 1965 to students of Howard University in Washington, DC. "[F]reedom is not enough," Johnson maintained.

"You do not wipe away the scars of centuries by saying: Now you are free to go where you want, and do as you desire, and choose the leaders you please." In the ongoing battle for civil rights, "[w]e seek not just legal equity but human ability, not just equality as a right and a theory but equality as a fact and equality as a result. . . . [E]qual opportunity," he told the students, "is essential, but not enough, not enough."[39]

Opponents of affirmative action preferences answer that Titles VI and VII establish the broad principle that individuals ought to be judged on their individual merits, regardless of personal characteristics over which they have no control. This principle, they say, ought to apply to whites as well as blacks, and to men as well as women. The goal should be a color-blind society, even if it is not perfectly achievable. This, they insist, was the original aim of the civil rights movement and the reason it was successful in a majority white nation. As evidence, they cite such leaders as

- Thurgood Marshall, the lead attorney for the NAACP Legal Defense Fund in the 1950s and later the first black member of the U.S. Supreme Court, who argued in the *Brown* case that "[d]istinctions by race are so evil, so arbitrary and insidious that a state bound to defend the equal protection of the laws must not allow them in any public sphere";[40]
- President John F. Kennedy, who sent Congress a far-reaching civil rights bill in 1963 and called on lawmakers "to join with the Executive and Judicial Branches in making it clear to all that race has no place in American life or law";[41]
- Martin Luther King Jr., who famously called for a society in which individuals would be judged not "by the color of their skin but by the content of their character";[42] and
- Supreme Court Justice William O. Douglas, a leading liberal voice on the Court, who wrote in a 1964 case that "[h]ere the individual is important, not his race, his creed, or his color."[43]

How has the Supreme Court dealt with this controversial issue? The highest court first ruled on affirmative action in 1978. Allan Bakke brought suit when the Medical School at the University of California at Davis denied him admission. The school had set aside 16 of its 100 seats in its entering class for minority students. Bakke charged that the school's policy denied him equal protection of the laws because his qualifications were superior to most of the minorities admitted.

Four members of the Court approved of the set-aside, and four held that any consideration of race violated the Civil Rights Act. Justice Lewis Powell, who agreed with neither position, controlled the outcome in *Regents of the University of California v. Bakke*.[44] He joined the latter group to overturn the formal quota—minorities could compete for all 100 seats but whites for only 84—and he joined the former group to conclude that some consideration of race was legitimate.

The divisions on the Court clearly defined three distinct positions on the legality of affirmative action.

- One position is that Title VI "is crystal clear: Race cannot be the basis of excluding anyone from participation in a federally funded program."[45] Whites as well as blacks must be free from discrimination.
- Another position is that race may be taken into account, at least to some extent, but formal set-asides, or quotas, go too far.
- The third position is that Title VI "does not bar the preferential treatment of racial minorities as a means of remedying past societal discrimination." In the words of Justice Harry Blackmun, "[i]n order to get beyond racism, we must first take account of race. There is no other way. And in order to treat some persons equally, we must treat them differently."[46]

These divisions on the Court persisted. In subsequent cases, the Court upheld some affirmative action programs but overturned others, often by 5–4 votes (see the box on page 194). A 1995 decision stands out for making it more difficult for government agencies to justify affirmative action. In *Adarand v. Pena*, the Court called into question, although it did not formally overturn, a federal affirmative action program through the Department of Transportation that gave contractors financial incentives to hire minority subcontractors. In sending

How the Supreme Court Has Ruled on Affirmative Action Programs

Programs that the Supreme Court sustained:

- A program in a steel company to set aside 50% of training slots for racial minorities (1979)
- A federal law requiring that 10% of grants from the Department of Commerce be awarded to minority business enterprises (1980)
- A 29% minority membership goal imposed by a lower court on a union (1986)
- A 50% minority promotion quota imposed on a state police department (1987)
- A county program to promote a woman over a man for a transportation supervisor job even though the man had more seniority and had scored somewhat higher on a competitive exam (1987)
- A policy of the Federal Communications Commission to give preferences to minorities in awarding broadcast licenses (1990)
- University of Michigan Law School's program to give preferences in admission to minority applicants (2003)

Programs that the Supreme Court overruled:

- An admission program at the University of California at Davis Medical School that reserved 16 of 100 seats in the entering class for minorities (1978)
- A judicially enforced consent decree that required the layoffs of white firefighters before blacks with less seniority (1984)
- A similar affirmative action plan that required the layoffs of white public school teachers before blacks with less seniority (1986)
- A 30% set-aside of city contracts in Richmond, Virginia, to minority businesses (1989)
- Admissions program at the University of Michigan College of Literature, Science, and the Arts to give a large quantitative advantage to minority applicants (2003)

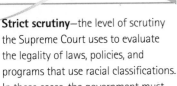

Strict scrutiny—the level of scrutiny the Supreme Court uses to evaluate the legality of laws, policies, and programs that use racial classifications. In these cases, the government must show that the program serves a "compelling government interest" and that the means it adopts are "closely related" and "narrowly tailored" to serve that interest.

Suspect class—the term the Supreme Court uses to characterize racial classifications in laws or government policies and programs. These cases require "strict scrutiny." (**See strict scrutiny**.)

Diversity rationale—the argument that racial, ethnic, and gender diversity in schools and the workplace is a worthy goal in itself and ought to be promoted by government. It is used to defend affirmative action policies.

the case back to the district court, the Supreme Court's majority ruled that all government programs that used racial classifications were subject to **strict scrutiny** by the courts. In such reviews, the government must show that the program serves a "compelling government interest" and that the means it adopts are "closely related" and "narrowly tailored" to serve that interest.[47]

For a half century or so, the Supreme Court had considered the use of race in laws, policies, or programs a **suspect class** when such a classification disadvantaged minorities. In *Adarand*, the Court extended this approach to programs intended to benefit racial minorities. The strict scrutiny standard puts a very high burden on the government, and in most (but not all) such cases the programs are overturned.

Some legal experts predicted that the principles put forth in *Adarand* would end government affirmative action. The University of Michigan cases in 2003 proved them wrong. Although the Court overturned the 20-point bonus to minority applicants to the university's liberal arts college, it upheld less rigid preferences in minority admissions to the law school on the ground that the school "has a compelling interest in attaining a diverse student body."[48] Yet in upholding the law school program, Justice Sandra Day O'Connor, writing for the Court, insisted that the race-conscious program be of limited duration because "[e]nshrining a permanent justification for racial preferences would offend . . . [the] fundamental equal protection principle." The majority expected that in 25 years "the use of racial preferences will no longer be necessary."[49]

Because the justices have divided sharply on many different kinds of affirmative action programs, it is difficult to identify clear judicial principles that distinguish acceptable from unacceptable policies. In general, the Court has been more willing to allow programs that involve hiring and training than those that determine firings and layoffs. And, as in the Michigan cases, it has been more likely to uphold programs that give some advantage to minorities (one factor among many) than those that set quotas or make race, ethnicity, or gender the decisive factor.

In recent years, advocates of affirmative action have increasingly relied on the **diversity rationale**. This holds that racial, ethnic, and gender diversity in schools and the workplace is a worthy goal in itself and ought to be promoted by government. Initially, proponents of affirmative action defended it as necessary to enforce nondiscrimination. For example, making a police department hire minorities in the same proportion as their share of a city's population made it difficult to favor whites. Some also argued that preferences were necessary to compensate for past discrimination, which suppressed minority representation in the professions, boardrooms, colleges and universities, and public employment. Although courts have sometimes looked favorably on this remedial rationale, they have usually required that these be *temporary* programs. The diversity rationale, in contrast, justifies affirmative action not to compensate for past wrongs but because of the value of racial and ethnic diversity itself. Preference programs adopting this rationale would not necessarily be temporary.

In 2009 and 2010, the Supreme Court issued important rulings on whether race may be taken into account in public hiring and promotion. Both were "disparate impact" cases that involved interpretations of the provisions in the 1991 Civil Rights Act that prohibited the use in hiring or promotion of standards or qualifications that had a different impact on different races unless the employer could show that these were "job related" and "consistent with business necessity."

In the first case, *Ricci v. DeStefano*, white and Hispanic firefighters sued New Haven, Connecticut, when the city threw out written and oral examinations for promotion to lieutenant and captain because no black firefighters scored high enough for promotion. Had the results been followed, 10 whites would have been eligible for promotion to lieutenant and 7 whites and 2 Hispanics for promotion to captain. Writing for the five-member majority, Justice Anthony Kennedy concluded that "race based action like the City's in this case is impermissible under Title VII unless the employer can demonstrate a strong bias in evidence that, had it not taken the action, it would have been liable under the disparate impact statute."[50] In the second case, *Lewis v. City of Chicago*, a unanimous Court ruled in favor of black applicants for firefighter jobs who had charged that the written hiring examination had unfairly discriminated against them.[51] Although this case focused on the time limits that applied to bringing such suits, many legal analysts puzzled over how to reconcile this decision with *Ricci*.

In addition to the federal courts, other agencies have decisively shaped affirmative action policies. These include, most importantly, the **Equal Employment Opportunity Commission (EEOC)** and the Office of Federal Contract Compliance Programs (OFCCP) of the U.S. Department of Labor. These agencies promote affirmative action in employment, especially among companies that receive federal contracts.

Affirmative action remains highly controversial, and the people in several states have voted to end it. In 1996, Californians voted 54%–46% to amend their state constitution by passing the California Civil Rights Initiative (Proposition 209). This brief law stipulated that the state of California and its political subdivisions (such as counties, cities, and towns) "shall not discriminate against, or grant preferential treatment to, any individual or group on the basis of race, sex, color, ethnicity, or national origin in the operation of public employment, public education, or public contracting." Although voters in Houston, Texas, defeated an anti–affirmative action measure in 1997, the citizens of the state of Washington passed a measure almost identical to California's in 1998, by a vote of 58%–42%.

More recently, in November 2006, voters in Michigan approved, 58%–42%, a measure to ban "affirmative action programs that give preferential treatment to groups or individuals based on their race, gender, color, ethnicity or national origin for public employment, education or contracting purposes." This effectively overturned the preference programs at issue in the Supreme Court decisions of 2003. (In July 2011, a federal appeals court panel overturned the citizen measure, and that decision is now being appealed.) In November 2008, Nebraska voters passed a similar measure, 58%–42%, but Coloradans defeated one, 49%–51%. Voters in Arizona banned preferential treatment in 2010 (60%-40%), and Oklahoma followed in 2012 (59%–41%).

Equal Employment Opportunity Commission (EEOC)—the federal agency, which began operating in 1965, charged with enforcing the employment nondiscrimination provisions of the Civil Rights Act of 1964 and other federal laws.

EQUALITY FOR WOMEN

MAJOR ISSUE

- How have Congress and the courts expanded the civil and political rights of women over the course of American history, and what controversies remain today?

As we saw in Chapter 1, when the American founders wrote that "all men are created equal," they used the word *men* generically to refer to human beings. "Natural liberty," Alexander Hamilton wrote, "is a gift of the beneficent Creator to the whole human race." Yet, at the time of the founding, women could not vote (except in New Jersey, where unmarried women could vote from 1776 to 1807). Also, because married women lost their separate legal identity to their husbands, they could not buy, own, or sell property in their own name, sue or be sued, or make contracts and wills. Single women and widows, however, had essentially the same property rights as men.

This distinction between married and unmarried women had been the rule under English law and, therefore, in the American colonies as well. Nonetheless, all the rights identified in the Constitution of 1787 (such as trial by jury in criminal cases, no ex post facto laws, and habeas corpus protections) and in the Bill of Rights (such as freedom of speech and protection against cruel or unusual punishments) applied to women just as to men.

The Beginning of the Women's Rights Movement

In March 1776, Abigail Adams wrote to her husband John, then serving at the Second Continental Congress in Philadelphia, complaining of the legal inequality of women: "[I]n the new Code of Laws which I suppose it will be necessary for you to make I desire you would Remember the Ladies, and be more generous and favourable to them than your ancestors. Do not put such unlimited power into the hands of the Husbands. Remember all Men would be tyrants if they could."[52]

Despite this plea, little was done to expand women's legal and political rights until 1838, when Kentucky granted unmarried women the right to vote in some local elections. The next year, states began passing **Married Women's Property Acts**, granting married women some or all of the property rights possessed by men. Between 1839 and 1895, all the states passed such laws. One of the most far-reaching was New York's reform of 1860. It guaranteed the right of married women to buy, own, and sell property, to enter into contracts in their own name, to sue in court, to keep their own wages, and to be a joint guardian of their children.

The **women's movement** for full political equality with men began in earnest in 1848 in Seneca Falls, New York, when Lucretia Mott and Elizabeth Cady Stanton organized the first public meeting to address the "social, civil and religious rights of women." More than 250 women and 40 men (including abolitionist leader Frederick Douglass) attended the **Seneca Falls Convention**. It adopted a "Declaration of Sentiments," closely modeled on the Declaration of Independence, that affirmed, "We hold these truths to be self-evident: that all men and women are created equal." It "demand[ed]" for women "the equal station to which they are entitled," including the rights to vote, own property (whether married or unmarried), attend college, pursue a career, and participate in religious institutions on the same basis as men.[53]

In 1851, Stanton and Susan B. Anthony began a 50-year collaboration fighting for women's rights. They founded a women's rights newspaper in 1868 and, a year later, the National Woman Suffrage Association (NWSA). In this same year, Lucy Stone and Julia Ward Howe founded the American Woman Suffrage Association (AWSA). The two groups pursued different political and legal strategies to achieve women's **suffrage**. In the 1860s, some prominent women's rights leaders opposed the adoption of the Fourteenth Amendment because in Section 2 it stated the presumption of universal male suffrage and, indeed, introduced the word *male* into the Constitution for the first time.

Married Women's Property Acts— laws passed in all the states between 1839 and 1895 to give married women some or all of the property rights possessed by married men.

Women's movement—the political and social movement that began at the Seneca Falls Convention in 1848 that sought full legal and political equality for women.

Seneca Falls Convention—held in 1848 in Seneca Falls, New York, the first public meeting to address the "social, civil and religious rights of women." It was attended by more than 250 women and 40 men and adopted a "Declaration of Sentiments," modeled on the Declaration of Independence.

Suffrage—the right to vote.

In 1869, the Wyoming Territory granted women voting rights on the same terms as men. The Utah Territory followed a year later. But when Wyoming applied to become a state in 1890, many in Congress opposed the state constitution because of its women's suffrage provision. In response, the territorial legislature sent a telegram to Washington stating, "we will remain out of the Union a hundred years rather than come in without the women." Congress relented and accepted Wyoming into the Union as the first state in which women had full voting rights.

During this period, some in the women's movement sought help from the courts, arguing that the right of women to vote derived from the citizenship provisions of the Fourteenth Amendment. In 1875, however, the Supreme Court ruled in *Minor v. Happersett* that the rights of citizenship (women were indeed citizens) did not include the right to vote: "For nearly ninety years the people have acted upon the idea that the Constitution, when it conferred citizenship, did not necessarily confer the right of suffrage."[54]

The Modern Women's Movement

In 1890, the two major women's rights groups, the NWSA and AWSA, merged to become the National American Woman Suffrage Association (NAWSA). Its leaders were Elizabeth Cady Stanton (its first president), Lucy Stone, and Susan B. Anthony (who served as president from 1892 to 1900). In 1893, New Zealand became the first nation to grant women the right to vote. Australia followed in 1902.

The right to vote was not the only issue that affected women. In the early 1900s, many states wrote laws to improve their condition in the workplace, such as limiting the hours they could work, prohibiting night work, and establishing a minimum wage for women (when one did not yet exist for men). In 1908, the Supreme Court upheld state laws limiting a woman's workday to 10 hours; and in 1937, overturning a previous decision, it upheld a separate state minimum wage for women.

In 1913, tensions within the women's rights movement resulted in the expulsion of militant suffragette Alice Paul from NAWSA over issues of tactics and focus. Three years later, Paul founded the National Women's Party, which rejected the state-by-state approach of the NAWSA in favor of fighting for a women's suffrage amendment to the U.S. Constitution. Soon NAWSA refocused its efforts on the passage of a federal constitutional amendment.

By 1919, women had the right to vote in about half the states, although in some of these they could vote only in presidential elections. In this year, women's suffrage finally garnered the support of the necessary two-thirds of the House and Senate, which sent to the states a proposed Nineteenth Amendment to the U.S. Constitution: "The right of citizens of the United States to vote shall not be denied or abridged by the United States or by any State on account of sex." In August 1920, Tennessee became the 36th state to endorse the amendment, making it part of the Constitution.

Just three years later, while attending the 75th anniversary of the Seneca Falls Convention in New York, Alice Paul drafted what became known as the Equal Rights Amendment (ERA): "Men and women shall have equal rights throughout the United States and every place subject to its jurisdiction." Not all women's advocates embraced the proposal. Some feared that it would invalidate protective employment legislation for women. It was later rewritten to read: "Equality of rights under the law shall not be denied or abridged by the United States or by any state on account of sex." The ERA was introduced into every session of Congress for half a century.

Although the Great Depression and World War II pushed women's rights issues into the background of national affairs, the civil rights movement of the 1950s and 1960s refocused attention on the subject. The 1960s saw the birth of a new women's movement, inspired by such books as Betty Friedan's *The Feminine Mystique*. *Women's liberation* became a popular

This marble statue of the three most influential leaders of the women's rights movement—(from left to right) Elizabeth Cady Stanton, Susan B. Anthony, and Lucretia Mott—is in the U.S. Capitol Building.

Architect of the Capitol

[LC-B201-3643-12] Library of Congress Prints and Photographs Division

Suffragists march for the right to vote in New York City in 1913. This movement achieved success in 1920, when the Nineteenth Amendment became part of the Constitution.

term, as women challenged laws and practices that many believed placed them in a subordinate position to men in American society.

Women scored two important victories in the 1960s. The first was the Equal Pay Act of 1963, which prohibited industries engaged in interstate commerce from paying men and women different amounts for "equal work on jobs the performance of which requires equal skill, effort, and responsibility, and which are performed under similar working conditions." The second was the inclusion of "sex" as a category of prohibited employment discrimination in Title VII of the Civil Rights Act of 1964. Later the federal courts would interpret this language broadly to prohibit "sexual harassment" against working women or the creation of a "hostile work environment."

In 1966, the National Organization for Women (NOW) was founded, and other groups devoted to women's rights followed. The ACLU became increasingly interested in the issue and established the Women's Rights Project. At the urging of these and other groups, Congress passed the Equal Rights Amendment in 1972 and, following standard practice, gave the states seven years to ratify. Within one year, 22 states did so; but after seven years, the number was stuck at 35, three short of the necessary three-fourths. Although Congress in 1978 gave a three-year extension for ratification, no new states endorsed the amendment, and it failed.

Women in Public Office: Famous Firsts

- In 1887, Susanna Medora Salter was elected mayor of Argonia, Kansas, becoming the nation's first elected woman mayor.
- In 1917, Jeannette Rankin of Montana became the first women to serve in the U.S. House of Representatives.
- In 1922, Rebecca Felton of Georgia became the first woman to serve in the United States Senate after the governor appointed her to fill a vacancy. She served just two days before a successor was elected.
- In 1924, Nellie Tayloe Ross of Wyoming was elected the nation's first woman governor. Although she was defeated for reelection in 1926, she later became vice chairwoman of the Democratic National Committee and served as director of the U.S. Mint from 1933 to 1952.
- In 1932, Hattie Wyatt Caraway of Arkansas became the first woman elected to the Senate. She had been appointed to that body the year before to fill out the term of her deceased husband.
- In 1933, Frances Perkins, nominated by newly elected president Franklin Roosevelt to be secretary of labor, became the first woman to serve in a presidential Cabinet.
- In 1979, the likeness of Susan B. Anthony appeared on the new dollar coin, the first time a woman appeared on U.S. currency.

- In 1981, Sandra Day O'Connor, nominated by President Ronald Reagan, became the first woman to serve on the Supreme Court.
- In 1984, Congresswoman Geraldine Ferraro was nominated by the Democratic Party to become the first female vice-presidential nominee of a major party.
- In 1993, Janet Reno became the first woman to serve as attorney general of the United States.
- In 1997, Madeleine Albright became the first woman to serve as secretary of state, the highest-ranking cabinet position.
- In 2001, Condoleezza Rice became the first woman to serve as national security adviser to the president. (She later served four years as secretary of state.)
- In 2002, Nancy Pelosi (D-CA) became leader of the Democratic Party in the U.S. House of Representatives, becoming the first woman to lead a major party in the Congress. After the Democratic Party in the House gained a majority in the November 2006 elections, Pelosi became the first woman Speaker of the House in January 2007.
- In 2008, New York senator Hillary Clinton became the first woman to come close to winning the presidential nomination of a major party, and Governor Sarah Palin of Alaska became the first woman to be the Republican vice-presidential nominee.

Not all women supported the ERA. Perhaps its most effective opponent was Phyllis Schlafly of Illinois, who led the "Stop the ERA" movement. Schlafly warned that the amendment would harm women by ending legal benefits for wives under the Social Security system and the legal exemption of women from mandatory military service during wartime. Many commentators believed that her efforts were decisive in stemming the momentum for ratification.

In the same year that Congress passed the ERA, it approved Title IX of the Education Amendments of 1972. Title IX provided that "[n]o person in the United States shall, on the basis of sex, be excluded from participation in, be denied the benefits of, or be subjected to discrimination under any education program or activity receiving Federal financial assistance." Title IX has had a large impact on college and university athletics, opening up varsity athletic opportunities for women at America's colleges and universities. Nonetheless, it has generated controversy among some coaches and participants in men's sports who contend that it has reduced opportunities for male athletes in such sports such as gymnastics and wrestling, as colleges and universities try to equalize the numbers of men and women playing varsity sports.

The Courts and Women's Rights

The federal courts have also been active on women's rights. In its earliest cases on the subject, the Court applied ordinary scrutiny in reviewing laws that made distinctions based on sex. Under this approach, such a law does not violate equal protection if it has a "rational basis." This **rational-basis test** is a fairly lenient standard, requiring no more than some reasonable grounds for the distinctions in the law. Rarely do the courts overturn a law when using this test.

Some advocates of women's rights have pushed the courts to treat sex distinctions as they treat racial distinctions: as a "suspect" classification requiring strict scrutiny. As noted in the discussion of affirmative action, to survive strict scrutiny, a law, policy, or program must serve a compelling government interest and be narrowly tailored to serve that interest.

Instead of adopting this standard, the Court introduced **intermediate or heightened scrutiny** in sex discrimination cases in the 1970s. According to the Court in *Craig v. Boren* (1976), classifications based on gender "must serve important governmental objectives, and must be substantially related to achievement of those objectives."[55] Applying heightened scrutiny, the Court overturned laws that favored men as executors of estates, that established different ages for child support obligations to sons and daughters, that set different drinking ages for men and women, and that provided Social Security benefits to widows but not widowers.

In other cases, the Court sought to equalize job opportunities for women by overturning mandatory pregnancy leaves (1974), by prohibiting laws that harmed women's employment opportunities through arbitrary height and weight requirements (1977), and by banning company policies that barred women of child bearing age from jobs that might harm a developing fetus (1991).

In a recent case that attracted widespread attention, a former employee of the Goodyear Tire & Rubber Co., Lilly Ledbetter, sued the company for sex discrimination that she claimed she had suffered many years before and that had suppressed her wages until her retirement in 1998. The problem was that the law that allowed such suits required that a complaint be filed with the EEOC within 180 days of the alleged discriminatory act. In *Ledbetter v. Goodyear Tire & Rubber Co.* (2007), the Court ruled 5-4 against Ledbetter, saying that the time limits for her claim had long since expired.[56]

One of the first acts of the new Congress that convened in January 2009 was to pass the Lilly Ledbetter Fair Pay Act, which overturned the *Ledbetter* decision by applying the 180-day time limit to each time an employee is paid if the compensation was affected by a discriminatory act, even if long in the past. In his ninth day in office, President Barack Obama signed the law in a public ceremony at the White House.

Women, the Military, and the Law

Until the twentieth century, the regular armed forces of the United States and the state militia were limited to men (although a handful of women served in the nation's wars disguised as men). The nation's military academies were also restricted to men. A small number of women served in World War I and a much larger number enlisted during World War II

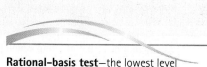

Rational-basis test—the lowest level of scrutiny used by the Supreme Court in addressing constitutional issues. When using this standard of review, the Court requires only that the law or government program at issue be rationally related to some legitimate government function or interest.

Intermediate or heightened scrutiny—the level of scrutiny the Supreme Court uses to evaluate the legality of laws or government policies and programs that distinguish between the sexes. In such cases, the government must show that the distinction serves important governmental objectives and is substantially related to the achievement of those objectives.

© Sandy Huffaker/Corbis

Women marines train at Camp Pendleton in southern California before deployment to Afghanistan.

FOCUS QUESTION

Should Congress and the military services be allowed to establish different rules for men and women regarding military service, such as a male-only draft during wartime and prohibitions on women in direct combat roles?

(1941–1945), when all the services created special corps for women to serve in various support capacities. About a third of a million women served during the war. Then, in 1975, Congress opened all the service academies to women. Currently, women constitute about 15% of all active-duty military personnel in the United States. Under federal law and policy, women may serve in combat positions aboard ship and on aircraft, but they may not serve in the infantry.

The Supreme Court has heard two important cases on women and the military. In the first, *Rostker v. Goldberg* (1981), the Court addressed a challenge to the Military Selective Service Act on equal protection grounds. The case began near the end of the Vietnam War when several men challenged the male-only draft as unconstitutional. After the draft was discontinued, President Jimmy Carter reinstated registration for young men in 1980. Goldberg renewed his suit for himself and others similarly situated.

Writing for the six-member majority in upholding the federal law, Justice William Rehnquist noted that the Constitution vested in Congress the powers "[t]o raise and support Armies," "[t]o provide and maintain a Navy," and "[t]o make Rules for the Government and Regulation of the land and naval Forces." In exercising these powers, Congress had restricted the draft and selective service registration to men. The Court, Rehnquist said, owed great deference to Congress's judgment, especially in an area of such importance where the justices had no particular expertise. "We must be particularly careful," he wrote, "not to substitute our judgment of what is desirable for that of Congress."[57]

In the second case, the Court overturned the male-only admission policy of the Virginia Military Institute (VMI), the nation's oldest state-funded military academy, even though Virginia proposed a parallel program for women at a private liberal arts college. Writing for the majority in *United States v. Virginia* (1996), Justice Ruth Bader Ginsburg held that the state had not shown the "exceedingly persuasive justification" necessary to defend the exclusion of women. Laws and policies may not deny women "simply because they are women, full citizenship stature—equal opportunity to aspire, achieve, participate in and contribute to society based on their individual talents and capacities."[58]

Civil rights laws have a broad reach, and the principles of equal opportunity and nondiscrimination are not limited to African Americans and women. Here we review civil rights developments and controversies regarding older Americans, individuals with disabilities, and gays and lesbians.

OTHER MINORITIES

MAJOR ISSUE

- How does modern civil rights law affect older Americans, individuals with disabilities, and gays and lesbians?

The Civil War amendments, the Reconstruction Acts, and modern civil rights legislation all sought to secure the civil and political rights of black Americans. Yet these laws used broad language not necessarily limited to discrimination against blacks. The Fourteenth

Amendment, for example, prohibits states from denying due process and equal protection to "any person." And the Civil Rights Act of 1964 prohibits both discrimination in public accommodations on the basis of "race, color, religion, or national origin" and discrimination in hiring and promotion on the basis of "race, color, religion, sex, or national origin." In 1975, Congress expanded the Voting Rights Act to prohibit discrimination against four "language minorities": "American Indian[s], Asian American[s], Alaskan Natives or [those] of Spanish heritage."

Court cases and administrative rulings in recent decades have embraced a broad interpretation of the protected categories. "Race," for example, includes groups that are "ethnically and physiognomically distinctive" (e.g., Arabs)[59] or individuals who share a common "ancestry or ethnic characteristics" (such as native Hawaiians).[60] Similarly, "national origin" includes "birthplace, ancestry, culture, or linguistic characteristics common to a specific ethnic group."[61] Also, under EEOC interpretations, employees cannot discriminate against someone because he or she has a name or a spouse "associated with a national origin group"; attends "schools, churches, temples or mosques, generally used by persons of a national origin group"; or belongs to an organization that is identified with or "[seeks] . . . to promote the interests of national origin groups."[62]

Few Americans today would dispute the wrongness of denying someone a job or promotion because of race, ethnicity, or gender. But what about older Americans and people with disabilities? Neither group was mentioned in the landmark civil rights laws of the 1960s. Does it violate equal rights to require workers to retire at a certain age? What if those workers are police officers, firefighters, or airplane pilots? Does it violate the nation's principles to refuse to hire a person who is disabled if the employer suspects that the job candidate will not perform as well as someone else? Does equality of rights require public authorities to make special efforts to provide people with disabilities access to public transportation and buildings? Finally, most Americans today would agree that government may not prohibit someone of one race from marrying someone of another race. But what if a male wants to marry a male, or a woman wants to marry a woman? In recent years, the American people, their elected officials, and state and federal judges have been grappling with these and related questions.

Older Americans

Although Congress in 1964 defeated an amendment to Title VII of the Civil Rights Act that would have prohibited employment discrimination based on age, three years later it passed the Age Discrimination in Employment Act (ADEA) to address the problem. Drawing from the language of Title VII, Congress made it illegal for an employer "to fail or refuse to hire or to discharge any individual or otherwise discriminate against any individual with respect to his compensation, terms, conditions, or privileges of employment, because of such individual's age." The original act covered only those 40–64 years old. Later, the upper limit was extended to 69; and then in 1986, the cap was removed entirely, thereby prohibiting mandatory retirements based on age. The law exempted police, firefighters, and commercial pilots.

The EEOC is the federal agency that enforces the ADEA. In recent years, it has received 20,000–24,000 complaints of illegal age discrimination each year. In 2011, it

- dismissed 16% of the cases because the charge was withdrawn, lack of jurisdiction, or other reasons;
- found no discrimination in 67% of the cases; and
- resolved the remaining 17% to the benefit of the complaining party, with the employer either ending the discriminatory practice or providing monetary compensation as part of a settlement (a total of $95.2 million).[63]

Companies sometimes reduce their costs by firing high-salaried employees. Because older workers tend to make more than younger ones, they may suffer more when companies retrench. Is this illegal age discrimination? The federal courts have ruled that the ADEA is not violated as long as there is no intent to discriminate because of age. According to a federal appellate court, the law was "not intended to be used as a means of reviewing the propriety of a business decision."[64]

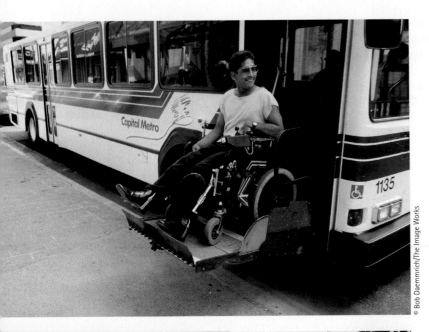

The Americans with Disabilities Act (ADA) effectively requires wheelchair access in all public transportation systems. These photos show wheelchair accessible buses in Texas (top) and Minnesota (bottom).

What about policies that benefit, rather than harm, older employees? In 2004, the Supreme Court heard for the first time a so-called reverse age discrimination case in which the General Dynamics Corporation offered less generous retirement benefits to those under 50 than those older. Workers 40–50, who are covered by ADEA, brought suit claiming illegal age discrimination. But the majority of the Court held that "the text, structure, purpose, and history of the ADEA . . . [show] that the statute does not mean to stop an employer from favoring an older employee over a younger one."[65]

People with Disabilities

Congress first addressed the issue of discrimination against disabled persons in the Rehabilitation Act of 1973. This law provided: "No otherwise qualified handicapped individual in the United States . . . shall, solely by reason of his handicap, be excluded from participation in, be denied the benefits of, or be subjected to discrimination under any program or activity receiving Federal financial assistance." By 1990, Congress had concluded that stronger legislation was required to meet the needs of the disabled. In passing the Americans with Disabilities Act (ADA), Congress found that 43 million Americans "have one or more physical or mental disabilities" and that these people are often isolated and segregated. Discrimination against them continues to be "a serious and pervasive social problem." Congress committed the nation "to assure equality of opportunity, full participation, independent living, and economic self-sufficiency for such individuals."[66] At the signing ceremony in July 1990, President George H. W. Bush praised the new law for ensuring that "every man, woman, and child with a disability can now pass through once-closed doors into a bright new era of equality, independence, and freedom."[67]

Specifically, the ADA prohibits discrimination in employment, in the programs and services of public entities (e.g., mass transit systems), and in public accommodations. It defines a disability as "(a) a physical or mental impairment that substantially limits one or more of the major life activities; (b) a record of such an impairment; or (c) being regarded as having such an impairment." It bars employers from refusing to hire or promote a "qualified individual with a disability" and requires them to make "reasonable accommodations" to workers with disabilities, such as providing wheelchair access and restructuring jobs, unless this imposes an "undue hardship." Also, the ADA prohibits employers from asking job applicants whether they have a disability. Employers may, however, ask applicants whether they can perform certain job-related tasks.

Recently, the EEOC has received 20,000–26,000 complaints each year of employer discrimination against people with disabilities. In 2011, in a pattern similar to its age discrimination enforcement, it

- dismissed 16% of the cases because the charge was withdrawn, lack of jurisdiction, or other reasons;
- found no discrimination in 64% of the cases; and

- resolved the remaining 21% of the cases to the benefit of the complaining party, with the employer either making changes to accommodate the worker or providing monetary compensation as part of a settlement (a total of $103.4 million).[68]

Under the ADA and the earlier Rehabilitation Act, colleges and universities, both public and private, must provide disabled students with appropriate academic adjustments, such as extended time for testing. If institutions provide housing to nondisabled students, they must provide comparable and accessible housing to students with disabilities at the same cost. A 1975 law—the Individuals with Disabilities Education Act—places additional obligations on public elementary and secondary schools. Until the early 1970s, many young people with disabilities did not receive special instructional services. In some cases, public schools simply closed their doors to them. Congress addressed this problem in 1975 by requiring public schools to offer disabled children a free appropriate public education. Under this law, public school systems must develop an Individualized Education Program (IEP) for each participating child. The IEP outlines the special education and related services necessary to meet the student's individual needs.

Gays and Lesbians

As we noted in the previous chapter, the Supreme Court ruled in 2003 that homosexuals have a "full right to engage in their conduct without intervention of the government." In a word, the state must leave them alone when it comes to private consensual sexual behavior. This does not mean, however, that the nation's civil rights laws extend to gays and lesbians, for Congress has consistently refused to add sexual orientation as a category of prohibited discrimination. Gays and lesbians have been more successful in the states, many of which now protect homosexuals against discrimination in employment and public accommodations. Yet, as we also saw in the last chapter, on two occasions the Court has ruled that, in some circumstances, private organizations have a First Amendment right of "expressive association" to exclude homosexuals, even if state law requires otherwise.

Perhaps the most contentious issue currently regarding gay rights is same-sex marriage. This subject broke into public consciousness in 1993 when the Hawaii Supreme Court ruled that the state's ban on same-sex marriage might violate the equal protection clause of the state's constitution. After a lower court ruled that the state had not demonstrated a compelling reason to prohibit same-sex marriage, large majorities in the state legislature (25–0 in the Senate and 44–6 in the House) proposed a state constitutional amendment to ban same-sex marriages. In November of 1997, 69% of the voters approved the amendment.

The developments in Hawaii attracted widespread national attention because of the "Full Faith and Credit" clause of Article IV of the U.S. Constitution. It reads, "Full Faith and Credit shall be given in each State to the Public Acts, Records, and judicial Proceedings of every other State." Opponents of same-sex marriage worried that if gay marriages became legal in one state, all other states would have to recognize them. In that case, gay couples who wanted to marry could simply travel to a state that allowed same-sex marriage and then return home as married, despite the laws of their home state.

To address this concern, Congress passed the Defense of Marriage Act (DOMA) by a vote of 342–67 in the House and 85–14 in the Senate. President Bill Clinton signed the measure into law on September 21, 1996. The law had two key provisions:

> No State, territory, or possession of the United States, or Indian tribe, shall be required to give effect to any public act, record, or judicial proceeding of any other State, territory, possession, or tribe respecting a relationship between persons of the same sex that is treated as a marriage under the laws of such other State, territory, possession, or tribe, or a right or claim arising from such relationship....
>
> In determining the meaning of any Act of Congress, or of any ruling, regulation, or interpretation of the various administrative bureaus and agencies of the United States, the word "marriage" means only a legal union between one man and one woman as husband and wife, and the word "spouse" refers only to a person of the opposite sex who is a husband or a wife.

Because the U.S. Constitution trumps legislation that violates it, it was not clear when the law passed whether its first provision would withstand judicial scrutiny, given the constitutional obligations of states to respect the "Public Acts, Records, and judicial Proceedings" of all the other states.

The issue heated up again in 1999. The constitution of Vermont stipulates that "government is, or ought to be, instituted for the common benefit, protection, and security of the people, nation, or community." In December, the state supreme court ruled that this provision required the state legislature either to include same-sex couples within the state's marriage laws or to create a parallel "domestic partnership" system that gave same-sex couples "the common benefits and protections that flow from marriage under Vermont law."

A few months later, the state legislature passed and Governor Howard Dean signed the nation's first **civil unions** law, which became effective on July 1, 2000. Although the law reaffirmed that civil marriage "consists of a union between a man and a woman," it extended to same-sex couples who formally entered into civil unions "all the same benefits, protections and responsibilities under law… as are granted to spouses in a marriage." These included, among others, property rights, inheritance rights, rights to sue for harm to a partner, adoption rights, family leave benefits, and immunity from compelled testimony against a partner. The California legislature passed a similar law in 2003 (effective January 1, 2005) to "extend the rights and duties of marriage to persons registered as domestic partners."

These actions seemed to embrace a practical compromise: only a man and a woman could "marry," but same-sex couples could register to enjoy all the legal rights and benefits of marriage. In November 2003, however, the Massachusetts Supreme Court ruled in a 4–3 decision that the state legislature had "no rational reason" for restricting marriage to heterosexual couples. It attributed the state's policy to "persistent prejudices" against homosexuals. The court concluded that the ban on same-sex marriages violated the state constitution, and it gave the state legislature 180 days to rewrite the marriage laws. The dissenters sharply disputed the court's reasoning, insisting that "[t]he power to regulate marriage lies with the Legislature, not with the judiciary." Instead of protecting individual rights, the court had become the "creator of rights."[69] On May 17, 2004, same-sex marriages began in Massachusetts.

Two years later, the highest courts of New York and Georgia reached the opposite conclusion, holding that same-sex marriage was a policy matter to be decided by the legislature. A state legislature, the New York court insisted, could have legitimate reasons for limiting marriage to a man and a woman. In particular, it could reasonably believe "that it is better, other things being equal, for children to grow up with both a mother and a father." According to the court, "[i]ntuition and experience suggest that a child benefits from having before his or her eyes, every day, living models of what both a man and a woman are like."[70]

The Massachusetts Supreme Court decision of 2003 touched off a grassroots campaign by opponents of same-sex marriage to amend state constitutions. They were able to get measures prohibiting gay marriage on the ballot in 27 different states in 2004–2008. Voters approved them in all 27, averaging 63% in favor. (Voters in Arizona defeated such an amendment in 2006 and then approved one in 2008.) By 2012, 29 states had constitutional provisions prohibiting same-sex marriage, and another 9 had state laws, but not constitutional provisions, defining marriage as between one man and one woman.[71]

Proponents of same-sex marriage also had successes. In the years after the Massachusetts Supreme Court decision, state supreme courts in California (2008), Connecticut (2008), and Iowa (2009) also mandated that same-sex marriages be permitted, as did legislatures in Vermont (2009), Maine (2009), New Hampshire (2009), New York (2011), Washington state (2012), New Jersey (2012), and Maryland (2012). Also, in 2009 the District of Columbia Council passed a same-sex marriage law. But not all of these rulings and laws went into effect. Voters in California amended their state constitution to prohibit same-sex marriage; voters in Maine overturned its legislature's decision; Governor Chris Christie vetoed the New Jersey statute; and the Washington state and Maryland laws of 2012 were subject to possible override by popular votes. (See Figure 6-2.)

By the summer of 2012, the constitutionality of limiting marriage to one man and one woman seemed headed to the U.S. Supreme Court. In February 2012, a federal appeals court ruled against the California initiative (Proposition 8) that banned same-sex marriage, and in May 2012 another federal appeals court ruled unconstitutional the part of the Defense

Civil union—domestic arrangement recognized by the laws in some states that grants same-sex couples most or all of the benefits, protections, and responsibilities enjoyed by spouses in a marriage. Also called a *domestic partnership*.

of Marriage Act (Section 3) that denied federal recognition to same-sex marriages. Then in November 2012 voters in Maine, Maryland, and Washington state approved same-sex marriage in popular referenda.

Previously, the Obama administration had refused to defend DOMA in court, arguing that Section 3 was unconstitutional. This required Congress to hire its own attorneys to defend the act. On May 9, 2012, President Obama became the first president to support same-sex marriage when he told a television reporter that "I think same-sex couples should be able to get married."[72]

The legal cases surrounding same-sex marriage presented several distinct issues. First, should the federal government

Status of Same-Sex Marriage Laws in the States, 2012

MA
RI
CT
NJ
DE
MD
DC

- Constitutional provisions defining marriage as between a man and a woman
- Only statutory provisions defining marriage as between a man and a woman
- Statutory or judicial recognition of same-sex marriage that has not yet taken effect*
- Same-sex marriages allowed
- No statutory or constitutional provisions on same-sex marriage

FIGURE 6–2 The status of the same-sex marriage laws in the 50 states as of November 2012.
SOURCE: http://www.ncsl.org/Portals/1/ImageLibrary/WebImages/Human%20Services/State-Laws-on-DOMA-Same-sex.gif

be required to recognize same-sex marriages done in the handful of states where it is legal? That is, is the Defense of Marriage Act unconstitutional in so far as it prohibits this recognition? Second, should states opposed to same-sex marriage be required under the "Full Faith and Credit" clause to recognize such marriages done elsewhere? For example, if two men marry in Massachusetts, where same-sex marriage has been legal since 2004, and move to North Carolina, where the voters amended their constitution to prohibit same-sex marriage in 2012 by a vote of 61–39%, must North Carolina recognize that marriage? Finally, and most far-reaching, does the U.S. Constitution (through, for example, the equal protection clause of the Fourteenth Amendment) require that all the states open marriage to those of the same sex?

Outside the United States, ten nations had extended marriage to same-sex couples by 2012: Argentina, Canada, South Africa, and seven European countries—Belgium, Iceland, Netherlands, Norway, Portugal, Spain, and Sweden. Are same-sex marriages in these countries recognized in other countries? Generally, the answer is no. To remove any ambiguity, Australia passed a law in 2004 defining marriage in Australia as "the union of a man and a woman to the exclusion of all others, voluntarily entered into for life." The law prohibited the recognition of same-sex marriages performed elsewhere.[73] The 27 member states of the European Union have debated, but not yet passed, a provision that would require each nation to recognize same-sex marriages conducted in any other EU state.

Another controversial issue involving gays and lesbians is military service. Prior to 1993, U.S. military policy prohibited the service of homosexuals. In 1992, presidential candidate Bill Clinton supported allowing gays and lesbians to serve openly in the military. Shortly after taking office, Clinton moved to change policy. Opposition in Congress led to the "Don't Ask, Don't Tell" compromise, which was incorporated into law and executive branch regulations. Starting in 1993, recruits were not to be asked about their sexual orientation, but servicemen and women who were openly homosexual would be discharged.

Opposition to "Don't Ask, Don't Tell" continued to grow and, in 2008, presidential candidate Barack Obama urged its repeal so that gays and lesbians could serve openly. Then, late in 2010, the Democratic Congress repealed "Don't Ask, Don't Tell" subject to certification by the president, secretary of defense, and chairman of the Joint Chiefs of Staff that allowing gays and lesbians to serve openly would not undermine "standards of military readiness, military effectiveness, unit cohesion, and recruiting and retention of the Armed Forces."[74] The three officials sent the appropriate certifications in July 2011, and the new policy went into effect in September.

FOCUS
QUESTION

Currently, a few states allow same-sex marriage but most do not. Apart from your personal preferences on the subject, do you believe that over the long term the United States can manage with different marriage rules in different states, or must there be one national standard?

CIVIL RIGHTS AND DELIBERATIVE DEMOCRACY

The long struggle over civil rights in the United States has involved both clashing interests and collective deliberation about justice and the common good. The American founders fully understood that not all those then living in the United States were enjoying their natural rights to life, liberty, and the pursuit of happiness. Many expected slavery to die out as the principles of freedom increasingly influenced human behavior. Instead, the slave interest grew, and more and more Americans subordinated moral principles to economic gain. By the 1850s, even some political leaders from free states expressed indifference to the spread of slavery. Abraham Lincoln, abolitionists, and the new Republican Party opposed this growing sentiment and worked to reinvigorate public understanding and commitment to the principles of freedom. The Civil War proved that the divisions over slavery were too deep to be resolved by what James Madison had called "the mild voice of reason."

In the decades after the Civil War, national majorities tried to secure the rights of citizenship for the former slaves, but they were thwarted by the power of majorities in the states of the former Confederacy and by Supreme Court decisions that limited federal power to combat private discrimination. Little progress was made until the civil rights movement of the 1950s and 1960s drove home to white Americans the moral imperative of achieving justice for their fellow citizens. No interpretation of the events of this period, which culminated in the great civil rights acts of 1964 and 1965, would be complete without recognizing the role that citizen deliberation about justice and the common good played in building national majorities for change.

National deliberation continues on the future of civil rights policy, especially on school desegregation, voting rights, and affirmative action. All three issues have sparked lively debate on the meaning of the civil rights achievements of the 1960s and the proper purposes of American government. That debate will continue.

The movement for women's rights in the United States, especially since the Seneca Falls Convention of 1848, provoked lengthy national deliberation about the meaning of citizenship and the rights it conveys. In the nineteenth century, men throughout the nation came to understand that all citizens, including married women, should have the right to own and convey property in their own name and to have access to the courts. And by the early twentieth century, national majorities agreed that female citizens should have an equal share in choosing their leaders.

The great debates over civil rights prodded Americans to think seriously about whether new policies were required to protect the rights and interests of groups in addition to blacks and women. With support from the executive branch, Congress prohibited employment discrimination against older Americans and people with disabilities, and it went further to require public agencies to take positive actions to bring the latter group more fully into the American mainstream.

For gays and lesbians the courts have played a major role in instigating change. Federal courts overturned state laws that criminalized homosexual behavior, but it was state courts that provoked the ongoing national debate on same-sex marriage. This controversy raises deep questions about whose deliberations should govern in American democracy. Popular initiatives, court decisions, and legislative judgments have all influenced same-sex marriage policy. In Chapter 15, we address more fully the proper role of the courts in influencing policy in American democracy.

Because of the success of the civil rights movement, nearly all adult American citizens now enjoy the rights to vote and hold office. (Some states deny these rights to convicted felons.) As full participants in the political community, Americans elect a half million public officials throughout the United States, vote on hundreds of initiatives and referenda, and make their views known to public officials in a myriad of other ways (see especially Chapters 7 and 10). As a consequence, public deliberation on the great issues of American politics now incorporates the vast and diverse American community.

IMPACT
of Social Media and Communications Technology

Social Media and Civil Rights

Social movements to promote rights depend on communication. The abolitionists of the nineteenth century were famous for their orators, such as former slave Frederick Douglass. But before he made speeches against slavery, Douglass penned an autobiography that communicated the horrors of slavery to a broad audience. Abraham Lincoln's speeches and debates against the extension of slavery to the territories were printed in newspapers throughout the country (often in full) and helped to convince many to remain committed to the principles of the Declaration of Independence. In the twentieth century, electronic mass media spread the message of civil rights leaders to millions. Not only could radio and television reach a mass audience instantaneously, these media also conveyed the force and power of a superbly delivered live address. However impressive the written text of a document like Martin Luther King's "I Have a Dream" speech, it must also be heard and seen to appreciate fully its impact.

Social media provide new modes for communicating political messages. Individuals, groups, and governments now employ social media to highlight rights abuses, to spread reform ideas, and even to defend government and military actions. (See, for example, the Bessette–Pitney blog for June 8, 2012).

CRITICAL THINKING

On balance, will the use of social media in the years ahead significantly advance the cause of civil rights and civil liberties around the world?

SUMMARY

- The nation's great moral leaders have taught that American citizens have an obligation to see to it that all enjoy their fundamental rights.
- Although many of the founders believed that slavery would die out in the new nation, it became increasingly profitable and spread throughout the South. Political leaders opposed to the spread of slavery founded the Republican Party in the 1850s. During the Civil War, congressional statutes in 1862 and Abraham Lincoln's Emancipation Proclamation of 1863 freed most of the slaves. The Thirteenth Amendment of 1865 freed the rest.
- In the years after the Civil War, national majorities tried to secure the rights of citizenship for the former slaves through constitutional amendments and new national laws. Southerners responded first with Black Codes and then Jim Crow laws that segregated the races.
- In 1941, President Franklin Roosevelt prohibited discrimination in federal agencies and defense industries, and in 1948 President Harry Truman ended segregation in the military. In 1954, the U.S. Supreme Court ruled in *Brown v. Board of Education* that segregated public schools violated the equal protection clause of the Fourteenth Amendment. The modern civil rights

- movement culminated in the landmark Civil Rights Act of 1964 and the Voting Rights Act of 1965.
- In recent decades, three issues have dominated legal controversies over the civil rights of African Americans and other racial/ethnic minorities: school desegregation, voting rights, and affirmative action.
- The women's movement for full political equality with men began in earnest in 1848 when the Seneca Falls Convention adopted a "Declaration of Sentiments" modeled on the Declaration of Independence. Women achieved voting equality with men in 1920 (the Nineteenth Amendment). In 1963, the Equal Pay Act prohibited wage discrimination, and a year later Congress included "sex" as a category of prohibited employment discrimination in Title VII of the Civil Rights Act of 1964.
- In 1967, Congress passed the Age Discrimination in Employment Act to protect workers between the ages of 40 and 64. Subsequent amendments removed the cap on age, thereby making mandatory retirements illegal (except for police, firefighters, and commercial pilots). In 1990, Congress passed the Americans with Disabilities Act to protect people with disabilities from discrimination and to move them more fully into the American mainstream.

- In 1996, Congress passed the Defense of Marriage Act, which stipulates that under federal law, marriage is "a legal union between one man and one woman." The law also affirms that states shall not be required to recognize same-sex marriages conducted in other states. By 2012, 29 states had amended their constitutions to limit marriage to one man and one woman, and in another 8 states, same-sex marriage was legal as a result of court decisions or legislation.

- Public deliberation on the great issues of American politics is no longer the preserve of a select few but incorporates the vast and diverse American community.

KEY TERMS

Affirmative action p. 192
Black Codes p. 180
Civil disobedience p. 184
Civil rights p. 175
Civil rights movement p. 184
Civil union p. 204
De facto segregation p. 187
De jure segregation p. 187
Desegregation p. 181
Discrimination p. 175
Diversity rationale p. 194
Emancipation Proclamation p. 180
Equal Employment Opportunity
    Commission (EEOC) p. 195

Equality of opportunity p. 187
Equality of results p. 187
Freedmen's Bureau p. 180
Grandfather clauses p. 181
Intermediate or heightened scrutiny
    p. 199
Jim Crow laws p. 181
Ku Klux Klan p. 180
Lincoln-Douglas debates p. 179
Literacy tests p. 181
Majority-minority district p. 190
March on Washington for Jobs
    and Freedom p. 185
Married Women's Property Acts p. 196

Montgomery bus boycott p. 184
Poll tax p. 181
Rational-basis test p. 199
Reconstruction p. 180
Segregation p. 175
Seneca Falls Convention p. 196
Separate but equal doctrine p. 182
Strict scrutiny p. 193
Suffrage p. 196
Suspect class p. 194
Underground Railroad p. 178
White primary p. 182
Women's movement p. 196

TEST YOUR KNOWLEDGE

1. By 1804, which states had abolished slavery or passed laws providing for gradual emancipation?
   a. the thirteen original states
   b. all the northern states
   c. all the southern states
   d. all the states admitted since the Constitution was signed
   e. only Virginia, Pennsylvania, and New York

2. The fugitive slave law enacted as a part of the Compromise of 1850 was
   a. a great step toward abolition.
   b. adamantly opposed by southerners.
   c. more favorable to slave owners than to the accused fugitive slave.
   d. never put into effect.
   e. the result of tireless efforts of abolitionists.

3. The 1857 Lecompton Constitution was a fraudulent document submitted by slavery advocates in
   a. California.
   b. Kansas.
   c. Missouri.
   d. Nebraska.
   e. the Wyoming territory.

4. Why did Abraham Lincoln issue the Emancipation Proclamation despite his initial position that the president did not have that authority?
   a. Congress demanded it.
   b. Ending slavery was his central campaign promise.
   c. He believed it was his moral obligation.
   d. It was a military decision designed to weaken the enemy.
   e. The Supreme Court granted him an allowance to overstep the bounds of his office in this extreme case.

5. The Ku Klux Klan Act of 1866 suspended
   a. habeas corpus.
   b. large gatherings after dark.
   c. martial law.
   d. segregation.
   e. state legislative sessions.

6. Majority-minority districts are those in which
   a. a racial minority represents a majority of voters.
   b. a minority of the majority actually votes.
   c. the majority elects a racial minority into office.
   d. the majority of a racial minority is eligible to vote.
   e. the majority oppresses a racial minority.

7. In the early years of American history, married women did NOT have the right to
   a. trial by jury.
   b. ex post facto laws.
   c. habeas corpus.
   d. own property.
   e. the freedom of speech.

8. Why did some women's rights leaders oppose the adoption of the Fourteenth Amendment?
   a. It did not go far enough in extending rights of citizenship to blacks.
   b. It presumed universal male suffrage, introducing the word *male* into the Constitution.
   c. It was not written by women.
   d. They did not want blacks to gain voting rights before women.
   e. They sought more than just voting rights.

9. How does the rational-basis test differ from strict scrutiny?
   a. Strict scrutiny is used by lower courts, while the Supreme Court depends on the rational-basis test.
   b. Strict scrutiny requires a special hearing, while the rational-basis test can be applied by any judge.
   c. The rational-basis test is a more stringent test than strict scrutiny.
   d. The rational-basis test is applicable only to laws with distinctions in gender, while strict scrutiny applies only to racial distinctions.
   e. The rational-basis test requires only some reasonable grounds for distinctions in laws, while strict scrutiny requires a compelling government interest.

10. The _____ clause of the Constitution raises the question of whether or not states have to recognize same-sex marriages from other states.
    a. commerce
    b. implied powers
    c. necessary and proper
    d. full faith and credit
    e. supremacy

FURTHER READING

Belz, Herman. *Equality Transformed: A Quarter-Century of Affirmative Action.* New Brunswick, NJ: Transaction, 1991.

Branch, Taylor. *Parting the Waters: America in the King Years, 1954–63.* New York: Simon and Schuster, 1989.

Connerly, Ward. *Creating Equal: My Fight against Race Preferences.* San Francisco: Encounter Books, 2000.

Douglass, Frederick. *Narrative of the Life of Frederick Douglass.* New York: Dover, 1995.

Foner, Eric. *Reconstruction: America's Unfinished Revolution, 1863–1877.* New York: Harper and Row, 1988.

Franklin, John Hope, and Alfred A. Moss Jr. *From Slavery to Freedom: A History of African Americans.* 8th ed. New York: Knopf, 2002.

King, Martin Luther, Jr. "I Have a Dream." Address delivered at the March on Washington for Jobs and Freedom, August 28, 1963, Washington, DC, www.mlk-kpp01.stanford.edu/kingweb/publications/speeches/address_at_march_on_washington.pdf, accessed July 12, 2009.

King, Martin Luther, Jr. "Letter from Birmingham Jail." In *American Political Rhetoric: A Reader*, 4th ed., ed. Peter Augustine Lawler and Robert Martin Schaefer. Lanham, MD: Rowman and Littlefield, 2001.

Kull, Andrew. *The Color-Blind Constitution.* Cambridge, MA: Harvard University Press, 1992.

Mansbridge, Jane J. *Why We Lost the ERA.* Chicago: University of Chicago Press, 1986.

Steele, Shelby. *The Content of Our Character: A New Vision of Race in America.* New York: St. Martin's Press, 1990.

Thernstrom, Abigail M. *Whose Votes Count: Affirmative Action and Minority Voting Rights.* Cambridge, MA: Harvard University Press, 1987.

Washington, Booker T. *Up from Slavery.* Oxford: Oxford University Press, 1995.

Whalen, Charles, and Barbara Whalen. *The Longest Debate: A Legislative History of the 1964 Civil Rights Act.* Cabin John, MD: Seven Locks Press, 1985.

WEB SOURCES

American Civil Rights Institute: www.acri.org—an organization founded by Ward Connerly in California to oppose affirmative action preferences in the states.

Joint Center for Political and Economic Studies: www.jointcenter.org—a Washington, DC–based research and public institution that focuses on the issues related to the well-being of African Americans.

The Leadership Conference on Civil and Human Rights: www.civilrights.org—a coalition of nearly 200 civil rights organizations.

National Association for the Advancement of Colored People: www.naacp.org—the nation's oldest and most influential civil rights organization.

NAACP Legal Defense and Educational Fund, Inc.: www.naacpldf.org—a legal organization devoted to issues of race, now a separate organization from the NAACP.

National Organization for Women: www.now.org—the nation's largest organization of feminist activists.

National Urban League: www.nul.org—one of the nation's oldest and largest community-based civil rights organizations (located in New York City).

U.S. Department of Education, Office for Civil Rights: www.ed.gov/about/offices/list/ocr/index.html—the civil rights enforcement arm of the Department of Education.

U.S. Department of Justice, Civil Rights Division: www.justice.gov/crt/index.php—the civil rights enforcement arm of the Department of Justice.

U.S. Equal Employment Opportunity Commission: www.eeoc.gov—the federal agency with principal responsibility for enforcing nondiscrimination in employment.

A supporter of President Obama expresses himself amid signs for Republican presidential candidates in the 2012 New Hampshire primary.

AP Photo/Charles Dharapak

Public Opinion and Political Participation

7

OBJECTIVES

After reading this chapter, you should be able to:

- Define the concept of public opinion, and tell how researchers measure it.
- Contrast short-term reactions to issues with more deliberative opinions.
- Explain the core beliefs that separate different ideologies in the United States.
- Summarize the major influences on public opinion about politics.
- Recognize different forms of political participation, and analyze how they contribute to deliberation.
- Assess inequalities in political participation.
- Discuss political participation as a responsibility of citizenship.

INTRODUCTION

Debating Stephen A. Douglas in 1858, Abraham Lincoln said, "With public sentiment, nothing can fail; without it, nothing can succeed. Consequently he who molds public sentiment goes deeper than he who enacts statutes or pronounces decisions."[1] In this chapter, we will look at the impact of public opinion and political participation on the political process. We will ask what it is, how it evolves, how we measure it, and how it translates into political action and policy through civic engagement and the deliberative process.

Public opinion—an aggregate of individual beliefs about political questions.

Public opinion is the sum total of individual beliefs about political questions. There are two kinds. The first involves the views that people voice as soon as a question comes up. These instant reactions may burn with feeling ("Throw the bums out!"), but they seldom stem from deep thought. Polls often tap such opinions. Most Americans are not thinking about politics most of the time, so the typical survey resembles a pop quiz on topics that students have not studied. When pollsters ask about world trade or campaign finance reform, people give the first answer that comes to mind. Observers have long worried that such rash expressions drive policy.

Americans are also capable of more deliberative opinion. Although they rarely dwell on details, they do reach lasting judgments about large questions. Scholars have shown that public opinion on many issues does not shift wildly, but rather that it responds sensibly to information and events.[2] For example, between the 1940s and the 1960s, sentiment shifted from passive acceptance to firm rejection of racial discrimination.[3]

Where do political opinions come from? Obviously, family and schooling have an impact. Although few people think exactly as their parents or teachers, the lessons they learn in their youth will color their opinions through old age. Individual self-interest also leaves its mark. James Madison wrote, "As long as the connection subsists between [a person's] reason and his self-love, his opinions and his passions will have a reciprocal influence on each other."[4] When people gain from tax cuts or spending programs, for instance, they tend to see such policies as good for the country. Political reasoning, however, often means more than self-serving rationalization. Particularly with the deliberative form of opinion, judgment may diverge from selfish interest. Few people crave combat, but most believe that national survival may require it. When the sentiment runs deep enough—as it did during World War II—many willingly risk their lives for their country.[5]

Political participation—activities aiming to shape the structure and policies of the government, as well as the choice of those who run it.

Americans usually find safer ways to put their thoughts into action. **Political participation** consists of activities aiming to shape the choice of leaders and policies.[6] Voting is a central form of political participation. Other forms of participation may involve influencing how fellow citizens vote—attending rallies, wearing campaign buttons, working for candidates, or making political contributions.

Some kinds of political participation have a less direct link to elections. People write to public officials, tweet political messages, or speak up at town hall meetings. These activities advance policy deliberation by drawing attention to issues or arguments. Ordinary citizens may persuade their officials on the merits of an issue, but the electoral connection still lies in the background. Elected officials will lose votes if they ignore what their constituents are saying. That prospect gives public opinion much of its political force, confirming what Lincoln said in 1858.

But why do citizens bother to participate at all? Self-interest is part of the reason, but it cannot explain it all. Although turnout is lower in the United States than in many other countries, millions of Americans vote for public offices that have little direct effect on them. Many rally around issues involving distant lands or future generations. Such participation stems from a broad sense of citizenship. Some take up political activity because they believe that certain causes or candidates will serve the public interest. Others see politics as a civic duty in itself.

When you voice an opinion about war or another political issue, your friends might ask you a couple of questions: "Why do you think that?" and "So what are you going to do about it?" This chapter is about both of these questions, explaining the origins of opinions and participation, and the links between them. It makes sense to consider these topics together. After all, we study opinions precisely because citizens act on them. Moreover, scholars often use the same kinds of tools for measuring opinion and participation.

MEASURING OPINION

MAJOR ISSUE

- How can we know the state of public opinion?

Opinion is a state of mind. Medical imaging may someday show how the brain mulls politics.[7] Until then, we must infer thoughts from acts. Lincoln and Douglas gauged sentiment by listening to audiences, reading mail, and studying newspapers. Politicians still do.

Such informal methods are frequently unreliable. Many people with strong opinions may lack the time to write, call, or show up at meetings. Conversely, floods of letters, e-mails, and phone messages might not represent spontaneous outpourings of public sentiment. Campaigns and interest groups often stir them up to create the appearance of a groundswell. They persuade people to get in touch with officials, newspapers, and radio call-in shows, even supplying model letters or phone scripts. They bus people to rallies and give them signs to wave. Most people, however, rarely write political letters or attend rallies. To understand these quiet Americans, politicians and reporters may talk with "the person in the street." The problem with this approach is that a few chats are more likely to reflect a particular time and place than to represent a cross section of the public. In midmorning, younger people are at work or in school, so retirees rule the street. Interviews at 10 a.m. will show more concern about social security than student aid.

Elections provide only a partial picture of opinion. First, the returns are silent about the thoughts of nonvoters. Second, although they reveal the voters' choices, they tell nothing about motives. Did the Republican takeover of the House in 2010 reflect support for their policies, doubts about President Obama, or something else? The electoral tallies did not say. Measuring public sentiment requires another tool: the public opinion poll.

Polls and Respondents

A **public opinion poll (or survey)** is a device that gauges public opinion by asking people a standard set of questions. In addition to opinions, pollsters may also ask about behavior (e.g., past votes) and intentions (e.g., future votes). No pollster can afford to survey all adults in a state, much less the country. The solution is to take a **random sample**, a relatively small group of people who represent the larger group that the pollster wants to study (e.g., all Americans, or residents of a state or district). A sample is "random" if everyone in the larger group has an equal chance of being in it. Nearly all households have phone service, so pollsters usually reach their samples through **random-digit dialing**, in which a computer picks phone numbers by chance. This technique is better than choosing numbers out of a directory since it allows pollsters to call people with unpublished numbers or new addresses.

Honest pollsters can only claim to get reasonably accurate results. The *New York Times* has explained its polling this way: "In theory, in 19 cases out of 20, overall results based on such samples will differ by no more than three percentage points in either direction from what would have been obtained by seeking out all American adults. For smaller subgroups, the margin of sampling error is larger."[8]

When a potential poll respondent answers the phone, the pollster asks screening questions to learn whether she or he belongs to the group under study. In an election survey, the pollster asks whether the person has registered to vote. If not, the interview might stop. Many of those eligible to vote do not cast ballots, so as Election Day draws close, pollsters may ask questions to spot **likely voters**, those with the greatest chance of casting a ballot. These questions, involving voting history and interest, differ from pollster to pollster, which is one reason why election surveys may yield different results.[9]

Questions

Obviously, a survey's meaning hinges on its questions. Small differences in wording can yield big differences in the numbers. Consider a 2003 survey of Americans about Islam

Public opinion poll (or survey)—a device for measuring public opinion, usually consisting of a standard set of questions that one administers to a sample of the public.

Random sample—a subset of people who are representative of a larger group because everyone in the larger group has an equal chance of selection.

Random-digit dialing—the process of finding poll respondents by calling phone numbers from random-number generators. The aim is to reach people with unpublished or recently assigned telephone numbers.

Likely voter—prior to the election, one with the greatest probability of casting a ballot. Pollsters have different methods for identifying likely voters.

Sven Martson/The Image Works

At the Quinnipiac University Polling Institute, a student calls randomly generated telephone numbers in a survey on current political questions.

FOCUS
QUESTION
Is the American public basically pro-choice or pro-life on abortion? Does it make sense to pose the question that way? If you find these labels to be inadequate, how would you describe public opinion on the issue?

Tracking poll—a survey that measures day-to-day changes in public opinion by updating the sample each day.

Exit poll—survey that measures the opinions of voters as they leave polling places.

and Muslims. When it asked about "Muslim-Americans," 51% were favorable and 24% were unfavorable. With "Muslims," the answers shifted to 47% favorable and 31% unfavorable. Respondents were even less favorable to "Islam," 40% to 34%.[10]

Complicated questions may confuse or mislead. One poll asked, "Does it seem possible or does it seem impossible to you that the Nazi extermination of the Jews never occurred?" More than a fifth said that it seemed possible, which shocked many observers, but experts noted the question's double negative ("impossible"/"never occurred"). When pollsters simplified the question, only 1% said that it seemed possible that the Holocaust never happened.[11]

Wording and detail have the biggest impact when people have mixed feelings. Abortion is a vivid example. In May 2011, Gallup asked, "With respect to the abortion issue, do you consider yourself to be pro-choice or pro-life?" Respondents chose the pro-choice side over the pro-life side, 49%–45%. The poll also asked, "Do you think abortions should be legal under any circumstances, legal only under certain circumstances, or illegal in all circumstances?" This time, 50% said "legal under certain circumstances" with 27% saying "legal under any circumstances" and 22% saying "illegal under all circumstances"; and 51%, believed abortion is "morally wrong," while 39% said it is "morally acceptable."[12] Later that year, Gallup found that "pro-choice" and "pro-life" Americans actually *agreed* on several major areas of abortion policy. Large majorities of both groups favored requiring informed consent for women and banning abortion in the third trimester.[13]

The order of the questions can affect results. A set of items about an incumbent's record may remind respondents about what they like or dislike about the person. Accordingly, a question about overall approval may get different results if it follows such a series instead of preceding it.[14] Pollsters can remedy such difficulties by rotating the order of questions or choices.

Types of Polls

A survey usually takes several days. Whatever sample size the pollsters want, they must make a greater number of calls because random-digit dialing will often connect with modems and fax machines. Even when they do reach a household, they might not get an answer. One day's interviews may give a faulty picture, as certain people are unavailable at certain times. Members of a faith may decline to pick up the phone on their holy days, and many football fans are unreachable during night games.

With such cautions in mind, survey researchers often use **tracking polls** to follow shifts in opinion during campaigns. Every day, a tracking poll surveys several hundred people; over two or three days, it should catch a good random sample. Each day, the tracking poll drops the oldest interviews to make room for the newest. On Thursday, the poll reports results from Tuesday and Wednesday. On Friday, the poll drops the Tuesday numbers and reports Wednesday–Thursday results, and so on. In theory, a tracking poll provides a "rolling average" that will register day-to-day changes. In practice, however, tracking polls sometimes take shortcuts, such as using small samples or failing to call back respondents who were not home. These shortcuts may undermine their reliability.[15]

News organizations use **exit polls** to explain election results. In a national exit poll, the organization samples polling places, where temporary workers ask voters to fill out questionnaires, such as the example in the photo. (The growing use of mail ballots means that pollsters cannot capture a full sample at polling places, and they must also take phone surveys of absentees.) In principle, this method has several advantages. First, by sampling people who have just left the booth, exit polls avoid the uncertainty of identifying likely voters. Second, exit polls find voters at the peak of their political knowledge and interest. Third, they involve thousands of respondents. Telephone polls usually have hundreds, which is enough for findings about the whole electorate but not for specific groups. Such a sample may only include 20 or so Asian Americans, too small a "subsample" to yield a meaningful result. With larger samples, exit polls enable analysts to draw more detailed portraits of the electorate.

News organizations sometimes invite everyone to respond to questions by phone, mail, or Internet. Although these pseudo-polls may get many responses, they are practically worthless. Respondents consist not of a random sample but only those who choose to take part. Activists often stuff the box. During the 2008 and 2012 nomination campaigns, Representative Ron Paul (R-TX) won online polls that followed Republican debates, even though most legitimate polls showed his support in single digits.

Focus groups are another device for studying opinion. Instead of large samples of people who answer from their homes, focus groups consist of small numbers who gather in one place. The analyst may have them discuss an issue, perhaps with cameras rolling behind a one-way mirror. Focus groups can help pollsters draft questionnaires or flesh out survey data, but candidates and news organizations sometimes use them as substitutes for polls, drawing conclusions from a few casual reactions.

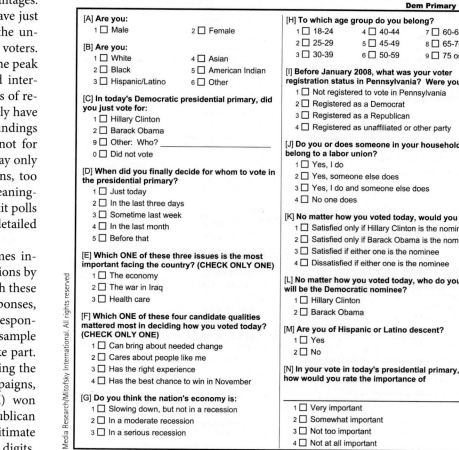

Pages from the National Election Pool's exit poll questionnaire for the 2008 Democratic presidential primary in Pennsylvania.

Problems with Polls

Even the best polls can run into trouble. High rates of nonresponse can skew the data, because the people who refuse to talk to pollsters may have different views from those who do. The problem may be getting worse.[16] Americans are using caller ID and voicemail, picking up only for familiar numbers or voices. After spending a day as a survey caller, one reporter recounted the following exchange:

> "Hi, this is Colleen with Texas Research. I'm not trying to sell you anything. . . ." (extended scream)

> "So, you're not willing to participate in the survey?" (scream continues)
> "Thanks for your time."[17]

Cellular phones mean further problems. Pollsters can save money by using automatic dialers, but federal law forbids the use of such devices for unsolicited calls to cellular

Focus group —a set of ordinary people who agree to gather for an in-depth group interview about their opinions.

Nonattitudes—answers that survey respondents give even when they have no real opinion on the question.

[O] If these are the only candidates on the ballot in November, for whom would you vote?
1 ☐ Hillary Clinton, the Democrat
2 ☐ John McCain, the Republican
3 ☐ Would not vote for president

[P] If these are the only candidates on the ballot in November, for whom would you vote?
1 ☐ Barack Obama, the Democrat
2 ☐ John McCain, the Republican
3 ☐ Would not vote for president

[Q] Do you or does someone else in your household own a gun?
1 ☐ Yes
2 ☐ No

[R] Did either of these candidates for president attack the other unfairly?
1 ☐ Only Hillary Clinton did
2 ☐ Only Barack Obama did
3 ☐ Both did
4 ☐ Neither did

[S] Which candidate do you think is in touch with people like you?
1 ☐ Only Hillary Clinton
2 ☐ Only Barack Obama
3 ☐ Both of them
4 ☐ Neither of them

[T] Which candidate do you think is honest and trustworthy?
1 ☐ Only Hillary Clinton
2 ☐ Only Barack Obama
3 ☐ Both of them
4 ☐ Neither of them

[U] In deciding your vote for president today, was the gender of the candidate:
1 ☐ The single most important factor
2 ☐ One of several important factors
3 ☐ Not an important factor

[V] In deciding your vote for president today, was the race of the candidate:
1 ☐ The single most important factor
2 ☐ One of several important factors
3 ☐ Not an important factor

[W] Which candidate would improve the country's economy?
1 ☐ Only Hillary Clinton
2 ☐ Only Barack Obama
3 ☐ Both of them
4 ☐ Neither of them

[X] Are you:
1 ☐ Protestant
2 ☐ Catholic
3 ☐ Mormon/LDS
4 ☐ Other Christian
5 ☐ Jewish
6 ☐ Muslim
7 ☐ Something else
8 ☐ None

[Y] How often do you attend religious services?
1 ☐ More than once a week
2 ☐ Once a week
3 ☐ A few times a month
4 ☐ A few times a year
5 ☐ Never

[Z] No matter how you voted today, do you usually think of yourself as a:
1 ☐ Democrat
2 ☐ Republican
3 ☐ Independent
4 ☐ Something else

[AA] On most political matters, do you consider yourself:
1 ☐ Very liberal
2 ☐ Somewhat liberal
3 ☐ Moderate
4 ☐ Somewhat conservative
5 ☐ Very conservative

[AB] What was the last grade of school you completed?
1 ☐ Did not complete high school
2 ☐ High school graduate
3 ☐ Some college or associate degree
4 ☐ College graduate
5 ☐ Postgraduate study

[AC] 2007 total family income:
1 ☐ Under $15,000
2 ☐ $15,000 - $29,999
3 ☐ $30,000 - $49,999
4 ☐ $50,000 - $74,999
5 ☐ $75,000 - $99,999
6 ☐ $100,000 - $149,999
7 ☐ $150,000 - $199,999
8 ☐ $200,000 or more

Please fold questionnaire and put it in the box. Thank you.

Pennsylvania (D-S-V1-2008)

Reverse side of questionnaire.

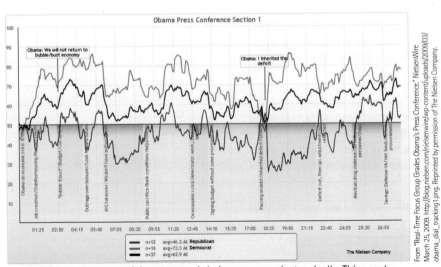

Obama Press Conference Section 1

In some focus groups, participants record their responses electronically. This graph shows how one group responded to a press conference by President Obama. (Higher scores mean more favorable reactions.)

phones. As more and more Americans rely on their cellular phone as their main line, pollsters may risk missing an important part of the population.[18] In 2008, the Gallup Poll announced that it would take the costly step of including "cell only" respondents in its samples.[19] Not all pollsters have followed suit, however.

False responses are another problem. People often overreport acceptable behavior and underreport unacceptable behavior. Some misremember what they did; others lie. Relying on head counts from churches, one study reckoned that worship attendance is only half as great as polls say.[20] Election pollsters have long noted that many nonvoters claim to have cast ballots. In comparison with vote totals, some polls have overstated turnout by as much as 24%.[21] When surveys involve elections, researchers can check their results against vote tallies, but when pollsters ask about beliefs, the only way to check one survey is to take a second, which may also yield false responses. Social scientists have techniques for foiling deception and uncovering "hidden" feelings, but they are scarcely foolproof.

A related challenge involves **nonattitudes**. People often answer questions when they have no opinion. A 1978 survey asked Cincinnati residents about the 1975 Public Affairs Act. About a third voiced an opinion— even though *there was no 1975 Public Affairs Act.* Researchers had made it up to test whether people would answer questions that they knew nothing about. In 1995, pollsters for the *Washington Post* repeated the test nationally. This time, 43% gave an opinion, with 24% agreeing with repeal and 19% disagreeing.[22] Pollsters can partially guard against the problem by asking people whether they have an opinion at all and reassuring them that it is okay not to. Even so, some will insist on offering nonattitudes.

In examining poll data, therefore, readers should remember a line from Alexis de Tocqueville: "When statistics are not based on strictly accurate calculations, they mislead instead of guide."[23]

KNOWLEDGE AND DELIBERATIVE OPINION

MAJOR ISSUE

- How can public officials distinguish fleeting opinions from lasting judgments, and how does this distinction affect their decisions?

Even real attitudes are not necessarily deep or well founded. Many surveys show serious gaps in public knowledge. Several months after the dramatic 2010 midterm elections, only 38% knew that Republicans controlled the House, but not the Senate or the whole Congress. Just 43% knew that John Boehner was Speaker, and 19% incorrectly thought that Nancy Pelosi still held that job.[24] As the Supreme Court was hearing oral arguments on the health care law in 2012, a survey showed a number of respondents either thought that the Court had overturned it (14%) or were unsure (28%).[25] When a 2010 poll presented respondents with a list of names, just over a quarter correctly identified John Roberts as the chief justice. More than half admitted that they did not know, while 8% chose former justice Thurgood Marshall, who had been dead for 17 years.[26]

Lack of knowledge can lead to inconsistent poll results. By a 2–1 margin, Gallup found in 2011 that Americans wanted to pay for jobs legislation by raising taxes on individuals making more than $200,000 a year.[27] Around the same time, another poll asked respondents about "the maximum percentage that the federal government should take from any individual's income" and then offered alternatives ranging from 10% to 50%. Nearly two-thirds of voters said the maximum tax rate should be 20% or lower.[28] Because the top marginal rate was actually 35%, a 20% maximum would have meant a big tax cut for high-income Americans, not an increase. People often fail to think through the consequences of their opinions, especially when the issue is remote or the question is abstract. Columnist Michael Kinsley notes that support for nuclear power plunged after much-publicized accidents at Three Mile Island in 1979 and Chernobyl in 1986. It gradually rose, then dropped again after a nuclear disaster at Fukushima, Japan, in March 2011. "This suggests that people want the advantages of nuclear power without the risks. This is an understandable position—but not a reasonable one."[29]

"The first lesson you learn as a pollster is that people are stupid," says Democratic pollster Tom Jensen. "I tell a client trying to make sense of numbers on a poll that are inherently contradictory at least once a week."[30] The great political scientist V. O. Key, however, offered an alternative view: "Voters are not fools."[31] Because of work and family, many people lack the time to study politics. Instead, they take reasonable shortcuts.[32] For instance, they make presidential choices by weighing the country's condition, the candidates' affiliations, and other bits of information. The electorate, Key said, acts as rationally as we can expect, "given the clarity of the alternatives presented to it and the character of the information available to it."[33]

Indeed, there are cases in which voters come to a judgment with eyes open to benefits and costs. Take capital punishment. Nearly everyone knows what it means, and since the late 1960s, public opinion has consistently favored it. In the late 1990s, the press carried stories about DNA tests that freed wrongly convicted prisoners. In 2008, 95% of the public acknowledged that the death penalty could lead to the execution of innocents.[34] Yet, as we see in Figure 7-1, support for capital punishment never dipped below 60%. Pollster Daniel Yankelovich writes, "Many experts disagree with the public's judgment on the death penalty, and I am not claiming that the public is correct either morally or factually. I *am* emphasizing the important fact that . . . the public is conscious here of the consequences of its views and is prepared to accept them."[35]

Politicians and Deliberative Opinion

In 2007, New Jerseyans agreed with their fellow Americans on the death penalty: by a margin of 53% to 39%, they opposed repeal.[36] At the same time, however, the state legislature passed a repeal measure, which the governor signed. This case illustrates two important

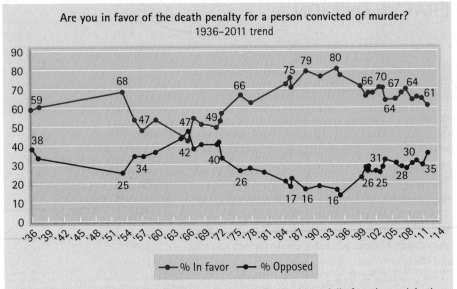

Are you in favor of the death penalty for a person convicted of murder?
1936–2011 trend

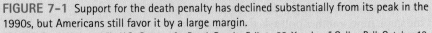

—●— % In favor   —●— % Opposed

FIGURE 7-1 Support for the death penalty has declined substantially from its peak in the 1990s, but Americans still favor it by a large margin.
SOURCE: Frank Newport, "In U.S., Support for Death Penalty Falls to 39-Year Low," Gallup Poll, October 13, 2011, at http://www.gallup.com/poll/150089/Support-Death-Penalty-Falls-Year-Low.aspx, accessed April 23, 2012. Reprinted with Permission.

points about the ways in which elected officials consult public opinion.

First, they do not automatically obey all the poll numbers that they see. In deliberating on policy decisions, they consider the merits of the issues. In this instance, the state had not put anyone to death in many years, but the death penalty had forced New Jersey to pay hundreds of millions for prosecutors, public defenders, courts, and death row facilities. Among other things, opponents of the death penalty argued that it had become too costly.[37]

Second, politicians know that public opinion has nuances. While supporting the death penalty, New Jerseyans preferred life imprisonment without parole for first-degree murderers. Most wanted to restrict the death penalty to the most heinous criminals, such as child killers.[38] Accordingly, the action of the governor and the legislature was less inconsistent with public opinion than it may seem at first. Furthermore, foes of the death penalty had managed to win elections in places that strongly supported it. New Jersey officials apparently concluded that repeal would not end their careers.

Recent presidencies provide additional insights into the complex relationship between politicians and public opinion. President Bill Clinton's critics accused him of bending his policies to polls. Clinton had a different account, using the example of a popular tax bill that he would veto:

> I can say, I'm going to veto this because it only helps less than 2 percent of the people and half of the relief goes to one-tenth of one percent of the people and it's an average $10 million. That is a populist explanation. I can say, I'm going to veto it because we only have so much money for tax cuts. . . . Or I could say, I think there should be estate tax relief [although] it's not fair to totally repeal it. . . . So I could make either of those three arguments. It's helpful to me to know what you're thinking. I know what I think is right. I'm not going to change what I think is right. But in order to continue to be effective, you have to believe I'm right. So that's kind of what I use polls for.[39]

Deliberative Polling

As suggested earlier, surveys often catch respondents by surprise. If pollsters gave people a chance to deliberate about the issues, would they get a clearer picture of what informed public opinion would be? Political scientist James Fishkin, director of Stanford's Center for Deliberative Democracy, has tried to find out with "deliberative polls." The Center describes the process this way:

> A random, representative sample is first polled on the targeted issues. After this baseline poll, members of the sample are invited to gather at a single place for a weekend in order to discuss the issues. Carefully balanced briefing materials are sent to the participants and are also made publicly available. The participants engage in dialogue with competing experts and political leaders based on questions they develop in small group discussions with trained moderators. Parts of the weekend events are broadcast on television, either live or in taped and edited form.

After the deliberations, the sample is again asked the original questions. The result-ing changes in opinion represent the conclusions the public would reach, if people had opportunity to become more informed and more engaged by the issues.[40]

One such poll took place in California in mid-2011. On certain issues, attitudes shifted quite a bit: for instance, support for lengthening the terms of state legislators nearly doubled. The process also improved the respondents' knowledge of state government. On average, correct answers to factual survey questions rose 18% over the course of the ses-sions.[41] "It was striking how smart and thoughtful the participants were," wrote journalist Joe Mathews.[42] He also reported that they had a hard time understanding California's com-plicated system of government, especially the relationship of localities to the state.

Deliberative polling has drawbacks. The "nonpartisan" briefing materials may omit views that would get a hearing in the real world. Libertarian writer Tim Cavanaugh wrote of those who contributed to the California poll: "In my experience 'nonpartisan' in contexts like this means 'encompassing both Republicans and Democrats' . . . I can say that not one group on the list comes within a country mile of my own view of the proper relationship of state power to individual liberty."[43] Moreover, group dynamics may take odd turns in de-liberative polls, and the presence of observers may distort responses. Finally, a few days of conferences cannot replace years of kitchen-table conversations. Nevertheless, deliberative polls do represent an attempt to move beyond snapshots of snap thoughts.

DELIBERATION AND IDEOLOGY

MAJOR ISSUE

- What core beliefs separate different ideologies in America?

Deliberation requires elements of agreement and disagreement. Unless people share some assumptions, they will just talk past one another. A debate about protecting equal rights will sputter if one of the parties believes in inequality. Conversely, discussion without disagree-ment will give neither heat nor light. Management theorist Peter Drucker wrote, "The first rule in decision-making is that one does not make a decision unless there is disagreement."[44]

Political Ideology

In public policy deliberation, disagreements often reflect different **political ideologies**—systems of belief about what government should do. Of the many ways to label political ideologies, the simplest is to contrast **liberals** and **conservatives**. Those who put themselves somewhere in between are **moderates**. A 2011 poll found that 21% of American adults considered themselves liberal, 41% conservative, and 36% moderate.[45] Conservatives tend to identify with the Republican Party, while liberals side with the Democrats.

As we use them today, the terms "liberalism" and "conservatism" have departed from their original meanings. Until the early 1900s, liberals favored less government regulation. The twentieth century saw greater support for government action as a counterweight to concentrations of economic power. Liberals came to see activist policies as a way to free people from this power. In a generic sense, "conservatism" has always referred to a reluc-tance to change. President Reagan, who personified conservatism in the late twentieth cen-tury, had a different view. He often quoted Thomas Paine: "We have it within our power to begin the world over again."[46] Many modern conservatives, for example, favor voucher systems that would fundamentally change education policy.

Liberals, Conservatives, Libertarians, Populists

One way to understand contemporary liberalism and conservatism is to look at three areas of argument: economics, social issues, and international relations.

Political ideology—a comprehensive system of belief about what government should do.

Liberal—in contemporary American usage, one who favors more government activity to foster economic equality, and less activity to promote traditional social values.

Conservative—in contemporary American usage, one who wants less government activity on economic issues, and more activity to promote traditional social values.

Moderate—one whose opinion falls between that of a liberal and a conservative.

On economics, liberals believe that the principle of equality should involve material conditions, for the poor cannot exercise their rights as effectively as the rich. They favor national policies to reduce inequalities of income and curb corporate power. Conservatives reply that these policies may slow economic growth and transfer power from an economic elite to a political elite. Liberals worry about corporate power and failures of the private economy, whereas conservatives warn against government power and the failures of public policy.[47]

On social issues, conservatives think that government should support traditional standards of behavior, while liberals stress individual choice. Conservatives support "religion-friendly" measures such as allowing the use of school facilities for vocal group prayer and providing government funds for faith-based community service. Liberals are more skeptical of such measures, holding that government should stay neutral in matters of religion. Most conservatives would tighten limits on abortion, whereas liberals usually oppose greater restrictions. Ideological positions are not always consistent on specific social issues. Conservatives generally think that government should be able to curb access to narcotics and pornography but are leery of restrictions on firearms. Liberals lean in the opposite direction.

On international relations, liberals in recent years have emphasized diplomacy, and conservatives emphasize military strength. Liberals give more weight to the opinions of other countries and international bodies such as the United Nations. Conservatives are more willing to assert American power.

American ideologies do not stop with liberalism and conservatism. **Libertarians** would limit government across the board. Like conservatives, they want to cut taxes and public spending; but like liberals, they oppose government intervention in issues such as abortion. **Populists** take the opposite view, favoring strong government action in both economics and social matters. Few recent polls have gauged the number of libertarians and populists. Although these ideologies are arguably more consistent than contemporary liberalism or conservatism, they have not found a firm political base. Ron Paul ran as the Libertarian Party candidate for president in 1988 and got less than one percent of the vote. In 2008 and 2012, he sought the Republican nomination. Despite raising substantial funds and gathering a passionate corps of volunteers, he did not win a single primary either time.

We should be cautious about applying ideological categories to the general public. Those who call themselves liberals or conservatives may have opinions at odds with a strict interpretation of their belief systems. Some conservatives oppose limits on abortion and favor recognition of same-sex marriage. Some liberals disagree with restrictions on the ownership of firearms. Such departures suggest that there is more to acquiring political opinions than pinning on an ideological label.

Events and trends in public policy can shift ideological lines. In light of the global threats of the past 80 years, few liberals would reduce the military to the very low levels of the 1930s. Similarly, few conservatives would completely scrap the social welfare programs that have grown during the same period. In 2008 and 2009, economic turmoil prompted Congress to enact huge increases in federal spending. For a while, it seemed that Americans approved of the expansion of government's role, but sentiment then turned against it. How will memories of current times affect the beliefs of future generations? This question is especially significant, for as we shall now see, history can exert a deep influence on political opinions.

Libertarian—one who favors less government activity across the board, including economic and social issues.

Populist—one who favors increased government activity both to regulate the economy and to protect traditional social norms.

FOCUS QUESTION

If there is another economic crisis like that of 2008–2009, will public opinion again turn in favor of government activism, or will it move in a different direction entirely?

WHAT INFLUENCES OUR OPINIONS ABOUT POLITICS?
MAJOR ISSUE

- What affects our views about politics?

Social scientists have identified broad patterns in the way people develop their political thought, but remember the difference between broad patterns and iron laws. There is a great deal of room for variation and change over time. Keep in mind that people can think for themselves.

Political Socialization

Political socialization is the process by which people gain their opinions and knowledge about politics. In childhood, the key agent of socialization is the family. Parents teach children their first lessons about life, including politics. From household conversations, children pick up many of their parents' political beliefs. More often than chance would explain, they will eventually belong to the same political party as adult family members.

Families also shape political beliefs in less direct ways. A family's social and economic background may affect children's thinking regardless of how often the parents talk politics. In 1927, debts forced a small-town druggist in South Dakota to sell his house. His 16-year-old son remembered years later, "It was the moment I ceased being a child, when I began to have an adult's awareness of the pain and tragedy in life. It was sharpened because about the same time other people in town began suffering similar losses of home and happiness."[48] The son was Hubert H. Humphrey, who went on to serve as U.S. senator and vice president. During his career, he championed liberal causes such as bank regulation. His father's experience gave him a special sympathy for victims of the Great Depression. Humphrey concluded that the market economy had failed them all and that government action was necessary to prevent such disasters.

When families choose a home, they are placing children in a certain political environment. Whether the locale is liberal or conservative, children may absorb the views of friends and neighbors. A family's religious faith also exposes children to political influences. In Humphrey's case, the family attended a Methodist church where the preaching of the Social Gospel buttressed his budding liberalism. Formal education is another force in socialization. Schools usually sidestep ideological struggles, but they have traditionally taught core principles. One example is Michigan's curricular framework, which says: "All students will explain the meaning and origin of the ideas, including the core democratic values expressed in the Declaration of Independence, the Constitution, and other foundational documents of the United States."[49] In the past decade, schools have stepped up efforts at civic education, with mixed results. Between 2006 and 2010, civic scores went up for fourth-graders, stayed the same for eighth-graders, and went down for twelfth-graders.[50]

As people age, other influences come into play. Those from modest backgrounds may grow rich, and their new friends and economic interests may nudge their political beliefs in a new direction. College students generally give little thought to property taxes, but they may later develop strong views when they buy real estate. It is hard to sort out these influences because there are so many links among them. Family background helps shape careers and marital choices. In turn, economic and marital status has much to do with where people live and whom they befriend.

Also, at any stage in a person's life, major historical events can have an effect. Perhaps the clearest example is the Great Depression, which greatly increased support for federal aid to the needy and led directly to the passage of programs such as Social Security. A decade

In the 2012 presidential campaign, families pass along their political beliefs to their children.

Political socialization—the long-term process by which people gain their opinions and knowledge about politics.

after September 11, 2001, the terror attacks kept their hold on the public mind. Nearly all survey respondents could recall what they were doing when the attacks took place. Most said that the day had a deep personal effect and that the attacks changed the nation.[51] The long-term impact is not as obvious, however. The attacks increased concern about terrorism and, in the short run, led to support for more homeland security spending and surveillance of suspected terrorists. But amid controversies about wiretapping and the treatment of detainees at Guantánamo Bay, polls showed divisions over antiterrorism policy.

Political Persuasion

Political writers and activists hope to sway the undecided and convert the opposition, but a mind is a difficult thing to change. Hand a political pamphlet to someone without interest in politics, and that person will likely throw it away without reading it. Politicians and other activists try to get around this barrier by taking part in events that are otherwise nonpolitical. Local candidates shake hands at county fairs and march in Memorial Day parades, while national candidates long for opportunities to appear on *The Daily Show*.

Selective exposure—the human tendency to seek out information sources that back one's existing beliefs and to spurn sources that dispute them.

Among those with an interest in politics, **selective exposure** poses another hurdle. This concept refers to the tendency to seek out information sources that back one's existing beliefs and to spurn sources that dispute them. Conservatives and liberals tend to favor programs and publications that are friendly to their ideologies. In a 2010 survey, Republicans outnumbered Democrats by 44% to 21% in the audience of the conservative-leaning Fox News Channel. Viewers of liberal-leaning MSNBC were strongly Democratic, 53% to 14%.[52] Another survey found that 18% of social network users had blocked, unfriended, or hidden someone because of that person's views or political Internet activity. In all, 28% of liberals had taken such steps, compared with 16% of conservatives and 14% of moderates.[53]

When political figures do catch the attention of people they might persuade, what methods work? Aristotle named three.[54] *Ethos* refers to the character of the person making the cases. The more authoritative the source, the more likely that people will believe the message. *Pathos* is an appeal to emotion. Political speakers and writers usually summon symbols or memories that evoke strong feelings. *Logos* is an appeal to reason. Cynics belittle the role of logic in political persuasion, but logic can indeed shape opinion, provided that the words are clear.

Racial issues show how public opinion can shift decisively over time. A 1944 poll asked white respondents whether blacks "should have as good a chance as white people to get any kind of a job, or do you think white people should have the first chance at any kind of job?" A 52% majority said that whites should have the first chance. In 1972, only 3% said so.[55] On questions ranging from intermarriage to education, support swung from segregation to integration. Sixty-four years after Americans said that whites should come first, they elected a black president.

Civil rights leaders sparked the transformation. Reverend Martin Luther King Jr., contributed ethos by building a broad coalition. As the photo suggests, he enlisted support from many segments of American society. His stirring oratory added elements of pathos and logos, invoking the nation's core values and appealing to broad national interests: "When the architects of our republic wrote the magnificent words of the Constitution and the Declaration of Independence, they were signing a promissory note to which every American was to fall heir. This note was

After his famous March on Washington on August 28, 1963, Reverend Martin Luther King Jr. and his supporters meet with President Kennedy at the White House. Left to right: Whitney Young Jr. (Urban League); Martin Luther King Jr. (SCLC); John Lewis (SNCC); Rabbi Joachim Prinz (American Jewish Congress); Dr. Eugene Carson Blake (National Council of Churches); A. Philip Randolph; President Kennedy; Walter Reuther (United Auto Workers); Vice President Lyndon Johnson (behind Reuther); Roy Wilkins (NAACP).

© Flip Schulke/CORBIS

a promise that all men—yes, black men as well as white men—would be guaranteed the unalienable rights of life, liberty, and the pursuit of happiness."[56]

Events deepened the movement's emotional grip. In 1946, the lynching of black veterans laid bare the gap between racial reality and the goals of World War II.[57] In the following decades, television audiences watched as civil rights demonstrators faced bloody mistreatment. And over several decades, a stream of books, official reports and congressional hearings detailed segregation's corrosive effects. The logos, or logic, of the issue did not turn on narrow self-interest because the movement for black civil rights directly benefited only one-eighth of the population. Supporters of civil rights instead spoke of injustice and the harm it did to America's global image.[58]

As a result, Americans deliberated about race and gradually concluded that the law should stop discrimination, and because of the new laws, whites had more contact with other racial groups in school and on the job. Although racial conflict did not disappear, daily life socialized Americans, especially the young, to regard official segregation as a thing of the past.

OPINIONS INTO ACTION
MAJOR ISSUE

- How does participation foster deliberation?

As we noted at the start of this chapter, political participation consists of activities aiming to shape the choice of leaders and policies. Thoughts and deeds have a close connection. When Americans take part in politics, they are turning their opinions into action. Indeed, action is the reason that we study opinion in the first place: it would be pointless to measure beliefs if citizens never acted on them. At the same time, we cite opinion to explain what people do in the political world; and to a large extent, we use the same kind of instrument—survey research—to find out what citizens think and how they act.

Forms of Participation

Talk is one simple and direct method of political participation.[59] In 2008, 45% said that they had talked to others in an effort to influence their vote, a figure that had ranged from a low of 15% in 1974 to a high of 48% in 2004.[60] Other forms of participation attract fewer Americans:

- Attended a political meeting, 5%–9%
- Worked for a party or a candidate, 2%–7%
- Gave money to help a campaign, 4%–16%

Displaying campaign paraphernalia is a way of expressing political beliefs and inviting political conversation. It also builds morale. Voters are likely to feel better about supporting a candidate if they see that candidate's name on lapels, backpacks, and bumpers. Between 1956 and 1972, the percentage saying that they had worn a button or put a bumper sticker on their car fluctuated between 9% and 21%. Between 1974 and 2000, the figure fluctuated between 5% and 11%. In 2004, it jumped back to 21%. This change reflected the passions of that campaign.

The 2008 election highlighted newer forms of participation. Three-quarters of Internet users went

From an emotional standpoint, the hardest job in a campaign is cleaning up the signs after a defeat. Christiana Dominguez, who took a semester off from law school to work in the Kerry campaign in 2004, here faces the day after in the Philadelphia headquarters.

AP Photo/Kevork Djansezian

online to take part in or learn about the campaign. This figure encompassed just over half of American adults, making 2008 the first time that a majority had used the Internet to connect to the electoral process. Some 38% of Internet users talked about politics online, and 59% used tools such as Twitter or e-mail to send or receive political messages.[61] College students, who typically have easy access to the Internet and spend much of their time with computers, were especially likely to engage in online participation (see Table 7-1). The Obama campaign made skillful use of such tools to gather contributions, recruit volunteers, and get voters to the polls. Thousands of college students joined the Facebook group "Students for Barack Obama" along with local Facebook chapters. The campaign set up profiles on other general sites such as MySpace and on more focused sites such as AsianAve.com and BlackPlanet.com. In all, Obama had more than 2 million friends on social networking sites.[62]

TABLE 7-1   ONLINE PARTICIPATION IN 2012

In the spring of 2012, Knowledge Networks conducted an online survey of 3,096 18- to 29-year-olds for Harvard's Institute of Politics. The table below compares answers from the total sample with those attending four-year colleges.

	Total %	4-Year College %
Percent with a Facebook account	84	89
Percent of Facebook users who have used their Facebook status to advocate a political position	17	21
Percent of Facebook users who have liked a political issue on Facebook	23	27
Percent with Twitter account	28	33
Percent of Twitter users who have used it to advocate political positions	15	20

SOURCE: Adapted from Harvard University, Institute of Politics, The 21st Biannual Youth Survey on Politics and Public Service, March 23–April 9, 2012. Copyright © 2012. Reprinted with permission.

MYTHS AND MISINFORMATION

Internet Petitions

Many people have received e-mail "petitions," which are actually chain letters. After Congress authorized President George W. Bush to attack Iraq, one such petition urged support for "Congresswoman Barbara Bell." According to the e-mail, she had led a walkout of female members from the House chamber. In fact, no one of that name has ever served in Congress, and there was no such walkout.[64] Another petition protested a Senate vote to allow illegal aliens to collect Social Security benefits. No such measure ever reached the Senate floor.[65]

Some Internet petitions appear on Web sites, and may provide organizations with a way to harvest e-mail addresses. During and after the 2008 presidential campaign, rumors spread that Barack Obama was born in Kenya and is therefore constitutionally ineligible to be president. Internet petitions demanded that he produce his birth certificate and that Congress investigate his national origins. By the middle of 2010, more than half a million people had reportedly put their names on one such petition. The demand was based on misinformation. As early as June 2008, the Obama campaign posted a copy of his certification of live birth. Also available online were announcements of his birth that appeared in local newspapers in 1961. Conservative blogger Ed Morrissey wrote: "Unless someone wants to argue that the [Honolulu] Advertiser decided to participate in a conspiracy at Obama's birth in 1961 to provide false citizenship on the off-chance that an infant from a union of a Kenyan father and a teenage mother would run for President, then I'd say the 'mystery' is over."[66] Yet the petitions continued. Even after President Obama persuaded Hawaii to release the "long form" of his birth certificate, still more petitions asked Congress to investigate the document as a forgery. Politicians have started to post petitions to their own Web sites, in hopes of influencing other members or the executive branch. But as with advocacy groups, such petitions may have another motive: creation of an electronic mailing list. Once people have "signed" a Web petition, they will probably start getting e-mails on that issue.

Americans can also try to influence public policy outside the election season. A 2008 study found that 44% of voting-age Americans had communicated in some way with a senator or House member in the past five years. Of those who had gotten in touch with Congress, 43% used online methods for their most recent contact: e-mail, an online petition (see Myths and Misinformation box), a contact form on the lawmaker's Web site, or a contact form on another site. Another 24% used the telephone, while only 18% chose postal mail.[63]

One study examined "offline" political activities such as joining a civic group, as well as online activities such as friending candidates on social networking sites. The study found that college graduates were 28% more likely to engage in two or more online or offline activities than those who had not gone beyond high school. A similar gap appeared between those making at least $100,000 a year and those making less than $20,000.[67] Together with the differences in voter turnout, these disparities give a political edge to those who already have social and economic advantages.[68]

As a form of participation, blogging combines the informality of talk with the lasting record of print. One survey showed that about 14% of online adults worked on their own blog in 2011.[69] Another study found that about 11% of blogs focused on government and politics.[70] From these figures, we can make a very rough guess that there are between 2 and 3 million political bloggers. Because they made up barely 2% of the electorate and because most blogs have small audiences, blogging may seem to be a minor form of participation, but many Americans regularly read blogs about politics or current events, and as we have seen (Table 7-1), many others use social media to communicate about politics.

FOCUS
QUESTION
How has technology changed the way we deliberate about politics?

Deliberation and Impact

Some forms of participation contribute only indirectly to political deliberation. A bumper sticker may get people talking about a candidate or issue, but it has little content in itself. Everyday conversations, however, often involve such serious topics as health care, education, or crime. Even though these exchanges may not mention government policies, they may still add up to a significant political force. For instance, millions of Americans have heard friends and neighbors complain about the long waits and short office visits at health care organizations. These discussions, in turn, help create a political climate for policy change.

Some methods of contacting officials have more impact than others. It takes little effort to sign issue petitions, form letters, and preprinted postcards. Accordingly, politicians and their staffs assume that the signatures do not represent deep sentiments, and these documents usually go straight to the recycling bin. Individual letters and e-mails get more serious attention. Because they take some time and thought to compose, they suggest that the sender really cares about the subject matter. In one study, most congressional aides said that if their boss had not already made a decision, individual messages would have "some" or "a lot of" influence. Aides also said that messages could be especially helpful in the early stages of decision. According to

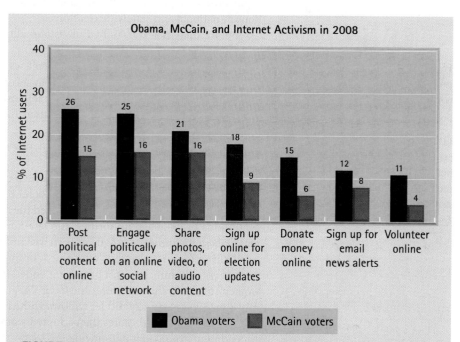

FIGURE 7-2 In the 2008 presidential election, McCain supporters were more likely than Obama supporters to use the Internet (83% vs. 76%). Nevertheless, online Obama supporters took part in a wider range of online political activities, such as posting comments, volunteering, or giving money.
SOURCE: From Internet and American Life Project. Copyright © 2009. Reprinted with permission.

the study, "Staff reported that well-reasoned letters from constituents often helped them assess the impact of pending legislation or proposals on a particular group, or on the district or state as a whole."[71]

Some evidence suggests that blogs may improve day-to-day political deliberation by giving voice to views that get less attention in the traditional media.[72] Social networking sites may also foster deliberation. During the 2008 campaign, for instance, my.barackobama.com enabled Obama supporters to exchange views on policy issues such as higher education (see Figure 7-2).

WHO VOTES?

MAJOR ISSUE

- In public deliberation, do certain groups have a greater voice than others?

Most forms of participation have some relationship to voting. The whole idea of taking part in campaigns is to sway elections. And when constituents write to an elected official, their voting power makes it more likely that their arguments will get a hearing. To understand how public sentiment drives public policy, therefore, we must know who votes and why. In turn, we must first study the rules that determine who may vote.

Expansion of Suffrage

Suffrage—the right to vote.

In the nation's early days, many American adults could not vote. Since then, the United States has expanded the right to vote, which we sometimes call **suffrage** or the franchise. Some states originally barred people from voting unless they held a substantial amount of property. By the end of the eighteenth century, the qualifications were low enough to include most white males.[73] In the decades that followed, most states scrapped these qualifications in national and statewide elections.

Before the Civil War, only a few states allowed African Americans to vote. In 1870, the Fifteenth Amendment forbade the denial of voting rights "on account of race, color, or previous condition of servitude." In many places, officials undercut this protection. **Poll tax** requirements meant that people had to pay a certain sum to vote, which kept poor people from the polls. Some states imposed **literacy tests** and examinations asking would-be voters to interpret complex legal language. Often, officials applied such tests to African Americans but not to whites.

Poll tax—a requirement to pay a certain sum of money in order to vote, which kept poor people from the polls. Poll taxes are now illegal.

Literacy test—a requirement that someone prove the ability to read before casting a vote. In practice, literacy tests were ruses to keep poor people and minorities from the polls. Federal law now forbids them.

In 1964, the Twenty-fourth Amendment banned the poll tax in federal elections; and two years later, the Supreme Court extended the ban to state and local elections.[74] In 1965, Congress passed the Voting Rights Act, which suspended literacy tests, banned other discriminatory practices, and authorized federal registrars to ensure the enfranchisement of African Americans. Congress has amended the act several times. In certain areas with concentrations of language minorities, the law now requires the printing of official election materials in the minority language as well as in English.

During the first elections after the adoption of the Constitution, only New Jersey let women vote (if unmarried), a practice it ended in 1807. Although some territories allowed women to vote in the years after the Civil War, no state did so until the admission of Wyoming in 1890. (Kentucky did let widows with children in school take part in school board elections.) A number of states then adopted women's suffrage, and in 1920, the Nineteenth Amendment extended it nationwide.

Four years later, Congress granted citizenship to all Native Americans born in the United States. Although this act enabled some Native Americans to vote, certain states barred them from the polls for several more decades.

Before the 1960s, residents of the nation's capital could not vote. The District of Columbia had no representation in Congress or the electoral college, and the Constitution put its government under congressional control. In 1961, the Twenty-third Amendment gave DC three electoral votes. Congress then allowed DC to elect a board of education (1968), a nonvoting delegate to the House (1970), and a city government (1973).

Until the 1960s, most states did not let people vote until they were 21. (The four exceptions were Kentucky, Georgia, Alaska, and Hawaii.) In 1970, Congress passed a law that lowered the voting age to 18. The Supreme Court ruled that Congress could change the voting age for federal races but not state and local elections.[75] Because it would be impractical to keep two registration rolls, state and federal lawmakers soon concluded that they should amend the Constitution. In 1971, the Twenty-sixth Amendment set the voting age at 18 in all elections.

In expanding the franchise, Americans have confirmed the ancient linkage between civic participation and military service. After the Civil War, support for black voting rights increased because African Americans had fought for the Union. During World War I, some 30,000 women served in the military, and millions more did civilian work. These efforts impressed many, including President Woodrow Wilson, who came out for women's suffrage. Similarly, the Indian Citizenship Act was in part a tribute to the heroism of Native American soldiers in World War I. Later in the twentieth century, supporters of voting rights legislation pointed to black soldiers who had fought in World War II. Supporters of the vote for the District of Columbia made the same point about Washington residents; and the Twenty-sixth Amendment passed during the Vietnam War, which gave new urgency to the old slogan "Old enough to fight, old enough to vote."

In one way, these laws shrank the franchise in the early twentieth century. During the nineteenth century, at least 22 states and territories gave the vote to noncitizens.[76] War played a role in the rise and fall of alien suffrage—the right of noncitizens of the United States to vote. The idea became popular after the Civil War because many noncitizens had served. It became unpopular in the early twentieth century, when anti-immigrant sentiment was rising. World War I effectively put an end to statewide alien voting, as many people feared enemy influence. The last state to drop it was Arkansas in 1926. Nevertheless, a few communities today let resident noncitizens vote in certain local elections.[77]

One formal limitation on citizen suffrage does exist. Except for Maine and Vermont, all states and the District of Columbia forbid voting by people serving prison sentences for felonies. Felons on parole (supervision in the community after release from prison) cannot vote in 35 states, 30 of which also forbid those on probation (supervision in the community instead of imprisonment) to vote.[78]

Registration

In every state except North Dakota, people must register to vote.[79] Many states used to require at least a year's residency, but in 1972, the Supreme Court ruled that anything more than three months would deprive people of their rights to vote and travel.[80] **Voter registration** requires citizens to enter their names on a government list before voting in elections. In 1993, Congress passed the National Voter Registration Act, or **Motor Voter**.[81] Under this law, states must offer voter registration when people apply for services such as driver's licenses. States must also accept mail-in voter registration. They may not take people off the rolls for failure to vote or set registration deadlines more than 31 days before an election. In 2010, nine states and the District of Columbia let people register on Election Day.[82]

Nevertheless, the United States remains unusual among democracies by putting the burden of registration on the voter instead of the government. Many countries have nationwide voter lists. For instance, Elections Canada maintains the National Register of Electors, a database that it updates from a variety of sources, including motor vehicle registrars.[83] The United States has no such national list. Each state maintains its own procedures.

The American system of registration and voting is subject to a good deal of criticism. One school of thought says that it is too vulnerable to fraud. In 2011 and 2012, accordingly, a number of states passed or considered legislation that would make voters show photo identification, or require proof of citizenship for registration or voting. Another school of thought says that the system already discourages people from voting and

Voter registration—the requirement in most states for citizens to enter their names on a government list before voting in elections.

Motor Voter—the 1993 National Voter Registration Act, which requires states to offer voter registration when people apply for services such as driver's licenses.

that such restrictions will further reduce turnout and increase the risk of discrimination against poor people, who sometimes lack the necessary documents. Both sides agree that there is inefficiency. One study found nearly 2 million dead people on the voter rolls, 3 million people with registrations in more than one state, and about 12 million voter records with the wrong address.[84]

Understanding Turnout

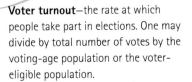

Voter turnout—the rate at which people take part in elections. One may divide by total number of votes by the voting-age population or the voter-eligible population.

Voting-age population—all residents over the age of 18.

Voter-eligible population—all those who have the right to vote.

Drop-off—the tendency for voter turnout to decline in nonpresidential elections.

Roll-off—the decline in the number of votes cast from high-profile races (e.g., president or governor) to low-profile races (e.g., coroner or sewer commissioner)

Critics of American election rules note that the United States has lower voter participation than most developed countries. There are two main ways to measure **voter turnout**, the rate at which people take part in elections. The first consists of dividing the number of votes in an election by the number of people who have registered to vote. Registered voters, who tend to be more motivated than the general population to begin with, are also more likely to vote. This measure then indicates the number of voters who follow through on their intent, but it fails to account for potential voters who failed to register at all. For that reason, scholars prefer another measure: dividing the number of votes by the **voting-age population** (VAP), all residents over the age of 18. In 2000, just over half of the U.S. voting-age population cast a ballot, compared with more than two-thirds of registered voters. By either measure, turnout in the United States is smaller than that of democracies that register nearly all adults.

Despite an upward trend since 1996, turnout among the VAP remains lower than in 1960. This difference is less ominous than it seems. The plunge between 1968 and 1972 occurred mainly because the Twenty-sixth Amendment added people from 18 to 20 to the VAP. Young people have lower turnout, so they brought down the overall figure. Also, the voting-age population includes many who cannot legally vote in federal elections: resident noncitizens and (in certain states) felons. Both groups have grown since the 1970s, increasing the VAP without increasing the electorate. If we look at the total number who have the right to vote, or the **voter-eligible population** (VEP), instead of the voting-age population, turnout grew from 1972 to 2008, moving from 56.2% to 61.6%[85] (see Figure 7-3).

Turnout rises in presidential elections and falls in nonpresidential elections, a pattern that political scientists have dubbed **drop-off**. During a presidential election, more people cast a ballot for president than for lower offices. In 2008, at least 9 million people voted for president but not for U.S. House.[86] Scholars refer to such differences as **roll-off**.

Despite changes such as the Motor Voter law, turnout remains lower than it could be. Why? Consider how individuals weigh the costs and benefits of voting. The "costs" do not necessarily involve money (at least since the end of poll taxes) but rather the time and trouble that go into voting. One cost is the act of registering, which most people must repeat with every change of address. Even in 2011, a year of low mobility, 45.3 million people had changed their U.S. address within the past year.[87]

Another cost consists of the effort to learn about all the contests: the more offices, the more work. Unlike nations where each voter has only a couple of races to decide every few years, the American system often serves up long ballots and frequent elections. A Michigan civic leader said, "I voted for a total of 50 state officials—4 executive officials, 2 legislators, 2 members of the state board of education, 2 each for the governing bodies of UM [University of Michigan], MSU [Michigan State University], and Wayne State, and 36 judges."[88] Such a menu can discourage would-be voters.

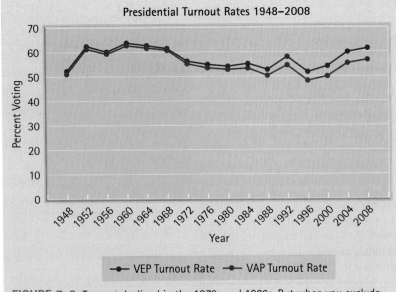

FIGURE 7-3 Turnout declined in the 1970s and 1980s. But when you exclude adults ineligible to vote from calculations, you find that the decline was not as great as it seems at first. Turnout is up since the 1990s.
SOURCE: Copyright © 2009 by Michael McDonald. Reprinted with permission.

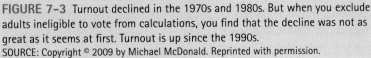

A major benefit of voting is the opportunity to make a difference.[89] People have a strong motive to go to the polls if their vote may be decisive and if the outcome will change public policy and affect them personally. The impact of a single vote depends on the size of the constituency and the competitiveness of the election. With a small electorate and a close race, each person could reckon that his or her vote could decide the winner. But especially in big constituencies that heavily favor one side or the other, the chances of casting the deciding vote are small. In a presidential election, those chances approach the vanishing point. Public-choice scholar Gordon Tullock refrains from voting because he believes that the relative insignificance of his ballot would not justify the time and effort it would take to cast it.[90] In other words, voting would be irrational for him.

Despite the real costs and debatable benefits, more than 130 million Americans took part in the 2008 presidential election.[91] Many voters saw important differences between Barack Obama and John McCain, and they took a strong interest in the election. Just before Election Day, the Pew Research Center found, 88% of registered voters said they were following campaign news very closely or fairly closely, which was the highest level of voter interest just before a presidential election since the Pew Research Center began tracking it in 1988.[92]

Why do so many citizens part company with Tullock? The answer is that they do not apply rigid cost-benefit analysis to the act of voting: instead, they see it as a responsibility. Civic leaders have long reminded Americans that voting is patriotic (see the photo) and that fellow Americans died for their right to vote. In a 2008 survey, 95% of voters agreed that it was their duty as a citizen to vote in every election, with 69% saying that they felt guilty when they did not get a chance to vote.[93] This sense of civic responsibility is strongest among "the greatest generation," those who

Is voting a means of promoting self-interest, or is it a duty of citizenship?

AP Photo/Marcio Jose Sanchez

In 2011, President Obama met Mark Zuckerberg at Facebook headquarters.

IMPACT
of Social Media and Communications Technology

Facebook and Voter Mobilization

At Facebook, Jonathan Chang wrote, shortly after the 2010 election:

> When Facebook users in the United States logged into Facebook on Election Day this year, they were greeted by a message alerting them of voting activity on Facebook. Users could click a button to announce to their friends that they had already voted and see which of their friends had done the same.
>
> . . .
>
> On our election-day display we showed users which of their friends had voted; but how much effect could this have on voter turnout? Could people see their friends voting and go out to do the same?[97]

There was indeed a relationship between the probability that a Facebook user would vote and the fraction of that person's friends who announced that they had voted. Chang said: "As more and more of your friends vote, not surprisingly, you are more likely to vote. Unfortunately, we cannot tell whether this effect is because of social influence, or if voting practice is simply clustered at a local level, but the fact that voting behavior is shared between friends is quite clear."

Apparently, one person who did not join in this voter mobilization was none other than Facebook founder Mark Zuckerberg. As the Bessette–Pitney blog noted on April 20, 2011, a local California paper found that Zuckerberg had not voted until 2008 and then failed to cast a ballot in the 2010 midterm.

CRITICAL THINKING
QUESTION

As we noted earlier, people tend to overreport socially acceptable behavior. So is it possible that a significant number of Facebook users were lying when they told their friends that they had voted? Discuss.

came of age during World War II. Accordingly, military veterans tend to vote at higher rates than nonveterans.[94]

People know that their fellow citizens regard voting as a duty. (See the Impact of Social Media and Communications Technology feature.) In one field experiment, scholars sent mailings to thousands of voters. There was much higher turnout among those whose mailings promised to tell their neighbors that they had voted.[95] This finding raises questions about reforms to increase turnout by making voting more convenient. In Switzerland, turnout actually dropped with the introduction of mail-in ballots. One scholar explained, "In Switzerland, like in many other countries, there exists a fairly strong social norm that a good citizen should go to the polls. As long as poll-voting was the only option, there was an incentive (or pressure) to go to the polls only to be seen handing in the vote.... With the introduction of postal voting, the signal from going to the polls got weakened."[96]

Voter Demographics

Different groups vote at different rates[98] (see Figure 7-4). Citizenship is one obvious reason for such differences. Among adult residents of the United States in 2008, noncitizens accounted for 6% of African Americans and 2% of non-Hispanic whites. But the figure was 32% for Asians and 37% for Hispanics. These rates are an important reason why Asians and Hispanics make up a smaller share of the electorate than of the population.

Even among citizens, however, non-Hispanic whites are more likely to vote than African Americans or Hispanics. The latter groups tend to have fewer years of schooling, which is one cause of the turnout gap. People with bachelor's degrees are twice as likely to vote as high school dropouts. Education accustoms people to handling paperwork and looking up information, thereby preparing them for the demands of voting.[99] Furthermore, schooling improves a person's income. People with higher incomes are more likely to own their homes, which gives them a greater stake in issues such as property taxation. Among people with the same level of education, the ethnic turnout gap is smaller, but persists. In recent years, political activists have sought to identify and mobilize potential voters in the African-American, Hispanic, and

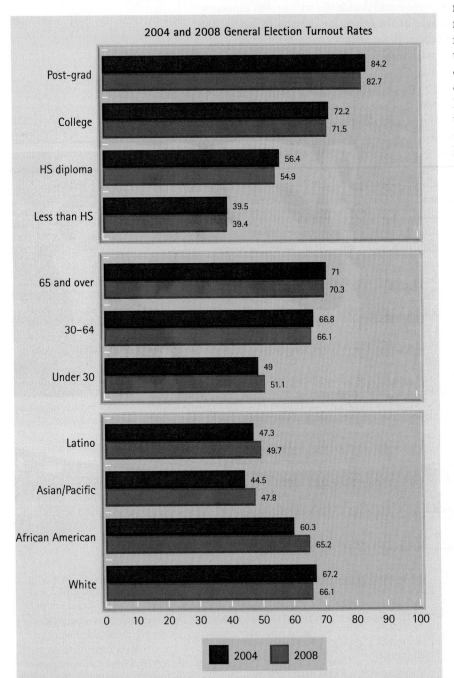

2004 and 2008 General Election Turnout Rates

Post-grad: 84.2 (2004), 82.7 (2008)
College: 72.2 (2004), 71.5 (2008)
HS diploma: 56.4 (2004), 54.9 (2008)
Less than HS: 39.5 (2004), 39.4 (2008)

65 and over: 71 (2004), 70.3 (2008)
30–64: 66.8 (2004), 66.1 (2008)
Under 30: 49 (2004), 51.1 (2008)

Latino: 47.3 (2004), 49.7 (2008)
Asian/Pacific: 44.5 (2004), 47.8 (2008)
African American: 60.3 (2004), 65.2 (2008)
White: 67.2 (2004), 66.1 (2008)

■ 2004   ■ 2008

FIGURE 7-4 This graph shows the percentage of the voter-eligible population (VEP) in each category casting ballots in 2004 and 2008. In both elections, turnout rose with age and education. Whites and African Americans were more likely to vote than Latinos or Asian/ Pacific Islanders. Although overall turnout did not change much between the two elections, there was one major exception: African-American turnout jumped nearly seven points, reaching near parity with white turnout.
SOURCE: Michael P. McDonald, "2008 Current Population Survey Voting and Registration Supplement," United State Election Project, April 6, 2009, at http://elections.gmu.edu/CPS_2008.html; Doug Hess, "Analysis of the 2008 Current Population Survey (CPS) Voter and Registration Supplement," Project Vote, April 8, 2009, at www.projectvote.org/newsreleases/429.html.

Asian communities. Turnout levels also track closely with age, at least up to 75, where in-firmities start keeping large numbers from the polls. In other words, the electorate is older, better educated, and more affluent than the population as a whole, and it has a smaller share of ethnic minorities.

As a result, say critics of the political process, sentiments that drive statutes and decisions are unrepresentative of the public as a whole. Politicians worry about Social Security and Medicare in part because the elderly vote at high rates. They also deal with issues that affect young adults, such as higher education. But the political motivation for those policy decisions comes less from the young voters themselves than from the concerns of their more politically active middle-aged parents.

PUBLIC OPINION, POLITICAL PARTICIPATION, AND DELIBERATIVE DEMOCRACY

As we have seen, laws and court decisions have made it easier to vote. Former Clinton speechwriter Eric Liu argues that it should be *harder* to vote:

> One of the prime reasons for the Voting Rights Act of 1964 was the sordid history of Jim Crow literacy tests used by whites at the ballot box to screen out and intimidate black voters. (Even worse, those tests often required would-be voters to read aloud from the Constitution.) As shameful and discriminatory as those tests were, just imagine now if there were a sincere and universal requirement of civic knowledge in order to vote. Think how few *non*-immigrants would pass.
>
> Today, public understanding of our past and our system of government is pitifully low: As Justice Sandra Day O'Connor has archly observed, far more Americans can name a judge on *American Idol* than a justice of the Supreme Court. Only a third can name all three branches of government. One simple remedy would be to update the citizenship test now given to naturalizing immigrants—and administer it to everyone. That would boost knowledge in a hurry.[100]

Obviously, the idea is whimsical. Yet it does make the point that citizenship involves duties as well as rights. One could contend that the right to vote entails a duty to cast an informed vote. Moreover, the right to hold and voice opinions means a responsibility to take account of the country's long-term well-being. As we saw at the beginning of the chapter, people often blur national interest and self-interest, but most understand that they are not always the same thing.

How should political leaders react to public opinion and participation? In 1999, journalist Peter Jennings asked Senator Daniel Patrick Moynihan if polls had contributed "to a lack of confidence in politicians in their own deliberative thinking process." Senator Moynihan replied, "Yeah, I think you wouldn't be mistaken, as a citizen, to ask, Are we really necessary?"[101] As the Jennings question suggests, a common criticism of elected officials is that they pay too much attention to the latest survey or tabulation of constituent letters. Most elected leaders would say that this criticism is too broad. Politicians are shrewd readers of survey research and political participation. They know that many polling numbers or mail counts may reflect snap judgments or nonattitudes, and they do not automatically treat these data as commands.

In his book *Profiles in Courage*, John F. Kennedy wrote of several figures in American history who acted against public opinion. He concluded that "democracy means much more than popular government and majority rule, much more than a system of political techniques to flatter or deceive powerful blocs of voters." True democracy, he continued, requires faith that the people will elect officials who exercise conscientious judgment, "faith that the people will not condemn those whose devotion to principle leads them to unpopular courses, but will reward courage, respect honor and ultimately recognize right."[102] In 1989, members of the late president's family established the Profile in Courage Award to celebrate the qualities that he had described. In 2001, the award went to former president

Gerald R. Ford. After succeeding to the presidency when Richard Nixon resigned in 1974, Ford pardoned Nixon for possible offenses in the Watergate scandal. Although the decision was unpopular—and contributed to Ford's defeat in the 1976 presidential election—many historians believe that it was an honorable effort to heal the country. Ironically, Nixon had been Kennedy's opponent in the 1960 presidential election.

Politicians cannot ignore opinion, either. If they buck strong currents of sentiment, they may sink to defeat. Therefore, they often trim their positions, clinging to some version of their principles that the public will take. Lincoln hated slavery but knew that few voters shared his passion. He publicly backed measures to stop its spread, in the hope of causing its "ultimate extinction." Yet it was well into the Civil War before he supported a constitutional amendment to abolish it. Had he supported abolition much earlier, he might have lost the presidency or at least would have found it harder to rally the Union. At the same time, by taking as strong a stance as he did, he helped move public opinion toward abolition. The famed ex-slave Frederick Douglass said of Lincoln:

> Had he put the abolition of slavery before the salvation of the Union, he would have inevitably driven from him a powerful class of the American people and rendered resistance to rebellion impossible. Viewed from the genuine abolition ground, Mr. Lincoln seemed tardy, cold, dull, and indifferent; but measuring him by the sentiment of his country, a sentiment he was bound as a statesman to consult, he was swift, zealous, radical, and determined.[103]

Deliberative democracy involves an ongoing dialogue between elected officials and citizens. If politicians *consult* opinion—rather than *parrot* it—then the modern technology of survey research and political participation can actually advance the cause of deliberative democracy.

SUMMARY

- In a democracy, public opinion plays a major role in driving public policy.
- Measuring public opinion is difficult. Random-sample surveys are the most reliable method for gauging public sentiment, but polling faces a variety of problems and challenges: drawing accurate samples, writing unbiased questions, reaching potential respondents at the appropriate times, dealing with people who refuse to answer, and sorting genuine opinions from deceptive or superficial responses.
- The last point is important, because some results capture fleeting reactions, while others tap lasting convictions.
- Survey results can be misleading when respondents are ill-informed about the question at hand. Those who analyze poll data should always keep in mind that the results may reflect this lack of information.
- Political figures sometimes use survey data to determine which positions to take. But they can also use polls to figure out how they should explain stands that they have already taken.
- Underlying many opinions are political ideologies, or systems of belief about what government should do. Opinions and ideologies are the product of many influences, such as family, schooling, the mass media, and persuasive leaders.
- Public sentiment translates into public policy through the medium of political participation. Over time, the expansion of voting rights has given opportunities for participation to more and more Americans. Not all eligible adults cast a ballot. Still, millions do vote, and civic duty is a major motivation. People participate in other ways as well, contributing to political mobilization and deliberation.
- Election laws can have a major impact on who registers and votes.
- Social media and communications technology have increased the number of ways in which citizens can participate in politics.
- Citizens and leaders alike must heed public opinion, but they do not necessarily bow to it in all circumstances.

KEY TERMS

Conservative p. 219
Drop-off p. 228
Exit poll p. 214
Focus group p. 215
Liberal p. 219
Libertarian p. 220
Likely voter p. 213
Literacy test p. 226
Moderate p. 219
Motor Voter p. 227

Nonattitudes p. 215
Political ideology p. 219
Political participation p. 212
Political socialization p. 221
Poll tax p. 226
Populist p. 220
Public opinion p. 212
Public opinion poll (or survey) p. 213
Random-digit dialing p. 213

Random sample p. 213
Roll-off p. 228
Selective exposure p. 222
Suffrage p. 226
Tracking poll p. 214
Voting-age population p. 228
Voter-eligible population p. 228
Voter registration p. 227
Voter turnout p. 228

TEST YOUR KNOWLEDGE

1. The sum total of individual beliefs about political questions is called
   a. political ideology.
   b. political participation.
   c. public opinion.
   d. roll-off.
   e. selective exposure.
2. A device that gauges public opinion by asking people a standard set of questions is called a(n)
   a. exit poll.
   b. opinion calculator.
   c. public opinion poll.
   d. random sample.
   e. tracking poll.
3. Polls conducted by news organizations that invite everyone to participate by phone, mail, or Internet are practically worthless because they
   a. do not consist of a random sample.
   b. do not reach enough respondents.
   c. largely falsify the results to support the current news story.
   d. primarily reach nonvoters.
   e. reach only those people who have little knowledge of the issues.

4. Survey questions about abstract issues most often show different public attitudes than questions about specific policies regarding those issues because
   a. analysts have not interpreted the data correctly.
   b. people can't make up their minds.
   c. people generally do not listen carefully to specific questions about policies.
   d. people often fail to think through the consequences of their opinions when answering abstract survey questions.
   e. pollsters have failed to formulate good questions.

5. Which political ideology seeks to limit government across the board?
   a. conservative
   b. liberal
   c. libertarian
   d. moderate
   e. populist

6. The tendency to seek out information sources that support one's existing belief system is called
   a. drop-off.
   b. political socialization.
   c. roll-off.
   d. selective exposure.
   e. suffrage.

7. Attending a political meeting, contributing time or money to a campaign, and simply talking to others about politics are forms of
   a. opinion polls.
   b. political participation.
   c. political parties.
   d. roll-off.
   e. selective exposure.

8. Which of the following groups was not allowed to vote until the 1960s?
   a. members of the military on active duty
   b. immigrants from western Europe
   c. Native Americans born in the United States
   d. residents of Washington, DC
   e. women

9. Voter registration requires citizens to
   a. appear before a judge to prove eligibility.
   b. enter their names on a government list before voting in elections.
   c. pay a poll tax before receiving approval to vote.
   d. present valid identification at the polls.
   e. publicly declare their allegiance to a candidate.

10. Asians and Hispanics make up a smaller portion of the electorate than of the general population because they are
    a. more likely to be noncitizens and therefore ineligible to vote.
    b. often not provided with ballots printed in their native languages.
    c. often turned away at the polls.
    d. often unable to pass the literacy tests.
    e. unable to pay the poll tax.

FURTHER READING

Asher, Herbert. *Polling and the Public: What Every Citizen Should Know*. 7th ed. Washington, DC: CQ Press, 2007.

Campbell, David E. *Why We Vote: How Schools and Communities Shape Our Civic Life*. Princeton, NJ: Princeton University Press, 2006.

DelliCarpini, Michael X., and Scott Keeter. *What Americans Know about Politics and Why It Matters*. New Haven, CT: Yale University Press, 1996.

Kahneman, Daniel. *Thinking, Fast and Slow*. New York: Farrar, Straus and Giroux, 2011.

Mayer, William G. *The Changing American Mind: How and Why Public Opinion Changed between 1960 and 1988*. Ann Arbor: University of Michigan Press, 1992.

Popkin, Samuel L. *The Reasoning Voter*. 2nd ed. Chicago: University of Chicago Press, 1994.

Weissberg, Robert. *Polling, Policy, and Public Opinion: The Case against Heeding the "Voice of the People."* New York: Palgrave Macmillan, 2002.

WEB SOURCES

Gallup www.gallup.com/—home page of the nation's best-known survey organization.

Pew Research Center for the People and the Press: www.people-press.org—national polling data, with an emphasis on media politics.

The Polling Report: www.pollingreport.com—compilation of recent poll data.

HuffPost Pollster—www.huffingtonpost.com/news/pollster/—data, graphics, and analysis by pollster Mark Blumenthal and others.

Teachers are an important interest group. Here, Miami teachers protest planned cuts in the local education budget.

Joe Raedle/Getty Images

Interest Groups

8

OBJECTIVES

After reading this chapter, you should be able to:

- Define what interest groups are.
- Explain different ways by which they take form and sustain themselves.
- Compare economic and policy groups, and discuss their role in deliberative democracy.
- Identify ways in which interest groups try to influence public policy.
- Analyze potential tensions between citizenship and interest group politics.

INTRODUCTION

Many political figures use the term *special interest* as a slur. "People want Washington to work on behalf of the American people, not on behalf of folks in Washington and special interests," said President Obama early in the 2012 campaign.[1] "My team is the American people, not the insiders in Washington," said Mitt Romney, "and I'll fight for the people of America, not special interests."[2]

Special interest—an unfavorable way to characterize those who stand to gain or lose more from a public policy.

For any policy or issue, a ***special interest*** consists of those who stand to gain or lose more than others. Everybody may dislike special interests, but everybody belongs to them, because any policy has different effects on different people. Child-care tax credits benefit parents. To make up the forgone tax revenue, the government sets higher rates, which childless people must pay. In this case, parents and nonparents both constitute "special interests." Similarly, students gain from government aid to higher education, but nonstudents must help pay for them.

Even policies that seem to affect everyone equally often have unequal impacts. Everybody breathes, so everyone has the same stake in federal clean air laws, right? Think again. In smoggy areas, the law requires expensive special gasoline, so commuters bear more cost than people who walk or bike to work. Coal-fired power plants pay more to curb pollution than hydroelectric plants, so people who use coal-generated electricity pay higher utility bills.

Interest group—an organization that seeks to influence public policy.

People sometimes speak of **interest groups** interchangeably with special interests, but these terms do not have quite the same meaning. Interest groups are organizations that try to influence public policy. Not every *potential* special interest has such a body. One can think of people who share a common concern but lack organization. Conversely, there are interest groups whose members have little tangible stake in the group's issues. Students for a Free Tibet wants the U.S. government to support Tibetan independence from China, even though many of its members may never have set foot in that land, and few will ever do so.[3] Rather than material wants, such groups act on the basis of altruism or idealism.

Faction—James Madison's term for a group that pursues interests harmful to those of another group or to the good of the country. In contemporary usage, it often refers to any interest group.

Critics of "special interests" may argue that interest groups undercut ideal citizenship and deliberation—and, indeed, Madison believed that they may do just that. He defined a **faction** as a group whose passions or interests are "adverse to the rights of other citizens, or to the permanent and aggregate interests of the community."[4] Nearly every interest group, some say, has goals or methods that disadvantage others. In 2008, Students for a Free Tibet staged protests against the torch relay for the Beijing Olympics, causing serious public relations problems for the United States Olympic Committee.

Many Americans worry that political debate is often a mismatch, in which the power of rich interest groups can drown out the voices of the poor. In the classic words of one scholar: "The flaw in the pluralist heaven is that the heavenly chorus sings with a strong upper-class accent."[5] Critics point to farm price supports, arguing that they enrich large agricultural corporations at the expense of consumers.

Another view is that citizenship and deliberation can benefit from the activities of interest groups. Tocqueville said that political associations teach citizens "to advance in methodical agreement toward a common aim."[6] According to this view, by working for narrower aims, people learn how to advance loftier ones. Interest groups also pour vast sums into educational and charitable activities. Indeed, your classroom may have been the gift of a corporate CEO. Even if the goal of such giving is to win good publicity or curry political favor, say defenders of interest groups, the ultimate effect is to serve the public interest.

REUTERS/Larry Downing

Near the White House, Students for a Free Tibet and other groups protest the visit of Chinese president Hu Jintao, January 2011.

Interest groups also hold that they advance deliberative democracy by educating citizens and public officials about policy issues. They dismiss the stereotype of the cigar-chomping, arm-twisting lobbyist as a myth, contending that most of their effort goes into data and arguments. The Edison Electric Institute, an organization of electric companies, issues detailed studies of energy and environmental issues.[7]

Defenders and critics can agree that interest groups have become more numerous and diverse. Between 1980 and 2010, the number of national nonprofit associations grew from 14,726 to 23,983.[8] This chapter will look at the role of interest groups in American politics. We will discuss their origins and development, types of interest groups, and the methods they use to influence policy; and finally, we evaluate the impact of interest groups on the political process and consider the need for reform. A good way to begin is by explaining how they spread.

CREATING AND SUSTAINING INTEREST GROUPS
MAJOR ISSUE

- Why do interest groups form?

When Tocqueville was writing in the 1830s, it was hard to form associations covering large areas. People had trouble uniting, he said, "for all being very small and lost in the crowd, they do not see one another at all and do not know where to find one another."[9] The press supplied one answer to the communication problem, but news could travel no faster than a horse or steamboat. Soon, however, the telegraph enabled far-flung interests to communicate instantaneously. The spread of railroads and hotels made it possible to hold meetings for people from all over the country.[10] During the twentieth century and into the twenty-first, advances in communication and transportation further reduced the barriers. Organizational work that once took months of letter writing and weeks of wagon travel now requires a few minutes at the computer keyboard.

MYTHS AND MISINFORMATION
Lincoln and Special Interests

Conservative and antitax groups sometimes suggest that Abraham Lincoln would have taken their side. They quote a passage that includes the following: "You cannot strengthen the weak by weakening the strong. You cannot lift the wage earner by pulling down the wage payer. You cannot help the poor man by destroying the rich." Lincoln never used those words. They came from William Boetcker, a minister who was born eight years after Lincoln died and who led an antistrike interest group called "The Citizens' Industrial Alliance." Boetcker never attributed the lines to Lincoln, but apparently some of his listeners did.[11]

Conversely, liberal groups sometimes claim Lincoln as a fellow foe of corporate lobbies. They cite this passage: "Corporations have been enthroned. An era of corruption will follow and the money power of the country will endeavor to prolong its reign by working upon the prejudices of the people until the wealth is aggregated in a few hands and the republic is destroyed." Journalist Joe Conason cited it in *It Can Happen Here* (2007) as did former vice president Al Gore in *The Assault on Reason* (2007).[12] In 2010, Senator Ben Cardin (D-MD) quoted Lincoln as uttering the passage "100 years ago," by which time Lincoln had been dead for 45 years.[13] In 2011 and 2012, members of the "Occupy" movement used it to attack big business.[14]

This quotation is also bogus. Apparently, members of the Populist movement concocted it in the late 1800s, and it has been in circulation ever since, with speakers and writers passing it to one another without checking its authenticity. Lincoln's personal secretary and biographer, John Nicolay, called it a "bald, unblushing forgery."[15] Indeed, the statement would have been inconsistent with Lincoln's pre-presidential career. Lincoln represented railroad companies in court. He also lobbied the U.S. House on behalf of canal developers and the Illinois Legislature on behalf of medical professionals.[16]

Government has grown alongside the interest group community, both as result and cause. During the country's early decades, the federal bureaucracy was small. National interest group activity was light, with few issues to talk about and few officials to talk to, but some groups began to press for new agencies to represent their interests. In 1862, the United States Agricultural Society and other groups persuaded Congress to establish the Department of Agriculture (which gained Cabinet status 27 years later). Contrary to myth (see the Myths and Misinformation feature), Lincoln was not an automatic foe of special interests, and he signed the measure. In the years since then, group pressure has also made way for the Departments of Commerce, Labor, Education, and Veterans Affairs.

The public sector has *created* new interests. Some groups represent members who gain direct benefits from government such as veterans and Social Security recipients. Some groups represent members who carry out government programs, such as public school teachers. Still others supply goods and services that government policy requires, such as diversity consultants (see the photo) and defense contractors. Each now has its own interest groups.

Before 1890, most Americans worked in farming,[17] but this situation changed as the new century drew near. The growth of organized labor followed the development of industries. Law, medicine, and other fields evolved into distinct professions, each with its own distinct interests. With more lines of business came more associations.[18] Continuing into the twenty-first century, this trend toward diversification has created economic interests, many stemming from new technologies. E-commerce was once science fiction; now it is a set of industries, each with its own issues. Meanwhile, waves of immigration have increased the nation's demographic diversity. Although English remains the nation's common tongue, millions speak another language at home. Linguistic and social variety has meant additional interests and their related organizations. For instance, the National Council of *La Raza* (the Race) is an important Hispanic group.

Sometimes, new interest groups arise from changes in beliefs. Pollution had befouled the nation long before the 1960s, but it took books such as Rachel Carson's *Silent Spring*—which inspired widespread public concerns with pesticides and pollution of the environment and led to the 1972 ban of the insecticide DDT—to make it an urgent political issue. This new perspective fed the growth in existing environmental groups and helped give birth to others. Meanwhile, other writers and activists persuaded Americans to spurn workplace discrimination against women. The 1966 founding of the National Organization for Women (NOW) was one result of this new attitude, and more groups followed.

Although technology has smashed many of the hurdles, one difficulty persists, which scholars call the **free-rider problem**. Membership in a group takes time (for attending meetings or even reading publications) and money (for dues and contributions). If a group seeks something that will help members and nonmembers alike, such as clean air, members might wonder why they should bother to join, thinking it may pay just to skip the hassle of membership and reap the rewards anyway. One solution is to establish a rule that makes people join. Labor unions try to insert such a requirement in their employment contracts. Another is to provide **selective incentives** that only members may enjoy, such as exclusive access to publications.[19] On its Web page, the Texas Organization of Nurse Executives (TONE) lists several incentives for joining and concludes that membership "is a smart investment in your career."[20]

Free-rider problem—the difficulty that exists when an organization seeks a good or policy change but cannot confine the benefits to its own members. If people can reap the benefits without bearing the costs of membership, they lack incentives to join.

Selective incentive—a good or service that only members of an organization may enjoy. A selective incentive is one remedy to the free-rider problem.

Courtesy of the American Association for Affirmative Action

The American Association for Affirmative Action is a trade association for diversity consultants and other professionals who run affirmative action programs.

ECONOMIC GROUPS

MAJOR ISSUE

- What are some types of economic groups, and what role do they play in policy deliberation?

Economic groups, including businesses, trade associations, and labor unions, pursue their own material welfare by seeking the following benefits:

- Direct monetary benefit, including jobs, contracts, purchases, subsidies, or tax breaks
- Restraints on competition that hamper rivals
- Relief from regulation, in the form of less red tape and fewer government requirements

Economic groups often equate the people's well-being with their own, or, as one auto executive put it in 1952: "What was good for our country was good for General Motors, and vice versa."[21]

Economic group—an interest group, such as a union or business, that explicitly pursues its own material welfare.

Business Firms

One political scientist has written of "the privileged position of business." Because a market economy rises or falls with private enterprise, he wrote, public officials tend to defer to the needs of business.[22] According to a common impression, a few billionaires rule the government. The actual picture is more complex. Far from being a narrow elite, the business sector represents a large part of the public, and its breadth is a source of power.

The United States is home to more than 7 million business establishments.[23] Their combined payrolls of 120 million jobs account for most working Americans. Of course, not all employees identify their own interests with those of their employers, and the relationship can be tense. In the end, though, workers usually gain when their companies prosper and always suffer when they fail. If a firm's existence is at stake, employees may join with management to seek government help. In the 1980s, the United Auto Workers (UAW) supported federal loan guarantees that helped save the Chrysler Corporation. In 1994, some 16,000 tobacco workers marched on Washington to protest an increase in tobacco taxes. "I'm marching for my livelihood," said one. "I've got to have that job."[24]

Stock ownership widened in the late twentieth century, then declined with the economic turmoil that started in 2008. Still, about half of American households now own stock, either directly or through individual retirement accounts, company pension funds, or mutual funds (see Figure 8-1). Because the value of their investment varies with the fortunes of companies with which they have holdings, shareholders sometimes take the corporate side in political disputes. During the federal government's antitrust action against Microsoft, the company's 3 million shareholders supplied it with a base of support. But widespread stock and bond ownership also means that executive misconduct or mismanagement may have harmed millions of Americans. The economic upheaval of recent years has caused many to take a harsher view of big business and the financial community. In 2011, 47% of Americans said that Wall Street hurts the U.S. economy more than it helps, while 38% said that it helps more than hurts.[25]

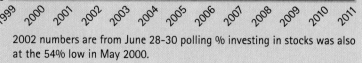

Percentage of Americans Investing in Stock, April of Each Year, 1999–2011
Do you, personally, or jointly with a spouse, have any money invested in the stock market right now—either in an individual stock, a stock mutual fund, or in a self-directed 401(k) or IRA?

2002 numbers are from June 28-30 polling % investing in stocks was also at the 54% low in May 2000.

FIGURE 8-1 Since 1999, Gallup has asked: "Do you, personally or jointly with a spouse, have any money invested in the stock market right now—either in an individual stock, a stock mutual fund, or in a self-directed 401-K or IRA?"
SOURCE: Dennis Jacobe, "In U.S., 54% Have Stock Market Investments, Lowest Since 1999," Gallup Poll, April 20, 2011, http://www.gallup.com/poll/147206/stock-market-investments-lowest-1999.aspx

Although business has a reputation for preferring smaller government, firms often profit from the *growth* of government. Throughout the Cold War (1945–1991), heavy industry made billions from defense spending, which led to President Dwight Eisenhower's famous warning against "unwarranted influence, whether sought or unsought, by the military-industrial complex."[26] Even after the Cold War, the ties remained close. A 2009 study by the Cato Institute, a free-market research organization, estimated that the government annually spends at least $90 billion on "corporate welfare," including direct cash payments to businesses (e.g., subsidies to farmers and grants to automobile companies) and indirect benefits such as loans, research, and marketing support.[27] The connection between business and government became dramatically deeper in 2008, when Congress approved $700 billion to rescue financial institutions. A few months later, a $787 billion economic stimulus bill greatly increased opportunities for contractors at all levels of government: construction, information technology, renewable energy, and many others.

While many businesses object to costly government rules, other businesses benefit from them. Bigger firms can better afford to comply with health and safety rules than smaller ones, giving them an edge.[28] In other cases, regulation increases demand for a business's services. Antipollution laws have enlarged the environmental services industry, with more than $300 billion in revenue and 1.7 million workers.[29]

Trade and Professional Associations

Hundreds of businesses have offices in Washington, DC, to represent their interests to the government, but they make up only a portion of economic interest groups. **Trade or industry associations** are another major part of that group. Businesses join trade associations when they have an interest in public policy but find it uneconomical to keep offices in the capital. For example, few individual farmers could afford Washington representation, so they have banded together in large national groups such as the American Farm Bureau Federation and the National Farmers Union.

Even firms with government relations offices join trade associations. When issues affect an entire industry, individual companies want a united front. The federal government has responsibility for fighting movie piracy at home and abroad. Accordingly, major film companies belong to the Motion Picture Association of America (MPAA; see the photo).

Such groups may perform public services as alternatives to government action. In response to demands for government censorship, for instance, MPAA established the rating system that curbs children's access to movies with adult content.

Professional associations usually consist of people with special training. These groups often start with the aim of gaining official recognition of their profession, including laws requiring a license or credential. They differ from most trade associations because they can sometimes impose formal discipline on their members. Professional associations argue that such requirements and procedures protect their clients. At the same time, they also hold down competition. In the state legislatures and in Congress, the American Medical Association (AMA) has fought independent medical providers, such as nurse midwives

Trade or industry association—
an organization that represents businesses in a particular field or industry.

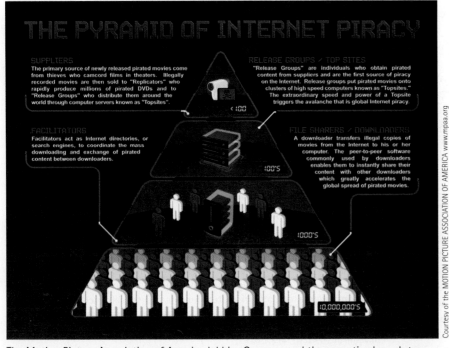

Courtesy of the MOTION PICTURE ASSOCIATION OF AMERICA www.mpaa.org

The Motion Picture Association of America lobbies Congress and the executive branch to fight the illegal copying of movies. It also files lawsuits against those who make the copies.

(who deliver babies) and chiropractors. Describing "alternative" providers as unqualified, the AMA has sought laws forbidding them to practice or at least denying them federal reimbursement. The AMA's detractors respond that barriers to entry have stifled consumer choice, leading to poorer health care at higher cost.[30]

The AMA is the lead organization for physicians, and the American Bar Association (ABA) plays a similar role for attorneys. Among trade associations, lead organizations include the National Association of Manufacturers for industrial companies, and both the U.S. Chamber of Commerce and the National Federation of Independent Business for small businesses. Within their fields, these groups have the largest memberships and the broadest scope of policy concerns. Beside the lead organizations stand many specialized groups. While the ABA serves lawyers in general, different kinds of lawyers have different interests. Members of the American Association for Justice (formerly the Association of Trial Lawyers of America), specialize in lawsuits, and members of the Federation of Insurance and Corporate Counsel defend clients against them. The National Association of Criminal Defense Lawyers seldom agrees with the National District Attorneys Association.

The free-rider problem poses difficulties for trade and professional associations. These groups seek policies that benefit everyone in their fields. Here is where selective incentives come into play. Associations supply members with research, training, and opportunities to "network" with other members. Many also help members in dealings with government.

Organized Labor

Labor unions in the United States have always faced steep challenges in gaining and keeping members. Well into the twentieth century, industrial employers used violence against unions. In 1935, American labor gained important federal protections with the passage of the **National Labor Relations Act**, or the **Wagner Act**. This law set up the National Labor Relations Board (NLRB) to protect union organizing and encourage collective bargaining. The act prohibited the setting up of company unions and firing workers who tried to organize their own unions. The Wagner Act, together with the growth of industry during and after World War II, helped bring union membership to one-third of nonagricultural employment by 1955. Membership then dropped off. Union leaders blamed the 1947 **Taft-Hartley Act**, which curbed their ability to counteract the free-rider problem. This law banned **closed shops**, in which employees must belong to the union at the time of hiring. It allowed **union shops**, where new employees must join the union within a certain period; but at the same time, it allowed states to enact **right-to-work laws**, which forbid union shops and thus let employees decline membership. The 22 states with right-to-work laws tend to have lower levels of union membership than states with union shops.

Other forces have also weakened the unions. In 1955, about 33% of nonagricultural jobs were in manufacturing, the old mainstay of organized labor. Forty years later, that proportion had plunged to less than 16%. Union membership fell accordingly, so that by 2011, less than one in eight nonagricultural employees in the United States belonged to a union.[31] Although other industrial countries have also seen declining rates of union membership, the figure in the United States is especially low. In 2010, for instance, it was less than half the rate of Britain and Canada.[32]

One area of growth consists of public employees. In 2009, for the first time in American history, a majority of union members were working in government instead of the private sector.[33] (Job losses in industry hastened the shift in the public/private balance, which had been under way for years.) Many of the public sector union members are white-collar professionals such as teachers.[34] In 2009, the outgoing general counsel of the National Education Association (NEA) candidly explained the group's effectiveness:

> Despite what some among us would like to believe it is not because of our creative ideas; it is not because of the merit of our positions; it is not because we care about children; and it is not because we have a vision of a great public school for every child.
>
> The NEA and its affiliates are effective advocates because we have power. And we have power because there are more than 3.2 million people who are willing to

National Labor Relations Act (Wagner Act)—the New Deal statute that set up the National Labor Relations Board (NLRB) to protect union organizing and encourage collective bargaining. The act forbade such unfair employer practices as setting up a company union and firing workers who organized unions.

Taft-Hartley Act—the 1947 law that curbed union power in several ways, including a ban on closed shops.

Closed shop—a requirement that employees join a labor union before the business hires them. The Taft-Hartley Act outlawed it.

Union shop—a requirement that an employee join a union after starting employment.

Right-to-work laws—laws in 22 states that forbid union shops.

pay us hundreds of million of dollars in dues each year because they believe that we are the unions that can most effectively represent them; the unions that can protect their rights and advance their interests as education employees.[35]

In recent years, blue-collar unions have aimed for a comeback. The 1.4-million-member International Brotherhood of Teamsters, which represents truck drivers, delivery service employees, and workers in other occupations, has striven to overcome a history of corruption.[36] That effort is part of a strategy to improve the union's image. Its leaders have talked about international human rights and launched services such as the James R. Hoffa Memorial Scholarship Fund. The Service Employees International Union (SEIU) has more than 2 million members, including nurses, health technicians, janitors, food service workers, and office workers.[37] It has worked to bring Hispanics and other ethnic groups into the labor movement.

The largest American labor group is the **American Federation of Labor–Congress of Industrial Organizations (AFL-CIO)**. It is not a union itself. Rather, it is an organization of 56 unions and their 12 million members.[38] The AFL-CIO tries to serve labor's interests through public relations, education of union organizers, and political activity. In recent years, some labor leaders have voiced disappointment in the AFL-CIO's efforts to sustain labor union membership. In 2005, the Teamsters, the SEIU, and five other major unions broke away from the AFL-CIO to form Change to Win, which focuses on union organizing.[39]

What does labor want? Samuel Gompers, an early union leader, said in 1890, "We do want more, and when it becomes more, we shall still want more. And we shall never cease to demand more until we have received the results of our labor."[40] Unions back laws that mean better pay, benefits, and workplace safety. Like other economic groups, they also try to use public policy to thwart competition. Industrial unions oppose measures that would lower trade barriers, unless they also improve wages and working conditions overseas. (Critics say that the American unions want to make foreign labor more costly and less competitive.) Public employee unions fight efforts to shift government services to private contractors. Teacher unions oppose programs that would let parents use tax money for nonpublic schools.

Economic groups can contribute to deliberation. As we have seen, they marshal information and arguments to gain support from policymakers and the general public. When rising energy prices led to calls for the breakup of energy companies, the U.S. Chamber of Commerce issued a 132-page report on antitrust law and the oil industry.[41] In the same vein, the National Education Association publishes detailed studies of issues such as the No Child Left Behind Act.[42]

Deliberation requires multiple points of view, but on any given issue, there is no guarantee that organized economic groups will represent more than one side. For instance, consider an industry group that presses for tax breaks or subsidies for its members. Even though each such measure might mean millions of dollars in spending or forgone revenue, that sum will make up only a tiny fraction of a multitrillion-dollar federal budget, and the cost to each taxpayer will not be noticeable. (A billion dollars came to less than three one-hundredths of 1% of federal spending in 2012.) So while the affected group has a strong incentive to argue for such measures, there may be no material incentive for another economic group to rebut them. Another type of organization can sometimes fill the void, however. We now turn out attention to policy groups.

American Federation of Labor–Congress of Industrial Organizations (AFL-CIO)—the leading group of American labor, an organization of 56 unions and their 11 million members.

Narrow interest groups sometimes benefit at the taxpayers' expense.

POLICY GROUPS

MAJOR ISSUE

- What are policy groups, and how do they affect policy deliberation?

Policy groups differ from economic groups in that their announced mission is to serve higher goals than their members' material interests. Observers sometimes refer to them as **ideological interest groups**, though they call themselves **public interest groups**. Some work on many issues. The American Conservative Union says that it "represents the views of Americans who are concerned with economic growth through lower taxes and reduced government spending and the issues of liberty, personal responsibility, traditional values and national security."[43] Americans for Democratic Action is "committed to liberal politics, liberal policies, and a liberal future" on a wide range of issues.[44] Other groups, such as the Children's Defense Fund, concentrate on more specific topics.

Sometimes, the boundary between economic and policy groups is vague. Consider the groups that oppose urban sprawl, the spread of homes and businesses into undeveloped land at the edge of cities. Much of the motivation behind the movement stems from a sincere belief that sprawl wastes resources, but self-interest also plays a part because stopping sprawl will benefit urban property owners (whose real estate values will rise) and downtown business owners (who will not have to face suburban competition).

Policy group—an interest group that purports to seek goals that benefit the broader public, not just its own members.

Ideological interest group—an interest group with a strong commitment to a particular political philosophy whether liberal, conservative, or libertarian.

Public interest group—a nonprofit organization whose primary goal is to seek benefits for the broader public, not just its own members.

Forms of Organization

Many policy groups are tax-exempt under Section 501(c)(4) of the Internal Revenue code. Such groups pay no income tax, but contributions to them are not tax-deductible. Although they may not give direct contributions to federal candidates, they may make independent expenditures in campaigns and advocate specific legislative positions.[45] One example is Citizens United, a conservative group that prevailed in the case of *Citizens United v. FEC*, which held that the federal government could not ban independent political expenditures by corporations and unions (see below). The most prominent 501(c)(4) is AARP (formerly the American Association of Retired Persons), whose 40 million members make it the largest interest group in the United States.[46]

Other groups are tax-exempt under Section 501(c)(3) of the same law. This status enables a group's supporters to deduct contributions from income tax and also makes it much easier to receive grants from private foundations. Such an organization may not do any electioneering or spend more than a small fraction of its resources advocating stands on particular measures. So how can these groups influence policy? The limits on advocacy do not apply to analyses of public issues, provided that they do not explicitly tell legislators how to vote. **Think tanks** are 501(c)(3) organizations that specialize in such work by issuing statements and reports, and by supporting the writing of books on policy topics. For instance, the Cato Institute looks at issues from a libertarian angle, faulting government intervention both in the economy and in individuals' private lives.

Think tank—a research organization, usually nonprofit, that issues statements and reports on policy issues.

Think tanks can foster deliberation by supplying intellectual fuel to staffers and lawmakers. The idea of establishing a Council of Economic Advisers in the White House started with a 1931 pamphlet from the Brookings Institution, a leading think tank in the nation's capital.[47] The conservative Manhattan Institute sponsored Charles Murray's controversial 1984 book, *Losing Ground*, which convinced many policymakers that federal welfare programs had worsened poverty. Although critics questioned the book's analysis, it helped lead to major welfare reform in 1988 and 1996.

Because most think tanks post their material on the Internet, anyone can now read reports on the very day that they come out. Scholars from these organizations also appear on cable television and talk radio. Think tanks can thus contribute to everyday conversations among activists and ordinary citizens, but the higher media profile has come at a price. A common criticism is that short-term thinking is crowding out long-term deliberation. One scholar says that the national media care for "the 30-second sound bite

ONCE WE PROGNOSTICATE HOW UPTURNS AND DOWNTURNS IMPACT SHORT AND LONG-TERM EARNING DATA, WE'LL GENERATE A POSITION PAPER...

GOBBLEDYGOOKOLOGIST

SCHWADRON

© Harley Schwadron. Reproduction rights available at www.CartoonStock.com

Not all think tanks specialize in sound bites. Some continue to produce lengthy technical documents, which draw the attention of cartoonists.

rather than an in-depth analysis of the issues and many websites publicize reports without critiquing the methodology or level of analysis. These practices serve to undermine the basic standards desirable for rigorous analysis of the issues."[48]

Some 501(c)(3) organizations mount "nonpartisan" voter registration and get-out-the-vote efforts in accord with federal rules, even if these drives focus on locales or demographic categories that favor one party. Republican and Democratic leaders alike have helped raise money for groups that tend to turn out votes for their own side.[49] For instance, President Clinton appeared at fund-raisers for the Southwest Voter Registration and Education Project, a group that increases participation among Mexican Americans, who mostly vote Democratic.

Yet another type of 501(c)(3) is a **foundation**. The usual purpose of a foundation is to make grants to organizations and individuals for scientific, educational, or other charitable purposes. Many foundations are nonpolitical, but some provide large sums to think tanks and other policy groups. Examples are the Ford Foundation, which supports liberal groups, and the Bradley Foundation, which supports conservative ones.

Economic or policy groups sometimes prefer to give money to federal candidates. For this purpose, they form **political action committees (PACs)**, which are not tax-exempt and must abide by the contribution limits and disclosure rules enforced by the Federal Election Commission (FEC). A policy group may be a conglomerate, with several kinds of organization. The Sierra Club, a major environmental group, is a 501(c)(4). The Sierra Club Foundation is a 501(c)(3) and thus can take tax-deductible contributions for public education, litigation, and training. The Sierra Club Political Committee supports candidates who favor the club's environmental stands and opposes those who take the other side.

Super PACs are a relatively new kind of political action committee made possible by the *Citizens United* case, as well as a 2010 federal court case called *SpeechNow.org v. Federal Election Commission*. A Super PAC (the formal term for which is "independent expenditure-only committee") may raise unlimited sums from individuals, unions, associations, and corporations, and spend unlimited sums to support or oppose political candidates. Super PACs must report contributions and expenditures to the Federal Election Commission, just as a traditional PAC would. But unlike traditional PACs, Super PACs may not give money directly to parties or candidates. (Our chapter on elections and campaigns will offer more detail on traditional PACs and Super PACs.)

Foundation—a nonprofit corporation or a charitable trust that makes grants to organizations or individuals for scientific, educational, cultural, religious, or other charitable purposes. Some foundations support policy groups.

Political action committee (PAC)—a political committee, other than a candidate's campaign committee or a party committee, that raises and spends money to elect or defeat candidates. Businesses and labor unions often form PACs because they cannot give money directly to federal candidates from their own treasuries.

Super PAC—a political action committee that can accept unlimited contributions from individuals, unions, corporations, and associations, and spend unlimited sums on independent expenditures in federal election campaigns, provided that it does not contribute to or coordinate with parties or candidates.

Membership and Funding

When Tocqueville wrote of associations, he was describing clusters of Americans who had regular local meetings. And until the late twentieth century, such associations were the building blocks of most national policy groups. Either a national group arose from existing local groups, or a national group admitted local chapters. The League of Women Voters began in 1920 at the convention of the National Women's Suffrage Association, which had

The Crossroads Groups

In 2010, a set of prominent Republicans formed one of the first Super PACs, American Crossroads. Although the group correctly asserted that it received contributions from hundreds of people during that year, more than three-quarters of its money came from a handful of wealthy individuals and corporations.

Soon afterwards, the founders of American Crossroads created a 501(c)(4) group, Crossroads Grassroots Policy Strategies, or Crossroads GPS. One purpose of the group was to engage in issue advocacy and research, but it could also play a part in electoral politics. Before *Citizens United*, a 501(c)(4) group could not run ads explicitly advocating the election or defeat of federal candidates. Now, it could do so, provided that such activity did not account for more than half of its spending. Unlike a traditional or Super PAC, a 501(c)(4) does not have to make public disclosure of its donors. "There are some donors who are interested in anonymity when it comes to advocating for specific issues," a Crossroads GPS spokesperson told the *Washington Post*.[50] "Whether it's legitimate or not, there is this near-hysteria, this belief that the Democrats are going to come after us," said one potential contributor.[51]

The two groups raised more than $70 million during the 2010 campaign, and their advertising helped Republicans regain a majority in the House. They remained active after the midterm race. "On the policy side, Crossroads GPS, we are working to stop President Obama's agenda. On the political side, American Crossroads, we're looking to replace him as president," said a spokesperson for both groups.[52]

Pro-transparency organizations criticized the Crossroads groups for taking so much money from corporate interests and for blurring the line between campaigning and true issue advocacy. They were especially critical of the "dark money" passing through Crossroads GPS. But Dan Eggen of the *Washington Post* reports an irony:

Most of the organizations behind the latest disclosure push—including Americans United for Change, Common Cause and Public Citizen—fall under a portion of the tax code that allows them to keep their donor details private. Some of the groups do reveal their biggest contributors voluntarily, but not at the level of detail required for political campaigns, super PACs and other explicitly election-oriented organizations.

The contrast underscores the muddiness surrounding much of the disclosure debate, because a broad array of the nonprofit groups that advocate for greater transparency in political donations are often not required to make such disclosures themselves.[53]

---

achieved its goal of a constitutional amendment securing voting rights for women. The League then focused on **grassroots** organization—working among the broad, general public. To this day, it works on local voter education.

In the 1960s and 1970s, a different pattern became common. Instead of starting with a confederation of local groups or a national convention of individuals, the new kind of group would start with a small number of leaders. Scholar Theda Skocpol calls these groups "associations without members."[54] Often working from Washington, DC, the organizers would solicit grants from individuals or foundations (hence the importance of 501(c)(3) status) and seek free publicity.[55] If successful, they would use much of their money for research and communication, plowing the rest back into more fundraising. Some groups also did grassroots organizing, but many did not. For example, the Mexican American Legal Defense & Education Fund, which promotes the civil rights of Hispanics, began in 1968 with money from the Ford Foundation and has never built local chapters.[56]

Face-to-face groups attract members with opportunities to make business contacts, gain friends, and even get dates. The new kind does not supply such benefits. According to scholar Robert Putnam, membership seldom involves much more than mailing checks. The bond between any two members of a such a group, he says, "is less like the bond between two members of a gardening club or prayer group and more like the bond between two Yankees fans on opposite coasts or perhaps two devoted L. L. Bean catalog users: they share some of the same interests but they are unaware of each other's existence."[57] And just as Yankee fans wear caps and shirts with their team's logo, so do members of the Sierra Club or the National Rifle Association. Group membership can be a form of self-branding.

Without the lure of personal relationships, how does a new-style national policy group attract and hold members? Often starting with money from foundations, it seeks people who share its philosophy. Usually, this process involves renting mailing lists from

Grassroots—the broad general public. Interest groups often seek grassroots support.

The Sierra Club offers a branded backpack as an incentive to join.

like-minded publications. Organizers of a liberal group, for instance, often find their best prospects among subscribers to liberal magazines. Then it sends them a mass-produced, direct-mail letter explaining its purpose and asking them to become "members" by sending money. Those who do respond—seldom more than a tiny fraction of the original addressees—enable the group to broaden its financial base. They also become the core of the group's future mailing list.

In recent years, associations have also used social media to gain the attention of potential members. Current members can re-post or re-tweet material to their friends and acquaintances, who in turn may "like" or "follow" the group and thus receive future communications. Over time, recruiters hope, these relatively passive forms of participation will prompt them to play a more active part, especially by sending membership dues.

Letters and online communication may not be quite enough to win membership, so policy groups offer their own selective incentives. For a membership fee of just $16 a year, AARP offers travel discounts, insurance, investment services, and tax assistance, among other things.[58] (Because the benefits are so extensive, and preceded most of AARP's legislative activity, some would classify the organization more as an economic group than a policy group.) Other incentives, such as branded merchandise (see the photo), depend for their value on the members' devotion to the cause. People display them not only for self-branding but as expressions of altruism and public spirit.

Even after they receive their seed money and start building membership, policy groups also receive grants. Labor unions have supported liberal organizations such as the Economic Policy Institute, and corporations have backed conservative ones such as the Heritage Foundation—though a large share of corporate money goes to liberal groups.[59] The federal government also gives grants to policy groups. A group may not use these funds to influence lawmakers, but federal dollars that it receives may "free up" money from other sources, which it may use for policy initiatives. Although Planned Parenthood is a leading provider of abortion services, it has received millions in federal grants, even under Republican presidents who opposed abortion.[60] Scholars have pointed out that the greater the number of members, the harder it is to consult with them, and that large membership organizations follow the lead of the Washington staff.[61] Supporters of interest groups argue that these studies underestimate the rank and file. If a company makes bad decisions, shareholders sell their stock; and if an association strays from its mission, members stop sending their dues. In 1988, AARP and other groups secured passage of legislation expanding Medicare to include unlimited annual hospital coverage for catastrophic illness, as well as other benefits such as outpatient prescription drugs. To fund the new benefits, Medicare recipients would have to pay higher premiums. To AARP's surprise, senior citizens rebelled. The next year, AARP did a U-turn and supported repeal of the measure.

Policy Groups and Political Controversies

FOCUS QUESTION

To what extent can policy groups distinguish the public interest from the economic interests of their supporters and financial backers?

The best-known policy groups focus on contentious domestic issues. For years, the National Rifle Association (NRA) blocked proposals to increase federal regulation of firearms. During the 1990s, it lost some battles to Handgun Control and other anti-firearm groups. General public opinion seemed to tilt against the NRA, but it still retained powerful resources, including 3 million highly motivated members, and the potential support of the 47% of Americans who report having a firearm on their property.[62] Since the start of the new century, NRA has regained some ground.

Abortion stirs even deeper passions among many. Leading organizations include the National Right to Life Committee, which favors curbs on abortion, and NARAL Pro-Choice America, which opposes them. (The latter's name was once the National Abortion

Rights and Reproduction Action League, but it has dropped the mention of abortion.) Many other groups also take part in the issue, including some whose names confound common expectations: Catholics for a Free Choice and Feminists for Life; and as Figure 8-2 suggests, the names of organizations do not always reveal their purpose.

Civil rights and civil liberties involve a large number of additional issues. The National Association for the Advancement of Colored People (NAACP) is the largest and oldest of the major civil rights organizations. Related groups include the Southern Christian Leadership Conference, founded by Martin Luther King Jr., and the National Urban League. These organizations originated in the struggle for African-American equality, but in recent decades other groups have formed to aid Hispanics, Asian Americans, people with disabilities, and women. The Leadership Conference on Civil Rights is an umbrella organization uniting dozens of such groups. On civil liberties, the most prominent organization is the American Civil Liberties Union (ACLU), which has often supported unpopular defendants in court cases involving free expression.

Most of these groups take liberal positions, but they have conservative and libertarian counterparts. The American Civil Rights Institute backs legislation to end racial preferences, while the Institute for Justice and the Washington Legal Foundation wage legal battles against preferences and other forms of government activism.

Policy and economic groups are key players in American politics. They supply much of the analysis and information on which public deliberation depends, and many of them give citizens a chance to express their views and take part in public life. In one way or another, they all try to influence what government does. Accordingly, it is important to know how they do this work.

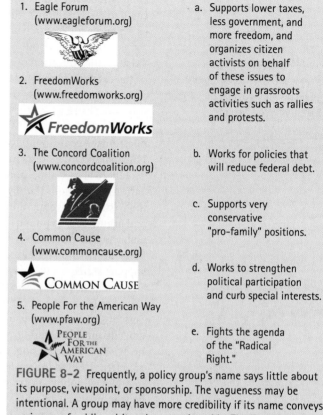

1. Eagle Forum
   (www.eagleforum.org)

2. FreedomWorks
   (www.freedomworks.org)

3. The Concord Coalition
   (www.concordcoalition.org)

4. Common Cause
   (www.commoncause.org)

5. People For the American Way
   (www.pfaw.org)

a. Supports lower taxes, less government, and more freedom, and organizes citizen activists on behalf of these issues to engage in grassroots activities such as rallies and protests.

b. Works for policies that will reduce federal debt.

c. Supports very conservative "pro-family" positions.

d. Works to strengthen political participation and curb special interests.

e. Fights the agenda of the "Radical Right."

FIGURE 8-2 Frequently, a policy group's name says little about its purpose, viewpoint, or sponsorship. The vagueness may be intentional. A group may have more credibility if its name conveys an image of public spirit and nonpartisanship. The first column in this figure lists some advocacy groups and think tanks. The second column, in different order, briefly describes what they stand for. See if you can match the items in the two columns.
(Answers: 1-c, 2-a, 3-b, 4-d, 5-e)
SOURCE: Courtesy of Eagle Forum www.eagleforum.org; Courtesy of FreedomWorks/www.freedomworks.org; Courtesy of The Concord Coalition; Courtesy of Common Cause; Courtesy of People for the American Way

METHODS OF INFLUENCE
MAJOR ISSUE

- How do economic and policy groups try to get their way, and do their techniques contribute to deliberative democracy?

People often assume that interest groups operate simply by giving money to politicians' campaigns. Indeed, they often do so, but political contributions are only one of the ways in which groups exercise influence.

Direct Lobbying

In the nineteenth century, people representing special interests would wait in the lobbies of Congress and the state legislatures to make their case to lawmakers passing through. This practice gave rise to the terms *lobbying* and **lobbyists**, referring to the direct advocacy of special interests and the people who do it. **In-house lobbyists** are on a group's payroll, while others work at outside law firms or consulting companies. Groups retain these **contract lobbyists** or "lobbyists for hire" either to take the place of in-house lobbyists or to

Lobbyist—an individual whose job is to influence policymakers on behalf of an interest group.

In-house lobbyist—a lobbyist on a group's payroll.

Contract lobbyist—a lobbyist who works at outside law firms or consulting companies and takes on interest groups as clients.

Direct lobbying—meetings or communications between interest group representatives and the officials they are trying to persuade.

supplement their efforts for special projects. In 2011, total expenditures on federal lobbying came to $3.32 billion.[63] The spending included salaries for lobbyists and their staffs, as well as expenses for research and communication.

"Lobbying is about education," says Jeffrey Seisler, CEO of Clean Fuels Consulting. "That is, the education of policymakers."[64] **Direct lobbying** consists of talking with officials of the executive branch, lawmakers, and their aides; offering issue analysis; and supplying drafts of proposed bills. These exchanges may take the form of low-key office visits and hallway conversations, or they may involve formal presentations before committees or regulatory boards. Either way, lobbyists have to learn all about their issues and be ready for tough questions. According to lobbyist Wright Andrews, "For every hour I actually spend on the Hill, I spend nine hours in the office on preparation."[65]

In 2011, a Gallup poll asked Americans to rank the honesty and ethical standards of various professions. Lobbyists tied with telemarketers for last place.[66] Yet the most effective lobbyists have a reputation in the political world for integrity. Policymakers use their facts and arguments in public forums, and if opponents can discredit this material, the result is embarrassment. Officials and staffers thus learn to rely on "straight shooters." To make sure their information remains dependable, good lobbyists often keep technical experts on their support staffs.

The deliberative process depends on those who do this job well. Lobbyist Bill Sarpalius, a former House member (D-TX), said, "Good lobbyists do their homework and help Members of Congress understand the impact of legislation, the outcomes of which American citizens must live with every day. Good lobbyists understand the industry or organization he or she is representing. Good lobbyists are great sources of information. Good lobbyists are factual. Good lobbyists are truthful."[67]

Not all lobbyists are good. In 2006, lobbyist Jack Abramoff pleaded guilty in federal court to several felony counts. He admitted that he had bribed officials and bilked his own clients. After news stories told how Abramoff had provided lawmakers with lavish travel and entertainment, Congress took steps to reform ethics rules, but the rules changes seemed unlikely to change the basics of Washington lobbying. "The Abramoff style is so far afield from the normal course of business as to be irrelevant to me and probably most people in my line of work," said lobbyist Joel Johnson, who had served in the Clinton White House.[68]

Revolving door—slang for the interchange of employees between government and the private sector.

Lobbyists must also know the key decision makers as well as the procedures of the agency or legislative body that makes the policy.[69] Academic training may confer policy expertise, but it takes practical experience to gain these other kinds of knowledge. Many lobbyists are former public officials or staffers, who have access to policymakers. "Go to work on Capitol Hill," a top lobbyist advises would-be colleagues. "Learn how the place works before you lobby—be an intern, be a legislative correspondent. Understand what a member of Congress or their staff needs."[70] Conversely, many congressional aides and officials of the executive branch have worked as lobbyists.[71] Accordingly, critics refer to a **revolving door** between the public and private sectors.

Congress has tried to slow down the revolving door by limiting what executive branch officials, lawmakers, and other government employees may do after they leave government service. Among other things, they must observe a waiting period before they can undertake certain lobbying activities. These "cooling-off periods" usually last a year or two, depending on the job or office. In some cases, the limitation is permanent. The aim is to keep

On January 3, 2006, lobbyist Jack Abramoff pleaded guilty to fraud, tax evasion, and conspiracy to bribe public officials.

AP Photo/Gerald Herbert

individuals from taking unfair advantage of the contacts and inside knowledge that come from public service. In 2009, President Obama issued an executive order further curbing the activities of former lobbyists who enter government service and of appointees who leave the government to lobby,[72] but within weeks of issuing the order, he waived it for three former lobbyists that he was naming to government posts, citing the need for their knowledge and expertise.[73]

Lobbyists say that the "revolving door" provides them with more expertise, enabling them to supply better information. More generally, lobbyists portray themselves as servants of deliberative democracy. Pointing to the information they supply, they may argue that they are helping policymakers reason on public policy. Of course, some policymakers may decide on the basis of political survival, but the merits still matter to them. They must offer policy justifications in order to sell their position to other policymakers and explain it to constituents. In this way, the self-interest of lobbyists and policymakers alike can foster deliberation.[74]

Critics see a flaw in that reasoning, since not all interests join the fray. Groups that cannot afford sophisticated lobbying will probably not gain access to policymakers. They may have a good case, but if officials never hear them, then their arguments go to waste and official "deliberation" is incomplete. Likewise, the specific interests of organized groups often speak more loudly than the diffuse interests of the general public. At congressional hearings, witnesses who favor more spending on programs greatly outnumber those who favor less.[75]

There is also a bias against the future. Policymakers sometimes deliver bounty to current voters at the expense of their descendants. Consider Social Security and Medicare, both of which do a great deal of good for today's senior citizens. Without benefit cuts, tax increases, or some mix of the two, these programs will run into hard times before future generations get to use them. Tax increases are usually unpopular, though, and any proposal to curb benefits will draw fire from groups such as AARP. People currently in college might gain from reform, but very few of them are focusing on these issues. (Unless you are a returning student well into middle age, it is unlikely that you and your friends spend much time talking about retirement.) Younger people have less money and vote at lower rates than older ones, so they have much less political clout.

FOCUS QUESTION

Will the rise of social media strengthen the influence of groups representing younger generations?

Grassroots, Air Wars, and Grasstops

Politicians worry about elections, so although good access and solid policy arguments are crucial, an interest group will have more impact if it enjoys grassroots power, the ability to influence the voters. This power requires a membership that is

- large,
- geographically dispersed, and
- intensely concerned about the group's issues.

When an important issue comes up for decision, leaders of the group try to mobilize the membership. Through newsletters, e-mails, or social media, they explain the issue's significance and ask members to get in touch with Congress. If this effort works, lawmakers receive so many messages and calls that they may bow to the group's wishes. Politicians reason that anyone who feels strongly enough to write or call will probably cast his or her next vote on the basis of the issue. (Petitions and preprinted postcards have scant effect, however, because they take so little effort.)

A good example of grassroots power is AARP, whose members care passionately about senior citizens' issues and vote in every state and congressional district. Although many people equate interest group power with campaign finance, AARP makes no contributions to candidates. It does not have to. Its millions of activists volunteer to write letters and swarm politicians' offices.[76] AARP and other interest groups regularly issue voter guides, listing where each elected official stood on key roll calls. The groups often summarize this information in vote ratings, which score lawmakers according to how often they sided with the group. Voter guides and vote ratings identify politicians as friends or foes, sending a message to a group's members and sympathizers.

Grasstops—an interest group tactic of enlisting the support of people with strong local influence or a personal connection to lawmakers.

A stealthier tactic is **grasstops** lobbying. For every lawmaker whose vote is at stake, a grasstops lobbying operation will use sophisticated databases to mobilize former staffers, friends, neighbors, or local political figures—anyone whose opinion would carry weight with the lawmaker. They may discuss the issue without ever disclosing what prompted them, so the lawmaker may not even know of the grasstops operation.

Interest groups have increasingly relied on the Internet (see the box on "The Impact of Social Media and Communications Technology"). Most major groups post issue material, and those that rely on member contributions usually make it easy to give online. "To be an effective advocate you have to use social media," said John Feehery of Quinn, Gillespie. "Whether you call yourself a lobbyist, a public affairs person or a strategist, if you don't include social media in your offering you're just not really playing."[77] Katherine Hamilton, a lobbyist at the same firm, said: "If you are a thought leader and you establish yourself through a blog, through tweeting, any kind of social media, you can present that as an asset to attract clients."[78]

Air war—an interest group effort to sway public opinion through broadcast advertisements.

Groups often wage **air war** by buying advertisements in the broadcast and print media. During the 108th Congress (2003–2004), interest groups spent over $404 million on such advertisements.[81] In an effort to reach a broader public, some of the spending went to national media. Other ad campaigns targeted policymakers and their staffs by focusing on Washington area television stations and publications that policymakers read. As with direct lobbying, there is disagreement about how issue advertising serves deliberative democracy. Some say that it gets the public to think about issues that they would otherwise overlook or that the mainstream press tends to ignore. Others call it a tool of manipulation, not deliberation. They argue that the advertising fails to foster evenhanded debate, noting that most issue ads came from corporations or groups of corporations.

YouTube and other online video sites have enabled other interests to get their message out. Groups opposed to the war in Iraq posted clips of television news stories about the conflict, as well as their own videos of congressional hearings and antiwar rallies. Such methods have limits in persuading the undecided, however. Unlike television ads, Web videos only reach people who seek them out or belong to e-mail lists.

IMPACT
of Social Media and Communications Technology

The SOPA/PIPA War

The 112th Congress considered legislation to crack down on foreign Web sites trafficking in pirated music and motion pictures. The House version was called the Stop Online Piracy Act (SOPA), while the Senate version had a more unwieldy name: the PROTECT IP Act (Preventing Real Online Threats to Economic Creativity and Theft of Intellectual Property Act, or PIPA for short). The legislation had support from the entertainment industry, including the Motion Picture Association of America and the Recording Industry Association of America. These groups had created a powerful coalition that included other industries and reached across party lines. By early 2012, it seemed likely that some form of the legislation would soon reach the president's desk.

But as the Bessette–Pitney blog noted on January 18, 2012, the legislation faced opposition from Silicon Valley interests, which argued that it would place unfair burdens on legitimate Web sites. To drive home the point, popular sites such as Craigslist and Wikipedia staged a brief "blackout" on January 18, the Internet's first such intentional stoppage. Instead of their usual content, many of these sites featured arguments against the legislation. Fight for the Future, the coalition against the legislation, claimed that it flooded Congress with millions of e-mails and over 100,000 calls.[79] House and Senate cosponsors of the legislation started to withdraw their names, and appropriately, they announced their change of heart on Facebook. Soon, both chambers of Congress indefinitely postponed action.

The action showed "that Americans actually still can dictate policy and not just lobbyists," Reddit co-founder Alex Ohanian told *Politico*. "It's motivating because this was a decentralized movement. Lots of people with great ideas started contributing and it started to get momentum. This idea went viral. It's powerful when you think we've now hit this critical mass. We can get a message out there that actually affects politicians."[80]

CRITICAL THINKING QUESTION

Did the outcome represent a triumph of popular will, or did it result from the ability of one industry to mobilize its resources more effectively than another industry?

Campaign Finance

Since 1907, federal law has forbidden business corporations from contributing directly to federal candidates. Labor unions have faced a similar ban since 1943. In that same year, however, the Congress of Industrial Organizations (a predecessor of the AFL-CIO) found a way around this barrier. From voluntary contributions by union members, it set up a separate fund that could give money to campaigns without tapping union treasuries. The CIO called this organization the Political Action Committee (PAC), a name that has since applied to all similar operations. After years of slow growth, PACs spread with the passage of the Federal Election Campaign Act of 1974, which capped individual contributions at $1,000 per candidate per election and PAC contributions at $5,000. (A 2002 law raised the individual cap to $2,000 and provided that it would rise with inflation. For the 2012 election, the cap was $2,500.) PACs offered congressional candidates a way to raise money in larger sums. For economic and policy groups, they offered a lawful way to stay in campaign politics.

A corporation, union, or trade association may set up a **connected PAC**, which may seek contributions only from people with connections to the parent organizations, such as members, employees, or shareholders. For example, the Democratic Republican Independent Voter Education Committee (DRIVE) is the PAC for the International Brotherhood of Teamsters. The organization that sponsors a connected PAC may directly pay its overhead expenses (e.g., office space and staff). **A nonconnected PAC** does not have ties to an existing organization and may seek contributions from anyone who may lawfully give to federal campaigns. Nonconnected PACs usually aim to support candidates with specific policy positions. EMILY's List, which backs pro-choice Democratic women, is the largest such PAC. This group, whose name is an acronym for "Early Money Is Like Yeast" (i.e., it makes the "dough" rise), is well known for **bundling** contributions. In this practice, the PAC asks its individual supporters to write checks to a candidate. It then collects the checks and delivers them in a "bundle," earning the candidate's gratitude. Because the payee is the candidate instead of the PAC, these contributions do not count against the PAC's contribution limit and indeed can add up to a figure well over that limit. Under the letter of the law, a bundle of 100 checks of $2,500 each is not a $250,000 contribution from the PAC but a set of separate contributions from 100 individuals.

Until 2002, another loophole consisted of **soft money** contributions to political parties. Although corporations and labor unions may not contribute directly to candidates for federal office, they (as well as individuals) could give unlimited amounts to political parties, ostensibly for nonfederal elections or for "party-building" activities. Campaign finance legislation banned the practice, but in 2010, the Supreme Court ruled that corporations and unions could make unlimited independent expenditures for or against candidates.[82] As noted earlier, this decision helped give rise to Super PACs.

Surprisingly, there is no scholarly consensus linking contributions to specific outcomes on Capitol Hill.[83] According to a pollster who surveyed members of the Washington political community: "We couldn't find any direct relationship between campaign donations and clout. The only place we could find a modest correlation with influence was in spending on lobbying."[84] So why do groups give money? Contributions are one way to gain access. All other things being equal, a politician is more likely to listen to a contributor than a noncontributor. Debbie Wasserman Schultz (D-FL) candidly acknowledged that if she finds 30 messages on her desk, "of the thirty, you're going to know ten of them. Anyone is going to

President Obama's proposal for changes in health coverage sparked an advertising war.

Connected PAC—a political action committee that is under the sponsorship of a corporation, union, or trade association and may solicit contributions only from people with connections to the sponsoring organization.

Nonconnected PAC—a political action committee that is not under the sponsorship of an existing organization and may seek contributions from anyone who may lawfully give to federal campaigns.

Bundling—the practice of gathering a large number of small contributions into one group. Although the recipient typically views the result as one large contribution, each check counts separately for the purposes of campaign finance limits.

Soft money—political spending that influences elections but is not subject to contribution or expenditure limits under campaign finance law.

TABLE 8-1	PACS

This table shows 2010 PAC contributions going to incumbents, challengers, and open-seat candidates for Congress. Incumbents consistently get most of the money from business and labor.

Sector	Total (in millions)	To Incumbents	To Challengers	To Open Seats
Agribusiness	$22.0	83%	5%	12%
Communication/Electronics	$25.0	91%	2%	7%
Construction	$15.0	79%	10%	12%
Defense	$14.0	92%	1%	7%
Energy/Natural Resources	$28.0	79%	8%	13%
Finance/Insurance/Real Estate	$62.0	84%	5%	11%
Health	$54.0	84%	5%	11%
Lawyers & Lobbyists	$15.0	86%	3%	11%
Transportation	$21.0	85%	5%	10%
Miscellaneous Business	$37.0	81%	7%	12%
Labor	$63.0	81%	6%	13%
Ideology/Single-Issue	$60.0	53%	24%	23%

SOURCE: Center for Responsive Politics, "PAC Dollars to Incumbents, Challengers, and Open Seat Candidates," www.opensecrets.org/bigpicture/pac2cands.php?cycle=2010, accessed June 1, 2012.

make phone calls to the people they know first. I'm going to call the people I know. Among the people I know are donors."[85] Still, the money is no substitute for good policy arguments and motivated constituencies. According to one health care executive, "The PAC gets you a place at the table, but you have to know which fork to use."[86]

If anything, it is the elected officials who have the leverage, using their policymaking power to pressure economic groups into making contributions. As Table 8-1 shows, incumbents get most PAC money. One former aide to a congressional campaign committee said of its chairman, "He has the [nerve] to let the business community know that if you don't give us the money, see what happens: We may not have the votes to pass your bills, but we sure as hell can kill them."[87]

Philanthropy

Philanthropy is another way interest groups wield influence. Charity may seem to be the most selfless of activities. Indeed, a genuine sense of social responsibility may lie behind many of the educational and philanthropic works of corporations, unions, and other interest groups. Yet other motivations are seldom far away. Public service may improve an organization's public image, an important goal when people have a bad opinion of it. For instance, many Americans believe that the managed care industry denies necessary health services to clients. Such attitudes encourage politicians to fight the industry. To improve their public image, managed care companies emphasize charitable activities. CIGNA Corporation said, "The mission of the CIGNA Contributions Program is to strengthen CIGNA by supporting organizations and activities that improve the overall climate for business."[88] Charitable contributions also create potential allies. If a group receives money, its members are more likely to side with their benefactor in political disputes. When AT&T sought federal approval for a controversial merger, for instance, it received statements of support from groups to which it had contributed, including the NAACP, the Gay & Lesbian Alliance Against Defamation (GLAAD), and the NEA.

Policymakers have pet charities. For interest groups seeking influence, giving to these charities is "a win-win," lobbyist Wright Andrews told the Associated Press. "Give to charities and get a tax deduction. There's no question it gives you better access. Access is power. It goes to having a direct impact on whether you get support or not."[89] Interest groups may focus on charities with which politicians have some connection. Senator John D. Rockefeller IV (D-West Virginia), has long ties to the Washington

Bach Consort. "This is a major, major—the major event for us," he told lobbyists and corporate executives at a 2010 fund-raiser. "Many of you are here, and who have contributed, you are special to us."[90]

Whereas direct contributions to federal candidates are subject to dollar limits and public disclosure, charitable contributions are unlimited and often go unreported.[91] So philanthropy frequently enables interests to curry favor with public officials out of public view. Critics say that such practices are a way of evading the spirit of campaign finance laws under the guise of good citizenship. Supporters of the practice take a more benign view. In many cases, charity does reflect a genuine belief in corporate citizenship, and even when the motive is not entirely noble, it may still be beneficial. Tocqueville spoke of "self-interest properly understood," the idea that "by serving his fellows man serves himself and that doing good is to his private advantage."[92] Corporate philanthropy and "community service" may reflect selfish calculations, but the *effect* is the same as if they had stemmed from sheer benevolence.

Legal Action

As mentioned before, interest groups have long made a practice of bringing their issues to court, as the NAACP Legal Defense and Educational Fund did with the landmark school segregation case of *Brown v. Board of Education*. Many of the Supreme Court's most important cases have involved sponsorship by an interest group.

Congress has encouraged litigation by interest groups. Since the 1970s Clean Air Act, every major environmental law has provided for "citizen suits." Under such provisions, individuals or interest groups may sue polluters who are breaking the law or regulators who are failing on the job. The idea began at a time when lawmakers distrusted the executive branch and wanted a backup enforcement mechanism in case officials got too cozy with industry. In 2000, the Supreme Court upheld a citizen suit that environmental groups had pressed under the Clean Water Act. Writing for the majority, Justice Ruth Bader Ginsburg said that members of the groups had had standing to sue. In dissent, however, Justice Antonin Scalia raised questions about citizen suits in general, saying that they give a private citizen the power to enforce the law, acting as "a self-appointed mini-EPA." Interest groups, he added, have great discretion in picking enforcement targets. The size of the potential penalties can give such groups massive bargaining power, "which is often used to achieve settlements requiring the defendant to support environmental projects of the plaintiffs' choosing. Thus is a public fine diverted to a private interest."[93] Although conservatives have often criticized interest group legal action for promoting judicial activism, they, too, have joined the fray. Conservative foundations and donors have helped finance suits against racial preferences, restrictions on school vouchers, limitations on religion, and infringements of property rights.

A related tactic is the filing of an ***amicus curiae***, or friend-of-the court brief. Those who file such briefs are not parties to the case but want to volunteer information and analysis to the court. The Court receives them in most cases that go to argument.[94] There is evidence that the briefs do influence court deliberations, so interest groups hire top attorneys to write them.[95] In a pair of affirmative action cases in 2003, supporters of existing programs deluged the Court with briefs. Referring to the briefs' binding, Justice John Paul Stevens said that the Court had relied on "the powerful consensus of the dark green briefs."[96]

Amicus curiae brief—a document filed by an individual or group that is not a party to a legal case, which provides information that aids the court in its deliberations (the term is Latin for "friend of the court"). Interest groups use such briefs to influence court decisions.

Protest

The civil rights movement pioneered the techniques of nonviolent protest, including organized demonstrations. The "March on Washington" has become a standard tactic of many organizations. The problem here is that the whole idea of protest is to capture public attention, and once it becomes routine, it stops being newsworthy. What is more, the objects of protest learn to adapt. Radical organizer Saul Alinsky recalled a corporate executive who displayed the blueprints to a new plant, telling him, "See the big hall? That's our sit-in room! When the sit-inners come they'll be shown in and there will be coffee, TV, and good toilet facilities—they can sit here until hell freezes over."[97]

Another protest tactic is the boycott, in which the group urges people not to do business with the target, whether a business or an entire state. Boycotts work when organizers can enlist a large share of the target's clientele. Martin Luther King Jr. rose to fame when he organized a boycott of segregated public buses in Montgomery, Alabama. Because his followers accounted for much of the bus ridership, the campaign had an impact. By contrast, national groups have often mounted boycotts of large, popular corporations to protest offenses ranging from objectionable music lyrics to unfair labor practices. Some boycotts have worked: in the 1980s, consumer pressure led companies to divest from South Africa, which was oppressing its black majority. Boycotts usually flop, however, because most consumers never even hear about them in the first place.

Protest has tended to be a tactic of the liberal side of the political spectrum. During the Obama administration, however, protest emerged on the right. The "tea party" movement arose in opposition to the 2009 economic stimulus bill, the president's health care plan, and other expansions of federal power. Recalling the 1773 Boston Tea Party, participants sent tea bags to elected officials as a symbol of their disapproval. The modern tea party protesters also staged spirited rallies and harshly confronted lawmakers at town hall meetings.

The movement was loose and decentralized, though it did receive some support from national organizations. In this and similar cases, however, critics contend that protests and other tactics are not truly a spontaneous outpouring of opinion. They say that this "grassroots" activity is artificial, so they dub it **Astroturf**. Beyond the question of methods, however, is the broader question of whether interest group politics supports or undermines good citizenship.

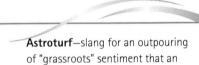

Astroturf—slang for an outpouring of "grassroots" sentiment that an interest group manufactures.

INTEREST GROUPS AND DELIBERATIVE DEMOCRACY

Any appraisal of the role of interest groups in deliberative democracy must grapple with the potential conflict between their goals and the broader public good. It must also consider whether good citizens can serve certain kinds of interests.

Foreign Interests

To influence policy in the United States, foreign governments hire lobbyists, who must register with the U.S. Department of Justice. In 2010, foreign governments spent $460 million on lobbying.[98] Some question whether former officials—or any American citizen, for that matter—should lobby for foreign businesses or governments. To the extent that American interests are in competition or conflict with those of other countries, the argument goes, such lobbying constitutes bad citizenship. In this sense, foreign lobbying would also undercut the main goal of American deliberative democracy, which is to serve the common interests of the United States. Defenders of foreign lobbying say that international voices aid deliberation by presenting policymakers with perspectives that they might not otherwise consider. The two sides would disagree sharply about trade policy. Evidence indicates that foreign lobbying has influenced the federal government to reduce trade barriers. Some would say that this trend is a sellout of American workers, while others would say that lower barriers may foster American economic growth.[99] Further complicating the issue is the meaning of "foreign." Many American firms "offshore" much of their work overseas. (If you call a customer service line, the person on the

A worker at a Toyota plant in Georgetown, Kentucky. The company is Japanese, but the workers are American.

other end may be in India.) Conversely, many foreign firms have extensive operations in the United States, employing large numbers of Americans.

Thorny questions also involve policy groups that support foreign governments or groups of people in other countries. As we saw at the start of this chapter, Students for a Free Tibet is an example. One view is that supporting such groups is inconsistent with the duties of citizens, since the foreign interests are seldom identical to those of the United States. In a highly controversial paper, scholars John Mearsheimer and Stephen M. Walt criticized "The Israel Lobby" for denying such conflict. "Indeed the mere existence of the Lobby suggests that unconditional support for Israel is not in the American national interest. If it was, one would not need an organized special interest group to bring it about. But because Israel is a strategic and moral liability, it takes relentless political pressure to keep US support intact."[100] Legal scholar Alan Dershowitz strongly dissented: "In other words, any group that needs a lobby must be working against 'American national interest.' . . . By their reasoning, the very existence of the ACLU proves that civil liberties are not in America's national interest!"[101]

An Inherent Conflict?

Some would disagree with Dershowitz, arguing that interest group activity *is* in conflict with citizenship and deliberative democracy. Critics of interest groups say that they encourage people to forget what they should do for their country and instead focus on what their country can do for them, in the form of prescription drug benefits, ethanol subsidies, and tax breaks. "AARP is concentrating the political mind on the elderly," says the executive director of the Concord Coalition, an antideficit group, but "nobody is representing those in future generations."[102]

Vassar professor Michael McCarthy says that while there is a place for lobbyists, they have a duty to consider the public good: "The task of practical wisdom and the purpose of legitimate political deliberation is to determine concretely, here and now, what national unity, justice, security, prosperity, and liberty really require in the thicket and turmoil of existing reality." This task, he adds, belongs not only to public officials, "but it is also the responsibility of democratic citizens as they interact with government through voluntary associations. It is also, we argue, the responsibility of professional lobbyists as they struggle to balance civic and professional obligations in their daily practice."[103]

Lobbyist Thomas Susman disagrees. He notes that many lobbyists are lawyers, and thus they must abide by codes and canons requiring them to put their clients' interests first. More important, he says, the common good may be a reliable guidepost for legislators, but not for lobbyists. "[I]s it my job, as a lobbyist, to determine whether the common good is best served by cheap power provided by hydroelectric plants that can make electricity more readily available to the poor, or by maintaining pristine waterways? I think that's Congress's role, not mine."[104]

Others would say that interest groups perform a vital role in promoting deliberation and citizen participation. After the NRA scored a legislative victory in the House of Representatives, the group won praise from George Stephanopoulos, television commentator and former aide to President Clinton. "You know, there's a lot of talk about extremists here. But let me make one small vote for the NRA. They're good citizens. You know what, they call their congressmen. They write, they vote, they contribute and they get what they want over time. Now, I disagree with what they're trying to do, but they mobilized well."[105] In response to criticism that they represent the privileged few, lobbyists say that the interest group community actually represents the broad general public, for as we have seen, millions of American citizens are shareholders, employees, and customers. And one survey has found that 84% of Americans belong to at least one voluntary association.[106]

Deliberation requires debate, which in turn requires disagreement. Interest groups supply those clashing viewpoints. Many policy groups sincerely aim for the public good instead of private benefit, yet they have very different views about which policies are best for their country. Their members' backgrounds and economic interests will color those views. Many business owners think that higher minimum wages are bad for the overall economy,

FOCUS QUESTION

In deliberations on public policy, does bias necessarily taint information and analysis from interest groups?

FOCUS QUESTION

How can interest groups both help and hinder the cause of good citizenship?

while union members think that they are good for social equity. Such differences are unavoidable. Also, serious abuses exist. As this chapter has shown, lawmakers have tried to curb those abuses by regulating lobbying and campaign finance. Debate continues about the propriety and adequacy of the rules. Yet for all the public cynicism about lobbyists and special interests, citizens do not simply shrug off corruption as "part of the game." Scandals helped lead voters to change party control of Congress in 2006 and 2010. Although sometimes slow to react, politicians try to avoid such backlash by taking action against offenders. Key members of Congress have lost leadership positions and committee chairs because of misconduct.

This chapter began with quotations from 2012 presidential candidates denouncing special interests. Yet both had ties to special interests. Mitt Romney drew some of his closest advisers from the ranks of Washington lobbyists.[107] President Obama repeatedly suggested that lobbyists should not have special access, but the *Washington Post* reported in 2012: "The White House visitor records make it clear that Obama's senior officials are granting that access to some of K Street's most influential representatives."[108] (Washington's K Street is home to many lobbying firms.) And when President Obama said people did not want Washington to work on behalf of special interests, he was addressing a $10,000-per-person fund-raising event at the home of a New York real estate developer.

Moreover, both candidates took contributions from individual members of economic or policy groups. How could they avoid doing so? The point here is not to fault the candidates but to stress that interest groups are inevitably a part of political life. They sometimes contribute to deliberation and sometimes detract from it. They foster good citizenship and public spirit but often encourage selfishness. Amid the debates about campaign finance and lobbying rules, one thing is clear: abolishing interest groups is no more practical than abolishing human nature. As Madison wrote, "The inference to which we are brought is that the *causes* of faction cannot be removed and that relief is only to be sought in the means of controlling its *effects*."[109]

SUMMARY

- Interest groups are organizations that try to influence public policy. Economic groups (e.g., businesses, unions, trade associations) openly pursue the material interests of their members. Private-sector unions have suffered membership declines in recent years, and most union members now belong to public-sector unions.
- Policy groups pursue broader goals, though their members may also have a material stake in their positions. The Internal Revenue code sets limits on what tax-exempt policy groups may do.
- Interest groups face a challenge in recruiting and holding members. One solution is to offer selective incentives, that is, goods or services that are available only to members.
- Direct lobbying involves face-to-face contact with policymakers, whereas grassroots lobbying involves the mobilization of group members in politicians' home constituencies, in hopes of generating the political support that makes direct lobbying more effective.
- Advertising and social media can also get a group's message out to a large audience.

- Political contributions may help a group get access to politicians, but campaign money does not bear a direct relationship to policy outcomes.
- The newest channel for political money consists of Super PACs, organizations that may take unlimited contributions from individuals, unions, and corporations, and make unlimited expenditures in federal elections, provided that they do not coordinate directly with candidates or political parties.
- Philanthropy is a way of currying favor with the general public and political elites.
- Legal action can be effective if the group has the time and resources for protracted court battles.
- Protest can be a tool for otherwise weak interests.
- Some say that interest-group activity serves narrow interests at the expense of the public interest. Others say that it promotes the public interest by fostering active citizenship and public deliberation. Actually, it does both, but there is no way to avoid it.

KEY TERMS

Air war p. 250

American Federation of Labor–
    Congress of Industrial
    Organizations (AFL-CIO) p. 242

Amicus curiae brief p. 253

Astroturf p. 254

Bundling p. 251

Closed shop p. 241

Connected PAC p. 251

Contract lobbyist p. 247

Direct lobbying p. 248

Economic group p. 239

Faction p. 236

Foundation p. 244

Free-rider problem p. 238

Grassroots p. 245

Grasstops p. 250

Ideological interest group
    p. 243

In-house lobbyist p. 247

Interest group p. 236

Lobbyist p. 247

National Labor Relations Act (Wagner
    Act) p. 241

Nonconnected PAC p. 251

Policy group p. 243

Political action committee (PAC)
    p. 244

Public interest group p. 243

Revolving door p. 248

Right-to-work laws p. 241

Selective incentive p. 238

Soft money p. 251

Special interest p. 236

Super PAC, p. 244

Taft-Hartley Act p. 241

Think tank p. 243

Trade or industry association p. 240

Union shop p. 241

TEST YOUR KNOWLEDGE

1. Interest groups maintain that one of their major contributions to deliberation is
   a. bringing suit against the government when rights are endangered.
   b. directing the flow of donations to the proper officials.
   c. donating to campaigns.
   d. educating policymakers about their issues.
   e. presiding over congressional hearings.

2. Many interest groups encourage membership by
   a. advertising monetary gain for active members.
   b. coercing employers into hiring only group members.
   c. offering political favors to elected officials who bring in new members.
   d. providing selective incentives to members.
   e. threatening those who choose not to join.

3. Employees must join the union within a certain period in a
   a. closed shop.
   b. foundation.
   c. PAC.
   d. right-to-work industry.
   e. union shop.

4. The National Rifle Association (NRA) is an example of a(n)
   a. economic group.
   b. foundation.
   c. policy group.
   d. professional association.
   e. trade association.

5. A lobbying tactic that enlists the help of those who may hold influence with lawmakers is a(n)
   a. air war.
   b. bundling operation.
   c. direct lobby.
   d. grassroots operation.
   e. grasstops operation.

6. In order to keep its members informed of the direction of policy in Congress, the AARP distributes
   a. lists of each politician's vote on key issues.
   b. policy packets to members of Congress.
   c. selective incentives to its members.
   d. voter registration cards.
   e. voting directives to its members.

7. Which of the following can a Super PAC *not* do?
   a. accept corporate contributions.
   b. run television ads.
   c. accept large individual contributions.
   d. contribute money to candidates.
   e. criticize officeholders.

8. EMILY's List is a PAC that often collects checks written directly to a candidate and then delivers them together to that candidate. This practice is called
   a. absorbing.
   b. bundling.
   c. connecting.
   d. funneling.
   e. lobbying.

9. In a recent case, an interest group hired lawyers to write a brief supplying the court with information and analysis. This brief is called a(n)
   a. *amicus curiae.*
   b. *ex post facto.*
   c. *habeas corpus.*
   d. lobby brief.
   e. PAC.

10. What is a central difficulty in identifying foreign interests?
   a. Foreign interests typically align with American interests, so most issues are not clearly foreign or domestic.
   b. Many American firms are financed by foreign nations.
   c. Many American firms send much of their work overseas, and many foreign firms have large operations and workforces in the United States.
   d. Many top executives of American firms are foreign citizens.
   e. Most interest groups have a department devoted to foreign affairs.

FURTHER READING

Andres, Gary G. *Lobbying Reconsidered: Under the Influence.* New York: Pearson Longman, 2009.

Harwood, John, and Gerald F. Seib. *Pennsylvania Avenue: Profiles in Backroom Power.* New York: Random House, 2008.

Lynch, Frederick R. *One Nation under AARP: The Fight over Medicare, Social Security, and America's Future.* Berkeley: University of California Press, 2011.

Olson, Mancur. *The Logic of Collective Action: Public Goods and the Theory of Groups.* Cambridge, MA: Harvard University Press, 1971.

Schattschneider, E. E. *The Semi-Sovereign People: A Realist's View of Democracy in America.* Hinsdale, IL: Dryden, 1960.

WEB SOURCES

Center for Responsive Politics: www.opensecrets.org— data on campaign finance and lobbying expenditures.

Foreign Agents Registration Act Reports: www.fara.gov— official information on foreign lobbying.

GuideStar: www.guidestar.org—national database of nonprofit organizations.

Lobby Disclosure Act Reports: www.senate.gov/legislative/ Public_Disclosure/LDA_reports.htm—official information on registered federal lobbyists.

President Obama receives a copy of Republican ideas from House Republican Leader John Boehner before speaking to House Republicans in Baltimore, on January 29, 2010.

SAUL LOEB

Political Parties

9

OBJECTIVES

After reading this chapter, you should be able to:

- Define political parties.
- Explain the historical development of the American party system.
- Discuss the meaning and impact of party identification.
- Analyze the various forms of party organization.
- Evaluate the role of parties in government.
- Appraise different arguments about virtues and defects of the party system.

INTRODUCTION

Strong partisanship—a firm adherence to one party over another—can be healthy for deliberation and citizenship. Political parties, wrote a Democratic newspaper in 1841, "are the schools of political science, and no principle can be safely incorporated into the fabric of national law until it has been digested, limited, and defined by the earnest discussions of contending parties."[1] At all levels of American life, party competition can foster debate on serious issues. When people think that the public good is at stake in a choice between parties, they are more likely to take part in public affairs;[2] yet partisan divides can arguably become unhealthy, resulting in policies that benefit partisan self-interest at the expense of the public interest. In recent years, many observers have warned of **partisan polarization**, the movement of parties away from each other and toward more extreme issue positions.

Partisan polarization—the movement of parties away from each other and toward more extreme issue positions.

The issues separating the parties have evolved, and the partisan split has widened and narrowed accordingly, and at any given time, the parties in government might be closer or farther apart than the parties in the electorate. Over the years, the makeup of the parties has changed. As Figure 9-1 shows, and as we shall explain later, the parties' geographic bases of support have reversed almost completely since 1896.

Differences cannot give rise to deliberation unless the conflicting parties talk to each other. If people regard partisan conflict as trivial bickering instead of reasoned debate, public life becomes much less attractive. To understand today's partisan divide, as well as its impact on deliberation and ultimately political outcomes, we must first learn about what parties are, how they function, and how they have evolved. This chapter will examine the function, structure, organization, and membership of political parties in the United States, paying close attention to the impact of polarization. It asks how well the parties represent the interests of their membership and the interests of the country over all.

POLITICAL PARTIES AND THEIR FUNCTIONS

MAJOR ISSUE

- What are political parties, and how do they function?

In the 2008 presidential election, 89% of Democrats voted for Barack Obama, while 90% of Republicans voted for John McCain.[3] Similar percentages voted for their party's nominees for the House. Nearly all members of Congress win office under a party label, as do most state legislators,[4] and among presidents, only George Washington did not have a party affiliation. Obviously, parties matter in American politics.

The Meaning of Party

Political party—a political group that seeks to elect its members to public office.

What is a **political party**? Like an interest group, it consists of a set of people who try to influence what government does. Political parties differ from interest groups in that they focus on elections, with the intent to put their own members into office under the party label. A party has three levels.

Party in the electorate—the voters who tend to support a given party.

Party organization—formal structure of party officers and workers who try to influence elections.

Party in government—those who win office under the party label.

- The **party in the electorate** consists of the voters who tend to support it.
- The **party organization** includes the formal structure of party officers and workers who try to influence elections.
- The **party in government** comprises those who win office under the party label.

The three levels overlap. The party in the electorate helps pick the party in government through primary elections. Members of the party organization recruit candidates, and officeholders have a great deal of say in staffing party organizations. Although anyone can identify with a political party, lawmakers and organizational leaders can set the terms under which voters take part in primary elections and other party activities. We shall examine these three levels in this chapter in a section dedicated to each one.

Electoral Vote in 1896 and 2004

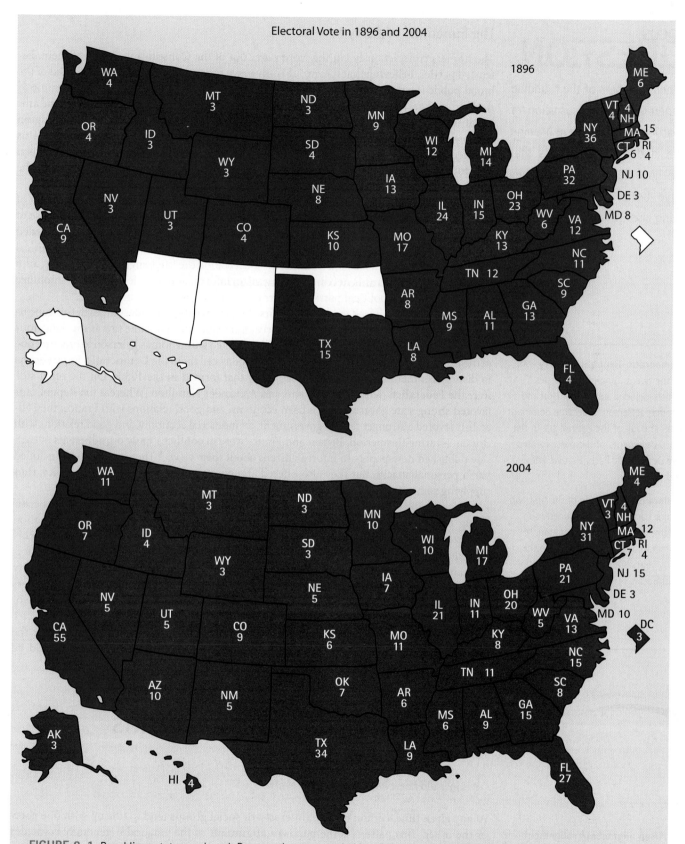

FIGURE 9–1 Republican states are in red; Democratic states are in blue. Between 1896 and 2004, the parties' geographic bases reversed. In 1896, Democrat William Jennings Bryan carried the South, the Plains States, and Mountain States, while Republican William McKinley carried the Northeast, Great Lakes States, and Pacific Coast. In 2004, George W. Bush carried the South, Plains, and Mountain States, while John Kerry won the Northeast and Pacific Coast. Bush made a crucial Great Lakes inroad with Ohio, which won him victory in the Electoral College.

SOURCE: www.politicalmaps.org/the-changing-electoral-map.

FOCUS
QUESTION

When members of the founding generation voiced suspicion of "parties," did they have in mind the kind of organizations that we have today, or might they have been thinking of something else?

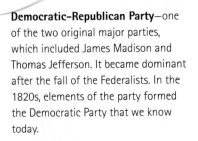

Democratic-Republican Party—one of the two original major parties, which included James Madison and Thomas Jefferson. It became dominant after the fall of the Federalists. In the 1820s, elements of the party formed the Democratic Party that we know today.

Federalist Party—one of the first two major parties, which included John Adams and Alexander Hamilton. It dominated American politics in the early years but fell into rapid decline at the start of the nineteenth century.

The Functions of Party

The framers conspicuously left the word *party* out of the Constitution. Many of them distrusted parties, believing that they would only serve narrow factional interests instead of the broad public interest. James Madison wrote of "the pestilential influence of party animosities."[5] In his Farewell Address, Washington warned that the spirit of party "kindles the animosity of one part against another, foments occasionally riot and insurrection." Washington acknowledged the argument that parties can serve as a check on the government. "This within certain limits is probably true; and in governments of a monarchical cast, patriotism may look with indulgence, if not with favor, upon the spirit of party. But in those of the popular character, in governments purely elective, it is a spirit not to be encouraged."[6]

The Constitution did not solve the problem of connecting citizens to the government of a far-flung democratic republic. Ordinary Americans needed some way of making sense of the issues and personalities of their state and federal governments. Political leaders needed some way of joining together and reaching voters. There was an obvious answer. Political scientist Zachary Courser said succinctly, "Because of the challenges of citizenship in a democracy, some means is necessary to organize, inform, and—at election time—mobilize citizens into action; political parties perform these functions admirably."[7]

James Madison himself was one of the first American national leaders to reach this conclusion. By the 1790s, he worried less about party animosities than what he saw as the dangerous trend toward a powerful central government. He worked with Thomas Jefferson to organize one of the first national parties, the Republicans. We today call them the **Democratic-Republicans** to distinguish them from the Republican Party that formed in the 1850s. On the other side were the **Federalists**, led by John Adams and Alexander Hamilton. Whereas the Republicans favored strong state governments, a farm economy, and good relations with France, the Federalists favored a stronger federal government, an industrial economy, and good relations with Britain. (During this period, Britain and France were in conflict.) Early on, adherents of each side published newspapers to inform citizens about their views.[8] These newspapers included harsh personal attacks, but they also offered arguments on the merits of public policy, thus supplying some of the raw material for debate and deliberation.

Democratic-Republican societies held public meetings and published addresses criticizing the Washington administration. In this way, they provided further information to citizens and gave them an organized way to participate in politics. The societies corresponded with one another and with national leaders, creating an embryonic party network. In some places, Democratic-Republican politicians worked systematically to identify sympathetic voters and get them to the polls.[9] Washington and his Federalist supporters openly questioned the legitimacy of party activity, but it was going to be a lasting feature of American political life.

While partisanship would endure, the identities of the parties would change over the course of history. Some changes would be gradual and marginal, while others would be abrupt and fundamental.

PARTY ALIGNMENTS AND REALIGNMENTS
MAJOR ISSUE

- How did the two-party system evolve?

Partisan alignment/realignment—an enduring pattern of party loyalty in the electorate. A **realignment** is a sudden and permanent shift in that pattern.

At any given time, certain regions, interests, or social groups tend to line up with one party or the other. This pattern is the **partisan alignment** of the era, and it generally coincides with the party with the most political power for that time period, the party most in control of government. Over time, the lines move as voters switch sides or new groups join the electorate. New parties may crop up and existing parties may grow, shrink, or disappear. Sudden **realignments**, or abrupt shifts in the lines, occurred with the Civil War and the Depression, but such events have been rare.[10]

Since the middle of the nineteenth century, the Republicans and Democratic parties have been hardy survivors. They have remained as the nation's two major parties, even though their size and makeup have shifted. **Third parties** have sometimes won a hefty share of the popular vote for an election or two. For reasons that we shall discuss later, none has sustained a challenge to the two-party system since the Republicans emerged as the Democrats' main rival in the 1850s. Other minor parties linger on the ballot without ever "graduating" to major party status. For that reason, the story of party alignments is mainly the story of two-party politics.

Early Party Era: The Federalists and the Democratic-Republicans

Writing to Madison in 1793, Jefferson applied a partisan spin in describing each side's base of support. On the Federalist side, he said, were the "fashionable circles" of major cities, merchants "trading on British capital," and those who had sided with the Crown during the Revolution. On his own Democratic-Republican side, Jefferson wrote, were "[t]radesmen, mechanics, farmers, and every other possible description of our citizens."[11] At first, the Federalists' superior economic resources gave them the upper hand. But they had weaknesses. They were not as adept at voter mobilization as the Democratic-Republicans, and during the Adams administration, congressional Federalists enacted the Sedition Act, which outlawed "false, scandalous, and malicious writing" against the government. Seeing a threat to legitimate dissent, Americans turned against the Federalists.

Jefferson defeated Adams in the presidential contest of 1800, which Jefferson later called "the Revolution of 1800."[12] This race brought the world's first transfer of party power as a result of a national election. Although Adams and the Federalists harbored hard feelings, they accepted the outcome. In his 1801 Inaugural Address, Jefferson sought to be conciliatory by saying that "every difference of opinion is not a difference of principle. We have called by different names brethren of the same principle. We are all Republicans, we are all Federalists."[13] The election also launched a shift in the party system. In the early nineteenth century, the Federalists crumbled. Their pro-British sentiments became increasingly unpopular as the nation came into conflict with Britain. During the "Era of Good Feeling" (roughly 1815–1825), there was little partisan polarization. The Democratic-Republicans made up the only true national party, though it did have internal divisions.

They picked their presidential candidates through a closed-door conference, or **caucus**, of their members of Congress. As all of the party's candidates won, "**King Caucus**" gained power. Congressional caucuses—not the electorate at large—effectively chose the president, a practice that the framers had opposed. In 1824, in a four-way race among candidates from party factions, caucus nominee William Crawford failed to win a majority in the Electoral College. Under the Twelfth Amendment, the House chose from among the three candidates with the most electoral votes: Crawford, John Quincy Adams, and Andrew Jackson, who had won a plurality of the popular vote. The fourth candidate, Henry Clay, threw his support to Adams, enabling him to win in the House. Adams's subsequent selection of Clay as secretary of state led to charges of a "corrupt bargain," though there was no proof of an explicit deal. In any case, the choice was controversial. It helped lead to Adams's 1828 reelection loss to Jackson.

Democrats and Whigs

As a hero of the War of 1812 and self-styled foe of the elite (though he was a rich slave-holder), Jackson was popular with the "common man." Once in office, Jackson, a Democrat, gained more power through **political patronage**, the granting of government jobs and favors to supporters. In this effort, he took advice from Martin Van Buren, who served as his secretary of state and later as vice president. "We must always have party distinctions," wrote Van Buren, who stressed that the Democrats should fight for farmers and working people.[14] Patronage created armies of campaign workers, ready to win votes in order to keep their jobs. Party workers may have been acting on selfish desires, yet they did engage their fellow citizens in public life. The political organizations encouraged other community

Third party—a political party other than the two major parties of the era. It may be either a short-lived movement that gains significant support or a longer-lasting movement that gets little.

Caucus—a meeting of political party members. Today, some states begin the process of selecting national convention delegates by holding caucuses of voters. In Congress, *caucus* also refers to the formal organization of House members or senators who belong to the same party.

King Caucus—in the early nineteenth century, referred to meetings of Democratic-Republican members of Congress who nominated presidential candidates.

Political patronage—the granting of jobs, contracts, and other official favors in return for loyalty to an individual leader or political party.

Whigs—major party that lasted from the 1830s to 1850s. It firmly supported economic development but split over the issue of slavery.

activities. "A political association draws a lot of people at the same time out of their own circle," wrote Tocqueville. "Once they have met, they always know how to meet again."[15]

The Jackson years saw the development of the national party convention. In September 1831, members of the Anti-Masonic Party, a fringe group believing that the fraternal order of Masons was an evil conspiracy, met in Baltimore to nominate a presidential candidate. In December of that year, the "National Republicans," the anti-Jackson group that had backed Adams in 1828, also met in Baltimore.

After Jackson's reelection in 1832, the National Republicans folded and new opposition arose. Accusing Jackson and then Van Buren of seeking monarchy, their foes started calling themselves "**Whigs**," after the seventeenth-century English party that favored Parliament over the Crown. The new party called for federal financing of canals and other "internal improvements." By the 1840s, the nation had a true two-party system, with each side representing a broad array of interests in every region. The Whigs drew more support from wealthier groups, while the Democrats did better among less affluent people and new immigrants, particularly Catholics.

Party names were still informal, with many on the Jackson–Van Buren side calling themselves "Republicans" or "Democrats" interchangeably. They came to prefer the latter term, dubbing the record of their 1840 meeting *Proceedings of the National Democratic Convention.*[16] Eight years later, the Democrats advanced party organization with the creation of the Democratic National Committee.

Republicans Rising

American Party—a short-lived political party of the 1840s and 1850s that opposed immigration. Its nickname was the "Know-Nothing Party." (In response to questions about their secret organizations, members reportedly promised to reply, "I know nothing.")

Know-Nothings—see American Party.

By the late 1840s, slavery was polarizing American political debate. Former president Van Buren ran against Lewis Cass (Democrat) and Zachary Taylor (Whig) in 1848 as the candidate of the "Free Soil Party," which opposed the extension of slavery into the new western territories. He scored 10% of the popular vote. Although the Free Soilers would then decline, this showing foreshadowed more turmoil. The Whigs groaned with conflict between pro- and anti-slavery factions. National party leaders had tried compromise and evasion, but these tactics no longer worked. Immigration added to the party's woes. The arrival of Catholics from Germany and Ireland led to a backlash among longer-established groups, who sought to close the borders and limit the immigrants' civil rights. When Lincoln and other Whig leaders fought this sentiment, some Whigs broke off to form the **American Party**. History remembers this group as the "**Know-Nothings**" because members reportedly promised to tell outsiders nothing about the party that they knew.[17]

In 1854, a new party arose with the goal of curbing slavery.[18] Organizers chose the name "Republican" because it alluded to Jefferson's ideas about equality.[19] In 1856, they nominated explorer John C. Fremont, who ran second to Democrat James Buchanan, with third place going to former president Millard Fillmore, candidate of both the Whig and American Parties. The Whigs then disintegrated, with pro-slavery members joining the Democrats and antislavery members joining the Republicans. The American Party soon collapsed as well. It could not settle internal divisions over slavery, and anti-immigrant passions cooled as immigration plunged.

With an anti-slavery party on the rise, party differences grew clear, even violent. In May 1856, Republican senator Charles Sumner of Massachusetts made a floor speech about slavery in Kansas. He used harsh personal terms to attack colleagues Stephen Douglas of Illinois and Andrew Butler of South Carolina.[20] Two days later, Representative Preston Brooks, Butler's cousin and a pro-slavery

Representative Preston Brooks (D-SC) attacks Senator Charles Sumner (R-MA) on the Senate floor May 22, 1856.

Democrat from South Carolina, entered the Senate chamber. Using his cane, he beat Sumner so badly that it took years for him to recover.

In 1860, the slavery issue split the Democrats into three factions, each of which ran its own candidate. The Republican nominee was Abraham Lincoln. Although Lincoln gained just under 40% of the popular tally, he won a majority in the Electoral College, while the other three split the rest. The election was the most polarizing in American history. The leaders of 11 southern states saw Lincoln's views as so hostile to their interests in slaveholding that they seceded from the Union, seven doing so before he even took office.

In a normal American election, the losers accept the outcome because they still have some common ground with the winners. In 1800, John Adams seethed at Thomas Jefferson but shared the principles of the Declaration and Constitution.[21] By the 1860 election, however, supporters of slavery had renounced the Declaration, and could not abide the election of Abraham Lincoln. Alexander Stephens, the vice president of the Confederacy, said that "the assumption of the equality of the races" had guided Thomas Jefferson. "This was an error," he added. "Our new government is founded upon exactly the opposite idea . . . that the negro is not equal to the white man; that slavery—subordination to the superior race—is his natural and normal condition."[22]

The Civil War launched a new alignment. During Reconstruction, Republicans had strong support from voters in the Northeast and Midwest, along with the newly enfranchised black voters of the South. (Three southern states—Texas, Mississippi, and Virginia—did not gain readmission to the Union until 1870.) In a deal to settle the disputed 1876 election, Democrats conceded to Republican candidate Rutherford B. Hayes in return for pulling federal troops from the South, thereby ending Reconstruction. White Democrats then found ways to keep blacks from voting, and the region became a Democratic stronghold that offset Republican advantages elsewhere. Between 1876 and 1892, the parties enjoyed nearly equal strength nationwide. Control of Congress seesawed, and no president came to office with more than half of the popular vote.[23] (And now that the Republican Party appeared to be a permanent fixture of American politics, newspapers started calling it by the nickname it retains today: Grand Old Party, or GOP.)

The war shaped party attachments for generations, especially in the South. Blaming Republicans for death and destruction, most southern voters (now almost all white) shunned the party until the mid-twentieth century. On many issues, though, party lines tended to blur. In 1888, British observer James Bryce listed a set of policy questions and wrote that neither party has "anything definite to say on these issues." Their interests consisted "of getting or keeping the patronage of the government."[24]

The emphasis on patronage was timely. The term "**political machine**" was becoming common, referring to a party organization that ran a state or local government by using patronage, constituent service, and in many cases, election fraud. (As the box shows, party organizations today tend to airbrush such things from their official histories.) Political machines most often took hold in big cities, and machine politics spread as the nation became more urban. In 1850, only six American cities had 100,000 people or more, but by 1900, 38 topped that level.[25] And while later political machines would be mostly Democratic, the second half of the nineteenth century saw Republican machines in Philadelphia and other major cities.

Political machine—a party organization, usually in a city, that uses patronage to ensure its local dominance.

Populists and Progressives

While urban America was growing, rural America was floundering. Crop and livestock prices generally went down, while the railroads were charging high rates for shipping these commodities. Thinking that both major parties were ignoring them, farmers rallied to the new **Populist Party** in 1892. The Populists supported nationalization of the railroads as well as the deliberate inflation of the currency. Inflation would have artificially raised their income, making it easier for them to pay their debts (which were not adjusted for inflation). In the 1892 presidential race, Populists won 8.5% of the popular vote. Four years later, Democratic nominee William Jennings Bryan ran on a pro-inflation platform, allying himself with the Populists. The Republicans stood against inflation and also held to

Populist Party—a political party of the 1890s that favored inflation to help farmers at the expense of city dwellers. Its members united with the Democrats in 1896 to nominate William Jennings Bryan for president.

MYTHS AND MISINFORMATION

Official Party Histories—Yada, Yada, Yada

In the official histories of the national parties, each side naturally tends to cast itself in the most favorable light—and to skip its more embarrassing chapters. Here, the Republican National Committee discusses the party's early years:

> It all started with people who opposed slavery. They were common, everyday people who bristled at the notion that men had any right to oppress their fellow man. In the early 1850's, these anti-slavery activists found commonality with rugged individuals looking to settle in western lands, free of government charges. "Free soil, free labor, free speech, free men," went the slogan. And it was thus in joint opposition to human enslavement and government tyranny that an enterprising people gave birth to the Republican Party.
>
> In 1856, the Republicans became a national party by nominating John C. Fremont for President. Four years later, with the election of Abraham Lincoln in 1860, the Republicans firmly established themselves as a major political party. The name "Republican" was chosen because

it alluded to equality and reminded individuals of Thomas Jefferson's Democratic-Republican Party.[26]

It then moves to a discussion of women's suffrage. The page omits anything about the impeachment of Andrew Johnson, the regression on civil rights that followed Reconstruction, or the scandal-ridden presidency of Ulysses S. Grant.

The Democrats are no more candid. In fact, they skip the nineteenth century completely, thereby avoiding the pre–Civil War period, when Democratic views of slavery ranged from the toleration of Senator Stephen A. Douglas of Illinois to the enthusiastic support of Representative Alexander Stephens of Georgia. Stephens became the Confederacy's vice president. Instead, the party history starts with 1920: "Under the leadership of Democratic President Woodrow Wilson, the U.S. Constitution was amended to grant women the right to vote. On August 18, 1920, Tennessee became the 36th state to ratify women's suffrage, and it became our nation's 19th amendment."[27] Actually, supporters of suffrage had picketed Wilson to protest his lack of activity for their cause.[28]

Progressive Party—a reformist party that nominated former president Theodore Roosevelt as its standard-bearer in the 1912 presidential election.

Primary/primary election—an election that determines who runs in the final or general election (see also the chapter on elections and campaigns).

Party ballots—a nineteenth-century method of voting in which each party printed a list of candidates. People would vote by placing a party's list in the ballot box.

Australian ballot—a government-published ballot that lists all lawful nominees for office. It allows the voters to make their choices in private and to choose nominees from different parties for different offices.

their support for a high tariff on imported goods, which most people thought would help American industry.

Bryan's 1896 defeat helped tip the party balance toward the Republicans. Inflation may have sounded good to debt-ridden farmers, but it scared wage earners, shopkeepers, pensioners, savers, and investors. The Democrats held the South and made some gains in the still sparsely populated western and Plains states. The GOP grew stronger in the rest of the country, including big cities. Bryan's platform also alarmed big business, making it easier for Republican leaders to collect campaign contributions. Not until 1932 would a Democratic presidential nominee gain a popular majority. Democrat Woodrow Wilson did win in 1912 and 1916, but with less than 50%.

Wilson prevailed in 1912 because of a split between William Howard Taft, the Republican incumbent, and former Republican president Theodore Roosevelt, the candidate of the **Progressive Party**. This short-lived party was an outgrowth of the larger Progressive movement, which fought the political machines. Progressives won the adoption of new procedures, including **primary elections** in which voters could choose party candidates. By 1920, most states had primary elections for at least some offices, though primaries would not dominate presidential nomination politics until the 1970s.[29]

Party organizations suffered from the political reforms of the late nineteenth and early twentieth centuries. Their leaders lost control of party nominations because of primaries, and they lost patronage power as states and localities adopted civil service reforms that distributed jobs on the basis of merit. The reforms may have led to greater efficiency and less corruption, but they also made political activity less attractive. "This civil service law is the biggest fraud of the age," said George Washington Plunkitt, a New York City machine politician. "It is the curse of the nation. There can't be no real patriotism while it lasts. How are you goin' to interest our young men in their country if you have no offices to give them when they work for their party?"[30]

Before the 1890s, state governments did not print election ballots, so voters would use **party ballots**, each listing only its own candidates. Party workers often followed voters to the ballot box, which was in the open, to make sure they deposited the "right" ballot. This system encouraged party-line voting. In the 1890s, states adopted the "**Australian ballot** system" (named for the country that developed it), in which people entered private booths to mark government-printed ballots listing all candidates. This system made it easier for **split-ticket voting**—that is, for voters to vote for different parties' candidates for different offices. It also discouraged voter intimidation, further weakening party organizations.

Meanwhile, social trends were seeding change in the party system. One was immigration. Between 1900 and 1925, more than 17 million people came to the United States, mostly from Eastern, Central, and Southern Europe. Although Congress restricted immigration in 1924, America had already changed. The census of 1930 showed that 15% of Americans were foreign-born, and 36% had at least one foreign-born parent, the highest such figures ever.[31] Immigration coincided with urbanization. With the census of 1920, for the first time in American history, urban areas had more people than rural areas. By 1930, 12.2% of Americans lived in cities of more than a million people—a level not exceeded before or since.[32]

New Deal

In the early decades of the twentieth century, party principles seemed to be in flux. Republican Theodore Roosevelt and Democrat Woodrow Wilson both pushed for active government. Wilson's 1916 Republican opponent, Charles Evans Hughes, had the endorsement of the Progressive Party. In 1924, the Democrats nominated John W. Davis, a corporate lawyer who would later go on to defend segregation in the case of *Brown v. Board of Education*. In 1928, the Republican candidate for president was Secretary of Commerce Herbert Hoover. Although many remember him as a foe of active government, his reputation at the time was that of a pro-government progressive. Democrats nominated Governor Alfred E. Smith of New York. As a New York City politician, foe of Prohibition, and the first Roman Catholic to win a major party nomination, Smith alienated the rural South. He fell to Hoover, losing several former Confederate states that Democrats had carried since Reconstruction. In the shadow of his defeat, however, grew the seeds of a Democratic comeback. Smith ran strongly in major cities and did well among recent immigrants, many of whom were fellow Catholics.

In 1929, the stock market crash marked the start of the Great Depression, which Americans blamed on the GOP. In 1932, they gave a landslide to the Democratic nominee, Governor Franklin D. Roosevelt of New York, and increased Democratic majorities in Congress. Roosevelt called his legislative program "the New Deal," so we apply the term **New Deal Coalition** to the diverse groups that joined under the Democratic banner—southerners, Jews, Catholics, African Americans, people with roots in Southern and Eastern Europe, union members, poor people, intellectuals, and artists. These groups overlapped: for instance, many southerners and African Americans were poor, many union members and Southern Europeans were Catholic, many Jews had roots in Eastern Europe, and so on. If one thing united them, it was the belief that they had been outsiders in a country whose elite consisted of northern and midwestern Protestants with roots in England and Northern Europe.

New Deal policies appealed to them. Economic programs such as the National Recovery Administration reached the whole range of disadvantaged groups. FDR also appealed to elements of his coalition in more specific ways.

- The South came back to the party after straying in 1928. As a Protestant and frequent visitor to Georgia (where he received polio therapy at Warm Springs), Roosevelt was more acceptable to southerners than Smith. Once in office, he solidified this support by backing such programs as the Tennessee Valley Authority, which brought electricity to much of the region.

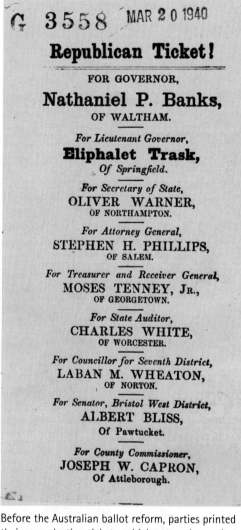

[LC-USZ26-814]/The Library of Congress

Before the Australian ballot reform, parties printed their own election tickets, which voters dropped into ballot boxes. Here is a Republican ticket for Massachusetts in the election of 1860.

Split-ticket voting—voting in any given election for candidates of different political parties for different offices (e.g., a Republican for governor, a Democrat for senator).

New Deal Coalition—the voter support base of the Democratic Party, which took form during Franklin Roosevelt's administration. The coalition included southerners, Jews, Catholics, African Americans, people with roots in Southern and Eastern Europe, union members, poor people, intellectuals, and artists.

- African Americans had voted Republican since the Civil War, but switched to the Democrats during the Depression.[33] Many were poor. Although the need for southern white support kept Roosevelt from endorsing civil rights laws, his New Deal economic programs did help African Americans.
- Immigration had increased the ranks of Jewish voters, who were political liberals. Many had voted Republican in previous decades, but the New Deal convinced them that the Democratic Party was their political home.[34]
- Roosevelt's National Recovery Administration encouraged labor union organization. In 1935, he signed the National Labor Relations Act, which protected the rights of union workers. Union membership increased and grateful union members supported the Democrats.
- Although Roosevelt did not have "Catholic-specific" policies, the New Deal was consistent with emerging Catholic social teaching.[35] He also reached out to Catholics through appointments. Whereas only four Catholics had served in the Cabinet since 1798, Roosevelt's first cabinet choices included two.[36] In 1932, famous radio priest Charles Coughlin fervently preached Roosevelt's cause in national broadcasts. (He later denounced Roosevelt as a tool of Wall Street.)
- Artists and intellectuals were few in number, but their works had influence on public opinion. FDR won them for the Democrats, too. He enlisted economists and other experts in his administration, and his Works Progress Administration (WPA) employed writers and painters.

Roosevelt built early alliances with urban political leaders, whose constituents included many of the recent immigrants from Southern and Eastern Europe. In the long run, however, the New Deal had the effect of further weakening the machines. Programs such as Social Security and organizations such as the National Labor Relations Board (NLRB) dealt directly with citizens, without political machines serving as intermediaries.[37]

The New Deal coalition outlived Roosevelt, who died in 1945. Democrats won seven of the nine presidential elections between 1932 and 1964, losing in 1952 and 1956 mainly because of Republican Dwight Eisenhower's popularity as leader of Allied forces in Europe during World War II. Meanwhile, they lost Congress only twice, and then regained House and Senate majorities two years later. With the important exception of the debate over domestic Communism, the period saw relatively little party polarization. Eisenhower tempered but never tried to undo the New Deal, and many Republicans backed liberal domestic initiatives. The main opposition to civil rights legislation came from southern Democrats. Most of their black constituents could not yet vote, and most of their white constituents supported segregation.

Scholars believed that the party system failed to present clear alternatives to the voters.[38] They did not think that the parties had to be radically different, but they did argue for more coherent policies that could prompt public debate and deliberation. At the same time, conservative Republicans and liberal Democrats wanted their parties to stake out bolder positions.[39] Scholars and activists both favored giving ordinary citizens more chance to take part in party affairs. To a large extent, these wishes would later come true.

Upheavals

In the 1964 presidential election, Democratic incumbent Lyndon Johnson won a record 61% of the popular vote, and his party padded its majorities in the House and

"Today's the Big Day, Folks. Vote Early and Often!"

Dr. Seuss Collection—Mandeville Special Collections, UC, San Diego

By 1941, political machines had become highly unpopular. Tammany Hall, New York's Democratic machine, was the target of a young political cartoonist named Theodore Geisel. The cartoonist would go on to greater fame as Dr. Seuss.

Senate. Yet just as Hoover's 1928 victory was the peak of a Republican era, Johnson's landslide was the beginning of the end of the New Deal coalition. Time was eroding some of its key elements. Large northern and midwestern cities had supplied many votes to Al Smith and Franklin Roosevelt, but now many were shrinking. Between 1950 and 1990, Detroit lost 44% of its population. Suburbs were growing, and they were more likely to vote Republican; organized labor started losing members, in part because of changes in employment patterns.

Perhaps most important, the South stopped being a Democratic fortress. Although Lyndon Johnson was the first president from a former Confederate state since the Civil War, he lost several southern states to Republican Barry Goldwater.[40] In part, this outcome reflected southern white opposition to the 1964 Civil Rights Act, which Johnson had pushed. Although most Republican lawmakers had voted for it, Senator Goldwater had voted against it on what he considered strictly constitutional grounds. Even apart from civil rights, the South was ready to go Republican. The Civil War had faded from living memory, so southerners stopped linking the party with the burning of Atlanta. Many Republican northerners had moved south. As the regional economy grew, affluent southerners began to question Democratic social programs.[41]

In 1968, Republican Richard Nixon campaigned heavily in the South. His rhetoric suggested a "go slow" approach to civil rights, though his actual policies proved to be different. In 1972, his campaign accused Democratic opponent George McGovern of weakness on national defense. The issue was potent in the South, with its many military installations.

A peculiar polarization was taking place. Although Republicans said that the Democratic presidential candidate was too liberal, their own policies were far from conservative. Nixon imposed peacetime wage-price controls, proposed a guaranteed annual income, and signed bold new environmental laws—all liberal actions. And though he widened the Vietnam War, he eventually withdrew combat troops. He also opened relations with China and pursued arms control with the Soviet Union. Party conservatives opposed these moves. One of these conservatives was Ronald Reagan, governor of California from 1967 to 1975. In 1976, Reagan nearly defeated Nixon's successor, Gerald Ford, in the race for the Republican nomination. Four years later, Reagan won the nomination and went on to defeat incumbent Democrat Jimmy Carter.

Reagan's positions helped build a new coalition. His support for a defense buildup and an assertive stance against the Soviet Union won him support from anti-Communist Democrats, especially those with roots in Eastern Europe. Conservative positions on social issues such as abortion appealed to traditional Catholics and evangelical Protestants, especially in the South. His policy of cutting taxes shored up support among business people and those earning high wages. With this coalition, Reagan won a landslide reelection in 1984. George H. W. Bush, his vice president, won a convincing victory in 1988 by promising to continue Reagan policies.

For a long time, however, Republicans fell short in congressional elections. After regaining the House in the 1954 election, Democrats kept it for 40 years. They also held a Senate majority for 34 of those years, and many regarded the six years of Republican control (1981–1987) as a fluke. Some held that Democrats ran more skillful candidates whose positions were more appealing to local electorates.[42] Gerrymandered districts and the power of incumbency also slowed Republican gains in the House. (See the chapter on elections and campaigns.) The result was **divided government**, where one party holds the presidency while the other party controls at least one chamber of Congress. Republicans seemed to be the "natural" presidential party, whereas Democrats seemed to be the "natural" congressional party.

Things changed in the 1990s. President George H. W. Bush's poor showing in 1992 (just 37% of the popular vote) cast doubt on a Republican "lock" on the White House. Two years later, the Democrats suddenly lost their "lock" on Capitol Hill. Southern voters shifted Republican in congressional elections, helping the GOP win House and Senate. The parties now seemed to be in an even balance.[43] Between 1992 and 2000, no presidential candidate won a majority of the popular vote. After an initial surge in 1994, Republicans held only a slim lead over Democrats in the nationwide vote for the House of Representatives.

Divided government—a situation in which one party holds the executive branch while the other holds at least one chamber of the legislative branch.

In 2004, for the first time in 52 years, Republicans won both control of Congress and a majority of the popular vote for president. Two years later, though, amid an unpopular war in Iraq and corruption scandals in Washington, Democrats retook control of the House and Senate. In 2008, Democrat Barack Obama won the presidency by a substantial margin, and his fellow Democrats increased their congressional majorities. Democrats hoped that the trend would continue because of increasing numbers of pro-Democratic voting groups.[44] But the Republican takeover of the House in 2010 suggested that Democratic hopes were premature at best.

Sources of Party Change

A single sentence cannot explain more than 200 years of change in the American party system, but it is possible to identify some of the forces at work. For example, ideas matter. In the twentieth century, Roosevelt and Reagan articulated ideas about government that moved millions of American voters. Granted, both presidents and their party successors made many compromises and sometimes strayed from their own principles. Nevertheless, one can see the sweep of party history as a grand deliberation involving party leaders and the general public. At certain times, one side wins the argument, as the New Deal Democrats did from the 1930s through the 1950s. At other times, events can change the terms of debate and thus the balance of power. On rare occasions, the event is so profound as to cause a sudden and radical shift. The Civil War and the Great Depression both transformed American society in fundamental ways and, accordingly, reconfigured the party system. Other changes are more gradual, such as the economic and demographic developments that helped move the South into the Republican column.

In the longer run, a cycle is in motion. Elections bring about changes in policy, which in turn change the party system. Although economic historians disagree on the point, Democrats say that the policies of the 1930s and 1940s led America to economic greatness—with ironic results. Tip O'Neill, a Massachusetts Democrat who served as Speaker of the House from 1977 to 1987, said, "We in the Democratic party raised millions out of poverty into the middle class and made them so comfortable they could afford to become Republicans."[45]

As the makeup of the citizenry evolves, so does the makeup of the parties. In the twentieth century, neither party could depend only on the farm vote, since the rural population was shrinking fast. Immigration provided Franklin Roosevelt with millions of recruits, though many of their grandchildren would sign up with Ronald Reagan.[46] The process continues. In the 1960s and 1980s, changes in immigration law opened the way for a massive influx from Asia and, more important, the Americas. Many of these new citizens are joining the electorate and voting Democratic.

Party change thus involves voters, election campaigns, and officeholders. Understanding their relationship requires a closer look at party in the electorate, party organization, and party in government.

PARTIES IN THE ELECTORATE

MAJOR ISSUE

- What is the composition of the major parties?

Party identification—a self-reported feeling of attachment to a political party.

Party registration—a formal declaration of party affiliation. In many states, it is necessary to register in a party in order to vote in party primaries.

Party identification is a key concept in understanding party in the electorate. It differs from **party registration**, a formal affiliation that lets a voter take part in the party's primary elections where the law requires. Rather, party identification is a sense of attachment that leads a voter to favor one party's candidates over another's.[47] Public opinion polls measure it through such questions as "Generally speaking, do you usually think of yourself as a Republican, a Democrat, an Independent, or what?" Polls also measure the intensity of party identification. If the person identifies with a party, the pollster may ask, "Would you call yourself a strong (Republican/Democrat) or a not very strong (Republican/ Democrat)?" If the respondent identifies as an independent, the pollster may try to find a partisan leaning by asking, "Do you think of yourself as closer to the Republican or Democratic party"

Party Identification

As Figure 9-2 shows, Democrats led through the 1940s. Their advantage grew in the late 1950s and early 1960s, ebbed in the mid-1960s, and rose again in the late 1970s. In the latter period, the Watergate scandal helped Democrats. During the 1980s and 1990s, Democratic identification dropped while the Republicans made gains. Democrats then built a lead that culminated in President Obama's election in 2008, only to lose some

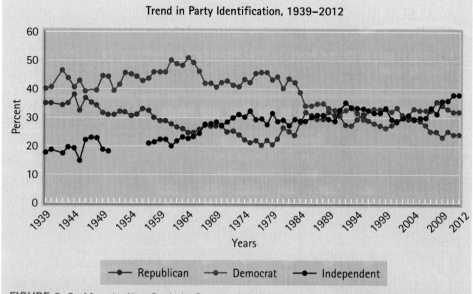

FIGURE 9-2 After the New Deal, the Democrats built a strong lead in party identification, but that advantage dwindled in the late 1980s and early 1990s. After reaching parity in 2002, however, the GOP lost ground. Democratic identification then sagged, too. (Data on independents not available between 1951 and 1956.)
SOURCE: Pew Research Center for the People and the Press, "Trend in Party Identification 1939–2012," June 1, 2012, www.people-press.org/2012/06/01/trend-in-party-identification-1939-2012/, accessed June 13, 2012. Copyright © 2012 by Pew Research Center. Reprinted with permission.

of their support in the years after. Meanwhile, a growing number of Americans called themselves independents, though many still leaned toward one party or the other.

For a while, the growing ranks of independents led some observers to question the importance of parties, but as we have already seen, there have been signs of party polarization. Rather than a massive shift, where people stand on the issues, there has been a "sorting out" of the parties, with fewer and fewer liberal Republicans or conservative Democrats.[48] Republican identifiers are now more uniformly conservative than before, and Democratic identifiers are more liberal. Party identification also makes more of a difference in how people see various issues (see Table 9-1).

This "sorting out" reflects the behavior of political leaders in Washington, DC. The Republican leaders are conservative, and their Democratic counterparts are liberal. Republicans have supported tax cuts that Democrats have opposed. Conversely, Democrats have sought to expand the federal role in health insurance, while Republicans have said that these plans would go too far. Democrats have been more willing to accept same-sex marriage, and Republicans have been more likely to support further limits on abortion. Republicans have supported an assertive foreign policy while Democrats have been more internationalist. (For more detail, see Chapter 8 on public opinion and participation.)

Voters on both sides are responding to the positions and cues coming from the White House and Capitol Hill. Many of these voters have not moved as far to the left or right as the party leaders. As political scientist Morris Fiorina writes, "Voters will be less enthusiastic about their choices and about election outcomes than previously, but given a choice between two extremes, they can only elect an extremist."[49] Although the two "poles" have roughly equal strength nationwide, the picture is different in the states. Following the color graphics that the television networks use, commentators have divided the country into red (Republican) states or blue (Democratic) states. The South and Plains states are red, while the Northeast and West Coast are blue. Parts of the industrial Midwest have emerged as a battleground.

Demography also plays a part in party identification.

FOCUS
QUESTION

When people call themselves "independent," what do they mean?

TABLE 9-1	PARTISAN POLARIZATION

According to polls by the Pew Research Center, Republicans and Democrats have come to have very different ideological leanings and views of political issues.

Government's Obligations to the Poor and Needy

Government should...
Take care of people who can't care for themselves

	1987	1994	1999	2003	2007	2012
	%	%	%	%	%	%
Total	71	57	62	66	69	59
Republican	62	45	52	54	58	40
Democrat	79	69	73	79	79	75
Independent	70	56	64	62	68	59
R-D gap	*-17*	*-24*	*-21*	*-25*	*-21*	*-35*

Guarantee food and shelter for all

	1987	1994	1999	2003	2007	2012
	%	%	%	%	%	%
Total	62	59	64	65	69	59
Republican	46	41	48	46	47	36
Democrat	73	71	72	81	83	78
Independent	62	61	68	64	71	58
R-D gap	*-27*	*-30*	*-24*	*-35*	*-36*	*-42*

Help more needy people even if debt increases

	1987	1994	1999	2003	2007	2012
	%	%	%	%	%	%
Total	53	41	49	54	54	43
Republican	39	26	35	39	34	20
Democrat	64	55	58	72	68	65
Independent	50	39	54	50	57	39
R-D gap	*-25*	*-29*	*-23*	*-33*	*-34*	*-45*

A Wide Partisan Divide over Peace through Strength

Percent agreeing that "The best way to ensure peace is through military strength"

	1997	1999	2002	2003	2007	2012
	%	%	%	%	%	%
Total	57	55	62	53	49	53
Republican	65	70	72	69	72	73
Democrat	56	53	55	44	40	44
Independent	54	50	62	51	46	52
R-D gap	*+9*	*-17*	*+17*	*+25*	*+32*	*+29*

SOURCE: Pew Research Center for the People and the Press, "Political Landscape More Favorable to Democrats," March 22, 2007, www.people-press.org/files/legacy-pdf/312.pdf; Pew Research Center for the People and the Press, "Partisan Polarization Surges in Bush, Obama Years," June 4, 2012, www.people-press.org/files/legacy-pdf/06-04-12%20Values%20Release.pdf, accessed June 13, 2012. Copyright © 2009 and 2012 by Pew Research Center. Reprinted with permission.

Age

In recent years, younger people have been increasingly likely to identify as independent. A 2012 Pew survey drives the point home.[50] Among Millennials, those born between 1981 and 1994, 45% said in 2012 that they were independents, up from 39% in 2008. At the same time, the Democratic share of Millennials dropped from 35% to 31%. A mere 18% were Republicans, though other survey data suggested that a fair number of independent Millennials "leaned" Republican. Among Gen Xers (born 1965–1980), the 2012 breakdown was 42% independents, 29% Democrats, and 24% Republicans. For Baby Boomers (born 1946–1964), as many identified as independents (34%) as Democrats, with Republicans accounting for 27%. The oldest generation in the survey—the Silent generation (born 1928–1945)—had an equal amount of Republicans and Democrats at 34%, with 27% as independents.

Why was there a generational difference? One reason may lie in social issues such as same-sex marriage, on which younger people tended to be more liberal than their elders. Whatever the reason, the big question for the future is whether an "age effect" or a "generation effect" is at work. An "age effect" means that people's attitudes reflect their stage in life and that their views will change as they get older. A "generation effect," by contrast, means that early views and affiliations tend to stick. Democrats hope that a generation effect will strengthen their party as Millennials and Gen Xers mature into greater political activity and start voting at higher rates. Republicans hope that an age effect will convert today's young Democrats into tomorrow's middle-aged Republicans as they pay taxes and encounter other effects of big government.

Income

Between the New Deal and the end of the twentieth century, pollsters found that the more money an individual made, the more likely he or she was to identify as a Republican.[51] This pattern reflected broad differences in party policies, with Republican leaders tending to favor lower taxes and Democratic leaders tending to favor policies to redistribute income. It bears repeating, though, that Republican officials often supported increases in social spending just as Democrats often supported tax cuts. It is also worth noting that the GOP lost some ground with affluent voters during the 2008 campaign.

Education

Higher levels of education mean higher income, so it makes sense that college graduates are more likely to be Republican than high school dropouts. There is a key exception to the pattern, however: people with postgraduate education are less likely to identify with the GOP than those whose schooling stopped with a bachelor's degree.[52] Many people with graduate degrees belong to professions (e.g., education) that have a direct tie to the activist government programs that Democrats favor.[53]

Ethnicity

In the 1950s, between 50% and 60% of black voters identified as Democrats. When Democratic president Lyndon Johnson and Republican nominee Barry Goldwater took opposing stands on federal civil rights legislation, that figure shot upward and stayed there. Since the 1960s, it has varied between 74% and 94%.[54] Hispanics also identify with the Democrats, increasingly so since the entry of new Hispanic voters in the 1990s. Like African Americans, many are poor and support more generous social programs. Cuban Americans are an exception to this pattern. Because of their intense opposition to the Castro regime, they vote for Republicans, whom they believe take a harder line on Communism.

Religion

Since the late nineteenth century, the Republicans have drawn substantial support from white mainline Protestants: Methodists, Lutherans, Presbyterians, Episcopalians, and Congregationalists.[55] (This support has scarcely been unanimous: Democrats have won a fair number of mainline Protestant votes.) During the last decades of the twentieth century, the party gained additional strength from an influx of white evangelical Protestants, who once sided with the Democrats. Meanwhile, Republicans also did better among non-Hispanic Catholics. The movement within both groups reflected their attraction to the conservative stands of Republican leaders on social and cultural issues. In a 2011 poll, 62% of very religious whites identified with or leaned toward the GOP, more than twice the share who identified or leaned Democratic. Nonreligious whites, by contrast, were 17% more likely to side with the Democrats.[56] Jewish voters have also maintained their long-standing allegiance with the Democrats.[57]

Gender

Republicans tend to do better among men than among women. Unmarried women are especially likely to be Democrats, while the gap between married men and married women is much smaller. Scholars have offered many explanations for the gender gap, including differences in economic status and divergent views on social welfare issues.[58] Among other things, single women tend to be poorer and more reliant on social programs.

Geography and demography work together, because groups cluster in certain locales, whose voting patterns reflect their presence. Many cities have large African-American neighborhoods, which overwhelmingly vote Democratic. The presence of many white evangelical Protestants helped tip the South to the Republicans.

There is more to the politics of a place than the census characteristics of its residents. History, tradition, and the physical environment may also shape partisan attachments.[59] For instance, Democrats do well in coastal areas, which include union members who work in ports and high-income professionals who favor strong environmental policies.

The combination of geography and demographic composition has given rise to "landslide counties," where one party gets at least 60% of the two-party presidential vote. In the 1976 election, only 27% of American voters lived in landslide counties.[60] In both 2004 and 2008, that figure was up to 48%. Such results may not favor grassroots deliberation and citizenship. When people in a locale overwhelmingly stand on one side of the partisan divide, those in the minority feel social pressure to stay quiet or scale back their political activity. One Democrat in a heavily Republican area told reporter Bill Bishop, "Discussions are cut short because people don't want to disagree or be disagreeable. So you don't have any real lively dialogue." A Republican in a Democratic area recounted similar experiences, saying, "We spend too much time in sealed environments where we can't find a nice way to say, 'I don't agree.'" Arguing that close party competition leads to better discussion and participation, political scientist James Gimpel told Bishop, "If you wanted to raise your kid to be a good citizen, you would want to raise them in a place that was fairly evenly divided."[61]

Party Registration and Primaries

In 29 states and the District of Columbia, voters register by party.[62] Usually, but not always, party declaration coincides with party identification. In states that require advance party registration, people may gradually change their sense of attachment without bothering to switch their formal affiliation. Some registered Republicans may think of themselves as Democrats, and vice versa.

In a strictly **closed primary**, only voters who register with the political party may vote in its primary. In a **semiclosed primary**, party members can only vote in their primary, but unaffiliated voters can vote in either party's primary. At the polls in some of these states, unaffiliated voters must choose one party's ballot or declare party preference in another way. In an **open primary**, any voter can take part in any party's primary. In a **top-two primary**, all candidates for all offices appear on the same ballot. All voters may take part, and the two candidates who get the most votes proceed to the general election regardless of party. In some cases, top-two primaries may result in general elections pitting two Republicans or two Democrats against each other.

Primaries demand more of citizens than partisan general elections. In the latter, voters can simply support the candidate of a particular party. In most primaries, they have to choose among candidates of the same party. (In top-two primaries, ballots may show the candidates' party affiliation, but there may be multiple candidates from the same party.) Candidates of the same party will generally have smaller issue differences than candidates of opposing parties. Moreover, voters are likely to have less information about candidates in primaries than in general elections.[63]

Closed primary—a primary in which only voters who formally register with the political party may vote.

Semiclosed primary—a primary in which party members can only vote in their primary, but unaffiliated voters can vote in either party's primary.

Open primary—a primary in which any voter can cast a ballot in any party's primary.

Top-two primary—a primary in which a single ballot displays all candidates. Voters may choose a Republican for one office, a Democrat for another, and so on. The two candidates with the most votes go on to the general election, regardless of party.

PARTY ORGANIZATION

MAJOR ISSUE

- What role do party organizations play in choosing candidates?

American party organization is a product of federalism, with 50 Republican and 50 Democratic state committees. Reflecting the diversity of local government structures, parties may have committees in villages, towns, cities, or counties. They may also have periodic conventions at the statewide level, as well as in legislative districts.

State and Local Parties

Whatever their structure, state and local party organizations are not as strong as they once were. As mentioned previously, the increased use of primary elections largely deprived them of their ability to choose candidates. In some states, however, committees or conventions can make it much easier for their preferred candidates to get onto the primary ballot.

Despite civil service reform, old-fashioned patronage did linger in some places. Late into the twentieth century, Chicago city workers knew that their chances for advancement hinged on their ability to round up Democratic votes. In a series of cases, however, the Supreme Court has curbed the ability of government officials to give jobs or contracts on the basis of political affiliation.[64]

Shorn of patronage and the ability to pick candidates, state and local party organizations have turned to providing assistance to campaigns. Most state party committees now have permanent headquarters (usually in the state capital) and professional staffs. They help candidates with polling and get-out-the-vote operations, and they provide the public with general information about the party.[65] The most important aid is financial. In most states, party organizations work under looser campaign finance laws than at the national level. Accordingly, they usually have more leeway in giving direct and indirect funding to state and local candidates. In supporting federal candidates, these organizations must abide by federal limits. But in a 1996 case, the Supreme Court ruled that state party organizations may spend unlimited sums in federal races, provided that they do not coordinate that spending with the candidates.[66]

National Party Committees

The Democratic and Republican National Committees both have large memberships, including dignitaries from every state. The committee members themselves seldom make key decisions, except to choose national party chairs when their side does not hold the White House. (By tradition, sitting presidents recommend the name of the national chair to their committee.) When we speak of national committees, we are actually speaking of party chairs and their staffs.[67] For most of the committees' history, dating back to the middle of the nineteenth century, that role was minor. Beginning in the 1960s, these organizations assumed a higher profile by raising money, providing technical assistance to state parties, and training candidates and campaign operatives.

In addition to the Republican National Committee and Democratic National Committee, Democrats and Republicans in the House and Senate have their own separate campaign organizations. These committees aim at gaining or holding party majorities. They answer not to the president or the national party chair, but to the party's members in the relevant chamber.[68] Generally, they cooperate with national committees of the same party, but because the separation of powers sometimes pits a president against fellow party members in Congress, their interests may clash. During the 1990 tax debate, President George H.W. Bush agreed to a tax increase and the Republican National Committee urged GOP lawmakers to support the president. The National Republican Congressional Committee told members and candidates that they should not hesitate to oppose him.[69] "We admire the president, we support the president," said one House Republican, "but we don't work for the president."[70]

National party committee chairs Reince Priebus (R-WI) and Debbie Wasserman Schultz (D-FL)

All of the party committees at the national level have become collectors and suppliers of money. Campaign expenditures by national party committees take three different forms:

- *Direct contributions*, in which the committee gives campaign funds to candidates for federal office. Under the Federal Election Campaign Act, party committees may provide each candidate up to $5,000 per election. Because the primary and general elections count separately, this limit effectively means up to $10,000 per candidate.

William B. Plowman/NBC/NBC NewsWire via Getty Images

TABLE 9-2	PARTY MONEY	
Total funds raised by national party organizations in the 2010 election cycle.		
Democratic Party		$814,988,123
Republican Party		$586,594,377
Democratic National Committee		$229,592,109
Republican National Committee		$198,791,545
Democratic Congressional Campaign Committee		$163,896,053
National Republican Congressional Committee		$133,779,119
Democratic Senatorial Campaign Committee		$129,543,443
National Republican Senatorial Committee		$ 84,513,719

SOURCE: Center for Responsive Politics, "Political Parties Overview, Election Cycle 2010," May 20, 2011, www.opensecrets.org/parties/index.php?cmte=&cycle=2010, accessed June 14, 2012.

(There is a separate limit for Senate candidates, shared between the party's national and senatorial committees. This limit is indexed for inflation and in 2012, it was $43,100.) Under federal law, the committees may only raise this money from individuals, campaigns, political action committees, or other party organizations. These contributions are in turn subject to strict limits.

- *Coordinated expenditures*, in which the party committee helps a candidate by paying for services such as polling but does not give the money directly to the candidate. The law adjusts these limits both for inflation and, in the case of Senate and presidential candidates, the size of the voting age population.
- *Independent expenditures*, in which the committee buys services that affect a campaign (usually advertisements) but that the committee does not coordinate with the candidate.

As Table 9-2 shows, the national parties are able to raise considerable amounts of money in spite of the contribution limits. And as the next chapter will explain in greater detail, these figures represent only a part of the campaign finance picture. As a result of court decisions, certain outside groups may raise and spend unlimited sums for campaigns, provided that they do not coordinate with candidates and party committees. Because many of the people staffing these groups have deep experience in the parties, they do not need direct marching orders: they can easily figure out what activities party officials would want them to undertake.[71]

National Party Conventions

Since the 1830s, American political parties have held national conventions to nominate their candidates for president and vice president, adopt a party platform, and conduct other party business. These gatherings take place in the summer of presidential election years and comprise thousands of delegates from every state as well as U.S. territories and the District of Columbia. Until the 1960s, state party organizations and their leaders controlled the selection of most delegates.[72]

After the 1968 election, the Democrats changed party rules so that ordinary citizens would have a hand in choosing most delegates, and Republicans followed suit. Since then, two methods of delegate selection have prevailed. In a presidential primary, party members (either those who have enrolled or those who have chosen the party's ballot on that day) vote for presidential candidates. As a result of that vote, delegates supporting that candidate go to the convention. In caucuses (which are different from *congressional* caucuses), people meet in public places to pick delegates to other meetings that in turn will choose delegates to the national convention.

The following chapter on elections and campaigns has more detail on primaries and caucuses. For now, our focus is on the convention. When party organizations ran the selection process, delegates often arrived without commitments to any candidate. They would bargain and deliberate among themselves, and they would often have to vote a number of times before a winner emerged. Critics of the old system said that it shut out the people, giving all the power to political bosses meeting in "a smoke-filled room." The phrase, suggesting political intrigue, dates back to the 1920 Republican Convention, where party leaders met privately. Smoking cigars and cigarettes, they settled on Warren G. Harding of Ohio.[73] Although most ratings put Harding among the worst presidents, the "smoke-filled rooms" could also encourage serious deliberation about a candidate's ability to campaign and govern. Two of our greatest presidents—Abraham Lincoln and Franklin Roosevelt—were also products of convention bargaining.

In the 1980s, Democrats tried to restore an element of deliberation and "peer review": they provided for "**superdelegates**," an informal term for delegates whose selection does not depend on primaries or caucuses. Superdelegates may vote for any candidate for the nomination. Most superdelegates gain their status automatically, as current or former party leaders and elected officials. Superdelegates account for about one-fifth of the total number of delegates. Republicans also have unpledged delegates, though they usually do not use the term "superdelegate." The GOP gives its state delegates much more leeway in the number and selection of unpledged delegates.

In today's system of primaries and caucuses, candidates can usually win enough delegates to secure the nomination before summer. Between 1980 and 2012, no national party convention started with serious doubt about the nominee, so the gatherings largely served to ratify the results of primaries. In the close 2008 Democratic contest between Senators Hillary Clinton and Barack Obama, there was speculation that the superdelegates would wait until the convention to make their choice, but most bowed to public opinion and sided with Obama.

Conventions still do other business, such as the adoption of **party platforms**, which are statements of party issue positions. The staffs of the candidates and the party organizations put great effort into drafting platforms, which are subject to change by the delegates. The outcome can offer clues about a party's direction. Still, no member of the party in government must follow the national party platform, and most ignore it. In fact, the presidential nominees themselves give scant attention to these documents, preferring to spell out their own beliefs. "I'm not bound by the platform," said 1996 Republican nominee Bob Dole. "I probably agree with most everything in it, but I haven't read it."[74]

So if conventions merely formalize the results of the primaries, and if platforms are not binding, what is the point of meeting? Media coverage is one answer. Yet even this function is losing importance as the television networks scale back convention coverage to an hour or so per night. Accordingly, the parties schedule their most broadly appealing speakers for those three hours.

In the old system, political leaders deliberated on the merits of would-be presidents. The leaders were practical politicians who worried about the candidates' chances of winning. Practicality forced them to think about the public good, because "electability" depended in part on the candidates' qualifications and ability to do a good job as president. Journalist Theodore H. White summed up the questions that Democratic delegates pondered in 1960 before they chose John F. Kennedy: "What manner of man should be selected to lead the country? What kind of opportunity might best straddle the past and turn to face the future?"[75] "Now," says scholar William Galston, "we have a system of presidential selection in which the element of deliberation is almost completely absent."[76]

Voters do deliberate during nomination battles, particularly when they meet and argue in party caucuses. Just as important, the new system provides greater opportunities for citizen activity. The old smoke-filled rooms involved very few people, whereas thousands volunteer in primary and caucus campaigns. Moreover, there is indeed an element of "peer review" in the preconvention phase, as candidates seek support from elected officials and other party leaders. Barack Obama won a majority of superdelegates not just because he did well in the polls but also because he had been calling them since March 2007.[77] Mitt Romney lost the Republican nomination in 2008, but never really stopped running. He campaigned vigorously for John McCain in the 2008 general election and for many Republicans in the

Superdelegate—an informal term for a Democratic National Convention delegate who is not chosen in a primary or caucus, and who may vote for any candidate for the nomination. Most superdelegates automatically gain their status by being current or former party leaders and elected officials.

Party platform—statement of party issue positions.

2010 midterm. He spent a great deal of time building goodwill among Republican leaders, and by the start of the 2012 nomination process, he had largely cornered the market on endorsements.[78] After he won enough delegates to secure the nomination, the Republican National Committee prepared to support him in the general election campaign . (See "the Impact of Social Media.")

PARTY IN GOVERNMENT

MAJOR ISSUE

- What is the relationship between party in the electorate and party in government?

The ultimate aim of any political party is to influence the government's composition and policies. Chapters on Congress and the presidency deal with the party in government, but a few additional details deserve attention here.

Federalism and Parties

Within each party, public officials take many different approaches to public issues. Federalism is one reason for this diversity. State and local officials deal with different sets of problems and institutional rules than do their national counterparts. In the last decades of the twentieth century, national policymakers in both parties lived with deficits, often proposing tax cuts or spending increases that would have enlarged them. Governors and state legislators lacked the same flexibility, for most states have constitutional requirements for balanced budgets. Consequently, state Republican officials sometimes supported tax increases and Democratic officials backed spending cuts, putting themselves at odds with their party's

IMPACT of Social Media and Communications Technology

Parties and Social Media in 2012

During the 2008 presidential campaign, Barack Obama made innovative use of the burgeoning technology of social media. Chris Hughes, one of Facebook's founders, left to work on Obama's digital campaign. The focus of the effort was My.BarackObama.com, where supporters could get information, volunteer for campaign duty, and create events. It was so successful that it became a template for both parties.

In 2012, the Republican National Committee launched a new Facebook app, the "Social Victory Center." (See Bessette-Pitney blog on May 3, 2012). "Politics is inherently social. You know, we have a strategy and a way to win, so it made a lot of sense for us to go to Facebook and not build this on GOP.com or a website or something like that, especially with Facebook's platform, which is all about sharing," said Andrew Abdel-Malik, of the RNC digital team.[79]

Users would register with their Facebook profile and contact information. In the "News" section, they would see GOP Web ads as well as news stories chosen by RNC staff and geared to the users' own location. That is, Texas voters would see Texas stories. The "Events" section would show nearby Republican events and candidate headquarters on a Google map. The "Discussion" section enabled users to deliberate about policy issues. The "Volunteer" section featured a map with the address and contact information for the local "Victory Center," or GOP field office.[80]

This app also allowed the party to collect data. "If you sign up to use one of these campaign apps on Facebook, you're given a little warning that says this app is now going to find out everything that you've made public about yourself on Facebook, as well as the names and IDs of all your friends," said Micah Sifry of the Personal Democracy Forum.[81] RNC was not shy about it. "Every article, every video, everything is tagged," said Abdel-Malik. "Whether it's an economy article or debt, so on and so forth. . . . Whatever it might be, we can collect those data points. And that's where things really start to get interesting."[82]

CRITICAL THINKING

Are party social media sites a way to encourage deliberation and participation from the bottom up, or to direct political activity from the top down?

International Perspectives

The Parliamentary Example

Some American observers have looked longingly at parliamentary systems, especially Britain's. Without a formal separation of powers, a majority party can set a clear policy, carry it out, and ask the voters to judge it on the results. In a 1980 book, economist Lester Thurow summed up the system's virtue: "Responsibility for success is clear, and failures can be punished."[84]

In the real world, these systems often stray from the ideal that Thurow described. Still, American parties are less "responsible" than their European counterparts. In Britain, leaders of each party start each election campaign by crafting a manifesto, a detailed plan of what they would do if they won. "Because it's done collectively, it means the ministers and prime ministers are bound by the manifesto," scholar Pippa Norris told reporter Adam Nagourney in 2005. "It's a real document, unlike the American platform."[85]

British campaigns last only a month. Such a system saves time and reduces fatigue, but at a cost in active citizenship. "In an election where they call it 30 days ahead of time, the system works against building citizen involvement," said Joe Trippi, a Democratic political consultant.[86]

British party leaders hone their skills in floor debate. During "Question Time," the opposition party poses tough inquiries to the prime minister or other officials. To survive Question Time, these leaders need a command of the issues as well as a quick tongue. Admirers of the system say that it produces better party leaders and improves deliberation, and thanks to television coverage, it also educates Britons about policy differences between the parties. There is nothing quite like it in the United States, except perhaps for press conferences.

"In our age of polarization, gladiator TV and unfortunate vitriol in our dialogue, regular 'question time' with the President is an idea worth trying," says Democratic media consultant Peter Fenn. "It gives the opportunity for civil dialogue and more thorough discussion of how to solve our most vexing problems."[87] Some take a more skeptical view. Scholar Michael Schudson writes, "The question period is a great deal more energetic and amusing—sometime uproarious—than the best presidential press conference, but it is even more stylized and hortatory. It is no more elevated, rational, or deliberative. It is more a scoring of points than a trading of views."[88]

CRITICAL THINKING QUESTION

Would an American version of "question time" contribute to deliberative democracy? Would it be consistent with the separation of powers?

---

philosophical direction. In 2009, for instance, California governor Arnold Schwarzenegger became a pariah among Republican activists when he agreed to a tax increase as part of a plan to close the state's enormous budget deficit.

Furthermore, state and local officials often work on issues that often have a more immediate impact on voters, so they often stray from party ideology. Republican governors have sponsored increases in education spending while Democratic mayors of big cities have carried out tough, conservative policies on crime control.

States vary in their economic, social, and political makeup. Politicians must respond to these circumstances, so parties in government may favor different positions in different parts of the country. In 2008, 38% of the nation's governors served states that voted for the opposite party in the presidential election. In these states, Republican governors tended to be more liberal than their party's norm, and Democratic governors tended to be more conservative.

Leadership and Unity

A brief comparison with parliamentary systems (see the International Perspectives feature) will deepen our understanding of American parties in government. As we have seen, divided government has often occurred in U.S. national politics since the 1950s, and a similar pattern has emerged in many states.[83] In most parliamentary systems, by contrast, divided government is impossible, because the head of the ruling party in Parliament automatically becomes the head of government. Cabinet posts go to other members of Parliament from that party, or from parties that agree to form a coalition with it. (One exception is France, which has both a popularly elected president and a Parliament with a prime minister at its head. Occasionally, the French have experienced divided government, which they call "cohabitation.")

British Prime Minister David Cameron speaks in the House of Commons during Question Time.

PA Wire URN:9682523 (Press Association via AP Images)

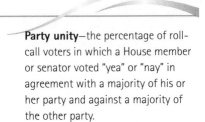

Party unity—the percentage of roll-call voters in which a House member or senator voted "yea" or "nay" in agreement with a majority of his or her party and against a majority of the other party.

Under certain circumstances, if the governing party loses a vote on the floor of Parliament, the government "falls" and new elections take place. Therefore, party leaders have a strong incentive to discipline their members through punishments and rewards. Those who vote with the party may eventually gain cabinet positions, while defectors may lose their chance for advancement and even renomination. (Primaries are largely unknown in parliamentary systems, where party leaders usually pick candidates in the general election.)

In the United States, such discipline is harder to impose. Elected officials serve fixed terms, so while a setback on a legislative vote may be embarrassing, it will not force new elections. Because of the local basis of American elections, national and state party leaders usually cannot deny renomination to straying lawmakers. In some states, legislative party discipline is stronger than in other states or in Congress. Even in the "strong party" states, however, legislative leaders sometimes clash with governors of their own party. More often, legislative and executive leaders recognize that party discipline can backfire. When lawmakers have to vote with their party against their constituents' interests or opinions, they may lose their seats in the next election, potentially depriving the party of a majority.

Nevertheless, recent congressional votes have shown high partisanship. Congressional Quarterly defines a **party unity** vote as one in which a majority of one party votes against a majority of the other. During the 1970s, annual party unity scores for both parties in both chambers averaged around 60% to 70%. In 2011, House Democrats averaged 87% to the Republicans' 91%. Senate Democrats averaged 92%, their highest ever, while Senate Republicans lagged a bit, with 86%.[89]

In the House, some of the change may reflect the majority party's ability to control the agenda and the minority's resentment of that control. Furthermore, many House members represent districts that are overwhelmingly Republican or Democratic. Senators generally represent larger and more diverse constituencies, yet as with House members, the nomination process may still tug them in a partisan direction. If a Republican moves too far to the left or a Democrat moves too far to the right, party activists may react by mounting a challenge in the primary. During the general election, voters in the middle may thus face a choice between a very conservative Republican and a very liberal Democrat.[90] Even if they prefer centrists, they might not have one to choose.[91]

Rancor has accompanied the polarization of the parties in government. Political leaders sometimes insult each other, even suggesting that people in the other party resemble Nazis.[92] Some scholars and political leaders worry that the effects of rancor go beyond hurt feelings. "As a condition for promoting deliberation, civility remains crucial," says political scientist Burdett Loomis, noting that the need for civility is especially necessary when legislative procedures require broad consensus.[93]

After his defeat in a 2012 primary, Senator Richard Lugar (R-IN) said that it had become difficult to achieve that consensus:

> Partisans at both ends of the political spectrum are dominating the political debate in our country. And partisan groups, including outside groups that spent millions against me in this race, are determined to see that this continues. They have worked to make it as difficult as possible for a legislator of either party to hold independent views or engage in constructive compromise. If that attitude prevails in American politics, our government will remain mired in the dysfunction we have witnessed during the last several years.[94]

Another viewpoint comes from conservative columnist Jonah Goldberg:

> Many of our greatest heroes were men and women who were willing to rock the boat. If consensus is such a high political value, then the abolitionists, suffragettes and civil rights marchers are all villains. Unity is not only overrated, it's often undemocratic. Decrying the "polarization" may be something decent people are supposed to do, like recycling or paying more for organic breakfast cereal that tastes like kitty litter. But the alternative is no great shakes. . . . When you hear that rhetoric, consider this as a translation: "Those who disagree with me should shut up and get on board the progress train."[95]

FOCUS
QUESTION
Does partisan polarization foster deliberation by clarifying differences, or hinder it by impeding dialogue?

Party Caucuses and Conferences

Because of various laws and rules, dating mainly from recent decades, most formal meetings of legislative bodies are open to the public. These "sunshine in government" reforms have enabled citizens to observe the workings of their government, especially when the meetings air on cable television or the Internet. Yet while making government more accountable, openness may have made it less deliberative. Under the eyes of voters, lobbyists, and researchers for their political opponents, lawmakers hesitate to voice unpopular beliefs or admit shortcomings in their own proposals. Instead, they feel pressure to "play to the galleries" with rhetoric that wins applause without contributing to substantive discussion.

Parties in government supply a partial solution to this problem. In both houses of Congress and in most state legislative chambers, lawmakers from each party meet in a separate caucus or conference to choose leaders and discuss policy. In some statehouses, these meetings are open to the public, but in most cases they are closed to everyone except lawmakers and aides. In the privacy of closed-door sessions, lawmakers are better able to reason on the merits of public policy without fear that their enemies will turn their words against them. In Congress, parties also have "policy committees," which enable members to discuss issues in smaller, more intimate settings. Such an exchange of views, said one lawmaker, "causes some members to start talking it over with their own associates and colleagues. It's part of the educational process, I think, and part of the formulative process sometimes."[96]

Some say, however, that these meetings, with only one party present, include only a limited range of views, and their internal discussions sometimes serve to deepen partisan tensions instead of easing them.

THIRD PARTIES
MAJOR ISSUE

- What roles have third parties played in American history?

The Democrats and Republicans have dominated this chapter, but there have been other parties in our political history. Some have had a major impact for an election or two, and then they faded. In 1912, former president Theodore Roosevelt ran as the candidate of the Progressive Party and outpolled Republican incumbent William Howard Taft, though both lost to Democrat Woodrow Wilson. Despite this showing, the Progressive Party failed to gain ground in elections for other offices and soon fell apart. In 1992, H. Ross Perot ran under various labels in different states and won 18.9% of the popular vote, the largest third-party share since 1912. Four years later, running as the Reform Party candidate, he won only 8.4%.

Other third parties remain on the ballot election after election, without soaring as high as the short-lived parties.[97] The Libertarian Party opposes social welfare programs, drug laws, and any defense expenditures beyond what is necessary to safeguard American borders from invasion.[98] Since its founding in 1971, the party has occasionally won a significant share of the vote in House races and has elected a handful of officials to minor offices, but has never won more than 1.1% of the vote in a presidential election.

Members of the Green Party have won hundreds of races, but mostly in nonpartisan elections in small constituencies.[99] The Green Party takes strongly liberal positions on many issues, though it also endorses decentralization of economic and political power. Its 2010 platform expressed three core values:

- Participatory Democracy, rooted in community practice at the grassroots level and informing every level, from the local to the international.
- Social Justice and Equal Opportunity emphasizing personal and social responsibility, accountability, and an informing ethic of Nonviolence.
- Ecological and Economic Sustainability, balancing the interests of a regulated market economy and community-based economics with effective care for the Great Economy in which we are embedded: the ecosystems of the Earth.[100]

Both the Libertarians and the Greens grapple with the "**spoiler**" **effect**, which is both the greatest strength and biggest weakness of third parties. A *spoiler* is a minor candidate who draws votes from one major candidate, thereby helping another. Greens tend to siphon from Democrats, as Libertarians do from Republicans. The prospect of a spoiler effect may lead major party candidates to move in the minor party's direction. But when a spoiler does change an election, the result may displease those who voted for the spoiler.

In 2000, Green presidential candidate Ralph Nader won 2.7% of the popular vote, mostly from those who thought Democrat Al Gore was not liberal enough. In Florida, Nader split off enough votes from Gore to tip the state to Republican George W. Bush, thereby allowing Bush to win the presidency. From then on, Democrats used the 2000 election to discourage liberals from backing Green candidates. A vote for the Greens, they said, would only help Republicans. The Libertarians may have played a similar role in a 2006 race. Incumbent Republican senator Conrad Burns lost a tight reelection contest in Montana, where the Libertarian vote was much bigger than his margin of defeat. His loss was enough to shift control of the Senate from Republicans to Democrats. In 2008, a candidate from the very conservative Constitution Party probably took enough votes from incumbent Republican senator Gordon Smith to shift the race to Democratic challenger Jeff Merkley.

Spoilers or not, third parties may foster public deliberation by drawing attention to issues and policy alternatives that the major parties ignore. In the early part of the century, Roosevelt's Progressive Party and the less successful Socialist Party both supported the minimum wage and other initiatives that later became accepted public policy. Perot's

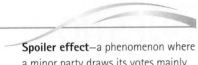

Spoiler effect—a phenomenon where a minor party draws its votes mainly from one major party, thereby tipping elections to the other major party.

Photo courtesy of James Harrison

Copyright © Jeff Greenberg/Photo Edit

The Green and Libertarian Parties have some things in common. Both attract a small but passionate following, and both have managed to elect public officials. They oppose the extension of American military power overseas and are deeply suspicious of domestic security measures that could jeopardize civil liberties. They also agree on certain issues involving personal conduct: both parties would ease drug laws. On other issues, however, their views diverge. Greens favor a far more expansive welfare state, while Libertarians would slash existing social programs. Greens want to raise more government revenue, particularly from the wealthiest Americans, while Libertarians would repeal the income tax. Greens favor aggressive government action against pollution, while Libertarians think that the solution lies in free markets and property rights.

1992 candidacy refocused the campaign on the issue of the national debt, and thereby encouraged Congress and the presidency to take stronger action.

Barriers to Third-Party Success

Why do third parties either flame out or fail to catch fire in the first place? When a minor party either gains a significant share of the vote or threatens to do so, one or both of the major parties may adopt its positions. Woodrow Wilson's domestic policy agenda deflated the Progressive Party, just as Bill Clinton's deficit reduction took away much of the rationale for the Perot movement.

A number of other obstacles hinder third parties:

- *The single-member-constituency-plurality system.* In most American elections, candidates vie for an individual office, which goes to the one with the most votes. In a proportional representation system, by contrast, parties win seats according to their share of the total vote. So whereas a party winning 25% of the national vote gets about 25% of the parliamentary seats in a proportional representation system, it might not win any congressional seats.[101]

- *The presidency and the Electoral College.* The White House is the greatest prize in American politics, but the Electoral College system tends to keep third parties from influencing the choice of its occupant. Third-party presidential candidates do poorly in the Electoral College unless they enjoy concentrated support in certain states. Despite winning nearly a fifth of the popular vote in 1992, Perot did not get a single electoral vote. This inability to "get on the scoreboard" discourages third-party candidates, contributors, and voters.

- *Ballot access.* The 50 states and the District of Columbia have different rules about how parties can get on the ballot. Generally, third parties have to collect signatures, pay fees, or get individuals to register as party members. These steps can be costly, and in many places third parties have to repeat them for each election unless they win a set percentage of the vote.[102]

- *Campaign finance.* Few individuals and even fewer interest groups will contribute to parties that seem to have little chance of winning. What is more, federal election law favors the major parties. Any party winning more than 25% of the popular vote (since 1912, only the Republicans and Democrats) gets a partial subsidy for its next national convention and full public funding for its next general election campaign. A "minor" party, winning between 5% and 25% of the vote, is entitled to much less.[103] Because the Reform Party won 8.4% of the vote in 1996, it qualified for $12.6 million in federal funds four years later. The Democratic and Republican parties each received $67.6 million.

- *Press and polls.* Reporters give these parties little coverage, which means that they draw little support, which reporters, in turn, cite as justification for slighting them. And when polls show a third party with a small share of the electorate, it loses support from people who do not want to waste their vote—and this loss of support further depresses their poll numbers.

- *Candidates.* Because of these obstacles, attractive candidates tend not to run on third-party tickets. And, in turn, the dearth of attractive candidates further hurts the prospects of third parties. In 2012, a bipartisan group of activists got considerable financial support for a third-party effort called Americans Elect. Even though it secured ballot access in more than half the states, the effort foundered when no candidate got enough support in its online selection progress. The group "took a 'Field of Dreams' approach: if you build it—a virtual nominating convention—they will come," said Will Marshall, president of the Progressive Policy Institute. "But political movements are built around compelling personalities or causes, not technology. Neither materialized in 2012."[104]

Would it be desirable to lower barriers to third parties? There is reason for doubt. First, some of them have strong justification apart from their impact on the party system. **Single-member districts** allow for a relationship between voters and lawmakers, who

Single-member district—district that elects only one member to a legislative body.

have to take local views and conditions into account.[105] Second, it is hard to see how basic institutions would work if third parties regularly captured large numbers of votes and seats. If a third party won enough electoral votes to deadlock the Electoral College, the election would go to the House. But if the third party also had enough House seats, the chamber might not be able to choose a president. Finally, a two-party system theoretically requires each side to build a broad coalition that encourages conciliation and compromise.

In practice, however, the two parties have become highly polarized. The effect of this polarization is a major topic of current debate and discussion.

POLITICAL PARTIES AND DELIBERATIVE DEMOCRACY

In 2009, Senator Arlen Specter, a liberal from Pennsylvania, switched parties to join the Democrats. He said that the GOP had become too conservative. Some Republican senators regretted their party's loss of a seat, but Jim DeMint of South Carolina actually welcomed it: "I would rather have 30 Republicans in the Senate who really believe in principles of limited government, free markets, free people, than to have 60 that don't have a set of beliefs."[106]

Markos Moulitsas, founder of the influential liberal blog the Daily Kos, also welcomes polarization: "We need to be down and dirty and absolutely tear them apart."[107] During his 2008 campaign, President Obama voiced a different view, promising to pursue liberal policies while quieting partisan rancor. His administration presented a decidedly mixed picture. Although he did name Republicans to some important posts, the two parties kept up their political sniping. Republicans continued harsh attacks on Democratic leaders, and Democrats attacked Republicans—with some of the fire coming from the White House itself.

On both sides, voices were arguing that parties ought to be "big tents," covering a range of different and even conflicting viewpoints. "Big tent" parties, they say, serve the cause of deliberative democracy by adding a layer of intraparty deliberation to the debate *between* the parties. Furthermore, the argument goes, such parties foster compromise and civility in place of the harsh partisanship that can break out when the parties are polar opposites. Finally, broad-based party coalitions ensure that no one is totally "in the cold" when one party or the other is in power.

As the Civil War demonstrated, extreme polarization can reach a point that threatens the nation itself. As one scholar put it: "[If] citizens differ among themselves on questions concerning the very basis of society, they cannot, in a moral sense, be fellow-citizens. Without agreement on fundamentals there can be no trust, and without trust there is no basis for citizenship."[108]

How does polarization affect deliberation? On the one hand, it tends to clarify policy alternatives, and need not end in gridlock. Even the most heated political conflicts can result in substantial policy change, as we saw during the first two years of the Republican Congress under President Clinton. Despite the harshness of the rhetoric on both sides, they balanced the budget and reached agreement on fundamental welfare reform. On the other hand, polarization can erode the mutual trust necessary for deliberation. Just when President Clinton and House Speaker Newt Gingrich had

Senator Jim DeMint (R-SC) speaks to the 39th Conservative Political Action Committee February 9, 2012.

quietly made progress on reforming Social Security and Medicare, the impeachment controversy wrecked any chance for serious congressional deliberation on these issues.[109]

A system with three or more major parties might enable voters to register their views more precisely. By giving voters a chance to back an alternative they like, instead of forcing them to choose "the lesser of two evils," a multiparty system might encourage participation and active citizenship. At the same time, however, it might aggravate the fragmentation of American life. An analogy with communications technology is appropriate. During the age of "mass media," network broadcasts and large-circulation periodicals provided Americans with common points of reference: ideas and trends that they all knew about and could discuss. In an age of "niche media"—hundreds of cable channels and millions of blogs—Americans are gaining more chances to enter the fray while losing common ground with fellow citizens. Similarly, the major parties have served to provide a common political home for diverse individuals and interests. Might their breakup further alienate Americans from one another?

Such a breakup seems very unlikely. Recent years have seen renewed strength for the major parties in government and in the electorate. Party organizations have also gained in importance, but their role has changed. In the nineteenth century, local party organizations depended on armies of volunteers who worked year-round. Scholar Michael Schudson pictures their impact: "[T]here is much more bustle around the polling place. The area is crowded with the banners of rival parties. Election day is not a convivial oasis, set off from other days, but the culmination of a campaign of several months and many barbecues, torchlight processions, and 'monster meetings.' If you were not active in the campaign, you may be roused on election day by a party worker to escort you on foot or by carriage."[110] As Tocqueville suggested, these efforts drew citizens out of their tight circles and taught them the art of association.

Today's party structures are professional operations that raise and disburse large sums of money, and mount elaborate national communication efforts. Their Web sites supply a good deal of information about policy issues. At ground level, however, voter contact depends less on the personal relationships of party workers than on computerized lists. In comparison with the past, parties may be better at providing material for public deliberation, but they may not be better at fostering active citizenship.

FOCUS QUESTION

In what ways do parties help and hinder the cause of active citizenship?

SUMMARY

- Since the middle of the nineteenth century, the Republicans and Democrats have been the dominant parties in the United States. The longevity of these parties is remarkable, though they have undergone substantial changes over the years.
- The party in the electorate consists of the voters who tend to support it. African Americans and Hispanics strongly tend to support the Democrats, while non-Hispanic whites lean to the GOP. For decades, pollsters have noticed that Republican identification goes up along the income scale.
- The party organization includes the formal structure of party officers and workers who try to influence elections. There is no single chain of command. American party organizations are fragmented, though the national

committees have played an important service role in recent years.
- The party in government comprises those who win office under the party label. As with party organization, federalism and the separation of powers prevent the parties in government from acting as unitary armies. In Congress, however, we have seen increasing polarization, with Republicans and Democrats voting in starkly different ways.
- Third parties seldom win elections, yet they have had significant effects. First, they sometimes change outcomes by drawing votes away from one of the major parties. Second, they may bring public attention to issues or positions that the major parties might otherwise ignore.

KEY TERMS

TEST YOUR KNOWLEDGE

1. The movement of parties away from each other and toward more extreme issue positions is called
   a. party caucusing.
   b. partisan polarization.
   c. partisan realignment.
   d. party identification.
   e. party politics.
2. The granting of government jobs and favors to supporters is called
   a. partisan alignment.
   b. partisan polarization.
   c. bribery.
   d. political machines.
   e. political patronage.
3. What party arose in 1854 with an anti-slavery platform?
   a. Democrats
   b. Know-Nothings
   c. Progressives
   d. Republicans
   e. Whigs
4. The Australian ballot system used
   a. government-printed ballots listing all candidates.
   b. open voting booths so each voter's choices were public.
   c. party ballots listing only the candidates from one party.
   d. political machines to get voters to the polls.
   e. voter intimidation to ensure the "right" ballots were cast.
5. Suppose a voter whose registration card is marked Republican feels a stronger attachment to the Democratic platform and tends to favor Democratic candidates. This leaning toward the Democratic Party is his party
   a. alignment.
   b. ballot.
   c. identification.
   d. poll.
   e. registration.
6. To what extent are members of the party in government bound by the party platform?
   a. All members of the party in government sign the platform in acknowledgement of its planks, but they are not required to follow it.
   b. Certain planks of the platform require an oath of loyalty from members of the party in government.
   c. In order to retain the party label, all members of the party in government are bound to the entirety of the platform.
   d. No member of the party in government must follow the platform.
   e. The highest-ranking members of the party in government are bound by the platform, but lower members are given more leeway.
7. Political parties differ from interest groups in that they
   a. do not back specific policy positions.
   b. do not try to expand their membership.
   c. do not try to influence what the government does.
   d. focus on elections and getting their own members elected to office.
   e. often seek to expand their membership.
8. The president and the Speaker of the House are a part of the party
   a. affiliation.
   b. in Congress.
   c. in government.
   d. in the electorate.
   e. organization.

9. The presidential race in which Jefferson defeated Adams was the world's first
   a. breakdown of government.
   b. defeat of an incumbent.
   c. democratically conducted national election.
   d. political coup.
   e. peaceful transfer of power as a result of a national election.

10. The granting of government jobs and favors to supporters is called
   a. partisan alignment.
   b. partisan polarization.
   c. bribery.
   d. political machines.
   e. political patronage.

FURTHER READING

Brownstein, Ronald. *The Second Civil War: How Extreme Partisanship Has Paralyzed Washington and Polarized America.* New York: Penguin, 2007.

Gimpel, James G., and Jason E. Schuknecht. *Patchwork Nation: Sectionalism and Political Change in American Politics.* Ann Arbor: University of Michigan Press, 2004.

Klinkner, Philip A. *The Losing Parties: Out-Party National Committees 1956–1993.* New Haven, CT: Yale University Press, 1994.

Kolodny, Robin. *Pursuing Majorities: Congressional Campaign Committees in American Politics.* Norman: University of Oklahoma Press, 1998.

Mayhew, David R. *Electoral Realignments: A Critique of an American Genre.* New Haven, CT: Yale University Press, 2002.

Sundquist, James L. *Dynamics of the Party System.* Rev. ed. Washington, DC: Brookings Institute, 1983.

Trende, Sean. *The Lost Majority: Why the Future of Government Is Up for Grabs—and Who Will Take It.* New York: Palgrave Macmillan, 2012.

WEB SOURCES

Democratic National Committee: www.democrats.org—the lead national organization of the Democratic Party.

Frontloading HQ: frontloading.blogspot.com/—a blog examining parties from the perspective of political science.

Green Party of the United States: www.gp.org—the Web site of the Green Party, which supports progressive positions on the environment and other issues.

Libertarian Party: www.lp.org—the Web site of the Libertarian Party, which supports minimal government.

Republican National Committee: www.gop.com—the lead national organization of the Republican Party.

Diane Boyd casts her primary
election ballot at Covenant
Baptist United Church of Christ in
Washington, DC, on April 3, 2012.

© Linda Davidson/The Washington Post via Getty Images

10 Elections and Campaigns

OBJECTIVES

After reading this chapter, you should be able to:

- Describe various kinds of elections in the United States.
- Explain the distinctiveness of presidential and congressional elections.
- Analyze how the mechanics of voting may affect turnout and outcomes.
- Summarize the reasons for electoral success and failure.
- Discuss the basics of how candidates finance and run their campaigns.
- Appraise the ways in which the current electoral process may foster or hinder deliberation and active citizenship.

INTRODUCTION

Why have elections at all? The obvious answer is that elections translate the public will into government policy. Nevertheless, it is possible to picture an alternative system to do the same thing. Some ancient Greek city-states chose public officials by lot. The modern equivalent would use the scientific sampling techniques that pollsters employ. Such a system might randomly select a group of citizens to serve as members of Congress or state legislators. Thus, we could have lawmakers whose views and personal characteristics reflected those of the public as a whole—and without all the expense and turmoil of political campaigns. Serious scholars have proposed variations of selection by lot.[1] Still, there are several reasons why elections are worth the trouble.

First, elections provide a way for the people to check and control their government. Elections are imperfect, but we can hardly assume that selection by lot would be better. Even if the lottery produced lawmakers who were an exact mirror image of the general population, power could go to their heads, or they could fall prey to corruption.

Second, we do not necessarily want officials to be a perfect cross section of the public. In *Federalist* no. 57, Madison said that the goal of republican government is to choose officials with "the most wisdom to discern, and most virtue to pursue, the common good of the society."[2] That is, the founders hoped that people would pick those with the best capacity to reason on the merits of public policy. Although one can think of exceptions, it is likely that most members of Congress and state legislators come to office with more political knowledge and experience than the average citizen.

Third, elections foster active citizenship. (Also see Chapter 7 on public opinion and participation.) Campaigns enable people to take part in public life in a variety of ways: attending rallies and political meetings, ringing doorbells and stuffing envelopes, wearing buttons and displaying bumper stickers, donating money, and joining candidates' Facebook groups. Others take more demanding roles by helping run campaigns and seeking office themselves. The multiple layers of federal, state, and local government create abundant opportunities. The United States has more than half a million elected offices.[3] Therefore, several million Americans have probably been political candidates at one time or another, at least for local positions such as school board. Many others have considered running.[4]

Fourth, election campaigns stimulate public deliberation. Candidates discuss issues in their speeches and advertisements. Often they debate their opponents directly. Officeholders explain what they have done during their terms, and most candidates talk about what policies they will pursue in the future. Reporters, commentators, and bloggers analyze what the candidates have said and identify what they have failed to discuss. All of this campaign activity and analysis, in turn, can spur countless informal conversations in kitchens, workplaces, and dorm rooms.[5]

As the chapter on public opinion and participation explains, however, many Americans forgo an active part in the electoral process. In addition, the electoral system may sometimes fall short in promoting deliberation and the selection of the best people. As we shall now see, many problems with the system are unintentional. Others stem from misconduct ranging from deceptive rhetoric to outright vote fraud. Concern with such behavior is nothing new. Madison wanted to keep "unworthy candidates" from practicing "the vicious arts by which elections are too often carried."[6] To grasp these issues, we must first understand the many forms that American elections can take.

VARIETIES OF AMERICAN ELECTIONS
MAJOR ISSUES

- Can people make good law through direct democracy?
- How does the conduct of elections affect voter and candidate behavior?

The American electoral system is complicated. Three reasons for this complexity are basic features of the nation's politics: the separation of powers, bicameralism, and federalism. Every four years, the nation elects the president, and every two years it chooses all House members and about one-third of the senators. Most races for state office take place in even-numbered years, but many local elections occur in odd years, as do statewide races in Virginia, New Jersey, Kentucky, Louisiana, and Mississippi. The number and type of offices that appear on the ballot (see below for an example) vary greatly from place to place. Some elections involve entire states, counties, cities, or towns. Others involve districts that cross local boundaries. Ballots for Congress and state office usually post the candidates' party affiliations, but there are exceptions. Some items on the ballot do not involve candidates at all. In two dozen states and many localities, citizens can put legislation on the ballot. In principle, at least, such measures are the most direct way by which the public can guide public policy.

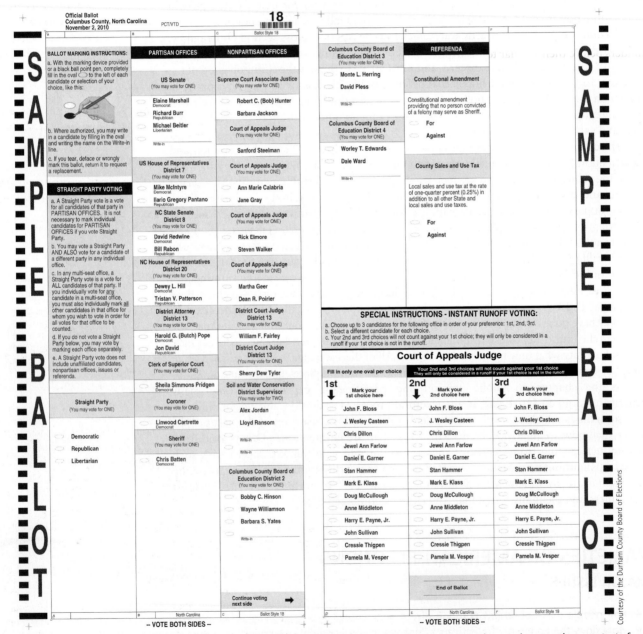

This sample ballot from North Carolina illustrates the complexity of choices that face American voters: partisan and nonpartisan contests for a variety of offices, as well as ballot measures.

Referendum, Recall, and Initiative

The framers believed that the deliberative work of legislation could not take place among a large mass of citizens. They thought that individuals were flawed and that crowds were dangerous. "Had every Athenian citizen been a Socrates," Madison wrote, "every Athenian assembly would still have been a mob."[7] Accordingly, the U.S. Constitution set up a representative government and did not provide for a popular vote on federal legislation. Many states, however, have long used procedures giving voters a more direct voice:

- The **initiative** (24 states): people may gather signatures to put proposed laws or constitutional amendments directly on the ballot for voters to approve or reject.
- The **popular referendum** (24 states): people may gather signatures to enable the voters to accept or reject measures that the legislature has passed.
- **Legislative referendum** (50 states): the state legislature, or other officials or public bodies, may submit measures to the people for their approval or rejection.[8]

Nineteen states provide for statewide **recall elections**, in which voters may oust officeholders before their regular terms expire.[9] To get a recall on the ballot, a certain percentage of voters must sign a petition. Because the number of required signatures is often high, statewide recall elections are rare. In 2003, California voters recalled Democratic governor Gray Davis and replaced him with Republican Arnold Schwarzenegger. In 2012, labor unions mounted a recall drive against Wisconsin's Republican governor Scott Walker after he signed legislation limiting collective bargaining for public employees. The recall made it to the ballot, but Walker won. In at least 29 states, recalls may take place in localities.[10] Supporters of direct democracy make the following points. Professional politicians make key decisions behind the scenes, draining the process of accountability. In many places, voters know little about their lawmakers' deeds or even identities. Many areas lack party competition, meaning that a lawmaker has little to fear from making bad policy. By lobbying politicians behind closed doors, special interests can thwart majority opinion and profit at the expense of the broader public good. Direct democracy enables citizens to bypass unresponsive politicians. One scholar says, "The initiative allows the majority to defend itself against powerful groups that receive favorable treatment in the legislature."[11] Although ballot measures are often controversial and complex, the decisions of voters are usually as defensible as those of the legislators. Perhaps most important, direct democracy can encourage citizen participation in politics (see photo) and widespread engagement in the deliberative process.

The case against direct democracy stresses the deliberative advantages of representative government. Although the process is imperfect, the need to build majorities encourages lawmakers to consider a variety of needs and interests. Most of their official actions are on public record, so they must be ready to defend what they have done. Direct democracy is different. Voters face an up or down vote on each measure, with no chance to amend it. Because their vote is secret, they face no individual sanction for foolish choices. Survey evidence suggests that the initiative process does not inspire voters to become better citizens by learning more about government.[12] Because ballot campaigns

Initiative—a procedure that allows citizens to draft their own legislation and get it on the ballot through a petition.

Popular referendum—a process whereby people may gather signatures to enable the voters to accept or reject measures that the legislature has passed.

Legislative referendum—a vote that takes place when a state legislature sends measures to the people for their approval.

Recall elections—special elections in which voters in some states may oust officeholders before their regular terms expire.

Justin Sullivan/Getty Images

In October 2010, medical marijuana activist and Oaksterdam University founder Richard Lee speaks during a news conference to bring attention to California State Proposition 19, a measure to legalize and tax marijuana in California. The measure lost.

Partisan election—a contest in which each candidate's party affiliation appears on the ballot.

Nonpartisan election—an election in which the candidate's party affiliation does not appear on the ballot.

Primary—an election that determines who runs in the final or general election.

General election—an election for final selection of a variety of offices. The general election for federal office is "on the first Tuesday after the first Monday" in November of even-numbered years.

Partisan primary—a primary in which voters nominate party candidates for the general election.

Runoff primary—a primary used in some states in which the top finishers face off if no one wins a majority (or some designated percentage) in the first-round partisan primary.

Instant-runoff voting—a system in which voters rank candidates in order of preference. If no candidate gets more than 50% of first-preference votes, the candidate with the fewest first-preference votes drops off and the votes for that candidate are redistributed according to the voters' next preference. The process repeats until a candidate wins a majority.

FOCUS QUESTION

Should we adopt instant-runoff voting on a larger scale? That is, would it be possible to apply the system to congressional, gubernatorial, and presidential elections?

At-large election—race in which candidates run not in districts but in an entire state, county, city, or town.

are so expensive, they give an advantage to rich interest groups and politicians.[13] The goal of signature requirements was to screen out measures lacking public support, but these requirements have given rise to initiative qualification firms. One handbook tells the paid collectors not to talk policy: "The goal of the table operation is to get petition signatures, not educate voters."[14]

Candidate Elections

Even in places that make the most extensive use of direct democracy, only a small fraction of policy issues go directly to the ballot box. Officials are responsible for a greater number of decisions. Elections for their offices may take different forms.

In a **partisan election**, the typical procedure of state and federal races, each candidate's party appears on the ballot. Many races for local or judicial office involve **nonpartisan elections**, where ballots list the candidates' names without their party affiliation. In the nineteenth century, areas with one strong party often developed political machines, or organizations that sealed their dominance through patronage (see Chapter 9 on parties). A major advantage of nonpartisan elections is that they foster voter deliberation by forcing voters to weigh the candidates' merits instead of their labels. Partisan debates usually cast little light on local issues because there is no Republican or Democratic way to carry out such jobs as street cleaning. Conversely, the advantage of partisan elections is that parties get people to the polls. Parties are arguably most useful in poor urban areas, where people might otherwise have no contact with politics.[15] Indeed, some evidence indicates that nonpartisan elections may depress turnout. (See Chapter 7 on public opinion and participation for more discussion of turnout.)[16]

Most American elections have two phases. The **primary** election is the preliminary phase, in which voters choose which candidates run in the final or **general election**. If the election is for a nonpartisan office, all candidates appear on the same ballot and voters may vote for any candidate. In a **partisan primary**, by contrast, candidates from different parties appear on different ballots. As Chapter 9 explains, states have different rules on who may vote in partisan primaries, but the basic idea is the same. In each party's primary, voters nominate its candidates for the general election. In areas of one-party dominance, the partisan primary usually amounts to election, and the other party seldom mounts a serious battle.

In most states, the primary election goes to the candidate with the most votes even if that number falls short of a majority. With many candidates in a race, it may be possible to win with a small share of the vote. This system favors candidates with a passionate core of support, which typically means liberals in the Democratic Party and conservatives in the Republican Party. Nevertheless, these candidates are sometimes too far from the center to do well in the general election. Some states, however, provide for a **runoff primary** between the top two candidates if no one gets a majority in the first round. Runoffs may foster moderation by favoring candidates with a broad base of support.[17]

San Francisco, Minneapolis, and some other localities use an alternative to primaries called **instant-runoff voting**.[18] This system lets voters rank candidates in order of preference (first, second, third, fourth and so on). Once the votes are in, election officials tabulate first choices, and if a candidate gets a majority, he or she wins the office. If nobody has a majority on the first count, the candidate with fewest first place choices drops off. Election officials retabulate the ballots, and voters who chose the eliminated candidate will have their ballots added to the totals of their second choice. The process continues until a candidate earns a majority of votes (see Figure 10-1). Supporters of instant-runoff voting say it better reflects voter preferences than other systems. Critics say that its complexity confuses voters.

Districts

In states and localities, elected executives usually compete in **at-large elections**, meaning that they run in the entire state, county, city, or town. Legislators are different. U.S. House members run in **single-member districts**.[19] That is, states divide themselves into constituencies, and each elects its own member. (The smallest states each get only one seat apiece.) Most state legislatures and major city councils also have single-member districts, although some legislatures have multimember districts, and many smaller communities choose council members at large. District sizes vary widely. New Hampshire's State House of Representatives has 400 members, meaning an average district has just 3,291 people. Despite its greater size, California has only 80 members in its lower chamber, so the average member of the California Assembly represents 141 times as many people as his or her New Hampshire counterpart.[20]

The U.S. House, said Madison, was to have "an immediate dependence on, and an intimate sympathy with, the people."[21] Over time, it has become harder for House members to maintain that sympathy. During the nineteenth century, Congress periodically voted to increase House membership along with population. After the 1910 census, it set the figure at 435, which it made permanent in 1929. Population growth has since more than doubled the average House constituency, from 283,000 in 1930 to 710,000 in 2010. Bigger districts have meant less voter contact with lawmakers and greater complexity in representing constituents. Some have argued that the House should have a larger number of smaller districts, but the risk is that a bigger House would be costlier and less deliberative.

The distribution of seats causes other problems. Under the principle of "**one person, one vote**," which holds that everyone should have equal voting power in district elections, the Supreme Court has said that all House districts *within each state* should have equal populations. This standard does not rule out variances *among* states. After each census comes **reapportionment**, whereby every state gets a share of seats according to population. Those with higher growth gain at the expense of others. Because states cannot get fractions of seats, the distribution comes out uneven.

Aside from such discrepancies, the phrase "one person, one vote" is still misleading. Apportionment depends on *total* resident population, including minors and aliens, as well as adult citizens who abstain from voting. Therefore, districts with equal *populations* may have unequal *electorates*. One perspective is that the practice unfairly benefits politicians and interest groups in low-turnout districts. Another viewpoint is that the Constitution protects residents, not just voters, and that such protection is vital in low-turnout areas, which tend to be poor and vulnerable. An additional wrinkle is that the census fails to get a full count of poor people, ethnic minorities, and immigrants. The census must try to include all residents, including aliens here illegally. Undocumented immigrants shun government officials, so counting them is difficult.

While the federal government is in charge of the census and apportionment, state governments do the **redistricting**, the redrawing of congressional and state legislative district lines. Although a growing number of states use commissions, the most common method is still for the legislature to write the plan, which the governor may sign or veto.[22] Redistricting has partisan effects, so politicians care about party control of legislatures and governorships. The courts have ended the old practice of deliberately giving districts unequal populations, but mapmakers can still engage in

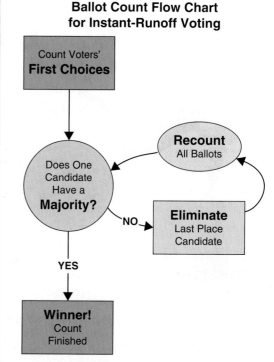

Ballot Count Flow Chart for Instant-Runoff Voting

In each round, your ballot counts for your favorite candidate who is still in the race.

FIGURE 10-1 An explanation of instant-runoff voting. SOURCE: Center for Voting and Democracy, 2011. http://www.fairvote .org/assets—resampled/Resized Image 300380-IRV-flow.jpg

© Bettmann/CORBIS

THE GERRY-MANDER.

After the 1810 census, the Democrat-Republicans, who controlled the Massachusetts Legislature, redrew state senate lines. Trying to keep their control, they created odd shapes such as the district shown here. Governor Elbridge Gerry signed the plan. Noting that this district resembled a salamander, foes called it a "Gerrymander." Note that Gerry pronounced his name with a hard *g* as in "gulf."

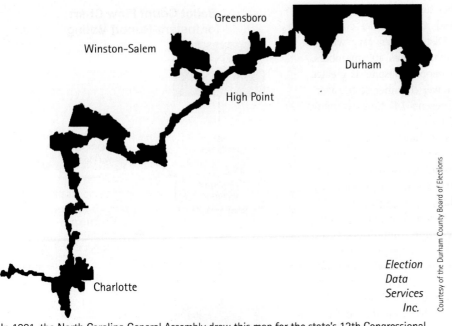

Greensboro

Winston-Salem

Durham

High Point

Charlotte

Election Data Services Inc.

Courtesy of the Durham County Board of Elections

In 1991, the North Carolina General Assembly drew this map for the state's 12th Congressional District. The intent was to bring as many African Americans as possible into the district. Court rulings later prompted the General Assembly to revise the map with a more compact shape.

gerrymandering. In this practice, the dominant side draws odd lines that favor its own candidates and does the following to the losing side:

- *packs* its vote into a few districts where lopsided elections waste its voting strength;
- *cracks*, or, fragments, its remaining vote among districts where the dominant side will win;
- *merges* the districts of its lawmakers so as to pit them against each other in primaries; or
- *isolates* its lawmakers from their bases of support by putting them in new districts with few voters from their previous ones.

Critics of gerrymandering argue that it reduces competition. But not everyone believes that competition necessarily serves good government. Close races increase the need for campaign money, which causes candidates to court special interests. California state senator Kevin Murray wrote that he represented a 65% Democratic district. Therefore, he said, "two out of three of my constituents are, presumably, happy with the guy they've got. If you redrew the district lines and turned it into a 50-50 district, only half would be happy—and the other half would not. What's so great about that?"[23]

For many years, states sometimes engaged in *racial* gerrymandering to dilute minorities' voting power.[24] Laws and court decisions eventually banned the practice. After the 1990 census, the U.S. Justice Department interpreted court rulings to make states maximize the number of **majority-minority districts**, where minority groups would dominate. Ironically, districts took on odd shapes as they reached for distant pockets of minority group members. One district in North Carolina wound through more than 100 miles to connect minority neighborhoods with a thin line. "I love the district because I can drive down I-85 with both car doors open and hit every person in the district," said one candidate.[25] In 1995, the Supreme Court ruled that such districts went too far by making race the "overriding and predominant" element. Writing for the majority, Justice Anthony Kennedy said that "carving electorates into racial blocs" undercuts the goal of nondiscrimination."[26] In dissent, Justice Ruth Bader Ginsburg wrote that such requirements were justified "to make once-subordinated people free and equal citizens."[27]

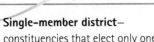

Single-member district— constituencies that elect only one member to a legislative body.

One person, one vote— a judicial principle holding that everyone should have equal voting power in district elections.

Reapportionment— a process that reallocates House seats to states in line with population changes. People often confuse this term with **redistricting**, which refers to the drawing of the district lines.

Redistricting— the drawing of boundaries for legislative districts, which usually takes place after the federal census.

Gerrymandering— the drawing of district lines, often in odd shapes, to benefit a party or constituency group.

Majority-minority district— an election district in which members of an ethnic or racial minority constitute a majority of votes.

Long and Short Ballots

Just as basic as the issue of competitiveness is the question of which offices should be elective in the first place. In the United States, the answer varies from place to place. Some states and localities have long ballots, with many elected officials. Texans choose their governor, lieutenant governor, attorney general, comptroller of public accounts, state treasurer, commissioner of the General Land Office, and commissioner of agriculture. In Tennessee, the governor is the only statewide elected official, apart from U.S. senators. Counties may elect officials such as treasurer, assessor, sheriff, and coroner. Many places elect judges.

In 2010, voters in Harris County, Texas, decided on dozens of offices, including 72 judges. *The Houston Chronicle* reported:

MYTHS AND MISINFORMATION

Campaign Legends

Many familiar stories about congressional and presidential campaigns turn out to be false.

The Shameless Extrovert

In 1950, Congressman George Smathers challenged incumbent Senator Claude Pepper in the Florida Democratic primary. According to a popular legend, Smathers took advantage of supposedly uneducated rural voters with a suggestive description of his foe:

> Are you aware that Claude Pepper is known all over Washington as a shameless extrovert? Not only that, but this man is reliably reported to practice nepotism with his sister-in-law, and he has a sister who was once a thespian in wicked New York. Worst of all, it is an established fact that Mr. Pepper before his marriage habitually practiced celibacy.[29]

Some books on political history have treated this story as fact. Actually, it was nothing more than a tall tale that reporters made up for their own amusement.

The Secret Plan

For decades, many books and articles have claimed that Richard Nixon in 1968 told voters that he had a "secret plan" to end the Vietnam War. Google "Nixon," "secret plan," and "Vietnam," and you will get tens of thousands of hits. But Nixon never used that phrase. Speechwriter Raymond Price explained:

That myth had its origin in the New Hampshire primary, when a wire-service reporter, new to the campaign, filed an article misinterpreting one line of Nixon's standard stump speech: that "a new administration will end the war and win the peace." We on the Nixon staff immediately pointed out, to all who would listen, that he had not claimed a "plan." Nixon himself told reporters that if he had one, he would have given it to President Johnson.[30]

"I Invented the Internet"

Ever since the 2000 presidential campaign, critics of former vice president Al Gore have lampooned him for claiming to have invented the Internet. The jibes, however, distort what he actually said:

> During my service in the United States Congress, I took the initiative in creating the Internet. I took the initiative in moving forward a whole range of initiatives that have proven to be important to our country's economic growth and environmental protection, improvements in our educational system.

Although the word *creating* may have been a stretch, Gore did indeed take the lead in turning a scientific communications network into the Internet that we know today. Robert Kahn and Vint Cerf, who did much of the design work on the Internet, said, "Al Gore was the first political leader to recognize the importance of the Internet and to promote and support its development."[31]

If it seems like that Harris County ballot you got in the mail is long, it is. Veteran election watchers say it is the longest they can recall.

The ballot is so long that it requires 61 cents to mail in your vote. Harris County Democratic Party Chairman Gerry Birnberg joked, "We're real close to a poll tax here."

Harris County Clerk Beverly Kaufman recently gave a vivid demonstration of the daunting list voters face Nov. 2 by unfolding a ballot that extended to nearly her height.

Voters are "overwhelmed," said the Houston-area League of Women Voters president, Nancy Parra.[28]

Longer ballots are arguably more democratic because they allow the people to choose more officials. Like ballot measures, they give rise to more campaigns and thus more opportunities for citizen activism. Nevertheless, they also pose challenges for citizen deliberation. Chief executives and legislators deal with many issues, and voters may know something about some of them, but what can the average voter know about a coroner's office?

PRESIDENTIAL AND CONGRESSIONAL RACES

MAJOR ISSUE

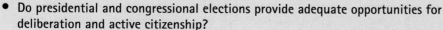

- Do presidential and congressional elections provide adequate opportunities for deliberation and active citizenship?

Presidential nomination candidates lavish attention on the early contests in Iowa and New Hampshire while often ignoring the last primaries. In a 2012 Iowa Republican caucus, voters deliberate about their choices.

In contrast with states and localities, the federal government has just four categories of elected office: president and vice president (who run together), House member, and senator. There are no federal initiatives, referenda, or recalls.

Presidential elections are unique. The president and vice president are the only officials who answer to a national electorate. Contests for the White House generally draw more voter interest and turnout than any other kind of election. General elections for the House and Senate take place in even-numbered years, either coinciding with presidential races or taking place halfway through a presidential term. As we shall see, there is a strong connection between presidential and congressional politics.

Nominations

Delegate—a person entitled to vote at a party convention for the nomination of candidates.

Since the 1830s, national party conventions have formally chosen the presidential nominees who run in the general election (see Chapter 9). Until the early twentieth century, state party leaders picked the **delegates**, the people who made up the conventions and thus formally chose the nominee. In 1904, Florida became the first state to choose delegates through primaries. Although some states followed its lead, party leaders still drove the process for decades. During this time, many candidates either shunned primaries or ran in a select few, to prove their appeal. In 1960, John F. Kennedy won the Democratic primary in West Virginia, the state with the lowest percentage of his fellow Roman Catholics. Kennedy ran in this primary to show party leaders that a Catholic could get Protestant votes.

In 1968, Democratic vice president Hubert Humphrey became the last major party candidate to win a presidential nomination without winning a primary. During the 1970s, new party rules and state laws enabled rank-and-file party voters to choose most of the delegates. In the most common method, the names of candidates appear on the state's primary ballot.

Instead of primaries, some states hold caucuses, where voters meet in schoolrooms and other public places to pick delegates to other meetings that in turn will choose delegates to the national convention. Some states have changed their delegate selection method from time to time, and some use a different method for each party. Caucuses require more time from the voters than primaries, so turnout tends to be lower. In 2012, for instance, twice as many people voted in the New Hampshire Republican primary as in the Iowa Republican caucuses, even though Iowa had more than twice the population of New Hampshire.[32]

FOCUS QUESTION

Does the contemporary system of presidential nominations produce better candidates than the old, boss-led system?

Aspects of the post-1960s system have prompted concern. First, winning a nomination has become costly. In 2011, before a single primary or caucus had taken place, the contenders for the 2012 Republican nomination had raised a grand total of $156 million.[33] In the 1970s, candidates could start with a modest war chest and then use early victories to attract contributions for the later primaries and caucuses. Today, however, candidates must raise huge sums ahead of time. Unable to do so, many drop out early. Some say that the process favors the best fund-raisers instead of the best leaders, while others respond that the money flows to those who have already built a strong base of support.

Second, the process is arguably less deliberative than in the old system. Party leaders carefully weighed the candidates' qualities, usually from firsthand acquaintance. Ordinary voters tend to know less about the candidates. Among Republican and Republican-leaning voters at the start of 2012, 76% knew that Newt Gingrich had been House speaker, but just 59% knew that Romney had been governor of Massachusetts, and only 51% knew that Representative Ron Paul (R-TX) opposed military involvement in Afghanistan.[34]

The Electoral College

Late in the summer, party conventions formally select the presidential nominees. Then comes the general election campaign, which is different in one crucial respect from other contests. We choose the president not by direct popular vote but through the **Electoral College**. The Constitution provides each state a number of **electors** equal to its number of House seats plus two senators. The Electoral College has 538 electors, corresponding to 435 House members, 100 senators, plus the 3 electors that the Twenty-third Amendment provides to the District of Columbia.

According to Alexander Hamilton, electors should be those "most capable of analyzing the qualities adapted to the station and acting under circumstances favorable to deliberation." Such a body, he said, "will be most likely to possess the information and discernment requisite to so complicated an investigation."[35] The Constitution does *not* require a popular vote on electors. In 2000, the Supreme Court observed, "The individual citizen has no federal constitutional right to vote for electors for the President of the United States unless and until the state legislature chooses a statewide election as the means to implement its power to appoint members of the electoral college."[36] In the first few elections, legislatures chose electors in about half the states. Even then, however, it was clear that the Electoral College would not be the deliberative body that Hamilton described: the election became a matter of party politics. By the 1830s, nearly all the states had provided for popular choice of the electors, which is true for every state today.

In each state, each candidate has a different slate of electors. In most states, party organizations or conventions nominate electors.[37] Only a few states put the names of would-be electors on the ballot. Everywhere else, voters only see the presidential candidates. In 48 states, if a candidate wins the popular vote—no matter how narrowly—the entire slate of electors is victorious. That is, all of the state's electoral votes go to this candidate. The two exceptions are Maine and Nebraska, which use the **district system for the Electoral College**. In these two states, the statewide winner gets two at-large electors, and the choice of the other electors depends on the popular vote within each congressional district. These states could thus have split slates of electors, which happened in Nebraska in 2008, when Barack Obama took one electoral vote even though McCain won statewide.

When presidential candidates and their advisers lay out campaign plans, the electoral college is uppermost in their minds. In deciding where to put their scarce campaign resources, campaigns can divide the states into three categories: those that they are very likely to win, those that they are very likely to lose, and those that could go either way. They spend relatively little time and money on the first two in order to concentrate on the third. In recent elections, these "battleground" or "swing" states have included Ohio, Florida, and Iowa, among others. On election night, observers focus less on the national popular vote than on the results in the swing states.

The electors meet on the first Monday after the second Wednesday in December. Although the term "electoral college" suggests a single body, the nation's electors never gather in one place. Instead, they meet in their own states (usually in the capital) and the District of Columbia. At these meetings, they officially cast their votes for president and vice president. (There is no constitutional requirement for a secret ballot, and many states used signed ballots.) The formal counting of the votes takes place during a joint session of Congress in January. A majority of electoral votes (currently 270) is necessary to elect the president and vice president. If no one wins that total, the House of Representatives would choose the president from the three candidates with the most electoral votes. In this process, which last came into play after the election of 1824, each state delegation would have one vote, with a majority necessary for election. Even though the president and vice president run together in the general election, different houses of Congress choose them in case of Electoral College deadlock. If no vice presidential candidate wins a majority of electoral votes, the Senate would choose from the top two candidates.

The Electoral College may deny victory to the popular-vote winner (see Table 10-1). In the 1824 election, the House chose John Quincy Adams even though Andrew Jackson had led the popular tally in states where voters chose electors. In 1876 and 1888, the loser of the popular vote won an electoral majority. Some analysts also contend that John Kennedy lost the popular vote in 1960. His name did not appear on the Alabama presidential ballot that year; instead, Alabamians voted for individual electors. Of the 11 who won, 5 had

Electoral College—the mechanism for formal election of the president and vice president. The Electoral College consists of 538 members, or electors. Each state has a number of electors equal to the number of its U.S. senators and House members. The District of Columbia has a number of electors equal to those of the smallest state. The electors meet in their own states and vote for president and vice president. To win, a candidate must have a majority of electoral votes (at least 270).

Elector—a person entitled to vote in the Electoral College.

District system for the Electoral College—a process currently in place in Maine and Nebraska, whereby the statewide presidential winner gets two at-large electors, and the choice of the other electors depends on the popular vote within each congressional district.

TABLE 10-1 PRESIDENTS WHO WON WITHOUT A POPULAR MAJORITY

This list shows the presidents who got less than 50% of the popular vote. In four cases, the opposing candidate got more popular votes: Adams in 1824, Hayes in 1876, Harrison in 1888, and Bush in 2000.

Year	President	Percentage
1824	John Q. Adams (D-R)	29.8%
1844	James K. Polk (D)	49.3
1848	Zachary Taylor (W)	47.3
1856	James Buchanan (D)	45.3
1860	Abraham Lincoln (R)	39.9
1876	Rutherford B. Hayes (R)	47.9
1880	James A. Garfield (R)	48.3
1884	Grover Cleveland (D)	48.8
1888	Benjamin Harrison (R)	47.8
1892	Grover Cleveland (D)	46.0
1912	Woodrow Wilson (D)	41.8
1916	Woodrow Wilson (D)	49.3
1948	Harry S Truman (D)	49.5
1960	John F. Kennedy (D)	49.7
1968	Richard M. Nixon (R)	43.4
1992	William J. Clinton (D)	43.0
1996	William J. Clinton (D)	49.0
2000	George W. Bush (R)	47.8

© Cengage Learning 2014

pledged to support the party nominee, and 6 were unpledged Democrats who then voted for segregationist Senator Harry F. Byrd (D-VA). Most reference books credit Alabama's entire popular Democratic vote to JFK, but by following the Electoral College split, one could assign him just 5/11 of the total. By this method, Alabama gave him 147,295 votes instead of 324,050. Instead of winning the nationwide popular vote by 119,450—the figure that most books cite—he actually lost to Nixon by 57,305.[38] This example shows that there is no official national popular vote total, only an official electoral vote.

Soon after Election Day of 2000, tallies showed that George W. Bush had run about half a million votes behind Vice President Albert Gore Jr. Even apart from the Florida recount controversy, many observers wondered how Americans would react to putting the loser of the popular vote into the White House. Just after the Supreme Court decision in *Bush v. Gore*, 80% of respondents told a CNN survey that they would regard Bush as a legitimate president.[39] Yet polls have consistently found majorities in favor of a direct popular vote.[40] Most people find force in the argument that the plurality's will should prevail. So why does the Electoral College live on? Each state has two electoral votes in addition to the number corresponding to House seats, so many people in less populous states think that it gives them extra influence. Because three-quarters of state legislatures (or of state ratifying conventions) are required to approve a constitutional amendment, small states could block the change.

Supporters of the Electoral College cite the national interest. They argue that it upholds the federal system by drawing attention to statewide issues. Candidates must contest a broad array of states, whereas a direct popular election would enable them to win by running up large majorities in a few urban areas.[41] Also, in closely divided states, the candidates have a strong incentive to deal with state and local officials and the issues they care about because in nearly all the states the winner of the popular vote, no matter how small the margin, wins all the electoral votes. This **winner-take-all system** also protects the two-party system by making it difficult for third and fourth parties to score electoral votes. In an argument relevant to the 2000 election, supporters say that a direct election would lead to endless recounts. Instead of challenging the outcome in one state, the loser could seek recounts nationwide.

Winner–take–all system—the system by which the presidential candidate who wins a plurality of a state's popular votes will win all of its electoral votes.

Opponents of the Electoral College say that it causes candidates to overlook large portions of the country. Campaigns write off states where one candidate has a large lead, and focus on a handful of large swing states. FairVote, an advocacy group that seeks to reform or abolish the Electoral College, analyzed appearances by major party candidates in the fall of 2008. It found that 57% took place in only four states with only 17% of the nation's eligible voters: Ohio, Florida, Pennsylvania, and Virginia.[42] Such strategies have consequences for active citizenship. In the battleground states, parties and campaigns mount stronger get-out-the-vote drives. There is less effort elsewhere. Between 2004 and 2008, turnout increased much more in the most competitive states than in the rest.[43] In the battleground states, citizens enjoy many opportunities to volunteer for campaign work. Citizens in the other states are largely spectators.

Congressional Elections

There is no Electoral College for the selection of lawmakers. Under the original Constitution, however, the people did not directly choose senators as they chose House members. That task belonged to the state legislatures. The idea was that this "select appointment" would produce senators of high quality and that the senators would represent the views and interests of state governments.[44] The Progressives challenged this view, arguing that senators had become pawns of special interests. In 1913, they won ratification of the Seventeenth Amendment, providing for the direct election of senators.

Candidates for both chambers of Congress must face the people, yet House and Senate elections are different. As we have seen, House members represent districts that may heavily favor one party or the other. Senators represent entire states that usually encompass a wider variety of voters and thus may be more competitive. Senators also tend to draw more prominent challengers, many of whom have served as House members, governors, or other high-profile officials.[45] Whereas House members serve two-year terms, senators serve six-year terms. With greater time in office, senators can focus more on public policy, but they may also lose touch with constituents and let their campaign muscles get flabby.[46] Accordingly, senators often have tougher reelection contests.

The outcomes of House and Senate races depend in part on national conditions. During a presidential race in which voters decide along party lines, the winning candidate may have a **coattail effect**, in which congressional candidates of the same party may get more votes than they would otherwise. (In other words, they ride on the presidential candidate's "coattails.") In even-numbered years when there is no presidential race come **midterm elections** (see Table 10-2). Since 1934, the president's party has lost House seats in every midterm—with two exceptions. In 1998, the public disapproved of Republican efforts to impeach President Clinton, and Democrats gained seats. In 2002, President Bush still enjoyed support stemming from his response to the 2001 terrorist attacks and Republicans picked up seats. The president's party usually loses Senate seats as well, though not as consistently. Scholars have offered various explanations. Some have pointed to economic conditions and presidential popularity, which may slump in the middle of a term.[47] Others say that the absence of presidential coattails leave some lawmakers vulnerable to defeat.[48] Still others say that it represents an effort to check presidential power.

So far, we have taken a broad overview of elections and their background. Now it is time to consider the mechanics of elections and campaigns. When it comes to voting, as will soon be clear, the word *mechanics* is not merely a figure of speech.

FOCUS QUESTION

Should we continue to use the Electoral College for selecting the president?

Coattail effect—the tendency for a popular candidate for higher office to draw votes for other candidates of the same party.

Midterm elections—elections that take place in even-numbered years when there is no presidential election. In a midterm election, the offices up for contest include all U.S. House seats, about one-third of U.S. Senate seats, as well as most governorships and state legislative seats.

THE AMERICAN ELECTORAL PROCESS
MAJOR ISSUE

- How does the American electoral process work?

On Election Night 2000, television networks first projected that Vice President Al Gore had won Florida. They later said that Texas governor George W. Bush had carried the state,

TABLE 10-2	LOSSES/GAINS BY THE PRESIDENT'S PARTY IN MIDTERM ELECTIONS		
		House	Senate
1934	D	9	10
1938	D	−71	−6
1942	D	−45	−9
1946	D	−55	−12
1950	D	−29	−6
1954	R	−18	−1
1958	R	−47	−13
1962	D	−5	3
1966	D	−47	−4
1970	R	−12	3
1974	R	−48	−5
1978	D	−15	−3
1982	R	−26	1
1986	R	−5	−8
1990	R	−7	−1
1994	D	−54	−10
1998	D	4	0
2002	R	8	1
2006	R	−30	−6
2010	D	−63	−4

SOURCE: Harold W. Stanley and Richard G. Niemi, *Vital Statistics on American Politics 2011–2012* (Washington, DC: CQ Press, 2011), 42.

thus winning a bare majority in the Electoral College. Then Bush's lead dwindled, and the networks reversed themselves again, saying the state was too close to call. Out of more than 5 million votes in Florida, only a few hundred separated the two candidates. For 36 days, Republicans and Democrats fought in court over which ballots should count. Finally, in the controversial case of *Bush v. Gore*, the U.S. Supreme Court voted 7–2 that Florida's method of recounting ballots violated the Constitution's equal protection clause. A 5–4 majority ruled that no more time was left for recounts, effectively sealing the election for Bush.

Scholars debate the wisdom of that decision, but everyone agrees that the fight underscored the importance of voting procedures. The next two presidential election outcomes were not in serious dispute, but there was little doubt that voting procedures could lead to messy elections in the future. To understand American elections, then, we have to know the rules for designing, casting, and counting the ballots.

Ballot Design

Since the introduction of the Australian ballot (see Chapter 9), American voters have used government-designed ballots in the privacy of booths. Ballot designs differ by state and often by county. Each design has advantages and drawbacks.

Hand-counted paper ballots were once common, and some rural areas still use them. Hand counts are slow, error prone, and open to fraud. Corrupt officials can either stuff the box for their candidates or spoil their opponents' ballots. To avoid such problems, many jurisdictions adopted mechanical lever machines for much of the twentieth century. Although an improvement on paper ballots, these machines had a large number of moving parts, which increased the risk of malfunction. In the 1960s, some jurisdictions started using punch cards, on which the voters pierce pre-scored holes. Sometimes, voters failed to punch all the way through, resulting in uncounted votes.[49] After the 2000 election, many jurisdictions switched to optically scanned paper ballots. With this method, voters fill in circles, as students do with the SAT. This system is more reliable, although light or stray marks can spoil these ballots.

The newest method is electronic voting, including touch screen systems (see the accompanying photo). So far, the record is mixed. Some places have had smooth counts, but as the *New York Times* reports, the machines may fail in odd ways: "[V]oters report that their choices 'flip' from one candidate to another before their eyes; machines crash or begin to count backward; votes simply vanish. (In the 80-person town of Waldenburg, Ark., touch-screen machines tallied zero votes for one mayoral candidate in 2006—even though he's pretty sure he voted for himself.)."[50] The possibility of hackers manipulating election outcomes has led to deep skepticism about electronic voting, and some jurisdictions have abandoned touch screens in favor of optical scan ballots.

Thus, the design of the ballot may influence the results. Many politicians think that an advantage goes to the candidate whose name appears first.[51] Some states try to avoid bias by listing the candidates for each office at random. In New York, each party's candidates appear on the same line, whose placement depends on the party's showing in the last race for governor. California lists candidates' occupations, while Arkansas lists their current public office, if any. This practice may benefit those who already hold office.

A Miami-Dade election official tests the accuracy of a touch screen voting machine on August 4, 2010, in Miami.

Photo by Joe Raedle/Getty Images

Convenience and Inconvenience

General elections for all federal offices and most state offices occur in even-numbered years on the first Tuesday after the first Monday in November. As we discuss in Chapter 7, most states require voters to register in advance—a hurdle that keeps a significant number of people from casting ballots. Because the election takes places on a weekday, many voters must take the trouble of getting to the booth early in the morning or in the evening. When they do reach polling places, they may find long lines—a serious problem for people whose responsibilities leave them with little time to spare.

In response, most states now let voters cast their ballots before Election Day without having to file an excuse. In some states, early voters may use booths at designated stations. Another alternative is the absentee or mail ballot, which the voter may fill out at home. By federal law, states must allow members of the armed forces, their families, and citizens living abroad to vote absentee in all federal elections.[52] Oregon has gone the farthest and now runs elections entirely by mail. Nationwide, **early voting** and absentee voting—or "convenience voting"—accounted for about 30% of the ballots in the 2010 election.[53]

For Americans overseas, however, mail voting still presents challenges. Despite federal and state efforts to improve the process, military personnel, students on

Early voting—a procedure by which people may cast ballots at designated stations before Election Day.

Lieutenant Lynn Shradley helps Sergeant David DaSilva, left, apply for an absentee ballot at an election fair at Fort Campbell, Kentucky, on September 9, 2004.

AP Photo/Christopher Berkey

study abroad programs, and other citizens living abroad have sometimes found that election officials do not respond to their requests for ballots, or that they received the wrong ballot, or that they received the right ballot but too late to send it back on time.[54]

Not everyone approves of convenience voting. Political scientist Norman Ornstein worries that it undercuts voter deliberation: "During the final stages of a campaign, when the pressure increases, more voters are apt to pay close attention. Debates are held, October surprises pop up. Candidates react differently under the pressure, and events can change the whole context of the election." He also thinks it is bad for citizenship: "It cheapens the voting process. Voting is one of the most precious privileges of a free society (as is the freedom not to vote). In America, individuals join their neighbors at a local polling place, underscoring their role as a part of a collective society, then go into a curtained booth to make their choices as free individuals."[55]

The reform group Common Cause takes a different view, arguing that more reliance on mail voting could boost turnout. It also contends that ballot box voting may hamper deliberation, since "voters naturally want to get the process over quickly and may not take as much time as they should to consider their choices." Mail voting, it says, gives voters "greater time to deliberate and research their choices."[56]

Despite the greater availability of mail ballots, most voters still cast their ballots on Election Day. During presidential elections, voting hours spark controversy. Because the United States spans five time zones, western polling places stay open long after they have closed in the East. The winner of the presidential election is often clear before millions of westerners have voted. Some observers have said that turnout suffers, because many people figure that the big race is already over. Uniform voting hours might help, but that approach would require either late closing times in the East or early opening times in the West. Canadian law forbids the transmission of election results from areas where polling places have closed to those where they are still open. In the United States, however, courts would probably rule such a ban an unconstitutional breach of press freedom. In any event, the Internet now makes it hard to enforce information blackouts.

WHAT WINS ELECTIONS?

MAJOR ISSUE

- **What contributes to success or failure on the campaign trail?**

The previous section laid out some of the rules of the game. Now we turn to the question of how the players win and lose. Focusing on campaign strategy and tactics, news accounts often suggest that candidates' fates are entirely in their own hands. By contrast, scholarly studies have explained elections by pointing to social and economic forces beyond the candidates' control. Neither perspective is complete. Election outcomes depend both on impersonal forces and on the very personal efforts of candidates and their supporters.

Party

Ticket splitting—the practice of voting for candidates of different parties for different offices in the same election.

Party identification offers very strong clues as to how people will vote (see Chapter 9). In the 2010 midterm election, 91% of self-identified Democrats voted for a Democratic House candidate while 94% of Republicans voted GOP.[57] Those who identify with a party often support its candidates for all offices. Sometimes, however, people will vote for one party's candidate for one office, another party's candidate for a second office, and so on. This **ticket splitting** appeared to be on the rise during the middle of the twentieth century but had declined by the early years of the twenty-first century. In 1988, 148 House districts voted for congressional and presidential candidates of different parties. Twenty years later, that figure was down to 83.[58]

In areas where the candidate's party is strong, the campaign will emphasize party ties and try to boost turnout by party members. Where the party is weak, the candidate will downplay party connections and use other appeals to seek votes from ticket-splitters.

Demographics

As Chapter 9 explains, characteristics such as gender and ethnicity affect partisan choice. The "gender gap" came into play during the 2008 election, when Obama had a 13-point lead among women but only a 1-point lead among men.[59] Gender and family status were a potent mix, with married men with children favoring McCain 54% to 45% and unmarried women with children favoring Obama 74% to 25%.[60] McCain got only 4% among African-American voters, while winning a majority of whites. As with recent elections, GOP support rose with worship attendance. Also as in other elections, the Republican vote tended to rise with income level, with an important exception: Obama won a majority of those making $200,000 a year or more, reflecting his appeal to highly educated professionals. (See Figure 10-2 for a 2008 exit poll.)

Knowing demographic patterns, campaigners engage in **mobilization**, the effort to motivate supportive voter groups to turn out in higher numbers. In the late twentieth century, Republicans mobilized conservative Christians and gun owners, while Democrats worked

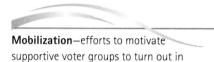

Mobilization—efforts to motivate supportive voter groups to turn out in higher numbers.

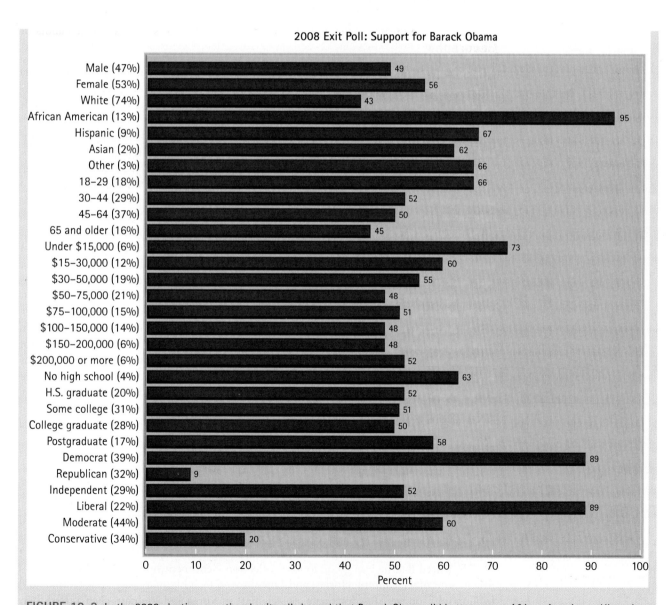

FIGURE 10-2 In the 2008 election, a national exit poll showed that Barack Obama did better among African Americans, Hispanics, women, lower-income groups, educated professionals, and younger voters. The figure shows the percentage of each category voting for Obama. (Figures in parentheses are each category's share of the electorate.)

with union members and ethnic minorities. Drawing on information about contributions and group memberships, computer databases now let campaigners spot individual households that they can sway. Recent campaigns have seen the rise of microtargeting, whereby these households got phone calls and mail pieces aiming at their specific interests. The Republicans seemed to have an advantage in 2004, but by 2008 the Democrats had surpassed them in microtargeting. A Republican consultant told the *New York Times*, "The quality and the quantity of their ground game is measurably better than the Republican campaign of 2004 or the McCain campaign. Obama has better deployed microtargeting and is using it more."[61]

Some worry that such techniques hurt citizen involvement. In the past, the limits of technology forced campaigns to seek votes more inclusively, hoping that a broad brush would sweep at least some votes their way.[62] Microtargeting focuses on some households while ignoring most others, yet national turnout did rise in both 2004 and 2008. Although the effect may have been greater in some places than in others, microtargeting probably contributed to the increase. Moreover, as we discuss in Chapter 7, the high-tech turnout efforts fostered active citizenship by enlisting large numbers of volunteers.

Geography

Whether because of economic circumstances, housing discrimination, or simple preference, members of demographic groups often tend to cluster in certain places. This clustering affects election results in those areas. For instance, African-American neighborhoods tend to vote heavily Democratic.

Geography shapes elections in other ways. Different areas have distinct political cultures and traditions that affect voting patterns. Even though Connecticut is affluent, its social liberalism helps Democrats. Conversely, Mississippi is the poorest state, but its social conservatism has helped the GOP carry it in most recent presidential elections. Geography also affects voters' opinions on the issues, especially when policies may benefit one area at the expense of another. Like Mississippi, West Virginia is a poor state, but it voted Republican in the presidential elections of 2000, 2004, and 2008. Democratic candidates have associated themselves with environmental policies that have arguably burdened coal mining, a major source of jobs and income for that state. Moreover, West Virginia has many hunters, who take issue with Democratic support for gun control, and its many conservative Christians tend to agree with Republicans on social issues. Figure 10-3 shows another effect of geography by adjusting an electoral map of Republican and Democratic states for population size.

In deciding where to spend campaign resources, strategists ponder these patterns. In 2008, Republicans ignored Illinois, a Democratic-leaning state that would surely vote for its native son, Barack Obama. Democrats, likewise, never made a serious effort in heavily Republican Utah. Instead, both parties focused on states that could have gone either way. Cross-pressures made Ohio and Pennsylvania key battlegrounds. Obama benefited from the presence of labor unions and ethnic minorities, whereas McCain drew strength from suburban and rural voters. In the end, Obama carried both, in part because of national forces that we shall now examine.

Good Times, Bad Times

Voters usually side with the party holding the White House but turn against it in bad times. Of the many dimensions of "good" or "bad" times, two are critical. First, Americans tend to spurn the presidential party when the nation is in a war or international crisis with no end in sight. In the summer of 1864, the Civil War seemed likely to drag on, and President Lincoln feared that he was going to lose reelection. Sentiment turned after the capture of Atlanta and other Union victories, and Lincoln won by a big margin. Harry Truman and Lyndon Johnson were less fortunate, as stalemate in Korea and Vietnam checkmated their hopes for reelection. Both opted not to run again.

In 1991, President George H. W. Bush led the United States to victory in the Gulf War. So why did he lose the 1992 election to Bill Clinton? "The economy, stupid" was the motto

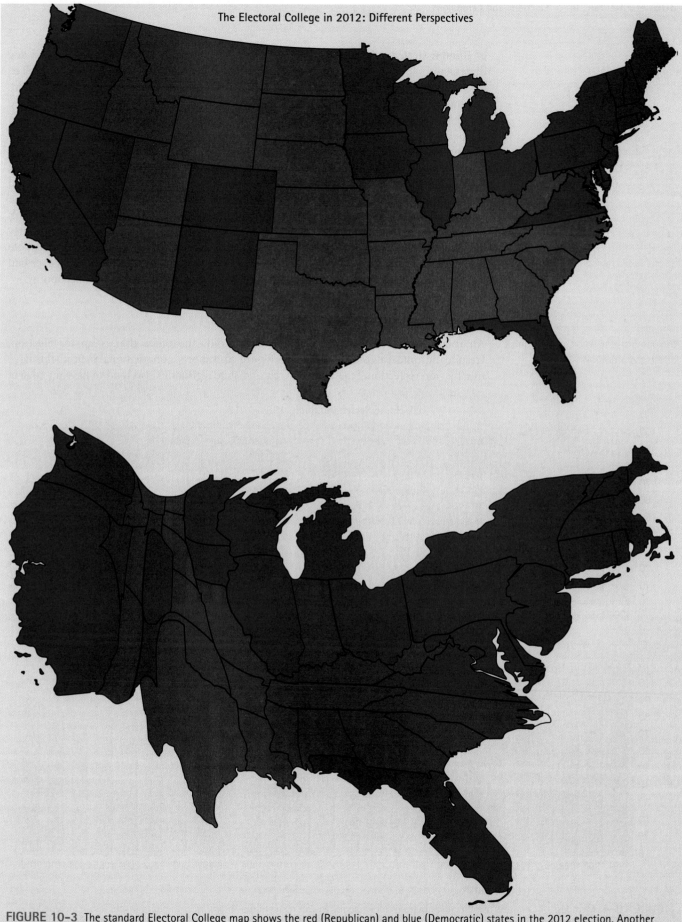

The Electoral College in 2012: Different Perspectives

FIGURE 10-3 The standard Electoral College map shows the red (Republican) and blue (Democratic) states in the 2012 election. Another perspective, however, adjusts the map, changing state sizes to reflect population size.
SOURCE: © 2012 M.E.J. Newman.

of Clinton strategist James Carville, and it provides a good summary of the second key dimension. When the economy is growing briskly, the incumbent party tends to do well in elections for most offices. When the economy is struggling, the other party tends to gain. The most dramatic case was the Great Depression, which brought Franklin Roosevelt to the White House and entrenched Democratic majorities in Congress for years. The recession of 1991–1992 was far milder and had actually ended by Election Day, but its memory was still too fresh for Bush to overcome.

In 2000, a panel of political scientists made forecasts of the presidential election. Basing their calculations on such elements as the strong economy, six of the seven predictions had Gore winning.[63] Although Bush won the White House, the models were not wildly wrong, as Gore did take 50.3% of the two-party vote. Eight years later, conditions were different. The economy was ailing, President Bush was deeply unpopular, and the Republican Party had held the presidency for eight years. Under such circumstances, Americans usually vote for change, and accordingly, most models forecast an Obama victory.[64] If McCain ever had a chance, he lost it in mid-September, when a financial crisis shook the world economy.

The Power of Incumbency

Incumbent—one who currently holds an elected office.

An **incumbent** is the person who currently holds the office that is up for election. Despite the upheavals of recent years, as Figure 10-4 shows, congressional incumbents have usually won reelection. Statewide officials and state legislators also tend to have an edge at

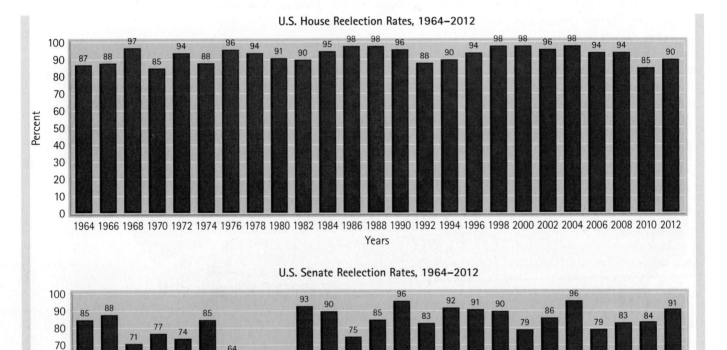

FIGURE 10-4 Members of Congress use the advantages of incumbency to win reelection at high rates. The data in the figure include primaries and general elections. The results for 2012 are current as of press time.

the polls.[65] One reason is obvious: victory in one election shows that a candidate has the skills and support necessary to succeed in the next.

As we shall also see, fund-raising is an example of an **incumbency advantage**. The trappings of office can help as well. For example, each member of the U.S. House may hire up to 18 full-time and 4 part-time employees.[66] Senators' personal staffs vary by state population. State legislatures vary a great deal in staff, though most have more than in past decades.[67] Although personal aides perform a variety of jobs, they have at least one goal in common: helping the official appeal to constituents. Efficient handling of correspondence is essential to this goal. When an office gets a letter or e-mail from an average constituent, it typically goes not to the elected official but to an entry-level aide who drafts the response or "personalizes" a form letter. An electronic printer then adds a genuine-looking signature. Most people do not know what happens backstage, so the "personal" response impresses them.

Officeholders and their staffs spend much of their time bringing government benefits to their constituency and helping individual voters with government problems, such as slow processing of a passport. Most elected officials now have Web sites inviting constituents to ask for help.

Incumbency advantage—the electoral benefits that come with holding office, such as visibility and staff.

Message

Obviously, a campaign needs a message: the reason why people should vote a certain way. As the discussion of incumbency suggests, officeholders may focus on their record of accomplishment. Such a message explains what the candidate has done for individuals and the broader community, with the understanding that he or she will keep up this level of performance during the next term of office. A pithy expression of this idea was the 1966 reelection slogan of Governor Nelson Rockefeller (R-NY): "He's done a lot. He'll do more."

Nonincumbent candidates may emphasize their qualifications. They want voters to know that they have the training and experience to do the job, which is why it may be a benefit or burden when official ballot materials list their occupation. At the presidential level, candidates want to assure voters that they could handle a crisis. "Think about it," said the narrator of a 1968 Nixon television ad, "who is the one man who has the experience and the qualifications to lead America in these troubled, dangerous times? Nixon's the one."[68] Stressing experience does not always work. Of the contenders for the 2012 Republican nomination, Jon Huntsman arguably had the strongest background: White House staff assistant, Deputy Assistant Secretary of Commerce, Deputy U.S. Trade Representative, ambassador to Singapore and China, CEO of a corporation, and governor of Utah. He scored about 2% in national polls of Republicans and exited the race in January without having won any primaries or caucuses.

Candidates want to show that they identify with their constituents and empathize with their problems. They march in local parades, assist in relief efforts when disaster strikes the community, and visit groups of senior citizens. Candidates may go to great lengths to display devotion to the constituency. In 1988, former general Pete Dawkins ran for the Senate from New Jersey, even though he had only moved there the year before. He claimed, "I've never found a single place that had as good people or as much promise as I've found right here in our Garden State." Suggesting that Dawkins was merely an opportunist who came to the state to seek office, his opponent ran ads saying, "C'mon Pete, be real."[69]

Issues are often a major part of a candidate's message. When they can afford it, candidates commission polls to identify the voters' concerns and beliefs, as well as the broad attitudes that underlie them. This information allows candidates to craft their issue positions to maximum benefit. As two distinguished political scientists write, "Candidates

RICHARD B. LEVINE/Newscom

The Obama-Biden Web site.

need to understand these beliefs if they are going to frame their policy issues appropriately. A pro-choice policy position might be framed in terms of individual freedom, for example; a flat-tax proposal might go to fundamental fairness."[70]

Candidates may discuss issues, but are they deliberating? Many people believe that television has made it difficult for candidates to do so. Regular news programs tend to give them little time to discuss policy. Most campaign advertisements run only 30 seconds, but brevity does not always mean lack of substance. With careful use of words and graphics, an ad can convey a good deal of information in 30 seconds. Moreover, campaigns usually run a number of broadcast ads, often with each conveying some additional information.

In races for the presidency and other offices, candidates take part in broadcast debates. Says political scientist Amy Gutmann, president of the University of Pennsylvania, "Nobody seems to be listening to anybody, let alone taking the views of their opponents into account in formulating their own positions. Deliberation is lacking in the presidential debates, in entertainment programming . . . and in most televised news interviews—by correspondents who answer their own questions and interviewees who answer none."[71] According to scholar Stephen Bates, debates matter because we experience them together: "By giving us a nearly universal political experience, debates have thus become a vehicle for our public deliberation."[72]

In many ways, technology has increased the volume of issue information. Thanks to C-SPAN, YouTube, and streaming video, viewers can see many campaign speeches in full length. Most candidates now have Web sites that include detailed position papers and video presentations. Some independent sites specialize in scrutinizing campaign material. The Annenberg Political Fact Check (www.factcheck.org) monitors the accuracy of broadcast ads, debate statements, speeches, interviews, and news releases. Candidates set up social networking sites to allow supporters to get in touch with one another and share ideas. Ordinary citizens debate issues on these sites, sometimes in great detail.

Attacks

Many worry about election tactics that focus on the opponent's faults. Most agree that negative campaigns can have an impact, but they disagree about their value. One argument is that negative campaigning turns people away from politics and thus depresses voter turnout.[73] At the same time, evidence indicates that negative campaigning may stimulate voter interest and increase turnout among partisans.[74] Many attack ads lack substance, but political scientist John Geer finds that "negative ads are 50% more likely to focus on policy than positive ads. Negative ads are also five times more likely to document their claims than positive ads. Finally, negative ads are two times more likely to be specific when mentioning issues than positive ads."[75]

Today's attacks are tame in comparison with those of the past. In 1800, some Federalists warned of the doom that would follow a victory by Thomas Jefferson: "Are you prepared to see your dwellings in flames, hoary hairs bathed in blood, female chastity violated, or children writhing on the pike and the halbert?"[76] In the 1858 Lincoln-Douglas debates, which many cite as the pinnacle of high-minded policy discussion, the candidates made harsh accusations about each other's records.

Even advocates of negative campaigning acknowledge that it can get out of hand. The American Association of Political Consultants has a

A 2012 Romney ad appealed to voters who had previously supported President Obama.

KAREN BLEIER/AFP/Getty Images

code of ethics, which includes promises to refrain from falsehoods and to document any criticism of an opponent.[77] The code has no enforcement mechanism, however. Some states have enacted voluntary codes of fair campaign practices, in which candidates may pledge to run on the issues and avoid character attacks. Such pledges have little effect. One California pollster said of his state's code, "Nobody gives a darn about it and nobody ever did."[78] Ironically, just about the only time the California code comes up in a statewide campaign is when one candidate attacks another for allegedly violating it.[79]

FOCUS

QUESTION

From the standpoint of democratic citizenship, what are the costs and benefits of negative campaigning?

CAMPAIGN FINANCE AND MANAGEMENT
MAJOR ISSUE

- How do candidates raise money and organize their campaigns?

It costs money to air ads and carry out other campaign tasks. It takes strong leadership to make sure that the campaign uses the money effectively and efficiently. An old military saying applies here as well: amateurs talk about strategy, while professionals talk about logistics—the day-to-day management of resources and people.

The amount of campaign spending and the structure of the organization will vary widely by the office at stake and the competitiveness of the race. A candidate for the city council of a very small community can probably run the campaign from a kitchen table while spending just a few thousand dollars. Candidates for higher office must spend much more, hiring staff, renting office space, and buying ads. In 2010, House incumbents seeking reelection spent an average of $1.5 million, while senators spent $11.2 million.[80] Spending for Senate campaigns can vary greatly depending on the size of the state, the closeness of the race, and the national prominence of the candidates. In 2010, Senate Majority Leader Harry Reid (D-NV) faced a tough reelection fight, and money for both sides flowed in from all over the country. In a relatively small state, Reid and Republican challenger Sharron Angle spent a combined $54 million, which was more than candidates spent in next-door California.[81] The 2008 elections for the House, Senate, and presidency cost a grand total of more than $5 billion, and analysts projected that the figure would nearly *double* in 2012.[82]

Where do candidates get all this money?

Where Campaign Financing Comes From

Campaign finance has long been the subject of federal regulation.[83] In 1907, Congress responded to business scandals by forbidding corporations and national banks to give money to federal campaigns. Other laws followed, though politicians and interest groups found loopholes. In 1971, Congress passed the Federal Election Campaign Act (FECA), requiring full disclosure of federal campaign contributions and expenditures. In 1974, after the Watergate scandal, Congress amended FECA to limit contributions to all federal candidates and political committees influencing federal elections. (*Hard money* is the term for contributions subject to these limits.) The law established the **Federal Election Commission (FEC)** to administer campaign finance regulation.

In the 1976 case of *Buckley v. Valeo*, the Supreme Court upheld contribution limits as a way to avoid real or apparent bribery.[84] The Court deemed several other provisions as unconstitutional abridgements of free speech. Specifically, the Court ruled against limits on **independent expenditures**, campaign spending that a group does not coordinate with a campaign, candidates' expenditures from personal funds, and overall campaign expenditures.

FECA set up guidelines for political action committees (PACs), which give to candidates and undertake other political activities. Corporations, labor unions, and other organizations may set up PACs and pay their overhead costs. Federal campaign contributions

Federal Election Commission (FEC)—the agency that administers federal campaign finance law.

Independent expenditure—the use of funds to support or oppose a federal candidate but coming from a source that does not directly coordinate its efforts with any of the parties or candidates.

Bipartisan Campaign Reform Act (BCRA)—a 2002 federal law that banned soft-money contributions to political parties. It also increased federal contribution limits and indexed them for inflation.

Issue advocacy advertisement—advertisements that urge the public to take action on an issue. Although they may mention federal candidates in a favorable or unfavorable light, they do not directly urge the candidates' election or defeat.

Super PAC—an independent expenditure-only political action committee that may raise unlimited funds from individuals, corporations, and unions. A Super PAC may make unlimited expenditures in federal election campaigns, provided that it does not directly coordinate its activities with the candidates or political parties it supports.

may not come from corporate or union treasuries. These funds must come from voluntary donations from members, employees, or shareholders.

In the late 1990s, those seeking new campaign finance rules focused on major loopholes. The first was "soft money," political funds outside FECA limits. Federal regulations allowed party committees to set up separate "federal" and "nonfederal" bank accounts. The nonfederal or soft money accounts were subject to state laws, often looser than federal law. Accordingly, national party committees could fill soft money coffers with corporate and union contributions, freeing other party funds for federal candidates. After a wave of corporate scandals in 2002, Congress passed the **Bipartisan Campaign Reform Act (BCRA)**, banning soft-money contributions to political parties (see Chapter 9).

The legislation also limited another loophole, **issue advocacy advertisements**. *Buckley v. Valeo* said that federal campaign finance curbs could not apply to advertisements unless they expressly advocated the election or defeat of federal candidates by using "magic words" such as "vote for," "elect," "or "reject."[85] So, an "issue advocacy" ad denouncing candidate X would not count as a regulated expenditure if, instead of saying "Vote Against X," it said, "Call X and tell her to stop wasting tax money." BCRA forbade corporations and unions to use their treasury funds to air broadcast ads referring directly to federal candidates within 60 days of a general election or 30 days of a primary election or caucus.

"We are under no illusion that BCRA will be the last congressional statement on the matter," wrote Justices John Paul Stevens and Sandra Day O'Connor in a 2003 case. "Money, like water, will always find an outlet."[86] And that case was not the last judicial statement on the matter: within a few years, other decisions chipped away at the law. The most significant development came with the controversial 2010 decision in *Citizens United v. FEC*. The justices struck down the BCRA "blackout," as well as the long-standing ban on independent campaign expenditures by corporations. The Court said that these prohibitions banned speech and therefore fell afoul of the First Amendment.[87] Because of the Court's ruling, which President Obama criticized, federal campaign finance law no longer keeps corporations or unions from using their own funds to advocate the election or defeat of a candidate.

The law still forbids them to use their own treasuries to make contributions to candidates and political parties. (The idea is that direct contributions raise concerns about corruption.) Instead, they either make independent expenditures on their own, or give to a new kind of group that enables them to pool their resources. In 2010, the Federal Election Commission allowed the formation of independent expenditure-only committees, or **Super PACs.** Unions, corporations, and individuals may make unlimited contributions to Super PACs, which can in turn make unlimited expenditures in federal elections. Super PACs may not directly coordinate their activities with candidates or parties, but there are a variety of ways in which they may legally figure out what candidates and parties want them to do.[88] Super PACs gave significant help to Republican congressional candidates in the 2010 midterm. The 2012 election saw the emergence of Super PACs to promote particular presidential candidates, including former governor Mitt Romney and President Barack Obama. Additional outside spending came from tax-exempt, nonprofit groups organized under Section 501(c)(4) of the internal revenue code. These groups can run campaign ads, provided that the cost does not exceed 50% of their total budgets. Whereas Super PACs have to disclose their donors to the Federal Election Commission, 501(c)(4) groups do not. Critics say that "secret funding" undermines accountability and opens the door to corrupt political influence. Supporters say that privacy protects contributors from harassment and intimidation.

Under the new rules as much as the old, incumbents raise money more easily than their challengers. Nevertheless, fund-raising takes time that lawmakers could otherwise use for deliberating on issues. Some argued that contribution limits worsened this problem. Despite a rising cost of living, the limits stayed the same for many years, meaning that incumbents had to reach more and more donors. BCRA raised the individual contribution limits from $1,000 per candidate per election to $2,000, and indexed this amount for inflation. (The PAC limit remained at $5,000). See Table 10-3.

Under the *Buckley* decision, government may not limit candidates from spending their personal funds. (The purpose of limits is to avoid corruption, and candidates cannot bribe themselves.) Since then, wealthy candidates have run self-financed campaigns at all levels.

| TABLE 10-3 | FEDERAL CONTRIBUTION LIMITS FOR 2011–2012 |

Donors	Recipients				Special Limits
	Candidate Committee	PAC	State, District, and Local Party Committee	National Party Committee	
Individual	$2,500 per election	$5,000 per year	$10,000 per year combined unit	$30,800 per year	Biennial limit of $117,000 ($46,200 to all candidates and $70,800 to all PACs and parties)
State, District, and Local Party Committee	$5,000 per election combined limit	$5,000 per year combined limit	Unlimited transfers to other party committees		
National Party Committee	$5,000 per election	$5,000 per year	Unlimited transfers to other party committees		$43,100 to Senate candidate per campaign
PAC Multicandidate	$5,000 per election	$5,000 per year	$5,000 per year combined limit	$15,000 per year	
PAC not Multicandidate	$2,500 per election	$5,000 per year	$10,000 per year combined limit	$30,800 per year	

SOURCE: www.fec.gov/ans/answers_general.shtml#How_much_can_I_contribute.

In 2010, former eBay CEO Meg Whitman spent $144 million—or about $35 per vote—on her losing race as a Republican candidate for governor of California.

Unlike congressional candidates, presidential candidates may receive public funds. The money comes from dollars that taxpayers check off on their federal tax returns.[89] If a candidate for a presidential nomination meets certain fund-raising criteria showing broad public support, he or she is eligible for **matching funds**. The federal government will match up to $250 of an individual's total contributions to an eligible candidate. In return, the candidate must agree to certain spending limits. In 2012, all the major candidates found the limits too confining and rejected matching funds.

The nominee of each political party is eligible for a large grant, which in 2008 came to $84.1 million. To get the money, a candidate must agree to forgo private contributions. Like every major party nominee between 1976 and 2004, John McCain accepted public funding for the general election. Barack Obama declined this funding and instead used private contributions in the fall campaign. This decision allowed him to outspend McCain heavily: in some states, he spent several times as much. In 2012, both major party candidates, President Obama and Mitt Romney, declined public funding.

State and local campaign finance rules vary widely. Some jurisdictions have tight contribution limits and disclosure requirements, while others have few restrictions. One theme of races at all levels is that candidates without money criticize fund-raising by their more fortunate foes. Another constant is that having money is more useful than making an issue of the other side's money. "The simple truth is that most voters think all of us in the political process are corrupt. It's an eye-roller," says one political consultant. "My advice always is to take the money because if you don't, you're broke."[90]

Matching funds—money that the federal government provides to presidential candidates to match the money they have raised on their own. Acceptance is voluntary and entails restrictions on fund-raising. Presidential candidates have increasingly decided to forgo matching funds.

Where the Money Goes

How do candidates and campaigns spend all this money? "Television ads" might be your guess. Presidential campaigns rely heavily on television, but the pattern is different for other races. The average Senate campaign puts about a third of its budget into television, compared with one-fifth for the average House campaign.[91] In races for state legislature and many local offices, the share is lower. The reason is cost. Broadcast stations charge a great deal for ads,

IMPACT
of Social Media and Communications Technology

Online Fundraising

With the emergence of eBay and Amazon in the mid-1990s, Americans became more comfortable with using their credit cards on the Internet. In 1999, the Federal Election Commission ruled that online campaign contributions would be eligible for federal matching funds. The next year, John McCain took advantage of this rule in his race for the Republican presidential nomination. Within 48 hours of his victory in the 2000 New Hampshire primary, more than a million dollars came through his Web site. Although the sum would be modest by today's standards (and included some money that he would have raised anyway), McCain's fund-raising performance taught the politicians that the Internet provided a way to raise a great deal of money from a great number of people—and to do it very quickly. "The Web was only an electronic billboard in the last two elections," said McCain webmaster Max Fose, "but this is the first time anyone ran a truly interactive campaign."[93]

In 2003, a little-known former governor of Vermont named Howard Dean entered the race for the 2004 Democratic presidential nomination. Few observers gave him much chance, but his opposition to the Iraq war stirred the Democratic "netroots." On its Web site, the campaign used a baseball bat (instead of the more traditional thermometer) to symbolize its fund-raising progress. Campaign manager Joe Trippi tells what happened next:

The next week was the most amazing thing I've ever seen in a campaign. All over the Internet, smaller, individual bats went up, as this huge network of grassroots organizations took it upon themselves to replicate the campaign at their own levels. All of the blogs that had followed the campaign began filling up their own bats, and the money began flowing in.[94]

Within three months, he raised $14.8 million, much of it online.[95] Four years later, the Obama campaign developed the techniques that the Dean campaign had pioneered, taking online fundraising to a much higher level. Over half a billion dollars—a majority of the campaign's total—came via the Internet.[96]

On June 14, 2012, the Bessette-Pitney blog reported on a new chapter in online fund-raising: the FEC voted unanimously to let individuals make political contributions through text messages. Time will tell whether this move would have as much impact as the original 1999 decision on online fund-raising.

CRITICAL THINKING QUESTION

Who benefits most from online fund-raising? Does it enhance the political role of the small donor?

Direct mail—campaign appeals, often asking for contributions, which go directly to voters via postal mail.

Campaign consultants—professionals who contract with political campaigns to provide management and other services.

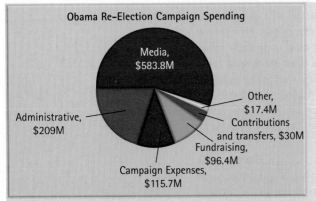

Obama Re-Election Campaign Spending

Media, $583.8M

Administrative, $209M

Other, $17.4M

Contributions and transfers, $30M

Fundraising, $96.4M

Campaign Expenses, $115.7M

FIGURE 10-5 The bulk of Obama's re-election campaign war chest went to media.
NOTE: Data cover expenditure reports through October 25, 2012.
SOURCE: Center for Responsive Politics, www.opensecrets.org/pres12/expenditures.php.

especially when they reach millions. A district may have only a sliver of a station's market, so why buy ads when most of the audience cannot vote in the race? **Direct mail** may make more sense, because campaigns can target it to households in their voting area.[92]

The more costly the race, the more likely it is that the candidate will hire **campaign consultants**, professional advisers who can run nearly every aspect of an election contest. The first professional campaign consultants started business during the 1930s, and by the end of the century, they had largely supplanted volunteers and party officials in the top posts of large campaigns. In addition to general consultants, there are also consultants for specific tasks, such as the following:

- *Media production and placement*—making print and broadcast advertisements and placing them where they will have the greatest effect. These expenditures tend to be high in presidential races (see Figure 10-5).
- *"New media"*—developing Web sites and social networking groups, posting video on sites such as YouTube.
- *Polling*—taking random samples of public opinion to find out how well the candidate is doing and reckon what approaches will gain more votes.
- *Direct mail and telephone voter contact*—sending messages to individual voters.
- *Press*—writing news releases and handling questions from reporters.
- *Fund-raising*—gathering money by direct mail, the Internet, or solicitation of political action committees and other large givers.

- *Field operations*—engaging in the true hand-to-hand combat of campaigns, including rallies and door-to-door canvasses.
- *Get-out-the-vote (GOTV)*—identifying supporters and making sure that they cast ballots either at the booth or by mail.
- *Research*—gathering material on issues and gaining intelligence about the opposition, and studying the vulnerabilities of one's own candidate.

The Center for Responsive Politics, which backs more curbs on campaign finance, says that the costs of consulting make money-hungry politicians beholden to special interest contributors."[97] Bradley Smith, a former member of the Federal Election Commission, replies that regulation itself is driving ordinary people out of politics. Prior to FECA, he says, citizens simply campaigned for candidates they liked. "They'd print their own literature, hold rallies, and so on. But now to do that, they'd first have to organize a committee and name a treasurer; and if they collect money at a county fair, they risk running afoul of the law. So that kind of grassroots politics is no more."[98]

ELECTIONS, CAMPAIGNS, AND DELIBERATIVE DEMOCRACY

What good does an election do? Needless to say, it results in the choice of public officials; but as the beginning of this chapter suggested, there are other ways to do that. Campaigns and elections are valuable because they also serve other purposes. Ideally, they enhance deliberation, both by candidates and by the people they seek to govern. They provide opportunities for active citizenship at all levels, and they enable the people both to provide the government with mandates for action and to check elected officials if they exceed or violate their mandate. As this chapter has described, however, the electoral system does not always live up to this ideal standard.

What Elections Do for Candidates and Voters

Elections concentrate the mind. They force citizens to review the public record, to reflect on the candidates' character and positions, and decide which people and policies would better serve the community, the state, or the country. The result is a more deliberative appraisal of the government's performance than one would normally find between elections.

As Chapter 7 on public opinion and participation makes clear, many citizens do not vote, and many voters are not diligent in studying campaign materials, but without campaigns and elections, the level of interest and knowledge would be far lower. Candidates who challenge current officeholders and policies strive to educate people about public problems. Incumbents and their allies draw attention to the good things that current policies have done. Thanks in part to 30-second ads, even the less attentive citizens end up learning something about these arguments.

Campaigns educate candidates, too. When they prepare for debates, interviews, and town hall meetings, they have to learn more about a broader range of issues than they would otherwise. In anticipating attacks, they confront their own faults. On the campaign trail, they encounter all kinds of people and may find out about issues that they had not previously considered. When John F. Kennedy campaigned in the 1960 West Virginia primary, the poverty he saw made a deep impression on him.

Elections and campaigns are about acting, not just learning. Seeking elective office gives a citizen a chance to serve the public. Analyses of political candidates sometimes assume "progressive ambition," or the notion that each office is but a step to the next one up. This notion applies only in certain cases. The great majority of elected offices in the United States—school boards and low-visibility local posts—do not attract would-be presidents. People run for these offices because they want to do something for their community.[99]

Although Bradley Smith may be right that regulation has closed the door on some forms of citizen activism, campaign technology has opened others. As mentioned before, citizens can now debate issues on candidate blogs, and YouTube has created avenues for campaign activism that no one expected a few years ago. With a video camera and modest computer equipment, anyone can make a campaign ad that millions could see. In 2008, the Obama campaign used social networking and other technologies to mobilize thousands of volunteers. With guidance and technical support from a vast network of paid organizers and local team leaders, volunteers rang doorbells, made phone calls, drove people to rallies and voting booths, and talked up their candidate in everyday settings. Obama supporters hoped that the impact of the mobilization would outlast the campaign itself. "They've invested in a civic infrastructure on a scale that has never happened," said a veteran organizer who helped train Obama staff. "It's been an investment in the development of thousands of young people equipped with the skills and leadership ability to mobilize people and in the development of leadership at the local level. It's profound."[100]

Mandates and Checks

Mandate—an election victory that indicates strong voter approval of the winner's plans and policies.

Successful candidates often claim to have a **mandate**, an endorsement of their policies, which in turn gives them the moral authority to put those policies into practice. New presidents or governors often refer to their mandate when seeking legislative approval for their programs. Political foes quarrel about the existence of a mandate. Scholars disagree about whether mandates even exist in the first place.[101] Those who deny the existence of mandates note the large number of citizens who do not vote. Getting an absolute majority of the voting-age population, however, is an impractically high standard. Lyndon Johnson won a historical landslide in 1964, but with a 62% turnout of the voting-age population, his 61% of the popular vote came to just 38% of the voting-age population. (That is, 62% times 61% equals 38%.) He needed 80% of the vote to get a majority of adults.

A mandate is questionable when the winning candidate is vague on key issues. But as we saw in Chapter 9, a major contemporary concern is not that the partisan differences are too fuzzy but that they are too sharp. On the one hand, when positions are clear and the margins are large, it is hard to deny a mandate. On the other hand, some political leaders have gone in directions that their voters did not expect or approve. In 1964, Lyndon Johnson talked about ambitious plans for domestic policy. His big victory and massive Democratic congressional gains gave him reason to claim a mandate for such plans. At the same time, however, he did not disclose what his advisers were telling him about the risks of American involvement in Vietnam. As historian Michael Beschloss says:

> Certainly Johnson was reluctant to make crucial decisions amid the heat and pressures of a campaign, if he could help it. But his approach kept Americans from fully knowing whom and what they were voting for in 1964. It also tragically foreclosed the possibility of a grand national debate that might have educated both Johnson and the American people as they faced one of the most important presidential decisions of the century—whether the United States should make a monumental commitment to war in Vietnam.[102]

The electorate giveth, and the electorate taketh away. If voters dislike the results of the previous mandate, they can vote out the incumbents in the next election. In the case of national politics, they do not even have to wait until the next presidential race. Midterm elections provide them with a means to reverse or modify the president's policies.[103] For instance, Republican losses in the 1982 midterm curbed President Reagan's ambitions for conservative domestic policy. In 2010, the Republican takeover of the House put enormous hurdles in the way of President Obama's ambitious domestic policy agenda.

The midterm policy effect has limits. A president has enormous institutional power over foreign policy and national security. A chief executive may stay the course in spite of an adverse midterm election. Although Democrats took control of Congress in 2006, for instance, President George W. Bush did not withdraw forces from Iraq.

As we saw earlier, the framers devised a system enabling institutions to check one another. Even ballot initiatives and other versions of direct democracy are subject to these institutional checks. Courts may overturn them, or the federal government may assert jurisdiction, as in the case of medical marijuana laws. Bureaucrats and legislators may balk at carrying out measures they disapprove. But these institutional arrangements are what Madison called "auxiliary precautions." He emphasized the role of elections when he wrote: "A dependence on the people is, no doubt, the primary control on the government."[104]

SUMMARY

- The United States has a complex election system because of federalism, bicameralism, and the separation of powers.
- Controversy has long surrounded election procedure and technology.
- Elections take a variety of forms: ballot measure contests, partisan and nonpartisan primaries, district and at-large races.
- Americans pay closest attention to presidential elections, which have rules of their own. Through primaries or caucuses, each state chooses delegates to national party conventions.
- In November, nominees face off in the general election, whose outcome depends on the Electoral College. Although the winner of the popular vote usually gets a majority in the Electoral College, the 2000 election served as a reminder that the results can diverge.

- Elections are expensive, and federal campaigns take place under intricate rules regarding contributions. The necessity of fund-raising and the difficulty of rule compliance may leave candidates with little time to focus on the issues, and they may hinder citizen involvement in some ways.
- Nevertheless, technology has opened new doors to participation and deliberation.
- Elections educate candidates and voters alike, and they allow the electorate both to empower officials and to check them.
- The importance of elections lies not just in the identity of the winners but in the ways that they win. Elections are an important occasion for policy deliberation, and campaigns provide many opportunities for active citizenship.

KEY TERMS

TEST YOUR KNOWLEDGE

1. Which is NOT a reason to have elections rather than the random selection of lawmakers?
   a. Election campaigns stimulate public deliberation.
   b. Elections are less costly than random selection would be.
   c. Elections foster more active citizenship.
   d. Elections provide a way for the people to check and control their government.
   e. It is not necessarily desirable for officials to be a perfect cross-section of the public.

2. How might nonpartisan elections foster voter deliberation?
   a. Each vote is made public so the voters can discuss them.
   b. The election is held after a town meeting in which citizens have discussed the issues.
   c. They force voters to weigh the candidates' merits rather than their party labels.
   d. They require the voter to give an explanation of his or her vote.
   e. They usually involve obscure items that force voters to do some research before casting their ballots.

3. A majority-minority district is based on
   a. district reporting measures.
   b. the racial identity of a majority of the potential voters.
   c. financial contributions within a state.
   d. merging ideas of the majority and minority.
   e. educational funding.

4. How many electoral votes are currently needed to elect the president and vice president?
   a. 240
   b. 270
   c. 300
   d. 420
   e. 470

5. Under the original Constitution, senators were selected when they were
   a. appointed by governors.
   b. elected by popular vote.
   c. elected by the House of Representatives.
   d. elected through an Electoral College.
   e. selected by state legislatures.

6. In mid-term elections since 1934, the president's party has typically
   a. gained House seats.
   b. gained Senate seats.
   c. lost House seats.
   d. maintained its number of congressional seats.
   e. won a majority in Congress.

7. Early voting is a response to the complaint that
   a. absentee votes are seldom counted.
   b. campaigns run too long.
   c. election officials are too vulnerable to corruption.
   d. voting on Election Day takes too much time.
   e. voting procedures favor western states.

8. The effort to motivate supportive voter groups to turn out in higher numbers is called
   a. early voting.
   b. front-loading.
   c. gerrymandering.
   d. microtargeting.
   e. mobilization.

9. In the case *Buckley v. Valeo*, the Supreme Court upheld contribution limits as a way to
   a. avoid real or apparent bribery.
   b. control campaign fraud.
   c. encourage political participation.
   d. level the playing field for third parties.
   e. spur public deliberation.

10. What is one limit of the midterm policy effect?
    a. New representatives chosen in midterm elections have little impact on the course of policies since there are only two years left in the president's term.
    b. Presidents often prefer that Congress be controlled by the opposing party.
    c. The executive can misinterpret the public's intentions.
    d. The president is generally unconcerned with his party's numbers in Congress.
    e. The president still has enormous power over foreign policy and national security.

FURTHER READING

Burton, Michael John, and Daniel M. Shea. *Campaign Craft: The Strategies, Tactics, and Art of Political Campaign Management.* 4th ed. Santa Barbara, CA: Praeger, 2010.

Ceaser, James W., Andrew E. Busch, and John J. Pitney Jr. *Epic Journey: The 2008 Elections and American Politics.* Lanham, MD: Rowman and Littlefield, 2009.

Ellis, Richard J. *Democratic Delusions: The Initiative Process in America.* Lawrence: University Press of Kansas, 2002.

Herrnson, Paul S. *Congressional Elections: Campaigning at Home and in Washington.* 6th ed. Washington, DC: CQ Press, 2012.

Niemi, Richard G., and Paul S. Herrnson. "Beyond the Butterfly: The Complexity of U.S. Ballots." *Perspectives on Political Science* 1 (June 2003): 317–326.

Popkin, Samuel L. *The Candidate: What It Takes to Win – and Hold – the White House.* New York: Oxford University Press, 2012.

WEB SOURCES

David Leip's Atlas of U.S. Presidential Elections: www.uselectionatlas.org—maps and historical data.

Factcheck.org: www.factcheck.org—analysis of statements by candidates and officials.

Federal Election Commission: www.fec.gov—data and disclosure on federal campaign finance.

OpenSecrets.org: www.opensecrets.org—data and analysis of campaign finance.

Voting America: www.americanpast.richmond.edu/voting—"cinematic" maps of electoral history.

In 1991, President George H. W. Bush banned the media from covering the return of overseas casualties to Dover Air Force Base. In 2009, the Obama administration changed the policy, allowing news media to photograph the flag-draped caskets of fallen U.S. troops returning home, if their familes agreed.

Mark Wilson/Getty Images

11 Mass Media

OBJECTIVES

After reading this chapter, you should be able to:

- Identify the major news media and describe how they have changed over time.
- Explain various ways in which the media affect politics.
- Discuss strengths and weaknesses of the American news media.
- Analyze ways in which government regulates and influences the news media.
- Recognize how public figures seek to shape news coverage.
- Appraise ways in which the media foster deliberation and citizenship.

INTRODUCTION

News is information about events that are recent, unusual, and important. Such a definition may sound simple, but it leads to more complex questions. Who brings the news? How do these people shape the kinds of information that reaches the public?

Little political news reaches us by our own firsthand experience. Average Americans have not met major political candidates, witnessed foreign battles, or inspected raw economic data. Instead, they count on **mass media**, the means of broadly distributing information. The mass media include newspapers, magazines, television, radio, and the Internet. These media also convey various kinds of entertainment, so we use the term "**news media**" for those segments that focus on news, particularly about politics. We use the terms "press" and "news media" interchangeably.

It is appropriate that we refer to news organizations as "media." In the physical world, a medium can filter another substance. Filtering and selection constitute a large part of a newsperson's job. There are only so many minutes in a broadcast and so many pages in a paper. With a sea of facts available, news outlets have the time or space for just spoonfuls. What they feature may drive political debate, while what they leave out will sink into the murk. So although the press may not dictate what we think, it does affect what we think *about*.

In selecting what to cover and how, journalists face competing pressures. On the one hand is the pressure to pump up revenues. When clicking through news channels, viewers are more likely to stop on stories of sex and violence than on explanations of the federal budget. More sex and violence means bigger audiences and more money. On the other hand, many journalists resist pandering. They gain their peers' esteem with stories that foster public deliberation. That is one reason why the press sometimes *does* cover complex policy issues.

Do journalists deliberately favor certain points of view? There is serious debate as to whether such bias exists and what side it may take, but undoubtedly political figures try to mold public opinion by molding media coverage. In that sense, there is a bias toward those who know how to sway the media.

Effective deliberation depends on accurate knowledge. Because of the Internet, cable television, and other technologies, Americans can tap far more sources of news and entertainment than ever before. But quantity does not equal quality. The media may sometimes offer a warped view of politics and public issues, and the pursuit of truth faces a variety of obstacles, including manipulation by politicians. With an eye to such issues, this chapter examines the role and structure of the media and their influence on the American political process. It asks how well today's media foster citizenship and deliberation.

News—information about events that are recent, unusual, and important.

Mass media—means of broadly distributing information or entertainment, including newspapers, magazines, television, radio, and the Internet.

News media—the means of transmitting news to broad populations, including television, radio, newspapers, magazines, and the Internet.

McNamee/Getty Images

President Obama speaks during a 2010 town hall on the BET, CMT, and MTV networks. He appeared before some 250 young people and answered questions from the studio audience as well as from viewers who submitted questions via Twitter.

A BRIEF HISTORY
MAJOR ISSUE

- How have technological and organizational changes shaped the mass media over time?

The mass media have played a central role in American politics since the Founding. Hamilton, Madison, and Jay published *The Federalist Papers* as a series of newspaper articles responding to Anti-Federalist essays, which also appeared in newspapers. This exchange was an early example of the ways in which the press can promote deliberation. In this case, deliberation resulted in the ratification of the Constitution, and soon afterward, Congress included freedom of press in the First Amendment. In 1792, it went further, giving newspapers direct assistance by providing them with low postal rates. A few years later, however, Congress undercut the press by passing the Sedition Act, which forbade "false, scandalous, and malicious writings" against the government (see Chapter 5). The act expired in 1801, but its short life signaled that politics and the media would have a turbulent relationship.

The Era of Ink

In the early days of the republic, newspapers had close ties to political parties. During the 1830s and 1840s, they sought larger readerships and greater profits, and they focused more on reporting. Improvements in papermaking and printing made it more cost-effective to produce newspapers in mass quantities. Other technological developments changed the way news organizations worked. Before the nineteenth century, it took a long time for writers to reach the scene of faraway news, and just as long for them to send their stories back. By the mid-1800s, however, railroads enabled journalists to travel quickly, and the telegraph allowed them to transmit stories instantaneously to their newspapers. During the Mexican-American War (1846–1848), the publisher of the *New York Sun* arranged to receive reporters' battle dispatches through a system of horse riders, railroads, and telegraphs. Other newspapers joined the venture, which was the forerunner of the Associated Press (AP), discussed later.[1]

A less-noted innovation helped reporters write word-for-word accounts of news events and interviews. In the 1840s, a new method of shorthand improved the speed and accuracy of transcription, so newspapers soon came to value reporters with shorthand skills. In the Lincoln-Douglas debates of 1858, the development of shorthand converged with the growth of railroads and the telegraph. At each debate site, *Chicago Tribune* reporter Robert Hitt would take down the exchanges in shorthand. Then he would catch the first train to Chicago and turn the shorthand into readable text during the journey. The *Tribune* could publish the full transcript within 36 hours.[2] (The rival *Chicago Times* did likewise.) And by telegraph, the text reached papers around the country in three days. Thanks to technological change, therefore, many Americans soon had access to a profound deliberation on the meaning of their country.

After the Civil War, daily newspaper circulation grew rapidly, rising from 2.6 million in 1870 to 15.1 million in 1900.[3] Publishers Joseph Pulitzer and William Randolph Hearst promoted this growth, helping turn newspapers into big business. Both emphasized sensational stories of sex and violence. Critics referred to such practices as "**yellow journalism**," after a cartoon character, the Yellow Kid. To this day, the term applies to excessive coverage of lurid events.

There was more to the press than yellow journalism. In 1896, Adolph Ochs bought the *New York Times* and set about to turn the struggling paper into a model of professionalism and impartiality. In the years ahead, it would regularly publish key speeches and other documents, thus becoming a primary source for scholarly research and public deliberation.

A group of reporters of the early 1900s wrote about corruption. President Theodore Roosevelt praised their work, up to a point: "There is filth on the floor and it must be scraped up with the muck-rake; and there are times and places where this service is the most needed of all the services that can be performed." But he cautioned that if they "gradually grow to feel that the whole world is nothing but muck, their power of usefulness is gone."[4] Despite the criticism, investigative reporters eventually embraced the word "**muckrakers**." We still use this term for journalists who expose misconduct in government and business.

In addition to newspapers, the muckrakers published their work in books and magazines, whose numbers increased during the late nineteenth and early twentieth centuries. Further improvements in publishing technology had brought down prices, making these

Yellow journalism—news coverage that emphasizes sex, crime, and scandal over substantive public policy.

Muckrakers—journalists who expose misconduct in government and business.

print media affordable for large numbers of Americans. Compulsory education expanded the market by increasing the number of Americans who could read. Between 1870 and 1910, the literacy rate grew from 80% to 92.3%.[5]

The Era of Sight and Sound

Until the early twentieth century, print was the only practical means of distributing news to far-flung audiences. After World War I, broadcasting became part of the mass media. Between 1922 and 1940, the number of households with radio sets grew from 60,000 to more than 28 million.[6] At first, each station aired only its own news and entertainment programs. In 1926, the National Broadcasting Company (NBC) formed the first permanent broadcast **network**, a system by which the company would simultaneously supply programs to stations in different cities. The Columbia Broadcasting System (CBS) soon followed. Through radio networks, broadcast journalists and public figures could now reach millions of Americans at once. Franklin Roosevelt was the first national politician who fully grasped this potential. During his presidency (1933–1945), he gave 30 "fireside chats," radio addresses on a variety of topics.[7] Unlike other politicians of the era, who often spoke into the radio microphone as if addressing a crowd, Roosevelt knew that he was talking to citizens in their living rooms. He used a conversational tone that led millions to feel a connection with him.

Network—a broadcast organization that simultaneously supplies radio or television programs to stations in different cities.

During the 1930s and 1940s, radio enabled the public to have a real-time experience of major events, such as the deadly 1937 fire that destroyed the airship *Hindenburg*. World War II gave a high profile to reporters who broadcast from Europe, such as Edward R. Murrow of CBS.

When they were not listening to the radio, Americans were flocking to movie theaters. Between 1922 and 1942, average weekly attendance more than doubled, from 40 million to 85 million.[8] (In the middle of this period, silent movies gave way to "talkies.") Some movies addressed political issues, but more often, politics entered the theater by way of newsreels. Coming before the main feature, these short documentaries usually covered several current news stories.

After the war, television cut deeply into movie attendance and eventually meant the end of newsreels. TV also displaced radio as the dominant broadcast news medium. In 1954, Murrow aired a tough documentary about Senator Joseph McCarthy, the Wisconsin senator who had made extravagant claims about Communist infiltration. (The 2005 movie *Good Night and Good Luck* dramatized the Murrow–McCarthy confrontation.) Public opinion was turning against McCarthy, and the Murrow broadcast hastened his fall, which ended in a Senate censure. Six years later, John Kennedy and Richard Nixon faced off in the first televised debates between presidential nominees. Kennedy looked more poised than Nixon, and the debates may have helped tip the close election to Kennedy.[9]

Edward R. Murrow reports from London during World War II.

The year 1963 was a milestone. CBS and NBC moved from 15-minute to 30-minute evening news programs, increasing their ability to cover politics. For the first time, pollsters reported, television topped newspapers and radio as Americans' main source of news.[10] Television made President Kennedy's assassination a shared national experience, and two days after his death, viewers witnessed the murder of assassin Lee Harvey Oswald during a live broadcast. Ever since then, Americans have turned on their televisions when there is word of a disaster or other breaking news event. For many, news means TV.

As we shall see, however, two features of the medium pose problems for news broadcasters. First is public ownership of the airwaves. Unlike print media, television stations must secure government licenses, which potentially give public officials a way to pressure television journalists. Second, the broadcast television networks, like the radio networks from which they grew, are mainly in the entertainment business. They make most of their money not by airing policy deliberation but by selling ads on comedies, dramas, and sports programs. When

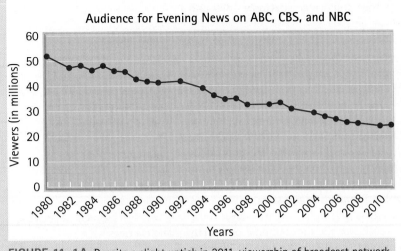

Audience for Evening News on ABC, CBS, and NBC

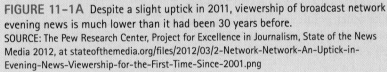

FIGURE 11-1A Despite a slight uptick in 2011, viewership of broadcast network evening news is much lower than it had been 30 years before.
SOURCE: The Pew Research Center, Project for Excellence in Journalism, State of the News Media 2012, at stateofthemedia.org/files/2012/03/2-Network-Network-An-Uptick-in-Evening-News-Viewership-for-the-First-Time-Since-2001.png

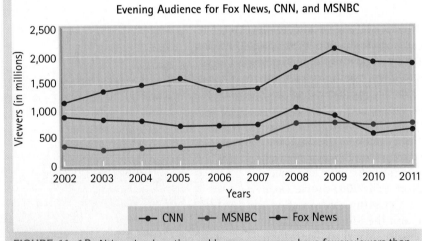

Evening Audience for Fox News, CNN, and MSNBC

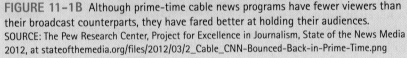

FIGURE 11-1B Although prime-time cable news programs have fewer viewers than their broadcast counterparts, they have fared better at holding their audiences.
SOURCE: The Pew Research Center, Project for Excellence in Journalism, State of the News Media 2012, at stateofthemedia.org/files/2012/03/2_Cable_CNN-Bounced-Back-in-Prime-Time.png

FOCUS
QUESTION

Franklin Roosevelt was a powerful presence on the radio. How would he have fared in an age of cable television?

there is competition for scarce resources such as money or airtime, the networks may favor entertainment over news.

The Era of Cable and Conglomerates

In the 1970s, cable television started providing large numbers of Americans with greater choices in news as well as entertainment. The year 1979 brought C-SPAN, a cooperative enterprise of the cable television industry. C-SPAN provided gavel-to-gavel coverage of the House of Representatives, and it would soon offer unedited coverage of congressional hearings and other public affairs events. (Several years later, C-SPAN 2 would cover the Senate.) In 1980, the Cable News Network (CNN) started operation as the first all-news television network. At first, the "big three" broadcast networks (NBC, CBS, and ABC) seemed to have little to fear, but CNN gradually gained an audience. A turning point came at the start of the 1991 Gulf War. CNN led the coverage because it had the only correspondents broadcasting live from Baghdad. In 1996 came two additional all-news cable networks, MSNBC and Fox News. The big three broadcast networks would continue to have larger audiences, but their numbers would decline (see Figure 11-1).

Politically aware Americans could now immerse themselves in television news. On C-SPAN and sometimes on the other cable news networks, viewers could watch speeches in their entirety. They would not have to rely on reporters and editors to select bits and pieces for them. In this sense, cable gave Americans unprecedented access to news and political information. Later on, some cable programs also blurred the line between news and entertainment. On Comedy Central, *The Daily Show with Jon Stewart* and *The Colbert Report* combined sketch humor and interviews with major political figures. In 2010, President Obama appeared on *The Daily Show*.

As cable TV was emerging, talk radio was also entering the national fray. FM radio had become widely available, and music programming was shifting to the better sound quality of the FM dial. Many AM stations switched to news and talk. Satellite technology made it more economical to transmit talk shows to stations throughout the country. The growth of toll-free telephone lines enabled people to make free long-distance calls to these shows.[11] Because anyone with a phone could now speak nationwide, it appeared that the mass media were becoming more diverse and decentralized.

However, other trends were at work in the media business. Between 1970 and 2009, the number of daily newspapers declined from 1,748 to 1,397.[12] Ninety-eight percent of cities now had only a single local paper.[13] In 2012, the *New Orleans Times-Picayune* announced plans to become a predominantly online publication and cut its print edition to three days a week, thus making New Orleans the largest American city without a daily print newspaper.[14] And the remaining local papers were often not under local control. **Newspaper chains**—businesses owning multiple papers—played a more important role in American journalism. By the first decade of the twenty-first century, the top ten chains accounted for more than half of daily newspaper circulation.[15] Moreover, both news and entertainment increasingly came under the control of **media conglomerates**, corporations owning several different kinds of media businesses (see Table 11-1). Toward the end of the decade, the trend reversed slightly—not because local journalism was flowering but

Newspaper chain—a business owning multiple newspapers.

Media conglomerate—a large corporation that owns a variety of media outlets.

TABLE 11-1 · WHO OWNS THE MEDIA?

	Broadcasting	Newspapers Magazines, and News Websites	Film	Books and Others
News Corp.*	Fox Network Fox News Channel FX 27 TV stations	*New York Post* *The Daily* *Times of London* *Wall Street Journal*	20th Century Fox Fox Searchlight	HarperCollins Zondervan
CBS	CBS Showtime CW 28 TV stations 117 radio stations			Simon & Schuster
Comcast	NBC MSNBC CNBC Bravo Telemundo The Weather Channel	Flipboard	Universal Studios	Universal Parks and Resorts
TimeWarner	CNN HBO TNT truTV	*Time* *Fortune* *Sports Illustrated* *Money* *People* *MAD* TheSmokingGun.com	Warner Brothers	
Walt Disney	ABC Disney Channel A&E (part) ESPN 10 TV stations 32 radio stations		Walt Disney Touchstone Miramax	Hyperion Baby Einstein Disney Resorts Hollywood Records
Gannett	23 TV stations	*USA Today* 81 other papers		
Viacom	BET		Paramount Pictures	
Clear Channel	Comedy Central MTV 850 radio stations Premiere Radio Networks			

To a large extent, the news and entertainment media are part of the same corporate families.

*In 2012, the News Corporation announced plans to split its news and entertainment operations into separate companies.

SOURCE: *Columbia Journalism Review*, "Who Owns What," at www.cjr.org/resources/index.php, accessed July 3, 2012.

because some chains broke up, went bankrupt, or sold their money-losing papers to private equity companies. Accordingly, there is widespread concern that fewer media voices are contributing to public deliberation. CNN founder Ted Turner said, "[O]nly a few corporations decide what we can choose. That is not choice. That's like a dictator deciding what candidates are allowed to stand for parliamentary elections, and then claiming that the people choose their leaders."[16]

The Era of the Internet

The most important recent development has been the growth of the Internet. In 1994, just 14% of Americans reported online activity. Seventeen years later, that figure was up to 78%.[17] With the expansion of the Internet came the development of online news and information. A key event occurred early in 1998, when the online *Drudge Report* broke the news of President Clinton's affair with a White House intern. Later that year, the independent counsel's report went online just as soon as hard copies were available. In that sense, the Internet helped open the way to a presidential impeachment.

During the early years of the mass Internet, most information flowed one way: from Web sites to users. More recently, advances in technology have allowed millions to post their own material. Initially, most of this material consisted of text. In February 2005, online video took a leap forward with the founding of YouTube. Users can easily upload video clips on www.youtube.com and share them through Web sites, mobile devices, blogs, and e-mail.

As of 2011, there were about 181 million blogs worldwide.[18] About 14% of American adults report working on blogs or online journals.[19] Even if just one-tenth of American bloggers focus on politics, then there are some 3 million political blogs in the United States. Most have tiny audiences, but a few dozen blogs do have impact. Among the most influential are the liberal *Daily Kos* (dailykos.com) and the conservative (Michelle Malkin (michellemalkin.com/).

Sometimes bloggers have drawn attention to stories that the "mainstream" media have arguably overlooked or bungled. In 2007, for instance, *Talking Points Memo* (www.talkingpointsmemo.com) gathered and posted information about the firing of several federal prosecutors. The story, which prompted critics to accuse the Bush administration of improper political influence, triggered a significant controversy. Although journalists may face serious time or space constraints in their regular reporting, many now keep blogs where they can offer additional details or viewpoints. Other blogs provide expert commentary on specific topics such as election law (electionlawblog.org) or public opinion (www.pollster.com/blogs).

The Internet has been good for journalism in other ways, too. Tablets and smartphones enable people to access news and information practically everywhere. A small but growing number of Americans get news recommendations from sites such as Facebook and Twitter.[20] Most American journalists now use blogs and other social media as sources for story ideas and angles.[21] There is a catch, however. Reporting is difficult, whereas tapping traditional news sources has become very easy. Most major news operations now put material online, usually for free. Years ago, for instance, only news organizations had direct access to the Associated Press and other wire services. Today, anyone can find AP stories at many sites or search them at news.google.com. Most blog posts consist of commenting on—or "chewing"—stories from existing news organizations. If the flow of information from such sources is shrinking, then the blogs have less to work with.

Although many question their accuracy, bloggers see themselves as an important corrective to the mainstream media.

Ironically, the Internet itself jeopardizes that flow. The availability of online content has caused huge economic problems for the news business (see Figures 11-2 and 11-3). When it comes to national and international news, each local paper must compete not only with nearby publications but with a multitude of online sources. In turn, these sources compete with one another, and with so many users posting broadcast news stories online, TV networks must compete with YouTube. Most journalists think that the wider range of news choices is a major reason why some news organizations have lost their audience.[22]

More basically, why would people pay for newspapers or magazines when they can get the same material online? And not only are Internet news sites competing for circulation, but Internet advertising has cut deeply into a key source of revenue. Newspapers once could make a great deal of money selling classified ads, particularly for real estate. Now home buyers can log on to real estate sites, while buyers and sellers of merchandise go through eBay. Retailers have also cut back on print advertising. Newspaper ad revenue amounted to $23.9 billion in 2011, less than half its peak of $48.7 billion in 2000.[23] As a result, many news organizations have had to slash budgets or close their doors. Thousands of journalists have lost their jobs, and newspapers have cut the scope of their coverage.

We will shortly return to "bottom-line" pressures. First, we need to ask a very basic question: How do the news media affect political life?

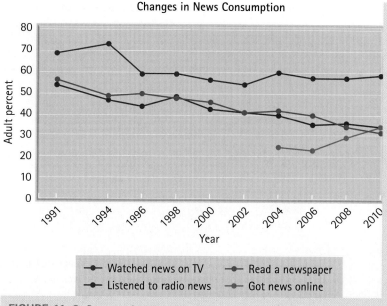

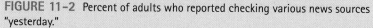

FIGURE 11-2 Percent of adults who reported checking various news sources "yesterday."
SOURCE: The Pew Research Center, www.people-press.org/2010/09/12/section-1-watching-reading-and-listening-to-the-news

MEDIA IMPACT

MAJOR ISSUE

- What role do the media play in the political process?

"In proportion as the structure of a government gives force to public opinion," said George Washington in his Farewell Address, "it is essential that public opinion should be enlightened." Civic virtue depended on this enlightenment, he said, so he urged his fellow citizens to "promote institutions for the general diffusion of knowledge."[24] He was thinking of schools and universities, but the mass media can serve this purpose as well. Writing of the connection of citizenship and the media, journalist and educator David T. Z. Mindich noted, "A thin citizenship is good for no one. When we don't pay attention, we fall for slogans and get swayed by lofty rhetoric with little regard for policy differences and voting records. Deep citizenship lets us hold leaders accountable by engaging in a deliberative process that goes deeper."[25]

Informing

Contemporary citizenship may appear to be thin because many Americans are ill informed about politics (see Chapter 7 on public opinion and participation). So are the news media failing to provide citizens with the information they need to deliberate about politics? News stories about international affairs and complex domestic issues have indeed fallen prey to media cutbacks. But even with reductions in reporting staff, newspaper pages,

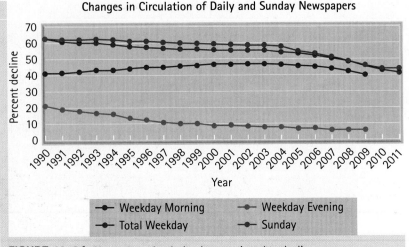

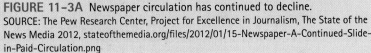

FIGURE 11–3A Newspaper circulation has continued to decline.
SOURCE: The Pew Research Center, Project for Excellence in Journalism, The State of the News Media 2012, stateofthemedia.org/files/2012/01/15-Newspaper-A-Continued-Slide-in-Paid-Circulation.png

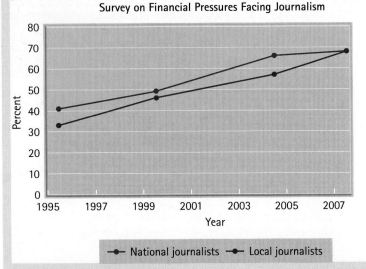

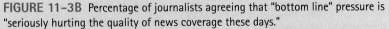

FIGURE 11–3B Percentage of journalists agreeing that "bottom line" pressure is "seriously hurting the quality of news coverage these days."
SOURCE: The Pew Research Center, Project for Excellence in Journalism, "The Web: Alarming, Appealing and a Challenge to Journalistic Values," p. 5, http://www.people-press.org/files/legacy-pdf/403.pdf

Agenda setting—influencing the range of issues up for public deliberation.

and broadcast airtime, the news media continue to supply basic information, and most Americans have access to the Internet, whether at home, work, or a public library.

Why are so many people not keeping up with current events? Some reasons are straightforward. It takes effort to learn about the news, and the demands of work and family leave a large number of people with little of the necessary time and energy. Formal education also makes it easier for people to seek out and absorb political information, and some Americans have had inadequate schooling.[26] Others may simply believe that politics is irrelevant to their lives. For most people, there is scant tangible payoff for following the news. In that sense, the remarkable thing is not that so many are underinformed but that a large number do read newspapers and watch news broadcasts. The sense of citizenship is an important motive. In one national survey, 77% said that "keeping fully informed about news and public issues" is an "extremely" or "very" important obligation of citizenship.[27]

Agenda Setting, Priming, and Framing

Following the news does not entail learning every possible detail of public policy, which would be an impossible task. The media emphasize certain issues over others, so we must consider **agenda setting**, the process by which topics come up for deliberation in the political world. Sometimes, large numbers of Americans may learn about a problem through firsthand experience. When gasoline prices suddenly go up, for instance, millions of drivers will notice when they pull up to the pump. More often, people rely on the mass media to bring issues to their attention.

Potential issues may lie dormant for years before the press picks them up. By the 1990s, for instance, many professional athletes were taking steroids to enhance their performance. Even though the effects (e.g., abrupt and massive muscle growth) were obvious to any careful observer, the problem got only modest attention during this time. In June 2002, *Sports Illustrated* ran a story (see the photo on page 327) in which a former National League MVP suggested that about half the players in professional baseball were using performance-enhancing drugs.[28] Suddenly, the press was full of stories about steroids in baseball and other sports. Congress held hearings, and lawmakers warned that if college and professional sports did not take action, federal regulation would soon follow. Despite the adoption of mandatory drug testing, the issue remains alive amid reports that drug abuse still occurs.

Just as the media may ignore certain problems, it may exaggerate others. Some say that this happened in the 1990s when networks and local stations gave heavy television coverage to crime. This increased public concerns and prompted politicians to respond with a variety of anticrime initiatives.[29] Critics of these measures point out that crime rates actually dropped during most of the decade, after peaking around 1992–1994—a trend that the media were slow to record. But others claim that the tough-on-crime measures introduced in the mid-1990s helped to drive down crime.

In addition to shaping the public agenda, the news media also affect the standards by which citizens appraise political figures and institutions. When the media stress certain issues, people will tend to use those issues as a basis for political judgment. Scholars refer to this process as **priming**.[30] For instance, if terrorism is the top issue in the press, then people will be more likely to support public figures who would be best at fighting it. **Framing** is closely related to priming. The term refers to the way in which the media define an issue by emphasizing or deemphasizing certain aspects of that issue. Framing has an impact on the way in which citizens and political leaders deliberate about policy questions. Consider a proposed tax cut. One could frame the issue as a matter of economic stimulus, thereby steering the debate toward estimates of its impact on investment and job creation. Alternatively, one could frame it as an issue of equity, thereby highlighting its potential impact on the relative tax burdens of the rich and poor.

The framing of political stories often stresses conflict instead of public policy. In covering elections, the news media frequently indulge in "**horse race journalism**," concentrating on which candidates are ahead or behind rather than explaining where they stand on the issues.[31] During the 2012 race for the Republican presidential nomination, 64% of campaign coverage revolved around polls, advertising, fund-raising, strategy, and the question of who was winning or losing. Domestic policy issues accounted for just 9% of the coverage and foreign policy was virtually invisible at a mere 1%.[32]

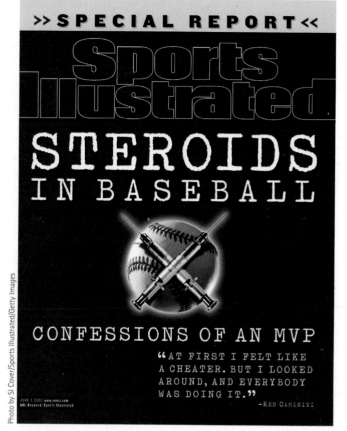

A 2002 cover story in *Sports Illustrated* generated widespread coverage in the mainstream press and spurred Congress to hold hearings on drug abuse in professional sports.

The horse race frame does little to serve good citizenship and deliberation. After all, does knowing that one candidate is a front-runner help anyone know what is good for the country and how to achieve it? Citizens say they want the kind of information that will help them be better citizens: more coverage of candidate issue positions and *less* coverage of the horse race and fund-raising.[33]

Even dealing with policy, the media may still frame stories less about content than conflict. During the 2000 presidential race, said Frank Bruni of the *New York Times*, some reporters would "goad one candidate into criticizing a second candidate's position on an issue, use that comment to coax a retort from the second candidate, then write about how the two had 'feuded' or 'sparred' on the campaign trail that day. Of course the candidates had—they were set up to do so."[34] When reporters keep asking newsmakers about a controversy, the questions themselves become the story. A typical headline might read "Questions about Voting Record Dog Candidate."[35]

Horse race journalism may not be good for citizenship. Evidence suggests that an emphasis on political maneuvering and conflict makes people more cynical about public life.[36] All other things being equal, cynical people are less likely to take part in political and civic affairs. Moreover, horse race journalism deprives citizens of information they need to deliberate about policy and candidate choice. According to journalism educator Jay Rosen, "the job of the campaign press is not to preempt the voters' decision by asking endlessly, and predicting constantly, who's going to win. The job is to make certain that what needs to be discussed will be discussed in time to make a difference—and then report on that."[37]

As we shall see later, political figures do not merely react to the media's agenda setting, priming, and framing. In various ways, they try to influence these processes in order to advance their own priorities.

Priming—the process by which the media emphasize some issues over others, thereby affecting the standards by which people make political judgments.

Framing—the way in which the media define an issue by emphasizing or deemphasizing certain aspects of that issue.

Horse race journalism—reporting that emphasizes the candidates' chances of election instead of their policies.

FOCUS QUESTION

The news media shape the issues about which we deliberate. Are there important issues that they tend to overlook?

Photo by SI Cover/Sports Illustrated/Getty Images

Direct Involvement

Sometimes media owners and executives openly use their news organizations to promote a cause. In the late nineteenth century, William Randolph Hearst stoked international conflict through sensationalized stories about alleged misdeeds by Spain. He got his wish with the Spanish-American War. A more recent and benign example is Robert Wright, chairman and chief executive officer of NBC/Universal. After his grandson received a diagnosis of autism, Wright became a champion of autistic people and their families. To increase autism awareness, he encouraged NBC, MSNBC, and CNBC to run numerous stories on the disorder.[38]

Editorial—an unsigned article expressing a view of publishers or editors.

Most newspapers and some news magazines run **editorials**, unsigned articles expressing the views of publishers or editors. During election season, the editorials may include endorsements of candidates and ballot measures. Many readers often skip editorials, which usually do not determine races for high-profile offices such as president or governor. But with lower-profile elections (e.g., municipal judge, county coroner), where voters have fewer cues to use, editorial endorsements can make a difference.[39] Journalist David Freelander writes of the local impact of the *New York Times*:

> The *Times*' coverage of local politics has shrunk in recent years with the closing of the Metro section, but the paper's ability to make or break candidates has grown. In conversations with nearly two dozen political operatives, office holders and candidates, the consensus was that the *Times* remains the biggest single factor in deciding who gets elected in this town. The paper's imprimatur carries more weight than even the biggest unions. Pollsters estimate that a *Times* endorsement can boost a candidate anywhere between 5 and 20 points.[40]

Major media figures occasionally seek office themselves. Horace Greeley, longtime editor of the *New York Tribune*, was the 1872 presidential nominee of the Democratic and Liberal Republican parties. (He lost to Republican incumbent Ulysses S. Grant.) Michael Bloomberg, founder of a multimedia news company, successfully ran for mayor of New York in 2001, 2005, and 2009. Journalists themselves, however, usually refrain from partisan activities in order to maintain an image of objectivity. The exceptions have been controversial. In 2010, MSNBC suspended host Keith Olbermann after news reports revealed that he had contributed money to Democratic candidates.[41] He left the network a year later.

Like other businesses, media companies try to influence public policy through lobbying operations. News outlets are often in the awkward position of covering the officials that their owners are trying to influence. Although there is little hard evidence that the companies slant the news to benefit their government relations efforts, critics still suggest that they have conflicts of interest. Potential conflicts multiply when the parent company is a conglomerate that does business in diverse fields. In 2012, television networks tended to give little coverage to the grassroots fight against online piracy legislation (see Chapter 8), and critics noted that the networks' parent companies had an economic stake in the legislation's passage.[42]

PROFESSIONALISM, ACCURACY, AND BIAS
MAJOR ISSUE

- How fair and accurate are the media in portraying current events?

Trust in the media may suffer from the conflicts that we just examined. The Gallup Poll has regularly asked this question: "In general, how much trust and confidence do you have in the mass media—such as newspapers, TV and radio—when it comes to reporting the news fully, accurately, and fairly?" In 1972, 68% reported "a great deal" or "a fair amount."[43] In 2011, that figure stood at just 44%.[44] Is the public judging the news media too harshly? To answer that question, we should consider the journalists' motivations and professional standards.

The Standards of the Profession

A few journalists achieve wealth, fame, and glamour. Most do not. They receive modest pay and recognition, and they report from unglitzy places such as courthouses, city halls, and state capitols. Amid recent turmoil in the media industry, they worry about making a secure living, and they sometimes face danger, especially when covering warfare or terrorism.[45] During the Iraq war, columnist Michael Kelly died when the army vehicle in which he was traveling careened off the road while evading enemy fire. Bomb blasts severely injured ABC reporter Bob Woodruff and CBS reporter Kimberly Dozier. In Pakistan, terrorists kidnapped *Wall Street Journal* reporter Daniel Pearl, and when the American government did not give in to their demands, they beheaded him. Late in 2008, Taliban terrorists kidnapped *New York Times* reporter David Rohde in Afghanistan. Out of concern for his safety, the *Times* kept the abduction a secret until he escaped seven months later. As the Afghanistan war heated up in 2009, CBS reporter Cami McCormick suffered serious wounds in a roadside bombing. In 2012, American journalist Marie Colvin was reporting on the civil war in Syria for the London *Sunday Times* when she died in a shelling attack. For years she had worn an eye patch because of injuries she had sustained while covering another civil war, in Sri Lanka.

There are hazards at home as well. In 1956, labor columnist Victor Riesel was probing mob control of New York unions when a gangster threw acid in his face, blinding him for life. Twenty years later, a car bomb killed Don Bolles of the *Arizona Republic*, who had reported on organized crime and crooked land deals.

Despite economic and physical dangers, large numbers of students keep applying to journalism schools. "I've never met a single person in 35 years who went into journalism out of pure economic reason," says Nicholas Lemann, dean of the Columbia School of Journalism. "It doesn't make us recession-proof, but it makes us less recession responsive."[46] So why do people enter the profession? Despite risks and economic concerns, a recent poll finds, most say that they would want their children to become journalists. Good citizenship is a key motivation. Answering an open-ended question about reasons to take up a news career, 37% cite the chance to make a difference and serve society. Another 23% say that journalism is an important, noble calling.[47] Another survey asked them to tell in their own words what distinguishes journalism. Most journalists and media executives mentioned its contributions to society, including providing the public with information.[48] More than three-quarters saw journalism as a **watchdog** against corruption and abuse, believing that investigative reporting deters official wrongdoing.

Watchdog role—the news media's part in exposing corruption and official misconduct.

That survey also showed wide agreement on the basic principles of journalism: getting the facts right, getting both sides of the story, providing interpretation while remaining politically neutral, and not publishing rumors. The Society of Professional Journalists has elaborated on these principles in a code of ethics.[49] There is no formal way to enforce this code. Unlike physicians and attorneys, newspeople do not need a license or a specific credential. Apart from the journalists' own sense of integrity and good citizenship, the main guardian of standards is professional reputation. When word gets out that reporters have cut corners or used sleazy tactics, they usually find it tougher to get work. Nevertheless, the profession has had to grapple with problems concerning accuracy and bias.

Mistakes

Deliberation requires consensus about at least some elements of basic information. People rely on the press to supply such information, so doubt about its accuracy hinders deliberation.

AP Photo/Lefteris Pitarakis

A memorial service program for journalist Marie Colvin, who died while covering a civil war in Syria.

Journalists literally run to report the Supreme Court health-care decision on June 28, 2012. Not all of them got it right.

Mark Wilson/Getty Images

Nearly everyone who has witnessed a news event will spot flaws in the press coverage. Deadline pressure leads to mistakes, especially when news organizations compete to break a story. During the few hours before deadline, reporters must speak to sources who may tell conflicting versions. Journalists seldom have time for deep research to confirm their background information; and then they have to write a thousand or more words, roughly equal to a four-page take-home essay. News organizations have long tried to remedy this problem by assigning reporters to **beats**: specific issues (e.g., the environment), institutions (e.g., the Senate), or geographic regions. Beat journalists develop the expertise to report with depth, accuracy, and speed. Beat reporting, however, has been a casualty of staff cutbacks. Reporters who once had one beat may now have two or three. In interviews with the Project for Excellence in Journalism, newspaper editors agreed the coverage had become skimpier.[50]

Errors are likely in the chaos of disaster. After the attacks on the World Trade Center on September 11, 2001, some news stories said that the death toll could reach 10,000. The reporters were just repeating guesses made by officials. The actual figure turned out to be

Beat—a specific issue (e.g., the environment), institution (e.g., the Senate), or geographic region in which a journalist may specialize.

IMPACT
of Social Media and Communications Technology

Instant Analysis of the Supreme Court Decision on Health Care

On June 28, 2012, the United States Supreme Court issued an important decision on the comprehensive health care law that Congress had passed two years earlier. The decision and the accompanying opinions took up nearly 200 pages of text. Chief Justice Roberts's majority opinion was fairly complicated, arguing that the constitutionality of the individual mandate to buy health insurance rested not on Congress's power to regulate interstate commerce, but on its power to levy taxes.

Television networks and online news organizations were under pressure to break the story quickly. As a result, some journalists reported the decision before they understood it.[51] For instance, a CNN producer inside the courtroom told a reporter that the justices had overturned the mandate. The reporter then repeated the misinformation on air, and the network's Web site followed suit. Less than an hour later, the Bessette-Pitney blog showed two banner headlines from CNN.com. The first read, "The Supreme Court has struck down the individual mandate." The second read, "Correction: The Supreme Court backs all parts of President Obama's signature health care law." The correction was not entirely correct itself, since the Court had invalidated a provision dealing with Medicaid. (See Bessette-Pitney blog post for July 3, 2012.)

Responding to the early false reports, several congressional opponents of the law issued tweets celebrating the decision. After news organizations made their corrections, the lawmakers deleted the tweets, but the Politwoops Web site (politwoops.sunlightfoundation.com/)

preserved them for posterity—and the lawmakers' lingering embarrassment. (See Bessette-Pitney blog of July 1, 2012.)

Richard Mourdock, a Republican Senate candidate from Indiana, acted in advance, preparing video statements in response to four possible outcomes. The idea was to wait until the Court acted, and then swiftly post the response that best fit the result. Instead, however, his campaign mistakenly put all four videos on YouTube several days ahead of the decision. The blunder drew widespread criticism.[52]

Of course, the coverage was not simply a series of errors. Bloomberg News correctly reported the decision within a minute after Chief Justice Roberts began reading his oral summary. Shortly after Fox News mistakenly declared that the justices had overturned the mandate, anchor Megyn Kelly (a lawyer by training) made an on-air correction, citing SCOTUSblog, a respected legal blog.

CRITICAL THINKING QUESTION

Picture yourself as a network correspondent shortly after 10:00 AM (EST) on the morning of June 28, 2012. You have the densely written decision in your hand. You know that your career may suffer if you let competitors scoop you on the story—or if you get it wrong. What do you do?

less than one-third as high. In 2005, Hurricane Katrina gave rise to wild stories, such as one about 30–40 bodies lying in a freezer at the Superdome. Nothing of the kind happened. The reporter later learned that the National Guardsmen, who were the source of the story, had not actually seen any bodies in a freezer but instead were repeating a rumor they had heard in a food line.[53]

Technology may tempt reporters into risky shortcuts. With search engines such as Google, journalists can quickly gather old stories. They may repeat information without checking it. Searches may thus turn up misinformation. Conversely, media critics and bloggers can use the same technology to find and expose mistakes.

Dishonesty

The media have not been immune to dishonesty. Most newsreels about World War I included fake footage, with actors standing in for real soldiers.[54] The same was true of early documentaries about World War II, though the practice became less common as the war went on. Today, the ethics code of the Radio and Television News Directors Association says that broadcast journalists should not present "re-enactments" of news events without labeling them as such.[55]

Major news organizations try to maintain high standards of integrity, but there have been some important lapses. In 2003, the *New York Times* received a complaint from a San Antonio paper that *Times* reporter Jayson Blair had plagiarized one of its stories. The investigation led the newspaper's staff to discover dozens of cases in which he had either concocted information or taken it from other sources without attribution. The incident stained the paper's reputation and led to the resignation of top editors.

In September 2004, CBS News aired a story raising questions about President George W. Bush's service in the Texas Air National Guard during the Vietnam War. On its Web site, CBS posted its evidence: memos that supposedly came from a superior officer. Within hours, bloggers noticed that the documents looked more like the product of a word processor than a 1970s typewriter (see the photo). News organizations soon followed, spotting inconsistencies in the documents' content and physical layout. CBS defended the story for a while, and then admitted that it could not authenticate the documents. The network apologized and commissioned an outside report. Although CBS did not mean to air dubious documents, the report concluded, its "myopic zeal" led to its failure to check the facts.[56] CBS identified the man who provided the documents, but their origins remain murky. As a result of the story, the network fired several employees. Dan Rather, longtime anchor of the CBS Evening News and the on-air reporter for the story, announced his retirement.

The Depths and the Shallows

Even when news organizations avoid blatant mistakes or lies, many question whether they provide the depth necessary for Americans to deliberate on public policy. National and local journalists generally accept the criticism that news organizations have cut back too much on the scope of coverage. Large majorities also acknowledge the complaint that the press pays too little attention to complex issues.[57] The problem is not a lack of motivation. But technology has not only increased competition among news organizations; it has given citizens many other ways to spend their time. Back in the 1960s, evening news broadcasts and special events (e.g., presidential press conferences) got large audiences because little else was airing at the same time. Now viewers can choose from hundreds of channels showing sports, movies, and other forms of entertainment. Other media suffer as well.

Business pressures thus come into play. Colorful figures such as Joseph Pulitzer may have stressed sensationalism, but they also had a passion for news. Conglomerates, by contrast, see their mission as peddling "eyeballs

111th Fighter Interceptor Squadron
P. O. Box 34567
Houston, Texas 77034

04 May 1972

MEMORANDUM FOR 1st Lt. George W. Bush, ███████, Houston, Texas 77027.

SUBJECT: Annual Physical Examination (Flight)

1. You are ordered to report to commander, 111 F.I.S., Ellington AFB, not later than (NLT) 14 May, 1972, to conduct annual physical examination (flight) IAW AFM 35-13.

2. Report to 111th F.I.S. administrative officer for schedule of appointment and additional instructions. Examination will be conducted in duty status.

JERRY B. KILLIAN
Lt. Colonel
Commander

U.S. National Guard

"[E]very single one of these memos to file is in a proportionally spaced font, probably Palatino or Times New Roman," one blog commenter said of the documents' appearance. "The use of proportionally spaced fonts did not come into common use for office memos until the introduction of laser printers, word processing software, and personal computers. They were not widespread until the mid to late 90's . . . I am saying these documents are forgeries, run through a copier for 15 generations to make them look old."

to advertisers"—that is, increasing their audience so that they can sell more print space or airtime. Many national and local journalists contend that conglomerates have hurt the news business.[58] They blame business executives for insisting on shorter, snappier stories. The executives are also shifting resources away from news. During the 1980s and 1990s, newspapers and networks closed many foreign bureaus to save money. Without their own full-time staff in place, they must rely on wire services or other news outlets.

The 30-minute network evening news broadcast is giving less and less time to information. The average number of minutes devoted to news, as opposed to advertising, fell from 22.5 in 1968 to 22.0 in 1980 to 19.2 in 1996.[59] Sound bites—audio clips from speeches or interviews—got shorter. In coverage of presidential elections, the average candidate sound bite shrank from more than 40 seconds during the 1960s to less than 10 seconds in the 1980s to less than 8 seconds in 2004.[60]

Coverage of international affairs has taken an especially big hit. On the one hand, it can be very costly for news organizations to maintain bureaus overseas. On the other hand, serious stories of faraway countries are less likely to attract audiences than celebrity news and gossip. Between 1985 and 2010, according to a study of major U.S. daily newspapers by the *American Journalism Review*, coverage of foreign news fell by 53%. The percentage of staff-produced foreign stories also dropped, from 15% in 1985 to 4% in 2010, and the globe fell off the front page. In 1985, 9% of foreign stories appeared on page 1, compared with 6% in 2010.[61]

Leslie Gelb, a former reporter and senior government official, explains the consequences for deliberation on international issues:

> You can say, "What the devil difference does it make?" The difference that it makes is that the United States is still the most important country in the world. Even China will say that America is the leader on any international issue. The interested public in America absolutely has to have reliable information about what's going on in all those countries. Otherwise, our leaders do dumb things, and the American people never know about it. It's just that important.
>
> Just look at getting into Iraq or into Afghanistan. There were very few people who knew these countries who could tell us what it would be like once the boots were on the ground there, or what we would be running into. We developed that capacity after the fact. . . . You need reporters on the ground who know those places who can do the reporting.[62]

Ideological Bias in the News?

Because of their commitment to presenting all sides of an issue, journalists seldom deliberately tilt their coverage in favor of liberals or conservatives, Republicans or Democrats. But what of subtle and unintentional bias? By definition, subtle bias is hard to measure, and research has shown that when people with opposing viewpoints see the same news report, each will think that it shows a bias in favor of the other side.[63] Accordingly, there is disagreement about the question.

Some conservatives say that the media show a *liberal bias*. They point to polls showing that the press is more liberal than the public (see Figure 11-4). Many journalists think of themselves as moderates, though conservatives contend that press coverage belies this image. MSNBC.com identified 143 journalists who made federal political contributions from 2004 through the start of the 2008 campaign. Of this number, 125 gave to Democrats and liberal causes, while 16 gave to Republicans and 2 gave to both parties.[64] One recent study finds that major newspapers and television news programs tend to cite liberal think tanks more

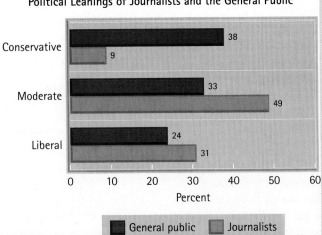

Political Leanings of Journalists and the General Public

FIGURE 11–4 Journalists comprise fewer conservatives and more liberals than the general public, although nearly half call themselves moderate.
SOURCE: Surveys of 673 journalists, March 7–May 2, 2005 and 1,500 adults March 3–April 5, 2005, Annenberg Public Policy Center, "Public and Press Differ About Partisan Bias, Accuracy and Press Freedom, New Annenberg Public Policy Center Survey Shows," May 24, 2005, at www.annenbergpublicpolicycenter.org/Downloads/IoD_Survey_Findings_Summer2005/Partisan_Bias_20050524.pdf, accessed July 7, 2012.

often than conservative ones and that media bias does indeed shape public opinion.[65] "Too often, we wear liberalism on our sleeve and are intolerant of other lifestyles and opinions," a *Washington Post* book review editor observed. "I've been in communal gatherings in *The Post*, watching election returns, and have been flabbergasted to see my colleagues cheer unabashedly for the Democrats."[66] Jon Stewart told Fox reporter Chris Wallace:

> I think that there is a—probably a liberal bias that exists within the media that is because of the medium in which it exists. I think that the majority of people working in it probably hold liberal viewpoints, but I don't think that they are as relentlessly activist as the conservative movement that has risen up over the last 40 years.
>
> And that movement has decided that they have been victims of a witch hunt. And to some extent they're right.
>
> People on the right are called racists and they're called things with an ease that I am uncomfortable with—and homophobic and all those other things. And I think that that is absolutely something that they have a real right to be angry about and to feel that they have been vilified for those things. And I've been guilty of doing some of those things myself.[67]

Some liberals speak of a *conservative* media bias. With the growth of Internet sites, talk radio, and all-news television have come more opportunities for opinion and analysis. While reporters try to stick to the middle, liberal analysts say, the key commentators are conservatives: talk-show host Rush Limbaugh, columnist George Will, and Internet journalist Matt Drudge. There are conservative-leaning newspapers (the *New York Post* and *Washington Times*), magazines (*The Weekly Standard* and *National Review*), and conservative-leaning religious and business channels. The Fox News Channel comes in for special criticism.[68] Roger Ailes, the founder and head of Fox News, was a longtime Republican operative, and critics say that his fingerprints are all over the network's news coverage. One study finds that Fox coverage helps persuade some of its viewers to vote Republican.[69] As First Lady, Hillary Rodham Clinton said that these outlets were part of a "vast right-wing conspiracy."

According to yet another school of thought, media bias is a matter of neither liberalism nor conservatism, but favoritism toward the United States and its government. Just before the Iraq war in 2003, a liberal advocacy group studied on-camera network news sources. Two-thirds were from the United States, and three-quarters of the American sources were current or former government officials.[70] After it became clear that Saddam Hussein did not currently have weapons of mass destruction, journalists regretted that they had not forcefully questioned American government assertions that he did.[71]

One reason for any pro-government bias could be the "revolving door" between the press and official Washington. (See Chapter 8 on interest groups for discussion of a similar "revolving door.") Over the years, many people have jumped between work in politics and the mass media. David Gergen worked for Republican presidents Nixon, Ford, and Reagan, then became a television commentator and editor for *U.S. News & World Report*. In 1993, he joined the staff of Democratic president Bill Clinton; after that stint, he returned to journalism. In 1989, *Washington Post* reporter David Broder openly worried about "a Washington Insiders' clique."[72] Twenty years later, amid newsroom job cuts, an unusually large number of journalists left their profession to work for the Obama administration and the Democratic congressional leadership.[73]

Yet another purported bias consists of support for big business. In one survey, most national and local journalists said that owners and advertisers do not have much influence over which stories their news organization covered or emphasized, but about a quarter did see owners or advertisers having a great deal or a fair amount of influence.[74] Those skeptical of a big-business bias would respond that the press has run many stories critical of corporate America, especially the tobacco industry.

Although perfect objectivity is impossible, deliberate bias may hamper deliberation, since one cannot reason on the merits of policy without knowing multiple perspectives and positions. And the public wants news that is more useful to deliberation: two-thirds of Americans say they prefer political news with no point of view to news that shares

FOCUS
FOCUS QUESTION

So that news audiences are aware of potential bias, should journalists publicly disclose their political preferences and affiliations?

their political views.[75] Journalists claim that they give the people what they want, through rigorous efforts to balance opposing viewpoints, but one argument holds that balance itself can be a form of bias. One study contended that major newspapers gave too much attention to the vocal minority of researchers who dissent from the scientific consensus on global warming.[76]

Bias, Citizenship, and Deliberation

Distorted or incomplete information can hamper deliberation. Perhaps the most striking recent example is the Iraq war. In the months before the war, much of the public debate assumed that Iraq had weapons of mass destruction. If the press had more vigorously questioned this assumption, then lawmakers and other public figures would have made more accurate arguments, and the debate might have taken a different course.

A subtler problem involves investigative reporting. Journalists strongly believe in their watchdog role, and they cite reporting on Watergate as a key example (see the Myths and Misinformation feature below). But they also recognize that scandal coverage can feed on itself.[77] That is, when a reporter recounts alleged misdeeds, other reporters and the politicians will pile on, often making inaccurate claims and stoking a controversy far out of proportion to the original offense. Such media-driven conflicts may distract attention from more serious issues or lead to ill-considered policies. The surge in media attention to toxic waste dumping led Congress to pass the 1980 Superfund cleanup legislation. Supporters of the bill dismissed concerns about its design. "The people are not interested in technicalities," said Representative James Jeffords (R-VT). "Let us help the people now and take care of the technicalities later."[78] The law proved costly and inefficient.[79]

Just as inaccurate information can undercut deliberation, some argue, media bias may undermine citizenship by deepening divisions in society. The Internet and talk radio now allow liberals and conservatives to receive most of their political information from like-minded sources. People may sort themselves into smaller groups, only hearing what reinforces their beliefs. A republic, writes legal scholar (and Obama administration official) Cass Sunstein, depends "on a set of common experiences and on unsought, unanticipated, and even unwanted exposures to diverse topics, people, and ideas. A system of 'gated communities' is as unhealthy for cyberspace as it is for the real world."[80] Commenting on the

MYTHS AND MISINFORMATION

Journalism in the Movies

Since the early days of talking pictures, Hollywood has produced many movies about journalism. Sometimes the depiction is heroic, sometimes villainous, but it is seldom completely accurate. Says Bill Goodykoontz of the *Arizona Republic*, "most of us have jobs that, if they were depicted with 100% authenticity, would be a crashing bore to sit through. Journalism is no different. . . . In other words, no one wants to see a movie about a roomful of people typing."[82]

Perhaps the best-known journalism movie of the late twentieth century was *All the President's Men* (1976), a gripping account of how two *Washington Post* reporters helped uncover the Watergate scandal. The film won several Academy Awards and gained a great deal of praise for the realistic look of its newsroom scenes. Yet like the book that inspired it, the film left the impression that the reporters exposed the scandal mostly by themselves. In fact, Congress, the FBI, and the courts all played key roles.[83]

The movie inserted a small but significant falsehood into discussions of Watergate. In memorable and melodramatic scenes, reporter Bob Woodward (Robert Redford) meets "Deep Throat" (Hal Holbrook), a mysterious source who tells him how to unravel the mystery: "Follow the money." That line has become a staple of political commentary. When journalist Daniel Schorr could not find it in the book that inspired the movie, he spoke to the screenwriter. "I can't believe I made it up," said William Goldman. "I was in constant contact with Woodward while writing the screenplay. I guess he made it up." Woodward thought that Goldman had made it up. Whoever wrote the line, concluded Schorr, "it was an invention."[84]

In 2005, when former FBI official Mark Felt revealed that he was Deep Throat, many news stories attributed the fictional line to him.

tendency for people to tune in commentators with whom they agree, conservative satirist P. J. O'Rourke asks, "I wonder; when was the last time a conservative talk show changed a mind?"[81] The danger is that people in the "gated communities" of biased communication may see people with other viewpoints as enemies rather than fellow citizens. As noted earlier, however, most Americans say that they prefer to get political news with no point of view rather than news that shares their political news.

GOVERNMENT AND MEDIA

MAJOR ISSUE

- How has government action curbed or protected political expression in the media?

In 2006, the Canadian magazine *Maclean's* published an article arguing that the rise of Islam threatened Western culture. Two years later, it faced a trial before the British Columbia Human Rights Tribunal on whether it had violated a provincial law. In Canada and a number of other liberal democracies, laws forbid the press to practice what the government defines as hate speech.[85] In the United States, by contrast, the First Amendment protects freedom of the press, even when the content is arguably hateful or false. (People who suffer harm as a result of false stories may sue for libel, but the government can neither suppress them nor impose criminal penalties after publication.) This protection, however, has not always been effective, and even today, difficult and controversial questions still surround the relationship of the government and the mass media.

Press Freedom, the Law, and the Courts

As we mentioned earlier, the Sedition Act of the late eighteenth century led to serious violations of freedom of the press. In 1918, during World War I, Congress passed another Sedition Act. Among other things, it forbade anyone to "willfully utter, print, write, or publish any disloyal, profane, scurrilous, or abusive language about the form of government of the United States, or the Constitution of the United States, or the military or naval forces of the United States." It also authorized the post office to deny deliveries to those who allegedly used the mails to undermine the government. The Wilson administration used this authority to suppress radical newspapers. Congress repealed the act in 1921, but a number of states had passed their own versions. In the 1925 case of *Gitlow v. New York*, the Supreme Court upheld a New York law that had led to the arrest of a socialist pamphleteer.[86] But for the first time, the Court said that the First Amendment applied to the states as well as the federal government. (See the discussion of the incorporation doctrine in Chapter 5 on civil liberties.)

In 1931, it relied on this reasoning to strike down a Minnesota law enabling the state government to stop publication of any "malicious, scandalous and defamatory newspaper, magazine or other periodical."[87] It held that the First Amendment prevented any level of government from exercising prior restraint of expression except under extraordinary circumstances. Forty years later, the Court drew on this precedent in a case involving the Pentagon Papers, a classified history of the Vietnam policy. The Nixon administration had tried to halt publication of the papers, but in *New York Times Co. v. United States*, the Court ruled that prior restraint in this case was unconstitutional.[88]

Control of the Broadcast Media

Despite constitutional protections for the news media in general, broadcast television and radio are subject to federal oversight because the public owns the airwaves. In the 1920s,

Federal Communications Commission (FCC)—the federal agency that regulates the electronic media.

Media market—the geographic area that receives broadcasts from a set of stations.

Equal time rule—the federal requirement that broadcasters who sell or give airtime to one candidate must provide the same opportunity for all other candidates for the same office.

Fairness doctrine—the 1949 FCC ruling that licensees were "public trustees" who must provide a forum for diverse views. In 1987, the FCC scrapped the doctrine, allowing for more opinionated programming.

the federal government regulated the growing radio industry because neighboring stations interfered with each other by broadcasting on the same frequencies. Congress updated federal regulation in 1934 by creating the **Federal Communications Commission (FCC)**. Congress empowered the FCC to license broadcasters in the name of "public interest, convenience, and necessity."

Federal laws and rules limit the ownership of broadcast media. No network may own television stations that together reach more than 39% of the nation's television households. There are restrictions on how many television and radio stations one owner may have within a single market. (A **media market** is the area that receives broadcasts from a set of stations.) And none of the four major broadcast networks (ABC, NBC, CBS, and Fox) may buy any of the others. The goal is to prevent monopolies.

Under the 1934 act creating the FCC, broadcasters who sold or gave airtime to one candidate would have to give the same chance for all other candidates for the same office. The FCC read this "**equal time**" rule to mean that broadcast campaign debates would have to be open to all minor party candidates. This interpretation discouraged broadcaster-sponsored debates between major party nominees. In 1983, however, the FCC ruled that broadcasters could sponsor debates between major party candidates alone.

In 1949, the FCC ruled that television and radio broadcasters were "public trustees" and therefore had a duty to present contrasting points of view whenever dealing with controversial public issues. Supporters said that this **fairness doctrine** enhanced deliberation by ensuring that the public could hear a variety of views. According to its critics, however, it chilled debate. Broadcasters feared that if they aired one view, they would have to give up valuable airtime for presentations of all other views whether or not the likely ratings would support the additional programming.[89] In 1987, the FCC scrapped the doctrine. Recently, some lawmakers have spoken of reviving the fairness doctrine, pointing to the proliferation of one-sided media outlets. Opponents of revival point to the large number of viewpoints available on radio, cable TV, and the Internet.

Unlike many nations, the United States does not have a government-owned network that offers domestic broadcasts. Nevertheless, the Corporation for Public Broadcasting does receive federal money, which it gives to local public television and radio stations and the Public Broadcasting Service (PBS), a private, nonprofit corporation.

The federal government also makes broadcasts overseas. With an annual budget of more than $190 million, the Voice of America (VOA) airs news and other programming in 45 languages through radio, satellite television, and the Internet.[90] The American Forces Radio and Television Service (AFRTS) provides radio and television to military and civilian defense personnel serving outside the United States.[91]

Government Information

Nearly every agency and elected official employs aides to provide information to the press. Although laws and rules require the release of certain kinds of material, press aides usually are quick to highlight good news and downplay bad news. Sometimes their practices spark controversy. After Congress passed a prescription drug benefit in 2003, the Department of Health and Human Services produced "video news releases" praising the new law. The videos resembled actual news stories, complete with interviews and voiceovers but without any identification of the source. If local stations broadcast the releases without adding a disclaimer, viewers would think they were watching "objective" news stories. The General Accounting Office said that the releases constituted "covert propaganda that violated federal law."[92] Agencies have usually avoided that problem by labeling their promotional materials.

Government can influence coverage not only through what it provides the news media, but also by what it withholds. The 1966 Freedom of Information Act (FOIA) gives people the right to access federal agency records. (There are similar laws on the state level as well.) Journalists make frequent use of FOIA. It has exceptions, however, and even where it applies, officials can be slow and grudging in response to information requests. President Obama came to office with a commitment to improve the transparency of government operations. Reporters gave him mixed grades on the subject. When an open-government group gave him an award, he accepted in an unannounced meeting that was closed to the press.[93]

Government influence on the media is an especially grave issue in time of war. During the war with Iraq, the Defense Department "embedded" reporters in military units. Each **embedded journalist** stayed with one unit for a lengthy period, gaining contextual knowledge that he or she might not otherwise get. The Pentagon has also trained journalists about survival skills and life in uniform. These efforts have led to better-informed reporting, but they may also shade the news in the military's favor.[94] Critics also argue that embedded journalism focuses narrowly on personal stories instead of larger questions of strategy.

During World War II, the military subjected correspondents to censorship for security reasons.

An excerpt from the Wikileaks embassy cables, printed in the Wednesday, December 1, 2010, edition of the *New York Times*.

Censorship was largely absent during Vietnam, but reporters argued that the government had plied them with misinformation. In recent military conflicts, the release of sensitive information has remained a point of contention between news organizations and the government. In 2010, the Wikileaks Web site posted thousands of pages of classified documents about the wars in Iraq and Afghanistan. It provided material in advance to selected news organizations, including the *New York Times*. Government officials condemned the publication of the documents, saying that it could put American lives at risk.

Embedded journalist—a reporter who stays with a single military unit for a long period.

INFLUENCING THE MEDIA

MAJOR ISSUE

- How do public figures try to influence media content?

Politicians and other public figures have certain ways of reaching the public directly, including mass mailings and the Internet. They can also get their message across by going on friendly talk radio programs and late-night television. But to communicate with the general public, they also need to influence news reporting.

Media Leaders

A few lead organizations influence the rest of media. Accordingly, newsmakers who want national or regional coverage will focus their efforts on these organizations.

Most newspapers do not have correspondents in Washington or foreign countries; instead, their national and international news comes from **wire services** such as Dow Jones and Reuters. The largest and most important is Associated Press (AP). One Democratic operative told the *Atlantic Monthly*, "If you want the biggest bang for the buck, you get it in the AP. They have fifteen hundred plus subscribers, so you get them to run it, and it runs everywhere. . . . And if they break it, the thinking is that it must be important and worth covering."[95]

Wire service—an organization that provides news stories to subscribers, including newspapers and broadcasters.

In the same way, newsmakers try to influence leading publications. Journalist David Shaw asked where reporters get their ideas. "From the *New York Times*. The same is true of many local newspapers, which are heavily influenced by what's on Page 1 of the *New York Times*—and which, in turn, influence what local radio and TV stations think is news."[96] Other publications have influence over specific kinds of stories. The *Washington Post* specializes in the politics in the nation's capital, just as the *Wall Street Journal* covers business. And certain regional publications carry weight in their states, such as the *Los Angeles Times* in California or the *Chicago Tribune* in Illinois.

On television, news and interview programs play an important role. If a newsmaker can make an important or provocative comment on one of these programs, reporters will pick it up and build a story around it. On the Internet, the *Drudge Report* is a key site. Writes one media critic:

> If the Drudge Report homepage links to a news or gossip article, the story is practically guaranteed a million page views. This power of deciding what to show to the millions of everyday Drudge Report viewers—in other words, deciding what is news—is where Drudge's power lies. And it's the very reason why politicians coddle Matt Drudge and try desperately to maintain good relations with him, feeding him newsworthy items and insider knowledge, which gives him even more power in shaping the political environment.[97]

Social media are also playing an ever-increasing role in driving the news agenda. Most news organizations and journalists use Twitter to gain exposure by tweeting links to their work. Reporters read one another's tweets, thereby stepping up the speed with which they pick up a "hot" story. Political figures and interest groups also put information on social media, in the hopes that journalists will see and respond to it.

Pictures, Attacks, Mistakes, and Spin

Once public officials have identified which media they seek to influence, what do they do? Roger Ailes, the founding chairman of the Fox News Channel, worked for George H. W. Bush's 1988 presidential campaign. After that election, Ailes said, "Let's face it, there are three things that the media are interested in: pictures, mistakes, and attacks. . . . It's my orchestra pit theory of politics. If you have two guys on stage and one guy says, 'I have the solution to the Middle East problem,' and the other guy falls in the orchestra pit, who do you think is going to be on the evening news?"[98] Knowing how the media respond, public figures act accordingly.

Would-be newsmakers mount events for media coverage. Examples include press conferences, marches, rallies, and protest demonstrations. The Ruckus Society, which trains protest groups, teaches organizers to "work backward" from the pictures they want. "Ask yourself: If the only coverage of this action is one wire service photo, what single image will best convey our message? Consider everything: lighting, camera angle, visibility of the target, size of the banner, even the clothes your activists are wearing."[99]

Manipulation involves much more than pictures. Political figures and their spokespeople try to **spin** the news—that is, influence what journalists cover and how they report it. Adept practitioners have gained the informal title of "spin doctor." One tool for spinning is the **news conference** (or **press conference**), a session at which a public figure answers questions from a number of journalists. A common tool for spinning is the **news release** (or **press release**), a statement from a newsmaker in the form of a news story, complete with a catchy lead paragraph, along with quotations and supporting facts. Small-town news outlets often reprint news releases as their own stories, with little editing. Larger organizations disdain such practices but still rely on news releases for raw material. When preparing spokespeople to talk to reporters, press aides try to anticipate what questions will come up. To steer the conversation, they write **talking points**, short bulleted lists of facts, phrases, and other background material that the spokespeople can draw upon.

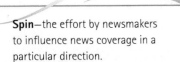

Spin—the effort by newsmakers to influence news coverage in a particular direction.

News conference (or press conference)—a session at which a public figure answers questions from a number of journalists.

News release (or press release)—a statement from a newsmaker in the form of a news story, complete with a catchy lead paragraph, along with quotations and supporting facts.

Talking points—short, bulleted lists containing suggested phrases and background material that an organization supplies to its supporters to prepare them for talking with reporters and the public.

In another method of spin control, **leaking**, political figures privately supply information to the press, usually with the agreement that their names will not appear. Sometimes leakers act without the knowledge of superiors. They may be trying to expose wrongdoing, scuttle policies they dislike, or smear their rivals. Often, however, leaks may come from the highest-ranking officials. In such cases, they may be floating **trial balloons**, informally bringing proposals to light in order to gauge political reactions. If a trial balloon leak reveals that a certain action would be unpopular, the leaker can ditch it without openly admitting that it was ever under consideration.

Leaks also come from **opposition researchers**, campaign operatives who specialize in finding information about the other side's candidate. Through press aides, they routinely provide clippings and documents to journalists, who use them in their own reporting. (Journalists seldom acknowledge the help from "oppo.") "Usually you can find stories that match up with the dynamics of different media outlets," said Democratic researcher Chris Lehane. "If you have videotape, you take it to a television outlet. If it's a complicated financial story, you take it to *The Wall Street Journal*. Something on special interests you take to the *New York Times*. It's all part of the process."[100]

Reporters face ethical dilemmas when they deal with political figures who are trying to manipulate them. If they accept the information, they may be advancing someone else's political strategy. If they reject it, they may be denying useful information to the public.

On August 28, 1963, a civil rights march on Washington attracted massive press attention.

MASS MEDIA AND DELIBERATIVE DEMOCRACY

As we have seen, commercial pressures may have harmed public deliberation by encouraging media owners to cut back on news content. There are possible remedies, however.

Civic Journalism

As we have seen, new technology has stepped up the pace of newsgathering and newsmaking. Journalists compete to see who can be first to get a story on the Internet or an all-news channel. While the volume of political exchange has increased, its quality may have diminished. Haste is the enemy of deliberation, and a rapid response is seldom a thoughtful response.

Efforts to make things better include **civic journalism**, a movement to enlist the news media in the service of deliberative democracy. This movement wants journalists to shift their focus from increasing circulation or audience share to fostering public discussion of community issues.[101] According to Jan Schaffer, the director of the Pew Center for Civic Journalism, "The goal is to produce news that citizens need to be educated about issues and current events, to make civic decisions, to engage in civic dialogue and action—and generally to exercise their responsibilities in a democracy."[102]

Most reporters applaud the effort to encourage serious stories, but other aspects of the movement create debate. At the local level, civic journalists often take polls to discover a community's concerns and then gear their coverage accordingly. Supporters say that it creates an informative dialogue between citizens and the press. Opponents dismiss it as

Leaking—the practice by which political figures privately supply information to the press, usually with the agreement that their names will not appear.

Trial balloon—proposals that newsmakers disclose to gauge the public's reaction.

Opposition researcher—a campaign operative who specializes in finding information about the other side's candidate.

Civic journalism—a movement urging journalists to shift their focus from increasing circulation or audience share to fostering public discussion of community issues.

a marketing gimmick in a deliberative disguise. "Why abandon the entire enterprise of informed, aggressive skepticism in the hope of pleasing an imagined public?" asked journalist David Remnick. "When journalists begin acting like waiters and taking orders from the public and pollsters, the results are not pretty."[103]

Self-Criticism

Ombudsman—a journalist who checks problems with accuracy, fairness, and taste in his or her own news organization's coverage, often publishing columns recommending remedies or responses.

Some news organizations have **ombudsmen** or "readers' advocates" to check problems with accuracy, fairness, and taste in their own news coverage. These professionals often publish columns recommending remedies or responses.[104] The ombudsman movement is still fairly small, but it reached a milestone when the *New York Times* named a "public editor" after the Jayson Blair scandal. One of his commentaries focused on the paper's coverage of social issues such as abortion and gay rights. "And if you think the *Times* plays it down the middle on any of them," he wrote, "you've been reading the paper with your eyes closed." He said that the paper presents "the social and cultural aspects of same-sex marriage in a tone that approaches cheerleading."[105]

Self-criticism has other venues as well. Some major news organizations have media critics, who write about news coverage in general and their own stories in particular. The *American Journalism Review* and the *Columbia Journalism Review* offer journalists and scholars a way to analyze reporting with an eye to improving its contributions to public deliberation. On a variety of Web sites devoted to politics and communications, bloggers post their own criticisms, suggestions, and analysis.

Amateurs and Professionals

Through blogs and YouTube, ordinary citizens are sometimes taking the news into their own hands. On the one hand, these efforts give people an opportunity to take part in public life and uncover information that advances deliberation on policy issues. A huge cache of primary-source material is available online, and video has been especially abundant since C-SPAN put its archives online in 2010. An amateur with time, patience, and knowledge of the material can dig up information that has eluded professional journalists. During the 2012 election, college student Andrew Kaczynski made a name for himself by finding revealing video of GOP presidential candidates and posting it on his YouTube channel.[106] (He went on to work for Buzzfeed.)

On the other hand, the amateur reporters often write poorly and lack training in the professional standards that career journalists try to uphold. Although there is an abundance of primary source information online—press conference transcripts, speech texts, government reports, statistical tables—it takes long study and experience to make sense of it. More important, some key information is not available online. It only comes to the surface when professional reporters make calls, knock on doors, and spend hours in musty archives.

Columnist Debra Saunders has explained why the Internet is not a genuine substitute for the mainstream media: "As for those who only read their news online, here's a news flash: News stories do not sprout up like Jack's bean stalk on the Internet. To produce news, you need professionals who understand the standards needed to research, report and write on what happened. If newspapers die, reliable information dries up." The Internet, she goes on, cannot be the solution when "all those shiny new Web sites are linking to fewer real news stories. What looks like more choice isn't. It's more doors leading to fewer rooms. When a newspaper dies, you don't get a comprehensive periodical to fill the void. You get an informational vacant lot into which passers-by can throw their junk."[107]

The result will be that citizens and officials will have less information for their deliberations. As Saunders explains, the impact will be particularly serious at the local level.

> [T]here also won't be as many stories about sanctuary city policies gone bad, the latest zany law out of San Francisco City Hall, or the growing bite that public employee pension systems are taking out of city and county services.

They don't understand that Fox News and talk radio aren't going to report on stories that require local beat reporting and time-consuming and expensive investigation. And there won't be as many nonideological stories—about crimes or zoning or state spending—until what was once a solvable problem festers, unreported, into a front-page disaster. By then, there may not be a front page.[108]

The picture is not entirely bleak. Some online news organizations are practicing traditional and professional journalism, though with new tools. It is also possible that newspapers and magazines may find ways to ease the economic problems that have plagued them over the past decade. The economic crisis that started in 2008 has put new pressure on them, though, so time is running short.

**FOCUS
QUESTION**

Do social media make it easier or harder to be a good citizen? That is, are they a political resource that empowers ordinary Americans, or a distraction that diverts attention from serious issues?

SUMMARY

- The news media influence what Americans know of the world around them. To understand American politics, we should ask what influences the content of these media.
- Critics fear that corporate control has stifled pluralism. Others say that the Internet has supplied ordinary citizens with new opportunities to get around, over, and under the "mainstream media."
- The federal government does regulate broadcast media, but no longer polices the news for fairness and balance. The presence of government regulation, however, does give politicians leverage over media companies and in turn prompts those companies to lobby the government.
- Pressure for speed and sensation may give rise to mistakes. Sometimes journalists even lie. Perhaps

more important is the question of depth: whether the media discuss public policy with enough detail to provide citizens with an adequate understanding of the issues.
- Many observers believe that the media show political bias, but consensus about its direction is lacking. Various observers see liberal, conservative, or establishmentarian bias, but it is obvious that the media tend to favor organizations and public figures who have mastered the art of manipulation.
- The news media help set the nation's issue agenda, but some worry that they clutter that agenda with trivial items that draw audiences. One response to this concern is the civic journalism movement, which aims to elevate deliberation in the media.

KEY TERMS

TEST YOUR KNOWLEDGE

1. The *Federalist Papers* were originally published as a
   a. book.
   b. memo to delegates at the Constitutional Convention.
   c. scholarly article in a professional journal.
   d. series of newspaper articles.
   e. series of pamphlets.
2. The sensational stories of sex and violence emphasized by Pulitzer and Hearst are early examples of
   a. agenda setting.
   b. embedded journalism.
   c. framing.
   d. priming.
   e. yellow journalism.
3. Broadcast television networks make most of their money from
   a. acting as government watchdogs.
   b. airing policy deliberation.
   c. engaging in yellow journalism.
   d. interviewing political candidates.
   e. selling ads on non-news-based programs.
4. Corporations who own several different kinds of media businesses are called
   a. embedded corporations.
   b. media conglomerates.
   c. muckrakers.
   d. networks.
   e. wire services.
5. The process by which topics come up for deliberation in the political world is called
   a. agenda-setting.
   b. embedding.
   c. framing.
   d. leaking.
   e. priming.
6. What reason do most journalists cite for entering their profession?
   a. citizenship
   b. economic gain
   c. fame
   d. exciting events
   e. relaxed atmosphere
7. A specific issue, institution, or geographic region in which a journalist specializes is called a(n)
   a. agenda.
   b. beat.
   c. editorial.
   d. ombudsman.
   e. wire.
8. In *Gitlow v. New York* the Supreme Court first ruled that
   a. Congress could not suppress radical newspapers.
   b. Congress has the power to regulate radical speech in times of war.
   c. the First Amendment applied to the states as well as the federal government.
   d. the First Amendment is applicable only to federal laws.
   e. the Sedition Act was unconstitutional.
9. Dow Jones and Reuters are examples of
   a. foreign bureaus.
   b. journalists' lobbies.
   c. journalists' unions.
   d. Wall Street investment firms.
   e. wire services.
10. The goal of an ombudsman is to
    a. check problems with accuracy, fairness, and taste in an organization's news coverage.
    b. ensure balanced reporting and adherence to the equal time rule.
    c. identify plagiarized articles.
    d. increase in-depth news coverage.
    e. increase the number of advertisers for a news organization.

FURTHER READING

Campbell, W. Joseph. *Getting It Wrong: Ten of the Greatest Misreported Stories in American Journalism.* Berkeley: University of California Press, 2010.

Downie, Leonard Jr., and Robert G. Kaiser. *The News about the News: American Journalism in Peril.* New York: Knopf, 2002.

Groseclose, Tim. *Left Turn: How Liberal Media Bias Distorts the American Mind.* New York: St. Martin's Press, 2011.

Iyengar, Shanto, and Jennifer A. McGrady. *Media Politics: A Citizen's Guide.* New York: Norton, 2007.

Salzman, Jason. *Making the News: A Guide for Activists and Nonprofits.* Boulder, CO: Westview, 2003.

WEB SOURCES

American Journalism Review: www.ajr.org—analysis of media coverage by scholars and journalists.

Buzzfeed: www.buzzfeed.com—a Web site that identifies and promotes videos and other material that is gaining attention on the Web.

Media Matters for America: www.mediamatters.org—a liberal watchdog group.

Media Research Center: www.mediaresearch.org—a conservative watchdog group.

Pew Research Center's Project for Excellence in Journalism: www.journalism.org—nonpartisan, empirical studies to evaluate the performance of the press.

Israeli Prime Minister Benjamin Netanyahu addresses a joint meeting of Congress on Capitol Hill on May 24, 2011. Joint meetings of the House and Senate always occur in the larger House chamber.

MANDEL NGAN/Getty Images

12 Congress

OBJECTIVES

After reading this chapter, you should be able to:

- Compare the delegate and trustee theories of representation and explain how the members of Congress were expected to combine elements of both.

- Analyze the most important differences between the House and Senate.

- Describe the constitutional powers of Congress.

- Evaluate the relative importance of political parties and committees to the structure and functioning of Congress.

- Describe the process by which a bill becomes a law.

- Assess the importance of the several major functions of Congress.

- Evaluate the power of the reelection incentive to mold behavior in Congress.

- Assess the performance of Congress as a deliberative, representative, ethical, and accountable institution.

INTRODUCTION

Representative Brian Baird (D-WA) once published a *Washington Post* op-ed titled "We Need to Read the Bills." After listing a series of measures that Congress had recently passed, Baird wrote, "If forced to tell the truth, most members of Congress would acknowledge that they did not fully or, in many cases, even partially read these bills before casting their votes."[1] The problem, in Baird's view, was not lack of interest by legislators but the sheer number and length of proposed laws, together with House rules that limited the time that lawmakers had to study a **bill** before voting on it.

A vivid example came in 2009, when Congress took up a $787 billion economic stimulus bill. The final version of the bill, which was over a thousand pages long, came out at 10:25 p.m. on February 12. The House began consideration of the measure at 11:20 the next morning, giving lawmakers just 13 hours to study the bill and also get some sleep. When debate commenced, several complained that no one had actually read the whole bill, and no one disputed them. But some members of Congress are not troubled by the failure of lawmakers to read the bills. As the chairman of the House Judiciary Committee, John Conyers (D-MI), told a Washington audience in 2009 when discussing a massive proposal to reform health care: "I love these members that get up and say, 'Read the bill.' What good is reading the bill if it's a thousand pages and you don't have two days and two lawyers to find out what it means after you read the bill?"[2]

Representatives and senators often get summaries of legislation weeks before voting. They do deliberate on bills in committees and subcommittees, on the House and Senate floors, and in other venues. Yet, like Baird, many lawmakers worry that Congress is not as deliberative as it could and should be. Some call the Senate the world's greatest deliberative body, but Senator Jeff Merkley (D-OR) says: "That is a phrase that I wince [at] each time I hear it, because the amount of real deliberation, in terms of exchange of ideas, is so limited."[3]

If Congress does have a deliberative deficit, what is the cause? Many Americans think that their lawmakers are slackers who crave vacations. Anyone who has seen Congress at work firsthand can attest that this image is wrong. Representative Xavier Becerra (D-CA) says: "I stay until the very wee hours, unfortunately. I have to walk out of the last open door at Longworth [Office Building]. I have nothing to go back to at my condo, so I stay and work."[4]

To exercise their best judgment on legislation, lawmakers must review and assess key information and arguments. Yet, other tasks may crowd out deliberation. To win reelection, the members of Congress must spend time raising money. To please their voters, they must meet with dozens or hundreds of local groups, both in Washington and back home; and as the federal government expands, they must keep a watchful eye over the increasingly powerful bureaucracy.

The framers feared that if Congress did not deliberate well, it could become a dangerous institution, as had many of the state legislatures during the first decade of independence. "The legislative department," James Madison wrote about the new state legislatures, "is everywhere extending the sphere of its activity, and drawing all power into its impetuous vortex."[5]

To keep the new Congress from going too far and too fast, the framers divided and checked its power. Some say that its cumbersome structure hobbles good ideas as well as bad. Others, in the Madisonian tradition, argue that bills *ought* to face high obstacles. At each stage in the process, supporters of new legislation must build support by making their best arguments, answering the opposition, and fashioning coalitions. Ideally, bad proposals would fail to clear at least one of the many hurdles in the way, while bills that advanced the public interest would survive. Madison hoped that "the mild voice of reason" would prevail; that Congress would express and act upon "the cool and deliberate sense of the community."[6]

Some believe that lawmakers should serve as **delegates** who follow majority opinion in their electorate. "Our message to Congress is simple and direct," Ross Perot said in 1993. "Respond to the will of the people."[7] A delegate does what **constituents** want regardless of the legislator's own beliefs about what policies would best serve the country. Others say that members of Congress should function as **trustees** who exercise their judgment independent of constituents' views. Willmoore Kendall, a modern exponent of this view, said that the framers left us "a form of government that was purely representative, a form of government in which

Bill—a draft of a proposed law.

Delegate—a type of representation in which legislators simply reflect the views of their constituents.

Constituent—a resident of the district or state represented by a member of the House or Senate.

Trustee—a type of representation in which legislators exercise judgment independent of their constituents' views.

there was no room . . . for policy decisions by the electorate."[8] The people should "make sound judgments regarding the virtue of their neighbors" but not "deliberate on matters of policy."[9]

The framers combined elements of both views, expecting members of the House to function more like delegates and senators more like trustees. Two-year terms and direct popular election would give House members "an immediate dependence on, and intimate sympathy with, the people."[10] The people and their representatives would have a "communion of interests and sympathy of sentiments."[11] But the framers also wanted lawmakers, especially senators, to exercise independent judgment. Chosen by state legislatures, and to serve six-year terms, senators, Madison wrote, would be able to defend the people "against their own temporary errors and delusions."[12]

The framers hoped that together the House and Senate would "refine and enlarge the public views." "[I]t may well happen," Madison explained, "that the public voice, pronounced by the representatives of the people, will be more consonant to the public good than if pronounced by the people themselves, convened for the purpose."[13] If the system worked well, the laws would reflect neither the enlightened views of a select few (the pure trustee theory) nor the raw sentiment of the political marketplace (the pure delegate theory) but the informed and considered views of the American people.

In this chapter, we analyze the nation's lawmaking body and its contribution to deliberative democracy. We begin with the constitutional provisions that established the structure and powers of Congress. We then detail how the modern Congress is organized and how it legislates. Later, we describe the important functions, in addition to lawmaking, that Congress carries out. We end with a discussion of how to evaluate the performance of the modern Congress.

As we will see, Congress does not operate in isolation from the other branches. Just as the presidency and the federal courts influence and limit congressional power, so also Congress checks executive and judicial power. As Supreme Court Justice Louis Brandeis (1916–1939) explained, the founders aimed "not to avoid friction, but by means of the inevitable friction incident to the distribution of the governmental powers among three departments, to save the people from autocracy."[14]

FOCUS QUESTION

Is it realistic to expect all members of the House and Senate to read all the bills before they vote? Is it sufficient if only the members of the reporting committee read the bills? Is it sufficient, for members not on the reporting committee, if a staff aide reads the bills and makes recommendations?

CONSTITUTIONAL STRUCTURE AND POWERS

MAJOR ISSUES

- How is the Congress structured, and what are its constitutional powers?
- Do bicameralism and separation of powers serve any purpose beyond mere delay?

From the start of the Constitutional Convention, most delegates agreed that the new national legislature should be **bicameral** (with two chambers). Later they named these the House of Representatives and the Senate. Many wrongly believe that the idea for the Senate came from the demands of small state delegates to have one legislative chamber where all states had equal power. But even before this controversy arose at the Convention, the delegates endorsed bicameralism to promote safer and more deliberative lawmaking.

The framers hoped that dividing the lawmaking body into two chambers, each with distinct qualities, would curb the legislative branch's natural dominance in a democracy.[15] Two separate bodies would need time and effort to agree on anything, making bad laws less likely. Also, with the House broadly representing public desires and the smaller Senate functioning "with more coolness, with more system, and with more wisdom, than the popular branch," bicameralism would promote sound legislation in the national interest.[16] (See the International Perspectives box on bicameralism in other democracies.)

Bicameral legislature—a legislative body that has two separate chambers or houses, often with equal authority to pass or amend legislation.

The House and Senate

Bicameralism shapes everything about Congress, even the architecture. The northern half of the Capitol building belongs to the Senate, the southern half to the House. Each body

International Perspectives

Bicameralism throughout the World

Bicameralism can be messy, yet it seems to be on the move across the globe. While 45 nations had two-chamber legislatures in the early 1970s, that number had risen to 67 by the start of the new century. In fact, most of the world's people live under bicameral systems (which are also found in all American state governments but one).

One chamber usually reflects population, with members winning election in constituencies of roughly the same size. By common usage, we refer to these bodies as "lower chambers." Bicameral systems vary in how they choose and apportion "upper chambers." Nineteen countries use direct elections. In the United States, each state elects two senators. Australia has 76 senators, 12 from each of the six states and 2 from each of the mainland territories. Unlike the United States, Australia uses proportional representation, so a party's share of seats in each constituency will roughly match its share of votes. Fourteen countries have appointive upper chambers. In Canada, the governor general names senators at the direction of the prime minister. Britain uses several methods to appoint members of the House of Lords. Other nations have various mixes of election and appointment.

Most upper chambers have legislative powers equal to those of the lower chambers. In some countries (such as Britain), the upper chamber can only amend or delay legislation.

Many nations have found that bicameralism brings benefits that offset its frustrations. Upper chambers can provide representation to geographical, ethnic, or occupational groups that might otherwise be in jeopardy. As a 2005 report from the Council on Foreign Relations noted, they can "restrain the power of majorities to trample the rights of minorities" and can potentially "prevent excesses by extremist groups."

More generally, upper chambers may create better deliberation. According to a forum of the world's senates: "The growing complexity and technical nature of issues, and the rapid growth in legislation justify the existence of a second chamber responsible both for examining legislation proposals and for reviewing texts adopted by the lower house."[17]

CRITICAL THINKING QUESTION

Upper chambers where either members are not popularly elected or membership is not based on population (as in the U.S. Senate) diminish to some extent majority control over the government. Reflecting on what you learn about the U.S. Senate in this chapter, evaluate the benefits of bicameralism in the United States. Can these benefits be extrapolated to other democracies?

---

has its own chamber, dining rooms, and office buildings. The physical divide is a symbol of other differences with roots in tradition and constitutional law.

Every state has two senators, and for half a century the Senate has had 100 members. Under the Constitution, each state gets House members according to its population, which the census measures every 10 years. The most populous state, California, currently has 53 members, while the least populous—Alaska, Delaware, Montana, North Dakota, South Dakota, Vermont, and Wyoming—each have one. In the 43 states with more than one House member, each represents a particular geographic district of nearly equal population. The Constitution itself does not require that a state be divided into districts; some states used to elect House members "at large," with each representing the entire state.

Although the Constitution set the original size of the House at 65, it allowed it to grow without specifying how large it could become. The Constitution only guarantees each state at least one seat and caps the total at one for every 30,000 residents. Congress repeatedly enlarged the House in the nineteenth century, but since the 1910 census, federal law has kept the size at 435.[18] Currently, each member of the House represents about 700,000 persons, although this number varies somewhat by state.

Under the Constitution, voters chose House members, while state legislatures originally chose senators. Madison said that legislative selection would ensure a Senate of high quality and give states a direct voice in the federal government.[19] In 1913, the states ratified the Seventeenth Amendment, providing for direct election of senators. All House seats come up for election in every even-numbered year; but because senators serve six-year terms, only one-third come up for election at a time. This guarantees that apart from deaths or resignations, two-thirds of the Senate membership will not change after any election. By design, this gives the Senate, but not the House, some insulation from rapid shifts in public opinion.

The difference in term length also has an effect. With two-year terms, "the House lives with minute-to-minute pressures and acts accordingly," said former senator Chuck Hagel (R-NE). With six-year terms, senators "take a longer view of things—and that goes for its leadership too."[20] Although House members might think that this senator exaggerated, few would deny that reelection pressures weigh more heavily on those serving in the House than on their counterparts in the Senate who are several years away from a reelection contest.

Senators represent entire states, unlike nearly all members of the House. Because states usually encompass a broader range of economic and social characteristics than House districts, senators face more diverse pressures and concerns. Moreover, because of smaller numbers, longer terms, and the higher age qualifications (30 as opposed to 25 for the House), senators enjoy more prestige. The clearest sign of this is the arrow of ambition. In the modern era, House members frequently run for the Senate (and now make up about half of that body), but senators do not voluntarily give up their seats to run for the House.[21]

In the much larger House of Representatives, members divide the work more narrowly, mainly through the committee system (discussed later), so they can focus on specific policies. In the smaller Senate, members are generalists, with less expertise in any issue. The expertise gap seldom overcomes the prestige gap. Former senator John Culver (D-IA) said that House members grow resentful when they work hard on an issue "and yet the television news will be full of a senator [who] won't know one end from the other about the problem, but he's the one who will be quoted."[22] Senators like to call their institution "the world's greatest deliberative body," but few in the House would agree.

The House's procedures focus power on majority party leaders and committee chairs (more on this later), whereas the Senate spreads power more evenly, allowing more debate in the full body. The Constitution does not spell out these differences.[23] Still, the framers thought that the House, the larger chamber, would come under more centralized control. Madison said that "in all legislative assemblies, the greater the number composing them may be, the fewer will be the men who will in fact direct their proceedings."[24] House members sometimes disdain the other body because of the lack of order and control. The Senate, as Representative John Dingell (D-MI) colorfully put it, "has the rules of monkey island at the San Francisco Zoo."[25]

"Even though the Senate is only 30 yards away across that Rotunda," said former House Speaker (1999–2007) Dennis Hastert (R-IL), "sometimes it's like they're 30 miles away."[26] That psychological distance has political consequences. Newt Gingrich (R-GA), who preceded Hastert as Speaker, once complained about the Senate's slowness to act on bills that had sped through the House. Years later, he took a more deliberative view: "If an idea isn't good enough to survive a couple of really tough fights in the Senate, maybe it isn't worth implementing after all."[27]

On a practical level, bicameralism means two sets of eyes to spot legislative problems and to deliberate about solutions. "Sometimes no one is focusing on the text," said one Senate aide. "Thank God for a bicameral legislature. Things can happen quickly, in the dark, in the long bills where no one has seen it."[28]

Constitutional Powers

The U.S. Constitution vests the Congress with several key powers. The most important of these is the power to make the nation's laws.

Lawmaking

After the Preamble, the Constitution begins, "All legislative Powers herein granted shall be vested in a Congress of the United States." The "herein granted"

A view of the Capitol area from the west. The Senate and its office buildings are to the north (left), and the House and its office buildings are to the south (right).

Architect of the Capitol

shows that the Constitution does not grant Congress all possible legislative powers, but only those later specified. This is what we mean when we say that the national government is one of limited powers.

These "enumerated powers," as detailed in Article I, Section 8, include, among others, the powers to raise revenues, to regulate interstate and foreign commerce, to coin and borrow money, to establish a federal court system, to declare war, and to raise armies and navies. The last item in Section 8 gives Congress the power to make all laws "necessary and proper for carrying into Execution the foregoing Powers." In *McCulloch v. Maryland* (1819), the Supreme Court ruled that this clause vests Congress with "implied powers," such as establishing a national bank (see Chapter 3). In the modern era, Congress has interpreted its enumerated powers quite broadly, and only rarely has the Supreme Court ruled that Congress exceeded its authority.

The Constitution gives the House of Representatives one special lawmaking power: only it can originate bills for raising revenues. Although the original proposal in the Constitutional Convention prohibited the Senate from amending revenue bills, the delegates dropped this restriction. Consequently, although the Senate must wait for the House to act first on tax bills, it may amend a House measure any way it wishes. In 1982, for instance, the Senate attached major tax increases to a relatively minor House bill on tariffs.

Impeaching and Removing Public Officials

Another important power that the Constitution vests in Congress is the power to impeach and remove from office "all civil Officers of the United States" for "Treason, Bribery, or other high Crimes and Misdemeanors" (Article II, Section 4). The House of Representatives has "the sole Power of Impeachment," meaning that a majority of the House may charge any executive or judicial officer with an offense serious enough to merit removal from office. The Senate has "the sole Power to try all Impeachments." If it convicts an individual by a two-thirds vote, the person is immediately removed from office. If it wishes, the Senate may impose an additional penalty: permanent disqualification from ever holding federal office again. (See the discussions of impeachment in Chapters 13 and 15.)

Expelling Members

Because members of the House and Senate are not considered "Officers of the United States," they are not subject to removal by the impeachment process. Nevertheless, by a two-thirds vote each chamber may "expel a Member." Altogether, the Senate has expelled 15 and the House 5. Most of these were for disloyalty during the Civil War. Since then, the Senate has expelled none and House only two. The most recent expulsion was of James Traficant (D-OH) in 2002 after his conviction for bribery, filing false tax returns, and other federal crimes. Some members of Congress facing likely expulsion have resigned first. One was Bob Ney (R-OH), who resigned from the House in 2006 after pleading guilty to involvement in a congressional bribery scheme. He then served 17 months in federal prison.

Ratifying Treaties and Confirming Appointments

The Constitution gives the Senate two important responsibilities denied to the House. It alone approves treaties (by a two-thirds vote) and confirms presidential nominations to the judiciary and high executive offices (by majority vote). (More on this in Chapters 13 and 15.) Although the House does not vote to approve treaties, it often must decide whether to pass legislation, including appropriations, to carry treaties into effect.

Although the Constitution does not give individual senators the power to veto presidential nominations, under the custom of **senatorial courtesy** the full body will not confirm presidential nominees for federal district judge, U.S. attorney, or federal marshal if the senior senator of the president's party from the state where the appointment is to be made objects. Knowing that their colleagues will not confirm an appointee they oppose, senators of the president's party can often persuade presidents to nominate individuals they recommend.

Proposing Constitutional Amendments

Congress plays a vital role in amending the Constitution. Under Article V, it proposes amendments by a two-thirds vote of each chamber. An alternative procedure is for two-thirds of

Senatorial courtesy—the custom in the Senate whereby the full body will not confirm presidential nominees for federal district judge, U.S. attorney, or federal marshal if the senior senator of the president's party from the state where the appointment is to be made objects.

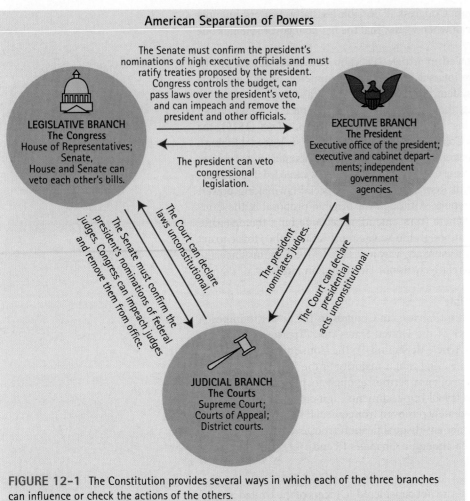

American Separation of Powers

The Senate must confirm the president's nominations of high executive officials and must ratify treaties proposed by the president. Congress controls the budget, can pass laws over the president's veto, and can impeach and remove the president and other officials.

LEGISLATIVE BRANCH
The Congress
House of Representatives;
Senate,
House and Senate can
veto each other's bills.

EXECUTIVE BRANCH
The President
Executive office of the president;
executive and cabinet departments; independent
government
agencies.

The president can veto congressional legislation.

The Court can declare laws unconstitutional.

The Senate must confirm the president's nominations of federal judges. Congress can impeach judges and remove them from office.

The president nominates judges.

The Court can declare presidential acts unconstitutional.

JUDICIAL BRANCH
The Courts
Supreme Court;
Courts of Appeal;
District courts.

FIGURE 12–1 The Constitution provides several ways in which each of the three branches can influence or check the actions of the others.
SOURCE: The Social Studies Help Center, www.socialstudieshelp.com/Lesson_13_Notes.htm

the state legislatures to request Congress to call a convention to propose amendments. This alternative has never been used; all 27 amendments were first proposed by Congress. Congress proposed six other amendments, but these failed in the states.

Besides exercising these explicit constitutional powers, Congress makes other contributions to the American political system. We review these contributions later in the chapter.

Congress and the Other Branches

The legislative branch keeps watch on the executive and judiciary. As we describe in the next chapter, Congress has often struggled with the White House over foreign policy, especially in the decades after the Vietnam War.[29] Although the president wields great authority as commander in chief, Congress declares war and authorizes some conflicts short of full-scale war, funds the military and determines its size and nature, and makes rules for the armed forces. On domestic matters, Congress has even more ability to thwart the president's desires. Noting congressional power over spending, taxes, and interstate commerce, Speaker Gingrich said, "All the advantages the Commander-in Chief gets in foreign policy the Congress gets in domestic policy."[30] (See Figure 12-1.)

The Senate plays a special role in checking the other branches. Because it has sole power to approve treaties, and because such approval requires a two-thirds vote, wise presidents consider Senate opinion on foreign policy. The Senate gains additional leverage through its authority to confirm presidential nominations to the federal courts, the Cabinet, and many major executive offices. Although outright rejections are rare, nominees sometimes withdraw their names before the Senate votes. In 2009, President Barack Obama nominated former Senate Democratic leader Tom Daschle from South Dakota to head the Department of Health and Human Services, but he soon pulled out amid criticism of his past tax problems.[31]

The Senate has exercised heightened scrutiny in recent decades. Fully 30% of all the Cabinet nominations that resulted in Senate rejection or withdrawal have occurred just since 1989. The Senate's new assertiveness has focused attention on the standards senators should use to judge nominees. With the Constitution silent on this point, some argue that the Senate should make an independent judgment on a nominee's merits, while others say it should defer to presidents unless it finds incompetence or misbehavior.

The framers designed the Constitution so that "[a]mbition . . . [would] counteract ambition."[32] They expected the members of each branch to develop a personal interest in protecting its constitutional rights and powers from encroachment by the others. Former representative Lee Hamilton (D-IN) says that the congressional oath of office insists "that legislators bear allegiance to the Constitution, which at its core provides for a Congress that is an equal and independent branch of the government."[33]

How, then, do the members of the House and Senate organize their institutions to carry out their constitutional responsibilities?

CONGRESSIONAL ORGANIZATION

MAJOR ISSUE

- How do parties and committees shape the work of Congress?

In addition to bicameralism, the most important organizational features of Congress are the influence of party leaders and the division of the two bodies into legislative committees and subcommittees. These features have changed over time, and they vary considerably between the House and Senate. As we will see, the organization of Congress has significant consequences for deliberation, lawmaking, and representation.

Party Control

Throughout the 1960s and 1970s, Democrats had firm majorities in the House and Senate. Republicans held a Senate majority for six years in the 1980s but never came close in the House. In 1994, Republicans won majorities in both chambers for the first time since the election of 1952 (see Figure 12-2). They held the House for the next 12 years. They also held the Senate, except for a brief period between mid-2001 and early 2003 (after a Republican senator left the party and gave the Democrats a majority). In 2006, concerns about corruption and the war in Iraq helped tip control of both chambers to the Democrats and in 2010, economic issues helped shift the House back to the GOP.

In each chamber, the majority party sets the agenda and gets the chairmanships of all the committees and subcommittees. Again, Lee Hamilton sums it up well:

> Party status affects pretty much everything. The majority not only gets nicer spaces and meeting rooms, it also gets to determine which members and staff will go on overseas fact-finding trips, and enjoys all sorts of little perks that make life on Capitol Hill more pleasant. And on congressional committees, the majority often takes two-thirds to three-fourths of the budget and will have three times the number of staff as the minority, so a shift in party control can be traumatic for those suddenly in the minority.[34]

When the sitting president is a member of the same party as the majority in the House or Senate, the party usually works to pass presidential proposals, and the minority usually tries to defeat or change them. Under **divided government**—when at least one house of Congress does not have a majority from the president's party—each congressional party has a split personality. The majority party in the House or Senate is in charge of that institution and tries to exercise its will, but if it is not the president's party (as in the House after the 2010 election), it may function as an opposition party trying to thwart presidential initiatives. The roles are reversed for a minority party in the House or Senate that is the same as the president's party. It may oppose the congressional majority party but support the president's efforts to direct American government.

It is no surprise that periods of divided government often result in neither the president nor the majority party in Congress getting its way. This may lead to what many call "gridlock," "deadlock," or "stalemate." But scholars have undercut the notion that divided government prevents major policy initiatives, for Congress has often passed important laws during times of divided control.[35] Examples include the Taft-Hartley Labor-Management Relations Act of 1947 (the key labor legislation of the modern era, which passed over President Harry Truman's veto), the Clean Air Act of 1970 (signed by President Richard Nixon), and

Divided government—a situation in which different parties control the presidency and at least one of the chambers of Congress.

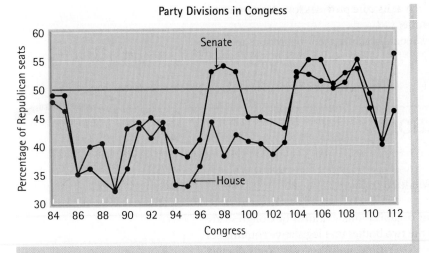

Party Divisions in Congress

FIGURE 12–2 This figure depicts the percentage of House and Senate seats in Republican hands from the 84th Congress (1955–1957) through the 112th Congress (2011–2013). The 50% line represents the crucial divide between majority and minority status. Figures are for the start of each Congress and do not include subsequent interelection changes (i.e., special elections or party switches). Senator James Buckley of New York, who won in 1970 on the Conservative Party line, counts as a Republican.

SOURCE: Office of the Clerk of the House of Representatives, "Party Divisions of the House of Representatives (1789 to Present)," at artandhistory.house.gov/house_history/partyDiv .aspx; U. S. Senate, "Party Division in the Senate, 1789-Present," at www.senate.gov/ pagelayout/history/one_item_and_teasers/partydiv.htm

the 2002 Homeland Security Act (eventually supported by President George W. Bush).

Over the years, Congress has become more polarized. In recent decades, liberal Democrats picked up many seats that had once belonged to moderate-to-liberal Republicans. Even after the massive GOP victory in 2010, Republicans held only two of New England's 22 House districts, and in that election, more than half of the 54 moderate-to-conservative "Blue Dog" House Democrats lost to Republicans, mostly strong conservatives. Consequently, the parties continued to have difficulty finding common ground.

Conflict between the parties has also grown more bitter. Floor debates sometimes involve personal invective, and wherever possible each side targets the other side's leaders for defeat. In 2008, Senate majority leader Harry Reid (D-NV) backed an effort to defeat Republican leader Mitch McConnell. A Republican official said, "McConnell never takes political attacks personally, but he is someone who has never hesitated to repay his opposition for their courtesy." The official explained that the party would seek a strong opponent to Reid in the next election.[36] Congressional politics is thus reminiscent of a scene in *The Godfather* in which Michael Corleone walks the deserted streets of a Sicilian village. "Where have all the men gone?" he asks. His guide explains, "They're dead from vendettas."[37]

Party Leaders

Just as the separation of powers affects the roles that congressional parties play, bicameralism influences the leadership structure in each chamber, the way that House and Senate leaders work, and the power they wield.

House of Representatives

Article I, Section 2 of the Constitution specifies that the House of Representatives shall choose "their Speaker and other Officers." The selection of Speaker is the first order of business in the House when a new Congress convenes on January 3 of odd-numbered years. Usually, this election is a formality, with Democrats voting for their candidate, previously chosen in a party caucus, and Republicans voting for theirs. Members almost always back their side's choice.

Unlike the speaker of the British House of Commons, a neutral umpire of debate, the U.S. **Speaker of the House** is a partisan figure as well as an institutional one. In recent decades, changes in Republican and Democratic rules have increased the Speaker's authority over procedural affairs and committee assignments. The goal has been to give the Speakers greater influence with party members, making them more effective leaders. In 2012, Speaker John Boehner described the complexity of the job: "[People] don't realize that I have about 200 responsibilities and roles. I've gotta be the big brother, the father, I gotta be the disciplinarian, the dean of students, the principal, the spouse—you can't believe all the roles that I have to play!"[38]

Some Speakers have been considerably more powerful than others and none more so than Joseph Cannon (R-IL), who presided over the House from 1903 to 1911. Nicknamed "Uncle Joe," Cannon became the most powerful Speaker in the history of the House. He used the formal authorities of the office—such as the power to recognize speakers during

Speaker of the House—the chief officer of the House of Representatives.

floor debate, to chair the Rules Committee, and to appoint the standing committees—to rule with an iron hand on behalf of his fellow Republicans. But in 1910, disaffected Republicans joined with Democrats to strip the Speaker of his chairmanship of the Rules Committee, transfer the power to appoint committees to the full House, and limit the Speaker's power to recognize members on the floor. This episode demonstrated that an energized majority of the full House could constrain the institution's leaders. Never again would a Speaker of the House of Representatives wield such unchecked power.[39]

Because the Speaker is also the institution's symbolic leader, he or she cannot concentrate entirely on partisan politics. In any case, time constraints require the delegation of authority. The House **majority leader** serves as the Speaker's top lieutenant, running the chamber's day-to-day business and planning its agenda.

The House **minority leader** does what the title suggests: speaks for the minority party in public forums and tries to outwit the majority on the floor. The minority party usually loses roll call votes, but it can sometimes bring its issues to public attention. If successful, the minority leader may help his or her party gain the majority in a future election. But if a party loses election after election, the leader may find individual members focusing less on that goal than on their own political survival.

Senate

Under the Constitution, the vice president presides over the Senate. Except for casting tie-breaking votes, however, vice presidents have little power in the chamber. When they do preside, custom normally dictates that they not take partisan advantage. Instead, they heed the **parliamentarian**, a staff expert on the rules. The Senate also chooses a **president pro tempore**, an honorary position that customarily goes to the longest-serving member of the majority party. Usually, however, junior members of the majority party preside over daily sessions.

The Senate majority leader, not the vice president or the president pro tempore, is that body's actual leader. Unlike the speakership, the post of majority leader is not a constitutional office. The majority leader speaks for the party, manages the chamber's business and the floor schedule, and (crucial from a procedural standpoint) has priority in seeking recognition on the Senate floor. Accordingly, the leader can offer amendments and motions before anyone else. In some ways the Senate majority leader is weaker than the Speaker of the House, for the House's procedures enable its leadership to override members who want to block action. Any member can create major procedural delays, which complicates the majority leader's job.

As in the House, the head of the minority party is the minority leader. This senator has similar responsibilities to speak for the party on public issues, to protect the party's interests in the chamber, and to affect legislation. Because of differences between the chambers, however, the Senate minority leader has much more influence within Congress. Under Senate rules, debate can continue indefinitely unless 60 senators vote to stop it. When senators continue speaking to prevent final action on a bill, this is called a **filibuster**. Because of these rules, a minority party with at least 41 seats can prevent passage of a bill and thereby wring concessions from the majority. Al Franken (D-MN) was seated in July 2009 after a lengthy dispute over the November 2008 election, becoming the 60th Democrat in the Senate. This marked the first time that either party had fallen below the 41-seat level since 1981. In recent decades, Senate minority leaders have been major legislative "players," much more so than their House counterparts.

Each party in each chamber has its own **whip**, who counts likely votes on upcoming measures. The whip maintains communication between party leaders and members, gathers support for party positions on the floor, coaxes wavering members to vote the party line, and crafts parliamentary strategy. Both whips lead an elaborate organization of members who count and harvest votes. The term "whip" comes from the British hunting term "whipper-in," the person who keeps hounds from straying in a fox hunt. It became a political word in England during the eighteenth century and later crossed the Atlantic.[40]

Many leaders have seen their jobs as managing deliberations within their chamber. Other leaders have taken a higher public profile, particularly when they were in the minority or when the other party held the White House. Speakers Tip O'Neill (D-MA) (1977–1987),

Majority leader—in the Senate, the highest-ranking member of the majority party; in the House the highest-ranking member after the Speaker.

Minority leader—in the Senate and the House, the highest-ranking member of the minority party.

Parliamentarian—a staff expert on the rules in the House of Representatives and Senate.

President pro tempore—under the Constitution, the officer who presides over the Senate when the vice president is not presiding. Now it is an honorary position that customarily goes to the longest-serving member of the majority party.

Filibuster—informal term for any attempt to block or delay Senate action on a bill or other matter by debating it at length, by offering numerous motions, or by other obstructive actions.

Whip—party leader whose job is to count votes and gather support from party lawmakers.

Newt Gingrich (R-GA) (1995–1999), and Nancy Pelosi (D-CA) (2007–2011) all became symbols of opposition to incumbent presidents of the other party.

Committees

Committees—groups of legislators in the House and Senate that deliberate on bills or other measures and make recommendations to the full body.

Within each house, **committees** screen bills and enable lawmakers to develop their own areas of expertise (which are broader in the Senate). As issues have changed over time, both houses have added new committees, dropped old ones, and restructured their jurisdictions. The committee structures of the House and Senate are similar but not identical, and each committee adopts its own rules. Generally, the parties are represented on the committees in the same proportion as their membership in the full body. Exceptions include the ethics committees in the House and Senate, which have equal numbers of Democrats and Republicans, and some important House committees on which the majority party has a disproportionately large representation.

Standing committee—a permanent body within Congress that evaluates proposals within its jurisdiction, chooses certain bills for consideration, and then revises and reports those bills to the full chamber. Also oversees specific agencies and programs.

Subcommittee—a unit of a congressional committee that handles a very specific area of policy and legislation.

There are several different kinds of committees. **Standing committees**, the most important, are permanent bodies that evaluate legislative proposals within their jurisdictions, choose certain bills for consideration, and then revise and report those bills to the full chamber. Standing committees also oversee specific agencies and programs. Most standing committees divide their work among **subcommittees**, which handle pieces of the committee's jurisdiction. **Select (or special) committees**, which may be permanent or temporary, are set up to mount an investigation or to handle an issue that the standing committees do not address effectively. **Joint committees**, with members from both the House and Senate, are typically permanent panels that carry out studies or administrative tasks. A **conference committee** is a temporary joint committee that settles differences between Senate and House versions of a bill.

Select (or special) committee—a permanent or temporary committee set up to mount an investigation or to handle a particular issue.

Joint committees—committees with members from both the House and Senate that carry out studies or administrative tasks.

Conference committee—a temporary joint committee that settles differences between Senate and House versions of a bill and recommends a compromise version to the House and Senate.

Leaders in the 113th Congress (2013–2015)

House

Speaker	John Boehner, R-Ohio
Majority Leader	Eric Cantor, R-Virginia
Majority Whip	Kevin McCarthy, R-California
Minority Leader	Nancy Pelosi, D-California
Minority Whip	Steny Hoyer, D-Maryland

Senate

President	Joseph Biden, Vice President of the United States
President Pro Tempore	Daniel Inouye, D-Hawaii
Majority Leader	Harry Reid, D-Nevada
Assistant Majority Leader (Whip)	Dick Durbin, D-Illinois
Minority Leader	Mitch McConnell, R-Kentucky
Assistant Minority Leader	John Cornyn, R-Texas

Note: This list represents the likely occupants of these positions after the 2012 election. At press time, there was still uncertainty about other leadership posts.

Because the Senate is so much smaller than the House, its members serve on many more committees and subcommittees. Also, the House designates some key committees as "exclusive committees," meaning that their members usually cannot serve on any other committees. With many fewer committee assignments, members of the House can develop greater expertise than their Senate colleagues. Each party in each chamber uses a special assignment committee to decide who will serve on which standing committees. Party leaders influence this process.

Committee chairs are among the most important and influential members of Congress. They set the committee's agenda, decide when to act, preside during meetings, and control the committee's budget. They have great power to advance major new initiatives through Congress and to thwart those they oppose. For about a century, the position of chair has usually gone to the majority party member who has served the longest continuously on the committee. This is called the **seniority** principle or the seniority system. (In addition to seniority on a committee, there is seniority in the full body: the length of continuous service in the House or Senate. Those with higher seniority in the chamber may get preferential treatment in committee assignments, office space, or other perquisites.)

The majority party members of the House or Senate formally select committee chairs through a secret vote. Since the 1960s, the parties have sometimes skipped seniority in order to choose a chair who was more energetic or better attuned to party philosophy than the most senior member. This happens more often in the House than in the Senate, though it is rare in both chambers. As one new committee chair said after leapfrogging over the most senior member, "Seniority is important, but it should not be a grant of property rights to be chairman for three decades or more."[41]

Committees may hold public hearings of several types. *Legislative hearings* address specific measures before the committee. *Oversight hearings* focus on how executive agencies are carrying out programs and identify problems that may require further legislation. *Investigative hearings* often look into scandals or disasters. While investigations may enable members to score partisan political points, they also bring important information to light. *Confirmation hearings* enable Senate committees to check out the president's nominees for key posts.

When running investigations or dealing with sensitive questions, committees may take testimony under oath. The act of swearing-in reminds witnesses of their obligation to tell the truth, and creates serious consequences for lying. Perjury in congressional testimony is a crime. In August of 2010, a federal trial jury indicted former baseball pitching star Roger Clemens for denying, before a congressional committee, that he had used performance enhancing drugs. In June 2012, however, a jury acquitted him of the charges. Such prosecutions are rare. "It's unusual for anyone to be prosecuted for testifying before Congress," says law professor Stephen Gillers, "mostly because people are careful and carefully advised."[42]

Committees and subcommittees are supposed to be Congress's workshops, the place where lawmakers undertake their most detailed policy deliberation. Hearings educate committee members about policy issues and the patterns of political support for proposed legislation. Lawmakers who do not serve on the committee may still benefit from hearings by having their aides read and digest the testimony for their own study.[43] Members of Congress pay attention to this material because they have to root their positions in respectable policy arguments. When they cannot find support in testimony or other sources, they sometimes change their positions. For instance, many lawmakers stopped supporting airline price regulation in the late 1970s when hearings showed that no prominent economists defended it.[44]

On some committees, such as Senate Foreign Relations, members concern themselves mainly with good public policy. On others, members focus on constituent demands. The House Transportation and Infrastructure Committee, for instance, attracts members who want roads and other public works in their own districts. (Thrift-minded lawmakers call them "the highwaymen.") In their pursuit of parochial interests, constituency committees often neglect broad public concerns, especially budgetary restraint.

Committees are supposed to serve as watchdogs over the bureaucracy. Often, however, agencies and their interest group allies "capture" committee members, persuading them to boost the programs they control. One study examined congressional hearings on government programs and found that over 95% of the witnesses testified in favor of the programs and that less than 1% testified against them.[45] This imbalance undercuts the process of deliberation, because lawmakers do not get full exposure to all points of view. Committee leaders interested in new legislative initiatives tend to pick witnesses who support, and will often benefit from, such proposals.

Through control over committee assignments, party leaders have gained greater influence over congressional committees. There are two schools of thought about this trend. Some believe that centralized control can keep committees from falling into the clutches of special interests. Others think that party leaders have undercut committee deliberation by undermining committee independence.

Seniority—refers to continuous service in either the House or Senate or continuous service on a committee. Committee chairmanships usually go to the senior committee member of the majority party.

FOCUS QUESTION

Which model of the committee system would better promote congressional effectiveness: (a) one in which the committees are extensions of the leadership and firmly under the control of the majority party in the body or (b) one in which committees are largely autonomous bodies that act independent of leadership control?

Congressional Staff

Congress is not just the 535 elected members of the House and Senate. It also includes about 13,000 staff who work for individual members, committees, or support organizations such as the Congressional Research Service (discussed later).

The vast majority of staff (about 11,000) work for individual legislators. House members may have up to 18 full-time and 4 part-time staffers. Senators have no set limit: their staff budgets depend on their states' population. A lawmaker's staff usually includes a chief aide (typically called an administrative assistant), a press secretary, legislative assistants (to work on bills), legislative correspondents (to draft responses to mail), and caseworkers (to help constituents deal with the federal government). House members and senators may distribute staff among their Washington and home offices as they choose. All members of the House maintain at least one office in the district, and some maintain several.

The committees of the House and Senate employ several thousand staff to write and study legislation. They work for either the majority or minority members of the committee, with most assigned to the majority. The top committee staff are often long-standing experts in the subject matter of the committee.

Many congressional observers worry that unelected staff in Congress have too much power. When a former congressional aide published an article criticizing dependence on staff, Representative Pat Schroeder (D-CO) gave a floor speech in rebuttal. The aide called to thank her for addressing his argument and got this response from her press secretary: "Oh, you don't want Mrs. Schroeder. You want Andy Feinstein of the Civil Service Subcommittee, who wrote her speech."[46]

Does staff help or hinder congressional deliberation? On the one hand, lawmakers benefit from their aides' experience and expertise. Thanks largely to staff work, Congress is probably the best-informed legislative body in the world. Staffers assigned to legislative work are in an excellent position to reason on the merits of public policy because they know so much and are free from the fund-raising, handshaking, and other political duties that take up so much of the lawmakers' own time. On the other hand, staff negotiation has replaced much of the face-to-face discussion and deliberation that once occurred among the members of Congress. And although legislative staffers have a command of data and scholarly studies, the lawmakers are the ones who have direct experience of their constituents' problems.

No responsibility of congressional staff is more important than helping the elected members pass sound legislation. In the next section, we examine how a bill becomes a law in the U.S. Congress.

Congressional Internships

Interning for Congress is an excellent way to learn about the operations of the legislative branch. Many colleges and universities have their own Washington semester programs. Even if yours does not, you can still apply directly either for a summer internship in Washington or for an internship at the local office of a House member or senator. Note that most of these positions are unpaid. Check with your institution about the possibility of getting academic credit.

Washington interns typically start with low-level tasks such as sorting mail or running the photocopier, but if you work hard and show initiative, you may quickly graduate to more substantial tasks, such as legislative research. In a local office, your focus will be on constituent service, but here, too, good work will usually bring you more responsibility.

Most lawmakers have internship information on their homepages. You may find a list of senators at www.senate.gov. If you do not know which House member represents a particular area, you may find out by entering the zip code at the House homepage (www.house.gov). Although lawmakers sometimes prefer interns from their own constituencies, many others are willing to consider applications from any qualified student. If you have a strong interest in a policy area, you might also check for internships with the appropriate congressional committees. You may find lists of committees at www.house.gov and at the Senate homepage just mentioned. Lawmakers and committees may also advertise for interns. One good place to check for such ads is www.hillzoo.com. The Senate Employment Bulletin (updated weekly) also includes internships; see www.senate.gov/employment/po/positions.htm.

SOURCE: From Schmidt/Shelley/Bardes, *American Government and Politics Today* 2009–2010 Edition, 14E. 2009 Wadsworth, a part of Cengage Learning, Inc. Reproduced by permission. www.cengage.com/permissions.

HOW A BILL BECOMES A LAW

MAJOR ISSUES

- How does the legislative process work?
- Who reads and writes the bills?

Although Congress, with its enumerated powers, looks weaker on paper than lawmaking bodies in other democracies, it wields more independent legislative power. As noted earlier, the courts in the modern era seldom stop Congress from legislating on whatever it wishes, and in contrast to parliamentary systems, the American Constitution makes each branch structurally independent. Unlike a parliament, the U.S. Congress is not under the direct control of the leader of the executive branch and his or her Cabinet. Even when it seems that Congress is following and the president is leading, the legislature may inspire presidential initiatives. After the attacks of September 11, 2001, lawmakers proposed a Department of Homeland Security. President George W. Bush balked at first but then embraced their proposal. Some decades earlier, President Lyndon Johnson incorporated into his Great Society agenda (discussed in Chapter 16) policy innovations previously proposed by Democrats in Congress.

Lame duck session—any session of Congress that occurs after a national election and before the new Congress has convened.

Although the legislative process in Congress can seem complicated, for successful proposals it proceeds in four basic steps: the drafting of a bill, consideration and modification by a committee, debate and decision by the full House or Senate, and, if the chambers pass similar but not identical measures, the fashioning of a compromise measure (see Figure 12-3).

Origins of Bills

The legislative process follows a two-year cycle beginning in the January after a congressional election. Each election results in a new Congress. The First Congress met between March 4, 1789, and March 3, 1791. The 112th Congress began in January 2011 and lasted until the beginning of January 2013. Prior to the passage of the Twentieth Amendment, Congress could meet in a so-called **lame duck session** for as long as four months after a November congressional election. Now a new Congress convenes in early January, limiting a possible lame duck session to about two months. If a legislative proposal fails to pass within a two-year period, its sponsors must resubmit it in the next cycle.

The seeds of legislation come from many places. Lawmakers may back proposals on the basis of private study

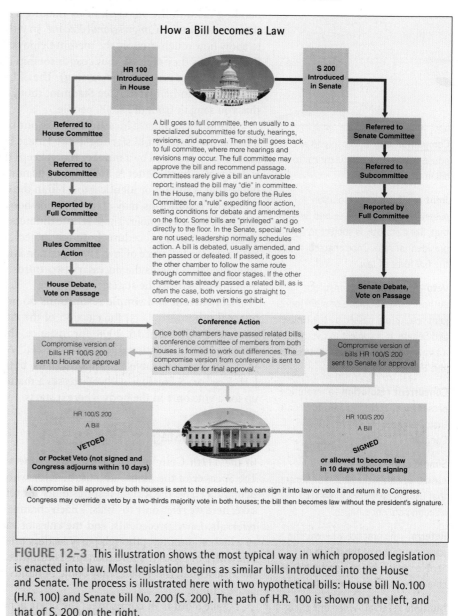

FIGURE 12–3 This illustration shows the most typical way in which proposed legislation is enacted into law. Most legislation begins as similar bills introduced into the House and Senate. The process is illustrated here with two hypothetical bills: House bill No.100 (H.R. 100) and Senate bill No. 200 (S. 200). The path of H.R. 100 is shown on the left, and that of S. 200 on the right.
SOURCE: Top Photo: Kenrick Griffith/Shutterstock.com; Bottom Photo: Jan Kratechvila/ Shutterstock.com

or personal experience. Senator Pete Domenici (R-NM) sponsored legislation to require health insurers to give mental illness the same coverage as other medical conditions. His interest in the issue stemmed from his daughter's battle with schizophrenia. "That changed my view of the health delivery system as far as mentally ill people," he said. "That's why I'm the leader in mental illness."[47] (Domenici himself fell prey to brain disease and retired from the Senate in 2008.) Proposals also come from the White House, executive agencies, or interest groups. Often such proposals include the legislative language itself.

Lawmakers seldom draft their own legislation. Two legal scholars asked Senate aides to describe their bosses' role. Here are typical responses that apply to both chambers:

- "Senators are generalists. Very few senators write their own language."
- "The vast majority of members deal at the conceptual level."
- "[Senators] rely upon staff. They set the goals and ask staff to 'work it out.'"[48]

When a lawmaker's staff has made revisions (with the help of the nonpartisan Office of Legislative Counsel), the measure is ready for introduction. In the House, members drop it into the "hopper," a wooden box on the House floor. Senators introduce measures either by handing them to the bill clerk or by making a statement on the Senate floor and entering the measure in the *Congressional Record*. In either house, the author may seek cosponsors to show how much support the measure enjoys. Most cosponsors have no hand in drafting the measures they endorse, but cosponsorship does supply a way to share credit (or blame if the legislation proves embarrassing). The old joke is that cosponsorship is like joining in the national anthem at Yankee Stadium: though your own role is minor, you can still say that you sang in front of 54,000 people.

In either chamber, a measure can take one of four basic forms. Bills are the main vehicle for enacting laws. A bill starting in the House bears the letters *H.R.* (for "House of Representatives"), followed by a number that it keeps through the rest of the process. A Senate bill is designated by the letter *S.*, followed by its number. A **companion bill** is a measure in one house that is similar or identical to a bill in the other.

Joint resolutions may start in either house and have the designation "H.J. Res." or "S.J. Res.," with a number. There is little difference between a bill and a joint resolution: both undergo the same procedure, both are subject to a presidential **veto** (discussed later), and both have the full force of law. The exception is a joint resolution proposing a constitutional amendment. If it wins the necessary two-thirds vote in both houses, it goes not to the president but directly to the states.

Concurrent and **simple resolutions** do not change the law of the land but deal with internal procedures (e.g., the election of the clerk of the House) or express congressional sentiments. On April 16, 2008, for instance, the House passed H. Res. 1112, recognizing 2008 as "the International Year of the Reef." A concurrent resolution ("H. Con. Res." or "S. Con. Res.") is subject to approval by both chambers, whereas a simple resolution ("H. Res." or "S. Res.") usually addresses a matter affecting only one house and thus comes up for a vote only in the body where it starts.

Committee Stage

In the 111th Congress (2009–2011) members introduced 13,683 bills and resolutions.[49] The Speaker of the House and the senator who is serving as presiding officer on any particular day have the formal responsibility for referring bills to committees. (For simplicity's sake, here we refer only to "bills.") Each chamber's parliamentarian takes care of routine bill **referrals**. Laws, precedents, and the rules of each house usually determine which bills go to which committees, though party leaders often make other arrangements. In a **multiple referral**, a bill goes to more than one committee. This procedure, which is more common in the House than the Senate, may come in handy when a complex bill cuts across committee jurisdictions.

Once a bill is in committee, the chair generally sends it to a subcommittee for consideration. For most bills, the process stops here. Why? Minority party members often introduce bills with little expectation of success, sometimes simply to generate debate,

Companion bill—a measure in one house that is similar or identical to a bill in the other.

Joint resolution—a resolution passed by both the House and Senate that, like a statute, is subject to a presidential veto. Once enacted, it has the full force of law.

Veto—the president's constitutional authority to disapprove of a bill (or joint resolution) passed by the House and Senate. It is subject to override by a two-thirds vote of both houses. See also **Pocket veto**.

Concurrent resolution—a resolution passed by both the House and Senate that expresses the sentiment of Congress.

Simple resolution—a resolution passed by either the House or Senate that usually addresses a matter affecting only one house.

Referral—the practice whereby the parliamentarian of the House or Senate sends a bill to a committee (or committees) for consideration.

Multiple referral—when one bill is sent to two or more committees for consideration.

to show their constituents that they are working hard on their behalf, or to do a favor for important supporters. Senators in the minority, however, do better than House members. Bills by majority party members may die because their sponsors really just want to make a gesture or because the chair has misgivings.

If a subcommittee chair wants to move a bill, the next step is usually to seek comments from executive agencies. Public hearings may produce further information. In preparing for hearings, lawmakers and staff invite testimony from other members of Congress, academic experts, federal officials, lobbyists, and private citizens. Hearings involve a good deal of choreography: aides often interview witnesses in advance and provide lawmakers with questions they might ask and answers that they are likely to get.[51] Before testifying, witnesses turn in written statements that become part of the public record.

Typically, legislative hearings gain attention only from officials and interest groups with a stake in the bill. Nevertheless, some hearings can produce moments of drama. Witnesses may tell of their struggles with crime, disease, or bureaucratic cruelty. Members of Congress may get into heated arguments with administration officials or corporate executives. In 1994, a House committee hearing chaired by Congressman Henry Waxman gained national attention when the CEOs of the nation's major tobacco companies denied under oath that tobacco was addictive. Waxman's Web site claimed that "it became clear to the American people that they were lying. This was the turning point in the battle against the tobacco industry."[52]

Celebrity witnesses usually draw greater media attention than policy experts. Having a prominent celebrity testify almost guarantees national publicity (see photos). On March 17, 2005, a House committee took testimony from 10 baseball stars and executives on steroid use in baseball. Mark McGwire, who ranks 10th in career home runs with 583, refused to answer questions about past steroid use: "My lawyers have advised me that I cannot answer these questions without jeopardizing my friends, my family, or myself."[53] Other stars denied steroid use, but one later tested positive and was suspended. Although no legislation resulted, the publicity called attention to a problem that had filtered down to youth athletics. The hearing generated pressure on baseball

Photo by Alex Wong/Getty Images

Comedian Stephen Colbert testifies in character before a subcommittee of the House Judiciary Committee on September 24, 2010. Some praised him for highlighting the plight of immigrant farm workers while others said that he made a mockery of Congress.

MYTHS AND MISINFORMATION

Legislating about a Myth

Deliberation requires an accurate understanding of an issue's factual basis. Sometimes lawmakers misunderstand the facts. During the 110th Congress (2007–2009), dozens of House members cosponsored a resolution opposing the construction of a "North American Free Trade Agreement (NAFTA) Superhighway System" that would unite Canada, the United States, and Mexico. Supporters of the measure said that the highway would be the first step toward a "North American Union" that would abolish American sovereignty. A candidate in South Carolina's 2008 Republican Senate primary said that the Union would create a joint currency called the "amero," after the "euro." There was just one problem with the controversy: no one in the federal government had suggested any such highway or political

union. Texas was considering a "Trans-Texas corridor" to the east of I-35 from Laredo to the Arkansas border, but those plans bore little relation to the behemoth that Internet postings described.

"There is absolutely no U.S. government plan for a NAFTA Superhighway of any sort," an assistant secretary of commerce told the *Seattle Times*. Senator Kit Bond (R-MO), a member of the Committees on Appropriations and Environment and Public Works, said that the idea stemmed from "unfounded theories" with "no credence."

Satirical commentator Stephen Colbert described the superhighway as a scheme "to make Canada, the U.S. and Mexico one country and force us to eat moose tacos." He concluded that the story must be true "*because I got it from the Internet.*"[50]

executives and players to toughen anti-steroid policies. Many agreed that the congressional spotlight served a useful public purpose.

Even when members know what witnesses will say, hearings still serve a deliberative purpose by creating a public record. After hearings, a subcommittee usually will hold a **markup** session, where members go through the bill line by line and often propose amendments. Reforms in the 1970s opened most of these meetings to the press and public. Those who serve in Congress are now more accountable for what they do, but some wonder whether greater openness has harmed deliberation (also discussed later). As one representative noted, "In the 1970s, we junior members argued strongly for openness, as did the media. But we discovered that people posture and abandon the responsibility of legislating."[54] Those who pay closest attention to markup sessions are lobbyists, who use the occasion to press for changes that serve their interests.

Markup—the process by which a committee or subcommittee proposes changes to a bill.

Photo by Win McNamee/Getty Images

On March 17, 2005, baseball players Curt Schilling (right), Rafael Palmeiro, Mark McGwire, Sammy Sosa (far left), and Jose Canseco (background) all appeared before a House committee investigating steroid use in Major League Baseball.

After markup, the subcommittee reports the bill and the amendments to the full committee, which may conduct further hearings and markups. The full committee then votes on its recommendation to the chamber. The chair has committee aides write a report on the bill's intent and scope. Such reports inform floor debate, because they are the official means by which a committee tells the full chamber what it has done and why. Later, judges and administrators may study these reports to discern the congressional intent behind a law.

Bills sometimes bypass serious committee consideration. In 1995, in their eagerness to pass their "Contract with America" agenda within a 100-day deadline, House Republicans often rushed bills through committee. Representative David Dreier (R-CA) said at the time, "The thing that has troubled me about the whole Hundred Days concept is that we're trying to do too much too quickly. We're going against the Founding Fathers. They wanted us to be deliberative."[55] Occasionally the leadership skips legislative committee action and brings a measure straight to the floor. At the start of the 2007 session, the new Democratic majority dispensed with hearings and markups, passing a set of bills within the first 100 hours.

Consideration by the Full Body

For most major bills, the House Rules Committee drafts special rules that may limit debate, assign control of debate time to certain members (called "managers"), and govern which amendments members may offer. The House must approve a special rule before it resolves itself into the "Committee of the Whole," which is just another name for the entire House operating under less rigid procedures. Special rules fall into several categories. **Open rules** permit any amendments that are otherwise in order. **Closed rules** forbid all amendments. Other special rules may allow certain amendments while barring others.

Open rule—a rule governing debate in the House of Representatives that allows any amendments to be considered.

Closed rule—a rule governing debate in the House of Representatives that prohibits amendments.

Especially for members who do not belong to the committee reporting the bill, floor amendments offer a way to change the legislation. They also let lawmakers force votes on questions their colleagues want to avoid. By restricting amendments, the majority can block these maneuvers, thus depriving the minority of what little influence it might have. "This particular rule is an outrage," said Martin Meehan (D-MA) when an appropriations bill came up and his party was in the minority.[56] In 2007, after Democrats had regained the majority, former Rules chair David Dreier (R-CA) said of the rule for a student loan bill, "The rule is an absolute outrage, the fact it denies any Democrat or Republican an opportunity to participate, and I urge opposition to it."[57] As these examples show, the minority in the House can do little to stop the majority from working its will.

Senate procedures, unlike those of the House, allow time-consuming parliamentary tactics and unlimited debate on most measures. Because a single senator can bring the chamber to a stop, the Senate operates mainly on unanimous consent. Senate custom, for example, allows a single senator to place a **hold** on a bill or presidential nomination, preventing further action. Uncontroversial measures ordinarily undergo little discussion and require no formal rules to govern debate. More significant measures require **unanimous consent agreements** that spell out the terms of debate and that are negotiated before debate begins. They are much like House special rules—except, of course, that a lone senator can scuttle them.

If senators cannot work out such an agreement, the bill faces a possible filibuster—the use of speeches and motions to keep the Senate from voting on a specific bill or presidential appointment, as described earlier in the chapter. These days, the Senate seldom sees "old-fashioned" filibusters, where one member holds the floor for many hours. (The record belongs to Senator Strom Thurmond of South Carolina, then a Democrat, who personally filibustered the 1957 civil rights bill for 24 hours and 18 minutes.) Since the 1970s, leaders have typically sought unanimous consent to "freeze" the filibustered bill, put it on a side-track, and take up other business. This "tracking system" lets the leaders keep the agenda moving while the filibustering senator stalls the one bill in question. Because filibusterers no longer have to endure a physical ordeal or face the wrath of a paralyzed Senate, the tracking system has actually encouraged filibusters.[58]

The Senate can end a filibuster through a **cloture** motion, which needs 60 votes to pass (three-fifths of the constitutional size of the Senate, now 100). If a united minority has more than 40 votes, it can defeat cloture, sustain a filibuster, and essentially kill the bill. Some have argued that the Senate should make cloture easier, noting that the filibuster is no longer a weapon of last resort but a common procedure that thwarts the majority's will.[59] Others back the current process, contending that the filibuster protects minority rights and encourages lawmakers to build broader majorities through compromise and deliberation.

The long-term trend in the use of filibusters is sharply upward. Although there is no official count of filibusters, cloture motions give a good approximation. In the ten years from 1971 through 1980, senators filed 160 cloture motions to end debate and were successful in 44 cases. In the ten years from 2001 through 2010, senators filed 477 cloture motions (about three times as many) and were successful in 204 cases.[60] This means that unsuccessful cloture motions (and therefore successful filibusters) grew from 116 in the earlier period to 273 thirty years later.

What of congressional floor debate in general? When ordinary Americans visit the Capitol, they expect to see a chamber full of lawmakers carefully listening to a clash of views. By contrast, says reporter Juliet Eilperin, debate "is now more Kabuki theater than germane discussion." Lawmakers prepare their speeches in advance and seldom engage one another in actual exchanges.[61] When he was a senator, Barack Obama said, "I'm surprised at the lack of deliberation in the world's greatest deliberative body. We have press releases passing in the night and floor statements nobody is listening to."[62] These statements, however, *do* serve an important function by putting members' arguments on the record. The contents of the *Congressional Record* enable scholars, judges, and ordinary citizens to see the rationale behind congressional decisions.

Members do not always base their voting decisions on thorough study of legislation. Complicated bills sometimes reach the floor only a few hours before the scheduled vote, making it impossible to read the text in time for the roll call (see photo). Even when lawmakers have three or more days to study a lengthy bill, the need to keep up with other bills may prevent them from doing so. The 111th Congress (2009–2011), for example, enacted 8,015 pages of statutes.[63]

It is impossible for individual legislators to digest thoroughly all the proposals on which they must vote. They rely heavily on their personal staff to advise them, and they often defer to committee or subcommittee members whose judgment they trust. After all, most deliberation on most bills occurs well before the measure makes it to the floor. This is especially

Hold—an informal practice in the Senate that allows a member to request the leader to hold up action on a bill, presidential nomination, or other matter.

Unanimous consent agreement—an agreement negotiated in the Senate before floor debate begins, to specify the terms of debate. These require the approval of all interested senators.

Cloture—the procedure used by the Senate to place a time limit on debate on a bill or other matter, thereby overcoming a filibuster. This requires approval by three-fifths of the full Senate, currently 60 votes.

House Minority Leader John Boehner (R-OH) (later the Speaker of the House) criticizes the Democrats' massive health care proposal in November of 2009 as a "government takeover of health care" and a "job killing bill."

true in the House of Representatives, where even major bills typically get only a few hours of floor debate. The Senate's tradition of lengthy floor debate makes senators less beholden to committees and subcommittees. Senators can also more easily add **riders** to bills. These legislative measures, often on other subjects, are added to popular bills because they might not pass on their own.

After the debate and the approval of any amendments, the chamber passes or defeats the bill. (In the House, the Committee of the Whole "rises and reports," and then the chamber votes on the measure as amended.) A passed bill then goes to the other chamber, which may amend the bill. If the changes are minor, the chamber that initially passed the bill may simply agree to them. The measure is then sent to the president for his signature or veto.

If the changes are major, a conference committee may work out the differences. In recent years, however, congressional leaders have increasingly bypassed the conference procedure through "ping-ponging." In this practice, one chamber amends a bill from another chamber, which in turn amends the amended version, and so on until they reach agreement. Party leaders in Congress direct the process, which tends to make the committee leaders, who typically serve on the conference committee, less important to the resolution. Former House aide Don Wolfensberger says that the trend "is one more sign of the decline of the committee system and its attributes of deliberation and expertise. It is especially troubling because the lack of conference deliberations shuts out majority and minority Members alike from having a final say on important policy decisions."[64]

Beyond the Floor

To become law, a bill must pass both chambers in exactly the same form, word for word. If it does, it goes to the president for his consideration. The president has three options. First, he may sign the bill, and it becomes law. Second, he may veto the bill. If he does, he must return the bill to the originating house "with his Objections" (Article I, Section 7). The purpose here is to promote a genuine deliberation between the branches, not merely a contest of wills. Congress may **override** a veto by a two-thirds vote of both houses.

Third, the president may do nothing. If he neither signs nor vetoes a bill within 10 days ("Sundays excepted") during a congressional session, it also becomes law. In this way, the president can allow a bill to become law without formally endorsing it. If, however, Congress adjourns during this 10-day period, withholding a signature constitutes a **pocket veto** and the bill dies. Unlike regular vetoes, pocket vetoes are not subject to override by Congress. This feature makes them attractive to presidents. In recent decades, Congress and presidents have clashed over whether the constitutional language—"unless Congress by their adjournment prevent [the bill's] return"—covers relatively short recesses of Congress during its two-year term. The Supreme Court has not definitively resolved this issue.

So Congress deliberates on the passage of the bill, and the president deliberates on whether to sign or veto it. In case of a veto, the Congress may again deliberate on the bill's merits. In the view of Alexander Hamilton, this system protects the community against bad laws. "The oftener a measure is brought under examination," he said, "the greater the diversity in the situations of those who are to examine it, the less must be the danger of those errors which flow from want of due deliberation, or of those missteps which proceed from the contagion of some common passion or interest."[65] Deliberation at many separate stages, Hamilton hoped, would promote reason over passion and the public good over narrow interest.

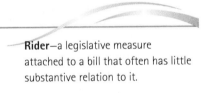

Rider—a legislative measure attached to a bill that often has little substantive relation to it.

FOCUS QUESTION

Should the filibuster rule in the Senate be eliminated so that a majority of members can always vote on a bill or presidential nomination?

Override—when the House and Senate by two-thirds votes approve a bill over the president's veto.

Pocket veto—when a president refuses to sign a bill within 10 days of Congress passing it and Congress has adjourned. Because a pocket veto cannot be overridden by Congress, presidential inaction kills the bill.

When a bill becomes law, it receives a number showing the Congress that passed it and a unique sequential identifying number. For example, President Obama's Affordable Care Act (discussed in Chapter 16) was P.L.111–148 because it was the 148th law passed by the 111th Congress. Volumes titled *Statutes at Large* present these laws (also known as statutes) chronologically. Another set of volumes, *U.S. Code*, arranges laws by subject matter and reflects changes that the statutes make in existing law. The *U.S. Code* now takes up more than 27,000 pages.

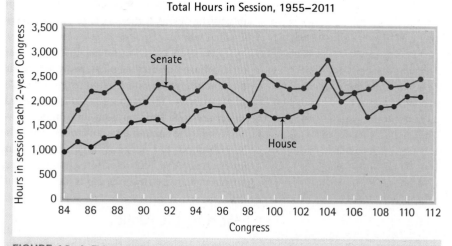

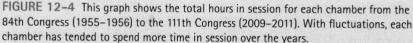

Total Hours in Session, 1955–2011

FIGURE 12-4 This graph shows the total hours in session for each chamber from the 84th Congress (1955–1956) to the 111th Congress (2009–2011). With fluctuations, each chamber has tended to spend more time in session over the years.
SOURCE: Norman J. Ornstein, Thomas E. Mann and Michael J. Malbin, *Vital Statistics on Congress 2001–2002* (Washington, AEI Press, 2002); Resumes of Congressional Activity, at www.senate.gov/pagelayout/reference/two_column_table/Resumes.htm

Legislative Workload

The legislative process takes up a huge share of a member's time. In recent years, legislative leaders have shortened the number of days each week that Congress is in session but lengthened the average legislative day. The result is that the total number of hours in session has gradually increased (see Figure 12-4). Legislators spend some part of this time, though well under half, on the floor monitoring or engaged in debate.

Although they do not listen to all floor speeches, members do rush back to the chamber for **roll call votes**, which are the recorded votes on major amendments and final passage of bills (done electronically in the House and by voice in the Senate). Most roll calls are not close, and many involve minor issues. Nevertheless, members feel political pressure to make recorded votes, because a high "absentee rate" can be a damaging campaign issue. As a result, lawmakers spend much of their day in motion, rushing between the Capitol and the office buildings. Responsible lawmakers also spend considerable time when Congress is in session attending committee hearings and markup sessions and meeting with staff on legislative matters.

Besides lawmaking, Congress carries out other functions that some claim are equally, or even more, important.

Roll call vote—a recorded vote on major amendments or final passage of a bill (done electronically in the House and by voice in the Senate).

OTHER IMPORTANT FUNCTIONS OF CONGRESS
MAJOR ISSUE

- Besides passing laws, what does Congress do?

Next to lawmaking, the most important functions of Congress are overseeing the administration, educating the public, and serving the needs of constituents. After examining these three, we assess how much the reelection incentive affects the functioning of Congress.

Overseeing the Administration

Over the years, Congress has established a vast federal bureaucracy, now numbering over two and a half million civilian employees. Most of this bureaucracy is part of the executive branch, which, of course, is headed by the president (see the discussion in Chapter 14). Yet despite the president's position as formal head of the executive branch, the members of

Congress generally believe that high-level appointees and career civil servants are responsible to the law and, therefore, to the lawmaking branch and not simply to the president's personal will.

Officially, Congress understands its job not as directing agencies but as overseeing their work to make sure they keep faith with congressional intent. Congress carries out this **oversight** function in several ways. First, it reviews the agencies whenever the executive branch seeks to renew authority for ongoing programs. Second, it assesses performance through its annual budget review. Third, standing committees oversee the operation of the government.

When the same party controlled both the executive and legislative branches during the presidency of George W. Bush, critics argued that Congress was failing in its oversight duties. After the 2006 election changed party control of Congress, Democrats in both chambers launched a series of investigations into the Bush administration.[66]

Oversight—congressional review of the activities of federal agencies and programs.

Educating the Public

Woodrow Wilson held that "[t]he informing function of Congress should be preferred even to its legislative function." Congress ought to instruct and guide the people in political affairs by keeping "all national concerns suffused in a broad daylight of discussion." It investigates the administration, Wilson wrote, less to improve the execution of the laws than to foster "the enlightenment of the people."[67] Rather than passively respond to public opinion, members of Congress try to shape it. They even help create public opinion by highlighting issues that would otherwise escape notice.[68]

Unlike the president and the Supreme Court, who deliberate and decide behind closed doors, the modern Congress conducts most formal business in the open. Radio and television have vastly expanded the audience for congressional activities. Some televised committee hearings have shaped the public's knowledge of national issues. Senate hearings in the 1950s on organized crime catapulted Senator Estes Kefauver (D-TN) into the national spotlight and created public pressure for federal action. Similarly, Americans paid close attention to investigations in the 1960s on hunger and in the 1970s on Watergate-related crimes. In October of 1991, the Senate confirmation hearing on the nomination of federal judge Clarence Thomas to the Supreme Court focused national attention on the issue of sexual harassment when a former employee of Thomas, Anita Hill, accused him of inappropriate conversations when they worked together.

Special order speech—a speech that members of the House of Representatives can give before or after each day's formal session in order to call attention to some matter.

Congress did not always embrace electronic broadcasting of its activities. The House banned the televising of floor debates until 1979 and the Senate until 1986. Now the C-SPAN cable network provides gavel-to-gavel coverage of floor proceedings in both the House (C-SPAN) and the Senate (C-SPAN 2).

Senators who wish to influence national opinion can speak on virtually any matter on the floor of the Senate and reach a larger audience through television. The House, given its size, cannot be so accommodating. Its members have made creative use of the periods before and after each day's formal session. During these periods, they give speeches on some matter to which they wish to call attention. **Special order speeches**, the name for these speeches that last up to an hour, may take on the trappings of a college lecture as members use charts and graphs to discuss the details of policy issues. Not coincidentally, the lawmaker who pioneered the use of special order speeches to promote the minority's legislative program was Newt Gingrich (R-GA), a former history professor.

Secretary of the Interior Ken Salazar testifies before a House Natural Resources Committee hearing on the BP oil spill on May 26, 2010. Greenpeace protesters hold up signs in back.

© Benjamin J. Myers/Corbis

In recent years, committees in the House and Senate have begun streaming live video coverage of hearings on the Internet and also archiving the hearings online. The authors of a recent study write that "[t]he privately-run cable network C-SPAN cannot cover every hearing, and it's unreasonable to expect people to travel to D.C. to be in attendance." In 2012, about three-fourths of all committee hearings in the House were streamed live and almost four-fifths were archived online.[69]

Members of Congress have other ways to reach broad audiences. They often appear on television interview shows and speak to groups with an interest in national policy. At home, they make use of local cable programs and radio call-in shows and conduct "town meetings." They also mail newsletters to the voters (at government expense), and all have Web pages.

Serving Constituents

Constituency service has become a major activity of lawmakers and aides. One form it takes is **casework**. The members help constituents with all kinds of federal matters, ranging from federally backed college loans to the burden of federal rules on a local business. Although this work seems remote from the great issues of the day, members have strong incentives to excel in this service. Unlike taking stands on controversial matters, which some voters will always oppose, constituency service is virtually risk free. It makes few if any enemies (except for constituents who cannot get what they want), and it creates beneficiaries who may reward the lawmaker with their votes.

Another form of constituency service consists of "bringing home the bacon" through highway funds, farm subsidies, and the like. If enough lawmakers support one another's desired projects, then majorities can emerge through vote trading, commonly called **logrolling**. The concept is well captured in the common Expression "you scratch my back and I'll scratch yours." The practice dates all the way back to the First Congress when Secretary of State Thomas Jefferson arranged a deal between a few southern and northern legislators in 1790. Some southern members of the House agreed to support the federal government's assumption of the state debts from the Revolutionary War in exchange for some northern representatives endorsing the movement of the nation's capital southward from New York City to the banks of the Potomac River at the border of Maryland and Virginia.

Logrolling sometimes results in so-called **pork barrel** legislation. In the nineteenth century, a pork barrel was a container for storing pig meat in brine. After refrigeration became common, it fell out of use. Now it refers to federal programs or subsidies that directly benefit constituents. Voters observe the benefits while discounting the costs. Rarely do legislators suffer for snagging federal pork. Lawmakers who procure such federal largesse and the constituents who benefit from it defend it as good public policy. A Florida senator described the behind-closed-doors process used in negotiating the details of the $800 billion economic stimulus package passed in 2009: "It was essentially about going around the table and instead of talking about the merits of the bill, it was what goodies they could get, what pet projects and the value and the price of it."[70] He voted against the bill, but most in the House and Senate favored it.

While the political benefits of constituency service are obvious, the substantive benefits are less clear. On the plus side, advocacy of constituent needs can check the bureaucracy. When policies from

FOCUS
QUESTION

Is there more that Congress should do to educate the American people about national issues and public policies? How can it best help to fashion "the cool and deliberate sense of the community"?

Constituency service—efforts undertaken by members of Congress to assist constituents, such as intervening with the bureaucracy and bringing home federal projects.

Casework—assistance to constituents in their dealings with federal agencies.

Logrolling—when two or more legislators trade votes for each other's proposals or exchange other legislative favors.

Pork barrel—a derogatory term for projects that benefit specific localities without serving the national interest.

Courtesy of the Office of Robert Menendez

Senator Robert Menendez (D-NJ) joins Governor Chris Christie (R-NJ) in cutting the ribbon for an "urban beach" in the Jersey City development of Newport. Menendez noted that federal dollars helped build the development.

Washington, DC, have unforeseen consequences back home, lawmakers may relay such information to the seat of government, perhaps leading to better policy.

A preoccupation with constituency service, however, may hamper sound lawmaking. The members are not only local representatives but national lawmakers who should promote the good of the country as a whole. Again and again, the authors of *The Federalist Papers* emphasized that the purpose of the new national government was to achieve a larger national good, using such terms as "the permanent and aggregate interests of the community," "the public good," "the good of the whole," "great and national objects," "the great and aggregate interests," "the national prosperity and happiness," "the great interests of the nation," "the common interest," "the common good of the society," and "the comprehensive interests of [the] country."[71]

This devotion to national objects prompted the U.S. Senate to write to President Washington in 1789, "It shall be our invariable aim to divest ourselves of local prejudices and attachments."[72] Rarely do modern senators (or representatives) talk this way. Legislators display insufficient civic virtue if they fail to balance local desires against national needs and interests. Pandering to local attachments does not cultivate good citizenship.

Does Congress lose sight of the broad national interest when its 535 members and their staff work hard to bring home the goods? In 2005, Congress passed a highway bill authorizing $286.4 billion in projects over six years. By one count, this bill contained 6,371 **earmarks**, provisions setting aside money for specific projects.[73] These earmarks were the pet projects of individual members and most had not been reviewed or debated in committee or on the floor. President Obama came to office vowing to fight earmarks but yielded to political reality when he signed a $410 billion spending bill with more than 9,000 earmarks.[74] Although public pressure led Congress to ban earmarks in 2011, legislators found creative means to direct public spending to pet projects. "We thought we'd gotten rid of earmarks," said the vice president of a budget watchdog group. "But it looks like Congress has just moved on to other methods that are less transparent than the old way."[75]

Earmark—a provision of a spending bill that sets aside funds for a specific purpose in a district or state.

Franking privilege—the right of members of Congress to send mail to their constituents without paying for the postage.

The Reelection Incentive and the Functioning of Congress

To accomplish long-term goals, members of Congress must win reelection.[76] Some focus on little else, but even the most selfless lawmakers must keep winning the favor of their constituents. Incumbents have numerous ways to communicate with their constituents and to provide them goods and services. The **franking privilege**, for example, allows members of Congress to send mail to their constituents without paying for the postage. Another advantage of incumbency is fund-raising. Lawmakers can usually raise more campaign money than their challengers, which is one reason why they seldom lose reelection.

Fund-raising comes at a cost to the deliberative process. Members of Congress spend a great deal of time phoning contributors. Because it is illegal to raise campaign money on federal property, they must go off the Capitol grounds to make these calls. They organize fund-raising events in Washington and at home, and they also attend the events of their party colleagues. Because of the high cost of campaigns, members start raising money for the next election almost as soon as the last one is over. With two-year terms, House members face even greater pressure than senators. An aide to a top House Democrat explained, "It would be nice to have a little break so people could do their job before they have to spend all their time calling people, asking them for money."[77]

Apart from distracting lawmakers from policy deliberation, does the pursuit of money distort the policies themselves? Some argue that powerful interest groups can buy influence through campaign contributions, but scholars have found only a weak link between campaign money and floor votes.[78] With an enormous range of interests to draw on, lawmakers of nearly every stripe can find enough contributions to fill their "war chests" (the funds used to campaign for reelection). Members obviously need to heed the major interests of their constituents. Lawmakers from rural areas thus tend to support subsidies for local crops, and those from smoggy areas will generally back tougher pollution controls. But beyond those constraints, members can pick which voices they want to hear.[79]

Some scholars believe that the reelection incentive is so powerful that it undermines serious deliberation within Congress about the broad public good. Others, however, have been impressed by how seriously many members of the House and Senate take their lawmaking responsibilities. One notes, for example, how former senator Edmund Muskie (D-ME, 1959–1980), a leader on environmental policy and his party's vice presidential candidate in 1968, cut back on Washington socializing to concentrate on his legislative homework. "Too often when I go to an embassy party or somewhere else," Muskie explained, "all during the evening I'm worried about that bill that I'd like to be working on, or a problem I'd like to be tackling. When I get home and go to bed, I pile the books up beside it and read until I fall asleep." To make more room for deliberation, Muskie cut back on the socializing. Muskie believed that "[t]he thing that draws people to this level of political office is the power to influence great events, great issues."[80] Reelection might well be the precondition for influencing great events, but it was not the end in itself.

In some cases, lawmakers even risk their jobs to do the right thing. John F. Kennedy's *Profiles in Courage*, published in 1955, won the Pulitzer Prize for recounting the courageous acts of eight U.S. sena-

Service in Congress sometimes involves physical danger as well as political risk. In 2011, a mentally-disturbed man shot Representative Gabrielle Giffords (D-Arizona) and several others while she was meeting constituents. She suffered brain damage and had to leave Congress. In this photo, President Obama embraces Representative Giffords at the 2012 State of the Union, just before her resignation took effect.

tors, several of whom suffered electoral defeat for doing what they thought was best for the country. Nearly half a century later, Kennedy's daughter, Caroline Kennedy, edited *Profiles in Courage for Our Time*, which highlighted the courageous acts of more than a dozen public figures, many of whom served in the Congress. Two of these were Senators John McCain (R-AZ) and Russell Feingold (D-WI), who took considerable political risks to push for campaign finance legislation that now bears their names: the McCain-Feingold Act of 2002. Feingold had read *Profiles in Courage* as a teenager: "I loved it . . . [T]his thin little book spoke volumes about what kind of a senator it is worthwhile to be."[81]

Although stories of courage by senators are better known, it is not unusual to find members of the House of Representatives voting for bills unpopular in their districts or against popular bills. One example, recounted by two congressional experts, is first-term congressman Ted Strickland (D-OH) who voted in August 1993 for President Bill Clinton's economic package to cut spending and raise taxes. It barely passed, 218 to 216. With every Republican voting against the bill, Democrats knew that they would be charged with voting for "the largest tax increase in history." Strickland understood the political risks, and his vote contributed to his defeat in the 1994 election.[82] (His political career recovered in 1996 when he retook his congressional seat. He served 10 more years in the House and then four years as governor of Ohio.)

Political courage, of course, is not the same thing as political wisdom. Courage may be necessary to get lawmakers to act on their understanding of the national interest, but it does not guarantee that they are right. How, then, should we judge Congress's contribution to American deliberative democracy? What standards should we use to evaluate congressional performance?

CONGRESS AND DELIBERATIVE DEMOCRACY

In evaluating Congress's contribution to American deliberative democracy, we must start with how well Congress deliberates on public policy. But we must also assess Congress as a representative, ethical, and accountable institution and how these qualities contribute to deliberation.

Deliberation

If Congress is to make laws for the broad national interest, it must have the qualities of a deliberative institution. Its members must reason with each other about the merits of public policy with the best information and arguments available. According to the nineteenth-century British political theorist John Stuart Mill, a good legislature is a "school of political capacity and general intelligence."[83] To a large extent, life on Capitol Hill revolves around gaining and using information. Congress has developed several agencies to help in this activity:

- The Congressional Research Service (CRS) supplies nonpartisan analysis on legislative issues. Its staff includes experts in law, economics, foreign affairs, the natural sciences, and many other fields. They perform in-depth policy analyses, help frame legislative proposals, and testify before congressional committees. One could say that CRS provides lawmakers with their study guides.[84]
- The Congressional Budget Office produces cost estimates and budget and economic projections that inform decisions about spending and taxes. Congress set it up in 1974 to provide it with a source of budget information independent of the White House.[85]
- The Government Accountability Office is Congress's investigative agency. It evaluates federal programs, audits federal expenditures, and issues legal opinions. Created by Congress in 1921 as the General Accounting Office, its mission gradually broadened over the decades, earning it a new name in 2004.[86]

Congress also receives expert analysis from committee staff. In most cases, different aides work for Republicans and Democrats, and their work has a partisan cast; but even here, there are exceptions. Serving both the House and Senate, the nonpartisan staff of the Joint Committee on Taxation prepares committee reports, helps draft and analyze tax bills, and studies various aspects of the federal tax system.

The existence of analytical organizations suggests that Congress cares about deliberation. As Barack Obama reflected on his Senate years in *The Audacity of Hope*, "Even when talking to colleagues with whom I most deeply disagreed, I was usually struck by their basic sincerity—their desire to get things right and leave the country better and stronger."[87] Among themselves, members of Congress distinguish "workhorses" (those who master the details of policy) from "show horses" (those who care more for appearances). Lawmakers trust the workhorses and tend to put them in leadership positions.

Yet even the strongest workhorse has a hard time carrying the deliberative load of modern legislation. There is seldom enough time in the day for members to read all the bills they must vote on, *and* attend all the committees and subcommittees on which they serve, *and* address the demands of their constituents.

So how well does Congress do? One recent study carefully examined House and Senate floor debate on several key issues. The authors concluded that the typical debate is roughly an even balance of fact and fiction: "Legislators frequently assert claims that are inaccurate or misleading, and reassert them after they have been effectively refuted. There is some good news: when one side to a debate perpetrates important distortions or omissions, the other side usually—though not always—offers a rebuttal."[88] The researchers did note some variations. They found that debate is more informative when the issue cuts across partisan and ideological lines, minimizing party polarization. (For more on polarization, see Chapter 9.) In such cases, members focus more on persuading undecided colleagues than on scoring political points.[89] The authors also found that Senate debates are generally longer and more informed than House debates.[90]

Earlier we noted that House members often have a very different view about deliberation in the upper chamber. They believe that they work harder and develop greater expertise on policy issues than their Senate colleagues. With so many more committee and subcommittee assignments, senators learn less about any particular subject and necessarily defer more to their staff.

So which institution is more deliberative? There is no simple answer to this question. The House has the advantage at the committee and subcommittee stage, and the Senate on the floor. Of course, what matters in the end is whether the combination of the efforts of the two chambers results in legislation well crafted to serve the national interest.

Representation

A deliberative democracy is not just deliberative; it is also democratic. All agree that Congress should represent the American people. The people cannot convene directly to draft laws, so they delegate this task to a small number of individuals who act on their behalf. But must the 535 voting members of Congress resemble the American people, and if so, how?

As Figure 12-5 shows, the modern Congress is not a mirror image of the people. Women are half of the U.S. population, but only 17% of the House and Senate. Hispanics are almost 16% of the population, but just 7% of the House and 2% of the Senate. African Americans are almost 14% of the population, but since Senator Obama became President Obama, there are none in the Senate. It follows that white males are a higher percentage of the Congress than they are of the American population. But this is also true of other groups: members of Congress are much more likely to have college degrees and to be lawyers than Americans in general.

Members of Congress do have a great variety of prior occupations. Although more than half of the representatives and senators in the 112th Congress (2011–2013) had previously been legislators in a state or territory and a fifth had been congressional staffers, 81 had been educators (including teachers, counselors, and coaches); 39, mayors; 26, prosecutors; 17, farmers; 17, medical doctors; 11, ranchers; 11, state governors; 10, judges; 9, accountants; 9, social workers; 9, engineers or scientists; 6, nurses; 6, reporters or journalists; 5, ordained ministers; 5, sheriffs or deputy sheriffs; 4, Peace Corps volunteers; 4, radio talk-show hosts; 4, pilots; and smaller numbers in other occupations.[91]

The debate over whether Congress should resemble the citizenry is as old as the Republic. Federalists and anti-Federalists clashed over this issue as soon as the Constitution was drafted. As we noted in Chapter 2, in the final days of the Convention, George Mason of Virginia predicted that the new House of Representatives would have "not the substance but the shadow only of representation." In the New York ratifying convention, Melancton Smith complained that the House would be so small (originally 65) that it would be composed almost entirely of the "first class in the community," those distinguished by "birth, education, talents and wealth." He preferred representatives who "resemble those they represent," who are "a true picture of the people." It is much better, he urged, to have a legislature dominated by "men of the middling class of life," such as small independent farmers, because they "are more temperate, of better morals and less ambition than the great." When these people "pursue their own interest, they promote that of the public."[92]

Although the Federalists insisted that the members of the House would share the "interests" and "sentiments" of the people, they did not expect the membership to mirror the population. Indeed, they wanted representatives, Madison wrote, who displayed superior "wisdom," "patriotism," and "love of justice."[93] James Wilson called for representatives "most noted for wisdom and virtue" and predicted that large electoral districts would favor candidates with "real weight of character."[94] As one scholar succinctly put it, "the Federalists saw the duty of representatives as extending

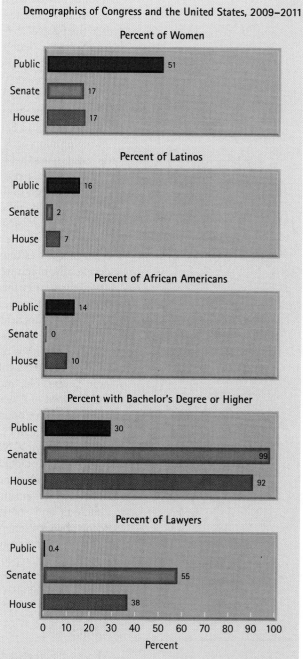

FIGURE 12-5 Congressional figures include five nonvoting members of the House. Census data for degrees includes population 25 and older.
SOURCE: Data on Congress (2011) from Jennifer E. Manning, "Membership of the 112th Congress: A Profile," Congress Research Service, March 1, 2011, at www.senate.gov/reference/resources/pdf/R41647.pdf; Census data for women (2010), Latinos/Hispanics (2009), and African-Americans (2009) at http://www.census.gov/compendia/statab/cats/population.html; Census data for educational attainment (2010) at http://www.census.gov/compendia/statab/cats/education.html; data on number of lawyers (2011) from the American Bar Association, "National Lawyer Population by State," at http://www.americanbar.org/content/dam/aba/migrated/marketresearch/PublicDocuments/2011_national_lawyer_by_state.authcheckdam.pdf

beyond the particular interests of their constituents to the common good."[95] In the words of Massachusetts Federalist Fisher Ames, "the representation of the people is something more than the people."[96]

If the main job of Congress is to mirror the local and partial interests that constitute American society, then Congress perhaps should "look like" the citizenry. But if the main purpose of Congress is to discern and promote the common good, as the Federalists urged, then it is more important to bring into the institution individuals whose experience and talents best suit them to the task. As we noted at the beginning of the chapter, the members of the House and Senate were not to be mere delegates from their localities, slavishly following opinion back home, but were also to exercise their own independent judgment on the great issues that faced the nation. Until the past few decades, the talent pool on which to draw for such lawmakers was almost exclusively white males; but between 1971 and 2011, female members of the House and Senate grew from 15 to 91, black members from 14 to 44, and Hispanic members from 6 to 31.[97]

In *The Federalist Papers*, Alexander Hamilton argued that even if it was a good idea to have "all classes of citizens" in the legislature, "this will never happen under any arrangement that leaves the votes of the people free."[98] In any particular election, the voters will decide how much weight to give demographic similarity, educational attainment, political experience, party membership, and the candidates' positions on the issues.

All would agree, after all, that certain qualities ought *not* to be the basis of representation. About 7% of Americans will spend time in federal or state prison, but would anyone recommend that felons get 29 House seats and 7 Senate seats?[99] At the same time, there are some characteristics Americans might want overrepresented in Congress, such as educational attainment. Almost all members of Congress have at least a college degree, compared with 30% of Americans over 25 years old; and fully two-thirds of House members have advanced degrees, compared with only 8% of Americans over 25. Many would say that it is good to have well-educated persons serving in Congress, even if this makes the institution unrepresentative of the population.

Some ancient democracies filled government posts by lot, giving every citizen an equal chance of serving. No one seriously proposes choosing the members of Congress this way, although this practice could result in a more "representative" body. Elections allow the citizens to give preference to those qualities they most want in their lawmakers, at least among the candidates on the ballot. Ideally, such representatives will not only share the people's "interests" and "sentiments" but will also deliberate together about the common good. As one scholar has written, representatives need some "constitutional distance" from their constituents so that they can exercise the independent judgment required for sound legislation.[100] But on issues the people feel strongly about, lawmakers may feel pressure to step off the high road and simply bow to the polls. Elected representatives are keenly aware that the voters will decide how well they represent their interests and concerns.

Ethics

Those who created the Congress hoped that its members would be virtuous. What did they mean by virtue, and why did they think it important? First, virtue meant devotion to "the common good of the society." Legislators who promoted only partial interests—their own district or state, certain classes or groups—or only their private advantage were not truly virtuous. This devotion to the common good, what they often simply called "patriotism," was necessary to prevent "temporary or partial considerations" from controlling legislative decisions.

Virtue also meant "love of justice." The United States was founded on a doctrine of natural rights; a just government secures these rights. Whenever groups with a passion or interest "adverse to the rights of other citizens" tried to warp the law to their ends, it would take justice-loving legislators to resist them.[101] If this love of justice was strong enough, legislators would sacrifice their self-interest—perhaps even their careers—for the sake of doing right.

Rarely today do discussions of congressional ethics address such exalted notions. Instead, they focus on sexual improprieties, corruption, and abuse of power. In 2006, Representative Randy "Duke" Cunningham (R-CA) went to prison for conspiracy and tax evasion. Cunningham sold favors to special interests, even writing a "bribe menu" listing payments for different levels of contracts. In June 2007, a federal grand jury indicted Congressman William Jefferson (D-LA) on corruption charges after the FBI discovered $90,000 in cash in his home freezer, allegedly from bribes. He was defeated for reelection the following year and convicted of 11 felony counts by a federal jury in 2009.

Corrupt behavior by national lawmakers has never been typical, and most observers of Congress believe that graft is rarer now than in the past. A more pervasive ethical problem involves a basic dilemma. Lawmakers should serve the broad public interest, but they cannot do as much if their party is in the minority, and they cannot do anything if they fail to win reelection. To win seats for themselves and their party colleagues, members often cater to narrow interests. They can rationalize this activity as the price of serving the national interest, but when does the price become too high? When does the pursuit of power eclipse the goals that power should serve?

Accountability

Elections link Congress's deliberations with the people's interests and sentiments. If elections are to be the means for holding the members of Congress accountable, then the people must be able to see what lawmakers are doing and reward or punish them accordingly. It follows that the congressional process must be open to public scrutiny.

The Constitution requires each house to keep and publish a "Journal of its Proceedings." A legislative journal typically includes all motions and vote results, but not a transcript of the debate. The Constitution further stipulates that one-fifth of those present may request a roll call vote for entry in the journal.[102] Otherwise, the Constitution leaves wide latitude to each house. As a result of rules adopted in the 1970s, more votes of individual members are now recorded and available for public inspection than in the past. This information includes many votes in committees as well as certain floor votes on amendments.

Since the mid-1990s, the Internet has heightened the level of scrutiny. The THOMAS Web site (thomas.loc.gov) enables anyone to get the full text of legislation, report language, and floor debates. As we noted earlier, many committees post text and video of their proceedings on their Web pages. In 2007, C-SPAN changed its copyright policy to allow people to post clips of congressional debate on sites such as YouTube.[103]

If accountability is a good thing, is more accountability better? Consider floor debate. In principle, televising floor debate makes the members more accountable to constituents. Yet television may also encourage grandstanding. Consider also the opening of committee markup sessions to public scrutiny. Although this move increases accountability, it also increases the power of lobbyists to influence committee decisions by putting them into the room where the decisions are happening. With recorded votes, it is increasingly difficult for members to cast a vote on the merits of a bill when this might be politically costly, and many bloggers try to pressure lawmakers to stick to rigid partisan or ideological positions. So, changes that have made Congress more accountable may also have made it less deliberative, less able to promote the broad national interest.

Openness can also foster accuracy. Lawmakers are more likely to avoid distortion if someone quickly exposes it to the public. The news media have generally not focused on this task, covering the broad outlines of congressional debate instead of the factual details. The Internet, however, is starting to fill the void. Many bloggers keep an eye on C-SPAN and rapidly comment on errors or misstatements.

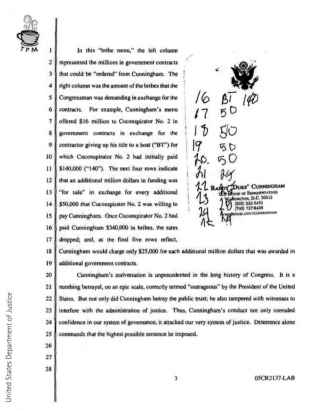

United States Department of Justice

This page from the prosecutors' sentencing recommendation for Representative Randy "Duke" Cunningham (R-CA) on February 18, 2006, shows Cunningham's "bribe menu."

IMPACT
of Social Media and Communications Technology

Broadcasting Congress

As we note in the Bessette/Pitney blog of April 18, 2012, most House committees now provide video broadcasts of hearings live over the Internet and also archive them online. We seem to be fast approaching the time when all committee and subcommittee hearings in Congress will be available for viewing in real time and anytime after they occur. Those who favor such developments argue the virtues of greater public accountability. Yet, there is no guarantee that greater public scrutiny and accountability will also foster sound deliberation about the broad public good.

CRITICAL THINKING
QUESTION

Will Congress's essential deliberative functions be enhanced, weakened, or not affected if all committee and subcommittee hearings and markup sessions are broadcast electronically while they occur and are archived online for public access?

The framers of the U.S. Constitution intended the new Congress to be an especially deliberative institution, one in which the members would "refine and enlarge the public views" by reasoning together about matters of national concern. Yet, as we have seen, assessing the deliberative character of the modern Congress is no simple matter. Although its committee structure, legislative procedures, and staff support all facilitate policy deliberation, other forces sap the members' time or create incentives to promote partial interests or private advantage at the expense of the broader public good.

SUMMARY

- The framers of the U.S. Constitution designed the new Congress so that its members would reason together about the broad public good and in so doing "refine and enlarge the public views." Congress would combine both the delegate and trustee theories of representation, with House members functioning more like delegates and senators more like trustees.

- Bicameralism would promote safer and more deliberative lawmaking. Because senators represent entire states and serve six-year terms, they have more prestige than House members, represent more diverse constituencies, face less reelection pressure early in their terms, and can take a somewhat longer-term view of the public good. Because the House is more than four times the size of the Senate, it operates under the centralized control of the majority party and its leaders. Individual senators have a much greater opportunity to influence policy than do their counterparts in the House.

- Congress's constitutional powers include lawmaking, impeaching and removing public officials, expelling its own members, ratifying treaties (Senate), confirming presidential nominations to the judiciary and high executive offices (Senate), and proposing constitutional amendments. In exercising these powers, the legislative branch keeps watch on the executive and judiciary.

- In additional to bicameralism, the most important organizational features of Congress are the influence of party leaders and the division of the two bodies into legislative committees and subcommittees. These features have changed over time and vary considerably between the House and Senate. They have large consequences for deliberation, lawmaking, and representation.

- Congress wields more independent legislative power than lawmaking bodies in other democracies. Unlike a parliament, it is not under the direct control of the leaders of the executive branch.

- In fashioning new laws, Congress proceeds in four basic steps: drafting a bill, considering and modifying it in committee, debating and voting on it in the full House and Senate, and fashioning a compromise measure when the two chambers disagree.

- Members of Congress spend a good deal of time with legislation, but they have other tasks as well: overseeing the executive branch, educating the public, and serving their constituents. To keep doing any of these things, they must win reelection, an effort that may consume a large share of their time and energy. This can also create incentives to promote partial interests or private advantage at the expense of the broader public good.

- In assessing Congress's contribution to deliberative democracy, we must examine it not only as a deliberative body but also as a representative, ethical, and accountable institution. These qualities sometimes come into tension, which makes the lawmaker's job even more difficult.

KEY TERMS

Bicameral legislature p. 346
Bill p. 345
Casework p. 365
Closed rule p. 360
Cloture p. 361
Committees p. 354
Companion bill p. 358
Concurrent resolution p. 358
Conference committee p. 354
Constituency service p. 365
Constituent p. 345
Delegate p. 345
Divided government p. 351
Earmark p. 366
Filibuster p. 353
Franking privilege p. 366

Hold p. 361
Joint committees p. 354
Joint resolution p. 358
Lame duck session p. 357
Logrolling p. 365
Majority leader p. 353
Markup p. 360
Minority leader p. 353
Multiple referral p. 358
Open rule p. 360
Override p. 362
Oversight p. 364
Parliamentarian p. 353
Pocket veto p. 362
Pork barrel p. 365
President pro tempore p. 353

Referral p. 358
Rider p. 362
Roll call vote p. 363
Select (or special) committee p. 354
Senatorial courtesy p. 349
Seniority p. 355
Simple resolution p. 358
Speaker of the House p. 352
Special order speech p. 364
Standing committee p. 354
Subcommittee p. 354
Trustee p. 345
Unanimous consent agreement p. 361
Veto p. 358
Whip p. 353

TEST YOUR KNOWLEDGE

1. Lawmakers who closely follow the majority opinion in their electorate are sometimes called
   a. constituents.
   b. delegates.
   c. justices.
   d. senators.
   e. trustees.
2. The number of representatives for each state is reevaluated every _____ years.
   a. two
   b. four
   c. six
   d. ten
   e. twelve
3. Under the original Constitution, senators were selected by
   a. state legislatures.
   b. Supreme Court justices.
   c. the House of Representatives.
   d. the president.
   e. the voters.
4. The establishment of a national bank is an example of Congress's
   a. constitutional duties.
   b. enumerated powers.
   c. implied powers.

   d. oversight of the executive branch.
   e. supremacy act.
5. Congress can propose amendments to the Constitution with a
   a. measure placed on the ballot in a federal election.
   b. simple majority in each chamber if approved by the president.
   c. two-thirds vote of each chamber.
   d. three-fourths vote of each chamber.
   e. two-thirds vote of one chamber and a majority vote in the other.
6. Which of the following is an honorary position?
   a. chair of the Rules Committee in the House
   b. majority leader in the House
   c. minority whip in the Senate
   d. parliamentarian
   e. president pro tempore of the Senate
7. Subcommittees go through bills line by line and propose amendments in
   a. agenda meetings.
   b. cloture sessions.
   c. legislative hearings.
   d. markup sessions.
   e. strategy sessions.

8. Legislative measures that lawmakers add to popular bills because they might not pass on their own are called
   a. cloture motions.
   b. companion bills.
   c. earmarks.
   d. filibusters.
   e. riders.

9. A pocket veto differs from a regular veto because it
   a. is not binding.
   b. is not subject to override by Congress.
   c. is subject to judicial review.
   d. must be approved by the voters.
   e. requires only a simple majority to override it.

10. Lawmakers are able to send mail to their constituents without paying postage because of the
    a. bicameral nature of Congress.
    b. concurrency of resolutions.
    c. franking privilege.
    d. lame duck session.
    e. logrolling incentive.

FURTHER READING

Connelly, William F. *James Madison Rules America: The Constitutional Origins of Congressional Partisanship.* Lanham, MD: Rowman and Littlefield, 2010.

Draper, Robert. *Do Not Ask What Good We Do: Inside the U.S. House of Representatives.* New York: Free Press, 2012.

Mayhew, David R. *America's Congress: Actions in the Public Sphere, James Madison through Newt Gingrich.* New Haven, CT: Yale University Press, 2000.

Mucciaroni, Gary, and Paul J. Quirk. *Deliberative Choices: Debating Public Policy in Congress.* Chicago: University of Chicago Press, 2006.

Polsby, Nelson W. *How Congress Evolves: Social Bases of Institutional Change.* New York: Oxford University Press, 2004.

Strand, Mark, Michael S. Johnson, and Jerome F. Climer. *Surviving inside Congress.* Washington, DC: Congressional Institute, 2008.

Wolfensberger, Donald R. *Congress and the People: Deliberative Democracy on Trial.* Washington, DC: Woodrow Wilson Center Press, 2000.

WEB SOURCES

Directory of the U.S. Congress: bioguide.congress.gov/biosearch/biosearch.asp—brief biographies of everyone who has ever served in the House or Senate.

C-SPAN: www.c-span.org—links to live coverage of the House and Senate, as well as many audio and video clips. An extensive archive of decades of video is at www.c-spanvideo.org/videoLibrary/.

LegiStorm: www.legistorm.com—information on staff salaries, congressional travel, and financial disclosures.

Open CRS: www.opencrs.com—access to studies by the Congressional Research Service.

THOMAS: thomas.loc.gov—legislative information from the Library of Congress.

Because the executive power is never "in recess" or "out of session," the president's personal residence is also his office.

Vaclav/Shutterstock.com.

The Presidency

13

OBJECTIVES

After reading this chapter, you should be able to:

- Summarize the key developments in the history of the American presidency and describe their importance.

- Describe the organization of the executive branch and explain how it influences presidential deliberation.

- Assess the importance of the independent exercise of power by presidents.

- Evaluate the effect of clashes between presidents, Congress, and the courts over foreign policy and war powers.

- Appraise the importance of Congress's power to hold presidents accountable for serious constitutional violations through impeachment and removal.

- Explain how presidents contribute to public deliberation, and evaluate its importance to American democracy.

- Assess how Americans judge presidential performance and presidential greatness.

INTRODUCTION

Presidents are unlike other politicians. Hunger for higher office cannot drive them because they have reached the top. They answer not to any single state or district, but to the whole country—and to history. During their first terms, they work for reelection; but in the second, they think more about their place in history. Whereas lawmakers usually retire into oblivion, presidents linger in the national memory. They wonder how that memory will judge them, so they ponder how they can leave a legacy of good works.

To accomplish such good works, they deliberate with aides and cabinet members within the White House and also with the other branches.[1] Although they sometimes make deals with lawmakers, they also try to persuade them with arguments about the merits of new policies. Indeed, much of the work at the White House goes into crafting policy arguments that will move lawmakers. In this way, presidents contribute to Congress's essential deliberative function (as described in the previous chapter). As for the judiciary, the clearest influence lies in the appointment of judges, but presidents also try to sway the courts through legal argumentation.

Presidents reason with the public as well. Amid the thunder of presidential rhetoric is a good deal of substance about the issues. In the 1960s, for example, President Lyndon Johnson fostered public deliberation on the need for new civil rights laws (see Chapter 6). Three decades earlier, as we will see in Chapter 16, President Franklin Roosevelt helped to convince Americans to expand social programs.

Staffers work hard to ensure the accuracy of presidential statements, because errors can have serious consequences. In his 2003 State of the Union address, President George W. Bush cited British intelligence that Saddam Hussein had sought material for nuclear weapons. The British did indeed have such a report, but it proved debatable. That passage of Bush's speech created years of political trouble.

In their various deliberations, presidents have unique advantages. They draw on the expertise of the executive branch, and they can get advice from nearly anyone because few hang up when the White House calls. Presidents also have unique problems. Most politicians can gain political intelligence by having casual chats with ordinary citizens. To see how highway policy is working, they can get behind the wheel and take a drive. Security precautions cut presidents off from such experiences, because they cannot leave the White House grounds without extensive preparations. A year after the 1981 attempt on his life, President Reagan said, "I sometimes look out the window at Pennsylvania Avenue and wonder what it would be like to be able to just walk down the street to the corner drugstore and look at the magazines. I can't do that anymore."[2]

According to Karl Rove, a former key adviser to President George W. Bush, "Sixteen hundred Pennsylvania Avenue is 18 acres of sheer Utopia, and like Utopia it can be isolated from reality quickly."[3] Aides (such as staffers in the White House who control access to the president) can worsen the isolation. "Just when a president needs straight talk the most, he's shielded from criticism on the inside," says veteran political operative Vic Gold. "This first principle of sycophancy—that the president can do no wrong—is so ingrained in the White House that even if the president admits he was wrong, his loyal aides will fall over themselves to deny it."[4] Other aides, however, take strong exception to this view. They best serve the president, they say, when they make sure their boss is fully informed of opposing points of view.

The scope and potential isolation of today's presidency would have astonished the framers of the

Official White House Photo by Pete Souza

President Barack Obama and Vice President Joe Biden, along with members of the national security team, receive an update on the mission against Osama bin Laden in the Situation Room of the White House, May 1, 2011.

Constitution. So would many other aspects of the office. No one at the time the office was created imagined that a single leader could broadcast to millions or give a coded message that could kill billions. Less amazing would have been the political friction that presidents must face. Beneath the trappings of twenty-first century politics lie institutional conflicts that began during the eighteenth century.

The ability to order a nuclear strike shows that presidents must have the capacity to act quickly and decisively as well as deliberatively. No other branch of government needs to act as quickly in a crisis. As we shall see, though the framers knew nothing about nuclear war, they recognized that effective government requires an energetic executive.

In this chapter, we begin by examining the constitutional design of the presidency and the development of the office and its powers since George Washington took the oath of office in 1789. We then examine the organization of the executive branch, the interaction between the presidency and the other branches of government, how presidents influence public deliberation on national issues, and why some presidents stand out as "great" or "near great" and others as only average or worse. We conclude by assessing how the presidency contributes to American deliberative democracy.

HISTORICAL DEVELOPMENT OF THE PRESIDENCY

MAJOR ISSUES

- How has presidential power expanded over time?
- Does the modern presidency fulfill the original design for the office? Does it carry out new and important functions?

"Energy in the Executive," wrote Publius, "is a leading character in the definition of good government."[5] It takes an energetic executive to protect against foreign attacks, to carry out the laws with firmness and consistency, and to protect property and liberty from assaults by ambitious individuals and factions. The ancient Roman republic achieved these goals by temporarily vesting all authority in a dictator during crises. The framers rejected this approach by creating a strong and independent president who was accountable through elections and, in extreme cases, could be removed from office by Congress. Short of removal, he was subject to other checks by Congress and the courts.

Creating the Presidency

As we saw in Chapter 2, the Articles of Confederation created a Congress but no national executive. Also, nearly all states during this period had weak governors who could not stand up to powerful legislatures. The result was ineffective government and, too often, legislative tyranny. "The legislative department is everywhere extending the sphere of its activity and drawing all power into its impetuous vortex," wrote Publius in *Federalist* 48. A strong, energetic executive would promote sound administration and provide a political check and balance to the new national legislature.

How did the framers provide the necessary energy to the national executive? First, they vested the executive power in a single individual. Article II opens, "The executive Power shall be vested in a President of the United States of America." The Constitution creates only one other executive official, the vice president, who exercises only legislative power (presiding over the Senate and casting tie-breaking votes there). The framers rejected both a committee executive—despite the urging of some at the Constitutional Convention—and an executive council, common in the states, that would have to approve executive decisions. This unified executive would act with more "[d]ecision, activity, secrecy, and dispatch" than a committee or one checked by a council.[6]

The president's powers and duties are considerable, including command of the military, the pardoning power, the treaty power (shared with the Senate), the power to appoint executive officials and federal judges (also shared with the Senate), the responsibility to recommend measures to Congress and to convene it on "extraordinary Occasions," the duty to "take Care that the Laws be faithfully executed," and a qualified veto over acts of Congress (subject to override by two-thirds of the House and Senate).

To promote independence from Congress, the framers denied the legislature any part in selecting the president except in case of an Electoral College deadlock (in most states at the time the legislature chose the governor), and they prohibited Congress from altering the president's salary during any one term (some state legislatures had altered the governor's salary to foster compliance). Ideally, the new chief executive would, in Publius's words, "dare to act his own opinion with vigor and decision."[7]

Finally, by making the president's term four years (longer than any state governor at the time) and placing no limits on how many terms a president could serve, the framers sought to give the president both a personal stake in protecting the prerogatives of the office and a powerful incentive to do a good job for the country. In virtually every respect, the president would be more unified, powerful, and independent than the state governors.

None of this means, of course, that the president would dominate Congress or the federal courts. Each branch would be supreme within its proper sphere of action, and the other branches might check the president in some ways. Congress might refuse to fund presidential programs, and the courts might overrule presidential acts as unconstitutional. (We discuss this power of "judicial review," which is not specifically mentioned in the Constitution, in Chapter 15.)

Prior to the American Founding, the common view was that strong executives were inconsistent with republican, or popular, governments. The framers believed otherwise. The new American president was, at the time, the most powerful executive ever created as a permanent office in a republic. Yet, the framers also recognized the dangers of executive tyranny; so the president was to be less powerful, and considerably more accountable, than a monarch. As Publius noted in *Federalist* 69, the British king, unlike the new president, had an absolute veto over legislative acts, could dissolve the legislature at any time, had sole authority to make treaties and take the nation to war, and could not be removed from office by the legislature no matter how dangerous or illegal his acts. The American presidency was a bold experiment to combine the advantages of executive energy with the virtues of popular government. (For a comparison of presidents and the chief executives in parliamentary governments, see the International Perspectives box.)

The framers attached one qualification to serve as president that applies to no other national office: the president must be a "natural born Citizen" (Article II, Section 1). This provision has made some major American political figures, who were naturalized citizens, ineligible for the presidency. Examples include former secretaries of state Henry Kissinger of the Nixon administration (born a German) and Madeleine Albright of the Clinton administration (born a Czechoslovakian); and former governors Arnold Schwarzenegger of California (born an Austrian) and Jennifer Granholm of Michigan (born a Canadian).

Records from the Constitutional Convention do not say why the delegates applied this special qualification to the presidency. One clue may lie in a letter from John Jay to George Washington, the president of the Convention. Jay, who was serving as superintendent of foreign affairs when the Convention met, said that it would be wise "to declare expressly that the command in chief of the American Army shall not be given to nor devolve on any but a natural-born Citizen."[9] To Jay, the presidency's military authority set it apart from other offices.

In January 2009, Barack Obama became the forty-third American to hold the office of president of the United States. (Because Grover Cleveland, who served two nonconsecutive terms in the nineteenth century, is counted twice in the conventional numbering, Obama is commonly referred to as the forty-fourth president.) Some of these 43 are famous for successfully leading the country through grave crises; others are little remembered for major accomplishments. Some have used every resource of the office to shape public opinion on the great issues of the day; others have made no such effort. Some have pushed the envelope of presidential power; others have taken a narrower view of their constitutional authority. Some have stamped the office with the force of their personalities; others have taken a more passive approach to governing.

In many democracies, the head of government is the prime minister, the leader of the majority party in parliament or of a majority coalition of parties. The prime minister names other members of parliament to serve in the cabinet and shares executive authority with them. Such overlap of the branches is not possible in the United States. Article I, Section 6 of the Constitution forbids anyone to hold executive and legislative office at the same time.

Prime ministers usually have long experience in parliament, allowing them to prove their abilities. But Americans rise to the presidency by winning primaries and general elections, not by building a record in Congress. In 2008, for example, Barack Obama earned the Democratic Party nomination for president after just three years in Congress. Several recent presidents had never before held federal office. In fact, many voters distrust Washington. Before 2008, no sitting member of Congress had won the White House since John F. Kennedy in 1960; and before Kennedy, it was Warren G. Harding, Republican senator from Ohio, in 1920.

Members of parliament seek party leaders who can shine in debate. In Britain and Canada, prime ministers must take questions from the opposing side, so they must have a quick wit and a command of policy. In the United States, such virtues matter less because presidents directly face their opponents only during televised campaign debates.

Critics of the American system sometimes quote what British statesman James Bryce wrote in 1888: that the British system had "more tendency to bring the highest gifts to the highest place than the artificial selection of America." Defenders say that the American system is more open to a wider array of life experiences and that Washington "outsiders" can bring changes that Washington "insiders" cannot.

Some Americans assume that the British system automatically produces strong parties, strong leaders, and clear mandates, but on seven occasions in the twentieth century, Britain had coalition or national governments in which a single party did not control the cabinet. Also, in no election during the century did the prime minister's party win a majority of the popular vote.[8]

CRITICAL THINKING
QUESTION

Would American government benefit from the adoption of one or both of the following features of parliamentary democracy: (1) allowing members of Congress to serve in the executive branch—for example, as heads of departments or presidential advisers or (2) requiring the president to appear before Congress once a week to answer questions?

By reviewing some of the highlights of the history of the American presidency, we can gain a fuller understanding of the leadership capacities of the office and the forces that shape presidential behavior. As we will see, many hold that the twentieth century saw the rise of a distinctly "modern presidency," although scholars debate just how much has changed since Washington first held the office. Few today, however, would disagree with Woodrow Wilson's description of the presidency as "the vital place of action in the system."[10]

George Washington and the Early Presidents

When George Washington took the oath of office on April 30, 1789, he acknowledged "the magnitude and difficulty of the trust to which the voice of my country called me." He proceeded to fulfill the high duties of the office. In international affairs, he kept the new nation out of European conflicts, despite considerable sentiment in Congress and among the people to side with France (the nation's ally in the Revolutionary War). In economic and commercial matters, his secretary of the treasury Alexander Hamilton fashioned the key policies and persuaded Congress to adopt them. In law enforcement, Washington vigorously upheld national law by calling up 13,000 members of the state militia to put down violent resistance in western Pennsylvania to a new federal tax on whiskey (the so-called **Whiskey Rebellion**). Near the end of his second term, Washington decided to retire to private life and thereby helped to set the "two-term precedent" that would last until 1940.

President John Adams largely continued Washington's policies, but dissension within the Federalist Party and growing opposition by the Democratic-Republicans, headed by Thomas Jefferson, led to his defeat in 1800. Because the new governing party had attacked the Federalists as "monarchists" and "monocrats," many expected Jefferson to weaken the

Whiskey Rebellion—the name given to the violent resistance of farmers in western Pennsylvania in 1792–1794 to a federal tax on distilled spirits.

presidency and give Congress a free hand to direct national affairs.[11] Instead, working through his party allies in the House and Senate, Jefferson exercised considerable influence over Congress. He even persuaded it, in 1807, despite widespread opposition, to prohibit American trade with European nations to reduce the likelihood of war.

Jefferson also forcefully exercised independent presidential powers. For example, he sent a naval squadron to the Mediterranean Sea without prior congressional approval to protect American merchant ships from the Barbary pirates (North African states); he authorized his foreign ministers to negotiate a treaty with France for the purchase of the Louisiana Territory despite his reservations about the constitutionality of adding territory to the nation; and, fearing war with Britain in 1807, he authorized the building of gunboats and the fortification of American ports without waiting for congressional appropriations.

Some charged that Jefferson exceeded his constitutional authority. After leaving office, he defended his acts in a private letter:

> A strict observance of the written laws is doubtless one of the high duties of a good citizen, but it is not the highest. The laws of necessity, of self-preservation, of saving our country when in danger, are of higher obligation. To lose our country by a scrupulous adherence to written law, would be to lose the law itself, with life, liberty, property and all those who are enjoying them with us; thus absurdly sacrificing the end to the means.[12]

Executive prerogative—the doctrine that an executive may sometimes have to violate the law to preserve the nation.

This notion that the president may sometimes have to violate the law to preserve the nation is called the doctrine of **executive prerogative**. It dates back to the philosopher John Locke's *Second Treatise of Government*, in which Locke described the "power to act according to discretion, for the public good, without the prescription of the law, and sometimes even against it."[13] We return to this issue of the prerogative power later in the chapter.

In 1808, Jefferson decided not to seek a third term, further cementing the two-term precedent. None of his immediate successors matched his popularity with the American people or his influence within the governing party. Congress became increasingly assertive, and the center of power in Washington moved to the House of Representatives.

The fight against the Barbary Pirates in 1801–1805 was the first offensive war waged by the United States after independence. It was also the nation's first confrontation with an Islamic power. This painting by Dennis Malone Carter shows Lieutenant Stephen Decatur (lower right center) in combat in waters off Tripoli, which is today the capital of Libya.

Courtesy of the Naval History and Heritage Command Washington, DC

Andrew Jackson and the Democratization of the Presidency

Andrew Jackson's eight years in office (1829–1837) halted the decline in presidential influence, at least temporarily. Jackson was a military hero from the War of 1812 who many believed had been cheated out of the presidency in 1824. With a reputation as a "man of the people," he was especially popular with small farmers and those living west of the Appalachians. By the late 1820s, nearly all the states had extended the vote to all free white males and allowed the people to choose presidential electors directly. The election of 1828 was a popular contest, and Jackson won in a landslide.

Jackson attacked government programs, such as the Bank of the United States, that "make the rich richer and the potent more powerful." Such programs, he said, harmed "the humble members of society—the farmers, mechanics, and laborers."[14] He vetoed a rechartering of the national bank and then interpreted his reelection in 1832 as "a decision of the people against the bank."[15] Not content to let the bank die when its charter expired in a few years, he ordered his secretary of the treasury to withdraw the federal funds from the bank to cripple it. When the secretary refused, he fired him and appointed another. When he also refused, Jackson replaced him as well, finally finding someone who would do his bidding.

Because the law had given the power to withdraw the federal deposits to the secretary of the treasury, and not to the president directly, Jackson's opponents charged that he had acted illegally. In March 1834, the Senate formally censured the president for "assum[ing] upon himself authority and power not conferred by the Constitution and laws, but in derogation of both." Jackson formally protested the Senate's actions and insisted that department heads were his "agents." Their job was to "aid him in the performance of his duties" because the Constitution vested the "whole executive power" in the president alone. "The president," he insisted, "is the direct representative of the American people, but the Secretaries are not."[16] In 1837, with Jackson supporters in the majority, the Senate voted to expunge the censure.

Jackson was the first president to use official messages to speak directly to the people over the heads of their members of Congress, the first to interpret reelection success as a popular endorsement of specific presidential policies, and the first to call himself the direct representative of the American people. Many viewed him as a "people's president" or even a "tribune of the people." His critics worried that he dangerously concentrated power in the presidency and that his direct popular appeals undermined Congress's capacity to deliberate on the merits of public policy free from the fear of political reprisals.

During this period, Jackson faced a crisis that nearly led to civil war. In 1832, the legislature of South Carolina "nullified" a federal law that it believed unfairly benefited New England manufacturers at the expense of the agrarian South by imposing high tariffs on imported goods. Facing possible secession, Jackson made clear that he would use force, if necessary, to preserve the Union. "The laws of the United States must be executed," he announced in a proclamation. "[M]y duty is emphatically pronounced in the Constitution."[17] The crisis was averted when Congress revised the tariff and South Carolina suspended its nullification.

This caricature of President Andrew Jackson as a monarch appeared after he vetoed the Bank Bill and ordered the federal deposits removed from the bank. The Constitution lies trampled underfoot.

With the exception of James Polk, who led the nation during the Mexican-American War of 1846–1848, Jackson's pre–Civil War successors were relatively weak, with none serving more than one term. During this period, Congress fashioned the nation's policies on slavery, commerce, and the westward expansion with relatively little input from presidents. In December 1860, with South Carolina on the verge of secession and other states soon to follow, President James Buchanan declared himself powerless to resist the dismemberment of the Union. The president's duty to enforce federal law, Buchanan believed, was now "impracticable."[18]

Abraham Lincoln and the Civil War

By the time Abraham Lincoln took the oath of office on March 4, 1861, seven states had seceded. Although Lincoln initially took no military action against the break-away states, he warned them in his First Inaugural Address that he would do all he could to preserve the Union: "You have no oath registered in heaven to destroy the Government, while I shall have the most solemn one to 'preserve, protect, and defend it.'"[19]

After southerners attacked Fort Sumter in Charleston harbor, South Carolina, in April, Lincoln responded forcefully. He called for a special session of Congress for July 4 (Congress was not scheduled to convene until December); called up 75,000 men from the state militia; blockaded southern ports; called for volunteers for large additions to the army and navy; and authorized the limited suspension of the writ of habeas corpus, thereby allowing federal authorities to apprehend suspected subversives and deny them access to the courts (see the discussion in Chapter 5).

Some believed that under the Constitution only Congress could suspend habeas corpus. Lincoln answered that the Constitution did not explicitly limit the power of suspension to Congress. The actual language is "The privilege of the Writ of Habeas Corpus shall not be suspended, unless when in Cases of Rebellion or Invasion the public Safety may require it" (Article I, Section 9). Lincoln insisted that it was particularly important for the president to suspend habeas corpus when southern sympathizers were trying to isolate the capital and prevent Congress from convening. But Lincoln also presented a broader justification, drawing on his duty to enforce federal laws and his oath to "preserve, protect and defend the Constitution":

> [A]re all the laws, but one, to go unexecuted, and the government itself go to pieces, lest that one be violated? Even in such a case, would not the official oath be broken, if the government should be overthrown, when it was believed that disregarding the single law, would tend to preserve it?[20]

To this day scholars debate Lincoln's actions. As we saw in Chapter 5, in 1861 the chief justice of the Supreme Court ordered the release of a person apprehended by the military (though Lincoln ignored the order); and one year after the war ended, the Supreme Court overturned a military trial Lincoln had authorized. What is clear is that Lincoln exercised extraordinary powers during extraordinary times and did so without permanently impairing civil liberties or institutionalizing presidential supremacy.

The Rise of the Modern Presidency

Indeed, Lincoln's immediate successors, like Andrew Jackson's, were relatively weak. Congress was the dominant branch of the national government in the decades after the Civil War. This began to change first with the election of William McKinley to the presidency in 1896 and then, more dramatically, with the rise of Theodore Roosevelt.

Theodore Roosevelt

When anarchist Leon Czolgosz assassinated President William McKinley in September 1901, Vice President Theodore Roosevelt succeeded to the presidency. A former assistant secretary of the navy, governor of New York, and leader of the volunteer cavalry known as the Rough Riders in the Spanish-American War, the new Republican president was forceful and charismatic. He attacked the power of large corporations, promoted federal regulation of the railroad industry, and set aside large tracts of federal land for national parks and forest preserves. He believed that the president was "a steward of the people bound actively and affirmatively to do all he could for the people." It was not only the president's "right but his duty to do anything that the needs of the Nation demanded unless such action was forbidden by the Constitution or by the laws."[21]

To promote his policies, Roosevelt cultivated public opinion, calling the presidency a "**bully pulpit**." In 1905, for example, he undertook several speaking tours to drum up public support for a law authorizing the Interstate Commerce Commission to regulate the rates railroads could charge. Going to the people in this way was a major innovation.

Modern Americans take the value of presidential rhetoric for granted. We expect our presidents to speak to us frequently about public matters. However, in the nineteenth century, presidents rarely did so outside of formal communications such as inaugural addresses, annual messages (which we now call **State of the Union addresses**), and veto messages; and not until the end of the nineteenth century did presidential candidates personally campaign for office. Many considered it demeaning for presidential candidates to personally ask for votes.

This reticence of presidents (and presidential candidates) to speak directly to the people reflected the framers' concern that presidents might use rhetoric to stir up popular passions to serve their political ambitions.

Bully pulpit—President Theodore Roosevelt's phrase to describe the rhetorical dimensions of the presidential office.

State of the Union address—an address delivered by the president to a joint session of Congress each year, usually in January, describing the state of the nation and proposing policy initiatives.

Demagogue—a dangerous popular leader who appeals to base emotions of the people or flatters them to gain power.

President Theodore Roosevelt uses the "bully pulpit" in Evanston, Illinois, in 1903.

© Bettmann/Corbis

Rhetoric had long been the tool of the **demagogue**, the dangerous popular leader who appealed to base emotions or flattery to gain power. In the first *Federalist* essay, Publius warned his readers about leaders who begin "their careers paying an obsequious court to the people, commencing demagogues and ending tyrants."[22]

Woodrow Wilson

Although Roosevelt began to make presidential policy rhetoric respectable, it was Democrat Woodrow Wilson (who served from 1913 to 1921) who provided a comprehensive theory that promoted rhetoric as essential to presidential leadership. The only president to earn a PhD, Wilson was a major scholar of American government and history (as a professor and president of Princeton University) well before he entered politics. Unlike the framers, he believed that it was "natural that orators should be the leaders of a self-governing people."[23] Political oratory, or rhetoric, would both stimulate public interest in government and provide the means for leaders to educate the citizenry. And because the president "is the representative of no constituency, but of the whole people," he better reflects national sentiment than members of Congress. Consequently, Wilson encouraged presidents to take a broad view of their powers and potential: "The President is at liberty, both in law and conscience, to be as big a man as he can."[24]

As president, Wilson worked to make the office the center of national policymaking. At his urging, Congress passed landmark legislation to regulate the money supply, to curb unfair practices in interstate commerce, and to strengthen the regulation of large corporations. In foreign affairs, he called for U.S. entry into World War I, telling a joint session of Congress, "The world must be made safe for democracy."[25] After the armistice of November 1918, he played a major role in negotiating the terms of the Versailles Treaty, which formally ended the war and established the League of Nations. His journey to France was the first time an American president had ever traveled overseas to negotiate with other foreign leaders. As we discuss later, however, his rhetorical campaign to persuade the American people and the Senate to support the Versailles Treaty proved unsuccessful.

In Wilson's writings and actions, we have the essential elements of the theory of the "modern presidency" that dominated so much thinking about the office in the twentieth century. This theory holds that

- the president is a better representative of national opinion than Congress;
- through his oratory, the president should educate the citizenry and shape national sentiment;
- the presidency should be the center of national policymaking; and
- the president should not be reluctant to call on the people to pressure Congress to pass his policies.

But if Wilson established the foundations of the modern presidency, it was Franklin Roosevelt who completed the structure.

Franklin D. Roosevelt

Elected three years into the Great Depression in 1932, Franklin Delano Roosevelt, a former assistant secretary of the navy under President Wilson and later the Democratic governor of New York, embraced Wilson's theory of the presidency and added to it great political skill and charisma. Casting off the two-term tradition, he ran for the presidency four times and received 57%, 61%, 55%, and 54% of the popular vote. He led the nation during both its worst economic downturn (the Great Depression) and, next to the Civil War, its largest military conflict (World War II). The first president to speak directly to the people on a regular basis, he gave 30 "fireside chats" (radio addresses from the White House) to calm public fears and explain his policies.

Roosevelt dominated the national scene. As he had announced in his First Inaugural Address, "I assume unhesitatingly the leadership of this great army of our people dedicated to a disciplined attack upon our common problems."[26] As we discuss in Chapters 16 and 17, he promoted dozens

After contracting polio in 1921, Franklin Roosevelt could not walk. During his presidency, however, the White House projected an image of vigor by hiding his disability. Newspapers refrained from publishing photographs that even suggested his condition. This photo is one of the very few in existence showing FDR in a wheelchair.

FOCUS
QUESTION

What purposes are served by presidential rhetoric in the modern era? At its best, what can it accomplish? Is it ever dangerous?

of new federal initiatives, collectively called the New Deal, that expanded federal authority over the economy and made the federal government directly responsible for the well-being of Americans. Later in this chapter we describe his leadership on national security matters.

Roosevelt interpreted his constitutional powers broadly—by, for example, trading 50 old destroyers to Britain in exchange for military bases in the Western Hemisphere when Britain was at war with Germany and the United States was officially neutral—and he won large delegations of authority from Congress. To many he embodied all the virtues of the modern presidency—popular leader, chief domestic policymaker, and steward of the nation's security—and set the standard for his successors.

After the defeat of fascism in 1945, the United States and its allies entered a "Cold War" with the Soviet Union and other Communist nations (see Chapter 1). Isolationism was no longer an option. Roosevelt's successors led the world's free nations in countering the Communist threat. They also embraced, in varying degrees, the federal government's new role as guarantor of the people's material well-being.

The Contemporary Presidency

Scholars debate whether the "modern presidency" is so modern after all. Washington, Jefferson, Jackson, and Lincoln all acted aggressively to meet the nation's needs. All interpreted the president's responsibilities broadly and found the powers necessary to meet those responsibilities.

In at least two respects, however, modern presidents, and public expectations, seem to go even further. First, with varying degrees of success, most presidents since FDR have happily embraced the role of legislative leader, seeking to direct the deliberations of Congress on a wide range of policies, foreign and domestic. In the nineteenth century, by contrast, presidents typically, though not always, deferred to Congress on domestic policy.

Second, as we have seen, modern presidents work hard to shape public opinion through their rhetoric in a way that was unprecedented in the nineteenth century. It is inconceivable today that a president could lead the nation in a major war without giving public speeches about the war. Yet, President James Madison, the first president to serve during a declared war, gave not a single public address on the War of 1812 (though he mentioned it in formal communications to Congress and in several proclamations).

Rethinking Presidential Power: Vietnam and Watergate

The 1960s and 1970s saw two events that led many to rethink the virtues of presidential power: the long and controversial Vietnam War, conducted by Democrat Lyndon Johnson and Republican Richard Nixon, and the Watergate and related scandals that led to Nixon's resignation. The nation's highest office, some charged, had become an "imperial presidency." Presidents, they said, exercised war powers vested in Congress by the Constitution, undermined the separation of powers, and used their powers to attack political opponents and subvert the legal process.

The Watergate scandal came to a head in July 1974, when, after a lengthy investigation, the House Judiciary Committee passed three articles of impeachment against President Nixon. These articles accused him of violating his oath of office and specifically charged him with:

- obstructing justice in the investigation of the June 1972 break-in of the headquarters of the Democratic National Committee in the Watergate hotel complex in Washington, DC;
- violating the constitutional rights of American citizens through his misuse of the Internal Revenue Service, the Federal Bureau of Investigation, and the Secret Service; and
- failing to provide papers and other materials subpoenaed by the House Judiciary Committee during its investigation.

Nixon's public and congressional support plummeted, and he resigned on August 9, 1974.

In response to these events, Nixon's immediate successors, Republican Gerald Ford and Democrat Jimmy Carter, embraced low-key governing styles and avoided constitutional controversies with Congress. Although Ford startled many by pardoning former president Nixon just a month after succeeding to the presidency (discussed later), he sought cooperation with Congress, not confrontation. President Carter symbolized his anti-imperial conception of the office by leaving his limousine on Inauguration Day and walking down Pennsylvania Avenue with his wife. He later delivered his first national television address from the White House wearing a cardigan sweater. Carter, however, had little success moving his legislative program through Congress; and for 444 days at the end of his term, radical students in Iran held more than 50 American officials hostage in Tehran. In April 1980, a rescue attempt failed in a sandstorm in an Iranian desert.

For many, the hostage crisis, coupled with growing economic distress, symbolized the failure of presidential leadership. Many journalists and scholars, reflecting on a succession of so-called failed presidencies, concluded that the American political system was no longer capable of effectively addressing the nation's needs.

Ronald Reagan

In his first term (1981–1985), Ronald Reagan, former movie actor and later two-term Republican governor of California, showed that the presidency was still capable of being "the vital place of action in the system." Taking office in the midst of a stagnant economy and double-digit inflation, he devoted much of his First Inaugural Address to criticizing the "unnecessary and excessive growth of government." He promised to launch "an era of national renewal" by returning power to states and localities, by "get[ing] government back within its means," and by "lighten[ing] our punitive tax burden."[27]

Drawing on a well of popular support, especially after recovering from an assassination attempt, Reagan pushed through Congress a 25% income tax cut in his first year, despite facing the opposition party in the House of Representatives. He was less successful in restraining the growth of federal domestic spending, which, together with increases in defense spending, resulted in large deficits. (See the Myths and Misinformation feature for a discussion of Reagan's impact on the size of the federal government.)

More so than any president since FDR, Reagan embraced rhetorical leadership. Many began to call him "The Great Communicator." Reflecting on Theodore Roosevelt's

---

MYTHS AND MISINFORMATION

Reagan and the Size of Government

President Reagan said, in his 1981 inaugural address, "In this present crisis, government is not the solution to our problem; government is the problem." His admirers quote that line to demonstrate his passion for cutting wasteful spending and excessive government power. His detractors quote it to portray him as an antigovernment extremist.

Most quotations of the line lop off the first four words, distorting its meaning. By "this present crisis," he meant the unusual mix of high unemployment and inflation that was plaguing the nation in 1981. Reagan was not speaking of government in general but of specific policies that were purportedly worsening these problems.

And those who quote "government is the problem" seldom mention what he said moments later: "Now, so there will be no misunderstanding, it is not my intention to do away with government. It is, rather, to make it work—work with us, not over us; to stand by our side, not ride on our back. Government can and must provide opportunity, not smother it; foster productivity, not stifle it."

Reagan's approach to government was more flexible than either side likes to admit. In his first year as governor of California, he learned that state finances were worsening badly. To balance the budget, he agreed to the largest tax increase in the state's history. In his first year as president, he did persuade Congress to cut income tax rates. During the following year, however, concern about deficits prompted him to sign the largest peacetime tax increase in American history up to that time. In the following years, he signed several other tax increases as well.

During Reagan's eight years in office, the highest marginal tax rates fell from 70% to 28%. Despite the reduction in marginal rates, in inflation-adjusted dollars federal revenues grew 19%. Spending, however, grew 22%, so the deficit got bigger.

The increase in spending may surprise those who remember Reagan as the scourge of big government. At the start of his administration, some of his supporters talked about eliminating some cabinet departments. By the end, all the departments were still standing, along with a new one: the Department of Veterans Affairs.[28]

description of the office as a bully pulpit, Reagan wrote, "I think this office does offer an opportunity for mobilizing public sentiment behind worthwhile causes."[29] One study of Reagan's rhetoric showed that in a typical month in 1982, he delivered 26 formal speeches in person, aired five weekly radio talks, and held five live press conferences.[30] Through his rhetoric, Reagan sought to generate public support for his policies and to influence public opinion at a deeper level. According to political scientist William Ker Muir, who wrote speeches for Vice President George H. W. Bush from 1983 to 1985, Reagan believed that "[t]he function of the presidency is to speak the truths of freedom and to make the people an enlightened citizenry."[31]

Democrats in Congress opposed many of Reagan's policies, and in his second term he was less successful. Also, the administration became mired in the Iran-Contra scandal (discussed later), which resulted in the criminal convictions of 11 administration officials for such crimes as lying to Congress, obstructing justice, and destroying documents. Appellate courts overturned the convictions of several, and Reagan's successor, President George H. W. Bush, pardoned the others. The scandal hurt Reagan's popularity, which recovered by the end of his second term.

Reagan's Successors

None of Reagan's immediate successors—George H. W. Bush, William Clinton, and George W. Bush—had as large an impact as he did on the American political system. Many speak of the "Reagan revolution" (both those who embraced it and those who did not), but no one talks about a "Bush revolution" (for either Bush) or a "Clinton revolution."

There is no doubt, however, that Reagan's successors had a decisive impact on foreign and national security policy. The first George Bush persuaded both houses of Congress and several dozen nations to go to war in the Persian Gulf to force Iraqi troops from Kuwait. President Clinton expanded the American military mission in Somalia, introduced peacekeeping forces into the former Yugoslavia, fought a three-month air war against Serbian forces in Kosovo, and sent troops to Haiti—all without prior congressional approval. And George W. Bush directed a war against the terrorists responsible for the attacks of September 11, 2001, and persuaded Congress to authorize the removal of Saddam Hussein from power in Iraq. Later, Democratic majorities in the House and Senate, who had come to power in the 2006 election, failed to force the administration to withdraw from Iraq. (More on national security policymaking later in this chapter and in Chapter 18.)

Because none of these presidents was nearly as dominant in domestic policy, scholars have reconsidered the "two presidencies" thesis, originally formulated in the 1960s. This idea holds that American presidents are more successful in directing foreign and national security policy than domestic policy either because they have greater success at persuading Congress or because they have more independent powers. Although Congress is now less deferential to presidents in foreign affairs than it was in the decades immediately after World War II, presidents can accomplish much through their independent powers, as we show later in the chapter.

Barack Obama

"[E]very so often," the new president told the nation in his inaugural address on January 20, 2009, "the oath of office is taken amidst gathering clouds and raging storms." President Obama then described the elements of the "crisis" that confronted the nation: "war against a far-reaching network of violence and hatred"; a "badly weakened" economy; "health care [that] is too costly"; "schools [that] fail too many"; ways of using energy that "strengthen our adversaries and threaten our planet"; and "a sapping of confidence across our land."[32]

In the first weeks and months, the president and his team refashioned national security policy (as we described in Chapter 5), shepherded a massive stimulus spending bill through Congress, engineered a federal "bailout" of the banking and auto industries, and set in motion a plan to dramatically expand the federal role in health care. Throughout all this, the president seemed to be everywhere, using televised news conferences, town meetings, and formal speeches to make his case to the American people. Although some of his signature initiatives—such as his "cap and trade" plan to regulate greenhouse gas emissions—stalled in Congress, others resulted in major new domestic legislation on health care and financial regulatory reform. (See also Chapters 16-18.)

During Obama's first two years in office, Democrats controlled the presidency, the House of Representatives, and the Senate. But in the 2010 election, Republicans gained a comfortable majority in the House. Divided government frustrated Obama's efforts to move his proposals through Congress. In the fall of 2011, as the president's chief of staff later reported, Obama instructed his aides "to scour everything and push the envelope in finding things we can do on our own."[33] In January of 2012, the president said, "I refuse to take 'no' for an answer.... When Congress refuses to act and—as a result—hurts our economy and puts people at risk, I have an obligation as president to do what I can without them."[34] In the second half of his term, the president "push[ed] the envelope" by ordering his Department of Justice not to defend the Defense of Marriage Act in court, making several controversial "recess appointments" (discussed on page 394), ordering air strikes in Libya without prior congressional approval, granting nearly two dozen states waivers to provisions of the No Child Left Behind Act, and announcing a new policy in June of 2012 not to deport most illegal immigrants 30 years old or younger who had been brought to the United States before the age of 16. Obama's actions sparked a renewed debate over the limits of presidential power.

Having explored how the history of the presidency illustrates the particular capacities and functions of the office, we now turn to the current structure and operation of the executive branch.

ORGANIZATION OF THE EXECUTIVE BRANCH
MAJOR ISSUE

- Alexander Hamilton warned of "plurality in the executive." Does the president risk this problem by delegating authority to aides and executive officials?

The Constitution vests "[t]he executive Power . . . in a President of the United States of America." Although it also mentions the vice president, "Heads of Departments," and "Ambassadors, other public Ministers and Consuls," it does not directly vest any of these executive officials with executive power. Yet, currently several thousand individuals assist the president in meeting his responsibilities. The presidency is more than just the president.

The Vice Presidency

If the president dies or resigns, the vice president becomes president. Originally, there was some question whether a vice president would actually become president or just serve as acting president until the next presidential election. But when President William Henry Harrison died after just a month in office in April 1841, Vice President John Tyler took the oath of office as president. Later vice presidents, faced with this situation, did the same. Nine vice presidents have become president through a vacancy in the office: eight times after a death, and once after a resignation.

Until 1967, no method to fill vice presidential vacancies existed, even though they had occurred 16 times.[35] Under the Twenty-fifth Amendment, the president may fill a vacancy by nominating a new vice president, who must win confirmation by a majority vote of the House and Senate. (No other office requires approval by both chambers.) If the presidency and vice presidency are vacant at the same time, a 1947 law spells out the line of succession, starting with the Speaker of the House.

The vice president scarcely had any power until recent decades. The only constitutional duty of the office is presiding over the Senate—a job with little real authority—and casting a tie-breaking vote. Unless the administration expects a close vote on an important matter, the vice president rarely presides over the Senate today. Vice presidents receive their pay from the Senate, not the executive branch, and until the mid-twentieth century, they did

Photo by the White House/Getty images

Vice President Dick Cheney talks with President George W. Bush as senior staff listen from the underground National Presidential Emergency Operations Center on September 11, 2001.

not even have office space in the White House complex.[36] For most of American history, presidents had few ties to their vice presidents and seldom sought their advice. In 1945, Vice President Harry Truman learned about the atomic bomb only after Franklin Roosevelt had died. Despite knowledge of his own ill health, FDR had not shared this secret with Truman.

Subsequent presidents realized that in a nuclear age, their vice presidents had to be ready to take over quickly. Vice presidents thus gained more access to classified information and, in varying degrees, started to take part in policy deliberations. They also served as administration spokesmen. Dick Cheney, vice president under George W. Bush, was the most influential occupant of the office to date. Because of Cheney's experience in government and business, Bush consulted with him on most major decisions. For months after the terror attacks of September 11, 2001, Cheney worked from secret locations to ensure continuity in case of an attack on the White House.

Executive Office of the President

In the nation's early decades, the work of the presidency largely belonged to a single man. Not until 1857 did Congress appropriate money for a White House staff—$2,500 for one clerk.[37] Lincoln had two, though one drew his salary from other government payrolls.[38] As the executive branch grew under Franklin Roosevelt, so did White House offices. In 1939, Roosevelt signed legislation enabling him to set up a formal staff organization, the **Executive Office of the President (EOP)**.

Executive Office of the President (EOP)—the formal staff structure of the White House.

Chief of staff—the highest-ranking staff aide to the president whose duties include supervising White House employees, overseeing the president's schedule, and advising the president on policy and politics.

Today, about 1,700 people work in the EOP, a figure that has remained fairly constant for the past several presidencies.[39] The president's top aide, the **chief of staff**, supervises White House employees, oversees the president's schedule, and advises the president on policy and politics.

At times the White House restricts routine access to the Oval Office, where the president works, to only a few people. The Eisenhower, Nixon, and George H. W. Bush administrations are examples. Such a system fosters deliberation when the top aides ensure that the president gets enough information. It falters when the president is closed off. As Charles Kolb, an aide to President George H. W. Bush, said of John Sununu, the chief of staff: "Few people wanted to incur Sununu's wrath, hence little in the way of innovative policy was actually undertaken inside the White House during the Bush years. People kept their mouths shut to avoid being yelled at."[40]

Other presidents have come to office preferring a "spokes of the wheel" arrangement. Jack Watson, chief of staff late in the Carter administration, describes the system: "The president is the hub, and he's going to have *x* number of advisors, six or eight or ten. And . . . he wants all of them reporting directly to him." Although some presidents, such as Franklin Roosevelt and John Kennedy, had success with a less formal staff structure, Watson concluded that the "spokes" model did not serve President Carter well: "The White House can't operate that way. It pulls the president into too much; he's involved in too many things. It also results in a lack of cohesion, a lack of organization and cutting in on decision making before the presidential level."[41]

Presidents also differ in the degree to which they delegate authority. Speechwriter James Fallows recalled President Carter: "He would leave for a weekend at Camp David laden with thick briefing books, would pore over budget tables to check the arithmetic, and, during his first six months in office, would personally review all requests to use the White House tennis court."[42] Although intelligent, President Carter could not keep up with the deluge of detail.

President Reagan delegated more and ran into different problems. During his second term, White House aides arranged to sell arms to Iran. The deal involved Iranian efforts to secure the release of Western hostages in the Middle East, as well as the diversion of the profits to rebels fighting the Marxist government of Nicaragua. Reagan knew little about the scheme, which sparked an uproar when it became public. A special review board appointed by Reagan observed that the president "put the principal responsibility for policy review and implementation on the shoulders of his advisors." With such a complex operation, he "should have ensured that the [staff] system did not fail him."[43]

The Cabinet

The president's **cabinet** includes the vice president and the heads of the 15 executive departments. The president may also grant cabinet rank to other officials, such as the director of the Environmental Protection Agency. In parliamentary systems, cabinets sometimes make important decisions as a group. In the United States, the cabinet has no such collective authority. Presidents can convene their cabinets for policy deliberations, but they seldom do so.[44] Instead, presidents seek advice from cabinet secretaries through individual meetings or smaller working groups. Presidents retain the final authority. As legend has it, President Abraham Lincoln once summarized a cabinet vote that went unanimously against him by saying, "Seven no and one aye—the ayes have it."

One might expect that department heads, called **secretaries**, automatically carry out the president's policies. They owe their jobs to the president, who may fire them at will. In practice, presidents have a thornier relationship with their department heads. Although presidents generally choose secretaries from their own party whom they expect to be loyal, they also consider other criteria. Department secretaries often get their jobs because they appeal to interest groups or have relevant experience. Many secretaries of agriculture grew up on farms, and most treasury secretaries have come from finance. Such ties may tug secretaries from the president's policies. Career bureaucrats may persuade the president's appointees to side with their department against the White House. As President Truman said about the prospect of Dwight Eisenhower becoming president, "He'll sit here, and he'll say, 'Do this! Do that!' *And nothing will happen.* Poor Ike—it won't be a bit like the Army. He'll find it very frustrating."[45]

Presidents often say that they want strong-minded secretaries. Up to a point, strong-mindedness may strengthen internal deliberation. At the same time, presidents need to keep their department heads in check because "loose cannons" can cause political trouble. The White House also has to coordinate the policies and activities of the departments because their jurisdictions overlap.

Presidents have several ways to control the cabinet. The White House includes a cabinet affairs office, whose staff maintains contact with the departments so that neither side undercuts the other. Also, the White House personnel office reviews hiring decisions for policy jobs. Even if a cabinet secretary strays, other political appointees in the department may remain loyal to the White House. Moreover, all budget requests, administrative rules, and legislative proposals from departments must go through the **Office of Management and Budget (OMB)**, which enforces presidential priorities throughout the executive branch.

President George W. Bush brought cabinet secretaries closer to home in a very literal sense. In his second term, he made them spend up to four hours a week in an office suite at the Eisenhower Executive Office Building, next to the White House. There they met with presidential aides to coordinate policy and public messages.[46] In the departments and agencies, officials with the title of "White House liaison" kept watch to see that official actions were consistent with the president's policies and political interests.[47]

The Special Case of National Security

National security presents special challenges because it involves diplomacy, intelligence, military force, economics, and international law. Officials in these fields handle secrets, which they hesitate to share even with other agencies. Looking back at the information

Cabinet—the collective name for the president's formal advisers. The cabinet includes the vice president, the heads of the 15 executive departments, and others to whom the president grants cabinet rank.

Secretary—the title given to the heads of executive departments.

Office of Management and Budget (OMB)—the agency within the Executive Office of the President that reviews budget requests, legislative initiatives, and proposed rules and regulations from the executive agencies.

AP Photo/Ron Edmonds

The nuclear "football," carried by a military officer. The football is a specially modified briefcase with a leather satchel with zippers and pouches for documents and a secure radio. Despite its portrayal in movies such as *Air Force One*, the military aide does not use a handcuff to hold it. The president would use its contents to wage nuclear war.

National Security Council (NSC)— the president's official forum for deliberating about national security and foreign policy, which includes the president as chair, the vice president, the secretary of state, the secretary of the treasury, and the secretary of defense.

Groupthink—the tendency for members of policymaking groups to go along with the prevailing view and mute their own misgivings.

available to different government organizations before December 7, 1941, President Truman reportedly said, "If we'd all had that information in one agency, by God, I believe we could have foreseen what was going to happen in Pearl Harbor."[48]

To remedy such problems, Congress set up the **National Security Council (NSC)** in 1947. The NSC is a forum for deliberating about national security and foreign policy. The president chairs the NSC, and regular attendees include the vice president, the secretary of state, the secretary of the treasury, and the secretary of defense.

Presidents usually prefer to set national security policy only after NSC deliberation, but they may have to make quick decisions. Wherever the president goes, a military officer holds the "football," a briefcase containing nuclear war plans. The president carries a card with coded numbers and words, which assure military commanders that radio orders are authentic. The president can communicate even when airborne. "Air Force One" is the radio call name for any Air Force plane carrying the president, but two special 747 jets fly usually under this name. Each has two kitchens and 4,000 square feet of workspace. Reportedly, the planes' wiring could survive the electromagnetic pulse of a nuclear blast, allowing the president to command the military during a nuclear war.[49]

White House Deliberation

Presidents usually endorse the idea of robust debate and deliberation among aides and cabinet secretaries. Some have abandoned this idea in practice, while others have tried to follow it. President Clinton drew criticism for fostering too much internal debate at the expense of decisiveness and clear policy. Nevertheless, presidents must beware of two obstacles to deliberation.

The first is **groupthink**.[50] Members of policymaking groups often feel social pressure to go along with the prevailing view. The desire for consensus may override the ability to weigh choices. In 1961, this tendency led President Kennedy and his advisers to go ahead with a faulty plan to invade Cuba with exiles from the island. The resulting disaster prompted Kennedy to review how he made decisions, and he did better with the Cuban Missile Crisis in 1962.

Groupthink can occur with any set of policymakers. Another problem is more specific to the presidency. Former President Carter once asked rhetorically, "Do you want those who will be sycophants, who will defer to you under any circumstances to gain your favor, or do you want people who will tell you the brutal truth even though they know it may not be the popular thing to say?"[51] The prestige of the office intimidates people and tempts them to defer to the president. By tradition, all rise when the president enters a room. Everyone addresses him as "Mr. President" (or presumably "Madam President" should a woman attain the office). Carter recalled, "Quite often, very articulate people would come in the Oval Office to ask a favor. And when they got there they couldn't speak, or they couldn't bring themselves to ask me to comply with their request. So I would say, 'What did you come for?' Well, they would just fumble around and then they would go out later and tell my staff member what they wanted."[52]

The problem can be serious when the president has a forceful personality. Chester Cooper, an NSC aide under President Johnson, remembered wanting to argue against administration policy on Vietnam. But when Johnson asked, "Mr. Cooper, do you agree?" Cooper answered, "Yes, Mr. President, I agree."[53]

Although the Constitution vests all executive power in the president, it does not, of course, vest all governing power in the president. Congress, as the lawmaking branch, makes its own claim to direct public policy, and the Supreme Court has the final word on the constitutionality of presidential and congressional acts. In the next section, we examine the interaction of the presidency with the two other branches and the struggle for dominance that sometimes results.

THE PRESIDENCY AND THE OTHER BRANCHES
MAJOR ISSUE

- What effect does the interaction of the presidency with the other branches have on the exercise of executive power and the functioning of the national government?

"Ambition must be made to counteract ambition," Publius famously wrote in *Federalist* 51. The framers expected, and wanted, the members of each branch to fight to uphold the prerogatives of their institution when threatened by another. Ideally, the officeholders would feel a personal interest in protecting "the constitutional rights of the place."[54] The framers particularly expected a lively interaction between the two representative policymaking institutions: Congress and the presidency. Here we focus on that interaction but also address some ways in which the Supreme Court has influenced the exercise of presidential power.

Congress has often thwarted presidential desires. Only a tiny fraction of federal employees (well under 1%) are subject to presidential hiring and firing (see Chapter 14). Others must pay close attention to congressional desires. And despite such terms as *Reaganomics* or *Clintonomics*, chief executives find that the economy does not bend to their will. Congress, after all, is the body that determines tax policies and spending levels.

Some scholars insist that presidents can get their way in Washington only by bargaining. A president must dicker, but it is misleading to portray the chief executive as a mere broker. Presidents try to persuade legislators, interest groups, and others on the merits of policy, and, as we will see, they also have power to act on their own in many situations, although Congress and the courts have ways of checking excesses.

Institutional loyalty (officials want their own branch to have the upper hand) and partisanship (politicians tend to back presidents of their own party) partially explain the preferences of public officials as to which branch should dominate policymaking. But sometimes political figures argue for principles derived from the constitutional distribution of power or they reach judgments about the public good that go beyond partisanship and institutional loyalty. In 1985, when a Republican held the White House and Democrats controlled the House, Senator Edward Kennedy (D-MA) said, "Congress has too much power over the purse, and the president has too little."[55] Ten years later, with a Democratic president and a GOP Congress, Senator John McCain (R-AZ) used the same words: "Congress has too much power over the purse and the president has too little."[56]

The Two-Way Street of Persuasion

The White House office of legislative affairs has day-to-day responsibility for dealing with Congress. The aides who work for the office try to persuade lawmakers to support the president's positions. Doing favors for members can create a "bank" of goodwill that they tap during roll calls. An aide to President Clinton said that the favors could involve many things: "White House tours, personnel concerns. I had a member today ask me if I could hand-deliver a letter to the president."[57]

The president may call lawmakers, though most administrations use this tactic sparingly. Lawrence O'Brien, who ran congressional affairs for Presidents Kennedy and Johnson, explained why a chief executive must be selective. "If a member reached the point of saying, 'Oh, hell, there's another call from the President,' then you lost the single, overriding resource you had available to you."[58]

In dealing with Congress, presidents and their subordinates use a mix of deliberation and bargaining, or, as O'Brien put it, "substance and shoe-leather."[59] On some issues, such as building public works, they may depend mostly on bargaining. On other issues, such as war and peace, they have to deliberate on the merits of public policy. In 1990, Americans were not demanding that their government fight Iraq's invasion of Kuwait. To win congressional approval for the use of force, President George H. W. Bush had to convince lawmakers that military action was necessary for national security. He made his case through private briefings and public testimony by cabinet members and military leaders. Although Democrats controlled both chambers, Congress voted to support the president's position.

Influence also works the other way, as members of Congress try to shape the president's policies. In 1960, Representative Henry Reuss (D-WI) and Senator Hubert Humphrey (D-MN) sponsored legislation to study prospects for sending volunteers to help poor countries. Humphrey persuaded Senator John F. Kennedy (D-MA) to discuss the idea during his presidential race. Kennedy thought the proposal would enhance the country's image and provide opportunities for active citizenship. Soon after taking office, he followed through by founding the Peace Corps.[60]

Vetoes

The veto, or disapproval of a measure that Congress has passed, is the president's most effective tool for influencing legislation. As we described in the previous chapter, all bills and joint resolutions that Congress passes, except those amending the Constitution, must go to the president before they become law. (Constitutional amendments require a two-thirds vote in each chamber and go directly to the states for ratification.) To promote deliberation between the branches, the Constitution requires that the president send Congress his reasons for vetoing a bill.

Prior to Andrew Jackson, presidents rarely vetoed bills (only nine times in 40 years) and usually because of constitutional concerns, but Jackson's 12 vetoes in 8 years made the use of the veto on policy grounds publicly acceptable. Veto messages can make convincing policy arguments, and they can also suggest ways in which Congress could adjust the measure to meet the president's objections. Presidents can usually make their vetoes stick. Not until 1845 did Congress first override a presidential veto. Since 1969, it has overridden only 18% of regular vetoes. Before then, the figure was just 5.7%.[61]

Vetoes are more likely when the president's party lacks a majority in one or both houses of Congress. This situation occurred for most of Eisenhower's presidency, as well as the entire tenures of Nixon, Ford, Reagan, and George H. W. Bush. These presidents vetoed more bills per term than Kennedy, Johnson, and Carter, who enjoyed Democratic majorities in both the House and Senate their entire time in office (see Figure 13-1).

When the other party rules Congress, presidents rely on their own party to sustain their vetoes. Said George H. W. Bush's chief of staff John Sununu, "We recognized because of the numbers that one of the things we had to establish was a capacity to have a credible veto. If George Bush did not have a credible veto, there is no way he could have influenced legislation."[62] If members of the opposition party doubt that they could win an override vote, they may negotiate their differences with the president. In this way, the threat of a veto enables the president to shape the details of legislation. Even though the first president Bush faced Democratic majorities in both branches for his entire term, Congress overrode only 1 of his 44 vetoes.

During his first two years in office, Bill Clinton had Democratic majorities on Capitol Hill, and he did

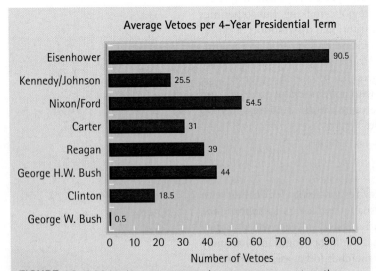

Average Vetoes per 4–Year Presidential Term

President	Number of Vetoes
Eisenhower	90.5
Kennedy/Johnson	25.5
Nixon/Ford	54.5
Carter	31
Reagan	39
George H.W. Bush	44
Clinton	18.5
George W. Bush	0.5

Number of Vetoes

FIGURE 13–1 Divided government tends to spawn more vetoes than united government, although the Clinton presidency was an exception. The figures represent averages for each four-year term. Johnson and Ford each became president during a term, so we combine them with their immediate predecessors. President Obama cast just two vetoes in his first three and a half years in office.

SOURCE: Authors' calculations from United States Senate, "Summary of Bills Vetoed, 1789-present," at www.senate.gov/reference/Legislation/Vetoes/vetoCounts.htm

not veto a single bill. When the Republicans took over Congress in the 1994 election, the veto became the focus of his legislative strategy. Former House Speaker Newt Gingrich recalls that House Republicans erred by underestimating the veto. "How could we have forgotten that? For me especially it was inexcusable, because when I was Republican whip during the [George H. W.] Bush Administration one of my duties had been precisely to help sustain presidential vetoes."[63]

A veto struggle in 1995 and 1996 led to a partial government shutdown, for which voters blamed the Republican Congress. Clinton gained a political advantage, and congressional Republicans became more cooperative. They remained skittish about repeating the shutdown battle.

Direct Authority

Presidents have several powers that they can exercise directly. For one, they can issue proclamations and executive orders. **Proclamations** often declare ceremonial occasions, such as National American Indian Heritage Month, although certain proclamations have policy implications. In 1793, President George Washington issued a proclamation that declared American neutrality in the war that had broken out in Europe. This informed the belligerents that the United States should enjoy the rights of a neutral nation under international law. The proclamation also warned Americans themselves not to violate the neutral status of the United States, by, for example, militarily assisting one of the sides. If they did, they would be subject to criminal prosecution.

Executive orders have the force of law and usually direct an executive agency to take specific steps. Such orders depend on some grant of authority in the Constitution or laws, but presidents have used them to set new policies. In 1961, for instance, President Kennedy introduced the term "affirmative action" to federal policy. Executive Order 10925 required federal contractors to take "affirmative action" to ensure equal treatment of employees and job applicants "without regard to their race, creed, color, or national origin."[64]

Present-day executive orders have consecutive numbers and appear in the *Federal Register*. Presidents may also make policy through documents bearing names such as "directives," "memoranda," or "determinations."[65] A recent study estimates that the executive branch has issued thousands of such orders and statements over the past century. According to a leading expert, since the 1970s, about 14 per year "constituted 'significant' policy making by the president." About three-fifths of these involved national security matters.[66]

Occasionally, presidents use executive orders to set policies that they are unable to get Congress to adopt through legislation, thus raising constitutional questions. Clinton White House aide Paul Begala expressed the administration's attraction to executive orders: "Stroke of the pen. Law of the land. Kind of cool."[67] But in 1996, a federal appeals court overturned a Clinton order that had prohibited the federal government from contracting with employers who had hired permanent replacement workers during a lawful strike. The court held that "the impact of the Executive Order is quite far-reaching" and that it violated existing federal law.[68]

When signing a bill, presidents may make a **signing statement** explaining their own interpretation of the measure and telling officials how to carry it out. Sometimes these statements challenge specific provisions on constitutional or other grounds. Prior to the Civil War, Presidents James Monroe, Andrew Jackson, and John Tyler issued such statements. More recently, Presidents George H. W. Bush, Bill Clinton, and George W. Bush each issued more than 100 statements that raised constitutional objections to provisions in bills they signed. The Clinton administration's Department of Justice defended the practice in a legal memorandum: "If the President may properly decline to enforce a law, at least when it unconstitutionally encroaches on his powers, then it arguably follows that he may properly *announce* to Congress and to the public that he will not enforce a provision of an enactment he is signing. . . . [This] can be a valid and reasonable exercise of Presidential authority."[69]

Although presidents insist that they are not required to enforce unconstitutional provisions of laws, critics charge that they have created, in effect, an unconstitutional **line-item veto**. This is a power possessed by many American governors to strike particular provisions without vetoing an entire bill.[70]

Proclamation—a formal statement issued by the president to the nation, often, but not always, to declare ceremonial occasions.

Executive orders—official documents, having the force of law, through which the president directs federal officials to take certain actions.

Signing statement—a statement issued by a president on signing a bill, which sometimes challenges specific provisions on constitutional or other grounds.

Line-item veto—a power, possessed by many American governors, to veto a particular item of a bill without vetoing the whole bill.

FOCUS QUESTION

Would the nation be well served if the president could veto specific items in congressional statutes without vetoing the entire bill?

Because signing statements had become particularly controversial under President George W. Bush, some thought that President Barack Obama—who had criticized Bush for using them "to accumulate more power in the presidency" and to "make laws as he's going along"—would change course.[71] But in just his second month in office, Obama issued a memorandum to the heads of executive departments defending the practice. Although he denied that a president may refuse to carry out a statutory provision because he did not like the policy, he maintained that "signing statements serve a legitimate function in our system, at least when based on well-founded constitutional objections." In limited circumstances, "they represent an exercise of the President's constitutional obligation to take care that the laws be faithfully executed."[72] Two days later, he issued a statement that objected to provisions of the Omnibus Appropriations Act, 2009, for interfering with his constitutional authority over foreign affairs, as commander in chief, over the heads of executive departments, over spending appropriated funds without prior approval of congressional committees, and over how to make budget requests to Congress.[73] Over the next three years, he issued nineteen more statements raising constitutional issues to bills he signed.[74]

Congress may reverse presidential orders through legislation and in this or other ways may resist presidential interpretations in signing statements. Other forms of direct presidential action are not subject to congressional review.

The Constitution empowers the president to issue pardons for federal offenses (though not for violations of state laws). Neither Congress nor the courts can take away a pardon. President Clinton issued controversial pardons during the last hours of his tenure, but critics could only complain. A president may pardon someone before conviction or even indictment. In 1974, President Ford pardoned former President Nixon for any Watergate offenses he may have committed before criminal cases against Nixon could start.

Presidents may also commute (reduce or abolish) the sentence of anyone convicted of a federal crime, but without pardoning the offender. This is what President George W. Bush did in 2007 when he overturned the 30-month prison sentence of Lewis "Scooter" Libby. A former chief of staff to Vice President Cheney, Libby had been convicted of perjury and obstruction of justice in the investigation of who leaked the name of a CIA agent.

Recess appointments are another direct power possessed by presidents. The Senate normally must confirm nominations to important policymaking jobs, but when the chamber is in recess, the president may make a temporary appointment that lasts through the next congressional session, or up to two years. Presidents have sometimes used recess appointments to bypass Senate resistance to a regular appointment. In 2005, after Democrats blocked the nomination of John Bolton to be ambassador to the United Nations, President George W. Bush gave him the post through a recess appointment, which lasted 16 months.

When Democrats gained a majority in the Senate in the 2006 election, they began to hold very brief pro-forma sessions (often with just one member present) every few days during the lengthy breaks when most members were out of town and no real business was being done. They said that because the Senate was technically not in recess, Bush could not make recess appointments. The Senate did not use such procedures during President Obama's first year in office. After the president made some controversial recess appointments, the Senate's Republican minority insisted on resuming pro-forma sessions late in 2010. But in early January 2012, President Obama made four recess appointments despite the ongoing pro-forma sessions of the Senate. Republicans cried foul, but the administration insisted that Congress was not, in fact, in session and the appointments were constitutional. Senate Republicans then took the matter into federal court.

Congress has sometimes cut back the president's direct power. Until a few decades ago, presidents had occasionally ordered **impoundments**, refusing to spend funds that Congress had appropriated. They defended such actions on grounds of economic efficiency in specific programs or the general need to hold down excess spending. In the early 1970s, many in Congress became convinced that President Nixon was impounding funds to thwart congressional policy. Congress responded by changing the law in 1974 so that presidents could only defer spending temporarily. Permanent impoundments would now require congressional approval.

Recess appointment—a temporary appointment that a president can make when the Senate is in recess. Such appointments do not require Senate approval and last until the end of the next Senate session, or up to two years.

Impoundment—presidential refusal to spend funds that Congress has appropriated—a power limited by Congress in 1974.

Finally, presidents sometimes reach agreements with foreign nations on matters that do not require formal treaties (and therefore Senate approval). These **executive agreements** cover such matters as basing American troops on foreign soil or resolving claims made by citizens of one country against the government of another. These agreements can be either *sole-executive agreements*, which presidents make on their own authority and do not bind Congress or future presidents, or *congressional-executive agreements*, which are approved by both the president and Congress and deal with matters typically decided by Congress, such as international trade. Policymakers often disagree as to whether a particular agreement between the United States and a foreign nation can be made by the president alone, requires majority approval of the House and Senate, or must be done as a formal treaty, thereby requiring approval of two-thirds of the Senate.

Executive agreement—an agreement reached between the president of the United States and a foreign nation on matters that do not require formal treaties (and therefore Senate approval). These may be either sole-executive agreements, which a president makes on his own authority, or congressional-executive agreements, which are approved by both the president and Congress.

Foreign Policy and the War Power

"It is of the nature of war," Publius wrote in *The Federalist*, "to increase the executive at the expense of the legislative authority."[75] Waging war requires the qualities of a unified, energetic executive that can act quickly, forcefully, decisively, and, at times, secretly. Congress, of course, plays a vital role in providing the troops, equipment, and financial resources necessary for war. But the president sets the broad war-fighting strategy, orders the deployment of troops, makes the key day-to-day decisions, and rallies the public to support the cause.

Presidents also dominate the conduct of foreign affairs more generally. The president, not Congress, has the constitutional responsibility to "receive Ambassadors" (which includes the power to recognize foreign governments) and thus to speak for the nation in the international arena. In the 1790s, French diplomat Edmond-Charles Genet, known as Citizen Genet, tried to bypass President Washington and go directly to Congress for American military aid to France. Secretary of State Thomas Jefferson, though sympathetic to the French cause, told Genet that "the President was the only channel of communication between the United States and foreign nations." It was from the president alone that foreign nations could learn "the will of the nation." Earlier, Jefferson had written that "[t]he transaction of business with foreign nations is executive altogether."[76]

Although presidents occasionally negotiate directly with foreign leaders or their representatives, they usually work through the secretary of state and the other officials of the U.S. Department of State, which now has some 30,000 employees in the United States and overseas. The law that created the department in 1789, originally as the Department of Foreign Affairs, emphasized presidential control by directing the secretary of the department to carry out the duties "enjoined on or intrusted to him by the President of the United States, agreeable to the Constitution" and to administer the department "in such manner as the President of the United States shall from time to time order or instruct."[77] When negotiations result in treaty proposals or commitments that require the expenditure of federal funds, then either the Senate (treaties) or full Congress (appropriations) must approve.

For much of the twentieth century, at least until the Vietnam War, the dominant view among scholars, journalists, and many others was that the president should control foreign and national security policy. The Supreme Court seemed to endorse this view in a 1936 case in which it approvingly described "the very delicate, plenary and exclusive power of the President as the sole organ of the federal government in the field of international relations."[78] Congress, however, need not defer to presidents. In 1919 and again in 1920, the Senate defeated the Versailles Treaty, negotiated by President Wilson and other allied leaders to end formally World War I and establish a League of Nations to prevent future wars.

The defeat of the League of Nations demonstrated the importance of the Senate's constitutional power to ratify treaties. (See Chapter 18 for more on the importance of the treaty power to influence foreign policy.) But it also convinced many that in a dangerous world the presidency was a more competent and forward-looking institution than Congress. Many drew the same lesson from President Franklin Roosevelt's handling of foreign policy in the years leading up to American involvement in World War II. In 1941, after war had broken out in Europe but before the United States was a participant, Roosevelt ordered the occupation and fortification of Greenland and Iceland (possessions of defeated Denmark) and ordered the American navy first to help the British find German submarines and then to attack German warships that threatened freedom of the seas. Historians believe it is unlikely that Congress would have formally approved these acts if Roosevelt had asked it to do so.

During the Cold War that dominated American foreign policy in the decades after World War II, Congress supported key presidential initiatives, including the Marshall Plan to rebuild Europe, the Korean War, and other policies to thwart Communist expansion. And in August 1964, after North Vietnamese forces attacked U.S. naval ships off the coast of Vietnam, nearly every member of Congress (416–0 in the House and 88–2 in the Senate) approved the **Gulf of Tonkin Resolution** giving President Lyndon Johnson broad authority to defend the peace and security of South Vietnam. The resolution announced that "the United States is . . . prepared, as the President determines, to take all necessary steps, including the use of armed force, to assist [South Vietnam]."[79]

As the war dragged on, public and congressional support ebbed. In January 1973, the parties to the conflict signed the **Paris Peace Accords** to end the conflict. Within two months, the last American combat troops withdrew. Then in June, Congress, by large majorities, prohibited any further American military involvement in Southeast Asia after August 15. In early 1975, a large North Vietnamese army invaded South Vietnam in violation of the Peace Accords. President Gerald Ford, hamstrung by the congressional prohibition, was unable to assist South Vietnam militarily, despite earlier oral and written promises by President Nixon that the United States would "take swift and severe retaliatory action" if North Vietnam violated the accords. South Vietnam fell in April.

In the years after the Vietnam War, Congress reasserted its influence on foreign and national security policy, often causing conflicts with the executive branch. Among other acts, it tried to rein in presidential warmaking with the **War Powers Resolution** (also called the War Powers Act) of 1973, passed over President Nixon's veto, and it prohibited the executive branch from aiding anti-Communist forces in Angola (1975–1976) and Nicaragua (mid-1980s).

The Constitution gives Congress the power "to declare War" and makes the president "Commander in Chief" of the armed forces. Many lawmakers thought that presidents had too often violated the Constitution by sending troops into combat without prior congressional authorization. In the War Powers Resolution (WPR), Congress tried to reassert its authority over decisions to send American troops into combat.

Gulf of Tonkin Resolution—the joint resolution passed by Congress in 1964 that authorized President Lyndon Johnson to use the armed forces to assist South Vietnam.

Paris Peace Accords—the agreement between the warring parties to end the fighting in Vietnam in 1973, violated by North Vietnam when it invaded the South with its regular army early in 1975.

War Powers Resolution—joint resolution passed by Congress in 1973 to limit the occasions when the president could order armed forces into combat, to require prior consultation with Congress before such actions and regular reporting afterward, and to force the withdrawal of troops within two to three months unless Congress specifically authorized further combat.

Key Provisions of the War Powers Resolution of 1973

- **Definition of the president's powers.** Defines the president's constitutional powers to send the armed forces into combat as including only actions after
    1. Congress has declared war;
    2. Congress has provided specific statutory authorization; or
    3. a foreign power has attacked "the United States, its territories or possessions, or its armed forces."

    (The WPR, however, does not expressly prohibit presidents from acting militarily in other situations.)
- **Consultation with Congress.** Requires the president to consult with Congress "in every possible instance" before sending the armed forces into combat.
- **Reporting to Congress.** Requires the president to report significant troop movements to Congress within 48 hours.
- **Withdrawing troops.** Orders the president to withdraw the armed forces from combat
    1. within 60 days (or 90 days if necessary for the safety of the troops) unless Congress has declared war or authorized further combat or
    2. whenever Congress so orders by concurrent resolution (effectively overturned by the Supreme Court in an unrelated case in 1983).[80]

Although Congress narrowly defined the conditions that allowed a president to send troops into combat—if formally authorized by Congress or if the nation or its troops were attacked—it did not expressly prohibit the president from acting militarily in other situations. Nonetheless, it did require consultation with Congress beforehand "in every possible instance" and regular reporting to Congress after the fact. It also limited military involvement to 60–90 days without congressional authorization and permitted Congress to end combat at any time though a concurrent resolution, which requires a majority of the House and Senate and cannot be vetoed by the president. (A decade later in an unrelated case, the Supreme Court ruled that it was unconstitutional to use concurrent resolutions to control presidential actions.)

In his veto message, President Nixon argued that the WPR was "both unconstitutional and dangerous to the best interests of our Nation."[81] It would undermine the nation's ability to respond flexibly to changing circumstances and it would embolden enemies by announcing that the president's authority to act militarily would cease after 60 days if Congress did nothing. Except for the concurrent resolution provision, the Supreme Court has never ruled on the constitutionality of the act, and no president has accepted it as binding, although presidents often file reports with Congress "in accordance with" it.

In 2004, the Congressional Research Service of the Library of Congress conducted a comprehensive review of the law's effectiveness. It found that "[t]he record . . . has been mixed, and after 30 years [the WPR] remains controversial."[82] As Table 13-1 shows, despite the WPR, presidents have often sent American forces into combat, or potential combat, without prior congressional approval. Some have concluded that this record shows the ineffectiveness of the War Powers Resolution, but others point out that most of these actions have at least respected the time limits of the WPR, taking no longer than a few months. The nation's three large-scale military operations since 1973 have all received prior congressional authorization: the Gulf War of 1991, the war against the Taliban regime in Afghanistan (2001–present), and the Iraq war (2003–2011).

Controversy over the force and meaning of the War Powers Resolution arose in 2011 when President Obama, without prior congressional authorization, authorized air strikes in Libya by both manned aircraft and unmanned drones to support NATO's military actions against the Kadafi regime. When American military involvement approached the 90-day limit of the WPR, Speaker of the House John Boehner sent the president a letter alerting him to the potential violation of the law. The next day the administration issued a report in which it claimed that the time limits of the WPR did not apply because the nation was not engaged in "hostilities" as that term was used in the WPR: "U.S. operations do not involve sustained fighting or active exchanges of fire with hostile forces, nor do they involve the presence of U.S. ground troops, U.S. casualties or a serious threat thereof, or any significant chance of escalation into a conflict characterized by those factors."[83]

After the terrorist attacks of September 11, 2001, the war on terror became the dominant focus of national security policy in the George W. Bush administration. Although Bush sought and received congressional authorization for military action against al Qaeda in 2001 and against Iraqi leader Saddam Hussein in 2002, he conducted many aspects of the war on terror without explicit congressional approval. This includes detaining suspected terrorists indefinitely at the U.S. Naval base at Guantánamo Bay, Cuba; ordering military trials for some suspected terrorists; authorizing the National Security Agency (NSA) to listen in on electronic communications between suspected terrorists overseas and Americans in the United States; and, perhaps, authorizing the analysis of millions of phone call records to discover patterns involving possible terrorist plots.

The administration defended these programs (except for the last, which it never officially acknowledged) as necessary for national security and as legitimate exercises of the president's constitutional authority. Officials argued that Congress had implicitly endorsed such steps in the **"Authorization for Use of Military Force"** of September 18, 2001. This authorized the president "to use all necessary and appropriate force against those nations, organizations, or persons he determines planned, authorized, committed, or aided the terrorist attacks that occurred on September 11, 2001, or harbored such organizations or persons."[84]

Authorization for Use of Military Force—the joint resolution passed by Congress in September 2001 that authorized the president "to use all necessary and appropriate force" against those responsible for the attacks of September 11, 2001.

| TABLE 13-1 | MAJOR AMERICAN COMBAT OPERATIONS ORDERED BY PRESIDENTS WITHOUT CONGRESSIONAL AUTHORIZATION SINCE PASSAGE OF THE WAR POWERS RESOLUTION IN 1973 |

Year	President	Military Action
1980	Carter	Unsuccessful attempt to rescue 53 American hostages in Iran.
1982	Reagan	Marine mission to Lebanon to support a multinational peacekeeping force. It came under hostile fire in August 1983, and 241 marines were killed in a bombing of their barracks in October.
1983	Reagan	Invasion of the small Caribbean island of Grenada to restore order after a violent coup and to protect 1000 American medical students on the island.
1986	Reagan	One-day bombing of military installations in Libya in retaliation for Libyan involvement in the bombing of a West Berlin discotheque, known to be frequented by off-duty American military, that killed two American soldiers and injured dozens more.
1989	Bush, G. H. W.	Invasion of Panama to capture strongman Manuel Noriega, who had been indicted in the United States for drug trafficking, and to restore the democratically elected leaders.
1992–1993	Bush, Clinton	American military mission in Somalia to support UN humanitarian efforts to feed starving residents. Clinton continued the Bush policy and authorized military efforts to capture a local warlord who was undermining relief efforts.
1993–1996	Clinton	Various military measures in Yugoslavia under the auspices of the UN and NATO to force Serbians into a peace agreement with Bosnians and Croatians.
1999	Clinton	Three-month NATO bombing campaign against Serbian military installations to protect the ethnic Albanian population in Kosovo.

Bush's critics challenged many of his actions and policies in federal court. In several important cases beginning in 2004 (discussed in Chapter 5), the Supreme Court ruled that (1) American citizens held as suspected terrorists must be given the opportunity to challenge the government's case before an impartial adjudicator; (2) unless Congress changed the law (as it later did), the administration could not try foreign nationals as terrorists before military tribunals; and (3) foreign nationals held as enemy combatants at the Guantánamo Bay Naval Base in Cuba had the right to contest their confinement through habeas corpus proceedings in federal courts. These were closely divided decisions with strong dissents.

As we discussed in Chapter 5, President Obama overturned several Bush policies in the war on terror (such as coercive interrogation techniques and the use of secret detention facilities overseas) but (eventually) accepted others (such as military trials of suspected terrorists and the use of investigative techniques authorized by the Patriot Act). On the military front, Obama withdrew all American forces from Iraq by the end of 2011. In Afghanistan, the president increased American forces from about 35,000 when he took office to a high of 100,000 by August of 2010.[85] In 2011, Obama announced the beginning of a drawdown of forces, scheduled to reach 68,000 by the end of 2012 and with most gone by 2014.

Obama also significantly expanded the use of unmanned drone aircraft to strike al Qaeda leaders, operatives, and facilities, especially in Pakistan and Yemen. Although the official figures are classified, estimates based on news reports place the number of Obama administration strikes in Pakistan

PETE SOUZA/MAI/Landov

Mindful of their role as commander in chief, presidents make a point to spend time with the American armed forces, both in the United States and overseas. Here President Obama visits with American troops in Iraq in April 2009.

through the summer of 2012 at over 250, resulting in more than 1,900 deaths (87 of these civilians). In Yemen, the number of strikes was 39 with 307 deaths (56 of these civilians).[86]

Investigation, Executive Privilege, and Impeachment

The president and Congress sometimes clash when lawmakers investigate ineffectiveness or wrongdoing in the executive branch or its failure to carry out congressional policy. Sometimes this takes the form of a battle over Congress's access to executive branch documents.

This issue first arose in 1792 when a House committee asked President Washington for documents related to a disastrous military expedition against American Indians. Washington convened his cabinet to discuss whether he should comply. According to Secretary of State Thomas Jefferson's notes, all agreed that the House had a right to request documents but that "the Executive ought to communicate such papers as the public good would permit, & ought to refuse those the disclosure of which would injure the public."[87] The president decided to provide what the committee requested.

Two years later, however, Washington censored the contents of some letters by the U.S. ambassador to France, which the Senate had requested; and the following year, he refused information requested by the House related to the negotiation of the unpopular Jay Treaty. So, although Washington provided most of what Congress wanted during his two terms, he established the precedent, known as the doctrine of **executive privilege**, that the president may legitimately refuse some requests for information.

In conflicts over executive privilege, Congress argues, on the one hand, that it needs information from the executive to carry out its responsibilities, and the president maintains, on the other hand, that the public interest requires, and the Constitution implicitly authorizes, restrictions on disclosure. Presidents give several reasons for withholding information, such as ensuring the success of military operations, guaranteeing the confidentiality of sensitive communications with foreign leaders or diplomats, promoting the effectiveness of criminal investigations or protecting innocent individuals falsely accused, and promoting frank advice from subordinates.

Occasionally, the clash between the branches becomes a crisis. When this happens, Congress can charge executive officials with contempt, though this is rare. In most cases, the parties compromise before the dispute gets that far. Congress usually gets what it wants in the end, although sometimes it agrees to executive requests to limit access to specific legislators or aides or to prohibit taking notes or making photocopies of sensitive documents.

The Supreme Court has never ruled directly on a clash over documents between the Congress and president. Its major executive privilege ruling, *U.S. v. Nixon*, came in 1974 when the special prosecutor in the Watergate investigation went to court to force Nixon to hand over tape recordings and other incriminating materials. Importantly, the Court recognized that executive privilege had "constitutional underpinnings" because presidents could not properly carry out their constitutional duties if subordinates, fearing disclosure, refused to give candid advice. Yet it ruled that the generalized claim of privilege had to yield to the criminal court's need for specific information necessary for a fair criminal trial. The outcome might have been different, the Court suggested, had Nixon claimed the need "to protect military, diplomatic, or sensitive national security secrets." "As to these areas of Art. II duties," the unanimous decision held, "the courts have traditionally shown the utmost deference to Presidential responsibilities."[88]

So, Nixon lost this claim and provided the recordings and other materials. One recording revealed him trying to obstruct the investigation of the Watergate break-in by ordering aides to tell the FBI it was a CIA operation. Nixon resigned soon after the disclosure of this "smoking gun" tape. But in ruling against Nixon's executive privilege claim, the Court acknowledged the importance of confidential communications for sound deliberation within the executive branch:

> A President and those who assist him must be free to explore alternatives in the process of shaping policies and making decisions and to do so in a way many

FOCUS QUESTION

Should the Constitution be amended to require formal congressional approval before the president sends American forces into combat overseas?

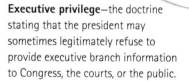

Executive privilege—the doctrine stating that the president may sometimes legitimately refuse to provide executive branch information to Congress, the courts, or the public.

would be unwilling to express except privately. These are the considerations justifying a presumptive privilege for Presidential communications. The privilege is fundamental to the operation of Government and rooted in the separation of powers under the Constitution.[89]

When presidents keep documents from Congress or the people, there is usually no easy way to determine whether the president is properly protecting his office or possibly covering up wrongdoing. President Obama ignited a controversy over this issue in June of 2012 when he formally asserted privilege to thwart a House committee's request for thousands of Department of Justice documents related to the ill-fated "Fast and Furious" program that allowed thousands of guns from the United States to fall into the hands of members of Mexican drug cartels. A few weeks later, the full House of Representatives voted 255-67 to hold Attorney General Eric Holder in contempt for refusing to provide the documents. This is the first time that the House held an attorney general in contempt. Seventeen Democrats joined the Republicans in supporting the contempt citation, while most Democrats walked out in protest. The administration insisted that it had already provided sufficient documents and that the Republicans were engaging in "political theater."[90]

Impeachment—a formal accusation by the House of Representatives (passed by a majority vote) that an officer of the United States has committed "Treason, Bribery, or other high Crimes and Misdemeanors." It results in removal if the Senate subsequently convicts by a two-thirds vote.

Nixon resigned from the presidency because he knew that if he did not, Congress would force him out of office through the **impeachment** process. This is Congress's harshest check on sitting officials. This procedure may apply to the president and other federal officers (including judges), but not members of Congress. Impeachment does not mean removal from office; rather, it is only the first step, much like indictment by a grand jury. The House has sole power over this phase, which requires a majority vote. If the House impeaches an official, the Senate conducts a trial. When the president is the defendant, as President Clinton was in 1999, the chief justice presides. A two-thirds vote is necessary for conviction, which triggers the official's removal.

The Senate has never convicted a president. In 1868, the House impeached Andrew Johnson, but the Senate failed to convict him by one vote. In 1974, the House Judiciary Committee approved three articles of impeachment against Richard Nixon, who resigned before the full House could vote. And in December 1998, the House approved two articles of impeachment against President Clinton, but in February 1999, only 45 senators voted to convict on the first article of impeachment and 50 on the second—well below the two-thirds required by the Constitution (67 of the current 100 senators).

The Constitution lists "Treason, Bribery, or other High Crimes and Misdemeanors" as the grounds for impeachment. Treason and bribery have specific meanings, but what are "High Crimes and Misdemeanors"? In the Clinton impeachment, a major issue was whether impeachable offenses must involve an abuse of official powers, as does bribery, or whether impeachment could reach to other abuses, such as obstructing justice in a civil suit unrelated to presidential powers. President Clinton's attorneys took the former position. Backers of his impeachment contended that impeachable acts reach to any conduct breaking the president's constitutional oath and his duty to "take Care that the Laws be faithfully executed."

Presidential Oath

Each president takes the following oath, which appears in Article II, Section 1 of the Constitution: "I do solemnly swear (or affirm) that I will faithfully execute the Office of President of the United States, and will to the best of my Ability, preserve, protect and defend the Constitution of the United States." The alternative of "affirm[ing]" was a nod to those with religious or philosophical objections to "swear[ing]." Although the framers had Quakers in mind, the two Quaker presidents—Herbert Hoover and Richard Nixon—both chose to "swear." The only president who "affirmed" was Franklin Pierce, an Episcopalian. Most presidents have concluded the oath with "so help me God," but these words are not in the Constitution. Also, most presidents have placed their hands on a Bible while taking the oath, but this gesture is also not mentioned in the Constitution.

The president's oath is different from that of every other federal official. The Constitution requires that other officials take an oath "to support this Constitution," and federal law spells out the actual language. Does the unique wording of the presidential oath have any significance? The president is often called the most powerful person in American government. This is because he heads the military, the intelligence agencies, and national law enforcement (FBI, DEA, etc.). *Most powerful* also means potentially the most dangerous. The president's special oath recognizes this danger and emphatically binds the president to the Constitution and the laws. Each of the three times that the House of Representatives (or its Judiciary Committee) has passed articles of impeachment against a president, it has charged him with violating his oath.

But the oath may have an even broader significance, as Abraham Lincoln thought. He cited it as one justification for his broad exercise of power at the start of the Civil War:

> I did understand however, that my oath to preserve the constitution to the best of my ability, imposed upon me the duty of preserving, by every indispensable means, that government—that nation—of which that constitution was the organic law. Was it possible to lose the nation, and yet preserve the constitution? By general law life *and* limb must be protected; yet often a limb must be amputated to save a life; but a life is never wisely given to save a limb. I felt that measures, otherwise unconstitutional, might become lawful, by becoming indispensable to the preservation of the constitution, through the preservation of the nation.[91]

For Lincoln, the president's special duty to "preserve, protect and defend the Constitution" gave him a special responsibility to preserve the nation in a crisis.

The Judiciary

Presidents seek to influence the judiciary by naming people with certain judicial philosophies to the federal courts. Judges have lifetime tenure, though, so a president cannot control them once they reach the bench. For example, President George H. W. Bush named David Souter to the Supreme Court in hopes that he would carry out a conservative judicial philosophy. Instead, Souter emerged as a reliable vote for the liberal side. Presidents try to avoid such surprises by reviewing the records of potential nominees. They rely on the office of counsel to the president, an in-house team of lawyers, to direct this process.

Presidents also try to sway the courts with legal arguments. The federal government has some involvement in about two-thirds of the cases that the U.S. Supreme Court decides on the merits.[92] The solicitor general, a presidential appointee in the Justice Department, is in charge of representing the government before the Supreme Court. Although solicitors general enjoy some independence, they generally follow presidential policy.

Some executives in the American political system are primarily administrators. A city manager, for example, is typically a professional administrator hired by an elected city council to carry out its policies. Although the American president is surely an administrator, he is also a political figure in his own right. Elected by the people, he has his own relationship with the broader political community.

THE POLITICAL PRESIDENCY
MAJOR ISSUE

- When and how do presidents deliberate with the general public?

A century ago, Woodrow Wilson famously wrote that the president "has no means of compelling Congress except through public opinion."[93] He meant that sometimes the president's arguments on the merits of public policy are not sufficient to persuade Congress. It may be necessary to mobilize public support for the administration's priorities and convince the people to pressure their representatives.

Links to Parties and Interest Groups

One way presidents try to influence public opinion is through party activists and interest groups. The White House office of political affairs keeps in touch with activists in the president's party, and the public liaison office deals with interest groups, often holding briefings and sending speakers to argue for presidential policies.

Executive offices face legal limits; they cannot, for instance, use government resources on election campaigns. For political tasks that their official staffs cannot legally carry out, presidents rely on private consultants and their parties' national committees. Presidents often campaign for members of Congress, in hopes of securing their loyalty. When a president flies on Air Force One to campaign for himself or others, committees must reimburse the government for the first-class airfare for the president and political operatives who come along. That reimbursement, however, makes up only a fraction of the cost of operating the plane.[94]

Unlike government staffs, parties and other political organizations can explicitly rally the public to put pressure on Congress. For instance, when President George W. Bush nominated Samuel Alito to the Supreme Court, the Republican National Committee e-mailed 10 million activists to ask them to sign an online petition in support of the nomination.[95] But in spite of the work of surrogates, much depends on the president's own words and direct communication with the people.

Communication and the Contemporary White House

Public communication is a major focus of the contemporary White House. The press secretary holds daily briefings of the White House press corps and advises the president on media relations. Other White House offices organize the chief executive's travel, provide photographs and videos, maintain the presidential Web site, and send informational e-mails to opinion leaders.

Every public utterance of the president invites intense scrutiny, especially from political foes. Consequently, White House aides strive to help the president stay "on message." Presidential press conferences require careful preparation by the president and the staff. Reporters do not submit questions in advance, but press secretaries and their assistants can usually anticipate what will come up. They suggest answers to the president, who practices in mock press conferences.

Although presidents may write some of their own remarks, they rely on speechwriters. Michael Gerson described his work for President George W. Bush: "I'm the head of speech writing and policy adviser, which really means I just get to go to the meetings I want to. I've got about six writers that work for me and researchers and fact-checkers and others, and we have anywhere from about one to three events a day for the president." He noted that drafts went to senior aides, who all got to comment and recommend changes, "and sometimes we get good speeches out of that process."[96]

Although this process sometimes frustrates speechwriters, senior aides need to review presidential speeches because they help set administration policy. Leon Panetta, who served as President Clinton's chief of staff (and later as head of the CIA and secretary of defense under President Obama), said, "Everybody thinks you make policy decisions and then you write a speech to announce a policy. It doesn't work that way. You schedule the speech and that's what forces the policy decisions to get made, the speech drives policy instead of the other way around."[97]

Speechwriting fosters deliberation by forcing presidents and advisors to think carefully about their policies. In 1987, the White House announced that President Reagan would speak at the Berlin Wall that divided Communist East Berlin and democratic West Berlin. Since the early 1960s, nearly 200 people had died there while trying to escape into the West. Speechwriter Peter Robinson got the job of writing the remarks, and he penned a challenge to the leader of the Soviet Union: "Mr. Gorbachev, tear down this wall!" The State Department and National Security Council staff both sought to remove the line for being too provocative. Far-ranging discussion occurred about the speech's relationship to policy goals. The president had the last word. He reportedly had this exchange with Deputy Chief of Staff Ken Duberstein:

Reagan: I'm the president, aren't I?

Duberstein: Yes sir, Mr. President, we're clear about that.

Reagan: So I get to decide whether the line about tearing down the wall stays in?

Duberstein: That's right, sir. It's your decision.

Reagan: Then it stays in.[98]

As this example suggests, presidents affect the speechwriting process in various ways. The nearby photo shows extensive revisions made by Reagan to the draft of an important speech in 1983 on the invasion of Grenada and the loss of American Marines in a Beirut bombing.

Presidents and Public Opinion

One purpose of presidential communication is to build support in the general public. Because politicians like to associate with popular figures, presidents may have more sway with Congress when their approval ratings are up. Members of Congress may also fear retribution at the polls if they oppose the policies of a popular president.

Pursuit of poll numbers can be frustrating, since words and images from the White House are not the only influences on public opinion. National security and the economy have greater impact. President George W. Bush came to office in 2001 not only with lingering controversy over his election but with a shaky economy as well. Accordingly, his initial ratings were modest (see Figure 13-2). After the attacks of September 11, 2001, approval soared in what is known as a **rally effect** (also called a "rally-around-the-flag effect")—a phenomenon that often occurs during crises, when Americans tend to rally around the commander in chief.[99] In this case, the rally effect lasted for months. With public support at his back, President Bush won passage of key national security legislation.

Presidents and their parties hire pollsters to provide detailed data on public opinion. The practice dates back to Franklin Roosevelt, who used surveys to gauge the strength of political opponents and the popularity of policy options. "As far as I am aware, Roosevelt never altered his goals because public opinion appeared against him or was uninformed," wrote FDR pollster Hadley Cantril. "Rather he utilized such information to try to bring the public around more quickly or more effectively to the course of action he felt was best for the country."[100] Decades later, when a reporter asked President Clinton about his reliance on polls, he suggested that he was following the Roosevelt precedent:

Roosevelt was the first President to be almost obsessive about polls. But I never was controlled by them because I always believed if you were right, you could find a way to change public opinion. . . .

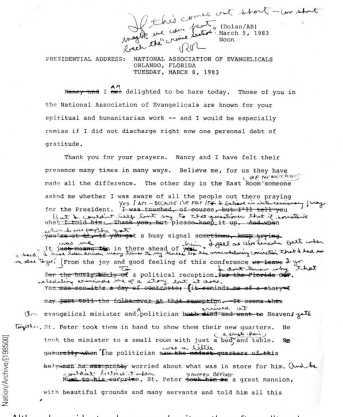

Nation/Archive/[198500]

Although presidents rely on speechwriters, they often edit and rewrite speech drafts. Despite a reputation for passivity, President Reagan was an active coauthor of his major addresses. Here is a draft page of his speech to the National Association of Evangelicals on March 8, 1983. This became popularly known as the "Evil Empire" speech. The alterations are Reagan's.

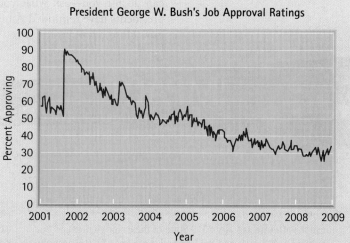

President George W. Bush's Job Approval Ratings

FIGURE 13-2 President George W. Bush's public support fluctuated with events in the domestic economy, terrorism, and the war in Iraq. This graph of his job approval in the Gallup poll shows a spike right after the attacks of September 11, 2001, and a smaller one in March 2003, at the beginning of the Iraq war. Crises typically raise presidential approval, but the effect is temporary.
SOURCE: www.gallup.com/poll/116677/Presidential-Approval-Ratings-Gallup-Historical-Statistics-Trends.aspx

Rally effect—the tendency for presidents to gain in public approval during crises. Also called the "rally-around-the-flag effect."

And one of the things that I used polls for was to understand how aware the public was of given issues or, if they disagree with me on an issue, what was the most effective argument I could make to try to persuade them. But I didn't—especially on issues affecting America's future, I never let the polls control me. . . . Bosnia, Kosovo, Haiti, those things were not popular. But I thought they were right, and I thought they could be made popular.[101]

As Clinton's comments suggest, presidents can use their communications machinery to lead public opinion, not just follow it. Even though his own approval had slipped from the 9/11 highs, President Bush mounted an extensive effort in early 2003 to persuade the public to back an invasion of Iraq. By March, public opinion was on his side. Yet this case also reminds us of the limits of presidential persuasion. Despite the rally effects of the invasion and Saddam's capture, public support for the war gradually waned. As major combat operations, costs, and casualties kept rising, so did criticism of Iraq policy. Public approval drifted downward, and by the end of his second term, Bush's approval ratings were near record lows since measurement began during FDR's administration. Similarly, President Obama learned the limits of presidential persuasion when more than 50 speeches did not generate broad public support for his health care reform (though it still passed Congress).

Presidents, Sacrifice, and Citizenship

A cynic would say that presidents tell Americans what they want to hear. Although much of the time they do, presidents sometimes deliver blunt talk. In his 1975 State of the Union address, President Ford said, "I must say to you that the state of the Union is not good: Millions of Americans are out of work. Recession and inflation are eroding the money of millions more. Prices are too high, and sales are too slow."[102]

When presidents strike a sour note, they generally use it to stress the need for action. In 1993, President Clinton said, "In the last month, we had 365,000 new jobs. That's the good news. The bad news is that more than half of them were part-time jobs, jobs that didn't contain a full income and couldn't provide for health care coverage for the family."[103] He then talked about his proposals for economic growth and health care.

Sometimes presidents ask for sacrifice. The most famous such call came in President Kennedy's inaugural address: "And so, my fellow Americans: ask not what your country can do for you—ask what you can do for your country."[104] Especially during wartime, presidents have reminded Americans that sacrifice is part of citizenship. As World War II grew close, Franklin Roosevelt spoke of legislation establishing "the obligation inherent in

IMPACT
of Social Media and Communications Technology

New Ways to Influence Public Opinion

The Obama administration has made extensive use of social media to communicate with the American people, especially with young persons. As we noted in our blog post of July 2, 2012, Obama fielded questions after his January 2012 State of the Union Address on YouTube and Google +. He and the First Lady both have Twitter accounts; the White House posts information on the president's travels and statements on Facebook in a series called "West Wing Week"; and people can receive a presidential photo every day in their inboxes by signing up through Flickr. Such new modes of communication are likely to be attractive to future presidents as well because they provide means of communicating with the American people on a daily basis without the filtering effect of the media. Although presidents occasionally speak directly to the people through televised addresses and press conferences, most of the time they, like other politicians, are dependent on the print and broadcast media to get their message out. And, like other politicians, they sometimes complain about inadequate or inaccurate coverage.

CRITICAL THINKING QUESTION

Will social media profoundly affect the way presidents influence public opinion in the twenty-first century?

our citizenship to serve our forces for defense through training in many capacities." It is not easy to ask Americans to leave their homes for national service, he said, but "the men and women of America have never held back even when it has meant personal sacrifice on their part if that sacrifice is for the common good."[105]

Opinion polls tell presidents on virtually a daily basis how popular they are with the American people and how successful they are in mobilizing support for their policies. History takes a longer view. An interesting case is Harry Truman, whose job approval rating in the Gallup Poll averaged less than 37% in his second term (1949–1953) and once dropped as low as 22% (February 1952). But after he left office, Truman's stature steadily grew. Both Democrats and Republicans now admire him for his efforts to contain Soviet expansion (the Truman Doctrine), to rebuild Europe devastated by war (the Marshall Plan), to relieve Berlin during the Soviet blockade of 1948–1949, to end segregation within the U.S. military, and to push for civil rights reforms despite the adamant opposition of southern Democrats. Truman is also admired for his personal integrity, his plain speaking, and his willingness to accept responsibility, famously keeping a sign on his desk: "The Buck Stops Here." Presidential rankings now place him at least "above average" and sometimes "near great" (see Figure 13-3). Apparently, immediate popularity is not an infallible guide as to whether a president has done a good or great job. How, then, should we make such judgments?

PRESIDENTIAL GREATNESS
MAJOR ISSUE

- ### What makes a president great?

When you ask someone to rank the greatness of American presidents, the answer will likely depend in part on the person's political leanings. In 1996, historian Arthur Schlesinger put the question to several dozen scholars and writers. Most were liberals who tended to prefer Democratic presidents, ranking Kennedy and Johnson above Reagan and George H. W. Bush. The Intercollegiate Studies Institute, a group of college students and faculty devoted to promoting the values of a free society, then polled a more conservative group, who gave better grades to Republicans, putting Reagan and Bush ahead of Kennedy and Johnson (see Figure 13-3).

The two groups tended to disagree most about recent presidents. The scholars may have been "backing their bets" by upgrading those whom they had supported in presidential elections. We should not be surprised if those with strong policy views—on the left or right—tend to judge presidents based on the fit between the president's accomplishments and their own policy preferences. Nonetheless, scholars generally agree on presidencies further back in history, suggesting that there is more to appraising presidents than mere partisanship.

	Scholars Rank the Presidents	
	Schlesinger Survey (liberal scholars)	ISI Survey (conservative scholars)
Great	Washington, Lincoln, F. D. Roosevelt	Washington, Lincoln
Near Great	Jefferson, Jackson, Polk, T. Roosevelt, Wilson, Truman	Jefferson, Jackson, Reagan, T. Roosevelt, F. D. Roosevelt, Eisenhower
High Average	Monroe, Cleveland, McKinley, Eisenhower, Kennedy, L. B. Johnson, J. Adams	J. Adams, J. Q. Adams, Cleveland, McKinley, Taft, Coolidge, Truman, Polk, Monroe
Low Average	Madison, J. Q. Adams, Van Buren, Hayes, Arthur, B. Harrison, Taft, Ford, Carter, Reagan, Bush, Clinton	Madison, Van Buren, Ford, B. Harrison, Hayes, Garfield, Arthur, Bush
Below Average	Tyler, Taylor, Fillmore, Coolidge	Tyler, Fillmore, Wilson, Kennedy, Nixon, Hoover
Failure	Pierce, Buchanan, A. Johnson, Grant, Harding, Hoover, Nixon	Buchanan, Grant, Harding, L. B. Johnson, Carter, Clinton, Pierce, A. Johnson

FIGURE 13–3 Surveys during the 1990s showed that liberal and conservative scholars had different assessments of American presidents.
SOURCE: From Gary L. Gregg II, "Liberals, Conservatives, and the Presidency," *Intercollegiate Review* (Spring 1998). Copyright © 1998 by Intercollegiate Studies Institute, Inc. Reprinted with permission.

Time and Chance

"Presidents are the custodians of the time in which they live as well as the instruments of the visions and dreams they have," said President Clinton in a 1997 interview. "So the first thing I had to start with was, you know, we don't have a war, we don't have a depression, we don't have a cold war."[106] As Clinton's remarks suggest, wars and other historical transformations supply presidents with their chance for greatness. George Washington presided over the difficult birth of the constitutional order. Abraham Lincoln saved the Union in the Civil War. Franklin Roosevelt confronted the Great Depression and World War II. Washington and Lincoln always rank at the top on presidential greatness scales, and Roosevelt either joins them or is not far behind.

Crises, however, need not end in glory. For instance, the scholars disagreed about Woodrow Wilson. He did lead the United States into World War I, which helped bring victory to the allies, but his critics say he lost the peace by negotiating a flawed treaty at Versailles and by botching his chance to win its approval by the Senate. More recently, George W. Bush led the nation into a war in Iraq, which lasted longer than World War II and drove down the president's popularity. It remains to be seen whether the war benefits the nation's long-term security and, if it does, whether Bush's stature will grow over time.

Courage and Conviction

Theodore Roosevelt ranked high with both groups of presidential evaluators even though he did not have to fight a war or an economic crisis. His stature reflects his strong ideas about the federal government's role at home and abroad and the energy with which he pursued his convictions. He went far in realizing his vision, ranging from the establishment of national parks to the construction of the Panama Canal.

Greatness also involves the ability to stay the course despite unpopularity and political risk. As the Civil War dragged on and casualties mounted, Abraham Lincoln refused to consider any peace deal with the Confederacy that would have continued slavery or weakened the Union. For most of 1864, Lincoln was sure that his firmness had doomed his chances with a war-weary electorate. "I am going to be beaten," he told an army officer, "and unless some great change takes place *badly* beaten."[107] A "rational" seeker of reelection would have followed the political winds. Lincoln hung on, and he prevailed after Union armies scored major victories in the fall of 1864.

Even lesser presidents have had their moments of courage. Shortly after taking office in 1974, President Ford faced the likelihood that his predecessor would stand trial for the Watergate scandal. After careful thought, Ford concluded that a Nixon trial would be a burden for the country and a distraction for the presidency. Ford scuttled any chance for criminal action against Nixon by granting him an unconditional pardon. Although the decision was unpopular and likely contributed to Ford's 1976 defeat, many observers now agree with it. In 2001, it earned Ford the John F. Kennedy Profile in Courage Award.[108]

In the book of the same name, Kennedy wrote of senators, but he could also have been thinking of presidents when he noted:

> The true democracy, living and growing and inspiring, puts its faith in the people—faith that the people will not simply elect men who will represent their views ably and faithfully, but also elect men who will exercise their conscientious judgment—faith that the people will not condemn those whose devotion to principle leads them to unpopular courses, but will reward courage, respect honor and ultimately recognize right.[109]

FOCUS QUESTION

Is the fascination of scholars, pundits, and presidents themselves with "presidential greatness" a good thing for the nation?

THE PRESIDENCY AND DELIBERATIVE DEMOCRACY

As we have seen, presidents contribute to American deliberative democracy in a variety of ways. They deliberate with advisers and aides, especially about decisions they can make on their own. Because of the president's preeminence in foreign affairs and national security policy, the quality of deliberations within the executive branch is crucial to the nation's well-being.

Presidents and their administrations also work hard to influence congressional deliberations through testimony in committee hearings, briefings at the White House, and informal contacts with the members of Congress. Because presidents have a much broader constituency than any single member of the House or Senate, they can often provide a broader perspective on the problems facing the nation and how to solve them.

Presidents also contribute to broader, community-wide deliberation on policy issues and, at times, on deeper principles of American democracy. American history shows many examples of presidents setting the terms of national debate and leaving a lasting impression on public opinion. As Abraham Lincoln said in the Lincoln-Douglas debates, "In this and like communities, public sentiment is everything. With public sentiment, nothing can fail; without it nothing can succeed. Consequently he who moulds public sentiment, goes deeper than he who enacts statutes or pronounces decisions."[110] Most presidents who rank high on the greatness scale have shaped public opinion, sometimes decisively, on the great issues of the day.

Moreover, as we noted at the beginning of the chapter, and as American history well documents, presidents must have the capacity to act quickly and decisively, as well as deliberatively. No other branch of government needs to act as quickly in a crisis, and no other branch has the same obligation to "preserve, protect and defend the Constitution of the United States." The nation's greatest presidents have been those who safely steered the ship of state through perilous times.

SUMMARY

- The framers designed an energetic executive who would be able to administer the laws firmly and consistently, to check Congress when necessary, and to protect the nation against foreign attacks. They also made the president accountable for his conduct through elections and, in extreme cases, impeachment and removal; and, short of impeachment, he was subject to other checks by Congress and the courts.

- Prior to the twentieth century, Presidents Washington, Jefferson, Jackson, and Lincoln stood out as leaders of the political system.

- In the early twentieth century, Woodrow Wilson urged that presidents become rhetorical leaders and that the office be "the vital place of action in the system." President Franklin Roosevelt brought this conception to fruition.

- In the 1960s and 1970s, the Vietnam War and the Watergate scandal led many to question the value and effectiveness of presidential leadership. But in the 1980s, Ronald Reagan showed that the office still had the capacity to shape American government and politics.

- The institution of the presidency includes the vice president's office, the Executive Office of the President, the cabinet, and the National Security Council.

- The president's most effective tool in influencing Congress is the veto. Presidents also exercise power directly through proclamations, executive orders, signing statements, recess appointments, and executive agreements.

- Presidents have dominated foreign affairs and national security policy. Waging war requires the qualities of a unified, energetic executive that can act quickly, forcefully, decisively, and, at times, secretly. Congress plays a vital role in providing the troops, equipment, and financial resources necessary for war.

- In recent decades, Congress and the Supreme Court have not simply deferred to the president in foreign and national security policy. In 1973, Congress passed the War Powers Resolution to limit the president's ability to engage American forces in hostilities. Nonetheless, presidents have frequently authorized smaller-scale or short-term military operations without prior congressional approval. During the George W. Bush administration, the Supreme Court limited the president's discretion in fighting the war on terror.

- In carrying out its own responsibilities, Congress often investigates the executive branch, and twice impeached, but did not convict, the president of "high Crimes and Misdemeanors" (Andrew Johnson and Bill Clinton). Richard Nixon resigned before likely removal by Congress.

- To get their way with other government officials, presidents often mobilize support among the general public and the political community. They use their communications machinery to lead public opinion, not just follow it.

- Although scholars disagree about the performance of recent presidents, they tend to agree about the rankings of past presidents. Presidents who rank highest have shaped public opinion, sometimes decisively, on the great issues of the day and have safely steered the ship of state through perilous times.

KEY TERMS

Authorization for Use of Military
    Force p. 397
Bully pulpit p. 382
Cabinet p. 389
Chief of staff p. 388
Demagogue p. 382
Executive agreement p. 395
Executive Office of the President
    (EOP) p. 388
Executive orders p. 393

Executive prerogative p. 380
Executive privilege p. 399
Groupthink p. 390
Gulf of Tonkin Resolution p. 396
Impeachment p. 400
Impoundment p. 394
Line-item veto p. 393
National Security Council (NSC) p. 390
Office of Management and Budget
    (OMB) p. 389

Paris Peace Accords p. 396
Proclamation p. 393
Rally effect p. 404
Recess appointment p. 394
Secretary p. 389
Signing statement p. 393
State of the Union address p. 382
War Powers Resolution p. 396
Whiskey Rebellion p. 379

TEST YOUR KNOWLEDGE

1. The framers helped secure the president's independence from Congress by prohibiting Congress from
   a. altering the president's salary during any one term.
   b. confirming Supreme Court appointees.
   c. overriding a presidential veto.
   d. removing the president from office.
   e. voting on matters of war.

2. Theodore Roosevelt changed the traditional understanding of the presidency when he
   a. depended on his rapport with lawmakers to get his policies through Congress.
   b. issued several hundred executive orders as a way of bypassing Congress.
   c. took more liberties with his position as commander in chief than his predecessors had done.
   d. took pains to cultivate public opinion and drum up public support for his policies.
   e. used radio addresses to sway the people and solidify his position as the leader on policy issues.

3. The only constitutional duty of the vice president is
   a. advising the president on matters of foreign policy.
   b. casting a tie-breaking vote in the House of Representatives.
   c. nominating Supreme Court justices.
   d. presiding over the Senate and casting tie-breaking votes.
   e. selecting presidential electors.

4. In some instances the president's entire cabinet or another group of advisers agrees to a course of action in order to achieve consensus, despite disagreement. This is called
   a. the consensus principle.
   b. demagoguery.
   c. groupthink.
   d. the deference principle.
   e. intimidation.

5. President Obama's recess appointments in January of 2012 were controversial because
   a. he made so many at one time.
   b. the individuals had already been voted down by the Senate.
   c. recess appointments are not mentioned in the Constitution.
   d. one of the appointments was to the Supreme Court.
   e. the Senate was technically not in recess but holding regular brief, pro-forma sessions.

6. The Gulf of Tonkin Resolution gave President Johnson the authority to
   a. declare war on Japan.
   b. defend South Vietnam.
   c. enter into arms negotiations with the Soviet Union.
   d. protect Korean interests in the region.
   e. regulate U.S. trade with Canada and Mexico.

7. Which of the following is not a provision of the War Powers Resolution of 1973:
   a. Congress must approve the introduction of military forces into hostilities in advance.
   b. The president must consult with Congress whenever possible before sending troops into combat.
   c. The president must report significant troop movements to Congress within 48 hours.
   d. The president must withdraw forces within 60 to 90 days unless Congress authorizes further combat.
   e. By a concurrent resolution, Congress may order the withdrawal of troops from combat at any time.

8. Which of the following statements best describes President Obama's military actions with respect to the wars in Iraq and Afghanistan?
   a. He significantly increased the number of troops in both countries before beginning a drawdown.
   b. He replaced ground actions in Afghanistan with unmanned drone attacks.

c. He withdrew all American forces from Iraq, but increased the number of troops in Afghanistan before beginning a drawdown.

d. He withdrew all American forces from Iraq, while reducing forces in Afghanistan from the 100,000 that President Bush had sent there.

e. He successfully used unmanned drone attacks in Iraq so that ground forces could be withdrawn.

9. How many presidents have been convicted by the Senate and removed from office?

a. none
b. one
c. two
d. three
e. four

10. Scholars tend to agree on presidential greatness when considering

a. modern presidents.
b. peacetime presidents.
c. presidents who were neither Democrats or Republicans.
d. early presidents.
e. wartime presidents.

FURTHER READING

Bessette, Joseph M., and Jeffrey K. Tulis. *The Constitutional Presidency*. Baltimore, MD: Johns Hopkins University Press, 2009.

Bessette, Joseph M., and Jeffrey Tulis, eds. *The Presidency in the Constitutional Order*. Baton Rouge: Louisiana State University Press, 1981. Reprinted with a new Introduction by Transaction Publishers in 2010.

Caro, Robert A. *Passage to Power: The Years of Lyndon Johnson*. New York: Knopf, Borzoi Books, 2012.

Corwin, Edward S. *The President: Office and Powers, 1787–1984*. 5th rev. ed. New York: New York University Press, 1984.

Greenstein, Fred I. *The Presidential Difference: Leadership Style from FDR to George W. Bush*. 2nd ed. Princeton, NJ: Princeton University Press, 2004.

Lowi, Theodore J. *The Personal President: Power Invested, Promise Unfulfilled*. Ithaca, NY: Cornell University Press, 1985.

Muir, William Ker Jr. *The Bully Pulpit: The Presidential Leadership of Ronald Reagan*. San Francisco: ICS Press, 1992.

Neustadt, Richard E. *Presidential Power and the Modern Presidents: The Politics of Leadership from Roosevelt to Reagan*. New York: Free Press, 1991.

Nichols, David K. *The Myth of the Modern Presidency*. University Park, PA: Pennsylvania State University Press, 1994.

Pious, Richard M. *The American Presidency*. New York: Basic Books, 1979.

Skowronek, Stephen. *The Politics Presidents Make: Leadership from John Adams to Bill Clinton*. Cambridge, MA: Belknap Press of Harvard University Press, 1997.

Sykes, Patricia Lee. *Presidents and Prime Ministers: Conviction Politics in the Anglo-American Tradition*. Lawrence: University Press of Kansas, 2000.

Troy, Tevi. *Intellectuals and the American Presidency: Philosophers, Jesters, or Technicians?* Lanham, MD: Rowman and Littlefield, 2002.

Tulis, Jeffrey K. *The Rhetorical Presidency*. Princeton, NJ: Princeton University Press, 1987.

WEB SOURCES

American Presidency Project: www.presidency.ucsb.edu/index.php—the most extensive electronic collection of presidential documents, maintained by the University of California, Santa Barbara.

National Archives: www.archives.gov—a guide to the documents and materials maintained by the National Archives.

Obameter: www.politifact.com/truth-o-meter/promises/obameter/—a site run by the *St. Petersburg Times* that tracks President Obama's campaign promises (more than 500).

USA.gov: www.usa.gov—the official Web portal for the U.S. government.

Voices of American Presidents: www.lib.msu.edu/cs/branches/vvl/presidents/—a collection of audio recordings of American presidents going back to Benjamin Harrison, maintained by Michigan State University.

White House Tapes: www. tapes.millercenter.virginia.edu—a collection of recordings of meetings and phone conversations secretly made by presidents, from Franklin Roosevelt through Richard Nixon.

White House: www.whitehouse.gov—the president's official Web site with links to presidential speeches and documents.

Some public servants are ready to put their lives at risk in the line of duty. Here, a new FBI agent undergoes training.

Courtesy of the Federal Bureau of Investigation

14 Bureaucracy and the Administrative State

OBJECTIVES

After reading this chapter, you should be able to:

- Define bureaucracy.
- Explain what bureaucrats do at headquarters and in the field.
- Discuss, in general terms, the size and organization of the federal bureaucracy.
- Analyze how bureaucrats and elected officials try to influence each other.
- Understand control and oversight of the bureaucracy.
- Appraise alternatives to current bureaucratic structures.

INTRODUCTION

On March 11, 2002, a Florida flight school got a notice from the Immigration and Naturalization Service (INS) that two of its enrollees now had student visas (see the photo). There was nothing unusual about the notice except for the identity of the enrollees. Exactly six months earlier, they had helped crash planes into the World Trade Center.

In one way, the episode embodies the faults of bureaucracy in general and the INS in particular. Not only had the government failed to spot terrorists seeking entry into the country; it sent the notice of their approval after they had died. Congress later scrapped the INS, splitting its responsibilities between two parts of the Department of Homeland Security.

The 9/11 attacks also showed another face of government service. Firefighters and other "first responders" ran toward the burning towers. Hundreds died. In the months afterward, authorities sped to clear the enormous wreckage. At the Pentagon, within a day of the attack, thousands of civilian and military personnel resumed their work in the undamaged sections. An air force sergeant said, "We just want to do our job."[1] By the first anniversary of the attacks, the Defense Department had rebuilt the crash site, under budget and ahead of schedule.

Government bureaucracy is sometimes slow and frustrating, sometimes swift and heroic. Whether for good or ill, it touches each of us. So what is it, and how did it become so strong? By a rough definition, **bureaucracy** is the sum of government organizations that carry out public policy. In that sense, every government in history has had a bureaucracy. By a more precise definition, from the sociologist Max Weber, bureaucracy also involves a division of labor, a hierarchy of authority, and impersonal rules. Upset with such rules, people often sneer at "bureaucracy." Here, we apply the term in a neutral sense. Likewise, we use the term "**bureaucrats**" for those who staff government organizations.

In drafting the Constitution, the framers made no mention of "bureaucracy" or "administration." Although they authorized the creation of the armed forces and the appointment of diplomats, they made only brief mention of "heads of Departments" and "inferior officers." They did not define what kinds of organizations those people would work in, or what their responsibilities would be.

For much of the nineteenth century, the federal civilian workforce was small, and its members got their jobs mainly through the patronage of politicians. In the twentieth century, merit hiring eventually replaced patronage while the federal workforce grew in size and professionalism. As the issues

Bureaucracy—the unelected organizations that carry out government policy; more generally, a form of organization with division of labor, a hierarchy of authority, and impersonal rules.

Bureaucrat—an unelected government employee who administers government policy by adhering to rules and procedures.

This is the INS notification of Mohomed Atta's student visa to a Florida flight school. Atta piloted one of the planes that crashed into the World Trade Center towers. Although the INS approved his application before 9/11, the formal notification did not go out until months afterward. The INS blamed a bureaucratic backlog.

U.S. Department of Justice

became more complex, lawmakers kept delegating authority to the bureaucracy. Indeed, it gained so much autonomy that scholars started to speak of an **administrative state**. So although bureaucrats are part of the executive branch, it makes sense to consider them separately from the institution of the presidency, which we discuss in the previous chapter.

The bureaucracy also draws power from alliances with congressional committees, interest groups, and think tanks. Bureaucrats deal with people who share their interest or expertise. Within each field, people know one another, work on similar issues, and read the same publications. In formal and informal settings, they can deliberate on concerns that may be too technical to draw popular attention. These concerns, however, may have a deep impact on the public's well-being. One danger is that the bureaucrats may be making decisions in isolation from the people whose lives they affect. Yet bureaucrats can also foster deliberative democracy by "speaking truth to power." Because most of them do not serve at the pleasure of politicians, they can supply honest information and analysis even when it is unpleasant.

What is the result of bureaucratic power? Some say that the administrative state has helped make America fairer and safer. Despite complaints about paperwork, they add, it has also left the country richer. Of many possible examples of bureaucratic success, one should be familiar to every reader of this book. In 1967, the Defense Advanced Research Projects Agency launched a computer network that got little media attention at the time. It later turned into the Internet.[2]

Administrative state—a government in which the nominal rulers (usually elected officials) have delegated much of their authority to bureaucrats.

Frontline worker—a government employee who has the physical task of carrying out public policy, often in direct contact with the general public.

WHAT BUREAUCRATS DO

MAJOR ISSUE

- How does bureaucracy affect everyday life?

Inspector Dean

The Millennium Plot failed because Customs Inspector Diana Dean did her job.

Federal law enforcement officers, Social Security claims representatives, and State Department consular officials are all **frontline workers**. Studies of bureaucracy also call them "field" staff, even though technology now enables many to work at headquarters. They have the physical task of carrying out public policy.[3] You meet them if you have a problem with a government agency, or if the agency deems you a problem. For instance, if you have a hard time getting a passport, you probably need to speak with an official of the Passport Services Directorate of the State Department's Bureau of Consular Affairs.

Frontline workers must answer to management, which sometimes has many layers. They must also follow elaborate guidelines. Yet even the biggest rulebook cannot anticipate every situation that these workers will face. They must use judgment, which is why the government seeks able people for these jobs. The terror war illustrates the importance of "judgment calls."

On December 14, 1999, a follower of Osama bin Laden drove onto a ferry from Canada into Washington State. Before going farther, he had to clear a U.S. checkpoint. "He approached in my lane, and I just started to ask him a couple of routine Customs questions," said Diana Dean, a veteran inspector.[4] When he grew edgy, Dean asked him to open his trunk. With two other inspectors, she found explosives. They also spotted a map with a circle around Los Angeles International Airport (LAX). These Customs officials had just foiled the "Millennium Plot" to carry out a deadly bombing on New Year's 2000.

Sometimes headquarters will foil a frontline worker. On November 19, 2009, a Nigerian businessman spoke to two CIA officers at the U.S. Embassy in his country. He was alarmed that the State Department was letting his son enter the United States, since he had become a militant and had spent time in Yemen, the site of terrorist training camps. The officers took the information seriously, cabling the Agency's Counterterrorism Center which, in turn, passed word to the National Counterterrorism Center, a separate organization that reports to the

Director of National Intelligence. Neither organization recommended putting the businessman's son on the no-fly list. On Christmas Day, 2009, the young man flew from Amsterdam to Detroit with explosives hidden in his clothing. He tried to blow up the plane, but the device failed and instead severely burned him. Why did the government let him get so far? Journalist David Ignatius writes: "The Counterterrorism Center is supposed to review more than 120 databases; senior officials there are supposed to process 10,000 to 12,000 pieces of information a day; large stations can receive several thousand cables a day. No wonder the real threats get lost in the noise."[5]

Information

In deliberating on policy issues, lawmakers and executive officials need numbers. Debates on education policy, for instance, hinge on measures of school performance, and under the No Child Left Behind Act schools face federal penalties if they fail to meet certain statistical goals. Because of the need for accurate data, the federal government spends more than $6 billion a year to gather, analyze, and publish statistics.[6] Dozens of agencies do this work. For some, such as the Bureau of Labor Statistics, it is the core of their mission.[7] This work may seem dry, but it may cause fights.

In 2005, the Bureau of Justice Statistics issued a report saying that police were equally likely to stop drivers of different racial and ethnic groups. But the report also found that, after a traffic stop, officers were much more likely to search or arrest African Americans and Hispanics. The bureau's director wanted to include the latter finding in a press release; his superiors disagreed and fired him. "There's always a natural and healthy tension between the people who make the policy and the people who do the statistics," he reflected. "That's there every day of the week, because some days you're going to have good news, and some days you're going to have bad news."[8]

Measurements of poverty or unemployment underlie billions in federal spending. If the measurements go wrong, then much of the money goes to waste. For instance, the government does not adjust poverty levels for regional living costs, so it may overstate problems in low-cost areas while understating them in expensive ones. Adequate data are essential to deliberation about the problem. "You can't fix a problem if you misunderstand it, so if we are serious about tackling poverty, we need to get serious about accurately measuring poverty," said New York City mayor Michael Bloomberg in 2008.[9] In 2011, the Census Bureau responded to such concerns by issuing a supplemental poverty measure, which took different data into account and showed a higher rate than the customary measure. Some liberals said that the supplemental measure understated poverty, while some conservatives said that it overstated poverty.

Statistical programs often raise privacy concerns, especially with respect to detailed questions on census forms. Census officials have long held that they have a spotless record of guarding privacy, and that the information is vital to deliberation on issues such as housing quality. Even so, there have been abuses. During World War II, the Census Bureau helped in the internment of Japanese Americans by providing officials with names and addresses. For decades the bureau flatly denied this activity, admitting only that it had turned over statistical data. Historians later published documents showing that these denials were false.[10]

For individuals and businesses, meeting government information requirements takes about 9 billion hours a year.[11] The owner of a small business that makes pipe organs once showed a congressional committee the piles of federal reports that he must file. He also noted two forms that the Environmental Protection Agency requires for a toxic substance inventory: "Through their Web site, which includes 195 pages of instruction on how to complete the two different forms, the EPA estimates that both forms will take approximately 82 hours combined, to complete. I currently charge clients $50.00 per hour for labor costs. That amounts to $4,100 additional cost to report on lead usage that is just barely over the minimum level for most in my industry."[12]

Frustrated citizens refer to such paperwork as **red tape**, after the ribbon that English officials once used to bind legal documents.[13] In response to those who would scrap all red

FOCUS QUESTION

Counterterrorism is one policy area where the sheer volume of information may overwhelm bureaucrats. Can you think of others? Is there any way to prevent this problem?

Red tape—official forms and procedures, which are often burdensome. The term stems from a British tradition of binding documents with red cloth tape.

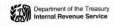

2009

Instructions for Form 1040-SS

U.S. Self-Employment Tax Return (Including the Additional Child Tax Credit for Bona Fide Residents of Puerto Rico)

Section references are to the Internal Revenue Code unless otherwise noted.

General Instructions

What's New

Maximum income subject to social security tax. For 2009, the maximum amount of self-employment income subject to social security tax is $106,800.

Optional methods to figure net earnings. For 2009, the maximum income for using the optional methods is $4,360.

Making work pay credit. For tax years 2009 and 2010, if you have earned income from work you may be able to take this credit. It is 6.2% of your earned income but cannot be more than $400 ($800 if married filing jointly). Bona fide residents of Puerto Rico, American Samoa, the Commonwealth of the Northern Mariana Islands, Guam, and the U.S. Virgin Islands will receive this credit from their territorial governments.

Government retiree credit. For 2009, you may be able to take this credit if you receive a government pension or annuity. Bona fide residents of American Samoa and Puerto Rico who are not required to file Form 1040 can use this form to claim the credit. See the instructions for line 10 on page SS-4 for more information.

⚠ **CAUTION** At the time these instructions went to print, Congress was considering legislation that would change how bona fide residents of American Samoa and Puerto Rico will claim the government retiree credit. To find out if legislation was enacted, go to www.irs.gov.

Reminders

Electronic filing. You may be able to e-file Form 1040-SS if you are claiming **only** the additional child tax credit. For general information about electronic filing, visit *www.irs.gov/efile* and click on "Individual Taxpayers."

Estimated tax payments. If you expect to owe self-employment (SE) tax of $1,000 or more for 2010, you may have to make estimated tax payments. Use Form 1040-ES, Estimated Tax for Individuals, to figure your required payments and for the vouchers to send with your payments.

Purpose of Form

This form is for residents of the U.S. Virgin Islands (USVI), Guam, American Samoa, the Commonwealth of the Northern Mariana Islands (CNMI), and the Commonwealth of Puerto Rico (Puerto Rico) who are not required to file a U.S. income tax return. One purpose of the form is to report net earnings from self-employment to the United States and, if necessary, pay SE tax on that income. The Social Security Administration (SSA) uses this information to figure your benefits under the social security program. SE tax applies no matter how old you are and even if you already are receiving social security or Medicare benefits.

See *Who Must File* below for additional uses of this form.

You may also be required to file an income tax return with the government of Guam, American Samoa, the USVI, the CNMI, or Puerto Rico. Check with your local tax office for more details.

Who Must File

You must file Form 1040-SS if:

1. You, or your spouse if filing a joint return, had net earnings from self-employment (from other than church employee income) of $400 or more (or you had church employee income of $108.28 or more—see *Church Employees* on this page);
2. You do not have to file Form 1040 with the United States; and
3. You are a resident of:
   a. Guam,
   b. American Samoa,
   c. The USVI,
   d. The CNMI, or
   e. Puerto Rico (you can file either Form 1040-PR (in Spanish) or Form 1040-SS).

💡 **TIP** Even if you have a loss or little income from self-employment, it may benefit you to file Form 1040-SS and use either "optional method" in Part VI. See Part VI on page SS-8.

If (2) and (3) above apply, you also must file Form 1040-SS (or you can use Form 1040-PR in Spanish if you are a resident of Puerto Rico) to:
• Report and pay household employment taxes;

• Report and pay employee social security and Medicare tax on (a) unreported tips, (b) wages from an employer with no social security or Medicare tax withheld, or (c) uncollected social security and Medicare tax on tips or group-term life insurance (see the instructions for Part I, line 5, on page SS-3);
• Claim excess social security tax withheld;
• Claim the additional child tax credit (bona fide residents of Puerto Rico only);
• Claim the health coverage tax credit (bona fide residents of Puerto Rico only); and
• Claim the government retiree credit (bona fide residents of American Samoa and Puerto Rico only).

Who Must Pay SE Tax?

Self-Employed Persons
You must pay SE tax if you had net earnings of $400 or more as a self-employed person. If you are in business (farm or nonfarm) for yourself, you are self-employed.

You must also pay SE tax on your share of certain partnership income and your guaranteed payments. See *Partnership Income or Loss* beginning on page SS-6.

Church Employees
If you had church employee income of $108.28 or more, you must pay SE tax on that income. Church employee income is wages you received as an employee (other than as a minister or member of a religious order) of a church or qualified church-controlled organization that has a certificate in effect electing exemption from employer social security and Medicare taxes.

If your only income subject to self-employment tax is church employee income, skip lines 1a through 4b in Part V. Enter "-0-" on line 4c and go to line 5a.

Ministers and Members of Religious Orders
In most cases, you must pay SE tax on wages and other income for services you performed as a minister, a member of a religious order who has not taken a vow of poverty, or a Christian Science practitioner. But if you filed Form 4361, Application for Exemption From Self-Employment Tax for Use by

Cat. No. 26341Y

The IRS has hundreds of different forms. Here is one page of instructions from one such form, IRS Form 1040-SS, U.S. Self-Employment Tax Return.

Administrative rules—formal regulations issued by executive branch agencies, usually to carry out legislation.

Administrative Procedure Act—the 1946 law that set out the process by which federal executive agencies propose and issue regulations.

Accountability—the state of being responsible for official acts in which success means recognition and reward, while failure means some form of punishment.

tape, agency officials note that every form starts with somebody's demand for it.[14] In the case of the inventory, EPA officials would say that small businesses account for a large share of toxic substances, and that the government must track these materials.

Administrative Rules

Many federal laws delegate important decisions to the bureaucracy. The Federal Land Policy and Management Act, for example, directs the Interior Department to "promulgate rules and regulations to carry out the purposes of this Act and of other laws applicable to the public lands."[15] *Rules* and *regulations* mean the same thing, so we will use the shorter word and speak of **administrative rules**.

Congress finds it hard to avoid delegation. In drafting bills about clean water, lawmakers would have to put a vast effort into listing every pollutant, and it would be impractical for them to pass another law whenever polluters put out a new one. For such specifics, Congress relies on executive officials. Delegation can also serve a political purpose. Vague legislation allows lawmakers to shift responsibility for irksome details. The 1996 Telecommunications Act has dozens of provisions telling the Federal Communications Commission (FCC) to heed the "the public interest," but it fails to define the term. Critics say that the standard is so broad that it invites abuse, whereas supporters say that congressional intent is clear.[16]

Federal agencies issue thousands of rules each year. The effects surround us. If you look inside your bicycle helmet, you should see a warning label that it cannot protect you against all possible impacts and that serious injury could occur. The Consumer Products Safety Commission requires that warning.[17] If you open a package of prunes and notice that they are all about the same size, you may thank the U.S. Department of Agriculture. Its rules specify, "Not more than 5%, by count, of the plums or prunes in any package may vary more than one-fourth inch in diameter."[18] If your school wants to receive federal funds for work-study programs or other purposes, it must have accreditation under the rules of the U.S. Department of Education.[19]

The **Administrative Procedure Act** lays out the steps of the rulemaking process. First, the agency must post a notice of the proposed rule in the *Federal Register,* a daily publication. Second, the agency must let interested individuals and groups present views and information. Third, the agency must publish the final rule in the *Federal Register*, along with an explanation of purpose and responses to public comments. Fourth, the final rule goes into effect no sooner than 30 days after publication.

This process aims for **accountability** and deliberation. By reading the *Federal Register* and offering opinions, citizens can presumably follow what the bureaucracy is doing and help officials reason about public policy. One catch is the sheer mass of rulemaking. The 2011 volume of the *Federal Register* totaled 81,247 pages, or an average of 223 pages a day (see Figure 14-1). Much of this material is complex and highly specialized. Consider this example: "(A) Luffing boom tower cranes shall have a boom angle indicator readable from the operator's station. (B) Hammerhead tower cranes manufactured more than one year after the effective date of this subpart shall have a hook radius indicator readable from the operator's station."[20]

One may remember James Madison's warning against "laws that are so voluminous that they cannot be read, or so incoherent that they cannot be understood."[21] The rulemakers would argue that Congress has ordered them to handle technical issues that require specialized language. If they included less detail, critics would accuse them of vagueness. Yet regulatory officials have acknowledged that they could make their work more readable. The Clinton administration launched a "plain language" initiative to cut gobbledygook in federal rules. The effort goes on, and it has had some success (see www.plainlanguage.gov), but many rules remain hard for nonspecialists to decipher.

The major nongovernmental players in rulemaking are interest groups (see Chapter 8). Businesses and labor unions track rules from the Occupational Safety and Health Administration, while farmers and ranchers watch the Department of Agriculture. By providing agencies with arguments and data, these groups do make a mark on policy.[22] One view is that this process can improve rulemaking, because interest groups can educate the bureaucracy. Another view is that the process is a closed system. Although rulemaking may affect everyone, only an elite few take part. Adherents of this view might quote Madison: "Every new regulation concerning commerce or revenue . . . presents a new harvest to those who watch the change and can trace its consequences."[23]

To improve openness and deliberation, the government now puts proposed rules on the Internet. Citizens can post comments and read what others have said. Ideally, this process will allow policymakers to weigh a greater variety of views while deliberating on policy.[24] Although public comments can be helpful, it is not yet clear that ordinary citizens know about the system.

The Constitution vests the lawmaking power in Congress. In 1825, Chief Justice John Marshall wrote that "the maker of the law may commit something to the discretion of the other departments, and the precise boundary of this power is a subject of delicate and difficult inquiry."[25] The Supreme Court has only twice overturned laws on grounds of unconstitutional delegation. In *Panama Refining Co. v. Ryan* (1935), the Court invalidated a part of a law authorizing the executive branch to forbid certain interstate shipments of oil.[26] In *Schechter Poultry Corp. v. United States* (1935), the Court struck down other provisions of the law allowing "codes of fair competition." Justice Cardozo wrote, "This is delegation running riot."[27] The Administrative Procedure Act has since supplied safeguards that the Court found lacking.

The administrative state's boundaries also cross into another branch of the government. When agencies find violations of rules, or when the affected parties dispute an agency's interpretation, the case often goes to an **administrative law judge (ALJ)**. Despite their title, ALJs are part of the executive branch, not the judiciary. They preside over hearings, develop records, apply legal expertise, and render decisions.

The administrative state has important economic impacts. The **Office of Management and Budget (OMB)** studied 95 major federal rulemaking actions between 1999 and 2009.

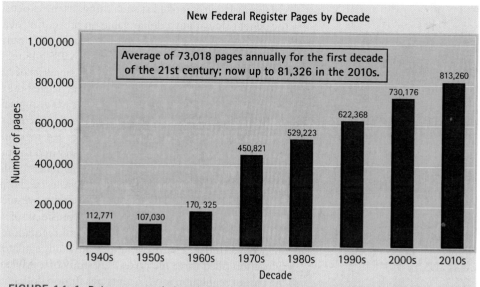

FIGURE 14–1 Rules may vary in length from just a few pages to several hundred. A very rough measure of the scope of regulation is the annual number of pages in the *Federal Register*. Although Democratic and Republican presidents alike have talked about curbing federal regulation, the trend has pointed upward since the 1950s. The figure for the 2010s is a projection based on a two-year average.
SOURCE: Clyde Wayne Crews Jr., *Ten Thousand Commandments 2012: An Annual Snapshot of the Federal Regulatory State* (Washington, DC: Competitive Enterprise Institute, 2012), cei.org/sites/default/files/Wayne%20Crews%20-%2010,000%20Commandments%202012_0.pdf, accessed July 13, 2012. The data exclude blank and jump pages.

Administrative law judge (ALJ)— a federal official who conducts hearings, makes findings, and offers recommendations for resolving disputes over an agency's actions.

Office of Management and Budget (OMB)—a White House office that drafts the president's budget message, prepares budget documents, advises the president on economic and regulatory matters, and oversees management of the federal government.

On the cost side, it looked at such things as the expense of pollution control equipment. On the benefit side, it put a dollar value on preventing death and injury, among other things. It estimated that total annual benefits of these rules ranged from $128 billion to $616 billion while the costs ranged from $43 billion to $55 billion.[28] Such figures are in dispute. Arguing that the OMB cost figure only involved a small set of rules, conservatives cited a 2010 report for the Small Business Administration that pegged the total cost of all rules at $1.75 trillion.[29] Conversely, an analyst for a liberal advocacy group said that the problem is not the cost of regulation: "Unfortunately, in many cases our current system is characterized by exactly the opposite problem: long delays before needed regulations are issued—often at substantial cost in lives and monetary costs to industry and the public."[30]

Colleges and universities must follow federal rules about student aid, labor relations, workplace safety, disposal of hazardous wastes, and other matters. In many ways, regulation has made these institutions safer, fairer, and more accessible to those with disabilities. But good things come at a cost. In 2011, the president of a small private college testified before a House committee that the list of federal regulations that apply to colleges covered nine single-spaced pages. The text of the rules and regulatory guidance from the Department of Education filled three file boxes.[31] A study of a private university in the Midwest reckoned the cost of regulation at 11.7 cents per tuition dollar.[32]

THE BUREAUCRACY'S STRUCTURE AND SIZE

MAJOR ISSUE

- Why is the bureaucracy so big and complicated?

Now that we have looked at what bureaucrats do, it is time to examine the organizations in which they work. Federal government organizations go by many names. The most familiar are the 15 departments whose secretaries belong to the president's cabinet. There are also independent agencies, including organizations such as the Environmental Protection Agency (EPA) and the National Aeronautics and Space Administration (NASA). Under law, there is little difference between a cabinet-level department and an independent agency. But cabinet status has political heft. Saying that their members should have a "seat at the cabinet table," veterans groups lobbied for a long time to "elevate" the Veterans Administration to the Department of Veterans Affairs. In 1988, Congress granted their wish.

Large government organizations may have many parts, which bear names such as *bureau, office,* or *administration*—and there are further subdivisions. The National Weather Service is part of the National Oceanic and Atmospheric Administration, which in turn is part of the Department of Commerce (see Figure 14-2).

Cabinet departments and independent agencies answer to the chief executive. Their heads are appointees of the president, who can fire them at will. **Independent regulatory commissions**, such as the FCC, are different. The president names the members and the chair, subject to Senate confirmation, but these officials serve fixed terms and are not subject to presidential dismissal, except for good cause, such as corruption. The basic idea is to shield members from political pressure, so they can deliberate in the public interest. These bodies set broad policies through administrative rules and enforce these policies in specific cases. The Supreme Court long ago upheld their constitutionality, saying that their duties are "neither political nor executive but predominantly quasi-judicial and quasi-legislative."[33]

The "quasi-judicial" and "quasi-legislative" tasks have been in the news. Crisis in the financial services industry led to charges of lax enforcement and prompted Congress to pass reform legislation in 2010. When the Federal Trade Commission (FTC) launched a "do not call" registry to block unwanted sales calls, telemarketers filed a lawsuit saying that it lacked authority. A court sided with the telemarketers, but Congress swiftly authorized the registry. Aggressive action by the independent regulatory commissions is nothing new. More than half a century ago, Justice Robert Jackson wrote that such bodies "have become a veritable fourth branch of the Government."[34]

Independent regulatory commission—a government organization that issues rules and conducts quasi-judicial proceedings. The president names the members and the chair of each commission, subject to Senate confirmation, but these officials serve fixed terms and are not subject to presidential dismissal without good cause.

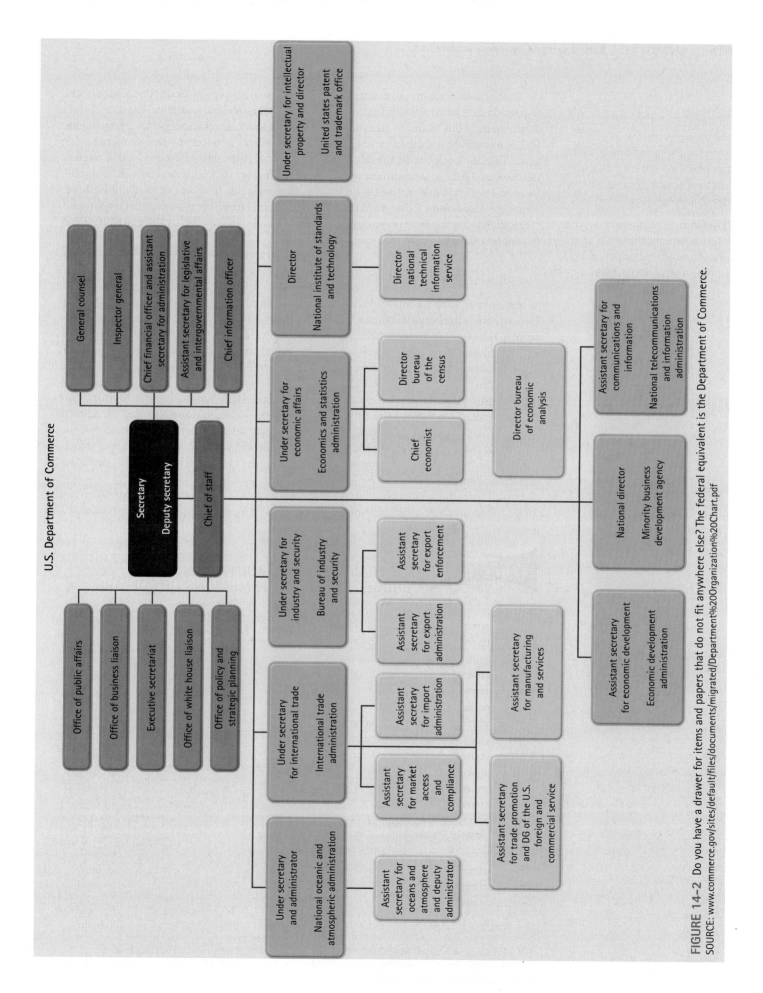

U.S. Department of Commerce

FIGURE 14–2 Do you have a drawer for items and papers that do not fit anywhere else? The federal equivalent is the Department of Commerce.

SOURCE: www.commerce.gov/sites/default/files/documents/migrated/Department%20Organization%20Chart.pdf

Government corporation—
a government-owned corporation that provides goods or services for which the private sector presumably cannot meet the need.

Government-sponsored enterprise (GSE)—a federally chartered but privately owned corporation that seeks to improve the flow of credit.

Congress has set up **government corporations** to supply goods or services when the free market seems to fall short. The U.S. Postal Service (USPS), which started as a cabinet department, is one example. Although many companies offer efficient package service, the USPS contends that it could not ensure low-cost delivery of letters to every American address. To keep USPS afloat, the law bans private competition for first-class mail. Congress has also established **government-sponsored enterprises (GSEs)**, privately held corporations that seek to improve the flow of credit. Two such corporations, the Federal National Mortgage Association ("Fannie Mae") and the Federal Home Loan Mortgage Corporation ("Freddie Mac"), arguably played a part in the financial crisis of 2008 by underwriting loans to people who could not afford them.

Jurisdiction

When a major issue has multiple dimensions, it is hard to map jurisdiction. "The Interior Department is in charge of salmon while they're in fresh water, but the Commerce Department handles them when they're in saltwater," said President Obama in his 2011 State of the Union address. "I hear it gets even more complicated once they're smoked."[35]

As Table 14-1 suggests, nearly every major federal organization has some stake in the issue of drug control. During the 1980s, many lawmakers said that lack of coordination hindered the war on drugs. They cited cases where the Drug Enforcement Administration (DEA) ignored leads from the Customs Service and where various agencies all claimed credit for the same seizures of drug profits, thereby inflating government statistics.[36] Congress then created the Office of National Drug Control Policy to coordinate federal efforts against drug abuse. Without direct authority over agency budgets, however, this office has had limited success.

Additional concerns about bureaucratic coordination arose after the terror attacks of 2001. "If you look at a diagram of all the entities in Washington addressing terrorism,"

TABLE 14-1	FEDERAL DRUG CONTROL FUNDING, 2011 BUDGET AUTHORITY IN MILLIONS OF DOLLARS
Department of Agriculture	15.3
Court Services and Offender Supervision Agency for the District of Columbia	52.8
Department of Defense	1,836.5
Department of Education	123.9
Federal Judiciary	1,126.9
Department of Health and Human Services	8,459.2
Department of Homeland Security	4,209.9
Department of Housing and Urban Development	464.2
Department of the Interior	18.4
Department of Justice	7,461.3
Department of Labor	6.6
Office of National Drug Control Policy	406.2
Small Business Administration	1.0
Department of State	773.9
Department of Transportation	30.6
Department of the Treasury	60.1
Department of Veterans Affairs	532.9
Total	$25,579.7

SOURCE: Office of National Drug Control Policy, *The National Drug Control Budget: FY 2013 Funding Highlights,* February 2012, www.whitehouse.gov/ondcp/the-national-drug-control-budget-fy-2013-funding-highlights, accessed August 20, 2012.

said one expert, "it looks like a bowl of spaghetti."[37] President George W. Bush established a White House "czar" for homeland security, but as with the "drug czar," lack of authority became a problem. Congress's answer was the largest reorganization since the birth of the Defense Department in 1947. The new Department of Homeland Security (DHS) combined 22 existing organizations. The reorganization created its own jurisdictional tangles. On the one hand, many other government organizations still dealt with aspects of homeland security. "Turf battles" were inevitable, and the new department has fought with the Defense Department, the FBI, and other government agencies.[38] On the other hand, DHS took in organizations with many duties unrelated to homeland security.

The Department of Homeland Security's National Operations Center, the nation's nerve center for information sharing and domestic incident management, which coordinates antiterrorism efforts of federal, state, territorial, tribal, and local governments, as well as the private sector.

One is the Coast Guard, which has five broad missions: maritime safety, maritime security, mobility of goods and people, protection of natural resources, and national defense. Since Congress established the Coast Guard in 1915, writes journalist Timothy Noah, it has been "the rolling stone of U.S. government agencies."[39] At first, one of its biggest jobs was to stop smugglers who were evading tariffs, so it was natural that Congress kept it in the Treasury Department. During World Wars I and II, it temporarily moved to the Navy Department (which later became part of the Defense Department). Treasury remained its home until 1967, when Congress put it in the new Transportation Department. There it stayed until the homeland security reorganization.

Coordination problems plagued the federal response to the 2010 oil spill in the Gulf of Mexico. There was initial confusion about the size and scope of the spill. "It's a lot like Custer," said former senator Bob Graham (D-FL), co-chair of a presidential commission that investigated the incident, referring to the 1876 battle that killed General George Armstrong Custer and most of his troops. "He underestimated the number of Indians on the other side of the hill and paid the ultimate price." Local official Billy Nungesser criticized coordination by the command post in Houma, Louisiana. "It became a joke," he said. "The Houma command was the Wizard of Oz, some guy behind the curtain."[40]

As we discussed in Chapter 3 on federalism, multiple layers of government make jurisdictional issues even more complex. State and local agencies may overlap with federal agencies, and with one another. In California, for instance, policy on elementary and secondary education may involve the federal Department of Education, the state Board of Education, the state superintendent of public instruction, the state secretary of education, and 977 different school districts.

Size of Government

In addition to jurisdictional questions, the sheer size of the federal government is an issue. Just before the financial crisis of 2008, federal spending took a *smaller* share of gross domestic product (20.8% in fiscal 2008) than it did two decades before (21.3% in fiscal 1988). When the crisis hit, however, gross domestic product shrank, and Congress stepped up spending in order to stimulate the economy. As a result, the figure exceeded 25%, the highest since World War II.[41] Although the United States has tended to spend less on government than many other nations, such changes may affect its relative standing.

Figures on government employment (see Figure 14-3) offer a different picture of the size of government. The federal civilian workforce actually shrank in the last decades of the twentieth century, then grew again in the early years of the twenty-first century. Meanwhile, state and local payrolls tended to increase until the post-2008 recession forced cutbacks. Much of the increase reflected federal mandates. Moreover, the federal government has increasingly relied on **outsourcing**, giving grants or contracts to the private sector. According to one estimate, more than 10 million jobs came from federal grants and contracts in 2005,

Outsourcing—in the context of public policy, the practice of carrying out government functions by giving grants or contracts to the private sector.

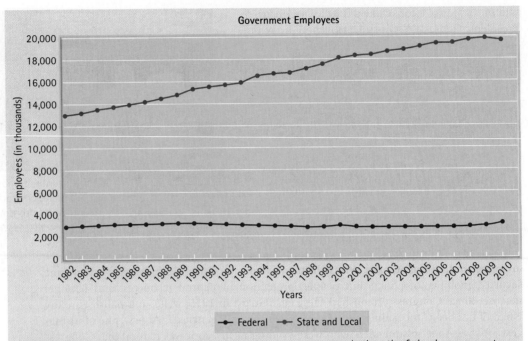

FIGURE 14-3 State and local governments employ many more people than the federal government.
SOURCE: U.S. Department of Commerce, United States Census Bureau, *2012 Statistical Abstract of the United States,* www.census.gov/compendia/statab/cats/state_local_govt_finances_employment.html; U.S. Department of Commerce, United States Census Bureau, Annual Survey of Government Employment & Payroll, August 30, 2011, www.census.gov/govs/apes, accessed July 13, 2012.

up from 7.5 million in 1990.[42] If you measure the size of the federal government by its civilian and military workforce plus its grantees and contractors, you get a very different picture. Between 1990 and 2005, this total increased from 12.6 million to 14.6 million.

Government programs grow for many reasons, including pressures from powerful constituency groups. Federal employees have themselves become an important political force, as we shall now see.

BUREAUCRATS AND BUREAUCRATIC POLITICS
MAJOR ISSUE

- How does government define, measure, and encourage good performance by its employees? And how do these employees seek to influence policy?

Merit system—a government personnel practice in which hiring and promotion hinges on individual qualification instead of political affiliation.

Spoils system—the practice of giving jobs or contracts on the basis of political ties instead of merit.

Pendleton Act (Civil Service Reform Act)—an 1883 federal law that set up a merit-based system for choosing government employees and supervising their work.

Presidential appointees fill only a few thousand of more than 2 million federal jobs. The rest serve under **merit systems**, which means that they do not lose their jobs simply because a new administration comes to power.

It was not always so. Under the **spoils system** of the nineteenth century, government posts went to the administration's political supporters, who were often unqualified. When the White House changed parties, novices replaced experienced workers. Corruption was common, and the problem got worse as federal civil employment grew from 26,274 in 1851 to 100,020 in 1881.[43] The latter year saw the assassination of President James A. Garfield. Newspapers reported that the assassin resented Garfield for spurning his pleas for a federal job. The stories fueled the movement for reform. Two years later, Congress passed the **Pendleton Act** (the Civil Service Reform Act), which required examinations for particular jobs. The law also set up the Civil Service Commission to run a personnel system on merit.

By the early twentieth century, merit hiring had become the norm for federal employees. As the bureaucracy grew, public servants gained protections against arbitrary firing, and the Civil Service Commission settled employee disputes. Critics said that one body should not set the rules and settle disputes arising from those rules.[44] In 1978, President Carter persuaded Congress to overhaul the federal employment system. The reform replaced the Civil Service Commission with new bodies, including the Office of Personnel Management, which would now set federal personnel policy.[45]

Until the middle of the twentieth century, most policymakers thought that government workers should not join unions. Major New Deal labor laws excluded public employees. In 1962, President Kennedy signed an executive order giving federal workers the right to unionize and bargain collectively. With another executive order in 1969, President Nixon strengthened those rights. The 1978 reform included a Federal Labor Relations Authority to administer relations with public-employee unions. These changes fostered the growth of these unions. In 2011, 33.2% of the federal workforce had union representation, compared with just 7.6% of private workers.[46]

The American Federation of Government Employees supported President Obama for reelection in 2012.

In dealing with employers, federal unions lack a tool that the private sector counterparts enjoy: the right to strike. In 1981, when air traffic controllers broke the "no-strike" condition of their employment, President Reagan fired them. But government workers do have unique leverage, because they help choose their ultimate bosses: elected officials. Together with retirees and adult kin, federal employees add up to a weighty voting bloc. They have particular clout in areas near major federal facilities. Lawmakers from these areas serve as advocates for the federal workforce.

In 1939, Congress passed the **Hatch Act**, which barred federal employees from most partisan political activities. In 1993, Congress amended the Hatch Act. While the law still forbids federal employees to engage in partisan activity on the job or to run in partisan elections, most may now use their off-duty hours on partisan campaigns. Accordingly, federal employee unions and their political action committees have become a major political force. Their get-out-the-vote drives played a part in helping Democrats win control of Congress in 2006 and the White House in 2008 (see the photo).

Federal unions hire lobbyists. Because of the workers' political power, these lobbyists can catch the eye of lawmakers. When homeland security became an issue, they helped ensure that airport screeners would be federal employees. They were less successful with the new Department of Homeland Security. Over their objections, President Bush got Congress to give the department unusual leeway in setting work rules.

Hatch Act—a law restricting the political activities of federal employees. In 1993, Congress relaxed the restrictions.

Performance

Federal employees are subject to firing for misconduct or poor work, but civil service protections often hinder dismissal. Employees have a right to appeal, which can take months. Government executives often fail to support supervisors who want to fire an employee because they would rather avoid the time and paperwork that such a move would take. Estimates of "poor performers" in the federal workplace range from 4% to 14%.[47] In a 2011 survey, only 31% of federal employees said that their work units would take steps against poor performers who could not or would not improve.[48] Although most federal workers are competent, the poor performers cause disproportionate trouble, undermining morale and marring the public image of civil servants. One bad scrape with a bureaucrat is more likely to stick in a citizen's memory than a dozen cases of good service.

Much the same is true with the issue of waste, fraud, and abuse. During the 1980s, a federal study panel catalogued horror stories such as the Pentagon's purchase of three-cent screws for $91 apiece. Many of the stories proved wrong. In the case of the screws, the report's writers did not know how to read the accounting books.[49] Nevertheless, government waste is hardly a trivial issue. The Government Accountability Office (GAO) estimates that the federal government made $115 billion in improper payments in fiscal year 2011.[50]

Questions about the bureaucracy's performance go beyond bad employees and needless expenses. How can citizens and elected officials tell how well a government organization is working? It is fairly straightforward to measure government activity by *inputs*, such as how much money goes into a program, or how many staffers it employs. Such figures tell little about *outcomes*—how the program helps or hurts people.[51] Performance measurements prompt disagreement. Many teachers fault educational testing, arguing that tests shed little light on how students fare. They also say that the testing itself is costly and distorts the educational mission of public schools. Answering such arguments, President George W. Bush told Congress in 2001, "If you test a child on basic math and reading skills, and you're teaching to the test, you're teaching math and reading. And that's the whole idea."[52]

When the government does find a reliable measurement for an outcome, then comes the problem of responsibility. In a federal system with 89,000 governments (e.g., states, counties, cities, school districts), where different levels share responsibility and where different agencies may deal with different aspects of a problem, it can be hard to assign credit or blame. If test scores drop, is the U.S. Department of Education responsible? Or does the problem lie with state education departments? Or local school boards?

The division of labor can also create confusion. At an Illinois town meeting with President Obama, a farmer raised concerns about rules on noise and dust. The president told him to get in touch with the U.S. Department of Agriculture (USDA). A reporter did so and found that it can be difficult to get an answer:

> **Wednesday, 2:40 p.m. ET:** After calling the USDA's main line, I am told to call the Illinois Department of Agriculture. Here, I am patched through to a man who is identified as being in charge of "support services." I leave a message.
>
> **3:53 p.m.:** The man calls me back and recommends in a voicemail message that I call the Illinois Farm Bureau—a nongovernmental organization.
>
> **4:02 p.m.:** A woman at the Illinois Farm Bureau connects me to someone in the organization's government affairs department. That person tells me they "don't quite know who to refer you to."
>
> **4:06 p.m.:** I call the Illinois Department of Agriculture again, letting the person I spoke with earlier know that calling the Illinois Farm Bureau had not been fruitful. He says "those are the kinds of groups that are kind of on top of this or kind of follow things like this. We deal with pesticide here in our bureau." "You only deal with pesticides?" I ask. "We deal with other things . . . but we mainly deal with pesticides here," he says, and gives me the phone number for the office of the department's director, where he says there are "policy people" as well as the director's staff.
>
> **4:10 p.m.:** Someone at the director's office transfers me to the agriculture products inspection department, where a woman says their branch deals with things like animal feed, seed, and fertilizer. "I'm going to transfer you to one of the guys at environmental programs."

Several more rounds of telephone calls followed, but the reporter never did get an answer to the question.[53]

Organizational Culture

A bureaucracy's performance depends in part on its **organizational culture**, its members' shared beliefs about how they should deal with problems and carry on their daily tasks. In other words, it is "the way we do things here."

During the 1960s, NASA showed how a strong organizational culture could succeed. From astronauts to janitors, nearly everyone at NASA harbored a passion for putting

FOCUS QUESTION

As in the case of dust and agriculture, is it always obvious as to which agency or level of government should have jurisdiction over an issue?

Organizational culture—shared beliefs within an organization about how its members should deal with problems and carry on their daily tasks. It is "the way we do things here."

Americans on the moon. NASA people thought that hard work could sweep away every obstacle. Gene Kranz, the flight director at NASA's Mission Control from 1962 to 1974, summed up the attitude: "Failure is not an option."

Failure becomes an option when an organizational culture fails to adapt to new circumstances. The "can-do" spirit worked when Congress was adding billions to the space program's budget. In the 1970s and 1980s, funding waned along with public enthusiasm and sense of mission. Although NASA had to make do with less money, its administrators still thought that they could meet an ambitious schedule for the space shuttle. Flight after flight took place without serious incident, which reinforced NASA's confidence. In 1986, however, *Challenger* blew up shortly after takeoff. To probe the fatal accident, President Reagan named a special commission, which criticized NASA. The agency made administrative changes, but its basic culture remained intact.

Seventeen years and dozens of additional flights had restored NASA's sense of invincibility when *Columbia* burned up on reentry in early 2003. Another investigative board faulted the "can-do" attitude. NASA workers could often beat deadlines, said the board, but "those same people (and this same culture) have difficulty admitting that something 'can't' or 'shouldn't' be done . . . or that resources are being stretched too thin. No one at NASA wants to be the one to stand up and say, 'We can't make that date.'"[54]

If organizational culture rendered NASA too bold, it has also made other bureaucracies too timid. Through 2005, Federal Emergency Management Agency (FEMA) did not see its role in a disaster as the command of "first responders." That was the job of state and local governments. Instead, FEMA would coordinate other federal bureaucracies while providing money and information to those on the scene. After Hurricane Katrina overwhelmed the police and fire departments of the Gulf Coast, FEMA was slow to move. The agency asked firefighters nationwide to volunteer for the recovery effort. When they answered the call, however, they learned that FEMA wanted them to hand out pamphlets, not join in emergency work. Before they could start, they had to undergo training about diversity, sexual harassment, and data input.[55]

One source of an organization's culture lies in the shared expertise of its members. Sometimes a certain profession naturally dominates a bureaucracy, as with lawyers at the Department of Justice or public health physicians at the Centers for Disease Control and Prevention (CDC). A profession's mind-set may lend clarity and direction to a bureaucracy, but it can also create conflict. The CDC defines the spread of sexually transmitted diseases as a public health problem that requires a medical response. Critics say that it overlooks moral concerns that are crucial to changing behavior.

When a bureaucracy has diverse tasks, it may have trouble maintaining a positive organizational culture. The Department of Homeland Security (DHS) comprises FEMA, the Coast Guard, the Secret Service, and other units that had little to do with one another before the reorganization. No single profession dominates DHS, and its disparate parts have different perspectives. Lacking a clear central mission, its employees suffer from low morale and deep doubts about the department's effectiveness (see Figure 14-4).

Iron Triangles, Issue Networks, Policy Communities

Bureaucrats spend much of their time with interest group representatives, lawmakers, and congressional committee staff. Obviously, all have an interest in the issues at hand. They may also have similar professional

NASA Headquarters—Greatest Images of NASA (NASA-HQ-GRIN)

In 1986, *Challenger* blew up during its ascent.

FOCUS
QUESTION

How can a given organizational culture be both a defect and a virtue at the same time?

Leah Hogsten/The Salt Lake Tribune

Seven weeks after Hurricane Katrina hit the Gulf Coast, a disabled Mississippi resident was still living in a tent and pondering correspondence from the Federal Emergency Management Agency.

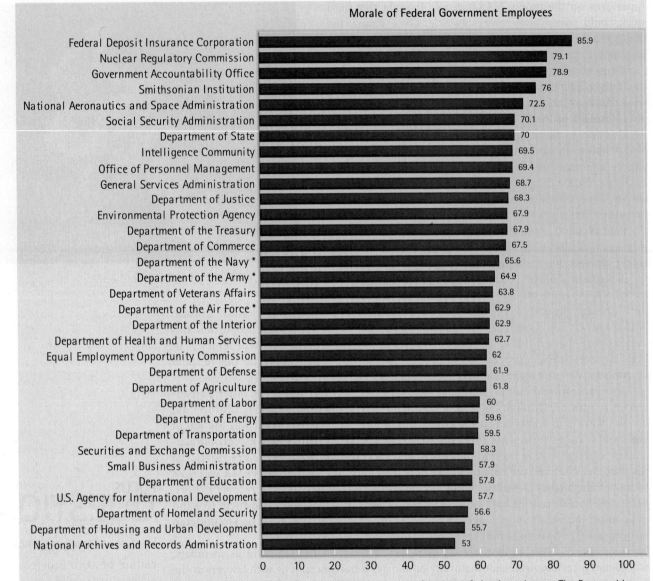

Morale of Federal Government Employees

Agency	Score
Federal Deposit Insurance Corporation	85.9
Nuclear Regulatory Commission	79.1
Government Accountability Office	78.9
Smithsonian Institution	76
National Aeronautics and Space Administration	72.5
Social Security Administration	70.1
Department of State	70
Intelligence Community	69.5
Office of Personnel Management	69.4
General Services Administration	68.7
Department of Justice	68.3
Environmental Protection Agency	67.9
Department of the Treasury	67.9
Department of Commerce	67.5
Department of the Navy *	65.6
Department of the Army *	64.9
Department of Veterans Affairs	63.8
Department of the Air Force *	62.9
Department of the Interior	62.9
Department of Health and Human Services	62.7
Equal Employment Opportunity Commission	62
Department of Defense	61.9
Department of Agriculture	61.8
Department of Labor	60
Department of Energy	59.6
Department of Transportation	59.5
Securities and Exchange Commission	58.3
Small Business Administration	57.9
Department of Education	57.8
U.S. Agency for International Development	57.7
Department of Homeland Security	56.6
Department of Housing and Urban Development	55.7
National Archives and Records Administration	53

FIGURE 14-4 In 2011, the Office of Personnel Management published a survey of 266,000 federal employees. The Partnership for Public Service used these data to calculate an index of workplace satisfaction. The higher the score, the more satisfied the employees.

SOURCE: http://bestplacestowork.org/BPTW/rankings/overall/large

Iron triangle—the political alliance of executive branch agencies, congressional committees, and interest groups.

Issue networks—loose groupings of people and organizations that seek to influence policy, including not only the members of the traditional iron triangle but also policy experts in universities, think tanks, and the media. Also called policy communities.

backgrounds, and some may have worked together in past jobs. Observers often refer to the relationship of bureaucracy, interest group, and congressional committee as an **iron triangle**. The term summons up an image of lasting unity, which is too simple. On certain issues, the relevant interest groups may work together while on others they may clash. With alliances in flux, it is more accurate to speak of **issue networks** or *policy communities*. These terms refer to loose groupings of people and organizations that seek to influence policy. They include not only the members of the traditional iron triangle but also policy experts in universities, think tanks, and the media. Environmental issues, for instance, involve multiple executive organizations, congressional committees, and levels of government. They engage many sets of competing economic interests: upstream polluters versus downstream fisheries, developers versus homeowner groups, high-sulfur coal versus low-sulfur coal. In the deliberative process, these interests may draw information and arguments from environmental research organizations and university scientists.

Bureaucrats may try to influence lawmakers and congressional staffers within their issue network. Surprisingly, a strict reading of the law would suggest that at least some of these efforts are legally questionable. A federal statute forbids bureaucrats from spending government funds to "influence in any manner a Member of Congress, to favor or oppose . . . any legislation or appropriation by Congress."[56] The law also bans bureaucrats from mounting substantial grassroots campaigns on pending bills.[57] In practice, this law has had little impact. Every major executive branch organization has a unit that seeks to influence Congress, usually with the name "Office of Congressional and Legislative Affairs." Nodding to the law, these offices typically do not say that they "lobby" but rather "make *accurate* information promptly available to Congress."[58] This information may take the form of letters, reports, briefings, and testimony. "Public affairs" offices do the same for the news media and social media (see The Impact of Social Media and Communications Technology feature). Accordingly, the Justice Department has never prosecuted anybody for violating the Anti-Lobbying Act.

An indirect channel of bureaucratic influence is the placement of detailees on Capitol Hill. Departments and agencies frequently "lend" or "detail" employees to congressional offices for temporary assignments. Supporters of the practice say that it provides lawmakers with technical help and allows them to understand the executive branch. It also enables bureaucrats to learn about Congress while befriending lawmakers and their aides. Critics say that it thus gives the bureaucracy an unfair "inside track."

Dissent and Resistance

In principle, career civil servants carry out the lawful directives of presidents and their appointees. How do they react when they disagree with those directives?

One option is to voice their views internally, either through private memoranda or discussions with administration officials. Such debate can enhance deliberation within the executive branch. Because of their expertise and insulation from public opinion, career

Bureaucrats Gain and Lose from Social Media

Government agencies make abundant use of social media to keep citizens up to date on their activities. For instance, the FBI Facebook page (www.facebook.com/FBI) provides information about ongoing investigations. On May 20, 2011, the Bessette-Pitney blog noted that the Centers for Disease Control had a blog post about a "zombie apocalypse," a lighthearted way of conveying a serious message about disaster preparation.

Sometimes the information bears directly on legislation pending before Congress. After the House passed an appropriations bill cutting certain programs of the Census Bureau, the director used his blog to argue that the move would have harmful consequences. On May 21, 2012, the Bessette-Pitney blog presented video of the director's case.

Social media can also cause trouble for bureaucrats. In a 2010 talk, the head of the EPA's Dallas office said that his method for dealing with noncompliant oil and gas companies was like that of the ancient Romans, who would go into small towns and crucify people at random. A video camera captured the talk, which went up on YouTube. Few noticed until 2012, when staffers for Senator James Inhofe (R-OK) spotted it and posted the controversial remark on the

senator's YouTube channel. As the Bessette-Pitney blog noted on April 30, 2012, the clip quickly went viral. After angry reactions from the energy industry, as well as lawmakers from oil-producing states, the official had to resign.

Around the same time, the office of House Committee on Oversight and Government Reform chair Darrell Issa (R-CA) posted "gag videos" by employees of the General Services Administration (GSA). In one video, a GSA employee sang a song bragging about the wasteful things he would do if he were in charge. In another, employees joked that their environmentally friendly initiatives were intended to get better media coverage for President Obama. (See Bessette-Pitney blog of April 9 and 10, 2012.)

CRITICAL THINKING QUESTION

How will the fear of a "YouTube moment" affect the ability of public officials to discuss issues freely in public forums?

bureaucrats can offer insights into the long-term effects of pending decisions.[59] Whereas political executives may want to act quickly, career bureaucrats can draw on long memories to note cases where quick action led to disaster. Accordingly, wise executives will include veteran bureaucrats at some stage of policy deliberation. During the Reagan administration, for instance, career attorneys at the Justice Department's Civil Rights Division frequently argued with the political appointee who headed the division.[60]

Another course is to go "outside" and work with others in the relevant issue network. To avoid open conflict with their superiors, dissenting bureaucrats may leak information to allies in Congress, the interest group community, or the press. Sometimes the fight breaks into the open. In 2003, two career employees of the National Park Service appeared at an environmental group's news conference. Wearing dark glasses, hats, and scarves, and speaking through an electronic "voice disguiser," they denounced the George W. Bush administration for its policies toward national parks.[61]

A final option is to resist implementation of a policy. Although cases of outright sabotage are rare, critics frequently charge bureaucrats with "dragging their feet" on policies that they would prefer not to carry out. Slowness in bureaucratic action can have many sources, including the requirements of the Administrative Procedure Act. It can thus be very hard to distinguish intentional foot-dragging from inevitable delay.

Bureaucrats' Sense of Citizenship

Civil service protection and the favor of politicians might tempt bureaucrats to get away with being less diligent. Yet according to a Brookings Institution survey, more than three-fourths of political appointees found the bureaucrats with whom they worked to be both responsive and competent. Figures were similar for Republican and Democratic administrations.[62]

So why do career officials cooperate so readily with political executives? One reason is that they are citizens as well as bureaucrats. Constant resistance and stalemate would hurt the system, and although bureaucrats take account of their self-interest, they do have some concern for the greater good. Like lawmakers and military officers, civil servants must swear an oath that they will "well and faithfully discharge" their official duties. In interviews with political scientist Marissa Martino Golden, two career civil servants explained their attitude toward political executives:

> "If they want policy changed and it's not outside the law and morality, you have a responsibility to assist them in implementing policies."

> "Once you have explained the implications as you see them, you have to carry out the policy to the best of your ability."[63]

CONTROL AND OVERSIGHT
MAJOR ISSUE

- How do individuals and institutions keep the bureaucracy within the bounds of law, ethics, and administration policy?

The federal bureaucracy is vast and complex. Most of its employees enjoy at least some measure of job security under the law. It can be hard for elected officials and ordinary citizens to make sure that the bureaucracy is doing what it is supposed to be doing. To aid in this task, a variety of formal and informal mechanisms exist to monitor and check bureaucratic activity.

Executive Branch

Although most federal employment comes under merit hiring, the president can place political appointees in key policymaking jobs. A list of these positions appears in a publication titled *United States Government Policy and Supporting Positions*, which most know as

"The Plum Book."[64] The people in these "plum" jobs can try to steer the bureaucracy in the direction that the president wants. Accordingly, the Office of Presidential Personnel screens candidates for these positions, with an eye to two key qualities.

The first is loyalty to the president's agenda. The White House seeks political appointees who agree with its policies. Sometimes their enthusiasm wanes as they come under the sway of career bureaucrats. To prevent such "capture," recent administrations have held regular briefings for their appointees.[65] A few appointees fail to get the message, and they have short, unhappy tenures. In early 2002, an assistant secretary of the army testified before the Senate Budget Committee that the president was asking for too little money for the Army Corps of Engineers. The Bush White House forced him to resign. "The president welcomes a healthy debate," explained the president's press secretary, "but once the debate is settled and the president has proposed a budget, the president does think it's reasonable for the people who work for him to support the budget."[66]

The second quality is knowledge. Donald Devine, former director of the Office of Personnel Management, put it this way: "It is critical to know the details of administration, because if he does not, the political leader will lose control of policy, which is his first responsibility."[67] Presidents often look for policy experts, but sometimes they turn to people who have a more general background in government or management, and who can master the policy details. In 2011, President Obama chose CIA director Leon Panetta to head the Defense Department. Apart from a stint in the army in his youth, Panetta did not have a background in the military, but he did have wide-ranging government experience and a reputation as a quick study.

Presidents have broad discretion in hiring and firing political appointees, but their choices sometimes draw criticism. President George W. Bush and Attorney General Alberto Gonzales came under attack for the dismissal of several federal prosecutors. One of the fired officials wrote that prosecutors are different from other political appointees: "Although we receive our appointments through the political process (I am a Republican who was recommended by Senator Pete Domenici), we are expected to be apolitical once we are in office."[68] He said that the administration had strayed from this tradition. He explained that he and others had lost their jobs because they had not been aggressive enough in pursuing allegations of misconduct by Democrats.

Besides personnel selection, the president has other tools for controlling the bureaucracy. In drafting spending plans, the Office of Management and Budget (OMB) evaluates how well federal agencies are adhering to the president's policies. A unit of OMB, the **Office of Information and Regulatory Affairs (OIRA)**, sets federal policy on statistics and reviews draft rules before publication. If a draft rule clashes with policy, OIRA can send it back for revision.

The system has not always worked. In 1981, the Agriculture Department issued a proposed rule that would have classified ketchup as a vegetable for the purposes of the federal school lunch program. The idea was to save money, but the effect was to subject the Reagan administration to mockery. The controversy surprised the White House, because Agriculture had not submitted the proposal for OIRA review. In the face of budget cuts, the department had issued it under an emergency procedure.[69] OMB director David Stockman quickly withdrew it, but the damage lingered. Ironically, the Agriculture Department won praise 17 years later, when it conferred vegetable status on salsa.[70]

White House liaisons offer the president another way to drive the bureaucracy. These officials are political appointees who serve in departments and agencies to make sure that they respond to the president's policies and interests (see Chapter 13).

Inspectors General

In 1978, Congress provided for offices of **inspector general (IG)** in federal organizations. These offices were to run independent investigations into bureaucratic operations and make recommendations to stop waste. The president names inspectors general at cabinet departments and major agencies, subject to Senate confirmation. Heads of other agencies pick their own inspectors general. There are 73 such offices, with about 14,700 staff.[71] Over the

---

Office of Information and Regulatory Affairs (OIRA)—a unit of the Office of Management and Budget that sets federal policy on statistics and reviews draft rules before publication.

Inspector general (IG)—an official within federal agencies who runs independent investigations into bureaucratic operations and makes recommendations to stop waste.

"These projected figures are a figment of our imagination. We hope you like them."

There is a basic irony about hiring bureaucrats to gather information about bureaucracy.

Whistleblower—a federal employee who reports waste, fraud, or misconduct.

Government Accountability Office (GAO)—formerly the General Accounting Office, an independent, nonpartisan agency that works for Congress. GAO investigates how the federal government spends taxpayer dollars.

Congressional Review Act—a federal law that requires agencies to send rules to Congress for review 60 days before they take effect.

years, these offices have reportedly saved billions of dollars and referred thousands of cases for legal action. They have also run into political storms. During the 2004 presidential campaign, Democratic candidate John Kerry attacked the George W. Bush administration by citing reports by the Department of Homeland Security's IG. In an interview three years later, the inspector general said that he supported President Bush. "I hoped he would be re-elected, but IGs can't time their reports to minimize political consequences to the administration that appoints them. If my job results in political perils for the president, so be it."[72] Several years later, Republicans criticized President Obama for slowness in filling IG vacancies.[73]

Inspectors general often receive their initial information from **whistleblowers**, public employees who suspect waste or misconduct and decide to report on it. Under federal law, superiors may not retaliate against whistleblowers.

Congress

In dealing with the bureaucracy, Congress has a split personality. As we have seen, members and their aides quietly collaborate with bureaucrats. In several ways, however, Congress also checks the administrative state.

Constituent complaints about an agency may spur members to look further. Congressional aides in Washington and in district offices spend a great deal of time tracking and questioning the actions of the federal bureaucracy. Committee hearings can hold bureaucrats to account, especially when Congress is reviewing budgets. The House and Senate Appropriations Committees annually require officials to tell how they spend public funds. By holding the purse strings, these committees can supervise the bureaucracy in great detail. During the 1980s, Representative Charles Wilson (D-TX) learned that the Central Intelligence Agency (CIA) was funding opposition to the Soviet occupation of Afghanistan but lacked a plan to drive out the invaders. He helped make the CIA take a more aggressive posture.[74] A popular movie recounted his efforts, though with a good deal of artistic license.

The **Government Accountability Office (GAO)**, a congressional agency, evaluates programs and audits expenditures. Lawmakers rely on GAO reports, which are available to the general public at www.gao.gov. The Congressional Research Service and the Congressional Budget Office also study the operations of the administrative state.

Congress can overturn actions of the bureaucracy through legislation. In 1996, lawmakers passed the **Congressional Review Act**, which requires agencies to send rules to Capitol Hill for review 60 days before they take effect. If Congress passes a joint resolution of disapproval, and it becomes law through presidential signature or veto override, the rule cannot go into effect. Without congressional permission, the agency cannot reissue the rule.[75] The law's critics say that it slows rulemaking and disrespects the judgment of career officials. Proponents respond, however, that it enables Congress to make the final decision on the need for specific rules. Although Congress has killed only one regulation this way (an extensive rule on workplace injuries), the very possibility of such action encourages regulators to keep congressional preferences in mind.

Courts

Congress not only checks the administrative state, but it has invited the judiciary to do so as well. Many federal environmental laws allow "citizen suits" against alleged polluters. The idea is to give people a way to enforce the law when the bureaucracy either cannot or will not act. During the 1990s, some court decisions raised doubts about citizen suits, but in 2000, the Supreme Court gave them qualified support.[76]

At one time, the judiciary hesitated to step into bureaucratic affairs. Courts now frequently review rules and other decisions of the administrative state. In 2007, for instance, the Supreme Court ruled that the EPA had violated federal law by declining to regulate tailpipe emissions of greenhouse gases.[77] Although judicial review guards against bureaucratic abuses, it may also cause officials to "cover themselves" against litigation with needless delay and red tape. There are limits to judicial intervention. In 1984, the Supreme Court ruled that when a statute is vague, the judiciary should follow the congressional intent on the issue in question. If intent is unclear, then the courts should defer to the bureaucracy's interpretation, as long as it stays within the letter of the law.[78]

One drawback of litigation is the reliance on courts to resolve technical issues. While bureaucrats often have the training and resources to deliberate about such matters, judges and jurors seldom do. Attorney Edward Warren described what happens: "What we are asking jurors to do is to decide between competing experts who are presenting testimony that is beyond their comprehension."[79]

Press and Public Opinion

One might think that the news media are a powerful check on the administrative state. The "glare of publicity" can arouse public opinion against bureaucratic overreaching or misconduct, and from time to time, scandals and other dramatic stories do catch public attention, particularly when they involve high-profile bureaucracies. During Hurricane Katrina, cable news networks pursued FEMA for its slow reaction. As bad as the situation was, some of the coverage exaggerated it (see the Myths and Misinformation feature below).

Most of the time, the media overlook the bureaucracy. Because of limited resources or lack of audience interest, news organizations have shied away from covering most administrative actions. According to one journalist, "Reporters so rarely go to the federal agencies anymore that many pressrooms have grown dusty and little-used, or, in some cases, have been completely eliminated."[83] Specialized publications and Web sites monitor the administrative state, but they cater to issue networks, not ordinary citizens.

MYTHS AND MISINFORMATION

Katrina

When Hurricane Katrina devastated New Orleans in 2005, it quickly became clear that officials at all levels of government had responded too slowly. The Federal Emergency Management Agency (FEMA) came under especially harsh criticism. While key problems went unreported, however, some media reports contained misinformation that magnified the failure, and in some ways, the press may have made things worse.

As thousands sought refuge in the city's Superdome and Convention Center, the media aired numerous horror stories:

- evacuees firing at helicopters trying to save them;
- gangs engaging in sexual assault against women and children;
- snipers shooting at doctors and soldiers from high-rise buildings;
- looters stealing all the firearms from a Walmart;
- sharks swimming through the flooded business district;
- death tolls surpassing 10,000.

The stories were either overblown or just false.[80] The death toll of about 1,000 was horrific enough, but it was only a fraction of the early estimates. One National Guardsman told a local paper, "Don't get me wrong, bad things happened, but I didn't see any killing and raping and cutting of throats or anything. . . . Ninety-nine percent of the people in the Dome were very well-behaved."[81]

Rumors forced officials to divert resources from genuine problems. Answering a report that the Superdome held 200 dead bodies, a FEMA official brought a refrigerated 18-wheel truck and three physicians to the scene. They found only six deaths, four of which were from natural causes.

Weeks after the disaster, the *Washington Post* concluded, "The sensational accounts delayed rescue and evacuation efforts already hampered by poor planning and a lack of coordination among local, state and federal agencies. People rushing to the Gulf Coast to fly rescue helicopters or to distribute food, water and other aid steeled themselves for battle. In communities near and far, the seeds were planted that the victims of Katrina should be kept away, or at least handled with extreme caution."[82]

Interest groups do manage to rouse public activism on certain bureaucratic issues. When the FCC considered a relaxation of media ownership rules, liberal groups such as Code Pink mounted a public relations offensive, complete with public demonstrations. The leaders of the campaign saw it as a way of bringing democracy to rulemaking. One of the commission's former lawyers, however, voiced concern that the opponents wanted the decision to hinge on the decibels of protest. "If these electioneering-style tactics become more common," wrote Randolph May, "the idea of substantive deliberation informed by agency expertise surely will suffer."[84]

This comment points to a dilemma that plagues efforts to check bureaucracy. On the one hand, we want administration to be open to the people and subject to their influence. On the other hand, we want bureaucrats to aid policy deliberation by offering their knowledge and candid advice. If they are under popular control, might they balk at saying something unpopular?

Markets

"Government by market" resolves the problem of bureaucratic control by dispensing with bureaucracy in the first place.[85] Instead of directly providing services or regulating private behavior, the government could try to achieve the same ends through economic incentives. One way to curb an undesirable activity such as pollution is to tax it. If the tax is high enough, polluters will have an incentive to curb emissions. Whereas traditional regulation tells polluters exactly how to achieve the goal, tax incentives let them design their own methods, which are presumably more efficient. Similarly, the government can provide tax breaks for desirable activities such as the installation of energy-saving equipment. Either way, the idea is the same: to harness private interest to the public good.[86]

Tax incentives can often make effective public policy but do not constitute a magic bullet. As we have already seen, taxes mean tax forms. To some extent, substituting tax incentives for other kinds of government action is swapping one spool of red tape for another, and unlike a program that depends on appropriations bills, a tax measure does not come up for review every year. Congress thus has less opportunity to study its effects and deliberate on possible changes.

Instead of relying on public employees to perform a task, the government could outsource it (i.e., contract it out to private businesses) or supply citizens with financial support to buy it. The idea here is that nonpublic providers can often give better service at lower cost because they respond to competition and the profit motive. They also may have less red tape than their public sector counterparts.

As we have seen, the government already does a good deal of outsourcing. One drawback has become apparent: less red tape may mean less oversight. During the conflict in Iraq, the federal government hired over 100,000 private contractors in Iraq—a number almost as high as the U.S. military force.[87] "No one knows to whom they are accountable," said political scientist Elaine Kamarck. "Is it the United States or their contract?"[88] One audit found that a contractor had spent millions on an Olympic-size swimming pool in a police training camp that the Iraqis had never used.[89]

THE SPECIAL CASE OF THE MILITARY
MAJOR ISSUE

- What is the military's role in policy deliberation?

The armed forces differ from the civilian bureaucracy in some ways but resemble it in others. Most civilian government jobs do not entail a willingness to lay down one's own life. Law enforcement officers and other first responders sometimes die in the line of duty, but even they do not have to undergo the long periods of separation and hardship that may be part of a military career, a different kind of public service. At the same time, though, the armed services are hierarchies with thick layers of impersonal rules. They have a system of social services that parallel those of civilian life, complete with schools, hospitals, and child care centers. Like other large organizations, the armed forces must meet payrolls and buy goods.

Comparing the Military with Civilian Bureaucracy

Like the civilian bureaucracy, the military has evolved from patronage to merit. In the mid-1800s, Congress required that applicants to the military academies to get nominations from their local lawmakers, who treated these appointments as political favors.[90] During the Civil War, politicians without military training could even get generalships for themselves. In the decades afterward, the armed forces increasingly emphasized their professionalism. Today, the service academies have rigorous admissions requirements, with congressional nominations as largely a formality.

During wartime, combat may provide the military with a brutally clear measure of success or failure. In peacetime, however, the military follows the civilian bureaucracy in the search for performance measurements. And just as civilian bureaucrats find ways to "game" the numbers, so do people in uniform. In his memoirs, Colin Powell recalls his time as a rising military officer in the 1970s:

> I had long since learned to cope with Army management fashions. You pay the king his shilling, get him off your back, and then go about doing what you consider important. If, for example, you are going to judge me on AWOL [absent without leave] rates, I'm going to send a sergeant out by 6:30 AM to bloodhound the kid who failed to show up for a 6:00 AM reveille. The guy's not considered AWOL until midnight. So drag him back before then and keep the AWOL rate down. I vigorously set out to better every indicator by which my brigade was statistically judged. And then went on to do the things that I thought counted.[91]

Observers have long noted the significance of the military's issue networks and iron triangles. In his 1961 farewell address, President Eisenhower spoke of the "conjunction of an immense military establishment and a large arms industry," which he famously dubbed "the military-industrial complex."[92] Defense issue networks derive intellectual firepower from think tanks that specialize in national security. Although members of the armed services have generally refrained from electoral politics, lawmakers heed the voting power of veterans, military families, and civilians who benefit from military facilities. Lawmakers and their staffs often have close ties to officers, in part because the armed services supply many of the detailees who work on Capitol Hill. Political scientist Norman Ornstein says that officers "leave far more able to understand the value of civilian control of the military and far more sophisticated and sensitive to the separation of powers and the role of Congress. Congress, in turn, learns a lot about the military, including the tremendous quality of people who are in it and that they have nuanced and sophisticated views of the world and their role in the system."[93] Nevertheless, potential for conflicts of interest exist, because detailees may tend to favor the interests of their own service branch.

Control and oversight are especially important in the case of the armed services because the nation's survival depends on their faithful performance. Unlike many other countries, the United States has never faced a real risk of a military coup, yet there have been problems in civil-military relations.[94] At the extreme, President Truman had to fire General Douglas MacArthur for violating orders during the Korean War. In other cases, the military has followed the lead of civilian authorities but with little enthusiasm. So as with civilian bureaucracies, elected officials have had to monitor military performance through congressional hearings and the other means that we discussed earlier. In this case, oversight is harder because military operations often take place overseas and usually require secrecy.

Because external controls may not always work, it is especially important for Americans in the military to uphold their oath to support and defend the Constitution. According to

FOCUS QUESTION

People in the military are supposed to obey their superiors, so does the military operate more efficiently than civilian bureaucracies?

Military and civilian personnel commemorate the reconstruction of the Pentagon.

one officer, the oath binds officers not to an individual but to a system:

> To support the Constitution is to be obedient to the lawful orders of the civilian government. All policies, instructions, regulations, and laws are derived from a legitimate authority clearly spelled out in the Constitution. Compliance with these orders, whether they pertain to hair styles or nuclear weapons, is a direct derivative of the officer's oath.[95]

Coordination and Deliberation

In 1980, President Carter ordered the military to rescue American hostages in Iran. The mission failed when a helicopter crashed into a refueling aircraft. Reviews later showed that planning for the mission had suffered from infighting and miscommunication among the uniformed services. Along with other problems over the years, the failed rescue prompted Congress to reorganize the Defense Department. A 1986 law set up several joint commands, in which all the services would report to one commander, who would answer to the secretary of defense. In the 1991 Gulf War, for instance, General Norman Schwarzkopf had control over the U.S. Army, Air Force, Navy, and Marines in the Middle East.

In past years, service chiefs had been advocates for their services. The army chief would seek more power and money for the army, while the navy chief would do the same for his service, and so on. The authors of the law wanted someone to speak for the national interest, so they named the chairman of the Joint Chiefs as the president's main military adviser. Before supplying advice to the White House, the chairman would consult the other chiefs.

In this post, General Powell (1989–1993) noticed that the service chiefs would revert to their advocacy roles during large formal meetings where others from their services were present. He started the practice of informal private meetings. "This was not great for history," he said, "but it was a superb way of getting the unvarnished, gloves-off, no-holds-barred personal views of the chiefs. They never shrank from defending their service views, but it was easier for them to get beyond those views when we were no longer a spectator sport. It was also easier to protect the privacy of our deliberations."[96]

BUREAUCRACY AND DELIBERATIVE DEMOCRACY

Shortly after taking office, President Obama issued a statement that applied the idea of deliberative democracy to the federal bureaucracy:

> Public engagement enhances the Government's effectiveness and improves the quality of its decisions. Knowledge is widely dispersed in society, and public officials benefit from having access to that dispersed knowledge. Executive departments and agencies should offer Americans increased opportunities to participate in policymaking and to provide their Government with the benefits of their collective expertise and information.[97]

Such efforts had been under way for some time, but new technologies offered the promise of an even greater public role in policy deliberation. Public participation, of course, is not enough. Effective policy deliberation also requires public servants of high quality, because it takes a great deal of intelligence, knowledge, and experience to reason on the merits of difficult policy issues. As we saw at the start of this chapter, some government tasks entail great risks and sacrifices. If the government relied purely on economic incentives, it would have to pay enormous sums to get people to undertake these tasks. In fact, though, public employees often accept such work for modest pay. They do so not only because of the job security that comes with government employment but also because of a sense of public service and citizenship. Surveys of federal job seekers have shown that many cite patriotism and a desire to serve others.[98] A 2008 survey asked foreign service officers about reasons for working in several dangerous countries. Of those who had served in these countries—or expressed a willingness to do so—a majority mentioned self-interested motives. Forty-seven percent cited patriotism.[99]

Similarly, young Americans have told pollsters that service is a better reason to enter government work than the pay and benefits. In 1997, 33% of young adults said that helping people and making a difference was the biggest attraction of a government career. Seven years later, that figure reached 47%. But the proportion of young people seeking government work went down in the first years of the twenty-first century, in part because fewer of them have encountered anyone who asked them to serve.[100]

More recently, there has been greater interest in public service. A 2008 poll found that if the request came from parents (33%) or the newly elected president (29%), many of those age 18–29 would give serious consideration to serving. Also, 70% found public service to be "very" or "fairly" appealing, a higher percentage than in the past.[101] This figure may reflect the impact of the 2008 presidential campaign, in which both nominees placed an unusual degree of emphasis on public service.

A word of caution is in order. Government agencies staffed with dedicated professionals provide valuable benefits to the country, but at some point a large administrative state could have corrosive effects on citizenship. Over 150 years ago, Alexis de Tocqueville warned that government could impose a "network of petty, complicated rules." Such power, he said, "hinders, restrains, enervates, stifles, and stultifies so much that in the end each nation is no more than a flock of timid and hardworking animals with the government as its shepherd."[102] At that point, "there are subjects still, but no citizens."[103] One counterweight to this tendency is the encouragement of public participation. By taking part in policy deliberations, Americans can act as citizens instead of subjects.

SUMMARY

- Bureaucracy carries out the work of government. Some bureaucrats interact with other citizens "in the field," while others work at headquarters. Much of their labor consists of gathering and spreading information.
- Another major task consists of devising administrative rules to carry out the sometimes vague mandates of lawmakers.
- Complexity is a common complaint about bureaucracy, but because of the size of the nation and the intricacy of its policy issues, it would be difficult to avoid elaborate organizational charts and conflicts over jurisdiction.
- Bureaucracies take on lives of their own. The people who staff them have their own perspectives, and may form alliances with interest groups and legislators. Sometimes they may balk at the direction of elected

executives, but a basic sense of duty may curb undue foot dragging.
- There are various ways of controlling and overseeing the bureaucracy. Elected officials may place loyalists in key posts. Inspectors general search for waste and abuse. Members of Congress hold investigations. Judicial action may check bureaucratic overreaching. The press may alert the public to problems.
- In several ways, the military represents a unique challenge for control and oversight, in part because much of its activity takes place outside the United States.
- If one thing is certain in American political life, it is that bureaucracy will not disappear. It will continue to need public-spirited recruits to staff it and vigilant citizens to control it.

KEY TERMS

TEST YOUR KNOWLEDGE

1. An organization with division of labor, hierarchy of authority, formal rules, and impersonal relationships is called
   a. a bureaucracy.
   b. Congress.
   c. frontline workers.
   d. the government corporation.
   e. the iron triangle.

2. Government employees who have the physical task of carrying out public policy are called
   a. administrators.
   b. bureaucratic commissioners.
   c. federal policy experts.
   d. frontline workers.
   e. policy managers.

3. How does the *Federal Register* attempt to contribute to deliberation?
   a. Citizens can read it to follow what the bureaucracy is doing and help officials reason about public policy.
   b. Lawmakers can read it for summaries of bills and potential issues that may arise from the legislation.
   c. It provides voters with information regarding the propositions on the ballot in elections.
   d. It serves as the focus of deliberation in the House of Representatives and Senate.
   e. The president and Congress are both able to exchange comments within its pages.

4. The government tried to improve openness and deliberation by
   a. assigning a press liaison to each department and agency.
   b. broadcasting departmental meetings on C-SPAN.
   c. conducting public opinion polls.
   d. issuing press releases that include select data.
   e. putting proposed rules on the Internet.

5. Members of independent regulatory commissions are NOT subject to presidential dismissal because they
   a. are better able to deliberate in the public interest when they are not governed by political pressures.
   b. are chosen by Congress.
   c. are elected officials and can only be removed from their positions by a recall election.
   d. are not government entities, but private enterprises.
   e. were created outside the bounds of the Constitution, so they cannot be subject to governmental intervention.

6. An example of a government-sponsored enterprise is the
   a. Environmental Protection Agency.
   b. Federal Communications Commission.
   c. Federal National Mortgage Association.
   d. Securities and Exchange Commission.
   e. United States Postal Service.

7. Under the spoils system, government posts went to
   a. men who had completed a higher education.
   b. military personnel.
   c. the administration's political supporters.
   d. the family members of congressmen.
   e. those whose experience was relevant to the position.

8. What unique leverage do government workers have in the workplace?
   a. They have annual contract negotiations.
   b. They have employee protection regulations.
   c. They have federal disability pay.
   d. They have the right to strike.
   e. Their bosses are elected officials.

9. The independent, nonpartisan agency that works for Congress and investigates how the federal government spends taxpayer dollars is called the
   a. Congressional Oversight Office.
   b. Department of Management and Budget.
   c. Government Accountability Office.

d. Government Budget Office.

e. Office of Federal Accountability.

10. How can a large administrative state have a negative impact on citizenship?

   a. A large administrative state requires less of its citizens and allows them to make more individual choices.

   b. Citizens are more likely to make choices based on their own personal interest rather than the national interest because they feel less connected to the government.

c. Citizens begin to rebel against the government because they resent the imposition of so many rules.

d. Citizens vote less because they feel left out of the deliberative process.

e. When rules become too numerous, citizens quit deliberating because they are too busy trying to follow all the rules.

FURTHER READING

Feaver, Peter D. *Armed Servants: Agency, Oversight, and Civil-Military Relations.* Cambridge, MA: Harvard University Press, 2003.

Golden, Marissa Martino. *What Motivates Bureaucrats? Politics and Administration during the Reagan Years.* New York: Columbia University Press, 2000.

Kamarck, Elaine C. *The End of Government . . . As We Know It: Making Public Policy Work.* Boulder, CO: Lynne Rienner, 2007.

Kerwin, Cornelius M. *Rulemaking: How Government Agencies Write Law and Make Policy.* 2nd ed. Washington, DC: CQ Press, 1999.

Osborne, David, and Ted Gaebler. *Reinventing Government: How the Entrepreneurial Spirit Is Transforming the Public Sector.* Reading, MA: Addison-Wesley, 1992.

Powell, Colin, with Joseph E. Persico. *My American Journey.* New York: Random House, 1995.

WEB SOURCES

Government Executive: www.govexec.com—a publication for and about public servants.

National Academy of Public Administration: www.napawash.org—a nonprofit that studies issues of government organization.

Regulations.gov: www.regulations.gov—official information about federal rules.

Transactional Records Access Clearinghouse: www.trac.syr.edu—comprehensive information about federal staffing, spending, and enforcement activities.

U.S. Government Manual: www.gpo.gov/fdsys/browse/collection.action?collectionCode=GOVMAN—a guide to the structure and personnel of the federal government.

This is the west facade, the main entrance, of the Supreme Court building. It faces the Capitol building. Prior to the opening of this building in 1935, the Court had met in various rooms in the Capitol.

Jonathan Larsen/Shutterstock.com

15 The Judiciary

OBJECTIVES

After reading this chapter, you should be able to:

- Explain why courts are so influential in the United States.
- Assess the argument that the power of judicial review is necessarily implied by the U.S. Constitution.
- Describe the structure and functioning of the federal court system and explain how the Supreme Court hears and decides cases.
- Evaluate the influence of the Supreme Court on government and politics throughout American history.
- Describe and appraise the arguments in the modern debate over judicial activism.
- Explain how the American people or their elected officials have tried to check the power of the federal courts.
- Assess the contribution of the Supreme Court to deliberative democracy in the United States.

INTRODUCTION

"There is hardly a political question in the United States which does not sooner or later turn into a judicial one."[1] This may sound like a commentary on modern America, but it is actually Alexis de Tocqueville's description of the United States in the 1830s.

Events in 2010–2012 proved the continuing relevance of Tocqueville's insight. Immediately after Congress passed a major restructuring of the health coverage system in the United States in the summer of 2010—the Patient Protection and Affordable Care Act (often simply called "Obamacare")—its opponents challenged its key provisions in federal court as unconstitutional. After lower courts split on the matter, the Supreme Court took the case. During the weeks leading up to the decision in June 2012, the fate of the law was the dominant national news story. The major networks covered the decision live on the morning of June 28, as correspondents raced through the 187-page opinion to find the actual holdings in this complex case. (See the discussion of the media coverage in Chapter 11.) While this was happening, several justices summarized their opinions from the bench but without live broadcast coverage (prohibited by Court rules). In their haste, many reporters got the actual decision wrong. When the smoke had cleared, the nation learned that five of the nine justices had upheld the act's requirement that Americans pay a penalty (interpreted by the justices as a tax) if they refused to buy health insurance. Although this was a major victory for the Obama administration, seven justices also overturned a key provision that allowed the federal government to withhold all of a state's federal Medicaid funding for the poor if the state refused to expand Medicaid eligibility. Once this major legal contest was settled, focus shifted to a reenergized political battle over health care in the presidential and congressional campaigns leading up to the November election.

Although Tocqueville would not have been shocked by how health care went from a political issue to a legal one, even he would likely be surprised at just how much judges influence American politics today. Just think of all the other political issues that courts now influence:

- Abortion rights
- Affirmative action programs in colleges, universities, and businesses
- Voting rights and the redrawing of legislative districts after the census every 10 years
- The rights of people with disabilities
- The death penalty
- The rights of criminal defendants
- The use of prayers or religious symbols on public property or by public officials
- The legal restriction of pornographic or obscene materials
- The right to own or carry firearms
- The power of governments to take private property through eminent domain
- Gay marriage
- The president's authority to detain suspected terrorists indefinitely and to try them in military courts

Why are American courts so influential? The short answer is the power of **judicial review**. This is the power to strike down laws that the courts determine violate the federal or state constitutions. Some of the best-known cases, discussed in previous chapters, are the Supreme Court's ruling in 1857 that Congress could not prohibit slavery in the federal territories (*Dred Scott v. Sandford*); its decision in 1954 that segregated public schools violate the Equal Protection Clause of the Fourteenth Amendment (*Brown v. Board of Education*); and its overturning of state abortion restrictions in 1973 (*Roe v. Wade*). State courts have also used judicial review to force far-reaching changes in public policy. In 2003, for example, the Massachusetts Supreme Court ruled that its state constitution required the legalization of same-sex marriage. A few other state supreme courts later did the same.

Early in the life of the nation, judicial review was in dispute. Some leaders opposed it for seemingly making the one unelected branch of the federal government supreme over the others, thus violating American separation of powers. Its defenders countered that it

Judicial review—the power of courts to strike down laws that they judge to be in violation of the federal or state constitutions.

Judicial activism—the charge that under the guise of interpreting the Constitution, federal judges read their own policy preferences into the fundamental law.

Strict construction—a method of interpreting the Constitution that claims to follow closely the actual words of the document as originally understood by those who wrote and ratified it.

Original intent—the doctrine that judges should interpret the Constitution based on the original intent of those who wrote and ratified it. See also **original meaning**.

Original meaning—the doctrine that judges should interpret the Constitution based on how it was understood by those who wrote and ratified it. See also **original intent**.

Evolving Constitution—the notion that the meaning of the Constitution changes, or evolves, over time to meet changing circumstances or norms. See also **living Constitution**.

Living Constitution—the notion that the Constitution is a living document that changes, or evolves, to meet changing circumstances. See also **evolving Constitution**.

makes the Constitution, and thereby the sovereign people, supreme over the will of elected officials—a fundamental principle of American constitutionalism.

Although the legitimacy of judicial review is little questioned today, its consequences are as controversial as ever. Some critics of judicial review charge that under the guise of interpreting the Constitution, federal judges read their own policy preferences into the fundamental law. They call this **judicial activism**. Some of these critics insist that judges should follow a **strict construction** of the Constitution by looking to the **original intent** of its framers or the **original meaning** of its provisions. The Constitution, they say, should be interpreted as understood by those who wrote it and ratified it.

Others, however, say that the framers of the Constitution had no single common intent on many issues, which is why they often used vague terms. Also, the nation and the world have changed so much since 1787 that original intent, even if we could discern it, should not bind us. They maintain that ours is an **evolving Constitution**—also called a **living Constitution**—that must be adapted to meet the needs of the times.

In interpreting the Constitution and laws, the Supreme Court is a preeminently deliberative institution. During the debate over the ratification of the Constitution, Alexander Hamilton wrote that the Court would exercise "neither FORCE nor WILL but merely judgment."[2] In resolving legal disputes, the Court would make decisions by reasoning about the meaning of the Constitution and the laws, not by responding to political pressures or representing any class or group.

In so doing, however, the Supreme Court would limit itself to well-defined legal disputes and would not supplant the broader policy deliberations of elected officials, who reason together on behalf of the people. As Nathaniel Gorham of Massachusetts put it at the Constitutional Convention (see Chapter 2), "As Judges they are not to be presumed to possess any particular knowledge of the mere policy of public measures."[3] Although judges ought not to make policy, they do contribute to deliberation about rights, justice, and the powers of government when they reason about the meaning of the Constitution and announce their judgments in written opinions. Thus, one expert calls the Supreme Court a "republican schoolmaster," and another says that it engages Americans in "a vital national seminar."[4]

We begin with the constitutional and legal foundations of the federal judiciary, focusing on its independence and authority within the political system. We then turn to the structure and functioning of the federal courts, their impact on American politics over the past two centuries, the modern debate over judicial activism, and ways in which the people or their elected officials can check the courts. We conclude by assessing how the Supreme Court contributes to deliberative democracy in the United States.

CONSTITUTIONAL AND LEGAL FOUNDATIONS

MAJOR ISSUE

- What is the source of the federal judiciary's independence and authority in the American constitutional system, and how can judicial review be justified in a democracy?

One of the principal accomplishments of the framers of the U.S. Constitution was to establish an independent judiciary. They insulated it to a considerable degree from political forces and made it a coequal branch of the national government.

The Case for an Independent Judiciary

In the English system of government at the time of the American founding, courts were formally part of the executive power. The king appointed judges, who served only as long as he pleased. By the late 1700s, however, political thinkers had developed a strong case for an independent judiciary. Most important was Montesquieu's argument in *The Spirit of the Laws* that people's lives and property would only be secure if tribunals independent of legislatures and executives decided the merits of legal claims.[5]

The American founders embraced Montesquieu's call for a separation of the powers of government. In the Declaration of Independence, they chastised the king for making judges "dependent on his Will alone, for the Tenure of their Offices, and the Amount and Payment of their Salaries." Yet Americans had their own lapses in establishing independent judiciaries. They failed, for example, to create a separate judicial branch in the Articles of Confederation, and they were generally unsuccessful in preventing powerful legislatures in the new state governments from undermining judicial independence. State legislatures used their control over salaries to bend judges to their will, and sometimes they simply exercised judicial powers in violation of their state's constitution.

Constitution of 1787

Drawing on the lessons of the previous decade, the delegates to the Constitutional Convention worked to establish an independent federal judiciary in the new Constitution. In Article III, they vested the "judicial Power of the United States" in "one supreme Court, and in such inferior Courts as the Congress may from time to time ordain and establish." Article II stipulates that the president will appoint all federal judges "by and with the Advice and Consent of the Senate." Senate approval, Hamilton wrote, "would be an excellent check upon a spirit of favoritism in the President, and would tend greatly to prevent the appointment of unfit characters."[6]

The Constitution leaves open the number of judges on the Supreme Court and the number and nature of lower federal courts. Congress decides these matters. To ensure judicial independence, the framers specified that federal judges serve "during good Behaviour"—meaning until they die, resign, or undergo impeachment and conviction—and that their salaries cannot be decreased (but may be increased) while they serve. The framers believed that a life term and a prohibition on cutting judicial salaries would allow judges to exercise their independent judgment.

The new federal judiciary was not intended to replace the state courts, which would continue to handle issues under state law, including most criminal prosecutions and most lawsuits between individuals. Rather, the federal courts would rule in cases involving federal law, treaties, and the national Constitution. The Constitution distinguishes between those cases in which the Supreme Court will have **original jurisdiction**, meaning the parties can go directly to the Supreme Court, and those in which the Supreme Court will have **appellate jurisdiction**, meaning the parties must first go to a lower court. Because of the importance of cases involving foreign nations and states, the Constitution gives the Supreme Court original jurisdiction in "Cases affecting Ambassadors, other public Ministers and Consuls, and those in which a State shall be Party." In all the other cases it has appellate jurisdiction, "with such Exceptions, and under such Regulations as the Congress shall make." As we shall see, some critics of judicial power have proposed using this provision to deny the Supreme Court jurisdiction over some controversial matters.

Judiciary Act of 1789

A major task of the First Congress, which convened in March 1789, was to set up a federal court system. In September, it added flesh to the skeleton of the Constitution with the **Judiciary Act of 1789**.

The new law established a more extensive court system than many had expected. It created a three-tiered structure that still exists in a modified form (see Figure 15-1 on page 443). At the bottom were the **district courts** (now formally called the **United States District Courts**), with one federal judge in each state except for Massachusetts and Virginia, which had two. Next were three **circuit courts** (now called the **United States Courts of Appeal**)— one for the Northeast, one for the middle states, and one for the South. These did not have

Original jurisdiction—the authority of a court to hear a case taken directly to it, as a new legal controversy.

Appellate jurisdiction—the authority of a court to review a decision reached by a lower court.

Judiciary Act of 1789—the law passed by the First Congress that created a three-tiered federal court structure.

District courts—see United States District Courts.

United States District Courts—the basic trial courts (civil and criminal) in the federal system, where the typical federal case begins.

Circuit court—the original name for the federal courts intermediary between the district courts and the Supreme Court. The name is still used informally to apply to the federal courts of appeal. See **United States Courts of Appeal**.

United States Courts of Appeal—the federal courts intermediary between the district courts and the Supreme Court, one for each of 12 regions of the country and one for the Federal Circuit, which handles specialized cases.

their own judges (although they do now) but were staffed by the district judge in the state where the circuit court met and two Supreme Court justices, who "rode circuit" throughout the region assigned to them. At the top was the Supreme Court, which was to have five "associate justices" and a "chief justice."

The district courts had jurisdiction over minor federal crimes and many civil matters (conflicts between private parties), especially involving maritime law. Circuit courts handled more serious crimes and could review decisions by the district courts. State courts, which would continue to decide cases arising under state law, would also hear "federal question" suits in which the Constitution, federal law, or treaties were at issue. Judgments in these cases were appealable to the U.S. Supreme Court, as were decisions by the federal circuit courts.

Here the authors of the Judiciary Act sought a balance. Although they established an extensive federal court system "so that the majesty and power of an otherwise small and distant, distrusted new national government might be brought closer to everyone's doorstep," they recognized a role for the state courts in handling matters of federal importance in the first instance.[7]

Judicial Review: Constitutional Foundations and the Early Debate

Neither the Constitution nor the Judiciary Act said anything about the courts' power to strike down federal or state laws as unconstitutional. Yet some members of the Constitutional Convention seemed to assume that the Supreme Court would have such a power. As Hamilton wrote in *Federalist 78*, Congress derives all its authority from the Constitution, which is the sovereign act of the people and, therefore, "fundamental law." Congress, thus, has no right to violate the Constitution's provisions. If it does, the courts must defend "the power of the people" against the legislature.[8] Despite Hamilton's public defense of judicial review, the Supreme Court did not exercise such authority until the landmark case *Marbury v. Madison* in 1803.

This complicated case began after Thomas Jefferson defeated incumbent President John Adams in the election of 1800. In those days, presidents served for nearly three months after the electoral vote was counted in December, even if they had lost. President Adams used this time to appoint Federalists to the judiciary—the so-called **midnight appointments**. One was William Marbury, nominated to serve as a justice of the peace in the District of Columbia. Although the Senate confirmed the appointment and the president signed the commission, Adams's secretary of state John Marshall failed to deliver the commission to Marbury before he left office. In the final days of his term, Adams also appointed Marshall to serve as chief justice of the United States.

These last-minute appointments incensed the incoming Democratic-Republicans. Because James Madison became Jefferson's secretary of state, it fell to him to deliver Marbury's commission. Yet, concerned that Adams had attempted to load the judiciary with Federalists, he refused to do so. Marbury then asked the Supreme Court to issue a **writ of mandamus**—a judicial command to a public official to do his or her duty—ordering Madison to deliver the commission.

In a 5–0 decision, Chief Justice Marshall maintained that although Marbury had a legal right to his judgeship, the Supreme Court had no authority to issue a writ of mandamus in this case. The provision of the Judiciary Act that authorized the Supreme Court to issue writs of mandamus, Marshall wrote, violated the Constitution's limited grant of original jurisdiction to the Court. Because the Constitution trumps legislation that violates it, the relevant provision of the Judiciary Act was void.

Much of Marshall's argument paralleled Hamilton's. The Constitution, "the fundamental and paramount law of the nation," had "defined and limited" the powers of Congress. Because the Constitution is the supreme law, "a legislative act contrary to the constitution is not law." "It is emphatically the province and duty of the judicial department," Marshall famously held, "to say what the law is." Marshall added that the Constitution requires judges (and all public officials) "to take an oath to support it." How could judges perform this duty, Marshall asked, if they allowed a law to stand that violated the Constitution? Finally,

Midnight appointments—the appointments to the federal judiciary that President John Adams and the lame-duck Federalist Congress made in the final months and weeks of Adams's one term as president.

Writ of mandamus—an order from a court to an officer of the government or to a lower court requiring the performance of some mandatory, or ministerial, duty.

Marshall noted that the Constitution states in Article VI that "the supreme Law of the Land" includes "not the laws of the United States generally, but those only which shall be made in pursuance of the constitution."[9]

Despite the Court's vigorous defense of judicial review, its decision required no action by the Jefferson administration. Marbury, it said, had a right to his office, but the Court had no authority to order Secretary of State Madison to deliver the commission. Had the Court issued such an order, historians note, the administration might not have carried it out. In the opinion of some commentators, Marshall found an ingenious way to assert the authority of the Court without facing the possibility of the president ignoring its order.

In response to *Marbury v. Madison*, President Jefferson denied (not publicly but in private letters) that the Supreme Court had the final say on the constitutionality of laws. In 1804, he wrote that allowing judges "to decide what laws are constitutional, and what not, not only for themselves in their own sphere of action, but for the legislature and executive also in their spheres, would make the judiciary a despotic branch."[10] In Jefferson's view, this violated the constitutional separation of powers. "The Constitution," he wrote three years later, "intended that the three great branches of the government should be coordinate, and independent of each other. As to acts, therefore, which are to be done by either, it has given no control to another branch." He expressed his long-standing wish "for a proper occasion to have the gratuitous opinion in Marbury vs. Madison brought before the public, and denounced as not law."[11]

Marbury v. Madison was the first of many landmark decisions of the Marshall Court. Marshall served as chief justice from 1801 to 1835, and no one who has donned the robes of a Supreme Court justice has had a greater impact on the Court or on American democracy. Born in Virginia in 1755, Marshall had served as an officer in the Continental Army during the Revolutionary War (and was at Valley Forge during the winter of 1777–1778), was a member of both the Virginia Assembly and the state ratifying convention that approved the Constitution in 1788, and undertook an important diplomatic mission to France during John Adams's administration. He served briefly in the House of Representatives and as secretary of state before Adams appointed him chief justice of the Supreme Court. Once on the Court, Marshall convinced his colleagues to speak with one voice on many of the controversial issues that came before the justices. He personally wrote key decisions on judicial review, implied powers, and national supremacy and eventually became known as "The Great Chief Justice."

Although it took half a century after *Marbury* before the Supreme Court again overturned a federal law, beginning in 1810 the Court issued a series of decisions that overturned state laws and state supreme court decisions as inconsistent with the U.S. Constitution. These decisions were even more controversial than *Marbury*. Critics charged that they violated federalism by making the federal courts supreme over state laws and state courts. Defenders insisted that the Supreme Court was merely enforcing the supremacy of the U.S. Constitution in the federal system. In the modern era, also, many of the Court's most controversial decisions have overturned state laws, not national laws.

Jefferson was not the only nineteenth-century president to challenge the Supreme Court as the final word on the meaning of the Constitution. In 1832, President Andrew Jackson vetoed a bill to recharter the Bank of the United States because in his view it was both unconstitutional and unwise. Yet 13 years before, in *McCulloch v. Maryland*, the Court had upheld the constitutionality of the bank (see the discussion in Chapter 3). Jackson defended the right of the Congress and the president to make up their own minds about the Constitution:

> [T]he opinion of the Supreme Court . . . ought not to control the coordinate authorities of this Government. The Congress, the Executive, and the Court must each for itself be guided by its own opinion of the Constitution. Each public officer who takes an oath to support the Constitution swears that he will support it as he understands it, and not as it is understood by others. . . . The opinion of the judges

Theodor Horydczak, Collection of the Supreme Court of the United States

Known as "The Great Chief Justice," John Marshall headed the Supreme Court from 1801 to 1835.

has no more authority over Congress than the opinion of Congress has over the judges, and on that point the President is independent of both.[12]

Twenty-five years later, the *Dred Scott* decision reignited the debate over the Supreme Court's authority. Abraham Lincoln, a former one-term congressman from Illinois with aspirations for higher office, attacked Chief Justice Roger B. Taney's reasoning in *Dred Scott* as based "on assumed historical facts which were not really true."[13] He often cited the strong dissents by Justices Benjamin Curtis and John McLean. Sometimes he quoted Andrew Jackson's comments about the duty of the members of each branch to interpret the Constitution.

In response, Senator Stephen Douglas of Illinois charged that opponents of the decision "aim[ed] a deadly blow to our whole Republican system of government" by undermining the authority of the Court "to determine, expound and enforce the law."[14] During the Lincoln-Douglas debates of 1858, he accused Lincoln of "mak[ing] war on the decision of the Supreme Court" and of engaging in "a crusade against the Supreme Court."[15] Douglas asked rhetorically, "By what tribunal will he reverse [the *Dred Scott* decision]? Will he appeal to a mob? Does he intend to appeal to violence, to Lynch law? Will he stir up strife and rebellion in the land and overthrow the court by violence?"[16]

In taking office on March 4, 1861, Lincoln gave his first explanation as president of the authority of the Supreme Court. He accepted that Court decisions on constitutional questions "must be binding in any case upon the parties to a suit as to the object of that suit," and "they are also entitled to very high respect and consideration in all parallel cases by all other departments of the Government." Yet, an erroneous decision "may be overruled and never become a precedent for other cases." "At the same time," Lincoln continued, "the candid citizen must confess that if the policy of the Government upon vital questions affecting the whole people is to be irrevocably fixed by decisions of the Supreme Court, the instant they are made in ordinary litigation between parties in personal actions the people will have ceased to be their own rulers, having to that extent practically resigned their Government into the hands of that eminent tribunal."[17] (As discussed in Chapter 6, it took the Fourteenth Amendment of 1868 to overturn the *Dred Scott* decision.)

Note that Lincoln did not challenge the legitimacy of judicial review in specific legal cases or the obligation of officials to abide by the Court's decisions. As president, he must abide by the specific holding in *Dred* Scott. But he need not agree with the decision; he could try to persuade others that the Court wrongly interpreted the Declaration and the Constitution; and he could hope to see the holding overruled by a future Court. (Later in the chapter, we discuss how the American separation of powers system gives the people and their elected officials some means for checking Supreme Court errors or excesses.)

Trial by Jury

Another important legal principle (besides judicial review) embodied in the nation's fundamental law is trial by jury. The jury trial has its roots in medieval England, and early Americans considered it necessary to achieve justice and check tyranny. Indeed, one reason they broke with England was because the king and Parliament had "deprive[ed] us, in many Cases, of the Benefits of Trial by Jury" (Declaration of Independence).

In the Constitution, the framers guaranteed trial by jury in federal criminal cases (Article III) but said nothing about civil cases. Anti-Federalists criticized this omission during the ratification debates. In response, the authors of the Bill of Rights extended jury trials to federal civil cases involving more than $20 (Seventh Amendment). They also guaranteed that in all federal criminal cases the defendant would have "the right to a speedy and public trial, by an impartial jury of the State and district wherein the crime shall have been committed" (Sixth Amendment). All of the original 13 states guaranteed jury trials in serious criminal cases, as did every other state upon entering the Union. Today, the United States uses juries in civil and criminal cases more than any other modern democracy (We will discuss jury trials in greater detail later in the chapter.).

THE STRUCTURE AND FUNCTIONING OF THE FEDERAL COURT SYSTEM

MAJOR ISSUE

- How do the federal courts carry out the judicial power?

Most Americans are familiar with the U.S. Supreme Court, which frequently issues holdings on important and controversial matters. Yet, only a tiny fraction of legal issues in the United States ever reach the Supreme Court, which sits atop the court system. The vast majority of legal cases achieve final resolution in state courts or in the lower federal courts. If we want to understand how the federal courts carry out the judicial power, we must start with the federal district courts.

Trial court—the court, such as federal district court, in which civil and criminal trials occur.

District Courts

The modern federal court system follows the basic three-tiered pyramid structure created by the Judiciary Act of 1789 (see Figure 15-1). At the bottom are the U.S. District Courts, which are organized into 94 judicial districts (see Figure 15-2). Each state has at least one federal judicial district; the larger states have up to four. In 2011, 673 judges served in district courts. Some states—such as Alaska, Idaho, Maine, Montana, Nebraska, New Hampshire, North Dakota, Rhode Island, South Dakota, Vermont, and Wyoming—have as few as 2 or 3 federal district judges; California, with the most, has 61.[18]

The district courts are the basic **trial courts** in the federal system. Judges handle both civil and criminal cases. In **civil cases**, one individual sues another person or an organization (or even the government, if the law allows) because of some alleged harm, such as a violation of a contract, a libel, or the sale of a defective product. In **criminal cases**, the government prosecutes an individual for violating a criminal statute, such as a law against violence, theft, corporate fraud, or drug trafficking. In the United States, more than 90% of all criminal cases go through state courts, not federal courts.

The chief federal prosecutor in each of the 94 judicial districts, the **United States Attorney**, is nominated by the president and confirmed by the Senate. The U.S. Attorney's offices are part of the Department of Justice,

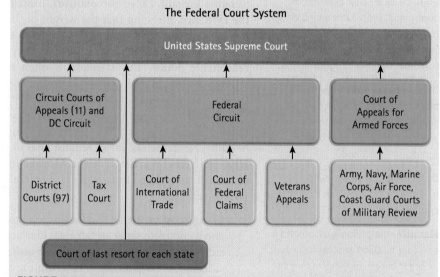

FIGURE 15-1 The United States Supreme Court tops the federal court system, but also takes cases from state supreme courts when federal issues are involved.
Note: District courts in this figure include three territorial courts that also hear federal cases.
SOURCE: www.law.syr.edu/media/documents/2008/2/IntroCourts.pdf, accessed July 9, 2012.

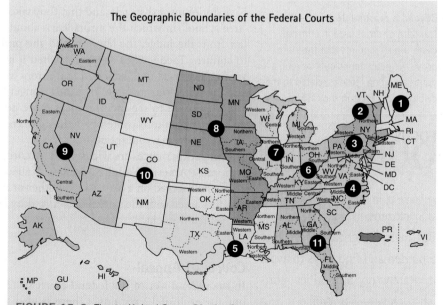

FIGURE 15-2 The 94 United States District Courts cover part or all of each of the 50 states. The Federal Circuit (Appellate) Courts are numbered 1 through 11, with another for the District of Columbia and one for the "Federal Circuit."
SOURCE: www.uscourts.gov/courtlinks, accessed July 9, 2012.

Civil case—case in which one individual sues another person or an organization (or even the government, if the law allows) because of some alleged harm, such as a violation of a contract, a libel, or the sale of a defective product.

Criminal case—case in which the government prosecutes an individual for violating a criminal statute, such as a law against violence, theft, corporate fraud, or drug trafficking.

United States Attorney—the chief prosecutor in each of the 94 federal judicial districts, nominated by the president and confirmed by the Senate.

Defendant—the person sued in a civil case or charged with a crime in a criminal case.

Plaintiff—the person who initiates a civil case by suing another individual, an organization, or the government.

Preponderance of the evidence—a standard of proof used in most civil cases, which requires that the weight of the evidence support the plaintiff's case, even if only slightly.

Beyond a reasonable doubt—the standard of proof used in criminal cases, which requires that the state prove the defendant's guilt beyond a doubt based on reasons related to the evidence and facts in the case.

FOCUS QUESTION

Jury duty is mandatory for most U.S. citizens, if called to serve. But many Americans view it as a burden and find ways to avoid it. Rarely do authorities punish such behavior. Would it be a good idea to strictly enforce the laws on jury service with fines or jail time?

but in many respects they operate independently of day-to-day supervision by "main Justice." Although they serve at the pleasure of the president, a controversy arose in President George W. Bush's second term when seven U.S. Attorneys were dismissed in December 2006. Some charged that the officials were fired for improper political reasons, such as failure to investigate Democratic politicians. Congressional investigations attracted widespread public attention, and the controversy contributed to the resignation of Attorney General Alberto Gonzales in September 2007.

Under the U.S. Constitution, **defendants** in federal criminal cases and the parties in a federal civil case have a right to a jury trial. If they do not assert that right, the judge may serve as the neutral fact finder and determiner of guilt or fault. In most civil cases, the party bringing the suit, called the **plaintiff**, must prove his or her case by a **preponderance of the evidence**, meaning that the weight of the evidence supports the plaintiff's case, even if only slightly. Because the consequences of a criminal case can be much more serious, prosecutors face a much higher burden: they must prove the defendant is guilty **beyond a reasonable doubt**. This standard is often misunderstood. It does not mean beyond a shadow of a doubt or any possible doubt, but beyond a doubt based on reasons related to the evidence and facts in the case (see the Myths and Misinformation feature on page 445.).

Despite the right to a jury trial, many civil cases are settled by the mutual agreement of the parties, and about 95% of all convictions in federal criminal cases result from a plea of guilty. Nevertheless, juries remain vital to the judicial system. The prospect of a trial is what motivates the settlement of civil and criminal cases, and many of the hardest and most notorious cases do go to trial. As one federal court puts it, the responsibility to serve as a juror is serious:

> Jurors must be men and women possessed of sound judgment, absolute honesty, and a complete sense of fairness. Jury service is a high duty of citizenship. Jurors aid in the maintenance of law and order and uphold justice among their fellow citizens. . . . In addition to determining and adjusting property rights, jurors may also be asked to decide questions involving a crime for which a person may be fined, placed on probation, or confined in prison. In a very real sense, therefore, the people must rely upon jurors for the protection of life, liberty and the pursuit of happiness.[20]

Tocqueville also praised juries. He wrote that jury service reminds citizens that "they have duties toward society and that they take a share in its government." The jury acts as a "free school" in which the jurors learn about their rights and gain practical lessons in the law from the judge, the lawyers, and the parties in the case.[21] One recent study seemed to confirm Tocqueville's argument when it showed that serving on a jury that reached a verdict increased the likelihood that jurors would vote in future elections. The researchers also found that jurors often "develop stronger faith in government and their fellow citizens, and they come to see themselves as more politically capable and virtuous."[22] Apparently, deliberating about the fate of a fellow citizen in a criminal case does stir the civic feelings that Tocqueville wrote about.

Such experiences are widespread. According to a report by the American Bar Association, most American adults have been called for jury service. Of those who got the call, nearly half served on a jury. And whether or not Americans have served, more than three-quarters agree with the statement: "Jury duty is an important civic duty I should meet even if it is inconvenient."[23]

Courts of Appeal

In the second tier of the federal court system are the United States Courts of Appeals, one for each of 12 regions. (There is also a Court of Appeals for the Federal Circuit, which handles appeals in certain specialized cases.) Because the first federal appeals courts were staffed in part by Supreme Court justices who "rode circuit," they are also called circuit courts. They range in size from 6 authorized judges for the First Circuit, which covers most of New England and Puerto Rico, to 29 judges for the Ninth Circuit,

MYTHS AND MISINFORMATION

The Meaning of "Beyond a Reasonable Doubt"

No one in the United States may be convicted of a criminal offense unless the prosecutor persuades the jury or judge that the defendant is guilty "beyond a reasonable doubt." Although these words do not appear in the Constitution, the Supreme Court has ruled that in criminal cases, this standard of proof is an essential element of the "due process" that the Fifth Amendment requires in federal courts and the Fourteenth Amendment requires in state courts. Yet despite the universal use of "beyond a reasonable doubt" in American criminal courts, the phrase is often misunderstood. The standard, as high as it is, does not demand the elimination of all possible doubt.

Black's Law Dictionary, a standard reference work for American law, defines "reasonable doubt" as "[t]he doubt that prevents one from being firmly convinced of a defendant's guilt, or the belief that there is a real possibility that a defendant is not guilty." When a judge instructs the jury in a criminal case before deliberations begin, he or she may provide some explanation of what "beyond a reasonable doubt" means. In California criminal courts, judges use the following standard language: "Proof beyond a reasonable doubt is proof that leaves you with an abiding conviction that the charge is true. The evidence need not eliminate all possible doubt because everything in life is open to some possible or imaginary doubt."

For federal criminal trials in the areas covered by the Federal Ninth Circuit (California and eight other western states), the U.S. Court of Appeals provides trial judges the following model instructions:

> Proof beyond a reasonable doubt is proof that leaves you firmly convinced that the defendant is guilty.

It is not required that the government prove guilt beyond all possible doubt. A reasonable doubt is a doubt based upon reason and common sense and is not based purely on speculation. It may arise from a careful and impartial consideration of all the evidence, or from lack of evidence.

The "beyond a reasonable doubt" standard of proof is the highest used in American courts and is much higher than the "preponderance of the evidence" commonly used in civil courts. It makes it difficult to convict defendants without compelling evidence of guilt. Apparently, however, this was not its original purpose when it entered British legal practice in the eighteenth century. According to Professor James Q. Whitman of Yale Law School:

> At its origins . . . the familiar "reasonable doubt" rule was not intended to perform the function we ask it to perform today: It was not primarily intended to protect the accused. Instead, it had a significantly different, and distinctly Christian, purpose: The "reasonable doubt" formula was originally concerned with protecting the souls of the jurors against damnation. Convicting an innocent defendant was regarded, in the older Christian tradition, as a potential mortal sin. The purpose of the "reasonable doubt" instruction was to address this frightening possibility, reassuring jurors that they could convict the defendant without risking their own salvation, as long as their doubts about guilt were not "reasonable."[19]

which covers California and 8 other western states.[24] (The Ninth Circuit is so large and handles so many cases that some have tried to get Congress to divide it into two separate circuits.) Vacancies are common in the circuit courts, especially because of increasing delays in the confirmation process in the Senate. For example, between 1972 and 1994, the duration of a vacancy in the federal appellate courts nearly tripled, from 125 days to 360.[25]

Generally, the losing party in a case decided in the district court has the right to appeal to the federal appeals court for its region. The government, however, may not appeal a finding of not guilty in a criminal trial. Typically, cases are handled by three-judge panels of the appellate court. The party appealing the case, called the **appellant**, files a written **brief** with the court making the case that the trial court made a legal error. Rarely does the appellate court review a factual finding by the trial court. The party who won in the trial court, called the **appellee**, then files a brief in response defending the decision at the lower court. Some cases are decided at this stage on the basis of the written briefs alone.

Other cases move to **oral arguments** before the panel of judges, in which each side gets a short period, usually 15–30 minutes, to make its case and to answer questions. A two-person majority of the panel is sufficient to decide the matter. In rare cases, the full court meeting "en banc" will review a panel's decision. Because the U.S. Supreme Court reviews only about 100 of the 27,000 cases decided each year by the federal appeals courts, these intermediate courts are the final word for nearly all the cases they decide.

Appellant—the party who appeals a case from a lower court, seeking reversal of the decision.

Brief—a document written for an appellate court that gives legal arguments for overturning or sustaining the decision of a lower court.

Appellee—the party who won in the lower court and responds to the appeal by the losing side by seeking a reaffirmation of the lower-court decision.

Oral arguments—arguments made in person before an appellate court, making the legal case for reversing or reaffirming a lower-court decision.

Supreme Court

The Supreme Court by statute has nine members. (The Constitution leaves the size of the Court to Congress.) It is headed by a **chief justice** and has eight associate justices. The Constitution specifies no qualifications—such as citizenship, residency, or age—for service on the Supreme Court or any other federal court. The president appoints all federal judges subject to confirmation by the Senate. The framers presumed that Supreme Court justices would be accomplished lawyers.

Determining the Court's Size

The original Judiciary Act set the size of the Court at six. With the exception of 1801–1802, when Congress reduced the number to five, the Court grew gradually until it reached 10 in 1863. Since 1869, the size has been nine. Although Congress may change the size of the Supreme Court, it has been nine for so long that this is now a settled feature of the constitutional system. (Later we discuss President Franklin Roosevelt's failed plan to increase the size of the Court in the 1930s.)

Hearing Appeals

The Supreme Court handles appeals from the federal appeals courts and from state supreme courts on matters that relate to federal law, treaties, or the U.S. Constitution. In only a small number of specified cases do the parties have a right to a Supreme Court review. In all the others, the Court decides whether to hear an appeal. In these cases the loser in the federal appeals court or a state supreme court files a **writ of certiorari** seeking a hearing before the highest court. The Court considers about 9,000 of these requests each year but grants fewer than 100 (see Table 15-1). If any four justices agree to "grant cert," the case proceeds. This is called the **rule of four**.

How does the Court decide which cases to review from the thousands it considers? One factor is to ensure uniformity of federal law by resolving conflicts among the federal appellate courts. Another is to settle a constitutional or legal matter of broad public importance. A third is to overrule a lower court that violated Supreme Court precedents. This last reason may seem surprising, but lower courts sometimes balk at following Supreme Court decisions despite its position at the top of the federal judiciary.

If the Supreme Court decides to hear a case, the parties file written briefs making their legal arguments. The Court may also allow others who are not parties to the case to file briefs on one side or the other. These are **amicus curiae briefs** (amicus curiae is Latin for "friend of the court"), often simply called "amicus briefs." This kind of brief, the Court explains in its rules, "may be of considerable help to the Court" by presenting "relevant matter not already brought to its attention by the parties."[26] Neither the federal government nor state governments need permission to file an amicus brief, but all others do. Amicus briefs give those who are not actual parties to a case an opportunity to influence the Court's deliberations through additional information and arguments. Occasionally, the Court will accept an amicus brief from a single individual, but usually such briefs are filed by organizations of various sorts (see the discussion in Chapter 8 and the box below on the Affordable Care Act case).

The official who represents the federal government in all matters before the Supreme Court is the **solicitor general** in the Department of Justice. This individual is responsible for filing the briefs that represent the position of the executive branch. Sometime after filing their briefs, the parties make oral arguments before the full Supreme Court, with each side

Chief justice—the head of the U.S. Supreme Court and the administrative head of the U.S. court system.

Writ of certiorari—a request by the losing side in a case decided by a federal appeals court or a state supreme court to have the U.S. Supreme Court review and overturn the decision.

Rule of four—the practice of the Supreme Court that it will hear a case if at least four justices agree to do so.

Amicus curiae brief—Latin for a "friend of the court" brief submitted by an individual or organization that has an interest in the outcome of the case but is not formally a party to it.

The high court sits for a new group portrait October 8, 2010. Back row, left to right: Associate Justice Sonia Sotomayor, Associate Justice Stephen Breyer, Associate Justice Samuel Alito Jr., and Associate Justice Elena Kagan. Front row, left to right: Associate Justice Clarence Thomas, Associate Justice Antonin Scalia, Chief Justice John G. Roberts, Associate Justice Anthony M. Kennedy, and Associate Justice Ruth Bader Ginsburg.

Solicitor general—a high-ranking official in the Department of Justice who represents the United States before the Supreme Court.

| TABLE 15-1 | THE SUPREME COURT WORKLOAD |

	Cases Reviewed	Cases Granted Oral Argument	Cases Decided by Signed Opinion	Number of Signed Opinions
1980	4,351	154	144	123
1990	5,478	125	121	112
1995	6,644	90	87	75
2000	7,760	86	83	77
2005	8,236	88	82	69
2007	8,419	75	72	67
2009	8,131	82	77	73
2010	7,868	86	83	75

NOTE: Because one opinion of the Supreme Court can cover several related cases that raise the same legal issue (called "companion cases"), the number of signed opinions is less than the number of cases with signed opinions.

SOURCE: U.S. Census Bureau, The 2012 *Statistical Abstract, The National Data Book*, Table 331, www.census .gov/compendia/statab/cats/law_enforcement_courts_prisons/courts.html, accessed July 3, 2012.

Opinion of the Court—in a Supreme Court case the opinion that explains and justifies the holding of the majority.

Majority opinion—an opinion of an appellate court, such as the U.S. Supreme Court, that garners the approval of a majority of the members of the court.

Dissenting opinion—in a Supreme Court case, an opinion written by a justice in the minority explaining why he or she disagrees with the majority.

Concurring opinion—in a Supreme Court case, an opinion written by a justice who agrees with the holding of the majority but for reasons in addition to, or different from, those stated in the opinion of the court.

usually assigned 30 minutes to make its case. Typically, the justices do not wait long before they begin questioning the speaker. These exchanges often signal how the Court is leaning on the case at hand.

According to veteran lawyer and judge Stanley Mosk, oral arguments foster deliberation in several ways. First, they enable ordinary citizens to hear judicial proceedings. Second, they let justices ask hypothetical questions to identify issues the opposing lawyers did not fully anticipate and to help determine how a decision might work in practice. "And finally, oral argument provides an important forum for an interchange of ideas between counsel and the judges, and between the judges themselves. The members of the court are given the opportunity to probe, to seek answers to questions that may have arisen in their minds. A justice may challenge his own temporarily formed opinion about the case by probing questions pro and con on the position he may have in mind."[27]

Reaching a Decision

Throughout its October–June term, the Court meets in conference on Wednesdays and Fridays to discuss and make provisional decisions on the cases argued in the days before. Only the justices may attend, and no official record is kept of what happens in these meetings. The chief justice frames the issues and leads the discussion. The associate justices then give their opinions in order of seniority. The purpose of these meetings, according to former chief justice William Rehnquist, "is not to persuade one's colleagues through impassioned advocacy to alter their views, but instead by hearing each justice express his own views to determine therefrom the view of the majority of the Court."[28]

Deliberation continues into the writing phase. If the chief justice is in the majority, he or she decides who will write the **opinion of the Court**. When the chief justice is not in the majority, the senior justice on the majority side decides who will write the opinion. Once the **majority opinion** is drafted, it is circulated to the other justices, who may write **dissenting** or **concurring opinions**. Justices write concurring opinions when they agree with the decision of the Court but perhaps for different reasons than the others in the majority.

Throughout this process, justices are free to change their minds. Occasionally, the minority at the time of the conference will become the majority when drafts of dissenting opinions persuade one or more justices on the other side. "I think it shows the system works," said Associate Justice Sandra Day O'Connor. "We are able on occasion to recognize that perhaps

Franz Jantzen, Collection of the Supreme Court of the United States

In the courtroom in the Supreme Court building, the nine justices sit in the raised seats in the front, with the chief justice in the middle. During oral arguments, the attorneys address the court from the podium in the center. Members of the public may sit for 10–15 minutes to observe the Court in session. Court rules prohibit video recording, photographs, and audio recordings, except for an official audio recording of oral arguments. The Oyez Project makes these recordings available at www.oyez.org.

Amicus Briefs in the Affordable Care Act Case

The most closely watched Supreme Court case in recent years was *National Federation of Independent Business v. Sibelius* (2012), which upheld the constitutionality of the Affordable Care Act (ACA). Dozens of organizations and individuals filed amicus briefs on one side or the other. Here is a list of some of these:

In Support of ACA	Opposed to ACA
AARP	Chamber of Commerce of the United States
American Civil Liberties Union	Family Research Council
NAACP Legal Defense and Educational Fund	National Restaurant Association
American Academy of Pediatrics	American Catholic Lawyers Association
American Nurses Association	American Life League
American Hospital Association	Cato Institute
American Cancer Society	Heritage Foundation
National Women's Law Center	Tax Foundation
A group of 500 state legislators	A group of 333 state legislators
Professors of economics, health law, and constitutional law	Professors of economics and constitutional law

SOURCE: American Bar Association, www.americanbar.org/publications/preview_home/11-398.html, accessed July 3, 2012.

Law clerk—in the Supreme Court, usually a recent top graduate of a prestigious law school who works for a year assisting a justice with legal research and, possibly, opinion writing.

Plurality opinion—in a Supreme Court case, the opinion written by the most justices who support the decision, when a majority of justices cannot agree on a single opinion.

Unanimous opinion—an opinion of an appellate court, such as the U.S. Supreme Court, that garners the approval of every member of the court.

Precedents—the body of court decisions on similar matters to an issue before the courts.

Case law—the body of authoritative prior court decisions.

a previously expressed view may not have been the best view."[29] In formulating their positions and writing opinions, the justices have the help of **law clerks** (up to four per justice), who are usually recent top graduates of prestigious law schools.

Justices may sign other opinions even if they write their own. If a majority of justices cannot agree on a single opinion, then the opinion that the most justices signed and that agrees with the Court's holding becomes the **plurality opinion**. In these cases the Court's actual decision is binding and stands as precedent, but the arguments of the plurality carry less weight than a majority opinion would. **Unanimous opinions** are the "weightiest" of all. This is why in many tough legal battles the justices will work to fashion a single unanimous judgment and opinion.

Before John Marshall entered the Court in 1801, it was common for each justice to write his own opinion. Marshall worked hard to get his colleagues to agree to a single unanimous opinion to promote public acceptance of its often controversial decisions. More recently, the Supreme Court issued unanimous opinions in *Brown v. Board of Education* (1954), which overturned state-enforced segregation in public schools, and in *U.S. v. Nixon* (1974), which led to President Richard Nixon's resignation by requiring him to turn over incriminating tape recordings to a federal prosecutor.

In their opinions, justices rely heavily on **precedents**—prior court decisions on similar matters—and **case law**—the body of authoritative prior court decisions. Even when they are breaking new ground, they show the links between the current decision and those of the past. In recent years, some justices have even cited precedents from foreign courts. In *Lawrence v. Texas*, for example, which struck down laws prohibiting homosexual conduct in 2003, Justice Anthony Kennedy, writing for the majority, drew support from a similar decision by the European Court of Human Rights. Supporters of the practice of citing foreign precedents say that foreign courts can be a good source of legal reasoning. Opponents say that the Court has no authority to interpret the United States Constitution by the light of the laws and constitutions of other nations. (See the International Perspectives box for a discussion of the International Criminal Court and the issues it raises for American sovereignty and foreign policy.)

This is the room in which the justices meet on Wednesdays and Fridays when the Court is in session to discuss cases and reach provisional decisions. No one but the justices themselves may be present during these conferences.

Steve Petteway, Collection of the Supreme Court of the United States

International Perspectives

The International Criminal Court

The International Criminal Court (ICC) was established in 2002 after the requisite 60 nations ratified the "Rome Statute of the International Criminal Court," which was drafted under the auspices of the United Nations in 1998. The ICC should not be confused with the International Court of Justice (ICJ), also called the World Court, which was established in 1946 as the principal judicial organ of the United Nations. The ICJ issues advisory opinions on matters of international law when requested by the UN or its agencies and rules on disputes between member states of the UN when they agree to its jurisdiction.

 The International Criminal Court was created to serve as a permanent tribunal to prosecute "genocide, crimes against humanity, and war crimes," replacing the need for such ad hoc tribunals as the Nuremberg tribunal of 1945–1949; the International Criminal Tribunal for the Former Yugoslavia, which has been operating since 1993; and the International Criminal Tribunal for Rwanda, which has been operating since 1994. It is officially located in The Hague, the Netherlands (as is the ICJ), is composed of 18 judges who serve for up to 9 years, and has an independent prosecutor who "conduct[s] investigations and prosecutions of crimes that fall within the jurisdiction of the Court." As of 2012, it had completed or was conducting formal investigations or prosecutions in seven African countries: Uganda; the Democratic Republic of the Congo; Sudan; the Central African Republic; the Republic of Kenya; Libya; and the Ivory Coast. It had also opened preliminary examinations of situations in Afghanistan, Georgia, Guinea, Colombia, Honduras, Korea, and Nigeria.

More than 100 nations have now ratified the treaty establishing the ICC, but not such large countries as the United States, Russia, India, and China. Although President Bill Clinton signed the treaty in 1998, he never presented it to the Senate for ratification, and his successor, George W. Bush, formally rescinded the signature.

 In 2003, the U.S. Congress passed the American Service-Members' Protection Act, which essentially reiterated the Bush administration's objections to the ICC. It deplored the fact that American citizens prosecuted by the ICC would be "denied procedural protections to which all Americans are entitled under the Bill of Rights to the United States Constitution, such as the right to trial by jury," and it announced that "[t]he United States will not recognize the jurisdiction of the International Criminal Court over United States nationals." Because of the fear that U.S. service members overseas could be prosecuted by the ICC, the United States has sought UN Security Council resolutions or bilateral agreements that would exempt the U.S. military on peacekeeping missions from ICC jurisdiction. This remains a matter of great controversy. The Obama administration has taken a friendlier attitude toward the ICC, cooperating in some of its efforts, but has not asked the Senate to ratify the treaty.[30]

CRITICAL THINKING QUESTION

Would the nation and the world be better served if the United States formally approved the International Criminal Court?

Special Courts

The federal court system also includes several specialized courts. Each federal judicial district, for example, has a bankruptcy court; altogether these courts process about a million bankruptcy applications each year. A Court of International Trade has jurisdiction over international trade and customs issues; and a Court of Federal Claims handles issues of federal contracts, the taking of private property by the federal government, and other claims against the United States. In 1951, Congress created a special court to handle appeals from military courts-martial. It is now called the U.S. Court of Appeals for the Armed Forces. It reviews courts-martial that result in a death sentence or another severe sanction.

Cases and Controversies

In Article III, the U.S. Constitution extends the judicial power to "Cases" and "Controversies" involving federal issues, conflicts between states, and disputes between citizens of different states. The courts have interpreted the constitutional language to mean that they only get involved when there is "a real conflict of interests or rights between contending parties."[31] Unlike some state courts, federal courts do not address hypothetical controversies or issue **advisory opinions** on legal or constitutional matters. The Supreme Court set this

Advisory opinion—an opinion by a court giving its advice or interpretation on a legal matter outside of a specific case or controversy. Federal courts do not issue advisory opinions.

precedent in 1793 when it refused to answer questions about international law and treaty obligations submitted by Secretary of State Thomas Jefferson on behalf of President George Washington. Chief Justice John Jay insisted that it was not proper for the justices to advise the executive branch on matters that might come before them. Ever since, the federal courts have refused to issue advisory opinions, although judges and justices have sometimes offered private advice to presidents.

How, then, do the courts determine whether a genuine case or controversy exists? They look at four key characteristics of the case: whether the parties have standing to sue, whether the matter is ripe for judicial resolution, whether events have rendered the controversy moot or irrelevant, and whether the case presents a political question within the jurisdiction of elected officials.

Standing

Standing—a party's right to bring a case to court and receive a judicial resolution, usually requiring that the party has suffered a real injury and does not simply have a generalized grievance against an individual, organization, or the government.

To have standing to sue, the party must have suffered a real injury. It is not enough to have a generalized grievance against an individual, organization, or the government. Citizens, for example, who believe that a public agency has exceeded its authority, illegally spent public funds, or in some other way violated the Constitution will not generally have standing to sue unless a federal law specifically gives them that legal right. In a highly publicized case in 2004, the Supreme Court ruled that a noncustodial father of an elementary school student did not have standing to sue a public school at which students recited the Pledge of Allegiance. The father had argued that the words "under God" in the Pledge violated the separation of church and state.

Ripeness

Ripeness—the doctrine that the courts will not hear cases brought prematurely—that is, before the dispute is well developed and ready, or ripe, for adjudication.

Even if a party has standing to sue, the courts will not hear the case prematurely. The dispute must be sufficiently well developed and specific that it is "ripe" for adjudication. The ripeness doctrine requires that the parties to a legal controversy exhaust their remedies through federal or state administrative procedures before asking the courts to get involved. It has also been used in separation of powers disputes in recent decades, especially when some members of Congress have gone to court to prevent presidents from undertaking military actions overseas. Several lower federal courts have dismissed such suits because Congress had not formally opposed the president. Until it did, the issue was not ripe for review.[32]

Mootness

Mootness—the doctrine that the courts will not decide a case if the dispute has been resolved or rendered irrelevant by subsequent events.

Even if a case is ripe for resolution, the courts will usually not decide it if events have rendered the dispute moot, or irrelevant. This happened when the first affirmative action case involving college or university admissions reached the Supreme Court. Marco DeFunis had sued the University of Washington Law School after it turned him down for admission in 1971, contending that minorities with lower qualifications had been admitted ahead of him. He won in lower federal court, was admitted to the law school, and had nearly graduated by the time his case, on appeal from the state of Washington, reached the Supreme Court. Rather than resolve the legal and constitutional issues, the Court declared the issue moot.

At other times, the Court has issued decisions on the merits that it could have avoided by invoking the mootness doctrine. A prominent example is the 1973 abortion decision *Roe v. Wade*, which took three years to get from initial suit to the Supreme Court. This was long after the plaintiff had given birth. The Court recognized that the federal appeals process will always take longer than a pregnancy, and it issued a ruling on the merits.

Political Questions

Political questions—the doctrine that the courts should not decide issues that the Constitution has given over to the discretion of the Congress or the president.

A final reason the courts occasionally give to justify not deciding an issue is the political questions doctrine. The Supreme Court first asserted this principle in *Marbury v. Madison* in 1803. Although executive officials have specific legal responsibilities that courts may order to be carried out, such as delivering a presidential commission, a president also has broader "political powers" that courts cannot control. In the words of Chief Justice John Marshall: "By the constitution of the United States, the president is invested with certain important political powers, in the exercise of which he is to use his own discretion, and is accountable only to his country in his political character, and to his own conscience." When the president exercises these powers, the courts cannot control him: "The subjects are political. They respect the nation, not individual rights, and being entrusted to the executive, the decision of the executive is conclusive."[33]

In 1849, the Court extended this doctrine to Congress in a case that arose out of Dorr's Rebellion in Rhode Island. In this uprising, citizens who did not own sufficient property to vote under the rules of the colonial charter that still governed the state tried to replace the charter with a new constitution. In *Luther v. Borden*, the Supreme Court held that in guaranteeing the states "a Republican Form of Government" in Article IV, the U.S. Constitution gives Congress the final say in determining whether a state government is republican. Congress's "decision is binding on every other department of the government, and could not be questioned in a judicial tribunal."[34]

Drawing on this doctrine, the modern Supreme Court has denied that it has the right to review (1) the Senate's power to remove a federal judge after an impeachment trial and (2) the president's authority to terminate a treaty, at least in the absence of formal congressional opposition to the termination. Although it is not used often, the doctrine of political questions remains controversial. Its critics dispute its constitutional basis and accuse the Court of using it to avoid making judgments about the powers of Congress and the president. Its defenders insist that the Constitution left some important matters exclusively to the political branches.

Together, the rule against advisory opinions and the doctrines of standing, ripeness, mootness, and political questions enable the federal courts to focus on disputes involving real harms to individuals, to defer to the political branches in appropriate cases, and, perhaps in some cases, to duck hot issues. These are tools of judicial self-restraint, which we will discuss later in this chapter.

THE COURTS AND AMERICAN POLITICS
MAJOR ISSUE

> • How has the Supreme Court influenced American politics throughout its history?

Because the U.S. Supreme Court heads a coequal branch of the federal government and has the final word on many issues, it has had a greater impact on its country's government and politics than any other national court. No history of American politics could be complete without assessing the impact of the Supreme Court.

The Foundations for National Power

During the first decades under the Constitution, the Supreme Court cemented its position as a coequal branch of the national government through the doctrine of judicial review, affirmed the supremacy of the federal Constitution and federal law over state constitutions and state law, and legitimized a broad interpretation of Congress's enumerated powers.

As we noted in Chapter 3, two particularly important cases were *McCulloch v. Maryland* (1819) and *Gibbons v. Ogden* (1824). The first upheld Congress's authority to establish a national bank as a "necessary and proper" measure for carrying out its enumerated powers. It also overturned the tax levied by Maryland on the federal bank, a tax that would have made the federal institution uncompetitive with state chartered banks. Through its decision, the Court enforced the supremacy of national law in the American federal system. Similarly, the *Gibbons* case broadly interpreted Congress's commerce power to include navigation, not merely the exchange of goods, and gave Congress's regulations preeminence over conflicting state laws.

In another important case, *Dartmouth College v. Woodward* (1819), the Court broadly interpreted the Constitution's prohibition on the states from passing laws "impairing the Obligation of Contracts." In this case, the Court prevented the New Hampshire state legislature from changing the charter issued by King George III in 1769 that created Dartmouth College. By treating corporate charters as contracts, the Court signaled that it was not reluctant to overrule state economic regulations, especially if these interfered with private institutions. In interpreting the federal government's economic powers broadly and in affirming the supremacy of the federal Constitution and laws, these cases (and others) provided the foundation for the growth of a strong central government.

Race and Reconstruction

In Chapter 4, we reviewed in detail the Supreme Court's hugely controversial decision in *Dred Scott v. Sandford* in 1857, which exacerbated tensions over slavery and may have helped to bring about the Civil War. In the years after the war, the task of Reconstruction set the nation's domestic agenda.

As we noted in Chapter 6, the Supreme Court issued several key decisions that narrowly interpreted the guarantees of the Civil War amendments (Thirteenth, Fourteenth, and Fifteenth) and the new civil rights acts. In the *Slaughterhouse Cases* of 1873, the Court held that the Fourteenth Amendment's command that the states not "abridge the privileges and immunities of citizens of the United States" did not encompass the basic rights over person and property that the state governments had always regulated. Instead, it referred only to rights specifically associated with national citizenship, such as asserting claims on the federal government and demanding its protection when traveling outside the country. Critics of the decision maintain that it weakened the ability of the federal government to secure the rights of the former slaves in the South.

Three years later, in *United States v. Cruikshank*, the Court ruled that the federal government had no authority to prosecute several white men in Louisiana for contributing to a massacre of more than 100 blacks. No specifically federal rights had been violated, the Court held, and the Fourteenth Amendment's guarantee of "due process" and "equal protection" applied only against state action—not private lawlessness. Only the state could prosecute such offenses.

In 1883, in the *Civil Rights Cases*, the Court reaffirmed that the guarantees of the Fourteenth Amendment did not apply to private discrimination. In so doing, it declared as unconstitutional provisions of the Civil Rights Act of 1875 that prohibited racial discrimination in "accommodations, advantages, facilities, and privileges of inns, public conveyances on land or water, theatres, and other places of public amusement."

Finally, in *Plessy v. Ferguson* in 1896, the Court endorsed the doctrine of "separate but equal" by ruling that the Fourteenth Amendment did not prohibit states from segregating the races, as long as they had access to comparable facilities. The consistent theme in these cases was that the federal government had little authority to affect race relations in the states, even when white majorities used their political power to disadvantage blacks.

Limiting the Power of Government to Regulate the Economy

In 1895, the Supreme Court signaled a new assertiveness in limiting the government's power over the economy when it overturned the federal income tax of 1894, which had imposed a 2% tax on incomes above $4,000. (Congress had previously taxed incomes during the Civil War, but these laws had lapsed.) The Court ruled 5–4 that an income tax was a "direct Tax" that, according to the Constitution, must be apportioned based on state population. To overturn this decision, the state legislatures ratified the Sixteenth Amendment in 1913, granting Congress unrestricted power to tax incomes. This was one of the few times in American history when the Constitution was amended to overturn a Supreme Court decision.

In the decades after the Civil War, large industrial organizations increasingly dominated the economy, and their employees often worked long hours in unsafe conditions.

Demands grew for government to regulate economic enterprise, but in 1905, the Supreme Court ruled that the Constitution limited what government could do. In the landmark case *Lochner v. New York*, it held that New York state could not prevent certain employers, including bakers, from requiring more than 60 hours of work per week. In this 5–4 decision, the majority held that the state law interfered with "the right of contract between the employer and employees." The right of individuals to sell their own labor or to purchase the labor of others was one of the liberties protected by the clause in the Fourteenth Amendment that prohibits a state from "depriv[ing] any person of life, liberty, or property, without due process of law." If a willing employer and a willing employee agreed to a work week longer than 60 hours, the state could not interfere.[35]

In a short and influential dissent, Justice Oliver Wendell Holmes Jr. charged the majority with embracing "an economic theory which a large part of the country does not entertain." Here Holmes was referring to "laissez-faire" principles, which hold that government regulation hampers economic growth. A majority of the people, Holmes said, have a right "to embody their opinions in law" even if this "interfere[s] with the liberty to contract." Laws that restrict economic activity on Sundays, that limit the interest rates that banks can charge for loans, and that mandate school attendance all restrict liberty for reasons thought important by the majority. Unless "fundamental principles" are at issue, Holmes insisted, the courts should not "prevent the natural outcome of a dominant opinion."[36]

In the following decades, the Supreme Court upheld some state and federal laws that regulated working conditions but overturned many others. Especially controversial were its decisions in 1918 to overturn a federal law prohibiting the interstate commerce of goods produced through child labor (although it had previously upheld state laws against child labor), and in 1923 to strike down a federal law mandating a minimum wage for women and children in the District of Columbia.[37] The Court overturned so many state and federal laws on the principles of the *Lochner* decision that this period became known as the **Lochner era**.

The controversy over the Court's role escalated when it struck down popular elements of Franklin Roosevelt's New Deal legislation in the 1930s. In *Panama Refining Co. v. Ryan* and *Schechter Poultry Corp. v. U.S.*, both in 1935, the Court threw out major provisions of Roosevelt's National Industrial Recovery Act, the administration's main effort to fix the Great Depression economy.[38] These and other decisions held that Congress had unconstitutionally delegated its legislative powers to the president and to industry groups and had in other ways exceeded its powers.

Lochner era—the period from 1905 until 1937 when the Supreme Court overturned many state and federal laws for interfering with the free-market economy. The name comes from the Supreme Court case *Lochner v. New York* of 1905.

Shifting Gears: Deferring to the Political Branches on Economic Matters

In response to the *Schechter* decision, President Roosevelt attacked the Court's "horse-and-buggy definition of interstate commerce." Early in 1937, he proposed adding one justice to the Court for each sitting justice over 70 years old who did not retire. With six justices over 70, he could have increased the Court to 15 members, ensuring a pro–New Deal majority. Opponents denounced this **court-packing plan**, and it failed to gain enough public and congressional support to pass. Later that same year, however, one justice changed his voting patterns, and suddenly the Court began producing 5–4 majorities in support of broad federal and state regulatory power. Pundits called this "the switch in time that saved nine." Subsequent retirements and new appointments solidified the liberal majority on the Court.

The case that best illustrates the transformation of the court is *Wickard v. Filburn* of 1942.[39] In this case, the owner of a small Ohio farm, Roscoe Filburn, was penalized for producing more wheat (239 bushels from 12 acres) than he was permitted under the Second Agricultural Adjustment Act of 1938. Filburn's wheat never left the farm; his family and dairy cattle consumed it all. Thus, the legal question was whether Congress's power to regulate interstate commerce ("Commerce . . . among the several States") extended even to a product that was grown and consumed entirely on a single farm. A unanimous

Court-packing plan—the common name for President Franklin Roosevelt's proposal to increase the size of the Supreme Court by up to six additional members.

A cartoonist accuses President Roosevelt of toppling American democracy by undermining the independence of Congress and the federal judiciary.

© 1937, Elderman/The Washington Post

Court ruled that because Filburn's overproduction reduced his demand for wheat in the marketplace, it affected the market price of wheat and therefore interstate commerce. "Home-grown wheat in this sense," the Court held, "competes with wheat in commerce."[40] Congress's regulation was thus constitutional.

If Congress may lawfully regulate the private production and consumption of wheat, virtually no economic activity would seem to be outside its power. The Lochner era was over. (As we saw in Chapter 3, however, the Supreme Court has occasionally struck down federal laws as beyond the federal commerce power because they regulate noneconomic matters, such as the possession of firearms near public schools.)

The Rights Revolution

Critics of the "activist" Supreme Court of the Lochner era applauded the Court's deference to the political branches on economic matters after 1937. In 1938, however, the Court began to develop principles that justified a more activist stance in reviewing federal and state legislation in other areas. In *United States v. Carolene Products Co.*, where the Court upheld a broad interpretation of Congress's commerce power, the majority opinion included a footnote (now famous as "footnote 4") that identified areas where the Court should not necessarily presume the constitutionality of legislation. These included laws that violated specific provisions of the Constitution (such as the Bill of Rights), that restricted participation in the political process and that reflected prejudice against religious, ethnic, or racial minorities.[41]

In the post–New Deal period, the Court has not been reluctant to overturn state and federal laws, practices, or policies in areas outside economic regulation. Examples include the following:

- Prohibiting states from segregating the races in public schools
- Prohibiting official prayer in public schools
- Requiring states to reorganize their legislatures to conform to the dictates of "one person, one vote"
- Limiting the power of government to restrict access to some sexually explicit materials
- Overturning state laws prohibiting abortion
- Expanding the rights of criminal defendants
- Requiring all the states with the death penalty to rewrite their capital punishment laws
- Narrowing the grounds on which a public figure could sue for libel
- Prohibiting the states and federal government from criminalizing the burning of the American flag
- Overturning state laws against homosexual acts
- Intervening in a recount ordered by a state supreme court in a presidential election (Florida in 2000)

Table 15-2 shows how much more likely the Supreme Court was to overturn state and federal laws in the twentieth century than it was in the nineteenth century.

Observers often refer to the Supreme Court by the name of its chief justice, such as the **Marshall Court** of 1801–1835 (named after John Marshall) and the Taney Court of 1836–1864 (named after Roger B. Taney). In the last half of the twentieth century, the Court that most aggressively expanded private rights was the **Warren Court** of 1953–1969, named after Chief Justice Earl Warren. When President Dwight Eisenhower nominated the Republican governor of California to be chief justice in 1953, few expected the "rights revolution" that followed, including landmark decisions on racial segregation, reapportionment, separation of church and state, the freedom of speech and press, and the rights of criminal defendants.

Marshall Court—the Supreme Court under the leadership of Chief Justice John Marshall, 1801–1835. Its decisions cemented the Court's position as a coequal branch of the national government, affirmed the supremacy of the federal Constitution and federal law over state constitutions and state law, and legitimized a broad interpretation of Congress's enumerated powers.

Warren Court—the Supreme Court under the leadership of Chief Justice Earl Warren, 1953–1969. It is famous for its rulings expanding rights.

TABLE 15-2	FEDERAL, STATE, AND LOCAL LAWS DECLARED UNCONSTITUTIONAL BY THE SUPREME COURT, 1790–1999		
Years	Federal Laws	State and Local Laws	Total
1790–1799	0	0	0
1800–1809	1	1	2
1810–1819	0	7	7
1820–1829	0	8	8
1830–1839	0	3	3
1840–1849	0	9	9
1850–1859	1	7	8
1860–1869	4	23	27
1870–1879	7	36	43
1880–1889	4	46	50
1890–1899	5	36	41
1900–1909	9	40	49
1910–1919	6	118	124
1920–1929	15	139	154
1930–1939	13	93	106
1940–1949	2	57	59
1950–1959	5	61	66
1960–1969	16	149	165
1970–1979	20	193	213
1980–1989	16	162	178
1990–1999	23	61	84

SOURCE: Harold W. Stanley and Richard G. Niemi, eds., *Vital Statistics on American Politics*, 3rd ed. (Washington, DC: CQ Press, 1992), 306; Lawrence Baum, *The Supreme Court*, 8th ed. (Washington, DC: CQ Press, 2004), 170, 173.

Many of the Warren Court's decisions were so controversial that some in Congress discussed impeaching the chief justice, and in 1968 Republican presidential candidate Richard Nixon promised to appoint "strict constructionists" to the Court. During his first term, Nixon made four appointments to the Court, including a new chief justice, Warren Burger. To the surprise of many, the Burger Court did not overturn the major precedents of the Warren Court and proved just as willing to overturn federal, state, and local laws. Nonetheless, the Burger Court did limit the potential reach of some Warren Court precedents, especially in cases involving the rights of criminal defendants, affirmative action, and regulation of obscenity and pornography.

Including Nixon's appointments, 16 new justices joined the Court between Earl Warren's retirement in 1969 and Elena Kagan's confirmation in 2010. Twelve of these were appointed by Republican presidents and two each by Democrats Bill Clinton and Barack Obama. Although the Supreme Court has not dismantled the legal foundations of the "rights revolution," most close observers would agree that dozens of important decisions handed down in recent decades might have turned out differently had Democratic presidents appointed 12 justices and Republican presidents only 4. Even a single change of justice can tip many issues, especially since 20%–30% of Supreme Court decisions in recent years have resulted from 5–4 votes. In just the years since 2006, for example, slim 5–4 majorities issued the following landmark rulings:

- Local school districts may not voluntarily use race to promote diversity in assigning students to schools.

© Bettmann/Corbis

Under Chief Justice Earl Warren, the Supreme Court launched a "rights revolution" in the 1950s and 1960s.

On the whole, has the impact of the Supreme Court on American politics and public policy been for good or for ill?

- The federal ban on partial-birth abortions is constitutional.
- The use of the death penalty against those who rape children is unconstitutional.
- Americans have a personal constitutional right to own firearms, which states must respect.
- Enemy combatants apprehended by the United States in the war on terrorism have a right to challenge their detention in habeas corpus proceedings in federal courts.
- The city of New Haven, Connecticut, cannot refuse to promote white and Hispanic firefighters who scored highest on an exam because no blacks were promoted based on the exam results.
- Under the First Amendment, Congress cannot restrict independent political expenditures by corporations and unions.
- States may not require life sentences for juveniles convicted of murder.
- Congress may require those who do not purchase health insurance to pay a financial penalty (technically a tax, according to the Court).

The Expansion of the Remedial Powers of the Federal Courts

The Supreme Court's landmark decision in *Brown v. Board of Education* in 1954 is rightly famous. Less well known is its follow-up decision a year later, *Brown II*. In this case, the Supreme Court gave the federal district courts primary responsibility for working with local officials to carry out the principles of *Brown*. In doing so, the courts would use their "equity power," which "has been characterized by a practical flexibility in shaping its remedies and by a facility for adjusting and reconciling public and private needs."[42] In later school desegregation cases, the Supreme Court endorsed a variety of judicial mandates—such as busing students and redrawing school attendance boundaries—as legitimate exercises of the equity power.

Equity power—the judicial power, derived from the British legal tradition, to issue injunctions or provide for other kinds of relief, especially when a strict application of the law would lead to unjust results.

The **equity power**, which derives from the British legal tradition, refers to the power of courts to issue injunctions or decrees to achieve a just outcome in a particular case. Originally, courts of equity in Britain were created to give an aggrieved party the opportunity to achieve justice when the strict application of the law, as applied in the regular common law courts, led to unfair results. Although the U.S. Congress never established separate federal courts of equity, the Constitution provides that the federal judicial power shall extend to cases "in Law and Equity" (Article III, Section 2).

During the ratification debates of 1787–1788, the "Federal Farmer," one of the leading Anti-Federalists, charged that vesting "general powers in equity" in the federal courts was "a very dangerous thing" because it would vest too much discretion in judges to decide anyway they wanted.[43] In *The Federalist Papers*, Alexander Hamilton, an accomplished lawyer, denied that the equity power conveyed a general, undefined discretionary authority on the courts. It was necessary, he said, in such cases as disputes over contracts where one party had an "undue and unconscionable advantage."[44]

Even today, scholars debate the breadth of the equity power. For the first century under the Constitution, federal courts seldom used it. Then in the late 1800s, federal courts began issuing injunctions to prohibit strikes. Congress responded in 1932 by passing a law that prohibited courts from issuing injunctions in labor disputes. Several decades later, the federal courts used their equity powers to desegregate public schools. Later, they began to regulate jails and prisons, public housing authorities, and mental health facilities when convinced that these had been operating in violation of constitutional principles. Sometimes they appointed "special masters" to bring these institutions up to constitutional standards.

Class action—a lawsuit in which one or a few individuals are certified by the court as representing many others in a similar situation and in which the resulting remedies, if any, apply to the entire class.

These interventions often resulted from **class action** lawsuits in which one or a few individuals are certified by the court as representing others in a similar situation. Court-imposed remedies apply to the entire class, not just those who brought the suit.

One of the most far-reaching and controversial examples of federal courts using their equity powers to order remedies occurred in Kansas City, Missouri, in the 1980s. Responding to a suit from parents of public school children, a federal district judge decided that the only way to integrate the schools in Kansas City, in which 68% of the students were black, was to attract white students from the surrounding suburbs into the city school system by converting most of the city schools into magnet schools.

The judge asked local school officials to think big about improvements and innovations. As the Supreme Court later noted, the judge ordered "massive expenditures" to finance large reductions in class size, salary increases to virtually all district employees, full-day kindergarten, an expanded summer school, tutoring programs, and "an early childhood development program."[45] Much of the money would go to capital improvements:

> High schools in which every classroom will have air conditioning, an alarm system, and 15 microcomputers; a 2,000-square-foot planetarium; greenhouses and vivariums; a 15-acre farm with an air-conditioned meeting room for 104 people; a Model United Nations wired for language translation; broadcast capable radio and television studios with an editing and animation lab; a temperature controlled art gallery; movie editing and screening rooms; a 3,500-square-foot dust-free diesel mechanics room; 1,875-square-foot elementary school animal rooms for use in a zoo project; swimming pools; and numerous other facilities.[46]

Three times the case reached the Supreme Court, and twice the Court allowed the judge's sweeping orders to stand. Although in 1990 the Court overturned the judge's imposition of a large property tax increase to fund the improvements, it allowed the judge to order local officials to raise the necessary funds. But in 1995, in a 5–4 decision, the Supreme Court ruled that the district judge had "transgressed the constitutional bounds of its remedial powers."[47] Shortly thereafter, the federal judge returned the control of the schools to local and state officials. When he did, the minority proportion of the school system was higher than when he first intervened.[48]

The Growing Importance of State Supreme Courts

In the first decades of the rights revolution, the U.S. Supreme Court led the way, but after the Burger Court failed to expand individual rights in cases on education, freedom of speech, and the rights of criminal defendants in the 1970s, some began to look anew to the state courts. In several speeches and writings, Supreme Court Associate Justice William J. Brennan called on the state courts to look to their state constitutions as "a font of individual liberties."[49]

Although state court judges are required to follow a Supreme Court interpretation of a provision of the U.S. Constitution, they are generally free to read similar (or even identical) language in their own constitutions—such as "due process" or "equal protection"—more expansively. Also, many state constitutions include broader language on rights than in the U.S. Bill of Rights or cover topics such as education not explicitly addressed in the U.S. Constitution. As Brennan noted, state court decisions based on interpretations of state constitutions "not only cannot be overturned by, they indeed are not even reviewable by, the Supreme Court of the United States. We are utterly without jurisdiction to review such state decisions."[50]

Many state supreme courts have followed Brennan's call. They have, among other actions, expanded the rights of criminal defendants beyond federal Supreme Court requirements; mandated the complete restructuring of public education funding to equalize resources across the state; and, in recent years, expanded the rights of gays to marry or enter into civil unions, which bestow the legal benefits of marriage without the name.

The Courts and the 2000 Presidential Election

In December 2000, the Supreme Court ignited a firestorm of controversy when it ordered Florida authorities to halt the recount of ballots in the disputed presidential election.[51] This case, *Bush v. Gore*, resulted in Texas governor George W. Bush winning Florida's 25 electoral votes and the presidency. Critics attacked the majority's legal reasoning, and some went further to charge political bias among the five justices, all appointed by Republican presidents. They were "determined," wrote one prominent law professor, "to ensure a Republican victory."[52] Another accused them of "sheer willfulness."[53]

So, what was the majority's legal argument? Many years before, the Supreme Court had established the principle of "one person, one vote." This meant, said the majority in *Bush v. Gore*, that "equal weight [should be] accorded to each vote and . . . equal dignity [is] owed to each voter."[54] The problem with the massive manual recount ordered by the Florida Supreme Court was that each county could set its own rules to determine voter intent when the counting machines did not record a vote for president on the punch-card ballot. This meant that identical punch cards might be recorded differently in different counties. The majority concluded that the recount procedures violated the equal protection clause of the Fourteenth Amendment and that there was not sufficient time, because of statutory deadlines for counting the electoral votes, to establish and enforce uniform procedures.

Due to intense public interest in *Bush v. Gore*, argued before the Supreme Court on December 11, 2000, the Court permitted the release of an audio recording of the oral arguments immediately after they ended. Because there was no videotape of the session, C-SPAN used an artist's sketch when it played the audio tape.

Seven of the nine justices agreed that there was an equal protection violation, but two of these strongly opposed ordering a halt to the recounts then underway. Altogether, four justices (two who found an equal protection violation and the two who did not) insisted that there was still time for constitutional recounts to be completed and that the principle of federalism required the U.S. Supreme Court to defer to the Florida Supreme Court's interpretation of Florida law. Three of these dissenters castigated the majority for implicitly challenging the "impartiality and capacity of the state judges." The Court's decision, they argued, "can only lend credence to the most cynical appraisal of the work of judges throughout the land."[55] Indeed, three members of the majority had specifically criticized the Florida Supreme Court for "impermissibly distort[ing]" Florida's election laws, noting that the U.S. Constitution gave ultimate authority to choose presidential electors to the state legislatures, not the courts. They even called one of the Florida Supreme Court's interpretations "absurd."[56]

Both sides in this contentious debate charged judicial activism. The critics of *Bush v. Gore* denounced the Court's intrusion into state election procedures as legally unjustified and possibly politically motivated. Supporters responded that the Court was simply overturning the unjustified activism of the Florida Supreme Court, while enforcing the equal protection guarantee of the Fourteenth Amendment. *Bush v. Gore* signals that the federal courts may play a larger role in monitoring elections in the future than they have in the past.

THE CONTINUING DEBATE OVER JUDICIAL ACTIVISM
MAJOR ISSUES

- How much should the Supreme Court influence public policy?
- Should the modern Court base its constitutional interpretations on the "original intent," or "original meaning," of the Constitution?

The Supreme Court's impact on American public policy raises fundamental questions about deliberative democracy in the United States. In a genuine deliberative democracy, the people rule themselves through elected officials who deliberate on their behalf. The courts have their own unique deliberative function—reasoning about how the laws and the Constitution apply in specific cases and controversies—but their deliberations ought not to replace the policy deliberations of legislatures and executives. It is no surprise that the debate over judicial activism is as old as the republic.

The Debate at the Founding

During the ratification debates over the Constitution, an Anti-Federalist writing under the pseudonym of Brutus (many believe he was a New York judge named Robert Yates) published seven essays on the dangers of the new federal judiciary. His principal concerns were that the Court would "explain the constitution according to the reasoning spirit of it, without being confined to the words or letter"; that it would use this freedom of interpretation to expand federal power at the expense of the states and localities; and that its decisions, no matter how erroneous, would be "final and irreversible" because the Court would be "independent of the people, of the legislature, and of every power under heaven."[57] Although the impeachment power could give Congress real control over the federal courts, Brutus predicted (correctly, it turns out) that "errors in judgment" would not be considered the kinds of "high Crimes and Misdemeanors" that justify removal from office.[58]

In *The Federalist Papers*, Alexander Hamilton responded to Brutus's fears. Hamilton argued, first, that the "long and laborious study" of the law that would qualify people to serve in the federal judiciary would also dispose them to "be bound down by strict rules and precedents."[59] By their training and disposition, judges were simply not likely to abuse their trust and become policymakers. Second, nothing in the Constitution "directly empowers the national courts to construe the laws according to the spirit of the Constitution."[60] Third, the judiciary will be too weak to encroach significantly on legislative power, for it is "the least dangerous" of the three branches.[61] Finally, Congress's power to impeach and remove judges "is alone a complete security" against the dangers of judicial usurpation.[62] Hamilton believed that the political branches would respond vigorously to a real abuse of judicial authority.

By giving federal judges life tenure and prohibiting Congress from reducing judicial salaries, the framers sought to insulate judges from political pressures so that they could decide each case on its legal merits. Ideally, the federal judiciary would be strong enough to resist unconstitutional actions by the political branches and also "to guard the Constitution and the rights of individuals" from temporary passions or "ill humors" that may affect the people themselves.[63] The Anti-Federalists asked whether judges could be this independent without falling prey to the temptation to interpret the Constitution and laws to produce the results they wished, thereby making laws rather than interpreting them.

The Debate Recurs

This debate over the proper role of the federal courts has popped up again and again in American history. In the first decades, Jefferson, Madison, and many others opposed the broad doctrine of judicial review set forth by John Marshall in *Marbury v. Madison*. During the same period, state officials challenged the principles of national supremacy that the Supreme Court enforced against state legislatures and state courts. In the late 1850s, Lincoln and fellow Republicans denounced the *Dred Scott* decision for misinterpreting the relationship of slavery to the Declaration of Independence and the Constitution. From the *Lochner* decision in 1905 through the Court's redirection in 1937, proponents of government regulation of the economy accused the members of the Court of reading their preferred economic philosophies into the Constitution. After the Court outlawed segregated public schools in 1954, segregationist lawmakers condemned it for substituting "naked power for established law."[64] More recently, critics of *Roe v. Wade* faulted the Court for making decisions that should be left to elected representatives. In the words of dissenting justice Byron White, the decision in *Roe* was "an exercise of raw judicial power."[65]

The Modern Debate

As we have seen, the loudest criticisms of the Supreme Court have sometimes come from Democrats and liberals, as during the first decades of the twentieth century, and sometimes from Republicans and conservatives, as during the Warren Court of the 1950s and 1960s. In the 1980s, Attorney General Edwin Meese attacked what he considered illegitimate judicial activism by calling for the Court to return to a "jurisprudence of original intent." In support, Meese quoted James Madison: "if the sense in which the Constitution was accepted and ratified by the Nation . . . be not the guide in expounding it, there can be no security for a consistent and stable, more than a faithful, exercise of its powers."[66] Meese charged that too many judges no longer looked to how the Constitution was understood by those who wrote and ratified it. Instead, judges draw on "extra-constitutional values" that they personally embrace.[67]

Originalism—the theory that in interpreting the Constitution judges should look to how it was understood by those who wrote and ratified it.

This is sometimes called the theory of **originalism**. Its proponents call for a return to the *original intent* of those who wrote and ratified the Constitution or to the *original meaning* of the Constitution. While some use these two phrases synonymously, others prefer *original meaning* over *original intent*. As Supreme Court justice Antonin Scalia, the Court's foremost defender of this approach, explained:

> The theory of originalism treats a constitution like a statute, and gives it the meaning that its words were understood to bear at the time they were promulgated. You will sometimes hear it described as the theory of original intent. You will never hear me refer to original intent, because as I say I am first of all a textualist, and secondly an originalist. If you are a textualist, you don't care about the intent, and I don't care if the framers of the Constitution had some secret meaning in mind when they adopted its words. I take the words as they were promulgated to the people of the United States, and what is the fairly understood meaning of those words.[68]

In 1985, Justice Brennan, one of the most influential justices of the last half of the twentieth century, criticized the originalist approach in a speech at Georgetown University. Mincing few words, he denounced the appeal to return to original intent as "arrogance cloaked as humility." "It is arrogant," he insisted, "to pretend that from our vantage we can gauge accurately the intent of the Framers on the application of principle to specific, contemporary issues." This is because the evidence of the framers' intent is often "sparse or ambiguous," frequently the framers themselves did not agree and "hid their differences in cloaks of generality," and the two centuries since the founding "cannot but work as a prism refracting all we perceive." Brennan charged that although the proponents of original intent claimed to favor "a depoliticization of the judiciary," in fact their choice "was not less political than any other" because they were against expanding rights and "turn[ed] a blind eye to social progress."[69]

Brennan gave the example of the death penalty to illustrate the breadth of his approach to constitutional interpretation. "As I interpret the Constitution," he said, "capital punishment is under all circumstances cruel and unusual punishment prohibited by the Eighth and Fourteenth Amendments." Brennan knew that those who wrote and ratified the Constitution did not agree with him; for the very same people who prohibited "cruel and unusual punishments" in the Eighth Amendment also made several specific references to capital punishment in the Fifth Amendment. That amendment refers to "a capital, or otherwise infamous crime," and it prohibits the government from taking "*life*, liberty, or property, without due process of law" (emphasis added). Capital crimes are by definition crimes that can result in a sentence to death, and prohibiting the government from taking someone's life without due process necessarily implies that government may take life if it follows proper procedures.

How, then, can capital punishment be unconstitutional? To Brennan, it violates the "sparkling vision of the supremacy of the human dignity of every individual" that guided those who wrote the Constitution, the Bill of Rights, and the Civil War Amendments. Although he recognized that "a majority of my fellow Justices" and "a majority of

The Collection of the Supreme Court of the United State

Associate Justice Antonin Scalia (1982–present) is the Court's foremost proponent of interpreting the Constitution as it was understood by those who wrote and ratified it in 1787–1788.

Miscellaneous Items, Prints & Photographs Division, Library of Congress, LC-US262-60138

Associate Justice William J. Brennan (1956–1990) was one of the Court's fiercest critics of the originalist approach to interpreting the Constitution.

my fellow countrymen" disagreed with him, he "hope[d] to embody a community striving for human dignity for all, although perhaps not yet arrived."[70]

To an originalist like Justice Scalia, the text of the Constitution is quite clear. The Fifth Amendment "clearly permits the death penalty to be imposed, and establishes beyond doubt that the death penalty is not one of the 'cruel and unusual punishments' prohibited by the Eighth Amendment." Scalia conceded that "[c]onvictions in opposition to the death penalty are often passionate and deeply held," but he insisted that this is "no excuse for reading them into a Constitution that does not contain them."[71] This contrast between Brennan and Scalia shows how differently two justices can read the same Constitution using different approaches.

Capital punishment is but one of the many issues that illustrate the importance of the debate over constitutional interpretation. How judges and justices approach constitutional interpretation can have profound, real-world consequences for the American people.

CHECKING THE COURTS
MAJOR ISSUES

- What are the ways in which the American people or their elected officials can check the power of the federal courts?
- Do any of these methods improperly undermine judicial independence?

Scholars, public officials, and judges disagree about how activist the courts should be in addressing social problems or expanding private rights. Yet most acknowledge that the courts sometimes err (e.g., *Dred Scott*, *Plessy v. Ferguson*) and that the body politic must have some way to deal with these mistakes. Most also agree that in a democracy unelected judges should not promote their policy preferences through their legal decisions. President Obama embraced this view in 2009 when he praised his nominee to the Supreme Court, federal judge Sonia Sotomayor, for her "recognition of the limits of the judicial role, an understanding that a judge's job is to interpret, not make, law; to approach decisions without any particular ideology or agenda, but rather a commitment to impartial justice; a respect for precedent and a determination to faithfully apply the law to the facts at hand."[72]

Judges themselves have warned about the dangers of unrestrained judicial power. No one did this more forcefully than Felix Frankfurter, who served on the Supreme Court from 1939 to 1962. A well-known advocate of progressive causes before joining the Court, Frankfurter urged his fellow justices to defer on most matters to representative institutions, state and federal. This is known as the doctrine of **judicial self-restraint**.

"I am not justified," Frankfurter wrote in an important 1943 dissent, "in writing my private notions of policy into the Constitution, no matter how deeply I may cherish them." "[O]ne's own opinion about the wisdom or evil of a law," he insisted, "should be excluded altogether when one is doing one's duty on the bench." A broad interpretation of the power of judicial review, Frankfurter cautioned, "prevent[s] the full play of the democratic process." Judges have no authority to overturn laws based on the "spirit of the Constitution" because "[s]uch undefined destructive power was not conferred on this Court by the Constitution."[73]

One way that judges and justices exercise restraint is deciding what cases to hear. As discussed earlier, they use the doctrines of standing, ripeness, mootness, and political questions to avoid hearing some cases. Another tool of judicial restraint is the doctrine of **stare decisis**, which is Latin for "let the decision stand." This principle calls for judges to look to precedents as a guide whenever possible. If every judge felt free to ignore prior decisions, the law would quickly lose stability and predictability.

Sometimes, however, precedents should be overturned; otherwise, judicial errors would become permanent. Under a rigid adherence to precedent, decisions such as

Judicial self-restraint—the doctrine that judges should exercise restraint in the kinds of cases they decide, deferring to the political branches on most matters.

Stare decisis—the principle, from the Latin for "let the decision stand," that calls for judges to look to past precedents as a guide whenever possible.

Brown v. Board of Education, which overturned *Plessy v. Ferguson*, would be impossible. Members of the Supreme Court often have to decide whether to follow precedents they disagree with or to overturn a prior decision with a new one that more accurately reflects their understanding of the Constitution or the laws. Indeed, between 1810 and 2001, the Supreme Court overruled, in whole or in part, one of its prior decisions 167 times.[74] Members of the lower federal courts, though, must follow Supreme Court precedents. Otherwise, the highest court would no longer be "Supreme."

What happens, then, if judges and justices do not restrain themselves? What if they violate Frankfurter's admonition and read their "own opinion about the wisdom or evil of a law" into the Constitution? The courts sometimes check the actions of the political branches, but what if the courts themselves need checking? Under the constitutional principles of separation of powers and checks and balances, are there legitimate ways for the Congress and president to check the federal courts without violating judicial independence? Here we briefly review seven ways for checking the courts that have been tried at one time or another in American history.

Revising the Laws

Because Supreme Court decisions on constitutional matters are so important, it is easy to forget that many Court decisions involve the interpretation of federal statutes, not the Constitution. In these cases, Congress can rewrite the relevant law if it disagrees with the Court's interpretation. Because there are so many hurdles that a new legislative proposal must surmount in Congress, passing a new law can be daunting. Yet, occasionally such efforts to overturn a Supreme Court interpretation succeed, as they did in January 2009 when Congress reacted against a 2007 Supreme Court decision by passing the Lilly Ledbetter Fair Pay Act (see Chapter 6).

Amending the Constitution

What if Congress disagrees with an interpretation not of a law but of the Constitution itself? Changing the Constitution, though possible, is much more difficult than rewriting laws. Only four times in American history has the Constitution been amended to overturn a Supreme Court decision:

- The Eleventh Amendment (1795), which prohibits a citizen of a foreign country or a state from suing another state in federal court, after the Supreme Court had ruled otherwise in 1793
- The Fourteenth Amendment (1868), which overturned the ruling in *Dred Scott* that blacks could not be citizens of the United States
- The Sixteenth Amendment (1913), which gave the federal government the power to lay income taxes, despite a prior Court ruling
- The Twenty-sixth Amendment (1971), which gave 18-year-olds the right to vote in federal and state elections, after the Court had ruled that Congress could not impose this requirement on the states

These four cases, however, are the exceptions that prove the rule: dozens of unsuccessful attempts have been made to overturn Supreme Court decisions interpreting the Constitution.

Limiting the Jurisdiction of the Courts

Under its constitutional power "To constitute Tribunals inferior to the supreme Court," Congress has broad power to control the jurisdiction of the lower federal courts, since these courts have only such authority as Congress vests in them. Congress has less control over the jurisdiction of the Supreme Court. Although Congress determines the size of the Court, the Constitution itself in Article III determines the kinds of cases it will hear and establishes its original jurisdiction. However, its appellate jurisdiction—when it reviews cases from lower courts—is subject to "such Exceptions, and . . . such Regulations as the Congress shall make."

Scholars and jurists debate just how far Congress may go in limiting the Supreme Court's appellate jurisdiction. Some argue that this power is without restriction. Others contend that Congress may not subvert the Supreme Court's constitutional position as head of the federal judiciary. Members of Congress have made several unsuccessful attempts to deny the Supreme Court appellate jurisdiction over issues such as school prayer.

In the past, the Court itself has given mixed signals on the authority of Congress to limit its jurisdiction. Thus, it is not at all clear how the modern Court would respond to an attempt by Congress to limit its authority to review constitutional decisions from lower federal courts.

Changing the Size of the Supreme Court

As we have seen, Congress determines the size of the Supreme Court. At times in the past, lawmakers changed its size for partisan or political reasons. In 1801, the lame-duck Federalist Congress reduced the size from six to five to deny incoming President Thomas Jefferson one potential appointment. In 1866, Congress decided to allow the Court to drop from 10 to 7 as justices died or retired so that President Andrew Johnson could not make new appointments. In 1869, with the size of the Court at eight and Johnson no longer in office, Congress increased the size to nine, where it has remained ever since. The failure of FDR's court-packing plan seemed to confirm the American public's view that Congress should not alter the size of the Court to influence its decisions.

Impeaching and Removing Judges

As "civil Officers of the United States," federal judges are subject to impeachment and removal from office for "Treason, Bribery, or other high Crimes and Misdemeanors" (Article II, Section 4). The House of Representatives has impeached 14 lower-court federal judges and 1 Supreme Court justice. Of the 14, the Senate convicted 8, removing them from office, and acquitted 3. Three resigned before trial. When the Senate votes to convict an impeached official, it has the option under the Constitution of disqualifying the individual from federal office permanently. Often it does not impose such a bar. Such was the case in 1989 when it removed federal judge Alcee Hastings from office. Three years later, Hastings won election to the House of Representatives from Florida.

The most recent impeachment was of District Court Judge G. Thomas Porteous Jr., in March, 2010, for accepting bribes and making false statements under penalty of perjury on financial disclosure forms. The House vote was unanimous. The Senate followed by unanimously convicting Porteous on one article of impeachment and by the necessary two-thirds vote on three others. It then voted 94-2 to permanently bar Porteous from federal office.

The impeachment power gives Congress the constitutional means to remove any federal judge or justice. But may it use this power to remove judges whose decisions it disapproves? The first two impeachments of judges seemed to settle this issue.

In 1803, the House of Representatives impeached federal judge John Pickering of New Hampshire for abuse of his judicial responsibilities due to intoxication and mental instability. At his trial in the Senate, Pickering's son presented evidence that his father was insane and thus not capable of committing "high Crimes or Misdemeanors." The Senate convicted Pickering by the requisite two-thirds vote when all the Republicans voted in favor and all the Federalists voted against. Three Republicans, however, left the chamber to avoid voting, presumably because they were inclined to acquit but did not want to split with their party colleagues.[75]

Despite the party-line vote in the Senate, there were good reasons to remove Pickering. Yet, immediately after the Senate convicted Pickering, Republicans in the House set their sights on a bigger target: Associate Justice Samuel Chase of the Supreme Court. Chase was a highly partisan Federalist who, while riding circuit, had presided over several controversial trials involving charges of treason and sedition. His opponents accused him of abusing his

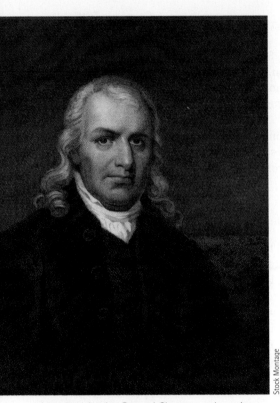

Stock Montage

Associate Justice Samuel Chase was the only member of the Supreme Court to be impeached by the House of Representatives (1804). He was acquitted by the Senate in 1805 and served until 1811, when he died in office.

judicial authority to bias the outcome in these cases, and of delivering "an intemperate and inflammatory political harangue" when charging a grand jury in Baltimore, Maryland.[76]

The House of Representatives passed eight articles of impeachment against Chase, none of which related to his service on the Supreme Court itself. On three of these, a majority of senators voted to convict but not the necessary two-thirds. The highest conviction vote of 19–15 came four votes short of removing Chase from office. All nine Federalist senators voted to acquit on each count, as did six Republican senators.[77]

Most constitutional historians agree that this was an effort by partisan Republicans to remove a partisan Federalist from the nation's highest court. Had it succeeded, the Republican Congress might have gone after other Federalist judges and justices, perhaps even Chief Justice John Marshall. President Jefferson himself had encouraged the impeachment of Chase when he admonished a House leader not to let Chase's behavior "go unpunished." "[T]o whom so pointedly as yourself," Jefferson wrote the House member, "will the public look for the necessary measures?"[78] Massachusetts senator John Quincy Adams saw the impeachment of Chase as nothing less than "a systematic attempt upon the independence and powers of the Judicial Department."[79]

In a book on the Chase impeachment, former chief justice William Rehnquist wrote that "[t]he acquittal of Samuel Chase by the Senate had a profound effect on the American judiciary." By ensuring "that impeachment would not be used in the future as a method to remove members of the Supreme Court for their judicial opinions, it helped to safeguard the independence of that body."[80] Indeed, Congress never again impeached a justice of the Supreme Court. Also, all of the lower federal judges removed since Pickering (including resignations after impeachment) had committed major offenses, seriously abused their judicial authority, or, in one case, joined the Confederacy.

Refusing to Enforce Judicial Decisions

In countering Anti-Federalist concerns about the new federal courts, Alexander Hamilton pointed out that the federal judiciary "must ultimately depend upon the aid of the executive arm even for the efficacy of its judgments."[81] This reminds us that judicial decisions are not self-executing. Courts have little influence if other public officials refuse to carry out their decisions. Rarely, however, does this happen in the United States.

One notable case occurred in 1832 after the state of Georgia convicted and imprisoned a missionary from Vermont for living among the Cherokee Indians in Georgia without a license from the governor. Writing for the Court in *Worcester v. Georgia*, Chief Justice Marshall held that the relevant state laws were "repugnant to the constitution, laws, and treaties of the United States" and therefore null and void.[82] The missionary's conviction, the Court ruled, must be "reversed and annulled."[83] Georgia officials, however, ignored the Court, and Worcester spent 10 more months in prison at hard labor. Moreover, President Andrew Jackson refused to assist the Court in enforcing its decision, reportedly saying, "John Marshall has made his decision; now let him enforce it."[84] (See also the discussion of this case in Chapter 4.)

A second important example, reviewed in Chapter 5, was President Lincoln's refusal in 1861 to abide by Chief Justice Roger B. Taney's order to release John Merryman from military custody. After Lincoln suspended habeas corpus around the railroad line from Philadelphia to Washington, officials apprehended Merryman for burning railroad bridges in Baltimore to prevent loyal troops from getting to the capital. In *Ex parte Merryman*, Taney ruled that only Congress could lawfully suspend habeas corpus. Lincoln ignored Taney's order as a legal matter and publicly defended his authority to suspend the writ in the message he sent to Congress when it convened in special session on July 4, 1861. Lincoln continued to authorize suspensions of the writ on his own authority, eventually

FOCUS QUESTION

If the Supreme Court ordered the release of a suspected terrorist from the detention facility at Guantánamo, Cuba, whom the president believed was a direct threat to national security, should the president refuse to enforce the Court's order? Would it matter if the vote on the Court was 9–0 or 5–4?

expanding coverage to the whole country. In March 1863, nearly two years after Taney's decision, Congress finally provided statutory authorization. We have no way of knowing whether Lincoln would have reacted differently had the Supreme Court as a whole ordered Merryman's release.

Choosing Certain Kinds of Judges

From the earliest days of the Republic, those with an interest in the decisions of the federal courts have recognized that presidents can influence the direction of the courts through their nominees to the bench. This is why, in the weeks after the Federalists were defeated in the election of 1800, President John Adams and his allies in Congress sought to expand the judiciary and fill vacancies with reliable Federalist attorneys. It is also why Congress has twice reduced the size of the Supreme Court, limiting new appointments by Jefferson and Andrew Johnson. Yet, for much of the twentieth century, nominations to the federal courts were not especially partisan and focused on the candidates' qualifications, character, and temperament, not on their likely decisions.

In March 1829, Chief Justice John Marshall (on the right in the center) administered the presidential oath to Andrew Jackson. Three years later, President Jackson refused to assist the Supreme Court in enforcing its decision, *Worcester v. Georgia*, reportedly saying, "John Marshall has made his decision; now let him enforce it."

Some argue that this is all the Senate, the body that confirms judicial nominations, should consider. They draw support from Hamilton's discussion in *Federalist* 76, where he wrote that the Senate confirmation process "would be an excellent check upon a spirit of favoritism in the President, and would tend greatly to prevent the appointment of unfit characters from State prejudice, from family connection, from personal attachment, or from a view to popularity."[85] Under this view, the Senate should confirm any presidential nominee who has substantial legal qualifications, who is honest, and who has demonstrated the temperament appropriate for service on the bench.

Others, however, insist that just as presidents consider judicial philosophy and likely future decisions when choosing nominees, so may the Senate in evaluating them. This dispute over the proper standards for evaluating nominees became a major public issue in 1987 when President Ronald Reagan nominated for the Supreme Court Robert Bork, a federal appellate judge and noted legal scholar. Reagan described Bork as "the most prominent and intellectually powerful advocate of judicial restraint, [who] shares my view that judges' personal preferences and values should not be part of their constitutional interpretations."[86]

Almost immediately after Reagan announced the nomination, Senator Edward Kennedy (D-MA) took to the Senate floor to denounce Bork:

> Robert Bork's America is a land in which women would be forced into back-alley abortions, blacks would sit at segregated lunch counters, rogue police could break down citizens' doors in midnight raids, schoolchildren could not be taught about evolution, writers and artists could be censored at the whim of the Government, and the doors of the Federal courts would be shut on the fingers of millions of citizens.[87]

In the following weeks, other senators and liberal groups repeated the charge that Bork was a legal radical who had no concern for racial minorities or the poor. The director of the American Civil Liberties Union warned that with Bork's confirmation "we risk nothing short of wrecking the entire bill of rights. . . . His confirmation would threaten our system of government."[88]

In two respects, the battle over Bork was a watershed in Supreme Court nominations. First, interest groups organized an extensive campaign to defeat the Supreme Court nominee. They mobilized civil rights organizations and labor unions, influenced newspaper editorial opinion, placed newspaper ads, and broadcast commercials against the nomination. Groups on the left and right have been active in confirmation contests ever since, although not usually as intensely.

Second, the debate over Bork focused not on competence, integrity, and judicial temperament, but on the nominee's views on a range of legal issues. This was an important new development. Prior to 1925, no Supreme Court nominee even appeared before the Senate Judiciary Committee, and the few the Senate invited politely declined. In the following decades a few did appear, but appearances did not become standard practice until 1955. Even then, nominees generally declined to answer questions on legal issues that might come before the Court.

Since the Bork nomination, increasing numbers of senators have expressed a willingness to vote against an otherwise qualified nominee because of decisions he or she might make on the highest court. In 2006, for example, a reporter asked Senator Dianne Feinstein (D-CA), a member of the Senate Judiciary Committee, whether she would vote to filibuster the nomination of Judge Samuel Alito to the Supreme Court: "If I believed he was going to go in there and overthrow *Roe*? . . . Most likely, yes."[89] In the Judiciary Committee, Senator Kennedy made clear that Alito's judicial record was the key to his opposition. He faulted the appellate court judge for his unwillingness to restrain executive power "when government officials intrude on individual rights"; for not being "open to the claims of vulnerable individuals asking only justice against powerful institutions"; for not supporting "the liberty and privacy of citizens seeking to protect their fundamental rights"; and for not upholding "equal justice under the law." Supporters such as Senator Orrin Hatch (R-UT) countered that Alito's critics "cannot support the kind of limited judiciary that he represents. A limited judiciary will not get them where they want to go. A limited judiciary leaves too many issues, too many questions, too many decisions to the people and to the people's elected representatives." What the debate was all about was "whether the American people and those they elect still have the power to make the law and define the culture, or whether judges, unelected judges, should do it for us instead."[90]

In the end, Alito, who had been nominated by Republican president George W. Bush, won confirmation, 58–42. All but one Republican voted in favor, and all but four Democrats voted against. Opposition in the full Senate, as on the Judiciary Committee, focused on the kinds of decisions Alito would likely make on the Supreme Court based on his 15-year record as a judge on the United States Court of Appeals for the Third Circuit, where he sat on thousands of cases and wrote hundreds of opinions.

The closely divided vote on Alito was a striking contrast to previous votes on Antonin Scalia in 1986 and Ruth Bader Ginsburg in 1993. Scalia, an outspoken conservative jurist and legal scholar, was approved 98–0. Ginsburg, a past general counsel for the ACLU and a prominent liberal judge, was approved 96–3. All the Democrats voted for the conservative Scalia, and nearly all the Republicans voted for the liberal Ginsburg. Indeed, between May 1970 and February 1988, five of the eight Senate votes on Supreme Court nominees were unanimous, and another was decided 89–1 (see Table 15-3).

The most recent Supreme Court nomination contest—that of Elena Kagan in 2010—showed a partisan division as deep as that over Alito. All but one of the Senate Democrats, members of the party of the president who nominated her, voted in favor (58–1); all but 5 of the Senate Republicans voted against (36–5). With Democrats holding a commanding 59–41 majority in the Senate, the nomination passed easily, 63–37. It appears that the era of the Senate voting strictly on the professional qualifications of Supreme Court nominees is over. Senators now focus on the kinds of decisions that a new justice will likely reach.

In 2009, President Obama sparked a controversy over the standards that presidents themselves should use in selecting Supreme Court nominees. When Justice David Souter retired, Obama praised him for "that quality of empathy, of understanding and identifying with people's hopes and struggles, [which is] an essential ingredient for arriving at just decisions and outcomes."[91] A few weeks later, in nominating Sonia Sotomayor to replace Souter, he praised her for "a common touch and a sense of compassion; an understanding of how the world works and how ordinary people live."[92] This was not the

Supreme Court nominee Elena Kagan appears before the Senate Judiciary Committee in June 2010.

TABLE 15-3	CONFIRMATION VOTES ON SUPREME COURT NOMINATIONS, 1954–2010

Nominee	Date of Nomination	Nominated by	Date of Confirmation Vote	Vote for Confirmation
Earl Warren	Jan. 11, 1954	Eisenhower	Mar. 1, 1954	Voice vote
John Harlan	Jan. 10, 1955	Eisenhower	Mar. 16, 1955	71–11
William Brennan	Jan. 14, 1957	Eisenhower	Mar. 19, 1957	Voice vote
Charles Whittaker	Mar. 2, 1957	Eisenhower	Mar. 19, 1957	Voice vote
Potter Stewart	Jan. 17, 1959	Eisenhower	May 5, 1959	70–17
Byron White	Apr. 3, 1962	Kennedy	Apr. 11, 1962	Voice vote
Arthur Goldberg	Aug. 31, 1962	Kennedy	Sept. 25, 1962	Voice vote
Abe Fortas	July 28, 1965	Johnson	Aug. 11, 1965	Voice vote
Thurgood Marshall	June 13, 1967	Johnson	Aug. 30, 1967	69–11
Warren Burger	May 23, 1969	Nixon	June 9, 1969	74–3
Clement Haynsworth	Aug. 21, 1969	Nixon	Nov. 21, 1969	45–55
G. Harrold Carswell	Jan. 19, 1970	Nixon	Apr. 8, 1970	45–51
Harry Blackmun	Apr. 15, 1970	Nixon	May 12, 1970	94–0
Lewis Powell	Oct. 22, 1971	Nixon	Dec. 6, 1971	89–1
William Rehnquist	Oct. 22, 1971	Nixon	Dec. 10, 1971	68–26
John Paul Stevens	Nov. 28, 1975	Ford	Dec. 17, 1975	98–0
Sandra Day O'Connor	Aug. 19, 1981	Reagan	Sept. 21, 1981	99–0
Antonin Scalia	June 24, 1986	Reagan	Sept. 17, 1986	98–0
Robert Bork	July 1, 1987	Reagan	Oct. 23, 1987	42–58
Anthony Kennedy	Nov. 30, 1987	Reagan	Feb. 3, 1988	97–0
David Souter	July 25, 1990	Bush, G. H. W.	Oct. 2, 1990	90–9
Clarence Thomas	July 8, 1991	Bush, G. H. W.	Oct. 15, 1991	52–48
Ruth Bader Ginsburg	June 14, 1993	Clinton	Aug. 3, 1993	96–3
Stephen Breyer	May 17, 1994	Clinton	July 29, 1994	87–9
John Roberts	Sept. 6, 2005	Bush, G. W.	Sept. 29, 2005	78–22
Samuel Alito	Nov. 10, 2005	Bush, G. W.	Jan. 31, 2006	58–42
Sonia Sotomayor	June 1, 2009	Obama	Aug. 6, 2009	68–31
Elena Kagan	May 10, 2010	Obama	August 5, 2010	63–37

SOURCE: "Supreme Court Nominations, Present–1789," www.senate.gov/pagelayout/reference/nominations/Nominations.htm, accessed July 8, 2012.

first time that Obama had highlighted the importance of having justices with empathy and compassion on the Supreme Court. While serving in the Senate in 2005, he had opposed John Roberts to be chief justice because of reservations about "the breadth and depth of [his] empathy." In the hard cases where the constitutional text of the language of the statute is not "directly on point," Obama maintained, "the critical ingredient is supplied by what is in the judge's heart."[93]

Critics charged that President Obama wanted justices who were disposed to side with the poor or minorities. They pointed to the official judicial oath—"I will administer justice without respect to persons, and do equal right to the poor and to the rich" (the full oath is below)—and some recalled what Roberts had said during his confirmation hearings in 2005. Pressed by Senator Richard Durbin (D-IL) about the advantages that rich and powerful people have in the legal process, Roberts responded, "And it's, again, what's carved above the doors to the Supreme Court: 'Equal justice under law.' And the judicial oath talks about doing justice without regard to persons, to rich and to poor. And that, of course, is critically important."[94]

Sotomayor, herself, in testifying on her nomination before the Senate Judiciary Committee in July 2009, rejected the president's reliance on "what is in the judge's heart":

I wouldn't approach the issue of judging in the way the president does. He has to explain what he meant by judging. I can only explain what I think judges should

FOCUS
QUESTION

Because modern justices of the Supreme Court live longer and serve longer than was probably contemplated by the framers, some scholars have proposed a single 18-year term. With staggered appointments, a vacancy would arise every 2 years and each president would get two appointments during a single 4-year term. Is this a good idea?

do, which is judges can't rely on what's in their heart. They don't determine the law. Congress makes the laws. The job of a judge is to apply the law. And so it's not the heart that compels conclusions in cases. It's the law. The judge applies the law to the facts before that judge.[95]

However presidents describe their criteria for choosing Supreme Court nominees, it is clear that presidential elections matter in shaping the Court. It is as unlikely today that a Republican president would appoint a Ruth Bader Ginsburg or an Elena Kagan to the Supreme Court as it is that a Democratic president would appoint an Antonin Scalia or a Samuel Alito. Although justices sometimes surprise the presidents who appointed them, a series of appointments by presidents of one party or the other can have a profound influence on the direction of Court. Indeed, but for the rare constitutional amendment, appointments may be the only effective way for the broader political community to influence the Supreme Court. The justices may not "follow the election returns," but in the long run, presidential and senatorial elections may decisively, if indirectly, shape the Court.

THE SUPREME COURT AND DELIBERATIVE DEMOCRACY

Columnist George Will has written, "The judiciary is the intellectual branch. The executive and legislative branches legitimately can act on motives that are validated by simple power calculations—by the pressure of a majority or a salient faction. The judiciary must ground its actions in reasonings about principles."[96]

Judges, justices, and their clerks put an enormous amount of effort into judicial opinions. These documents may run for dozens of pages and include hundreds of highly detailed legal citations. What is the point of all this work? As Hamilton argued, the courts gain their influence not through force or will, but judgment. Their legal judgments are directly binding only on the parties to the specific case, but the reasoning behind their decisions may well influence other judges handling similar cases.

In Supreme Court decisions, majority opinions carry more weight than dissents. Nevertheless, the dissenting justices work just as hard on their opinions as those in the majority. Charles Evans Hughes, who had served as an associate justice and would soon become chief justice, wrote in 1928, "A dissent in a court of last resort is an appeal to the brooding spirit of the law, to the intelligence of a future day, when a later decision may possibly correct the error into which the dissenting judge believes the court to have been betrayed."[97] Sometimes dissents become the basis for future majority opinions, but whatever their fate, they contribute greatly to the judiciary's deliberative character. They give judges, lawyers, and citizens access to the exchange of views that led to a decision. As legal scholar Kevin Stack writes: "Dissenting opinions preserve the dialogue of previous Courts concerning questions of law. . . . [They are] valuable as carriers of judicial conversation through time; they connect the dialogue of generations of Justices and judges with one another."[98]

Majority and minority opinions also inform the deliberations of the broader political community on rights, justice, and the powers of government. Presidents, lawmakers, scholars, and interest group advocates all draw on the writings of justices. Indeed, what was arguably the greatest of all American political exchanges—the Lincoln-Douglas debates of 1858—focused to a large degree on the merits of a Supreme Court case, *Dred Scott v. Sandford*.

To influence their colleagues and other public officials, justices have to reason logically on the merits. A slipshod opinion—or worse, one that merely stakes out a partisan stance—may eventually prove unpersuasive and fail the test of time. Justices have good reason to act "faithfully and impartially," just as required by the oath that all federal judges must take:

I, _____, do solemnly swear (or affirm) that I will administer justice without re-spect to persons, and do equal right to the poor and to the rich, and that I will faithfully and impartially discharge and perform all the duties incumbent upon me as _____ under the Constitution and laws of the United States; and that I will support and defend the Constitution of the United States against all enemies, for-eign and domestic; that I will bear true faith and allegiance to the same; that I take this obligation freely, without any mental reservation or purpose of evasion; and that I will well and faithfully discharge the duties of the office on which I am about to enter. SO HELP ME GOD. (U.S. Code, Title 28, Sec. 453 and Title 5, Sec. 16)

The judicial responsibility sometimes pits the federal courts against the political branches. One of Hamilton's arguments for the power of judicial review was the need for the Supreme Court "to guard the Constitution and the rights of individuals" from "ill hu-mors" that might affect the people until "better information, and more deliberate reflection" could prevail. An independent judiciary, then, guards the people, at least temporarily, from deficiencies in their own deliberations. This does not mean, however, that judicial delibera-tions ought to displace those of the political branches on policy matters. The federal courts are very different institutions from the popularly elected and accountable Congress and presidency.

First, the courts do not represent public opinion in the way that the political branches do. No one would call a nation a democracy if unelected and unaccountable courts made all the important decisions. If courts become policymakers, they threaten to lose their public legitimacy.

Second, by virtue of their structure and procedures, courts have less institutional ca-pacity and expertise than the political branches to make judgments about specific public policies. Many (perhaps most) federal judges have neither training nor practical experience in public policy issues. Also, unlike many who serve in legislatures and executive branches,

IMPACT
of Social Media and Communications Technology

Should Justices Tweet?

The Supreme Court forbids tweeting from its courtroom (see the Bessette-Pitney blog of April 1, 2012). Nonetheless, thousands of people interested in the Court's decisions have used Twitter to dis-seminate information or communicate their opinions. On the first day of the Supreme Court's oral arguments on the constitutionality of the Affordable Care Act, in March of 2012, interested people sent more than 72,000 tweets. But what about the justices themselves? Should they use such social media as Twitter and Facebook to communicate with the public?

In recent years, justices Sonia Sotomayor and Stephen Breyer have both argued that it would be inappropriate for members of the Supreme Court to communicate with the public in this way (see the Bessette-Pitney blog of April 6, 2012). Asked by students at the Uni-versity of Pennsylvania Law School whether justices should use social media to educate the public about the workings of the Court, Soto-mayor was unequivocal: "We can't do that as judges," she said. "We can't engage the public in a seminar about health law." Judges, she held, cannot exchange ideas with the public and debate issues the way elected officials do. Referring to teaching law courses, presiding

over moot courts, and giving public lectures, she noted that "We're all participating publicly, just maybe not in the way the public would like us to." Breyer, testifying before a congressional committee, admitted using Twitter to monitor international events, but was opposed to justices having followers on Twitter or Facebook: "It's not a good idea on balance," he said. "Judges wear black robes so that they will resist the temptation to publicize themselves, because we really speak for the law and that is to be anonymous."

CRITICAL THINKING
QUESTION

Are justices Sotomayor and Breyer right that certain modes of communication are appropriate for Supreme Court justices—such as written opinions, law courses, and public lectures—but others are not—such as Facebook and Twitter? What is the connection between the job of a judge and the way judges should communi-cate with the public?

they are typically generalists, not specialists. Whereas a committee chair in the House or Senate or members of a federal agency might focus for years on specific policy issues, federal district judges must preside over civil and criminal cases of all kinds. As Justice Ruth Bader Ginsburg wrote for the Court in a 2011 decision, "Federal judges lack the scientific, economic, and technological resources an agency can utilize in coping with issues [like environmental pollution]."[99] (Judges in specialty courts, such as bankruptcy or tax courts, can develop greater expertise.)

Finally, at the core of much political deliberation is the need to make trade-offs among competing goals or values. Is a city better off, for example, spending an extra million dollars to improve its schools, to reduce crime, or to upgrade its public transportation? Generally, courts deciding one case at a time are in no position to make such judgments. We expect judges to apply the law and the Constitution in particular cases or controversies, not to make broad policy judgments about how best to achieve the common good. Deliberative democracy presumes that such decisions are best made by elected officials deliberating on behalf of the people they serve.

It is no wonder that the place of powerful, independent courts in American democracy is such a contentious topic and is likely to remain so in the years ahead.

SUMMARY

- The power of judicial review, by which courts can strike down laws that they believe violate the federal or state constitutions, gives courts in the United States a large impact on public policy.
- Through life terms and restrictions on congressional control over salaries, the framers insulated the judiciary to a considerable degree from political forces and made it a coequal branch of the national government.
- In 1789, the First Congress established a three-tiered federal court system that, in modified form, still exists today. In *Marbury v. Madison* (1803), the Supreme Court unanimously struck down a provision of the Judiciary Act, thus establishing the Court's authority to void acts of Congress that violated the U.S. Constitution.
- Only a tiny fraction of legal issues handled by courts in the United States ever reach the Supreme Court, which sits atop the judicial hierarchy. The vast majority of cases achieve final resolution in state courts or in the lower federal courts.
- The federal courts decide cases or controversies that involve real conflicts of interest or rights between the parties. They do not issue advisory opinions.
- During the first decades under the Constitution, the Supreme Court cemented its position as a coequal branch of the national government, affirmed the supremacy of the federal Constitution and federal law over state constitutions and state law, and legitimized a broad interpretation of Congress's enumerated powers.
- After the Civil War, the Supreme Court issued key decisions that narrowly interpreted the guarantees of the Civil War amendments and the new federal civil rights acts.

- In the early twentieth century, the Court restricted the power of the states and the federal government to regulate economic activity. This changed in 1937, when the Court began to interpret the commerce power broadly to uphold New Deal regulations.
- In the 1950s and 1960s, the Court initiated a "rights revolution," with landmark decisions on racial segregation, reapportionment, separation of church and state, the freedom of speech and press, and the rights of criminal defendants. In the last half of the twentieth century, the federal courts became increasingly influential as they used their equitable remedial powers to regulate school systems, jails and prisons, public housing authorities, and mental health facilities.
- The debate over judicial activism began with the contest between Federalists and Anti-Federalists and continues today with the dispute over whether judges should interpret the Constitution by looking to the original intent, or original understanding, of those who wrote and ratified it.
- Citizens and their elected officials have employed various means to check perceived abuses by the courts: revising the laws, amending the Constitution, limiting the jurisdiction of the courts, changing the size of the Supreme Court, impeaching and removing federal judges, refusing to enforce judicial decisions, and choosing certain kinds of judges.
- The federal courts influence American deliberative democracy principally through their reasoned opinions, which can contribute to community-wide deliberation on rights, justice, and the powers of government.

KEY TERMS

Advisory opinion p. 449
Amicus curiae brief p. 446
Appellant p. 445
Appellate jurisdiction p. 439
Appellee p. 445
Beyond a reasonable doubt p. 444
Brief p. 445
Case law p. 448
Chief justice p. 446
Circuit court p. 439
Civil case p. 444
Class action p. 456
Concurring opinion p. 447
Court-packing plan p. 453
Criminal case p. 444
Defendant p. 444
Dissenting opinion p. 447
District courts p. 439
Equity power p. 456

Evolving Constitution p. 438
Judicial activism p. 438
Judicial review p. 437
Judicial self-restraint p. 461
Judiciary Act of 1789 p. 439
Law clerk p. 448
Living Constitution p. 438
Lochner era p. 453
Majority opinion p. 447
Marshall Court p. 454
Midnight appointments p. 440
Mootness p. 450
Opinion of the Court p. 447
Oral arguments p. 445
Original intent p. 438
Original jurisdiction p. 439
Original meaning p. 438
Originalism p. 460
Plaintiff p. 444

Plurality opinion p. 448
Political questions p. 450
Precedents p. 448
Preponderance of the evidence p. 444
Ripeness p. 450
Rule of four p. 446
Solicitor general p. 446
Standing p. 450
Stare decisis p. 461
Strict construction p. 438
Trial court p. 443
Unanimous opinion p. 448
United States Attorney p. 444
United States Courts of Appeal p. 439
United States District Courts p. 439
Warren Court p. 454
Writ of certiorari p. 446
Writ of mandamus p. 440

TEST YOUR KNOWLEDGE

1. The case for an independent judiciary was largely made in *The Spirit of the Laws* by
   a. Baron de Montesquieu.
   b. Benjamin Franklin.
   c. John Locke.
   d. Thomas Hobbes.
   e. Thomas Jefferson.

2. The number of judges on the Supreme Court is determined by
   a. Congress.
   b. the Constitution.
   c. the electorate.
   d. the president.
   e. the size of the general population.

3. The Supreme Court first exercised judicial review in which landmark case?
   a. *Brown v. Board of Education*
   b. *Lochner v. New York*
   c. *Marbury v. Madison*
   d. *Plessy v. Ferguson*
   e. *Roe v. Wade*

4. The chief federal prosecutor in charge of each judicial district is called a(n)
   a. appellant.
   b. associate justice.
   c. chief justice.
   d. solicitor general.
   e. United States attorney.

5. What qualifications does the Constitution specify for service on any federal court?
   a. Nominees must be at least 35 years of age.
   b. Nominees must be natural-born citizens.
   c. Nominees must be permanent residents of the district in which they would serve.
   d. Nominees must have lived in the United States at least ten of their adult years.
   e. The Constitution specifies no qualifications for service on any federal court.

6. Citizens who are not actual parties to a case are able to influence the Court's deliberations through
   a. advisory opinions.
   b. amicus curiae briefs.
   c. class action suits.
   d. writs of certiorari.
   e. writs of mandamus.

7. Which of the following is NOT one of the four key characteristics justices use to determine whether a genuine case or controversy exists?
   a. equity
   b. mootness
   c. political question
   d. ripeness
   e. standing

8. What was the consistent theme of major Supreme Court decisions in the decades following the Civil War?
   a. State governments can do little to use political power to disadvantage black persons.
   b. The Constitution requires a broad interpretation of the Thirteenth, Fourteenth, and Fifteenth Amendments.
   c. The federal government can do little to affect race relations in the states.
   d. The federal government is the only authority on the implementation of the Thirteenth, Fourteenth, and Fifteenth Amendments.
   e. The judiciary is supreme over the other branches of government in matters of economic development.

9. Which amendment was NOT added to overturn a Supreme Court decision?
   a. Eleventh, prohibiting a citizen of a foreign country from suing a state
   b. Fourteenth, declaring that blacks could be citizens
   c. Sixteenth, granting Congress the power to levy an income tax
   d. Nineteenth, giving women the right to vote
   e. Twenty-Sixth, giving 18-year-olds the right to vote

10. What was significant about Robert Bork's nomination to the Supreme Court?
    a. It represented one of the least divisive confirmation hearings in the Senate's history.
    b. It was the only debate to lead to a unanimous confirmation of a Supreme Court nominee.
    c. This was the first time since 1950 that a nominee refused to appear before the Senate Judiciary Committee.
    d. This was the first time a nomination debate focused on the nominee's view on legal issues, rather than solely on his competence, integrity, and judicial temperament.
    e. This was the last confirmation hearing conducted by the House of Representatives.

FURTHER READING

Abraham, Henry. *The Judicial Process: An Introductory Analysis of the Courts of the United States, England, and France.* 7th ed. New York: Oxford University Press, 1998.

Abraham, Henry. *Justices, Presidents and Senators: A History of the U.S. Supreme Court Appointments from Washington to Clinton.* Rev. ed. Lanham, MD: Rowman and Littlefield, 1999.

Baum, Lawrence. *The Supreme Court.* 8th ed. Washington, DC: CQ Press, 2004.

Bickel, Alexander. *The Least Dangerous Branch: The Supreme Court at the Bar of Politics.* New Haven, CT: Yale University Press, 1986.

Bork, Robert. *The Tempting of America: The Political Seduction of the Law.* New York: Free Press, 1990.

Breyer, Stephen. *Active Liberty: Interpreting Our Democratic Constitution.* New York: Knopf, 2005.

Gastil, John, E. Pierre Deess, Philip J. Weiser, and Cindy Simmons. *The Jury and Democracy: How Jury Deliberation Promotes Civic Engagement and Political Participation.* New York: Oxford University Press, 2010.

Hall, Kermit L., ed. *The Oxford Companion to the Supreme Court of the United States.* New York: Oxford University Press, 1992.

Horowitz, Donald L. *The Courts and Social Policy.* Washington, DC: Brookings Institution, 1977.

Kelly, Alfred H., Winfred A. Harbison, and Herman Belz. *The American Constitution: Its Origins and Development.* 7th ed. 2 vols. New York: Norton, 1991.

McDowell, Gary L. *Equity and the Constitution: The Supreme Court, Equitable Relief, and Public Policy.* Chicago: University of Chicago Press, 1982.

Rehnquist, William H. *The Supreme Court.* Revised and updated ed. New York: Random House, Vintage Books, 2002.

Rosenberg, Gerald. *The Hollow Hope: Can Courts Bring about Social Change?* Chicago: University of Chicago Press, 1991.

Rossum, Ralph A., and G. Alan Tarr. *American Constitutional Law.* 2 vols. Thousand Oaks, CA: Wadsworth, 2006.

Scalia, Antonin. *A Matter of Interpretation: Federal Courts and the Law.* Princeton, NJ: Princeton University Press, 1997.

Tribe, Lawrence H. *God Save This Honorable Court: How the Choice of Justices Shapes Our History.* New York: Random House, 1985.

Wolfe, Christopher. *The Rise of Modern Judicial Review: From Constitutional Interpretation to Judge-Made Law.* New York: Basic Books, 1986.

WEB SOURCES

ABA Standing Committee on Federal Judiciary: www.abanet.org/scfedjud—the ABA committee that evaluates nominees to the federal courts.

American Bar Association: www.abanet.org—a voluntary professional association that represents 400,000 attorneys in the United States.

Cornell Law School Legal Information Institute: www.law.cornell.edu—an extensive online collection of legal materials maintained by the Cornell Law School.

Federalist Society for Law and Public Policy Studies: www.fed-soc.org—a group of conservative and libertarian lawyers, law professors, and law school students who focus on legal education and the legal order.

FindLaw: www.findlaw.com—an extensive online collection of legal materials. State and federal court cases and laws are at: www.findlaw.com/casecode.

International Criminal Court: www.icc-cpi.int—the official Web site for the International Criminal Court.

National Center for State Courts: www.ncsc.org—an organization that seeks to improve the administration of justice in state courts.

Office of the Solicitor General: www.usdoj.gov/osg—the office in the U.S. Department of Justice that represents the government in matters before the Supreme Court.

Oyez Project: www.oyez.org—a multimedia archive devoted to the Supreme Court of the United States and its work.

Supreme Court of the United States: www.supremecourtus.gov—the official Web site for the Supreme Court.

U.S. Courts: www.uscourts.gov—the Web site for the federal judiciary.

U.S. Senate Committee on the Judiciary: judiciary.senate.gov—the official Web site for the Senate committee that conducts all confirmation hearings for nominees to the federal courts.

President Obama signing the
Affordable Care Act in March 2010.

Doug Mills/The New York Times/Redux

16 Social Policy and the Welfare State

OBJECTIVES

After reading this chapter, you should be able to:

- Describe the importance of FDR's approach to laying the foundations
  of the welfare state.

- Identify the major developments in American social policy from the New Deal
  through the present.

- Explain why President Clinton and Congress reformed the welfare system
  in the 1990s.

- Assess the arguments for and against the Affordable Care Act of 2010.

- Evaluate the prospects for the long-term viability of Social Security and
  Medicare.

- Identify the key innovations of the school choice movement and evaluate their
  importance to improving education in the United States.

INTRODUCTION

When Democrat Franklin D. Roosevelt, then serving as governor of New York, ran for the presidency in 1932, the country was in the third year of a severe economic downturn, now known as the **Great Depression**. Industrial production had fallen by half since the summer of 1929, and plummeting prices for agricultural commodities had devastated the rural economy. Banks closed and thousands lost their savings. One-quarter of the workforce was unemployed; millions were homeless; and breadlines stretched for miles in the nation's cities. Roosevelt addressed the crisis is a remarkable campaign speech in September at the Commonwealth Club in San Francisco.

Roosevelt explained that during the nation's westward expansion in the previous century, Americans had equal opportunity, and the purpose of government was to help industry develop. In the late 1800s, however, the era of free land on the frontier came to a close, and the large industrial organization became the dominant force in the economy. Within a few decades, these organizations became the "despot of the twentieth century," threatening millions with "starvation and penury" and destroying equality of opportunity.[1]

So much had changed, Roosevelt told his audience, that citizens could no longer enjoy their rights to life, liberty, and the pursuit of happiness without major new government programs. At one time, the right to life required government to protect people from murder. Now it included the "right to make a comfortable living" and required government to see to it that everyone possessed "a portion of that plenty sufficient for his needs, through his own work."[2] At one time, the right to property meant protection from theft or fraud. Now, it obligated government to guarantee bank deposits so that savings would be secure.[3] At one time, the rights to liberty and the pursuit of happiness required government to allow people to live their lives as they wished. Now it required public authorities to restrict the liberty of "the speculator, the manipulator, even the financier."[4]

Thus, Roosevelt promised not just to combat the distress caused by the depression but to redefine the relationship of the federal government to the American citizenry. For the first time, Washington would be directly responsible for ensuring the material well-being of the people. By electing Roosevelt to the presidency four times and by sending large majorities of Democrats to the House and Senate in the 1930s, Americans embraced Roosevelt's conception of the **welfare state**, also called the **social welfare state**. By these terms, we mean a government that works to ensure the material and economic well-being of its citizens.

Roosevelt's **New Deal**—the term he used to describe his social programs—ushered in a dramatic increase in federal spending as the national government embraced its new responsibilities. In 1932, the entire federal budget was just over $5 billion. Of this, about $2.3 billion was for all domestic expenditures—that is, all expenditures excluding national defense (including veterans' expenditures), international relations (State Department), and costs associated with the national debt. Eighty years later, in 2012, the federal government spent $3.8 trillion, and domestic expenditures amounted to $2.8 trillion. Adjusting for inflation (a dollar was worth a lot more in 1932 than in 2010), total federal spending in 2012 was about 45 times as much as in 1932, and domestic spending was 73 times as much.[5] (The nation's population in 2012 was about two and half times that in 1932.)

Table 16-1 lists the principal domestic expenditures in 2012 by category. **Social Security** (mainly income support for seniors), other income security, **Medicare** (health coverage for the elderly and disabled), and other health expenses together accounted for over $2.2 trillion (58% of the budget) and dwarfed other domestic expenditures. (National defense expenditures in 2012 totaled $716 billion, or 19% of the budget.) As we will see, more money is spent on programs for the middle class than for the poor.

In this chapter, we address modern social policy in the United States. After providing some background on the connection between American civic culture and social welfare, we outline the growth and rationale of the welfare state since FDR's New Deal. We then examine four major modern developments and controversies: the welfare reform of the 1990s, former president George W. Bush's attempt to introduce private accounts into Social

Great Depression—the major downturn in the American economy that began in 1929 and lasted through the 1930s.

Welfare state—a term to describe a government that sees its responsibility as providing for the material well-being of the citizens and that spends a significant amount of its resources to this end.

Social welfare state—see **Welfare state**.

New Deal—the term to describe the economic and social welfare policies of President Franklin Roosevelt in the 1930s.

Social Security—a system of old-age insurance that provides monthly benefits to retired workers and their spouses.

Medicare—a federal program established in 1965 to assist those over 65 with hospital and doctors' expenses.

TABLE 16-1	MAJOR DOMESTIC EXPENDITURES BY THE FEDERAL GOVERNMENT, 2012	
Category of Spending	Expenditures (in billions)	Percent of all Federal Spending
Social Security	$778.6	20.5%
Income security*	580.0	15.3
Medicare	484.5	12.8
Health†	361.6	9.5
Educ., training, employ., soc. services	139.2	3.7
Transportation	102.6	2.7
Administration of justice	62.0	1.6
Natural resources and environment	42.8	1.1
Community and regional development	31.7	0.8
General science, space, and technology	31.0	0.8
Energy	23.0	0.6
Agriculture	19.2	0.5

*Includes retirement, disability insurance, unemployment compensation, housing assistance, and food and nutrition assistance.

†Includes Medicaid, health research and training, and occupational health and safety.

NOTE: Data are estimates for the fiscal year October 1, 2011–September 30, 2012.

SOURCE: Office of Management and Budget, Historical Tables, Table 3.2, at http://www.whitehouse.gov/omb/budget/Historicals, accessed July 16, 2012.

Security, the major expansion of the federal role in health care during the administrations of George W. Bush and Barack Obama, and the growth of school choice programs throughout the United States in recent years. We conclude by examining the relationship of social policy and the welfare state to citizenship and deliberation.

THE GROWTH AND RATIONALE OF THE WELFARE STATE

MAJOR ISSUES

- What is the connection between American civic culture and social policy?
- How and why has the welfare state grown since the early twentieth century?

Ever since the colonial period, essential elements of American civic culture have shaped how government in the United States approaches education and social welfare.

Civic Culture and Social Policy

As we saw in Chapter 4, civic culture shapes public policy in the United States in a variety of ways. A major constituent of that civic culture is religious faith, and one area where the influence of religion has been especially strong is education.

Many private universities, especially older ones, have a religious history. Except for the University of Pennsylvania, every major American college before the Revolution had religious origins. Examples include Harvard, Yale, and Dartmouth (all Congregationalist), Brown (Baptist), Columbia (Anglican), and Princeton (Presbyterian).

The linkage of faith and education in America extends to all levels. The first important national law dealing with education, the **Northwest Ordinance** of 1787, acknowledged its motive: "Religion, morality, and knowledge, being necessary to good government and the

Northwest Ordinance—a 1787 law that provided for the administration of what is now the industrial Midwest and set rules for admission of states in the region. The law explicitly cited the advancement of religion as a rationale for public education.

happiness of mankind, schools and the means of education shall forever be encouraged."[6] In the early nineteenth century, American public or "common" schools had a Protestant cast, often requiring daily readings from the King James Bible. In some places, Catholic schools also got public funds. In the 1840s, Irish Catholic immigration triggered nativist and anti-Catholic sentiment, which in turn resulted in state laws forbidding public aid to religious schools.[7] With Catholic education either unavailable or unaffordable, many Catholic parents had to send their children to public schools, where their beliefs came under challenge. In 1859, a Boston teacher beat an 11-year-old Catholic after the child refused to recite from the King James Bible. A local court upheld the beating.[8] In the years after the Civil War, as more and more states adopted compulsory attendance laws, the Catholic Church responded by founding more parochial schools.

In 1915, Catholic schools faced a new foe, the Ku Klux Klan, which now targeted Catholics and immigrants as well as African Americans. In 1922, it persuaded the Oregon legislature to pass the Compulsory School Bill, which required students to attend public schools. The Supreme Court invalidated the law, saying that the fundamental idea of liberty "excludes any general power of the state to standardize its children by forcing them to accept instruction from public teachers only."[9]

In recent decades, the ill will between Protestants and Catholics has ebbed, and the issue of faith-based education has taken on a new meaning. Pointing to problems in public schools, some argue that government should provide families with scholarships or vouchers for tuition at private institutions, including religious schools. Later in the chapter we examine the controversy over educational vouchers.

Private and parochial schools have a great deal of latitude in curriculum, but religion has also played a controversial role in public school coursework. In 1925, Tennessee teacher John Scopes stood trial for violating a state ban on the teaching of evolution. Although Scopes lost, evolutionism gained ground. A court reversed the conviction on a technicality, the state never enforced the law again, and the press hammered the creationist side. Nevertheless, the conflict continued. In 1968, the U.S. Supreme Court struck down an anti-evolution statute, calling it an "attempt to blot out a particular theory because of its supposed conflict with the Biblical account, literally read."[10] For similar reasons, it later rejected a Louisiana law requiring schools to teach creation science if they taught evolution.[11] Darwin, however, still struggles in the court of public opinion. By a margin of 58%–35%, Americans favor teaching creationism alongside evolution in public schools.[12] A 2012 poll found that 46% of Americans adhere to the strict creationist view that God created humans in their present form within the past 10,000 years. Another 32% believe that humans developed over millions of years but that God guided the process. Only 15% hold the strict evolutionist view that humans evolved without divine guidance.[13] In a 2010 survey of international public opinion, the United States ranked far ahead of all other Western industrial countries in support for creationism.[14]

Religious institutions have also been intimately involved with helping the needy. From colonial times, American houses of worship provided charity to the poor, often mixing material help with biblical instruction and work requirements.[15] In the late nineteenth century, liberal Protestants tried to broaden the scope of religious compassion. This **Social Gospel** movement urged churches to step up charitable work; it also advocated reforms such as the abolition of child labor. Although it lasted only a few decades as a distinct religious movement, it has had lasting influence. Believing that reform required better knowledge, movement leaders pushed for the growth of social sciences. Current or former clergy accounted for 40% of attendees of the American Economic Association's first meeting in 1885.[16] Richard T. Ely, the group's main founder, said, "It rests with us so to direct inevitable changes that we may be brought nearer that kingdom of righteousness for which all good Christians long and pray."[17]

Theodore Roosevelt's 1912 Progressive campaign for president had a Social Gospel flavor, with delegates to the party's convention singing "Onward Christian Soldiers." Roosevelt called his acceptance speech "a confession of faith."[18] Jane Addams, a Social Gospel Christian who founded settlement houses for the poor, called the Progressive Platform "all I have been fighting for a decade."[19] When Franklin Roosevelt became president two decades

Social Gospel—a Protestant Christian movement of the late 1800s and early 1900s that stressed the application of Christian principles to problems such as poverty.

later, key figures in his administration included relief administrator Harry Hopkins and Labor Secretary Frances Perkins, whose policies reflected their roots in the Social Gospel.

Later generations of activists also attested to its impact. Martin Luther King Jr. said, "I am a profound advocate of the social gospel."[20] Democratic presidential nominees George McGovern (1972) and Walter Mondale (1984) were ministers' sons who learned the Social Gospel in their youth. Secretary of State Hillary Rodham Clinton has often spoken of her Social Gospel beliefs.[21] As a young community organizer, President Obama called local activism "a powerful tool for living the social gospel."[22]

In 2012, Representative Paul Ryan (R-WI), then the chairman of the House Budget Committee and a leading opponent of President Obama's social policies (and later the Republican candidate for vice president), cited his commitment to the principle of subsidiarity, which is an important element of the social teaching of his Catholic faith: "To me, the principle of subsidiarity, which is really federalism, meaning government closest to the people governs best, having a civil society . . . where we, through our civic organizations, through our churches, through our charities, through all of our different groups where we interact with people as a community, that's how we advance the common good." "[T]he preferential option for the poor," he continued, "which is one of the primary tenets of Catholic social teaching, means don't keep people poor, don't make people dependent on government so that they stay stuck at their station in life, help people get out of poverty onto [a] life of independence." Other Catholics, however, interpret the church's social teaching differently. "Many Catholics," responded a Democratic Party official, "oppose the Ryan budget not in spite of our Catholic faith, but because of it."[23]

As this brief sketch demonstrates, American civic culture has long embraced the notion that the community should help the needy. For most of U.S. history, private organizations, such as churches and charities, and local governments were the principal sources of such aid. This began to change in the first decades of the twentieth century as many states adopted programs to aid poor children and their mothers. But not until the 1930s did the American people look to Washington, DC, to play a direct role.

Federal Deposit Insurance Corporation (FDIC)—the federal agency created in the 1930s to insure private savings in federally chartered banks.

Securities and Exchange Commission (SEC)—the federal agency created in the 1930s to regulate the stock market and some activities of publicly held corporations.

Jobless men line up to receive cabbage and potatoes from a federal relief agency in Cleveland, Ohio, in 1933, during the Great Depression.

FDR's New Deal

Many New Deal programs were temporary measures to relieve the distress caused by the Great Depression. These included the National Recovery Administration (NRA), which sought to stabilize prices and wages through cooperative agreements among government, business, and labor; the Public Works Administration (PWA), which funded thousands of public projects across the nation; and the Works Progress Administration (WPA), which employed several million out-of-work Americans on a variety of public building projects, arts and literacy programs, and the distribution of food and clothing.

Other programs, however, outlasted the Depression and gave the federal government an active role in regulating the economy and promoting the material well-being of Americans. These included the first national minimum wage law ($0.25 per hour), the creation of the **Federal Deposit Insurance Corporation (FDIC)** to insure private savings in federally chartered banks, and the establishment of the **Securities and Exchange Commission (SEC)** to regulate the stock market and some activities of publicly held corporations. Perhaps the most important and far-reaching innovation was the Social Security Act of 1935, which Roosevelt described in his signing statement as "a cornerstone in a structure which is being built . . . [to] take care of human needs."[24]

The Social Security Act consolidated a few existing programs to promote infant and maternal health and established three major new programs:

- An unemployment program, funded by a new federal tax on employers, to provide temporary cash benefits to laid-off workers.
- A public assistance program to supply cash payments to dependent children, the blind, and the elderly poor. This program, later called **Aid to Families with Dependent Children (AFDC)**, became what most Americans think of as "**welfare.**"
- Most importantly, a system of old-age insurance to provide monthly benefits to retired workers and their spouses. This third program, which we commonly call "Social Security," was to be funded by a **payroll tax**, divided equally between the employer and employee. Originally, the tax was 1% on both the employer and employee on the first $3,000 of salary. (In 2012, it was 6.2% on each on income up to $110,100.)

Social Security was the cornerstone of the new welfare state but not the entire building. In his State of the Union Address in January, 1944, deep into World War II, President Roosevelt said that too many Americans were "ill-fed, ill-clothed, ill-housed, and insecure." Although Americans possessed political rights such as freedom of speech, freedom of worship, and trial by jury, these were not enough to assure "equality in the pursuit of happiness." Needy people were not truly free and were "the stuff of which dictatorships are made." Roosevelt called for "a second Bill of Rights" to promote "security and prosperity . . . for all."

He listed the following specific rights:

- The right to a useful and remunerative job in the industries or shops or farms or mines of the Nation;
- The right to earn enough to provide adequate food and clothing and recreation;
- The right of every farmer to raise and sell his products at a return that will give him and his family a decent living;
- The right of every businessman, large and small, to trade in an atmosphere of freedom from unfair competition and domination by monopolies at home or abroad;
- The right of every family to a decent home;
- The right to adequate medical care and the opportunity to achieve and enjoy good health;
- The right to adequate protection from the economic fears of old age, sickness, accident, and unemployment; and
- The right to a good education.

"After the war is won," Roosevelt told his fellow citizens, "the nation must implement these rights and thereby move forward to new goals of human happiness and well being."[25]

What does it mean to say that someone has a right to adequate clothing, a decent home, or proper medical care? We have seen in earlier chapters that rights imply duties. If one person has a right to life, then everyone else has a duty not to kill him without just cause (such as in self-defense or during a just war). If one person has a right to liberty, then everyone else has a duty not to interfere with that liberty unless there is some legitimate reason to do so (such as constraining the "liberty" to drive through red lights).

What, then, of an individual's right to a decent home? Does this impose a duty on everyone else to provide that person a decent home? A right, as we saw in Chapter 5, is something to which one has a just claim or something that one may properly claim as his due. Does this mean, then, that

Aid to Families with Dependent Children (AFDC)—the federal assistance entitlement program based on the Social Security Act of 1935 that provided income to poor families (commonly called "welfare"). It was replaced in 1996 by Temporary Assistance to Needy Families (TANF).

Welfare—the common term for the old Aid to Families with Dependent Children program, replaced in 1996 by Temporary Assistance to Needy Families (TANF).

Payroll tax—the tax on payroll used to fund Social Security and part of Medicare, equally divided between the employer and employee.

195886/National Archives

The federal government advertises one of the benefits provided by the new Social Security Act of 1935.

Negative rights—rights to do certain things—such as speaking or worshipping freely—without interference from the government; includes traditional civil rights and civil liberties.

Positive rights—social or economic rights that some say oblige government to provide for the well-being of the citizens.

FOCUS
QUESTION

Practically speaking, does it make a difference whether social programs are described and defended in terms of rights or simply as social goods?

Fair Deal—the term for President Harry S Truman's social programs, especially his proposal for national health insurance.

Modern Republicanism—President Dwight D. Eisenhower's term for Republican Party acceptance of Social Security, unemployment insurance, labor laws, farm programs, and other features of the welfare state.

every American has a just claim to a decent home? Is this something that everyone may properly claim as his or her due?

Some theorists distinguish between **negative rights** and **positive rights**. Negative rights are rights to do certain things—such as speaking or worshipping freely—without interference from the government. These rights imply *freedom from* government intrusion or control. We discussed these traditional civil rights and civil liberties in Chapters 5 and 6. Positive rights, in contrast, refer to social or economic goods that some say government is obliged to provide its citizens. These rights imply *freedom to* enjoy certain goods, such as decent housing, education, and medical care.

Roosevelt could have promoted the various social goods in his "second Bill of Rights" without using the language of rights. He could have argued that a compassionate and generous nation should help its citizens secure good jobs, decent housing, and adequate medical care. It should help when old age, sickness, accidents, or unemployment robs people of income and drives them into poverty. It should make available to all its citizens a good public education. But by saying that Americans had a right to all these things, Roosevelt was implying that government had a moral obligation to provide them. If Americans embraced this understanding, it would be difficult for future leaders who might think differently to undo the large expansion of government ushered in by the New Deal.

Veterans returning from World War II had a special claim on their fellow citizens for assistance in returning to civilian life. In 1944, Congress passed the GI Bill of Rights (technically the Servicemen's Readjustment Act) to assist the several million Americans who had served in uniform. It provided medical assistance, low-cost mortgages, unemployment insurance, and educational subsidies. Its educational benefits were so popular that more than 2 million attended colleges and universities at government expense. To accommodate the influx, many large schools became even larger, and new ones were established.

The GI Bill was an engine of social and economic opportunity for millions of young men and women. The mortgage assistance it offered help to fuel the vast expansion of suburbs in the postwar years. In 2008, Congress passed the Post-9/11 GI Bill, expanding educational benefits for those who had served since the attacks of September 11, 2001.

Truman's Fair Deal

Democrat Harry S Truman, who succeeded to the presidency upon FDR's death in April 1945, served nearly two full terms. In his first year, he called on Congress to make FDR's economic Bill of Rights "the essence of postwar American economic life."[26] His program became known as the **Fair Deal**. Soon he asked Congress to provide universal health insurance coverage funded through the federal government.[27]

Truman, however, was less successful than FDR in getting his proposals through Congress, especially because Republicans gained strength in the House and Senate during his first term and were in the majority in both bodies in 1947–1948. Congress failed to pass Truman's health care initiative and other major new domestic programs. It did, however, create the National School Lunch Program in 1946, which committed the federal government to subsidizing school lunches for millions of American children. And three years later, it passed the landmark Housing Act of 1949, which called for "a decent home and suitable living environment" for all Americans. Under the new law, the federal government funded slum clearance and urban redevelopment, increased federal mortgage assistance, and built new public housing.

Eisenhower and Modern Republicanism

Republican Dwight D. Eisenhower won the presidency in 1952, and his party gained slim majorities in both houses of Congress. Although some thought the party that had opposed the New Deal and Fair Deal would now dismantle the welfare state, the new president showed little such inclination. Describing his principles as those of "**modern Republicanism**," he wrote, "Should any political party attempt to abolish social security, unemployment insurance, and eliminate labor laws and farm programs, you would not hear of that party again in our political history."[28] Eisenhower even supported an increase in the minimum wage and the expansion of Social Security. In 1953, he acknowledged and emphasized the federal government's new social welfare responsibilities by establishing the Cabinet-level Department of Health, Education, and Welfare. It was renamed the Department of Health and Human Services in 1979 when the separate Department of Education was created.

In October 1957, the Soviet Union orbited the first artificial satellite, Sputnik. Fearing that the American educational system was falling behind, Congress passed the National Defense Education Act of 1958, which expanded federal support for schools and students with an emphasis on scientific, mathematical, and technical training. With this partial exception, no large-scale expansion of the welfare state occurred during Eisenhower's presidency. The 1960s would bring change.

Johnson's Great Society

Although Democratic president John F. Kennedy, elected in 1960, proposed major new programs in housing, health, and unemployment, most of his more ambitious proposals did not pass while he served. His assassination in November 1963 and Vice President Lyndon Johnson's succession to the presidency added new momentum to the domestic agenda. In his State of the Union Address in January 1964, Johnson outlined perhaps the most far-reaching domestic agenda ever announced by a U.S. president. He called on lawmakers "to build more homes, more schools, more libraries, and more hospitals than any single session of Congress in the history of our Republic."[29]

War on Poverty—President Lyndon Johnson's term for a wide range of federal policies to combat poverty in America.

Johnson declared "unconditional **war on poverty**" and pledged that "we shall not rest until the war is won." It was not enough, he said, to provide jobs and money. Public policy had to get at the root causes of poverty, such as the lack of "education and training," "medical care and housing," and "decent communities in which to live and bring up . . . children." The goal was "not only to relieve the symptom of poverty, but to cure it and, above all, to prevent it."

Great Society—President Lyndon Johnson's term for his social programs to reduce poverty, address the problems of the cities, promote natural beauty, and enhance a sense of community.

The president then called for more than a dozen new programs to combat economic distress in Appalachia, reduce youth unemployment, distribute more food to the needy, extend the coverage of minimum wage laws, improve the quality of teaching, build more libraries, provide hospital insurance for older citizens, provide more housing for the poor and elderly, improve mass transit, reduce taxes, and provide for the hospital costs of the elderly.[30]

Four months later, Johnson announced an even more ambitious goal in his **Great Society** speech at the University of Michigan. The Great Society was more than the "rich society" or the "powerful society":

> The Great Society is a place where every child can find knowledge to enrich his mind and to enlarge his talents. It is a place where leisure is a welcome chance to build and reflect, not a feared cause of boredom and restlessness. It is a place where the city of man serves not only the needs of the body and the demands of commerce but the desire for beauty and the hunger for community.[31]

The decay of urban centers, the "despoiling" of the suburbs, and disappearance of open land were "eroding the precious and time honored values of community with neighbors and communion with nature." This was leading to "loneliness and

AP Photo

In January 1964, President Lyndon Johnson, right, meets with black leaders to discuss his War on Poverty. From the far left: Roy Wilkins, executive director of the NAACP; James Farmer, national director of the Congress of Racial Equality; Martin Luther King Jr., head of the Southern Christian Leadership Conference; and Whitney Young of the Urban League.

The Pruitt-Igoe housing project in St. Louis was a vast complex of 33 11-story apartment buildings on 57 acres built in the early 1950s as part of the federal housing program. By the 1960s it was heavily vandalized and crime infested. Authorities judged it a complete failure by 1972 and demolished three of its buildings. The rest were razed a year later.

boredom and indifference," seeming to condemn Americans to "a soulless wealth." Too many Americans were unhappy, even amidst plenty. Although Johnson, unlike FDR, did not quote the Declaration of Independence, he seemed to be saying that too many Americans were pursuing happiness but not achieving it. To remedy this situation, the president would assemble teams of experts to address the problems of cities, the environment, and education.[32]

Johnson's commitment to the war on poverty and the Great Society, assisted by large majorities of Democrats in the House and Senate, led to an expansion of the welfare state that rivaled the New Deal. Key programs included the following:

- Economic Opportunity Act of 1964, which established the Office of Economic Opportunity in the White House to create, fund, and coordinate antipoverty programs such as VISTA (Volunteers in Service to America), the Job Corps, the Neighborhood Youth Corps, Head Start, Foster Grandparents, Legal Services, Summer Youth Programs, and Senior Centers
- Food Stamp Act of 1964, which created a program to provide coupons to needy Americans to purchase food at retail outlets (replacing the direct distribution of surplus commodities)
- Elementary and Secondary Education Act of 1965, which provided new federal funding for elementary and secondary schools and especially (through Title I) to schools in poor neighborhoods
- Medicare Act of 1965, which for the first time provided federal assistance to those over 65 for hospital and doctor's expenses—partially funded through mandatory contributions from employers and employees (**Medicaid**, a companion program involving both the states and the federal government, was created at the same time to meet the medical needs of the poor.)

By the end of Johnson's presidency, the character of the American welfare state was well defined.

Medicaid—a program established in 1965, as a companion program to Medicare, to meet the medical needs of the poor. It is administered by the states and funded by both the states and the federal government.

Modern Social Welfare Policy

In the decade following the Great Society, Congress passed two new major social welfare programs. One was **Supplemental Security Income (SSI)**, signed by President Richard Nixon in 1972. This provides monthly cash benefits to those over 65, the blind, and the disabled who have little income. In 2012, the monthly benefit was $698 for an individual and $1,048 for a couple.[33] Many states add their own supplements to the federal benefit. The other program was the **Earned Income Tax Credit (EITC)** enacted in 1975 during the presidency of Gerald Ford. This provides a special federal tax credit to low-wage workers based on income and family size. Many who pay little or no federal income taxes receive checks under this legislation. EITC has grown to be a major antipoverty program, disbursing a total of $60 billion to 27 million tax filers in 2010.[34] Later, President George W. Bush persuaded Congress in 2003 to add a prescription drug benefit to Medicare, and President Barack Obama in 2010 secured passage of a major health care reform bill.

Some social welfare programs (e.g., Medicaid) are directed specifically at the needs of the poor. These are called **means-tested programs** because eligibility depends on low income or few tangible assets. Other programs (e.g., Social Security and Medicare) are aimed at the much larger middle class. Their benefit levels do not depend on the income

Supplemental Security Income (SSI)—a federal program established in 1972 that provides monthly cash benefits to those over 65, the blind, and the disabled who have little income.

Earned Income Tax Credit (EITC)—a federal program enacted in 1975 that provides a special income tax credit to low-wage workers based on income and family size.

Means-tested program—a social welfare program that disburses benefits to those who have low income or few tangible assets.

of the recipient. Because they have many more recipients, they cost more overall than antipoverty programs.

Many programs provide benefits as **entitlements**, meaning that those who meet the qualifications under the law are entitled to benefits. Entitlement spending is difficult to control because unless the underlying law is changed the amount paid out each year is determined simply by the number eligible for benefits. For this reason, entitlement spending is sometimes called "uncontrollable spending" and is contrasted with "discretionary spending." Nothing, however, prevents Congress from rewriting federal law to control entitlement spending (however difficult this may be politically).

Entitlement—a government benefit to which one is entitled by meeting certain qualifications spelled out in law.

In a 2006 special report, the Congressional Research Service identified 84 means-tested programs that cost governments in the United States a total of $583 billion in 2004: $427 billion in federal funds and $156 billion in state and local funds. The total was 16.1% of all government spending in 2004: 18.6% of federal spending and 11.8% of spending by state and local governments.[35] These numbers give a good sense of how much governments in the United States spend directly to help the poor. (This does not include spending by private individuals and groups; see Chapter 4.)

Table 16-2 lists the biggest of these programs with their costs and number of recipients. Medicaid was the most expensive ($300.3 billion) and had the widest reach (enrolling 56 million Americans during the year). The next in order of cost were Supplemental Security Income ($39.8 billion), the Earned Income Tax Credit ($34.0 billion), food stamps ($31.0 billion), and low-income housing assistance ($22.4 billion). After Medicaid, the programs with the most recipients were food stamps (24.9 million recipients each month), the Earned Income Tax Credit (19.2 million families), and the school lunch program (16.9 million children each day). (See also the Myths and Misinformation feature on page 484.)

TABLE 16-2   LARGEST MEANS-TESTED PROGRAMS, EXPENDITURES BY FEDERAL, STATE, AND LOCAL GOVERNMENTS, 2004 (RANKED BY COST)

Program	Cost	Number of Recipients
Medicaid	$300,300,000,000	56,100,000 (number enrolled at any time during the year)
Supplemental Security Income	39,839,000,000	7,139,000 (average monthly)
Earned Income Tax Credit (refundable part)	34,012,000,000	19,163,000 (families)
Food stamps	30,993,000,000	24,900,000 (average monthly)
Section 8 low-income housing assistance	22,356,000,000	3,387,000 (families or dwelling units)
Temporary Assistance for Needy Families (TANF): cash payments	14,067,000,000	4,746,000 (average monthly)
Federal Pell grants (financial assistance for college)	12,006,000,000	5,344,000 (participants in school year)
Child care and development block grant	9,380,000,000	1,732,000 (average monthly)
Child tax credit (refundable part)	9,113,000,000	12,571,000 (average monthly)
Medical care for veterans (without a service-connected disability)	8,725,000,000	1,630,000 (per year)
Foster care	8,564,000,000	233,000 (average monthly)
Head Start (education, health, and nutrition assistance to preschool children)	8,469,000,000	906,000 (during school year)
Public housing	7,488,000,000	1,189,000 (families or dwelling units)
School lunch program	6,816,000,000	16,930,000 (average daily number)
State Children's Health Insurance (SCHIP)	6,633,000,000	6,799,000 (at any time during the year)
TANF services	6,250,000,000	n.a.
Federally subsidized student college loans	5,261,000,000	6,869,000 (during school year)

NOTE: Data are for all programs that cost at least $5 billion.

SOURCE: Congressional Research Service Report for Congress, RL33340, "Cash and Noncash Benefits for Persons with Limited Income: Eligibility Rules, Recipient and Expenditure Data, FY2002–FY2004," March 27, 2006, 163–177, http://assets.opencrs.com/rpts/RL33340_20060327.pdf, accessed July 17, 2012.

MYTHS AND MISINFORMATION

Spending for the Poor

Discussions of social welfare policy frequently include assertions that the federal government has cut antipoverty spending. Historian Howard Zinn writes that when President Reagan increased military spending, he "tried to pay for this with cuts in benefits for the poor." At various times, pundits have said that cuts also came during the administrations of Jimmy Carter, George H. W. Bush, Bill Clinton, or George W. Bush.

As we note in this chapter, means-tested programs are those that provide benefits to individuals and families with income or assets below a certain level. If we want to answer the question, "How much does the federal government spend on the poor?" the best single measure is spending on means-tested programs in constant dollars (which controls for the effects of inflation). Figure 16-1 shows that despite relatively constant expenditures in President Carter's administration (1977–1981) and President Reagan's first term (1981–1985), total federal spending for these programs has been increasing for decades.

So why do we often hear talk of cuts? Sometimes, Congress has curbed the growth of such programs below projections, and some critics argue that these programs have not kept pace with social needs.[36]

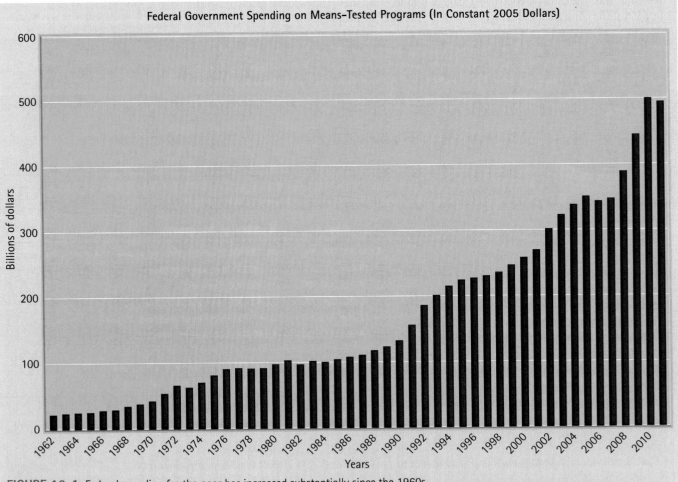

Federal Government Spending on Means-Tested Programs (In Constant 2005 Dollars)

Billions of dollars (y-axis) / *Years* (x-axis)

FIGURE 16-1 Federal spending for the poor has increased substantially since the 1960s.
SOURCE: U.S. Government Printing Office, Budget of The United States Government, Fiscal Year 2013, Historical Tables, 8.2, at www.gpo.gov/fdsys/browse/collection.action?collectionCode=BUDGET&browsepath=Fiscal+Year+2013&searchpath=Fiscal+Year+2013&leafLevelbrowse=false&isCollapsed=false&isopen=true&packageid=BUDGET-2013-TAB&ycord=710, Accessed October 6, 2012.

The two largest federal programs in 2004 that were not means tested—that is, were available to eligible recipients regardless of income—were Social Security, at $496 billion, and Medicare, at $269 billion. These programs totaled $765 billion, almost twice as much as all the means-tested programs combined. (As Table 16-1 shows, in 2012, Social Security cost $779 billion and Medicare $485 billion, for a total of $1.26 trillion—a 65% increase in eight years.)

Note, however, that means-tested programs are **noncontributory programs**. That is, the recipients draw benefits without contributing directly to the programs; funds come from general revenues. They are also called **redistribution programs** because they redistribute income, or wealth, from the nonpoor to the poor. Social Security, by contrast, is a **contributory program**, paid for each year by contributions from current and future recipients (but see the later discussion). Medicare has both characteristics: it is partly paid for by contributions (taxes, monthly premiums, and copayments) and partly from general revenues.

Despite the American people's broad acceptance of the basic features of the welfare state, controversies continue to arise. Next we discuss four key debates over social policy. We begin with welfare reform.

Noncontributory program—a program under which recipients draw benefits without contributing directly to the program; funds come from general revenues.

Redistribution program—a noncontributory program that redistributes income or wealth from taxpayers generally to the poor.

THE WELFARE DEBATE

MAJOR ISSUES

- Why did Congress replace the AFDC entitlement program with the TANF block grant?
- What effect did the change have on welfare rolls?

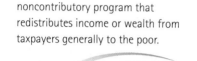

Contributory program—a program, such as Social Security, that is paid for by contributions from current or future recipients.

Until a major reform in 1996, "welfare" generally referred to the monthly cash assistance provided by the Aid to Families with Dependent Children (AFDC) program, which grew out of one provision of the Social Security Act of 1935. To say that a family was "on welfare" usually meant that it was a recipient of AFDC. In 1960, about 3 million adults and children received AFDC benefits. In just over a decade, this number more than tripled, to more than 10 million. After remaining fairly stable for 17 years, the number began to move upward in 1990, peaking at more than 14 million in 1993 (see Figure 16-2). These trends seemed to contradict the hopes of the architects of the Great Society, who sought to combat the "root causes" of poverty by moving the poor toward self-sufficiency and into the middle class.

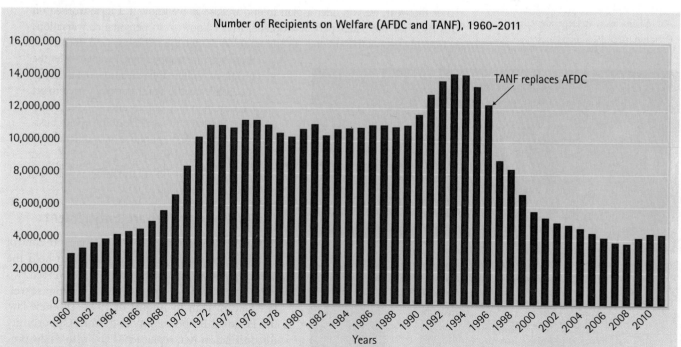

FIGURE 16-2 Welfare caseloads have dropped by large amounts since the mid-1990s.
SOURCE: U.S. Department of Health and Human Services, Administration for Children & Families, AFDC and TANF caseload data at archive .acf.hhs.gov/programs/ofa/data-reports/caseload/caseload_archive.html and www.acf.hhs.gov/programs/ofa/resource/caseload2011, accessed October 6, 2012.

Families poor enough to receive AFDC often qualified for other means-tested programs as well, especially food stamps, Medicaid, and housing assistance. By the mid-1980s, some social scientists began to wonder whether the upsurge in social welfare expenditures in the 1960s and 1970s was itself exacerbating the problem by creating a dependency on public aid. Some argued that in many cases the combination of programs produced a package of benefits that could not be matched by the wages that a welfare recipient could likely earn in an entry-level job, thus discouraging entry into the workforce. In his influential *Losing Ground: American Social Policy, 1950–1980*, Charles Murray argued that "[w]e tried to provide more for the poor and produced more poor instead."[37] His controversial argument led to a renewed debate about the poverty problem and public assistance.

Politicians began to take note. In May 1992, Vice President Dan Quayle delivered a speech in California that addressed the causes of riots that had erupted in Los Angeles after a jury had acquitted four police officers of nearly all charges in the beating of a black man after a high-speed chase. Quayle asked, "What were the underlying causes of the riots?"

> I believe the lawless social anarchy which we saw is directly related to the breakdown of family structure, personal responsibility and social order in too many areas of our society. For the poor the situation is compounded by a welfare ethos that impedes individual efforts to move ahead in society, and hampers their ability to take advantage of the opportunities America offers.[38]

Although Quayle's speech is remembered mainly for his criticism of a fictional television newswoman, Murphy Brown, for having a child out of wedlock, it made "family values" a subject of political discussion and called attention to the issue of welfare dependency.

The year before, Arkansas's Democratic governor Bill Clinton had announced his candidacy for the presidency by promising to make welfare reform a major theme of his campaign: "The government owes our people more opportunity, but we all have to make the most of it through responsible citizenship. We should insist that people move off welfare rolls and onto work rolls."[39] Throughout the campaign he promised to "end welfare as we know it" and received favorable notice for stressing responsibility and citizenship. Clinton returned to the issue in his first address to Congress in February 1993:

> Later this year, we will offer a plan to end welfare as we know it. I have worked on this issue for the better part of a decade. And I know from personal conversations with many people that no one, no one wants to change the welfare system as badly as those who are trapped in it. I want to offer the people on welfare the education, the training, the child care, the health care they need to get back on their feet, but say after two years they must get back to work, too, in private business if possible, in public service if necessary. We have to end welfare as a way of life and make it a path to independence and dignity.[40]

The End of the Welfare Entitlement

In the 1994 elections, Republicans gained control of the House and Senate and worked to hold the president to his promises. After Clinton vetoed two Republican proposals, he signed a compromise welfare reform plan in August of 1996. The new law, the Personal Responsibility and Work Opportunity Reconciliation Act, replaced AFDC with a new program, **Temporary Assistance to Needy Families (TANF)**. The law ended the entitlement to welfare by providing the states with block grants (see

Temporary Assistance to Needy Families (TANF)—the block grant program created in 1996 to replace Aid to Families with Dependent Children (AFDC).

President Bill Clinton signs the Personal Responsibility and Work Opportunity Reconciliation Act in 1996.

Stephen Jaffe/Reuters/Landor

Chapter 3) to fund needy families in state-run programs. It set a lifetime five-year limit on benefits, imposed new work requirements, expanded funds for child care, toughened child support enforcement, and stipulated that unwed mothers under 18 had to live with an adult to receive aid. Although Clinton objected to some provisions of the bill, he praised the new law for making public assistance "a second chance, not a way of life." The new program, he said, would replace "a never-ending cycle of welfare" with "the dignity, the power, and the ethic of work."[41]

Welfare reform was controversial within the Democratic Party and among organizations that often allied with it. Senator Tom Daschle (D-SD), leader of the Democrats in the Senate, denounced the measure

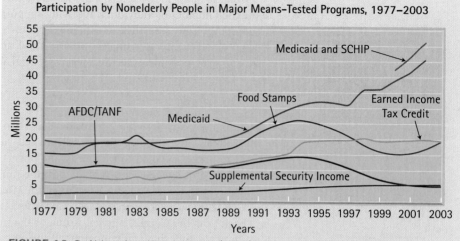

FIGURE 16-3 Although welfare caseloads (AFDC/TANF) have dropped during the past decade, other programs have grown.
SOURCE: Congressional Budget Office, "Changes in Participation in Means Tested Programs," April 20, 2005, p. 3, at www.cbo.gov/sites/default/files/cbofiles/ftpdocs/63xx/doc6302/04-20-means-tested.pdf, accessed July 25, 2012.

because "[t]oo many kids will still be punished." Senator Daniel Patrick Moynihan (D-NY), a former Harvard University social scientist and expert on welfare, said that he could not "conceive that the party of Social Security and of civil rights could support this legislation which commences to repeal, to undermine both."[42] Moynihan described the proposal as "the most brutal act of social policy since reconstruction." And Marian Wright Edelman, the president of the Children's Defense Fund, called the law an "outrage . . . that will hurt and impoverish millions of American children."[43]

Effects of Welfare Reform

Experts, advocates, and public officials continue to debate the law's effects. Defenders point to the large reduction in welfare caseloads from over 12 million when the reform passed to 3.9 million in 2007, a drop of two-thirds. (Caseloads then rose slightly to 4.4 million in 2011; see Figure 16-2.) This downward trend, they maintain, shows the success of the new law in moving former welfare recipients into jobs. Others claim, however, that a growing economy and the expansion of the EITC program may account for much of the reduction in caseloads.[44] Critics of the new law also charge that a reduction in those receiving assistance is not necessarily a good thing if needy families are being denied aid.

A 2005 analysis by the Congressional Budget Office (CBO) showed that of the five major antipoverty programs funded by the federal government, TANF, or "welfare," was the only one that saw an overall decline between 1977 and 2003 (see Figure 16-3). The number of food stamp recipients began to decline in 1994 but started trending upward in 2001. The other three programs—Supplemental Security Income, the EITC, and Medicaid—all grew during this period, with the EITC remaining fairly level after 1994. In the decade and a half since 1994, the number of participants grew in all the programs other than TANF, but at different rates. Most dramatic was the increase in the number of food stamp recipients, which more than doubled in 17 years.[45]

	1994	2009–2012
Medicaid	45 million	54 million (2010)
Food Stamps	20 million	45 million (2011)
TANF	5 million	4 million (2011)
Earned Income Tax Credit	20 million	27 million (2009)
Supplemental Security Income	5 million	8 million (2012)

Because many individuals qualify for more than one program, there is no official count of the total number of individuals receiving support under at least one means-tested federal program over time. Nonetheless, with most means-tested programs growing in size and Medicaid and food stamps dwarfing the others, it is clear that, despite the welfare reform of 1996, many more low-income Americans receive federal aid now than at any time in the past.

Poverty Trends

Traditionally, means-tested programs have had two purposes: to relieve human distress and to move recipients out of poverty and into self-sufficiency. Yet, despite the expansion of federal resources devoted to the needy, the poverty rate in the United States, after falling significantly in the 1960s, has remained in the range of 11% to 15% for four decades (see Figure 16-4). Indeed, in the first decade of the twenty-first century, it grew from 11.3% to 15.1%, reaching a level it had not seen since 1993.

Each year the Census Bureau estimates the number of Americans in poverty by determining whether the family income falls below a certain level, depending on family size. These income levels are based mainly on what it costs a family to have an inexpensive but adequately nutritious diet, assuming further that a family spends one-third of its income on food. In 2010, the poverty level for a family of four was calculated to be $22,491.[46]

Those on both sides of the debate over federal antipoverty programs criticize these figures, arguing that they distort deliberations on social policy. Some say that the census sets the poverty line too low, thereby underestimating the number of people who are truly poor. Others say that the data exaggerate poverty by not including as income such "in-kind" benefits as food stamps, medical aid, and subsidized housing. They also note that almost half of those officially classified as poor own their own homes, nearly three-fourths own a car, and nearly all have at least one color television.[47]

Scholars and policymakers vigorously debate the causes of poverty in America. Despite much disagreement, most recognize that one factor that correlates very highly with the

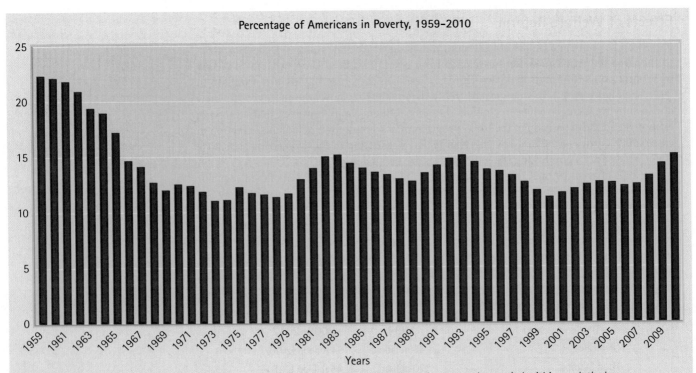

FIGURE 16-4 After dropping considerably in the 1960s, the percentage of Americans in poverty has varied within a relatively narrow range in the years since.

SOURCE: U.S. Census Bureau, Income, Poverty, and Health Insurance Coverage in the United States: 2010, Table B-1, p. 62, at www.census.gov/prod/2011pubs/p60-239.pdf, accessed October 6, 2012.

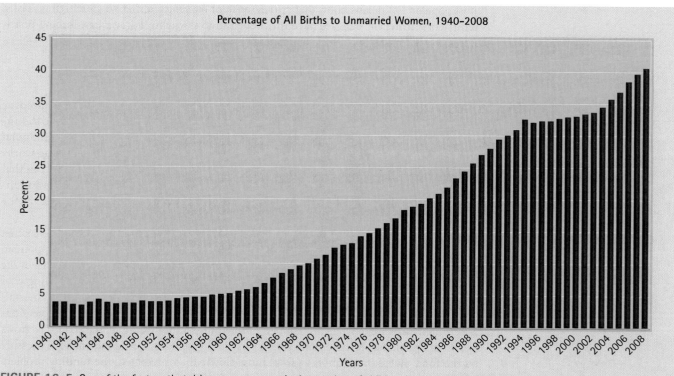

FIGURE 16–5 One of the factors that drives poverty rates is the number of children born out of wedlock.
SOURCE: U.S. Census Bureau, Statistical Abstract of the United States 2003, Births to Teenagers and Unmarried Women: 1940–2002, at www.census.gov/statab/hist/HS-14.pdf, accessed July 25, 2012; The 2009 Statistical Abstract, Table 85, www.census.gov/compendia/statab/tables/09s0085.pdf, accessed June 10, 2009; and The 2012 Statistical Abstract, Table 86, at www.census.gov/compendia/statab/2012/tables/12s0086.pdf, accessed July 25, 2012.

poverty rate is the number of single-parent households. It stands to reason that two parents will, on average, net more family income than one. Either both will generate income outside the home, or one parent will stay home, eliminating the need for child-care expenses. It is no surprise, then, that studies consistently show that single-parent families are much more likely to be poor than two-parent families. In 2010, according to the Census Bureau, the poverty rate for female-headed households with no husband present was 31.6%, compared to 15.8% for male-headed households with no wife present and only 6.2% for households headed by a married couple.[48] Given this strong association between family structure and poverty, the trends are not encouraging. In 1960, only one of every twenty births in the United States was to an unwed mother, but by 2008 the figure had increased eightfold, reaching two of every five births (see Figure 16-5).

Despite the importance of the issues involved in the welfare debate, the actual costs of AFDC and TANF pale in comparison to the nation's largest domestic program: Social Security.

FOCUS QUESTION

Can poverty in the United States be significantly reduced if two-fifths of all births continue to be to unwed mothers?

THE SOCIAL SECURITY DEBATE

MAJOR ISSUES

- Does the Social Security system face a crisis in the future?
- What are the key issues in the debate over private accounts?

In 2011, the federal government disbursed $732 billion to 54 million Americans through the Social Security system; 64% were retired workers, 19% were disabled workers, 12% were the survivors of deceased workers, and 9% were the spouses or children of retired or disabled workers.[49] Not only is Social Security the largest single government program (slightly larger than national defense, which cost $717 billion in 2011); it is perhaps the most popular. Politicians know that criticizing it, or offering alternatives, is extremely risky. Yet its costs in recent decades have threatened to overwhelm its revenues, forcing politicians to place it on the public agenda.

How Social Security Is Funded

Social Security trust fund—the fund into which Social Security taxes are deposited and then used to buy federal securities (government IOUs).

Unlike privately financed individual retirement accounts, employer and employee contributions to Social Security are not held in reserve as an investment for the individual to draw on once retired. Instead, all contributions go into a common **Social Security trust fund**, which disburses benefits to current retirees. In effect, the working generation pays for the benefits of the retired generation, with the expectation that the same will happen when it retires. In principle, this system can continue indefinitely as long as there are enough current workers paying sufficient taxes to cover the costs of current retirees.

Federal law requires that the trustees of the Social Security trust fund—three cabinet secretaries, the commissioner of Social Security, and two public representatives appointed by the president—prepare a public report each year that projects the financial status of the trust fund over the next 75 years. These projections rely on assumptions regarding economic growth, wage growth, inflation, unemployment, fertility, immigration, and mortality. Because no one can know whether these assumptions will hold true, the projections are a rough estimate of what will happen in the future. If, for example, the economy grows faster than predicted, Social Security revenues would increase, easing the financial pressure on the fund. But if the economy grows more slowly than predicted, the funding problem will just get worse (see Figure 16-6).

Table 16-3 shows the projected revenues and expenses of the Social Security trust fund from 2020 through 2090. In the mid-1970s, the trust fund began to take in less each year than it paid out. This funding crisis led Congress and President Ronald Reagan to create a blue-ribbon panel in the early 1980s to recommend reforms. The **Greenspan Commission** (named for chairman Alan Greenspan) recommended, and Congress enacted, a variety of measures to put the program on a sounder financial footing: higher Social Security taxes, the first-time coverage of federal employees, and a gradual increase in the retirement age (for full benefits) from 65 to 67.

Greenspan Commission—the 15-member National Commission for Social Security Reform, chaired by Alan Greenspan and established by Congress in 1981 to address the funding imbalance in the Social Security system.

The results were immediate. From 1984 on, the trust fund took in more than it paid out every year. But currently, costs exceed revenues, and according to the trustees of the system this will continue indefinitely. If there are no changes in the law, the annual deficit will grow from $115 billion in 2020 to $8.4 trillion in 2090.

| TABLE 16-3 | PROJECTED REVENUES, COSTS, AND ANNUAL BALANCE FOR THE SOCIAL SECURITY TRUST FUND, 1960–2080 |

Year	Revenues	Cost	Annual Balance (or deficit)
2020	1,151	1,266	−115
2030	1,786	2,292	−506
2040	2,782	3,635	−854
2050	4,301	5,534	−1,233
2060	6,607	8,533	−1,925
2070	10,158	13,235	−3,077
2080	15,615	20,645	−5,030
2090	24,013	32,367	−8,354

NOTE: The data are intermediate projections.

SOURCE: *The 2012 Annual Report of the Board of Trustees of the Federal Old-Age and Survivors Insurance and Federal Disability Insurance Trust Funds*, Table VI.F9 (p. 208), www.ssa.gov/oact/tr/2012/tr2012.pdf, accessed July 19, 2012.

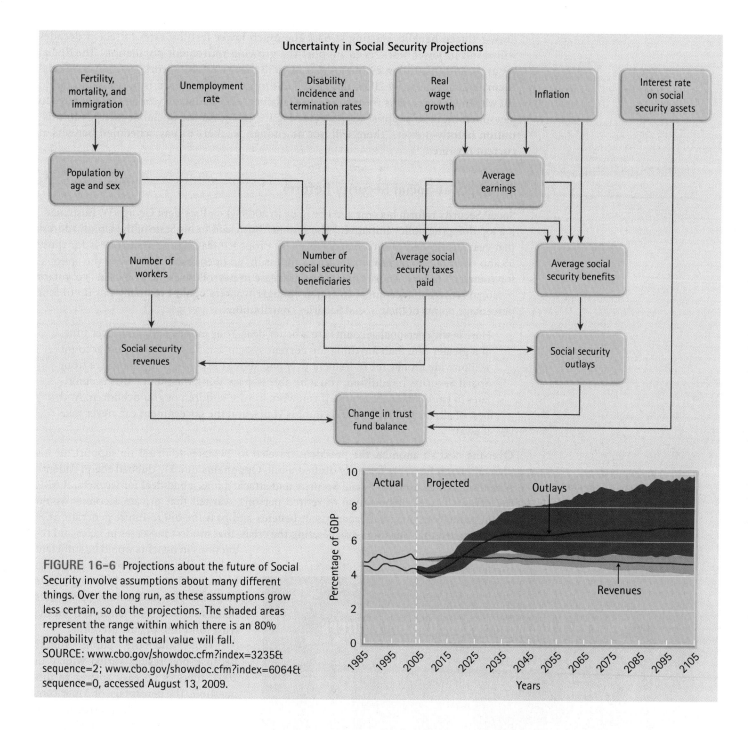

FIGURE 16-6 Projections about the future of Social Security involve assumptions about many different things. Over the long run, as these assumptions grow less certain, so do the projections. The shaded areas represent the range within which there is an 80% probability that the actual value will fall.
SOURCE: www.cbo.gov/showdoc.cfm?index=3235&sequence=2; www.cbo.gov/showdoc.cfm?index=6064&sequence=0, accessed August 13, 2009.

When Social Security taxes exceed payments to individuals, the excess revenue goes into the Social Security trust fund. By law, these funds go to buy securities from the federal government. The government then uses these funds to contribute to the operating costs of federal agencies. In effect, one part of the federal government—the Treasury Department—promises to pay another part of the federal government—the Social Security trust fund—the funds it borrowed, with appropriate interest, when the trust fund needs them. As of 2010, the trust fund held about $2.6 trillion in federal securities.[50] Now that Social Security expenses exceed revenues, the trust fund must cash in securities each year, requiring the government to dip into its general revenues.

Demographic forces are partially responsible for the dire long-term prospects for funding Social Security. The large population of baby boomers born just after World War II will start to become eligible for full benefits in the next few years. (Retirees may draw reduced benefits starting at 62.) The much lower fertility rates of recent decades will result in fewer workers to support the growing retirement population. The Social Security Administration estimates that in 1950 there were 16.5 workers for every Social Security beneficiary. By 2006, the ratio had dropped to 3.3, and it is projected to fall to 2.0 within 40 years. This means that unless benefits are reduced, workers would have to pay much more to support retirees (see Figure 16-7). As the Social Security Administration bluntly puts it, "there will not be enough workers to pay scheduled benefits at current tax rates."[33]

Attempts at Social Security Reform

Social Security reform became a major issue in 2005 when President George W. Bush made it a top domestic policy initiative. "The system," Bush said in his State of the Union address that year, "is headed toward bankruptcy." He proposed leaving the system as is for those 55 and older but offered to work with Congress in "an open, candid review of the options" for younger workers. After ruling out an increase in payroll taxes, he proposed "voluntary personal retirement accounts" in which younger workers could eventually put up to four percentage points of their Social Security contribution:

> Here is why personal accounts are a better deal. Your money will grow, over time, at a greater rate than anything the current system can deliver—and your account will provide money for retirement over and above the check you will receive from Social Security. In addition, you'll be able to pass along the money that accumulates in your personal account, if you wish, to your children or grandchildren. And best of all, the money in the account is yours, and the government can never take it away.[51]

Over the next six months, the president traveled to 29 states to drum up support for his plan, although he never formally drafted a bill. Opponents quickly dubbed the president's plan the "privatization" of Social Security and attacked it as a bad deal for workers. AARP, the nation's largest organization of retired persons, warned that private accounts would "drain money out of Social Security, cut benefits and pass the bill to future generations."[52] Others argued that Bush was exaggerating the crisis, that modest increases in taxes and reductions in benefits would be sufficient to keep the system solvent. They also highlighted the large "start-up" costs of Bush's plan as millions of workers opted to divert contributions from the trust fund into private accounts.

What did the public think? Because poll results varied widely in 2005, there is no easy answer to this question. The percentage of Americans voicing support for the president's plan between March and July 2005 ranged from a high of 60% to a low of 33%, depending on how the question was asked. The most negative response came to a question that mentioned that the proposal "would reduce the guaranteed benefits [people] get when they retire." The most positive response was to a question about whether individuals should have the "choice" to invest in stocks or mutual funds.[53] Pollsters have long known that even slight changes in wording can significantly affect results.

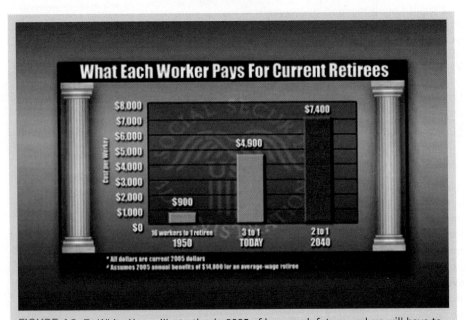

FIGURE 16-7 White House illustration in 2005 of how much future workers will have to pay to maintain current benefit levels for retirees on Social Security if current demographic trends continue.

One interesting issue in the debate was whether younger people, who tend to have less confidence in the long-term viability of Social Security than do older Americans, were more favorable to Bush's proposal. In late 2004, the National Annenberg Election Survey showed a strong correlation between support for Bush's proposal and age.[54]

Age	Percent Who Favored the Proposal
18–29	66%
30–44	63
45–54	57
55–64	51
65–75	41
76+	33

Interestingly, all age groups that would have been eligible to participate in the new plan (those under 55) showed substantial majorities in favor. The respected Gallup polling organization also found an age effect: "Americans under age 50 are much more likely to support private investment plans than are those age 50 and older."[55]

President Bush was not successful in building public support for private accounts. Polls showed that support was higher when he first began talking about private accounts in the 2000 presidential campaign than it was in 2005. Also, during his six-month public opinion offensive, some polls showed either little change in public support or a decline (see Table 16-4). With little public pressure to keep the issue alive, interest in Congress waned and the proposal for private accounts quietly died. Because much of the money in private accounts would presumably be invested in the stock market, big drops in the value of stocks at the end of Bush's second term further weakened the case for change in the minds of many.

Despite the failure of Bush's proposal, few maintain that the Social Security program can be sustained without major change. As each year goes by, expenses will further outpace revenues, unless changes are made to the law. Either more revenue will have to be found (by raising Social Security taxes or drawing on the general revenues of the federal government) or expenditures will have to be reduced (by cutting benefit levels or postponing the retirement age).

One consequence of the uncertainty surrounding the future of Social Security is that more and more Americans have looked to individual retirement accounts (IRAs), such as

TABLE 16-4   PUBLIC SUPPORT FOR PRESIDENT BUSH'S PROPOSED REFORM OF THE SOCIAL SECURITY SYSTEM, JANUARY–JULY 2005

Organization	January	February	March	April	May	June	July
NBC/*Wall Street Journal*	40	40		35	36		33
PSRA/Pew*		4	44/46[†]		47		
Gallup/CNN/*USA Today*	40	40/36[†]	33	33			
Gallup/CNN/*USA Today*			45	39	44	44	
ABC News/*Washington Post*			56	45	48		
Quinnipiac		51	49				
CBS News/*New York Times*	45	43		45	47	45	
Fox News/Opinion Dynamics		48		53			

*Princeton Survey Research Associates/Pew Research Center.

[†]Two polls in the same month.

NOTE: Table shows the results for all polls that used exactly the same question at different times between January and July 2005. Most surveys have a sampling error of ±3%.

SOURCE: AEI Public Opinion Study, "Attitudes about Social Security Reform (updated August 2, 2005)," 19–23, www.aei.org/files/2005/08/02/20050802_SOCIALSECURITY0802.pdf, accessed July 25, 2012.

401(k) plans (named after a provision of the internal revenue code) to meet their retirement needs. Under federal law, employees can put thousands of dollars into personal accounts, which are sometimes matched by their employers, without paying taxes on the money contributed or on the investment earnings of the account. Income taxes are paid when the money is withdrawn—no sooner than age 59½. In 2009, about 39% of U.S. households owned some kind of IRA. Assets totaled $4.1 trillion, up from $637 billion in 1990.[56] Tax laws that promote saving for retirement appeal to the principle of self-reliance, encouraging citizens to defer some current spending for the sake of their long-term well-being.

The second-most expensive federal domestic program is Medicare, health coverage for those 65 and older. It is growing at a more rapid rate than Social Security and, if projections are right, presents an even larger long-term funding problem. Congress expanded Medicare coverage in 2003 and then further expanded the federal role in health in 2010 with the passage of the Patient Protection and Affordable Care Act.

THE HEALTH CARE DEBATE

MAJOR ISSUES

- What are the challenges to the long-term viability of Medicare?
- How did the Affordable Care Act seek to improve health coverage in the United States?

When Medicare began in 1965, health costs for those 65 and older went mainly for hospitalization and doctors' services. In the years since, prescription drugs for such conditions as high blood pressure and high cholesterol became increasingly important to seniors' health. Drug costs increasingly burdened the elderly, and many looked to Medicare for help. Responding to this growing sentiment, both major party candidates in the 2000 presidential campaign—Democrat Al Gore Jr. and Republican George W. Bush—advocated adding prescription drug benefits to Medicare. Many believed that the money would come from predicted surpluses in federal revenues (the federal budget had surpluses of $123 billion in 1999 and $230 billion in 2000).

Once elected, Bush made the prescription drug benefit a major domestic priority. In his view, it embodied the principles of "compassionate conservatism" on which he had run. "No senior in America," he said in his first speech to Congress, "should have to choose between buying food and buying prescriptions."[57]

The Medicare Expansion

Despite some heated conflicts among the nation's lawmakers, Congress passed the Medicare Prescription Drug, Improvement, and Modernization Act in 2003. The new law

- helped all seniors with their prescription drug costs,
- covered most drug costs for low-income seniors,
- authorized a limited number of pilot programs in which private medical plans (the Medicare Advantage program) could compete with the original Medicare fee-for-service program,
- created new voluntary health savings accounts,
- expanded funding for rural health services, and
- provided new coverage for preventive care.

During the congressional debates of 2003, the White House estimated the 10-year cost of the program as $400 billion, but by 2010 the trustees of the Medicare trust fund were estimating a cost of $763 billion for 2010–2019.[58] This was the largest addition to social welfare spending since Lyndon Johnson's Great Society. Most of the cost was for the new prescription drug benefit. Seniors would enroll not directly with the government but with private insurance companies, which would contract with the federal government. Participants would pay an initial monthly premium of $35 (but this could increase over time) and the program would cover approximately three-quarters of annual drug costs up to $2,250 and nearly all the costs above $5,100. Beyond minor copays, participants would face a maximum out-of-pocket cost of $3,600 per year.

In his signing statement, President Bush called the law "a great achievement of a compassionate government."[59] Although Democrats in Congress had supported the addition of prescription drug benefits to Medicare, the specifics of Bush's proposal had sharply divided the two parties, especially in the House, and also caused fissures within each party. Some Republicans opposed any expansion of the government's role—"Republicans do not stand for growing government," said Representative Walter B. Jones (R-NC)[60]—and most Democrats opposed the introduction of private companies into the Medicare system—"And a cruel hoax it is indeed. . . . It is an elimination of Medicare," said Nancy Pelosi (D-CA), leader of the House Democrats (and later Speaker of the House of Representatives).[61]

In the end, the bill barely made it through the House, but passed more comfortably in the Senate. In signing the act into law on December 8, 2003,

Paul J. Richards/AFP/ Getty Images

Speaking to retirees in Sun City, Florida, in 2006, President Bush praises the 2003 law that added prescription drug benefits to Medicare.

President Bush emphasized the new choices seniors would have: "We show our respect for seniors by giving them more choices and more control over their decision making. We're putting individuals in charge of their health care decisions. And as we move to modernize and reform other programs of this government, we will always trust individuals and their decisions, and put personal choice at the heart of our efforts."[62]

By 2008, 25 million Americans were enrolled in the new Medicare prescription drug program. The monthly premium was $28, about a third lower than originally projected, at least partly because of the widespread use of cheaper generic drugs. The Centers for Medicare and Medicaid Services, which administers the program, reported that most participants were happy with it.[63]

Funding Medicare in the Twenty-first Century

Revenues to fund the various programs that are part of Medicare come from (1) the payroll tax of 1.45% on both the employer and the employee, (2) general revenues, and (3) premiums and copayments by the enrollees. The aging of the baby boomers and acceleration in medical costs make the long-term prospects of adequately funding Medicare even bleaker than for Social Security. As the trustees of the Medicare trust fund warned in 2008, "Medicare's financial difficulties come sooner—and are much more severe—than those confronting Social Security."[64]

Medicare Part A, which covers hospitalization costs and is funded exclusively through the payroll tax, already pays out more each year than it collects in revenues. According to the trustees' projections, the shortfall in Part A will increase every year throughout the century, reaching $119 billion in 2020, $1.1 trillion in 2040, $4.0 trillion in 2060, and $12.4 trillion in 2080.[65] This last figure is almost two and a half times greater than the projected Social Security deficit for that year. Altogether, Medicare costs will grow from 3.2% of the nation's gross domestic product (GDP) in 2007 to 4.4% in 2020, 7.6% in 2040, 9.2% in 2060, and 10.7% in 2080.[66] Currently, all federal spending for all purposes is 24% of GDP. It is little wonder that so many experts agree that current tax and benefit levels for Medicare (and Social Security) cannot be sustained indefinitely.

In December of 2011, Democratic senator Ron Wyden of Oregon and Republican representative Paul Ryan of Wisconsin, chairman of the House Budget Committee, presented a bipartisan plan to reform Medicare and control its costs. Decrying the "heated partisan rhetoric" that too often surrounds the Medicare debate and the tendency of politicians to exploit Medicare "to frighten and entice voters," they proposed:

- no changes for those currently 55 and older;
- beginning in 2022, giving seniors a choice among traditional Medicare and approved private plans that would provide equivalent or better benefits;
- providing seniors "premium support" for purchasing private plans roughly equivalent to what the government now pays for Medicare;
- imposing a limit on out-of-pocket expenses to protect seniors from catastrophic health care costs; and
- capping increases in Medicare spending to 1% over growth in GDP plus inflation.[67]

During the 2012 presidential campaign, Republican candidate Mitt Romney proposed a plan that was quite similar to the Wyden-Ryan proposal. Leading Democrats and President Obama fired back. On the campaign trail in Florida, where seniors are a large percentage of the electorate, Obama said that Romney would turn Medicare into a voucher system. "So, if that voucher isn't worth enough to buy the health insurance that's on the market, you're out of luck," he told an audience in Jacksonville.[68] Then, referring to Romney's support for maintaining the top marginal tax rate at 35% (on the books since 2001) rather than returning to the earlier rate of 39.6%, Obama said, "It's wrong to ask seniors to pay more for Medicare just so millionaires and billionaires can pay less in taxes."[69] The Romney camp responded that the president had not "offered a serious plan of his own to save Medicare" and that Romney's plan would "preserve Medicare for today's seniors while strengthening it for future generations."[70]

Affordable Care Act

"Today, after almost a century of trying; today, after over a year of debate; today, after all the votes have been tallied—health insurance reform becomes law in the United States of America. Today."[71] So said President Barack Obama to an audience at the White House on March 23, 2010, when he signed the Patient Protection and Affordable Care Act (usually referred to simply as the Affordable Care Act [ACA] or, to its critics, "Obamacare"). The act represented a major expansion of federal involvement in the health care of Americans. Its two main purposes were (1) to make health insurance affordable to the approximately 50 million U.S. residents who were not poor enough for Medicaid, nor old enough for Medicare, and either could not afford, or chose not to buy, health insurance; and (2) to reduce the growth rate in overall health care spending in the United States.[72]

To achieve these goals, the act, when fully implemented by 2014, would:

- prohibit insurers from placing annual and lifetime dollar limits on essential services;
- require insurers to keep dependent children on their parents' policies until their 26th birthday;
- require insurers to accept applicants with preexisting conditions and prohibit them from charging these individuals more and from dropping policyholders when they get sick;
- require all new plans to cover an array of preventive services with no deductibles or copays;
- require individuals who refuse to purchase insurance to pay a penalty up to 2.5% of their income;
- expand Medicare in participating states to all those with incomes up to 133% of the poverty line (with the federal government paying 100% of the increased cost for the first few years and 90% thereafter);
- offer small businesses tax credits to help them extend health coverage to their employees;
- impose a $2000 penalty per employee on businesses with more than 50 full-time workers who do not offer health insurance;
- establish health insurance exchanges in the states through which individuals could compare and purchase insurance;
- subsidize the purchase of health insurance for individuals in households with income up to 400% of the poverty line; and
- establish an Independent Payment Advisory Board (IPAB) to develop proposals to restrain the growth in Medicare spending, which would go into effect unless overturned by Congress.

FOCUS
QUESTION

What is the best way to address the long-term funding problems facing Social Security and Medicare?

In March of 2012, the Congressional Budget Office estimated that the gross annual cost of the new coverage provisions (as the law was phased in) would increase from $3 billion in 2012 to $265 billion in 2022. Subtracting the new revenues the law would generate (including the penalties on uninsured individuals and on employers who refused to provide coverage), the net cost each year would grow from $3 billion in 2012 to $169 billion in 2022.[73]

The Affordable Care Act was and remains hugely controversial. It passed the House and Senate with no Republican votes (a first for a major piece of social legislation) and Republicans made it a big issue in the congressional election of 2010 and the presidential election of 2012. Many commentators credit it with helping Republicans gain 63 seats in the House and six in the Senate in 2010.

Republicans continue to attack the new law as a government takeover of health care that will drive up deficits and limit the freedom of doctors, insurance companies, and patients. They charge that new costs on employers will force them to drop health coverage for their workers, that the law will drive up the cost of insurance for all Americans, that it gives too much power over health care to an unaccountable body (IPAB), that it unfairly penalizes those healthy young adults who opt not to buy insurance, and that it will impose crushing new costs on the federal government by adding trillions to the national debt over the coming decades. Democrats insist that it will control long-term health care costs, reduce the national deficit in the long-term, and significantly reduce the number of American residents without health insurance coverage. They also argue that opponents exaggerate the number of employers who will drop health insurance coverage for their employees.

As noted in previous chapters, in June of 2012 the Supreme Court upheld (by a 5–4 vote) the penalty that the act imposes on those who refuse to purchase health insurance (interpreted by the Court as a tax) but overturned (by a 7–2 vote) the provision that allowed the federal government to deny states all their Medicaid funding if they refused to expand Medicaid rolls. Opponents of the act had hoped that the Court would throw out the entire law, but when it did not, the controversy returned with renewed vigor to the political arena. In the weeks after the Court's decision, several Republican governors announced that their states would not participate in the expansion of Medicaid and the Republican-dominated House of Representatives voted 244–185 to repeal the law (with all the Republicans and five Democrats supporting repeal). The repeal effort then died in the Democratic-controlled Senate.

Welfare, Social Security, Medicare, and Medicaid are federal programs that grew out of FDR's New Deal of the 1930s and Lyndon Johnson's Great Society of the 1960s. Well before the federal government embraced a social welfare role, states and localities sought to improve the welfare of Americans and make them better citizens by providing children a free public education. In the next section, we examine the modern movement to combat perceived deficiencies in the public school system by increasing educational choices for parents of school-age children.

THE SCHOOL CHOICE MOVEMENT
MAJOR ISSUE

- What are the elements of the modern school-choice movement and what controversies has it raised?

The modern school choice movement was spawned in 1990 in Milwaukee, Wisconsin, through an unlikely political alliance. State Representative Annette Polly Williams, an African-American product of Milwaukee public schools, joined forces with Republican governor Tommy Thompson and Republican state legislators to secure the passage of the **Milwaukee Parental Choice Program**.

As Williams explained in an interview in 2002, she was discouraged by the quality of Milwaukee public schools and not persuaded that busing black children to white schools was the solution: "Desegregation does not mandate education. I didn't feel that our children

Milwaukee Parental Choice Program—the nation's first publicly funded school voucher program.

Courtesy of Representatives Annette Polly Williams

School voucher advocate Polly Williams meets with student leaders at a conference in Tennessee.

should have to leave their community and go into another community just to be educated." She and other parents

had been fighting for years to improve the public schools but it was falling on unresponsive ears. The system's attitude seemed to be, "What do parents know? They're not educated, so they don't know what's best." We said the parents should have more input in what was going on. We began asking, "How do we get more power to the parents to initiate what they think is best for their children?"[74]

Williams and her staff drafted a bill that would have the state provide scholarships for low-income Milwaukee parents to enroll their children at private, nonsectarian schools of their choice. The bill targeted low-income families because "those are the students and families who need help the most and who always get left out. We were putting power in the hands of low-income parents to make sure they really did benefit." Williams was happy to cross the aisle and join forces with Republicans in the state legislature. "We called it the Unholy Alliance," she recounted. "I knew that my side of the aisle did not support the parental choice legislation. In fact, the Democratic Party, the teachers' union, and the liberal establishment did not support the parental choice legislation."[75]

Originally limited to 1,000 students (in a system of about 100,000), the program expanded to 15,000 in 1995 and allowed parents to choose religious schools. In 2006, the legislature raised the cap to 22,500 students. By the 2011–2012 academic year, the program was serving 23,198 students who used grants of $6,442 to attend 106 different private schools.[76]

Types of School Voucher Programs

Educational voucher—money provided by governments (often termed "scholarships") to parents of school-age children to cover some or all of the cost of their children attending a private (and sometimes public) school of their choice.

School voucher—see **Educational voucher**.

The scholarships that the Wisconsin program provided are often called **educational vouchers** or **school vouchers**. Several different types of school voucher programs exist. Depending on the state or city, vouchers to attend private schools are provided to:

- low-income families (Cleveland, Ohio; Milwaukee and Racine, Wisconsin; Washington, DC; and the state of Louisiana) or those who attend failing public schools (Ohio);
- parents of disabled students who do not like the public school to which they are assigned (Arizona, Florida, Georgia, Mississippi [children with dyslexia] North Carolina, Ohio [children with autism], Oklahoma, Utah); and
- families who live in rural areas far from public schools (Maine, Vermont).

Moreover, some states give tax credits to support parents who send their children to private schools. Although these are not technically voucher programs, they serve the same end indirectly. Such tax credits include:

- credits to reduce personal state income taxes for some part of the cost of private school tuition (Iowa, Illinois, Indiana, Louisiana, Minnesota);
- credits to reduce personal income taxes for making a contribution to an organization that distributes private school scholarships (Arizona, Georgia, Indiana, Iowa, Louisiana, Virginia); and
- credits to corporations to reduce state corporate taxes for making a contribution to an organization that distributes private school scholarships (Arizona, Florida, Indiana, New Hampshire, Pennsylvania, Rhode Island, Virginia).[77]

Some voucher advocates, like the late free-market economist Milton Friedman, who established a foundation to promote vouchers, propose a much broader program: universal vouchers that all children could use. In November 2000, California voters rejected, 71%–29%, a universal voucher proposal that would have provided parents $4,000 per child each year (about half of what the state was then spending per child in the public schools) to attend a private school. Currently, no American jurisdiction has such a program. Nonetheless, voucher programs have spread in recent years. One commentator called 2011 the "Year of the Voucher" because legislatures in 12 states had either started new programs or expanded existing ones.[78]

Opponents attack vouchers for diverting public funds to private institutions, and thereby potentially damaging public schools. When the Supreme Court upheld the constitutionality of a Cleveland, Ohio, program in 2002 that allowed vouchers to be used at religious schools, Senator Edward Kennedy (D-MA) said, "It's flat wrong to take scarce taxpayer dollars away from public schools and divert them to private schools." Even if vouchers are constitutional, they "are still bad policy for public schools, and Congress must not abandon its opposition to them." The vice president of the Cleveland teacher's union predicted that the Court's decision would lead to "the devastation of our public schools." Attorney General John Ashcroft responded that the decision was "a great victory . . . particularly for many minority, low-income students who have been trapped in failing public schools." And President George W. Bush commented that "[s]chool choice offers proven results of a better education, not only for children enrolled in the specific plan, but also for children whose public schools benefit from the competition."[79]

Other Kinds of School Choice

Voucher advocates defend such programs as part of a broader movement for "**school choice.**" Many who advocate for school choice insist that large increases in funding for public schools over the past half century have not resulted in higher quality education (see Figure 16-8). What is necessary, they insist, are more choices for parents and more competition for traditional public schools.

School choice can take many forms, most of which are less controversial than vouchers. These include:

- **charter schools**, which are relatively autonomous public schools that are exempt from many state rules and often employ innovative teaching techniques;
- **magnet schools**, public schools that often draw students from a wide area by specializing in such subjects as science, technology, or the performing arts;
- intradistrict school choice, which allows parents to enroll their children in any public school in the district with space;
- parent-trigger laws that allow a majority of parents unhappy with a public school to turn it into a charter school, replace the staff, or shut it down; and
- home schooling, in which parents educate their children directly (estimated currently at about 2 million children).

Perhaps the fastest growing of these innovations is the charter school movement. Charter schools promise improvements in student performance in exchange for relative

School choice—a contemporary movement to give parents more choice as to where to send their children to school; includes charter schools, magnet schools, choice among regular public schools, various types of educational vouchers to allow students to attend private schools, tax credits or deductions for private school tuition, and home schooling.

Charter school—relatively autonomous public school that is exempt from many state rules and often employs innovative teaching techniques.

Magnet school—a specialized public school (often emphasizing science, technology, or the performing arts) that draws students from a wide area.

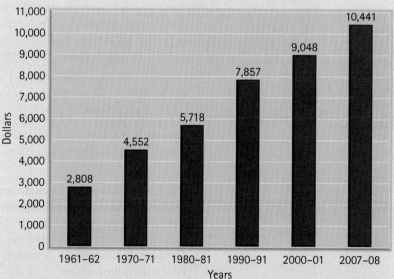

FIGURE 16-8 In the past half century, spending per pupil in public elementary and secondary schools has more than tripled. Figures are in inflation-adjusted (constant 2008–2009) dollars.
SOURCE: National Center for Education Statistics, Fast Facts, Expenditures, at nces.ed.gov/fastfacts/display.asp?id=66, accessed July 25, 2012.

President Barack Obama and First Lady Michelle Obama visit the Capital City Public Charter School in Washington, DC, in February 2009.

autonomy from the many rules and regulations that govern regular public schools. Charter schools began in Minnesota in 1991 and spread rapidly to other states. Currently, more than 1.6 million children attend almost 5,000 public charter schools in 39 states and Washington, DC. More than 500 new schools open each year. Minorities make up three-fifths of charter school students, and children from low-income families make up two-fifths.[80]

President Barack Obama strongly endorsed charter schools early in his administration. In just his second week in office, he and his wife, Michelle Obama, visited a high-performing charter school in Washington, DC. He told the teachers and students at Capital City Public Charter School: "We're very proud of what's been accomplished at this school and we want to make sure that we're duplicating that success all across the country."[81] According to the White House, "President Obama will encourage the growth of successful, high-quality charter schools, and challenge states to reform their charter rules and lift limits that stifle growth and success among excellent schools."[82] A few months later, the president proclaimed the first week in May "National Charter Schools Week," praising public charter schools "for their dedication and commitment to achievement in education. They are models of excellence and are promoting the interests of our children, our economy, and our Nation as a whole."[83]

The Ongoing Debate

Although the movement for charter schools has garnered support across the political spectrum, state policymakers debate whether to limit the number of charter schools, how much to fund them, and how to hold them accountable for their promises to improve educational performance. Other elements of the school choice movement remain controversial, such as giving tax breaks for attending private schools or providing vouchers to do so.

The Democratic and Republican party platforms of 2004 show the differences in how the two major parties approach the school-choice issue, especially regarding vouchers. In the words of the Democratic Party platform:

> Instead of pushing private school vouchers that funnel scarce dollars away from the public schools, we will support public school choice, including charter schools and magnet schools that meet the same high standards as other schools.[84]

In contrast, the Republican Party praised a newly enacted voucher demonstration plan in the District of Columbia (though it avoided the term *voucher*) and called for greater school choice:

> The Republican Party strongly supports school choice, because choice creates competition and competition puts the focus on quality. . . . President Bush and the Republican Congress enacted the D.C. School Choice initiative—the first federally funded school choice demonstration program. We commend the President and Congress for making DC's schoolchildren the most important special interest in education improvement."[85]

The DC Opportunity Scholarship Program provided tuition grants of $7,500 per year to 1,700 students of poor families to attend private schools. This is about half of what the District pays per student in the public schools. In his 2009 budget, President Obama proposed ending the program for new students, which would result in its gradual phase-out. In Congress, Democrats generally opposed the program while Republicans strongly supported it. Although a deal was reached for a new five-year authorization in 2011, the president's 2013 budget included no funds for the program. President Obama, according to a White House spokesperson in 2009, "has repeatedly said that school vouchers are not a long-term solution to our educational challenges."[86] In May of 2012, the then presumptive Republican presidential nominee Mitt Romney strongly endorsed the DC program and promised as president to "expand it to offer more students a chance to attend a better school. It will be a model for parental choice programs across the nation."[87] Currently, there are about four applicants for each scholarship.

SOCIAL POLICY AND DELIBERATIVE DEMOCRACY

In the first decades of the twentieth century, some political leaders cautioned against expanding the government's domestic role. An early opponent of the welfare state was Elihu Root, who served in the cabinets of Presidents William McKinley and Theodore Roosevelt and later was a senator from New York. Root worried that if the people became too dependent on government, this might undermine "individual initiative, energy, enterprise, [and] courage." A "paternal government," Root feared, would make the people "incapable of free self-government and fit only to be governed." "[N]o free government can endure," he said, if its citizens lack "independence of character."[88]

Here, Root was repeating some of the concerns that the Frenchman Alexis de Tocqueville had voiced about 80 years before. Near the end of *Democracy in America*, Tocqueville had warned that a democratic government might become "an immense protective power" that provided for the people's pleasures and controlled their fate. Such a power would be "absolute, thoughtful of detail, orderly, provident, and gentle." Unlike good parents, which it might seem to resemble, it could keep its subjects "in perpetual childhood":

> It does not break men's will, but softens, bends, and guides it; it seldom enjoins, but often inhibits, action; it does not destroy anything, but prevents much being born; it is not at all tyrannical, but it hinders, restrains, enervates, stifles, and stultifies so much that in the end each nation is no more than a flock of timid and hardworking animals with the government as its shepherd.[89]

Like Root, Tocqueville believed that free government cannot succeed without independent, responsible citizens: "No one should ever expect a liberal, energetic, and wise government to originate in the votes of a people of servants."[90]

As we have seen, the debates of the 1990s echoed some of these earlier concerns that social welfare programs, no matter how well intended, may undermine the qualities of self-reliance and good citizenship. Yet despite the reform of AFDC, the American people embrace the government's social welfare role. Indeed, the welfare state was still young when President Eisenhower warned his party colleagues that any effort to dismantle the new social programs of the 1930s and 1940s would result in a political disaster for the party. Whatever reservations Republicans might have had with the programs of FDR and Truman, political calculation dictated an accommodation.

Social policy in the United States in the twenty-first century serves two popular purposes: helping those in need and reducing risk in daily life. As we have seen, federal, state, and local governments now spend over half a trillion dollars each year on programs for low-income Americans, including medical coverage, cash income, food stamps, housing assistance, school lunches, and other programs. This amounts to about one in six of all the dollars spent by governments in the United States.

Yet, today the federal government alone spends about twice as much as this on two programs that benefit mainly the middle class: Social Security and Medicare. The debate in 2003 over adding a prescription drug benefit to Medicare underscored the popular commitment to government assistance. Few in Congress challenged the notion that the federal government should help the nonpoor elderly with prescription drug costs, despite projections of massive deficits in Medicare for decades to come.

KEY SOCIAL POLICY LAWS

Social Security Act of 1935

GI Bill of Rights of 1944

National School Lunch Program of 1949

Housing Act of 1949

National Defense Education Act of 1958

Economic Opportunity Act of 1964

Food Stamp Act of 1964

Elementary and Secondary Education Act of 1965

Medicare Act of 1965

Personal Responsibility and Work Opportunity Reconciliation Act of 1996

Medicare Prescription Drug, Improvement, and Modernization Act of 2003

Patient Protection and Affordable Care Act of 2010

FOCUS QUESTION

Is the growing dependency of Americans on government programs a genuine problem for the future of the nation, or not?

Although Americans no longer deliberate over whether government should provide for the material well-being of its citizens, they vigorously debate how to do so. Should workers be allowed to divert some of their Social Security taxes to private accounts? Should private companies be permitted to compete with traditional fee-for-service Medicare in providing for the medical needs of the elderly? Should public funds be used to defray the cost of children attending private schools? And however one answers these questions, there is another that cannot be avoided: Where will the resources come from to cover all the promises that government has made? These and many other issues continue to divide citizens and elected officials alike. As the demands of the welfare state escalate the fiscal pressures on government in the years ahead, public deliberation on social policy will surely intensify.

IMPACT
of Social Media and Communications Technology

The Life of Julia

As noted in the Bessette/Pitney blog of July 27, 2012, the Obama reelection campaign posted an interactive timeline showing how a fictional woman, Julia, benefited from government programs supported by the president (and contrasting Obama's policies with those of Republican presidential candidate Mitt Romney). The timeline begins at age 3, when Julia enters a Head Start program "to help get her ready for school" so that she "will start kindergarten ready to learn and succeed," and ends at age 67 when she "receives monthly benefits that help her retire comfortably . . . allow[ing] her to volunteer at a community garden." (See www.barackobama.com/life-of-julia.) Critics mocked the timeline. House Budget Committee Chairman Paul Ryan called it "creepy" and "demeaning": "It suggests that this woman can't go anywhere in life without Barack Obama's government-centered society. It's kind of demeaning to her." Two other critics purchased the domain name "thelifeofjulia.com" and posted a parody of the Obama site. On this site, which looks remarkably like the original, Julia at age 3 enters a Head Start program

"despite the fact that Head Start costs taxpayers as much as 3 times what private daycare or preschool does while showing no positive lasting effect" and ends at retirement age when the Social Security program is bankrupt and "Julia starts gardening and painting fences to make ends meet." What's more, the government will not approve knee replacement surgery for the elderly Julia necessary to cure a painful arthritic condition and Julia's son "is unable to help with medical costs because he has been unable to hold a steady job due to the poor economy his mother's generation left him."[91]

CRITICAL THINKING QUESTION

Was the Obama campaign's "Life of Julia" an effective use of the new technology to promote the benefits of the welfare state? Was the critics' parody an effective response?

SUMMARY

- President Franklin D. Roosevelt's New Deal programs, launched in the depths of the Great Depression, redefined the relationship of the federal government to the American people. For the first time Washington would be directly responsible for ensuring citizens' material well-being.

- Roosevelt promoted social goods—such as good jobs, decent housing, and medical care—as rights to which Americans were entitled. This implied that government had a responsibility to provide them.

- Social programs expanded in the decades after World War II, especially during the administration of President Lyndon Johnson in the 1960s.

- In 1996, Congress replaced AFDC, which provided monthly cash payments to needy families, with Temporary Assistance to Needy Families. The new law placed a lifetime five-year limit on benefits, imposed new work requirements, expanded funds for child care, toughened child support enforcement, and stipulated that unwed mothers under 18 had to live with an adult to receive aid. By 2007, the number of recipients had dropped by about two-thirds.

- In his second term, President George W. Bush proposed allowing Americans under 55 to put up to four percentage points of their Social Security contribution into a private savings account, but he was unable to convince enough Americans to support it. Polls showed, however, that those under 55 liked the idea.

- In 2003, Congress passed Bush's proposal to add prescription drug coverage to Medicare, the nation's second-largest social program. In 2010, Congress passed President Obama's proposal to expand health insurance coverage to most of the 50 million U.S. residents who lacked it.

- Both Social Security and Medicare face serious long-term financing problems. Medicare alone, according to the projections of its trustees, will consume 10% of the nation's GDP before the end of the century. Experts tend to agree that current tax and benefit levels for Medicare and Social Security cannot be sustained indefinitely.

- The modern school-choice movement began in 1990 in Milwaukee, Wisconsin, when the state legislature passed a law to give low-income Milwaukee parents scholarships to enroll their children at private schools. A variety of voucher programs now exist throughout the United States. Vouchers are part of a broader movement for school choice that has led to such innovations as charter schools, magnet schools, state income tax credits for private school tuition, and choice among public schools within a district.

- Although Americans no longer deliberate over whether government should provide for the material well-being of its citizens, they vigorously debate how to do so and how to fund the promises that government has made.

KEY TERMS

Aid to Families with Dependent
    Children (AFDC) p. 479
Charter school p. 499
Contributory program p. 485
Earned Income Tax Credit
    (EITC) p. 482
Educational voucher p. 498
Entitlement p. 483
Fair Deal p. 480
Federal Deposit Insurance
    Corporation (FDIC) p. 478
Great Depression p. 475
Great Society p. 481
Greenspan Commission p. 490

Magnet school p. 499
Means-tested program p. 482
Medicaid p. 482
Medicare p. 475
Milwaukee Parental Choice Program
    p. 497
Modern Republicanism p. 480
Negative rights p. 480
New Deal p. 475
Noncontributory program p. 485
Northwest Ordinance p. 476
Payroll tax p. 479
Positive rights p. 480
Redistribution program p. 485

School choice p. 499
School voucher p. 498
Securities and Exchange Commission
    (SEC) p. 478
Social Gospel p. 477
Social Security p. 475
Social Security trust fund p. 490
Social welfare state p. 475
Supplemental Security Income (SSI) p. 482
Temporary Assistance to Needy Families
    (TANF) p. 486
War on Poverty p. 481
Welfare p. 479
Welfare state p. 475

TEST YOUR KNOWLEDGE

1. The federal program of health insurance for the elderly and disabled is called
   a. HMO.
   b. Medicaid.
   c. Medicare.
   d. Social Security.
   e. welfare.

2. Which of the following is NOT one of FDR's New Deal programs?
   a. Earned Income Tax Credit
   b. Social Security
   c. the Federal Deposit Insurance Corporation
   d. the Public Works Administration
   e. the Securities and Exchange Commission

3. Which of the following is an example of a "negative right"?
   a. job
   b. an education
   c. decent housing
   d. free speech
   e. medical care

4. President Dwight D. Eisenhower's term for Republican Party acceptance of social security, unemployment insurance, labor laws, farm programs, and other features of the welfare state was
   a. Socialism.
   b. Democratic-Republicanism.
   c. moderate Republicanism.
   d. liberal conservatism.
   e. modern Republicanism.

5. The _____ Act was NOT a part of Johnson's expansion of the welfare state.
   a. Economic Opportunity
   b. Elementary and Secondary Education
   c. Food Stamp
   d. Medicare
   e. National Defense of Education

6. Over the past 40 years, the percentage of Americans living in poverty, as measured by the federal government, has
   a. steadily declined.
   b. dropped by about half.
   c. remained fairly steady within a narrow range.
   d. steadily increased.
   e. doubled.

7. Among the following social programs, which increased the most since 1994?
   a. Medicaid
   b. Food Stamps
   c. TANF
   d. Earned Income Tax Credit
   e. Supplemental Security Income

8. Which social programs in the United States present the greatest funding challenges for the coming decades?
   a. Medicaid and Earned Income tax Credit
   b. Medicare and Social Security
   c. Medicare and Earned Income Tax Credit
   d. Food Stamps and Medicare
   e. Food Stamps and Social Security

9. Which of the following is NOT a provision of the Affordable Care Act, as passed by Congress in 2010.
   a. funding for new public hospitals to serve the needs of those not poor enough for Medicaid but too poor to afford health insurance
   b. a requirement that health insurers accept those with preexisting conditions
   c. funding to expand Medicare to all those with incomes up to 133% of the poverty line
   d. a requirement that individuals purchase health insurance or pay a penalty
   e. a $2000 penalty per employee on businesses with more than 50 full-time workers who do not offer health insurance

10. Which of the following is NOT a type of school-choice program currently available somewhere in the United States?
    a. vouchers that allow all parents of school-age children within a state to send their child to a public or private school
    b. relatively autonomous public schools that are exempt from many state rules and often employ innovative teaching techniques
    c. public schools that draw students from a wide area by specializing in such subject as science, technology, or the performing arts
    d. policies that allow parents to enroll their children in any public school in the district if there is space
    e. laws that allow a majority of parents unhappy with a public school to turn it into a charter school, replace the staff, or shut it down

FURTHER READING

Davies, Gareth. *From Opportunity to Entitlement: The Transformation and Decline of Great Society Liberalism.* Lawrence: University Press of Kansas, 1996.

Derthick, Martha. *Policymaking for Social Security.* Washington, DC: Brookings Institution, 1979.

Milton and Rose D. Friedman Foundation. *The ABCs of School Choice.* Indianapolis, IN: Author, 2005–2006.

Moynihan, Daniel Patrick. *Family and Nation.* New York: Harcourt, 1986.

Murray, Charles. *Losing Ground: American Social Policy, 1950–1980.* New York: Basic Books, 1984.

Murray, Charles. *Coming Apart: The State of White America, 1960–2010.* New York: Crown Forum, 2012.

Sundquist, James. *Politics and Policy: The Eisenhower, Kennedy, and Johnson Years.* Washington, DC: Brookings Institution, 1968.

Teles, Steven. *Whose Welfare? AFDC and Elite Politics.* Lawrence: University Press of Kansas, 1998.

Wilson, William Julius. *The Truly Disadvantaged: The Inner City, the Underclass, and Public Policy.* Chicago: University of Chicago Press, 1987.

WEB SOURCES

American Enterprise Institute for Public Policy Research: www.aei.org—a conservative think tank in Washington, DC, that specializes in social policy.

Brookings Institution: www.brookings.edu/ —a liberal think tank in Washington, DC, that specializes in social policy.

Center on Budget and Policy Priorities: www.cbpp.org—a liberal/progressive think tank in Washington, DC, that specializes in social policy and poverty.

Centers for Medicare and Medicaid Services: www.cms.hhs.gov—the agency in the Department of Health and Human Services that administers the Medicare and Medicaid programs.

Children's Defense Fund: www.childrensdefense.org—a nonprofit organization that advocates for the needs of children.

Heritage Foundation: www.heritage.org—a conservative think tank in Washington, DC, that emphasizes free enterprise, limited government, individual freedom, and traditional American values.

Manhattan Institute: www.manhattan-institute.org/— a New York City–based conservative think tank that focuses on law enforcement, social policy, and legal policy.

Milton and Rose D. Friedman Foundation: www.edchoice.org/— the institute founded by Milton and Rose Friedman to promote school vouchers.

Milwaukee Parental Choice Program: dpi.wi.gov/sms/choice.html—the Web site for Milwaukee's educational voucher program.

National Alliance for Public Charter Schools: www.publiccharters.org—a nonprofit organization committed to advancing the charter schools movement.

National Center for Policy Analysis: www.ncpa.org—a conservative/free market think tank based in Dallas, Texas, that promotes reforms in health care, taxes, Social Security, welfare, criminal justice, education, and environmental regulation.

Urban Institute: www.urban.org—an independent research organization established by the Lyndon Johnson administration to research issues regarding social policy and urban affairs.

U.S. Social Security Administration: www.ssa.gov—the Web site for the agency that administers the Social Security system.

High unemployment means long lines. Here, job seekers wait to apply for an opening with Major League Baseball's Miami Marlins on November 15, 2011 in Miami, Florida.

Joe Raedle/Getty Iamges

17

Economic Policy

OBJECTIVES

After reading this chapter, you should be able to:

- Outline the history of economic policy and its relationship to citizenship.
- Describe the elements of fiscal policy.
- Explain why the tax system is so complex.
- Analyze the mechanics of monetary policy.
- Summarize the elements of regulatory policy, especially in matters of finance.
- Understand the politics of trade policy.
- Discuss how policymakers and citizens deliberate on economic policy.

INTRODUCTION

In deliberating about economic issues, most people agree on certain goals:

- economic growth, which we usually measure through change in **gross domestic product (GDP)**, the total value of goods and services that people produce in the nation;
- low **unemployment**, the percentage of people who are seeking work but failing to find it; and
- low **inflation**, the general rise in prices.

To achieve these goals, the federal government takes action in three broad areas. **Fiscal policy** concerns spending and taxes. **Monetary policy** involves the supply of money and the level of interest rates. **Regulatory and trade policy** encompasses a variety of ways by which government policies affect markets for goods and services.

These policy areas came into play when a severe economic crisis began in 2008: GDP shrank, unemployment grew, and millions worried about their futures. The story is complicated, but some details are worth noting. In the years before the crisis, mortgage lenders made loans to many people with poor credit. As long as home values were going up, people who got behind in their payments could sell their houses at a profit and pay off their loans; but when home values started falling in 2006, more and more borrowers defaulted. Many of these loans were adjustable rate mortgages with low "teaser" rates that enabled borrowers to pay their mortgages—at first. The problem arose when the mortgage automatically reset to much higher interest rates and borrowers found themselves trapped in homes with falling values and no way to refinance. This problem had a big effect on the financial community because of "mortgage-backed securities." Investment firms would buy a large number of mortgages from lenders, thus creating a pool of mortgages. They could then sell shares in these pools to investors. As long as homeowners kept up with their payments, the investors got a stream of payments, but when the defaults started, the payments dried up. Major financial firms had themselves borrowed huge sums to invest in the mortgage-backed securities, and so now they had trouble paying *their* creditors. The result was a chain reaction that choked off credit and panicked the business world.

The Federal Reserve, which has responsibility for monetary policy, sought to restore credit by increasing the money supply and pushing interest rates downward. Meanwhile, Congress and President George W. Bush agreed on a $700 billion plan to shore up the financial industry. Soon after President Barack Obama took office, he persuaded Congress to pass a $787 billion economic stimulus bill. The aim was to get money into people's pockets so they could spend it on goods and services. The businesses that provide these goods and services could then afford to keep or hire employees, who in turn could spend their paychecks. In the years to follow, however, progress was frustratingly slow.

The crisis should prompt sober reflection on the role of citizenship and deliberation in the nation's economy. Although most borrowers and lenders behaved responsibly, some acted without concern for how their actions might affect others, and there were substantial cases of outright fraud. Yet while Congress and the White House understandably felt pressure to act quickly, they may not have given due deliberation to the issues before them. With minimal hearing and debate in the fall of 2008, the $700 billion bill passed just two weeks after the Bush administration had proposed it. The figure itself did not result from profound internal deliberation. "It's not based on any particular data point," a Treasury spokesperson said at the time. "We just wanted to choose a really large number."[1] As Chapter 12 on Congress explained, lawmakers did not read the stimulus bill, either.

These measures were dramatic, but they were scarcely the first major federal interventions in the economy. Government has been shaping economic activity ever since the nation began, so it makes sense to begin by looking at the origins of that relationship.

Gross domestic product (GDP)—the total value of the nation's production of goods and services in a given year.

Unemployment—joblessness or, for the purpose of the federal government, the percentage of job seekers who cannot find work.

Inflation—a general rise in prices over time.

Fiscal policy—federal policy concerning overall levels of spending and taxes.

Monetary policy—federal policy concerning the supply of money and the level of interest rates.

Regulatory and trade policy—a variety of ways by which government tries to police markets for goods and services.

A BRIEF HISTORY OF ECONOMIC POLICY

MAJOR ISSUE

- How have intellectual trends and historical circumstances (such as war) affected economic policy?

Throughout American history, economic policy has borne the mark of war and its aftermath. Mobilizing for war often means large increases in taxes, spending, debt, and coordination of economic activity. The federal government responds to wartime needs with policy innovations that may long outlast the war itself.

Battles of thought have mattered as much as battles of steel. Economist John Maynard Keynes wrote that economic ideas "are more powerful than is commonly understood." He added that practical people "who believe themselves to be quite exempt from any intellectual influence, are usually the slaves of some defunct economist."[2] When people deliberate about policy, they draw on these ideas, often without full knowledge of where they came from.

Founding an Economy

Some writers apply the term "laissez-faire" (French for "allow to do") to the federal government's economic stance during the nation's early decades. Insofar as the term suggests inactivity, it is misleading. Because property rights need government safeguards, the Constitution empowered Congress to punish counterfeiting, write uniform bankruptcy laws, and protect intellectual property through patents and copyrights. It also provided for regulation of commerce "with foreign Nations, and among the several States, and with the Indian Tribes." And the provision for "post offices and post roads" signaled that the federal government would foster economic growth with efficient systems of communication and transportation. As Madison wrote of this power: "Nothing which tends to facilitate the intercourse between the States can be deemed unworthy of the public care."[3] During the first half of the nineteenth century, the federal government did give some support to "internal improvements" such as roads and canals, but such projects ran into widespread skepticism about a powerful national government.[4]

Controversy also beset other aspects of economic policy. In 1791, Treasury Secretary Alexander Hamilton got Congress to approve a 20-year charter for the first Bank of the United States. Although a private institution, the bank provided a central depository for public funds, making it easier to handle Revolutionary War debts. It worked well, but rural voters resented its power and Congress failed to renew its charter in 1811. The difficulty of financing the War of 1812 revived support for the idea, and Congress authorized a second Bank of the United States in 1816. Three years later came the nation's first major financial crisis, the Panic of 1819, which caused bank failures and foreclosures. Many victims of the panic, particularly in rural areas, blamed the tight credit policies of the Bank. Like the first Bank, it eventually fell to public opposition, this time under the leadership of President Andrew Jackson. Its charter expired in 1836.

Civil War and Progressivism

Tariff—a tax on imported goods for the purposes of either raising revenue or protecting domestic industries.

Although slavery was the main issue dividing North from South, economic policy deepened the split. The industrial North backed high protective **tariffs**, taxes on imported goods that competed with the North's products. The South depended on farm exports and opposed tariffs because other nations would respond by slapping their own tariffs on those exports. The Civil War swung the balance of power over economic policy to the North.[5] The 1860s saw the rise of the Republicans, who at the time favored a larger government role in the economy. Congress passed a land-grant college act, a homestead act for settlement of the West, and legislation providing loans and land grants for a transcontinental railroad. To pay for the war, lawmakers passed new taxes, including the nation's first-ever income tax. Most of the wartime taxes were gone by the early 1870s, but they had set a precedent for a stronger federal government.

Another change came in the field of money and banking. Before the Civil War, the federal government issued coins but not paper money. Banks lent money by issuing their own notes, promising holders that they could trade the notes back for gold or silver. By the war's start, thousands of different bank notes were circulating. Since the fall of the second Bank of the United States, state governments had supervised banks, but they could not stem the confusion. As a result, banks and businesses failed, counterfeiting boomed, and panicky citizens hoarded gold and silver coins. Financing a costly war and facing a shortage of hard currency, Congress passed laws providing for a uniform national currency and a new system of nationally chartered banks.[6] These laws remained in place after peace came.

In the early years of the twentieth century, the Progressive movement left a lasting influence not only on the electoral process but also on economic policy. The Progressives believed that the federal government should foster greater equality of incomes and check the power of large business interests. Progressive innovations included the following:

2nd Liberty Loan of 1917/Sackett & Wilhelms Corp. N. Y. [LC-USZC4-9944]/The Library of Congress

This poster, which also appeared in Yiddish and Italian, appealed to the patriotism of recent immigrants.

- the Sixteenth Amendment, which empowered Congress to tax incomes. In 1894, following the precedent from the Civil War, Congress had passed an income tax. The Supreme Court then invalidated it. The Constitution, said the Court, forbade the federal government to collect "direct" taxes, except in proportion to state populations.[7] In 1909, Congress sent the new amendment to the states, and ratification was complete by 1913.
- the Federal Reserve System. Until the early twentieth century, private banks largely determined the supply of money. In 1913, President Woodrow Wilson proposed greater government power, "so that the banks may be the instruments, not the masters, of business and of individual enterprise and initiative."[8] Congress soon created the Federal Reserve as the nation's central bank.
- new regulations on business. Theodore Roosevelt, who championed much of this legislation, saw it as a matter of good citizenship. He said that "the man who has forethought as well as patriotism, should heartily welcome every effort, legislative or otherwise, which has for its object to secure fair dealing by capital, corporate or individual, toward the public and toward the employee."[9] New laws strengthened government oversight of railroads and aimed to protect consumers from unhealthy products. The Clayton Antitrust Act and the Federal Trade Commission Act (both 1914) sought to curb monopolies and other misdeeds by big business.

World Wars and Their Aftermath

Woodrow Wilson came to office as a champion of Progressive reform, but in his second term, America's entry into World War I overshadowed domestic issues. The war cost billions of dollars. Relying on the Sixteenth Amendment, Wilson persuaded Congress to

TO BE FILLED IN BY COLLECTOR.

Form 1040.

TO BE FILLED IN BY INTERNAL REVENUE BUREAU.

List No. ....

.... District of ....

Date received ....

INCOME TAX.

THE PENALTY
FOR FAILURE TO HAVE THIS RETURN IN
THE HANDS OF THE COLLECTOR OF
INTERNAL REVENUE ON OR BEFORE
MARCH 1 IS $20 TO $1,000.
(SEE INSTRUCTIONS ON PAGE 4.)

File No. ....

Assessment List ....

Page .... Line ....

UNITED STATES INTERNAL REVENUE.

RETURN OF ANNUAL NET INCOME OF INDIVIDUALS.
(As provided by Act of Congress, approved October 3, 1913.)

RETURN OF NET INCOME RECEIVED OR ACCRUED DURING THE YEAR ENDED DECEMBER 31, 191...
(FOR THE YEAR 1913, FROM MARCH 1, TO DECEMBER 31.)

Filed by (or for) .... of ....
(Full name of individual.) (Street and No.)

in the City, Town, or Post Office of .... State of ....
(Fill in pages 2 and 3 before making entries below.)

1. GROSS INCOME (see page 2, line 12) .... $

2. GENERAL DEDUCTIONS (see page 3, line 7) .... $

3. NET INCOME .... $

Deductions and exemptions allowed in computing income subject to the normal tax of 1 per cent.

4. Dividends and net earnings received or accrued, of corporations, etc., subject to like tax. (See page 2, line 11).......... $

5. Amount of income on which the normal tax has been deducted and withheld at the source. (See page 2, line 9, column A)..

6. Specific exemption of $3,000 or $4,000, as the case may be. (See Instructions 3 and 19)..

Total deductions and exemptions. (Items 4, 5, and 6)........ $

7. TAXABLE INCOME on which the normal tax of 1 per cent is to be calculated. (See Instruction 3).. $

8. When the net income shown above on line 3 exceeds $20,000, the additional tax thereon must be calculated as per schedule below:

				INCOME.		TAX.	
1 per cent on amount over $20,000 and not exceeding $50,000....				$		$	
2 " " 50,000 " " 75,000....							
3 " " 75,000 " " 100,000....							
4 " " 100,000 " " 250,000....							
5 " " 250,000 " " 500,000....							
6 " " 500,000							
Total additional or super tax						$	
Total normal tax (1 per cent of amount entered on line 7).....						$	
Total tax liability............						$	

National Archives

After ratification of the Sixteenth Amendment, Congress passed an income tax law. It only covered net taxable incomes over $3,000 ($65,000 in 2009 dollars) and applied to less than 1% of the population. Rates started at 1% and rose to 7% for taxpayers with income over $500,000 (about $11 million in 2009 dollars). This is the 1913 version of Form 1040.

enact large tax increases. His administration also financed war debts in a new way. In past conflicts, rich people had bought government bonds and reaped large profits afterward. William G. McAdoo, Wilson's treasury secretary, worked to sell small bonds to ordinary people and eventually got half of American families to buy them. These "Liberty Loans" were the forerunners of U.S. Savings Bonds. "We capitalized on the profound impulse called patriotism," said McAdoo. "It is the quality of coherence that holds a nation together; it is one of the deepest and most powerful of human motives."[10]

During the war, Congress found it hard to track the government's finances. Up to that point, the president had never had to make an estimate of overall federal spending and revenues. For years, therefore, reformers had advocated a more systematic approach to government finance. In 1921, three years after the war, Congress passed the Budget and Accounting Act requiring the president to turn in an annual budget proposal. To help the White House draw it up, the law created the Bureau of the Budget (now the Office of Management and Budget). It also set up the General Accounting Office to inform Congress of how the government was spending the money. (In 2004, Congress renamed it the Government Accountability Office.) After the budget process had been in place for a few years, President Calvin Coolidge called it a success: "In these days of effort to make each dollar count we have learned the lesson of mature thought and mature deliberation."[11]

Deficit—an amount by which spending exceeds revenues in any given year.

Economic policy and thought took a new turn with the Great Depression. Facing massive unemployment, President Franklin Roosevelt's New Deal programs increased federal spending on public works and other job-creating programs. This spending helped create an annual **deficit**—the gap that occurs when the government spends more than it takes in. Until the 1930s, economists generally condemned deficits. British scholar John Maynard Keynes revolutionized economic thinking by saying that private investment might not always create enough jobs. In bad times, he said, government should revive the economy by running deficits on purpose. Although Keynes did not inspire the New Deal, his theories eventually provided a rationale for what the federal government was already doing.[12] (Indeed, his followers argued that deficits should have been even bigger.) More broadly, his school of thought convinced many policymakers that government should plan and monitor the economy.

By requiring a huge mobilization, World War II furthered the cause of planning. Facing likely disruptions in resources and the labor force, Washington controlled wages and prices. It even used coupons to ration sugar, gasoline, and other goods. Federal spending shot up, so by 1945, outlays were nearly seven times greater than in 1940. To pay for the war effort, Congress in 1942 lowered the threshold for the income tax, raising billions of dollars by bringing millions of Americans onto the tax rolls. The following year, Congress authorized **tax withholding**, under which employers would take or "withhold" federal income tax out from every paycheck and send it to the government. Tax collection became easier and Washington's cash flow became steadier; and by spreading payments over 26 or 52 pay periods, critics later argued, the withholding system made tax increases less noticeable and thus easier to pass.

Enthusiasm for economic planning continued after the war. Congress passed the Employment Act of 1946, which declared a policy "to promote maximum employment, production, and purchasing power."[13] The law required the president to give Congress an annual economic report. The law also set up the Council of Economic Advisers (CEA) in the White House to draft the report and provide the president with economic analysis on a range of issues. CEA's purpose was to offer professional advice to the president and, through the annual report, to supply Congress with detailed information on the economy. Although the council has sometimes served as an advocate for administration policies, its members have usually had an incentive to do serious analysis. In most cases, they have served for a couple of years and then returned to university professorships, so they wanted to maintain their professional reputations. According to Alan Greenspan, who chaired CEA in the 1970s and would later head the Federal Reserve, CEA's most important role is deliberative: "to scuttle many of the more adventuresome ideas that inevitably bubble up through the machinery of government. . . . A few of these ideas are genuinely good. However, many of them are ill-advised and not well thought through and fail miserably the test of benefits exceeding costs. Often, it falls to the CEA to point out the flaws and derail these ideas."[14]

Tax withholding—the system by which employers take money out of employees' paychecks and deposit it for the government. The government credits this money against the employees' tax liability when they file their returns. Employers withhold money for federal income taxes, social insurance taxes, and state and local income taxes in some states and localities.

An Age of Uncertainty

For decades, support for government planning ran strong among academics and policymakers. The 1970s raised doubts. Economists had assumed that inflation and unemployment pushed in opposite directions, so that increasing one would reduce the other. Then came a mix of high inflation, economic stagnation, and unemployment, which renewed interest in alternative viewpoints. Economists Friedrich Hayek and Milton Friedman had long argued that government planning threatened individual liberty and would throttle economic growth. Although many of their colleagues had been skeptical, they gained a wider audience in the 1970s, and both won the Sveriges Riksbank Prize in Economic Sciences, better known as the Nobel Prize in Economics.

Toward the end of the decade, some political leaders embraced **supply-side economics**. According to the supply-siders, high taxes hurt economic growth by discouraging savings and investment. They said that cutting tax rates would spur economic activity, meaning bigger profits and payrolls. Ronald Reagan championed the idea during his 1980 presidential campaign, and after his election, he persuaded Congress to slash income tax rates. Supporters of the measure argued that economic growth would expand the tax base, thereby offsetting at least some of the forgone tax revenue stemming from the cut in rates. By the mid-1980s, the United States did have strong economic growth, but it was not great enough to prevent large deficits.[15]

Before we discuss more recent developments in the economy, we should take a closer look at the mechanics of how the government raises and spends tax money.

Supply-side economics—a school of thought holding that high taxes hurt economic growth by discouraging savings and investment. Supply-siders argue that cutting tax rates can spur economic activity, meaning bigger profits and payrolls and perhaps even greater revenues.

FISCAL POLICY: TAXES

MAJOR ISSUE

- What are the costs and benefits of the federal government's complex system of income taxes?

Fiscal policy, as we have said, involves taxes and spending. We start with the former, which can be both constructive and destructive. Tax revenue allows the government to build universities, vaccinate babies, and send people into space. "Nobody likes paying taxes, particularly in times of economic stress," President Obama said in 2009. "But most Americans meet their responsibilities because they understand that it's an obligation of citizenship, necessary to pay the costs of our common defense and our mutual well-being."[16] Under certain circumstances, however, taxes can also slow economic growth and put severe burdens on businesses and individuals.

The Power of Taxation

Most people would like to reduce their own tax burden while still enjoying the benefits that come from the taxes that everybody else pays. Taxes thus change behavior. Accordingly, lawmakers will put high taxes on things they want to discourage (e.g., smoking and drinking) while easing the burden on things they want to foster (e.g., home ownership). Such uses of tax policy may be a way to achieve social goals, but they also have drawbacks. For example, many people and businesses engage in lawful tax avoidance, minimizing the activities, investments, and expenditures that carry high taxes in favor of those with low taxes. With the help of attorneys and accountants, taxpayers may avoid much more than lawmakers intend. Some commit the crime of tax evasion, shirking their share through deceptions such as falsifying documents. Tax avoidance and evasion have long histories.

There are several different kinds of taxes. The biggest source of federal revenue is one that most adult Americans know all too well: the income tax.

Individual Income Taxes

In addition to wages and salaries, Americans must also pay income taxes on tips, bonuses, commissions, and interest from bank accounts. Every year, taxpayers must add up their income and report it to the Internal Revenue Service (IRS), which runs the federal tax system. When withheld taxes do not cover the full amount they owe, they must pay the difference. When they owe less than the amount withheld, they get a refund. (Some taxpayers view a refund as a benefit, but they are just getting back money that they have lent to the government—without interest.)

The **marginal income tax rate** is the rate on one's last dollar of taxable income. Currently there are six such rates, ranging from 10% to 35%.[17] Each rate applies to a different bracket, or range of taxable incomes. Many people mistakenly believe that you owe the same rate on all of your taxable income. In fact, you pay 10% on income within the first bracket, 15% on the next, and so on. The key word here is *taxable*. Americans normally do not have to pay federal income tax on every dollar they gain. The law allows for **exemptions**, specific amounts that taxpayers may subtract from their taxable income. Taxpayers can claim one exemption for every person in their household. The amount, which rises with inflation and drops for high-income taxpayers, was $3,800 in 2012. Taxpayers may also reduce their taxable income with **tax deductions** for certain expenses. For instance, homeowners may deduct interest on mortgages.

Exemptions and deductions cut people's tax bills by reducing the amount of income on which they must pay tax. If your income is well into the 25% bracket, a deduction of $1,000 saves you $250 in tax. By contrast, **tax credits** are sums that people may subtract directly from their taxes. In 2012, for example, the American Opportunity Credit was worth up to $2,500 to pay for certain education expenses.[18]

Marginal income tax rate—the tax rate on one's last dollar of taxable income. Currently there are six such rates, ranging from 10% to 35%.

Tax exemption—a reduction in the amount of income subject to tax. There are two types: personal and dependency. The exemption amount changes from year to year.

Tax deduction—an amount (often a personal or business expense) that reduces income subject to tax.

Tax credit—a dollar-for-dollar reduction in tax liability, usually for a specific purpose such as child care.

What counts as income? Who qualifies for which tax breaks? Precise answers will be complicated. A nation of more than 300 million people presents Congress and the IRS with a mind-bending array of situations. Consider what happens when a child is the victim of a kidnapping. At one point, the IRS ruled that parents could not take an exemption for the child after the year of the abduction. Following public complaints, Congress allowed such exemptions. Because of so many circumstances, tax laws and rules take up thousands of pages.

This complexity is a problem in itself. The instructions for the standard individual income tax return (Form 1040) run over a hundred pages. The federal tax code has more than 2 million words.[19] The IRS offers free help, but it confirms the adage "You get what you pay for." In 2003, one study found that when taxpayers called the IRS about tax law, they got wrong answers about 19% of the time. By 2011, IRS had improved its telephone service and was wrong only 7% of the time.[20] Much good information is online, but so are many urban legends about taxes (see the Myths and Misinformation feature).

The **alternative minimum tax (AMT)** is another source of complexity. During the 1960s, the press ran stories of rich people who used lawful tax maneuvers to avoid paying any income tax. In 1969, Congress reacted by passing AMT to keep individuals from exploiting deductions and credits to cut their income tax below what is appropriate for their income. The AMT is a parallel tax system, with its own rates, exemptions, and credits.[22] Taxpayers first calculate their regular income tax and then calculate their AMT. They owe whichever is greater. Unlike the regular income tax, the AMT does not make adjustments for inflation. So although it originally aimed at the wealthy, it now hits millions of middle-class taxpayers who must now do their taxes twice and often owe thousands of dollars more than they would under the regular income tax.

Because the system is so complex, taxpayers must put a great deal of time and effort into collecting data and filling out forms. Many buy special software or pay tax professionals to do the work. Even apart from the taxes themselves, the mere act of complying with tax

Alternative minimum tax (AMT)—a parallel tax system with a more limited set of tax deductions and credits than the regular income tax. Those potentially subject to the tax must calculate their regular income tax, then their AMT. They pay whichever is greater.

FOCUS
QUESTION

Who gains and loses from the complexity of the federal tax code?

MYTHS AND MISINFORMATION

Income Tax Tales

Surf the Web for information about income taxes, and you will find sites making outlandish arguments that you may owe little or no tax. The IRS warns that people can get into deep trouble if they use such arguments to justify nonpayment.

Some common arguments include the following.

The Sixteenth Amendment, which empowers Congress to tax incomes, is invalid because the states did not properly ratify it. Tax protesters argue that there were technical flaws and clerical errors in the state ratifying resolutions. Legal scholars, however, hold that these flaws did not affect the validity of the ratifications. They also point to a Supreme Court case (*Coleman v. Miller*, 307 U.S. 433, in 1939), indicating that only Congress may decide whether enough states have ratified an amendment. In this case, Congress did so in 1913.

Federal law does not actually require anyone to file a return. This argument hinges on a nonsensically literal reading of the law. The federal tax code does not include the exact phrase "You must file a return." Nevertheless, Section 1 of the federal tax code reads as follows: "There is hereby imposed on the taxable income of . . . " and then presents tables showing the tax rates on various categories. Section 6011 authorizes the IRS to issue rules requiring the filing of returns. Section 6012 identifies those who must file.

Filing a tax return is "voluntary." Individuals and businesses fill out their own tax forms, and the IRS checks up on only a small percentage. Serious tax evasion seems to be rare, so the IRS has praised Americans for their "voluntary compliance." Some tax protesters take the word *voluntary* out of context to mean "optional," but tax law is "voluntary" only in the sense that traffic law is "voluntary." Most people stop for red lights even when the police are not around—but running a red light is still illegal, and you will get a ticket if an officer catches you.

African-American taxpayers can claim a "reparations tax credit" to compensate for the effects of slavery. Some scholars and activists have argued that Congress ought to enact reparations for the descendants of American slaves. According to one urban legend, the reparations have already arrived in the form of a tax credit. Some con artists even charge large fees to help people receive it. But Congress has not passed such a measure. Unless it does, no one may lawfully take a reparations tax credit.

There are legal ways to reduce tax liability. But as the IRS warns: "If an idea to save on taxes seems too good to be true, it probably is."[21]

law costs somewhere between $163 and $228 billion a year.[23] Even those who administer and write the tax laws seek help with their own taxes. In 2010, the head of the Internal Revenue Service acknowledged that he needed a professional to do his taxes. "Uh, I've used one for years," said Commissioner Douglas Shulman. "I find it convenient and I find the tax code complex, so I use a preparer."[24] Most members of the House Ways and Means Committee and Senate Finance Committee, which have jurisdiction over taxes, rely on tax professionals.[25] When a reporter sought lawmakers who prepared their own returns, he did find Senator Mike Enzi (R-WY), who is a certified public accountant.[26] To some extent, lawmakers' reliance on paid preparers may just reflect constraints on their own time. Yet the sheer complexity of the tax code may vex the wisest public officials. In 2009, several of President Obama's choices for high office got into political trouble because of tax mistakes. Many have wondered whether policymakers can deliberate effectively on tax issues that they do not fully understand.

Progressive taxes—taxes that take proportionately more from the income of higher-income people than from lower-income people.

The aim of graduated rates is to make the system **progressive**, ensuring that more affluent taxpayers pay a greater fraction of their income. Those with higher incomes do pay higher average rates, and their share of the total tax burden exceeds their share of total income (see Figure 17-1). Many low-income people qualify for the Earned Income Tax Credit (EITC), which helps struggling individuals and families. Low-income workers who take this credit may get more in refunds than they paid in taxes.

In the past, rates were higher. The top marginal rate reached an all-time high of 94% in the wartime year of 1945. It fell after victory, but stayed at 91% for much of the 1950s and early 1960s. On the eve on Ronald Reagan's election, it stood at 70%. Through credits and deductions, however, most rich people could shelter much of their income from such a bite. Both liberals and conservatives asked whether it made sense to set high marginal rates only to see people escape them through loopholes. In 1986, President Reagan and Congress

Tax Burden

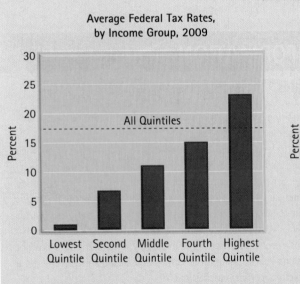

Average Federal Tax Rates, by Income Group, 2009

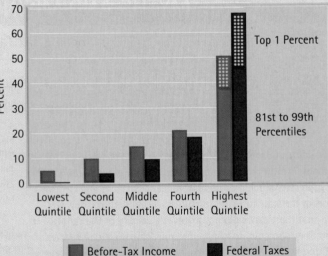

Shares of Before-Tax Income and Federal Taxes, by Income Group, 2009

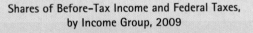

Before-Tax Income   Federal Taxes

FIGURE 17-1 In 2012, the Congressional Budget Office estimated the effective individual tax rate falling on various income groups. (The "effective" rate is what remains after deductions, exemptions, and credits.) This estimate included income, payroll, excise, and corporate taxes. CBO also estimated each group's share of the total tax burden. The "lowest quintile" is the bottom fifth of income, the second is the second fifth, and so on. Also note that those in the highest-income category not only pay the highest rate but also bear most of the burden, even in comparison with their share of total pretax income. The figures for income tax alone would show even greater concentration of the burden on upper-income groups.

SOURCE: Congressional Budget Office, "The Distribution of Household Income and Federal Taxes, 2008 and 2009," July 2012 at www.cbo.gov/sites/default/files/cbofiles/attachments/43373-AverageTaxRates_Screen.pdf accessed July 24, 2012.

agreed on landmark legislation to scrap billions in tax breaks in return for lower rates, but policymakers soon started to raise rates and create new breaks.

Reformers have proposed replacing the current structure with a **flat tax**. In its simplest form, the idea is to do away with all deductions and credits, and tax all income at one rate. A flat tax would drastically simplify the system, making it easier to understand and slashing the cost of compliance. Proposals for a flat tax have run into objections. Tax preferences encourage such social goods as home ownership, and from a political standpoint, millions benefit from current deductions and credits. Former IRS commissioner Sheldon Cohen said, "The tax code, once you get to know it, embodies all the essence of life: greed, politics, power, goodness, charity. Everything's in there. That's why it's so hard to get a simplified tax code. Life just isn't simple."[27]

Virginia's 529 sponsors a NASCAR race. Kurt Busch won in 2012.

More recently, Congress again cut tax rates, but it also added new preferences that nudge the system further from a flat tax. One such provision should be of special interest to students. Many families now save for college with "529 plans" (the name comes from the section of federal tax law that Congress added to create them). Although taxpayers cannot take federal tax deductions for the money they put into such plans, they do not have to pay federal income tax on their plans' investment earnings. When students reach college age, families may make tax-free withdrawals to pay for educational costs. Every state has its own 529 plan, and some let their residents take deductions from state income tax for contributions to their own state plans. Congress could abolish the 529 plans, but that could disrupt college financial planning for millions. Lawmakers who voted for such a move would be unpopular.

Flat tax—a proposal to tax all income at a single rate.

Corporate Income Taxes

The corporate income tax applies to businesses with a corporate charter. Unlike the individual income tax, it does not apply to gross income but to net income or profits, with deductions for business costs. Corporate income taxes have averaged just below 2% of GDP since the 1990s, more than in the 1980s but substantially less than in previous decades. These taxes account for about 10%–15% of total federal revenues, compared with 28% in the 1950s.[28]

In part, these trends reflect the aggressive use of tax laws. Some corporations set up headquarters in places such as the Cayman Islands, which let companies avoid U.S. taxes on their foreign operations. Representative Rosa DeLauro (D-CT) said, "We cannot afford to reward companies who shun their responsibilities of American citizenship at the expense of loyal American businesses and contractors."[29] During the 2012 campaign, the Obama campaign criticized Republican candidate Mitt Romney for investing money offshore. Republicans replied that top Democratic fundraisers had similar investments.[30]

A larger question involves the role of corporate taxation itself. Some argue that raising corporate taxes would make the tax system fairer by shifting more of the burden from the poor to the rich. They note examples of large corporations that pay no tax while working-class people struggle. A counterargument is that increases in these taxes would backfire. Corporations would pass the cost to workers through lower wages, to consumers through higher prices, and to shareholders through lower returns. Although the rich own more stock than the poor, any tax impact on shareholders would reverberate widely. About half of American families own stock, either directly or through retirement plans and the like. Even college students have a stake in the corporate world. Most colleges have endowments, 77 of which topped a billion dollars in 2008.[31] Much of this money lies in corporate stock. When corporations take an economic hit, endowments may shrink, and less money is available for students. Institutions of higher education suffered greatly from the steep market declines of 2008.

Payroll Taxes

Payroll taxes (or social insurance taxes), which finance Social Security and Medicare, make up a growing share of federal revenues. Most Americans pay more in payroll taxes than in individual income taxes.[32] The government takes 6.2% out of your paycheck for Social Security and 1.45% for Medicare. Your employer must also pay an equal amount on your behalf.

Unlike income taxes, payroll taxes do not have exemptions, deductions, credits, or rates that go up with income. On the Social Security portion, you pay only on wages up to a certain amount ($110,100 in 2012). Because people do not have to pay on any part of their wages above this cap, the poor pay a greater share of their income to Social Security than the rich. In other words, the tax is **regressive**. Why did the federal government finance Social Security this way? If the money to fund Social Security came from the income tax, the program's founders believed, people would see it as a handout. Lawmakers structured it so that people could feel that they had earned their benefits, even though current workers pay for the benefits of current retirees. Accordingly, they dubbed the financing law "The Federal Insurance Contribution Act" (FICA). President Franklin Roosevelt said, "[T]hose taxes were never a problem of economics. They are politics all the way through. We put those payroll contributions there so as to give the contributors a legal, moral, and political right to collect their pensions and their unemployment benefits. With those taxes in there, no damn politician can ever scrap my social security program."[33]

Roosevelt's comment was not completely accurate about the law. In 1960, the Supreme Court ruled that individuals do not have a property right to Social Security benefits.[34] Although the Social Security Administration must carry out the law fairly, Congress may change or abolish the law at any time. FDR was right about the politics. Any cut in current Social Security benefits would be political poison.

Other Taxes

Excise taxes supply the federal government with a relatively small part of its revenue. These taxes apply to specific goods and services, usually by the unit (e.g., gallon, pound, or pack). **Sales taxes** apply to most items, with rates as a percentage of the price. Many states and localities have general sales taxes, but the federal government does not; and along with many states, the federal government places steep excise taxes on alcoholic beverages and tobacco. In part, these "sin taxes" aim to discourage drinking and smoking. They have succeeded to an extent, though the authorities must fight efforts at evasion: bootlegging of whiskey and "butt-legging" of cigarettes. The federal excise tax for gasoline is 18.4 cents per gallon. Congress has set aside most of the tax for the federal highway trust fund, with a small share to mass transit. The more one drives, the reasoning goes, the more one should pay to support the highway system, and, as with Social Security, the presence of an "earmarked" tax creates political support for the program.

The **estate tax** is a tax on people's right to transfer property at death. It involves an accounting of the fair market value of everything they own when they die. It applies only to large estates ($5 million or more as of 2012). There has long been debate about its appropriate level, and those seeking to reduce or end it prefer to call it the "death tax."

Taxes and Freedom

Every year, the Tax Foundation calculates "Tax Freedom Day," the date on which Americans have earned enough to pay off their total tax bill for the year. In 2012, Tax Freedom Day fell on April 17.[35] Before then, many conservatives argue, Americans were working for the government. Afterward, they were free to work for themselves. According to liberal groups such as the Center on Budget and Policy Priorities, Tax Freedom Day is a misleading gimmick.[36] They dispute the data and argue that taxes serve the cause of freedom by supporting programs that promote economic opportunity.

Regressive tax—the opposite of a progressive tax, taking proportionately more from lower-income people.

Excise tax—a tax on specific goods and services, usually by the unit (e.g., gallon, pound, or pack).

Sales tax—tax on the purchase of a wide range of items, with rates as a percentage of the price.

Estate tax—a tax on your right to transfer property at your death. Those who want to reduce or eliminate it sometimes call it the "death tax."

There are other debates about taxes and freedom. Some argue that tax preferences liberate people from a rigid approach that would otherwise treat many people unfairly. Critics contend that the tax code directly jeopardizes political freedom. To keep their tax-exempt status, many organizations have to steer clear of certain kinds of political activity. As we explain in the chapter on interest groups, there are lawful ways around these restrictions. Nevertheless, political activists often call for investigations of tax-exempt groups that they deem to be their enemies.

Federal debt—the total value of outstanding securities that the federal government has issued.

FISCAL POLICY: SPENDING AND THE BUDGET
MAJOR ISSUE

• How do the executive and legislative branches deliberate about fiscal policy?

The president and Congress annually work on a budget for the federal government. In deliberating, they must ponder two sets of considerations. The first is the economic impact. How will changes in spending and taxation (see Figure 17-2) affect economic growth, unemployment, and inflation? What are the effects of deficits or surpluses? How will the **federal debt** (the sum of unpaid deficits) affect the long-term economic outlook?

The second set of considerations involves the budget's components. In addition to raising revenue, as we have seen, Congress writes tax laws to foster or discourage certain activities. On the spending side, the government funds programs not only to pump money into the economy but also to achieve other policy goals. Although the Department of Defense creates jobs, its main purpose is to protect the nation against attack. Often these two sets of goals may clash. Balancing the budget may require cuts in agency spending. Conversely, some non-economic goals may be so important that the government pursues them at the risk of economic trouble.

The Budget Process

At the beginning of each calendar year, the Office of Management and Budget (OMB) issues the president's budget proposal for the following fiscal year, which starts on October 1 (Table 17-1). The proposal is the product of months of deliberation involving OMB and the government's departments and agencies. OMB weighs their competing demands in light of the president's fiscal priorities.

FIGURE 17-2 A pay stub from Montana shows taxes and other items withheld from a paycheck.
SOURCE: www.challenge.treas.gov/educator_toolkit/documents/Family_economics_and_financial_education/understanding_your_paycheck_lesson_plan_1.31.1.pdf.

TABLE 17-1	BUDGET TIMELINE

Deadline	Action to be Completed
First Monday in February	President submits budget to Congress.
February 15	CBO submits reports on economic and budget outlook to budget committees.
Six weeks after president's budget is submitted	Committees submit reports on views and estimates to respective Budget Committee.
April 1	Senate Budget Committee reports budget resolution.
April 15	Congress completes action on budget resolution.
June 10	House Appropriations Committee reports last regular appropriations bill.
June 30	House completes action on regular appropriations bills and any required reconciliation legislation.
July 15	President submits mid-session review of his budget to Congress.
October 1	Fiscal year begins.

SOURCE: Bill Henniff et al., "Introduction to the Federal Budget Process," Congressional Research Service, December 2, 2010, opencrs.com/document/98-721/2010-12-02/download/1005/, accessed July 23, 2012.

After approval by the president, OMB sends the proposal to Congress, which starts work on a budget resolution. This document spells out spending and revenue targets for the coming fiscal year as well as projections for future years. The House and Senate Budget Committees draft the resolution after taking testimony and receiving information from other committees, as well as analysis and cost estimates from the Congressional Budget Office. Under the law, both chambers should pass the resolution by April 15, although Congress has often skipped this deadline. (In 2010, 2011, and 2012, budget resolutions did not reach final passage at all.) The budget resolution does not go to the president. It neither supplies money nor changes revenue levels, but instead guides Congress as it deliberates on spending and tax bills. If such a measure seems to violate the terms of the budget resolution, a House member or senator may raise a budget "point of order" on the floor to block it. The House, however, can waive such points of order by a simple majority vote on a resolution from its Rules Committee. In the Senate, it takes 60 votes to waive budget points of order.

The House and Senate Appropriations Committees both have a dozen subcommittees, each of which works on a measure to fund specific areas of the government. The full committees and their subcommittees hold hearings to learn how government organizations have spent money in the past (see Figure 17-3) and what they plan for the coming year. After the budget resolution has set spending ceilings, these bodies develop the 12 appropriations bills. If Congress does not pass these bills by October 1, it must pass a **continuing resolution** to supply stopgap funding.

Appropriations bills usually supply budget authority for only one fiscal year at a time. Tax measures, by contrast, stay in effect until Congress changes them or unless it adds an expiration date. The same is true of entitlements (see Chapter 16 on social welfare policy). The term refers to Social Security, Medicare, and other programs that require payments to anyone who meets certain eligibility standards. Budget resolutions usually direct congressional committees to draft changes in tax and entitlement laws. The Budget Committees then bundle these changes into a **reconciliation** bill. The full House and Senate vote on this bill, which is sometimes the year's key fiscal measure. In 1993, Congress passed a reconciliation bill with big tax increases, mainly on higher incomes. President Clinton had to fight to win enactment of the bill, which passed by only one vote in both the House and Senate.

When all the legislative action is over, revenues never exactly match expenditures. In recent decades, the government has occasionally taken in more than it has spent. More often, it has run deficits, leading to debt. The Treasury Department borrows this money mainly by issuing **securities**: Treasury bills, Treasury notes, and Treasury bonds. Bearing the full

Continuing resolution—a stopgap measure that provides for spending until Congress passes a regular appropriations bill.

Budget reconciliation bill—a measure that changes existing law in order to carry out instructions in a budget resolution.

Securities—a broad term for stocks, bonds, and other investment instruments.

faith and credit of the United States, these securities make a safe investment. Buyers include individuals, corporations, states, localities, and foreign governments.

When you borrow money for a car or a house, the bank or other lender can take away the property if you fall behind in your payments. The federal government does not borrow that way. Its "full faith and credit" backs payments of the principal and interest on all its public debt securities. Buyers of these securities know that, in case of default, they could not repossess fighter jets, presidential limousines, or the Washington Monument. They simply count on Washington's promise to pay

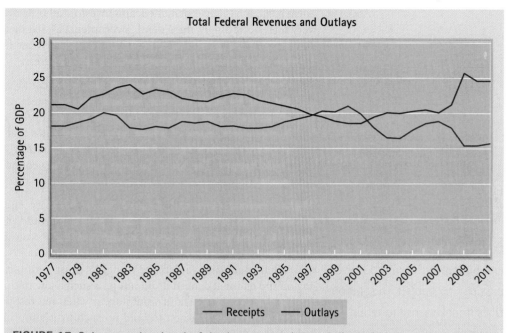

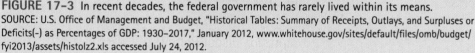

FIGURE 17-3 In recent decades, the federal government has rarely lived within its means.
SOURCE: U.S. Office of Management and Budget, "Historical Tables: Summary of Receipts, Outlays, and Surpluses or Deficits(-) as Percentages of GDP: 1930–2017," January 2012, www.whitehouse.gov/sites/default/files/omb/budget/fyi2013/assets/histolz2.xls accessed July 24, 2012.

IMPACT
of Social Media and Communications Technology

Catching Waste and Abuse

In deliberating on what to do after the 2009 economic stimulus became law, Congress and the administration needed to find out where stimulus spending actually went and what effect it had. Aware of the need to guard against waste and abuse, President Barack Obama pledged an all-out effort to ensure that government would spend every dollar wisely. But the sheer size of the stimulus posed an immense challenge for deliberation and oversight. The Office of Management and Budget, the Congressional Budget Office, the Government Accountability Office, various congressional committees, and the newly created Recovery Act Accountability and Transparency Board (RAATB) all played a part in tracking stimulus spending. Nevertheless, with so much money going to so many places, even their combined efforts were not enough. Ordinary Americans would have to join the effort.

What could citizens do? On its Web page (www.recovery.gov), RAATB supplied a number of links that allowed people to report suspected cases of waste and abuse. The GAO also set up a FraudNet reporting system, enabling citizens to file their reports by Web form, e-mail, toll-free phone, or fax. A number of state governments and private organizations also set up similar systems. One such organization was "Stimulus Watch" (stimuluswatch.org/2.0/), which described its operations this way: "StimulusWatch.org was built to help the

new administration keep its pledge and to hold public officials to account. We do this by allowing you, citizens around the country with local knowledge about the proposed projects in your city, to find, discuss and rate those projects."

Critics of the administration started their own watchdog projects. Crossroads GPS created Wikicountability.org, a collaborative Web site, to create a database of freedom of information requests about the actions of the Obama administration. And after the 2010 midterm election brought a Republican majority to the House, the homepage of the House Oversight and Government Reform Committee (oversight.house.gov) featured a link where government employees could "blow the whistle on fraud and abuse in your agency or other organization."

For more details, see the Bessette-Pitney blog post of July 25, 2012.

CRITICAL THINKING
QUESTION

Did any of these efforts result in substantial savings to the federal government? If so, how? If not, why not?

them back. It has never defaulted, and investors all over the world regard these securities as very safe. Accordingly, the federal government can sell them at a relatively low interest rate.

What if the government broke its promise? What if it failed to pay? President Bill Clinton once answered this question in a radio address.

> Our unbroken record of keeping our word could end, with taxpayers bearing the cost for years to come, because interest rates would go up on United States obligations. And interest rates could also go up for businesses, consumers, and homeowners, many of whom have interest rates that vary according to the government's interest rates. And for tens of millions of Americans, the unthinkable could happen. The Social Security checks they count on would not be able to be mailed out.[37]

Higher interest rates and delayed Social Security checks would also cut economic growth. If tax revenue fell, the debt problem would get worse, slowing growth even more. At some point, this spiral would stop, but it would have done serious harm in the meantime.

What could cause a default? Congress must periodically pass laws that raise the ceiling on the national debt. If it did not pass such a law in time to keep the government from hitting that ceiling, a default would occur when interest payments could not go out. Lawmakers sometimes threaten to hold up such legislation in order to bargain for their own priorities.

Limits of Fiscal Policy

At one time, policymakers hoped that the federal government could use fiscal policy to "fine-tune" the economy.[38] When growth was slow and unemployment was high, the thinking went, it could run deficits to spur activity. Conversely, it could run surpluses to ease inflationary pressures. Over time, though, economists and public officials have learned that fiscal policy is a blunt instrument rather than a precision instrument.

The image of "fine-tuning" suggests that the government can always respond swiftly to emerging trends. As we have just seen, fiscal policymaking involves many people, organizations, and interests. Multiple discussions and hearings can foster thorough deliberation but seldom lead to quick decisions. A presidential proposal usually takes months to get into the law, and even after a policy becomes official, it takes more time to have an impact. The government does not lay out all the money at once. Months will pass as officials draft contracts or cut checks. Accordingly, there may be a year or more between the time an economic problem crops up and the time the government's response takes effect. By that point, economic conditions may have shifted and the response may no longer work. Experts refer to this time gap as **policy lag**.

When policymakers think that the nation is in crisis, they may act more swiftly. Within weeks of taking office in 2009, President Obama won congressional approval of a $787 billion economic stimulus, including new spending and tax breaks. Despite the sense of urgency, however, only a small portion of the spending could take place right away. Proponents of the economic stimulus spoke of "shovel-ready projects," which would get under way upon passage, but because of delays with construction permits and other red tape, President Obama later admitted, "there's no such thing as shovel-ready projects."[39]

Another limit on fiscal policy is that most federal spending is usually outside the annual appropriations process. For instance, government must pay interest on the debt, which may amount to hundreds of billions of dollars each year. **Mandatory spending** consists mainly of entitlement programs, which keep writing checks until Congress decides otherwise (see Figure 17-4). The law provides an annual cost-of-living adjustment (COLA) for Social Security retirement benefits. Benefits automatically rise with price levels. Although it is legally possible to pass a bill reducing COLAs or cutting entitlement programs, it is politically difficult. The same applies to much of **discretionary spending**, the remainder of the budget. Politicians hate to cut funding for the Federal Bureau of Investigation, for example, or for many of the other items under this heading.

FOCUS QUESTION

Congress has gone through several budget cycles without even passing a budget resolution. Does it make sense to retain the process?

Policy lag—the time period between the creation of a policy and its implementation.

Mandatory spending—federal spending that is not subject to the annual appropriations process. It consists mainly of entitlement programs and interest payments on the debt.

Discretionary spending—federal outlays that are subject to the annual process of appropriations, unlike mandatory spending.

Uncertainty is yet another constraint.[40] In drafting plans for the next fiscal year, officials must make assumptions about the economy. Tax collections will hinge on the overall level of wages, salaries, interest income, and corporate profits, which all reflect the level of economic activity. Social Security COLAs move with the inflation rate. Programs for the poor may spend more or less money depending on levels of poverty or joblessness. If assumptions about these conditions prove wrong, then spending or revenues could be hundreds of billions of dollars different from the estimates.

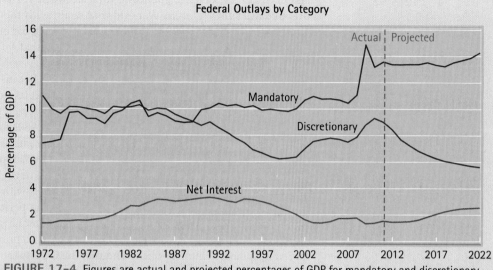

Federal Outlays by Category

FIGURE 17-4 Figures are actual and projected percentages of GDP for mandatory and discretionary spending, as well as interest on the debt.

SOURCE: Congressional Budget Office, "Economic and Budget Outlook, Fiscal Years 2012 to 2022," January 31, 2012, www.cbo.gov/sites/default/files/cbofiles/attachments/01-03-2012_Outlook.pdf accessed July 24, 2012.

Economists and policymakers use sophisticated models to forecast the economy. They also develop scenarios to map out the possible impact of unexpected events. In light of all the uncertainty, it is remarkable that they perform as well as they do. But as OMB director David Stockman admitted in the first year of the Reagan administration: "None of us really understands what's going on with all these numbers."[41]

Stockman's complaint took on new meaning with the start of the economic crisis in 2008. As the plight of financial institutions quickly worsened, the secretary of the treasury warned Congress of catastrophe if it did not act right away. Not only did the lawmakers have little chance for deliberation, but they also had to act before they knew much about the scope of the problem and the effectiveness of possible solutions. "A major source of uncertainty in the outlook is the degree and persistence of turmoil in financial markets and the resulting impact on the future course of the economy," reported the Congressional Budget Office. "[T]he scale of the problems and the worldwide linkages of financial markets are significantly different from what they were in previous episodes of financial stress in the United States." Together with the unprecedented dimensions of the federal government's response, CBO concluded, these problems "make it particularly difficult for analysts to use historical patterns to forecast the near future."[42]

Deficits, Surpluses, and the Debt

The federal government ran a deficit in every fiscal year between the late 1960s and the late 1990s. For a brief period at the close of the twentieth century, the nation enjoyed surpluses. Since the 2002 fiscal year, the budget has been back in deficit.

For the most part, deficits have not been a deliberate goal. Although they may stimulate economic growth in the short run, few would argue that they do good over the long run. Each year's deficit increases the debt, which in turn means that the government will have to pay even more interest in the future. This burden will fall on the next generations of taxpayers, many of whom are now in cribs. Indeed, politicians often decry deficits by stressing how much they will cost our children.

So why do deficits happen? As we have already suggested, some goals may override fiscal ones. During his 1961 inaugural address, President John F. Kennedy pledged "that we shall pay any price, bear any burden, meet any hardship, support any friend, oppose any foe to assure the survival and the success of liberty."[43] During the 1960s and early 1970s, defense spending took between 7.4% and 9.4% of GDP. The figures dropped after the Vietnam War and rose again with the Reagan defense buildup of the 1980s. The end of the Cold War in 1991 made way for cuts, bringing defense spending down to just 3.0% in 1999. Not coincidentally, that year marked the first surplus in decades.

Peace did not last, and neither did the surplus. Because of the war on terror, Congress approved spending increases for defense. The 2003 invasion of Iraq made further demands. President George W. Bush, meanwhile, pressed Congress to continue his policy of tax cuts. Both sides in the debate pointed to the 1980s for evidence. Democrats said that President Reagan caused the deficit to mushroom by pushing tax cuts and defense increases at the same time. Republicans said that the Reagan's "supply-side" tax cuts fostered a long period of economic growth that in turn generated new tax revenues. The argument was murky because Congress followed the tax cuts of 1981 with a series of tax increases between 1982 and 1993. Democrats noted that another long period of growth followed the 1993 round of tax increases. They credited President Clinton's spending programs in education and job training, which they called "investments." Republicans said that the growth occurred in spite of Clinton's policies and that the GOP takeover of Congress in 1994 blocked even greater increases in taxes and spending.

In 2008, the fiscal policy picture changed starkly with the economic crisis. When people lost their jobs and companies went out of business, they stopped paying income or corporate taxes. The government had already spent huge sums to stimulate the economy, and much greater increases in spending lay in the future. Shortly before he took office, president-elect Obama said, "[W]e're already looking at a trillion-dollar budget deficit or close to a trillion-dollar budget deficit, and that potentially we've got trillion-dollar deficits for years to come, even with the economic recovery that we are working on at this point."[44]

The Obama administration sought to pay for the spending by raising taxes and framed its policy as a matter of good citizenship. Vice President Biden said that the affluent would be willing to give up tax cuts out of love of country. "Rich folks are just as patriotic as poor folks; they're not asking for this extra help."[45] President Obama said that he was asking "the wealthiest Americans who enjoyed the biggest tax cuts over the past decade to just pay a little bit more. And, you know, here's the thing. There are plenty of patriotic, successful Americans who want to make this contribution. They're willing to do it because they remember how they got successful."[46]

John F. Kennedy's famous line, applied to taxes.

MONETARY POLICY

MAJOR ISSUE

- How does the Federal Reserve seek to maintain economic stability?

The response to the economic crisis went beyond the decisions about taxes and spending that make up fiscal policy. Another crucial element was monetary policy, which involves the supply of money and interest rates. We now turn to that subject.

Organization and Policy

The **Federal Reserve System**, the "Fed," helps manage the supply of money and credit. A seven-member Board of Governors runs the system, which includes 12 regional federal reserve banks and 25 branches. Subject to Senate approval, the president names the governors, who serve overlapping 14-year terms (see Figure 17-5). The governors enjoy some political insulation because the president cannot fire them before the end of their terms. They also have some independence from Congress because the Fed does not rely on appropriations. It gets operating expenses from fees and investment income.

The Federal Reserve System's main goal is economic stability.[47] When the economy is sputtering and unemployment is high, the Fed may seek lower interest rates. With easier money, businesses

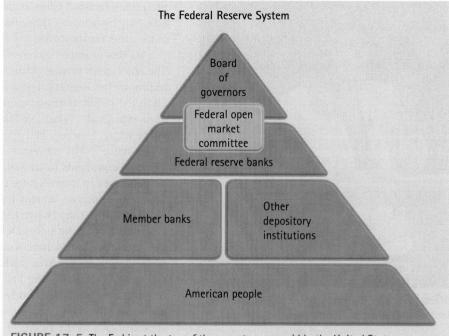

The Federal Reserve System

FIGURE 17–5 The Fed is at the top of the monetary pyramid in the United States. SOURCE: "The Federal Reserve System," web.archive.org/web/20070711084643/http://www .federalreserveeducation.org/fed101_html/structure/, accessed July 24, 2012.

borrow to expand their activities, thereby creating jobs. Similarly, consumers respond to low rates by stepping up purchases of costly items that require loans, such as homes and cars. When inflation looms, however, the Fed may seek higher rates to reverse these effects and "cool off" the economy.

Many people think that the Fed dictates the interest rate. This belief is erroneous in two ways. First, there is no such thing as "the" interest rate. Depending on the size and purpose of the loan, as well as the characteristics of the borrower, rates differ a great deal. Second, the Fed does not set rates for consumers and businesses; but it does have ways of influencing these rates. Its main tool involves the **federal funds rate**, which member banks charge for overnight loans to one another.[48] Over time, most other interest rates move along the same general path as the federal funds rate.

The Fed's policymaking branch, the **Federal Open Market Committee (FOMC)**, holds the key to the federal funds rate. The FOMC's voting members are the Fed's seven governors, the president of the Federal Reserve Bank of New York, and presidents of four other reserve banks who serve on a one-year rotating basis. The chair of the Board of Governors usually chairs the FOMC as well. The committee meets eight times a year to set a target for the federal funds rate. At the end of each meeting, it announces its decision in a public statement, which gets a great deal of press attention.

The FOMC's decision does not change the rate automatically. After the FOMC makes its decision, the New York Federal Reserve Bank buys and sells securities to nudge the rate toward the target.[49] When the New York Fed buys, it pays with checks. The sellers then deposit the checks in their banks, and the Fed credits the amount to the banks' required reserves. By increasing total reserves, this step reduces the need for overnight borrowing, thereby bringing down the federal funds rate. Conversely, when the New York Fed sells securities, it pushes the rate upward. The Federal Reserve's economic power has limits. Upheavals in the global economy can overwhelm its decisions, and interest rates reflect more than monetary policy. When the federal government runs deficits, it must increase its borrowing, and over time the competition for scarce capital tends to raise long-term interest rates. Soon after the 1992 election, Fed chairman Alan Greenspan convinced

Federal Reserve System—the "Fed," the central bank of the United States. It has the primary responsibility for monetary policy.

Federal funds rate—the rate that banks charge for overnight loans to one another. The Federal Reserve sets targets for this rate to influence interest rates in general.

Federal Open Market Committee (FOMC)—the group that makes monetary policy for the Federal Reserve System. Its voting members are the members of the Fed's Board of Governors and the presidents of five federal reserve banks, including the Federal Reserve Bank of New York.

Maria Bartiromo of CNBC is one of the major figures in broadcast economic journalism.

FOCUS QUESTION

Does the Federal Reserve System put too much power into the hands of unelected officials?

president-elect Bill Clinton that deficit reduction would strengthen the economy by bringing those rates down.[50] Greenspan's advice helped lead to the 1993 tax increases.

As this example shows, the chair of the Fed wields major influence. The chair gives private counsel to the White House and regularly offers testimony to Congress. Those words may rock financial markets. Accordingly, the public testimony contains a great deal of hedging. Greenspan once explained, "What I've learned at the Federal Reserve is a new language which is called 'Fed-speak.' You soon learn to mumble with great incoherence."[51] His successor, Ben Bernanke, learned a lesson when his informal comments to television reporter Maria Bartiromo about a possible increase in interest rates caused stock prices to plunge.[52]

Critics such as Senator Rand Paul (R-KY) worry that the Fed lacks accountability. They charge that its officials and staff reflect the financial community, not the poor. Defenders note that all the central banks of the developed world have some degree of political insulation. Without it, the banks could never push up interest rates, even if inflation were a dire threat. Moreover, the Fed's insulation is far from absolute. Because it is not a constitutional body, Congress could change its operations by passing a law. Over time, a president can influence its policies through appointments to the Board of Governors. In periods of growth and low inflation, such as the 1990s, there is little public call for change in the Fed. In hard times, it needs friends in high places.

During the early 1980s, for instance, it kept interest rates high to beat down inflation. In the resulting recession, when unemployment topped 10%, many political leaders wanted to force a change of course. President Reagan publicly supported the Fed and reappointed its chair in 1983. By the next year, inflation was falling, growth was soaring, and Reagan won 49 states in his bid for reelection.

Deliberation and the Fed

Members of the Federal Open Market Committee prepare diligently for their deliberations. One regional president explained in 2002, "My homework for an FOMC meeting begins with a review of the hard data: statistics on prices and wages, jobs, housing starts, production and so on. Decisions are based primarily on these data. But because these numbers often trail current conditions, I seek out personal accounts, media reports and similar anecdotal information to get a glimpse of what's happening now."[53]

At the closed meeting itself, Fed staffers report on the business and financial situation around the world. Before voting on a target for the federal funds rate, the members discuss the data and their options. FOMC makes the vote public right after the meeting, and releases the minutes a few days later. When the House and Senate pass tax and spending bills, by contrast, C-SPAN broadcasts the debate live, and the *Congressional Record* is soon online. Lawmakers have sometimes urged FOMC to follow its lead and open its meetings. In his memoirs, Greenspan disagreed: "If its discussions were made public, with the details of who said what to whom, the meetings would become a series of bland, written presentations. The advantages to policy formulation of unfettered debate would be lost."[54] FOMC does release a full transcript five years after each meeting, when the information is no longer as sensitive.

Crisis and Monetary Policy

Signs of financial trouble appeared as early as the summer of 2007, and the Fed responded by seeking to bring down interest rates. In early 2008, the Fed guaranteed $29 billion to support the rescue of Bear Stearns, a leading investment bank. The situation grew dramatically worse in September, and the Fed again propped up a major corporation by lending billions to the American International Group (AIG) insurance company. In October, as conditions got even worse, it bought tens of billions in short-term corporate debt in order to stimulate lending and restore confidence. The corporate bailouts occurred because policymakers considered certain firms "too big to fail." That is, their collapse would have catastrophic consequences for the entire financial system. In January 2009, Fed chairman Bernanke said that it was unacceptable for the government to prop up big companies that had taken big risks during economic expansion. "The existence of too-big-to-fail firms also violates the presumption of a level playing field among financial institutions. In the future, financial firms of any type whose failure would pose a systemic risk must accept especially close regulatory scrutiny of their risk-taking."[55]

In December 2008, the Fed made the extraordinary decision to bring the federal funds rate close to zero. Unable to cut the rate any further and facing an economy that continued to worsen, the Fed then took other steps to revive economic activity. It announced that it would buy over $1 trillion in mortgage-backed securities to keep mortgage rates low, and it would also buy up to $200 billion in Fannie Mae and Freddie Mac debt. The goal was to shore up the housing market, which had crashed. To bring down other long-term interest rates, it planned to buy up to $300 billion in Treasury securities. As of 2012, however, such steps had only limited success. Although the economy had not slipped into another recession, unemployment remained high by historical standards, and a robust recovery was not yet at hand.

REGULATORY AND TRADE POLICY
MAJOR ISSUES

- What is the appropriate role for the government in policing economic activity?
- Do international trade agreements infringe on American sovereignty?

Government regulates business in several broad ways. Civil rights laws apply to many private decisions on hiring and promotion (see Chapter 6). Health, safety, and environmental regulations affect a wide array of practices ranging from the massive (installation of pollution control equipment in power plants) to the modest (requirements that food service workers wash their hands). You may find a discussion of such rules in Chapter 14 on bureaucracy and the administrative state. Here we look at regulation of the marketplace.

Regulating the Marketplace

Financial regulation has four main goals:

- Protect consumers from fraud, deception, or unfair practices.
- Ensure the integrity and fairness of markets to prevent fraud and manipulation.
- Monitor the safety and soundness of institutions.
- Ensure the stability of the overall financial system.[56]

Complex arrays of government agencies pursue these goals. State banking departments charter state banks while the Office of the Comptroller of the Currency (OCC) does the same for national banks. The title of "state" or "national" depends on where the bank got its charter, not on its location or methods of operation. OCC, part of the Treasury Department, is the primary regulator of national banks. Regulation of state banks is the shared responsibility of state banking departments, the Fed, and the Federal Deposit Insurance Corporation (FDIC). Consumers are more familiar with FDIC for another reason: it insures bank accounts so as to maintain confidence in the system and prevent the "runs"

The Occupy Wall Street movement protested corporate misconduct and what it considered government's failure to fight it aggressively enough.

on banks that ruined many Americans during the Great Depression. The Securities and Exchange Commission regulates the New York Stock Exchange and other securities markets. According to its Web site, SEC's mission is to "protect investors, maintain fair, orderly, and efficient markets, and facilitate capital formation."[57] The newest federal agency in this field is the Consumer Financial Protection Bureau (CFPB). In the wake of the economic crisis, Congress set up the CFPB to enforce federal consumer financial protection laws involving products and services such as mortgages and credit cards.

Free-market advocates warn against excessive regulation, arguing that government itself helped create the crisis. According to economic historian Lawrence H. White, the growth of risky mortgage lending came after the Federal Housing Administration loosened down payment standards, and the Department of Housing and Urban Development pressured lenders to extend mortgages to borrowers who would not have qualified before. He also pointed to Freddie Mac and Fannie Mae, which had funded hundreds of billions in loans to dubious borrowers.[58] Taking a different angle, a report in the *New York Times* blamed President Bush for encouraging loans to low-income home buyers without sufficient regulation to prevent abuse.[59]

In some ways, regulation is less extensive than it used to be. Decades ago, the federal government maintained strict oversight of air travel, trucking, and telecommunications. Public policy discouraged competition and controlled prices. During the 1970s, however, a bipartisan consensus emerged that such policy hurt consumers by limiting choices and keeping prices artificially high.[60] The executive and legislative branches then deregulated these industries, with major economic benefits.

Trade

Protectionism—a policy of erecting trade barriers to shield domestic business from international competition.

International trade has long been a source of conflict among different regions and businesses. Generally, those who profit from exports back free trade, whereas those who fear foreign competition back trade barriers, or a policy of **protectionism**. The high-water mark of protectionism came with the Smoot-Hawley Act of 1930, which raised tariffs in an effort to help American businesses during the Depression. It backfired, causing other nations to keep out American goods and thereby making hard times worse.

After the Depression and World War II, the lessons of Smoot-Hawley helped give free trade the upper hand. In 1947, the United States joined 22 other nations in signing the General Agreement on Tariffs and Trade (GATT), a mutual effort to reduce trade barriers. The next five decades saw seven more rounds of GATT talks, with the last (1986–1994) encompassing 123 nations. That round culminated in the founding of the World Trade Organization (WTO). Its 155 member nations agree on rules for trade, take part in procedures to settle disputes, and hold talks on easing barriers even further.[61] The United States has also reached separate agreements with individual countries. In 1993, Congress approved the North American Free Trade Agreement (NAFTA) to foster trade among Mexico, the United States, and Canada. The pact cut or ended most tariffs on trade among the three countries. In 2005 came a similar agreement with the nations of Central America and the Dominican Republic.

At a time of globalization, when so much economic activity moves across national boundaries, free trade remains controversial. Some blame it for job losses, saying that Americans have a hard time competing with cheap labor in developing countries. Others argue that American labor remains competitive because of its productivity. A closely related issue is **offshoring**, the practice by which American or multinational firms delegate work to lower-wage laborers overseas. For instance, when you call a company's customer service line, you may be talking to someone in India. Offshoring has increasingly become a topic of campaign discussion. There are limited data on its effects, however, and its impact on unemployment is unclear.[62]

International trade involves issues such as human rights. When Congress considered normal trade relations with China, opponents said that the measure would reward Beijing for suppressing religion and political dissent. Representative David Bonior (D-MI) said, "You can't have a system of free markets where people aren't free." On the other side, Representative David Dreier (R-CA) said that "trade promotes private enterprise, which creates wealth, which improves living standards and undermines political oppression."[63] The measure passed.

On both ends of the political spectrum is the worry that international trade agreements may threaten American sovereignty. In 2002, President George W. Bush imposed tariffs on foreign steel. In 2003, after the WTO had ruled that it could trigger tariffs against U.S. goods, he withdrew them. WTO also ruled against American tax breaks for exporters, which Congress then repealed as part of a corporate tax bill. Such moves drew fire from Ralph Nader on the left and Pat Buchanan on the right:

> **Nader:** Sovereignty shredding, you know. The decisions are now in Geneva, bypassing our courts, our regulatory agencies, our legislatures.
> **Buchanan:** I find it amazing that Congress sits there and they get an order from the WTO, and they capitulate. What happened to bristling conservative defiance, "don't tread on me" patriotism?[64]

Conversely, another argument asserts that WTO benefits the United States. Foreign tariffs are higher than American ones, so a global reduction will make American exports more competitive. WTO strongly contends that the concerns about sovereignty are overblown.[65] The WTO cannot directly change American law. Its rulings may sometimes influence the decisions of the federal government, but responding to international pressure is hardly a new practice. Like other nations, the United States has always had to take foreign reactions into account in setting trade policy.

In negotiating trade agreements, the president has sometimes been able to rely on **Trade Promotion Authority**. Under this procedure, the lawmakers may accept or reject the agreement but cannot amend it. Otherwise, they might make changes that would help their constituents at the risk of breaking the deal with the other countries. By blocking debate on alternatives, say critics, this process hampers deliberation.[66] Its defenders say that it improves deliberation by focusing Congress on the broad national interest instead of the narrow economic concerns of states or districts. Congress let the Trade Promotion Authority lapse in 1994, revived it in 2002, and let it lapse again in 2007.

Mark Henley/Panos Pictures

Many American consumer goods come from China, where labor is cheap.

Offshoring—the practice by which American or multinational firms delegate work to lower-wage laborers overseas.

Trade Promotion Authority—special procedures meant to speed up the regular process when Congress considers trade agreements. These special procedures limit debate and prohibit amendments.

International Perspectives

Economic and Political Freedom

The Fraser Institute, a free-market Canadian research organization, annually publishes an index of economic freedom. The index ranks more than 100 nations according to size of government; security of property rights; access to sound money; freedom of international exchange; and regulation of credit, labor, and business. Freedom House, a human rights organization with headquarters in the United States, annually rates countries according to their protection of political rights and civil liberties. It uses three broad categories: "Free," "Partly Free," or "Not Free." Table 17-2 shows the strong correlation between economic freedom and political freedom. (For more on the Freedom House rankings, see Chapter 1.)

CRITICAL THINKING
QUESTION

Does economic freedom foster political freedom, or does it work the other way around?

TABLE 17-2 FREEDOM INDEXES

Top Countries in Index of Economic Freedom		Bottom Countries in Index of Economic Freedom	
Political Freedom		**Political Freedom**	
Singapore	Partly free	Algeria	Not free
New Zealand	Free	Ukraine	Partly free
Switzerland	Free	Ethiopia	Not free
Australia	Free	Sierra Leone	Partly free
Canada	Free	Mozambique	Partly free
Chile	Free	Nepal	Partly free
United Kingdom	Free	Niger	Partly free
Mauritius	Free	Algeria	Not free
United States	Free	Chad	Not free
Bahrain	Not free	Burundi	Partly free
Finland	Free	Congo, Rep.	Not free
Slovak Republic	Free	Guinea-Bissau	Partly free
United Arab Emirates	Not free	Central Af. Rep.	Partly free
Denmark	Free	Congo, Dem.Rep.	Not free
Estonia	Free	Angola	Not free
Hungary	Free	Venezuela	Partly free
Cyprus	Free	Myanmar/Burma	Not free
Austria	Free	Zimbabwe	Not free

SOURCES: Freedom House, "Freedom in the World: Table of Independent Countries," www.freedomhouse.org/sites/default/files/inline_images/TableofIndependentCountriesFIW2011.pdf, accessed July 23, 2012; James Gwartney, Robert Lawson, and Joshua Hall, *Economic Freedom of the World, 2011 Annual Report,* The Fraser Institute, www.freetheworld.com/2011/reports/world/EFW2011_complete.pdf, accessed July 23, 2012. (The Fraser Institute listed Hong Kong as first in economic freedom, but because it is not an independent country, it did not appear in the Freedom House rankings.)

ECONOMIC DEBATE AND DELIBERATIVE DEMOCRACY

Any deliberation depends on a shared understanding of basic information. James R. Schlesinger, an economist who headed the Departments of Defense and Energy, once told a congressional committee, "Everyone is entitled to his own opinion. No one is entitled to his own facts."[67] Because of the Internet, economic data are more widely available than ever before, but more information does not automatically produce better policy. With its unprecedented character and scope, the 2008 crisis forced many economic analysts to resort to the cliché of "uncharted waters." Good data help us see how many people are out of work, but they do not always tell us how to bring back jobs.

Deliberation also depends on shared goals. Nearly everyone agrees that low unemployment is desirable, and, as suggested at the start of this chapter, everyone also wants moderate prices and a growing GDP. In deliberating about economic policy, however, Americans disagree about the means to these ends. One view is that the government should aggressively manage the economy because problems such as joblessness reflect basic flaws in private enterprise. Therefore, government should respond with regulations, job training programs, and the like. A counterview is that government planners do not know enough to guide the billions of dealings that take place each day, and the unanticipated consequences of big government will overwhelm the benefits.[68] The 2008 presidential campaign saw a minor controversy when an Ohioan—who then briefly became famous as "Joe the Plumber"—asked Barack Obama about tax policy. Obama responded, "I think when you spread the wealth around, it's good for everybody." Republican candidate John McCain argued that Obama's programs would stifle economic growth and drive up

In a tight job market, college graduates do not always start with jobs that match their education. This Boston University alumnus works at a coffeehouse while waiting for a substitute teaching job.

pork barrel spending, and he dismissed "spreading the wealth" as a form of socialism. Columnist Michael Kinsley replied that "the principle that the unequal distribution of wealth is a legitimate concern and government policies should mitigate it has been part of American democracy since at least the New Deal."[69]

Deliberations about economic policy involve disagreements about the relationship between government action and citizenship. According to a task force of the American Political Science Association, political and social inequalities reinforce each other. Government action, it argued, is necessary to counterbalance special interest power: "[B]road efforts to spread opportunity and assure security for large numbers of Americans can also have the salutary side-effect of enhancing democratic citizenship. People are more likely to get involved when they have faith that government can and will address the needs and values of the majority."[70] On the other side, policy scholar Arthur Brooks argues that an emphasis on government action squelches active citizenship. "This view discourages a personal sense that an individual's time and treasure can meaningfully help solve social problems, and it diminishes individual charity."[71]

This disagreement relates to a larger debate about economic freedom, which entails the ability to work and trade without government interference. Most scholars see a link between economic freedom and political liberty (see the International Perspectives box). But which comes first? According to economist Milton Friedman, economic freedom "also promotes political freedom because it separates economic power from political power and in this way enables the one to offset the other."[72] According to political scientist Charles

Lindblom, political liberty came first and was a condition for economic freedom, not the other way around. Regimes with such liberty, he writes, "were established to win and protect certain liberties: private property, free contract, and occupational choice."[73]

Principled disagreements underlie deliberations about economic policy; but as a practical matter, we must also remember that politicians may change course in the face of political and economic pressures. Bill Clinton had ambitious plans for government activism, but after the GOP takeover of Congress, he declared that "[t]he era of big government is over." George W. Bush spoke the language of economic conservatism but ended up presiding over significant growth in federal spending, and at the end of his tenure, he supported massive interventions to contain the economic crisis. In his last press conference, he said, "I readily concede I chucked aside some of my free market principles when I was told by chief economic advisors that the situation we were facing could be worse than the Great Depression."[74]

It is an exaggeration to picture the economy as dancing to Washington's tune. Although the federal budget makes up a large part of the economy, the private sector is even bigger. The United States is part of a global market in which American government policy is just one of many influences. Robert Reich, who served as President Clinton's secretary of labor, says, "Job numbers are largely a function of population and the business cycle, and the business cycle has its own rhythm."[75] Private economist Robert Barbera adds that "the notion that presidents create and lose jobs is the most grotesque mischaracterization of the economic backdrop" that he has seen.[76]

Moreover, as this chapter has shown, there is no single government policy on the economy. Fiscal, monetary, trade, and regulatory policies all involve different decision makers. Because all these policies are working at once, it may be hard to sort out which one has which effect. Consider the boom of the 1990s: Did it stem from President Clinton's deficit cutting? Or was it the monetary policy of Alan Greenspan? Or did congressional Republicans do the trick by restraining regulation and tax increases?

Dollars and cents are not the only way to appraise economic policy. Toward the end of this chapter, we saw a table in the International Perspectives box on the relationship between economic and political freedom. By this standard, one may judge government actions by whether they increase or decrease individual liberty. For instance, critics say that the federal income tax endangers our privacy and distorts our daily economic decisions. As we discuss in Chapter 14, federal rules force Americans to spend much of their time coping with red tape. From a different perspective, however, others say that energetic government action can free Americans from the ill effects of market competition. This debate will probably never end.

SUMMARY

- In deliberating about economic issues, most people agree on certain goals: economic growth, low unemployment, and low inflation.
- Fiscal policy concerns taxes and spending.
- Most tax revenue comes in the form of personal income taxes (which are progressive) and social insurance taxes (which are generally regressive).
- Policymakers use the tax system both to raise revenue for the government and to influence the behavior of individuals and businesses.
- Spending consists of discretionary outlays, which are subject to the annual appropriations process of Congress, and mandatory spending, which continues until Congress changes the law that authorizes it.

- Because of the lag between policy decisions and their effects, as well as the difficulty of coordinating spending and revenue decisions, it is very difficult to influence the economy through fiscal policy.
- Monetary policy involves the supply of money and the level of interest rates. But as interest rates sank to very low levels after the 2008 economic crisis, the Federal Reserve had to contemplate new approaches to monetary policy.
- Regulatory and trade policy encompasses a variety of ways by which government policies affect markets for goods and service.

KEY TERMS

TEST YOUR KNOWLEDGE

1. Economic growth is usually measured through change in
   a. free-trade alliances.
   b. general population.
   c. gross domestic product.
   d. tax revenues.
   e. voter registration.

2. The provision in the Constitution that Congress could establish "post offices and post roads" signaled that the federal government would foster economic growth through
   a. efficient systems of communication and transportation.
   b. international alliances.
   c. private postal institutions.
   d. regulation of commerce between states.
   e. stamps and other postal services.

3. Although most wartime taxes of the Civil War were gone by the early 1870s, they set a precedent for
   a. a federal sales tax.
   b. a laissez-faire economic approach.
   c. a stronger federal government.
   d. supply-side economics.
   e. the national bank.

4. What new method did the Wilson administration employ to finance war debts?
   a. Congress established a national bank.
   b. Congress instituted a war-time tax.
   c. Congress levied the first federal income taxes.
   d. The administration borrowed heavily from foreign investors.
   e. The government sold small bonds to ordinary people.

5. What deliberative purpose does the Council of Economic Advisors serve?
   a. Congress must clear all its spending bills with the council.
   b. It offers the president objective advice and supplies Congress with detailed information about the economy.
   c. It oversees the development of the federal budget each year and supplies the president with an account of all new spending bills.
   d. It writes the tax codes.
   e. The CEA establishes the federal budget.

6. What is the biggest source of federal revenue?
   a. corporate taxes
   b. payroll taxes
   c. Social Security payments
   d. tariffs
   e. income taxes

7. Once the president approves a budget proposal, it is submitted to
   a. Congress.
   b. the Federal Reserve.
   c. the Office of Management and Budget.
   d. the Secretary of the Treasury.
   e. the vice president.

8. What is one way in which the Federal Reserve's Board of Governors is politically insulated?
   a. Members are elected by the people rather than appointed by the president.
   b. The members rely on Congress for their salaries.
   c. The members serve life terms.
   d. The president cannot fire any member before the end of the 14-year term.
   e. They receive their authority from the international economic community.

9. The policy of erecting trade barriers to shield domestic business from international competition is called
   a. protectionism.
   b. isolationism.
   c. sovereignty.
   d. progressive policy.
   e. supply-side economics.

10. A stopgap measure that provides for spending until Congress passes a regular appropriations bill is called a
   a. budget reconciliation bill.
   b. budget resolution.
   c. continuing resolution.
   d. discretionary spending bill.
   e. policy lag.

FURTHER READING

Alter, Jonathan. *The Promise: President Obama, Year One.* New York: Simon and Schuster, 2010.

Derthick, Martha, and Paul J. Quirk. *The Politics of Deregulation.* Washington, DC: Brookings Institution, 1985.

Friedman, Milton. *Capitalism and Freedom.* Chicago: University of Chicago Press, 1962.

Morgenson, Gretchen, and Joshua Rosner. *Reckless Endangerment.* New York: Times Books, 2011.

Stein, Herbert. *Presidential Economics: The Making of Economic Policy from Roosevelt to Reagan and Beyond.* New York: Simon and Schuster, 1984.

Weisman, Steven R. *The Great Tax Wars.* New York: Simon and Schuster, 2002.

Woodward, Bob. *Maestro: Greenspan's Fed and the American Boom.* New York: Simon and Schuster, 2000.

WEB SOURCES

Board of Governors of the Federal Reserve System: www.federalreserve.gov—official information on monetary policy.

Office of Management and Budget: www.whitehouse.gov/omb—a wealth of contemporary and historical budget data.

Recovery.gov: www.recovery.gov—the official site of President Obama's economic program.

Tax Policy Center: www.taxpolicycenter.org/index.cfm—a joint program of the Urban Institute and the Brookings Institution to provide data and analysis on tax policy.

USBudget Watch: usbudgetwatch.org—a project of the Pew Charitable Trusts to provide detailed information on the economic stimulus package and other fiscal issues.

Protesters in Quetta, Pakistan, burn an American flag and display portraits of Osama bin Laden on the first anniversary of his death.

© Musa Farman/EPA/Corbis

National Security and Foreign Policy

18

OBJECTIVES

After reading this chapter, you should be able to:

- Summarize the history of U.S. foreign policy and its relationship to citizenship.
- Compare the conflicting traditions of American foreign policy.
- Describe the organizations that develop and execute foreign policy.
- Analyze the political struggle for control of foreign policy.
- Discuss how policymakers and citizens deliberate on foreign policy.

INTRODUCTION

The invaders entered Washington, DC, on a hot summer afternoon. On reaching the Capitol, they lit torches and set it aflame. With the night sky glowing, they marched down Pennsylvania Avenue to the White House, which the First Lady had just fled. After some looting, they set fire to the White House, too.

This scenario does not come from a cheap novel. It happened during the War of 1812. British forces under Admiral George Cockburn got to the capital city on August 24, 1814. The destruction avenged an 1813 attack on the Canadian city of York (now Toronto), in which Americans had burned public and private buildings.[1] The British left Washington within two days, and the war ended a few months later, but it would take years to fix the wreckage.

The United States faced direct threats in the twentieth century as well. During World War I, Germans put mines in American waters, sinking a warship just off Long Island. In 1941, Japanese forces attacked Pearl Harbor, Hawaii (which was then a territory, not yet a state). During the following year, they invaded and occupied two islands in Alaska (also a territory at the time). Meanwhile, German submarines attacked throughout the Atlantic coastline, the Gulf of Mexico, and the Caribbean. Before the Allies organized convoys in mid-1942, the Germans had sunk 397 vessels.[2] The attacks came so close that people on the coast could hear blasts and see burning wrecks at night. Dead bodies washed up on beaches.

These cases make a point. Long before the twenty-first century war on terror, Americans had to worry about **national security**. This broad term refers to safety from external hazards to the nation's territory, sovereignty, and freedom of action, as well as to its people's lives and property.[3] National security is the most basic duty of government, because everything else hinges on it. In particular, it has always been the first object of **foreign policy**, the set of programs and principles directing the government's interactions with the rest of the world. Wars and other momentous actions beyond the nation's borders usually reflect the belief that national security is at stake. For years after the Gulf War of 1991, intelligence reports said that Iraqi dictator Saddam Hussein was developing chemical and biological weapons that could endanger Americans. In 2003, the United States invaded Iraq—and then learned that the reports had been wrong.

Foreign policy is more than defense against immediate threats. In fits and starts since the early twentieth century, the United States has also sought to advance democracy, economic freedom, and human rights.[4] These goals have national security implications because free countries are less likely than tyrannies to threaten the United States.

Whatever its motivation, foreign policy requires quiet deliberation and long-term planning. In the 1830s, Alexis de Tocqueville worried that the United States would fall short. "[I]n the control of society's foreign affairs, democratic governments do appear decidedly inferior to others. [A] democracy finds it difficult to coordinate the details of a great undertaking and carry it through with determination in spite of obstacles. It has little capacity for combining measures in secret and waiting patiently for the result."[5] Some would argue that the politics of foreign policy has confirmed Tocqueville's fears. A report of the Council on Foreign Relations, a nonpartisan research group, says that harsh politics quashes deliberation. "Democrats and Republicans are secluded in separate foxholes as they develop policy initiatives with little input from those in the opposing party. . . . Over time, the political game has overtaken the deliberative policy process, which results in a dumbing-down of policy."[6]

The United States also has great advantages. Its economic strength has enabled it to undertake tasks that no other country would try, such as the rebuilding of Europe after World War II. Although it has sometimes skimped on preparedness, as in the Depression era, U.S. armed forces have rebounded from repeated setbacks. American traditions of individualism and adaptability have given its citizen soldiers a major edge over forces from less flexible societies.[7]

National security—safety from external hazards to the nation's territory, sovereignty, and freedom of action, as well as to its people's lives and property.

Foreign policy—the programs and principles that direct the government's interactions with the rest of the world.

The issues of national security and foreign policy cover a range of political, military, and economic matters. Americans serve their country overseas in many ways—as combat soldiers, economists, farm experts, and physicians. To understand this complex field, we should first see how the nation's global role has developed over the years. Although the United States did not gain a central role in world affairs until the twentieth century, foreign affairs have been a key concern of the federal government from the very beginning, and even though they agree on the importance of foreign policy, political leaders have disagreed about the principles that should govern it. We shall also examine the institutions that develop and carry out foreign policy and try to protect national security.

A BRIEF HISTORY OF U.S. FOREIGN AND DEFENSE POLICIES

MAJOR ISSUE

- Was isolationism the American norm before World War II? How has national security policy changed during the war on terror?

Concern about international politics was present at the birth of the United States. The Declaration of Independence was in part a foreign policy document, aiming to justify rebellion and gain the support of other nations. The first paragraph addressed not the king but the rest of humankind: "To prove this, let facts be submitted to a candid world." After the Revolution, security concerns drove efforts to scrap the weak structure of the Articles of Confederation. Britain controlled the lands to the north, while Spain ruled Florida and lands to the west. Potential attacks from these countries made a potent case for a stronger national government. Accordingly, many of the *Federalist* essays focused on defense.[8] As the new constitutional order came into place, Americans continued to deliberate on the nation's place in the world.

From the Founding to the Twentieth Century

Some writers assume that **isolationism** soon became the American norm. They point to George Washington, who said in his 1796 Farewell Address that the United States should "steer clear of permanent alliances with any portion of the foreign world." But his point was that a new nation should avoid European disputes, not that it should shun other countries. He backed international trade, and he looked forward to the day when the United States would be strong enough to "choose peace or war, as our interest, guided by justice, shall counsel."[9] In the decades afterward, the United States faced tensions with France and Britain, including the War of 1812 and the "Quasi-War," a limited naval conflict with France in the late 1790s. In an 1823 message to Congress, President James Monroe spelled out what we know as the **Monroe Doctrine**, declaring a national policy to keep European powers from interfering further in the Western Hemisphere and reaffirming that the United States would stay out of European affairs.

From the Revolution to the Civil War, territorial expansion involved peaceful diplomacy, as in the Louisiana Purchase of 1803, and the use of force, as in the Mexican-American War of 1846–1848. Both were subject to serious deliberation, with members of Congress questioning whether the Constitution empowered the government to buy new territory or whether the United States had good cause to fight Mexico. In 1848, Abraham Lincoln was a member of the U.S. House, and he said that the war with Mexico was "unnecessarily and unconstitutionally commenced by the president."[10] Twelve of America's first 15 presidents had backgrounds in national security or foreign policy, having served as generals, secretaries of state, or diplomats.[11]

Isolationism—avoidance of involvement in international affairs.

Monroe Doctrine—President James Monroe's 1823 proclamation that North and South America should be closed to further European colonization and free from European interference over the continents' sovereign nations. It also stated that the United States would not interfere in European affairs.

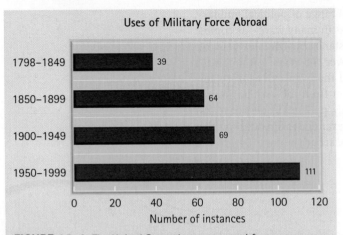

Uses of Military Force Abroad

	Number of instances
1798–1849	39
1850–1899	64
1900–1949	69
1950–1999	111

FIGURE 18–1 The United States has sent armed forces overseas on hundreds of occasions. This graph depicts these incidents by half-century. These data supply only a rough picture of American foreign involvement because they do not account for the size of the conflicts: World War II counts as much as a minor skirmish. Nevertheless, the numbers undercut the idea that the United States detached itself from the world before the middle of the twentieth century. Between 1999 and 2010, there were an additional 50 uses of force—more than in the first half-century of the country's existence.
SOURCE: Richard F. Grimmett, *Instances of Use of United States Armed Force Aboard, 1798–2010* (Washington: Congressional Research Service, March 20, 2011) at www.fas.org/sgp/crs/natsec/R41677.pdf assessed July 30, 2012

During the Civil War, Lincoln strove to avoid conflicts with European powers and to block diplomatic recognition of the Confederacy. In the aftermath of the Civil War, the United States stayed out of European affairs while expanding activities in Latin America and Asia. Even this "isolationist" period witnessed serious American activity, including the use of force (see Figure 18-1). The United States gained Alaska, Hawaii, Puerto Rico, Guam, and the Philippines, the last three through victory in the Spanish-American War of 1898. In the fall of 1905, President Theodore Roosevelt mediated the Russo-Japanese War, for which he won the Nobel Peace Prize. And the United States sent forces overseas—especially to the Caribbean and Central America—more often than the image of "isolation" would suggest.

World Wars and the Cold War

By the early twentieth century, the United States had become a major world economy. In 1917, it joined the fight against Germany in World War I, but after the war the Senate rejected U.S. participation in the League of Nations, which was a defeat for President Woodrow Wilson. Although some histories depict them as isolationist, many opponents of the League favored international engagement but worried that the treaty would threaten congressional war powers by committing the nation to defend other members. The United States did promote arbitration treaties, naval arms control, and even a pact to outlaw war.[12] For the most part, however, the United States stood aloof from major international developments.

Although Franklin D. Roosevelt ran for reelection in 1940 on the pledge to stay out of war, he knew that a Nazi victory in the European war that began in 1939 would endanger the United States. The president's dilemmas dissolved in December 1941, when Japan attacked Pearl Harbor and its German ally declared war on the United States. With an army of fewer than 200,000 soldiers, the United States was unready, but once on a war footing, the American economy soon put out huge quantities of weapons and supplies. American power was crucial to the 1945 victory over the fascist powers.

Despite rapid demobilization and a wrenching national debate over America's global role, the nation emerged as the leader of the world's liberal democracies. The Soviet Union was a continent-sized rival whose Marxist ideology opposed American ideals of liberty and equality. Unlike Adolf Hitler, Soviet leaders did not want war with the United States, but President Harry Truman argued that they did seek to impose their power over the world. The American response was a policy of **containment**. In this policy, the United States and its allies sought to build up their political, economic, and military strength to halt Soviet expansion and foster negotiations on favorable terms. In the long run, they hoped that thwarting expansionist aims would force political change within the Soviet Union.[13] The Cold War, this period of tension between the United States and the Soviet Union, would last for more than 40 years.

The Cold War was not the only issue in the decades following World War II, but for almost half a century the Soviet Union posed the greatest menace. The American–Soviet relationship was the hinge of world politics, often affecting other issues, such as the Arab-Israeli conflict and the decision to reopen relations with the People's Republic of China. Throughout the Cold War, the twin goals for the United States were to contain Soviet expansionism and to avoid nuclear war. To carry out these goals, Congress restructured much of the government. The biggest change came with the **National Security Act of 1947**, which created:

Containment—the policy of preventing further expansion of the Soviet Union's influence in the hope of fostering its eventual downfall.

National Security Act of 1947—a law that reorganized the foreign policy and military establishments after the Second World War. The act created the National Security Council (NSC), the Central Intelligence Agency (CIA), the United States Air Force, and the office of Secretary of Defense.

- the office of the secretary of defense, who would oversee the armed forces;
- the United States Air Force, previously the U.S. Army Air Forces, now a separate branch of the armed services;

- the Central Intelligence Agency (CIA), a civilian organization for the collection and evaluation of foreign intelligence to aid in foreign policy deliberation;
- the National Security Council, a body of key policymakers, which would use its own staff to coordinate federal agencies and offices dealing with foreign policy and defense and which would answer directly to the president.

In the name of containment, the United States waged two costly military interventions (Korea and Vietnam) and several lesser ones. It built a network of alliances and security arrangements. It kept up peacetime armed forces that were large by American historical standards, including a nuclear arsenal that cost up to $50 billion per year. It also fought the Soviet Union by proxy, giving military and financial aid to foreign forces resisting the Soviet Union and its allies. Several years after the 1979 Soviet invasion of Afghanistan, the United States provided crucial support to Afghan rebels in the form of money and weapons. The rebellion bled the Soviet Union's economy and compelled its forces to withdraw by 1989.

During this decade, the Soviet Union faced economic crisis. Under General Secretary Mikhail Gorbachev, it suddenly changed course, granting more freedom at home and easing its grip on subjugated nations. Peaceful revolutions in Poland and other Eastern European countries sped the breakup of the Soviet empire. In 1989, two years after President Reagan had stood at the Berlin Wall and challenged the Soviet leaders to tear it down, they opened its gates. At the end of 1991, the Soviet Union was officially dissolved and the Cold War ended. President Reagan's admirers say that the West's victory had stemmed from his military buildup and tough stance against Soviet expansionism. Others say that the Cold War ended because of Gorbachev's reforms and his country's internal weaknesses, and that Reagan policies had little to do with it.

Iraq and Terror

The year 1991 also brought the Gulf War, in which the United States and its allies reversed Iraq's invasion of Kuwait. Saddam Hussein retained control of Iraq, however, and in 1993, Kuwaiti authorities foiled an Iraqi attempt to kill former president George H. W. Bush with a car bomb while he was visiting Kuwait City. President Bill Clinton struck back by firing 23 cruise missiles at Iraqi targets. Meanwhile, knowing that Saddam had used chemical weapons and tried to develop nuclear bombs, the United Nations created a commission to inspect Iraqi weapons facilities. Saddam resisted the inspectors and finally stopped cooperating in 1998. President Clinton responded with air strikes. He warned that a failure to respond would mean a greater Iraqi threat: "Saddam will strike again at his neighbors. He will make war on his own people. And mark my words, he will develop weapons of mass destruction."[14] President Clinton signed a law committing the nation to seek Saddam's removal and the establishment of democracy in Iraq.[15]

After World War II, East Germany was a Communist dictatorship under Soviet domination, while West Germany became a free-market democracy. Within East Germany, the city of Berlin had two parts: West Berlin was an enclave with a West German government, and East Berlin belonged to East Germany. In 1961, East Germany built a wall around West Berlin, to keep East Germans from escaping to freedom. In 1987, President Reagan spoke in front of the Berlin Wall and challenged the Soviet leader: "Mr. Gorbachev, tear down this wall!" Reagan's remark was controversial at the time. House Speaker Jim Wright said that he "spoiled the chance for a dramatic breakthrough in relations between our two countries." Two years later, however, the Soviet Union finally let people cross freely, and in 1990, the former president lent a hand in tearing down the wall.

President Clinton's Iraq policy did not involve ground forces and cost no American lives. He was particularly reluctant to put troops at risk after a 1993 incident in which 18 Army Rangers had died in Somalia and mobs had dragged bodies through the streets. During the same decade, the United States took action in Haiti and Kosovo, with no American combat deaths. Meanwhile, the focus of public opinion moved inward. In a 2001 poll, only 3% cited a defense or international issue as the country's most important problem.[16] After titanic struggles against Nazism and Communism, national security seemed much less urgent.

Urgency returned on the morning of September 11, 2001. Hijackers belonging to the radical Islamic group al Qaeda took control of four commercial airliners. They crashed two of the planes into the twin towers of the World Trade Center in New York City; a third hit the Pentagon; a fourth went down in a Pennsylvania field after passengers fought back. In all, 2,986 people died, including the hijackers. Subsequent investigations revealed that al Qaeda and its leader, Osama bin Laden, had spent years setting up the attacks.

The war on terror now replaced containment as a guiding principle of foreign policy. Nine days after the attacks, President George W. Bush addressed Congress and issued a blunt warning to the world: "Either you are with us, or you are with the terrorists. From this day forward, any nation that continues to harbor or support terrorism will be regarded by the United States as a hostile regime."[17] On October 7, 2001, the United States made its first strike in Afghanistan, where al Qaeda had made its headquarters with the aid of an Islamist regime known as the Taliban. Working with local forces, the American military destroyed al Qaeda training camps and ousted the Taliban, although bin Laden got away. During a 2002 address, Bush said, "We must take the battle to the enemy, disrupt his plans, and confront the worst threats before they emerge."[18] Commentators often referred to this concept of **preemption** as the "Bush doctrine" (although they applied the title to several other ideas as well).[19] Critics argued that while early action might be justifiable to stop an imminent attack, this policy stretched the concept too far. One scholar wrote that other countries would cite it as "a cover for settling their own national security scores."[20]

Preemption—President George W. Bush's policy of taking military action against hostile regimes or groups to forestall attacks against the United States or its interests.

President Bush soon put the doctrine to work in Iraq. As they had been doing since the early 1990s, intelligence services reported that Saddam Hussein was developing weapons of mass destruction.[21] President Bush persuaded Congress to authorize the use of force. With the help of Britain and other countries, American forces invaded Iraq in March 2003.

Major combat ended within weeks. Although Iraq then made progress toward democracy, several developments turned the American public against the war. First, it soon became clear that the intelligence had been wrong: Any Iraqi weapons of mass destruction were long gone, and Saddam did not appear to be on the verge of getting new ones. Second, the Bush administration faced charges that it had manipulated the intelligence, selectively publicizing items that supported the case for war while ignoring cautions about the quality of the information and the likelihood of trouble in post-invasion Iraq.[22] Third, ongoing attacks by insurgents pushed the American body count far above the toll stemming from the March 2003 invasion itself.

A 2007 surge of military forces in Iraq reduced the violence and increased the chances that the United States could eventually withdraw combat forces without disaster. At the start of 2009, President Barack Obama said, in his inaugural

At Dover Air Force Base, Chaplain Col. Dennis Goodwin, left, directs a prayer over the transfer case containing the remains of a U.S. Army captain who died in Afghanistan.

AP Photo/Jose Luis Magana

address, that the United States would "begin to responsibly leave Iraq to its people."[23] He completed the withdrawal in December 2011.

While the new president changed course in Iraq, he maintained military efforts in Afghanistan and stressed that he would continue to fight terrorism. In his inaugural, he said, "Our nation is at war against a far-reaching network of violence and hatred. . . . We will not apologize for our way of life, nor will we waver in its defense. And for those who seek to advance their aims by inducing terror and slaughtering innocents, we say to you now that our spirit is stronger and cannot be broken—you cannot outlast us, and we will defeat you." Although the fighting in Afghanistan continued, he later announced plans for an eventual end to an American combat role. In the broader war on terror, the United States had a major victory on May 2, 2011, when American commandos killed Osama bin Laden in his Pakistan hideout.

**FOCUS
QUESTION**

What do you consider to be the overriding goals of American foreign policy in the second decade of the twenty-first century?

CONFLICTING TRADITIONS IN NATIONAL SECURITY
MAJOR ISSUE

- **What competing ideas and sentiments influence American foreign policy?**

Deliberations over Iraq policy showed conflicting strains of thought behind American foreign policy. As we shall now see, these strains of thought have been present for a long time.

Moralism versus Pragmatism

In the seventeenth century, colonists came to New England to escape religious persecution and create what John Winthrop called a "city on a hill." Eighteenth-century revolutionaries aimed at fulfilling the ideals of equality, liberty, and self-governance. Both experiences fostered "**American exceptionalism**"—in this context, the notion that Americans, more than other peoples, cherish morality in public affairs (see Chapter 4). In colonial days, this attitude baffled the British. After an adjustment in tea taxes failed to quiet the colonists, Benjamin Franklin wrote, "They have no idea that any people can act from any other principle than that of interest; and they believe that threepence in a pound of tea . . . is sufficient to overcome all the patriotism of an American."[24]

American exceptionalism includes two strains of moralism. The older of the two, stretching back to the country's early days, involves an aversion to the seamy side of international politics and a desire to defend the nation's way of life. Another strain, which emerged late in the nineteenth century, involves an idealistic desire to remake the world.[25] At the end of the First World War, President Wilson did not want simply to restore peace; he wanted to establish democracy and self-determination throughout Europe. Such moralism in foreign policy has taken on a distinctly religious tone. During the Allied invasion of Europe on June 6, 1944, President Franklin D. Roosevelt offered a prayer on the radio:

American exceptionalism—the idea that the United States is fundamentally different from other nations and that it places higher value on morality in its foreign relations.

> Almighty God: Our sons, pride of our Nation, this day have set upon a mighty endeavor, a struggle to preserve our Republic, our religion, and our civilization, and to set free a suffering humanity. . . . For these men are lately drawn from the ways of peace. They fight not for the lust of conquest. They fight to end conquest. They fight to liberate. They fight to let justice arise, and tolerance and good will among all Thy people. They yearn but for the end of battle, for their return to the haven of home.
>
> Some will never return. Embrace these, Father, and receive them, Thy heroic servants, into Thy kingdom.
>
> And for us at home—fathers, mothers, children, wives, sisters, and brothers of brave men overseas—whose thoughts and prayers are ever with them—help us, Almighty God, to rededicate ourselves in renewed faith in Thee in this hour of great sacrifice.[26]

Pragmatism—a practical focus on costs and benefits—tempers the force of idealism, the pursuit of higher goals. American presidents have often stepped back from righteous fights for which the nation was unprepared. During World War II, the United States may have aspired to protect democracy and religious freedom, but it also had to work with Soviet dictator Joseph Stalin. Soon after the war, the United States rearmed former enemies in the common struggle against Communist expansion, and during the Cold War, Americans worked with governments that fell short of democratic standards. Because the United States sets a high rhetorical standard, policies that seem morally suspect—collaboration with friendly dictators, misdeeds in wartime—trigger charges of hypocrisy. For example, President Obama pressed for democracy and the rule of law in Afghanistan. The American presence came under international criticism, though, when newspapers published photographs of American troops posing with the dismembered remains of Afghan insurgents. Secretary of Defense Leon Panetta said: "These days it takes only seconds—seconds for a picture, a photo, to suddenly become an international headline. And those headlines can impact the mission that we're engaged in. They can put your fellow service members at risk. They can hurt morale. They can damage our standing in the world, and they can cost lives."[27] Accordingly, as the International Perspectives box and Figure 18-2 show, much of the world takes a skeptical view of American influence.

These incidents, along with disagreements over American foreign policy, fuel disapproval of the United States in a number of countries. Yet in others, many people still see it as a force for good. One reason is foreign aid. Since the middle of the twentieth century, the United States has spent billions on economic and humanitarian assistance. Such programs have ranged from the Marshall Plan, which helped rebuild Europe after World War II, to relief for the victims of the 2011 tsunami in Japan. Both idealism and pragmatism have motivated this spending. On the one hand, American policymakers have genuinely wanted to help people in need. President Truman recalled the Marshall Plan: "Well, there wasn't anything selfish about it. We weren't trying to put anything over on people. We were in a position to keep people from starving and help them preserve their freedom and build up their countries, and that's what we did."[29] On the other hand, the goodwill resulting from foreign aid can serve the purposes of U.S. foreign policy. For instance, the Marshall Plan enhanced American stature in Europe, thereby containing Soviet influence.

As a percentage of national income, the U.S. government spends less on foreign aid than developed countries such as Norway and Sweden.[30] Even at such levels, U.S. foreign aid has drawn intense criticism for wastefulness. In 2009, Secretary of State Hillary Clinton made a striking admission about assistance to Africa: "I don't know where a lot of it ends up. . . . Fifty cents out of every dollar [is] not even in the pipeline to end up serving the people it should serve."[31]

American idealism and citizenship reach beyond official policy. Individual citizens, businesses, and voluntary organizations provide people in other countries with much more aid than the federal government.[32] Groups such as Catholic Relief Services, CARE (Committee for American Relief Everywhere), and Save the Children have helped millions in poor nations. American institutions of higher education give more in scholarships to students from developing countries than Australia, Norway, or Spain gives in official foreign aid.[33]

Military interventions have often had a humanitarian side. As a matter of official policy, the armed forces have helped many civilian populations, and so have individual Americans in uniform. Historian Stephen Ambrose put it well in his description of the world of 1945. In most places, he wrote, the sight of a 12-man squad of soldiers meant looting and destruction. "There was a single exception and that exception was a squad of 12 GIs. Wherever they were, in France, Italy, Belgium, Holland, even in Germany, even after September of 1945 in Japan, the sight of those 12 American teenagers meant cigarettes, candy, C-rations and freedom. We had sent the best of our young men halfway around the world, not to conquer, not to terrorize, but to liberate."[34] In recent decades, the nation has used the military for humanitarian purposes in such places as the former Yugoslavia, Somalia, and Haiti.

International Perspectives

Views of U.S. Influence in the World

A 2010–2011 BBC World Service poll of 27 countries found that views of the United States had improved significantly over the past four years, in part stemming from approval of President Obama. In 20 of the countries more people had a positive view than a negative view. Nevertheless, large numbers of people across the globe still thought that the United States has a negative influence. These results may have reflected a widespread belief that the United States looks out only for itself. In a 2012 international survey, respondents in most countries said that U.S. foreign policy did not take account of their countries' interests. In the United States, by contrast, 77% said that their government paid either a great deal or a fair amount of attention to the interests of other nations. And in 17 of the 20 countries surveyed, more than half disapproved of a major element of American antiterrorism policy: drone strikes targeting extremist leaders and groups in countries such as Pakistan, Yemen, and Somalia.[28]

CRITICAL THINKING
QUESTION

Why do some countries take a more positive view of the United States than others?

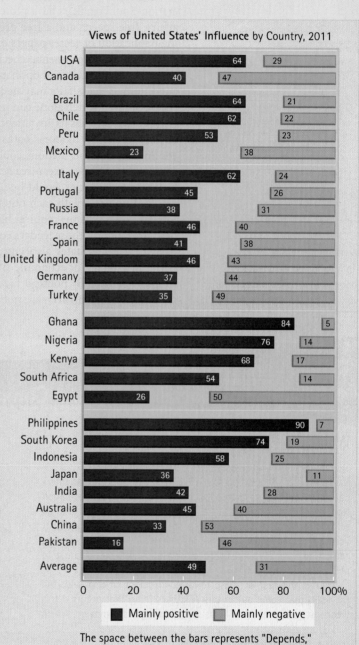

Views of United States' Influence by Country, 2011

Country	Mainly positive	Mainly negative
USA	64	29
Canada	40	47
Brazil	64	21
Chile	62	22
Peru	53	23
Mexico	23	38
Italy	62	24
Portugal	45	26
Russia	38	31
France	46	40
Spain	41	38
United Kingdom	46	43
Germany	37	44
Turkey	35	49
Ghana	84	5
Nigeria	76	14
Kenya	68	17
South Africa	54	14
Egypt	26	50
Philippines	90	7
South Korea	74	19
Indonesia	58	25
Japan	36	11
India	42	28
Australia	45	40
China	33	53
Pakistan	16	46
Average	49	31

■ Mainly positive   ■ Mainly negative

The space between the bars represents "Depends," "Neither/neutral," and "DK/NA."

FIGURE 18-2 Views of the United States were more positive than negative in 2011, but with large numbers expressing a negative view. SOURCE: From World Public Opinion. Reprinted with permission. BBC World Service, "View of US Continue to Improve in 2011, BBC Country Rating Poll." March 2011. www.worldpublicopinion.org/pipa/pdf/mar11/BBCEvalsUS_Mar11_rpt.pdf

Openness versus Secrecy

Voicing a typically American sentiment, President Wilson called for "open covenants of peace, openly arrived at."[35] Free-wheeling deliberation and the free flow of information are the lifeblood of democracy. Because democracies celebrate the "right to know," a free press must dig up information about public policy, including defense and foreign policy.

Openness in foreign affairs has some advantages. When more people take part in deliberations, policymakers have more information and hear more viewpoints. As in domestic affairs, free speech and a free press expose ineptitude and wrongdoing. In a case involving publication of secret papers on the Vietnam War, Justice Potter Stewart wrote, "In the absence of the governmental checks and balances present in other areas of our national life, the only effective restraint upon executive policy and power in the areas of national defense and international affairs may lie in an enlightened citizenry—in an informed and critical public opinion which alone can here protect the values of democratic government."[36]

Secrecy also has its advantages, which is why the government may require military and civilian personnel to swear oaths not to divulge confidential information. Justice Stewart continued that other nations could not deal with our government without confidentiality. "And within our own executive departments, the development of considered and intelligent international policies would be impossible if those charged with their formulation could not communicate with each other freely, frankly, and in confidence."[37] Deliberation about foreign policy options requires blunt assessments of foreign leaders, which officials would hesitate to offer if those leaders could soon read them.

The United States also engages in **covert operations**, secret attempts to influence political, military, or economic situations abroad. Covert operations may include financial support for friendly political factions and the quiet use of force against terrorists. Covert operations are controversial, not only because they are secret but also because they have

Covert operation—a secret attempt to influence political, military, or economic situations abroad, often involving the use of force.

IMPACT
of Social Media and Communications Technology

WikiLeaks

Several posts on the Bessette-Pitney blog (e.g., July 27, 2010; March 19, 2011) have discussed WikiLeaks (wikileaks.org), an international Web site that publishes private and classified information from a variety of sources. In mid-2010, WikiLeaks posted a large set of documents about the war in Afghanistan. In the fall of that year, it released many Iraq war documents and State Department cables. In April 2011, it started publishing secret files relating to prisoners at Guantánamo Bay.

After the first of these releases, President Obama said: "All the leaks that came out in this WikiLeaks thing that occurred this week just confirmed what I was saying during the campaign. Which was, from 2004 onward, Afghanistan was under resourced."[41] Later releases triggered a stronger reaction. In November 2010, the White House issued a statement:

> To be clear—such disclosures put at risk our diplomats, intelligence professionals, and people around the world who come to the United States for assistance in promoting democracy and open government. These documents also may include named individuals who in many cases live and work under oppressive regimes and who are trying to create more open and free societies. President Obama

supports responsible, accountable, and open government at home and around the world, but this reckless and dangerous action runs counter to that goal. By releasing stolen and classified documents, WikiLeaks has put at risk not only the cause of human rights but also the lives and work of these individuals.[42]

WikiLeaks paid a steep price for the disclosures. The governments of the United States and other countries took various actions against the organization. (Swedish authorities issued an arrest warrant for founder Julian Assange, albeit for an unrelated offense.) Companies such as Mastercard, Visa, and PayPal stopped doing business with WikiLeaks, severely reducing its flow of revenues.

CRITICAL THINKING

How can ordinary citizens appraise claims about the impact of the WikiLeaks disclosures? That is, if we do not have access to secret information, how can we know whether the leaks were as harmful as officials say?

often failed or backfired. Yet in testimony before a bipartisan commission on intelligence, witnesses said that "the United States should maintain a capability short of military action to achieve its objectives when diplomacy alone cannot do the job."[38] In his 2003 State of the Union Address, President George W. Bush alluded to the covert use of force: "All told, more than 3,000 suspected terrorists have been arrested in many countries. Many others have met a different fate. Let's put it this way—they are no longer a problem to the United States and our friends and allies."[39] President Obama took a direct hand in continuing this policy. In 2012, the *New York Times* reported on weekly counterterrorism meetings during which the president studied charts listing potential targets.

President Obama has placed himself at the helm of a top secret "nominations" process to designate terrorists for kill or capture, of which the capture part has become largely theoretical. He had vowed to align the fight against al Qaeda with American values; these charts, introducing people whose deaths he might soon be asked to order, have underscored just what a moral and legal conundrum this can be.

President Obama was the liberal law professor who campaigned against the Iraq war and torture, and then insisted on approving every new name on an expanding "kill list," poring over terrorist suspects' biographies on what one official calls the macabre "baseball cards" of an unconventional war. When a rare opportunity for a drone strike at a top terrorist arises, but his family is with him, it is the president who has reserved to himself the final moral calculation.[40]

Civilian Control versus Military Prestige

Experiences with British military power during the Revolution left Americans uneasy about military affairs. Anti-Federalists often attacked the Constitution for allowing standing armies in peacetime. Although the framers did not ban a standing army, Article I, Section 8 of the Constitution said that appropriations for the army could not exceed two years. There was less fear of misuse of sea power, so there were no barriers to multiyear budgeting for the navy.[43]

The military is subject to civilian control through the president's constitutional authority as commander in chief. Under federal law, no one may serve as secretary of defense within 10 years after leaving active duty as a military officer.[44] Congress has waived this provision only once, to allow George C. Marshall to serve as secretary of defense during the Korean War. His case was exceptional. Marshall, who was U.S. Army chief of staff during World War II, had already proved his civilian credentials as Truman's secretary of state. In 1953, he received the Nobel Peace Prize for the Marshall Plan, the effort to rebuild Europe after the war.

Yet while maintaining civilian control, Americans have given great respect and deference to the military. Since 1973, Gallup has

FOCUS QUESTION

In what ways did President Obama continue President Bush's national security policy? In what ways did he change it? Why?

During the 1960s, the U.S. government sought to destabilize or depose the Castro regime in Cuba. A U.S. Army document listed a variety of tactics for doing so. As this declassified excerpt suggests, some plans never made it off the drawing board.

asked Americans how much confidence they have in a variety of U.S. institutions. In 2012, respondents were most confident in the military (75%), which had placed first every year since 1989 except 1997, when it ranked slightly behind small business.[45] In reaction to complaints that civilian bureaucrats had second-guessed the military during the Vietnam War, recent administrations have given commanders more leeway to set strategy and tactics. Right after the Persian Gulf War, President George H. W. Bush said, "We would not have enjoyed such success if someone had tried to micromanage the war from Washington, DC."[46]

Munich versus Vietnam

At the 1938 Munich Conference, Britain and France tried to appease Hitler by giving in to his territorial demands. The effort backfired, leading to Nazi takeovers of Czechoslovakia and Poland. For future generations, *appeasement* became a dirty word, and the avoidance of "Munichs" became a goal of American foreign policy. Some policymakers cited the Munich analogy as a reason to pursue the Vietnam War.

As that conflict dragged on in the late 1960s and early 1970s, doubts about foreign policy activism grew among lawmakers, intellectuals, and ordinary citizens. The "Munich syndrome" did not disappear, but next to it now stood a "Vietnam syndrome," the fear that a new conflict would become long, bloody, and futile. Through the 1980s, the United States did use military force in Grenada, Panama, and other places, but the operations had limited duration and scope. In early 1991, the Persian Gulf War loomed as the largest conflict since Vietnam. During congressional debates, opponents of military action cited Vietnam while supporters cited Munich. A few months later, the fast and successful conclusion to the conflict appeared to quell the Vietnam syndrome. In 2001, the syndrome declined further with the initial victory of the Afghanistan campaign. Later in the decade, however, Vietnam analogies again became common as the Iraq conflict proved far more costly than policymakers had expected. Although the Afghan conflict did not involve nearly as many American deaths as the Vietnam War, it lasted even longer. In a 2011 poll, 58% agreed that "the war in Afghanistan has turned into a situation like the United States faced in the Vietnam War."[47]

Unilateralism versus Multilateralism

As we saw earlier, the United States was never completely isolationist. Instead, a strong tradition in its foreign policy was **unilateralism**—the practice of avoiding permanent alliances and acting independently of other nations.[48] This tradition was particularly strong through the early twentieth century and, among other things, helped defeat the League of Nations. With World War II and its aftermath, the United States started to embrace **multilateralism**—the practice of coordinating foreign policy with other countries on a long-term basis. Today, the United States takes part in some 300 international organizations, including the United Nations (UN), the North Atlantic Treaty Organization (NATO), the International Monetary Fund (IMF), the World Bank, and the World Trade Organization (WTO).[49]

Supporters of active U.S. involvement in world affairs dominate both parties, although serious disagreements exist over the extent to which the United States should rely on multilateral institutions. The basic dilemma is simple. On the one hand, policies in concert with other nations are more likely to appear legitimate, and such policies can lower costs and risks for the United States. On the other hand, it can be hard to reach agreements among many nations; collective decision making is always difficult and may limit the ability of the United States to act with a free hand.

In his 2004 State of the Union address, President Bush tried to resolve the dilemma by citing aspects of both traditions. "From the beginning, America has sought international support for operations in Afghanistan and Iraq, and we have gained much support." Then he drew a unilateralist line. "There is a difference, however, between leading a coalition of many nations, and submitting to the objections of a few. America will never seek a permission slip to defend the security of our people."[50] In his 2008 campaign, Barack Obama

FOCUS
QUESTION

How does the war in Afghanistan compare to the war in Vietnam? What are the similarities and differences?

Unilateralism—the practice of avoiding permanent alliances and acting independently of other nations.

Multilateralism—the practice of coordinating foreign policy with other countries on a long-term basis.

criticized the administration for stressing unilateralism over multilateralism and promised a new approach. In 2011, when he announced air strikes to protect Libyan civilians from dictator Moammar Kadafi, he said: "It is not an action that we will pursue alone. Indeed, our British and French allies and members of the Arab League have already committed to take a leadership role in the enforcement of this resolution, just as they were instrumental in pursuing it."[51]

ORGANIZATION AND COORDINATION IN THE EXECUTIVE BRANCH
MAJOR ISSUE

- Who makes foreign policy, and how do they organize their deliberations?

Americans have not only deliberated about the content of foreign policy but also about its processes. That is, we debate how administrations should plan and carry out their policies.

The President

The president is the key figure in foreign policy and national security. With the partial exception of war powers, presidential primacy has long had wide acceptance. As early as 1800, leading Federalist John Marshall, who would soon become secretary of state and later serve as chief justice, called the president "the sole organ of the nation in its external relations, and its sole representative with foreign nations."[52] Political rival Thomas Jefferson concurred, arguing that "the transaction of business with foreign nations is executive altogether."[53] Scholars agree that the increasing prominence of foreign affairs was a major cause of the growth of presidential power in the twentieth century. Presidential preeminence is evident in foreign policy doctrines bearing the names of Truman, Eisenhower, Nixon, Carter, Reagan, and Bush.[54]

Despite periods of divided government (different parties in control of the Congress and presidency) and the congressional activism of the post-Vietnam/Watergate period, presidents bring substantial assets to foreign policy decision making. As with executive powers more broadly, the president's role stems from the words of the Constitution and the president's own character and style.

Under the Constitution, Congress has the exclusive power of declaring war. Only five times has the United States fought under a congressional declaration of war: the War of 1812, the Mexican-American War, the Spanish-American War, World War I, and World War II.[55] On many other occasions, however, the president has used his constitutional power as commander in chief of the armed forces to wage military conflicts. As we saw in Chapter 13, after the withdrawal of American combat forces from Vietnam in 1973, Congress tried to curb presidential warmaking by passing the War Powers Resolution over President Nixon's veto. This law requires the president to consult with Congress "in every possible instance" before starting hostilities and to withdraw forces from combat within 60–90 days unless Congress approves. Nevertheless, presidents have continued to use military deployments and the threat of force as tools of foreign policy. And since 1973, Congress has specifically authorized the use of force on three occasions: the Persian Gulf War in 1991, the war on terror in 2001, and the Iraq War in 2002.

Presidents use their powers of appointment and treaty making, as well as their status as chief executive, to put their own stamp on foreign and defense policies.[56] Article II, Section 3 of the Constitution empowers the president to "receive Ambassadors and other public Ministers," which may seem merely ceremonial. According to a generally accepted interpretation, however, this power means that the president decides whether to recognize foreign governments after a revolution or regime change. More generally, it implies the power to define U.S. policy and run the day-to-day business of foreign affairs. Unlike Congress, the chief executive leads a bureaucracy that is responsible for defense and foreign affairs, and so has ready access to information. Unlike Congress, a single leader can act with dispatch, consistency, and secrecy, especially in a crisis.

The National Security Council

The secretaries of state and defense both belong to the National Security Council (NSC). The 1947 National Security Act created the NSC to harmonize foreign, economic, intelligence, and defense policy. Other members include the president and vice president, plus any other officials that the president names. Each member brings different organizational perspectives, with the secretary of defense representing the military, the secretary of state speaking for the diplomats, and so on. Presidents have often used NSC meetings to harness these clashing viewpoints into productive deliberation. As President Eisenhower said, "[T]he NSC debates never failed to give me a deeper understanding of questions. In several instances, I might add, such deliberations persuaded me to reverse some of my preconceived notions."[57]

National Security Adviser—the Assistant to the President for National Security Affairs, who runs the day-to-day operations of the National Security Council. Some advisers have confined themselves to coordination, whereas others have been forceful policy advocates.

The position of Assistant to the President for National Security Affairs—or **National Security Adviser**—began in 1951. The adviser's appointment is not subject to congressional approval and the adviser typically does not give congressional testimony. Advisers aid in White House deliberations by offering analyses that are free from agency interests. Dick Cheney, former White House chief of staff and future vice president, said in 1986 that the adviser "is in a position to bring to all the internal debate and controversy that's bound to reign between those departments the kind of broad, generalist view that only the president shares, and is vital to have."[58]

Civilian Departments and Agencies

The national security bureaucracy is as vast as the subject. Consider the Department of State. Contemporary secretaries of state like Colin Powell, under President George W. Bush, or Hillary Clinton, under President Obama, are typically distinguished individuals. The secretary's main job is to act as the president's principal adviser on foreign affairs. The secretary also leads the State Department bureaucracy, including embassies around the world and missions to international organizations. Most ambassadors are career diplomats, but presidents often give these jobs to people from outside the Department. Some of these appointments are rewards for political support (the Bahamas embassy is a plum assignment); others represent efforts to control the implementation of foreign policy. Presidents have frequently clashed with the State Department's career officials. In 2000, al Qaeda bombed an American naval vessel, the USS *Cole*, while it was in Yemen. President Clinton vowed to punish the bombers and specifically directed the FBI to investigate, but in the following year, the U.S. ambassador to Yemen barred the leader of the FBI team from returning to the country. The ambassador, a career diplomat, was reportedly engaged in a personal feud and a turf battle over the investigation.[59]

AP Photo/Sayyid Azim

Although some diplomatic jobs are glamorous, working in American embassies can be difficult and dangerous. On August 7, 1998, followers of Osama bin Laden bombed the U.S. embassies in Nairobi, Kenya, and Dar es Salaam, Tanzania, killing 258 people and injuring more than 5,000.

Some specialized foreign policy agencies have ties to the State Department, though they are independent of it. The U.S. Agency for International Development (USAID) runs nonmilitary aid programs. The National Endowment for Democracy (NED) supplies advice and assistance to newly democratizing states. NED focuses on the nuts and bolts of democratization, giving advice about such concrete matters as how to run elections or draft laws to protect freedom of the press.

Three cabinet departments, Commerce, Treasury, and Agriculture, frequently take part in international economic policy. The Treasury Department plays a central role in efforts to manage the global economy. Its Office of Terrorism and Financial Intelligence seeks to shut off the money flow to rogue nations, terrorists, money launderers, and drug traffickers.[60] Commerce works to promote American exports. Together with State and Defense, Commerce shares responsibility for reviewing export applications

TABLE 18-1   ACTIVE-DUTY MILITARY PERSONNEL AND EXPENDITURES

	Active-Duty Personnel	Defense Expenditures (in billions of 2005 dollars)
1970	3,064,760	465.1
1975	2,128,120	331.0
1980	2,050,627	331.7
1985	2,151,032	433.7
1990	2,043,705	462.4
1995	1,518,224	377.6
2000	1,384,338	362.0
2005	1,378,014	493.6
2010	1,430,985	610.0
2011	1,468,364	606.6

NOTE: After the end of the Cold War, defense spending and the ranks of the armed forces both shrank. In the early years of the twenty-first century, the war on terror and the Iraq war led to a large increase in spending but not in personnel.

SOURCE: "Active Duty Military Personnel 1940–2011," www.infoplease.com/ipa/A0004598.html; Department of Defense, "Active Duty Military Personnel Strengths by Regional Area and by Country (309a), September 30, 2010," http://siadapp.dmdc.osd.mil/personnel/MILITARY/history/hst1009.pdf, accessed August 30, 2012; U.S. Office of Management and Budget, *Budget of the United States Government, Fiscal Year 2012*, Historical Tables, www.whitehouse.gov/sites/default/files/omb/budget/fy2013/assets/hist08z8.xls, accessed July 27, 2012.

for technologies with both civilian and military applications. Defense officials routinely accuse Commerce of favoring exports over security needs. Commerce officials claim that restrictions are often pointless since firms from other Western countries would just step in and sell the same technologies. In 2002, Congress established the Department of Homeland Security. Its many diverse functions include safeguarding the nation against terrorist incidents (see Chapter 14 on bureaucracy).

The Military

Across the Potomac River in Arlington, Virginia, stands the Department of Defense (DOD) headquarters. The Pentagon covers 29 acres, with 17.5 miles of corridors and 23,000 employees. The DOD trains the nation's armed forces and, at the direction of the president and Congress, plans and carries out American military operations. It also maintains a global system of bases and a supporting network of communications and intelligence systems. As with secretaries of state, secretaries of defense often play a very important part in setting policy, either by virtue of their expertise or by dint of their close ties to the president.[61]

Aside from the Coast Guard, part of the Department of Homeland Security, the nation's armed services report to the secretary of defense. The U.S. Army is the largest of the armed services, with about half a million active-duty personnel (see Table 18-1). It defends the nation's land mass, fights the nation's wars overseas (most recently in Iraq and Afghanistan), and operates bases in dozens of countries.[62] Many active-duty officers are graduates of the U.S. Military Academy at West Point, New York.

The U.S. Navy operates around the world with 286 ships and more than 3,700 aircraft.[63] Most of the latter operate from aircraft carriers, which often sail to regions where dangerous situations loom or are under way. The U.S. Naval Academy at Annapolis, Maryland, provides the navy with many of its officers. The academy does the same for the U.S. Marine Corps, which is part of the Department of the Navy. The Corps places a unique emphasis on speed and maneuver. It maintains expeditionary forces ready to land on beaches and enables the United States to respond quickly to unfolding crises.

The U.S. Air Force defends the United States through control of air and space. It can deliver forces anywhere in less than 48 hours. In addition to combat, it carries out peace-keeping and humanitarian missions. The U.S. Air Force Academy is in Colorado Springs, Colorado.

Since the end of the draft in 1972, all members of the armed forces have been volunteers. In addition to those who make the military their main occupation, the armed forces can also tap the Reserves and National Guard. During normal times, members of both work in civilian jobs, committing one weekend a month and two weeks a year to training and service. Reservists are always under the president's authority. National Guard units normally serve under the command of state governors, but the president can call them into active national duty. When the president declares a national emergency, Reserve and Guard units may serve on active duty for up to two years. Many have fought in Iraq and Afghanistan, often more than once.

The conflicts in Iraq and Afghanistan are the latest reminders that serving in the military means accepting the risk of death (see Figure 18-3). War deaths are particularly tragic because they happen at such an early age. Over half the Americans who died in Iraq were under 25.

The Intelligence Community

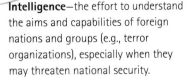

Intelligence—the effort to understand the aims and capabilities of foreign nations and groups (e.g., terror organizations), especially when they may threaten national security.

There is no single definition of foreign policy **intelligence**.[64] Among other things, intelligence seeks to understand the aims and capabilities of foreign nations and groups (e.g., terror organizations), especially when they may threaten national security.

When most people think of intelligence, they picture spies for the Central Intelligence Agency (CIA). Secret agents do supply the CIA with a good deal of information, and they sometimes use exotic devices, just as their Hollywood counterparts do. But much intelligence comes from other sources, especially now that so much information is available electronically. Many CIA employees do the unglamorous work of studying foreign language documents, news clips, and Web sites. According to one CIA analyst, "The world today abounds in open information to an extent unimaginable to intelligence officers of the Cold War. When the Soviet Union sent the first man into space in 1961, secretive officials revealed little and lied even about the location of the launch site. In contrast, television reports, Internet sites, and newspaper articles heralded China's first manned flight into orbit last year."[65]

The CIA is only one part of a much larger intelligence community. Altogether, intelligence agencies spend around $55 billion annually.[66] The biggest are the National Security Agency (NSA) and the National Reconnaissance Office (NRO). The NSA monitors foreign communications systems and handles code breaking. The NRO gathers and analyzes data from spy satellites. The State Department has its own

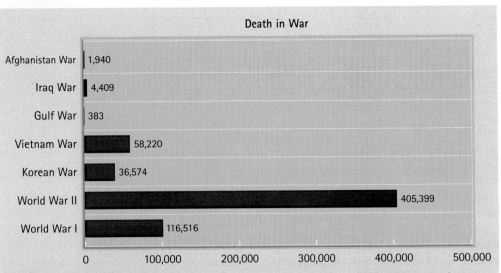

FIGURE 18-3 The figures include American service personnel who have died in major wars since the start of the twentieth century. Data are for combat and noncombat casualties. The Iraq and Afghanistan figures are for deaths as of July 30, 2012.

SOURCE: U.S. Department of Defense, "Principal Wars in Which the United States Participated: U.S. Military Personnel Serving and Casualties," siadapp.dmdc.osd.mil/personnel/CASUALTY/WCPRINICPAL.pdf; U.S. Department of Defense, "Casualty Status," July 30, 2012, www.defense.gov/news/casualty.pdf, accessed July 30, 2012.

intelligence branch, and each of the armed services has an intelligence arm in addition to the Defense Department's overarching Defense Intelligence Agency.

Deliberation about foreign policy depends on good intelligence. Sometimes, however, intelligence has been incomplete or wrong. Before Pearl Harbor, intelligence analysts received conflicting signals about Japanese aims, and they could not sort out true signs from false ones.[67] In 1950, the invasion of South Korea shocked American policymakers who did not think that North Korea would make such a move.[68] A greater shock came 51 years later, with the attacks on the Pentagon and the World Trade Center. In the months before September 11, 2001, different intelligence services had different hints of the terrorists' plans but could not assemble them into a coherent picture.

Yet another surprise came from Iraq. Before the 2003 invasion, the government assumed that Saddam Hussein had restarted his nuclear weapons program and was developing stockpiles of chemical and biological weapons. "All of this was based on the assessments of the U.S. Intelligence Community," a government commission observed. "And not one bit of it could be confirmed when the war was over." Although other nations also thought that Iraq had weapons of mass destruction, said the commission, "in the end it was the United States that put its credibility on the line, making this one of the most public—and most damaging—intelligence failures in recent American history."[69]

With both the 9/11 attacks and Iraq, failure had a variety of causes. One was bureaucratic. Comprising 17 government organizations, the intelligence community is hard to manage. According to the commission that studied the 9/11 attacks, "Information was not shared, sometimes inadvertently or because of legal misunderstandings. Analysis was not pooled. Effective operations were not launched. Often the handoffs of information were lost across the divide separating the foreign and domestic agencies of the government."[70] In the decade before the attacks, a dozen high-level studies had recommended reforms in intelligence and counterterrorism.[71] In 1999, the Hart-Rudman Commission made an unnerving forecast of what would happen two years later: "States, terrorists, and other disaffected groups will acquire weapons of mass destruction and mass disruption, and some will use them. Americans will likely die on American soil, possibly in large numbers."[72]

In 2004, Congress set up the Office of the Director of National Intelligence. The whole community would report to the director, who in turn could supply

Agents use the hollow container, which seems to be a silver dollar, to hide messages or film. And why does the CIA need a robot catfish? According to Dr. Donald Kerr, who was the CIA's deputy director for science and technology, "This is the kind of thing we might use when we think about how do you get a censored package or collect materials close to a source where you don't want to reveal your presence. And so we concealed the device as a fish; it moves in a quite realistic way."

the White House with comprehensive intelligence. The idea was that more coherent analysis would improve deliberation. Critics soon began to wonder. "Did 'the system work' on May 1, 2010, when Faisal Shahzad attempted to detonate explosives in Times Square?" asked the Bipartisan Policy Center. "Or was a lot of luck involved because of the plot's rushed nature?"[73]

Although the executive branch tends to dominate decisions about intelligence and other aspects of foreign policy, it hardly acts alone.

CONGRESS, COURTS, INTEREST GROUPS, AND PUBLIC OPINION

MAJOR ISSUE

- How should Congress, the courts, interest groups, and public opinion influence decisions on foreign policy and national security?

Few deny that the president has unique strengths in handling international crises, but not all power resides in the White House. Congress has its say in foreign policy, and both the president and the lawmakers must answer to the voters. Courts and interest groups also play a part in shaping decisions on foreign policy and national security. Presidents sometimes complain about these influences, but broad deliberation and accountability are essential because concentrated power invites abuse.

Congress

The Constitution gives Congress several powers that are relevant to the making of foreign policy.[74] The power of the purse enables lawmakers to determine what forces are available to the Defense Department and to keep the president from spending money on policies that Congress disapproves. In 1973, for example, Congress cut off funds for military operations in Southeast Asia, effectively ending American involvement there. Congress uses its power over foreign commerce because trade involves hundreds of billions of dollars and millions of jobs. Lawmakers often heed claims from business and labor groups who say that they suffer from other nations' trade practices. Congress as a whole (by simple majorities) must also approve multilateral trade agreements, such as the Central American Free Trade Agreement (CAFTA) or agreements under the World Trade Organization.

The Senate can also use its confirmation power to influence policy. For example, President George W. Bush could not overcome a Senate filibuster of John Bolton, his nominee for ambassador to the United Nations. Although he was able to grant Bolton a temporary recess appointment, the controversy was a clear sign that Senate Democrats were less willing to grant the president a free hand. Key senators sometimes hold up nominations as a way of influencing policy, either by killing the nomination outright or by wringing policy concessions from the president in exchange for approval.

The Senate also has a big role in foreign policy because of its treaty power.[75] Because treaties must gain the approval of two-thirds of attending senators, the Senate can kill treaties relatively easily.[76] Since the founding, though, more than 1,500 treaties have gained approval, and only 21 have failed in a Senate vote.[77] The numbers fail to tell the whole story, however. Some of the treaties that lost in the Senate have involved key issues, such as the League of Nations. In 1999, the Senate defeated U.S. participation in the Comprehensive Test Ban Treaty, a top priority for President Clinton.

The small number of treaties that have fallen in the Senate is also misleading because presidents seldom submit treaties likely to fail. President Jimmy Carter refrained from sending a major arms control treaty to the Senate, and President Bill Clinton did the same with the 1997 Global Warming Convention, because the treaties faced certain defeat.

The Senate has choices other than simply accepting or rejecting a treaty. It can attach amendments, which require new talks with the other signing nations. It can also pass reservations, understandings, or declarations. Such statements do not change the treaty itself and do not automatically trigger renegotiation, but they do shape American policy and the ways in which the government carries out the treaty.[78]

As we noted in Chapter 13, many agreements with foreign nations do not require formal treaties (and therefore approval by two-thirds of the Senate). The president makes some of these "executive agreements" on his own authority, and some the House and Senate subsequently approve by majority votes. In 1972, Congress passed the Case Act, which requires the secretary of state to provide Congress with the text of executive agreements.[79]

The Case Act was part of a congressional effort to reassert itself in foreign affairs. In the 1970s, Congress set out to balance the president's superior access to information, which had long provided a rationale for presidential primacy. Congress expanded its own support agencies; demanded more testimony from national security officials, including millions of pages of reports and answers to congressional inquiries; and more than doubled the number of staff available to congressional committees and individual lawmakers.

[LC-US262-8828]/Library of Congress

THE LAMB FROM THE SLAUGHTER.

On November 19, 1919, the Senate rejected the Treaty of Versailles and its provision for a League of Nations. The Treaty's chief Senate critic was Henry Cabot Lodge, chair of the Foreign Relations Committee. In this political cartoon, Lodge escorts the battered Treaty from the Senate Foreign Relations Committee.

By veto-proof majorities, Congress stopped all U.S. military activities in Southeast Asia (1973), imposed an arms embargo on Turkey in response to the Turkish invasion of Cyprus (1974), banned covert aid to anti-Communist factions in the civil war in Angola (1975–1976), prohibited U.S. aid to Contra rebels in Nicaragua (on and off from 1982), and imposed economic sanctions on South Africa over Reagan administration objections (1986). Congress also placed restrictions or mandates on broad ranges of policy—war powers, intelligence, and covert operations.

The presidency of George W. Bush confirmed what Alexander Hamilton wrote: "It is of the nature of war to increase the executive at the expense of the legislative authority."[80] Although many lawmakers became critical of the administration's handling of Iraq and the war on terror, they continued to finance these operations.

The basic picture was similar under the Obama administration. Rejecting the views of lawyers at the Pentagon and the Justice Department, the president decided that he had the power to conduct air operations in Libya without congressional authorization.[81] Opinion on Capitol Hill was divided, but Congress did not cut off funding. In the end, the Libyan rebels prevailed and killed Kadafi.

An even more basic issue is whether Congress deliberates properly about foreign policy. Lawmakers face multiple demands on their time, which distract them from studying international affairs. In the fall of 2002, the Bush administration provided Congress with a classified assessment of the evidence for weapons of mass destruction in Iraq. To see the 92-page document, senators and House members had to walk to a guarded vault in a Senate office building. They could not take notes or bring staff. At most, only six senators and few House members read beyond a five-page summary.[82] Had more lawmakers read the document itself, they might have raised more questions about its accuracy.

The sheer number of members of Congress is a problem for deliberation. John Hamre, undersecretary of defense from 1993 to 1997, testified before the Senate Appropriations Committee: "There are 54 members on the House Armed Services Committee. All of the energy of the leadership is devoted to running the committee. You cannot do deliberation with a committee of 50. Have you ever testified over there in front of them? By the time you get through the second row, boy, you have run out of good questions, but you have not run out of questions."[83]

Political polarization has also affected deliberation, for both good and ill. Sharp partisan disagreement encourages each side to lay out its reasoning and identify weaknesses in the other side's arguments. On the same day in May 2009, for instance, President Obama and former Vice President Cheney gave detailed speeches explaining their divergent viewpoints on terrorism. This long-range "debate" generated productive discussion about the treatment of terror suspects. Sometimes, however, the focus of discussion shifts away from the merits of public policy. A report by the Council on Foreign Relations says that the problem is less a matter of increased partisanship than "decreased deliberation and interaction between parties."[84] The Council emphasizes that the deliberation does not have to be passionless, but it must entail a genuine exchange of views. Instead, the Council and other critics contend, members of Congress too often attack one another on national security without actually debating the issues.

Courts

Federal courts are active in domestic affairs but have generally deferred to the other two branches in foreign affairs, especially during wartime. The Supreme Court did not interfere with Lincoln's exercise of war powers during the Civil War or the Roosevelt administration's removal of Japanese Americans from the west coast during World War II. The Supreme Court spurned challenges to the constitutionality of the Vietnam-era draft by denying standing to draftees, taxpayers, and others. The Court often invoked the doctrine of "political questions," saying that matters of national security belonged to the president and Congress.

The courts, however, have not been entirely passive. After the Civil War, the Supreme Court ruled in one case that Lincoln had pushed his powers beyond constitutional limits. And in the 1952 *Youngstown* case, the Court declared that President Truman's seizure of the steel mills was unconstitutional despite the administration's claim that an industry-wide strike threatened access to military equipment during the Korean War.[85] In the 1971 "Pentagon Papers" case, the Supreme Court voided efforts by the Justice Department to prevent the *New York Times* from publishing excerpts from a classified (and illegally leaked) Pentagon study of U.S. policy in Vietnam. It held that freedom of the press trumped national security claims, especially in a case involving prior restraint (i.e., prevention of publication).[86] In a 2004 case involving an American who allegedly fought for the Taliban, the Court ruled that he should have the chance to challenge his detention. Justice Sandra Day O'Connor wrote that "a state of war is not a blank check for the President when it comes to the rights of the Nation's citizens."[87] In three additional cases that grew out of the war on terror, the Court ruled against executive branch actions or policies (see Chapter 5).

Even when the executive and legislative branches battle over foreign policy powers, the courts hesitate to step in. In 1979, Senator Barry Goldwater filed suit against President Carter for cancelling the mutual defense treaty between the United States and Taiwan. Goldwater argued that just as the Senate must approve treaties, so it must agree to their abrogation. (The Constitution itself is silent on the question.) Various members of Congress later sued Presidents Reagan, Bush, and Clinton for violating the War Powers Resolution. In all of these cases, federal courts dismissed the suits, meaning that the judiciary would neither settle disputes over the law's application nor rule on its constitutionality.

A 1978 law established two special courts, the U.S. Foreign Intelligence Surveillance Court (FISC) and the U.S. Foreign Intelligence Surveillance Court of Review (Court of Review), composed of federal judges to evaluate applications for court orders authorizing electronic surveillance of those suspected of threatening national security. The idea behind the law was to strike a balance between civil liberties and the need for intelligence. In response to a 2005 news story that the National Security Agency had conducted wiretaps without FISC approval, Congress revised the law but left its basic structure in place. In any case, FISC has apparently not been a huge barrier to the executive branch. Since 1979, it has approved more than 99% of the applications presented by the intelligence community.[88]

Interest Groups

Do narrow interests shape foreign and defense policies at the expense of the national interest? Some contend that foreign governments and businesses exert undue influence on American public policy. (See Chapter 8 on interest groups.) Other targets of criticism include big domestic corporations, especially those in the military-industrial complex that President Eisenhower warned against. One difficulty in assessing the impact of American businesses is that these interests often point in the same direction as American strategic interests. Additionally, business is seldom monolithic. Exporting industries favor liberal trade policies, whereas those fearful of competition are protectionist.

If private interests do not control American foreign policy, business and other groups sometimes have considerable influence. In the long congressional fight over the extension of normal trade relations with China, lobbying by business was instrumental in securing victory over opponents of liberalized trade who stressed Beijing's human rights violations and its role in exporting missiles and materials for weapons of mass destruction. Ethnic lobbies representing Jews, African Americans, Armenians, Greeks, and Poles have also tried to sway American policy about regions of concern to these groups.

Many groups take part in foreign policy debates neither to make money nor to serve foreign interests. Rather, they have strong beliefs about the principles that should guide foreign policy. For instance, human rights organizations have left their mark. Laws now require annual State Department reports on human rights around the world and link some American foreign aid to human rights records. Some groups and individuals, such as the singer Bono, have argued on humanitarian grounds for relieving the debt burden of poor nations.[89] Others have argued with equal sincerity that debt relief will fail without economic reform.[90]

In light of the role of religion in American politics (see Chapter 4), it is not surprising that religious advocacy groups have long played a major part in foreign policy. A recent study of such groups found that more than three-quarters of them are involved in at least one international policy issue. More than half of the groups said they deal with international human rights in some way. Many others tackle such issues as international poverty, demilitarization, and religious freedom.[91]

Public Opinion and the Media

Except when American lives or interests are directly at stake, many people in the United States neither know nor care much about global affairs. In a 2009 international survey, for example, 62% of Americans could not identify the Kyoto Accords as a climate-change treaty, compared with just 20% of Finns and Danes, and 39% of Britons.[92] One reason for the lack of interest and understanding is that the media skip large parts of the globe in their reporting. In 1994, when genocide killed hundreds of thousands in Rwanda, the American media were slow to catch on. Meanwhile, events elsewhere preoccupied political leaders, resulting in little pressure to act. President Clinton later recalled, "With a few thousand troops and help from our allies, even making allowances for the time it would have taken to deploy them, we could have saved lives. The failure to try to stop Rwanda's tragedies became one of the greatest regrets of my presidency."[93]

The general public arguably does an uneven job of deliberating about foreign policy. Tocqueville wrote, "The people feel more strongly than they reason; and if present ills are great, it is to be feared that they will forget the greater evils that perhaps await them in case of defeat."[94] But the people do the fighting and dying in foreign wars, and although they might not know the details of foreign policy, one could make the case that they do have good judgment on broad issues.

As we discussed earlier, secrecy may cramp public deliberation on national security. Ordinary Americans cannot intelligently discuss whether the government is spending too much or too little on the National Security Agency because the figure is secret. In the months before the invasion of Iraq in 2003, the claim that Saddam Hussein was developing weapons of mass destruction rested on classified intelligence reports. As we have seen, these reports were flawed, but few people had a chance to see them. If more people had gained access to

TABLE 18-2	POLARIZATION ON FOREIGN POLICY

A Partisan Divide over Peace through Strength

	The best way to ensure peace is through military strength					
	1987	1992	1997	2002	2007	2012
Total	54	54	57	62	49	53
Republican	67	65	65	72	72	73
Democrat	50	51	56	55	40	44
Independent	50	48	54	62	46	52
Rep–Dem diff.	*+17*	*+14*	*+9*	*+17*	*+32*	*+29*

NOTE: Much more than in the 1990s, Republicans and Democrats disagree as to the value of military strength for ensuring peace.

SOURCE: Pew Research Center, American Values Survey Question Database, www.people-press.org/values-questions/q40p/best-way-to-ensure-peace-is-through-military-strength/#party, accessed July 29, 2012.

more information, would the outcome have been different? No one can say for sure, but the nation might have had more informed and thoughtful public debates on the issue.

Despite limits on public knowledge, presidents and lawmakers fret over polls, and certain foreign policy debates take place in the glare of public attention. Public opinion can be very important in wartime. The "rally effect" dominates in crises or in the early stages of military conflict, when the public tends to "rally around the flag" and back the president. Right after President Reagan launched an invasion of Grenada in 1983, Democratic leaders were highly critical, but in the face of apparent military success and polls showing strong support for the president, they quickly fell silent. Presidents know, however, that public opinion will sour if conflicts drag on and casualties mount. Growing disillusionment with Vietnam encouraged President Lyndon Johnson to halt the bombing of North Vietnam and President Richard Nixon to reduce U.S. involvement. Public disaffection emboldened congressional opponents of the war to sponsor more antiwar bills, which gained ever-larger vote counts after 1970. In the spring of 1973, as noted earlier, Congress stopped funding for U.S. combat operations in Southeast Asia. In May 2003, with the end of major combat in Iraq, 69% of Americans approved of President George W. Bush's handling of the situation there, compared with 26% who disapproved. But after five years and more than 3,000 American deaths, the numbers nearly reversed: in November 2008, 65% disapproved and only 32% approved.[95]

Opinion on foreign policy reflects partisan polarization. In a 2010 survey, 62% of Democrats thought that the United States should be more willing to make decisions within the United Nations even if this means that the United States will sometimes have to go along with a policy that is not its first choice. Just 35% of Republicans agreed.[96] For other differences, see Table 18-2.

From op-ed pieces, to blogs, to noisy marches, to full-page ads in newspapers, those seeking to shape national debates use the media to reach a broad audience. Opponents of the Iraq War used all of these methods on lawmakers who had supported the Bush policy. Although these activities did influence some House members and senators, they did not persuade the Bush administration to withdraw.

Americans are not the only ones to use the media. In the early 1960s, when Buddhist monks in South Vietnam burned themselves to protest the U.S.-backed government in Saigon, they made sure that American TV cameras were present and that protest signs were in English. In the six years after the American invasion of Iraq, violence claimed the lives of 139 reporters from several countries, more than the number who died during the Vietnam War.[97] One report indicated that the killers had deliberately targeted the victims in many cases.[98] By killing journalists, the insurgents ensured that their actions would get attention. Said one American officer, "Insurgents count on the media to carry their story."[99]

FOREIGN POLICY, NATIONAL SECURITY, AND DELIBERATIVE DEMOCRACY

To deliberate effectively, people must know what they are talking about. In this respect, the United States has serious challenges when it comes to foreign policy and national security. As the Myths and Misinformation feature suggests, there is much room for improvement in Americans' knowledge of foreign languages and cultures.

Several reasons may account for this shortcoming. Elementary and secondary schools may be doing an uneven job of teaching world history. Popular culture is part of the problem, too: whereas people in other countries routinely see American movies and television programs, most Americans see only home-grown fare. Americans lag in language skills, with only 9% able to speak both their native language and another language fluently. By contrast, a survey by the European Union shows that half of European citizens speak a second language. The highest rate of bilingualism was in Luxembourg, where 99% of respondents said they could master conversation in a second language.[100] Even though the Internet potentially enables anyone to get real-time news from international papers and news services, Americans have limited direct access to what people in other countries are saying and thinking. For the most part, they have to rely on English-language news sources, and as we see in the chapter on the mass media, American news organizations are slashing their international bureaus.

The shortage of language skills affects the operation of government. With too few Arabic speakers, the intelligence community had a long backlog of untranslated wiretaps of suspected al Qaeda members. On September 10, 2001, the National Security Agency intercepted al Qaeda messages saying "Tomorrow is zero hour" and "The match is about to begin." The translations did not take place until several days later.[106] These messages did not indicate the location or manner of the attack, so prompt translations would not have been enough to avert the disaster. But in combination with other bits of information, might they have provided important clues? Such questions nag the intelligence community.

Foreign travel is one possible remedy for such problems. The more time Americans spend abroad, the more opportunity they have to learn about other languages and cultures. Despite an encouraging upward trend, only a small percentage of college students do study

MYTHS AND MISINFORMATION

The Public and Foreign Policy

Polls have consistently shown that Americans have serious misunderstandings about world affairs. Some examples:

- In a 2011 survey presenting respondents with several different religious symbols, just 42% correctly identified the star and crescent with Islam.[101] In the same survey, only 38% named David Cameron as the British Prime Minister.
- In a 2005 poll, only 20% could name two of the countries (other than the United States) with troops in Iraq. (By comparison, 71% of Swiss respondents could do so.) In the same survey, only 18% could name the secretary-general of the United Nations (Kofi Annan at the time), compared with 76% of the Swiss.[102]
- In a 2006 National Geographic survey of young Americans, 63% could not find Iraq on a map of the Middle East. Three-quarters could not find Indonesia on a map, even after the 2004 tsunami.

Three-quarters thought that English is the world's most common native language, instead of Mandarin Chinese.[103]

Misunderstandings may make a difference in the public's preferences on foreign policy. A 2010 survey asked a sample of Americans to estimate how much of the federal budget goes to foreign aid. The median estimate was 25%, even though the actual figure—including both humanitarian and military assistance—was roughly 1%.[104] In 2003, a group of researchers conducted a "deliberative poll." They interviewed a sample of Americans and then invited the respondents to gather for a weekend. Respondents received balanced briefing materials on foreign policy issues, and then they met in small groups to deliberate about the issues. The deliberations had an impact on knowledge and attitudes. By the end of the weekend, most respondents knew how little of the budget goes to foreign aid, and support for increasing it went from 20% to 53%.[105]

abroad, and mostly for short durations. Members of Congress often go to other countries, but such trips may carry political risk: even with strong justification for the travel, political opponents may attack the lawmakers for vacationing at taxpayer expense.

Another problem for deliberation stems from excessive reliance on historical analogies that may not fit the situation. Before the 1991 Gulf War and the 2003 invasion of Iraq, supporters of the impending action likened Saddam Hussein to Hitler and warned of appeasement. Opponents raised the example of the Vietnam War. In future conflicts, no doubt, debaters will in turn draw comparisons to Iraq. "It is great for sound bites but it is completely misleading," said Jeffrey Record, a professor of strategy at the United States Air Force's Air War College. "Reasoning by historical analogy is inherently dangerous. It is especially dangerous in the hands of policymakers whose command of history is weak and who are pushing specific policy agendas."[107] Policymakers could use more sophisticated training in historical analysis. Rather than simply reach for the most convenient historical analogy, they should carefully weigh similarities and differences between problems of the present and the past.

Even if ordinary voters and high officials enhanced their deliberative abilities, however, the world of foreign policy and national security would still involve a great deal of uncertainty. For several years after the attacks of September 11, 2001, there were no major terror incidents on American soil. Did the absence of attacks result from the covert operations that President Bush had hinted at? Or were the terrorists merely lying low, meticulously planning even bigger murders? Officials with access to classified information might know the answer—or perhaps not. As the case of Iraq teaches, classified information can be dead wrong. It can also be incomplete. In 2002, Secretary of Defense Donald Rumsfeld said:

> Reports that say that something hasn't happened are always interesting to me, because as we know, there are known knowns; there are things we know we know. We also know there are known unknowns; that is to say we know there are some things we do not know. But there are also unknown unknowns—the ones we don't know we don't know. And if one looks throughout the history of our country and other free countries, it is the latter category that tend [sic] to be the difficult ones.[108]

As we have seen, one can make a case that deliberation may suffer as a result of conflict between parties and branches of government. Amid heated debate over the intervention in Libya, former Secretary of State James Baker and former Representative Lee Hamilton wrote: "With our country engaged in three critical military conflicts, the last thing that Congress and the White House should be doing is squabbling over which branch of government has the final authority to send American troops to war."[109] Scholars Benjamin Kleinerman and Vincent Phillip Muñoz took a different view:

> The presidency is designed for action. Congress is designed for deliberation. At times, presidential decisiveness will necessarily come into conflict with legislative deliberativeness. This need not trouble us. If a situation calls more for "energy" and speed, the president will likely win. If the situation calls for more deliberation and more circumspection, Congress will likely win. The struggle for constitutional authority, which Baker and Hamilton lament, is actually the healthy exercise of two different constitutional virtues—both of which need a hearing.[110]

AP Photo/Kenneth Lambert, File

Shortly after the attacks of September 11, 2001, someone sent envelopes of deadly anthrax to members of Congress. Marines took part in testing congressional buildings.

At times, thoughtful individuals have feared that the virtues of American democracy might prove fatal weaknesses in the face of international threats. First the Nazis, then the Soviets, could mobilize vast resources for militaristic purposes. Neither tolerated any opposition. Both used military force when and where they saw fit. No meddlesome legislature, courts, media, or public opinion hampered foreign policy or military operations. For that matter, no institutional constraints limited even the most ruthless of policies. Yet the totalitarian powers lost. Nazi Germany overreached, falling victim to flawed strategy borne of Hitler's madness. The Soviet challenge also failed, in large part because of the inherent flaws of Communism and the inability of the Soviet economy to keep up with that of the West.

In his inaugural address, President Obama struck a hopeful note about the nation's ability to prosper in a dangerous world:

> Recall that earlier generations faced down fascism and communism not just with missiles and tanks, but with sturdy alliances and enduring convictions. They understood that our power alone cannot protect us, nor does it entitle us to do as we please. Instead they knew that our power grows through its prudent use; our security emanates from the justness of our cause, the force of our example, the tempering qualities of humility and restraint.[111]

FOCUS QUESTION

The basic theme of this book has been that Americans believe in ideals greater than their own self-interests. How does this final chapter illustrate this theme?

SUMMARY

- Although Americans have sometimes had mixed feelings about involvement in international affairs, the United States has never been truly isolationist, and since the middle of the twentieth century, it has been one of the world's great powers.
- For many years, the Cold War dominated debates on foreign policy. In the past two decades, terrorism has emerged as a major concern.
- In part because of the nation's religious traditions, moralism has long been an important part of foreign policy thinking. But pragmatic concerns about the national interests have also shaped policy.
- The United States values openness and transparency, but these ideals often come into conflict with the need to keep military and diplomatic secrets.
- Under the Constitution and laws of the United States, civilians have the last word on national security, but the military's expertise and prestige give it important advantages.
- Two conflicting fears haunt deliberations on national security: the fear of appeasement ("the Munich

syndrome") and the fear of bloody military stalemate ("the Vietnam syndrome").
- The United States sometimes acts in concert with other nations (multilateralism) and sometimes acts alone (unilateralism).
- Presidents have traditionally taken the lead in foreign policy, and in recent decades they have been able to rely on an elaborate national security establishment stretching from the National Security Council on the White House grounds, to various civilian agencies, to American armed forces around the globe. They also count on the intelligence community for foreknowledge of world events, but intelligence has not always been correct.
- The Congress, the courts, interest groups, and public opinion all exert serious influence in this area. In deliberating about foreign policy, officials, activists, and ordinary citizens must draw on their stock of knowledge about world affairs. Too often, this stock has been skimpy.

KEY TERMS

American exceptionalism p. 539
Containment p. 536
Covert operation p. 542
Foreign policy p. 534
Intelligence p. 548

Isolationism p. 535
Monroe Doctrine p. 535
Multilateralism p. 544
National security p. 534
National Security Act of 1947 p. 536

National Security Adviser p. 546
Preemption p. 538
Unilateralism p. 544

TEST YOUR KNOWLEDGE

1. _____ refers to safety from external hazards to the nation's territory, sovereignty, and freedom of action, as well as to its people's lives and property.
   a. Containment
   b. Intelligence
   c. Multilateralism
   d. National security
   e. Unilateralism

2. The Declaration of Independence was a foreign policy document because it
   a. established the fundamental laws by which the government would design its foreign policy.
   b. outlined the plan for a new government.
   c. specifically requested military and financial support from other nations.
   d. addressed a national government.
   e. was intended to justify rebellion and gain the support of other nations.

3. The long period of tension between the United States and the former Soviet Union is known as
   a. détente.
   b. Russian expansion.
   c. the Cold War.
   d. the Gulf War.
   e. the Russo-American War.

4. The committee in the executive branch that advises the president on defense and foreign policy and coordinates government agencies on national security is called the
   a. Central Intelligence Committee.
   b. Department of Defense.
   c. Foreign Policy Advisory Committee.
   d. Homeland Security Council.
   e. National Security Council.

5. After the attacks of September 11, 2001, _____ replaced containment as the guiding principle of American foreign policy.
   a. exceptionalism
   b. isolationism
   c. multilateralism
   d. unilateralism
   e. the war on terror

6. A strain of American exceptionalism that emerged in the late-nineteenth century involves the desire to
   a. contain the expansionist tendencies of the Soviet Union.
   b. establish an international economic forum.
   c. prevent the dominance of other nations.
   d. remain independent of all international affairs.
   e. remake the world.

7. What limitations did the Constitution place on the army?
   a. A standing army was specifically prohibited.
   b. Army appropriations could not exceed two years.
   c. The army could only be called into action by state legislatures.
   d. The army should be entirely made up of volunteers.
   e. The size of the army was to be directly proportional to the size of the civilian population.

8. The fear that new conflicts could become long, bloody, and futile is often called
   a. American exceptionalism.
   b. isolationism.
   c. pragmatism.
   d. the Munich syndrome.
   e. the Vietnam syndrome.

9. The power to declare war belongs exclusively to
   a. Congress.
   b. the Joint Chiefs of Staff.
   c. the National Security Council.
   d. the president.
   e. the Supreme Court.

10. How can the president bypass the Senate's power over treaties?
   a. The president can negotiate executive agreements instead of treaties.
   b. The president can appeal to the Supreme Court to uphold a treaty without the consent of the Senate.
   c. The president can obtain a writ of consensus from the Senate before negotiating the treaty.
   d. The president can personally sign the treaty, in which case Senate approval is not necessary.
   e. The secretary of state can negotiate the treaty, which would not then be subject to Senate approval.

FURTHER READING

Commission on the Intelligence Capabilities of the United States Regarding Weapons of Mass Destruction. *Report to the President of the United States*, March 31, 2005, www.fas.org/irp/offdocs/wmdcomm.html.

Hanson, Victor Davis. *Carnage and Culture: Landmark Battles in the Rise of Western Power*. New York: Doubleday, 2001.

McDougall, Walter A. *Promised Land, Crusader State: The American Encounter with the World since 1776.* New York: Houghton Mifflin/Mariner Books, 1997.

National Commission on Terrorist Attacks upon the United States. *The 9/11 Commission Report,* July 22, 2004, www.9-11commission.gov/report/911Report_Ch11.htm.

Shane, Scott. "Secret 'Kill List' Proves a Test of Obama's Principles and Will." *New York Times,* May 29, 2012, www.nytimes.com/2012/05/29/world/obamas-leadership-in-war-on-al-qaeda.html.

Wohlstetter, Roberta. *Pearl Harbor: Warning and Decision.* Stanford, CA: Stanford University Press, 1962.

WEB SOURCES

Department of Defense: www.defense.gov—the official site of the U.S. Defense Department, gateway to a wealth of information on national security.

The National Security Archive: www.gwu.edu/~nsarchiv/—online access to historical documents.

Pew Global Attitudes Project: pewglobal.org—worldwide public opinion surveys.

United States Intelligence Community: www.intelligence.gov/index.shtml—links to the various agencies that gather foreign intelligence.

U.S. State Department: www.state.gov—the lead agency on foreign policy.

Appendix A

The Declaration of Independence

IN CONGRESS, JULY 4, 1776*

The unanimous Declaration of the thirteen united states of America

When in the Course of human events, it becomes necessary for one people to dissolve the political bands which have connected them with another, and to assume among the powers of the earth, the separate and equal station to which the Laws of Nature and of Nature's God entitle them, a decent respect to the opinions of mankind requires that they should declare the causes which impel them to the separation.

We hold these truths to be self-evident, that all men are created equal, that they are endowed by their Creator with certain unalienable Rights, that among these are Life, Liberty and the pursuit of Happiness.—That to secure these rights, Governments are instituted among Men, deriving their just powers from the consent of the governed,—That whenever any Form of Government becomes destructive of these ends, it is the Right of the People to alter or to abolish it, and to institute new Government, laying its foundation on such principles and organizing its powers in such form, as to them shall seem most likely to effect their Safety and Happiness. Prudence, indeed, will dictate that Governments long established should not be changed for light and transient causes; and accordingly all experience hath shewn, that mankind are more disposed to suffer, while evils are sufferable, than to right themselves by abolishing the forms to which they are accustomed. But when a long train of abuses and usurpations, pursuing invariably the same Object evinces a design to reduce them under absolute Despotism, it is their right, it is their duty, to throw off such Government, and to provide new Guards for their future security.—Such has been the patient sufferance of these Colonies; and such is now the necessity which constrains them to alter their former Systems of Government. The history of the present King of Great Britain is a history of repeated injuries and usurpations, all having in direct object the establishment of an absolute Tyranny over these States. To prove this, let Facts be submitted to a candid world.

He has refused his Assent to Laws, the most wholesome and necessary for the public good.

He has forbidden his Governors to pass Laws of immediate and pressing importance, unless suspended in their operation till his Assent should be obtained; and when so suspended, he has utterly neglected to attend to them.

---

* Early versions of the Declaration of Independence differ in capitalization and punctuation. This is the official version of the text maintained by the National Archives in Washington, DC. It is available at www.archives.gov/exhibits/charters/declaration_transcript.html.

He has refused to pass other Laws for the accommodation of large districts of people, unless those people would relinquish the right of Representation in the Legislature, a right inestimable to them and formidable to tyrants only.

He has called together legislative bodies at places unusual, uncomfortable, and distant from the depository of their public Records, for the sole purpose of fatiguing them into compliance with his measures.

He has dissolved Representative Houses repeatedly, for opposing with manly firmness his invasions on the rights of the people.

He has refused for a long time, after such dissolutions, to cause others to be elected; whereby the Legislative powers, incapable of Annihilation, have returned to the People at large for their exercise; the State remaining in the mean time exposed to all the dangers of invasion from without, and convulsions within.

He has endeavoured to prevent the population of these States; for that purpose obstructing the Laws for Naturalization of Foreigners; refusing to pass others to encourage their migrations hither, and raising the conditions of new Appropriations of Lands.

He has obstructed the Administration of Justice, by refusing his Assent to Laws for establishing Judiciary powers.

He has made Judges dependent on his Will alone, for the tenure of their offices, and the amount and payment of their salaries.

He has erected a multitude of New Offices, and sent hither swarms of Officers to harrass our people, and eat out their substance.

He has kept among us, in times of peace, Standing Armies without the Consent of our legislatures.

He has affected to render the Military independent of and superior to the Civil power.

He has combined with others to subject us to a jurisdiction foreign to our constitution, and unacknowledged by our laws; giving his Assent to their Acts of pretended Legislation:

For Quartering large bodies of armed troops among us:

For protecting them, by a mock Trial, from punishment for any Murders which they should commit on the Inhabitants of these States:

For cutting off our Trade with all parts of the world:

For imposing Taxes on us without our Consent:

For depriving us in many cases, of the benefits of Trial by Jury:

For transporting us beyond Seas to be tried for pretended offences

For abolishing the free System of English Laws in a neighbouring Province, establishing therein an Arbitrary government, and enlarging its Boundaries so as to render it at once an example and fit instrument for introducing the same absolute rule into these Colonies:

For taking away our Charters, abolishing our most valuable Laws, and altering fundamentally the Forms of our Governments:

For suspending our own Legislatures, and declaring themselves invested with power to legislate for us in all cases whatsoever.

He has abdicated Government here, by declaring us out of his Protection and waging War against us.

He has plundered our seas, ravaged our Coasts, burnt our towns, and destroyed the lives of our people.

He is at this time transporting large Armies of foreign Mercenaries to compleat the works of death, desolation and tyranny, already begun with circumstances of Cruelty & perfidy scarcely paralleled in the most barbarous ages, and totally unworthy the Head of a civilized nation.

He has constrained our fellow Citizens taken Captive on the high Seas to bear Arms against their Country, to become the executioners of their friends and Brethren, or to fall themselves by their Hands.

He has excited domestic insurrections amongst us, and has endeavoured to bring on the inhabitants of our frontiers, the merciless Indian Savages, whose known rule of warfare, is an undistinguished destruction of all ages, sexes and conditions.

In every stage of these Oppressions We have Petitioned for Redress in the most humble terms: Our repeated Petitions have been answered only by repeated injury. A Prince whose character is thus marked by every act which may define a Tyrant, is unfit to be the ruler of a free people.

Nor have We been wanting in attentions to our Brittish brethren. We have warned them from time to time of attempts by their legislature to extend an unwarrantable jurisdiction over us. We have reminded them of the circumstances of our emigration and settlement here. We have appealed to their native justice and magnanimity, and we have conjured them by the ties of our common kindred to disavow these usurpations, which, would inevitably interrupt our connections and correspondence. They too have been deaf to the voice of justice and of consanguinity. We must, therefore, acquiesce in the necessity, which denounces our Separation, and hold them, as we hold the rest of mankind, Enemies in War, in Peace Friends.

We, therefore, the Representatives of the united States of America, in General Congress, Assembled, appealing to the Supreme Judge of the world for the rectitude of our intentions, do, in the Name, and by Authority of the good People of these Colonies, solemnly publish and declare, That these United Colonies are, and of Right ought to be Free and Independent States; that they are Absolved from all Allegiance to the British Crown, and that all political connection between them and the State of Great Britain, is and ought to be totally dissolved; and that as Free and Independent States, they have full Power to levy War, conclude Peace, contract Alliances, establish Commerce, and to do all other Acts and Things which Independent States may of right do. And for the support of this Declaration, with a firm reliance on the protection of divine Providence, we mutually pledge to each other our Lives, our Fortunes and our sacred Honor.

John Hancock

Georgia

Button Gwinnett

Lyman Hall

George Walton

North Carolina

William Hooper

Joseph Hewes

John Penn

South Carolina

Edward Rutledge

Thomas Heyward, Jr.

Thomas Lynch, Jr.

Arthur Middleton

Maryland

Samuel Chase

William Paca

Thomas Stone

Charles Carroll of Carrollton

Virginia

George Wythe

Richard Henry Lee

Thomas Jefferson

Benjamin Harrison

Thomas Nelson, Jr.

Francis Lightfoot Lee

Carter Braxton

Pennsylvania

Robert Morris

Benjamin Rush

Benjamin Franklin

John Morton

George Clymer

James Smith

George Taylor

James Wilson

George Ross

Delaware

Caesar Rodney

George Read

Thomas McKean

New York

William Floyd

Philip Livingston

Francis Lewis

Lewis Morris

New Jersey

Richard Stockton

John Witherspoon

Francis Hopkinson

John Hart

Abraham Clark

New Hampshire

Josiah Bartlett

William Whipple

Matthew Thornton

Massachusetts

Samuel Adams

John Adams

Robert Treat Paine

Elbridge Gerry

Rhode Island

Stephen Hopkins

William Ellery

Connecticut

Roger Sherman

Samuel Huntington

William Williams

Oliver Wolcott

Appendix B

The Constitution of the United States*

We the People of the United States, in Order to form a more perfect Union, establish Justice, insure domestic Tranquility, provide for the common defence, promote the general Welfare, and secure the Blessings of Liberty to ourselves and our Posterity, do ordain and establish this Constitution for the United States of America.

ARTICLE. I.

Section. 1.

All legislative Powers herein granted shall be vested in a Congress of the United States, which shall consist of a Senate and House of Representatives.

Section. 2.

The House of Representatives shall be composed of Members chosen every second Year by the People of the several States, and the Electors in each State shall have the Qualifications requisite for Electors of the most numerous Branch of the State Legislature.

No Person shall be a Representative who shall not have attained to the Age of twenty five Years, and been seven Years a Citizen of the United States, and who shall not, when elected, be an Inhabitant of that State in which he shall be chosen.

[Representatives and direct Taxes shall be apportioned among the several States which may be included within this Union, according to their respective Numbers, which shall be determined by adding to the whole Number of free Persons, including those bound to Service for a Term of Years, and excluding Indians not taxed, three fifths of all other Persons.][1] The actual Enumeration shall be made within three Years after the first Meeting of the Congress of the United States, and within every subsequent Term of ten Years, in such Manner as they shall by Law direct. The Number of Representatives shall not exceed one for every thirty Thousand, but each State shall have at Least one Representative; and until such enumeration shall be made, the State of New Hampshire shall be entitled to chuse three, Massachusetts eight, Rhode-Island and Providence Plantations one, Connecticut five, New-York six, New Jersey four, Pennsylvania eight, Delaware one, Maryland six, Virginia ten, North Carolina five, South Carolina five, and Georgia three.

When vacancies happen in the Representation from any State, the Executive Authority thereof shall issue Writs of Election to fill such Vacancies.

The House of Representatives shall chuse their Speaker and other Officers; and shall have the sole Power of Impeachment.

---

* This is the official version of the Constitution—with the original capitalization, spelling, and punctuation—maintained by the National Archives in Washington, DC. It is available at www.archives.gov/exhibits/charters/constitution_transcript.html.
[1] Changed by Section 2 of the Fourteenth Amendment.

Section. 3.

The Senate of the United States shall be composed of two Senators from each State, [chosen by the Legislature thereof][2] for six Years; and each Senator shall have one Vote.

Immediately after they shall be assembled in Consequence of the first Election, they shall be divided as equally as may be into three Classes. The Seats of the Senators of the first Class shall be vacated at the Expiration of the second Year, of the second Class at the Expiration of the fourth Year, and of the third Class at the Expiration of the sixth Year, so that one third may be chosen every second Year; [and if Vacancies happen by Resignation, or otherwise, during the Recess of the Legislature of any State, the Executive thereof may make temporary Appointments until the next Meeting of the Legislature, which shall then fill such Vacancies.][3]

No Person shall be a Senator who shall not have attained to the Age of thirty Years, and been nine Years a Citizen of the United States, and who shall not, when elected, be an Inhabitant of that State for which he shall be chosen.

The Vice President of the United States shall be President of the Senate, but shall have no Vote, unless they be equally divided.

The Senate shall chuse their other Officers, and also a President pro tempore, in the Absence of the Vice President, or when he shall exercise the Office of President of the United States.

The Senate shall have the sole Power to try all Impeachments. When sitting for that Purpose, they shall be on Oath or Affirmation. When the President of the United States is tried, the Chief Justice shall preside: And no Person shall be convicted without the Concurrence of two thirds of the Members present.

Judgment in Cases of Impeachment shall not extend further than to removal from Office, and disqualification to hold and enjoy any Office of honor, Trust or Profit under the United States: but the Party convicted shall nevertheless be liable and subject to Indictment, Trial, Judgment and Punishment, according to Law.

Section. 4.

The Times, Places and Manner of holding Elections for Senators and Representatives, shall be prescribed in each State by the Legislature thereof; but the Congress may at any time by Law make or alter such Regulations, except as to the Places of chusing Senators.

The Congress shall assemble at least once in every Year, and such Meeting shall [be on the first Monday in December],[4] unless they shall by Law appoint a different Day.

Section. 5.

Each House shall be the Judge of the Elections, Returns and Qualifications of its own Members, and a Majority of each shall constitute a Quorum to do Business; but a smaller Number may adjourn from day to day, and may be authorized to compel the Attendance of absent Members, in such Manner, and under such Penalties as each House may provide.

Each House may determine the Rules of its Proceedings, punish its Members for disorderly Behaviour, and, with the Concurrence of two thirds, expel a Member.

Each House shall keep a Journal of its Proceedings, and from time to time publish the same, excepting such Parts as may in their Judgment require Secrecy; and the Yeas and Nays of the Members of either House on any question shall, at the Desire of one fifth of those Present, be entered on the Journal.

Neither House, during the Session of Congress, shall, without the Consent of the other, adjourn for more than three days, nor to any other Place than that in which the two Houses shall be sitting.

Section. 6.

The Senators and Representatives shall receive a Compensation for their Services, to be ascertained by Law, and paid out of the Treasury of the United States. They shall in all Cases,

---

[2] Changed by the Seventeenth Amendment.
[3] Changed by the Seventeenth Amendment.
[4] Changed by Section 2 of the Twentieth Amendment.

except Treason, Felony and Breach of the Peace, be privileged from Arrest during their Attendance at the Session of their respective Houses, and in going to and returning from the same; and for any Speech or Debate in either House, they shall not be questioned in any other Place.

No Senator or Representative shall, during the Time for which he was elected, be appointed to any civil Office under the Authority of the United States, which shall have been created, or the Emoluments whereof shall have been encreased during such time; and no Person holding any Office under the United States, shall be a Member of either House during his Continuance in Office.

Section. 7.

All Bills for raising Revenue shall originate in the House of Representatives; but the Senate may propose or concur with Amendments as on other Bills.

Every Bill which shall have passed the House of Representatives and the Senate, shall, before it become a Law, be presented to the President of the United States: If he approve he shall sign it, but if not he shall return it, with his Objections to that House in which it shall have originated, who shall enter the Objections at large on their Journal, and proceed to reconsider it. If after such Reconsideration two thirds of that House shall agree to pass the Bill, it shall be sent, together with the Objections, to the other House, by which it shall likewise be reconsidered, and if approved by two thirds of that House, it shall become a Law. But in all such Cases the Votes of both Houses shall be determined by yeas and Nays, and the Names of the Persons voting for and against the Bill shall be entered on the Journal of each House respectively. If any Bill shall not be returned by the President within ten Days (Sundays excepted) after it shall have been presented to him, the Same shall be a Law, in like Manner as if he had signed it, unless the Congress by their Adjournment prevent its Return, in which Case it shall not be a Law.

Every Order, Resolution, or Vote to which the Concurrence of the Senate and House of Representatives may be necessary (except on a question of Adjournment) shall be presented to the President of the United States; and before the Same shall take Effect, shall be approved by him, or being disapproved by him, shall be repassed by two thirds of the Senate and House of Representatives, according to the Rules and Limitations prescribed in the Case of a Bill.

Section. 8.

The Congress shall have Power To lay and collect Taxes, Duties, Imposts and Excises, to pay the Debts and provide for the common Defence and general Welfare of the United States; but all Duties, Imposts and Excises shall be uniform throughout the United States;

To borrow Money on the credit of the United States;

To regulate Commerce with foreign Nations, and among the several States, and with the Indian Tribes;

To establish an uniform Rule of Naturalization, and uniform Laws on the subject of Bankruptcies throughout the United States;

To coin Money, regulate the Value thereof, and of foreign Coin, and fix the Standard of Weights and Measures;

To provide for the Punishment of counterfeiting the Securities and current Coin of the United States;

To establish Post Offices and post Roads;

To promote the Progress of Science and useful Arts, by securing for limited Times to Authors and Inventors the exclusive Right to their respective Writings and Discoveries;

To constitute Tribunals inferior to the supreme Court;

To define and punish Piracies and Felonies committed on the high Seas, and Offences against the Law of Nations;

To declare War, grant Letters of Marque and Reprisal, and make Rules concerning Captures on Land and Water;

To raise and support Armies, but no Appropriation of Money to that Use shall be for a longer Term than two Years;

To provide and maintain a Navy;

To make Rules for the Government and Regulation of the land and naval Forces;

To provide for calling forth the Militia to execute the Laws of the Union, suppress Insurrections and repel Invasions;

To provide for organizing, arming, and disciplining, the Militia, and for governing such Part of them as may be employed in the Service of the United States, reserving to the States respectively, the Appointment of the Officers, and the Authority of training the Militia according to the discipline prescribed by Congress;

To exercise exclusive Legislation in all Cases whatsoever, over such District (not exceeding ten Miles square) as may, by Cession of particular States, and the Acceptance of Congress, become the Seat of the Government of the United States, and to exercise like Authority over all Places purchased by the Consent of the Legislature of the State in which the Same shall be, for the Erection of Forts, Magazines, Arsenals, dock-Yards, and other needful Buildings;—And

To make all Laws which shall be necessary and proper for carrying into Execution the foregoing Powers, and all other Powers vested by this Constitution in the Government of the United States, or in any Department or Officer thereof.

Section. 9.

The Migration or Importation of such Persons as any of the States now existing shall think proper to admit, shall not be prohibited by the Congress prior to the Year one thousand eight hundred and eight, but a Tax or duty may be imposed on such Importation, not exceeding ten dollars for each Person.

The Privilege of the Writ of Habeas Corpus shall not be suspended, unless when in Cases of Rebellion or Invasion the public Safety may require it.

No Bill of Attainder or ex post facto Law shall be passed.

[No Capitation, or other direct, Tax shall be laid, unless in Proportion to the Census or enumeration herein before directed to be taken.][5]

No Tax or Duty shall be laid on Articles exported from any State.

No Preference shall be given by any Regulation of Commerce or Revenue to the Ports of one State over those of another; nor shall Vessels bound to, or from, one State, be obliged to enter, clear, or pay Duties in another.

No Money shall be drawn from the Treasury, but in Consequence of Appropriations made by Law; and a regular Statement and Account of the Receipts and Expenditures of all public Money shall be published from time to time.

No Title of Nobility shall be granted by the United States: And no Person holding any Office of Profit or Trust under them, shall, without the Consent of the Congress, accept of any present, Emolument, Office, or Title, of any kind whatever, from any King, Prince, or foreign State.

Section. 10.

No State shall enter into any Treaty, Alliance, or Confederation; grant Letters of Marque and Reprisal; coin Money; emit Bills of Credit; make any Thing but gold and silver Coin a Tender in Payment of Debts; pass any Bill of Attainder, ex post facto Law, or Law impairing the Obligation of Contracts, or grant any Title of Nobility.

No State shall, without the Consent of the Congress, lay any Imposts or Duties on Imports or Exports, except what may be absolutely necessary for executing it's inspection Laws: and the net Produce of all Duties and Imposts, laid by any State on Imports or Exports, shall be for the Use of the Treasury of the United States; and all such Laws shall be subject to the Revision and Controul of the Congress.

No State shall, without the Consent of Congress, lay any Duty of Tonnage, keep Troops, or Ships of War in time of Peace, enter into any Agreement or Compact with another State, or with a foreign Power, or engage in War, unless actually invaded, or in such imminent Danger as will not admit of delay.

---

[5] Changed by the Sixteenth Amendment.

ARTICLE. II.

Section. 1.

The executive Power shall be vested in a President of the United States of America. He shall hold his Office during the Term of four Years, and, together with the Vice President, chosen for the same Term, be elected, as follows:

Each State shall appoint, in such Manner as the Legislature thereof may direct, a Number of Electors, equal to the whole Number of Senators and Representatives to which the State may be entitled in the Congress: but no Senator or Representative, or Person holding an Office of Trust or Profit under the United States, shall be appointed an Elector.

[The Electors shall meet in their respective States, and vote by Ballot for two Persons, of whom one at least shall not be an Inhabitant of the same State with themselves. And they shall make a List of all the Persons voted for, and of the Number of Votes for each; which List they shall sign and certify, and transmit sealed to the Seat of the Government of the United States, directed to the President of the Senate. The President of the Senate shall, in the Presence of the Senate and House of Representatives, open all the Certificates, and the Votes shall then be counted. The Person having the greatest Number of Votes shall be the President, if such Number be a Majority of the whole Number of Electors appointed; and if there be more than one who have such Majority, and have an equal Number of Votes, then the House of Representatives shall immediately chuse by Ballot one of them for President; and if no Person have a Majority, then from the five highest on the List the said House shall in like Manner chuse the President. But in chusing the President, the Votes shall be taken by States, the Representation from each State having one Vote; A quorum for this purpose shall consist of a Member or Members from two thirds of the States, and a Majority of all the States shall be necessary to a Choice. In every Case, after the Choice of the President, the Person having the greatest Number of Votes of the Electors shall be the Vice President. But if there should remain two or more who have equal Votes, the Senate shall chuse from them by Ballot the Vice President.][6]

The Congress may determine the Time of chusing the Electors, and the Day on which they shall give their Votes; which Day shall be the same throughout the United States.

No Person except a natural born Citizen, or a Citizen of the United States, at the time of the Adoption of this Constitution, shall be eligible to the Office of President; neither shall any Person be eligible to that Office who shall not have attained to the Age of thirty five Years, and been fourteen Years a Resident within the United States.

[In Case of the Removal of the President from Office, or of his Death, Resignation, or Inability to discharge the Powers and Duties of the said Office, the Same shall devolve on the Vice President, and the Congress may by Law provide for the Case of Removal, Death, Resignation or Inability, both of the President and Vice President, declaring what Officer shall then act as President, and such Officer shall act accordingly, until the Disability be removed, or a President shall be elected.][7]

The President shall, at stated Times, receive for his Services, a Compensation, which shall neither be increased nor diminished during the Period for which he shall have been elected, and he shall not receive within that Period any other Emolument from the United States, or any of them.

Before he enter on the Execution of his Office, he shall take the following Oath or Affirmation:—"I do solemnly swear (or affirm) that I will faithfully execute the Office of President of the United States, and will to the best of my Ability, preserve, protect and defend the Constitution of the United States."

Section. 2.

The President shall be Commander in Chief of the Army and Navy of the United States, and of the Militia of the several States, when called into the actual Service of the United States; he may require the Opinion, in writing, of the principal Officer in each of the executive

---

[6] Changed by the Twelfth Amendment.
[7] Changed by the Twenty-fifth Amendment.

Departments, upon any Subject relating to the Duties of their respective Offices, and he shall have Power to grant Reprieves and Pardons for Offences against the United States, except in Cases of Impeachment.

He shall have Power, by and with the Advice and Consent of the Senate, to make Treaties, provided two thirds of the Senators present concur; and he shall nominate, and by and with the Advice and Consent of the Senate, shall appoint Ambassadors, other public Ministers and Consuls, Judges of the supreme Court, and all other Officers of the United States, whose Appointments are not herein otherwise provided for, and which shall be established by Law: but the Congress may by Law vest the Appointment of such inferior Officers, as they think proper, in the President alone, in the Courts of Law, or in the Heads of Departments.

The President shall have Power to fill up all Vacancies that may happen during the Recess of the Senate, by granting Commissions which shall expire at the End of their next Session.

Section. 3.

He shall from time to time give to the Congress Information of the State of the Union, and recommend to their Consideration such Measures as he shall judge necessary and expedient; he may, on extraordinary Occasions, convene both Houses, or either of them, and in Case of Disagreement between them, with Respect to the Time of Adjournment, he may adjourn them to such Time as he shall think proper; he shall receive Ambassadors and other public Ministers; he shall take Care that the Laws be faithfully executed, and shall Commission all the Officers of the United States.

Section. 4.

The President, Vice President and all civil Officers of the United States, shall be removed from Office on Impeachment for, and Conviction of, Treason, Bribery, or other high Crimes and Misdemeanors.

ARTICLE. III.

Section. 1.

The judicial Power of the United States shall be vested in one supreme Court, and in such inferior Courts as the Congress may from time to time ordain and establish. The Judges, both of the supreme and inferior Courts, shall hold their Offices during good Behaviour, and shall, at stated Times, receive for their Services a Compensation, which shall not be diminished during their Continuance in Office.

Section. 2.

The judicial Power shall extend to all Cases, in Law and Equity, arising under this Constitution, the Laws of the United States, and Treaties made, or which shall be made, under their Authority;—to all Cases affecting Ambassadors, other public Ministers and Consuls;—to all Cases of admiralty and maritime Jurisdiction;—to Controversies to which the United States shall be a Party;—to Controversies between two or more States;—[between a State and Citizens of another State],[8]—between Citizens of different States,—between Citizens of the same State claiming Lands under Grants of different States, [and between a State, or the Citizens thereof, and foreign States, Citizens or Subjects.][9]

In all Cases affecting Ambassadors, other public Ministers and Consuls, and those in which a State shall be Party, the supreme Court shall have original Jurisdiction. In all the other Cases before mentioned, the supreme Court shall have appellate Jurisdiction, both as to Law and Fact, with such Exceptions, and under such Regulations as the Congress shall make.

The Trial of all Crimes, except in Cases of Impeachment, shall be by Jury; and such Trial shall be held in the State where the said Crimes shall have been committed; but when not committed within any State, the Trial shall be at such Place or Places as the Congress may by Law have directed.

---

[8] Changed by the Eleventh Amendment.
[9] Changed by the Eleventh Amendment.

Section. 3.

Treason against the United States, shall consist only in levying War against them, or in adhering to their Enemies, giving them Aid and Comfort. No Person shall be convicted of Treason unless on the Testimony of two Witnesses to the same overt Act, or on Confession in open Court.

The Congress shall have Power to declare the Punishment of Treason, but no Attainder of Treason shall work Corruption of Blood, or Forfeiture except during the Life of the Person attainted.

ARTICLE. IV.

Section. 1.

Full Faith and Credit shall be given in each State to the public Acts, Records, and judicial Proceedings of every other State. And the Congress may by general Laws prescribe the Manner in which such Acts, Records and Proceedings shall be proved, and the Effect thereof.

Section. 2.

The Citizens of each State shall be entitled to all Privileges and Immunities of Citizens in the several States.

A Person charged in any State with Treason, Felony, or other Crime, who shall flee from Justice, and be found in another State, shall on Demand of the executive Authority of the State from which he fled, be delivered up, to be removed to the State having Jurisdiction of the Crime.

[No Person held to Service or Labour in one State, under the Laws thereof, escaping into another, shall, in Consequence of any Law or Regulation therein, be discharged from such Service or Labour, but shall be delivered up on Claim of the Party to whom such Service or Labour may be due.][10]

Section. 3.

New States may be admitted by the Congress into this Union; but no new State shall be formed or erected within the Jurisdiction of any other State; nor any State be formed by the Junction of two or more States, or Parts of States, without the Consent of the Legislatures of the States concerned as well as of the Congress.

The Congress shall have Power to dispose of and make all needful Rules and Regulations respecting the Territory or other Property belonging to the United States; and nothing in this Constitution shall be so construed as to Prejudice any Claims of the United States, or of any particular State.

Section. 4.

The United States shall guarantee to every State in this Union a Republican Form of Government, and shall protect each of them against Invasion; and on Application of the Legislature, or of the Executive (when the Legislature cannot be convened), against domestic Violence.

ARTICLE. V.

The Congress, whenever two thirds of both Houses shall deem it necessary, shall propose Amendments to this Constitution, or, on the Application of the Legislatures of two thirds of the several States, shall call a Convention for proposing Amendments, which, in either Case, shall be valid to all Intents and Purposes, as Part of this Constitution, when ratified by the Legislatures of three fourths of the several States, or by Conventions in three fourths thereof, as the one or the other Mode of Ratification may be proposed by the Congress; Provided that no Amendment which may be made prior to the Year One thousand eight hundred and eight shall in any Manner affect the first and fourth Clauses in the Ninth Section of the first Article; and that no State, without its Consent, shall be deprived of its equal Suffrage in the Senate.

---

[10] Changed by the Thirteenth Amendment.

ARTICLE. VI.

All Debts contracted and Engagements entered into, before the Adoption of this Constitution, shall be as valid against the United States under this Constitution, as under the Confederation.

This Constitution, and the Laws of the United States which shall be made in Pursuance thereof; and all Treaties made, or which shall be made, under the Authority of the United States, shall be the supreme Law of the Land; and the Judges in every State shall be bound thereby, any Thing in the Constitution or Laws of any State to the Contrary notwithstanding.

The Senators and Representatives before mentioned, and the Members of the several State Legislatures, and all executive and judicial Officers, both of the United States and of the several States, shall be bound by Oath or Affirmation, to support this Constitution; but no religious Test shall ever be required as a Qualification to any Office or public Trust under the United States.

ARTICLE. VII.

The Ratification of the Conventions of nine States, shall be sufficient for the Establishment of this Constitution between the States so ratifying the Same.

Attest William Jackson Secretary

Done in Convention by the Unanimous Consent of the States present the Seventeenth Day of September in the Year of our Lord one thousand seven hundred and Eighty seven and of the Independence of the United States of America the Twelfth In witness whereof We have hereunto subscribed our Names,

G. Washington
Presidt and deputy from Virginia

Delaware
Geo: Read
Gunning Bedford jun
John Dickinson
Richard Bassett
Jaco: Broom

Maryland
James McHenry
Dan of St Thos. Jenifer
Danl. Carroll

Virginia
John Blair
James Madison Jr.

North Carolina
Wm. Blount
Richd. Dobbs Spaight
Hu Williamson

South Carolina
J. Rutledge
Charles Cotesworth Pinckney
Charles Pinckney
Pierce Butler

Georgia
William Few
Abr Baldwin

New Hampshire
John Langdon
Nicholas Gilman

Massachusetts
Nathaniel Gorham
Rufus King

Connecticut
Wm. Saml. Johnson
Roger Sherman

New York
Alexander Hamilton

New Jersey
Wil: Livingston
David Brearley
Wm. Paterson
Jona: Dayton

Pennsylvania
B Franklin
Thomas Mifflin
Robt. Morris
Geo. Clymer
Thos. FitzSimons
Jared Ingersoll
James Wilson
Gouv Morris

AMENDMENTS TO THE CONSTITUTION OF THE UNITED STATES

Amendment I (1791)

Congress shall make no law respecting an establishment of religion, or prohibiting the free exercise thereof; or abridging the freedom of speech, or of the press; or the right of the people peaceably to assemble, and to petition the government for a redress of grievances.

Amendment II (1791)

A well regulated militia, being necessary to the security of a free state, the right of the people to keep and bear arms, shall not be infringed.

Amendment III (1791)

No soldier shall, in time of peace be quartered in any house, without the consent of the owner, nor in time of war, but in a manner to be prescribed by law.

Amendment IV (1791)

The right of the people to be secure in their persons, houses, papers, and effects, against unreasonable searches and seizures, shall not be violated, and no warrants shall issue, but upon probable cause, supported by oath or affirmation, and particularly describing the place to be searched, and the persons or things to be seized.

Amendment V (1791)

No person shall be held to answer for a capital, or otherwise infamous crime, unless on a presentment or indictment of a grand jury, except in cases arising in the land or naval forces, or in the militia, when in actual service in time of war or public danger; nor shall any person be subject for the same offense to be twice put in jeopardy of life or limb; nor shall be compelled in any criminal case to be a witness against himself, nor be deprived of life, liberty, or property, without due process of law; nor shall private property be taken for public use, without just compensation.

Amendment VI (1791)

In all criminal prosecutions, the accused shall enjoy the right to a speedy and public trial, by an impartial jury of the state and district wherein the crime shall have been committed, which district shall have been previously ascertained by law, and to be informed of the nature and cause of the accusation; to be confronted with the witnesses against him; to have compulsory process for obtaining witnesses in his favor, and to have the assistance of counsel for his defense.

Amendment VII (1791)

In suits at common law, where the value in controversy shall exceed twenty dollars, the right of trial by jury shall be preserved, and no fact tried by a jury, shall be otherwise reexamined in any court of the United States, than according to the rules of the common law.

Amendment VIII (1791)

Excessive bail shall not be required, nor excessive fines imposed, nor cruel and unusual punishments inflicted.

Amendment IX (1791)

The enumeration in the Constitution, of certain rights, shall not be construed to deny or disparage others retained by the people.

Amendment X (1791)

The powers not delegated to the United States by the Constitution, nor prohibited by it to the states, are reserved to the states respectively, or to the people.

Amendment XI (1795)

The judicial power of the United States shall not be construed to extend to any suit in law or equity, commenced or prosecuted against one of the United States by citizens of another state, or by citizens or subjects of any foreign state.

Amendment XII (1804)

The electors shall meet in their respective states and vote by ballot for President and Vice-President, one of whom, at least, shall not be an inhabitant of the same state with themselves; they shall name in their ballots the person voted for as President, and in distinct ballots the person voted for as Vice-President, and they shall make distinct lists of all persons voted for as President, and of all persons voted for as Vice-President, and of the number of votes for each, which lists they shall sign and certify, and transmit sealed to the seat of the government of the United States, directed to the President of the Senate;—The President of the Senate shall, in the presence of the Senate and House of Representatives, open all the certificates and the votes shall then be counted;—the person having the greatest number of votes for President, shall be the President, if such number be a majority of the whole number of electors appointed; and if no person have such majority, then from the persons having the highest numbers not exceeding three on the list of those voted for as President, the House of Representatives shall choose immediately, by ballot, the President. But in choosing the President, the votes shall be taken by states, the representation from each state having one vote; a quorum for this purpose shall consist of a member or members from two-thirds of the states, and a majority of all the states shall be necessary to a choice. [And if the House of Representatives shall not choose a President whenever the right of choice shall devolve upon them, before the fourth day of March next following, then the Vice-President shall act as President, as in the case of the death or other constitutional disability of the President.][11] The person having the greatest number of votes as Vice-President, shall be the Vice-President, if such number be a majority of the whole number of electors appointed, and if no person have a majority, then from the two highest numbers on the list, the Senate shall choose the Vice-President; a quorum for the purpose shall consist of two-thirds of the whole number of Senators, and a majority of the whole number shall be necessary to a choice. But no person constitutionally ineligible to the office of President shall be eligible to that of Vice-President of the United States.

Amendment XIII (1865)

Section 1.
Neither slavery nor involuntary servitude, except as a punishment for crime whereof the party shall have been duly convicted, shall exist within the United States, or any place subject to their jurisdiction.

Section 2.
Congress shall have power to enforce this article by appropriate legislation.

---

[11] Superseded by Section 3 of the Twentieth Amendment.

Amendment XIV (1868)

Section 1.

All persons born or naturalized in the United States, and subject to the jurisdiction thereof, are citizens of the United States and of the state wherein they reside. No state shall make or enforce any law which shall abridge the privileges or immunities of citizens of the United States; nor shall any state deprive any person of life, liberty, or property, without due process of law; nor deny to any person within its jurisdiction the equal protection of the laws.

Section 2.

Representatives shall be apportioned among the several states according to their respective numbers, counting the whole number of persons in each state, excluding Indians not taxed. But when the right to vote at any election for the choice of electors for President and Vice President of the United States, Representatives in Congress, the executive and judicial officers of a state, or the members of the legislature thereof, is denied to any of the male inhabitants of such state, being twenty-one years of age, and citizens of the United States, or in any way abridged, except for participation in rebellion, or other crime, the basis of representation therein shall be reduced in the proportion which the number of such male citizens shall bear to the whole number of male citizens twenty-one years of age in such state.

Section 3.

No person shall be a Senator or Representative in Congress, or elector of President and Vice President, or hold any office, civil or military, under the United States, or under any state, who, having previously taken an oath, as a member of Congress, or as an officer of the United States, or as a member of any state legislature, or as an executive or judicial officer of any state, to support the Constitution of the United States, shall have engaged in insurrection or rebellion against the same, or given aid or comfort to the enemies thereof. But Congress may by a vote of two-thirds of each House, remove such disability.

Section 4.

The validity of the public debt of the United States, authorized by law, including debts incurred for payment of pensions and bounties for services in suppressing insurrection or rebellion, shall not be questioned. But neither the United States nor any state shall assume or pay any debt or obligation incurred in aid of insurrection or rebellion against the United States, or any claim for the loss or emancipation of any slave; but all such debts, obligations and claims shall be held illegal and void.

Section 5.

The Congress shall have power to enforce, by appropriate legislation, the provisions of this article.

Amendment XV (1870)

Section 1.

The right of citizens of the United States to vote shall not be denied or abridged by the United States or by any state on account of race, color, or previous condition of servitude.

Section 2.

The Congress shall have power to enforce this article by appropriate legislation.

Amendment XVI (1913)

The Congress shall have power to lay and collect taxes on incomes, from whatever source derived, without apportionment among the several states, and without regard to any census of enumeration.

Amendment XVII (1913)

The Senate of the United States shall be composed of two Senators from each state, elected by the people thereof, for six years; and each Senator shall have one vote. The electors in each state shall have the qualifications requisite for electors of the most numerous branch of the state legislatures.

When vacancies happen in the representation of any state in the Senate, the executive authority of such state shall issue writs of election to fill such vacancies: Provided, that the legislature of any state may empower the executive thereof to make temporary appointments until the people fill the vacancies by election as the legislature may direct.

This amendment shall not be so construed as to affect the election or term of any Senator chosen before it becomes valid as part of the Constitution.

Amendment XVIII (1919)

[**Section 1.**

After one year from the ratification of this article the manufacture, sale, or transportation of intoxicating liquors within, the importation thereof into, or the exportation thereof from the United States and all territory subject to the jurisdiction thereof for beverage purposes is hereby prohibited.

Section 2.

The Congress and the several states shall have concurrent power to enforce this article by appropriate legislation.

Section 3.

This article shall be inoperative unless it shall have been ratified as an amendment to the Constitution by the legislatures of the several states, as provided in the Constitution, within seven years from the date of the submission hereof to the states by the Congress.][12]

Amendment XIX (1920)

The right of citizens of the United States to vote shall not be denied or abridged by the United States or by any state on account of sex.

Congress shall have power to enforce this article by appropriate legislation.

Amendment XX (1933)

Section 1.

The terms of the President and Vice President shall end at noon on the 20th day of January, and the terms of Senators and Representatives at noon on the 3d day of January, of the years in which such terms would have ended if this article had not been ratified; and the terms of their successors shall then begin.

Section 2.

The Congress shall assemble at least once in every year, and such meeting shall begin at noon on the 3d day of January, unless they shall by law appoint a different day.

Section 3.

If, at the time fixed for the beginning of the term of the President, the President elect shall have died, the Vice President elect shall become President. If a President shall not have been chosen before the time fixed for the beginning of his term, or if the President elect shall have failed to qualify, then the Vice President elect shall act as President until a President shall have qualified; and the Congress may by law provide for the case wherein neither a President elect nor a Vice President elect shall have qualified, declaring who shall then act as President, or the manner in which one who is to act shall be selected, and such person shall act accordingly until a President or Vice President shall have qualified.

Section 4.

The Congress may by law provide for the case of the death of any of the persons from whom the House of Representatives may choose a President whenever the right of choice shall

---

[12] Repealed by the Twenty-first Amendment.

have devolved upon them, and for the case of the death of any of the persons from whom the Senate may choose a Vice President whenever the right of choice shall have devolved upon them.

Section 5.
Sections 1 and 2 shall take effect on the 15th day of October following the ratification of this article.

Section 6.
This article shall be inoperative unless it shall have been ratified as an amendment to the Constitution by the legislatures of three-fourths of the several states within seven years from the date of its submission.

Amendment XXI (1933)

Section 1.
The eighteenth article of amendment to the Constitution of the United States is hereby repealed.

Section 2.
The transportation or importation into any state, territory, or possession of the United States for delivery or use therein of intoxicating liquors, in violation of the laws thereof, is hereby prohibited.

Section 3.
This article shall be inoperative unless it shall have been ratified as an amendment to the Constitution by conventions in the several states, as provided in the Constitution, within seven years from the date of the submission hereof to the states by the Congress.

Amendment XXII (1951)

Section 1.
No person shall be elected to the office of the President more than twice, and no person who has held the office of President, or acted as President, for more than two years of a term to which some other person was elected President shall be elected to the office of the President more than once. But this article shall not apply to any person holding the office of President when this article was proposed by the Congress, and shall not prevent any person who may be holding the office of President, or acting as President, during the term within which this article becomes operative from holding the office of President or acting as President during the remainder of such term.

Section 2.
This article shall be inoperative unless it shall have been ratified as an amendment to the Constitution by the legislatures of three-fourths of the several states within seven years from the date of its submission to the states by the Congress.

Amendment XXIII (1961)

Section 1.
The District constituting the seat of government of the United States shall appoint in such manner as the Congress may direct:

A number of electors of President and Vice President equal to the whole number of Senators and Representatives in Congress to which the District would be entitled if it were a state, but in no event more than the least populous state; they shall be in addition to those appointed by the states, but they shall be considered, for the purposes of the election of President and Vice President, to be electors appointed by a state; and they shall meet in the District and perform such duties as provided by the twelfth article of amendment.

Section 2.
The Congress shall have power to enforce this article by appropriate legislation.

Amendment XXIV (1964)

Section 1.
The right of citizens of the United States to vote in any primary or other election for President or Vice President, for electors for President or Vice President, or for Senator or Representative in Congress, shall not be denied or abridged by the United States or any state by reason of failure to pay any poll tax or other tax.

Section 2.
The Congress shall have power to enforce this article by appropriate legislation.

Amendment XXV (1967)

Section 1.
In case of the removal of the President from office or of his death or resignation, the Vice President shall become President.

Section 2.
Whenever there is a vacancy in the office of the Vice President, the President shall nominate a Vice President who shall take office upon confirmation by a majority vote of both Houses of Congress.

Section 3.
Whenever the President transmits to the President pro tempore of the Senate and the Speaker of the House of Representatives his written declaration that he is unable to discharge the powers and duties of his office, and until he transmits to them a written declaration to the contrary, such powers and duties shall be discharged by the Vice President as Acting President.

Section 4.
Whenever the Vice President and a majority of either the principal officers of the executive departments or of such other body as Congress may by law provide, transmit to the President pro tempore of the Senate and the Speaker of the House of Representatives their written declaration that the President is unable to discharge the powers and duties of his office, the Vice President shall immediately assume the powers and duties of the office as Acting President.

Thereafter, when the President transmits to the President pro tempore of the Senate and the Speaker of the House of Representatives his written declaration that no inability exists, he shall resume the powers and duties of his office unless the Vice President and a majority of either the principal officers of the executive department or of such other body as Congress may by law provide, transmit within four days to the President pro tempore of the Senate and the Speaker of the House of Representatives their written declaration that the President is unable to discharge the powers and duties of his office. Thereupon Congress shall decide the issue, assembling within forty-eight hours for that purpose if not in session. If the Congress, within twenty-one days after receipt of the latter written declaration, or, if Congress is not in session, within twenty-one days after Congress is required to assemble, determines by two-thirds vote of both Houses that the President is unable to discharge the powers and duties of his office, the Vice President shall continue to discharge the same as Acting President; otherwise, the President shall resume the powers and duties of his office.

Amendment XXVI (1971)

Section 1.
The right of citizens of the United States, who are 18 years of age or older, to vote, shall not be denied or abridged by the United States or any state on account of age.

Section 2.
The Congress shall have the power to enforce this article by appropriate legislation.

Amendment XXVII (1992)

No law, varying the compensation for the services of the Senators and Representatives, shall take effect, until an election of Representatives shall have intervened.

Appendix C

		Term of Service	Age at Inauguration	Political Party	College or University	Occupation or Profession
1.	George Washington	1789–1797	57	None		Soldier, Planter
2.	John Adams	1797–1801	61	Federalist	Harvard	Lawyer
3.	Thomas Jefferson	1801–1809	57	Democratic-Republican	William and Mary	Planter, Lawyer
4.	James Madison	1809–1817	57	Democratic-Republican	Princeton	Lawyer
5.	James Monroe	1817–1825	58	Democratic-Republican	William and Mary	Lawyer
6.	John Quincy Adams	1825–1829	57	Democratic-Republican	Harvard	Lawyer
7.	Andrew Jackson	1829–1837	61	Democrat		Lawyer, Soldier
8.	Martin Van Buren	1837–1841	54	Democrat		Lawyer
9.	William H. Harrison	1841	68	Whig	Hampden-Sydney	Soldier
10.	John Tyler	1841–1845	51	Whig	William and Mary	Lawyer
11.	James K. Polk	1845–1849	49	Democrat	U. of N. Carolina	Lawyer
12.	Zachary Taylor	1849–1850	64	Whig		Soldier
13.	Millard Fillmore	1850–1853	50	Whig		Lawyer
14.	Franklin Pierce	1853–1857	48	Democrat	Bowdoin	Lawyer
15.	James Buchanan	1857–1861	65	Democrat	Dickinson	Lawyer
16.	Abraham Lincoln	1861–1865	52	Republican		Lawyer
17.	Andrew Johnson	1865–1869	56	Democrat		Tailor
18.	Ulysses S. Grant	1869–1877	46	Republican	U.S. Mil. Academy	Soldier
19.	Rutherford B. Hayes	1877–1881	54	Republican	Kenyon	Lawyer
20.	James A. Garfield	1881	49	Republican	Williams	Minister, Teacher
21.	Chester A. Arthur	1881–1885	51	Republican	Union	Lawyer
22.	Grover Cleveland	1885–1889	47	Democrat		Lawyer
23.	Benjamin Harrison	1889–1893	55	Republican	Miami	Lawyer
24.	Grover Cleveland	1893–1897	55	Democrat		Lawyer
25.	William McKinley	1897–1901	54	Republican	Allegheny College	Lawyer
26.	Theodore Roosevelt	1901–1909	42	Republican	Harvard	Author
27.	William H. Taft	1909–1913	51	Republican	Yale	Lawyer
28.	Woodrow Wilson	1913–1921	56	Democrat	Princeton	Educator
29.	Warren G. Harding	1921–1923	55	Republican		Newspaper editor
30.	Calvin Coolidge	1923–1929	51	Republican	Amherst	Lawyer
31.	Herbert C. Hoover	1929–1933	54	Republican	Stanford	Engineer
32.	Franklin D. Roosevelt	1933–1945	51	Democrat	Harvard	Lawyer
33.	Harry S Truman	1945–1953	60	Democrat		Businessman
34.	Dwight D. Eisenhower	1953–1961	62	Republican	U.S. Mil. Academy	Soldier
35.	John F. Kennedy	1961–1963	43	Democrat	Harvard	Author
36.	Lyndon B. Johnson	1963–1969	55	Democrat	Southwest Texas State	Teacher
37.	Richard M. Nixon	1969–1974	56	Republican	Whittier	Lawyer
38.	Gerald R. Ford	1974–1977	61	Republican	Michigan	Lawyer
39.	James E. Carter, Jr.	1977–1981	52	Democrat	U.S. Naval Academy	Naval Officer, Businessman
40.	Ronald W. Reagan	1981–1989	69	Republican	Eureka College	Broadcaster, Actor
41.	George H. W. Bush	1989–1993	64	Republican	Yale	Businessman
42.	William Jefferson Clinton	1993–2001	46	Democrat	Georgetown	Lawyer
43.	George W. Bush	2001–2009	54	Republican	Yale	Businessman
44.	Barack Obama	2009–	47	Democrat	Columbia	Lawyer

* Never joined a church.

Presidents of the United States

	Religion	Born	Died	Age at Death	Vice President	
1.	Episcopalian	Feb. 22, 1732	Dec. 14, 1799	67	John Adams	(1789–1797)
2.	Unitarian	Oct. 30, 1735	July 4, 1826	90	Thomas Jefferson	(1797–1801)
3.	*	April 13, 1743	July 4, 1826	83	Aaron Burr	(1801–1805)
					George Clinton	(1805–1809)
4.	Episcopalian	Mar. 16, 1751	June 28, 1836	85	George Clinton	(1809–1812)
					Elbridge Gerry	(1813–1814)
5.	Episcopalian	April 28,1758	July 4, 1831	73	Daniel D. Tompkins	(1817–1825)
6.	Unitarian	July 11, 1767	Feb. 23, 1848	80	John C. Calhoun	(1825–1829)
7.	Presbyterian	Mar. 15, 1767	June 8, 1845	78	John C. Calhoun	(1829–1832)
					Martin Van Buren	(1833–1837)
8.	Dutch Reformed	Dec. 5, 1782	July 24, 1862	79	Richard M. Johnson	(1837–1841)
9.	Episcopalian	Feb. 9, 1773	April 4, 1841	68	John Tyler	(1841)
10.	Episcopalian	Mar. 29, 1790	Jan 18, 1862	71		
11.	Methodist	Nov. 2, 1795	June. 15, 1849	53	George M. Dallas	(1845–1849)
12.	Episcopalian	Nov. 24, 1784	July 9, 1850	65	Millard Fillmore	(1849–1850)
13.	Unitarian	Jan. 7, 1800	Mar. 8, 1874	74		
14.	Episcopalian	Nov. 23, 1804	Oct. 8, 1869	64	William R. King	(1853)
15.	Presbyterian	April 23, 1791	June 1, 1868	77	John C. Breckinridge	(1857–1861)
16.	*	Feb. 12, 1809	April 15, 1865	56	Hannibal Hamlin	(1861–1865)
					Andrew Johnson	(1865)
17.	*	Dec. 29, 1808	July 31, 1875	66		
18.	Methodist	April 27, 1822	July 23, 1885	63	Schuyler Colfax	(1869–1873)
					Henry Wilson	(1873–1875)
19.	*	Oct. 4, 1822	Jan. 17, 1893	70	William A. Wheeler	(1877–1881)
20.	Disciples of Christ	Nov. 19, 1831	Sept. 19, 1881	49	Chester A. Arthur	(1881)
21.	Episcopalian	Oct. 5, 1829	Nov. 18, 1886	57		
22.	Presbyterian	Mar. 18, 1837	June 24, 1908	71	Thomas A. Hendricks	(1885)
23.	Presbyterian	Aug. 20, 1833	Mar. 13, 1901	67	Levi P. Morton	(1889–1893)
24.	Presbyterian	Mar. 18, 1837	June 24, 1908	71	Adlai E. Stevenson	(1893–1897)
25.	Methodist	Jan. 29,1843	Sept. 14, 1901	58	Garret A. Hobart	(1897–1899)
					Theodore Roosevelt	(1901)
26.	Dutch Reformed	Oct. 27, 1858	Jan. 6, 1919	60	Charles W. Fairbanks	(1905–1909)
27.	Unitarian	Sept. 15, 1857	Mar. 8, 1930	72	James S. Sherman	(1909–1912)
28.	Presbyterian	Dec. 29, 1856	Feb. 3, 1924	67	Thomas R. Marshall	(1913–1921)
29.	Baptist	Nov. 2, 1865	Aug. 2, 1923	57	Calvin Coolidge	(1921–1923)
30.	Congregationalist	July 4, 1872	Jan. 5, 1933	60	Charles G. Dawes	(1925–1929)
31.	Friend (Quaker)	Aug. 10, 1874	Oct. 20, 1964	90	Charles Curtis	(1929–1933)
32.	Episcopalian	Jan. 30, 1882	April 12, 1945	63	John N. Garner	(1933–1941)
					Henry A. Wallace	(1941–1945)
					Harry S Truman	(1945)
33.	Baptist	May 8, 1884	Dec. 26, 1972	88	Alben W. Barkley	(1949–1953)
34.	Presbyterian	Oct. 14, 1890	Mar. 28, 1969	78	Richard M. Nixon	(1953–1961)
35.	Roman Catholic	May 29,1917	Nov. 22, 1963	46	Lyndon B. Johnson	(1961–1963)
36.	Disciples of Christ	Aug. 27, 1908	Jan. 22, 1973	64	Hubert H. Humphrey	(1965–1969)
37.	Friend (Quaker)	Jan. 9, 1913	April 22, 1994	81	Spiro T. Agnew	(1969–1973)
					Gerald R. Ford	(1973–1974)
38.	Episcopalian	July 14, 1913	Dec. 26, 2006	93	Nelson A. Rockefeller	(1974–1977)
39.	Baptist	Oct. 1, 1924			Walter F. Mondale	(1977–1981)
40.	Presbyterian	Feb. 6, 1911	June 5, 2004	93	George H. W. Bush	(1981–1989)
41.	Episcopalian	June 12, 1924			J. Danforth Quayle	(1989–1993)
42.	Baptist	Aug. 19, 1946			Albert A. Gore	(1993–2001)
43.	Methodist	July 6, 1946			Richard B. Cheney	(2001–2009)
44.	United Church of Christ	Aug. 4, 1961			Joseph Biden	(2009–)

Glossary

Accountability—the state of being responsible for official acts in which success means recognition and reward, while failure means some form of punishment.

Active consent—the consent to government that people demonstrate in democracies by participating in the political system, especially by voting.

Administrative law judge (ALJ)—a federal official who conducts hearings, makes findings, and offers recommendations for resolving disputes over an agency's actions.

Administrative Procedure Act—the 1946 law that set out the process by which federal executive agencies propose and issue regulations.

Administrative rules—formal regulations by executive branch agencies, usually to carry out legislation.

Administrative state—a government in which the nominal rulers (usually elected officials) have delegated much of their authority to bureaucrats.

Advisory opinion—an opinion by a court giving its advice or interpretation on a legal matter outside of a specific case or controversy. Federal courts do not issue advisory opinions.

Affirmative action—governmental policies that either (1) require special efforts to recruit minorities or women in employment, education, or public contracts or (2) grant preferences to minorities or women in employment, education, or public contracts.

Agenda setting—influencing the range of issues up for public deliberation.

Aid to Families with Dependent Children (AFDC)—the federal assistance entitlement program based on the Social Security Act of 1935 that provided income to poor families (commonly called "welfare"). It was replaced in 1996 by Temporary Assistance to Needy Families (TANF).

Air war—an interest group effort to sway public opinion through broadcast advertisements.

Al Qaeda—an international terrorist organization based on extremist Islamic beliefs and founded in the late 1980s by Osama bin Laden. It was responsible for the attacks on the United States of September 11, 2001.

Alternative minimum tax (AMT)—a parallel tax system with a more limited set of tax deductions and credits than the regular income tax. Those potentially subject to the tax must calculate their regular income tax, then their AMT. They pay whichever is greater.

American exceptionalism—the belief that the United States is different from other countries in its founding principles, that it should serve as an example to other nations, and that it has a special mission to spread freedom and democracy throughout the world.

American Federation of Labor–Congress of Industrial Organizations (AFL-CIO)—the leading group of American labor, an organization of 56 unions and their 11 million members.

American Party—a short-lived political party of the 1840s and 1850s that opposed immigration. Its nickname was the "Know-Nothing Party." (In response to questions about their secret organizations, members reportedly promised to reply, "I know nothing.")

Amicus curiae brief—a document filed by an individual or group that is not a party to a legal case, which provides information that aids the court in its deliberations (the term is Latin for "friend of the court").

Annapolis Convention—a gathering of delegates from five states that met in Annapolis, Maryland, in September 1786 to address commercial problems. It called on Congress to convene a constitutional convention to provide for a more effective national government.

Anti-Federalists—the name given to those who opposed the ratification of the Constitution of 1787.

Appellant—the party who appeals a case from a lower court, seeking reversal of the decision.

Appellate jurisdiction—the authority of a court to review a decision reached by a lower court.

Appellee—the party who won in the lower court and responds to the appeal by the losing side by seeking a reaffirmation of the lower-court decision.

Articles of Confederation—the first national constitution for the United States. In force from 1781 to 1789, it created a single-branch national government (Congress) in which each state had one vote.

Assimilation—the blending of diverse immigrant groups into one people by the adoption of common language, customs, and values.

Astroturf—slang for an outpouring of "grassroots" sentiment that an interest group manufactures.

At-large election—race in which candidates run not in districts but in an entire state, county, city, or town.

Australian ballot—a government-published ballot that lists all lawful nominees for office. It allows the voters to make their choices in private and to choose nominees from different parties for different offices.

Authorization for Use of Military Force—the joint resolution passed by Congress in September 2001 that authorized the president "to use all necessary and appropriate force" against those responsible for the attacks of September 11, 2001.

Beat—a specific issue (e.g., the environment), institution (e.g., the Senate), or geographic region in which a journalist may specialize.

Beyond a reasonable doubt—the standard of proof used in criminal cases, which requires that the state prove the defendant's guilt beyond a doubt based on reasons related to the evidence and facts in the case.

Bicameral legislature—a legislative body that has two separate chambers or houses, often with equal authority to pass or amend legislation.

Bill—a draft of a proposed law.

Bill of attainder—an act by a legislature convicting someone of a crime and imposing a punishment without a trial before a court.

Bill of Rights—the first 10 amendments to the U.S. Constitution, which became effective in 1791.

Bipartisan Campaign Reform Act (BCRA)—a 2002 federal law that banned soft-money contributions to political parties. It also increased federal contribution limits and indexed them for inflation.

Birthright citizenship—when a nation automatically grants citizenship to everyone born in the country (except for the children of foreign diplomats).

Black Codes—laws passed by many of the southern states immediately after the Civil War to restrict the rights and freedom of the former slaves, tying them to the soil, and imposing more severe criminal punishments on blacks than on whites.

Block grant—grant in which the federal government lays out broad terms on how the state and local governments should spend the money.

Border Patrol—the agency within the U.S. Department of Homeland Security that enforces immigration laws at the borders of the United States.

Brief—a document written for an appellate court that gives legal arguments for overturning or sustaining the decision of a lower court.

Budget reconciliation bill—a measure that changes existing law in order to carry out instructions in a budget resolution.

Bully pulpit—President Theodore Roosevelt's phrase to describe the rhetorical dimensions of the presidential office.

Bundling—the practice of gathering a large number of small contributions into one group. Although the recipient typically views the result as one large contribution, each check counts separately for the purposes of campaign finance limits.

Bureaucracy—the unelected organizations that carry out government policy; more generally, a form of organization with division of labor, a hierarchy of authority, and impersonal rules.

Bureaucrat—an unelected government employee who administers government policy by adhering to rules and procedures.

Bureau of Immigration—the agency created within the Treasury Department in 1891 to gain greater control over immigration into the United States.

Cabinet—the collective name for the president's formal advisers. The cabinet includes the vice president, the heads of the 15 executive departments, and others to whom the president grants cabinet rank.

Campaign consultants—professionals who contract with political campaigns to provide management and other services.

Case law—the body of authoritative prior court decisions.

Casework—assistance to constituents in their dealings with federal agencies.

Categorical grant—grant that spells out in detail the specific categories in which state and local governments must spend the money.

Caucus—a meeting of political party members. Today, some states begin the process of selecting national convention delegates by holding caucuses of voters. In Congress, *caucus* also refers to the formal organization of House members or senators who belong to the same party.

Charter school—relatively autonomous public school that is exempt from many state rules and often employs innovative teaching techniques.

Checks and balances—the principle of the U.S. Constitution that gives each of the three major branches of government the means to control partially the power exercised by another, largely to resist encroachments on its own powers.

Chief justice—the head of the U.S. Supreme Court and the administrative head of the U.S. court system.

Chief of staff—the highest-ranking staff aide to the president whose duties include supervising White House employees, overseeing the president's schedule, and advising the president on policy and politics.

Circuit court—the original name for the federal courts intermediary between the district courts and the Supreme Court. The name is still used informally to apply to the federal courts of appeal. See **United States Courts of Appeal.**

Citizenship—a legal status that accords full membership in a political community.

Citizenship oath—the oath of allegiance to the United States that candidates for naturalization must take in a public ceremony.

Civic culture—a widely shared set of beliefs and traditions concerning political activity and community service.

Civic duty—any obligation that citizens owe to the broader political community.

Civic journalism—a movement urging journalists to shift their focus from increasing circulation or audience share to fostering public discussion of community issues.

Civic virtue—a virtue that is an essential element of good citizenship, including self-restraint, self-reliance, civic knowledge, and civic participation and service.

Civil case—case in which one individual sues another person or an organization (or even the government, if the law allows) because of some alleged harm, such as a violation of a contract, a libel, or the sale of a defective product.

Civil disobedience—the nonviolent breaking of a law to protest injustice and to press for social or political change.

Civil liberties—personal freedoms that government may not legitimately infringe on, such as practicing one's religion, speaking freely, communicating opinions through print and electronic media, and being secure in one's person and property from arbitrary or oppressive government action.

Civil religion—a nondenominational belief that accepts the existence of fundamental principles of right and wrong and embraces a conviction that Americans should seek the protection of a higher power. It also includes the notion of American exceptionalism and a special attachment to national rituals and symbols. (See also **American exceptionalism**.)

Civil rights (original meaning)—the rights that are accorded to citizens in a particular political community and that are regulated by the state, such as the right to sue in court, to defend one's person and property, to drive an automobile, etc.

Civil rights (modern meaning)—the rights to live one's life and engage in the political process free from discrimination on such grounds as race, sex, religion, age, or disability.

Civil rights movement—in the broadest sense, the efforts dating back to the abolitionists of the early nineteenth century to secure equal rights for blacks in the United States. In the modern era, this term refers to the broad-based social movement that began with the Montgomery bus boycott of 1955 and involved such nonviolent "direct action" techniques as marches, demonstrations, boycotts, and sit-ins at segregated lunch counters.

Civil union—domestic arrangement recognized by the laws in some states that grants same-sex couples most or all of the benefits, protections, and responsibilities enjoyed by spouses in a marriage. Also called a *domestic partnership*.

Class action—a lawsuit in which one or a few individuals are certified by the court as representing many others in a similar situation and in which the resulting remedies, if any, apply to the entire class.

Clear and present danger test—a doctrine promulgated by the Supreme Court in 1919, according to which the government may restrict speech when the words "create a clear and present danger that they will bring about the substantive evils that Congress has a right to prevent."

Closed primary—a primary in which only voters who formally register with the political party may vote.

Closed rule—a rule governing debate in the House of Representatives that prohibits amendments.

Closed shop—a requirement that employees join a labor union before the business hires them. The Taft-Hartley Act outlawed it.

Cloture—the procedure used by the Senate to place a time limit on debate on a bill or other matter, thereby overcoming a filibuster. This requires approval by three-fifths of the full Senate, currently 60 votes.

Coattail effect—the tendency for a popular candidate for higher office to draw votes for other candidates of the same party.

Cold War—the period between the end of World War II (1945) and the collapse of Communism in Eastern Europe and the Soviet Union (1989–1991) when world politics was dominated by the clash between liberal democracies, led by the United States, and Communist nations, led by the Soviet Union.

Commerce clause—Article I, Section 8, of the Constitution, empowering Congress to regulate commerce with foreign nations and among the states. It has supplied the basis for federal regulation of business as well as other domestic policy initiatives.

Committee of Detail—the five-member committee of the Constitutional Convention that met in late July and early August 1787 to fashion the resolutions passed by the Convention, up to that point, into a draft constitution. Along with the Committee of Style, it was one of the two most important committees at the Convention.

Committee of Style—the five-member committee of the Constitutional Convention that met during the last week of the Convention in September 1787 to give final form to the Constitution. Along with the Committee of Detail, it was one of the two most important committees at the Convention.

Committees—groups of legislators in the House and Senate that deliberate on bills or other measures and make recommendations to the full body.

Common Sense—an influential pamphlet written by Thomas Paine and published in Philadelphia in January 1776 that urged the American colonists to break away from British rule and become an independent nation.

Communism—an ideology and form of government in which the state takes ownership of "the means of production" (industry and agriculture); outlaws political parties other than the Communist Party; suppresses religious worship to various degrees; and prohibits public opposition to the regime.

Companion bill—a measure in one house that is similar or identical to a bill in the other.

Concurrent resolution—a resolution passed by both the House and Senate that expresses the sentiment of Congress.

Concurring opinion—in a Supreme Court case, an opinion written by a justice who agrees with the holding of the majority but for reasons in addition to, or different from, those stated in the opinion of the court.

Confederal system—a political system in which states delegate a limited range of powers to a central government for certain purposes, such as the issuing of money. Examples include the United States under the Articles of Confederation and the contemporary European Union.

Confederation—a system of government in which a weak central authority acts on behalf of powerful independent states.

Confederation Congress—the name often given to the Congress established by the Articles of Confederation in 1781 to distinguish it from the Continental Congress, which it replaced.

Conference committee—a temporary joint committee that settles differences between Senate and House versions of a bill and recommends a compromise version to the House and Senate.

Congressional Review Act—a federal law that requires agencies to send rules to Congress for review 60 days before they take effect.

Connected PAC—a political action committee that is under the sponsorship of a corporation, union, or trade association and may solicit contributions only from people with connections to the sponsoring organization.

Connecticut Compromise—see **Great Compromise**.

Consent of the governed—the principle that no one has the right to govern another without that other person's consent.

Conservative—in contemporary American usage, one who wants less government activity on economic issues, and more activity to promote traditional social values.

Constituency service—efforts undertaken by members of Congress to assist constituents, such as intervening with the bureaucracy and bringing home federal projects.

Constituent—a resident of the district or state represented by a member of the House or Senate.

Constitutional Convention—the gathering of delegates from 12 states (all but Rhode Island) that met in Philadelphia from May 25 to September 17, 1787, and wrote the Constitution.

Constitutional monarchy—rule by a monarch, such as a king, who is restrained by a constitution that defines his powers.

Containment—the policy of preventing further expansion of the Soviet Union's influence, in the hope of fostering its eventual downfall.

Continuing resolution—a stopgap measure that provides for spending until Congress passes a regular appropriations bill.

Contract lobbyist—a lobbyist who works at outside law firms or consulting companies and takes on interest groups as clients.

Contributory program—a program, such as Social Security, that is paid for by contributions from current or future recipients.

Cosmopolitanism—in contrast to patriotism, the belief that one's main allegiance should not be to one country but to the world community.

Court-packing plan—the common name for President Franklin Roosevelt's proposal to increase the size of the Supreme Court by up to six additional members.

Covert operation—a secret attempt to influence political, military, or economic situations abroad, often involving the use of force.

Criminal case—case in which the government prosecutes an individual for violating a criminal statute, such as a law against violence, theft, corporate fraud, or drug trafficking.

Critical period—the period of economic, financial, and political distress between the effective end of the Revolutionary War (1781) and the establishment of a new government under the Constitution (1789).

Cultural relativism—the notion that moral standards are purely derivative from the values of a particular culture or society: no society's standards can be said to be "better" or "worse" than those of another. (See also **Moral relativism**.)

De facto segregation—segregation of races or ethnic groups that occurs in society even though not caused by law or official governmental policy.

De jure segregation—segregation mandated by law or official governmental policy.

Declaration of Independence—document approved by the Second Continental Congress on July 4, 1776, that articulated the principles of natural rights and consent of the governed, detailed the numerous ways in which King George III of Britain had violated the colonists' rights, and declared the former 13 colonies to be independent of Britain.

Defendant—the person sued in a civil case or charged with a crime in a criminal case.

Deficit—an amount by which spending exceeds revenues in any given year.

Deism—a belief that God created the world but does not intervene in its affairs.

Delegate—a person entitled to vote at a party convention for the nomination of candidates; also, a type of representation in which legislators simply reflect the views of their constituents.

Deliberation—reasoning on the merits of public policy, searching for the public interest or common good.

Deliberative democracy—a democracy whose institutions are designed to promote the rule of reasoned and informed majorities, usually through representative institutions.

Demagogue—a dangerous popular leader who appeals to base emotions of the people or flatters them to gain power.

Democracy—a form of government in which the people rule themselves either directly or through freely elected representatives.

Democratic-Republican Party—one of the two original major parties, which included James Madison and Thomas Jefferson. It became dominant after the fall of the Federalists. In the 1820s, elements of the party formed the Democratic Party that we know today.

Denaturalization—the process by which naturalized American citizens lose their citizenship because they obtained their original naturalization through fraud or illegality.

Department of Homeland Security— the federal agency created in 2002 to defend the nation from threats such as terrorism and natural disasters.

Desegregation—legal and other efforts to undo segregation of races or ethnic groups.

Devolution—a term that became common in the 1990s for the shift of power from the federal government to states and localities.

Direct democracy—a form of government, originally found in ancient Greece, in which the people directly pass laws and make other key decisions.

Direct incitement test—a doctrine promulgated by the Supreme Court in the twentieth century, according to which the government may suppress political speech that directly incites violence, but not the "advocacy of forcible overthrow as an abstract doctrine."

Direct lobbying—meetings or communications between interest group representatives and the officials they are trying to persuade.

Direct mail—campaign appeals, often asking for contributions, which go directly to voters via postal mail.

Discretionary spending—federal outlays that are subject to the annual process of appropriations, unlike mandatory spending.

Discrimination—treating individuals differently and unfairly because of characteristics over which they have no control, such as race, ethnicity, or gender.

Dissenting opinion—in a Supreme Court case, an opinion written by a justice in the minority explaining why he or she disagrees with the majority.

District courts—see **United States District Courts**.

District system for the Electoral College—a process currently in place in Maine and Nebraska, whereby the statewide presidential winner gets two at-large electors, and the choice of the other electors depends on the popular vote within each congressional district.

Diversity rationale—the argument that racial, ethnic, and gender diversity in schools and the workplace is a worthy goal in itself and ought to be promoted by government. It is used to defend affirmative action policies.

Divided government—when different political parties control the executive branch and at least one chamber of the legislature in a separation of powers, or presidential, system of government.

Drop-off—the tendency for voter turnout to decline in nonpresidential elections.

Dual citizenship—citizenship in two nations simultaneously. It is sometimes called "dual nationality."

Dual federalism—an arrangement whereby the national government would focus on foreign affairs, national security, interstate relations, and other topics of national reach, leaving many domestic policy issues to the states.

Due process of law—procedural protections that the Fifth and Fourteenth amendments require government to follow before depriving anyone of life, liberty, or property. These include at least fair notice and an opportunity to contest charges before a neutral tribunal.

Duties of citizenship—the obligations that citizens owe to one another or the community as a whole, such as obeying the law.

E pluribus unum—Latin motto on the scroll carried in the mouth of the eagle on the Great Seal of the United States: "Out of many, one."

Early voting—a procedure by which people may cast ballots at designated stations before Election Day.

Earmark—a provision of a spending bill that sets aside funds for a specific purpose in a district or state.

Earned Income Tax Credit (EITC)—a federal program enacted in 1975 that provides a special income tax credit to low-wage workers based on income and family size.

Economic group—an interest group, such as a union or business, that explicitly pursues its own material welfare.

Editorial—an unsigned article expressing a view of publishers or editors.

Educational voucher—money provided by governments (often termed "scholarships") to parents of school-age children to cover some or all of the cost of their children attending a private (and sometimes public) school of their choice.

Electoral College—the name later given to the method of electing presidents outlined in the Constitution of 1787 whereby electors, equal to the number of representatives and senators in each state, would be appointed as the state legislature saw fit and would meet in their states to vote for two persons for president, one of whom could not be a resident of their state (modified by the Twelfth Amendment in 1804).

Elector—a person entitled to vote in the Electoral College.

Elite theory—the view that government is controlled by a relative handful of elites in government, business, the professions, and the media who often think alike and work together to promote their mutual interests.

Ellis Island—site of the federal government's first immigrant processing center through which 12 million immigrants passed between 1892, when it opened, and 1924, when it was last used for the mass processing of immigrants.

Emancipation Proclamation—President Abraham Lincoln's executive order, effective January 1, 1863, that freed all the slaves then behind Confederate lines.

Embedded journalist—a reporter who stays with a single military unit for a long period.

Enlightenment—an intellectual movement of the 1700s that stressed the power of reason and took a scientific approach to morality.

Entitlement—a government benefit to which one is entitled by meeting certain qualifications spelled out in law.

Enumerated powers—the 17 express powers that Article I, Section 8, of the Constitution specifically grants to Congress.

Equal Employment Opportunity Commission (EEOC)—the federal agency, which began operating in 1965, charged with enforcing the employment nondiscrimination provisions of the Civil Rights Act of 1964 and other federal laws.

Equality of opportunity—the principle that laws and government programs should seek to provide men and women of all races and ethnic groups an equal chance to succeed.

Equality of results—the principle that government should concern itself not just with equality of opportunity, but with whether men and women of different races and ethnic groups have equal educational and economic success.

Equal time rule—the federal requirement that broadcasters who sell or give airtime to one candidate must provide the same opportunity for all other candidates for the same office.

Equity power—the judicial power, derived from the British legal tradition, to issue injunctions or provide for other kinds of relief, especially when a strict application of the law would lead to unjust results.

Establishment clause—provision of the First Amendment that prohibits Congress from making a law "respecting an establishment of religion."

Estate tax—a tax on your right to transfer property at your death. Those who want to reduce or eliminate it sometimes call it the "death tax."

Evolving Constitution—the notion that the meaning of the Constitution changes, or evolves, over time to meet changing circumstances or norms. See also **living Constitution**.

Ex post facto law—a law that makes an act criminal after it was committed or increases the penalty after the fact.

Excise tax—a tax on specific goods and services, usually by the unit (e.g., gallon, pound, or pack).

Exclusionary rule—the rule imposed by the Supreme Court that prohibits the use in court of evidence improperly obtained, no matter how relevant to demonstrating guilt.

Executive agreement—an agreement reached between the president of the United States and a foreign nation on matters that do not require formal treaties (and therefore Senate approval). These may be either sole-executive agreements, which a president makes on his own authority, or congressional-executive agreements, which are approved by both the president and Congress.

Executive Office of the President (EOP)—the formal staff structure of the White House.

Executive orders—official documents, having the force of law, through which the president directs federal officials to take certain actions.

Executive prerogative—the doctrine that an executive may sometimes have to violate the law to preserve the nation.

Executive privilege—the doctrine stating that the president may sometimes legitimately refuse to provide executive branch information to Congress, the courts, or the public.

Exit poll—survey that measures the opinions of voters as they leave polling places.

Expressive conduct—conduct by which people sometimes express their political feelings without using speech as such: for example, burning the American flag as a sign of protest. Also called "symbolic speech."

Faction—James Madison's term for a group that pursues interests harmful to those of another group or to the good of the country. In contemporary usage, it often refers to any interest group.

Fair Deal—the term for President Harry S Truman's social programs, especially his proposal for national health insurance.

Fairness doctrine—the 1949 FCC ruling that broadcast licensees were "public trustees" who must provide a forum for diverse views. In 1987, the FCC scrapped the doctrine, allowing for more opinionated programming.

Federal Communications Commission (FCC)—the federal agency that regulates the electronic media.

Federal debt—the total value of outstanding securities that the federal government has issued.

Federal Deposit Insurance Corporation (FDIC)—the federal agency created in the 1930s to insure private savings in federally chartered banks.

Federal Election Commission (FEC)—the agency that administers federal campaign finance law.

Federal funds rate—the rate that banks charge for overnight loans to one another. The Federal Reserve sets targets for this rate to influence interest rates in general.

Federalist Papers—85 essays in defense of the proposed Constitution and published in New York City newspapers between October 1787 and May 1788 under the pseudonym "Publius." They were written by Alexander Hamilton, James Madison, and John Jay and were originally titled _The Federalist_.

Federalist Party—one of the first two major parties, which included John Adams and Alexander Hamilton. It dominated American politics in the early years but fell into rapid decline at the start of the nineteenth century.

Federalists—originally, the name given to those who supported the ratification of the Constitution of 1787. Later, it was the name for members of one of the first two political parties in the United States. See **Federalist Party**.

Federal Open Market Committee (FOMC)—the group that makes monetary policy for the Federal Reserve System. Its voting members are the members of the Fed's Board of Governors and the presidents of five Federal Reserve Banks, including the Federal Reserve Bank of New York.

Federal Reserve System—the "Fed," the central bank of the United States. It has the primary responsibility for monetary policy.

Federal system—a political system in which a national government shares powers with states or provinces. Each level has definite powers and may act directly on individuals within its jurisdiction. Examples include the contemporary United States, Germany, and Canada.

Fighting words—words that, according to the Supreme Court (1942), "tend to incite an immediate breach of the peace" and thus are not protected by the First Amendment.

Filibuster—informal term for any attempt to block or delay Senate action on a bill or other matter by debating it at length, by offering numerous motions, or by other obstructive actions.

First Great Awakening—a religious revival of the 1700s that stressed a personal experience of God and helped develop a national identity among the American colonists.

Fiscal policy—federal policy concerning overall levels of spending and taxes.

Flat tax—a proposal to tax all income at a single rate.

Focus group—a set of ordinary people who agree to gather for an in-depth group interview about their opinions.

Foreign policy—the programs and principles that direct the government's interactions with the rest of the world.

Foundation—a nonprofit corporation or a charitable trust that makes grants to organizations or individuals for scientific, educational, cultural, religious, or other charitable purposes. Some foundations support policy groups.

Framing—the way in which the media define an issue by emphasizing or deemphasizing certain aspects of that issue.

Franking privilege—the right of members of Congress to send mail to their constituents without paying for the postage.

Freedmen's Bureau—an agency in the Department of War created by Congress in 1865 to promote the welfare and legal rights of the newly freed slaves.

Freedom of expression—a broad term to characterize what many believe the First Amendment was designed to protect, incorporating freedom of speech and press as well as expressive conduct.

Free exercise clause—provision of the First Amendment that prohibits Congress from "prohibiting the free exercise" of religion.

Free-rider problem—the difficulty that exists when an organization seeks a good or policy change but cannot confine the benefits to its own members. If people can reap the benefits without bearing the costs of membership, they lack incentives to join.

Frontline worker—a government employee who has the physical task of carrying out public policy, often in direct contact with the general public.

Fugitive slave clause—the provision of the Constitution (Article IV, Section 2) that stipulated that slaves who escaped to another state must be returned to their masters.

"Full faith and credit" clause—Article IV, Section 1, of the Constitution, which requires each state to recognize and honor the actions of the other states.

General election—an election for final selection of a variety of offices. The general election for federal office is "on the first Tuesday after the first Monday" in November of even-numbered years.

General revenue sharing—a program to distribute federal tax money to states and localities with few restrictions. The program ended in 1986.

Gentleman's Agreement of 1907—an understanding negotiated between President Theodore Roosevelt and the Japanese government, according to which Japan would restrict passports for its citizens to work in the United States, and the United States would allow the Japanese already in the country to remain and to bring in their families.

Gerrymandering—the drawing of district lines, often in odd shapes, to benefit a party or constituency group.

Government Accountability Office (GAO)—formerly the General Accounting Office, an independent, nonpartisan agency that works for Congress. GAO investigates how the federal government spends taxpayer dollars.

Government corporation— a government-owned corporation that provides goods or services for which the private sector presumably cannot meet the need.

Government-sponsored enterprise (GSE)—a federally chartered but privately owned corporation that seeks to improve the flow of credit.

Grandfather clauses—laws passed in the South in the late nineteenth century that exempted an individual from literacy tests or poll taxes if his grandfather or any ancestor could vote before the passage of the Fifteenth Amendment (1870). These were designed to enfranchise poor and illiterate whites.

Grassroots—the broad general public. Interest groups often seek grassroots support.

Grasstops—an interest group tactic of enlisting the support of people with strong local influence or a personal connection to lawmakers.

Great Compromise—the compromise between the large and small states at the Constitutional Convention, according to which population would be the basis for representation in the first branch of the new national legislature and equality of the states in the second. It also required that bills for raising revenues and appropriating funds originate in the first branch. Also called the **Connecticut Compromise**.

Great Depression—the major downturn in the American economy that began in 1929 and lasted through the 1930s.

Great Seal of the United States—adopted by the Congress of the Articles of Confederation in 1782 for use on official government documents. It includes the Latin motto "E pluribus unum."

Great Society—President Lyndon Johnson's term for his social programs to reduce poverty, address the problems of the cities, promote natural beauty, and enhance a sense of community.

Green card—a federally issued identification card (which used to be green but is no longer) that attests to the permanent legal status of an alien, or foreigner, within the United States.

Greenspan Commission—the 15-member National Commission for Social Security Reform, chaired by Alan Greenspan and established by Congress in 1981 to address the funding imbalance in the Social Security system.

Gross domestic product (GDP)—the total value of the nation's production of goods and services in a given year.

Group theory—the view that a large number of diverse groups control government and politics and promote policies to serve their particular interests. (Also called "pluralist theory.")

Groupthink—the tendency for members of policymaking groups to go along with the prevailing view and mute their own misgivings.

Gulf of Tonkin Resolution—the joint resolution passed by Congress in 1964 that authorized President Lyndon Johnson to use the armed forces to assist South Vietnam.

Habeas Corpus Act of 1679—a law passed by the British Parliament that codified the right to a writ of habeas corpus.

Hatch Act—a law restricting the political activities of federal employees. In 1993, Congress relaxed the restrictions.

Hold—an informal practice in the Senate that allows a member to request the leader to hold up action on a bill, presidential nomination, or other matter.

Horse race journalism—reporting that emphasizes the candidates' chances of election instead of their policies.

Ideological interest group—an interest group with a strong commitment to a particular political philosophy whether liberal, conservative, or libertarian.

Illegal immigrant—a foreigner who is illegally in the United States because (1) he or she entered the country illegally or (2) after a legal entry overstayed his or her visa. Also called *illegal alien*, *undocumented immigrant*, and *undocumented worker*.

Impeachment—a formal accusation by the House of Representatives (passed by a majority vote) that an officer of the United States has committed "Treason, Bribery, or other high Crimes and Misdemeanors." It results in removal if the Senate subsequently convicts by a two-thirds vote.

Implied powers—powers of the national government that the Constitution does not directly mention but that one may reasonably infer from the enumerated powers.

Importation of slaves clause—the provision of the Constitution (Article I, Section 9) that prevented Congress from prohibiting the importation of slaves before 1808.

Impoundment—presidential refusal to spend funds that Congress has appropriated, a power limited by Congress in 1974.

Incorporation doctrine—the judicial doctrine that the due process clause of the Fourteenth Amendment in effect incorporates most of the specific rights in the Bill of Rights against the states.

Incumbency advantage—the electoral benefits that come with holding office, such as visibility and staff.

Incumbent—one who currently holds an elected office.

Independent expenditure—the use of funds to support or oppose a federal candidate but coming from a source that does not directly coordinate its efforts with any of the parties or candidates.

Independent regulatory commission—a government organization that issues rules and conducts quasi-judicial proceedings. The president names the members and the chair of each commission, subject to Senate confirmation, but these officials serve fixed terms and are not subject to presidential dismissal without good cause.

Individualism—self-reliance and personal independence, usually in preference to government action.

Inflation—a general rise in prices over time.

In-house lobbyist—a lobbyist on a group's payroll.

Initiative—a proposed state law or constitutional amendment that appears on the ballot for a popular vote if enough registered voters sign petitions so requesting. (See also **Referendum**.)

Inspector general (IG)—an official within federal agencies who runs independent investigations into bureaucratic operations and makes recommendations to stop waste.

Instant-runoff voting—a system in which voters rank candidates in order of preference. If no candidate gets more than 50% of first-preference votes, the candidate with the fewest first-preference votes drops off and the votes for that candidate are redistributed according to the voters' next preference. The process repeats until a candidate wins a majority.

Intelligence—the effort to understand the aims and capabilities of foreign nations and groups (e.g., terror organizations), especially when they may threaten national security.

Interest group—an organization that seeks to influence public policy.

Intermediate or heightened scrutiny—the level of scrutiny the Supreme Court uses to evaluate the legality of laws or government policies and programs that distinguish between the sexes. In such cases, the government must show that the distinction serves important governmental objectives and is substantially related to the achievement of those objectives.

Iron triangle—the political alliance of executive branch agencies, congressional committees, and interest groups.

Isolationism—avoidance of involvement in international affairs.

Issue advocacy advertisement—advertisements that urge the public to take action on an issue. Although they may mention federal candidates in a favorable or unfavorable light, they do not directly urge the candidates' election or defeat.

Issue networks—loose groupings of people and organizations that seek to influence policy, including not only the members of the traditional iron triangle but also policy experts in universities, think tanks, and the media. Also called policy communities.

Jim Crow laws—laws passed in the South in the 1870s and 1880s that mandated the segregation of the races in virtually all social relations, such as transportation, housing, restaurants, churches, hospitals, cemeteries, and entertainment.

Joint committees—committees with members from both the House and Senate that carry out studies or administrative tasks.

Joint resolution—a resolution passed by both the House and Senate that, like a statute, is subject to a presidential veto. Once enacted, it has the full force of law.

Judicial activism—the charge that under the guise of interpreting the Constitution, federal judges read their own policy preferences into the fundamental law.

Judicial review—the power of courts to strike down laws that they judge to be in violation of the federal or state constitutions.

Judicial self-restraint—the doctrine that judges should exercise restraint in the kinds of cases they decide, deferring to the political branches on most matters.

Judiciary Act of 1789—the law passed by the First Congress that created a three-tiered federal court structure.

Kentucky Resolutions—resolutions authored by Thomas Jefferson and passed by the Kentucky legislature in 1798 that criticized the Alien and Sedition Acts.

King Caucus—in the early nineteenth century, referred to meetings of Democratic-Republican members of Congress who nominated presidential candidates.

Know-Nothing Party—an anti-Catholic and anti-immigrant party of the 1850s (also known as the American Party). It opposed Catholic candidates for political office because of their supposed ties to the pope in Rome, and it proposed requiring immigrants to wait 21 years before applying for citizenship.

Ku Klux Klan—the name for both (1) a white supremacist organization founded in Tennessee in 1866 to terrorize and intimidate southern blacks and their white sympathizers and (2) an organization founded in Georgia in 1915 to promote white supremacy, anti-Catholicism, anti-immigration, and anti-Semitism.

Lame duck session—any session of Congress that occurs after a national election and before the new Congress has convened.

Law clerk—in the Supreme Court, usually a recent top graduate of a prestigious law school who works for a year assisting a justice with legal research and, possibly, opinion writing.

Leaking—the practice by which political figures privately supply information to the press, usually with the agreement that their names will not appear.

Legislative referendum—a vote that takes place when a state legislature sends measures to the people for their approval.

Lemon test—the legal test promulgated by the Supreme Court in 1971 that held that a law that raises establishment clause issues may withstand challenge only if

- it has a secular legislative purpose,
- its main effect neither advances nor inhibits religion, and
- it does not foster an excessive government entanglement with religion.

Libel—a defamatory statement made in writing (see also **Slander**).

Liberal democracy—a democracy that works to secure the rights of its citizens and thus to promote their liberty, or freedoms.

Liberal—in contemporary American usage, one who favors more government activity to foster economic equality, and less activity to promote traditional social values.

Libertarian—one who favors less government activity across the board, including economic and social issues.

Likely voter—prior to the election, one with the greatest probability of casting a ballot. Pollsters have different methods for identifying likely voters.

Lincoln-Douglas debates—seven debates held throughout Illinois in the Senate contest of 1858 between Democratic incumbent Stephen Douglas and Republican challenger Abraham Lincoln.

Line-item veto—a power, possessed by many American governors, to veto a particular item of a bill without vetoing the whole bill.

Literacy test—a requirement that someone prove the ability to read before casting a vote. In practice, literacy tests were ruses to keep poor people and minorities from the polls. Federal law now forbids them.

Living Constitution—the notion that the Constitution is a living document that changes, or evolves, to meet changing circumstances. See also **evolving Constitution**.

Lobbyist—an individual whose job is to influence policymakers on behalf of an interest group.

Lochner era—the period from 1905 until 1937 when the Supreme Court overturned many state and federal laws for interfering with the free-market economy. The name comes from the Supreme Court case *Lochner v. New York* of 1905.

Logrolling—when legislators (or others) trade support for one another's proposals.

Loyalists—Americans who remained loyal to the British government during the Revolutionary War.

Magnet school—a specialized public school (often emphasizing science, technology, or the performing arts) that draws students from a wide area.

Majority faction—defined by James Madison in *Federalist 10* as a majority of the people brought together by a common passion or interest adverse to the rights of other citizens or to the permanent and aggregate interests of the community.

Majority leader—in the Senate, the highest-ranking member of the majority party; in the House the highest-ranking member after the Speaker.

Majority-minority district—voting district in which minorities represent a majority of the residents.

Majority opinion—an opinion of an appellate court, such as the U.S. Supreme Court, that garners the approval of a majority of the members of the court.

Mandate—federal requirement that state and local governments take certain actions; also, an election victory that indicates strong voter approval of the winner's plans and policies.

Mandatory spending—federal spending that is not subject to the annual appropriations process. It consists mainly of entitlement programs and interest payments on the debt.

March on Washington for Jobs and Freedom—a peaceful mass demonstration for civil rights and economic opportunity in Washington, DC, in August 1963 attended by more than 250,000 individuals, mostly black Americans.

Marginal income tax rate—the tax rate on one's last dollar of taxable income. Currently under federal law there are six such rates, ranging from 10% to 35%.

Markup—the process by which a committee or subcommittee proposes changes to a bill.

Married Women's Property Acts—laws passed in all the states between 1839 and 1895 to give married women some or all of the property rights possessed by married men.

Marshall Court—the Supreme Court under the leadership of Chief Justice John Marshall, 1801–1835. Its decisions cemented the Court's position as a coequal branch of the national government, affirmed the supremacy of the federal Constitution and federal law over state constitutions and state law, and legitimized a broad interpretation of Congress's enumerated powers.

Martial law—rule by military authorities (in place of civilian officials) in time of war or civil disorder.

Mass media—means of broadly distributing information or entertainment, including newspapers, magazines, television, radio, and the Internet.

Matching funds—money that the federal government provides to presidential candidates to match the money they have raised on their own. Acceptance is voluntary and entails restrictions on fund-raising. Presidential candidates have increasingly decided to forgo matching funds.

Mayflower Compact—the Pilgrims' covenant for governing the Plymouth colony. Although neither a declaration of independence nor a constitution, it came to symbolize how Americans could join for common purposes.

Means-tested program—a social welfare program that disburses benefits to those who have low income or few tangible assets.

Media conglomerate—a large corporation that owns a variety of media outlets.

Media market—the geographic area that receives broadcasts from a set of stations.

Medicaid—a program established in 1965, as a companion program to Medicare, to meet the medical expenses of the poor. It is administered by the states and funded by both the states and the federal government.

Medicare—a federal program established in 1965 to assist those over 65 with hospital and doctors' expenses.

Melting pot—the metaphor that conveys the notion that newcomers to the United States should leave behind old identities and adopt new ones; that many diverse peoples should blend together into a single American people.

Memorial and Remonstrance—document written by James Madison in 1785 opposing the use of tax money to support Christian religious instruction and making the case for freedom of religion.

Merit system—a government personnel practice in which hiring and promotion hinges on individual qualifications instead of political affiliation.

Mexican repatriation—policy adopted during the Great Depression to force between 300,000 and 500,000 Mexican immigrants to return to their homes.

Midnight appointments—the appointments to the federal judiciary that President John Adams and the lame-duck Federalist Congress made in the final months and weeks of Adams's one term as president.

Midterm elections—elections that take place in even-numbered years when there is no presidential election. In a midterm election, the offices up for contest include all U.S. House seats, about one-third of U.S. Senate seats, as well as most governorships and state legislative seats.

Milwaukee Parental Choice Program—the nation's first publicly funded school voucher program.

Minority leader—in the Senate and the House, the highest-ranking member of the minority party.

Miranda warnings—the warnings required by the Supreme Court that police must give when arresting a suspect: particularly the right to remain silent and to have the assistance of an attorney (also called "Miranda rights").

Missouri Compromise of 1820—a national compromise over the slavery issue in 1820 whereby Missouri entered the Union as a slave state, Maine entered as a free state, and slavery was "forever prohibited" in the remaining territory of the Louisiana Purchase north of the latitude line 36°30', which was the southern border of Missouri.

Mobilization—efforts to motivate supportive voter groups to turn out in higher numbers.

Moderate—one whose opinion falls between that of a liberal and a conservative.

Modern Republicanism—President Dwight D. Eisenhower's term for Republican Party acceptance of Social Security, unemployment insurance, labor laws, farm programs, and other features of the welfare state.

Monetary policy—federal policy concerning the supply of money and the level of interest rates.

Monroe Doctrine—President James Monroe's 1823 proclamation that North and South America should be closed to further European colonization and free from European interference over the continents' sovereign nations. It also stated that the United States would not interfere in European affairs.

Montgomery bus boycott—a boycott of city buses in Montgomery, Alabama, in 1955 to protest segregated seating. This action launched the modern civil rights movement.

Mootness—the doctrine that the courts will not decide a case if the dispute has been resolved or rendered irrelevant by subsequent events.

Moral relativism—the notion that moral standards are purely subjective: up to each individual to decide. (See also **Cultural relativism**.)

Motor Voter—the 1993 National Voter Registration Act, which requires states to offer voter registration when people apply for services such as driver's licenses.

Muckrakers—journalists who expose misconduct in government and business.

Multiculturalism—the view that American society is best thought of as a collection of different cultures, each with its own values, traditions, and practices, and that no one culture should dominate.

Multilateralism—the practice of coordinating foreign policy with other countries on a long-term basis.

Multiple referral—when one bill is sent to two or more committees for consideration.

Nationalization of the Bill of Rights—refers to the incorporation of the Bill of Rights against the states as a result of Supreme Court decisions in the twentieth century. See also **Incorporation doctrine**.

National Labor Relations Act (Wagner Act)—the New Deal statute that set up the National Labor Relations Board (NLRB) to protect union organizing and encourage collective bargaining. The act forbade such unfair employer practices as setting up a company union and firing workers who organized unions.

National origins quota system—the policy adopted in the Immigration Act of 1924 that limited immigration of each nationality group to 2% of the number residing in the United States in 1890, thus favoring immigrants from northern and western Europe.

National Security Act of 1947—a law that reorganized the foreign policy and military establishments after the Second World War. The act created the National Security Council (NSC), the Central Intelligence Agency (CIA), the United States Air Force, and the office of Secretary of Defense.

National Security Adviser—the Assistant to the President for National Security Affairs, who runs the day-to-day operations of the National Security Council. Some advisers have confined themselves to coordination, whereas others have been forceful policy advocates.

National Security Council (NSC)—the president's official forum for deliberating about national security and foreign policy, which includes the president as chair, the vice president, the secretary of state, the secretary of the treasury, and the secretary of defense.

National security—safety from external hazards to the nation's territory, sovereignty, and freedom of action, as well as to its people's lives and property.

Nativism—opposition to immigration by native-born Americans, giving rise to such movements as the Know-Nothing Party of the 1850s.

Naturalization—the process by which a foreigner becomes a citizen of a nation.

Naturalized citizen—someone who moves from one country to another and becomes a citizen of the new country.

Natural rights—rights to which all people are entitled by their very nature as human beings, such as those cited in the Declaration of Independence: "Life, Liberty, and the Pursuit of Happiness."

"Necessary and proper clause"—the final clause of Article I, Section 8, of the Constitution, which empowers Congress to make all laws "necessary and proper" in order to carry out the federal government's duties. This "elastic clause" is the constitutional basis for implied powers.

Negative rights—rights to do certain things—such as speaking or worshipping freely—without interference from the government; includes traditional civil rights and civil liberties.

Network—a broadcast organization that simultaneously supplies radio or television programs to stations in different cities.

New Deal—the term to describe the economic and social welfare policies of President Franklin Roosevelt in the 1930s.

New Deal Coalition—the voter support base of the Democratic Party, which took form during Franklin Roosevelt's administration. The coalition included southerners, Jews, Catholics, African Americans, people with roots in Southern and Eastern Europe, union members, poor people, intellectuals, and artists.

New Federalism—President Nixon's plan to turn more authority over to state and local governments. Other presidents have also used the term.

New Jersey Plan—a plan of government supported by the small states at the Constitutional Convention as a counterproposal to the Virginia Plan. It preserved the basic structure of the government under the Articles of Confederation (with equal state vote) but added new powers to regulate trade, raise revenues, and allow the Congress to create executive and judicial branches.

News—information about events that are recent, unusual, and important.

News conference (or press conference)—a session at which a public figure answers questions from a number of journalists.

News media—the means of transmitting news to broad populations, including television, radio, newspapers, magazines, and the Internet.

Newspaper chain—a business owning multiple newspapers.

News release (or press release)—a statement from a newsmaker in the form of a news story, complete with a catchy lead paragraph, along with quotations and supporting facts.

Nonattitudes—answers that survey respondents give even when they have no real opinion on the question.

Nonconnected PAC—a political action committee that is not under the sponsorship of an existing organization and may seek contributions from anyone who may lawfully give to federal campaigns.

Noncontributory program—a program under which recipients draw benefits without contributing directly to the program; funds come from general revenues.

Nonpartisan election—an election in which the candidate's party affiliation does not appear on the ballot.

Nullification—the idea that a state may refuse to acknowledge or enforce federal laws within its boundaries.

Obscenity—sexually explicit and patently offensive materials that may be suppressed by public authorities, as defined by the Supreme Court in *Miller v. California* (1973).

Office of Information and Regulatory Affairs (OIRA)—a unit of the Office of Management and Budget that sets federal policy on statistics and reviews draft rules before publication.

Office of Management and Budget (OMB) (original meaning)—a White House office that drafts the president's budget message, prepares budget documents, advises the president on economic and regulatory matters, and oversees management of the federal government.

Office of Management and Budget (OMB) (modern meaning)—the agency within the Executive Office of the President that reviews budget requests, legislative initiatives, and proposed rules and regulations from the executive agencies.

Offshoring—the practice by which American or multinational firms delegate work to lower-wage laborers overseas.

Ombudsman—a journalist who checks problems with accuracy, fairness, and taste in his or her own news organization's coverage, often publishing columns recommending remedies or responses.

One person, one vote—a judicial principle holding that everyone should have equal voting power in district elections.

Open primary—a primary in which any voter can cast a ballot in any party's primary.

Open rule—a rule governing debate in the House of Representatives that allows any amendments to be considered.

Opinion of the Court—in a Supreme Court case the opinion that explains and justifies the holding of the majority.

Opposition researcher—a campaign operative who specializes in finding information about the other side's candidate.

Oral arguments—arguments made in person before an appellate court, making the legal case for reversing or reaffirming a lower-court decision.

Organizational culture—shared beliefs within an organization about how its members should deal with problems and carry on their daily tasks. It is "the way we do things here."

Original intent—the doctrine that judges should interpret the Constitution based on the original intent of those who wrote and ratified it. See also **original meaning**.

Originalism—the theory that in interpreting the Constitution judges should look to how it was understood by those who wrote and ratified it.

Original jurisdiction—the authority of a court to hear a case taken directly to it, as a new legal controversy.

Original meaning—the doctrine that judges should interpret the Constitution based on how it was understood by those who wrote and ratified it. See also **original intent**.

Outsourcing—in the context of public policy, the practice of carrying out government functions by giving grants or contracts to the private sector.

Override—when the House and Senate by two-thirds votes approve a bill over the president's veto.

Oversight—congressional review of the activities of federal agencies and programs.

Paper money laws—laws passed by several states during the 1780s that allowed citizens to borrow paper money from the government and use it as legal tender, especially to pay taxes and debts.

Paris Peace Accords—the agreement between the warring parties to end the fighting in Vietnam in 1973, violated by North Vietnam when it invaded the South with its regular army early in 1975.

Parliamentarian—a staff expert on the rules in the House of Representatives and Senate.

Parliamentary government—the type of representative democracy in which the people vote for representatives to the lawmaking body and then the head of the majority party (or coalition of parties) becomes the chief executive. Many of the top executive officials also serve in the legislature.

Partisan alignment/realignment—an enduring pattern of party loyalty in the electorate. A **realignment** is a sudden and permanent shift in that pattern.

Partisan election—a contest in which each candidate's party affiliation appears on the ballot.

Partisan polarization—the movement of parties away from each other and toward more extreme issue positions.

Partisan primary—a primary in which voters nominate party candidates for the general election.

Party ballots—a nineteenth-century method of voting in which each party printed a list of candidates. People would vote by placing a party's list in the ballot box.

Party identification—a self-reported feeling of attachment to a political party.

Party in government—those who win office under the party label.

Party in the electorate—the voters who tend to support a given party.

Party organization—formal structure of party officers and workers who try to influence elections.

Party platform—statement of party issue positions.

Party registration—a formal declaration of party affiliation. In many states, it is necessary to register in a party in order to vote in party primaries.

Party unity—the percentage of roll-call voters in which a House member or senator voted "yea" or "nay" in agreement with a majority of his or her party and against a majority of the other party.

Patriotism—both an emotional and a rational attachment to the nation, a public spirit strong enough to inspire sacrifice.

Payroll tax—the tax on payroll used to fund Social Security and part of Medicare, equally divided between the employer and employee.

Peace Corps—a federal agency that sends civilian volunteers to help people in poor countries with education, agriculture, public health, and economic development.

Pendleton Act (Civil Service Reform Act)—an 1883 federal law that set up a merit-based system for choosing government employees and supervising their work.

Pilgrims—Calvinists who had broken with the Church of England and who settled in Massachusetts after arriving on the Mayflower in 1620.

Plaintiff—the person who initiates a civil case by suing another individual, an organization, or the government.

Pluralist theory—the view that a large number of diverse groups control government and politics and promote policies to serve their particular interests. (Also called *group theory*.)

Plurality opinion—in a Supreme Court case, the opinion written by the most justices who support the decision, when a majority of justices cannot agree on a single opinion.

Pocket veto—when a president refuses to sign a bill within 10 days of Congress passing it and Congress has adjourned. Because a pocket veto cannot be overridden by Congress, presidential inaction kills the bill.

Policy group—an interest group that purports to seek goals that benefit the broader public, not just its own members.

Policy lag—the time period between the creation of a policy and its implementation.

Political action committee (PAC)—a political committee, other than a candidate's campaign committee or a party committee, that raises and spends money to elect or defeat candidates. Businesses and labor unions often form PACs because they cannot give money directly to federal candidates from their own treasuries.

Political culture—a distinctive and widely shared set of beliefs on how to practice governmental and political activities.

Political ideology—a comprehensive system of belief about what government should do.

Political machine—a party organization, usually in a city, that uses patronage to ensure its local dominance.

Political participation—activities aiming to shape the structure and policies of the government, as well as the choice of those who run it.

Political party—a political group that seeks to elect its members to public office.

Political patronage—the granting of jobs, contracts, and other official favors in return for loyalty to an individual leader or political party.

Political questions—the doctrine that the courts should not decide issues that the Constitution has given over to the discretion of the Congress or the president.

Political rights—the rights to influence governmental decisions in a democracy by voting for representatives and holding office. One can be a citizen (such as a convicted felon or a minor) without enjoying political rights.

Political socialization—the long-term process by which people gain their opinions and knowledge about politics.

Poll tax—a tax assessed before someone can vote. Poll taxes are now illegal.

Popular referendum—a process whereby people may gather signatures to enable the voters to accept or reject measures that the legislature has passed.

Popular sovereignty—the principle that all political power derives from the people.

Populist—one who favors increased government activity both to regulate the economy and to protect traditional social norms.

Populist Party—a political party of the 1890s that favored inflation to help farmers at the expense of city dwellers. Its members united with the Democrats in 1896 to nominate William Jennings Bryan for president.

Pork barrel—a derogatory term for projects that benefit specific localities without serving the national interest.

Positive rights—social or economic rights that some say oblige government to provide for the well-being of the citizens.

Precedents—the body of court decisions on similar matters to an issue before the courts.

Preemption—President George W. Bush's policy of taking military action against hostile regimes or groups to forestall attacks against the United States or its interests.

Preemption statute—federal law that empowers the national government to override state and local authority over a public policy issue.

Preponderance of the evidence—a standard of proof used in most civil cases, which requires that the weight of the evidence support the plaintiff's case, even if only slightly.

Presidential government—the American system of representative democracy (also called a separation of powers system) in which the chief executive is independently elected and cannot be dismissed by the legislature. No executive official may also serve in the legislature.

President pro tempore—under the Constitution, the officer who presides over the Senate when the vice president is not presiding. Now it is an honorary position that customarily goes to the longest-serving member of the majority party.

Primary—an election that determines who runs in the final or general election.

Priming—the process by which the media emphasize some issues over others, thereby affecting the standards by which people make political judgments.

Prior restraint—prohibiting the publication of materials because of their harmful effects. Under English common law, government could not prevent the publication of materials but could punish the publisher after the fact.

Proclamation—a formal statement issued by the president to the nation, often, but not always, to declare ceremonial occasions.

Progressive movement—a political reform movement of the late nineteenth and early twentieth centuries that attacked political corruption and the failure of government to address social ills.

Progressive Party—a reformist party that nominated former president Theodore Roosevelt as its standard-bearer in the 1912 presidential election.

Progressive taxes—taxes that take proportionately more from the income of higher-income people than from lower-income people.

Protected speech—speech that government may not prohibit or punish under the First Amendment guarantee of "freedom of speech."

Protectionism—a policy of erecting trade barriers to shield domestic business from international competition.

Prudence—as used in the Declaration of Independence, refers to wisdom about practical affairs. It is the virtue associated with having good judgment and making sound decisions in government and politics.

Public interest group—a nonprofit organization whose primary goal is to seek benefits for the broader public, not just its own members.

Public opinion—an aggregate of individual beliefs about political questions.

Public opinion poll (or survey)—a device for measuring public opinion, usually consisting of a standard set of questions administered to a sample of the public.

Puritans—Calvinists who wanted to "purify" the Church of England without immediately abandoning it. Puritans settled in the northeastern United States. Their strict moral code and emphasis on education left lasting marks on American thought.

Rally effect—the tendency for presidents to gain in public approval during crises. Also called the "rally-around-the-flag effect."

Random-digit dialing—the process of finding poll respondents by calling phone numbers from random-number generators. The aim is to reach people with unpublished or recently assigned telephone numbers.

Random sample—a subset of people who are representative of a larger group because everyone in the larger group has an equal chance of selection.

Ratification—the process by which popularly elected conventions in the states formally approved the proposed Constitution of 1787.

Rational-basis test—the lowest level of scrutiny used by the Supreme Court in addressing constitutional issues. When using this standard of review, the Court requires only that the law or government program at issue be rationally related to some legitimate government function or interest.

Rational choice theory—a theory of politics based on the premise that citizens and public officials act rationally to serve their personal interests.

Reapportionment—a process that reallocates House seats to states in line with population changes. People often confuse this term with **redistricting**, which refers to the drawing of the district lines.

Recall elections—special elections in which voters in some states may oust officeholders before their regular terms expire.

Recess appointment—a temporary appointment that a president can make when the Senate is in recess. Such appointments do not require Senate approval and last until the end of the next Senate session, or up to two years.

Reconstruction—the 12 years after the Civil War (1865–1877) when national policy, directed principally by the Republican-dominated Congress, sought to reintegrate the 11 states of the Confederacy back into the Union and to provide for the civil and political rights of the newly freed slaves.

Red tape—official forms and procedures, which are often burdensome. The term stems from a British tradition of binding documents with red cloth tape.

Redistribution program—a noncontributory program that redistributes income or wealth from taxpayers generally to the poor.

Redistricting—the drawing of boundaries for legislative districts, which usually takes place after the federal census.

Referendum—a proposed law or constitutional amendment, usually written by legislators, that is sent to the people for a vote. (See also **Initiative**.)

Referral—the practice whereby the parliamentarian of the House or Senate sends a bill to a committee (or committees) for consideration.

Refugee—someone who has fled his or her country because of the fear of persecution.

Regressive tax—the opposite of a **progressive tax**, taking proportionately more from lower-income people.

Regulatory and trade policy—a variety of ways by which government tries to police markets for goods and services.

Renunciate—someone who voluntarily renounces his or her American citizenship.

Representative democracy—a form of government in which (a) candidates for office and political parties compete for popular support, (b) the people choose their leaders through free elections, and (c) elected officials are held accountable for their conduct in office.

Republic—as the American founders used the term, equivalent to a representative democracy.

Reserved powers—under the Tenth Amendment, the powers not delegated to the United States by the Constitution, or prohibited by it to the States, that are reserved to the states or to the people.

Revolving door—slang for the interchange of employees between government and the private sector.

Rider—a legislative measure attached to a bill that often has little substantive relation to it.

Right of expatriation—the right of men and women to renounce their allegiance to a nation and move elsewhere.

Right-to-work laws—laws in 22 states that forbid union shops.

Ripeness—the doctrine that the courts will not hear cases brought prematurely, that is, before the dispute is well developed and ready, or ripe, for adjudication.

Roll call vote—a recorded vote on major amendments or final passage of a bill (done electronically in the House and by voice in the Senate).

Roll-off—the decline in the number of votes cast from high-profile races (e.g., president or governor) to low-profile races (e.g., coroner or sewer commissioner).

Rule of four—the practice of the Supreme Court that it will hear a case if at least four justices agree to do so.

Rule of law—the principle that rulers should govern through law and not arbitrarily, that all persons should be treated equally before the law, and that individual rights are the foundation of the law and not the creation of the law.

Runoff primary—a primary used in some states in which the top finishers face off if no one wins a majority (or some designated percentage) in the first-round partisan primary.

Sales tax—tax on the purchase of a wide range of items, with rates as a percentage of the price.

School choice—a contemporary movement to give parents more choice as to where to send their children to school; includes charter schools, magnet schools, choice among regular public schools, various types of educational vouchers to allow students to attend private schools, tax credits or deductions for private school tuition, and home schooling.

School voucher—see **Educational voucher**.

Seamen's protection certificates—documents issued by the federal government to sailors, both white and black, to certify that they were citizens of the United States.

Second Great Awakening—a religious revival of the late 1700s and early 1800s. In contrast to the First Great Awakening, this movement stressed social improvement in addition to personal conversion. It inspired efforts to curb alcohol abuse and end slavery.

Secretary—the title given to the heads of executive departments.

Securities—a broad term for stocks, bonds, and other investment instruments.

Securities and Exchange Commission (SEC)—the federal agency created in the 1930s to regulate the stock market and some activities of publicly held corporations.

Seditious libel—the crime under British law that made it illegal to criticize the government in a way that undermined public support and respect; the truth of the charges was not a defense.

Segregation—a term referring to the separation of the races in housing, the use of public accommodations, employment, or education. See *De facto* **segregation** and *De jure* **segregation**.

Selective exposure—the human tendency to seek out information sources that back one's existing beliefs and to spurn sources that dispute them.

Selective incentive—a good or service that only members of an organization may enjoy. A selective incentive is one remedy to the free-rider problem.

Selective incorporation—the doctrine that much, but not all, of the Bill of Rights applies to the states.

Select (or special) committee—a permanent or temporary committee set up to mount an investigation or to handle a particular issue.

Semiclosed primary—a primary in which party members can only vote in their primary, but unaffiliated voters can vote in either party's primary.

Senatorial courtesy—the custom in the Senate whereby the full body will not confirm presidential nominees for federal district judge, U.S. attorney, or federal marshal if the senior senator of the president's party from the state where the appointment is to be made objects.

Seneca Falls Convention—held in 1848 in Seneca Falls, New York, the first public meeting to address the "social, civil and religious rights of women." It was attended by more than 250 women and 40 men and adopted a "Declaration of Sentiments," modeled on the Declaration of Independence.

Seniority—refers to continuous service in either the House or Senate or continuous service on a committee. Committee chairmanships usually go to the senior committee member of the majority party.

Separate but equal doctrine—the doctrine promulgated by the Supreme Court in *Plessy v. Ferguson* that under the equal protection clause of the Fourteenth Amendment, state governments could separate the races as long as they had access to equal facilities.

Separation of powers—an essential principle of the first American state constitutions and the U.S. Constitution according to which the legislative, executive, and judicial powers of government are assigned to three distinct institutions.

Shays's Rebellion—a forcible uprising of mainly poor farmers in central and western Massachusetts between August 1786 and February 1787. The rebels, led by former Continental Army officer Daniel Shays, closed courts to prevent the foreclosure of farms or the imprisonment of farmers for debt.

Signing statement—a statement issued by a president on signing a bill, which sometimes challenges specific provisions on constitutional or other grounds.

Simple resolution—a resolution passed by either the House or Senate that usually addresses a matter affecting only one house.

Single-member district—district that elects only one member to a legislative body.

Slander—a defamatory statement made through speech (see also **Libel**).

Social Security—a system of old-age insurance that provides monthly benefits to retired workers and their spouses.

Social Security trust fund—the fund into which Social Security taxes are deposited and then used to buy federal securities (government IOUs).

Social welfare—the function of government to foster a healthy economy and to enhance the material well-being of citizens, both the poor and the nonpoor.

Social welfare state—a society and government that make it a high priority to promote the social welfare of the people (see **Social welfare**).

Soft money—political spending that influences elections but is not subject to contribution or expenditure limits under campaign finance law.

Solicitor general—a high-ranking official in the Department of Justice who represents the United States before the Supreme Court.

Speaker of the House—the chief officer of the House of Representatives.

Special interest—an unfavorable way to characterize those who stand to gain or lose more from a public policy.

Special order speech—a speech that members of the House of Representatives can give before or after each day's formal session in order to call attention to some matter.

Spin—the effort by newsmakers to influence news coverage in a particular direction.

Split-ticket voting—voting in any given election for candidates of different political parties for different offices (e.g., a Republican for governor, a Democrat for senator).

Spoiler effect—a phenomenon where a minor party draws its votes mainly from one major party, thereby tipping elections to the other major party.

Spoils system—the practice of giving jobs or contracts on the basis of political ties instead of merit.

Standing—a party's right to bring a case to court and receive a judicial resolution, usually requiring that the party has suffered a real injury and does not simply have a generalized grievance against an individual, organization, or the government.

Standing committee—a permanent body within Congress that evaluates proposals within its jurisdiction, chooses certain bills for consideration, and then revises and reports those bills to the full chamber. Also oversees specific agencies and programs.

Stare decisis—the principle, from the Latin for "let the decision stand," that calls for judges to look to past precedents as a guide whenever possible.

State—the name given to the former American colonies when they collectively declared independence from British rule in 1776.

State of nature—the doctrine developed particularly by English philosophers Thomas Hobbes and John Locke that refers to a state of society that preceded civil society. In a state of nature, there is no common authority to settle disputes and thus no one to protect the weaker from the stronger.

State of the Union address—an address delivered by the president to a joint session of Congress each year, usually in January, describing the state of the nation and proposing policy initiatives.

Strict construction—a method of interpreting the Constitution that claims to follow closely the actual words of the document as originally understood by those who wrote and ratified it.

Strict scrutiny—the level of scrutiny the Supreme Court uses to evaluate the legality of laws, policies, and programs that use racial classifications. In these cases, the government must show that the program serves a "compelling government interest" and that the means it adopts are "closely related" and "narrowly tailored" to serve that interest.

Subcommittee—a unit of a congressional committee that handles a very specific area of policy and legislation.

Suffrage—the right to vote.

Superdelegate—an informal term for a Democratic National Convention delegate who is not chosen in a primary or caucus, and who may vote for any candidate for the nomination. Most superdelegates automatically gain their status by being current or former party leaders and elected officials.

Super PAC—a political action committee that can accept unlimited contributions from individuals, unions, corporations, and associations, and spend unlimited sums on independent expenditures in federal election campaigns, provided that it does not contribute to or coordinate with parties or candidates.

Supplemental Security Income (SSI)—a federal program established in 1972 that provides monthly cash benefits to those over 65, the blind, and the disabled who have little income.

Supply-side economics—a school of thought holding that high taxes hurt economic growth by discouraging savings and investment. Supply-siders argue that cutting tax rates can spur economic activity, meaning bigger profits and payrolls, and perhaps even greater revenues.

Supremacy clause—the portion of Article VI saying that the Constitution, as well as all treaties and federal laws, "shall be the supreme Law of the Land."

Suspect class—the term the Supreme Court uses to characterize racial classifications in laws or government policies and programs. These cases require "strict scrutiny." (See **strict scrutiny**.)

Symbolic speech—conduct by which people sometimes express their political feelings without using speech as such; for example, burning the American flag as a sign of protest. Also called "expressive conduct."

Tacit consent—the consent that people may give to government even if they do not actively participate.

Taft-Hartley Act—the 1947 law that curbed union power in several ways, including a ban on closed shops.

Talking points—short, bulleted lists containing suggested phrases and background material that an organization supplies to its supporters to prepare them for talking with reporters and the public.

Tariff—a tax on imported goods for the purposes of either raising revenue or protecting domestic industries.

Tax credit—a dollar-for-dollar reduction in tax liability, usually for a specific purpose such as child care.

Tax deduction—an amount (often a personal or business expense) that reduces income subject to tax.

Tax exemption—a reduction in the amount of income subject to tax. There are two types: personal and dependency. The exemption amount changes from year to year.

Tax withholding—the system by which employers take money out of employees' paychecks and deposit it for the government. The government credits this money against the employees' tax liability when they file their returns. Employers withhold money for federal income taxes, social insurance taxes, and state and local income taxes in some states and localities.

Temporary Assistance to Needy Families (TANF)—the block grant program created in 1996 to replace Aid to Families with Dependent Children (AFDC).

Think tank—a research organization, usually nonprofit, that issues statements and reports on policy issues.

Third party—a political party other than the two major parties of the era. It may be either a short-lived movement that gains significant support or a longer-lasting movement that gets little.

Three-fifths clause—the provision of the Constitution (Article I, Section 2) that stipulated that slaves would count as three-fifths of a person when determining population for apportioning seats in the House of Representatives and direct taxes among the states.

Ticket splitting—the practice of voting for candidates of different parties for different offices in the same election.

Top-two primary—a primary in which a single ballot displays all candidates. Voters may choose a Republican for one office, a Democrat for another, and so on. The two candidates with the most votes go on to the general election, regardless of party.

Totalitarian—a political system or ideology that places no limits on the reach of governmental power over the individual.

Tracking poll—a survey that measures day-to-day changes in public opinion by updating the sample each day.

Trade or industry association—an organization that represents businesses in a particular field or industry.

Trade Promotion Authority—special procedures meant to speed up the regular process when Congress considers trade agreements. These special procedures limit debate and prohibit amendments.

Treaty of Guadalupe Hidalgo—the treaty between the United States and Mexico that ended the Mexican-American War in 1848. It provided that the approximately 100,000 residents of the lands ceded by Mexico would become American citizens unless they decided to retain their Mexican citizenship.

Trial balloon—proposals that newsmakers disclose to gauge the public's reaction.

Trial court—the court, such as federal district court, in which civil and criminal trials occur.

Trustee—a type of representation in which legislators exercise judgment independent of their constituents' views.

Unanimous consent agreement—an agreement negotiated in the Senate before floor debate begins, to specify the terms of debate. These require the approval of all interested senators.

Unanimous opinion—an opinion of an appellate court, such as the U.S. Supreme Court, that garners the approval of every member of the court.

Underground Railroad—an informal network of secret routes, safe houses, and transportation run by abolitionists to help slaves escape from the South to Canada in the period before the Civil War.

Unemployment—joblessness or, for the purpose of the federal government, the percentage of job seekers who cannot find work.

Unfunded mandate—law or rule requiring states and localities, or the private sector, to perform functions for which the federal government does not supply funding.

Unilateralism—the practice of avoiding permanent alliances and acting independently of other nations.

Union shop—a requirement that an employee join a union after starting employment.

Unitary system—a political system in which all authority lies in a central government, and other governments within the nation can do only what the central government allows. Examples include France and Japan.

United States Attorney—the chief prosecutor in each of the 94 federal judicial districts, nominated by the president and confirmed by the Senate.

United States Courts of Appeal—the federal courts intermediary between the district courts and the Supreme Court, one for each of 12 regions of the country and one for the Federal Circuit, which handles specialized cases.

United States District Courts—the basic trial courts (civil and criminal) in the federal system, where the typical federal case begins.

Unprotected speech—speech that the government may prohibit or punish because it is not included in the First Amendment guarantee of "freedom of speech," such as obscenity, libelous speech, and "fighting words."

U.S. Citizenship and Immigration Services—the bureau within the Department of Homeland Security that adjudicates immigration and naturalization issues and provides services to immigrants.

Veto—the president's constitutional authority to disapprove of a bill (or joint resolution) passed by the House and Senate. It is subject to override by a two-thirds vote of both houses. See also **Pocket veto**.

Virginia Plan—the plan for a strong national government of three independent branches—legislature, executive, and judiciary—introduced by Virginia governor Edmund Randolph at the beginning of the Constitutional Convention. It rejected amending the Articles of Confederation and proposed instead a wholly new government.

Virginia Resolutions—resolutions authored by James Madison and passed by the Virginia legislature in 1798 that criticized the Alien and Sedition Acts.

Voter-eligible population—all those who have the right to vote.

Voter registration—the requirement in most states for citizens to enter their names on a government list before voting in elections.

Voter turnout—the rate at which people take part in elections. This is calculated by dividing the total number of votes either by the voting-age population or by the voter-eligible population.

Voting-age population—all residents over the age of 18.

Wall of separation—Thomas Jefferson's phrase for the meaning of the establishment clause of the First Amendment; later accepted by the Supreme Court as indicating the original meaning of the establishment clause.

War on Poverty—President Lyndon Johnson's term for a wide range of federal policies to combat poverty in America.

War Powers Resolution—joint resolution passed by Congress in 1973 to limit the occasions when the president could order armed forces into combat, to require prior consultation with Congress before such actions and regular reporting afterward, and to force the withdrawal of troops within two to three months unless Congress specifically authorized further combat.

Warren Court—the Supreme Court under the leadership of Chief Justice Earl Warren, 1953–1969. It is famous for its rulings expanding rights.

Watchdog role—the news media's part in exposing corruption and official misconduct.

Welfare—the common term for the old Aid to Families with Dependent Children program, replaced in 1996 by Temporary Assistance to Needy Families (TANF).

Welfare state—a term to describe a government that sees its responsibility as providing for the material well-being of the citizens and that spends a significant amount of its resources to this end.

Whigs—major party that lasted from the 1830s to 1850s. It firmly supported economic development but split over the issue of slavery.

Whip—party leader whose job is to count votes and gather support from party lawmakers.

Whiskey Rebellion—the name given to the violent resistance of farmers in western Pennsylvania in 1792–1794 to a federal tax on distilled spirits.

Whistleblower—a federal employee who reports waste, fraud, or misconduct.

White House Office of Faith-Based and Neighborhood Partnerships—an office that President Obama established to assist religious organizations and secular nonprofits in providing social services.

White primary—a primary election introduced in southern states in the late nineteenth century limited to white voters.

Winner-take-all system—the system by which the presidential candidate who wins a plurality of a state's popular votes will win all of its electoral votes.

Wire service—an organization that provides news stories to subscribers, including newspapers and broadcasters.

Women's movement—the political and social movement that began at the Seneca Falls Convention in 1848 that sought full legal and political equality for women.

Writ of certiorari—a request by the losing side in a case decided by a federal appeals court or a state supreme court to have the U.S. Supreme Court review and overturn the decision.

Writ of habeas corpus—protects individuals from arbitrary arrest by authorizing a judge to free someone from confinement if there are not sufficient legal grounds for holding him or her.

Writ of mandamus—an order from a court to an officer of the government or to a lower court requiring the performance of some mandatory, or ministerial, duty.

Yellow journalism—news coverage that emphasizes sex, crime, and scandal over substantive public policy.

Endnotes

Chapter 1

1. Harold D. Lasswell, *Politics: Who Gets What, When, How* (New York: McGraw-Hill, 1936).

2. Kevin L. Falk and Thomas M. Kane, "The Maginot Mentality in International Relations Models," *Parameters*, Summer 1998, at www.carlisle.army.mil/usawc/Parameters/98summer/falk.htm, accessed May 8, 2009.

3. John F. Kennedy, *Profiles in Courage* (New York: Harper, 1961), 20.

4. Tom Tyler, "Obeying the Law in America: Procedural Justice and the Sense of Fairness" at http://usinfo.org/enus/government/branches/tyler.html, accessed April 15, 2012.

5. Aristotle, *Politics*, Book III, translated by Benjamin Jowett in *Introduction to Aristotle*, ed. Richard McKeon (New York: The Modern Library, 1992), 619.

6. David Truman, *The Governmental Process: Political Interests and Public Opinion*, 2nd ed. (New York: Knopf, 1971, first published in 1951), 368.

7. Ibid., 51.

8. David Mayhew, *Congress: The Electoral Connection* (New Haven, CT: Yale University Press, 1974), 122.

9. Morris Fiorina, *Congress: Keystone of the Washington Establishment*, 2nd ed. (New Haven, CT: Yale University Press, 1989, first published in 1977), 47.

10. For articles and books on deliberation and deliberative democracy or that critique the reduction of politics to self-interest, see especially Joseph M. Bessette, "Deliberative Democracy: The Majority Principle in Republican Government," in *How Democratic is the Constitution?* ed. Robert A. Goldwin and William A. Schambra (Washington, DC: American Enterprise Institute, 1980); Jane J. Mansbridge, *Beyond Adversary Democracy* (Chicago: University of Chicago Press, 1983); Steven Kelman, *Making Public Policy: A Hopeful View of American Government* (New York: Basic Books, 1987); James Q. Wilson, "Interests and Deliberation in the American Republic, or, Why James Madison Would Never Have Received the James Madison Award," in *PS: Political Science and Politics* 23(4), December 1990; Jane J. Mansbridge, ed., *Beyond Self-Interest* (Chicago: University of Chicago Press, 1990); James S. Fishkin, *Democracy and Deliberation: New Directions for Democratic Reform* (New Haven, CT: Yale University Press, 1991); Joseph M. Bessette, *The Mild Voice of Reason: Deliberative Democracy and American National Government* (Chicago: University of Chicago Press, 1994); James S. Fishkin, *The Voice of the People: Public Opinion and Democracy* (New Haven, CT: Yale University Press, 1995); John Elster, ed., *Deliberative Democracy* (Cambridge: Cambridge University Press, 1998); Amy Gutmann and Dennis Thompson, *Why Deliberative Democracy?* (Princeton, NJ: Princeton University Press, 2004); Gary Mucciaroni and Paul J. Quirk, *Deliberative Choices: Debating Public Policy in Congress* (Chicago: University of Chicago Press, 2006).

11. Available at http://avalon.law.yale.edu/17th_century/mayflower.asp, accessed April 15, 2012.

12. Ralph Waldo Emerson, "Historical Discourse at Concord [Massachusetts]," September 12, 1835, at www.rwe.org/comm/index.php?option=com_content&task=view&id=72&Itemid=250, accessed April 15, 2012.

13. Quoted in Thomas G. West, *Vindicating the Founders: Race, Sex, Class, and Justice in the Origins of America* (Lanham, MD: Rowman & Littlefield, 1997), 122.

14. Data on voting rights and property qualifications are from West, *Vindicating the Founders*, 114.

15. Alexander Hamilton, James Madison, and John Jay, *The Federalist Papers*, ed. Clinton Rossiter, with a new introduction and notes by Charles R. Kesler (New York: New American Library, Signet Classic, 2003), no. 10, 76.

16. Ibid., no. 58, 358.

17. Ibid., no. 10, 72.

18. Ibid., 76.

19. Ibid., 76.

20. Ibid., no. 63, 382.

21. Ibid., no. 10, 76–77.

22. Ibid., 78.

23. Ibid., no. 51, 322.

24. Ibid., no. 63, 382.

25. Ibid., no. 71, 431, emphasis in the original.

26. Ibid., 431.

27. Ibid., no. 63, 383.

28. Initiative and Referendum Institute, *Initiative Use*, January 2008, available at www.iandrinstitute.org/,

accessed October 18, 2008. Although the citizens of South Dakota gained the right to place initiatives on the ballot in 1898, it was 1904 before an initiative appeared before voters in a state (in Oregon).

29. Terry Teachout, "Serenading a Tyrant: Should the New York Philharmonic Go to North Korea?" *Wall Street Journal*, October 27, 2007, W14.

30. *Federalist*, no. 70, 428.

31. Edward P. Djerejian, Assistant Secretary for Near East Affairs, "U.S. Policy Goals in the Near East," address before the National Association of Arab Americans, Washington, DC, September 11, 1992, at www.findarticles.com/p/articles/mi_m1584/is_n37_v3/ai_12800521/pg_7, accessed April 15, 2012.

32. The quotations are in Pauline Maier, *American Scripture: Making the Declaration of Independence* (New York: Vintage Books, 1998), 27–28.

33. Thomas Paine, *Common Sense*, ed. Isaac Kramnick (London: Penguin Books, 1986), 79, 80.

34. The original source of the inaccurate account is unknown. The correct version is based on the biographical sketches in Robert G. Ferris, ed., *Signers of the Declaration* (Washington, DC: U.S. Department of the Interior, National Park Service, 1975). See also the corrected version at www.snopes.com/history/american/pricepaid.asp?print=y, accessed April 15, 2012.

35. Thomas Jefferson, "Letter to Henry Lee," May 8, 1825, in *The Life and Selected Writings of Thomas Jefferson*, ed. Adrienne Koch and William Peden (New York: Random House, 1944), 719.

36. *Webster's Ninth New Collegiate Dictionary* (Springfield, MA: Merriam-Webster, 1991), 1066.

37. *Federalist*, no. 23, 149.

38. Abraham Lincoln, "Letter to Henry L. Pierce, & Others" April 6, 1859, available at http://teachingamericanhistory.org/library/index.asp?document=101, accessed April 15, 2012.

39. These expressions are quoted in West, *Vindicating the Founders*, 73–74. The sources are at ibid., 194, n. 8.

40. "Speech on the Dred Scott Decision," Springfield, Illinois, June 26, 1857, emphasis in the original; available at www.teachingamericanhistory.org/library/index.asp?document=52, accessed April 15, 2012.

41. John Locke, *Two Treatises of Government*, ed. Peter Laslett (New York: New American Library, Mentor Book, 1965), "Second Treatise of Government," section 222, 461.

42. "Letter to Dr. Benjamin Rush," January 16, 1811, available at http://etext.virginia.edu/etcbin/toccer-new2?id=JefLett.sgm&images=images/modeng&data=/texts/english/modeng/parsed&tag=public&part=205&division=div1, accessed April 15, 2012.

43. Thomas Hobbes, *Leviatian*, ed. Richard Tuck (Cambridge: Cambridge University Press, 1991), Part One, chap. 13, 89.

44. Locke, "Second Treatise," section 21, 323, emphasis in the original.

45. "Letter to Dr. Walter Jones," January 2, 1814, available at http://etext.virginia.edu/etcbin/toccer-new2?id=JefLett.sgm&images=images/modeng&data=/texts/english/modeng/parsed&tag=public&part=224&division=div1, accessed April 15, 2012.

46. "Letter to Henry L. Pierce, & Others."

47. "Speech on the Dred Scott Decision."

48. Republican Party Platform of 1856, June 17, 1856, available at www.presidency.ucsb.edu/ws/index.php?pid=29619, accessed April 15, 2012.

49. "Speech on the Repeal of the Missouri Compromise," Peoria, Illinois, October 16, 1854, available at http://teachingamericanhistory.org/library/index.asp?document=51, accessed April 15, 2012.

50. Martin Luther King Jr., "I Have a Dream" Speech, August 28, 1963, at http://avalon.law.yale.edu/20th_century/mlk01.asp, accessed April 15, 2012.

51. Thomas Jefferson, "Letter to Roger C. Weightman," June 24, 1826, at http://etext.virginia.edu/etcbin/toccer-new2?id=JefLett.sgm&images=images/modeng&data=/texts/english/modeng/parsed&tag=public&part=285&division=div1, accessed April 15, 2012.

52. Quoted in "Iraqis Sign Interim Constitution," John Daniszewski, *Los Angeles Times*, March 9, 2004, A10.

53. See West, *Vindicating the Founders*, 113–115.

54. Available at www.marxists.org/archive/marx/works/1848/communist-manifesto/ch04.htm, accessed November 12, 2007.

55. Quoted in "Big Brother Still Knows Best but Now Keeps Some Distance," David Lamb, *Los Angeles Times*, August 18, 2000, A5.

56. "Arab Spring" in Britannica Online Encyclopedia, at http://www.britannica.com/EBchecked/topic/1784922/Arab-Spring, accessed April 12, 2012; Matthew Kaminski, "Islamists Inside the Gates," *Wall Street Journal*, April 10, 2012, at http://online.wsj.com/article/SB10001424052702303299604577327770236632262.html; Pew Research Center, Global Attitudes Project, "Most Embrace a Role for Islam in Politics," December 2, 2010, available at http://pewglobal.org/files/2010/12/Pew-Global-Attitudes-Muslim-Report-FINAL-December-2-2010.pdf, accessed April 12, 2012.

57. Freedom House, *Freedom in the World 2012*, pp. 3–4, available at http://www.freedomhouse.org/sites/default/files/inline_images/FIW%202012%20Booklet--Final.pdf, accessed April 13, 2012.

58. Middle East Media Research Institute, *Special Dispatch Series - No. 1285*, September 8, 2006, available at www.memri.org/bin/articles.cgi?Page=archives&Area=sd&ID=SP128506, accessed April 15, 2012.

59. John Adams, "Thoughts on Government," April 1776, available at http://www.constitution.org/jadams/thoughts.htm, accessed April 12, 2012.

60. Massachusetts Constitution of 1780, Part the First, Article XXX; available at www.teachingamericanhistory.org/library/index.asp?document=266, accessed April 15, 2012.

61. Kepher Otieno, "Separation of Powers Now Comes to the Fore," *The Standard*, February 19, 2011, available at http://www.standardmedia.co.ke/politics/InsidePage.php?id=2000029563&cid=289&currentPage=1, accessed April 13, 2012.

62. Montesquieu, *The Spirit of the Laws*, ed. and trans. Anne M. Cohler, Basia Carolyn Miller, and Harold Samuel Stone (Cambridge: Cambridge University Press, 1989), 28, emphasis in the original.

63. Jeffrey Fleishman, "Kadafi's Last Refuge, Fear, Is Collapsing," *Los Angeles Times*, February 21, 2011, available at http://articles.latimes.com/2011/feb/21/world/la-fg-libya-kadafi-20110222, accessed April 13, 2012.

64. Raja Abdulrahim, "In Freed Benghazi, Libya's Second City, Strong Calls for Kadafi's Overthrow," *Los Angeles Times*, February 24, 2011, available at http://articles.latimes.com/2011/feb/24/world/la-fg-libya-benghazi-20110225, accessed April 13, 2012.

65. George Washington, "Farewell Address," available at http://avalon.law.yale.edu/18th_century/washing.asp, accessed April 15, 2012.

66. "Letter to Colonel Edward Carrington," January 16, 1787, available at http://etext.virginia.edu/etcbin/toccer-new2?id=JefLett.sgm&images=images/modeng&data=/texts/english/modeng/parsed&tag=public&part=52&division=div1, accessed April 15, 2012.

67. "Report of the Commissioners for the University of Virginia," August 4, 1818, in *The Portable Thomas Jefferson*, ed. Merrill D. Peterson (New York: Viking Press, 1975), 334.

68. James Madison, "Letter to W. T. Barry," August 4, 1822, available at http://press-pubs.uchicago.edu/founders/documents/v1ch18s35.html, accessed April 15, 2012.

Chapter 2

1. Alexander Hamilton, James Madison, and John Jay, *The Federalist Papers*, ed. Clinton Rossiter, with a new introduction and notes by Charles R. Kesler (New York: New American Library, Signet Classic, 2003), No. 1, 27.

2. George Washington, Thanksgiving Proclamation, October 3, 1789, available at www.presidency.ucsb.edu/ws/index.php?pid=65502, accessed April 16, 2012.

3. George Washington, "Circular to the States," August 27, 1780, available at oll.libertyfund.org/?option=com_staticxt&staticfile=show.php%3Ftitle=848&chapter=101800&layout=html&Itemid=27, accessed April 16, 2012.

4. Andrew C. McLaughlin, *A Constitutional History of the United States* (New York: Appleton-Century, 1935), 145.

5. Thomas Jefferson, "Notes on the State of Virginia," in *The Portable Thomas Jefferson* (New York: Viking Penguin, 1975), 164, emphasis in the original.

6. George Washington, "Letter to James Madison," November 5, 1786, available at teachingamericanhistory.org/library/index.asp?document=325, accessed April 16, 2012.

7. "Abigail Adams to Jefferson," January 29, 1787, in *The Complete Adams-Jefferson Letters*, ed. Lester J. Cappon (Chapel Hill: University of North Carolina Press, 1987), 168.

8. James Madison, "Vices of the Political System of the United States," available at press-pubs.uchicago.edu/founders/documents/v1ch5s16.html, accessed April 16, 2012.

9. James Madison, "Letter to Thomas Jefferson," October 24, 1787, available at press-pubs.uchicago.edu/founders/documents/v1ch17s22.html, accessed April 16, 2012.

10. Madison, "Vices of the Political System of the United States."

11. The Virginia Plan and Randolph's speech introducing it can be found in *The Records of the Federal Convention of 1787*, ed. Max Farrand, 4 vols. (New Haven, CT: Yale University Press, 1966), I:18–22 (May 29).

12. Ibid., 18–19.

13. *Federalist*, no. 40, 221. Madison here quotes from the Declaration of Independence.

14. Farrand, *Records*, I:293 (June 18).

15. Ibid., I:291 (June 18).

16. Ibid., I:283 (June 18).

17. Ibid., I:242 (June 15).

18. Ibid., I:492 (June 30).

19. Ibid., I:493 (June 30) and I:514 (July 2).

20. Ibid., I:483 (June 30), emphasis in the original.

21. Ibid., I:476 (June 29).

22. Ibid., I:468 (June 29).

23. Ibid., I:488 (June 30).

24. See Madison's discussion of the informal meeting of the delegates who were opposed to an equal vote in the Senate, at ibid., II:19–20 (July 16).

25. Ibid., II:33 (July 17).

26. Ibid., II:57 (July 19).

27. Ibid., II:114 (July 25).

28. Ibid., II:31 (July 17).

29. Ibid., I:48 (May 31).

30. Ibid., I:151 (June 7).

31. Ibid., II:73 (July 21).

32. Ibid., II:644 (September 17).

33. Noah Webster's *An American Dictionary of the English Language*, first published in 1828, is available at cbtministries.org/default/index.cfm/resources/1828-websters-dictionary, accessed April 16, 2012.

34. See the U.S. Office of Personnel Management, "The Oath of Office and the Constitution" at www.opm.gov/constitution_initiative/oath.asp, accessed April 16, 2012.

35. Farrand, *Records*, II:648 (September 17).

36. Ibid., II:90 (July 23).

37. Ibid., II:469 (August 30).

38. Ibid.

39. Ibid., II:476 (August 31).

40. Charles R Kesler, "Introduction," in *The Federalist Papers*, x.

41. Thomas Jefferson, "Letter to James Madison," November 18, 1788, available at teachingamericanhistory.org/library/index.asp?document=2502, accessed April 16, 2012.

42. *Federalist,* no. 23, 149, 152.

43. *Federalist,* no. 25, 162.

44. *Federalist,* no. 51, 318–319.

45. Ibid., 319.

46. Farrand, *Records,* II:632 (September 15).

47. "Centinel, Letter I," October 1787, in *The Anti-Federalist: An Abridgment of The Complete Anti-Federalist,* ed. Herbert J. Storing (Chicago: University of Chicago Press, 1985), 15.

48. "Essays of Brutus," I, in *The Anti-Federalist,* 113.

49. Montesquieu, *The Spirit of the Laws,* ed. and trans. Anne M. Cohler, Basia Carolyn Miller, and Harold Samuel Stone (Cambridge: Cambridge University Press, 1989), 35–36.

50. Quoted in Herbert J. Storing, *What the Anti-Federalists Were For* (Chicago: University of Chicago Press, 1981), 76.

51. *Federalist,* no. 9, 68.

52. *Federalist,* no. 10, 75.

53. Ibid., 72.

54. Ibid., 74.

55. Ibid., 77.

56. Ibid., 78.

57. *Federalist,* no. 51, 321.

58. Ibid., 322.

59. *Federalist,* no. 39, 242.

60. *Federalist,* no. 57, 348.

61. *Federalist,* no. 64, 389.

62. *Federalist,* no. 55, 343.

63. *Federalist,* no. 85, 521.

64. *Federalist,* no. 49, 311.

65. Thomas Jefferson, "Letter to Samuel Kercheval," July 12, 1816, in *The Portable Thomas Jefferson,* ed. Merrill D. Peterson (New York: Viking Press, 1975), 558–560.

66. *Federalist,* no. 49, 311–312.

67. President George Washington, Farewell Address, September 17, 1796, available at avalon.law.yale.edu/18th_century/washing.asp, accessed April 15, 2012.

68. "The Failed Amendments," available at www.usconstitution.net/constamfail.html, accessed April 17, 2012.

69. This account is from Robert A. Goldwin, *From Parchment to Power: How James Madison Used the Bill of Rights to Save the Constitution* (Washington, DC: AEI Press, 1997), and Herbert J. Storing, "The Constitution and the Bill of Rights" in *Toward a More Perfect Union: Writings of Herbert J. Storing,* ed. Joseph M. Bessette (Washington, DC: AEI Press, 1995).

70. Thomas Jefferson, "Letter to James Madison," December 20, 1787, available at teachingamericanhistory.org/library/index.asp?document=2550, accessed April 17, 2012.

71. *Federalist,* no. 84, 514.

72. Quoted in Goldwin, *From Parchment to Power,* 80.

73. The speaker is Congressman Aedanus Burke as quoted in Herbert J. Storing, "The Constitution and the Bill of Rights," 113.

74. Quoted in Goldwin, *From Parchment to Power,* 130.

75. Goldwin, *From Parchment to Power,* 173.

76. Ibid., 175.

77. This information on the slave trade is from W. E. B. DuBois, *The Suppression of the African Slave-Trade to the United States, 1638–1870* (New York: Dover, 1970, originally published in 1896).

78. Quoted in ibid., 7.

79. Quoted in ibid., 13–14.

80. "The Will of George Washington," Mount Vernon, July 9, 1799, available at www.gwpapers.virginia.edu/documents/will/text.html; accessed April 17, 2012.

81. Farrand, *Records,* II:95 (July 23).

82. Ibid., II:364 (August 21).

83. Ibid., II:370 (August 22).

84. Ibid.

85. Ibid., II:371 (August 22).

86. Ibid.

87. Ibid., II:372 (August 22).

88. Ibid., II:373 (August 22).

89. Ibid., II:417 (August 25).

90. Remarks by National Security Adviser Condoleezza Rice to Veterans of Foreign Wars, August 25, 2003, available at georgewbush-whitehouse.archives.gov/news/releases/2003/08/20030825-1.html, accessed April 18, 2012.

91. *Federalist,* no. 54, 336.

92. Farrand, *Records,* II:628 (September 15). The brackets indicate that Madison added the word *legal* some years after he first took the notes.

93. Abraham Lincoln, "Cooper Union Address," New York City, February 27, 1860, available at www.showcase.netins.net/web/creative/lincoln/speeches/cooper.htm, accessed April 17, 2012.

94. Quoted in Herbert J. Storing, "Frederick Douglass," in *Toward a More Perfect Union,* 159.

95. Frederick Douglass, "What to the Slave Is the Fourth of July," July 5, 1852, Rochester, NY, available at www.teachingamericanhistory.org/library/index.asp?document=162, accessed April 17, 2012.

96. Quoted in Herbert J. Storing, "Slavery and the Moral Foundations of the American Republic," in *Toward a More Perfect Union,* 138.

97. Thurgood Marshall, "Remarks at the Annual Seminar of the San Francisco Patent and Trademark Law Association," Maui, Hawaii, May 6, 1987, available at www.thurgoodmarshall.com/speeches/constitutional_speech.htm, accessed April 17, 2012.

98. Clarence Thomas, "The Virtue of Practical Wisdom," February 9, 1999, available at www.claremont.org/publications/pubid.524/pub_detail.asp, accessed May 12, 2009.

99. Quoted in Clinton Rossiter, *1787: The Grand Convention* (New York: Mentor Books, 1966), 11.

100. Farrand, *Records*, II:667.

101. George Washington, letter to Lafayette, February 7, 1788, available at www.gwpapers.virginia.edu/documents/constitution/1788/lafayette1.html, accessed April 17, 2012.

Chapter 3

1. Hubert H. Humphrey, remarks on the civil rights platform plank at the Democratic National Convention, Philadelphia, July 14, 1948, at www.americanrhetoric.com/speeches/PDFFiles/Hubert%20Humphrey%20-%201948%20DNC.pdf, accessed April 7, 2012.

2. President Barack Obama, remarks at the signing of a presidential memorandum regarding federal benefits, June 17, 2009, www.whitehouse.gov/the_press_office/Remarks-by-the-President-at-the-Signing-of-a-Presidential-Memorandum-Regarding-Federal-Benefits-and-Non-Discrimination, accessed April 7, 2012.

3. Forum of Federations, "Federalism by Country," at www.forumfed.org/en/federalism/by_country/index.php, accessed April 7, 2012.

4. United States Department of Commerce, Bureau of the Census, *Statistical Abstract of the United States 2012* (Washington, DC: Government Printing Office, 2011), 267.

5. Death Penalty Information Center, "Facts about the Death Penalty," March 29, 2012, at www.deathpenaltyinfo.org/FactSheet.pdf, accessed April 7, 2012.

6. U.S. Government Accountability Office, *Illicit Tobacco: Various Schemes Are Used to Evade Taxes and Fees*, GAO-11-313 March 2011, at www.gao.gov/assets/320/316372.pdf, accessed April 7, 2012.

7. Quoted in Judy Rakowsky, "Informant or Killer? US, Boston Disagree," *Boston Globe*, November 28, 1997, A1.

8. Akhil Reed Amar, *America's Constitution: A Biography* (New York: Random House, 2005), 106.

9. Alexander Hamilton, James Madison, and John Jay, *The Federalist Papers*, ed. Clinton Rossiter with a new introduction and notes by Charles R. Kesler (New York: Signet, 2003), no. 51, 320.

10. Michael S. Greve, *Real Federalism: Why It Matters, How It Could Happen* (Washington, DC: AEI Press, 1999), 2–3.

11. Alexis de Tocqueville, *Democracy in America*, ed. J. P. Mayer and trans. George Lawrence (Garden City, NY: Anchor Books, 1969), 63.

12. European Union, *The European Union: A Guide for Americans*, 2011, at www.eurunion.org/eu/images/stories/guideforamer2011.pdf, accessed April 7, 2012.

13. *New State Ice Co. v. Liebman*, 285 U.S. 262, 311 (1932). Writers often attribute the phrase "laboratories of democracy" to Brandeis, but it is a paraphrase instead of a direct quotation.

14. *Federalist*, no. 46, 292.

15. James Madison, *The Debates in the Federal Convention of 1787*, June 30, 1787, at avalon.law.yale.edu/18th_century/debates_630.asp, accessed April 7, 2012.

16. *Federalist*, no. 45, 289.

17. Herbert J. Storing, *What the Anti-Federalists Were For: The Political Thought of the Opponents of the Constitution* (Chicago: University of Chicago Press, 1981), 21.

18. Cato [pseudonym, probably George Clinton], fourth letter, November 8, 1787, *The Founders' Constitution*, at press-pubs.uchicago.edu/founders/documents/a2_1_1s6.html, accessed August 14, 2012.

19. Walter A. McDougall, *Promised Land, Crusader State: The American Encounter with the World since 1776* (Boston: Houghton Mifflin, 1997), 218–219.

20. *Gibbons v. Ogden*, 22 U.S. (9 Wheat.) 1, at 204–205 (1819).

21. *McCulloch v. Maryland*, 17 U.S. (4 Wheat.), 216, 421 (1819).

22. Ibid., 436.

23. *Gibbons*, 22 U.S. (9 Wheat.), 203.

24. Authors' calculations from United States Department of Commerce, Bureau of the Census, *Historical Statistics of the United States: Colonial Times to 1970* (Washington, DC: Government Printing Office, 1975), 8, 1103; United States Office of Personnel Management, "Historical Federal Workforce Tables," www.opm.gov/feddata/HistoricalTables/TotalGovernmentSince1962.asp, accessed April 7, 2012.

25. Draft of Kentucky Resolution, October 1798, at avalon.law.yale.edu/18th_century/jeffken.asp; Kentucky Resolution of 1799 at avalon.law.yale.edu/18th_century/kenres.asp; Virginia Resolution of 1798 at avalon.law.yale.edu/18th_century/virres.asp, accessed April 7, 2012.

26. South Carolina Ordinance of Nullification, November 24, 1832, at avalon.law.yale.edu/19th_century/ordnull.asp, accessed April 7, 2012.

27. Andrew Jackson, "Proclamation Regarding Nullification," December 10, 1832, at avalon.law.yale.edu/19th_century/jack01.asp, accessed April 7, 2012.

28. *Federalist*, no. 27, 173.

29. Andrew Jackson, "Proclamation Regarding Nullification."

30. Tocqueville, *Democracy in America*, 394.

31. *Ableman v. Booth* 62 U.S. 506, 517 (1858).

32. Declaration of the Immediate Causes Which Induce and Justify the Secession of South Carolina from the Federal Union, December 24, 1860, at avalon.law.yale.edu/19th_century/csa_scarsec.asp, accessed April 7, 2012.

33. For the weaknesses of the "state rights" theory as an explanation for the war's outcome, see James M. McPherson, *Drawn with the Sword: Reflections on the American Civil War* (New York: Oxford University Press, 1996), 118–121.

34. James B. McPherson, *Abraham Lincoln and the Second American Revolution* (New York: Oxford University

Press, 1991), 38–40; James M. McPherson, *Battle Cry of Freedom: The Civil War Era* (New York: Ballantine Books, 1989), 448.

35. *City of Rome v. United States,* 446 US 156 (1980).

36. McPherson, *Abraham Lincoln and the Second American Revolution,* viii. The changes in usage, of course, were neither instant nor absolute.

37. James Bryce, *The American Commonwealth* (Indianapolis, IN: Liberty Fund, 1995), Vol. I:371.

38. *The Civil Rights Cases,* 109 U.S. 3 (1883).

39. Ralph A. Rossum, *Federalism, the Supreme Court, and the Seventeenth Amendment: The Irony of Constitutional Democracy* (Lanham, MD: Lexington, 2001), 93–94.

40. Ralph Rossum, "A Short History of a Big Mistake," *The American Interest* 1 (Summer 2006): 82–93.

41. Alan I. Abramowitz and Jeffrey A. Segal, *Senate Elections* (Ann Arbor: University of Michigan Press, 1992), 18–19.

42. Randall G. Holcombe, "The Growth of the Federal Government in the 1920s," *Cato Journal* 16 (Fall 1996), at www.cato.org/pubs/journal/cj16n2-2.html, accessed April 7, 2012.

43. *N.L.R.B. v. Jones & Laughlin Steel Corp.,* 301 U.S. 1, 36 (1937).

44. *Wickard v. Filburn,* 317 U.S. 111, 119 (1942).

45. *U.S. v. Darby,* 312 U.S. 100, 124 (1941).

46. David Osborne, *Laboratories of Democracy: A New Breed of Governor Creates Models for National Growth* (Boston: Harvard Business School Press, 1990), 315.

47. The Citizens Conference on State Legislatures, *The Sometime Governments: A Critical Study of the 50 American Legislatures* (New York: Bantam Books, 1973).

48. John E. Chubb, "Federalism and the Bias for Centralization," in *The New Direction in American Politics,* ed. John E. Chubb and Paul E. Peterson (Washington, DC: Brookings Institution, 1985), 278.

49. Richard M. Nixon, Address to the Nation on Domestic Programs, August 8, 1969, at www.presidency.ucsb.edu/ws/?pid=2191, accessed April 7, 2012.

50. James Hosek and Robert Levine, "An Introduction to the Issues," in *The New Fiscal Federalism and the Social Safety Net: A View from California,* ed. James Hosek and Robert Levine (Santa Monica, CA: RAND, 1996), at www.rand.org/pubs/conf_proceedings/CF123/hosek.levine/index.html, accessed April 7, 2012.

51. Ronald W. Reagan, Remarks at the Annual Legislative Conference of the National Association of Counties, March 4, 1985, at www.presidency.ucsb.edu/ws/?pid=38280, accessed April 9, 2012.

52. Robert J. Dilger and Richard S. Beth, "Unfunded Mandates Reform Act: History, Impact, and Issues" (Washington, DC: Congressional Research Service, 2011), at assets.opencrs.com/rpts/R40957_20110419.pdf, accessed April 7, 2012

53. *McDonald v. Chicago,* 561 U.S. 3025 (2010).

54. Damon W. Root, "Stop Smearing Federalism," *Reason,* November 10, 2010, at reason.com/archives/

2010/11/10/stop-smearing-federalism, accessed April 7, 2012.

55. *Florida et al. v. U.S. Dept. of Health and Human Services et al.,* brief of state petitioners on Medicaid, January 10, 2012, at www.oyeztoday.org/healthcare/States%20brief%20as%20petitioner%20(Medicaid).pdf, accessed April 8, 2012.

56. *Florida et al. v. U.S. Dept. of Health and Human Services et al.,* transcript of oral argument, March 28, 2012, at www.supremecourt.gov/oral_arguments/argument_transcripts/11-400.pdf, accessed April 8, 2012.

57. *National Federation of Independent Business v. Sebelius,* 567 U. S. ____ (2012), at www.supremecourt.gov/opinions/11pdf/11-393c3a2.pdf, accessed July 12, 2012.

58. *National League of Cities v. Usery,* 426 U.S. 833, 852 (1976).

59. *Garcia v. San Antonio Metro. Transit Auth.,* 469 U.S. 528, 556 (1985).

60. *Congressional Record* (daily), November 8, 2011, S7193.

61. *Congressional Record* (daily), May 19, 2010, S3971.

62. State Senator Geoff Michel, quoted in Norman Draper, "No Child Left Behind: GOP Senators Want It to Be History," *Minneapolis Star-Tribune,* January 1, 2008, at www.startribune.com/politics/state/12963721.html, accessed April 8, 2012.

63. U.S. Department of Education, "Use of Technology in Teaching and Learning," http://www.ed.gov/oii-news/use-technology-teaching-and-learning, accessed April 14, 2012.

64. North Carolina Virtual Public School, "History," at http://www.ncvps.org/index.php/about-us/history/, accessed April 14, 2012.

65. I. Elaine Allen and Jeff Seaman, *Going the Distance: Online Education in the United States, 2011* (Wellesley, MA: Babson Survey Research Group, 2011), at http://www.onlinelearningsurvey.com/reports/goingthedistance.pdf, accessed April 14, 2012.

66. Office of the Governor, "Gov. Perry: Texas Knows Best How to Educate Our Students," January 13, 2010, at governor.state.tx.us/news/press-release/14146/, accessed April 8, 2012.

67. *Federalist,* no. 17, 115.

68. Congress, House, Committee on Judiciary, Subcommittee on Crime, Terrorism, and Homeland Security, *Over-Criminalization of Conduct, Over-Federalization of Criminal Law,* 111th Cong, 1st sess., July 22, 2009, 2.

69. *United States v. Lopez,* 514 U.S. 549, 567–568 (1995).

70. *Printz v. United States,* 521 U.S. 898, 935 (1997).

71. *United States v. Morrison et al.,* 529 U.S. 598, 613 (2000).

72. *Gonzales, Attorney General et al. v. Oregon et al.,* 546 U.S. 243 (2006).

73. Ibid.

74. *Alberto R. Gonzales, Attorney General et al., Petitioners v. Angel McBlary Raich et al.,* 545 U.S. 1 (2005).

75. Debra J. Saunders, "Obama, The Happy Drug Warrior," *San Francisco Chronicle,* April 8, 2012, at www.sfgate.

com/cgi-bin/article.cgi?file=/c/a/2012/04/06/INAT1M-NV8R.DTL, accessed April 8, 2012.

76. *Alden et al. v. Maine,* 527 U.S. 706 (1999).

77. *Federal Maritime Commission v. South Carolina State Ports Authority et al.,* 535 U.S. 743 (2002).

78. *Congressional Record* (daily), October 20, 2005, H8993; *BMW of North America, Inc. v. Gore,* 517 U.S. 559, 571 (1996).

79. *Congressional Record* (daily), October 20, 2005, H8996.

80. *Congressional Record* (daily), June 6, 2006, S5452–S5453.

81. Maggie Gallagher, "Latter Day Federalists," *The Weekly Standard,* March 29, 2004, at www.weeklystandard .com/Content/Public/Articles/000/000/003/880whlda .asp?pg=2, accessed April 8, 2012.

82. Transcript: Robin Roberts ABC News Interview With President Obama, May 9, 2012, at abcnews.go.com/ Politics/transcript-robin-roberts-abc-news-interview-president-obama/story?id=16316043, accessed July 12, 2012.

83. In a Supreme Court case upholding an individual right to keep and bear arms, the majority cited this definition. *DC v. Heller,* 554 U.S. 290 (2008), at www.supremecourt .gov/opinions/07pdf/07-290.pdf, page 23, accessed April 8, 2012.

84. The Army National Guard, "About Us," at www.arng. army.mil/aboutus/Pages/default.aspx, accessed April 8, 2012.

85. *Perpich v. Department of Defense,* 496 U.S. 334 (1990).

86. Select Bipartisan Committee to Investigate the Preparation for and Response to Hurricane Katrina, *A Failure of Initiative,* February 15, 2006, 206–207, at www .gpoaccess.gov/katrinareport/mainreport.pdf, accessed April 8, 2012.

87. Public Policy Polling, "Louisianans Support Off-Shore Drilling," June 14, 2010, publicpolicypolling.blogspot .com/2010/06/fallout-from-spill.html, accessed April 8, 2012.

88. David Brooks, "Trim the 'Experts,' Trust the Locals," *New York Times,* June 18, 2010, www.nytimes .com/2010/06/18/opinion/18brooks.html, accessed April 8, 2012.

89. Zachary Newkirk, "Tiny Towns Spend Big Bucks on Lobbyists to Reap Federal Government Riches," Open Secrets Blog, May 4, 2011, at www.opensecrets.org/news/2011/05/ tiny-towns-spend-big-on-lobbyists-to-reap-federal-government-riches.html, accessed April 8, 2012.

90. Ibid.

91. Summer Lollie, "State and Local Governments Aggressively Lobby the Federal Government in Hope of Federal Aid," Open Secrets Blog, July 2, 2010, at www .opensecrets.org/news/2010/07/state-and-local-governments-agressi.html, accessed April 8, 1992.

92. Ibid.

93. *Kelo et al. v. City of New London et al.,* 545 U.S. 469 (2005), at www.law.cornell.edu/supct/pdf/04-108P.ZO, accessed April 8, 2012.

94. National Conference of State Legislatures, "Eminent Domain Overview," 2012, at www.ncsl.org/issues-research/ env-res/eminent-domain-overview.aspx, accessed April 8, 2012.

95. Clint Bolick, *Grassroots Tyranny: The Limits of Federalism* (Washington, DC: Cato Institute, 1993).

96. Daniel Patrick Moynihan, "The Devolution Revolution," *New York Times,* August 6, 1995, D15.

97. Tom Carper, "Race to the Top," *Blueprint,* January/ February 2002, at www.dlc.org/ndol_ci.cfm?kaid=114& subid=143&contentid=250085, accessed April 8, 2012.

98. Matthew Potoski, "Clean Air Federalism: Do States Race to the Bottom?" *Public Administration Review* 61 (May/June 2001): 335–342.

99. Pew Center on Global Climate Change, "Climate Change 101: State Action," January 2011, at www.pewclimate.org/docUploads/climate101-state.pdf, accessed April 8, 2012.

100. Reporters Committee for Freedom of the Press, "Open Government Guide," 2011, at www.rcfp.org/open-government-guide, accessed April 8, 2012.

101. Steve Rogers, "Collective Accountability in State Legislative Elections," paper presented at the 2012 State Politics and Policy Conference, Houston, Texas, February 16–18, 2012, at 2012sppconference.blogs.rice.edu/files/ 2012/02/RogersSPPC-2012.pdf, accessed April 8, 2012.

102. National Conference of State Legislatures, "2010 Constituents per State Legislative District Table," at www.ncsl.org/legislatures-elections/legislatures/2010-constituents-per-state-legislative-district.aspx, accessed April 8, 2012.

103. State Senator Steve Kelly, in "Legislating in the Information Age," hearing of the U.S. House Committee on Rules, July 16, 1999, at web.archive.org/web/20101205095107/ http://rules.house.gov/archives/rules_tran05.htm, accessed April 8, 2012.

104. Pew Center for the People and the Press, "Public Knowledge of Current Affairs Little Changed by News and Information Revolutions," April 15, 2007, at www .people-press.org/reports/display.php3?ReportID=319, accessed April 8, 2012.

105. Michael X. Delli Carpini and Scott Keeter, *What Americans Know about Politics and Why It Matters* (New Haven, CT: Yale University Press, 1996), 314.

106. Mark Baldassare et al., "PPIC Statewide Survey: Californians and Their Government," May and June 2007, at www.ppic.org/main/allpubs.asp?sort=type#a12, accessed June 2, 2009.

107. "Oregon Public Knowledge Concerning State Revenues and Expenditures," *Linkages,* Spring 1999, at www.web .archive.org/web/20060907095300/www.oregonstate.edu/ Dept/pol_sci/pgre/link17.htm, accessed April 8, 2012.

108. Mark Baldassare et al., "PPIC Statewide Survey: Californians and Their Government, January 2012, at www.ppic.org/content/pubs/survey/S_112MBS.pdf, accessed April 8, 2012.

109. Alan Rosenthal, *Heavy Lifting: The Job of the American Legislature* (Washington, DC: CQ Press, 2004), 112.

110. Quoted in Ronald Brownstein, "A Wave of Activism in States May Signal a Surge Nationwide," *Los Angeles Times*, December 5, 2005, A9.

111. Congressional Budget Office, "Causes and Lessons of the California Electricity Crisis," September 2001, at http://www.cbo.gov/sites/default/files/cbofiles/ftpdocs/30xx/doc3062/californiaenergy.pdf, accessed April 9, 2012.

112. Quoted in Osborne, *Laboratories of Democracy*, 1.

113. President Bill Clinton, Remarks to the Forum of Federations Conference in Mont-Tremblant, Canada, October 8, 1999, at www.presidency.ucsb.edu/ws/?pid=56687, accessed April 9, 2012.

114. Caitlin Ginley, "Grading the Nation: How Accountable Is Your State?" Center for Public Integrity, March 19, 2012, at www.iwatchnews.org/2012/03/19/8423/grading-nation-how-accountable-your-state, accessed April 9, 2012.

115. Jeremy M. Creelan and Laura M. Moulton, *The New York State Legislative Process: An Evaluation and Blueprint for Reform* (New York: Brennan Center for Justice, 2004), at brennan.3cdn.net/1f4d5e4fa546eaa9cd_fxm6iyde5.pdf, accessed April 9, 2012.

116. Heather K. Gerken, "A New Progressive Federalism," *Democracy: A Journal of Ideas* 24 (Spring 2012), at www.democracyjournal.org/24/a-new-progressive-federalism.php, accessed April 9, 2012.

117. Tocqueville, *Democracy in America*, 244.

Chapter 4

1. Alexander Hamilton, James Madison, and John Jay, *The Federalist Papers*, ed. Clinton Rossiter with a new Introduction and Notes by Charles R. Kesler (New York: New American Library, Signet Classics, 2003), no. 2, 32.

2. Quoted in Arthur Mann, *The One and the Many: Reflections on the American Identity* (Chicago: University of Chicago Press, 1979), 83.

3. Abraham Lincoln, "Speech at Chicago, Illinois, July 10, 1858," available at teachingamericanhistory.org/library/index.asp?document=153, accessed April 20, 2012.

4. Mann, *The One and the Many*, 56, 68. The second quote is Mann's paraphrase of Richard Hofstadter.

5. Quoted in ibid., 83.

6. President Barack Obama, "Remarks by the President at a Memorial Service for Richard Holbrooke," January 14, 2011, at www.whitehouse.gov/the-press-office/2011/01/14/remarks-president-memorial-service-richard-holbrooke, accessed April 23, 2012.

7. Claudia Rosett, "China's Scare Tactics," *Wall Street Journal*, August 3, 2001.

8. The quotation, data, and comparisons are from Mann, *The One and the Many*, 75–76, updated through 2010.

9. Max Farrand, ed., *The Records of the Federal Convention of 1787*, 4 vols. (New Haven, CT: Yale University Press, 1966), II:268 (August 13).

10. Quoted in Leonard Dinnerstein and David M. Reimers, *Ethnic Americans: A History of Immigration*, 4th ed. (New York: Columbia University Press, 1999), 7.

11. *Notes on the State of Virginia*, 1784, in *The Life and Selected Writings of Thomas Jefferson*, ed. Adrienne Koch and William Peden (New York: Modern Library, 1944), 216–218.

12. Dinnerstein and Reimers, *Ethnic Americans*, 27.

13. Ibid., 21, 22, 32, 45.

14. Ibid., 41.

15. John F. Kennedy, speech to the Greater Houston Ministerial Association, September 12, 1960, available at www.npr.org/templates/story/story.php?storyId=16920600, accessed April 20, 2012.

16. *USA Today*, On Politics, "Santorum Stands by John F. Kennedy Criticism," February 27, 2012, available at content.usatoday.com/communities/onpolitics/post/2012/02/rick-santorum-john-f-kennedy-separation-church-state-/1#.T5GdxcjhePw, accessed April 20, 2012.

17. Dinnerstein and Reimers, *Ethnic Americans*, 74.

18. The text of the law is at www.ourdocuments.gov/doc.php?doc=47&page=transcript, accessed April 20, 2012.

19. Dinnerstein and Reimers, *Ethnic Americans*, 50–51.

20. Ibid., 54.

21. Ibid., 79.

22. President John F. Kennedy, "Letter to the President of the Senate and to the Speaker of the House on Revision of the Immigration Laws," July 23, 1963, at www.presidency.ucsb.edu/ws/index.php?pid=9355&st=&st1#axzz1sWmp2jzx, accessed April 20, 2012.

23. Department of Homeland Security, "Yearbook of Immigration Statistics, 2010," Table 2, at www.dhs.gov/files/statistics/publications/LPR10.shtm, accessed April 20, 2012.

24. See Figures 4-2 and 4-3 in the text.

25. See travel.state.gov/visa/immigrants/types/types_1326.html and the appropriate links, accessed April 20, 2012.

26. Voice of America, "US Apologizes for Visa Lottery Error," at www.voanews.com/english/news/usa/US-Mistakenly-Tells-22000-They-Were-Eligible-for-Visas-121790664.html, accessed May 18, 2012.

27. U.S. Citizenship and Immigration Services, "Questions and Answers: Refugees," at www.uscis.gov/portal/site/uscis/menuitem.5af9bb95919f35e66f614176543f6d1a/?vgnextchannel=385d3e4d77d73210VgnVCM1000000082ca60aRCRD&vgnextoid=e4eabcf527f93210VgnVCM100000b92ca60aRCRD, accessed April 20, 2012.

28. Department of Homeland Security, "Yearbook of Immigration Statistics: 2010: Refugees and Aslyees," Table 13, at www.dhs.gov/files/statistics/publications/YrBk10RA.shtm, accessed April 20, 2012.

29. Department of Homeland Security, "Estimates of the Unauthorized Immigrant Population Residing in the United States: January 2011," at www.dhs.gov/xlibrary/assets/statistics/publications/ois_ill_pe_2011.pdf, accessed April 21, 2012. See also Federation for American

Immigration Reform, "How Many Illegal Immigrants? (2011)," at www.fairus.org/issue/how-many-illegal-immigrants, accessed April 21, 2012.

30. Congress of the United States, Congressional Budget Office, *The Impact of Unauthorized Immigrants on the Budgets of State and Local Governments*, December 2007, at www.cbo.gov/ftpdocs/87xx/doc8711/12-6-Immigration.pdf, accessed April 23, 2012.

31. Testimony of Alan Bersin, Commissioner, U.S. Customs and Border Protection, before the House Appropriations Committee, Subcommittee on Homeland Security, April 14, 2010, at www.dhs.gov/ynews/testimony/testimony_1274108577939.shtm, accessed April 23, 2012.

32. UPI, "Obama: Immigrants need path to citizenship," September 18, 2011, at www.upi.com/Top_News/US/2011/09/28/Obama-Immigrants-need-path-to-citizenship/UPI-83191317229024/, accessed April 23, 2012.

33. *Arizona v. United States*, 567 U.S. _____ (2012).

34. "Naturalization," in *The Heritage Guide to the Constitution*, ed. David F. Forte and Matthew Spalding (Washington, DC: Regnery, 2005), 109.

35. See Randall Kennedy, "Dred Scott and African American Citizenship," in *Diversity and Citizenship: Rediscovering American Nationhood*, ed. Gary Jeffrey Jacobsohn and Susan Dunn (Lanham, MD: Rowman & Littlefield, 1996), 105.

36. Quoted in ibid., 119, n. 38.

37. Quoted in ibid., 118, n. 33.

38. For a detailed discussion of the facts and various court decisions in this case, see Don E. Fehrenbacher, *Slavery, Law, and Politics: The Dred Scott Case in Historical Perspective* (Oxford, UK: Oxford University Press, 1981).

39. *Scott v. Sandford*, 60 U.S. 393 (1857), 410. Although the defendant's name was Sanford, it was misspelled by the Court.

40. Ibid., 407.

41. Ibid., 572–573.

42. These newspaper quotations are from Fehrenbacher, *Slavery, Law, and Politics*, 230–231.

43. *U.S. v. Wong Kim Ark*, 169 U.S. 649 (1898).

44. In recent years, some scholars have argued that, properly understood, the Fourteenth Amendment does not confer citizenship on the children of illegal immigrants. See, for example, Edward Erler, "Birthright Citizenship and Dual Citizenship: Harbingers of Administrative Tyranny" in *Imprimis* 37, no. 7 (July 2008), at www.hillsdale.edu/hctools/ImprimisTool/archives/2008_07_Imprimis.pdf, accessed April 24, 2012.

45. United States Census Bureau, *We the People: American Indians and Alaska Natives in the United States*, February 2006, at www.census.gov/prod/2006pubs/censr-28.pdf, accessed April 24, 2012.

46. *Cherokee Nation v. Georgia*, 30 U.S. 1 (1831), 15.

47. Ibid., 17.

48. *Worcester v. Georgia*, 31 U.S. 515 (1832), 542, 557.

49. We do not know for sure whether President Jackson actually said this. Horace Greeley, the prominent American newspaper editor and politician, first reported the quotation, citing as his source a congressman from Massachusetts. Yet Robert Remini, a leading historian of the Jacksonian era, denies that Jackson ever said it. See Robert Remini, "Andrew Jackson and Indian Removal" at www.southernhistory.net/modules.php?op=modload&name=News&file=article&sid=9233&mode=thread&order=0&thold=0, accessed April 24, 2012.

50. This information is from Kettner, *Development of American Citizenship*, 292–293.

51. Mann, *The One and the Many*, 90.

52. *Lone Wolf v. Hitchcock*, 187 U.S. 553 (1903), 565.

53. Willard Hughes Rollings, "Citizenship and Suffrage: The Native American Struggle for Civil Rights in the American West, 1830–1965," *Nevada Law Journal* 5 (Fall 2004): 127.

54. Cornell University Law School, Legal Information Institute, "American Indian Law" at www.topics.law.cornell.edu/wex/American_Indian_law, accessed November 7, 2008.

55. Mann, *The One and the Many*, 73.

56. "Fighting for Their Citizenship," *Los Angeles Times*, April 1, 2003.

57. *U.S. Statutes at Large*, vol. 15:223–224 (Boston: Little, Brown, 1869), at constitution.org/uslaw/sal/015_statutes_at_large.pdf, accessed April 27, 2012.

58. Although the federal government does not report total numbers of renunciates, private organizations have compiled data from lists of individual renunciates published in the *Federal Register*. See, for example, renunciationguide.com/Data-On-Renunciants.html, accessed April 27, 2012.

59. Bloomberg, "Facebook Co-Founder May Gain Choosing Singapore over U.S.," May 11, 2012, available at www.bloomberg.com/news/2012-05-12/facebook-co-founder-may-gain-choosing-singapore-over-u-s.html, accessed May 18, 2012.

60. *Afroyim v. Rusk*, 387 U.S. 253 (1967), 268.

61. *Vance v. Terrazas*, 444 U.S. 252 (1980), 261.

62. U.S. Department of Justice, *United States Attorneys' Bulletin* 54, no. 1 (January 2006), "Office of Special Investigations," p. 1, at www.justice.gov/criminal/hrsp/archives/2006/01-06USABulletin.pdf, accessed April 27, 2012.

63. The debate between Barone and Fonte was published by the American Enterprise Institute and was posted at www.theamericanenterprise.org/taedec00b.htm, accessed July 20, 2001. All the following quotes are from this debate.

64. See, for example, Jacob L. Vigdor, "Measuring Immigrant Assimilation in the United States," Manhattan Institute, Civic Report No. 53 (May 2008), at www.manhattan-institute.org/html/cr_53.htm, accessed April 27, 2012.

65. Ibid.

66. Karin Brulliard, "At Odds over Immigrant Assimilation," *Washington Post*, August 7, 2007, at www.washingtonpost.com/wp-dyn/content/article/2007/08/06/AR2007080601581.html, accessed April 27, 2012.

67. Center for Immigration Studies, "Assimilation and Citizenship," at www.cis.org/Assimilation, accessed November 8, 2008.

68. President Barack Obama, "Inaugural Address," January 20, 2009, at www.presidency.ucsb.edu/ws/?pid=44, accessed May 21, 2012.

69. Pew Research Center, "The American–Western European Values Gap," November 17, 2011, revised February 29, 2012, www.pewglobal.org/2011/11/17/the-american-western-european-values-gap, accessed May 21, 2012.

70. Andrew Kohut and Bruce Stokes, *America against the World* (New York: Times Books, 2006), 133.

71. David Blanchflower and Andrew Oswald, "Measuring Latent Entrepreneurship across Nations," January 2000, www.dartmouth.edu/~blnchflr/papers/EntrepLeague.pdf, accessed May 21, 2012.

72. Seymour Martin Lipset and Gary Marks, *It Didn't Happen Here: Why Socialism Failed in the United States* (New York: Norton, 2000).

73. President Barack Obama, remarks on General Motors restructuring, June 1, 2009, www.whitehouse.gov/the_press_office/Remarks-by-the-President-on-General-Motors-Restructuring/, accessed May 21, 2012.

74. Robert H. Wiebe, *The Search for Order, 1877–1920* (New York: Hill and Wang, 1967), 174.

75. Pew Research Center for the People and the Press, "Democrats' Edge among Millennials Slips," February 18, 2010, pewresearch.org/assets/pdf/1497.pdf; Lydia Saad, "Among Recent Bills, Financial Reform a Lone Plus for Congress," Gallup Poll, September 13, 2010, www.gallup.com/poll/142967/Among-Recent-Bills-Financial-Reform-Lone-Plus-Congress.aspx, accessed May 21, 2012.

76. Elizabeth Mendes, "In U.S., Fear of Big Government at Near-Record Level," Gallup Poll, December 12, 2011, www.gallup.com/poll/151490/Fear-Big-Government-Near-Record-Level.aspx, accessed May 21, 2012.

77. Tom W. Smith, "Belief about God across Time and Countries," National Opinion Research Center, April 18, 2012, www.norc.org/PDFs/Beliefs_about_God_Report.pdf, accessed May 21, 2012.

78. Pew Research Center, "The American–Western European Values Gap."

79. Alexis de Tocqueville, *Democracy in America*, ed. J. P. Mayer and trans. George Lawrence (Garden City, NY: Anchor Books, Doubleday, 1969), 292.

80. John Adams, "Reply to the Massachusetts Militia," October 11, 1798, in *The Works of John Adams, Second President of the United States*, ed. Charles Francis Adams (Boston: Little, Brown, 1854), IX:229.

81. Tocqueville, *Democracy in America*, 444–445.

82. John J. Pitney Jr., "The Tocqueville Fraud," *The Weekly Standard*, November 13, 1995, www.tocqueville.org/pitney.htm, accessed May 21, 2012.

83. *Congressional Record*, September 11, 1940, 11902. The authors thank Bill Mullins for drawing our attention to the Ashurst speech.

84. *Congressional Record*, November 20, 2003, H11874.

85. *Congressional Record*, November 7, 2003, H11129.

86. Senator Barack Obama, "'Call to Renewal' Keynote Address," June 28, 2006, sojo.net/blogs/2012/02/21/transcript-obamas-2006-sojournerscall-renewal-address-faith-and-politics, accessed May 21, 2012.

87. Mayflower Compact, November 11, 1620, avalon.law.yale.edu/17th_century/mayflower.asp, accessed May 21, 2012.

88. Mark A. Noll, *Christians in the American Revolution* (Washington, DC: Christian University Press, 1977), 30.

89. See especially the concise analysis in Robert Booth Fowler and Allen D. Hertzke, *Religion and Politics in America* (Boulder, CO: Westview Press, 1995), 4–8.

90. Sydney E. Ahlstrom, *A Religious History of the American People* (New Haven, CT: Yale University Press, 1972), 349–350. Although Whitefield was English, he had his greatest impact in North America, and is buried in Newburyport, Massachusetts.

91. David L. Holmes, *The Faiths of the Founding Fathers* (New York: Oxford University Press, 2006), Chap. 4.

92. Donald S. Lutz, "The Relative Influence of European Writers on Late Eighteenth-Century American Political Thought," *American Political Science Review* 78 (March 1984): 192.

93. M. E. Bradford, *Founding Fathers: Brief Lives of the Framers of the United States Constitution* (Lawrence: University Press of Kansas, 1994), xvi.

94. Quotations from the petition and the debate are from *Annals of Congress*, House, 1st Congress, 2nd session, February 11, 1790, 1224–1229, www.memory.loc.gov/ammem/amlaw/lwac.html, accessed May 22, 2012. See also Joseph J. Ellis, *Founding Brothers: The Revolutionary Generation* (New York: Knopf, 2001), Chap. 3.

95. Eric Foner, *The New American History* (Philadelphia: Temple University Press, 1997), 87.

96. *Congressional Globe*, Senate, 33rd Congress, 1st sess., March 14, 1854, 621.

97. David Ewart, *A Scriptural View of the Moral Relations of African Slavery* (Charleston, SC: Walker, Evans, 1859), ia600307.us.archive.org/32/items/scripturalviewof00ewar/scripturalviewof00ewar.pdf, accessed May 22, 2012.

98. Frederick Douglass, "What to the Slave Is the Fourth of July?" July 5, 1852, www.mit.edu/~thistle/v12/2/douglass.html, accessed May 22, 2012.

99. John Hope Franklin and Alfred A. Moss, *From Slavery to Freedom: A History of African Americans* (New York: A.A. Knopf, 2000), 258.

100. Martin Luther King Jr., "I Have a Dream," August 28, 1963, www.americanrhetoric.com/speeches/mlkihaveadream.htm, accessed May 22, 2012.

101. Martin Luther King Jr., "I've Been to the Mountaintop," April 3, 1968, www.americanrhetoric.com/speeches/mlkivebeentothemountaintop.htm, accessed May 22, 2012.

102. Reuven Kimelman, "The Jewish Basis for Social Justice," in *Religion, Race and Justice in a Changing*

America, ed. Gary Orfield and Holly J. Lebowitz (New York: Century Foundation Press, 1999).

103. John Smestad Jr., "The Role of Archbishop Joseph F. Rummel in the Desegregation of Catholic Schools in New Orleans," *Student Historical Journal* (Loyola University of New Orleans), 1993–1994, at www.loyno .edu/~history/journal/1993-4/Smestad.html, accessed June 8, 2009.

104. *Congressional Record*, June 10, 1964, p. 13309.

105. W. J. Rorabaugh, *The Alcoholic Republic* (New York: Oxford University Press, 1981), 10.

106. James M. McPherson, *Battle Cry of Freedom: The Civil War Era* (New York: Ballantine, 1988), 134.

107. Alcoholics Anonymous, "The Twelve Steps of Alcoholics Anonymous," www.aa.org/lang/en/en_pdfs/smf-121_en.pdf, accessed May 22, 2012.

108. *Warner v. Orange County Department of Probation*, 968 F. Supp. 917, 922 (1997).

109. *Reynolds v. United States,* 98 U.S. 145 (1878).

110. American Civil Liberties Union, "*Roe v. Wade* at 25," 1998, www.web.archive.org/web/20010913214628/www .aclu.org/issues/reproduct/roeoped.html, accessed May 22, 2012.

111. Tom W. Smith and Seokho Kim, "National Pride in Cross-national and Temporal Perspective," *International Journal of Public Opinion Research* 18 (Spring 2006): 127–136.

112. Pew Research Center, "Beyond Red and Blue: The Political Typology," May 11, 2011, www.people-press.org/ files/legacy-pdf/Beyond-Red-vs-Blue-The-Political-Typology.pdf, accessed May 22, 2012.

113. Mordechi Sorkin, "Afghanistan," September 14, 2007, www.solomon2.blogspot.com/2007/10/six-years-later-motis-thoughts.html, accessed May 22, 2012.

114. Robert N. Bellah, "Civil Religion in America," in *Beyond Belief: Essays on Religion in a Post-Traditional World* (New York: Harper and Row, 1970).

115. John F. Kennedy, Remarks at a Dinner of the Big Brothers of America, June 7, 1961; Ronald W. Reagan, Remarks at a Dinner Marking the 10th Anniversary of the Heritage Foundation, October 8, 1983, www.presidency.ucsb.edu/ index.php, accessed May 22, 2012.

116. Matthew 5:14; John Winthrop, "A Modell of Christian Charity," 1630, www.history.hanover.edu/texts/winthmod .html, accessed February 19, 2009.

117. John F. Kennedy, "Inaugural Address," January 20, 1961, www.presidency.ucsb.edu/ws/index.php?pid=8032, accessed May 22, 2012. See also Bellah, "Civil Religion in America," 169.

118. Some would argue that the Constitution does indeed mention God at the end of Article VII, which dates the document on "the Seventeenth Day of September in the Year of our Lord one thousand seven hundred and Eighty seven." A list of state constitutional references to God is at "Brief for the United States as Respondent Supporting Petitioners," Elk Grove *Unified*

School District and David W. Gordon, Superintendent, Petitioners v. Michael A. Newdow et al., web.archive.org/ web/20071205221714/http://supreme.lp.findlaw.com/ supreme_court/briefs/02-1624/02-1624.mer.usa.html, accessed May 22, 2012.

119. Rhode Island Constitution, www.rilin.state.ri.us/ RiConstitution/ConstFull.html, accessed May 22, 2012.

120. *Journals of the Continental Congress*, June 20, 1782, www.memory.loc.gov/cgi-bin/ampage?collId= lljc&fileName=022/lljc022.db&recNum=348&item Link=?%230220349&linkText=1, accessed May 22, 2012. The phrase comes from Virgil's *Georgics*. See also Jon Meacham, *American Gospel: God, the Founding Fathers, and the Making of a Nation* (New York: Random House, 2006), 81–83.

121. Pauline Maier, *American Scripture: Making the Declaration of Independence* (New York: Knopf, 1997), xiv.

122. Pew Research Center for the People and the Press, "Proud Patriots—and Harsh Critics of Government," July 1, 2010, pewresearch.org/pubs/1649/proudest-patriots-most-critical-of-government-and-obama, accessed May 22, 2012.

123. S.J. Res. 19, 112th Congress, www.gpo.gov/fdsys/pkg/ BILLS-112sjres19is/pdf/BILLS-112sjres19is.pdf, accessed May 22, 2012.

124. William Safire, "On Desecration," *New York Times Magazine*, July 31, 2005, www.nytimes.com/2005/07/31/ magazine/31ONLANGUAGE.html, accessed May 22, 2012.

125. Abraham Lincoln, "First Inaugural Address," March 4, 1861, www.presidency.ucsb.edu/ws/?pid=25818, accessed May 22, 2012.

126. Abraham Lincoln, "Gettysburg Address," November 19, 1863, www.presidency.ucsb.edu/ws/?pid=73959, accessed May 22, 2012.

127. Kennedy, "Inaugural Address."

128. Gary Becker, comment on military pay, June 4, 2007, web.archive.org/web/20100609061635/http://www .becker-posner-blog.com/archives/2007/06/comment_ on_mili.html, accessed May 22, 2012.

129. Pew Research Center, "War and Sacrifice in the Post-9/11 Era," October 5, 2011, www.pewsocialtrends.org/ files/2011/10/veterans-report.pdf, accessed May 22, 2012.

130. General Colin Powell, "Equal Opportunities in the Armed Forces," November 10, 1998, www.web.archive .org/web/20020426075227/www.mod.uk/issues/equal_ opportunities/powell98.htm, accessed May 22, 2012.

131. Barack Obama, "The America We Love," speech in Independence, Missouri, June 30, 2008, www.realclearpolitics .com/articles/2008/06/the_america_we_love.html, accessed May 22, 2012.

132. Jeff Zeleny, "The Politician and the Absent American Flag Pin," *New York Times*, October 5, 2007, www.nytimes.com/2007/10/05/us/politics/05obama .html, accessed May 22, 2012.

133. Martha Nussbaum, "Patriotism and Cosmopolitanism," *Boston Review*, October/November1994, bostonreview .net/BR19.5/nussbaum.html, accessed May 22, 2012.

134. Richard Cohen, "The Myth of American Exceptionalism," *Washington Post*, May 9, 2011, www.washingtonpost.com/opinions/the-myth-of-american-exceptionalism/2011/05/09/AF2rm0bG_story.html, accessed May 22, 2012.

135. George Kateb, "On Patriotism," Cato Unbound, March 10, 2008, www.cato-unbound.org/2008/03/10/george-kateb/on-patriotism/, accessed May 22, 2012. See also George Kateb, *Patriotism and Other Mistakes* (New Haven, CT: Yale University Press, 2006).

136. Walter Berns, *Making Patriots* (Chicago: University of Chicago Press, 2001), 9.

137. James Madison, *The Debates in the Federal Convention of 1787*, August 9, 1787, avalon.law.yale.edu/18th_century/debates_809.asp, accessed May 22, 2012.

138. Walter Berns, remarks at conference on educating citizens for democracy, June 13, 2001, www.web.archive.org/web/20030312075552/www.empower.org/patriotism/berns.pdf, accessed May 22, 2012.

139. Charities Aid Foundation, "International Comparisons of Charitable Giving," November 2006, www.cafonline.org/PDF/International%20Comparisons%20of%20Charitable%20Giving.pdf, accessed May 22, 2012.

140. Susan J. Ellis and Katherine H. Noyes, *By the People: A History of Americans as Volunteers*, rev. ed. (San Francisco: Jossey-Bass, 1990), 43–44.

141. Arthur M. Schlesinger [Sr.], "Biography of a Nation of Joiners," *American Historical Review* 50 (October 1944): 5.

142. Theda Skocpol, Ziad Munson, Andrew Karch, and Bayliss Camp, "Patriotic Partnerships: Why Great Wars Nourished American Civic Voluntarism," in *Shaped by War and Trade: International Influence on American Political Development*, ed. Ira Katznelson and Martin Shefter (Princeton, NJ: Princeton University Press, 2002), 142–143. See also Ahlstrom, *Religious History*, 422–428.

143. Ibid., 678–679.

144. Robert D. Putnam, *Bowling Alone: The Collapse and Revival of American Community* (New York: Simon and Schuster, 2000), 268–270.

145. United States Department of Labor, Bureau of Labor Statistics, "Volunteering in the United States, 2011," February 22, 2012, www.bls.gov/news.release/volun.nr0.htm, accessed May 22, 2012.

146. Everett Carll Ladd, *The Ladd Report* (New York: Free Press, 1999).

147. Charities Aid Foundation, *World Giving Index 2011*, December 20, 2011, www.cafonline.org/pdf/World_Giving_Index_2011_191211.pdf, accessed May 22, 2012.

148. Karlyn Bowman, Andrew Rugg, and Emily Simmonds, "Polls on Patriotism and Military Service," American Enterprise Institute, June 2011, www.aei.org/files/2011/06/28/PATRIOTISM-2011.pdf, accessed May 22, 2012.

149. Arthur C. Brooks, *Who Really Cares* (New York: Basic Books, 2006), Chap. 2.

150. Nelson Polsby, *Political Innovation in America: The Politics of Policy Initiation* (New Haven, CT: Yale University Press, 1984), 92–93.

151. Texas Troops to Teachers, "Front and Center," July 17, 2011, www.texastroopstoteachers.org/frontandcenter.html, accessed May 22, 2012.

152. Philip Walzer, "Study: Ex-Military Often Make Better Teachers," *Virginian-Pilot*, October 3, 2005, www.redorbit.com/news/education/261257/study_exmilitary_often_make_better_teachers/index.html, accessed May 22, 2012.

153. Adrian Dungan and Michael Parisi, "Individual Income Tax Returns, Preliminary Data, 2010," *Statistics of Income Bulletin*, Winter 2012, www.irs.gov/pub/irs-soi/12inwinbulincomeprlim10.pdf, accessed May 22, 2012.

154. 8 USC 1424, us-code.vlex.com/vid/opposed-who-favor-totalitarian-forms-19271779; 8 CFR 316.2., www.uscis.gov/ilink/docView/SLB/HTML/SLB/0-0-0-1/0-0-0-11185/0-0-0-30650/0-0-0-30665.html.

Chapter 5

1. *Webster's Ninth New Collegiate Dictionary* (Springfield, MA: Merriam-Webster, 1991), 1015.

2. James Madison, letter to Thomas Jefferson, October 17, 1788, at www.constitution.org/jm/17881017_bor.htm, accessed January 15, 2008.

3. *Kelo v. City of New London*, 545 U.S. 469 (2005).

4. Robert A. Goldwin, *From Parchment to Power: How James Madison Used the Bill of Rights to Save the Constitution* (Washington, DC: AEI Press, 1997), 175.

5. Walter Berns, *Taking the Constitution Seriously* (Lanham, MD: Madison Books, 1987), 126–127.

6. *Barron v. Baltimore*, 32 U.S. 243 (1833), 249.

7. *Chicago, Burlingham & Quincy Railroad Company v. Chicago*, 166 U.S. 226 (1897).

8. *Gitlow v. New York*, 268 U.S. 652 (1925).

9. *Palko v. Connecticut*, 302 U.S. 319 (1937), 325, 328.

10. *Benton v. Maryland*, 395 U.S. 784 (1969).

11. A scriptural source for the ban on oaths is the *New Testament* Letter of James (5:12): "But above all things, my brethren, swear not, neither by heaven, neither by the earth, neither by any other oath: but let your yea be yea, and [your] nay, nay; lest ye fall into condemnation."

12. James Madison, "Memorial and Remonstrance," June 20, 1785, at www.law.ou.edu/hist/remon.html, accessed July 12, 2001.

13. Thomas Jefferson, "Letter to Messrs. Nehemiah Dodge and Others, a Committee of the Danbury Baptist Association, in the State of Connecticut," January 1, 1802, at www.loc.gov/loc/lcib/9806/danpre.html, accessed May 4, 2012.

14. *Reynolds v. United States*, 98 U.S. 145 (1879), 164.

15. Massachusetts Constitution of 1780, Part the First, Article III, at teachingamericanhistory.org/library/index.asp?document=266, accessed May 4, 2012.

16. Ibid., Part the Second, Chapter VI, Article I.

17. See, for example, Daniel L. Dreisbach, "Thomas Jefferson, a Mammoth Cheese, and the 'Wall of Separation Between Church and State,'" in *Religion and the New Republic: Faith in the Founding of America*, ed. James H. Hutson (Lanham, MD: Rowman and Littlefield, 2000), 78–82.

18. George Washington, "Thanksgiving Proclamation," October 3, 1789, at www.presidency.ucsb.edu/ws/index .php?pid=65502&st=&st1=#axzz1twhuabiy, accessed May 4, 2012.

19. James Madison, Presidential Proclamation, July 9, 1812, available at www.presidency.ucsb.edu/ws/index .php?pid=65944, accessed January 21, 2008.

20. *Holy Trinity Church v. United States*, 143 U.S. 457 (1892), 471.

21. Harry S Truman, "Exchange of Messages with Pope Pius XII," August 28, 1947, at www.presidency.ucsb .edu/ws/?pid=12746, accessed May 4, 2012.

22. *Everson v. Board of Education*, 330 U.S. 1 (1947), 15, 18.

23. *Zorach v. Clauson*, 343 U.S. 306 (1952), 313–314.

24. *Engel v. Vitale*, 370 U.S. 421 (1962).

25. *Abington School District v. Schempp*, 374 U.S. 203 (1963).

26. *Lemon v. Kurtzman*, 403 U.S. 602 (1971), 613.

27. *Lee v. Weisman*, 505 U.S. 577 (1992), 598.

28. *Santa Fe Independent School District v. Doe*, 530 U.S. 290 (2000), 312, 318.

29. *Good News Club v. Milford Central School*, 533 U.S. 98 (2001).

30. *Zelman v. Simmons-Harris*, 536 U.S. 639 (2002).

31. *Christian Legal Society v. Martinez*, 561 U.S. _____ (2010); Justice Ginsburg for the majority; Justice Alito for the dissenters.

32. *Elk Grove v. Newdow*, 542 U.S. 1 (2004).

33. Stephen L. Carter, *God's Name in Vain: The Wrongs and Rights of Religion in Politics* (New York: Basic Books, 2001), 77.

34. *Associated Contract Loggers, Inc., et al. v. United States Forest Service et al.*, 84 F. Supp. 2d 1029 (2000), 1034.

35. *Reynolds v. U.S.*, 98 U.S. 145 (1879), 164.

36. United States Department of State, Bureau of Public Affairs, "The Great Seal of the United States," 12, 6, at www.state.gov/www/publications/great_seal.pdf, accessed May 7, 2012.

37. President Barack Obama, "Remarks at an Easter Prayer Breakfast," April 19, 2011, at www.presidency.ucsb.edu/ ws/index.php?pid=90283, accessed May 7, 2012.

38. *Wisconsin v. Yoder*, 406 U.S. 205 (1972), 208.

39. *Employment Division, Department of Human Resources of Oregon v. Smith*, 494 U.S. 872 (1990), 879.

40. The Religious Freedom Restoration Act can be found at www.law.cornell.edu/uscode/42/usc_sup_01_42_ 10_21B.html, accessed May 7, 2012.

41. The 1997 case was *City of Boerne v. Flores*, 521 U.S. 507, and the 2006 case was *Gonzales v. O Centro Espírita Beneficente União do Vegetal*, 126 S.Ct. 1211.

42. *Hosanna-Tabor Evangelical Lutheran Church and School v. Equal Employment Opportunity Commission*, 565 U.S. _____ (2012).

43. William Blackstone, *Commentaries on the Laws of England*, 4 vols., Facsimile of the First Edition of 1765–1769 (Chicago: University of Chicago Press, 1979), IV:151–152.

44. *Schenck v. United States*, 249 U.S. 47 (1919), 52.

45. *Chaplinsky v. New Hampshire*, 315 U.S. 568 (1942), 571–572.

46. *Schenck v. United States*, 249 U.S. 47 (1919), 52.

47. *Gitlow v. New York*, 268 U.S. 652 (1925), 668, 673.

48. *Near v. Minnesota*, 238 U.S. 697 (1931), 703, 716.

49. The Smith Act can be found at immigration.procon .org/files/Immigration%20Images/SmithAct1940.pdf, accessed May 9, 2012.

50. *Dennis v. United States*, 341 U.S. 494 (1951), 509, 517.

51. *Yates v. United States*, 354 U.S. 298 (1957), 320.

52. *Brandenburg v. Ohio*, 395 U.S. 444 (1969), 446.

53. *Snyder v. Phelps et al.*, 562 U.S. _____ (2011).

54. *Stromberg v. People of the State of California*, 283 U.S. 359 (1931), 361.

55. *Tinker v. Des Moines School District*, 393 U.S. 503 (1969), 506, 514.

56. *Bethel School Dist. No. 403 v. Fraser*, 478 U.S. 675 (1986), 682.

57. *Morse et al. v. Frederick*, 551 U.S. 393 (2007), 405.

58. *Texas v. Johnson*, 491 U.S. 397 (1989), 414, 419, 429, 435.

59. *Virginia v. Black*, 538 U.S. 343 (2003), 365–366.

60. *United States v. O'Brien*, 391 U.S. 367 (1968), 376, 377.

61. *New York Times v. Sullivan*, 376 U.S. 254 (1964), 271, 280.

62. *Barnes v. Glen Theatre, Inc.*, 501 U.S. 560 (1991), 575.

63. *Roe v. Wade*, 410 U.S. 113 (1973).

64. *Griswold v. Connecticut*, 381 U.S. 479 (1965), 484

65. Ibid., 521.

66. *Doe v. Bolton*, 410 U.S. 179 (1973), 222.

67. The 2008 Democratic Party platform is at www.presidency.ucsb.edu/ws/index.php?pid= 78283#axzz1uQlbJRTR, accessed May 9, 2012, and the 2008 Republican Party platform is at www.presidency .ucsb.edu/ws/index.php?pid=78545#axzz1uQlbJRTR, accessed May 9, 2012.

68. *Webster v. Reproductive Health Services*, 492 U.S. 490 (1989).

69. *Planned Parenthood v. Casey*, 505 U.S. 833 (1992).

70. *Stenberg v. Carhart*, 530 U.S. 914 (2000), 927.

71. *Gonzales v. Carhart*, 550 U.S. 124 (2007).

72. President Barack Obama, Memorandum on Mexico City Policy and Assistance for Voluntary Population Planning, January 23, 2009, at www.presidency.ucsb .edu/ws/index.php?pid=85685, accessed May 10, 2012.

73. *Bowers v. Hardwick*, 478 U.S. 186 (1986), 190, 196.

74. *Hurley v. Irish-American Gay Group of Boston*, 515 U.S. 557 (1995), 570, 573.

75. *Boy Scouts of America v. Dale*, 530 U.S. 640 (2000), 648.

76. Justice John Paul Stevens, dissenting opinion, ibid., 700.

77. *Romer v. Evans*, 517 U.S. 620 (1996), 635, 636.

78. *Lawrence v. Texas*, 539 U.S. 558 (2003), 578, 602.

79. *Roth v. United States*, 354 U.S. 476 (1957), 489.

80. *A Book Named "John Cleland's Memoirs of a Woman of Pleasure" v. Attorney General of Massachusetts*, 383 U.S. 413 (1966), 418, 419.

81. *Jacobellis v. Ohio*, 378 U.S. 184 (1964), 197.

82. *Miller v. California*, 413 U.S. 15 (1973), 25, 32. See also the companion case, *Paris Adult Theatre v. Slaton*, 413 U.S. 49 (1973).

83. *Jenkins v. Georgia*, 418 U.S. 153 (1974), 161.

84. See *Renton v. Playtime Theatres*, 475 U.S. 369 (1986).

85. *New York v. Ferber*, 458 U.S. 747 (1982).

86. Ibid., 758.

87. *Ashcroft v. Free Speech Coalition*, 535 U.S. 234 (2002).

88. See *Reno v. American Civil Liberties Union*, 521 U.S. 844 (1997).

89. Quoted in Ralph A. Rossum and G. Alan Tarr, *American Constitutional Law*, 2 vols., 5th ed. (New York: St. Martin's/Worth, 1999), II:204.

90. *American Booksellers Association v. Hudnut*, United States Court of Appeals, Seventh Circuit, 771 F.2d 323 (1985), 325.

91. *United States v. Stevens*, 559 U.S. _____ (2010).

92. The text of the bill is available at www.govtrack.us/congress/bills/111/hr5566/text, accessed May 16, 2012.

93. *Brown v. Entertainment Merchants Association*, 564 U.S. _____ (2011).

94. Ibid.

95. *District of Columbia v. Heller*, 554 U.S. _____ (2008).

96. Ibid.

97. *McDonald v. City of Chicago*, 561 U.S. _____ (2010).

98. See the discussion in Rossum and Tarr, *American Constitutional Law*, II:269–275.

99. *Pennsylvania v. Mimms*, 434 U.S. 106 (1977), 108–109.

100. *Elkins v. United States*, 364 U.S. 206 (1960), 222.

101. *Brown v. State of Mississippi*, 297 U.S. 278 (1936), 285–286.

102. *Miranda v. Arizona*, 384 U.S. 436 (1966), 478–479.

103. Ibid., 455, 458.

104. Ibid., 518.

105. The quotation is from *Duckworth v. Eagan*, 492 U.S. 195 (1989), 203.

106. *Gideon v. Wainwright*, 372 U.S. 335 (1963), 344.

107. *Wilkerson v. Utah*, 99 U.S. 130 (1878), 135–136.

108. *Trop v. Dulles*, 356 U.S. 86 (1958), 100–101.

109. *Furman v. Georgia*, 408 U.S. 238 (1972), 309.

110. *Gregg v. Georgia*, 428 U.S. 153 (1976).

111. *Coker v. Georgia*, 433 U.S. 584 (1977); *Atkins v. Virginia*, 536 U.S. 304 (2002); *Roper v. Simmons*, 543 U.S. 551 (2005); *Kennedy v. Louisiana*, 129 S.Ct. 1 (2008).

112. Quoted in *Hirabayashi v. United States*, 320 U.S. 81 (1943), 93.

113. *Terminiello v. City of Chicago*, 337 U.S. 1 (1949), 37.

114. *Hamdi v. Rumsfeld*, 542 U.S. 507 (2004), 536.

115. Alfred H. Kelly, Winfred A. Harbison, and Herman Belz, *The American Constitution: Its Origins and Development*, 2 vols., 7th ed. (New York: Norton, 1991), I:137.

116. *Ludecke v. Watkins*, 335 U.S. 160 (1948).

117. *Ex parte Merryman*, 17 Fed. Case No. 9, 487 (1861).

118. Lincoln, "Message to Congress in Special Session," July 4, 1861, at www.presidency.ucsb.edu/ws/index.php?pid=69802, accessed May 23, 2012.

119. 12 Stat. 755 (1863).

120. See, for example, Mark E. Neely Jr., *The Fate of Liberty: Abraham Lincoln and Civil Liberties* (New York: Oxford University Press, 1991), esp. 113–138.

121. *Ex parte Vallandigham*, 68 U.S. 243 (1863).

122. *Ex parte Milligan*, 71 U.S. 2 (1866), 120–121.

123. Ibid., 122.

124. Ibid., 141.

125. *Schenck v. United States*, 249 U.S. 47 (1919), 52.

126. *Debs v. United States*, 249 U.S. 211 (1919), 214–215.

127. *Abrams v. United States*, 260 U.S. 616 (1919), 624.

128. Ibid., 630.

129. See especially William H. Rehnquist, *All the Laws but One: Civil Liberties in Wartime* (New York: Knopf, 1998), 182–183.

130. *Hirabayashi v. United States*, 320 U.S. 81 (1943), 93, 94–95.

131. *Korematsu v. United States*, 323 U.S. 214 (1944), 216, 217, 218.

132. *Ex parte Endo*, 323 U.S. 283 (1944).

133. *Ex parte Quirin*, 317 U.S. 1 (1942).

134. *New York Times v. United States*, 403 U.S. 713 (1971).

135. Ibid., 756, 758–759.

136. *Hamdi v. Rumsfeld*, 542 U.S. 507 (2004), 535.

137. Ibid., 532, 531.

138. *Hamdan v. Rumsfeld*, 548 U.S. 557 (2006).

139. *Boumediene v. Bush*, 553 U.S. _____ (2008).

140. President Barack Obama, Executive Order 13491—Ensuring Lawful Interrogations, January 22, 2009, at www.presidency.ucsb.edu/ws/index.php?pid=85669&st=&st1=, accessed March 2, 2009; see also President Barack Obama, *National Security Strategy*, May 2010, at www.whitehouse.gov/sites/default/files/rss_viewer/national_security_strategy.pdf, accessed October 25, 2010.

141. "Holder: Clear authority to kill US citizens," *The Hill*, March 5, 2012, at thehill.com/homenews/administration/214295-holder-clear-authority-to-kill-citizens, accessed May 23, 2012.

Chapter 6

1. Constitution of the American Anti-Slavery Society, December 4, 1833, at www.afgen.com/slavery2.html, accessed June 6, 2012.

2. "Declaration of Sentiments" of the Seneca Falls Convention of 1848, at www.fordham.edu/halsall/mod/Senecafalls.html, accessed June 6, 2012.

3. "Speech on the Repeal of the Missouri Compromise," Peoria, Illinois, October 16, 1854, at www.teachingamericanhistory.org/library/index.asp?document=51, accessed June 6, 2012.

4. Martin Luther King Jr., "I Have a Dream," address delivered at the March on Washington for Jobs and Freedom, August 28, 1963, Washington, DC, at avalon.law.yale.edu/20th_century/mlk01.asp, accessed June 6, 2012. The video recording of the speech is available at www.teachertube.com/viewVideo.php?video_id=94828.

5. President Lyndon B. Johnson, "Special Message to the Congress: The American Promise," March 15, 1965, at www.presidency.ucsb.edu/ws/?pid=26805, accessed June 6, 2012.

6. Quoted in *The Collected Works of Abraham Lincoln*, ed. Roy P. Basler, 9 vols. (New Brunswick, NJ: Rutgers University Press, 1953), III: 537, n26.

7. The speech, delivered on February 6, 1837, is at www.en.wikisource.org/wiki/Slavery_a_Positive_Good, accessed June 6, 2012.

8. Abraham Lincoln, "Speech on the Kansas-Nebraska Act," October 16, 1854, www.vlib.us/amdocs/texts/kansas.html, accessed June 6, 2012.

9. Republican Party Platform of 1856, at www.presidency.ucsb.edu/ws/?pid=29619, accessed June 6, 2012.

10. Abraham Lincoln, "Speech on the *Dred Scott* Decision," June 26, 1857, at www.ashbrook.org/library/19/lincoln/dredscott.html, accessed June 6, 2012.

11. First debate between Abraham Lincoln and Stephen A. Douglas, Ottawa, Illinois, August 21, 1858, at www.nps.gov/liho/historyculture/debate1.htm, accessed June 6, 2012.

12. Abraham Lincoln, "Emancipation Proclamation," January 1, 1863, at www.presidency.ucsb.edu/ws/?pid=69880, accessed June 6, 2012.

13. *Slaughterhouse Cases*, 83 U.S. 36 (1873).

14. *United States v. Cruikshank*, 92 U.S. 542 (1876). See *The Oxford Companion to the Supreme Court of the United States*, ed. Kermit L. Hall (New York: Oxford University Press, 1991), 209.

15. *Civil Rights Cases*, 109 U.S. 3 (1883).

16. *Plessy v. Ferguson* (1896), 163 U.S. 537 (1896), 559.

17. Quoted in *From Slavery to Freedom: A History of African Americans*, 8th ed., ed. John Hope Franklin and Alfred A. Moss (New York: Knopf, 2002), 384.

18. Harry S Truman, Executive Order 9981, July 26, 1948, www.presidency.ucsb.edu/ws/?pid=60737, accessed June 6, 2012.

19. *Brown v. Board of Education*, 347 U.S. 483 (1954) 495.

20. *Brown v. Board of Education* (*Brown* II), 349 U.S. 294 (1955), 301.

21. Southern Manifesto, at georgiainfo.galileo.usg.edu/manifesto.htm, accessed June 6, 2012.

22. Martin Luther King, Jr., "Letter from Birmingham Jail," April 16, 1963, at www.africa.upenn.edu/Articles_Gen/Letter_Birmingham.html, accessed June 6, 2012.

23. Ibid. Note that not all versions of the "Letter from Birmingham Jail" contain the language "one has a moral responsibility to disobey unjust laws."

24. President Lyndon B. Johnson, "Special Message to the Congress: The American Promise," March 15, 1965, www.presidency.ucsb.edu/ws/?pid=26805, accessed June 6, 2012.

25. *Swann v. Charlotte-Mecklenburg Board of Education*, 402 U.S. 1 (1971), 15.

26. *Milliken v. Bradley*, 418 U.S. 717 (1974).

27. *Missouri v. Jenkins*, 515 U.S. 70 (1995), 115, 119, 120–122.

28. *Swann v. Charlotte-Mecklenburg*, 31–32.

29. *Parents Involved in Community Schools v. Seattle School District No. 1 et al.*, 127 S. Ct. 2738 (2007), 2757, 2768.

30. Ibid., 2837.

31. Ibid. 2789, 2790, 2791.

32. U.S. Commission on Civil Rights, *The Voting Rights Act: Ten Years After*, January 1975, Table 3, p. 43.

33. *U.S. Code*, Title 42, Chapter 20, Subchapter I-A, Section 1973.

34. *Shaw v. Reno*, 509 U.S. 630 (1993), 642.

35. Samuel Leiter and William M. Leiter, *Affirmative Action in Antidiscrimination Law and Policy: An Overview and Synthesis* (Albany: State University of New York Press, 2002), 194, emphasis in the original.

36. *Northwest Austin Municipal Utility District Number One v. Holder*, 557 U.S. _____ (2009), Opinion of the Court, slip opinion, 16.

37. Justice Sandra Day O'Connor's opinion for the Court in *Shaw v. Reno*, 509 U.S. 630 (1993), 657.

38. The law school case is *Grutter v. Bollinger*, 539 U.S. 306, decided on June 23, 2003. The college case is *Gratz v. Bollinger*, 539 U.S. 244, decided on the same day.

39. President Lyndon B. Johnson, "Commencement Address at Howard University," June 4, 1965, at www.presidency.ucsb.edu/ws/?pid=27021, accessed June 7, 2012.

40. Quoted in Ward Connerly, *Creating Equal: My Fight against Race Preferences* (San Francisco: Encounter Books, 2000), 3.

41. John F. Kennedy, "Special Message to Congress on Civil Rights and Job Opportunities," June 19, 1963, at www.presidency.ucsb.edu/ws/?pid=9283, accessed February 15, 2004.

42. "I Have a Dream."

43. *Wright v. Rockefeller*, 376 U.S. 52 (1964), 66.

44. *University of California Regents v. Bakke*, 438 U.S. 265 (1978).

45. Ibid., 418.

46. Ibid., 328, 407.

47. *Adarand Constructors Inc. v. Pena*, 515 U.S. 200 (1995).

48. *Grutter v. Bollinger*, 308.

49. Ibid., 342, 343.

50. *Ricci v. DeStefano*, 557 U.S. _____ (2009).

51. *Lewis v. Chicago*, 560 U.S. _____ (2010).

52. Abigail Adams, Letter to John Adams, March 31, 1776, at press-pubs.uchicago.edu/founders/documents/v1ch15s9.html, accessed June 6, 2012.

53. The Declaration of Sentiments is available at www.fordham.edu/halsall/mod/senecafalls.html; accessed June 6, 2012.

54. *Minor v. Happersett*, 88 U.S. 162 (1874), 177.

55. *Craig v. Boren*, 429 U.S. 190 (1976), 197. See also *Reed v. Reed*, 404 U.S. 71 (1971), and *Frontiero v. Richardson*, 411 U.S. 677 (1973).

56. *Ledbetter v. Goodyear Tire and Rubber Co.*, 550 U.S. 618 (2007).

57. *Rostker v. Goldberg*, 453 U.S. 57 (1981), 59, 68.

58. *United States v. Virginia*, 518 U.S. 515 (1996), 531, 532.

59. *Saint Francis College v. Al-Khazraji*, 481 U.S. 604 (1987), 607.

60. *Rice v. Cayetano*, 528 U.S. 495 (2000), 515.

61. EEOC, "Federal Laws Prohibiting Job Discrimination: Questions and Answers," www.eeoc.gov/facts/qanda.html, accessed September 22, 2003.

62. 29 *Code of Federal Regulations* 1606.1, www.frwebgate.access.gpo.gov/cgi-bin/get-cfr.cgi, accessed September 22, 2003.

63. U.S. Equal Employment Opportunity Commission, "Age Discrimination in Employment Act (includes concurrent charges with Title VII, ADA and EPA) FY 1997–FY 2011, at www1.eeoc.gov//eeoc/statistics/enforcement/adea.cfm?renderforprint=1, accessed June 5, 2012.

64. See *Slather v. Sather Trucking Corporation*, 78 F.3d 415 (8th Cir. 1996).

65. *General Dynamics Land Systems v. Cline*, 540 U.S. 581 (2004), 600.

66. *U.S. Code*, Title 42, Section 12101.

67. President George H. W. Bush, "Remarks on Signing the Americans with Disabilities Act of 1990," July 26, 1990, at www.presidency.ucsb.edu/ws/?pid=18711, accessed June 6, 2012.

68. U.S. Equal Employment Opportunity Commission, "Americans with Disabilities Act of 1990 (ADA) Charges (includes concurrent charges with Title VII, ADEA, and EPA) FY 1997–FY 2011," at www.eeoc.gov//eeoc/statistics/enforcement/ada-charges.cfm?renderforprint=1, accessed June 5, 2012.

69. *Goodridge v. Department of Public Health*, 440 Mass. 309 (2003), 341, 351.

70. New York Court of Appeals, *Daniel Hernandez v. Victor Robles*, 885 N.E.2d 1(N.Y. 2006), 7.

71. National Conference of State Legislatures, "Defining Marriage: Defense of Marriage Acts and Same-Sex Marriage Laws," at www.ncsl.org/issues-research/human-services/same-sex-marriage-overview.aspx, accessed June 5, 2012.

72. The White House Blog, "President Obama Supports Same-Sex Marriage," at www.whitehouse.gov/blog/2012/05/09/president-obama-supports-same-sex-marriage, accessed June 6, 2012.

73. The law, titled "Marriage Amendment Act 2004," is at www.comlaw.gov.au/Details/C2004A01361, accessed June 6, 2012.

74. Don't Ask, Don't Tell Repeal Act of 2010 at thomas.loc.gov/cgi-bin/query/z?c111:S.4023:, accessed June 7, 2012.

Chapter 7

1. First Lincoln-Douglas debate, Ottawa, Illinois, August 21, 1858, www.founding.com/founders_library/pageID.2276/default.asp, accessed April 18, 2012.

2. The distinction between snap judgments and deliberative opinion corresponds roughly to what psychologist Daniel Kahneman calls the mind's System 1 and System 2. See Daniel Kahneman, *Thinking, Fast and Slow* (New York: Farrar, Straus and Giroux, 2011). See also: Benjamin I. Page and Robert Y. Shapiro, *The Rational Public: Fifty Years of Trends in Americans' Policy Preferences* (Chicago: University of Chicago Press, 1992).

3. William G. Mayer, *The Changing American Mind: How and Why Public Opinion Changed between 1960 and 1988* (Ann Arbor: University of Michigan Press, 1992), 22–28; Page and Shapiro, *The Rational Public*, 67–81.

4. Alexander Hamilton, James Madison, and John Jay, *The Federalist Papers*, ed. Clinton Rossiter with a new introduction and notes by Charles R. Kesler (New York: Signet, 2003), no. 10, 73.

5. Robert Weissberg, *Polling, Policy, and Public Opinion: The Case against Heeding the "Voice of the People"* (New York: Palgrave Macmillan, 2002), 69.

6. M. Margaret Conway, *Political Participation in the United States*, 3rd ed. (Washington, DC: CQ Press, 2000), 3.

7. Some scholars have used brain imaging to gain a "picture" of political thought, although the science behind such studies has been controversial so far. Peter K. Hatemi and Rose McDermott, "Broadening Political Psychology," *Political Psychology* 33 (February 2012): 11–25, at onlinelibrary.wiley.com/doi/10.1111/j.1467-9221.2011.00867.x/full, accessed April 20, 2012.

8. "How the Poll Was Conducted," *New York Times*, April 18, 2012, www.nytimes.com/2012/04/19/us/how-the-poll-was-conducted.html, accessed April 20, 2012.

9. The screening questions may produce unreliable answers unless researchers cross-check them against actual voting records—a tedious and costly process. Todd Rogers and Masa Aida, "Why Bother Asking? The Limited Value of Self-Reported Vote Intention," December 13, 2011, papers.ssrn.com/sol3/papers.cfm?abstract_id=1971846, accessed April 20, 2012.

10. Pew Research Center for the People and the Press, "Religion and Politics: Contention and Consensus," July 24, 2003, www.people-press.org/2003/07/24/religion-and-politics-contention-and-consensus/, accessed April 20, 2012.

11. Herbert Asher, *Polling and the Public: What Every Citizen Should Know*, 7th ed. (Washington, DC: CQ Press, 2007), 59–60.

12. Lydia Saad, "Americans Still Split Along 'Pro-Choice,' 'Pro-Life' Lines," Gallup Poll, May 23, 2011, www.gallup.com/poll/147734/Americans-Split-Along-Pro-Choice-Pro-Life-Lines.aspx, accessed April 21, 2012.

13. Lydia Saad, "Plenty of Common Ground Found in Abortion Debate," Gallup Poll, August 8, 2011, www.gallup.com/poll/148880/Plenty-Common-Ground-Found-Abortion-Debate.aspx, accessed April 21, 2012.

14. Asher, *Polling and the Public*, 69–72.

15. Michael W. Traugott and Paul J. Lavrakas, *The Voter's Guide to Election Polls*, 4th ed. (Lanham, Maryland: Rowman and Littlefield, 2008), 19–20.

16. Jibum Kim et al., "Trends in Surveys on Surveys," *Public Opinion Quarterly* 75 (Spring 2011): 165–171, poq.oxfordjournals.org/content/75/1/165.full.pdf, accessed April 25, 2012.

17. Colleen McCain Nelson, "Tough Calls: Political Polling," *Dallas Morning News*, October 22, 2002, community.seattletimes.nwsource.com/archive/?date=20021110&slug=polltakers10, accessed April 25, 2012.

18. Scott Keeter, Leah Christian, and Michael Dimock, "The Growing Gap between Landline and Dual Frame Election Polls," Pew Research Center, November 22, 2010, pewresearch.org/pubs/1806/growing-gap-between-landline-and-dual-frame-election-polls, accessed April 25, 2012.

19. Mark Blumenthal, "Gallup Adds Cell Phone Interviewing," January 14, 2008, www.pollster.com/blogs/gallup_adds_cell_phone_intervi.php, accessed April 25, 2012.

20. C. Kirk Hadaway, Penny Long Marler, and Mark Chaves, "What the Polls Don't Show: A Closer Look at U.S. Church Attendance," *American Sociological Review* 58 (December 1993): 741–752.

21. Barry C. Burden, "Voter Turnout and the National Election Studies," *Political Analysis* 8 (2000): 389–398.

22. George F. Bishop et al., "Pseudo-Opinions on Public Affairs," *Public Opinion Quarterly* 44 (Summer 1980): 198–209; Richard Morin, "The 1975 Public Affairs Act: Never Was—but Not Forgotten," *Washington Post*, February 26, 1995, C5.

23. Alexis de Tocqueville, *Democracy in America*, ed. J. P. Mayer and trans. George Lawrence (Garden City, NY: Anchor Books, Doubleday, 1969), 218.

24. Pew Research Center for the People and the Press, "Well Known: Clinton and Gadhafi; Little Known: Who Controls Congress," March 31, 2011, www.people-press.org/2011/03/31/well-known-clinton-and-gadhafi-little-known-who-controls-congress, accessed April 25, 2012.

25. Kaiser Health Tracking Poll, March 2012, www.kff.org/kaiserpolls/upload/8285-F.pdf, accessed April 25, 2012.

26. Pew Research Center for the People and the Press, "The Invisible Court," August 3, 2010, pewresearch.org/pubs/1688/supreme-court-lack-of-public-knowledge-favorability, accessed April 25, 2012.

27. Frank Newport, "Americans Favor Jobs Plan Proposals, Including Taxing Rich," Gallup Poll, September 20, 2011, www.gallup.com/poll/149567/Americans-Favor-Jobs-Plan-Proposals-Including-Taxing-Rich.aspx, accessed April 25, 2012.

28. Jon McHenry, "Obama and Voters Define 'Fair Share' Differently," *Resurgent Republic*, September 20, 2011, www.resurgentrepublic.com/posts/obama-and-voters-define-fair-share-differently, accessed April 25, 2012.

29. Michael Kinsley, "The Right Tea Party Opinion? 'I Don't Know,'" *Los Angeles Times*, December 2, 2011, www.latimes.com/news/opinion/commentary/la-oe-kinsley-crowd-sourcing-versus-polling-20111202,0,2725604.story; Michael Cooper and Dalia Sussman, "Nuclear Power Loses Support in New Poll," *New York Times*, March 22, 2011, www.nytimes.com/2011/03/23/us/23poll.html, accessed April 25, 2012.

30. Alexander Burns, "How Much Do Voters Know?" *Politico*, March 13, 2012, www.politico.com/news/stories/0312/73947.html, accessed April 25, 2012.

31. V. O. Key, Jr., *The Responsible Electorate* (New York: Random House, Vintage Books, 1966), 7.

32. Samuel L. Popkin, *The Reasoning Voter*, 2nd ed. (Chicago: University of Chicago Press, 1994), 9.

33. Key, *The Responsible Electorate*, 7.

34. Harris Interactive, "Over Three in Five Americans Believe in Death Penalty," March 18, 2008, www.harrisinteractive.com/vault/Harris-Interactive-Poll-Research-Over-Three-in-Five-Americans-Believe-in-Death-Penalty-2008-03.pdf. Accessed August 21, 2012.

35. Daniel Yankelovich, *Coming to Public Judgment* (Syracuse, NY: Syracuse University Press, 1991), 26.

36. Quinnipiac University survey of 1,085 New Jersey voters, December 5–9, 2007, Quinnipiac University, www.quinnipiac.edu/institutes-and-centers/polling-institute/new-jersey/release-detail?ReleaseID=1126, accessed April 26, 2012.

37. "Governor Jon Corzine's Remarks on Eliminating Death Penalty in New Jersey," December 17, 2007, www.deathpenaltyinfo.org/node/2236, accessed April 26, 2012.

38. Quinnipiac poll, December 5–7, 2007.

39. President Bill Clinton, "Remarks to Ministers' Leadership Conference, Willow Creek Community Church, South Barrington, Illinois," August 10, 2000, www.presidency.ucsb.edu/ws/?pid=1485, accessed April 26, 2012.

40. James S. Fishkin, "Deliberative Polling: Toward a Better-Informed Democracy," Center for Deliberative Democracy, cdd.stanford.edu/polls/docs/summary/, accessed April 26, 2012.

41. Center for Deliberative Democracy, "What's Next California? A California Statewide Deliberative Poll for California's Future," October 2011, cdd.stanford.edu/polls/california/2011/final/nextca-final-report.pdf, accessed April 26, 2012.

42. Joe Mathews, "What I Saw at the Deliberative Poll," *Fox and Hounds*, June 28, 2011, www.foxandhoundsdaily.com/2011/06/9136-what-i-saw-deliberative-poll, accessed April 26, 2012.

43. Tim Cavanaugh, "Deliberative Polling is a Fool's Errand," Zocalo Public Square, June 22, 2011, zocalopublicsquare.org/thepublicsquare/2011/06/22/can-deliberative-polling-work/read/up-for-discussion, April 26, 2012.

44. Peter F. Drucker, *The Effective Executive* (New York: Harper and Row, Harper Colophon, 1985), 148.

45. Lydia Saad, "U.S. Political Ideology Stable with Conservatives Leading," Gallup Poll, August 1, 2011, www.gallup.com/poll/148745/political-ideology-stable-conservatives-leading.aspx, accessed April 26, 2012.

46. Ronald Reagan, "Remarks at the Annual Convention of the National Association of Evangelicals in Orlando, Florida," March 8, 1983, www.presidency.ucsb.edu/ws/?pid=41023, accessed April 26, 2012.

47. Charles Wolf Jr., "A Theory of Non-market Failures," *The Public Interest* 55 (Spring 1979): 114–133, www.nationalaffairs.com/doclib/20080528_197905507atheoryofnonmarketfailurescharleswolfjr.pdf, accessed April 26, 2012.

48. Hubert H. Humphrey, "My Father," *Atlantic Monthly*, December 1966, www.theatlantic.com/issues/66nov/humphrey.htm, accessed April 26, 2012. We thank Andy Brehm for pointing out this passage.

49. Michigan Curricular Framework, michigan.gov/documents/Social_Studies_Standards_122084_7.pdf, accessed April 26, 2012.

50. National Center for Education Statistics, United States Department of Education, *The Nation's Report Card: Civics 2010*, May 2011, nationsreportcard.gov/civics_2010/civics_2010_report, accessed April 26, 2012.

51. Pew Research Center for the People and the Press, "United in Remembrance, Divided over Policies," September 1, 2011, www.people-press.org/2011/09/01/united-in-remembrance-divided-over-policies, accessed April 26, 2012.

52. Pew Research Center for the People and the Press, "Americans Spending More Time Following the News," September 12, 2010, www.people-press.org/files/legacy-pdf/652.pdf, accessed April 26, 2012.

53. Pew Internet and American Life Project, "Social Networking Sites and Politics," March 12, 2012, www.pewinternet.org/~/media//Files/Reports/2012/PIP_SNS_and_politics.pdf, accessed April 26, 2012.

54. Aristotle, *Rhetoric*, trans. W. Rhys Roberts, www.classics.mit.edu/Aristotle/rhetoric.1.i.html, accessed June 12, 2009.

55. National Opinion Research Center data, in Mayer, *The Changing American Mind*, 366.

56. Martin Luther King Jr., "I Have a Dream," August 28, 1963, www.americanrhetoric.com/speeches/mlkihaveadream.htm/, accessed April 26, 2012.

57. Carl M. Cannon, *The Pursuit of Happiness in Times of War* (Lanham, MD: Rowman and Littlefield, 2004), 168–174.

58. Mary L. Dudziak, "*Brown* as a Cold War Case," *Journal of American History* 91 (June 2004), www.historycooperative.org/journals/jah/91.1/dudziak.html, accessed April 26, 2012.

59. Jane Mansbridge, "Everyday Talk in the Deliberative System," in *Deliberative Politics: Essays on Democracy and Disagreement*, ed. Stephen Macedo (New York: Oxford University Press, 1999), 211–239.

60. National Election Studies, "The NES Guide to Public Opinion and Electoral Behavior," www.electionstudies.org/nesguide/toptable/tab6b_1.htm, accessed April 26, 2012.

61. Aaron Smith, "The Internet's Role in Campaign 2008," Pew Internet and American Life Project, April 2009, www.pewinternet.org/~/media//Files/Reports/2009/The_Internets_Role_in_Campaign_2008.pdf, accessed April 26, 2012.

62. Nicholas Warshaw, "Inside Obama for America: Behind the Organization of the Greatest Campaign in American Political History," B.A. thesis, Claremont McKenna College, 2009.

63. Kathy Goldschmidt and Leslie Ochreiter, "Communicating with Congress: How the Internet Has Changed Citizen Engagement" (Washington, DC: Congressional Management Foundation, 2008), www.congressfoundation.org/storage/documents/CMF_Pubs/cwc_citizenengagement.pdf, accessed April 26, 2012.

64. Urban Legends and Folklore, "'Women United against War' Petition," January 30, 2003, urbanlegends.about.com/library/bl-wuaw-petition.htm, accessed April 27, 2012.

65. Urban Legends and Folklore, "Petition: No Social Security for Illegal Immigrants," March 4, 2009, www.urbanlegends.about.com/library/bl_social_security_petition.htm, accessed April 27, 2012.

66. Ed Morrissey, "Does This Kill the Obama Birth Certificate Myth?" July 28, 2008, hotair.com/archives/2008/07/23/does-this-kill-the-obama-birth-certificate-myth, accessed April 27, 2012.

67. Aaron Smith et al., "The Internet and Civic Engagement," Pew Internet and American Life Project, September 2009, www.pewinternet.org/~/media//Files/Reports/2009/The%20Internet%20and%20Civic%20Engagement.pdf, accessed April 27, 2012.

68. Steven J. Rosenstone and John Mark Hansen, *Mobilization, Participation, and Democracy in America* (New York: Longman, 2003), Chap. 8.

69. Kathryn Zickuhr, "Generations 2010," Pew Internet and American Life Project, December 16, 2010, pewinternet.org/Reports/2010/Generations-2010.aspx (see link for updated survey data), accessed April 27, 2012.

70. Amanda Lenhart and Susannah Fox, "Bloggers: A Portrait of the Internet's New Storytellers," Pew Internet and American Life Project, July 19, 2006, www.pewinternet.org/~/media/Files/Reports/2006/PIP%20Bloggers%20Report%20July%2019%202006.pdf.pdf, accessed April 27, 2012.

71. Brad Fitch and Kathy Goldschmidt, "Communicating with Congress: How Capitol Hill Is Coping with the Surge

in Citizen Advocacy" (Washington, DC: Congressional Management Foundation, 2005), www.congressfoundation.org/storage/documents/CMF_Pubs/cwc_capitol-hillcoping.pdf ,19–20, accessed April 27, 2012.

72. Kevin Wallsten, "Political Blogs and the Bloggers Who Blog Them: Is the Political Blogosphere an Echo Chamber?" paper presented at the annual meeting of the American Political-Science Association, Washington, DC, September 1–4, 2005, www.journalism.wisc.edu/~dshah/blog-club/Site/Wallsten.pdf, accessed April 27, 2012.

73. Thomas G. West, *Vindicating the Founders: Race, Sex, Class, and Justice in the Origins of America* (Lanham, MD: Rowman and Littlefield, 1997), 115–119.

74. *Harper v. Virginia Bd. of Elections*, 383 U.S. 663 (1966).

75. *Oregon v. Mitchell*, 400 U.S. 112 (1970).

76. Virginia Harper-Ho, "Noncitizen Voting Rights: The History, the Law and Current Prospects for Change," *Law and Inequality* 18 (Summer 2000): 271–322.

77. Immigrant Voting Project, "Noncitizen Voting Rights Legislation around the United States: (Proposed and Enacted)," www.immigrantvoting.org/legislation/legislation.html, accessed April 27, 2012.

78. The Sentencing Project, "Felony Disenfranchisement Laws in the United States," July 2012, www.sentencing-project.org/doc/publications/fd_bs_fdlawsinus_Aug2012.pdf, accessed August 20, 2012.

79. North Dakota, Office of the Secretary of State, "North Dakota: The Only State without Voter Registration," vip.sos.nd.gov/pdfs/Portals/votereg.pdf, accessed April 27, 2012.

80. *Dunn v. Blumstein*, 405 U.S. 330, at 348 (1972).

81. 42 USC 1973gg-5(a), (b).

82. Demos, "Voters Win with Same-Day Registration," May 2011, www.demos.org/sites/default/files/publications/Voters_Win_2010_demos.pdf, accessed April 27, 2012.

83. Elections Canada Online, "Description of the National Register of Electors," www.elections.ca/content.aspx?section=vot&dir=reg/des&document=index&lang=e, accessed April 27, 2012.

84. Pew Center on the States, "Inaccurate, Costly, and Inefficient: Evidence that America's Voter Registration System Needs an Upgrade," February 14, 2012, www.pewstates.org/research/reports/inaccurate-costly-and-inefficient-85899378437, accessed April 27, 2012.

85. Michael P. McDonald and Samuel Popkin. "The Myth of the Vanishing Voter," *American Political Science Review* 95 (December 2001): 963–974; Michael P. McDonald, "2008 General Election Turnout Rates," elections.gmu.edu/Turnout_2008G.html, accessed April 27, 2012.

86. Jeff Trandahl, "Statistics of the Presidential and Congressional Election of November 4, 2008," July 10, 2009, clerk.house.gov/member_info/electionInfo/2008election.pdf, accessed April 27, 2012.

87. U.S. Census, "Mover Rate Reaches Record Low, Census Bureau Reports," November 15, 2011, www.census.gov/newsroom/releases/archives/mobility_of_the_population/cb11-193.html, accessed April 27, 2012.

88. Earl M. Ryan, "Rescuing Voting from the Long Ballot," Citizens Research Council of Michigan, January 13, 1999, www.crcmich.org/PUBLICAT/1990s/1999/A2speech.html, accessed April 27, 2012.

89. Anthony Downs, *An Economic Theory of Democracy* (New York: Harper and Row, 1957).

90. WGBH Lab, "Voting, Schmoting" (online video), August 14, 2008, www.pbs.org/vote2008/video/2008/08/voting_schmoting.html, accessed April 27, 2012.

91. National Archives and Records Administration, "2008 Presidential Election: Popular Vote Totals," www.archives.gov/federal-register/electoral-college/2008/popular-vote.html, accessed April 27, 2012.

92. Pew Research Center for the People and the Press, "Election Weekend News Interest Hits 20-Year High," November 6, 2008, www.people-press.org/2008/11/06/election-weekend-news-interest-hits-20-year-high/, accessed April 27, 2012.

93. The figures were similar to those from 2004. See Pew Research Center for the People and the Press, "Likely Rise in Voter Turnout Bodes Well for Democrats," July 10, 2008, www.people-press.org/2008/07/10/likely-rise-in-voter-turnout-bodes-well-for-democrats/, accessed April 27, 2012.

94. Jeremy M. Teigen, "Enduring Effects of the Uniform: Previous Military Experience and Voting Turnout," *Political Research Quarterly* 59 (2006): 601–607.

95. Alan S. Gerber, Donald P. Green, and Christopher W. Larimer, "Social Pressure and Voter Turnout: Evidence from a Large-Scale Field Experiment," *American Political Science Review* 102 (February 2008): 33–48.

96. Patricia Funk, "Theory and Evidence on the Role of Social Norms in Voting," paper presented at the annual meeting of the Public Choice Society, San Antonio, March 6–9, 2005, www.pubchoicesoc.org/papers2005/Funk.pdf, accessed April 27, 2012.

97. Jonathan Chang, "How Voters Turned Out on Facebook," November 4, 2010, www.facebook.com/notes/facebook-data-team/how-voters-turned-out-on-facebook/451788333858, accessed April 27, 2012.

98. Data on voter demographics come from U.S. Census, "Voting and Registration in the Election of November 2008," May 2010, www.census.gov/prod/2010pubs/p20-562.pdf, accessed April 27, 2012.

99. Raymond E. Wolfinger and Steven J. Rosenstone, *Who Votes?* (New Haven, CT: Yale University Press, 1980), 35–36.

100. Eric Liu, "Should All Americans Have to Earn Their Citizenship?" *The Atlantic*, February 2, 2012, www.theatlantic.com/national/archive/2012/02/should-all-americans-have-to-earn-their-citizenship/252433/, accessed April 27, 2012.

101. Quoted in Don Van Natta Jr., "Silent Majorities; Polling's 'Dirty Secret': No Response," *New York Times*, November 21, 1999, D1.

102. John F. Kennedy, *Profiles in Courage* (New York: Harper, 1961), 244.

103. Frederick Douglass, "Oration in Memory of Abraham Lincoln," April 14, 1876, www.teachingamericanhistory.org/library/index.asp?document=39, accessed April 27, 2012.

Chapter 8

1. Barack Obama, "Remarks at an Obama Victory Fund 2012 Fundraiser in New York City," November 30, 2011, www.presidency.ucsb.edu/ws/?pid=97333, accessed May 23, 2012.

2. Mitt Romney, "Press Release - Mitt Romney: My Team is the American People," February 23, 2012, www.presidency.ucsb.edu/ws/?pid=99864, accessed May 23, 2012.

3. Students for a Free Tibet home page, www.studentsforafreetibet.org/, accessed May 23, 2012.

4. Alexander Hamilton, James Madison, and John Jay, *The Federalist Papers*, ed. Clinton Rossiter, with a new introduction and notes by Charles R. Kesler (New York: Signet, 2003), no. 10, 72.

5. E. E. Schattschneider, *The Semi-sovereign People: A Realist's View of Democracy in America* (Hinsdale, IL: Dryden, 1960), 35.

6. Alexis de Tocqueville, *Democracy in America*, ed. J. P. Mayer and trans. George Lawrence (Garden City, NY: Anchor Books, Doubleday, 1969), 521–522.

7. Edison Electric Institute, "Our Issues," at www.eei.org/ourissues/Pages/default.aspx, accessed May 23, 2012.

8. United States Department of Commerce, Bureau of the Census, *Statistical Abstract of the United States 2012* (Washington, DC: Government Printing Office, 2011), 788.

9. Tocqueville, *Democracy in America*, 518.

10. Daniel J. Boorstin, *The Americans: The National Experience* (New York: Random House, Vintage Books, 1965), 143.

11. Edward Steers Jr., *Lincoln Legends* (Lexington: University Press of Kentucky, 2007), 91–92.

12. Joe Conason, *It Can Happen Here* (New York: Thomas Dunne Books, 2007), 133; Al Gore, *The Assault on Reason* (New York: Penguin, 2007), 88; Andrew Ferguson, "What Al Wishes Abe Said," *Washington Post*, June 10, 2007, B5.

13. United States Senate, Committee on the Judiciary, hearing on the nomination of Elena Kagan to the United States Supreme Court, June 29, 2010, CQ Transcripts.

14. Mark Engler, "Occupiers from Around the Country Descend on Iowa Caucuses," Alternet, December 30, 2011, www.alternet.org/occupywallst/153613/occupiers_from_around_the_country_descend_on_iowa_caucuses, accessed May 23, 2012.

15. Paul F. Boller Jr. and John George, *They Never Said It: A Book of Fake Quotes, Misquotes, and Misleading Attributions* (New York: Barnes and Noble, 1989), 85.

16. David Herbert Donald, *Lincoln* (New York: Simon and Schuster, Touchstone, 1996), 154–155; Wayne C. Temple, "A. Lincoln, Lobbyist," *Journal of the Abraham Lincoln Association* 21 (Summer 2000), hdl.handle.net/2027/spo.2629860.0021.205, accessed May 23, 2012; Allen D. Spiegel and Florence Kavaler, "The Role of Abraham Lincoln in Securing a Charter for a Homeopathic Medical College," *Journal of Community Health* 27 (October 2002).

17. Between 1880 and 1890, the share of the labor force working in agriculture plunged from 51% to 43%. Authors' calculation from United States Department of Commerce, Bureau of the Census, *Historical Statistics of the United States: Colonial Times to 1970* (Washington, DC: Government Printing Office, 1975), 139.

18. Robert H. Wiebe, *The Search for Order 1877–1920* (New York: Hill and Wang, 1967), 123.

19. Mancur Olson, *The Logic of Collective Action: Public Goods and the Theory of Groups* (Cambridge, MA: Harvard University Press, 1971), 51.

20. Texas Organization of Nurse Executives, "Benefits of Membership," www.texasnurse.org/displaycommon.cfm?an=1&subarticlenbr=10, accessed May 23, 2012.

21. Charles Wilson, quoted in William Manchester, *The Glory and the Dream: A Narrative History of America 1932–1972* (New York: Bantam, 1975), 648.

22. Charles Lindblom, *Politics and Markets: The World's Political-Economic Systems* (New York: Basic Books, 1977), 179.

23. United States Department of Commerce, *Statistical Abstract*, 500.

24. Quoted in Mimi Hall and Del Jones, "Tobacco: Up in Smoke?" *USA Today*, March 10, 1994, 1B.

25. Pew Research Center, "'Staunch Conservatives' Are Wary of Wall Street," May 26, 2011, www.people-press.org/2011/05/26/staunch-conservatives-are-wary-of-wall-street, accessed May 24, 2012.

26. Dwight D. Eisenhower, "Farewell Radio and Television Address to the American People, January 17, 1961," www.presidency.ucsb.edu/ws/?pid=12086, accessed May 24, 2012.

27. *Cato Handbook for Congress,* 7th ed. (Washington, DC: Cato Institute, 2009), www.cato.org/pubs/handbook/hb111/hb111-26.pdf, accessed May 24, 2012.

28. W. Mark Crain, "The Impact of Regulatory Costs on Small Firms," *Small Business Research Summary* (September 2005), at www.sba.gov/advo/research/rs264tot.pdf, accessed May 24, 2012.

29. U.S. Department of Commerce, *Statistical Abstract,* 232.

30. Shirley Svorny, "Medical Licensing: An Obstacle to Affordable, Quality Care," Cato Institute, Policy Analysis 621 (September 17, 2008), www.cato.org/publications/policy-analysis/medical-licensing-obstacle-affordable-quality-care, accessed May 24, 2012.

31. U.S. Department of Labor, Bureau of Labor Statistics, "Union Members in 2011," January 27, 2012, www.bls.gov/news.release/union2.nr0.htm, accessed May 24, 2012.

32. Organization for Economic Cooperation and Development, "Trade Union Density," stats.oecd.org/Index.aspx?DataSetCode=UN_DEN, accessed May 24, 2012.

33. Steven Greenhouse, "Most U.S. Union Members Are Working for the Government, New Data Shows," *New York Times,* January 23, 2010, www.nytimes.com/2010/01/23/business/23labor.html, accessed May 24, 2012.

34. Daniel DiSalvo, "The Trouble with Public Sector Unions," *National Affairs 5* (Fall 2010), www.nationalaffairs.com/publications/detail/the-trouble-with-public-sector-unions, accessed May 29, 2012.

35. Remarks of Bob Chanin, General Counsel of the National Education Association, July 6, 2009, www.youtube.com/watch?v=bqn1rvv7Fis, accessed May 29, 2012.

36. International Brotherhood of Teamsters, "Teamster Structure," www.teamster.org/content/teamsters-structure, accessed May 29, 2012. For a description of Attorney General Robert F. Kennedy's fight against Teamster corruption, see Evan Thomas, *Robert Kennedy: His Life* (New York: Simon and Schuster, 2000).

37. Service Employees International Union, "Fast Facts," www.seiu.org/a/ourunion/fast-facts.php, accessed May 29, 2012.

38. American Federation of Labor Congress of Industrial Organizations, "About the AFL-CIO," www.aflcio.org/About, accessed May 29, 2012.

39. Change to Win, "About Us," www.changetowin.org/about, accessed May 29, 2012.

40. *Louisville Courier Journal,* May 2, 1890, www.history.umd.edu/Gompers/quotes.htm, accessed May 29, 2012.

41. U.S. Chamber of Commerce, *A Dozen Facts You Should Know about Antitrust and the U.S. Oil Industry,* June 2007, www.uschamber.com/publications/reports/0706oil_antitrust.htm, accessed May 29, 2012.

42. National Education Association, "Research and Reports," www.nea.org/home/NoChildLeftBehindAct.html, accessed May 29, 2012.

43. American Conservative Union, "The American Conservative Union," conservative.org/about-acu/, accessed May 29, 2012.

44. Americans for Democratic Action, "Who Are We?" www.s242798577.onlinehome.us/pages/about/ada-history.php, accessed May 29, 2012.

45. Although the Internal Revenue Code does not prohibit 501(c)(4) corporations from contributing directly to federal candidates and party committees, federal *election* law does impose such a ban on all corporations.

46. In 1999, the organization shortened its name to just the four letters. The reference to "retired persons" was no longer accurate because many of its members were still working. Frederick R. Lynch, *One Nation under AARP:* *The Fight over Medicare, Social Security, and America's Future* (Berkeley: University of California Press, 2011), 130–131.

47. Nelson W. Polsby, *Policy Innovation in America: The Politics of Policy Initiation* (New Haven, CT: Yale University Press, 1984), 101.

48. James G. McGann, *Scholars, Dollars and Policy Advice* (Philadelphia: Think Tanks and Civil Societies Program of the Foreign Policy Research Institute, August 2004), www.social-sciences-and-humanities.com/PDF/scholars-dollars.PDF, accessed May 29, 2012.

49. Trevor Potter, "Where Are We Now? The Current State of Campaign Finance Law," in *Campaign Finance Reform: A Sourcebook,* ed. Anthony Corrado et al. (Washington, DC: Brookings Institution, 1997), 19.

50. Dan Eggen and T. W. Farnam, "New Super PACs' Bringing Millions into Campaigns," *Washington Post,* September 28, 2010, www.washingtonpost.com/wp-dyn/content/article/2010/09/27/AR2010092706500.html, accessed May 29, 2012.

51. Kenneth P. Vogel, "Secrecy Flip-Flop Fueled Crossroads," *Politico,* October 25, 2010, www.politico.com/news/stories/1010/44104.html, accessed May 29, 2012.

52. Rachel Louise Ensign, "The New Rules for Political Donations," *Wall Street Journal,* April 30, 2012, online.wsj.com/article/SB100014240527023038165045773197235 11631462.html, accessed May 29, 2012.

53. Dan Eggen and T. W. Farnam, "Pro-Disclosure Groups Often Don't Disclose Themselves," *Washington Post,* March 13, 2012, www.washingtonpost.com/politics/the-influence-industry-pro-disclosure-groups-often-dont-disclose-themselves/2012/03/13/gIQAs9X9CS_story.html, accessed May 29, 2012.

54. Theda Skocpol, "Associations without Members," *The American Prospect,* November 30, 2002, prospect.org/article/associations-without-members, accessed May 30, 2012.

55. Theda Skocpol, *Diminished Democracy: From Membership to Management in American Civic Life* (Norman: University of Oklahoma Press, 2003), 204–211.

56. Peter Skerry, *Mexican Americans: The Ambivalent Minority* (Cambridge, MA: Harvard University Press, 1995), 325.

57. Robert D. Putnam, *Bowling Alone: The Collapse and Revival of American Community* (New York: Simon and Schuster, 2000), 52.

58. Lynch, *One Nation under AARP,* 137.

59. James Piereson, "The Next Generation," *Philanthropy,* September/October 2004, www.philanthropyroundtable.org/topic/excellence_in_philanthropy/the_next_generation, accessed May 30, 2012.

60. During the 2009–2010 fiscal year, Planned Parenthood and its affiliates received $467.4 million in government grants and contracts, or nearly half of their total revenues. Planned Parenthood Federation of America, *Annual Report 2009–2010,* www.plannedparenthood.org/

about-us/annual-report-4661.htm, accessed May 30, 2012.

61. Cary Coglianese, "Unequal Representation: Membership Input and Interest Group Decision-Making," Harvard University, John F. Kennedy School of Government, Politics Working Group, Working Paper 96-2 (1996), www.web.archive.org/web/20060317212350/www.ksg .harvard.edu/prg/cary/unequal.htm, accessed May 30, 2012.

62. National Rifle Association, "A Brief History of the NRA," www.nrahq.org/history.asp, accessed May 30, 2012; Lydia Saad, "Self-Reported Gun Ownership in U.S. Is Highest Since 1993," Gallup Poll, October 26, 2011, www.gallup .com/poll/150353/Self-Reported-Gun-Ownership-Highest-1993.aspx, accessed May 30, 2012.

63. Center for Responsive Politics, "Lobbying Database," www.opensecrets.org/lobby/index.php, accessed May 31, 2012.

64. Cillian Donnelly, "Lobbying: A Word in Your Ear," *Together*, May/June 2008, www.cleanfuelsconsulting. org/Portals/0/docs/TOGETHER%20%20Lobbyists%20 6.2008.pdf, accessed May 31, 2012.

65. Quoted in Kim I. Eisler, "Show Me the Money," *Washingtonian* (January 1998), 78.

66. Jeffrey M. Jones, "Record 64% Rate Honesty, Ethics of Members of Congress Low," Gallup Poll, December 12, 2011, www.gallup.com/poll/151460/Record-Rate-Honesty-Ethics-Members-Congress-Low.aspx, accessed May 31, 2012.

67. Bill Sarpalius, "Not Every Lobbyist Is Like Jack Abramoff," *Roll Call*, February 16, 2005.

68. Quoted in Jeffrey H. Birnbaum and Dan Balz, "Case Bringing New Scrutiny to a System and a Profession," *Washington Post*, January 4, 2006, A1.

69. Anthony J. Nownes, *Total Lobbying: What Lobbyists Want (and How They Try to Get It)* (New York: Cambridge University Press, 2006), 57–68.

70. Quoted in Jeffrey H. Birnbaum, "Lobbying, Best Learned on the Inside," *Washington Post*, May 1, 2005, K1.

71. Legistorm, "Former Lobbyists Working for Congress Outnumber Elected Lawmakers," September 13, 2011, www.legistorm.com/blog/former-lobbyists-working-for-congress-outnumber-elected-lawmakers.html; Center for Responsive Politics, "Obama Officials Who Have Spun through the Revolving Door," www.opensecrets .org/obama/rev.php, accessed May 31, 2012.

72. Executive Order—Ethics Commitments by Executive Branch Personnel, January 21, 2009, www.whitehouse .gov/the_press_office/Ethics-Commitments-By-Executive-Branch-Personnel/, accessed May 31, 2012.

73. Jake Tapper, "Obama White House Discloses Two More Lobbyist Waivers Granted," Political Punch, March 10, 2009, abcnews.go.com/blogs/politics/2009/03/obama-white-hou/, accessed May 31, 2012.

74. Joseph M. Bessette, *The Mild Voice of Reason: Deliberative Democracy and American National Government* (Chicago: University of Chicago Press, 1994), 142–143.

75. James L. Payne, *The Culture of Spending* (San Francisco: ICS Press, 1991), 13.

76. Julie Kosterlitz, "The World According to AARP," *National Journal*, March 10, 2007, 35.

77. Keenan Steiner, "For Clues about Who They're Meeting, Check Lobbyists Tweeting," Sunlight Foundation, November 9, 2011, unlightfoundation.com/ blog/2011/11/09/for-clues-about-who-theyre-meeting-check-lobbyists-tweeting, accessed June 1, 2012.

78. Ibid.

79. Jim Puzzanghera and Richard Verrier, "Websites Flexing Muscle in Push against Online Piracy Bills," *Los Angeles Times*, January 18, 2012, articles.latimes.com/2012/jan/ 18/business/la-fi-ct-piracy-battle-20120118Fight for the Future, "SOPA Timeline," sopastrike.com/timeline, accessed June 1, 2012.

80. Jennifer Martinez, "Reddit Founder: SOPA Showed Democracy Works," *Politico*, February 8, 2012, www.politico.com/news/stories/0212/72610.html, accessed June 1, 2012.

81. Erika Falk, Erin Grizard, and Gordon McDonald, "Legislative Issue Advertising in the 108th Congress," *Harvard International Journal of Press/Politics* 11 (Fall 2006), hij.sagepub.com/content/11/4/148.full.pdf+html, accessed June 1, 2012.

82. *Citizens United v. Federal Election Commission*, 558 U.S. 50 (2010).

83. Gregory Wawro, "A Panel Probit Analysis of Campaign Contributions and Roll-Call Votes," *American Journal of Political Science* 45 (July 2001): 563–579; James M. Devault, "CAFTA, Campaign Contributions, and the Role of Special Interests," *Economics and Politics* 22 (November 2010): 282–297, onlinelibrary.wiley.com/doi/ 10.1111/j.1468-0343.2009.00362.x/full, accessed June 1, 2012.

84. Quoted in Jeffrey H. Birnbaum, "How to Buy Clout in the Capital," *Fortune*, December 6, 1999, www.web .archive.org/web/20000817030750/www.fortune.com/ fortune/1999/12/06/lob3.html, accessed June 1, 2012.

85. John Harwood and Gerald F. Seib, *Pennsylvania Avenue: Profiles in Backroom Power* (New York: Random House, 2008), 85.

86. Stuart Byer, quoted in John J. Pitney Jr., "The FHP Health Care PAC," in *Risky Business? PAC Decisionmaking in Congressional Elections*, ed. Robert Biersack, Paul S. Herrnson, and Clyde Wilcox (Armonk, NY: Sharpe, 1994), 155.

87. Quoted in Art Levine, "The Adventures of . . . Money Man!" *The American Prospect*, April 24, 2000, prospect .org/article/adventures-money-man, accessed June 1, 2012.

88. CIGNA Corporation, "CIGNA 2002 Contributions Report," www.web.archive.org/web/20051023225441/ www.cigna.com/general/about/community/contr2002 .pdf, accessed June 1, 2012.

89. Larry Margasak, "Boeing Supported Politicians' Pet Charities to Help Win Contract," Associated Press, July 12, 2011, www.dailybreeze.com/ci_18464369, accessed June 4, 2012.

90. Quoted in Eric Lipton, "Congressional Charities Pulling In Corporate Cash," *New York Times,* September 5, 2010, www.nytimes.com/2010/09/06/us/politics/06charity .html, accessed June 4, 2012.

91. Federal law does require lobbyists to disclose contributions to charities "established, financed, maintained or controlled" by legislative or executive branch officials. But the law does not apply where the link between the official and the charity is informal. Keenan Steiner, "Some Lobbyists' Gifts to Lawmakers' Pet Causes Remain in the Dark," Sunlight Foundation, July 12, 2011, reporting.sunlight-foundation.com/2011/some-lobbyists-gifts-lawmakers-pet-causes-remain-dark, accessed June 4, 2012.

92. Tocqueville, *Democracy in America*, 525.

93. *Friends of the Earth, Inc. et al. v. Laidlaw Environmental Services (Toc), Inc.* 528 U.S. 167 (2000), Justice Scalia, dissenting, supreme.justia.com/cases/federal/us/528/167/ case.html, accessed June 4, 2012.

94. Paul M. Collins Jr., *Friends of the Supreme Court: Interest Groups and Judicial Decision Making* (New York: Oxford University Press, 2008), 46–48.

95. Ibid., 103.

96. Quoted in Tony Mauro, "Court Watch," *Legal Times*, October 6, 2003, 9.

97. Saul Alinsky, *Rules for Radicals* (New York: Vintage Books, 1989), 163.

98. In 2009, the figure was even higher, at $486.9 million. Alex Knott, "Lobbying by Foreign Countries Decreases," *Roll Call*, September 15, 2011, www.rollcall .com/issues/57_29/Lobbying_by_Foreign_Countries_ Decreases-208745-1.html, accessed June 4, 2012.

99. Kishore Gawande, Pravin Krishna, and Michael J. Robbins, "Foreign Lobbies and US Trade Policy," National Bureau of Economic Research Working Paper 10205, January 2004, www.nber.org/papers/w10205, accessed June 4, 2012.

100. John J. Mearsheimer and Stephen M. Walt, "The Israel Lobby and US Foreign Policy," Kennedy School of Government, March 2006, mearsheimer.uchicago .edu/pdfs/A0040.pdf, accessed June 4, 2012.

101. Alan Dershowitz, "Debunking the Newest—and Oldest—Jewish Conspiracy: A Reply to the Mearsheimer-Walt 'Working Paper,'" Kennedy School of Government, April 2006, www.docstoc.com/docs/618300/Debunking-the-Newest—and-Oldest—Jewish-Conspiracy, accessed June 4, 2012.

102. Kosterlitz, "The World According to AARP," 35.

103. Michael McCarthy, "Lobbying and the Search for the Common Good," October 24, 2002, woodstock.george-town.edu/resources/articles/the-ethics-of-lobbying .html, accessed June 4, 2012.

104. Thomas Susman, "Lobbying: Ethical, Though Not Bound by the 'Common Good,'" October 24, 2002, woodstock.georgetown.edu/resources/articles/the-ethics-of-lobbying.html, accessed June 4, 2012.

105. ABC, *This Week*, June 20, 1999, Transcript # 9906 2005-j12.

106. Keith Hampton, Lauren Sessions Goulet, Lee Rainie, and Kristen Purcell, "Social Networking Sites and Our Lives," Pew Internet and American Life Project, June 16, 2011, www.pewinternet.org/Reports/2011/ Technology-and-social-networks/Part-4/Civic-Engagement.aspx, accessed June 4, 2012.

107. Michael D. Shear, "Veteran Lobbyist to Advise Romney Campaign," *New York Times,* January 2, 2012, thecaucus.blogs.nytimes.com/2012/01/02/veteran-lobbyist-to-advise-romney-campaign, accessed June 4, 2012.

108. T. W. Farnam, "White House Visitor Logs Provide Window into Lobbying Industry," *Washington Post*, May 20, 2012, www.washingtonpost.com/politics/white-house-visitor-logs-show-lobbying-going-strong/2012/05/20/ gIQA2ok4dU_story.html, accessed June 4, 2012.

109. *Federalist,* no. 10, 48.

Chapter 9

1. Quoted in Sidney M. Milkis, *Political Parties and Constitutional Government: Remaking American Democracy* (Baltimore: Johns Hopkins University Press, 1999), 25.

2. Theda Skocpol, *Diminished Democracy: From Membership to Management in American Civic Life* (Norman: University of Oklahoma Press, 2003), 235.

3. National Election Pool exit poll of 17,836 respondents, November 4, 2008, www.cnn.com/ELECTION/2008/ results/polls/#USP00p1, accessed June 13, 2012.

4. Nebraska has the nation's only nonpartisan state legislature. That body also has the distinction of being the only legislature with a single chamber.

5. Alexander Hamilton, James Madison, and John Jay, *The Federalist Papers*, ed. Clinton Rossiter, with a new introduction and notes by Charles R. Kesler (New York: Signet, 2003), no. 37, 227.

6. George Washington, "Farewell Address, 1796," avalon.law .yale.edu/18th_century/washing.asp, accessed June 13, 2012.

7. Zachary C. Courser, "Voting Alone: Anti-Partyism, Political Independence and the Diminution of Political Participation," Ph.D. diss., University of Virginia, 2008, 14.

8. Sean Wilentz, *The Rise of American Democracy* (New York: Norton, 2005), 49–50.

9. Ibid., 74, 86.

10. David R. Mayhew, *Electoral Realignments: A Critique of an American Genre* (New Haven, CT: Yale University Press, 2002).

11. Thomas Jefferson, letter to James Madison, May 12, 1793, www.archive.org/stream/cu31924027055676/ cu31924027055676_djvu.txt, accessed June 13, 2012.

12. Thomas Jefferson, "Letter to Judge Spencer Roane," September 6, 1819, in *The Portable Thomas Jefferson*, ed. Merrill D. Peterson (New York: Viking, 1975), 562.

13. Thomas Jefferson, First Inaugural Address, March 4, 1801, avalon.law.yale.edu/19th_century/jefinau1.asp, accessed June 13, 2012.

14. Martin Van Buren, letter to Thomas Ritchie, January 13, 1827, www.scribd.com/doc/39551297/Martin-Van-Buren-to-Thomas-RitchieWashington, accessed June 13, 2012.

15. Alexis de Tocqueville, *Democracy in America*, ed. J. P. Mayer and trans. George Lawrence (Garden City, NY: Anchor Books, Doubleday, 1969), 521.

16. Richard C. Bain, *Convention Decisions and Voting Records* (Washington, DC: Brookings Institution, 1960), 28.

17. A. James Reichley, *The Life of the Parties* (Lanham, MD: Rowman and Littlefield, 2000), 88.

18. Members of the new party had diverse opinions on other economic and social issues. They essentially agreed to disagree. "We require no conformity of opinion on other subjects of National or State policy," said the Massachusetts Republican platform of 1855, quoted in James L. Sundquist, *Dynamics of the Party System*, rev. ed. (Washington, DC: Brookings Institution, 1983), 79.

19. The party's first official history read, "The Republican Party in the United States is a reformation and continuation of the political association which exalted Thomas Jefferson to the presidency, in the morning of the present century, and exists for similar purposes." Benjamin Franklin Hall, *The Republican Party and Its Candidates* (New York: Miller, Orton, and Mulligan, 1856), 13. Jefferson was a slaveholder, and his party was strong in the slaveholding South. The party name was a reference to the Jefferson of the Declaration.

20. James M. McPherson, *Battle Cry of Freedom: The Civil War Era* (New York: Ballantine Books, 1989), 149–152.

21. Harry V. Jaffa, *A New Birth of Freedom: Abraham Lincoln and the Coming of the Civil War* (Lanham, MD: Rowman and Littlefield, 2000), Chap.1.

22. Alexander Stephens, "The Cornerstone Speech," Savannah, Georgia, March 21, 1861, in *American Political Rhetoric: A Reader*, 4th ed., ed. Peter Augustine Lawler and Robert Martin Schaefer (Lanham, MD: Rowman and Littlefield, 2001), 241–242.

23. Democrat Samuel Tilden won 51% in 1876 but lost the electoral vote to Rutherford B. Hayes under dubious circumstances. In every other election of the period, minor candidates won between 3% and 10% of the popular vote.

24. James Bryce, *The American Commonwealth* (Indianapolis, IN: Liberty Fund, 1995 [1888]), 699.

25. *World Almanac and Book of Facts 2000* (Mahwah, NJ: World Almanac Books, 1999), 390–391.

26. Republican National Committee, "Who We Are," www.gop.com/index.php/issues/who_we_are/, accessed June 13, 2012.

27. Democratic National Committee, "Our Party, Our History," www.democrats.org/about/our_history, accessed June 13, 2012.

28. Library of Congress, "Brief Timeline of the National Women's Party 1912–1997," memory.loc.gov/ammem/collections/suffrage/nwp/brftime3.html, accessed June 13, 2012.

29. L. Sandy Maisel, *Parties and Elections in America: The Electoral Process*, 3rd ed. (Lanham, MD: Rowman and Littlefield, 1999), 193.

30. William L. Riordan, *Plunkitt of Tammany Hall* (New York: Dutton, 1963 [1905]), 11.

31. Michael Barone, *Our Country: The Shaping of America from Roosevelt to Reagan* (New York: Free Press, 1990), 20.

32. Barone, *Our Country*, 23–24; U.S. Department of Commerce, United States Department of Commerce, Bureau of the Census, *Historical Statistics of the United States: Colonial Times to 1970* (Washington, DC: Government Printing Office, 1975), 11.

33. Everett Carll Ladd Jr., and Charles D. Hadley, *Transformations of the American Party System* (New York: Norton, 1971), 57–60.

34. Ibid., 60–64.

35. A. James Reichley, *Religion in American Public Life* (Washington, DC: Brookings Institution, 1985), 219–220.

36. Gary Scott Smith, *Faith and the Presidency* (New York: Oxford University Press, 2006), 205.

37. Martin Shefter, *Political Parties and the State: The American Historical Experience* (Princeton, NJ: Princeton University Press, 1994), 81–86.

38. "Toward a More Responsible Two-Party System: A Report of the Committee on Political Parties" *American Political Science Review* 44, no. 3 (1950), Part 2, Supplement, www.apsanet.org/~pop/APSA_Report.htm, accessed June 13, 2012.

39. Ronald Brownstein, *The Second Civil War: How Extreme Partisanship Has Paralyzed Washington and Polarized America* (New York: Penguin, 2007), 71–72.

40. Woodrow Wilson grew up in Virginia but was governor of New Jersey when he ran for president in 1912.

41. Sundquist, *Dynamics of the Party System*, 283–284.

42. Gary C. Jacobson, *The Electoral Origins of Divided Government* (Boulder, CO: Westview Press, 1990).

43. Michael Barone, "The 49% Nation," in Michael Barone, Richard E. Cohen, and Grant Ujifusa, *The Almanac of American Politics 2002* (Washington, DC: National Journal, 2001), 21.

44. An early prediction of this trend came in: John B. Judis and Ruy Teixeira, *The Emerging Democratic Majority* (New York: Scribner, 2002).

45. Quoted in Martin F. Nolan, "Playing the Capital Gains Card," *Boston Globe*, September 7, 1992, 12.

46. An excellent impressionistic story of this change is Samuel G. Freedman, *The Inheritance: How Three Families and America Moved from Roosevelt to Reagan and Beyond* (New York: Simon and Schuster, 1996).

47. Angus Campbell et al., *The American Voter* (New York: Wiley, 1964), 67.

48. Morris P. Fiorina, Samuel J. Abrams, and Jeremy C. Pope, *Culture War? The Myth of a Polarized America* (New York: Pearson Longman, 2005), 25.

49. Ibid., 80.

50. Pew Research Center for the People and the Press, "Partisan Polarization Surges in Bush, Obama Years," June 4, 2012, www.people-press.org/files/legacy-pdf/06-04-12%20Values%20Release.pdf, accessed June 13, 2012.

51. Marjorie Randon Hershey, *Party Politics in America*, 15th ed. (New York: Pearson, 2013), 131.

52. Michael Dimrock, "Money Walks," Pew Research Center for the People and the Press, April 12, 2007, www.pewresearch.org/pubs/451/money-walks, accessed August 25, 2012.

53. Judis and Teixeira, *The Emerging Democratic Majority*, 39–49.

54. National Election Studies data, www.electionstudies.org/nesguide/2ndtable/t2a_2_1.htm, accessed August 25, 2012.

55. Barry A. Kosmin and Seymour P. Lachman, *One Nation under God: Religion in Contemporary American Society* (New York: Harmony, 1993), 190–193.

56. Frank Newport, "More Than 6 in 10 Very Religious Whites Identify With GOP," Gallup Poll, October 31, 2011, www.gallup.com/poll/150443/Religious-Whites-Identify-GOP.aspx, accessed June 13, 2012.

57. After 2008, there was some slight movement of Jewish voters toward the Republicans, but most remained Democrats. Pew Forum on Religion and Public Life, "Trends in Party Identification of Religious Groups," February 2, 2012, www.pewforum.org/Politics-and-Elections/Trends-in-Party-Identification-of-Religious-Groups-affiliation.aspx, accessed June 13, 2012.

58. Nancy Burns et al., "Explaining Gender Gaps and Racial Divides in Partisanship," paper presented at the annual meeting of the American Political Science Association, Seattle, August 29, 2011, papers.ssrn.com/sol3/papers.cfm?abstract_id=1901628, accessed June 14, 2012.

59. James G. Gimpel and Jason E. Schuknecht, *Patchwork Nation: Sectionalism and Political Change in American Politics* (Ann Arbor: University of Michigan Press, 2004), 3.

60. Bill Bishop, "No We Didn't: American Hasn't Changed as Much as Tuesday's Results Indicate," *Slate*, November 10, 2008, www.slate.com/blogs/bigsort/2008/11/04/no_we_didn_t_america_didn_t_change_as_much_as_tuesday_s_results_would_indicate.html, accessed June 14, 2012.

61. Bill Bishop, "Minority Views Increasingly Unheard," *Austin American-Statesman*, August 29, 2004, www.statesman.com/specialreports/content/special reports/greatdivide/082904minority.html, accessed June 14, 2012.

62. For state-by-state party registration totals as of October 2010, see Michael P. McDonald, "Partisan Voter Registration Totals," *Huffington Post*, October 13, 2010, www.huffingtonpost.com/michael-p-mcdonald/partisan-voter-registrati_b_761713.html, accessed June 14, 2012. Utah does not post party registration data online, so most compilations omit it.

63. Malcolm Ritter, "GOP Voters Confused? Experts Say Give Them a Break," Associated Press, February 24, 2012, articles.boston.com/2012-02-24/news/31096645_1_general-election-voting-in-primary-elections-primary-voters, accessed June 14, 2012.

64. *Elrod v. Burns*, 427 U.S. 347 (1976); *Branti v. Finkel*, 445 U.S. 507 (1980); *Rutan v. Republican Party of Illinois*, 497 U.S. 62 (1990); *O'Hare Truck Service, Inc. v. City of Northlake*, 518 U.S. 712 (1996).

65. Matthew J. Burbank, Ronald J. Hrebenar, and Robert C. Benedict, *Parties, Interest Groups, and Political Campaigns* (Boulder, CO: Paradigm, 2008), 40–45.

66. *Colorado Republican Federal Campaign Committee v. Federal Election Commission*, 518 U.S. 604 (1996).

67. Brian F. Schaffner, *Politics, Parties, and Elections in America*, 7th ed. (Boston: Wadsworth, 2011), 79–81.

68. Robin Kolodny, *Pursuing Majorities: Congressional Campaign Committees in American Politics* (Norman: University of Oklahoma Press, 1998), 7.

69. William F. Connelly Jr. and John J. Pitney Jr., *Congress' Permanent Minority? Republicans in the US House* (Lanham, MD: Rowman and Littlefield, 1994), 121.

70. Representative Mickey Edwards (R-Oklahoma), quoted in John E. Yang and Tom Kenworthy, "House GOP Takes Stand against Any Tax Increases," *Washington Post*, July 19, 1990, A7.

71. Kenneth P. Vogel and Ben Smith, "When 'Coordinate' Is a Dirty Word," *Politico*, May 31, 2011, www.politico.com/news/stories/0511/55911.html, accessed June 14, 2012.

72. James W. Ceaser, *Reforming the Reforms: A Critical Analysis of the Presidential Selection Process* (Cambridge, MA: Ballinger, 1982), 21.

73. Ralph G. Martin, *Ballot and Bandwagons* (Chicago: Rand McNally, 1964), 201–202.

74. Quoted in Mark Z. Barabak and Amy Bayer, "An Interview with the Republican Challenger," *San Diego Union-Tribune*, August 11, 1996, A1.

75. Theodore H. White, *The Making of the President 1960* (New York: Signet, 1967), 178.

76. William A. Galston, "Presidential Nominations: Improving the Performance of American Political Parties," in *American Political Parties and Constitutional Politics*, ed. Peter W. Schramm and Bradford P. Wilson (Lanham, MD: Rowman and Littlefield, 1993), 68.

77. Roger Simon, "Relentless," *The Politico*, August 25, 2008, www.politico.com/news/stories/0808/12732.html, accessed, June 14, 2012.

78. Nate Silver, "Romney Dominating Race for Endorsements," *New York Times*, November 25, 2011, fivethirtyeight.blogs.nytimes.com/2011/11/25/romney-dominating-race-for-endorsements, accessed June 14, 2012.

79. Bryan Naylor, "That New Friend You Made on Facebook? He Might Be Named Mitt or Barack," National Public Radio, May 3, 2012, www.npr.org/blogs/itsallpolitics/2012/05/03/151879422/that-new-friend-you-made-on-facebook-he-might-be-named-mitt-or-barack, accessed June 14, 2012.

80. Alex Fitzpatrick, "Republicans Launch Facebook App to Defeat Obama," *Mashable*, May 1, 2012, mashable .com/2012/05/01/republicans-facebook-app, accessed June 14, 2012.

81. Naylor, "That New Friend."

82. Fitzpatrick, "Republicans Launch Facebook App."

83. Morris Fiorina, *Divided Government* (New York: Macmillan, 1992), Chap. 3.

84. Lester Thurow, *The Zero-Sum Society* (New York: Basic, 1980), 212.

85. Adam Nagourney, "Maybe the British Do Democracy Better," *New York Times*, May 1, 2005, section 4, 7.

86. Ibid.

87. Michael Schudson, *The Good Citizen: A History of American Civic Life* (Cambridge, MA: Harvard University Press, 1998), 238.

88. "Is It Time to Make 'Question Times' a Regular Feature of Our Democracy?" *Politico*, February 3, 2010, www.politico.com/arena/archive/question-time .html, accessed June 14, 2012.

89. Emily Ethridge, "2011 Vote Studies: Party Unity," *Congressional Quarterly Weekly Report*, January 15, 2012, 111.

90. Jon R. Bond and Richard Fleisher, eds., *Polarized Politics: Congress and President in a Partisan Era* (Washington, DC: CQ Press, 2000); David C. King, "Congress, Polarization, and Fidelity to the Median Voter," Kennedy School of Government Working Paper, March 10, 2003, www.hks.harvard.edu/fs/dking/Extreme_Politics.pdf, accessed June 15, 2012.

91. Fiorina, *Culture War*, Chap. 7.

92. Mark Leibovich, "The Comparison that Ends the Conversation," *Washington Post*, June 22, 2005, C1.

93. Burdett A. Loomis, ed., *Esteemed Colleagues: Civility and Deliberation in the U.S. Senate* (Washington, DC: Brookings Institution, 2000), 10.

94. "Text: Senator Richard Lugar's Two Primary Election Statements," *Evansville Courier-Press*, May 8, 2012, www.courierpress.com/news/2012/may/08/text-sen-richard-lugars-two-primary-election-state, accessed June 15, 2012.

95. Jonah Goldberg, "Unity Is Overrated," *National Review Online*, March 14, 2007, www.nationalreview.com/ articles/220283/unity-overrated/jonah-goldberg, accessed June 15, 2012.

96. Quoted in Barbara Sinclair, *Majority Leadership in the U.S. House* (Baltimore: Johns Hopkins University Press, 1983), 74.

97. J. David Gillespie, *Politics at the Periphery: Third Parties in Two-Party America* (Columbia: University of South Carolina Press, 1993), Chap. 5.

98. Libertarian Party, National Platform, May 2012.

99. Green Party of the United States, "Green Officeholders," June 15, 2012, www.gp.org/elections/officeholders, accessed June 15, 2012.

100. Green Party of the United States, 2010 Platform, www.gp.org/committees/platform/2010/introduction .php, accessed June 15, 2012.

101. Steven J. Rosenstone, Roy L. Behr, and Edward H. Lazarus, *Third Parties in America*, 2nd ed. (Princeton, NJ: Princeton University Press, 1996), 16.

102. Diana Dwyre and Robin Kolodny, "Barriers to Minor Party Success and Prospects for Change," in *Multiparty Politics in America*, ed. Paul S. Herrnson and John C. Green (Lanham, MD: Rowman and Littlefield, 1997), 175–177.

103. Ibid., 179.

104. Quoted in Chris Cillizza and Aaron Blake, "Americans Elect and the Death of the Third Party Movement," *Washington Post*, May 18, 2012, www.washington-post.com/blogs/the-fix/post/americans-elect-and-the-death-of-the-third-party-movement/2012/05/17/ gIQAIzNKXU_blog.html, accessed June 15, 2012.

105. John F. Bibby and L. Sandy Maisel, *Two Parties—Or More? The American Party System*, 2nd ed. (Boulder, CO: Westview Press, 2003), 112.

106. Quoted in Timothy P. Carney, "Did DeMint's Endorsement of Toomey Set Off Specter?" *Washington Examiner*, April 28, 2009, www.washingtonexaminer.com/ politics/beltway-confidential/2009/04/did-demints-endorsement-toomey-set-specter/136018, accessed June 15, 2012.

107. Quoted in Brownstein, *The Second Civil War*, 335–336.

108. Harry V. Jaffa, "The Nature and Origins of the American Party System," in *Political Parties USA*, ed. Robert Goldwin (Chicago: Rand McNally, 1964), 67.

109. Steven M. Gillon, *The Pact* (New York: Oxford University Press, 2008).

110. Michael Schudson, "Changing Concepts of Democracy," MIT Forum, www.web.mit.edu/comm-forum/ papers/schudson.html, accessed August 25, 2012.

Chapter 10

1. See, for instance, Kevin O'Leary, *Saving Democracy: A Plan for Real Representation in America* (Stanford, CA: Stanford University Press, 2006).

2. Alexander Hamilton, James Madison, and John Jay, *The Federalist Papers*, ed. Clinton Rossiter with a new introduction and notes by Charles R. Kesler (New York: Signet, 2003), no. 57, 348.

3. Harold W. Stanley and Richard G. Niemi, *Vital Statistics on American Politics 2007–2008* (Washington, DC: CQ Press, 2008), 66.

4. Richard L. Fox and Jennifer L. Lawless, "To Run or Not to Run for Office: Explaining Nascent Political Ambition," *American Journal of Political Science* 49 (July 2005): 642–659.

5. The formal term for such informal talk is "discursive participation." Lawrence R. Jacobs, Fay Lomax Book, and Michael X. Delli Carpini, *Talking Together: Public Deliberation and Political Participation in America* (Chicago: University of Chicago Press, 2009).

6. *Federalist*, no. 10, 77.

7. *Federalist*, no. 55, 340.

8. Initiative and Referendum Institute, www.iandrinstitute .org/statewide_i&r.htm, accessed June 26, 2012.

9. National Conference of State Legislatures, "Recall of State Officials," June 6, 2012, www.ncsl.org/legislatures-elections/elections/recall-of-state-officials.aspx, accessed June 26, 2012.

10. National Conference of State Legislatures, "Recall of Local Officials," February 28, 2011, www.ncsl.org/legislatures-elections/elections/recall-of-local-officials .aspx, accessed June 26, 2012.

11. John G. Matsusaka, *For the Many or the Few: The Initiative, Public Policy, and American Democracy* (Chicago: University of Chicago Press, 2004), 13.

12. Daniel Schlozman and Ian Yohai, "How Initiatives Don't Always Make Citizens: Ballot Initiatives in the American States, 1978–2004," *Political Behavior* 30 (December 2008), www.springerlink.com/content/ j4723672581727hx/, accessed June 26, 2012.

13. David S. Broder, *Democracy Derailed: Initiative Campaigns and the Power of Money* (New York: Harcourt Brace, 2000).

14. Quoted in Richard J. Ellis, *Democratic Delusions: The Initiative Process in America* (Lawrence: University Press of Kansas, 2002), 70.

15. See other arguments for and against nonpartisan elections at National League of Cities, "Partisan vs. Non-Partisan Elections," 2010, www.nlc.org/build-skills-networks/ resources/cities-101/partisan-vs–non-partisan-elections, accessed June 26, 2012.

16. Brian F. Schaffner, Matthew Streb, and Gerald Wright, "Teams without Uniforms: The Nonpartisan Ballot in State and Local Elections," *Political Research Quarterly* 54 (March 2001): 7–30.

17. David C. King, "Centrism and the Quality of Representation in the U.S. Congress," Harvard University, Kennedy School of Government, November 14, 2000, www.hks.harvard.edu/fs/dking/Centrism.pdf, accessed June 28, 2012.

18. Center for Voting and Democracy, "What Is IRV?" 2011, www.fairvote.org/what-is-irv/#.T-pPjRe-VIE, accessed June 26, 2012.

19. The Constitution does not require single-member districts. In 1842, Congress enacted such a requirement (5 Stat. 491). After a brief lapse, Congress reinstated the requirement in 1862. A 1929 reapportionment statute omitted it, leaving states free to elect House members at large. In the 88th Congress (in the early 1960s), 22 of the 435 representatives served at large. In 1967, Congress enacted a permanent requirement (PL 90-196) for single-member House districts. Source: Center for Voting and Democracy, "History of Single Member Districts for Congress," archive.fairvote.org/reports/1995/chp2/mast. html, accessed June 27, 2012.

20. National Conference of State Legislatures, "2010 Constituents Per Legislative District Table," 2012, www.ncsl .org/legislatures-elections/legislatures/2010-constituents-per-state-legislative-district.aspx, accessed June 27, 2012.

21. *Federalist,* no. 52, 324.

22. National Conference of State Legislatures, "Redistricting Law 2010," November 2009, www.comptroller1 .state.tn.us/lg/PDF/NCSL%20Redistrictiing%202010 .pdf, accessed June 27, 2012.

23. Kevin Murray, "Competition Isn't Everything," *Los Angeles Times,* February 2, 2005, B13.

24. Frank R. Parker, *Black Votes Count: Political Empowerment in Mississippi after 1965* (Chapel Hill: University of North Carolina Press, 1990), 41–51.

25. Michael Barone and Grant Ujifusa, *The Almanac of American Politics 1996* (Washington, DC: National Journal, 1995), 1016.

26. *Miller v. Johnson,* 515 U.S. 900 (1995).

27. Ibid.

28. Chris Moran, "Ballot for Harris Co. Voters Is Longer Than Ever," *Houston Chronicle,* October 11, 2010, www.chron. com/news/houston-texas/article/Ballot-for-Harris-Co-voters-is-longer-than-ever-1597294.php, accessed June 27, 2012.

29. David Mark, *Going Dirty: The Art of Negative Campaigning* (Lanham, MD: Rowman and Littlefield, 2009), 32.

30. Ray Price, "A Nixon Myth" (letter), October 13, 2002, www.nytimes.com/2002/10/13/opinion/l-a-nixon-myth-335983.html, accessed June 27, 2012.

31. Scott Rosenberg, "Did Gore Invent the Internet?" *Salon.com,* October 5, 2000, www.salon.com/2000/10/ 05/gore_internet/, accessed June 27, 2012.

32. United States Election Project, "2012 Presidential Nomination Contest Turnout Rates," April 25, 2012, elections.gmu.edu/Turnout_2012P.html, accessed June 27, 2012.

33. Federal Election Commission, "Presidential Pre-Nomination Campaign Receipts Through December 31, 2011," www.fec.gov/press/bkgnd/pres_cf/pres_cf_odd_ doc/presreceiptsye2011.pdf, accessed June 27, 2012.

34. Pew Research Center, "Many Voters Unaware of Basic Facts about GOP Candidates," January 12, 2012, www.people-press.org/files/legacy-pdf/1-12-12%20 Knowledge%20release.pdf, accessed June 27, 2012.

35. *Federalist,* no. 68, 410.

36. *Bush v. Gore,* 531 U.S. 98, www.law.cornell.edu/supct/ html/00-949.ZPC.html, accessed June 27, 2012.

37. John C. Fortier, ed., *After the People Vote,* 3rd ed. (Washington, DC: AEI Press, 2004), 83–84.

38. Brian J. Gaines, "Popular Myths about Popular Vote–Electoral College Splits," *PS: Political Science and Politics* 34 (March 2001): 71–75.

39. Cable News Network, "Poll: Majority of Americans Accept Bush as Legitimate President," December 13, 2001, www.cnn.com/2000/ALLPOLITICS/stories/12/13/ cnn.poll/, accessed June 27, 2012.

40. Lydia Saad, "Americans Would Swap Electoral College for Popular Vote," Gallup Poll, October 24, 2011, www .gallup.com/poll/150245/americans-swap-electoral-college-popular-vote.aspx, accessed June 27, 2012.

41. Tara Ross, *Enlightened Democracy: The Case for the Electoral College* (Dallas, TX: Colonial Press, 2004), 81.

42. FairVote, "2008's Shrinking Battleground and Its Stark Impact on Campaign Activity," December 4, 2008, www.fairvote.org/tracker/?page=27&pressmode=show specific&showarticle=230, accessed June 27, 2012.

43. Ibid.

44. *Federalist*, no. 62, 375.

45. Paul S. Herrnson, *Congressional Elections: Campaigning at Home and in Washington*, 6th ed. (Washington, DC: CQ Press, 2012), 267.

46. See the incisive portrait of one-term senator Wyche Fowler (D-GA) in Richard F. Fenno Jr., *Senators on the Campaign Trail: The Politics of Representation* (Norman: University of Oklahoma Press, 1996), Chaps. 5–6.

47. Gary C. Jacobson, *The Politics of Congressional Elections*, 6th ed. (New York: Pearson Longman, 2004), 155.

48. James E. Campbell, *The Presidential Pulse of Congressional Elections*, 2nd ed. (Lexington: University Press of Kentucky, 1997).

49. R. Michael Alvarez, "Ballot Design Options," University of Maryland Center for American Politics and Citizenship, February 17, 2002, www.capc.umd.edu/rpts/MD_EVote_Alvarez.pdf, accessed June 27, 2012.

50. Clive Thompson, "Can You Count on Voting Machines?" *New York Times Magazine*, January 6, 2008, www.nytimes.com/2008/01/06/magazine/06Vote-t.html, accessed June 27, 2012.

51. Richard G. Niemi and Paul S. Herrnson, "Beyond the Butterfly: The Complexity of U.S. Ballots," *Perspectives on Political Science* 1 (June 2003): 320.

52. The Uniformed and Overseas Citizen Absentee Voting Act of 1986, 42 USC 1973ff.

53. Michael McDonald, "2010 Turnout Rate and Early Voting Forecasts," November 3, 2010, elections.gmu.edu/2010_vote_forecasts.html, accessed June 27, 2012.

54. John Dolan, "Military Vote a Priority in November," *Dayton Daily News*, June 26, 2012, www.daytondailynews.com/news/dayton-news/military-vote-a-priority-in-november-1396457.html, accessed June 27, 2012.

55. Norman J. Ornstein, "Early Voting Necessary but Toxic in Large Doses," *Roll Call*, September 22, 2004, www.economist.com/node/3219156, accessed June 27, 2012.

56. Common Cause, "Getting It Straight for 2008: What We Know about Vote by Mail Elections, and How to Conduct Them Well," January 2008, www.commoncause.org/atf/cf/%7Bfb3c17e2-cdd1-4df6-92be-bd4429893665%7D/WHAT%20WE%20KNOW%20ABOUT%20VOTE%20BY%20MAIL.PDF, accessed June 27, 2012.

57. National Election Pool exit poll of 17,504 respondents, November 2, 2010, www.cnn.com/ELECTION/2010/results/polls/#USH00p1, accessed June 27, 2012.

58. Harold W. Stanley and Richard G. Niemi, *Vital Statistics on American Politics 2011-2012* (Washington, DC: CQ Press, 2011), 38.

59. National Election Pool exit poll of 17,836 respondents, November 4, 2008, www.cnn.com/ELECTION/2008/results/polls/#USP00p1, accessed June 27, 2012.

60. Ibid.

61. Leslie Wayne, "Democrats Take Page from Their Rival's Playbook," *New York Times*, October 31, 2008, www.nytimes.com/2008/11/01/us/politics/01target.html, accessed June 27, 2012.

62. Steven E. Schier, *By Invitation Only: The Rise of Exclusive Politics in the United States* (Pittsburgh: University of Pittsburgh Press, 2000), 90–91.

63. Robert G. Kaiser, "Academics Say It's Elementary: Gore Wins," *Washington Post*, August 31, 2000, A12.

64. "Symposium: Forecasting the 2008 National Elections," *PS: Political Science and Politics* 51 (October 2008): 679–732.

65. Robert E. Hogan, "Challenger Emergence, Incumbent Success, and Electoral Accountability in State Legislative Elections," *Journal of Politics* 66 (November 2004): 1283–1303; Stephen Ansolabehere and James M. Snyder Jr., "The Incumbency Advantage in U.S. Elections: An Analysis of State and Federal Offices, 1942–2000," March 15, 2002, www.web.mit.edu/polisci/research/representation/incumb_advantage_elj.pdf, accessed July 3, 2009.

66. Roger Davidson, Walter J. Oleszek, and Frances Lee, *Congress and Its Members*, 13th ed. (Washington, DC: CQ Press, 2012), 132.

67. National Conference of State Legislatures, "Size of State Legislative Staff: 1979, 1988, 1996, 2003, 2009," June 2009, www.ncsl.org/legislatures-elections/legisdata/staff-change-chart-1979-1988-1996-2003-2009.aspx, accessed June 27, 2012.

68. "Decisions" (1968 Nixon television spot), www.livingroomcandidate.org/commercials/1968/decisions, accessed June 27, 2012.

69. Clifford D. May, "Jersey Race Is Taking Brutal Turn," *New York Times*, September 22, 1988, www.nytimes.com/1988/09/22/nyregion/jersey-race-is-taking-brutal-turn.html, accessed June 27, 2012.

70. Michael John Burton and Daniel M. Shea, *Campaign Craft: The Strategies, Tactics, and Art of Political Campaign Management*, 4th ed. (Santa Barbara, CA: Praeger, 2010), 97.

71. Amy Gutmann, "Deliberation in Education and the Media: Rising to the Challenge?" Annenberg Distinguished Lecture, University of Pennsylvania, October 26, 2004, www.upenn.edu/president/meet-president/annenberg-lecturel, accessed June 28, 2012.

72. Stephen Bates, "The Future of Presidential Debates," 1993, www.web.archive.org/web/20040427131613/www.annenberg.nwu.edu/pubs/debate/debate08.htm, accessed June 28, 2012.

73. Stephen Ansolabehere and Shanto Iyengar, *Going Negative: How Attack Ads Shrink and Polarize the Electorate* (New York: Simon and Schuster,1995).

74. Richard L. Lau, Lee Sigelman, and Ivy Brown Rovner, "The Effects of Negative Political Campaigns: A Meta-Analytic Reassessment," *Journal of Politics* 69, (November 2007): 1176–1209.

75. John G. Geer, "Campaign Negativity Can Be Positive," *Politico*, June 19, 2007, www.politico.com/news/stories/0607/4548.html, accessed June 28, 2012. See also John G. Geer, *In Defense of Negativity* (Chicago: University of Chicago Press, 2006).

76. *Commercial Advertiser* (New York), October 8, 1800, 2.

77. American Association of Political Consultants, "Code of Ethics," www.theaapc.org/default.asp?contentID=701, accessed June 28, 2012.

78. Martin Wisckol, "Politicians Ignoring Ethics Oath," *Orange County Register*, January 6, 2002, Local 1.

79. For example, see: Andy Barr, "Steve Poizner Urges Whitman Investigation," *Politico*, February 1, 2010, www.politico.com/news/stories/0210/32330.html, accessed June 28, 2012.

80. Center for Responsive Politics, "Incumbent Advantage," May 20, 2011, www.opensecrets.org/bigpicture/incumbs.php?cycle=2010&party=A&type=A, accessed June 28, 2012.

81. Center for Responsive Politics, "Most Expensive Races," May 20, 2011, www.opensecrets.org/bigpicture/topraces.php?cycle=2010&display=currcands, accessed June 28, 2012.

82. Center for Responsive Politics, "U.S. Election Will Cost $5.3 Billion, Center for Responsive Politics Predicts," October 22, 2008, www.opensecrets.org/news/2008/10/us-election-will-cost-53-billi.html; Cotton Delo, "Super PACs Could Drive Total 2012 Election Spending to $9.8 Billion," *Ad Age*, March 7, 2012, adage.com/article/campaign-trail/total-2012-election-spending-hit-9-8b/233155, accessed June 28, 2012.

83. Federal Election Commission, *Thirty Year Report*, September 2005, www.fec.gov/info/publications/30year.pdf, accessed June 28, 2012.

84. *Buckley v. Valeo*, 424 U.S. 1 (1976).

85. Ibid., fn. 52.

86. *McConnell v. Federal Election Commission*, 530 U.S. 93 (2003), www.law.cornell.edu/supct/html/02-1674.ZS.html, accessed June 28, 2012.

87. *Citizens United v. Federal Election Commission*, 558 U.S. 50 (2010).

88. John J. Pitney Jr., "The Iron Law of Emulation: American Crossroads and Crossroads GPS," in *Interest Groups Unleashed*, ed. Paul S. Herrnson, Christopher J. Deering, and Clyde Wilcox (Washington; CQ Press, 2012).

89. The checkoff neither increases the amount of taxes owed nor decreases any refund.

90. Darry Sragow, quoted in George Skelton, "California's Show-Me-the-Money Governor," *Los Angeles Times*, July 22, 2002.

91. Herrnson, *Congressional Elections*, 90.

92. Stephen Ansolabehere, Erik C. Snowberg, and James M. Snyder Jr., "Television and the Incumbency Advantage in US Elections," August 2005, www.hss.caltech.edu/~snowberg/papers/Ansolabehere-Snowberg-Snyder%20TV%20and%20Incumbency%20Advatage.pdf, accessed June 28, 2012.

93. Richard Rapaport, "Net vs. Norm," *Forbes ASAP*, May 29, 2000, www.forbes.com/asap/2000/0529/053_print.html, accessed June 28, 2012.

94. Joe Trippi, *The Revolution Will Not Be Televised* (New York: ReganBooks, 2004), 131.

95. Burton and Shea, *Campaign Craft*, 155.

96. Jose Antonio Vargas, "Obama Raised Half a Billion Online," *Washington Post*, November 20, 2008, voices.washingtonpost.com/44/2008/11/obama-raised-half-a-billion-on.html, accessed June 28, 2012.

97. Center for Responsive Politics, "Campaign Finance Reform: What's the Issue?" www.web.archive.org/web/20080202163236/www.opensecrets.org/news/campaignfinance/index.asp, accessed June 28, 2012.

98. Bradley A. Smith, "The Trouble with Campaign Finance Regulation," *Imprimis*, April 2002, 4.

99. Melissa Deckman, "Gender Differences in the Decision to Run for School Board," *American Politics Research* 35 (July 2007): 541–563.

100. Alec MacGillis, "Obama Camp Relying Heavily on Ground Effort," *Washington Post*, October 12, 2008, www.washingtonpost.com/wp-dyn/content/article/2008/10/11/AR2008101102119.html, accessed June 28, 2012.

101. Robert A. Dahl, "Myth of the Presidential Mandate," *Political Science Quarterly* 105 (Fall 1990): 355–372.

102. Michael Beschloss, ed., *Taking Charge: The Johnson White House Tapes*, 1963–1964 (New York: Simon and Schuster, 1997), 256–257.

103. Andrew E. Busch, *Horses in Midstream: U.S. Midterm Elections and Their Consequences*, 1894–1998 (Pittsburgh: University of Pittsburgh Press, 1999).

104. *Federalist,* no. 51, 319.

Chapter 11

1. Associated Press, "AP History: The News Cooperative Takes Shape," web.archive.org/web/20110729010041/http://ap.org/pages/about/history/history_first.html, accessed July 2, 2012.

2. Allen C. Guelzo, *Lincoln and Douglas: The Debates That Defined America* (New York: Simon and Schuster, 2008), 117.

3. U.S. Department of Commerce, Bureau of the Census, *Historical Statistics of the United States, Colonial Times to 1970* (Washington, DC: Government Printing

Office, 1975), 810, www2.census.gov/prod2/statcomp/documents/CT1970p2-01.pdf, accessed July 2, 2012.

4. Theodore Roosevelt, "The Man with the Muck-Rake," April 14, 1906, www.americanrhetoric.com/speeches/teddyrooseveltmuckrake.htm, accessed July 7, 2009.

5. U.S. Department of Commerce, Bureau of the Census, *Historical Statistics*, 382.

6. Ibid., 796.

7. There is some disagreement among historians as to which radio addresses to count as "fireside chats." See Franklin D. Roosevelt Presidential Library and Museum, "Fireside Chats of Franklin D. Roosevelt," docs.fdrlibrary.marist.edu/FIRESI90.HTML, accessed July 2, 2012.

8. U.S. Department of Commerce, Bureau of the Census, *Historical Statistics*, 400.

9. The debates were only one of many influences on the 1960 outcome. Nevertheless, evidence suggests that they gave Kennedy an advantage. See James N. Druckman, "The Power of Television Images: The First Kennedy-Nixon Debate Revisited," *Journal of Politics* 65 (May 2003): 559–571.

10. Roper surveys in William G. Mayer, "Poll Trends: Trends in Media Usage," *Public Opinion Quarterly* 57 (Winter 1993): 603.

11. Ellen Hume, "Talk Show Culture," www.ellenhume.com/node/22, accessed July 3, 2012.

12. Harold W. Stanley and Richard G. Niemi, *Vital Statistics on American Politics 2011-2012* (Washington, DC: CQ Press, 2011), 159-160.

13. Doris A. Graber, *Mass Media and American Politics*, 8th ed. (Washington, DC: CQ Press, 2011), 39.

14. John McQuaid, "Why a Weak Website Can't Replace a Daily Newspaper in New Orleans," *The Atlantic*, June 12, 2012, www.theatlantic.com/national/archive/2012/06/why-a-weak-website-cant-replace-a-daily-newspaper-in-new-orleans/258393, accessed July 3, 2012.

15. Richard Campbell, Christopher R. Martin, and Bettina Fabos, *Media and Culture with 2013 Update: An Introduction to Mass Communication* (Boston: Bedford/St. Martin's, 2013), 242.

16. Ted Turner, "My Beef with Big Media," *Washington Monthly*, July/August 2004, www.washingtonmonthly.com/features/2004/0407.turner.html, accessed July 3, 2012.

17. Kathryn Zickuhr and Aaron Smith, "Digital Differences," Pew Internet and American Life Project, April 12, 2012, pewinternet.org/&tidle;/media//Files/Reports/2012/PIP_Digital_differences_041312.pdf, accessed July 3, 2012.

18. "Buzz in the Blogosphere: Millions More Bloggers and Blog Readers," NielsenWire, March 8, 2012, blog.nielsen.com/nielsenwire/online_mobile/buzz-in-the-blogosphere-millions-more-bloggers-and-blog-readers/, accessed July 3, 2012.

19. Kathryn Zickuhr, "Generation 2010," Pew Internet and American Life Project, December 16, 2010, pewinternet.org/Reports/2010/Generations-2010/Trends/Blogging.aspx, accessed July 5, 2012. They account for about half of the world's bloggers. "State of the Blogosphere 2011," November 4, 2011, technorati.com/social-media/article/state-of-the-blogosphere-2011-part1, accessed July 5, 2012. Why is there a difference between the blog count and the number of people who report blogging? Many blogs are the products of public or private organizations, and many individuals keep multiple blogs.

20. Amy Mitchell, Tom Rosenstiel, and Leah Christian, "What Facebook and Twitter Mean for News," State of the News Media 2012, March 19, 2012, stateofthemedia.org/2012/mobile-devices-and-news-consumption-some-good-signs-for-journalism/what-facebook-and-twitter-mean-for-news, accessed July 5, 2012.

21. Oriella PR Network, "The Influence Game: How News Is Sourced and Managed Today," June 20, 2012, www.oriellaprnetwork.com/sites/default/files/research/Oriella%;20Digital%;20Journalism%;20Study%;202012%;20Final%20US.pdf, accessed July 5, 2012.

22. Pew Research Center for the People and the Press, "Financial Woes Now Overshadow All Other Concerns for Journalists," March 17, 2008, www.people-press.org/2008/03/17/financial-woes-now-overshadow-all-other-concerns-for-journalists/, accessed July 5, 2012.

23. Rick Edmonds, Emily Guskin, Tom Rosenstiel, and Amy Mitchell, "Newspapers: Building Digital Revenue Proves Painfully Slow," State of the News Media 2012, April 11, 2012, stateofthemedia.org/2012/newspapers-building-digital-revenues-proves-painfully-slow, accessed July 5, 2012.

24. George Washington, "Farewell Address," 1796, avalon.law.yale.edu/18th_century/washing.asp, accessed July 5, 2012.

25. David T. Z. Mindich, "Journalism and Citizenship: Making the Connection," *Nieman Reports*, Winter 2008, www.nieman.harvard.edu/reportsitem.aspx?id=100678, accessed July 5, 2012.

26. Michael X. Delli Carpini and Scott Keeter, *What Americans Know about Politics and Why It Matters* (New Haven, CT: Yale University Press, 1996), 188–194.

27. Meg Bostrom, "Rediscovering the Mission: Analysis of a Priming Survey Exploring Views of Government," October 2005, www.frameworksinstitute.org/assets/files/PDF_govt/surveyReport.pdf, accessed July 5, 2012.

28. Bryan E. Denham, "Sports Illustrated, the Mainstream Press and the Enactment of Drug Policy in Major League Baseball," *Journalism* 5 (2004): 51–68.

29. Dennis T. Lowry, Tarn Ching, Josephine Nio, and Dennis W. Leitner, "Setting the Public Fear Agenda: A Longitudinal Analysis of Network TV Crime Reporting, Public Perceptions of Crime, and FBI Crime Statistics," *Journal of Communication* 53 (March 2003): 61–73; Shanto Iyengar and Jennifer A. Grady, *Media Politics: A Citizen's Guide* (New York: Norton, 2007), 211–212.

30. Iyengar and Grady, *Media Politics*, 215.

31. Stephen J. Farnsworth and S. Robert Lichter, *The Nightly News Nightmare: Television's Coverage of U.S. Presidential Elections, 1988–2008*, 3d ed. (Lanham, MD: Rowman and Littlefield, 2011), 8–9.

32. Tom Rosenstiel, Mark Jurkowitz, and Tricia Sartor, "How the Media Covered the 2012 Primary Campaign," April 23, 2012, www.journalism.org/analysis_report/romney_report, accessed July 5, 2012.

33. Pew Research Center for the People and the Press, "Political Divide in Views of Campaign Coverage," June 1, 2007, www.people-press.org/report/333/political-divide-in-views-of-campaign-coverage, accessed July 5, 2012.

34. Frank Bruni, *Ambling into History: The Unlikely Odyssey of George W. Bush* (New York: HarperCollins, 2002), 81.

35. Matthew Robinson, *Mobocracy: How the Media's Obsession with Polling Twists the News, Alters Elections, and Undermines Democracy* (New York: Prima/Forum, 2002), 95.

36. Farnsworth and Lichter, *The Nightly News Nightmare*, 133.

37. Jay Rosen, "Why Horse Race Journalism Works for Journalists but Fails Us," AlterNet, January 22, 2008, www.alternet.org/media/74488?page=entire, accessed July 5, 2012.

38. "NBC's Autism Week," *Adventures in Autism*, February 20, 2005, adventuresinautism.blogspot.com/2005/02/nbcs-autism-week.html, accessed July 5, 2012.

39. Sean McCleneghan and Ruth Ann Ragland, "Municipal Elections and Community Media," *Social Science Journal* 39, no. 2 (2002): 203–219.

40. David Freedlander, "The Editorial Plea: How the *New York Times* Decides Who Wins and Loses Local Elections," *Politicker*, May 2, 2012, politicker.com/2012/05/the-editorial-plea-how-the-new-york-times-decides-who-wins-and-loses-local-elections, accessed July 5, 2012.

41. Simmi Aujla, "Keith Olbermann Suspended after Donating to Democrats," *Politico*, November 7, 2010, www.politico.com/news/stories/1110/44734.html, accessed July 5, 2012.

42. Alex Fitzpatrick, "Prime-Time TV Network News Ignoring SOPA," Yahoo News, January 11, 2012, news.yahoo.com/prime-time-tv-network-news-ignoring-sopa-report-134836459.html, accessed July 5, 2012.

43. Gallup Poll, "Media Use and Evaluation," www.gallup.com/poll/1663/Media-Use-Evaluation.aspx, accessed July 5, 2012.

44. Lymari Morales, "Majority in US Continues to Distrust Media, Perceive Bias," Gallup Poll, September 22, 2011, www.gallup.com/poll/149624/Majority-Continue-Distrust-Media-Perceive-Bias.aspx, accessed July 5, 2012.

45. Julie Moos, "Journalism Continues to Be a Risky Occupation," March 2, 2011, www.poynter.org/uncategorized/15646/journalism-continues-to-be-a-risky-occupation/, accessed July 5, 2012.

46. Lauren Streib, "Journalism Bust, J-School Boom," *Forbes*, April 6, 2009, www.forbes.com/2009/04/06/journalism-media-jobs-business-media-jobs.html, accessed July 5, 2012.

47. Pew Research Center for the People and the Press, "Financial Woes."

48. Pew Research Center for the People and the Press, "Striking the Balance, Audience Interests, Business Pressures and Journalists' Values," March 30, 1999, www.people-press.org/1999/03/30/striking-the-balance-audience-interests-business-pressures-and-journalists-values/, accessed July 5, 2012.

49. Society of Professional Journalists, Code of Ethics, 1996, www.spj.org/ethicscode.asp, accessed July 6, 2012.

50. Project for Excellence in Journalism, "The Changing Newsroom: Changing Content," July 21, 2008, www.journalism.org/node/11963, accessed July 6, 2012.

51. The discussion in this box draws on: Tom Goldstein, "We're Getting Wildly Differing Assessments," SCOTUSblog, July 7, 2012, www.scotusblog.com/2012/07/were-getting-wildly-differing-assessments/#more-148757; and Michael Hastings, "CNN News Staffers Revolt over Blown Coverage," Buzzfeed, June 28, 2012, www.buzzfeed.com/mhastings/cnn-news-staffers-revolt-over-blown-coverage, accessed July 9, 2012.

52. Ashley Killough, "Mourdock Takes Heat over YouTube Blunder," CNN Political Ticker, June 26, 2012, politicalticker.blogs.cnn.com/2012/06/26/mourdock-takes-heat-over-youtube-blunder, accessed July 6, 2012.

53. Brian Thevenot, "Myth-Making in New Orleans," *American Journalism Review*, December/January 2006, www.ajr.org/article.asp?id=3998, accessed July 6, 2012.

54. Steven Schoenherr, "History of the Newsreel," February 2, 2008, web.archive.org/web/20080512055855/http://history.sandiego.edu/gen/filmnotes/newsreel.html, accessed July 6, 2012.

55. Radio and Television News Directors Association, "Code of Ethics and Professional Conduct," September 14, 2000, www.rtnda.org/pages/media_items/code-of-ethics-and-professional-conduct48.php?id=48, accessed July 6, 2012.

56. Dick Thornburgh and Louis D. Boccardi, "Report of the Independent Review Panel," January 5, 2005, www.image.cbsnews.com/htdocs/pdf/complete_report/CBS_Report.pdf, accessed July 7, 2009.

57. Pew Research Center for the People and the Press, "Financial Woes."

58. Leonard Downie Jr. and Robert G. Kaiser, *The News about the News: American Journalism in Peril* (New York: Knopf, 2002), 24.

59. Karen Slattery, Mark Doremus, and Linda Marcus, "Shifts in Public Affairs Reporting on the Network Evening News: A Move toward the Sensational," *Journal of Broadcasting & Electronic Media* 45 (June 2001): 290–302.

60. Erik P. Bucy and Maria Elizabeth Grabe, "Taking Television Seriously: A Sound and Image Bite Analysis of

Presidential Campaign Coverage, 1992–2004," *Journal of Communication* 57, no. 4 (2007): 652–675.

61. Priya Kumar, "Shrinking Foreign Coverage," *American Journalism Review*, December/January 2011, www.ajr.org/article.asp?id=4998, accessed July 6, 2012.

62. Quoted in Jodi Enda, "Retreating from the World," *American Journalism Review*, December/January 2011, www.ajr.org/Article.asp?id=4985, accessed July 6, 2012.

63. Iyengar and Grady, *Media Politics*, 59.

64. Bill Dedman, "Journalists Dole Out Cash to Politicians (Quietly)," MSNBC.com, June 25, 2007, www.msnbc.msn.com/id/19113485/, accessed July 6, 2012.

65. Tim Groseclose, *Left Turn: How Liberal Media Bias Distorts the American Mind* (New York: St. Martin's, 2011).

66. Marie Arana, quoted in Howard Kurtz, "Suddenly, Everyone's a Critic," *Washington Post*, October 3, 2005, C1.

67. Glynnis MacNicol, "Jon Stewart on Fox News Sunday," Business Insider, June 20, 2011, www.businessinsider.com/jon-stewart-fox-news-sunday-bias-wallace-video-2011-6, accessed July 6, 2012.

68. Steve Rendall and Julie Hollar, "Still Failing the 'Fair and Balanced' Test," *Extra!* August 2004, www.fair.org/extra/0407/special-report.html, accessed July 6, 2012.

69. Stefano DellaVigna and Ethan Kaplan, "The Fox News Effect: Media Bias and Voting," *Quarterly Journal of Economics* 122 (August 2007): 1187–1234.

70. Fairness and Accuracy in Reporting, "In Iraq Crisis, Networks Are Megaphones for Official Views," March 18, 2003, www.fair.org/activism/iraq-sources-networks.html, accessed July 6, 2012.

71. Howard Kurtz, "The Post on WMDs: An Inside Story," *Washington Post*, August 12, 2004, A1.

72. David Broder, "Thin-Skinned Journalists," *Washington Post*, January 11, 1989, A21.

73. Jim Rutenberg, "Ex-Journalists' New Jobs Fuel Debate on Favoritism," *New York Times*, February 2, 2009, www.nytimes.com/2009/02/03/us/politics/03reporters.html, accessed July 6, 2012.

74. Pew Research Center for the People and the Press, "Financial Woes."

75. Pew Research Center for the People and the Press, "Cable Leads the Pack as Campaign News Source," February 7, 2012, www.people-press.org/files/legacy-pdf/2012%;20Communicating%;20Release.pdf, accessed July 6, 2012.

76. Jules Boykoff and Maxwell Boykoff, "Balance as Bias: Global Warming and the U.S. Prestige Press" *Global Environmental Change* 15 (July 2004): 125–136.

77. Pew Research Center for the People and the Press, "Striking the Balance."

78. *Congressional Record* (daily), December 3, 1980, H11799.

79. U.S. General Accounting Office, "Superfund: Extent to Which Most Reforms Have Improved the Program Is Unknown," GAO/RCED-00-118, May 2000, www.gao.gov/archive/2000/rc00118.pdf, accessed July 6, 2012.

80. Cass Sunstein, *Echo Chambers: Bush v. Gore, Impeachment, and Beyond* (Princeton, NJ: Princeton Digital Books Plus, 2001), www.pup.princeton.edu/sunstein/echo.pdf, accessed July 6, 2012.

81. P. J. O'Rourke, "I Agree with Me," *The Atlantic*, July/August 2004, 50.

82. Bill Goodykoontz, "The Scoop on Journalism in the Movies," *Arizona Republic*, April 11, 2009, www.azcentral.com/thingstodo/movies/articles/2009/04/11/2009/0411reporters0412.html, accessed July 6, 2012.

83. W. Joseph Campbell, *Getting It Wrong: Ten of the Greatest Misreported Stories in American Journalism* (Berkeley: University of California Press, 2010), Chap. 7.

84. Daniel Schorr, "Following 'Follow the Money,'" *Los Angeles Times*, June 15, 1997, M2.

85. Frederick Schauer, "The Exceptional First Amendment," John F. Kennedy School of Government, Harvard University, February 2005, web.hks.harvard.edu/publications/getFile.aspx?Id=167, accessed July 6, 2012.

86. *Gitlow v. New York*, 268 U.S. 652 (1925).

87. *Near v. Minnesota*, 283 U.S. 697 (1931).

88. *New York Times v. United States*, 403 U.S. 713 (1971).

89. Thomas W. Hazlett and David W. Sosa, "Was the Fairness Doctrine a 'Chilling Effect'? Evidence from the Post-deregulation Radio Market," *Journal of Legal Studies* 26 (January 1997): 279–301.

90. Voice of America, www.voa.gov/index.cfm, accessed July 6, 2012.

91. American Forces Radio and Television Service, afrts.dodmedia.osd.mil, accessed July 6, 2012.

92. General Accounting Office, "Department of Health and Human Services, Centers for Medicare & Medicaid Services—Video News Releases," May 19, 2004, www.gao.gov/decisions/appro/302710.pdf, accessed July 6, 2012.

93. Abby Phillip, "Shh! Obama Gets Anti-Secrecy Award," *Politico*, March 30, 2011, www.politico.com/politico44/perm/0311/not_a_secret_anymore_a00ccd98-0d9e-4822-8936-168f3a51b959.html, accessed July 6, 2012.

94. David Ignatius, "The Dangers of Embedded Journalism," *Washington Post*, May 2, 2010, www.washingtonpost.com/wp-dyn/content/article/2010/04/30/AR2010043001100.html, accessed July 6, 2012.

95. Joshua Green, "Playing Dirty," *Atlantic Monthly*, June 2004, www.theatlantic.com/doc/200406/green, accessed July 6, 2012.

96. David Shaw, "An Editor Intoxicated by Power," *Los Angeles Times*, June 7, 2003, Part 5, 1.

97. Chris McCarthy, "Matt Drudge: America's Most Influential Political 'Reporter,'" Associated Content, October 25, 2007, www.associatedcontent.com/article/427502/matt_drudge_americas_most_influential.html?cat=75, accessed July 6, 2012.

98. Quoted in David R. Runkel, ed., *Campaign for President: The Managers Look at '88* (Dover, MA: Auburn House, 1989), 136.

99. The Ruckus Society, "The Ruckus Society Media Training Manual," http://ruckus.org/section.php?id=18, accessed July 6, 2012.

100. Quoted in Joshua Green, "Playing Dirty," *The Atlantic*, June 2004, 78.

101. Albert W. Dzur, "Public Journalism and Deliberative Democracy," *Polity* 34 (Spring 2002): 315.

102. Jan Schaffer, "The Role of Newspapers in Building Citizenship," Fifth Brazilian Newspaper Congress, São Paulo, Brazil, September 13, 2004, www.pewcenter.org/doingcj/speeches/s_brazil.html, accessed July 6, 2012.

103. David Remnick, "Scoop," *The New Yorker*, January 26, 1996, www.newyorker.com/archive/1996/01/29/1996_01_29_038_TNY_CARDS_000374666, accessed July 6, 2012.

104. Organization of News Ombudsmen, "About Us," newsombudsmen.org/about, accessed July 6, 2012.

105. Daniel Okrent, "Is the *New York Times* a Liberal Newspaper?" *New York Times*, July 25, 2004, Sect. 4, 2.

106. Jason Zengerle, "Playing with Mud," *New York*, December 11, 2011, nymag.com/news/intelligencer/andrew-kaczynski-2011-12, accessed July 6, 2012.

107. Debra Saunders, "Cutting Off Your News to Spite Your Face," *San Francisco Chronicle*, February 26, 2009, www.sfgate.com/cgi-bin/article.cgi?f=/c/a/2009/02/25/EDFU164VIO.DTL, accessed July 6, 2012.

108. Debra Saunders, "The Death Knell of What We Need to Know," *San Francisco Chronicle*, August 10, 2008, www.sfgate.com/cgi-bin/article.cgi?f=/c/a/2008/08/10/IN4K125G6K.DTL, accessed July 6, 2012.

Chapter 12

1. Brian Baird, "We Need to Read the Bills," *Washington Post*, November 27, 2004, A31.

2. Quoted in Eva Rodriguez, "Read Before You Vote, Congressman," *Washington Post*, July 28, 2009, at voices.washingtonpost.com/postpartisan/2009/07/read_before_you_vote.html, accessed June 11, 2012. The video is at www.youtube.com/watch?v=ACbwND52rrw" www.youtube.com/watch?v=ACbwND52rrw

3. Quoted in George Packer, "The Empty Chamber," *The New Yorker*, August 9, 2010, www.newyorker.com/reporting/2010/08/09/100809fa_fact_packer, accessed October 25, 2010.

4. Quoted in Lauren Victoria Burke and Bob Cusack, "The 25 Hardest Working Lawmakers," *The Hill*, June 9, 2010, thehill.com/capital-living/102101-the-25-hardest-working-members-of-congress, accessed October 26, 2010.

5. Alexander Hamilton, James Madison, and John Jay, *The Federalist Papers*, ed. Clinton Rossiter with a new introduction and notes by Charles R. Kesler (New York: Signet, 2003), no. 48, 306.

6. *Federalist*, no. 42, 264; no. 63, 382.

7. Quoted in David Jackson, "Poll Finds Texans Rate Perot Higher Than President," *Dallas Morning News*, June 1, 1993, 3A.

8. Willmoore Kendall, *The Conservative Affirmation in America* (Chicago: Regnery Gateway, 1985), 16.

9. Willmoore Kendall, "The Two Majorities," in *Congress and the President: Allies and Adversaries*, ed. Ronald C. Moe (Pacific Palisades, CA: Goodyear, 1971), 285.

10. *Federalist*, no. 52, 24.

11. *Federalist*, no. 57, 350.

12. *Federalist*, no. 63, 382.

13. *Federalist*, no. 10, 76–77.

14. *Myers v. United States*, 272 U.S. 52 (1926), 293.

15. Richard F. Fenno, *The United States Senate: A Bicameral Perspective* (Washington, DC: American Enterprise Institute, 1982), 1.

16. Max Farrand, ed., *The Records of the Federal Convention of 1787*, 4 vols. (New Haven, CT: Yale University Press, 1966), I: 151 (June 7), James Madison.

17. Council on Foreign Relations, "In Support of Arab Democracy: Why and How," 2005, at www.cfr.org/content/publications/attachments/Arab_Democracy_TF.pdf; Forum of the World's Senates, "Bicameralism around the World: Position and Prospects," 2000, at www.senat.fr/senatsdumonde/introenglish.html; Parliament of Australia, "The Senate," at www.aph.gov.au/About_Parliament/Senate; United Kingdom, Parliament, "How Do You Become a Member of the House of Lords?" at www.parliament.uk/about/mps-and-lords/about-lords/lords-appointment/, accessed June 13, 2012.

18. Although Congress set a figure of 435 after the 1910 census, this figure did not officially become permanent until the 1929 Apportionment Act. See Charles A. Kromkowski and John A. Kromkowski, "Why 435? A Question of Political Arithmetic," *Polity* 24 (Fall 1991): 129–145.

19. *Federalist*, no. 62, 375.

20. Quoted in Helen Dewar, "Lott Appears Safe from Challenges as Senate Reorganizes," *Washington Post*, November 18, 1998, A7.

21. Fenno, *The United States Senate*, 9.

22. Quoted in Ross K. Baker, *House and Senate*, 4th ed. (New York: Norton, 2008), 42–43.

23. Sarah A. Binder and Steven S. Smith, *Politics or Principle? Filibustering in the United States Senate* (Washington, DC: Brookings Institution, 1997), 20.

24. *Federalist*, no. 58, 358.

25. Quoted in Kurt Shillinger, "House-Senate Rivalry Takes Shape in GOP Era," *Christian Science Monitor*, March 14, 1995, 1.

26. Quoted in Charles Babington and Mike Allen, "GOP Odd Couple Reflect Chambers They Lead," *Washington Post*, February 26, 2005, A01.

27. Newt Gingrich, *Lessons Learned the Hard Way: A Personal Report* (New York: HarperCollins, 1998), 7.

28. Quoted in Victoria F. Nourse and Jane S. Schacter, "The Politics of Legislative Drafting: A Congressional

Case Study," *New York University Law Review* 77 (June 2002): 593.

29. James L. Sundquist, *The Decline and Resurgence of Congress* (Washington, DC: Brookings Institution, 1981), chap. 10.

30. Quoted in Elizabeth Drew, *Showdown: The Struggle between the Gingrich Congress and the Clinton White House* (New York: Simon and Schuster, 1996), 336.

31. United States Senate, "Nominations," www.senate.gov/artandhistory/history/common/briefing/Nominations.htm, accessed June 13, 2012.

32. *Federalist*, no. 51, 319.

33. Lee Hamilton, "Being a Team Player Shouldn't Be a Compliment on Hill," *Roll Call*, May 31, 2005, 8.

34. Lee Hamilton, "Why Holding the Majority Matters," Center on Congress, August 28, 2008, at www.centeroncongress.org/radio_commentaries/why_holding_the_majority_matters.php, accessed March 19, 2009.

35. James L. Sundquist, *Politics and Policy: The Eisenhower, Kennedy, and Johnson Years* (Washington, DC: Brookings Institution, 1968); and David R. Mayhew, *Divided We Govern: Party Control, Lawmaking, and Investigations, 1946–1990* (New Haven, CT: Yale University Press, 1991).

36. John Stanton, "Senate Leaders' Rapport in Tatters," *Roll Call*, November 20, 2008, at www.rollcall.com/issues/54_59/news/30337-1.html, accessed August 3, 2012.

37. Quoted in James W. Ceaser, Andrew E. Busch, and John J. Pitney Jr., *Epic Journey: The 2008 Elections and American Politics* (Lanham, MD: Rowman and Littlefield, 2009), 183–184.

38. "Speaking with the Speaker, *Wall Street Journal*, March 9, 2012, at online.wsj.com/article/SB10001424052970204781804577269861424319908.html, accessed June 13, 2012.

39. "Joseph Gurney Cannon," in *Encyclopedia of American History, Bicentennial Edition*, ed. Richard B. Morris (New York: Harper and Row, 1976), 996–997.

40. William Safire, *Safire's New Political Dictionary* (New York: Random House, 1993), 870–871.

41. Patrick O'Connor, "Waxman Dethrones Dingell as Chairman," *Politico*, November 21, 2008, at www.politico.com/news/stories/1108/15822.html, accessed April 27, 2009.

42. Quoted in Adam Liptak, "Prosecutions for Perjury in Legislative Settings Are Unusual," *New York Times*, March 31, 2004, at www.nytimes.com/2004/03/31/politics/31PERJ.html, accessed June 13, 2012.

43. R. Douglas Arnold, *The Logic of Congressional Action* (New Haven, CT: Yale University Press, 1990), 85–86.

44. Martha Derthick and Paul Quirk, *The Politics of Deregulation* (Washington, DC: Brookings Institution, 1985), 120–121.

45. James L. Payne, *The Culture of Spending: Why Congress Lives beyond Our Means* (San Francisco: ICS Press, 1991), 12.

46. Mark Bisnow, *In the Shadow of the Dome: Chronicles of a Capitol Hill Aide* (New York: Morrow, 1990), 309.

47. Quoted in Mary Lynn F. Jones, "Life Experiences Shape Members' Causes," *The Hill*, March 6, 2002, 52.

48. Nourse and Schacter, "The Politics of Legislative Drafting," 586.

49. Résumés of Congressional Activity, at www.senate.gov/reference/resources/pdf/Resumes/111_1.pdf, and www.senate.gov/reference/resources/pdf/Resumes/111_.pdf, accessed June 14, 2012.

50. Philip Dine, "Urban Legend of 'North American Union' Feeds on Fears," *Seattle Times*, May 19, 2007, at www.seattletimes.nwsource.com/html/nationworld/2003713518_rumor19.html; "Legitimate Senate Campaign Issue or 'Internet Rumor'?" at www.alipac.us/f9/legitimate-senate-campaign-issue-internet-rumor-110220/; Michael Dobbs, "A 'Superhighway' to Nowhere," *Washington Post Online*, December 3, 2007, at voices.washingtonpost.com/fact-checker/2007/12/a_superhighway_to_nowhere.html, accessed June 2, 2008.

51. Walter J. Oleszek, *Congressional Procedures and the Policy Process*, 6th ed. (Washington, DC: CQ Press, 2004), 92.

52. Previously available at www.house.gov/waxman/issues/health/tobacco_back.htm, accessed May 24, 2008.

53. "McGwire Offers No Denials at Steroid Hearings," *New York Times*, March 18, 2005, at www.nytimes.com/2005/03/18/sports/baseball/18steroids.html, accessed June 14, 2012.

54. Rep. Phil Sharp (D-IN), quoted in Richard E. Cohen, *Washington at Work: Back Rooms and Clean Air*, 2nd ed. (Boston: Allyn and Bacon, 1995), 149.

55. Quoted in Drew, *Showdown*, 99.

56. *Congressional Record* (daily), July 23, 1997, H5657.

57. Ibid., January 17, 2007, H590.

58. Binder and Smith, *Politics or Principle*, 15.

59. Ibid., 115.

60. United States Senate, Senate Action on Cloture Motions, at www.senate.gov/pagelayout/reference/cloture_motions/clotureCounts.htm, accessed June 14, 2012.

61. Juliet Eilperin, *Fight Club Politics: How Partisanship Is Poisoning the House of Representatives* (Lanham, MD: Rowman and Littlefield, 2006), 35–36.

62. Quoted in Perry Bacon, "Obama Speaks," *Time*, February 13, 2006, at www.time.com/time/nation/article/0,8599,1159021,00.html, accessed June 14, 2012.

63. *Statutes at Large*, vol. 123 (2009) and 124 (2010), constitution.org/uslaw/sal/sal.htm, accessed June 16, 2012.

64. Don Wolfensberger, "Have House-Senate Conferences Gone the Way of the Dodo?" Woodrow Wilson International Center for Scholars, April 28, 2008, at www.wilsoncenter.org/publication/have-house-senate-conferences-gone-the-way-the-dodo, accessed June 14, 2012.

65. *Federalist*, no. 73, 442.

66. John Bresnahan, "The Oversight Congress: How Democrats Gain," *Politico*, May 22, 2007, at www.politico.com/news/stories/0507/4138.html, accessed June 14, 2012.

67. Woodrow Wilson, *Congressional Government: A Study in American Politics* (Cleveland, OH: Meridian Books, World, 1956; originally published in 1885), 195, 196, 198.

68. David R. Mayhew, *America's Congress: Actions in the Public Sphere, James Madison through Newt Gingrich* (New Haven, CT: Yale University Press, 2000), 96–102.

69. "Committees Make Leap to Online Video, but Approps Doesn't Get the Picture," Sunlight Foundation, April 17, 2012, at sunlightfoundation.com/blog/2012/04/17/committees-make-leap-to-online-video-but-approps-doesn't-get-the-picture/, accessed June 14, 2012.

70. James Freeman, "Your Tax Dollars Not at Work," *Wall Street Journal*, January 26, 2012.

71. *Federalist*, no. 10, 72, 74, 75, 77; no. 46, 293; no. 57, 348; no. 62, 377.

72. "Address of the Senate to George Washington, President of the United States," in James D. Richardson, *A Compilation of the Messages and Papers of the Presidents, 1789–1897*, 10 vols. (Washington, DC: U.S. Government Printing Office, 1896–1899), 1:55.

73. "Database of Earmarks in Conference Agreement to the Transportation Bill: State by State Comparison," Taxpayers for Common Sense, July 29, 2005, at www.taxpayer.net/Transportation/safetealu/states.htm, accessed June 2, 2008.

74. David Herszenhorn and Ron Nixon, "Old Problems Resurface in New Earmark Rules," *New York Times*, March 18, 2009, at www.nytimes.com/2009/03/18/washington/18earmarks.html, accessed March 18, 2009.

75. Ron Nixon, "Congress Appears to Be Trying to Get around Earmark Ban," *New York Times*, February 5, 2012, at www.nytimes.com/2012/02/06/us/politics/congress-appears-to-be-trying-to-get-around-earmark-ban.html?pagewanted=all, accessed June 14, 2012.

76. David R. Mayhew, *Congress: The Electoral Connection* (New Haven, CT: Yale University Press, 1974), 16.

77. Steve Elmendort, quoted in Juliet Eilperin, "Capitol Hill Fundraising Cycle Has No End; Newly Sworn Legislators Are Already Working on Filling Reelection War Chests," *Washington Post*, January 28, 2001, A8.

78. Anthony Nownes summarizes the relevant literature in *Total Lobbying* (New York: Cambridge University Press, 2006), 80–83.

79. The classic statement of this view came in Raymond A. Bauer, Ithiel de Sola Pool, and Lewis Anthony Dexter, *American Business and Public Policy*, 2nd. ed. (Chicago: Aldine, 1972), chap. 30.

80. Quoted in Joseph M. Bessette, *The Mild Voice of Reason: Deliberative Democracy and American National Government* (Chicago: University of Chicago Press, 1994), 116, 120.

81. Caroline Kennedy, ed., *Profiles in Courage for Our Time* (New York: Hyperion, 2002), 248.

82. Michael John Burton and Daniel M. Shea, *Campaign Mode: Strategic Vision in Congressional Elections* (Lanham, MD: Rowman and Littlefield, 2003), 47–65.

83. John Stuart Mill, *Considerations on Representative Government*, ed. Currin V. Shields (Indianapolis, IN: Bobbs-Merrill, 1958), 219.

84. Congressional Research Service, "About CRS," at www.loc.gov/crsinfo/about/, accessed June 14, 2012.

85. Congressional Budget Office, "Our Agency," at www.cbo.gov/about/our-agency, accessed June 14, 2012.

86. Government Accountability Office, "About GAO," at www.gao.gov/about/index.html, accessed June 14, 2012.

87. Barack Obama, *The Audacity of Hope* (New York: Crown, 2006), 104.

88. Gary Mucciaroni and Paul J. Quirk, *Deliberative Choices: Debating Public Policy in Congress* (Chicago: University of Chicago Press, 2006), 197.

89. Ibid., 187.

90. Ibid., 194.

91. Jennifer E. Manning, "Membership of the 112th Congress: A Profile," Congress Research Service, March 1, 2011, at www.senate.gov/reference/resources/pdf/R41647.pdf, accessed June 14, 2012.

92. Melancton Smith, "New York Ratifying Convention, June 20–21, 1788," in *The Founder's Constitution*, 5 vols., ed. Philip B. Kurland and Ralph Lerner (Indianapolis, IN: Liberty Fund, 1987), I: 410–411, also at http://press-pubs.uchicago.edu/founders/documents/v1ch13s37.html, accessed June 11, 2012.

93. *Federalist*, no. 10, 76.

94. Quoted in Herbert J. Storing, *What the Anti-Federalists Were For* (Chicago: University of Chicago Press, 1981), 44.

95. Ibid., 45.

96. Quoted in ibid., 45.

97. Mildred Amer and Jennifer E. Manning, "Membership of the 111th Congress: A Profile," Congressional Research Service, June 29, 2009, at www.senate.gov/CRSReports/crs-publish.cfm?pid=%260BL)PL%3B%3D%0A; Jennifer E. Manning, "Membership of the 112th Congress: A Profile," Congress Research Service, March 1, 2011, at www.senate.gov/reference/resources/pdf/R41647.pdf; Jennifer E. Manning and Colleen J. Shogan, "African American Members of the United States Congress: 1870-2012," at www.senate.gov/CRSReports/crs-publish.cfm?pid='0E%2C*PLW%3C%20P%20%20%0A; and Jennifer E. manning and Colleen J. Shogan, "Women in the United States Congress: 1917-2012," at www.fas.org/sgp/crs/misc/RL30261.pdf, accessed June 14, 2012.

98. *Federalist*, no. 35, 211.

99. Bureau of Justice Statistics, "Prevalence of Imprisonment in the U.S. Population, 1974–2001," August 2003, at bjs.ojp.usdoj.gov/content/pub/pdf/piusp01.pdf, accessed June 14, 2012.

100. Gary L. Gregg II, *The Presidential Republic* (Lanham, MD: Rowman and Littlefield, 2006), 60. See also Harvey Mansfield's discussion of "constitutional space" in *America's Constitutional Soul* (Baltimore: Johns Hopkins University Press, 1991), 16.

101. *Federalist,* no. 10, 72.

102. Article I, Section 5.

103. Noam Cohen, "In Policy Shift, C-Span Clears Some Clips for Web Use," *New York Times*, March 8, 2007, C2.

Chapter 13

1. Jeffrey K. Tulis, "Deliberation between Institutions," in *Debating Deliberative Democracy*, ed. James S. Fishkin and Peter Laslett (Oxford: Blackwell, 2003).

2. "Excerpts from President's Interview on Radio after Weekly Address," *New York Times*, December 19, 1982, Sec. 1, 26.

3. Karl Rove, remarks at the University of Utah, November 13, 2002, at hnn.us/articles/1529.html, accessed June 20, 2012.

4. Vic Gold, "Stay in Touch," *Washingtonian*, March 1993.

5. Alexander Hamilton, James Madison, and John Jay, *The Federalist Papers*, ed. Clinton Rossiter, with an introduction and notes by Charles R. Kesler (New York: New American Library, Mentor Book, 2003), no. 70, 421–422.

6. Ibid., 423.

7. Ibid., no. 71, 431.

8. Sources: Patricia Lee Sykes, *Presidents and Prime Ministers: Conviction Politics in the Anglo-American Tradition* (Lawrence: University Press of Kansas, 2000); James Bryce, *The American Commonwealth* (Indianapolis, IN: Liberty Fund, 1995); James W. Ceaser, *Liberal Democracy and Political Science* (Baltimore: Johns Hopkins University Press, 1990), 203.

9. Quoted by Forrest McDonald, Testimony before the House Committee on the Judiciary, Subcommittee on the Constitution, July 24, 2000, at commdocs.house .gov/committees/judiciary/hju67306.000/hju67306_0 .HTM, accessed June 22, 2012.

10. Woodrow Wilson, *Constitutional Government in the United States* (New York: Columbia University Press, 1961, first published in 1908), 73.

11. See, for example, John Marshall's letter to Alexander Hamilton, January 1, 1801, quoted in Henry Adams, *History of the United States of America during the Administrations of Thomas Jefferson*, vol. 1 (New York: Library of America, 1986), 132.

12. Letter to John B. Colvin, September 20, 1810, quoted in Jeremy David Bailey, "Executive Prerogative and the 'Good Officer' in Thomas Jefferson's Letter to John B. Colvin," *Presidential Studies Quarterly* 34, no. 4 (December 2004): 734–735.

13. John Locke, *Second Treatise of Government*, chap. 14, "Of Prerogative," at www.constitution.org/jl/2ndtr14 .htm, accessed June 22, 2012.

14. Veto of the bill rechartering the Bank of the United States, July 10, 1832, at avalon.law.yale.edu/19th_ century/ajveto01.asp, accessed June 22, 2012.

15. President Andrew Jackson, "Removal of the Public Deposits," September 18, 1833, in *A Compilation of the Messages and Papers of the Presidents, 1789–1897*, 10 vols., ed. James D. Richardson (Washington, DC: Government Printing Office, 1896–1899), III: 7.

16. President Andrew Jackson, "Message to the Senate Protesting Censure Resolution," April 15, 1834, at www.presidency.ucsb.edu/ws/index.php?pid=67039, accessed June 22, 2012.

17. President Andrew Jackson, "Proclamation," December 10, 1832, www.presidency.ucsb.edu/ws/index.php?pid=67078, accessed June 22, 2012.

18. James Buchanan, "Fourth Annual Message to Congress," December 3, 1860, at www.presidency.ucsb.edu/ws/ print.php?pid=29501, accessed June 22, 2012.

19. Abraham Lincoln, "First Inaugural Address," March 4, 1861, at www.presidency.ucsb.edu/ws/index.php? pid=25818, accessed June 22, 2012.

20. Abraham Lincoln, "Message to Congress in Special Session," July 4, 1861, www.presidency.ucsb.edu/ws/index .php?pid=69802, accessed June 22, 2012.

21. Theodore Roosevelt, *An Autobiography* (New York: Macmillan, 1913), at www.bartleby.com/55/10.html, accessed June 22, 2012.

22. *Federalist,* no. 1, 29.

23. Woodrow Wilson, *Congressional Government: A Study in American Politics* (Cleveland: Meridian Books, World, 1956, first published in 1885), 144.

24. Wilson, *Constitutional Government in the United States*, 68, 70.

25. Woodrow Wilson, "Address to a Joint Session of Congress Requesting a Declaration of War against Germany," April 2, 1917, www.presidency.ucsb.edu/ws/ index.php?pid=65366, accessed June 22, 2012.

26. Franklin D. Roosevelt, "First Inaugural Address," March 4, 1933, www.presidency.ucsb.edu/ws/index .php?pid=14473, accessed June 22, 2012.

27. Ronald Reagan, "First Inaugural Address," January 20, 1981, www.presidency.ucsb.edu/ws/index.php?pid=43130, accessed June 22, 2012.

28. Sources: ibid.; United States Office of Management and Budget, *Budget of the United States Government: Historical Tables Fiscal Year 2005* (Washington, DC: Government Printing Office, 2004), 25.

29. Quoted in William Ker Muir Jr., *The Bully Pulpit: The Presidential Leadership of Ronald Reagan* (San Francisco: ICS Press, 1992), 7.

30. Ibid., 22–23. The month was May.

31. Ibid., 103.

32. Barack Obama, "Inaugural Address," January 20, 2009, www.presidency.ucsb.edu/ws/index.php?pid=44, accessed June 22, 2012.

33. William Daley quoted in Charlie Savage, "Shift on Executive Power Lets Obama Bypass Rivals," *New York Times*, April 22, 2012, at www.nytimes.com/2012/04/23/ us/politics/shift-on-executive-powers-let-obama-bypass-congress.html, accessed June 22, 2012.

34. Ibid.

35. Thomas H. Neale, *Presidential and Vice Presidential Succession: Overview and Current Legislation* (Washington, DC: Congressional Research Service, 2004), at www.fas.org/sgp/crs/misc/RL31761.pdf, accessed June 22, 2012.

36. Vice President Dick Cheney, "Remarks at a Dinner for Tom Coburn," Tulsa, Oklahoma, September 24, 2004, at www.prnewswire.com/news-releases/remarks-by-vice-president-cheney-at-a-dinner-for-senatorial-candidate-tom-coburn-73919777.html, accessed June 22, 2012; White House, "Eisenhower Executive Office Building," at www.whitehouse.gov/about/eeob/, accessed June 22, 2012.

37. John P. Burke, "Administration of the White House," at millercenter.org/academic/americanPresident/policy/whitehouse, accessed June 22, 2012.

38. Ronald D. Rietveld, "The Lincoln White House Community," *Journal of the Abraham Lincoln Association* 20 (Summer 1999), at www.historycooperative.org/journals/jala/20.2/rietveld.html, accessed June 22, 2012.

39. Lyn Ragsdale, *Vital Statistics on the Presidency* (Washington, DC: CQ Press, 1996), 260–261; United States Office of Personnel Management, Employment and Trends September 2009, at www.opm.gov/feddata/html/2009/September/table2.asp, accessed June 22, 2012.

40. Charles Kolb, *White House Daze: The Unmaking of Domestic Policy in the Bush Years* (New York: Free Press, 1994), 183.

41. Quoted in Samuel Kernell and Samuel L. Popkin, *Chief of Staff: Twenty-five Years of Managing the Presidency* (Berkeley: University of California Press, 1986), 71–72.

42. James Fallows, "The Passionless Presidency," *Atlantic Monthly*, May 1979, 38.

43. John Tower, Edmund Muskie, and Brent Scowcroft, *The Tower Commission Report* (New York: Times Books/Bantam, 1987), 79.

44. Bradley H. Patterson Jr., *The White House Staff* (Washington, DC: Brookings Institution, 2000), 27–28.

45. Quoted in Richard E. Neustadt, *Presidential Power: The Politics of Leadership* (New York: Wiley, 1960), 9.

46. Michael A. Fletcher, "Bush Is Keeping Cabinet Secretaries Close to Home," *Washington Post*, March 31, 2005, A1.

47. John Solomon, Alec MacGillis, and Sarah Cohen, "How Rove Directed Federal Assets for GOP Gains," *Washington Post*, August 19, 2007, A1.

48. Quoted in Alan G. Whittaker, Frederick C. Smith, and Elizabeth McKune, *The National Security Policy Process: The National Security Council and Interagency System* (Washington, DC: National Defense University, 2005), 6.

49. Michael John Burton, "The 'Flying White House': A Travel Establishment within the Presidential Branch," *Presidential Studies Quarterly* 36 (June 2006): 303.

50. Irving L. Janis, *Victims of Groupthink* (Boston: Houghton Mifflin, 1972).

51. Quoted in *West Wing,* documentary special, April 24, 2002, at www.youtube.com/watch?v=5YwtyhZs2dU, accessed June 22, 2012.

52. Ibid.

53. Quoted in Greenstein, *The Presidential Difference*, 219.

54. *Federalist,* no. 51, 319.

55. *Congressional Record* (daily), July 23, 1985, S9872.

56. Ibid., March 20, 1995, S4157

57. Susan Brophy, quoted in Kevin Merida, "Winding Down from a Whirlwind: Clinton's Lobbyists Know Success, Frustration of Dealing with Hill," *Washington Post*, November 23, 1993, A19.

58. Transcript, "Lawrence F. O'Brien Oral History Interview II," October 29, 1985, by Michael L. Gillette, Internet Copy, LBJ Library, at www.lbjlib.utexas.edu/Johnson/archives.hom/oralhistory.hom/OBrienL/OBRIEN02.pdf, accessed July 11, 2009.

59. Transcript, "Lawrence F. O'Brien Oral History Interview VIII," April 8, 1986, by Michael L. Gillette, Internet Copy, LBJ Library, at www.lbjlib.utexas.edu/Johnson/archives.hom/oralhistory.hom/OBrienL/OBRIEN08.pdf, accessed July 11, 2009.

60. Nelson W. Polsby, *Policy Innovation in America: The Politics of Policy Initiation* (New Haven, CT: Yale University Press, 1984), 91–99.

61. Mitchel A. Sollenberger, *Congressional Overrides of Presidential Vetoes* (Washington, DC: Congressional Research Service, 2004), at www.senate.gov/reference/resources/pdf/98-157.pdf, accessed June 22, 2012.

62. Quoted in Terry Sullivan, ed., *The Nerve Center: Lessons in Governing from the White House Chiefs of Staff* (College Station: Texas A & M University Press, 2004), 34.

63. Newt Gingrich, *Lessons Learned the Hard Way* (New York: HarperCollins, 1998), 10.

64. Executive Order 10925, March 6, 1961, at www.thecre.com/fedlaw/legal6/eo10925.htm, accessed June 22, 2012.

65. Kevin M. Stack, "The Statutory President," *Iowa Law Review* 90 (January 2005): 554–555.

66. Kenneth R. Mayer, *With the Stroke of a Pen: Executive Orders and Presidential Power* (Princeton, NJ: Princeton University Press, 2001), 83–86.

67. James Bennet, "True to Form, Clinton Shifts Energies Back to U.S. Focus," *New York Times*, July 5, 1998, Sec. 1, 10.

68. *Chamber of Commerce of the United States v. Reich*, 74 F.3d 1322 (1996).

69. "The Legal Significance of Presidential Signing Statements," memorandum prepared by Walter Dellinger, Assistant Attorney General, for Bernard N. Nussbaum, Counsel to the President, November 3, 1993, at www.usdoj.gov/olc/signing.htm, accessed July 11, 2009.

70. For a summary of the history of presidential signing statements, see the report by the American Bar Association Task Force on Presidential Signing Statements and the Separation of Powers Doctrine, August 2006, at www.americanbar.org/content/dam/aba/migrated/leadership/2006/annual/dailyjournal/20060823144113.authcheckdam.pdf, accessed June 22, 2012.

71. The quotations are from a campaign appearance in 2008. The video is at www.bessettepitney.net/2011/04/president-obama-and-signing-statements.html, accessed June 22, 2012.

72. President Barack Obama, "Memorandum for the Heads of Executive Departments and Agencies," March 9, 2009, at www.whitehouse.gov/the_press_office/Memorandum-for-the-Heads-of-Executive-Departments-and-Agencies-3-9-09, accessed July 16, 2009.

73. Barack Obama, "Statement on Signing the Omnibus Appropriations Act, 2009, March 11, 2009, at www.presidency.ucsb.edu/ws/index.php?pid=85848, accessed June 22, 2012.

74. The list is at www.presidency.ucsb.edu/signingstatements.php#axzz24DGHwWzE, accessed August 21, 2012.

75. *Federalist*, no. 8, 62.

76. Cornell University, Legal Information Institute, CRS Annotated Constitution, at www.law.cornell.edu/anncon/html/art2frag32_user.html#art2_hd137, accessed June 22, 2012.

77. Library of Congress, *A Century of Lawmaking for a New Nation*, at memory.loc.gov/cgi-bin/ampage?collId=llsl & fileName=001/llsl001.db & recNum=152, accessed June 22, 2012.

78. *United States v. Curtiss-Wright Export Corporation*, 299 U.S. 304 (1936), 320.

79. The Gulf of Tonkin Resolution can be found at www.hbci.com/~tgort/tonkin.htm, accessed June 22, 2012.

80. The War Powers Resolution is Public Law 93-148 and can be found at www.en.wikisource.org/wiki/War_Powers_Resolution, accessed June 22, 2012.

81. Nixon's veto message of October 24, 1973, is at www.presidency.ucsb.edu/ws/index.php?pid=4021, accessed June 22, 2012.

82. CRS Report to Congress, "The War Powers Resolution: After Thirty Years," March 11, 2004, at www.fas.org/man/crs/RL32267.html, accessed June 22, 2012.

83. Department of State and Department of Defense, "United States Activities in Libya," June 15, 2011, at www.nytimes.com/interactive/2011/06/16/us/politics/20110616_POWERS_DOC.html?ref=politics, accessed June 22, 2012.

84. Public Law 107-40, at avalon.law.yale.edu/sept11/sjres23_eb.asp, accessed June 22, 2012.

85. Brookings, "Afghanistan Index," May 16, 2012, Figure 1-1, p. 4, at www.brookings.edu/~/media/programs/foreign%20policy/afghanistan%20index/index20120516.pdf, accessed June 24, 2012.

86. The Long War Journal, "Charting the data for U.S. airstrikes in Pakistan, 2004-2012," at www.longwarjournal.org/pakistan-strikes.php and "Charting the data for U.S. air strikes in Yemen, 2002-2012," at www.longwarjournal.org/multimedia/Yemen/code/Yemen-strike.php, accessed June 24, 2012.

87. Jefferson's notes of the cabinet meeting of April 2, 1792, quoted in *George Washington and the Origins of the American Presidency*, ed. Mark J. Rozell, William D. Pederson, and Frank J. Williams (Westport, CT: Praeger Publishers, 2000), 147.

88. *U.S. v. Nixon*, 418 U.S. 683 (1974), 706, 710.

89. Ibid., 708.

90. "Press Briefing by Press Secretary Jay Carney," June 21, 2012, at www.whitehouse.gov/photos-and-video/video/2012/06/21/press-briefing#transcript, accessed June 24, 2012.

91. Abraham Lincoln, "Letter to Albert G. Hodges," April 4, 1864, www.showcase.netins.net/web/creative/lincoln/speeches/hodges.htm, accessed June 24, 2012.

92. United States Department of Justice, Office of the Solicitor General, "About the Office," at www.justice.gov/osg/about-osg.html, accessed June 24, 2012.

93. Woodrow Wilson, *Constitutional Government in the United States* (New York: Columbia University Press, 1961, originally published in 1908), 70–71.

94. Mark Rodeffer and Claire Brinberg, "How It Works: The Perks of Presidential Travel," May 6, 2004, at www.edition.cnn.com/2004/ALLPOLITICS/03/22/perks/, accessed June 214, 2012.

95. Chris Cillizza, "RNC Rallies the Base for Alito," The Fix, October 31, 2005, at voices.washingtonpost.com/thefix/politics-and-the-court/rnc-rallies-the-base-for-alito.html, accessed June 24, 2012.

96. Michael Gerson, "The Danger for America Is Not Theocracy," December 2004, www.beliefnet.com/story/159/story_15943_1.html, accessed July 11, 2009.

97. Quoted in Sullivan, *The Nerve Center*, 117.

98. Peter Robinson, *It's My Party: A Republican's Messy Love Affair with the GOP* (New York: Warner Books, 2000), 17.

99. Marc J. Hetherington and Michael Nelson, "Anatomy of a Rally Effect: George W. Bush and the War on Terrorism," *PS: Political Science and Politics* 36 (January 2003): 37–42.

100. Hadley Cantril, *The Human Dimension: Experiences in Policy Research* (New Brunswick, NJ: Rutgers University Press, 1967), 41.

101. President William J. Clinton, interview with Mark Knoller of CBS radio in Dover, New Hampshire, January 11, 2001, at www.presidency.ucsb.edu/ws/index.php?pid=64800, accessed June 24, 2012.

102. Gerald R. Ford, "Address before a Joint Session of the Congress Reporting on the State of the Union," January 15, 1975, www.presidency.ucsb.edu/ws/index.php?pid=4938accessed June 24, 2012.

103. William J. Clinton, "Remarks to the Business Community in Atlanta," March 19, 1993, at www.presidency.ucsb.edu/ws/index.php?pid=46358, accessed June 24, 2012.

104. John F. Kennedy, "Inaugural Address," January 20, 1961, at www.presidency.ucsb.edu/ws/index.php?pid=8032, accessed June 24, 2012.

105. Franklin D. Roosevelt, "Address at Dedication of Great Smoky Mountains National Park," September 2, 1940, at www.presidency.ucsb.edu/ws/index.php?pid=16002, accessed June 22, 2012.

106. Quoted in Richard L. Berke and John M. Broder, "A Mellow Clinton at Ease in His Role," *New York Times*, December 7, 1997, 1.

107. Quoted in James M. McPherson, *Battle Cry of Freedom: The Civil War Era* (New York: Ballantine, 1989), 771.

108. John F. Kennedy Library and Museum, "President Ford Receives John F. Kennedy Profile in Courage Award," May 21, 2001, at www.jfklibrary.org/Education+and+Public+Programs/Profile+in+Courage+Award/Award+Recipients/Gerald+Ford/Award+Announcement.htm, accessed June 24, 2012.

109. John F. Kennedy, *Profiles in Courage* (New York: Harper, 1962), 244.

110. Abraham Lincoln, "First Lincoln-Douglas Debate," August 21, 1858, www.nps.gov/liho/historyculture/debates.htm, accessed June 24, 2012.

Chapter 14

1. Quoted in Steven Lee Myers and Diana Jean Schemo, "Amid the Soot and Uncertainty, Officials Try to Portray Business as Usual," *New York Times,* September 13, 2001, A15.

2. Paul Light, *Government's Greatest Achievements* (Washington, DC: Brookings Institution, 2002), 120–121.

3. Herbert Kaufman, *The Forest Ranger: A Study in Administrative Behavior* (Baltimore: Johns Hopkins University Press, 1960), 3–4.

4. Quoted in *Sixty Minutes II*, "The Millennium Plot," December 26, 2001, www.cbsnews.com/stories/2001/10/03/60II/main313398.shtml, accessed July 11, 2012.

5. David Ignatius, "Two Attacks Highlight Counterterrorism's Bureaucratic Bog," *Washington Post*, January 6, 2010, www.washingtonpost.com/wp-dyn/content/article/2010/01/05/AR2010010502986.html, accessed July 11, 2012.

6. U.S. Office of Management and Budget, *Statistical Programs of the United States Government Fiscal Year 2012* (Washington, DC: Government Printing Office, 2011), 9, www.whitehouse.gov/sites/default/files/omb/assets/information_and_regulatory_affairs/12statprog.pdf, accessed July 11, 2012.

7. For a comprehensive list of federal agencies with statistical programs, see www.fedstats.gov/agencies/index.html.

8. Lawrence A. Greenfield, quoted in Eric Lichtblau, "Profiling Report Leads to a Clash and a Demotion," *New York Times*, August 24, 2005, A1.

9. Quoted in Rourke L. O'Brien and David S. Pedulla, "Beyond the Poverty Line," *Stanford Social Innovation Review*, Fall 2010, www.ssireview.org/articles/entry/beyond_the_poverty_line, accessed July 11, 2012.

10. William Seltzer and Margo Anderson, "Census Confidentiality under the Second War Powers Act (1942–1947)," paper prepared for presentation at the session on "Confidentiality, Privacy, and Ethical Issues in Demographic Data," Population Association of America Annual Meeting, March 29–31, 2007, New York, www.uwm.edu/~margo/govstat/Seltzer-AndersonPAA-2007paper3-12-2007.doc, accessed August 20, 2012.

11. United States Office of Management and Budget, Office of Information and Regulatory Affairs, "Information Collection Budget of the United States Government, 2011," September 15, 2011, www.whitehouse.gov/sites/default/files/omb/inforeg/icb/2011_icb.pdf, accessed July 11, 2012.

12. Victor Schantz, testimony before the House Government Reform Subcommittee on Energy Policy, Natural Resources and Regulatory Affairs, Washington, DC, April 11, 2003, www.web.archive.org/web/20050519201157/www.reform.house.gov/UploadedFiles/4-11-03_Testimony_Schantz.pdf, accessed July 11, 2012.

13. Herbert Kaufman, *Red Tape: Its Origins, Uses, and Abuses* (Washington, DC: Brookings Institution, 1977), 1.

14. Ibid., 29.

15. 43 U.S.C. 1740.

16. Braden Cox, "The Public Interest Tax on Communications," Competitive Enterprise Institute, April 15, 2005, web.archive.org/web/20081128094216/http://cei.org/gencon/016%2C04489.cfm, accessed July 11, 2012; Michael Copps, "The Price of Free Airwaves," *New York Times*, June 2, 2007, www.nytimes.com/2007/06/02/opinion/02copps.html, accessed July 11, 2012.

17. 16 CFR 1203.6.

18. 7 CFR 51.1527.

19. 34 CFR 602.

20. *Federal Register,* no. 197, 73 (October 9, 2008), 59946.

21. Alexander Hamilton, James Madison, and John Jay, *The Federalist Papers*, ed. Clinton Rossiter with a new introduction and notes by Charles R. Kesler (New York: Signet, 2003), no. 62, 379.

22. Cornelius M. Kerwin, *Rulemaking: How Government Agencies Write Law and Make Policy*, 2nd ed. (Washington, DC: CQ Press, 1999), 197–201.

23. *Federalist,* no. 62, 379.

24. Curtis Copeland, "Electronic Rulemaking in the Federal Government, Congressional Research Service," May 16, 2008, www.fas.org/sgp/crs/misc/RL34210.pdf, accessed July 11, 2012.

25. *Wayman v. Southard*, 23 U.S. 1, 46 (1825).

26. *Panama Refining Co. v. Ryan*, 293 U.S. 388 (1935).

27. *A.L.A. Schechter Poultry Corporation v. United States*, 295 U.S. 495, 551 (1935).

28. U.S. Office of Management and Budget, Office of Information and Regulatory Affairs, "Draft 2012 Report to Congress on the Benefits and Costs of Federal Regulations and Unfunded Mandates on State, Local, And Tribal Entities," March 2012, www.whitehouse.gov/sites/default/files/omb/oira/draft_2012_cost_benefit_report.pdf, accessed July 11, 2012.

29. Nicole Crain and W. Mark Crain, "The Impact of Regulatory Costs on Small Firms," report prepared for the Small Business Administration, Office of Advocacy, September 2010, archive.sba.gov/advo/research/rs371tot.pdf, accessed August 20, 2012.

30. Ben Peck, "The Cost of Regulatory Delay," Demos, August 12, 2011, www.demos.org/publication/cost-regulatory-delay, accessed July 11, 2012.

31. Testimony of Christopher B. Nelson before the Committee on Education and the Workforce U.S. House of Representatives, March 1, 2011, edworkforce.house.gov/UploadedFiles/03.01.11_nelson.pdf, accessed July 11, 2012.

32. Bonnie Hunter and Donald D. Gehring, "The Cost of Federal Legislation on Higher Education: The Hidden Tax on Tuition. *NASPA Journal* 42 (2004), journals.naspa.org/jsarp/vol42/iss4/art5/, accessed July 11, 2012.

33. *Humphrey's Executor v. United States*, 295 U.S. 602 (1935).

34. *Federal Trade Commission v. Ruberoid Co.*, 43 U.S. 470, 487 (1952).

35. President Barack Obama, "Address before a Joint Session of the Congress on the State of the Union," January 25, 2011, www.presidency.ucsb.edu/ws/?pid=88928, accessed July 11, 2012.

36. Joseph R. Biden Jr., "To End Turf Wars That Foil Drug Control," *New York Times*, January 4, 1983, A19.

37. Loch Johnson, quoted in "Domestic Security Czar to Tame 'Bowl of Spaghetti,'" CNN.com, September 21, 2001, www.cnn.com/2001/US/09/21/rec.homeland.defense, accessed July 11, 2012.

38. Zachary Fryer Briggs, "'Turf War' Slows New US Cyber Rules," *Defense News*, May 7, 2012, www.defensenews.com/article/20120507/C4ISR01/305070015/-8216-Turf-War-8217-Slows-New-U-S-Cyber-Rules, accessed July 11, 2012.

39. Timothy Noah, "Tom Ridge's Navy," *Slate*, June 10, 2002, www.slate.com/articles/news_and_politics/chatterbox/2002/06/tom_ridges_navy.html, accessed July 11, 2012.

40. Seth Borenstein and Dina Cappiello, "Spill Panel: Federal Confusion Lost Public Trust," Associated Press, September 27, 2010, www.huffingtonpost.com/2010/09/27/gulf-oil-spill-commission_0_n_740988.html, accessed July 12, 2012.

41. United States Office of Management and Budget, *Historical Tables, Budget of the United States Government, Fiscal Year 2013*, www.whitehouse.gov/sites/default/files/omb/budget/fy2013/assets/hist01z2.xls, accessed July 12, 2012.

42. Paul C. Light, "The New True Size of Government," Robert F. Wagner School of Public Service, New York University, August 2006, www.wagner.nyu.edu/performance/files/True_Size.pdf, accessed July 12, 2012.

43. Harold W. Stanley and Richard G. Niemi, *Vital Statistics on American Politics 2007–2008* (Washington, DC: CQ Press, 2008), 272.

44. Ben Erdreich, quoted in Susannah Zak Figura, "Historical Roots," *Government Executive*, May 1, 1999, www.govexec.com/magazine/1999/05/historical-roots/6018/, accessed July 12, 2012.

45. Public Law 95-454.

46. U.S. Department of Labor, Bureau of Labor Statistics, "Union Affiliation of Employed Wage and Salary Workers by Occupation and Industry," January 27, 2012, www.bls.gov/news.release/union2.t03.htm, accessed July 12, 2012.

47. Government Accountability Office, *Poor Performers in the Federal Workplace*, GAO-05-812R, June 21, 2005, www.gao.gov/new.items/d05812r.pdf, accessed August 20, 2012.

48. United States Office of Personnel Management, "2011 Federal Employee Viewpoint Survey," www.fedview.opm.gov/2011/Reports, accessed July 12, 2012.

49. Steven Kelman, *Making Public Policy: A Hopeful View of American Government* (New York: Basic Books, 1987), 274–276.

50. Government Accountability Office, "Improper Payments: Moving Forward with Governmentwide Reduction Strategies," GAO-12-405T, February 7, 2012, www.gao.gov/products/GAO-12-405T, accessed July 12, 2012.

51. David Osborne and Ted Gaebler, *Reinventing Government* (Reading, MA: Addison-Wesley, 1992), chap. 5.

52. President George W. Bush, address to a joint session of Congress, February 27, 2001, www.presidency.ucsb.edu/ws/index.php?pid=29643, accessed July 12, 2012.

53. M. J. Lee, "Obama's Unhelpful Advice," *Politico*, August 18, 2011, www.politico.com/politico44/perm/0811/call_uncle_sam_5c130fdd-0e34-4b04-99e1-3d923ea3919e.html, accessed July 13, 2012.

54. Columbia Accident Investigation Board, *Report*, August 2003, 138, www.caib.nasa.gov/news/report/pdf/vol1/full/caib_report_volume1.pdf, accessed July 13, 2012.

55. Rex Bowman, "Firefighters Answered FEMA Call, but Now They're Biding Time," *Richmond Times-Dispatch*, September 22, 2005, A7.

56. 18 USC 1913.

57. U.S. Department of Agriculture Office of Ethics, "USDA Guidance Regarding Anti-Lobbying Laws," July 17, 2008, www.usda-ethics.net/rules/rule9.htm, accessed July 13, 2012.

58. William D. Jones Jr., *Congressional Involvement and Relations*, 4th ed. (Fort Belvoir, VA: Defense Systems Management College Press, 1996), 45.

59. Joseph M. Bessette, *The Mild Voice of Reason: Deliberative Democracy and American National Government* (Chicago: University of Chicago Press, 1994), 229–230.

60. Marissa Martino Golden, *What Motivates Bureaucrats? Politics and Administration during the Reagan Years* (New York: Columbia University Press, 2000), 91–92.

61. Elizabeth Shogren, "Park Workers 'Openly' Opposing Bush Policies," *Los Angeles Times*, November 14, 2003, part 1, 27.

62. George C. Edwards III, "Why Not the Best? The Loyalty-Competence Trade-off in Presidential Appointments," *Brookings Review* 19 (Spring 2001), www.brookings.edu/articles/2001/spring_governance_edwards.aspx, accessed July 9, 2009.

63. Golden, *What Motivates Bureaucrats?* 155.

64. U.S. Senate Committee on Governmental Affairs, *United States Government Policy and Supporting Positions (2008 Edition) Committee on Governmental Affairs*, 110th Congress, 2d Session, www.gpo.gov/fdsys/pkg/GPO-PLUMBOOK-2008/html/GPO-PLUMBOOK-2008.htm, accessed July 13, 2012.

65. Bradley H. Patterson Jr., *The White House Staff: Inside the West Wing and Beyond* (Washington, DC: Brookings Institution, 2000), 232–234.

66. Ari Fleisher, quoted in Michael Grunwald, "Members of Congress Rally around Ousted Corps Chief," *Washington Post*, March 2, 2002, A31.

67. Donald J. Devine, "Political Administration: The Right Way," in *Steering the Elephant: How Washington Works*, ed. Robert Rector and Michael Sanera (New York: Universe Books, 1987), 130.

68. David C. Iglesias, "Why I Was Fired," *New York Times*, March 21, 2007, www.nytimes.com/2007/03/21/opinion/21iglesias.html, accessed July 13, 2012.

69. Mary Thornton and Martin Schram, "U.S. Holds the Ketchup in Schools," *Washington Post*, September 26, 1981, A1.

70. Edward Walsh, "USDA Launches Salsa into School Lunches," *Washington Post*, July 2, 1998, A19.

71. Council of the Inspectors General on Integrity and Efficiency, *Progress Report to the President, Fiscal Year 2011*, www.ignet.gov/randp/FY2011-Annual-Progress-Report-to-the-President.pdf, accessed July 13, 2012.

72. Clark Kent Ervin, quoted in Peter H. Stone, "Government Oversight: The Watchdogs," *National Journal*, May 12, 2007, 35.

73. Timothy R. Smith, "Panel Chides Obama for Inspector-General Vacancies," *Washington Post*, May 10, 2012, www.washingtonpost.com/politics/panel-chides-obama-for-inspector-general-vacancies/2012/05/10/gIQAld6eGU_story.html, accessed July 13, 2012.

74. George Crile, *Charlie Wilson's War* (New York: Atlantic Monthly Press, 2003).

75. Morton Rosenberg, "Congressional Review of Agency Rulemaking: An Update and Assessment of the Congressional Review Act after a Decade" (Washington, DC: Congressional Research Service, May 8, 2008), www.fas.org/sgp/crs/misc/RL30116.pdf, accessed July 13, 2012.

76. *Friends of the Earth v. Laidlaw Environmental Services*, 528 U.S. 167 (2000).

77. *Massachusetts v. Environmental Protection Agency*, 549 U.S. 497 (2007).

78. *Chevron U.S.A. v. Natural Resources Defense Council*, 467 U.S. 387 (1984).

79. The Manhattan Institute, "Regulation through Litigation: Assessing the Role of Bounty Hunters and Bureaucrats in the American Regulatory Regime," February 23, 2000, www.manhattan-institute.org/html/mics2a.htm, accessed July 13, 2012.

80. Susannah Rosenblatt and James Rainey, "Katrina Takes a Toll on Truth, News Accuracy," *Los Angeles Times*, September 27, 2005, A16.

81. Brian Thevenot and Gordon Russell, "Rumors of Death Greatly Exaggerated," *New Orleans Times-Picayune*, September 26, 2005, www.web.archive.org/web/20070807163100/www.nola.com/newslogs/tporleans/index.ssf?/mtlogs/nola_tporleans/archives/2005_09_26.html, accessed July 13, 2012.

82. Robert E. Pierre and Ann Gerhart, "News of Pandemonium May Have Slowed Aid," *Washington Post*, October 5, 2005, A8.

83. Lucinda Fleeson, "Where Are the Watchdogs?" *American Journalism Review*, July/August 2001, www.ajr.org/article.asp?id=29, accessed July 13, 2012.

84. Randolph J. May, "Tumultuous Times at the FCC," *Washington Times*, September 4, 2003, A19.

85. Elaine C. Kamarck, *The End of Government . . . As We Know It* (Boulder, CO: Lynne Rienner, 2007), 127–142.

86. Charles L. Schultze, *The Public Use of Private Interest* (Washington, DC: Brookings Institution, 1977).

87. Renae Merle, "Census Counts 100,000 Contractors in Iraq: Civilian Number, Duties Are Issues," *Washington Post*, December 5, 2006, D1.

88. Kamarck, *The End of Government*, 38.

89. Statement of Stuart W. Bowen Jr., Special Inspector General for Iraq Reconstruction before the House Oversight and Government Reform Committee, "U.S. Contracting in Iraq," February 15, 2007, www.sigir.mil/files/testimony/SIGIR_Testimony_07-005T.pdf, accessed July 13, 2012.

90. Samuel P. Huntington, *The Soldier and the State: The Theory and Politics of Civil-Military Relations* (Cambridge, MA: Belknap Press of Harvard University Press, 1957), 205–206.

91. Colin Powell, with Joseph E. Persico, *My American Journey* (New York: Random House, 1995), 220.

92. Dwight D. Eisenhower, "Farewell Address," January 17, 1961, www.presidency.ucsb.edu/ws/index.php?pid=12086, accessed July 13, 2012.

93. Norman J. Ornstein, "Defense, OPM Detailees Too Valuable to Limit," Roll Call, October 29, 2003, www.aei.org/article/politics-and-public-opinion/elections/defense-opm-detailees-are-too-valuable-to-limit/, accessed July 13, 2012.

94. Peter D. Feaver, *Armed Servants: Agency, Oversight, and Civil-Military Relations* (Cambridge, MA: Harvard University Press, 2003), 10–11.

95. Robert C. Carroll, "Ethics of the Military Profession," *Air University Review*, November–December 1974, www.airpower.au.af.mil/airchronicles/aureview/1974/nov-dec/carroll.html, accessed July 13, 2012.

96. "An Interview with Colin Powell: The Chairman as Principal Military Adviser," *Joint Force Quarterly* 13 (Autumn 1996): 32, www.dtic.mil/doctrine/jel/jfq_pubs/0813 .pdf, accessed July 13, 2012.

97. President Barack Obama, "Transparency and Open Government," January 21, 2009, www.presidency.ucsb .edu/ws/?pid=85677, accessed July 13, 2012.

98. U.S. Office of Personnel Management, "OPM Director Kay James Releases Survey Indicating Patriotism Runs High among Federal Job Applicants" July 1, 2004, www.opm.gov/news/opm-director-kay-james-releases-survey-indicating-patriotism-runs-high-among-federal-job-applicants,479.aspx, accessed July 13, 2012.

99. American Foreign Service Association, "FCS Assignments & Services Survey 2007: Results Overview," January 31, 2008, www.afsa.org/FCS/afsa08survey.pdf, accessed July 13, 2012.

100. Data come from a Peter D. Hart Research Associates survey among 455 Americans aged 17–24 for the Council for Excellence in Government. The survey took place by telephone February 22–24, 2004. Source: Council on Excellence in Government, "Calling Young People to Government Service: From 'Ask Not . . .' to 'Not Asked,'" March 2004, www.web.archive.org/ web/20060927143803/www.excelgov.org/admin/ FormManager/filesuploading/FINAL_Richardson_ Poll_Report.pdf, accessed July 13, 2012.

101. Data come from a Gallup online survey of 895 respondents, April 14–21, 2008. Source: Council on Excellence in Government, "The Appeal of Public Service: Who . . . What . . . and How?" May 2008, www.govexec .com/pdfs/050608b1.pdf, accessed July 13, 2012.

102. Alexis de Tocqueville, *Democracy in America*, ed. J. P. Mayer and trans. George Lawrence (Garden City, NY: Anchor Books, Doubleday, 1969), 692.

103. Ibid., 94.

Chapter 15

1. Alexis de Tocqueville, *Democracy in America*, ed. J. P. Mayer and trans. George Lawrence (Garden City, NY: Anchor Books, Doubleday, 1969), 270.

2. Alexander Hamilton, James Madison, and John Jay, *The Federalist Papers*, ed. Clinton Rossiter, with an introduction and notes by Charles R. Kesler (New York: New American Library, Signet Classic, 2003), no. 78, 464.

3. *The Records of the Federal Convention of 1787*, ed. Max Farrand, 4 vols. (New Haven, CT: Yale University Press, 1966), II:73 (July 21).

4. Ralph Lerner, "The Supreme Court as Republican Schoolmaster," in *The Supreme Court Review: 1967*, ed. Philip B. Kurland (Chicago: University of Chicago Press, 1967); and Richard Funston, *A Vital National Seminar: The Supreme Court in American Political Life* (Palo Alto, CA: Mayfield, 1978).

5. Montesquieu, *The Spirit of the Laws*, ed. and trans. Anne M. Cohler, Basia Carolyn Miller, and Harold Samuel Stone (Cambridge, England: Cambridge University Press, 1989), 157.

6. *Federalist,* no. 76, 456.

7. Wythe Holt, "Judiciary Act of 1789," in *The Oxford Companion to the Supreme Court of the United States,* ed. Kermit L. Hall (New York: Oxford University Press, 1992), 472.

8. *Federalist,* no. 78, 466.

9. *Marbury v. Madison,* 5 U.S. 137 (1803), 176, 177, 180.

10. Thomas Jefferson, "Letter to Abigail Adams," September 11, 1804, quoted at www.earlyamerica.com/ review/fall98/original.html, accessed August 7, 2009.

11. "Letter to George Hay," June 2, 1807, quoted at www.oll.libertyfund.org/Texts/Jefferson0136/Works/ Vol10/0054–10_Pt06_1807.html, accessed August 7, 2009.

12. Andrew Jackson, "Veto Message," July 10, 1832, at www.presidency.ucsb.edu/ws/index.php?pid=67043, accessed October 27, 2009.

13. "Speech on the Dred Scott Decision," June 26, 1857, at teachingamericanhistory.org/library/index.asp? document=52, accessed June 27, 2012.

14. Quoted by Lincoln in "Speech on the Dred Scott Decision," ibid.

15. Third debate, September 15, 1858, at www.teachingamericanhistory.org/library/index .asp?document=1046; Seventh Debate, October 15, 1858, at www.teachingamericanhistory.org/library/ index.asp?document=1055, both accessed June 27, 2012.

16. Sixth debate, October 13, 1858, at www.teaching americanhistory.org/library/index.asp?document=1051, accessed August 9, 2009.

17. "First Inaugural Address," March 4, 1861, at www.presidency.ucsb.edu/ws/index.php?pid=25818, accessed June 27, 2012.

18. *Judicial Business of the United States Courts, 2011,* Administrative Office of the U.S. Courts, Table X-1A, at www.uscourts.gov/uscourts/Statistics/JudicialBusiness/ 2011/JudicialBusiness2011.pdf, accessed June 27, 2012.

19. Byran A. Garner, ed., *Black's Law Dictionary*, 7th ed. (St. Paul, MN: West Group, 1999), 1272; Judicial Council of California, *Criminal Jury Instructions 2006*, Instruction 103, at www.courts.ca.gov/partners/documents/ calcrim_juryins.pdf, accessed July 2, 2012; *Ninth Circuit Model Criminal Jury Instructions*, Instruction 3.5, "Reasonable Doubt—Defined," at archive.ca9 .uscourts.gov/web/sdocuments.nsf/0/e8b8a21279bf9 f74882564b400081023?OpenDocument, accessed July 2, 2012; James Q. Whitman, "The Origins of 'Reasonable Doubt,'" Yale Law School Faculty Scholarship Series, 2005, Paper 1, at digitalcommons.law.yale .edu/cgi/viewcontent.cgi?article=1000&context=fss_ papers, accessed July 2, 2012.

20. United States District Court, Middle District of Alabama, "Handbook for Trial Jurors Serving in the

United States District Courts," at www.almd.uscourts .gov/jurorinfo/docs/Handbook_for_Trial_Jurors.pdf, accessed July 3, 2012.

21. Tocqueville, *Democracy in America*, 274–275.

22. John Gastil, E. Pierre Deess, Philip J. Weiser, and Cindy Simmons, *The Jury and Democracy: How Jury Deliberation Promotes Civic Engagement and Political Participation* (New York: Oxford University Press, 2010), 10. See also "Chapter 3: From Jury Box to Ballot Box."

23. American Bar Association, "Jury Service: Is Fulfilling Your Civic Duty a Trial?" July 2004, at www.abanow.org/wordpress/wp-content/files_flutter/ 1272052715_20_1_1_7_Upload_File.pdf, accessed July 3, 2012.

24. "Chronological History of Authorized Judgeships in the U.S. Courts of Appeals," Administrative Office of the U.S. Courts, at www.uscourts.gov/JudgesAndJudgeships/ AuthorizedJudgeships/HistoryOfJudgeshipsCourtsAppeals.aspx, accessed July 3, 2012.

25. David C. Nixon and David L. Goss, "Confirmation Delay for Vacancies on the Circuit Court of Appeals," *American Politics Research* 29, no. 3 (May 2001): 251.

26. Supreme Court Rules, "Part VII. Practice and Procedure," Rule 37, at www.law.cornell.edu/rules/supct/37 .html, accessed July 3, 2012.

27. Stanley Mosk, "In Defense of Oral Argument," *Journal of Appellate Practice and Process* 1 (Winter 1999): 26–27.

28. Quoted in Robert J. Janosik, "The Conference," in *The Oxford Companion to the Supreme Court*, 174.

29. WETA-TV, "This Honorable Court," a documentary on the Supreme Court that aired on the Public Broadcasting System in May 1988.

30. For the International Criminal Court, see its Web site at www.icc-cpi.int/menus/icc/home. The American Service-Members' Protection Act is at www.state.gov/ t/pm/rls/othr/misc/23425.htm, both accessed July 3, 2012.

31. Ralph A. Rossum and G. Alan Tarr, *American Constitutional Law: Cases and Interpretation*, 2nd ed. (New York: St. Martin's Press, 1987), 50.

32. See the discussion of *Dellums v. Bush* (1990) and *Doe v. Bush* (2003) in Michael John Garcia, "War Powers Litigation Initiated by Members of Congress Since the Enactment of the War Powers Resolution," Congressional Research Service, February 17, 2012, at www.fas.org/sgp/crs/natsec/RL30352.pdf, accessed July 3, 2012.

33. *Marbury v. Madison*, 5 U.S. 137 (1803), 165–166.

34. *Luther v. Borden*, 48 U.S. 1 (1849), 42.

35. *Lochner v. New York*, 198 U.S. 45 (1905), 53.

36. Ibid., 75, 76.

37. *Hammer v. Dagenhart*, 247 U.S. 251 (1918), and *Adkins v. Children's Hospital*, 261 U.S. 525 (1923).

38. *Panama Refining Co. v. Ryan*, 293 U.S. 388 (1935); *Schechter Poultry Corp. v. U.S.*, 295 U.S. 495 (1935).

39. *Wickard v. Filburn*, 317 U.S. 111 (1942).

40. Ibid., 128.

41. *United States v. Carolene Products Co.*, 304 U.S. 144 (1938), 152–153.

42. *Brown v. Board of Education*, 349 U.S. 294 (1955), 300.

43. Herbert J. Storing, ed., *The Complete Anti-Federalist*, 7 volumes (Chicago: University of Chicago Press, 1981), 2:244.

44. *Federalist*, no. 80, 479.

45. *Missouri v. Jenkins*, 515 U.S. 70 (1995), 79, 75.

46. *Missouri v. Jenkins*, 495 U.S. 33 (1990), 77.

47. *Missouri v. Jenkins*, 515 U.S. 70 (1995), Justice O'Connor concurring, at 111.

48. *Jenkins v. State of Missouri*, 959 F.Supp. 1151 (W.D.Mo.,1997), 1165.

49. William J. Brennan Jr., "State Constitutions and the Protection of Individual Rights," *Harvard Law Review* 90, no. 3 (January 1977): 491.

50. Ibid., 501.

51. *Bush v. Gore*, 531 U.S. 98 (2000).

52. Alan M. Dershowitz, *Supreme Injustice: How the High Court Hijacked Election 2000* (New York: Oxford University Press, 2001), 52.

53. Bruce Ackerman, "Off Balance," in *Bush v. Gore: The Question of Legitimacy*, ed. Bruce Ackerman (New Haven, CT: Yale University Press, 2002), 195.

54. *Bush v. Gore*, 531 U.S. 98 (2000), 104.

55. Ibid., 128 (Justice Stevens, joined by Justices Ginsburg and Breyer).

56. Ibid., 115, 119 (Justice Rehnquist, joined by Justices Scalia and Thomas).

57. Storing, *Complete Anti-Federalist*, 2:419, 439, 438.

58. Ibid., 440.

59. *Federalist*, no. 78, 470.

60. *Federalist*, no. 81, 481, emphasis in the original.

61. *Federalist*, no. 78, 464.

62. *Federalist*, no. 81, 484.

63. *Federalist*, no. 78, 468.

64. "Southern Manifesto," introduced in Congress on March 12, 1956, and signed by 19 senators and 77 members of the House of Representatives, at sti.clemson.edu/holding-area/general-info/1956-southern-manifesto-2.html, accessed July 5, 2012.

65. White's dissent from the Court's ruling in *Roe v. Wade* was made in the companion case *Doe v. Bolton*, 410 U.S. 179 (1973), 222.

66. Edwin Meese III, "Toward a Jurisprudence of Original Intent," *Harvard Journal of Law and Public Policy* 11, no. 1 (Winter 1988): 6–7.

67. Ibid., 5.

68. Antonin Scalia, "A Theory of Constitutional Interpretation," speech at the Catholic University of America, October 18, 1996, at web.archive.org/ web/19970108070805/http://www.courttv.com/ library/rights/scalia.html, accessed July 5, 2012.

69. William J. Brennan Jr., "Speech to the Text and Teaching Symposium," Georgetown University, Washington,

DC, October 12, 1985, reprinted in *American Political Rhetoric: A Reader*, ed. Peter Augustine Lawler and Robert Martin Schaefer, 4th ed. (Lanham, MD: Rowman and Littlefield, 2001), 121–122.

70. Ibid., 125–126.

71. *Callins v. Collins*, 510 U.S. 1142 (1994), 1141, 1142.

72. President Barack Obama, "Remarks in Nominating Judge Sonia Sotomayor to the United States Supreme Court," May 26, 2009, at www.presidency.ucsb.edu/ws/index.php?pid=86204, accessed July 5, 2012.

73. *West Virginia State Board of Education v. Barnette*, 319 U.S. 624 (1943), 647, 650, 666.

74. The list of these 167 decisions is maintained by the United States Government Printing Office as part of "The Constitution of the United States of America: Analysis, and Interpretation - 2002 Edition," at www.gpo.gov/fdsys/granule/GPO-CONAN-2002/GPO-CONAN-2002–12/content-detail.html, accessed August 30, 2012. The list itself is "Supreme Court Decisions Overruled by Subsequent Decision," at www.gpo.gov/fdsys/pkg/GPO-CONAN-2002/pdf/GPO-CONAN-2002–12.pdf, accessed July 8, 2012. The list includes another 53 decisions in which the Supreme Court did not expressly overrule a previous decision but "the overruling [is] deduced from the principles of related cases."

75. William H. Rehnquist, *Grand Inquest: The Historic Impeachments of Justice Samuel Chase and President Andrew Johnson* (New York: Quill, Morrow, 1999), 127–128.

76. Ibid., 93.

77. Ibid., 104–105, 107–108.

78. Quoted in ibid., 22.

79. Quoted in ibid., 107.

80. Ibid., 114.

81. *Federalist*, no. 78, 464.

82. *Worcester v. Georgia*, 31 U.S. 515 (1832), 561.

83. Ibid., 563.

84. As to whether President Jackson actually said this, see footnote 49 in Chap. 4.

85. *Federalist*, no. 76, 456.

86. Quoted in Robert H. Bork, *The Tempting of America: The Political Seduction of the Law* (New York: Free Press, 1990), 267–268.

87. Senator Edward Kennedy, speech on the Senate floor, June 23, 1987, at en.wikisource.org/wiki/Robert_Bork's_America, accessed July 5, 2012.

88. Quoted in Bork, *The Tempting of America*, 287.

89. Quoted in Josh Gerstein, "Filibuster Is Eyed as Curtain Rises on Alito Hearing," *New York Sun*, January 9, 2006, at www.nysun.com/article/25507, accessed August 7, 2009.

90. Kennedy's and Hatch's statements are in "Senate Judiciary Committee Vote for the Nomination of Judge Samuel A. Alito, Jr. to Be Associate Justice on the U.S. Supreme Court," January 24, 2006, at www.rnla.org/blog/JudiciaryCommitteeFinalStatements1-24-06.pdf, accessed July 29, 2006.

91. President Barack Obama, "Remarks on the Retirement of Supreme Court Justice David Souter," May 1, 2009, at www.presidency.ucsb.edu/ws/index.php?pid=86087, accessed July 8, 2012.

92. President Barack Obama, "Remarks in Nominating Judge Sonia Sotomayor to the United States Supreme Court," May 26, 2009, at www.presidency.ucsb.edu/ws/index.php?pid=86204, accessed July 8, 2012.

93. The speech was reprinted in the *Wall Street Journal* on June 2, 2009, p. A21, at online.wsj.com/article/SB124390047073474499.html, accessed July 8, 2012.

94. Reprinted in the *New York Times*, September 15, 2005, at www.nytimes.com/2005/09/15/politics/politicsspecial1/15text-roberts.html?pagewanted=27, accessed July 8, 2012.

95. Reprinted by the *Los Angeles Times*, July 14, 2009, at latimesblogs.latimes.com/washington/2009/07/sotomayor-hearings-complete-transcript-4.html, accessed July 8, 2012.

96. George F. Will, "Bork: Up against a Stall Defense," *Washington Post*, August 2, 1987, C7.

97. Quoted in Henry J. Abraham, *The Judicial Process*, 6th ed. (New York: Oxford University Press, 1993), 203.

98. Kevin M. Stack, "The Practice of Dissent in the Supreme Court," *Yale Law Journal* 105 (June 1996): 2257.

99. *American Electric Power Co. v. Connecticut*, 564 U.S. _____ (2011).

Chapter 16

1. Franklin D. Roosevelt, "Commonwealth Club Campaign Speech," September 23, 1932, in *American Political Rhetoric: A Reader*, 5th ed., ed. Peter Augustine Lawler and Robert Martin Schaefer (Lanham, MD: Rowman and Littlefield, 2005), 192, 193, 194, 195. (Also at www.americanrhetoric.com/speeches/fdrcommonwealth.htm, accessed July 25, 2012.)

2. Ibid., 195.

3. Ibid.

4. Ibid., 196.

5. The source of the data is the same as Table 16-1, adjusted by the Bureau of Labor Statistics inflation calculator (based on the Consumer Price Index), at www.bls.gov/data/inflation_calculator.htm, accessed July 19, 2012.

6. U.S. Congress, *An Ordinance for the Government of the Territory of the United States Northwest of the River Ohio*, July 13, 1787, at avalon.law.yale.edu/18th_century/nworder.asp, accessed July 27, 2012.

7. Kurt T. Lash, "The Second Adoption of the Establishment Clause: The Rise of the Nonestablishment Principle," *Arizona State Law Journal* 27 (Winter 1995): 1123–1124.

8. Ibid., 1124.

9. *Pierce v. Society of the Sisters of the Holy Names of Jesus*, 268 U.S. 510, 535 (1925).

10. *Epperson v. Arkansas*, 393 U.S. 97, 109 (1968).

11. *Edwards v. Aguillard*, 482 U.S. 578 (1987).

12. Scott Keeter, "On Darwin's Birthday, Americans Still Divided about Evolution," Pew Research Center, February 5, 2009, at www.pewresearch.org/pubs/1107/polling-evolution—creationism, accessed July 27, 2012.

13. Frank Newport, "In U.S., 46% Hold Creationist View of Human Origins," Gallup Poll, June 1, 2012, at www.gallup.com/poll/155003/Hold-Creationist-View-Human-Origins.aspx, accessed July 27, 2012.

14. Three Islamic countries (Saudi Arabia, Turkey, and Indonesia) and two developing countries (Brazil and South Africa) did show more support for creationism than the United States. Ipsos survey of 18,531 adults aged 18–64 in the United States and Canada, and age 16–64 in all other countries, between September 7, 2010 and September 23, 2010, released April 25, 2011, at www.ipsos-na.com/download/pr.aspx?id=10670, accessed July 27, 2012.

15. Marvin Olasky, *The Tragedy of American Compassion* (Washington, DC: Regnery, 1992), chaps. 1 and 2.

16. Robert William Fogel, *The Fourth Great Awakening and the Future of Egalitarianism* (Chicago: University of Chicago Press, 2000), 125.

17. Quoted in Dorothy Ross, *The Origins of American Social Science* (New York: Cambridge University Press, 1991), 107.

18. Theodore Roosevelt, "A Confession of Faith," August 6, 1912, at www.theodore-roosevelt.com/images/research/speeches/trarmageddon.pdf, accessed July 27, 2012.

19. Quoted in A. James Reichley, *Faith in Politics* (Washington, DC: Brookings Institution, 2002), 203.

20. Quoted in Clayborne Carson, ed., *The Autobiography of Martin Luther King, Jr.* (New York: IPM/Warner Books, 1998), at mlk-kpp01.stanford.edu/index.php/king-papers/article/chapter_3_crozer_seminary/, accessed July 27, 2012. Video available at www.youtube.com/watch?v=WGuDpBANETg.

21. Kenneth Woodward, "Soulful Matters," *Newsweek*, October 31, 1994, 22.

22. Barack Obama, "Why Organize? Problems and Promise in the Inner City," *Illinois Issues*, 1990, at www.gatherthepeople.org/Downloads/WHY_ORGANIZE.pdf, accessed July 27, 2012.

23. Tom Mak, "Paul Ryan: Faith in the Budget Plan," *Politico*, April 10, 2012, at www.politico.com/news/stories/0412/74990.html, accessed July 19, 2012.

24. Franklin D. Roosevelt, "Statement on Signing the Social Security Act," August 14, 1935, at www.presidency.ucsb.edu/ws/index.php?pid=14916, accessed July 25, 2012.

25. Franklin D. Roosevelt, "Message on the State of the Union," January 1944, at www.presidency.ucsb.edu/ws/index.php?pid=16518, accessed July 25, 2012.

26. Harry S Truman, "Special Message to the Congress Presenting a 21-Point Program for the Reconversion Period," September 6, 1945, at www.presidency.ucsb.edu/ws/index.php?pid=12359, accessed July 25, 2012.

27. See Truman's "Special Message to the Congress Recommending a Comprehensive Health Program," November 19, 1945, at www.trumanlibrary.org/publicpapers/index.php?pid=483&st=&st1=, accessed July 25, 2012.

28. Dwight D. Eisenhower, "Letter to Edgar Newton Eisenhower," November 8, 1954, at www.eisenhowermemorial.org/presidential-papers/first-term/documents/1147.cfm, accessed July 25, 2012.

29. Lyndon B. Johnson, "Annual Message to Congress on the State of the Union," January 8, 1964, at www.presidency.ucsb.edu/ws/index.php?pid=26787, accessed July 25, 2012.

30. Ibid.

31. Lyndon B. Johnson, "Remarks at the University of Michigan," May 22, 1964, at www.presidency.ucsb.edu/ws/index.php?pid=26262&st=&st1=, accessed July 25, 2012.

32. Ibid.

33. Social Security Administration, Social Security Online, "SSI Federal Payment Amounts," at www.socialsecurity.gov/OACT/COLA/SSIamts.html, accessed July 16, 2012.

34. Internal Revenue Service, "EITC Statistics," at www.eitc.irs.gov/central/eitcstats/, accessed July 25, 2012.

35. See the source for Table 16-2. For total government spending: U.S. Government Printing Office, Budget of the United States Government, Fiscal Year 2013, Historical Tables, Table 15.2, at www.gpo.gov/fdsys/browse/collection.action?collectionCode=BUDGET&browsePath=Fiscal+Year+2013&searchPath=Fiscal+Year+2013&leafLevelBrowse=false&isCollapsed=false&isOpen=true&packageid=BUDGET-2013-TAB&ycord=770, accessed July 25, 2012.

36. Howard Zinn, *The Twentieth Century: A People's History* (New York: HarperPerennial, 1998), 346; Office of Management and Budget, *Budget of the United States Government, Fiscal Year 2009, Historical Tables*, Table 8.2, at www.gpoaccess.gov/usbudget/fy09/hist.html, accessed July 25, 2012.

37. Charles Murray, *Losing Ground: American Social Policy, 1950–1980* (New York: Basic Books, 1984), 9.

38. Dan Quayle, "Address to the Commonwealth Club of California," May 19, 1992, sometimes titled the "Speech on Family Values" or the "Murphy Brown Speech," at www.vicepresidentdanquayle.com/speeches_Standing-Firm_CCC_1.html, accessed July 25, 2012.

39. William J. Clinton, "Announcement Speech," Old State House, Little Rock, Arkansas, October 3, 1991, at www.4president.org/speeches/billclinton1992announcement.htm, accessed July 25, 2012.

40. President William J. Clinton, "Address before a Joint Session of Congress on Administration Goals," February 17, 1993, at www.presidency.ucsb.edu/ws/index.php?pid=47232, accessed July 25, 2012.

41. President William J. Clinton, "Remarks on Signing the Personal Responsibility and Work Opportunity Reconciliation Act of 1996 and an Exchange with Reporters," August 22, 1996, at www.presidency.ucsb.edu/ws/index.php?pid=53218, accessed July 25, 2012.

42. The Daschle and Moynihan quotations are from the Senate floor debate of July 23, 1996, as reported in *CQ Weekly*, July 27, 1996, "More Voices on Welfare," 2118.

43. The second quotation from Moynihan and the quotation from Edelman are from Robert Rector and Patrick F. Fagan, "The Continuing Good News about Welfare Reform," February 6, 2003, at www.heritage.org/Research/Welfare/bg1620.cfm, accessed July 25, 2012.

44. See, for example, Douglas J. Besharov, "The Past and Future of Welfare Reform," in *The Public Interest*, Winter 2003, 9.

45. The data for 2009–2012 are available at the following sites. Medicaid: www.cms.gov/Research-Statistics-Data-and-Systems/Research/ActuarialStudies/downloads/MedicaidReport2011.pdf; Food Stamps: www.fns.usda.gov/pd/34snapmonthly.htm; TANF: www.acf.hhs.gov/programs/ofa/data-reports/caseload/2011/2011_recipient_tan.htm; SSI: www.taxpolicycenter.org/taxfacts/displayafact.cfm?DocID=37&Topic2id=30&Topic3id=39 (EITC); www.ssa.gov/policy/docs/statcomps/ssi_monthly/2012-06/table01.html, accessed July 10, 2012.

46. U.S. Bureau of the Census, *Income, Poverty, and Health Insurance Coverage in the United States: 2010*, Appendix B, p. 61, at www.census.gov/prod/2011pubs/p60-239.pdf, accessed July 25, 2012.

47. See, for example, The Heritage Foundation report, *Understanding Poverty in America*, Robert E. Rector and Kirk A. Johnson, January 5, 2004, at www.heritage.org/Research/Welfare/bg1713.cfm, accessed August 11, 2009.

48. Ibid., Table 4, p. 16.

49. Social Security Administration, "Fast Facts & Figures about Social Security, 2011," p. 14, at www.ssa.gov/policy/docs/chartbooks/fast_facts/2011/fast_facts11.pdf, accessed July 20, 2012.

50. Social Security Administration, "Financial data for the Social Security Trust Funds," at www.ssa.gov/oact/progdata/qop.html, accessed July 20, 2012.

51. President George W. Bush, "Address before a Joint Session of the Congress on the State of the Union," February 2, 2005, at www.presidency.ucsb.edu/ws/index.php?pid=58746, accessed July 25, 2012.

52. AARP, "Social Security: Where We Stand; An Open Letter to AARP Members," June 2005, at www.aarpsegundajuventud.org/english/social/2005-JJ/05AM_socsecaarp.html, accessed August 11, 2009.

53. AEI Public Opinion Study, "Attitudes about Social Security Reform (updated August 2, 2005)," 19–24, at www.aei.org/files/2005/08/02/20050802_SOCIALSECURITY0802.pdf, accessed July 25, 2012.

54. Ibid., 25.

55. www.gallup.com/poll/1693/Social-Security.aspx, accessed July 25, 2012.

56. See Investment Company Institute, "Frequently Asked Questions about Individual Retirement Accounts (IRAs)," at www.ici.org/faqs/faqs_iras, accessed July 25, 2012.

57. President George W. Bush, "Address before a Joint Session of the Congress on Administration Goals," February 27, 2001, at www.presidency.ucsb.edu/ws/index.php?pid=29643, accessed July 25, 2012.

58. Calculated from Table III.C19. of the *2010 Annual Report of the Boards of Trustees of the Federal Hospital Insurance and Federal Supplementary Medical Insurance Trust Funds*, August 2010, 141, at www.cms.gov/ReportsTrustFunds/downloads/tr2010.pdf, accessed July 25, 2012.

59. President George W. Bush, "President Signs Medicare Legislation," December 8, 2003, at www.presidency.ucsb.edu/ws/index.php?pid=768, accessed July 25, 2012.

60. Mary Agnes Carey, "Medicare Deal Goes to Wire in Late-Night House Vote," *CQ Weekly Online*, November 22, 2003, 2879–2883.

61. House floor debate, June 26, 2003.

62. President George W. Bush, "President Signs Legislation," December 8, 2003, at www.whitehouse.gov/news/releases/2003/12/20031208?2.html, accessed November 25, 2006.

63. See the press releases of January 31, 2008, and August 14, 2008, of the Centers for Medicare and Medicaid Services of the Department of Health and Human Services, at www.cms.hhs.gov/apps/media/press/release.asp?Counter=2868&intNumPerPage=10&checkDate=&checkKey=2&srchType=2&numDays=0&srchOpt=0&srchData=part+d&keywordType=All&chkNewsType=1%2C+2%2C+3%2C+4%2C+5&intPage=&showAll=1&pYear=&year=0&desc=&cboOrder=date; and www.cms.hhs.gov/apps/media/press/release.asp?Counter=3240&intNumPerPage=10&checkDate=&checkKey=2&srchType=2&numDays=0&srchOpt=0&srchData=part+d&keywordType=All&chkNewsType=1%2C+2%2C+3%2C+4%2C+5&intPage=&showAll=1&pYear=&year=0&desc=&cboOrder=date, accessed July 25, 2012.

64. "Status of the Social Security and Medicare Programs: A Summary of the 2007 Annual Reports," at www.ssa.gov/OACT/TRSUM/trsummary.html, accessed August 11, 2009.

65. *The 2008 Annual Report of the Board of Trustees of the Federal Old-Age and Survivors Insurance and Federal Disability Insurance Trust Funds,* Table VI.F9 (p. 190), at www.ssa.gov/OACT/TR/TR08/index.html, accessed July 25, 2012.

66. *2008 Annual Report of the Boards of Trustees of the Federal Hospital Insurance and Federal Supplemental*

Medical Insurance Trust Funds, Table III.A2 (p. 35), at www.cms.hhs.gov/reportstrustfunds/downloads/tr2008.pdf, accessed July 25, 2012.

67. Senator Ron Wyden and Representative Paul Ryan, "Guaranteed Choices to Strengthen Medicare and Health Security for All," December 15, 2011, at http://budget.house.gov/uploadedfiles/wydenryan.pdf, accessed July 25, 2012.

68. Carol E. Lee and Arian Campo-Flores, "Florida Poses New Worry for Obama," *Wall Street Journal,* July 20, 2012, A4.

69. Ibid., and Michael A. Memoli and Seema Mehta, "Obama says Romney put Medicare's future at risk," *Los Angeles Times,* July 20, 2012, AA2.

70. At www.mittromney.com/news/press/2012/07/president-obamas-failed-record-medicare, accessed July 25, 2012.

71. President Barack Obama, "Passage of Health Care Marks a New Season in America," March 23, 2012, at www.realclearpolitics.com/articles/2010/03/23/passage_of_health_care_marks_a_new_season_in_america_104879.html, accessed July 25, 2012.

72. On the number of U.S. residents lacking health insurance, see U.S. Bureau of the Census, *Income, Poverty, and Health Insurance Coverage in the United States: 2010,* September 2011, Table C-1, p. 77, at www.census.gov/prod/2011pubs/p60-239.pdf, accessed July 20, 2012.

73. Congressional Budget Office, "Updated Estimates for the Insurance Coverage Provisions of the Affordable Care Act," March 2012, at cbo.gov/sites/default/files/cbofiles/attachments/03-13-Coverage%20Estimates.pdf, accessed July 20, 2012.

74. The Heartland Institute, "The Model for the Nation: An Exclusive Interview with Annette Polly Williams," August 2002, at www.heartland.org/Article.cfm?artId=10124, accessed July 25, 2012.

75. Ibid.

76. For information on the Milwaukee Parental Choice Program, see its Web site: dpi.wi.gov/sms/choice.html, accessed July 20, 2012. For Annette Polly Williams's own account of how she started the Milwaukee Parental Choice program, go to www.heartland.org/Article.cfm?artId=10124, accessed July 25, 2012.

77. See Friedman Foundation for Educational Choice, School Choice Programs, at www.edchoice.org/School-Choice/School-Choice-Programs.aspx, accessed July 25, 2012.

78. Marcus A. Winters, "The Year of the Voucher," *City Journal,* vol. 21, no. 4 (Autumn 2011), at www.city-journal.org/2011/21_4_snd-vouchers.html, accessed July 20, 2012.

79. All the quotations are from CNN, "Supreme Court Affirms School Voucher Program," June 27, 2002, at articles.cnn.com/2002-06-27/justice/scotus.school.vouchers_1_school-voucher-program-milwaukee-and-florida-parochial-school-tuition/3?_s=PM:LAW, accessed July 25, 2012.

80. National Alliance for Charter Public Schools, "Facing the Opposition: Speaking Up for Public Charter Schools," at www.publiccharters.org/editor/files/NAPCS%20Documents/FacingtheOppositionSpeakingUpforPublicCharterSchools.pdf, and "Schools Overview," at dashboard.publiccharters.org/dashboard/schools/page/overview/year/2012, accessed July 20, 2012. Posted by the White House on February 4, 2009, at www.whitehouse.gov/blog_post/how_our_schools_should_be/, accessed July 25, 2012.

81. White House press release, March 10, 2009, at www.whitehouse.gov/the_press_office/Fact-Sheet-Expanding-the-Promise-of-Education-in-America, accessed July 25, 2012.

82. President Barack Obama, "National Charter Schools Week, 2009," at www.whitehouse.gov/the_press_office/Presidential-Proclamation-National-Charter-Schools-Week, accessed July 25, 2012.

83. *Democratic Party Platform of 2004,* at www.presidency.ucsb.edu/ws/index.php?pid=29613, accessed July 25, 2012.

84. *Republican Party Platform of 2004,* at www.presidency.ucsb.edu/ws/index.php?pid=25850, accessed July 25, 2012.

85. "Fenty Pushes for School Vouchers," *Washington Times,* March 13, 2009, at www.washingtontimes.com/news/2009/mar/13/fenty-pushes-for-school-vouchers/?page=all, accessed July 25, 2012.

86. Mitt Romney, Speech to the U.S. Chamber of Commerce, May 23, 2012, at www.mittromney.com/blogs/mitts-view/2012/05/us-chamber-commerce-remarks-chance-every-child, accessed July 27, 2012.

87. Elihu Root, *Addresses on Government and Citizenship* (Freeport, NY: Books for Libraries Press, 1969 reprint of 1916 edition), 86.

88. Alexis de Tocqueville, *Democracy in America,* ed. J. P. Mayer and trans. George Lawrence (Garden City, NY: Anchor Books, Doubleday, 1969), 692.

89. Ibid., 694.

90. Justin Sink, "Paul Ryan: Obama's 'Julia' Website 'Creepy' and 'Demeaning,'" *The Hill*'s Blog Briefing Room, May 4, 2012, at thehill.com/blogs/blog-briefing-room/news/225553-paul-ryan-obama-julia-website-creepy-demeaning, accessed July 25, 2012. "The Life of Julia" on the official Obama campaign site is at www.barackobama.com/life-of-julia. The parody is at thelifeofjulia.com.

Chapter 17

1. Brian Wingfield and Josh Zumbrun, "Bad News for the Bailout," *Forbes.com,* September 23, 2008, at www.forbes.com/2008/09/23/bailout-paulson-congress-biz-beltway-cx_jz_bw_0923bailout.html, accessed July 16, 2012.

2. John Maynard Keynes, *The General Theory of Employment, Interest and Money* (New York: First Harvest/ Harcourt, 1964 [1936]), 383.

3. Alexander Hamilton, James Madison, and John Jay, *The Federalist Papers*, ed. Clinton Rossiter with a new introduction and notes by Charles R. Kesler (New York: Signet, 2003), no. 42, 239.

4. John Lauritz Larson, "'Bind the Republic Together': The National Union and the Struggle for a System of Internal Improvements," *Journal of American History* 74 (September 1987): 363–387.

5. James M. McPherson, *Abraham Lincoln and the Second American Revolution* (New York: Oxford University Press, 1990), chap. 2.

6. U.S. Department of the Treasury, Office of the Controller of the Currency, "National Banking System Created 1832–1864," at www.occ.treas.gov/exhibits/histor3 .htm, accessed August 27, 2012; Federal Reserve Bank of San Francisco, "A Brief History of Our Nation's Paper Money," at www.frbsf.org/publications/federalreserve/ annual/1995/history.html, accessed July 16, 2012.

7. *Pollock v. Farmers' Loan & Trust Co.*, 157 U.S. 429 (1895).

8. Woodrow Wilson, address to Congress, June 23, 1913, at www.presidency.ucsb.edu/ws/index.php?pid=65369, accessed July 16, 2012.

9. President Theodore Roosevelt, "Address to the New York State Agricultural Association," Syracuse, New York, September 7, 1903, at www.presidency.ucsb.edu/ws/ index.php?pid=24504, accessed July 16, 2012.

10. Quoted in Steven R. Weisman, *The Great Tax Wars* (New York: Simon and Schuster, 2002), 324.

11. President Calvin Coolidge, "Address at the Twelfth Regular Meeting of the Business Organization of the Government," Washington, DC, January 29, 1927, at www.presidency.ucsb.edu/ws/index.php?pid=415, accessed July 16, 2012.

12. Roosevelt himself had little interest in economic theory and was skeptical about Keynes. The latter exerted more influence on FDR's lower-level aides and on subsequent generations of policymakers. See James MacGregor Burns, *Roosevelt: The Lion and the Fox* (New York: Harcourt, Brace and World, 1956), 330–334.

13. Public Law 79–304, 15 U.S.C. 1021.

14. Remarks by Chairman Alan Greenspan before the Truman Medal Award and Economics Conference, Kansas City, Missouri, October 26, 2005, at www.federalreserve.gov/BoardDocs/Speeches/ 2005/20051026/default.htm, accessed July 16, 2012.

15. Martin Anderson, *Revolution* (New York: Harcourt, Brace, Jovanovich, 1988), 152.

16. President Barack Obama, remarks on tax reform, Washington, DC, May 4, 2009, at www.presidency .ucsb.edu/ws/?pid=86102, accessed July 18, 2012.

17. U.S. Internal Revenue Service, "2012 Form 1040-ES: Estimated Tax for Individuals," at www.irs.gov/pub/ irs-pdf/f1040es.pdf, p. 6, accessed July 18, 2012.

18. U.S. Internal Revenue Service, "American Opportunity Tax Credit," November 9, 2011, at www.irs.gov/uac/ American-Opportunity-Tax-Credit, accessed October 10, 2012.

19. Brian Palmer, "How Many Words Are in the Tax Code?" *Slate*, October 26, 2011, at www.slate.com/articles/news_ and_politics/explainer/2011/10/how_many_words_ are_in_the_tax_code_.html, accessed July 18, 2012.

20. U.S. Government Accountability Office, "Tax Administration: IRS's 2003 Filing Season Showed Improvements," October 2003, at www.gao.gov/new .items/d0484.pdf, accessed July 19, 2012; U.S. Government Accountability Office, "2011 Tax Filing: Processing Gains, But Taxpayer Assistance Could Be Enhanced by More Self-Service Tools," December 2011, www.gao.gov/assets/590/587061.pdf, accessed July 19, 2012.

21. Christopher S. Jackson, "The Inane Gospel of Tax Protest: Resist Rendering unto Caesar—Whatever His Demands," *Gonzaga Law Review* 32 (1996/1997): 291–329; Internal Revenue Service, "The Truth about Frivolous Tax Arguments," February 16, 2012, at www.irs.gov/pub/irs-utl/friv_tax.pdf, accessed July 18, 2012; Brian Doherty, "It's So Simple It's Ridiculous: Taxing Times for 16th Amendment Rebels," *Reason*, May 2004, at www.reason.com/news/show/117168 .html, accessed July 18, 2012; Internal Revenue Service, "Frivolous Arguments to Avoid When Filing a Return or Claim for a Refund," April 10, 2006, at www.irs.gov/irb/2006-15_IRB/ar12.html, accessed July 18, 2012.

22. Internal Revenue Service, Topic 556, "Alternative Minimum Tax," at www.irs.gov/taxtopics/tc556.html, accessed July 18, 2012. See also Michael Peel, "Alternative Minimum Tax (AMT) Reform," senior thesis, Claremont McKenna College, 2007.

23. Taxpayer Advocate Service, "2010 Annual Report to Congress," at www.irs.gov/pub/irs-utl/2010arcmsp1_ taxreform.pdf, accessed July 18, 2012; David Keating, "A Taxing Trend: The Rise in Complexity, Forms, and Paperwork Burdens," National Taxpayers Union, April 17, 2012, at www.ntu.org/news-and-issues/taxes/tax-reform/ ntupp130.html, accessed July 18, 2012.

24. Patricia Murphy, "IRS Commissioner Does Not Do His Own Taxes," *Politics Daily*, January 12, 2010, at www.politicsdaily.com/2010/01/12/irs-commissioner-admits-he-does-not-do-his-own-taxes, accessed July 18, 2012.

25. Mary Dalrymple, "Lawmakers Just Write the Tax Laws," Associated Press, April 16, 2006, at legacy.utsandiego .com/uniontrib/20060417/news_1n17taxes.html, accessed July 18, 2012.

26. Jonathan Strong, "Tax Writers Can't Figure Out the Tax Code, Either," *Daily Caller*, March 26, 2010, at daily caller.com/2010/03/26/tax-writers-cant-figure-out-the-tax-code-either, accessed July 18, 2012.

27. Sheldon Cohen, quoted in Jeffrey H. Birnbaum and Alan S. Murray, *Showdown at Gucci Gulch: Lawmakers, Lobbyists, and the Unlikely Triumph of Tax Reform* (New York: Random House, 1987), 289.

28. U.S. Office of Management and Budget, *Budget of the United States Government 2013 Historical Tables*, at www.whitehouse.gov/sites/default/files/omb/budget/fy2013/assets/hist02z2.xls, accessed July 19, 2012.

29. *Congressional Record* (daily), July 15, 2004, H5875.

30. "Obama Ad Says Romney Stashed Money in Cayman Island," Politifact, July 14, 2012, www.politifact.com/truth-o-meter/statements/2012/jul/17/barack-obama/obama-ad-says-romney-stashed-money-cayman-islands, accessed July 19, 2012; Betsy Woodruff, "Obama's Offshore Team," *National Review Online*, July 18, 2012, at www.nationalreview.com/articles/309763/obama-s-offshore-team-betsy-woodruff, accessed July 19, 2012.

31. National Association of College and University Business Officers, "U.S. and Canadian Institutions Listed by Fiscal Year 2011 Endowment Market Value," March 19, 2012, at www.nacubo.org/Documents/research/2011NCSEPublicTablesEndowmentMarketValues319.pdf, accessed July 19, 2012.

32. Congressional Budget Office, "The Distribution of Household Income and Federal Taxes, 2008 and 2009," July 10, 2012, at www.cbo.gov/sites/default/files/cbofiles/attachments/43373-Supplemental_Tables_Final.xls, Table 8, accessed July 19, 2012.

33. Quoted in Arthur M. Schlesinger Jr., *The Age of Roosevelt: The Coming of the New Deal* (Boston: Houghton Mifflin, 1958), 308–309.

34. *Flemming v. Nestor*, 363 U.S. 603 (1960).

35. William McBride, "Tax Freedom Day 2012," Tax Foundation, April 2, 2012, at taxfoundation.org/article/special-report-no-198-tax-freedom-day-2012, accessed July 19, 2012.

36. Chuck Marr and Chye-Ching Huang, "Tax Foundation Figures Do Not Represent Typical Households' Tax Burdens," Center on Budget and Policy Priorities, April 2, 2012, at www.cbpp.org/cms/index.cfm?fa=view&id=3738, accessed July 19, 2012.

37. Bill Clinton, presidential radio address on balancing the budget, January 27, 1996, at www.presidency.ucsb.edu/ws/index.php?pid=53258, accessed July 23, 2012.

38. Economist Walter Heller coined the term "fine-tuning." Herbert Stein, head of the Council of Economic Advisers under President Nixon, said that the term "later became a symbol of much that was thought to be wrong with the policy." Herbert Stein, *Presidential Economics: The Making of Economic Policy from Roosevelt to Reagan and Beyond* (New York: Simon and Schuster, 1984), 95.

39. "Interview Excerpts: President Obama," *New York Times*, October 12, 2010, at www.nytimes.com/2010/10/17/magazine/17obama-transcript.html, accessed July 19, 2012.

40. U.S. Congressional Budget Office, *The Budget and Economic Outlook: Fiscal Years 2005 to 2016* (Washington, DC: Government Printing Office, 2006), 119–123.

41. Quoted in William Greider, *The Education of David Stockman and Other Americans* (New York: Dutton, 1982), 33.

42. U.S. Congressional Budget Office, *The Budget and Economic Outlook: Fiscal Years 2009 to 2010* (Washington, DC: Government Printing Office, 2009), 4.

43. John F. Kennedy, "Inaugural Address," January 20, 1961, at www.presidency.ucsb.edu/ws/index.php?pid=8032, accessed October 10, 2012.

44. "Obama's Media Availability," *New York Times*, January 6, 2009, at www.nytimes.com/2009/01/06/us/politics/06text-obama.html, accessed July 23, 2012.

45. Carrie Dann, "Biden Revives 'Patriotic' Tax Argument," MSNBC.com, May 10, 2012, at firstread.msnbc.msn.com/_news/2012/05/10/11642446-biden-revives-patriotic-tax-argument, accessed July 23, 2012.

46. Barack Obama, "Remarks at a Campaign Rally in Cedar Rapids, Iowa," July 10, 2012, at www.presidency.ucsb.edu/ws/?pid=101349, accessed July 23, 2012.

47. Remarks by Chairman Ben S. Bernanke at the Center for Economic Policy Studies and on the occasion of the seventy-fifth anniversary of the Woodrow Wilson School of Public and International Affairs, Princeton University, Princeton, New Jersey, February 24, 2006, at www.federalreserve.gov/boardDocs/Speeches/2006/200602242/default.htm, accessed July 23, 2012.

48. Federal Reserve Board, "Open Market Operations," at www.federalreserve.gov/FOMC/fundsrate.htm, accessed July 23, 2012.

49. Federal Reserve Bank of New York, "Fedpoint: Open Market Operations," at www.ny.frb.org/aboutthefed/fedpoint/fed32.html, accessed July 23, 2012.

50. Bob Woodward, *Maestro: Greenspan's Fed and the American Boom* (New York: Simon and Schuster, 2000), 94–97.

51. Quoted in Bill Mintz, "Greenspan Makes It Perfectly Obscure," *Houston Chronicle*, June 22, 1995, Business 1.

52. Nell Henderson, "Fed Chief Calls His Remarks a Mistake," *Washington Post*, May 24, 2006, D1.

53. William Poole, "Untold Story of FOMC: Secrecy Is Exaggerated," *The Regional Economist*, July 2002, at www.web.archive.org/web/20060215215526/www.stlouisfed.org/publications/re/2002/c/pages/pres_message.html, accessed July 23, 2012.

54. Alan Greenspan, *The Age of Turbulence* (New York: Penguin, 2007), 151.

55. Ben S. Bernanke, "The Crisis and the Policy Response," Stamp Lecture, London School of Economics, London, January 13, 2009, at www.federalreserve.gov/newsevents/speech/bernanke20090113a.htm, accessed July 23, 2012.

56. U.S. Government Accountability Office, "Financial Regulation a Framework for Crafting and Assessing Proposals to Modernize the Outdated U.S. Financial Regulatory System," January 2009, at www.gao.gov/new .items/d09216.pdf, accessed July 23, 2012.

57. Securities and Exchange Commission, "The Investor's Advocate: How the SEC Protects Investors, Maintains Market Integrity, and Facilitates Capital Formation," at www.sec.gov/about/whatwedo.shtml, accessed July 23, 2012.

58. "John Harwood Interviews Barack Obama," *New York Times*, January 7, 2009, at www.nytimes.com/ 2009/01/07/us/politics/07text-harwood.html, accessed July 14, 2009.

59. Lawrence H. White, "How Did We Get into This Financial Mess?" Cato Institute Briefing Paper, November 18, 2008, at www.cato.org/pubs/bp/bp110 .pdf, accessed July 23, 2012; also see: Gretchen Morgenson and Joshua Rosner, *Reckless Endangerment* (New York: Times Books, 2011).

60. Jo Becker, Sheryl Gay Stolberg, and Stephen Labaton, "The Reckoning: White House Philosophy Stoked Mortgage Bonfire," *New York Times*, December 21, 2008, www.nytimes.com/2008/12/21/business/21admin .html, accessed July 23, 2012.

61. Martha Derthick and Paul J. Quirk, *The Politics of Deregulation* (Washington, DC: Brookings Institution, 1985).

62. World Trade Organization, "Understanding the WTO," at www.wto.org/english/thewto_e/whatis_e/tif_e/tif_e.htm, accessed July 23, 2012.

63. Dave Altig, "Is Offshoring Behind US Employment's Current Problems?" Federal Reserve Bank of Atlanta, May 4, 2011, at acroblog.typepad.com/macroblog/2011/05/ is-offshoring-behind-us-employments-current-problems .html, accessed July 23, 2012.

64. Online NewsHour, "Debating China Trade," May 19, 2000, at www.pbs.org/newshour/bb/asia/china/pntr/de-bate_5-19.html, accessed July 23, 2012.

65. Pat Buchanan and Ralph Nader, "Ralph Nader: Conservatively Speaking," *The American Conservative*, June 21, 2004, at www.amconmag.com/2004_06_21/cover .html, accessed July 23, 2012.

66. World Trade Organization, "Criticism Yes, Misinformation No," at www.wto.org/english/thewto_e/ minist_e/min99_e/english/misinf_e/09sov_e.htm, accessed July 23, 2012.

67. John Gershman, "Democracy and the Making of Foreign Policy," February 3, 2006, at www.fpif.org/fpiftxt/3103, accessed July 14, 2009.

68. Quoted in John Collins, *Military Geography for Professionals and the Public* (Washington, DC: National Defense University, 1998), at ia700506.us.archive.org/3/ items/militarygeograph00collrich/militarygeograph-00collrich_djvu.txt, accessed July 23, 2012. Some sources attribute the line to Senator Daniel Patrick Moynihan, but the evidence indicates that Schlesinger used it first.

69. Charles Wolf Jr., "A Theory of Non-Market Failures," *The Public Interest* 55 (Spring1979): 114–133; George J. Stigler, "The Theory of Economic Regulation," *Bell Journal of Economics* 2 (Spring 1971): 3–21.

70. Michael Kinsley, "Obama, The Wealth-Spreader," *Time*, October 31, 2008, at www.time.com/time/magazine/ article/0,9171,1855360,00.html, accessed July 23, 2012.

71. Task Force on Inequality and American Democracy, American Political Science Association, "American Democracy in an Age of Rising Inequality," 2004, at www.apsanet.org/imgtest/taskforcereport.pdf, accessed July 23, 2012.

72. Arthur C. Brooks, *Who Really Cares* (New York: Basic Books, 2006), 180.

73. Milton Friedman, *Capitalism and Freedom* (Chicago: University of Chicago Press, 1962), 9.

74. Charles E. Lindblom, *Politics and Markets* (New York: Basic Books, 1977), 164.

75. Press conference by President George W. Bush, January 12, 2009, at www.presidency.ucsb.edu/ws/ index.php?pid=85430, accessed July 23, 2012.

76. Quoted in Roger Lowenstein, "Help Wanted," *New York Times Magazine*, September 5, 2004, 54.

77. Ibid.

Chapter 18

1. Willis Thornton, "The Day They Burned the Capitol," *American Heritage*, December 1954, www.americanheritage.com/content/day-they-burned-capitol, accessed July 26, 2012.

2. A. Timothy Warnock, *Air Power versus U-Boats* (Air Force History and Museums Program, 1999), www.afhso.af.mil/shared/media/document/AFD-100525-066.pdf, accessed July 26, 2012.

3. United States Intelligence Community, "Intelligence Terms and Definitions," www.web.archive.org/ web/20070927034719/www.intelligence.gov/0-glossary .shtml#4, accessed July 26, 2012.

4. Walter A. McDougall, *Promised Land, Crusader State: The American Encounter with the World since 1776* (New York: Houghton Mifflin/Mariner Books, 1997), chap. 8.

5. Alexis de Tocqueville, *Democracy in America*, ed. J. P. Mayer and trans. George Lawrence (Garden City, NY: Anchor Books, Doubleday, 1969), 228–229.

6. Nancy E. Roman, "Both Sides of the Aisle: A Call for Bipartisan Foreign Policy" (Washington, DC: Council on Foreign Relations, September 2005), www.cfr.org/content/publications/attachments/ Bipartisan_CSR.pdf, accessed July 26, 2012.

7. Victor Davis Hanson, *Carnage and Culture: Landmark Battles in the Rise of Western Power* (New York: Doubleday, 2001).

8. Patrick Garrity, "Foreign Policy and *The Federalist*," in *Saving the Revolution: The Federalist Papers and the*

American Founding, ed. Charles R. Kesler (New York: Free Press, 1987), 83–99.

9. George Washington, "Farewell Address," 1796, avalon .law.yale.edu/18th_century/washing.asp, accessed July 26, 2012.

10. Abraham Lincoln, "Speech in the U.S. House of Representatives on the War with Mexico," January 12, 1848, in Don E. Fehrenbacher and Alfred Whital Stern, eds., *Lincoln: Speeches and Writings* (New York: Library of America, 1989), 161.

11. George Washington, Andrew Jackson, William Henry Harrison, Zachary Taylor, and Franklin Pierce had all been generals. Thomas Jefferson, James Madison, James Monroe, John Quincy Adams, Martin Van Buren, and James Buchanan had served as secretary of state. John Adams had served as minister to France, the Netherlands, and Great Britain.

12. Critics say the Kellogg-Briand pact was naive. But there was shrewdness behind the treaty, as Secretary of State Kellogg deflected French proposals for a Franco-American alliance against Germany by advocating a broader treaty in which all signatories renounced war as an instrument of policy against all other signatories. For political reasons, the French could hardly refuse this high-minded but harmless multilateral treaty.

13. Elizabeth Edwards Spalding, *The First Cold Warrior: Harry Truman, Containment, and the Remaking of Liberal Internationalism* (Lexington: University of Kentucky Press, 2006), 177–197.

14. President Bill Clinton, address to the nation announcing military strikes on Iraq, December 16, 1998, www.presidency.ucsb.edu/ws/index.php?pid=55414, accessed July 26, 2012.

15. Iraq Liberation Act of 1998, Public Law 105-338.

16. Pew Research Center for the People and the Press, "From News Interest to Lifestyles, Energy Takes Hold," May 24, 2001, www.people-press.org/files/legacy-pdf/11.pdf, July 26, 2012.

17. President George W. Bush, address to a joint session of Congress, September 20, 2001, www.presidency.ucsb .edu/ws/index.php?pid=64731, accessed July 26, 2012.

18. President George W. Bush, graduation speech at West Point, June 1, 2002, www.presidency.ucsb.edu/ws/index.php?pid=62730, accessed July 26, 2012.

19. Charles Krauthammer, "Charlie Gibson's Gaffe," *Washington Post*, September 13, 2008, A17, www.washingtonpost.com/wp-dyn/content/article/2008/09/12/AR2008091202457.html, accessed July 26, 2012.

20. Ivo H. Daalder, "Policy Implications of the Bush Doctrine on Preemption," Council on Foreign Relations, November 16, 2002, www.cfr.org/international-law/policy-implications-bush-doctrine-preemption/p5251, accessed July 26, 2012.

21. Commission on the Intelligence Capabilities of the United States Regarding Weapons of Mass Destruction, *Report to the President of the United States*, March 31, 2005, www.fas.org/irp/offdocs/wmd_report.pdf, accessed July 26, 2012.

22. Paul R. Pillar, "Intelligence, Policy, and the War in Iraq," *Foreign Affairs*, March/April 2006, www.foreignaffairs .org/20060301faessay85202/paul-r-pillar/intelligence-policy-and-the-war-in-iraq.html, accessed July 26, 2012.

23. President Barack H. Obama, "Inaugural Address," January 20, 2009, www.presidency.ucsb.edu/ws/index .php?pid=44, accessed July 26, 2012.

24. Benjamin Franklin, *Memoirs of Benjamin Franklin* (New York: Derby and Jackson, 1859), 284; see also McDougall, *Promised Land, Crusader State*, 21.

25. McDougall, *Promised Land, Crusader State*, 206.

26. President Franklin D. Roosevelt, "Prayer on D-Day," June 6, 1944, www.presidency.ucsb.edu/ws/?pid=16515, accessed July 28, 2012.

27. Leon Panetta, remarks at Fort Benning, May 4, 2012, www.defense.gov/speeches/speech.aspx?speechid=1668, accessed July 26, 2012.

28. BBC World Service, "Views of US Continue to Improve in 2011 BBC Country Rating Poll," March 7, 2011, www.worldpublicopinion.org/pipa/pdf/mar11/BBCEvalsUS_Mar11_rpt.pdf; Pew Research Center, "Global Opinion of Obama Slips, International Policies Faulted," June 13, 2012, www.pewglobal .org/2012/06/13/global-opinion-of-obama-slips-international-policies-faulted, accessed July 27, 2012.

29. Merle Miller, *Plain Speaking: An Oral Biography of Harry S Truman* (New York: Berkley Medallion, 1974), 263–264.

30. Organization for Economic Cooperation and Development, "Development: Aid to Developing Countries Falls Because of Global Recession," April 4, 2012, www.oecd.org/document/3/0,3746, en_21571361_44315115_50058883_1_1_1_1,00.html, data at webnet.oecd.org/oda2011, accessed July 27, 2012.

31. U.S. House Committee on Foreign Affairs, "New Beginnings: Policy Priorities in the Obama Administration," Federal News Service transcript, April 22, 2009; video at www.c-spanvideo.org/appearance/555888254, accessed July 27, 2012.

32. Center for Global Prosperity, *Index of Global Philanthropy and Remittances 2012* (Washington, DC: Hudson Institute, 2012), www.hudson.org/files/publications/2012IndexofGlobalPhilanthropyandRemittances.pdf, accessed July 27, 2012.

33. Carol Adelman, "The Privatization of Foreign Aid," *Foreign Affairs* 82 (November/December 2003), www.hudson.org/index.cfm?fuseaction=publication_details&id=3479, accessed July 27, 2012.

34. Stephen E. Ambrose, "A Hard Look at Heroes," *Denver Post*, June 7, 1998, G1.

35. President Woodrow Wilson's Fourteen Points, January 8, 1918, avalon.law.yale.edu/20th_century/wilson14.asp, accessed July 27, 2012.

36. *New York Times Co. v. United States*, 403 U.S. 713, 728 (1971).

37. Ibid.

38. Commission on the Roles and Capabilities of the United States Intelligence Community, *Preparing for the 21st Century: An Appraisal of U.S. Intelligence* (Washington, DC: Government Printing Office, 1996), www.gpo.gov/fdsys/pkg/GPO-INTELLIGENCE/content-detail.html, accessed July 27, 2012.

39. President George W. Bush, State of the Union address, January 28, 2003, www.presidency.ucsb.edu/ws/index.php?pid=29645, accessed July 27, 2012.

40. Scott Shane, "Secret 'Kill List' Proves a Test of Obama's Principles and Will," *New York Times*, May 29, 2012, www.nytimes.com/2012/05/29/world/obamas-leadership-in-war-on-al-qaeda.html, accessed July 27, 2012.

41. President Barack Obama, Interview on ABC's *The View*, July 28, 2010, www.presidency.ucsb.edu/ws/?pid=88313, accessed July 27, 2012.

42. "Statement by the Press Secretary on WikiLeaks," November 28, 2010, www.presidency.ucsb.edu/ws/?pid=89638, accessed July 27, 2012.

43. Akhil Reed Amar, *America's Constitution: A Biography* (New York: Random House, 2005), 45, 116.

44. 10 U.S.C. 113.

45. Jeffrey M. Jones, "Confidence in U.S. Public Schools at New Low," Gallup Poll, June 20, 2012, www.gallup.com/poll/155258/Confidence-Public-Schools-New-Low.aspx, accessed July 27, 2012.

46. President George H. W. Bush, "Remarks at the Community Welcome for Returning Troops in Sumter, South Carolina," March 17, 1991, www.presidency.ucsb.edu/ws/index.php?pid=19397, accessed July 27, 2012.

47. CNN/ORC survey of 1,007 American adults, October 14–16, 2011, i2.cdn.turner.com/cnn/2011/images/10/28/rel17h.pdf, accessed July 27, 2012.

48. McDougall, *Promised Land, Crusader State*, 40.

49. NATO is the military alliance linking the United States with Canada and 23 European nations. The IMF deals with exchange rates of the world's currencies, and it makes loans to countries with balance-of-payments problems or other major economic difficulties. The World Bank lends billions for development projects in developing countries. The WTO, formerly the General Agreement on Tariffs and Trade, sponsors rounds of trade talks to promote global trade and provides a mechanism to enforce international trade rules.

50. President George W. Bush, address before a joint session of the Congress on the State of the Union, January 20, 2004, www.presidency.ucsb.edu/ws/index.php?pid=29646, accessed July 15, 2009.

51. President Barack Obama: "Remarks on the Situation in Libya," March 18, 2011, www.presidency.ucsb.edu/ws/?pid=90162, accessed July 27, 2012.

52. 10 Annals of Congress 596, 613 (1800), www.memory.loc.gov/cgi-bin/ampage?collId=llac&fileName=010/llac010.db&recNum=304, accessed July 15, 2009.

53. Thomas Jefferson to George Washington, "Opinion on Right of Senate to Negate Diplomatic Grades Specified by President, with Copy," April 24, 1790, at www.memory.loc.gov/cgi-bin/query/r?ammem/mtj:@field(DOCID+@lit(tj060030)), accessed July 27, 2012.

54. See Cecil V. Crabb Jr., *The Doctrines of American Foreign Policy: Their Meaning, Role, and Future* (Baton Rouge: Louisiana State University Press, 1982).

55. During the two world wars, the declarations followed presidential requests. In the War of 1812 and the Spanish-American War (1898) reluctant presidents (Madison and McKinley) essentially followed the lead of Congress. In a fifth case, the Mexican-American War of 1846–1848, President James Polk's actions led to armed clashes, and Congress recognized the existence of a state of war.

56. Jeffrey Record, *Revising U.S. Military Strategy: Tailoring Means to Ends* (Washington, DC: Pergamon-Brassey's, 1984).

57. Quoted in Fred I. Greenstein and Richard H. Immerman, "Effective National Security Advising: Recovering the Eisenhower Legacy," *Political Science Quarterly* 115 (Autumn 2000): 344.

58. Quoted in Samuel Kernell and Samuel L. Popkin, *Chief of Staff: Twenty-five Years of Managing the Presidency* (Berkeley: University of California Press, 1986), 123.

59. James Risen, "U.S. Envoy to Yemen Reportedly Barred FBI," *New York Times*, July 6, 2001, www.nytimes.com/2001/07/06/world/us-envoy-to-yemen-reportedly-barred-fbi.html, accessed July 27, 2012.

60. United States Department of the Treasury, Office of Terrorism and Financial Intelligence, www.treasury.gov/about/organizational-structure/offices/Pages/Office-of-Terrorism-and-Financial-Intelligence.aspx /, accessed July 27, 2012.

61. Harold Brown, Jimmy Carter's secretary of defense, is an example of expertise. A nuclear physicist and weapons designer, Brown had previously served eight years at the Pentagon, including a stint as secretary of the U.S. Air Force. Caspar Weinberger, secretary of defense under Reagan, offers a good example of influence stemming primarily from a close relationship with the president. Although neither a defense expert nor a master of details, Weinberger shared Reagan's anti-Communist stance and his enthusiasm for missile defense. Additionally, Reagan was comfortable working with Weinberger.

62. United States Army, "About the Army: Personnel," www.goarmy.com/about/personnel.jsp, accessed July 27, 2012.

63. United States Navy, "Status of the Navy," www.navy.mil/navydata/navy_legacy_hr.asp?id=146, accessed July 27, 2012.

64. Michael Warner, "Wanted: A Definition of 'Intelligence,'" *Studies in Intelligence* 46 (2002), www.cia.gov/library/center-for-the-study-of-intelligence/csi-publications/csi-studies/studies/vol46no3/article02.html, accessed July 27, 2012.

65. Stephen C. Mercado, "Sailing the Sea of OSINT in the Information Age," *Studies in Intelligence* 48 (2004), www.cia.gov/library/center-for-the-study-of-intelligence/csi-publications/csi-studies/studies/vol48no3/article05.html, accessed July 27, 2012.

66. Office of the Director of National Intelligence, "DNI Releases FY2011 Appropriate Budget Figure for the National Intelligence Program," October 28, 2011, dni.gov/press_releases/20111028_release_budget.pdf, accessed July 27, 2012. Until 2007, the figure was classified, but a new law provided for its publication. The components of the budget remain secret.

67. Roberta Wohlstetter, *Pearl Harbor: Warning and Decision* (Stanford, CA: Stanford University Press, 1962).

68. P. K. Rose, "Two Strategic Intelligence Mistakes in Korea, 1950," *Studies in Intelligence* 11 (Fall–Winter 2001), www.cia.gov/library/center-for-the-study-of-intelligence/csi-publications/csi-studies/studies/fall_winter_2001/article06.html, accessed July 27, 2012.

69. Commission on the Intelligence Capabilities of the United States Regarding Weapons of Mass Destruction, *Report to the President of the United States*, March 31, 2005, www.gpo.gov/fdsys/pkg/GPO-WMD/pdf/GPO-WMD.pdf, accessed July 27, 2012.

70. National Commission on Terrorist Attacks upon the United States, *The 9/11 Commission Report*, July 22, 2004, www.911commission.gov/report/911Report_Ch11.htm, accessed July 27, 2012.

71. Amy B. Zegart, "An Empirical Analysis of Failed Intelligence Reforms Before September 11," *Political Science Quarterly* 121 (Spring 2006): 33–60.

72. U.S. Commission on National Security/21st Century, *New World Coming: American Security in the 21st Century*, September 15, 1999, www.fas.org/man/docs/nwc/nwc.htm, accessed July 27, 2012.

73. Peter Bergen and Bruce Hoffman, "Assessing the Terrorist Threat," Bipartisan Policy Center, September 10, 2010, bipartisanpolicy.org/sites/default/files/NSPG%20Final%20Threat%20Assessment.pdf, accessed July 27, 2012.

74. U.S. Constitution, Article I, Section 8.

75. Article II, Section 2 says, "By and with the advice and consent" of the Senate, the president has the power to make treaties "provided two thirds of the Senators present concur."

76. Technically, the Senate does not have the power to "ratify" treaties. The president does so by depositing an international "instrument of ratification," which makes the treaty binding on the United States. The president cannot, however, ratify a treaty until it gains Senate approval.

77. United States Senate, "Treaties," www.senate.gov/artandhistory/history/common/briefing/Treaties.htm, accessed July 27, 2012.

78. David P. Auerswald, "Advice and Consent: The Forgotten Power," in *Congress and the Politics of Foreign Policy*, ed. Colton C. Campbell, Nicol C. Rae, and John F. Stack Jr. (Upper Saddle River, NJ: Prentice Hall, 2003).

79. 1 U.S.C. 112b(a). Also see United States Department of State, "Reporting International Agreements to Congress under Case Act," www.state.gov/s/l/treaty/caseact, accessed July 27, 2012.

80. Alexander Hamilton, James Madison, and John Jay, *The Federalist Papers*, ed. Clinton Rossiter with a new introduction and notes by Charles R. Kesler (New York: Signet, 2003), no. 8, 62.

81. Charlie Savage, "2 Top Lawyers Lost to Obama in Libya War Powers Debate," *New York Times*, June 17, 2011, www.nytimes.com/2011/06/18/world/africa/18powers.html, accessed July 27, 2012.

82. Dana Priest, "Congressional Oversight of Intelligence Criticized: Committee Members, Others Cite Lack of Attention to Reports on Iraqi Arms, Al Qaeda Threat," *Washington Post*, April 27, 2004, A1.

83. United States Senate, Committee on Appropriations, *Review of the 9/11 Commission's Intelligence Recommendations*, September 21–22, 2004, Senate Hearing 108-614, www.gpo.gov/fdsys/pkg/CHRG-108shrg95943/html/CHRG-108shrg95943.htm, accessed July 27, 2012.

84. Roman, "Both Sides of the Aisle."

85. *Youngstown Co. v. Sawyer*, 343 U.S. 579 (1952).

86. *New York Times Co. v. United States*, 403 U.S. 713 (1971).

87. *Hamdi v. Rumsfeld*, 542 U.S. 507 (2004).

88. Electronic Privacy Information Center, "Foreign Intelligence Surveillance Act Orders 1979–2011," epic.org/privacy/wiretap/stats/fisa_stats.html, accessed July 27, 2012.

89. Bono's organization was DATA, for Debt, AIDS, Trade, and Africa. In 2008, it merged with another organization, ONE. Source: www.one.org, accessed July 28, 2012.

90. Ana Eiras, "Economic Freedom, Not Debt Relief, Is the Real Cure for Poverty," June 16, 2005, www.ephrem.org/dehai_news_archive/2005/jun05/0474.html, accessed July 28, 2012.

91. Pew Forum on Religion and Public Life, "Lobbying for the Faithful: Religious Advocacy Groups in Washington, DC," November 21, 2011, www.pewforum.org/Government/Lobbying-for-the-faithful—issue-agendas.aspx#global, accessed July 28, 2012.

92. James Curran et al., "Media System, Public Knowledge and Democracy: A Comparative Study," *European Journal of Communication* 24 (March 2009): 14.

93. Bill Clinton, *My Life* (New York: Knopf, 2004), 593.

94. Tocqueville, *Democracy in America*, 223.

95. See *Newsweek* and McClatchy surveys at www.pollingreport.com/iraq.htm; and www.pollingreport.com/iraq2.htm, accessed July 28, 2012.

96. Chicago Council on Foreign Affairs, "Constrained Internationalism: Adapting to New Realities," September 2010, www.thechicagocouncil.org/UserFiles/File/POS_Topline%20Reports/POS%202010/Global%20Views%202010.pdf, accessed July 28, 2012.

97. Committee to Protect Journalists, "Iraq: Journalists in Danger," 2009, www.cpj.org/reports/2008/07/journalists-killed-in-iraq.php, accessed July 29, 2012.

98. Reporters without Borders, Slaughter in Iraq, March 2006, www.rsf.org/IMG/pdf/Survey_RSF_Iraq_06.pdf, accessed July 29, 2012.

99. Lieutenant Colonel Barry Johnson, quoted in David Axe, "Fear and Loathing in Baghdad," *Salon*, January 20, 2006, www.salon.com/news/feature/2006/01/20/media_in_iraq, accessed July 29, 2012.

100. Half of Europe's Citizens Know Two Languages," Associated Press, September 24, 2005, www.freerepublic.com/focus/f-news/1490953/posts; "Europeans and Languages," European Commission, September 2005, www.ec.europa.eu/public_opinion/archives/ebs/ebs_237.en.pdf, accessed July 30, 2012.

101. Pew Research Center, "What the Public Knows—In Words and Pictures," November 7, 2011, www.people-press.org/2011/11/07/what-the-public-knows-in-words-and-pictures, accessed July 29, 2012.

102. Shanto Iyengar and Kyu Hahn, "'Dark Areas of Ignorance' Revisited: Comparing International Affairs Knowledge in Switzerland and the US," 2009, pcl.stanford.edu/research/2009/iyengar-darkareas.pdf, accessed July 29, 2012.

103. National Geographic Education Foundation, National Geographic–Roper Public Affairs 2006 Geographic Literacy Study, May 2006, www.nationalgeographic.com/roper2006/pdf/FINALReport2006GeogLitsurvey.pdf, accessed July 29, 2012.

104. World Public Opinion, "American Public Vastly Overestimates Amount of U.S. Foreign Aid," November 29, 2010, www.worldpublicopinion.org/pipa/articles/brunitedstatescanadara/670.php, accessed July 29, 2012.

105. Henry E. Brady, James S. Fishkin, and Robert C. Luskin, "Informed Public Opinion about Foreign Policy: The Uses of Deliberative Polling," *Brookings Review*, Summer 2003, 16–19; www.brookings.edu/research/articles/2003/06/summer-elections-brady, accessed July 29, 2012.

106. Eric Lichtblau, "FBI Said to Lag on Translating Terror Tapes," *New York Times*, September 28, 2004, www.nytimes.com/2004/09/28/politics/28fbi.html, accessed July 30, 2012.

107. David D. Kirkpatrick, "This War Is Not Like the Others—or Is It?" *New York Times*, August 26, 2007, www.nytimes.com/2007/08/26/weekinreview/26kirkpatrick.htm, accessed July 30, 2012.

108. Secretary Rumsfeld press briefing, February 12, 2002, www.defenselink.mil/transcripts/transcript.aspx?transcriptid=2636, accessed July 30, 2012.

109. James A. Baker III and Lee H. Hamilton, "Breaking the War Powers Stalemate," *Washington Post*, June 9, 2011, www.washingtonpost.com/opinions/breaking-the-war-powers-stalemate/2011/06/08/AGX0CrNH_story.html, accessed July 30, 2012.

110. Benjamin Kleinerman and Vincent Phillip Muñoz, "Did the Founders Create War Powers?" *The Weekly Standard*, June 17, 2011, www.npr.org/2011/06/17/137242737/weekly-standard-did-founders-create-war-powers, accessed July 30, 2012.

111. Obama, "Inaugural Address."

Index